The Broadview Anthology of

BRITISH LITERATURE

Volume 5
The Victorian Era

The Broadview Anthology of British Literature

The Medieval Period
The Renaissance and the Early Seventeenth Century
The Restoration and the Eighteenth Century
The Age of Romanticism
The Victorian Era
The Twentieth Century and Beyond

The Broadview Anthology of

BRITISH LITERATURE

Volume 5
The Victorian Era

GENERAL EDITORS

Joseph Black, University of Massachusetts
Leonard Conolly, Trent University
Kate Flint, Rutgers University
Isobel Grundy, University of Alberta
Don LePan, Broadview Press
Roy Liuzza, University of Tennessee
Jerome J. McGann, University of Virginia
Anne Lake Prescott, Barnard College
Barry V. Qualls, Rutgers University
Claire Waters, University of California, Davis

b

broadview press

LIBRARY AND ARCHIVES CANADA CATALOGUING IN PUBLICATION

The Broadview anthology of british literature / general editors, Joseph Black ... [et al].

Includes bibliographical references and index.
Contents: v.1. The Medieval period. —v.2. The Renaissance and the early seventeenth century. —v. 3. The Restoration and the eighteenth century.—v.4. The age of Romanticism.—v.5. The Victorian era.—v.6. The twentieth century and beyond
ISBN 1-55111-609-x (v.1), —ISBN 1-55111-610-3 (v.2), —ISBN 1-55111-611-1 (v. 3), —ISBN 1-55111-612-x (v.4),— ISBN 1-55111-613-8 (v.5),—ISBN 1-55111-614-6 (v.6)

1. English literature. I. Black, Joseph Laurence, 1962–

PR1109.B77   2006   820.8   C2006-900091-3

Broadview Press is an independent, international publishing house, incorporated in 1985. Broadview believes in shared ownership, both with its employees and with the general public; since the year 2000 Broadview shares have traded publicly on the Toronto Venture Exchange under the symbol BDP.

We welcome comments and suggestions regarding any aspect of our publications—please feel free to contact us at the addresses below or at broadview@broadviewpress.com.

North America
PO Box 1243,
Peterborough, Ontario
Canada K9J 7H5

2215 Kenmore Road,
Buffalo, NY, USA 14207
Tel: (705) 743-8990;
Fax: (705) 743-8353
email: customerservice@broadviewpress.com

UK, Ireland, and continental Europe
NBN International
Estover Road
Plymouth
UK PL6 7PY
Tel: +44 (0) 1752 202301;
Fax: +44 (0) 1752 202331;
Fax Order Line: +44 (0) 1752 202333;
Cust Ser: enquiries@nbninternational.com
Orders: orders@nbninternational.com

Australia and New Zealand
New South Books,
University of New South Wales
Sydney, NSW, 2052
Australia
Tel: 61 2 9664 0999;
Fax: 61 2 9664 5420
email: info.press@unsw.edu.au

www. broadviewpress.com
Broadview Press gratefully acknowledges the financial support of the Government of Canada through the Book Publishing Industry Development Program (BPIDP) for our publishing activities.

Cover design by Lisa Brawn

PRINTED IN CANADA

Contributing Editors and Writers

Managing Editor	Don LePan
Editorial Coordinator	Jennifer McCue
Developmental Editor	Laura Cardiff
General Academic and Textual Editors	Colleen Franklin, Morgan Rooney
Design Coordinator	Kathryn Brownsey

Contributing Editors

Katherine O. Acheson
Sandra Bell
Emily Bernhard Jackson
Joseph Black
Robert Boenig
Michael Calabrese
Laura Cardiff
Noel Chevalier
Mita Choudhury
Thomas J. Collins
Leonard Conolly
Dianne Dugaw
Michael Faletra
Christine Fitzgerald
Stephen Glosecki
Amanda Goldrick-Jones

Douglas Hayes
John Holmes
Michael Keefer
Scott Kleinman
Gary Kuchar
Don LePan
Roy Liuzza
Marie Loughlin
D.L. Macdonald
Hugh Magennis
Anne McWhir
Tobias Menely
Britt Mize
David Oakleaf
Jude Polsky

Anne Lake Prescott
Joyce Rappaport
Herbert Rosengarten
Jason Rudy
Janice Schroeder
John T. Sebastian
Emily Steiner
David Swain
Andrew Taylor
Peggy Thompson
Fred Waage
Craig Walker
Claire Waters
David Watt
James Winny

Contributing Writers

Laura Cardiff
Jude Polsky
Victoria Abboud
Jane Beal
Jennifer Beauvais
Rachel Bennett
Emily Bernhard Jackson
Rebecca Blasco
Julie Brennan
Andrew Bretz
Emily Cargan
Adrienne Eastwood
Wendy Eberle-Sinatra
Peter Enman
Joanne Findon

Jane Grove
Camille Isaacs
Erik Isford
Stephanie King
Gabrielle L'Archeveque
Don LePan
Anna Lepine
John McIntyre
Carrie Nartkler
Byron Nelson
Robin Norris
Kenna Olsen
Kendra O'Neal Smith
Laura Pellerine
Jason Rudy

Anne Salo
Janice Schroeder
Carrie Shanafelt
Nicole Shukin
James Soderholm
Anne Sorbie
Martha Stoddard-Holms
Jenna Stook
Candace Taylor
David van Belle
Shari Watling
Matthew Williams
bj Wray
Nicole Zylstra

Layout and Typesetting

Kathryn Brownsey   Susan Chamberlain

Illustration Formatting and Assistance

Cheryl Baldwin   Lisa Brawn

PRODUCTION COORDINATORS

Barbara Conolly
Judith Earnshaw

Leonard Conolly
Chris Griffin

Tara Lowes

PERMISSIONS COORDINATORS

Emily Cargan

Jennifer Elsayed
Amy Nimegeer

Chris Griffin

PROOFREADERS

Jennifer Bingham
Martin Boyne
Lucy Conolly
Lynn Fraser

Anne Hodgetts
Amy Neufeld
Lynn Neufeld

EDITORIAL ADVISORS

Rachel Ablow, University of Rochester
Rita Bode, Trent University
Susan Brown, University of Guelph
Catherine Burroughs, Wells College
Elizabeth Campbell, Oregon State University
Nancy Cirillo, University of Illinois, Chicago
David Cowart, University of South Carolina
Alex Dick, University of British Columbia
Len Diepeveen, Dalhousie University
Daniel Fischlin, University of Guelph
Robert Forman, St. John's University
Barbara Gates, University of Delaware
Chris Gordon-Craig, University of Alberta
Stephen Guy-Bray, University of British Columbia
Elizabeth Hodgson, University of British Columbia
John Holmes, University of Reading
Michael Keefer, University of Guelph
Gordon Kipling, University of California, Los Angeles
Emily Kugler, University of California, San Diego
William Liston, Ball State University
Peter Mallios, University of Maryland
Rod Michell, Thompson Rivers University
Byron Nelson, West Virginia University
Michael North, University of California, Los Angeles
Lesley Peterson, University of North Alabama
John Pollock, San Jose State University
Jason Rudy, University of Maryland
Carol Senf, Georgia Tech
Sharon Smulders, Mount Royal College
Goran Stanivukovic, St. Mary's University
Julian Yates, University of Delaware

CONTENTS

Preface

A Fresh Approach

To those with some awareness of the abundance of fresh material and lively debate in the field of English Studies in recent generations, it may seem surprising that this abundance has not been more fully reflected in the number of available anthologies. Thirty years ago there were two comprehensive anthologies designed for courses surveying British Literature: *The Norton Anthology of English Literature* and one alternative. In recent years there have been still two choices available—the *Norton* and one alternative. Over that time span *The Longman Anthology of British Literature* replaced *The Oxford Anthology of English Literature* in the role of "alternative," but there has been no expansion in range of available choices to match the expansion of content and of approach that has characterized the discipline itself. The number of available handbooks and guides to writing has multiplied steadily (to the point where there are literally hundreds of available choices), while the number of comprehensive anthologies of British literature has remained at two.

For those of us who have been working for the past three years on *The Broadview Anthology of British Literature*, it is not difficult to understand why. The very expansion of the discipline has made the task of assembling and editing an anthology that fully and vibrantly reflects the ways in which the British literary tradition is studied and taught an extraordinarily daunting one. The sheer amount of work involved is enormous, but so too is the amount of expertise that needs to be called on. With that background very much in mind, we have charted a new course in the preparation of *The Broadview Anthology of British Literature*. Rather than dividing up the work among a relatively small number of academics, and asking each of them to handle on their own the work of choosing, annotating, and preparing introductions to texts in their own areas of specialization, we have involved a large number of contributors in the process (as the pages following the

title page to this volume attest), and encouraged a high degree of collaboration at every level. First and foremost have been the distinguished academics who have served as our General Editors for the project, but in all there have literally been hundreds of people involved at various stages in researching, drafting headnotes or annotations, reviewing material, editing material, and finally carrying out the work of designing and typesetting the texts and other materials. That approach has allowed us to draw on a diverse range of talent, and to prepare a large anthology with unusual speed. It has also facilitated the maintenance of a high degree of consistency. Material has been reviewed and revised in-house at Broadview, by outside editors (chief among them Colleen Franklin, an academic with a wide-ranging background and also a superb copy editor), by a variety of academics with an extraordinarily diverse range of backgrounds and academic specialities, and by our team of General Editors for the project as a whole. The aim has been not only to ensure accuracy but also to make sure that the same standards are applied throughout the anthology to matters such as extent and coverage in author introductions, level of annotation, tone of writing, and student accessibility.

Our General Editors have throughout taken the lead in the process of making selections for the anthology. Along the way we have been guided by several core principles. We have endeavored to provide a selection that is broadly representative, while also being mindful of the importance of choosing texts that have the capacity to engage readers' interest today. We have for the most part made it a policy to include long works in their entirety or not at all; readers will find complete in these pages works such as *Utopia*, *Confessions of an English Opium Eater*, *In Memoriam* and *A Room of One's Own* that are often excerpted in other anthologies. Where inexpensive editions of works are available in our series of paperback Broadview Editions, we have often decided to omit them here, on the grounds that those wishing to teach one or more such works may easily order them in a combination package with the anthology; on these grounds we have decided against including *Frankenstein*, *Pride and Prejudice*, or *Heart of Darkness*. (For both Mary Shelley and Jane Austen we have made exceptions to our general policy regarding excerpts, however, including selections from *The Last Man* to represent Shelley and the first four chapters of *Pride and Prejudice*, together with a complete shorter work, *Lady Susan*, to represent Austen.)

Any discussion of what is distinctive about *The Broadview Anthology of British Literature* must focus above all on the contents. In every volume of the anthology there is material that is distinctive and fresh–including not only selections by lesser-known writers but also less familiar selections from canonical writers. The anthology takes a fresh approach too to a great many canonical texts. The first volume of the anthology includes not only Roy Liuzza's translation of *Beowulf* (widely acclaimed as the most engaging and reliable translation available), but also new translations by Liuzza of many other works of Old English poetry and prose. Also included in the first volume of the anthology are a new verse translation of *Judith* by Stephen Glosecki, and new translations by Claire Waters of several of the *Lais* of Marie de France. The second volume includes *King Lear* not only in the full Folio version but also with three key scenes from the Quarto version; readers are thus invited to engage firsthand with the question of how textual issues may substantially affect larger issues of meaning. And so on through all six volumes.

In a number of these cases the distinctive form of the anthology facilitates the presentation of content in an engaging and practical fashion. Notably, the adoption of a two-column format allows for some translations (the Marie de France *Lais*, the James Winny translation of *Sir Gawain and the Green Knight*) to be presented in parallel column format alongside the original texts, allowing readers to experience something of the flavor of the original, while providing convenient access to an accessible translation. Similarly, scenes from the Quarto version of *King Lear* are presented alongside the comparable sections of the Folio text, and passages from four translations of the Bible are laid out parallel to each other for ready comparison.

The large trim-size, two-column format also allows for greater flexibility in the presentation of visual materials. Throughout we have aimed to make this an anthology that is fully alive to the connections between literary and visual culture, from the discussion of the CHI-RHO page of the Lindisfarne Gospels in the first volume of the anthology (and the accompanying color illustration) to the inclusion in Volume 6 of a number of selections (including Graham Greene's "The Basement Room," Hanif Kureishi's "My Son the Fanatic," Tom Stoppard's "Professional Foul," and several skits from "Monty Python's Flying Circus") that may be discussed in connection with film or television versions. Along the way appear several full-page illustrations from the Ellesmere manuscript of Chaucer's *Canterbury Tales* and illustrations to a wide variety of other works, from *Robinson Crusoe* and *Gulliver's Travels* to *A Christmas Carol* and *The Road to Wigan Pier*.

CONTEXTUAL MATERIALS

Visual materials are also an important component of the background materials that form an important part of the anthology. These materials are presented in two ways. Several "Contexts" sections on particular topics or themes appear in each volume of the anthology, presented independent of any particular text or author. These include broadly based groupings of material on such topics as "Religion and Spiritual Life," "Print Culture," "India and the Orient," "The Abolition of Slavery," "The New Art of Photography," and "The End of Empire." The groups of "In Context" materials each relate to a particular text or author. They range from the genealogical tables provided as a supplement to *Beowulf*; to materials on "The Eighteenth-Century Sexual Imagination" (presented in conjunction with Haywood's *Fantomina*); to a selection of materials relating to the Peterloo massacre (presented in conjunction with Percy Shelley's "The Mask of Anarchy"); to materials on "'The Vilest Scramble for Loot' in Central Africa" (presented in conjunction with Conrad's "An Outpost of Progress"). For the most part these contextual materials are, as the word suggests, included with a view to setting texts in their broader literary, historical, and cultural contexts; in some cases, however, the materials included in "Contexts" sections are themselves literary works of a high order. The autobiographical account by Eliza M. of nineteenth-century life in Cape Town, for example (included in the section in Volume 5 on "Race and Empire"), is as remarkable for its literary qualities as it is for the light it sheds on the realities of colonial life. In the inclusion of texts such as these, as well as in other ways, the anthology aims to encourage readers to explore the boundaries of the literary and the non-literary, and the issue of what constitutes a "literary text."

WOMEN'S PLACE

A central element of the broadening of the canon of British literature in recent generations has of course been a great increase in the attention paid to texts by women writers. As one might expect from a publisher that has played an important role in making neglected works by women writers widely available, this anthology reflects the broadening of the canon quantitatively, by including a substantially larger number of women writers than have earlier anthologies of British literature. But it also reflects this broadening in other ways. In many anthologies of literature (anthologies of British literature, to be sure, but also anthologies of literature of a variety of other sorts) women writers are set somewhat apart, referenced in introductions and headnotes only in relation to issues of gender, and treated as important only for the fact of their being women writers. *The Broadview Anthology* strenuously resists such segregation; while women writers are of course discussed in relation to gender issues, their texts are also presented and discussed alongside those by men in a wide variety of other contexts, including seventeenth-century religious and political controversies, the abolitionist movement and World War I pacifism. Texts by women writers are front and center in the discussion of the development of realism in nineteenth-century fiction. And when it comes to the twentieth century, both Virginia Woolf and Dorothy Richardson are included alongside James Joyce as practitioners of groundbreaking modernist narrative techniques.

"BRITISH," "ENGLISH," "IRISH," "SCOTTISH," "WELSH," "OTHER"

The broadening of English Studies, in conjunction with the expansion and subsequent contraction of British power and influence around the world, has considerably complicated the issue of exactly how inclusive anthologies should be. In several respects this anthology (like its two main competitors) is significantly more inclusive than its title suggests, including a number of non-British writers whose works connect in important ways with the traditions of British literature. We have endeavored first of all to portray the fluid and multilingual reality of the medieval period through the inclusion not only of works in Old and Middle English but also, where other cultures interacted with the nascent "English" language and "British" culture, works in Latin, in French, and in Welsh. In later periods the word "British" becomes deeply problematic in different respects, but on balance we have preferred it to the only obvious alternative, "English." There are several objections to the latter in this context. Perhaps most obviously, "English" excludes authors or texts not only from Ireland but also from Scotland and from Wales, both of which retain to this day cultures quite distinct from that of the English. "English literature," of course, may also be taken to mean "literature written in English," but since the anthology does not cover *all* literature written in English (most obviously in excluding American literature), the ambiguity would not in this case be helpful.

The inclusion of Irish writers presents a related but even more tangled set of issues. At the beginning of the period covered by the six volumes of this anthology we find works, such as the *Book of Kells*, that may have been created in what is now England, in what is now Scotland, in what is now Ireland—or in some combination of these. Through most of the seventeenth, eighteenth, and nineteenth centuries almost the whole of Ireland was under British control—but for the most part unwillingly. In the period covered in the last of the six volumes Ireland was partitioned, with Northern Ireland becoming a part of the United Kingdom and the

Republic of Ireland declared independent of Britain on 6 December 1921. Less than two months earlier, James Joyce had completed *Ulysses*, which was first published as a complete work the following year (in Paris, not in Britain). It would be obviously absurd to regard Joyce as a British writer up to just before the publication of *Ulysses*, and an Irish writer thereafter. And arguably he and other Irish writers should never be regarded as British, whatever the politics of the day. If on no other grounds than their overwhelming influence on and connection to the body of literature written in the British Isles, however, we have included Irish writers—among them Swift, Sheridan, Wilde, Shaw, Beckett, Bowen, Muldoon, and Heaney as well as Joyce —throughout this anthology. We have also endeavored to give a real sense in the introductions to the six volumes of the anthology, in the headnotes to individual authors, and in the annotations to the texts themselves, of the ways in which the histories and the cultures of England, Ireland, Scotland and Wales, much as they interact with one another, are also distinct.

Also included in this anthology are texts by writers from areas that are far removed geographically from the British Isles but that are or have been British possessions. Writers such as Mary Rowlandson, Olaudah Equiano, and Phillis Wheatley are included, as they spent all or most of their lives living in what were then British colonial possessions. Writers who came of age in an independent United States, on the other hand, are not included, unless (like T.S. Eliot) they subsequently put down roots in Britain and became important British literary figures. Substantial grey areas, of course, surround such issues. One might well argue, for example, that Henry James merits inclusion in an anthology of British literature, or that W.H. Auden and Thom Gunn are more American poets than British ones. But the chosen subject matter of James's work has traditionally been considered to mark him as having remained an American writer, despite having spent almost two-thirds of his life in England. And both Auden and Gunn so clearly made a mark in Britain before crossing the Atlantic that it would seem odd to exclude them from these pages on the grounds of their having lived the greater part of their adult lives in America. One of our competitors includes Sylvia Plath in their anthology of British literature; Plath lived in England for only five of her thirty years, though, and her poetry is generally agreed to have more in common with the traditions of Lowell, Merwin and Sexton than with the currents of British poetry in the 1950s and '60s.

As a broad principle, we have been open to the inclusion of twentieth and twenty-first century work in English not only by writers from the British Isles but also by writers from British possessions overseas, and by writers from countries that were once British possessions and have remained a part of the British Commonwealth. In such cases we have often chosen selections that relate in one way or another to the tradition of British literature and the British colonial legacy. Of the Judith Wright poems included here, several relate to her coming to terms with the British colonial legacy in Australia; similarly, both the Margaret Atwood and the Alice Munro selections include work in which these Canadian authors attempt to recreate imaginatively the experience of British emigrants to Canada in the nineteenth century; the Chinua Achebe story in the anthology concerns the divide between British colonial culture and traditional Nigerian culture; and so on. For convenience we have also grouped most of the post-World War II non-British authors together, following the "Contexts: The End of Empire" section. (Other than that, the table of contents for the anthology is arranged chronologically according to the birthdate of each author.)

THE HISTORY OF LANGUAGE, AND OF PRINT CULTURE

Among the liveliest discussions we had at meetings of our General Editors were those concerning the issue of whether or not to bring spelling and punctuation into accord with present-day practice. We finally decided that, in the interests of making the anthology accessible to the introductory student, we should *in most cases* bring spelling and punctuation in line with present-day practice. An important exception has been made for works in which modernizing spelling and punctuation would alter the meaning or the aural and metrical qualities. In practice this means that works before the late sixteenth century tend to be presented either in their original form or in translation, whereas later texts tend to have spelling and punctuation modernized. But where spelling and punctuation choices in later texts are known (or believed on reliable authority) to represent conscious choice on the part of the author rather than simply the common practice of the time, we have in those cases, too, made an exception and retained the original spelling and punctuation. (Among these are texts by Edmund Spenser, by William Cowper, by William Blake, John Clare, and several other poets of the Romantic era, by George Bernard Shaw, and by contemporary figures such as Linton Kwesi Johnson.)

Beyond this, we all agreed that we should provide for readers a real sense of the development of the language and of print culture. To that end we have included in each volume examples of texts in their original form—in some cases through the use of pages shown in facsimile, in others by providing short passages in which spelling and punctuation have not been modernized. A list of these appears near the beginning of each volume of the anthology.

We have also included a section of the history of the language as part of the introduction to each volume. And throughout the anthology we include materials—visual as well as textual—relating to the history of print culture.

A Dynamic and Flexible Anthology

Almost all major book publishing projects nowadays are accompanied by an adjunct website, and most large-scale anthologies are accompanied by websites that provide additional background materials in electronic form. The website component of this anthology, on the other hand, is precisely that—a *component* of the anthology itself. The notion of a website of this sort grew organically out of the process of trying to winnow down the contents of the anthology to a manageable level—the point at which all the material to be included would fit within the covers of bound books that would not be overwhelmingly heavy. And we simply could not do it. After we had made a very substantial round of cuts we were still faced with a table of contents in which each volume was at least 200 or 300 pages longer than our agreed-upon maximum. Our solution was not to try to

cut anything more, but rather to select a range of material to be made available in a website component of the anthology. This material is in every way produced according to the same high standards of the material in the bound books; the editorial standards, the procedures for annotation, the author introductions, and the page design and layout—all are the same. The texts on the web, in short, are not "extra" materials; they are an integral part of the full anthology. In accordance with that principle, we have been careful to include a wide range of texts by lesser-known writers within the bound books, and a number of texts by canonical writers within the web component of the anthology.

The latter may be used in a variety of ways. Most obviously, readings from the web component are available to any purchaser of the book. Instructors who adopt *The Broadview Anthology of British Literature* as a course text are also granted permission to reproduce any web material for which Broadview holds copyright in a supplementary coursepack. An alternative for instructors who want to "create their own" anthology is to provide the publisher with a list of desired table of contents; Broadview will then make available to students through their university bookstore a custom-made coursepack with precisely those materials included. Other options are available too. Volumes of the anthology itself may of course be shrink-wrapped together at special prices in any desired combination. They may also (for a modest additional charge) be combined in a shrink-wrapped package with one or more of the over 200 volumes in the Broadview Editions series.

We anticipate that over the years the web-based component of the anthology will continue to grow—every year there will be a greater choice of web-based texts in the anthology. And every year too we anticipate additional web "extras" (discussed below). But we never foresee a day when the web will be the only option; we expect physical books always to remain central to Broadview's approach to publishing.

The Broadview List

One of the reasons we have been able to bring a project of this sort to fruition in such a relatively short time is that we have been able to draw on the resources of the full Broadview list: the many titles in the Broadview Editions series, and also the considerable range of other Broadview anthologies. As the contributors' pages and the permissions acknowledgments pages indicate, a number of Broadview authors have acted as contributing editors to this volume, providing material from other volumes that has been adapted to suit the needs of the present anthology; we gratefully acknowledge their contribution.

As it has turned out, the number of cases where we have been able to draw on the resources of the Broadview list in the full sense, using in these pages texts and annotations in very much the same form in which they appear elsewhere, has been relatively small; whether because of an issue such as the level of textual modernization or one of style of annotation, we have more often than not ended up deciding that the requirements of this anthology were such that we could not use material from another Broadview source as-is. But even in these cases we often owe a debt of gratitude to the many academics who have edited outstanding editions and anthologies for Broadview. For even where we have not drawn directly from them, we have often been inspired by them— inspired to think of a wider range of texts as possibilities than we might otherwise have done, inspired to think of contextual materials in places where we might otherwise not have looked, inspired by the freshness of approach that so many of these titles exemplify.

EDITORIAL PROCEDURES AND CONVENTIONS, APPARATUS

The in-house set of editorial guidelines for *The Broadview Anthology of British Literature* now runs to over 40 pages, covering everything from conventions for the spacing of marginal notes, to the use of small caps for the abbreviations CE and BCE, to the approach we have adopted to references in author headnotes to name changes. Perhaps the most important core principle in the introductions to the various volumes, in the headnotes for each author, in the introductions in "Contexts" sections, and in annotations throughout the anthology, is to endeavor to provide a sufficient amount of information to enable students to read and interpret

these texts, but without making evaluative judgements or imposing particular interpretations. In practice that is all a good deal more challenging than it sounds; it is often extremely difficult to describe why a particular author is considered to be important without using language that verges on the interpretive or the evaluative. But it is fine line that we have all agreed is worth trying to walk; we hope that readers will find that the anthology achieves an appropriate balance.

ANNOTATION: It is also often difficult to make judgments as to where it is appropriate to provide an explanatory annotation for a word or phrase. Our policy as been to annotate where we feel it likely that most first- or second-year students are likely to have difficulty understanding the denotative meaning. (We have made it a practice not to provide notes discussing connotative meanings.) But in practice the vocabularies and levels of verbal facility of first- and second-year students may vary enormously, both from institution to institution and within any given college or university class. On the whole, we provide somewhat more annotation than our competitors, and somewhat less interpretation. Again, we hope that readers will find that the anthology has struck a appropriate balance.

THE ETHICS AND POLITICS OF ANNOTATION: On one issue regarding annotation we have felt that principles are involved that go beyond the pedagogical. Most anthologies of British literature allow many words or phrases of a racist, sexist, anti-Semitic, or homophobic nature either to pass entirely without comment, or to be glossed with apologist comments that leave the impression that such comments were excusable in the past, and may even be unobjectionable in the present. Where derogatory comments about Jewish people and money-lending are concerned, for example, anthologies often leave the impression that money-lending was a pretty unsavory practice that Jewish people entered by choice; it has been all too rare to provide readers with any sense of the degree to which English society consistently discriminated against Jews, expelling them entirely for several centuries, requiring them to wear physical marks identifying their Jewish status, prohibiting them from entering most professions, and so on. *The Broadview*

Anthology endeavors in such cases, first of all, not to allow such words and phrases to pass without comment; and second, to gloss without glossing over.

DATES: We make it a practice to include the date when a work was first made public, whether publication in print or, in the case of dramatic works, made public through the first performance of the play. Where that date is known to differ substantially from the date of composition, a note to this effect is included in parentheses. With medieval works, where there is no equivalent to the "publication" of later eras, where texts often vary greatly from one manuscript copy to another, and where knowledge as to date of original composition is usually imprecise, the date that appears at the end of each work is an estimate of the date of the work's origin in the written form included in the anthology. Earlier oral or written versions are of course in some cases real possibilities.

TEXTS: Where translations appear in this anthology, a note at the bottom of the first page indicates what translation is being used. Similar notes also address overall textual issues where choice of copy text is particularly significant. Reliable editions of all works are listed in the bibliography for the anthology, which is included as part of the website component rather than in the bound books, to facilitate ready revision. (In addition to information as to reliable editions, the bibliography provides for each author and for each of the six periods a select lists of important or useful historical and critical works.) Copyright information for texts not in the public domain, however, is provided within the bound books in a section listing Permissions Acknowledgments.

INTRODUCTIONS: In addition to the introductory headnotes for each author included in the anthology, each "Contexts" section includes a substantial introduction, and each volume includes an introduction to the period as a whole. These introductions to the six volumes of the anthology endeavor to provide a sense not only of the broad picture of literary developments in the period, but also of the historical, social, and political background, and of the cultural climate. Readers should be cautioned that, while there is inevitably some overlap between information presented here and information presented in the author headnotes, an effort has been made to avoid such repetition as much as possible; the general introduction to each period should thus be read in conjunction with the author headnotes. The general introductions aim not only to provide an overview of ways in which texts and authors included in these pages may connect with one another, but also to give readers a sense of connection with a range of other writers and texts of the period.

READING POETRY: For much of the glossary and for the "Reading Poetry" section that appears as part of the appendices to each volume we have drawn on the superb material prepared by Herbert Rosengarten and Amanda Goldrick-Jones for *The Broadview Anthology of Poetry*; this section provides a concise but comprehensive introduction to the study of poetry. It includes discussions of diction, imagery, poetic figures, and various poetic forms, as well as offering an introduction to prosody.

MAPS: Also appearing within each of the bound books are maps especially prepared for this anthology, including, for each volume, a map of Britain showing towns and features of relevance during the pertinent period; a map showing the counties of Britain and of Ireland; maps both of the London area and of the inner city; and world maps indicating the locations of some of the significant places referenced in the anthology, and for later volumes showing the extent of Britain's overseas territories.

GLOSSARY: Some other anthologies of British literature include both glossaries of terms and essays introducing students to various political and religious categories in British history. Similar information is included in *The Broadview Anthology of British Literature*, but we have adopted a more integrated approach, including political and religious terms along with literary ones in a convenient general glossary. While we recognize that "googling" for information of this sort is often the student's first resort (and we recognize too the value of searching the web for the wealth of background reference information available there), we also recognize that information culled from the Internet is often far from reliable; it is our intent, through this glossary, through our introductions and headnotes, and through the wealth of accessible annotation in the anthology, to provide as part of the anthology a reliable core of information in the most convenient and accessible form possible.

OTHER MATERIALS: A chart of Monarchs and Prime Ministers is also provided within these pages. A range of other adjunct materials may be accessed through *The Broadview Anthology of British Literature* website. "Texts and Contexts" charts for each volume provide a convenient parallel reference guide to the dates of literary texts and historical developments. "Money in Britain" provides a thumbnail sketch of the world of pounds, shillings, and pence, together with a handy guide to estimating the current equivalents of monetary values from earlier eras. And the website offers, too, a variety of aids for the student and the instructor. An up-to-date list of these appears on the site.

ACKNOWLEDGMENTS

The names of those on the Editorial Board that shaped this anthology appear on the title page, and those of the many who contributed directly to the writing, editing, and production of the project on the following two pages. Special acknowledgment should go to Jennifer McCue, who as Editorial Coordinator has been instrumental in tying together all the vast threads of this project and in making it a reality; to Laura Cardiff and Jude Polsky, who have carried larger loads than any others in drafting introductory materials and annotations, and who have done so with great skill and unfailing grace; to Kathryn Brownsey, who has been responsible for design and typesetting, and has continued to do a superb job and to maintain her good spirits even when faced with near-impossible demands; to Colleen Franklin, for the range of her scholarship as well as for her keen eye as our primary copy editor for the entire project; to Emily Cargan, Jennifer Elsayed and Amy Nimegeer who have together done superb work on the vast job of clearing permissions for the anthology; and to Michelle Lobkowicz and Anna Del Col, who have ably and enthusiastically taken the lead with marketing matters.

The academic members of the Advisory Editorial Board and all of us in-house at Broadview owe an enormous debt of gratitude to the hundreds of academics who have offered assistance at various stages of this project. In particular we would like to express our appreciation and our thanks to the following:

Rachel Ablow, University of Rochester
Bryan Alexander, Middlebury College
Sharon Alker, Whitman College
James Allard, Brock University
Laurel Amtower, San Diego State University
Rob Anderson, Oakland University
Christopher Armitage, University of North Carolina, Chapel Hill
Clinton Atchley, Henderson State University
John Baird, University of Toronto
William Baker, Northern Illinois University
Karen Bamford, Mount Allison University
John Batchelor, University of Newcastle
Lynn Batten, University of California, Los Angeles
Alexandra Bennett, Northern Illinois University
John Beynon, California State University, Fresno
Robert E. Bjork, Arizona State University
Rita Bode, Trent University
Robert Boenig, Texas A & M University
Rick Bowers, University of Alberta
David Brewer, Ohio State University

William Brewer, Appalachian State University
Susan Brown, University of Guelph
Sylvia Brown, University of Alberta
Sheila Burgar, University of Victoria
Catherine Burroughs, Wells College
Rebecca Bushnell, University of Pennsylvania
Elizabeth Campbell, Oregon State University
Cynthia Caywood, University of San Diego
Jane Chance, Rice University
Ranita Chatterjee, California State University, Northridge
Nancy Cirillo, University of Illinois, Chicago
Eric Clarke, University of Pittsburgh
Jeanne Clegg, University of Aquila, Italy
Thomas J. Collins, University of Western Ontario
Kevin Cope, Louisiana State University
David Cowart, University of South Carolina
Catherine Craft-Fairchild, University of St. Thomas
Carol Davison, University of Windsor
Alex Dick, University of British Columbia
Len Diepeveen, Dalhousie University

Mary Dockray-Miller, Lesley College
Frank Donoghue, Ohio State University
Chris Downs, Saint James School
Julie Early, University of Alabama, Huntsville
Siân Echard, University of British Columbia
Garrett Epp, University of Alberta
Daniel Fischlin, University of Guelph
Verlyn Flieger, University of Maryland
Robert Forman, St. John's University
Roberta Frank, Yale University
Jeff Franklin, University of Colorado, Denver
Maria Frawley, George Washington University
Mark Fulk, Buffalo State College
Andrew Galloway, Cornell University
Michael Gamer, University of Pennsylvania
Barbara Gates, University of Delaware
Daniel Gonzalez, University of New Orleans
Jan Gorak, University of Denver
Chris Gordon-Craig, University of Alberta
Ann-Barbara Graff, Georgia Tech University
Michael Griffin, formerly of Southern Illinois
    University
Elisabeth Gruner, University of Richmond
Stephen Guy-Bray, University of British Columbia
Ruth Haber, Worcester State College
Margaret Hadley, University of Calgary
Robert Hampson, Royal Holloway University of
    London
Michael Hanly, Washington State University
Lila Harper, Central Washington State University
Joseph Harris, Harvard University
Anthony Harrison, North Carolina State University
Douglas Hayes, Winona State University
Jennifer Hellwarth, Allegheny University
Peter Herman, San Diego State University
Kathy Hickock, Iowa State University
John Hill, US Naval Academy
Thomas Hill, Cornell University
Elizabeth Hodgson, University of British Columbia
Joseph Hornsby, University of Alabama
Scott Howard, University of Denver
Tara Hyland-Russell, St. Mary's College
Catherine Innes-Parker, University of Prince Edward
    Island
Jacqueline Jenkins, University of Calgary

John Johansen, University of Alberta
Richard Juang, Susquehanna University
Michael Keefer, University of Guelph
Sarah Keefer, Trent University
Jon Kertzer, University of Calgary
Helen Killoran, Ohio University
Gordon Kipling, University of California, Los Angeles
Anne Klinck, University of New Brunswick
Elizabeth Kraft, University of Georgia
Mary Kramer, University of Massachusetts, Lowell
Linda Leeds, Bellevue Community College
Mary Elizabeth Leighton, University of Victoria
William Liston, Ball State University
Sharon Locy, Loyola Marymount University
Peter Mallios, University of Maryland
Arnold Markley, Penn State University
Pamela McCallum, University of Calgary
Kristen McDermott, Central Michigan University
John McGowan, University of North Carolina
Thomas McLean, University of Otago, New Zealand
Rod Michell, Thompson Rivers University
Kitty Millett, San Francisco State University
Richard Moll, University of Western Ontario
Monique Morgan, McGill University
Lucy Morrison, Salisbury University
Byron Nelson, West Virginia University
Carolyn Nelson, West Virginia University
Claudia Nelson, Southwest Texas State University
Holly Faith Nelson, Trinity Western University
John Niles, University of Wisconsin, Madison
Michael North, University of California, Los Angeles
Mary Anne Nunn, Central Connecticut State University
David Oakleaf, University of Calgary
Tamara O'Callaghan, Northern Kentucky University
Karen Odden, Assistant Editor for *Victorian Literature
    and Culture* (formerly of University of Wisconsin,
    Milwaukee)
Erika Olbricht, Pepperdine University
Patrick O'Malley, Georgetown University
Patricia O'Neill, Hamilton College
Delilah Orr, Fort Lewis College
Cynthia Patton, Emporia State University
Russell Perkin, St. Mary's University
Marjorie G. Perloff, Stanford University
Summer Pervez, University of Ottawa

John Peters, University of North Texas
Alexander Pettit, University of North Texas
Jennifer Phegley, The University of Missouri,
    Kansas City
John Pollock, San Jose State University
Mary Poovey, New York University
Gautam Premnath, University of Massachusetts, Boston
Regina Psaki, University of Oregon
Katherine Quinsey, University of Windsor
Geoff Rector, University of Ottawa
Margaret Reeves, Atkinson College, York University
Cedric Reverand, University of Wyoming
Gerry Richman, Suffolk University
David Robinson, University of Arizona
Laura Rotunno, Pennsylvania State University, Altoona
Nicholas Ruddick, University of Regina
Jason Rudy, University of Maryland
Donelle Ruwe, Northern Arizona University
Michelle Sauer, Minot State University
SueAnn Schatz, Lock Haven University of Pennsylvania
Dan Schierenbeck, Central Missouri State University
Norbert Schürer, California State University,
    Long Beach
David Seed, University of Liverpool
Carol Senf, Georgia Tech University
Judith Slagle, East Tennessee State University
Sharon Smulders, Mount Royal College
Malinda Snow, Georgia State University
Goran Stanivukovic, St. Mary's University
Richard Stein, University of Oregon
Eric Sterling, Auburn University Montgomery
James Stokes, University of Wisconsin, Stevens Point
Mary-Ann Stouck, Simon Fraser University

Nathaniel Strout, Hamilton College
Lisa Surridge, University of Victoria
Beth Sutton-Ramspeck, Ohio State University
Nanora Sweet, University of Missouri, St. Louis
Dana Symons, Simon Fraser University
Andrew Taylor, University of Ottawa
Elizabeth Teare, University of Dayton
Doug Thorpe, University of Saskatchewan
Jane Toswell, University of Western Ontario
Herbert Tucker, University of Virginia
John Tucker, University of Victoria
Mark Turner, King's College, University of London
Eleanor Ty, Wilfrid Laurier University
Deborah Tyler-Bennett, Loughborough University
Kirsten Uszkalo, University of Alberta
Lisa Vargo, University of Saskatchewan
Gina Luria Walker, New School, New York City
Kim Walker, Victoria University of Wellington
Miriam Wallace, New College of Florida
Hayden Ward, West Virginia State University
Ruth Wehlau, Queen's University
Lynn Wells, University of Regina
Chris Willis, Birkbeck University of London
Lisa Wilson, SUNY College at Potsdam
Anne Windholz, Augustana College
Susan Wolfson, Princeton University
Kenneth Womack, Pennsylvania State University
Carolyn Woodward, University of New Mexico
Julia Wright, Wilfrid Laurier University
Julian Yates, University of Delaware
Arlene Young, University of Manitoba
Lisa Zeitz, University of Western Ontario

John Everett Millais, *Ophelia* (1851 52). The drowning of Ophelia (from Shakespeare's *Hamlet*) was a frequent subject in Victorian painting; the best known representation is that of Millais. As the scene is described in Act 4, Scene 7 of the play, the mentally-ill Ophelia comes to a stream "with fantastic garlands" of flowers. Distracted, she falls into the "weeping brook." For a while before she drowns "her clothes spread wide" hold her up.

Henry Wallis, *Chatterton* (1856). The suicide of Thomas Chatterton (1752–70), of arsenic poisoning after years of living close to starvation as a struggling poet, captured the Victorian imagination even more strongly than it had the Romantic one. Wallis's painting was widely praised when exhibited in 1856 at the Royal Academy; John Ruskin described it in his notes on the exhibit as "faultless and wonderful."

Thomas Jones Barker, *The Secret of England's Greatness* (detail), c. 1863. Barker's painting depicts the Queen presenting a Bible. The recipient and the specific occasion remain unidentified; in the background are Prince Alberta; Elizabeth, Duchess of Wellington (who served as Mistress of the Robes to the Queen); Lord Palmerston (then serving as Prime Minister); and Lord John Russell (then serving as Foreign Secretary). An engraving of the painting was published under the fuller title, *The Bible: the Secret of England's Greatness.*

Franz Xavier Winterhalter, *The Royal Family in 1846* (detail), 1846.

George Clausen, *The Stone Pickers*, 1887.

Ford Madox Brown, *Work*, c. 1852–c. 1865. This famous painting, which took over twelve years to complete, brings together Victorians from an extraordinary range of backgrounds. The central group of excavators was the painting's starting point—the inspiration coming from the artist observing work on the construction of the London sewers. Less well-off members of society include the flower seller to the left and the motherless children in the foreground, cared for by an older sibling. To the right are two "brain-workers" admired by the artist, Rev. F.D. Maurice (founder of the Working Man's College, where Brown was an art instructor) and Thomas Carlyle. In the background members of the gentry on horseback observe the scene.

William Holman Hunt, *The Awakening Conscience*, 1853–54. This canvas presents an elaborately coded story. In a letter to *The Times* of London, John Ruskin (signing himself as "The Author of *Modern Painters*") described the reaction of viewers—and elucidated the painting's intended significance: "… assuredly it is not understood. People gaze at it in a blank wonder, and leave it hopelessly; so that, although it is almost an insult to the painter to explain his thoughts in this instance, I cannot persuade myself to leave it thus misunderstood. The poor girl has been singing with her seducer; some chance words of the song "Oft in the stilly night" have struck upon the numbed places of her heart; she has started up in agony; he, not seeing her face, goes on singing, striking the keys carelessly with his gloved hand." As Ruskin discerned, the woman is evidently the mistress rather than the wife of the man; she wears a ring on every finger of her left hand except the fourth. The piece that has been played, "Oft in the stilly night," is a song in which a woman looks back to the innocence of her childhood. The doubling of the female figure through the use of the mirror suggests the possibility of a brighter future if she follows her awakened conscience and gives up the life of a "kept woman."

G.W. Joy, *General Gordon's Last Stand*, c. 1893. Gordon, who had held an administrative post in the Sudan in the 1870s (and played an important role during that period in ending the slave trade in the area) was sent again to the Sudan in 1884 on a mission to rescue garrisons of British troops that had been cut off after a rebellion by Mohammed Ahmad (known to the British as "the Mahdi"). Gordon's forces were besieged in Khartoum for ten months and finally overwhelmed, and he was killed during the battle (though almost certainly in the streets of the city, not as he is shown in Joy's iconic painting of the imagined scene). The incident became a *cause célèbre* in Britain, and there were many calls to avenge Gordon's death, but it was not until fourteen years later that the British under General Kitchener re-established British control of the Sudan.

Trade Emblem, Amalgamated Society of Engineers, Machinists, Millwrights, Smiths, and Pattern Makers, c. 1860.

Alfred Concanen, *Modern Advertising: A Railway Station in 1874*, 1874. This colored lithograph appeared as a fold-out frontispiece in the book *A History of Advertising from the Earliest Times*.

John O'Connor, *From Pentonville Road Looking West*, 1884. In the background is St. Pancras, one of the greatest of Victorian railway stations.

Advertisement, 1890s, "Cook's Tours in Scotland." Featured at lower left is the Firth of Forth Bridge (also known as the Forth Rail Bridge). The bridge, built in the wake of the collapse of the Firth of Tay Bridge, in which 75 lives had been lost, pioneered new techniques of cantilever construction; on its completion in 1890 it was by far the longest bridge in the world.

Benjamin Duterrau, *The Conciliation*, 1840. The painting shows a Methodist lay preacher instructing native Tasmanians.

THE OLD FLAG.
THE OLD POLICY,
THE OLD LEADER.

Canadian election poster, 1891. The "Old Leader" was Sir John A. Macdonald, Canadian Prime Minister from 1867 to 1873 and again from 1878 to 1891. "The Old Policy" was Macdonald's National Policy, under the terms of which industries in the Dominion were protected by a tariff on imports from the United States, but "imperial preference" exempted goods from Britain and her possessions from any tariff.

The Victorian Era

The word "Victorian" conjures up a series of images that both accurately describe and misrepresent the literature and culture of nineteenth-century Britain. Stiff collars and stiff upper lips, draped table legs, exceedingly long novels and gritty urban squalor have become the iconic images of Victorian Britain. But these images reveal only one dimension of what is a much more complex picture. While it is certainly the case that Victorians tended to place a high value on such qualities as honor, duty, moral seriousness and sexual propriety, it is a mistake to assume that most were humorless or repressed. And while many of the best known Victorian novels run to many hundreds of pages, we need to remember that Victorian audiences read them in weekly or monthly installments, or in shorter volumes. Although brutal factory conditions, pitiful wages, and crowded cities impoverished many millions of people, the Victorian period also saw the passage of progressive labor laws, unprecedented wealth creation for some, and the first public sewage systems in Britain.

It is fair to say that there was never a single "Victorian mindset" or "Victorian value system" but a range of them, and that they shifted throughout the century. Nor is there a consensus about when the Victorian era began and ended. Some point to the passage of the Reform Bill of 1832 as the dawn of a new era, or to the abolition of slavery in the British Empire, in 1833. Others argue for the unity of a longer period, beginning perhaps with the end of the Napoleonic Wars in 1815, perhaps even earlier (some see the seeds of "Victorianism" being planted as early as the late eighteenth century, with the re-emergence of Evangelicalism), and ending with the outbreak of World War I in 1914. The obvious choice is to date the period starting with Victoria's ascension to the throne in 1837 to her death in 1901, but there is good reason not to identify the period solely on the basis of her reign.

Franz Xavier Winterhalter, *Queen Victoria*, 1842.

Photographer unknown, *Her Majesty the Queen*, 21 June 1887.

Photographer unknown, *Queen Victoria*, c. 1897.
A picture of Albert is in the background.

Although a great deal of overlap can be found between the Romantic and Victorian periods, most agree that the 1830s was a pivotal decade, marked by the transition of the monarchy from William IV to Victoria and by the spread of a spirit of political and social reform that would characterize the next several decades. During the 1850s and 60s, Britain emerged from a depressed economy and experienced a level of political and social stability that made these decades the most prosperous of the century; the mid-Victorian period is now often regarded as a kind of high-water mark for Victorian culture. The 1870s and 1880s saw some decline in the strength of the economy and in Britain's imperial dominance abroad, despite its continued acquisition of colonial possessions. These decades were marked by the glimmerings of another wave of social change. The fin-de-siècle spirit of the 1890s saw many challenges to the values and conventions of the preceding decades in literature, politics, and everyday life.

A GROWING POWER

During Victoria's reign, Britain was the richest nation and the most powerful empire on the globe, with unchallenged military supremacy until the latter decades of the century and an imperial reach that covered one quarter of the earth's surface by 1897. As the world's first industrialized country, Britain experienced both the benefits and the horrors of enormous growth throughout the nineteenth century. The census of 1801 put the population of the country at eleven million people. At the end of the century that number had increased by almost three hundred percent to thirty-seven million. Just as striking was the movement of this population, from 75 percent rural distribution in the early decades to nearly the same percentage residing in urban districts by the end of the century. Northern industrial cities grew particularly fast: Manchester, a town of no more than 15,000 people in 1750, had grown to 75,000 by 1800, and to 125,000 by 1820; by 1850 its population was over 300,000. Between 1815 and 1914 more than 20 million people emigrated from Britain to other parts of the world, over half of them to the United States, but millions, too, to Australia and to Canada. (The writings of Susanna Moodie, excerpted in this volume, provide a vivid sense of the immigrant

Fleet Street, London, c. 1890.

Construction of the sewer beneath Fleet Street, London, early 1860s. By 1858 the stench of sewage from the Thames had become so overwhelming that the Houses of Parliament at Westminster found it impossible to meet; construction of a city-wide underground system of sewers, under the direction of Joseph Bazalgette, began the following year.

Building the Holborn Viaduct across the Fleet valley (*Illustrated Times*, 18 September 1869). The viaduct, carrying both road and rail traffic, was a vast project carried out by the Corporation of the City of London between 1863 and 1869.

experience in what was then the British colony of Upper Canada.)

The shift from an agrarian to an industrial wage economy meant an increase in income for many people, creating a sector of the population that was neither rich nor poor and was frequently coming to be termed "middle class." A spirit of entrepreneurship and market thinking dominated by upwardly mobile males was replacing an entrenched system of aristocratic patronage and paternalism in the world of business and trade. The Reform Bill of 1832 granted political representation in Parliament to certain sectors of the middle-class male population for the first time (although even with its passage, only one in six adult males could vote, and the suffrage was still linked to property ownership). Rail travel, the advent of the telegraph, daily newspapers, and the manufacture and import of goods via steamship from all over the globe collapsed time and space, and flooded the homes of the affluent with new luxuries and conveniences. The Great Exhibition of 1851, the first world's fair, showcased Britain's industrial dominance with exhibits of new consumer goods and remarkable technologies. The event symbolized Britain's reputation as the "workshop of the world." For many the overall mood was positive, and Thomas Macaulay's confident assertions on the nation's progress in his bestselling *History of England* rang true for much of his audience.

Alfred Morgan, *An Omnibus Ride to Piccadilly Circus—Mr. Gladstone Travelling with Ordinary Passengers*, 1885. The previous year Prime Minister William Gladstone's government had extended the franchise to working class males, through the Reform Bill of 1884.

GRINDING MILLS, GRINDING POVERTY

The paradox of the economic life of the time was summed up by Thomas Carlyle in 1843: "England is full of wealth," he wrote, "of multifarious produce, supply for human want in every kind; yet England is dying of inanition." For millions of people, low wages, unemployment, and fluctuations in trade created widespread misery in crowded industrial cities such as Manchester and Birmingham. According to one estimate, 70 percent of the population at mid-century was considered poor. The new law divided and categorized the poor as either "deserving" (the elderly and the physically infirm) or "undeserving" (the able-bodied but unemployed). The poor were now eligible to receive public assistance only in the notorious workhouses, also known as the "Poor Law Bastilles" since they ended up punishing and stigmatizing the poor rather than relieving them. In addition, inadequate housing and slum conditions led to frequent outbreaks of illness and disease. Four cholera epidemics between 1831 and 1866 killed more than 140,000 people, inaugurating Britain's first wide-scale public health movement. Scores of statistical investigations, surveys, and government reports known as "Blue Books" on the condition of inner-city neighbourhoods culminated in the Public Health Acts of 1848 and the 1870s. Factories and mines producing iron, cotton, and coal were unregulated, employing men, women, and children in conditions that were often dirty and dangerous. A series of Factory Acts between 1802 and 1847 attempted to force employers to limit work hours (working fourteen hours a day was not uncommon) and prohibit the employment of children under the age of nine in certain industries.

In her poem, "The Cry of the Children," Elizabeth Barrett Browning drew attention to the problem of child labor, helping to create humanitarian awareness on the part of middle-class readers by asking "How long, O cruel nation, / Will you stand to move the world, on a child's heart." Thomas Hood's "The Song of the Shirt" focused on the plight of the genteel but impoverished female needleworker who toils alone in grim conditions for meager wages. Cast in the elevated and stylized "voices" of their victimized speakers, such poems were both wildly popular and highly sentimental, qualities that have until recently served to exclude them from serious study by scholars of English literature. Yet these poems did as much or more than government reports and statistical surveys to shed light on major social issues. So too did Carlyle's *Past and Present*, which called England to responsibility for the many starving workers in the land of "plenty":

We have more riches than any Nation ever had before: we have less good of them than any Nation had before. ... We have forgotten everywhere that

Cash-payment is not the sole relation of human beings; we think, nothing doubting, that it absolves and liquidates all other engagements.

Such voices spoke up in support of the destitute and the working classes; increasingly, over the course of the century, the voices of working class people themselves were also heard. The 1828 publication of Robert Blincoe's *Memoir* of his appalling early life in the mills had a lasting impact; in addition to a direct effect on its readers, Blincoe's memoir provided much of the raw material for Frances Trollope's novel *Michael Armstrong: Factory Boy* (1840), and may also have inspired Dickens's *Oliver Twist*. Blincoe's memoir was followed by a number of other autobiographical narratives of working-class hardship (that of William Dodd notable among them). Ellen Johnson published a more wide-ranging memoir, *Autobiography of a Factory Girl* (1867), together with her poems and songs. Another prominent working class poetic voice was that of Ebenezer Elliott, the "Corn-Law Rhymer" from Yorkshire who became an active force first in the Chartist movement and then in the struggle to repeal the Corn Laws (discussed below). In his *Corn-Law Rhymes* (1831) and in subsequent work Elliott attacked

> The deadly will that takes
> What labour ought to keep;
> It is the deadly power that makes
> Bread dear and labour cheap.

How best to respond to the force of this "deadly power"? If some emphasized the need to continually press for political reform, others appealed emotionally for hearts to change—and still others formulated new philosophical approaches to the underlying moral and socio-economic questions. Perhaps the most important of these was Utilitarianism, a broad-reaching philosophy that had first been developed in the late eighteenth century (primarily by Jeremy Bentham), and that was expounded in a more careful, subtle, and thoroughgoing fashion by John Stuart Mill in the nineteenth. Utilitarian thought began to shape governmental policy, including the New Poor Law, in the middle decades of the nineteenth century—and continues to be a shaping force in the social policy of most developed nations

Thomas Iron Works, London, 1867.

today. In its crude form Utilitarianism holds (in the words of Bentham's 1776 "A Fragment on Government") that "it is the greatest happiness of the greatest number that is the measure of right and wrong." In other words, the central guiding principle of social morality should be the pursuit of the what is good for all members of society, with no one person or group's interests given special weight. But how does one calculate "the greatest happiness of the greatest number"? Can social, legal, economic and political problems be resolved by a "moral arithmetic" that evaluates human pain and pleasure according to entirely rationalist principles? According to some crude versions of utilitarian philosophy (though certainly not that of Mill), the answer is yes; imagination, feeling, and individual desire are obsolete impediments to the operation of the "laws" of social improvement, which may be derived from empirical observation and calculation.

Hatting mill, Manchester, 1890s.

Writers such as Elizabeth Barrett Browning, Dickens, Carlyle, and John Ruskin were intensely critical of Utilitarianism, taking its crudest forms as representative and regarding it as a morally and spiritually bankrupt response to the human condition. Dickens, in particular, caricatured utilitarian thinking with telling directness in his portrayal of Thomas Gradgrind in *Hard Times*. (It may perhaps be wondered, however, if the intensity of the opposition of such writers to Utilitarianism also related in part to a fear of the consequences if utilitarian notions were extended to their logical conclusion; certainly to Mill "the greatest number" included not only white people in poverty in England but also brown people and black people in poverty the world over, whereas Dickens, Carlyle and Ruskin, for all their sympathy for the British poor, looked at best with condescension and at worst with outright loathing on people of other races.) In any case, as the works of writers such as Dickens, Barrett Browning, and Elizabeth Gaskell amply demonstrated, opposition to the cruelties of poverty could be expressed as plausibly and at least as powerfully by means of emotional and aesthetic appeals through literature as it could by means of the philosophical arguments of the Utilitarians.

Corn Laws, Potato Famine

As the powerful and privileged attempted to confront the range of social crises facing a newly industrialized nation, economic depression, unemployment, political instability in Europe and a series of crop failures in the 1840s—a decade often dubbed the "Hungry Forties"—caused a disproportionate level of suffering for the poor. Artificial shortages of grain in the country inflated the price of bread beyond the reach of the working class, causing periodic bread riots and a discontented work force. These shortages were in part the result of the Corn Laws, which imposed heavy tariffs on imports of grain, and were intended to protect British agricultural interests and limit dependence on foreign supplies of cereal grains. The Corn Laws were repealed in 1846 under the pressure of the Anti-Corn-Law League, an alliance of free trade advocates and liberal, laissez-faire[1] trade reformers.

In the wake of the repeal of the Corn Laws, three successive crop failures in Ireland led to one of the worst humanitarian disasters of the century, the Irish potato

---

[1] The phrase "laissez-faire" (French, literally "allow to do") came to be used in the late eighteenth century as a shorthand for the belief that government is best advised to intervene as little as possible in the workings of the economy.

famine of 1845–47. Prime Minister Robert Peel's government attempted to alleviate the situation by importing emergency shipments of grain from the United States in 1845, but when Peel's government was replaced by Lord John Russell's Whig administration in 1846, Russell in effect put a stop to emergency aid; the laissez-faire interests of Russell and his supporters led to the transfer of responsibility for famine relief to the inadequate jurisdiction of the Irish Poor Law. By 1847 somewhere between 850,000 and 1,500,000 Irish—from ten to over fifteen per cent of the population—had died of starvation. English government policy toward Ireland, its nearest colonial possession, was in this instance one of neglect amounting to extraordinary cruelty.

Inevitably, hostility towards the English, and with it Irish nationalist sentiment, was greatly intensified by the potato famine. The seeds of the Irish independence movement had been effectively sown—and sown not only in Ireland but also in the United States, where hundreds of thousands of Irish emigrated during this period. As they prospered in America they provided more and more support for the Fenian movement that sprang up in the 1850s in support of Irish independence (and that launched attacks in the 1860s and 1870s not only in England but also against British possessions in New Brunswick, Upper Canada, and Manitoba), and for subsequent political groups with like aims. But the road to Irish independence was an extraordinarily rocky one: the Irish won the right to be represented in the British House of Commons, but their greatest Parliamentary spokesman, Charles Parnell, after surviving dozens of scurrilous attempts to discredit him, was finally brought down when his affair with a divorced woman became a public scandal; British Prime Minister William Gladstone became a convert to the cause of Home Rule for the Irish and passed a bill authorizing it through the House of Commons in 1886, only to have the measure killed in the House of Lords; a similar bill in 1893 suffered the same fate; another bill to enact Home Rule was put aside with the outbreak of the First World War in 1914; and in the end, independence was only achieved after the violent struggles of the 1916 Easter Uprising and the War of Independence of 1919–22. Even then, the British retained possession of a substantial area in northern Ireland.

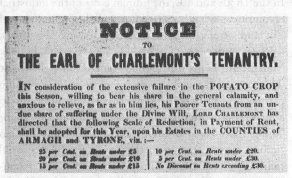

Notice of a rent abatement by an Irish landlord, 1846.

Evicted family, Glenbeigh, Ireland, 1888. In the 1880s an economic depression coincided with the election of a substantial number of Irish Home Rule Members of Parliament (under Charles Parnell's leadership), and with a campaign by the Land League to resist the practice of evicting impoverished tenant farmers unable to pay their rent.

"The Two Nations"

In the 1830s and 40s, the human costs of the industrial revolution—what became known as the "Condition of England" question—were scrutinized by legislators, workers, and writers. Carlyle, Dickens, Gaskell, Harriet Martineau, Benjamin Disraeli and Henry Mayhew documented the daily existence of poor and working people, and criticized the laws that were intended to address their suffering. The "social problem novel" or "industrial novel," an important subgenre of Victorian fiction, drew attention to class conflict and the social ramifications of laissez-faire economic policies. Examples include Charles Kingsley's *Alton Locke*, Charles Dickens's *Hard Times*, and Elizabeth Gaskell's *Mary Barton* and *North and South*. In his 1845 novel, *Sybil* future Prime Minister Benjamin Disraeli coined the phrase "the Two Nations" to describe the disparity in Britain between rich and poor. Novelists felt that their work could provoke social reform by exposing their middle-class audiences to the plight of the working classes, who were often portrayed as either vulnerable and victimized by forces beyond their control, or as a violent, angry "mass"; intervention by those of goodwill from other social classes is often implicitly recommended in such fiction as a way of ameliorating the situation. The middle-class narrator of Gaskell's 1848 novel *Mary Barton*, for example, adopts the role of mediator between Manchester's workers and their industrial "masters" in an attempt to foster understanding and prevent political insurrection.

Non-fiction writing such as Henry Mayhew's may have been as important as that of any novelist in nurturing the seeds of social change. Mayhew's interviews with working people and street folk for the *Morning Chronicle* newspaper opened a window for its readers onto the daily existence of an often voiceless underclass. They contained no overt political commentary or reform agenda, however. Friedrich Engels, by contrast, in his chronicle of urban squalor *The Condition of the Working Class in England in 1844*, not only described the extraordinary scale of the human suffering he witnessed, but also placed the blame squarely on the shoulders of a class system created by industrial capitalism: "Power

Jabez Hughes, *Benjamin Disraeli*, c. 1877. Disraeli, who led the Conservative Party from 1868 to 1880 (serving as Prime Minister briefly in 1868 and then again from 1874 to 1880), was seen as something of an exotic within the English establishment. His parents were Jewish, but he was baptized as an infant and remained a practicing Anglican throughout his life. Disraeli's prolific literary career, which began with the publication of his first novel, *Vivian Grey*, in 1826, made him a well-known man of letters. A fashionable figure, Disraeli was derided by his strait-laced rival, Liberal leader William Gladstone, as "Asiatic"—a word often used in Victorian times as a synonym for "indulgent and irresponsible." But Disraeli remained a popular figure with much of the general population as well as with much of the establishment—and with the Queen.

lies in the hands of those who own, directly or indirectly, foodstuffs and the means of production. The poor, having no capital, inevitably bear the consequences of defeat in the struggle." (Engels's treatise, first published in Germany in 1845, was not translated into English until 1892.)

It was not only middle-class writers and observers who were bringing attention to the great divide between Britain's rich and poor. Chartism, a movement that initiated a series of political campaigns in the 1830s and 40s, was a concrete expression of the desire of working-class people to resist economic and social disparity and press for political reform. The People's Charter of 1838, from which the movement took its name, petitioned the government to adopt a range of key reforms, including annual elections, universal male suffrage, the abolition of property qualifications for Members of Parliament, and the secret ballot. The mouthpiece of the Chartist movement was the *Northern Star* newspaper, one of

The Matchgirl Strike Committee, 1888. A threatened strike by Bryant and May Match Company employees —most of them girls of no more than 15, earning starvation wages and exposed to hazardous phosphorous fumes—became a *cause célèbre* in 1888, and forced the company to change its practices. The action was led by Annie Besant (who had initially become famous during her 1877 trial for obscenity —the charge being based on the distribution of her pamphlet offering practical advice on contraception).

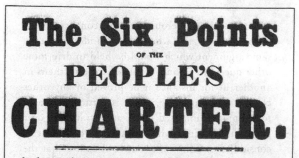

The Six Points
OF THE
PEOPLE'S
CHARTER.

1. A VOTE for every man twenty-one years of age, of sound mind, and not undergoing punishment for crime.

2. THE BALLOT.—To protect the elector in the exercise of his vote.

3. NO PROPERTY QUALIFICATION for Members of Parliament —thus enabling the constituencies to return the man of their choice, be he rich or poor.

4. PAYMENT OF MEMBERS, thus enabling an honest tradesman, working man, or other person, to serve a constituency, when taken from his business to attend to the interests of the country.

5. EQUAL CONSTITUENCIES, securing the same amount of representation for the same number of electors, instead of allowing small constituencies to swamp the votes of large ones.

6. ANNUAL PARLIAMENTS, thus presenting the most effectual check to bribery and intimidation, since though a constituency might be bought once in seven years (even with the ballot), no purse could buy a constituency (under a system of universal suffrage) in each ensuing twelvemonth; and since members, when elected for a year only, would not be able to defy and betray their constituents as now.

Chartist poster, 1838.

many working-class periodicals that flourished in the early decades of the nineteenth century. The Chartist petitions were signed by up to five million people and presented to Parliament by a coalition of workers in 1839, 1842, and 1848, but were rejected each time. A number of middle-class writers sympathetic to the claims of the working classes were nevertheless suspicious of the Chartist movement, particularly in light of the political revolutions taking place in continental Europe in the late 1840s. In his longing for the imagined social order of a feudal past, Carlyle denounced the "mad Chartisms" of the "anarchic multitude," comparing them to the events of the French Revolution and the Reign of Terror. With the defeat of the third petition,

Chartism collapsed, but it had helped instigate a new level of class consciousness among ordinary people, and is now considered to be the first independent working-class movement in Britain.

In the 1880s and 90s various socialist movements emerged, partly on the strength of Karl Marx's theories of capital, which he formulated under the dome of the British Library after moving to London in 1849. The Fabian Society was one of the most influential socialist organizations. Its membership was mainly drawn from the middle class, and included George Bernard Shaw, Sidney Webb and Beatrice Potter Webb, Edith Nesbit, and Annie Besant. The Fabians' tactics were reforming rather than revolutionary; they advocated public ownership of utilities, affordable housing, improved wages, and greater access to higher education for all. Trade unions and labor movements grew gradually in scope and strength throughout the century, with the Trade Union Act of 1871 granting legal status to unions for the first time. Newly mobilized workers in the 1880s organized to mount a series of strikes with varying degrees of success. Two of the most highly publicized of these were the matchgirls' strike in 1888 and the London dock workers' strike of 1889. Union membership doubled in these years, partly because of the success of these labor actions.

THE POLITICS OF GENDER

Gender consciousness was also central to Victorian England's political scene. At the beginning of the Victorian period, middle-class women were shut out of most remunerative employments and institutions of higher education, could not vote, and had few legal rights. By the end of the century the situation did not look radically different (universal female suffrage, for example, was not achieved in Britain until 1928), but several key developments heralded the changes to come in the twentieth century. The first major challenges by Victorian "strong-minded women" to patriarchal control were in the area of marriage law. The common law doctrine of coverture ensured that a woman's legal identity was subsumed in that of her husband upon marriage. In effect, the law of coverture regarded the husband and wife as "one person": the husband. This

meant that upon marriage a husband had full control of his wife's personal property and any earnings she acquired during the marriage; he had absolute authority over their home and children; and he could legally use physical force to discipline the members of his family. If he deserted his wife, she could not sue for divorce and had no custody rights to their children. No viable legal mechanism was available to an average woman to contest her husband's decisions, since husband and wife were "one body" under the law. The essayist Frances Power Cobbe was among the most effective in pointing out the illogic of such arrangements, as well as the terrible toll they exacted. In contemplating, for example, the situation of "the poor woman whose husband has robbed her earnings, who leaves her and her children to starve, and then goes unpunished because the law can only recognize the relation of husband and wife as ... one before the law," Cobbe observed in her provocative 1868 essay "Criminals, Idiots, Women, and Minors" that

> It is one of the numerous anomalies connected with women's affairs, that when they are under debate the same argument which would be held to determine other questions in one way is felt to settle theirs in another. If for instance it be proved of any other class of the community, that it is particularly liable to be injured, imposed upon, and tyrannized over (e.g., the children who work in factories), it is considered to follow as a matter of course that the law must step in for its protection. But it is the alleged *helplessness* of married women which, it is said, makes it indispensable to give all the support of the law, *not* to them, but to the stronger persons with whom they are unequally yoked.

Under pressure from organized networks of reformers, several key pieces of legislation were passed that challenged married women's legal disabilities. In addition, the Matrimonial Causes Act of 1878 accorded some legal protection to female victims of domestic violence, and the Infant Custody Acts of 1839 and 1886 granted a woman custodial rights to her children. Although full equality within marriage was not realized in law until the twentieth century, the passage of this legislation

TAXATION WITHOUT REPRESENTATION.

POLITICAL CANDIDATE: "As your husband is dead, madam, and women do not vote, it is no use my staying."

TAX COLLECTOR: "As your husband is dead, madam, and women have to pay taxes, you will have to pay the tax instead of him."

Cartoon from *Votes for Women III* (7 January 1910).

The movement to win the vote for women began in the 1850s, and articles and petitions on the issue appeared with increasing frequency thereafter. Many of the early arguments drew parallels with other efforts to extend the franchise; as Mary Margaret Dilke observed in an 1889 article, "it is really an interesting study to notice how every argument used to delay the enfranchisement of working men and farm labourers reappears to do duty against women. How often has the question been asked, 'What does Hodge know about finance and foreign policy, colonial affairs and commercial interests?'"

As the suffrage movement grew, differences of opinion developed over the appropriate level of militancy to adopt and over whether the movement should press for universal suffrage or only for certain categories of women to be allowed to vote. The granting of the vote eventually came in two stages, with certain classes of propertied women granted the right to vote in 1918 (the same year the vote was granted to all men of 21 years or more), and all women over the age of 21 finally being granted the franchise in 1928.

began to chip away at male patriarchal privilege, and challenged the legal and religious "justifications" for women's oppression within the family. In her 1851 essay "The Enfranchisement of Women" Harriet Taylor

Mill addressed those "justifications" one by one, and then cut to the heart of the matter: "The real question is, whether it is right and expedient that one half of the human race should pass through life in a state of forced subordination to the other half." *The Subjection of Women*, John Stuart Mill's famous extended essay on the topic,[1] grew out of Taylor Mill's essay (the two worked largely collaboratively); that work set out with utmost clarity the ideal that is still being striven for today: "the principle which regulates the existing social relations between the two sexes—the legal subordination of one sex to the other—is wrong in itself and now one of the chief hindrances to human improvement ... it ought to be replaced by a principle of perfect equality, admitting no power or privilege on the one side, nor disability on the other."

The principles of which Cobbe and Mill and Taylor Mill spoke were, of course, not only matters of law and politics; they pervaded every aspect of British life, from employment, to educational access, to a variety of cultural matters. The principle of "perfect equality" was far from being realized in any of these areas even at century's end. But by 1900 some at least were beginning to feel that the slow movement towards acceptance of the principles of gender equality had become inexorable.

EMPIRE

Victorian Britain's internal politics, enormous wealth, and its sense of national and global identity cannot be adequately understood in isolation from its imperial rule abroad. In an address at Oxford in 1870, John Ruskin urged England to "found colonies as fast and as far as she is able, ... seizing every piece of fruitful waste ground she can set her foot on, and there teaching these her colonists that their first aim is to be to advance the power of England by land and sea." And under Victoria's reign such power did indeed grow steadily, with eighteen major territories added to the British Empire (which included India, Canada, Australia, New Zealand, and much of East Africa and the Caribbean).

If the Empire arose largely from the desire to increase trade and maximize commercial interests, it also increasingly took hold of the political and cultural imagination. The often brutal effects of colonial domi-

nation were rationalized by a pseudo-science purporting to demonstrate the inferiority of dark-skinned peoples, by a felt sense of racial and cultural superiority over other peoples. A paternalistic sense of responsibility for the peoples of the "inferior races" became known as the "white man's burden" in Rudyard Kipling's famous phrasing. Or, as evolutionary theorist Alfred Russel Wallace put it, "the relation of a civilized to an uncivilized race, over which it rules, is exactly that of parent to child, or generally adults to infants." In missionary work, travel and exploration, scientific writing, advertising, visual art, and literature, the culture and logic of imperial rule were formulated as part of the everyday "common sense" of the age.

Not everyone was in complete agreement about Britain's imperial policies and practices. Impassioned public debates about the moral and economic injustice of slavery had culminated in the abolition of the slave trade in 1807 and of slavery in all British possessions in 1833. Britain continued to rely on cheap imports of raw materials from its Caribbean colonies, however, and conditions for free workers were sometimes little better than they had been for slaves. Attention to British rule in the "West Indies" was renewed in 1865 during the controversy that attended Governor Edward Eyre's actions, when black Jamaicans attempted to liberate a black prisoner from a courthouse. Violent clashes between the rebels and white authorities resulted in martial law and the execution of 600 black Jamaicans. The opinions of two of the century's most respected public intellectuals, Thomas Carlyle and John Stuart Mill, represented the opposing poles of the public's response, with Carlyle supporting Eyre's imposition of a harsh law and order regime, and Mill calling for Eyre to be tried for murder.

The "Indian Mutiny" of 1857–58 presented a major challenge to British rule in India, which until that point was still largely under the control of the East India Company. Sepoys (Indian men employed as soldiers by the British) staged a rebellion at Meerut early in 1857, killing British officers. The violence spread throughout

---

[1] *The Subjection of Women* was not published until 1869, though it had been completed many years earlier; Mill waited for a moment at which he felt the essay would exert a particularly strong effect on public opinion.

northern territories and to Delhi, with massacres of British men, women, and children taking place at Cawnpore and Lucknow. British reprisals were swift and bloody, and led to summary executions, looting, and massacres of Indian civilians. The Indian resistance was motivated by religious, cultural and political opposition to British policies, and had a lasting impact on British rule in India. Governance was transferred from the East India Company to the Crown in 1858. In England, the press was filled with lurid reports of the violence, resulting in greater public fascination with India than ever before. Countless eyewitness accounts, sermons, plays, novels, and poems—some still being written sixty years after the events—expressed moral outrage about the insurgency. There were also those, such as Benjamin Disraeli, who tried to contextualize the violence by criticizing Britain's exploitative attitudes and practices in India, but they remained very much a minority.

Famine Victims, Madras, c. 1877. Famine was a recurrent reality in India throughout the nineteenth century, but the famine of the 1870s was particularly harsh. It gave rise to considerable controversy in Britain, with some (such as Florence Nightingale) pressing for investment in health, sanitation, and irrigation as well as short-term relief measures; others (in sympathy with the harsh approach taken by the Viceroy, Edward Bulwer-Lytton), saw such measures as too expensive or too "lenient."

Edward Bulwer-Lytton, Viceroy of India, Calcutta, 1877.

Britain participated in few major wars during Victoria's reign; when it did, the results were often less than heroic. In the Crimean War of 1854–56, Britain joined Turkey and France in fighting Russian encroachment into the Middle East, but the war did little to change the balance of power in Europe, and resulted in the deaths of 21,000 British troops, 16,000 of whom died of disease. (When the deplorable conditions of the military's hospitals became public knowledge through reports in the newspaper the *Times*, Florence Nightingale was despatched to the Crimea to superintend Britain's female nurses.) In the Anglo-Zulu War of 1878–79, the Zulus of southern Africa enjoyed considerable initial success against British forces before being subdued, and in the Anglo-Afghan War of 1878–80, the

Florence Nightingale in the Crimea, c. 1856.

Queen Victoria and her servant, Abdul Karim, 1893.

British suffered various reversals before achieving a tenuous hold over Afghanistan. The Boer War of 1899–1902, in South Africa, was fought between the British and the Boers (white settlers of Dutch descent, also known as Afrikaners) over gold and diamond fields. For the Boers, the war was part of a larger struggle to prevent the influence of foreign powers on agricultural lands they had claimed. A guerilla war ensued, and Britain's image as the greatest military power in the world suffered when the army was unable to defeat the vastly outnumbered Boers.

In England, popular support for the Empire reached its zenith in the 1880s and 90s as Britain accelerated the pace of its drive to increase its imperial acquisitions to compete with European powers and with the United States. Queen Victoria's Golden and Diamond Jubilees, during which she celebrated the fiftieth and sixtieth anniversaries of her sovereignty, provided grand occasions for the expression of national pride. As the *Times* crowed, Britain was "the mightiest and most beneficial Empire ever known in the annals of mankind." Much popular reading in these decades was devoted to either a celebration of Empire or warnings of its imminent demise. Boys' adventure stories in such publications as

The Boy's Own Annual featured tales of manly prowess in the service of Empire and promoted the values of honor, courage, and duty to Queen and country. Travel and exploration narratives recounted the heroic journeys of Richard Burton and David Livingstone, among others, while travel journals by intrepid "lady explorers," including Mary Kingsley and Isabella Bird, unsettled conventional notions of Victorian femininity and satisfied the public taste for true stories with fictionalized elements.

Yet the Imperial romances of some authors were a symptom of the anxieties surrounding Britain's increasingly tenuous grip on its empire. Whereas early and mid-century Victorian fiction tends to imagine the Empire as a fairly static, unknown space to which characters can be exiled in the interests of narrative closure, late-century fiction often represents the Empire in darker, gothic terms. Incorporating supernatural and psychological elements in their work, writers such as H. Rider Haggard, Arthur Conan Doyle, Rudyard Kipling, and Robert Louis Stevenson used colonial settings to explore themes of racial degeneration and human "savagery." In his 1899 novella, *Heart of Darkness*, Joseph Conrad, a Polish émigré to England, drew on his experience in the merchant marine in his portrayal of imperial greed, exploitation, and corruption among ivory traders in the Congo. Even Kipling, called the "Laureate of Empire" for his energetic—and often jingoistic—portrayals of the glories of British imperialism, was not always unequivocal in his attitudes towards the Empire: in his 1897 poem "Recessional," he sounded a famous warning against Imperial hubris: "Far-called, our navies melt away; / On dune and headland sinks the fire: / Lo, all our pomp of yesterday / Is one with Nineveh and Tyre!"

Engraving by G. Durand, after a sketch by H. M. Stanley, "The Meeting of Livingstone and Stanley in Central Africa" (from *The Graphic*, 3 August 1872).

By 1869, it had been three years since the renowned missionary and explorer David Livingstone had embarked on an expedition in search of the source of the Nile River. American journalist Henry Morgan Stanley was commissioned in that year by a New York newspaper to find Livingstone; the story of the two finally meeting on the shores of Lake Tanganyika in 1871 became legendary. As Stanley described it, "I ... would have embraced him, only, he being an Englishman, I did not know how he would receive me; so I did what cowardice and false pride suggested was the best thing—walked deliberately to him, took off my hat, and said, 'Dr. Livingstone, I presume?'
'Yes,' said he, with a kind smile, lifting his cap slightly."

Faith and Doubt

One of the most unsettling developments for average citizens during the Victorian period was the growing opposition to the authority of Christian faith and the established church. A rapidly changing social order, accompanied by the predominance of scientific rationalism and empiricist method, destabilized Christian certainty, creating a rising tide of secularism and religious skepticism. As critic J.A. Froude put it in 1841, "the very truths which have come forth have produced doubts … this dazzle has too often ended in darkness." The poet Arthur Hugh Clough was a central figure in the expression of the religious doubt of the age; his verse conveys a strong sense of the passion that could accompany such feelings:

> My heart was hot within me; till at last
> My brain was lightened when my tongue had said—
> Christ is not risen!
> Christ is not risen, no—
> He lies and moulders low.

Biblical scholars in England and Europe in the early decades of the century had begun to question the Scriptures as a source of literal truth, and to present the figure of Jesus Christ as a mortal rather than a divine being. The German "higher critics" of the Bible, especially D.F. Strauss in his *Das Leben Jesu* (translated by George Eliot, 1844–46), were influential in this "scientific" discussion of Biblical texts. Influential Victorian thinkers such as Carlyle, Eliot, and Martineau wrote of personal religious crises, and wrestled publicly with doubts about the value and meaning of Christian belief. As Matthew Arnold wrote in 1880, "There is not a creed which is not shaken, nor an accredited dogma which is not shown to be questionable, not a received tradition which does not threaten to dissolve." In the climate of uncertainty as to whether the divine could be knowable, Carlyle's arrival, in *Sartor Resartus*, at an affirmation of "natural supernaturalism" offers a telling statement of the almost desperate determination to find the divine in both nature and other human beings.

Traditional religious belief received its greatest challenge in the Victorian period from the evidence of the fossil record and Darwinian explanations of the origins of the universe and human beings' place within it. Charles Darwin's theories of evolution and natural selection in *On the Origin of Species* (1859) and *The Descent of Man* (1871) rejected the Christian idea that human beings had been created in God's image, and were of a different order than the rest of the natural world. In *Descent*, Darwin provoked and challenged his audience by declaring, "He who is not content to look, like a savage, at the phenomena of nature as disconnected, cannot any longer believe that man is the work of a separate act of creation."

And religious controversy and doubt extended further still. Not only were the divinity of Christ, the literal truth of the Bible, and the processes of creation at issue; so too was the very existence of a creator or divine being. One of Darwin's strongest supporters, the scientist Thomas Henry Huxley, coined the term "agnostic" in 1869 at a party held in connection with the forming of the Metaphysical Society, a learned society which met regularly for over a decade to discuss theological issues, and whose members also included Tennyson, Ruskin, and Gladstone. The term agnostic named a person of a sort unimaginable in most earlier ages—one who neither believes nor disbelieves in the existence of God, holding instead that it is simply impossible for humans to possess knowledge of such matters. (Among Victorian authors George Eliot is perhaps the most prominent to have described herself as an agnostic.) It is to such beliefs—or the lack thereof—that Matthew Arnold refers when he writes in "Dover Beach" of the ebbing tide of the "Sea of Faith." Whereas in the twentieth century that ebbing tide was sometimes welcomed as representing a freeing of human potential, to Victorians it tended usually to be heard in the way that Arnold heard it, inextricably associated with an "eternal note of sadness."

The Established Church of England and Scotland (the Anglican denomination) remained a powerful entity throughout the Victorian era, but by century's end its power was more social than political. As had been the case since the time of Henry VIII's break with Rome in the 1530s, the Church was headed by the reigning monarch, the "Defender of the Faith." Until the late 1820s, only Anglicans could be admitted to

Parliament; until 1871, non-Anglicans were barred from taking degrees at Oxford and Cambridge. The Established Church was profoundly influenced by the gradual severance of church-state relations, and the increasing popularity of Evangelicalism, a broad-based movement comprising numerous Protestant denominations such as Methodism and Presbyterianism. These "Dissenting" or "nonconformist" faiths transformed religious practice in Britain, stressing the importance of an individual's personal relationship with God, of prudence and temperance, of conversion, of missionary work, and of humanitarian activism. In 1878, the Methodist minister William Booth founded the Salvation Army, which ministered to the poor in London's East End and became the center of social purity campaigns stressing chastity and public decency for both sexes. In general, Evangelical congregations were less hierarchical in organization than the traditional Anglican Church, were anti-Catholic in orientation, and attracted both middle- and working-class believers who felt that Anglicanism had lost its spiritual power and become a mere appendage of the state.

Henry Taunt, "Bible Stall at the St. Giles Fair, Oxford," 1880.

Evangelicalism—and the resistance to it—within the Church of England resulted in a split between Anglican Evangelicals (commonly referred to as Low Church), progressives (Broad Church, sometimes called Latitudinarians), and Anglo-Catholics (High Church). An important High Church reaction to Evangelicalism took place in the 1830s and 40s through the Oxford Movement, also called Tractarianism, led by Oxford theologians and intellectuals (chief among them John Henry Newman, John Keble, and Edward Pusey). Celebrating the mystical and aesthetic elements of worship, they advocated an increased emphasis on religious ritual and a strict observance of clerical hierarchy within the Anglican communion. Newman's conversion to Roman Catholicism in 1845 spelled the end of the Oxford Movement, and heralded a significant Catholic revival that saw many intellectuals rejecting Protestantism to embrace the Catholic faith and tradition. This was a significant religious as well as political development, since Catholics in England and especially in Ireland had for centuries been the objects of persecution. The Catholic Emancipation movement of the 1820s presaged the loosening of political and legal restrictions against members of the Catholic church, the majority of whom were barred from voting, holding office, running for Parliament, or attending the universities.

English Jews were also denied full rights of citizenship until a series of measures granted them access to Parliament, the military, the legal establishment, and institutions of higher learning. Anti-Semitic stereotypes were legion in Victorian novels such as *Oliver Twist*. In at least a few cases the writings of non-Jewish novelists challenged the stereotypes—sometimes tentatively—in ways that to some extent still participated in the culture of prejudice (as in Anthony Trollope's wide-ranging novel of capitalism, marriage, and religion, *The Way We Live Now*), sometimes more clearly and unequivocally (as in George Eliot's *Daniel Deronda*). And a significant body of Anglo-Jewish literature by writers such as Israel Zangwill and Amy Levy expressed a range of Jewish responses to social prejudice on the part of England's Christian majority.

Illustrations by George Cruikshank to Charles Dickens's *Oliver Twist* (1838). The captions identify the figures in the above illustrations as "Fagin and the boys" and as "Monks [another character in the novel] and the Jew." As presented by Dickens and Cruikshank, the character of Fagin is a caricature of evil—and of Jewishness. In passages such as the following Dickens's descriptions of Fagin give expression to some of the most extreme anti-Semitic stereotypes: "It seemed just the night when it befitted such a being as the Jew to be abroad. As he glided stealthily along, creeping beneath the shelter of the walls and doorways, the hideous old man seemed like some loathsome reptile, engendered in the slime and darkness through which he moved: crawling forth by night, in search of some rich offal for a meal." By repeatedly naming him as "the Jew" Dickens crudely implied that the characteristics of Fagin were also those of Jews in general. Dickens received complaints from readers on this score, and over time he altered his views. Beginning with the edition of 1867 he made revisions to *Oliver Twist*, changing to "Fagin" the previous references to "the Jew." The last novel Dickens completed, *Our Mutual Friend* (1864–65), is notable not least of all for the inclusion of a Jewish character (Riah) who is portrayed by Dickens in a distinctly positive light.

Although the religious establishment suffered many challenges to its power, it would be a mistake to assume that secularism, utilitarianism, and Darwinian theory stamped out religious faith or traditional religious practice: far from it. The Victorian period can be fairly characterized as an age of religious doubt that was also marked by intense religious feeling. As novels such as Anthony Trollope's *Barsetshire Chronicles* vividly convey, religious affiliation (irrespective of the strength of one's actual faith) shaped most people's sense of personal identity. And the quest for spiritual meaning was itself the driving force behind some of the most moving literary works of the age. Tennyson's elegy *In Memoriam* chronicles the spiritual crisis of one man in the aftermath of his friend's death. By the end of the poem, the speaker has reconciled his religious doubts and scientific skepticism to re-embrace a Christian vision of the afterlife. In the closing lines of the poem the speaker exalts "That God, which ever lives and loves, / One God, one law, one element, / And one far-off divine event, / To which the whole creation moves."

VICTORIAN DOMESTICITY

The center of British religious, cultural, and emotional life in the nineteenth century was the family. As industrialization transformed the household from a workspace into its "opposite," the home came to be regarded as an almost sacred space, to be shielded from the aggressive competitiveness of the public world of work. The family, especially among the rising middle class, was increasingly nuclear in structure; the extended networks of friends and relations that had formed strong household connections in pre-industrial society became more and more tenuous. Increasingly, the social arrangement perceived as ideal among the better-off social classes consisted of a male breadwinner, employed outside the home, and his female helpmeet, who nurtured the children, managed the servants, and served as a paragon of domestic virtue. One of the key signs of a man's professional success was his wife's "idleness" within the home. The separation of work and family life was reflected in city planning with the construction of the first modern suburbs, supported by public transportation systems. Middle-class domestic architecture en-

couraged the display of wealth and the division of sexual labor amongst family members by dividing houses into "public" and "private" spaces. The middle-class family model became the ideal for the working class as well, although economic necessity continued to force many working-class wives and children to contribute to household earnings through paid labor, both inside and outside the home.

The domestic ideal and the emphasis on the family circle was shaped and promoted within the most privileged sphere of society. Throughout her reign, Queen Victoria was a paragon of good manners, restraint, and

Illustration, *Wonders of a Toy-Shop*, c. 1852. Though it is sometimes claimed that children were treated as "little adults" in the nineteenth century, that was far less frequently the case than it had been a century or two earlier. In many respects, indeed, the nineteenth century marks the coming into prominence of "childhood" as a cultural entity. The changing attitudes towards children working in factories was one manifestation of change. Another was the evolution of "toy"—a word used before the nineteenth century to refer to a wide variety of trifles, but increasingly in the nineteenth century applied to playthings for children; toyshops specializing in such items became more and more widespread over the course of the Victorian period.

moral uprightness. In this she stood in contrast both to the escapades and excess that had surrounded the monarchies of her predecessors, George IV and William IV, and to the moral hypocrisy that characterized the reign of her son, Edward VII. In 1840, three years after her coronation, she married her first cousin, Prince Albert of Saxe-Coburg-Gotha. Together they had nine children, and Victoria became the nation's most revered icon of domestic femininity and maternal fecundity. She was a firm believer in separate spheres of influence and authority for men and women, and voiced a then-conventional feminine distaste for power: "I am every day more convinced," she at one point declared, "that we women, if we are to be good women, feminine and amiable and domestic, are not fitted to reign." The royal family exemplified an ideal of Victorian domesticity, with Albert exercising much influence over his wife's decisions, and Victoria displaying unwavering devotion to the practical, manly Albert. Yet for all her outwardly conventional feminine attitudes, Victoria privately expressed ambivalence towards childbirth and marriage; she once complained in a letter to her daughter that giving birth made her feel like "a dog or a cow." In 1853 she agreed to undergo anesthesia during the birth of her son Leopold. This was a controversial new medical procedure, not least of all because it challenged the curse laid upon Eve (and therefore all women) in Genesis 1: "In sorrow shalt thou bring forth children."

When Albert died of typhoid in 1861, the entire nation went into a state of mourning. Victoria was overwhelmed with grief, and for fifteen years after his death she was rarely seen in public, except at the unveiling of the many public monuments she arranged to have erected to his memory. Eventually many began to regard her seclusion as self-indulgent and excessive, and her popularity among her subjects suffered for several years. Yet Victoria's long widowhood was in many ways a sign of the times; it both reflected and influenced the Victorian vogue for elaborate mourning rituals and conventions governing the public observance of death.

Life expectancy during the Victorian period was almost certainly higher than it was in the late eighteenth century, and it did improve over the period, but for most of the century it was nevertheless extraordinarily low by the standards of the developed world today—

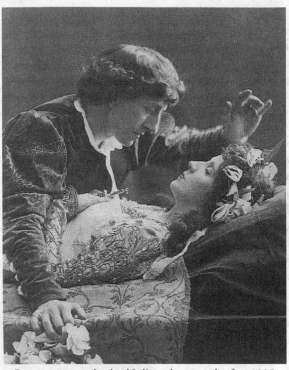

Romeo gazes at the dead Juliet: photograph of an 1895 production of Shakespeare's *Romeo and Juliet*, with Mrs. Patrick Campbell as Juliet.

probably no higher than forty years in many areas of the country. The death of relatively young people was far more common than it is today—not only deaths of children but also of young adults—of diseases such as "consumption" (tuberculosis), for example, and of cholera, and very commonly, mothers dying in childbirth. And it is no exaggeration to say that death became a commercial industry in the nineteenth century; funerals provided a public occasion to mourn the passing of a loved one as much as they offered an opportunity for rich and middle-income people to display wealth. Strict observance of funerary rituals in details of dress and deportment became a social necessity, and commemorative memorabilia, such as tea sets, photographs, and mourning jewelry (often made from the hair of the deceased) could be found in most homes. Many families were prepared to spend the bulk of their savings on the funerals of loved ones. For the poor, the story was of course much different. The indigent were buried with little or no ceremony in unmarked paupers' graves. Many working class families contributed to burial clubs, an early form of insurance that guaranteed that at least a modest amount of money would be set aside for a respectable funeral for family members.

Advertisement from *The Lady*, 4 October 1900.

The obsession with death in the Victorian period is reflected in much of the literature of the period; in Gaskell's novel *Mary Barton*, no fewer than thirteen deaths either take place or are recounted within the first ten chapters. Tennyson's elegy to his beloved friend Arthur Henry Hallam in *In Memoriam* is as much a celebration of death as it is a lament for the loss of a loved one. Countless Victorian novels feature prolonged death scenes, with grieving or greedy family members keeping vigil by the bedside of the dying. One of Dick-

ens's most beloved characters, Little Nell (*The Old Curiosity Shop*) was modeled on his sister-in-law, Mary Hogarth, whose death had affected him deeply. Little Nell's death prompted an outpouring of grief from readers, many of whom wrote letters to Dickens in between installments of the novel imploring him to spare her. The beautiful, often eroticized corpse was a favorite image in both visual art and poetry. In Christina Rossetti's "After Death," a female speaker observes her lover's attitude towards her corpse, and realizes, "He did not love me living; but once dead / He pitied me; and very sweet it is / To know he still is warm tho' I am cold."

Though mortality rates, especially among infants, remained high throughout the century, there were significant medical advances in disease control and sanitation. Prominent among these was the verification of the bacterial theory of disease. Until late in the century most medical practitioners and lay people believed that disease was spread through miasma—the spread of harmful odors through the atmosphere. Susceptibility was routinely blamed on moral and social factors such as poverty, overcrowding, and sexual behaviors. During the cholera epidemics of the 1840s, researchers began to make links between incidents of the disease and water sources. Joseph Lister's work in the 1850s and 60s confirmed the existence of microorganisms, yet the miasma theory of disease was so entrenched that it was not until late in the century that bacterial theory was fully accepted. By 1890 the pathogens for several diseases, including tuberculosis, cholera, typhoid, rabies, and diphtheria, had been identified. Surgical practice was also transformed by Lister's work on antiseptic treatments and the adoption of anesthetics, particularly ether and chloroform.

CULTURAL TRENDS

When the Duke of Wellington died in 1852, a million and a half people lined the streets of London to pay their last respects to the military hero who had defeated Napoleon at Waterloo. The deaths of the eminent were marked by elaborate, theatrical state funerals that fed an increasing appetite for public spectacles, epitomized by the Great Exhibition of 1851. The culture of Victorian

Britain was very much a visual one, with public amusements, popular shows, traveling exhibitions, circuses, sporting events, holiday resorts, and public gardens to cater to every stratum of a society that had a growing amount of both disposable income and leisure time. London's theaters drew thousands of spectators every night to witness ingenious visual effects created by London's theater impresarios; live animals, underwater sequences, mob scenes, flying machines, sumptuous interiors, and innovations in lighting stoked the public mania for stage realism. (Perhaps not by coincidence, this era of special-effects theatricality is now generally said to have marked a nadir in the history of English drama as a literary genre.) Music halls aimed at lower- middle- and working-class audiences featured a miscellany of comic songs, dance numbers, and magic shows by popular performers. Many public museums and galleries—which today draw thousands of visitors annually—were established in the Victorian period following the Great Exhibition, including the Victoria and Albert Museum, the National Portrait Gallery, and the Tate Gallery (founded by sugar magnate Henry Tate). Madame Tussaud's Wax Museum found a permanent home in London in 1835. From the 1870s and 80s onwards fashionable new shopping arcades and department stores filled with enticing consumer goods made shopping a respectable pastime for middle-class women.

"View of the Grand Entrance to the Great Exhibition, 1851" (from *The Official Illustrated and Descriptive Catalogue*, 1852). The idea for what became the Great Exhibition grew out of a proliferation of smaller exhibitions of the products of craft and industry in the 1840s, and out of an awareness that Paris was contemplating its own large-scale international exhibition. Organized largely by Henry Cole, with the strong support of Prince Albert, the "Great Exhibition of the Works of Industry of All Nations" was held in Hyde Park in 1851. The Crystal Palace, centerpiece of the Exhibition, was later dismantled and re-assembled at Sydenham in south London as a home for permanent exhibitions, where it stood until it was destroyed by fire in 1936.

Mass visual culture was inaugurated in the nineteenth century with the advent of a range of technologies including the kaleidoscope, the daguerreotype, the photograph, and the cinema. As on the stage, visual technologies exploited light and movement in an effort to create the illusion of reality and transport viewers across time and space. Panoramas and dioramas[1] featured foreign cities, battlefields, landscapes, and natural disasters, and anticipated the "moving pictures" of the cinema. Innovations in print technology and the explosion of illustrated print material from the 1830s onwards signaled the public's increasing demand for the pictorial representation of daily events. The popular *Illustrated London News*, established in 1842, was the world's first illustrated weekly paper to hit newsstands, and used increasingly sophisticated technologies—from woodcuts to steel engravings to photographs—in its pictorial coverage of events at home and abroad. Serial novels published in periodicals were accompanied by wood-engraved illustrations intended to heighten the reader's appreciation of the narrative; popular engraver-illustrators such as George Cruikshank and Hablot K. Browne ("Phiz"), both of whom illustrated for Dickens, were initially as celebrated as the author himself.

Victorian painters benefitted both from the emergence of a wealthy middle class able to purchase art for their homes and from the public's fascination with visual representation of contemporary life and historical drama. Scenes of everyday life with a narrative dimension and a moral message were especially popular with the viewing public. Like Victorian novelists and poets, many Victorian visual artists came to document the hardships of an industrial culture and landscape, depicting agricultural laborers, factory workers, and the unemployed in a highly realistic, yet often sentimental mode that has come to be known as social realism. Childhood innocence and scenes of domestic harmony were also common themes for many Victorian artists; new and inexpensive methods of art reproduction meant that such pictures could be sold cheaply to a wide audience that was interested in seeing the values of home and family reflected on its walls. Panoramic views of Victorian life in all its colorful variety were also popular: William Powell Frith's *Derby Day* (1858) and *Railway Station* (1877) portrayed scenes of ordinary Victorians in such realistic detail that they caused a great sensation when they were first exhibited at the Royal Academy. Founded in the eighteenth century under George III, the Royal Academy of Arts was institutionalized as the most important mediator of public taste in art in the Victorian period. It offered a free training school to many of the century's most significant artists, and its annual exhibitions of what it deemed the best works of the year drew thousands of spectators and buyers—as well as accusations of bias and preferential treatment on the part of those whose work had been excluded from the exhibitions or poorly hung.

The most influential movement in Victorian painting was the Pre-Raphaelite Brotherhood, composed of artists John Everett Millais, William Holman Hunt, Thomas Woolner, James Collinson, Frederick George Stephens, and the brothers of Christina Rossetti, artist and poet Dante Gabriel Rossetti, and critic William Michael Rossetti. At mid-century these artists began producing works that challenged the dominant taste for neoclassical style and subject matter by painting in the manner of medieval, pre-Renaissance artists. Close attention to natural detail, flattened perspective, vivid colors, an interest in literary subject matter, and erotically-charged images of spiritual and religious devotion were some of the hallmarks of the group. Their paintings of female figures as either ravishing "femmes fatales" or dreamy heroines in historical dress are today instantly recognizable (and are much reproduced). These paintings conveyed both women's power and vulnerability in nineteenth-century culture, and were sometimes twinned, in D.G. Rossetti's work especially, with a companion poem or with a quotation from a literary work. ("The Blessed Damozel" is one such example, in which the separation of two lovers by death in the poem is conveyed with two separate panels in the painting.) "Pre-Raphaelite," indeed, denotes a style of poetry as well as of painting; sensuous detail and a tendency to link earthly beauty to the divine are as characteristic of the poetry of Rossetti as they are of his paintings.

---

[1] In a diorama, spectators view a partially translucent painting in a specially designed building, with variations of light cast upon the image to simulate the movement of light in a daytime scene. The diorama was first exhibited in London in 1823.

William Powell Frith, *The Railway Station* (detail), 1862.
The painting depicts a scene at Paddington Station in London.

The Pre-Raphaelites should in part be considered alongside the Gothic Revival, a wave of interest in a Medieval and Gothic aesthetic that had begun in the Romantic period and influenced Victorian painting, architecture, design, literature, and religious practice. The idealization of the Middle Ages is exemplified in the writing of Thomas Carlyle, John Ruskin, William Morris, and Alfred Tennyson. Ruskin, an art critic who championed the work of the Pre-Raphaelites, argued in *The Stones of Venice* for the moral superiority of the Gothic style, in part because it was the product of artisan-workers who were free to use their creativity in their work, and so express their individual and spiritual nature. Ruskin urged his readers to re-examine the "ugly goblins" and "stern statues" of Gothic cathedrals, for "they are the signs of the life and liberty of every work-men who struck the stone; a freedom of thought, and rank in scale of being, such as no laws, no charters, no charities can secure." The Arts and Crafts Movement of the last few decades of the century, led by William Morris and influenced by Ruskin's ideas, was dedicated to the production of hand-crafted furniture, glassware, books, and art objects. Design firms such as Morris and Co. and the Century Guild revived the medieval guild system of production, rejecting the mass-produced manufactures of the assembly line in favor of the freedom and spontaneity of craft and its makers. In their critique of the ravages of industrial technology and the drudgery of mechanized labor, the practitioners of Gothic Revival imagined, and to some extent invented, the idea of the medieval past as a time of moral and religious stability, devotion to craft, and harmony with the rhythms of the natural world.

Arthur Hughes, *The Long Engagement* (detail). Hughes (1832–1915) was one of the most prominent of the second wave of Pre-Raphaelite painters.

The Palace of Westminster, home to both Houses of Parliament, was redesigned and rebuilt following the fire of 1834, in a vast project not completed until 1860. It is one of the most striking examples of the Gothic style applied to a secular construction.

Technology

The technological invention that typified the industrial age was the steam engine, a source and symbol of power both on land and at sea. Although the steam engine had been in use since the early eighteenth century, it was not until the nineteenth that steam technology helped transform an entire economy and a way of life. Steam engines were adapted for use in the production of coal, textiles, heavy metals, and printing presses, and were thus indispensable to Britain's industrial growth. Steamships powered the British Empire, with several major shipping lines established in the 1840s to serve routes to India, Africa, East Asia, and Australia. Railway steam locomotives epitomized the coming of the Victorian era, with the first local lines built in 1837 and 1838 as Victoria assumed the throne. In the "railway mania" of the 1840s, over eight thousand miles of new track were approved, and by 1900 over 900 million passengers were using Britain's rail system annually. London's underground rail system opened its first line in 1863 (horse-drawn transportation, however, continued to dominate the streetscape until the end of the century). The convenience and speed of rail travel caught on quickly with everyone from the Queen to the ordinary worker. Rail companies established excursions to special events, such as horse races or the seaside, inaugurating local and national tourism on a mass scale. From the 1850s onward railway stations became essential to the book trade and the spread of leisure reading; book stalls catering to thousands of daily commuters began to stock their shelves with newspapers, magazines, and cheap, popular fiction, which became known as "railway literature."

Robert Howlett, "Isambard Kingdom Brunel and the Launching Chains of the Great Eastern," 1857. The ship (designed largely by Brunel) remained the largest in the world throughout its 31 years on the seas. Brunel, the leading engineer of the age, also played an important role in designing such Victorian landmarks as the Crystal Palace, the new Houses of Parliament, Paddington Station, and the Clifton Suspension Bridge at Bristol.

CULTURAL IDENTITIES

The adoption of new technologies, the reorganization of employment, and the shift in power from the monarchy to the institutions of the modern liberal state revolutionized people's experience of work, family life, civic duty, and leisure time in the Victorian era. Such developments are almost always accompanied by shifts in the way people understand themselves as individuals in relation to their society. In the nineteenth century, the conditions and practices of one's class, gender, race, and sexuality began to take on new importance and to attract a new kind of attention. Changes in living conditions developed in connection with prescribed gender roles, which began to seem "natural" and

"innate" because they supported the logic of industrial capital and bourgeois family life. (This process did not begin in, but was rather extended and revised throughout, the Victorian period.) Victorians tended to think about identity in terms of oppositions: male and female, rich and poor, black and white, and, later in the century, homosexual and heterosexual. For example, the ideology of separate spheres for men and women proposed that gender and sexual identity were fixed categories, and that a "true womanhood" was the inherent opposite of a normative manliness. Yet in the literary works of the period, we see the line between these "opposites" constantly being crossed.

The "Angel in the House" (the phrase originated with a popular long poem by Coventry Patmore) became a common label for the Victorian ideal of respectable middle-class femininity. Quiet beauty, purity, devotion and selflessness were some of the essential features of the domestic wife and mother, who was described and exalted in advice literature and popular domestic novels aimed at women readers. "She must be enduringly, incorruptibly good," advised John Ruskin, "instinctively, infallibly wise—wise, not for self-development, but for self-renunciation; wise, not that she may set herself above her husband, but that she may never fall from his side." The absolute other to this paragon of virtue was the "fallen woman," a label that encompassed any form of female sexual experience deemed improper or immoral. Prostitutes, rape victims, unmarried mothers, adulteresses, homeless women, the insane, and any woman who displayed rebellious passions could be labeled "fallen." Yet the boundary between the domestic angel and the fallen woman was extraordinarily narrow; one false step and innocence became wickedness, followed by ostracism from society, poverty, and almost certain death for the transgressor, at least according to dominant narratives of fallenness. On the other hand, some fallen women were portrayed as penitent victims who embodied the feminine ideal even more fully than their uncorrupted female counterparts. Writers such as Elizabeth Gaskell, Christina Rossetti, George Eliot, Mary Elizabeth Braddon, Augusta Webster, and Thomas Hardy explored the tropes of purity and fallenness, bringing "pure" and "impure" women into each other's (and the reader's) proximity in order to probe the limits of the feminine ideal.

The male counterpart to the domestic angel was the Victorian gentleman, an heir of the chivalric ideal updated for the industrial age. In *The Idea of a University*, John Henry Newman characterized the gentleman as tender, merciful, prudent, patient, forbearing, resigned, and disciplined. Yet despite Newman's apparent confidence in this description, gentlemanliness was difficult to define: was it based on a man's mode of income or on his behavior? Was it a hereditary, professional, or moral category, or some combination? While eminent men were celebrated with great gusto in biography and prose works such as Carlyle's *On Heroes and Hero Worship*, men were also often regarded as morally inferior to women because of their greater contact with the competition and corruption of the public world. (On the other hand, women could just as easily be pressed into the role of evil temptress in accounting for a man's fall from grace.) Tennyson's dramatic monologue "Ulysses" wrestles with two competing versions of masculinity: the thwarted Romantic hero who longs for adventure and freedom from domestic encumbrance, and the reliable, managerial male who faithfully adheres to professional duty.

The concepts of the Victorian lady and gentlemen were also class categories, and served to both reinforce and blur distinctions between various socioeconomic groups. The boarding schools for the sons and daughters of the elite and the middle classes promulgated notions of proper female and male conduct in their curricula; increasingly, it was understood that one was not simply born a lady or a gentleman, but must learn to become one through rigorous training and constant self-scrutiny. As the terms "lady" and "gentleman" gradually lost their association with rank, socioeconomic boundaries became increasingly difficult to distinguish, and novelists began to focus on the gendered and class behaviors of individuals for their narrative content. In Charlotte Brontë's *Jane Eyre*, the moral awakening of the male hero, Edward Rochester, is achieved via the superior moral guidance of the "servant" governess, Jane Eyre, who, in avoiding becoming Rochester's mistress, teaches him the true nature of domestic love and Christian sacrifice, becoming his wife at his rebirth. In Dickens's novels, including *David Copperfield* and *Great Expectations*, the gentlemanly status of the male protagonists is achieved through diligence and perseverance rather than by birthright. The best-selling advice book for men, *Self Help* (1859) by Samuel Smiles, stressed thrift, hard work, and optimism as essential qualities of the "self-made man," who, no matter what his social status, could achieve respectability and success, in part by following the example of heroic men whose accomplishments Smiles recounted. Advice books, novels, and poems about the progress towards—or the fall from—"true" womanhood or manliness demonstrate that gendered and classed identities were cultural constructs that seemed "natural." The lady, the gentleman, the fallen woman, the hero—these gendered and class types, rationalized through the ideology of separate spheres, were cultural myths through which individuals made sense of their relationship to the social order.

As the century drew to a close, new styles of masculinity and femininity emerged to compete with the prevailing gender models of the previous decades. One of these new types was the "New Woman," a term that described a figure of greater sexual, economic, and social independence than the "Angel in the House." Although the term denoted a lifestyle and a literary category more than a political perspective, the figure of the New Woman was in part a product of the gains feminists had made by the 1880s and 90s in the areas of higher education, employment, political and legal rights, and civic visibility. The New Woman thus served as a flashpoint for opinion makers on either side of the "Woman Question." Smoking, swearing, riding a bicycle, debating in public, wearing men's clothes, and refusing marriage were some of the trademarks of the New Woman, who figured in novels, short stories, and popular journalism as someone either to emulate or to condemn. George Gissing, George Moore, and Thomas Hardy, among other male novelists, created memorable New Woman characters who grapple with the competing demands of personal autonomy and social expectation. The novels of Sarah Grand, such as *The Heavenly Twins* and the semi-autobiographical *The Beth Book*, present New Woman characters who triumph over social convention and the sexual double standard.

Advertisement for Swift Cycles, c. 1895.

For Grand and other feminist writers (such as Mona Caird and Olive Schreiner), the portrayal of the New Woman hinged on a critique of the male sexual privilege that had already come under fire in the 1870s and 80s during the social purity campaigns and the resistance to the Contagious Diseases Acts. This legislation, enacted in the 1860s, allowed for the forcible confinement and internal examination of prostitutes by doctors in order to prevent the spread of venereal disease, first among the military, and then within civilian communities. Underwriting these Acts was the assumption that because male sexual urges were "uncontrollable," prostitution was a necessary evil that should be regulated because it could not be eradicated. The campaign

against the Acts, led by the charismatic Josephine Butler, condemned the sexual double standard and the humiliation of poor and vulnerable women by police and doctors. Butler compared the compulsory medical examinations to "instrumental rape." The Acts were struck down in 1886 after much public controversy; the movement to repeal them, led mostly by middle-class women, marked the first instance in which women publicly debated the subject of sex on a broad scale. It was also one of the most visible of the many social purity campaigns of the 1870s, 80s, and 90s, in which moral reformers engaged in the rescue and "reformation" of prostitutes and other "fallen women," and urged men to take a vow of chastity. The mandate of the National Vigilance Association, for example, was to "create a universal ethic of chastity, for all men and women alike." In calling for a single standard of behavior, many of the social purity groups espoused moral coerciveness and interventionist policies, which often ended up stigmatizing and further repressing the women and girls they were attempting to help.

The preoccupations of the purity campaigners were part of a renewed cultural and scientific interest in human sexuality among Victorians from at least the early 1870s and the publication of Darwin's *Descent of Man*. In that book Darwin applied the theories from his *On the Origin of Species* to human evolution and behavior, positing that sexual selection among men and women accounted for their mental and physical differences. These "natural differences" were drawn straight from the catalogue of Victorian gender stereotypes, which held that men were inherently courageous, virile, and combative, and women intuitive, passive, and altruistic. The "complementarity" of these traits ensured the survival of the human "race," which evolutionists, anthropologists, and psychologists understood as a hierarchy: white European males at the top, followed by women, children, and the "primitive races." But, scientists wondered, how to explain the fact that some white males—seemingly nature's most civilized specimen—occasionally exhibited traits that resembled those of the women, children, primitives, and even the animals who were his biological and mental inferiors? Such questions were compounded by fears that Britain's empire was crumbling because the purity of the "white race" was being diluted through crossbreeding and racial mingling among English imperialists and the "savages" they ruled in the benighted labyrinths of the Empire. Closer to home, the poverty, crime and vice of England's urban districts was often racialized: "As there is a darkest Africa is there not also a darkest England?" asked William Booth, founder of the Salvation Army. "Civilisation, which can breed its own barbarians, does it not also breed its own pygmies? May we not find a parallel at our own doors, and discover within a stone's throw of our cathedrals and palaces similar horrors to those which Stanley has found existing in the great Equatorial forest?"

Social Darwinist theories of atavism (the reappearance of "primitive" characteristics in "advanced" populations) and degeneration (retrograde evolution) were formulated in the second half of the century to account for the "tendencies" of criminals, alcoholics, the poor, the mentally and physically disabled, and homosexuals. It was not until the 1880s that the term "homosexual" entered the English language; before that time homosexual acts among men were illegal (sodomy was punishable by death until 1861), but there was no concept of "the homosexual"—either male or female— as a distinct identity or way of being. With the emergence of a gay male subculture in London in the 1870s and 80s, homosexuals—also called "sexual inverts"—became subject to increased scientific and legal scrutiny.

The Criminal Law Amendment Act of 1885, which raised the age of sexual consent from thirteen to sixteen under pressure from the social purity campaigners, contained a clause—known as the Labouchère Amendment, after Member of Parliament Henry Labouchère, who had introduced it—that mandated imprisonment for any man found guilty of "gross indecency"— effectively, any sexual act[1]—with another man, even if the "indecency" were conducted entirely in private. Although "the lesbian" emerged as an identity in the 1890s, women were not subject to the same kinds of persecution as gay men, in part because of the belief that women were unmotivated by sexual desire, and that their passionate female "friendships" were innocent, temporary diversions from their true calling as wives and mothers. The Labouchère Amendment served to demonize gay men as "degenerates" whose "unnatural" desires threatened the stability of marriage, the future of the race, and the strength of the Empire. Feminized male types—the dandy, the aesthete, the fop—surfaced in visual art and literature alongside the masculinized New Woman figure to characterize a climate of sexual and gender experimentation at the fin-de-siècle that was celebrated by a few and denounced by many. As the popular satirical magazine *Punch* joked, "A new fear my bosom vexes; / Tomorrow there may be no sexes!"

"Two Seated Sicilian Youths," photograph from c. 1893 (Victoria and Albert Museum).

In 1895 celebrity playwright Oscar Wilde, who had been making little attempt to hide his homosexuality, was brought to trial under the terms of the Labouchère Amendment and sentenced to two years in prison for "gross indecency." The highly publicized Wilde trials brought the moral panic of the preceding two decades to a crisis point. Yet Wilde's trial testimony, his writing, and that of his contemporaries such as John Addington

---

[1] Some such acts were already illegal: in particular, "buggery" (a British term for anal sex), whether between two males or between a man and a woman, had been illegal since the Buggery Act of 1553.

Symonds, Algernon Charles Swinburne, "Michael Field," Sarah Grand, Mona Caird, Vernon Lee, and Edward Carpenter signaled a new level of consciousness about sexual and gender identity. With remarkable candor the sexologist Havelock Ellis wrote, "we may not know exactly what sex is, ... we do know that it is mutable, with the possibility of one sex being changed into the other sex, that its frontiers are often mutable, and that there are many stages between a complete male and a complete female." Ellis broke new ground with his multi-volume *The Psychology of Sex* (1897–1910), an early volume of which, *Sexual Inversion* (1897), was particularly noteworthy for treating homosexuality in a purely descriptive fashion, rather than as a pathology. (In other volumes Ellis took a similar approach to many other topics, including "auto-erotism" [masturbation] and sado-masochism.) Sexuality and sexual practice had become topics of public conversation in a way that belies twentieth-century stereotypes of Victorian culture as sexually conservative or naïve. The apparent "repression" of sexual behaviors deemed improper or immoral only seemed to prohibit what was in fact an intense interest in the passions, proclivities, and practices of "other" Victorians.

REALISM

"Art is the nearest thing to life," wrote George Eliot in "The Natural History of German Life." "It is a mode of amplifying experience and extending our contact with our fellow-men beyond the bounds of our personal lot. All the more sacred is the task of the artist when he undertakes to paint the life of the People." Written in 1856, Eliot's essay anticipated the masterpieces of realist fiction she would begin writing in just a few years—*Adam Bede, The Mill on the Floss,* and *Middlemarch* among them. For Eliot, as for many of her contemporaries, the true, even "sacred" purpose of art was to present an objective representation of real life that reflected the habits, desires, and aspirations of readers. For many novelists, realism seemed to be the form best suited to this purpose. In addition, Victorian poetry, especially at mid-century, was influenced by the predominance of realist fiction; long narrative poems such as Tennyson's *Idylls of the King* and Robert Browning's

The Ring and the Book appropriated novelistic forms of storytelling, while combining trenchant social critique with formal experimentation. In Elizabeth Barrett Browning's "verse novel" and female Bildungsroman, *Aurora Leigh,* the speaker, Aurora Leigh herself, defines and defends her poetic practice of social engagement with the contemporary world, sounding very much like Eliot: "Nay, if there's room for poets in this world / A little overgrown (I think there is), / Their sole work is to represent the age, / Their age, not Charlemagne's ... / ... this is living art, / Which thus presents and thus records true life."

Much realist fiction of the Victorian period tends to center on the everyday experiences, moral progress, and inner struggles of an ordinary individual, while giving a sense of the connections between that individual and his or her broader social networks. Many realist novels, such as those by Anthony Trollope, William Thackeray, Dickens, and Eliot contain multiple plot lines and a range of characters across socio-economic strata, representing both the cohesiveness and the disintegration of various social communities in an industrialized, commercializing society. Detailed descriptions of landscapes, city streets, and domestic interiors and close attention to the emotionally complex motivations of characters— these too are characteristic of the realism of the Victorian novel. This broad vision is typically viewed from a single narrative perspective, whether that of the novel's protagonist or of an omniscient narrator.

Why did realism hold such appeal for Victorian novelists and their audiences? One explanation is that the revolutions of the nineteenth century created a climate in which people longed for a sense of verisimilitude in their literature in order to guide them through the changes and upheavals, both private and public, which they themselves faced. Many Victorian readers sought moral and ethical guidance from their authors, who assumed—or were thrust into—the role of "secular clerics" with varying degrees of confidence and authority. Realist fiction, along with other forms of writing such as biography, criticism, poetry, and history, was accepted as having a pedagogical function; such texts not only taught readers how to navigate the changes they were experiencing, but also how to imagine sympathetically the authenticity of others' experience. "We want to be taught to feel," wrote Eliot, "not for the heroic artisan or the sentimental peasant, but for the peasant in all his coarse apathy, and the artisan in all his suspicious selfishness."

In rejecting the heroic and the sentimental, Eliot positioned the realist novel in opposition to the heightened, "falsifying" sensibilities of the romantic mode, as did many others. In 1785, Clara Reeve had observed that "the Novel is a picture of real life and manners, and of the times in which it was written. The Romance in lofty and elevated language, describes what never happened nor is likely to happen"; the same could be said of most Victorian fiction. Yet many of the best-known Victorian novels contain elements of the fantastic, the supernatural, or the mysterious: Dickens' *Oliver Twist* and, indeed, many of his novels set out to document the ravages of industrial poverty, but his plots depend on outrageous coincidence, and his stories are peopled with broadly-drawn character types befitting the romantic mode. His many orphans make this figure of the homeless child the Victorian rewriting of Wordsworth's child figures; Dickens's orphans inevitably confront the urban nightmares of Victorian life with well-nigh angelic purity (and, in Oliver's case, perfectly grammatical English). The novels of Charlotte and Emily Brontë memorably combine psychological realism with gothic elements such as female imprisonment and suggestions of ghostly presences. The persistence of romantic elements in Victorian realist novels not only unsettles the confidence of our formal definitions, but also prompts us to consider just whose versions of "the real" were recognized as the most truthful.

Inevitably, realism's dominance in literature and in visual art came under attack. As early as the 1850s, but more widely in the 1880s and 90s, visual artists, writers, and critics began to question the moral imperatives of realist art in a series of movements that have come to be referred to under the umbrella term "aestheticism." In poetry, drama, criticism, and fiction, aestheticism stressed experimentation in form and composition, independence of imagination and expression, and freedom of content, however perverse, morbid, or tawdry. In rebelling against the harsh brutalities of British industrial culture, the Aesthetes sought a "pure" art and formal beauty dissociated from the concerns and surroundings of the everyday. The Aesthetes were not interested in instructing or edifying a mass readership; rather, they advocated aesthetic withdrawal in order to pursue the essential forms of art. "Art for art's sake," translated from the French by art critic Walter Pater, became the rallying cry of the Aesthetes. "Art never expresses anything but itself," declares one of Oscar Wilde's speakers. "It has an independent life, just as Thought has, and develops purely on its own lines. It is not necessarily realistic in an age of realism, nor spiritual in an age of faith. So far from being a creation of its own time, it is usually in direct opposition to it." By the 1890s, the Aesthetic Movement had been charged with elitism, hedonism, self-absorption, and homosexuality. Aestheticism by that time had shifted into Decadence, a term of either censure or praise, depending on who wielded it. The Decadents extended the precepts of aestheticism in their affirmation of the perversity, artificiality, and overindulgence of a culture and a century that was nearing its end.

Page of advertisements from the eighth number of the 1846 serial publication in ten numbers of Dickens's *Oliver Twist*. (Pages of advertisements appeared at the front and back of each number.)

THE VICTORIAN NOVEL

The dominant Victorian literary form was the novel. Although the genre of the novel emerged well in advance of the Victorian period, the literary legitimacy and cultural authority the novel wields today were solidified in the nineteenth century. The novel was a dynamic form, shifting according to popular taste and critical assessments of its potential value to readers, who were offered an ever-expanding list of authors and subgenres from which to choose. The early and mid-Victorian novels of Dickens, Thackeray, and Trollope were wildly successful, both with the critical establishment and the reading public. Women novelists, including the Brontës, Eliot, Braddon, Gaskell, Charlotte Yonge, and Ellen Price Wood were some of the most respected and prolific novelists of the century, and paved the way for legions of other women to enter the field of fiction writing. Although the profession of "novelist" achieved new respectability in the period for both men and women alike, the novel continued in some circles to be maligned as lightweight and "pernicious," associated with frivolous lady scribblers and their female readers. As George Henry Lewes, George Eliot's partner, observed, "Of all departments of literature, Fiction is the one to which, by nature and by circumstance, women are best adapted … the very nature of fiction calls for that predominance of Sentiment which we have already attributed to the feminine mind."

The taste for particular subjects and approaches shifted regularly: the "silver fork" novels of the 1820s and 30s centered on the extravagances and corruptions of the rich and fashionable, while the "social problem" novels of the 1840s depicted the minute details of life at the very opposite end of the social scale. Domestic novels by both the famous and the obscure focused on the quotidian; George Eliot's *Middlemarch*, rich in psychological complexity and moral analysis, is one of the most outstanding examples of domestic fiction of the Victorian period. A heightened form of this domestic-centered fiction were the "sensation" novels which flourished in the 1860s and 1870s. Strong on dramatic incident and scandalous subject matter such as bigamy, murder, madness, and crime, sensation novels lifted the lid off the hidden corruptions and dirty secrets of the outwardly respectable middle class; Wilkie Collins, Braddon, and Wood were some of the leading practitioners of this wildly popular and much maligned sub-genre. The immense popular appeal of sensation novels helped inaugurate the concept of a "mass readership," much to the chagrin of the critical elite, who bemoaned the "degradation" of literature as the century drew to a close. In the latter decades of the century, mystery novels, detective fiction, horror, and adventure stories soared in popularity, partly on the strength of an expanding audience of lower-income readers, rising literacy rates, and cheaper methods of book production. The counterpart to these often lurid and shocking tales were the naturalistic novels of Thomas Hardy, George Gissing, and George Moore, whose late-century fiction offers bleak, social Darwinist portraits of urban class struggle, slum life, rural poverty, and sexual frustration.

Cover, *Famous Crimes*, Police Budget Edition, c. 1890. Sensationalized stories of crime and horror, priced at one penny each and known as "penny dreadfuls," became hugely popular in the late nineteenth century.

If the vogue for particular kinds of subject matter in novels shifted regularly, so too did their modes of publication, distribution, and consumption. One significant mode of publication was the three-volume edition, or "triple-decker." Readers who could not afford to buy the volumes themselves borrowed one volume at a time from lending libraries for a fee, generating huge profits for the most successful of these, Mudie's Select Library and W.H. Smith and Son. The triple-decker format was eventually supplanted by cheap single-volume editions that were sold in national book chains and at rail stations. Another mode of publication, and the one that made the novel a household word, was the monthly or weekly serial. Monthly installments of a few chapters, often accompanied by illustration and advertisements, were initially published and purchased in separate parts with paper wrappers, and generally appeared over a period of nineteen months. By the 1860s they were more often appearing in monthly or weekly literary magazines. Dickens's enormously successful *Pickwick Papers* appeared serially in 1836–37, launching the serial format as the most important publishing medium for Victorian fiction. (Long poems and works of non-fiction prose were also sometimes published serially; important examples include Robert Browning's *The Ring and the Book* and Matthew Arnold's *Culture and Anarchy*.) Serialization allowed readers with modest incomes to purchase new works when bound volumes were beyond their financial reach. Furthermore, the regular continuation of a novel over a period of months or years meant that novels and novel reading became woven into the fabric of daily life, mingling with news, opinion, and readers' personal experience.

POETRY

The novel's predominance and popularity have often meant that the significance of Victorian poetry is overlooked. Victorian poets throughout the century were greatly influenced by poets of the Romantic period, but key departures in form, content, and purpose set the Victorians apart from their predecessors. One of the most important of Victorian innovations was the development of the dramatic monologue, a lyric poem in the voice of a speaker who is not the poet, and who occasionally addresses a silent auditor. Although the Victorians did not invent the dramatic monologue, Robert Browning and Alfred Tennyson are typically credited with developing it into a form expressive of psychological complexity. Victorian psychologists were interested in exploring the boundary between sanity and madness, and the possibility of a lucid yet mentally unbalanced narrating persona appealed to Browning and Tennyson, who used the dramatic monologue to expose not only the unstable character of their speakers' passions, but also the social and cultural contexts that either produced or reflected their instability. Browning, in particular, chose a range of unstable, deluded, or even mentally deranged speakers whose self-perception is ironically distanced from the reader's, thus participating in pre-Freudian ideas about the divided self. The dramatic monologue was also employed by Elizabeth Barrett Browning, D.G. Rossetti, Augusta Webster, Thomas Hardy, Rudyard Kipling, and by many twentieth-century poets.

Many other poetic forms also flourished in the period. Epic poems are—perhaps surprisingly in an "age of realism"—a staple of the Victorian literary landscape, from Tennyson's *Idylls of the King* to George Eliot's *The Spanish Gypsy* and William Morris's *The Earthly Paradise*. Sonnet sequences too were a popular form, particularly among women poets; notable examples include George Eliot's *Brother and Sister Sonnets*, Christina Rossetti's *Monna Innominata*, Augusta Webster's *Mother and Daughter Sonnets*, and—most popular of all—Elizabeth Barrett Browning's *Sonnets from the Portuguese*. Through the work of these writers and a host of others—from Felicia Hemans and Letitia Landon at the beginning of the period to Charlotte Mew and Mathilde Blind at its end—the "poetess" became an accepted part of the literary landscape

The lyric introspection and self-exploration that is the hallmark of much Romantic verse was augmented in both form and content by a Victorian poetry of social engagement that strove to contextualize a speaker's moral and spiritual questions within the vicissitudes of contemporary life. In Tennyson's monologue *Maud*, the tormented speaker's mental deterioration and reawakening are represented as continuous with the effects of industrialization and England's entry into the Crimean War. In Augusta Webster's dramatic monologue *A Castaway* a high-class prostitute's self-scrutiny illustrates the relationship between political economy and the commodification of female identity, with "coin" as a central metaphor.

Not all poets accepted the view that poetry should speak to the issues and concerns of the present. In 1853, Matthew Arnold wrote that poets should respond to their world by mining "those elementary feelings which subsist permanently in the race, and are independent of time." In some of his later poetry Arnold turned to classical rather than contemporary subjects as a way of rejecting what he saw as the crass materialism and spiritual futility of modern life. Yet for all his melancholia, Arnold did not advocate artistic isolation; whereas many poets of the second half of the century called for the independence of art from the imperative to offer moral instruction, Arnold continued to feel that aesthetic endeavor also implied ethical responsibility.

In contrast, Swinburne's poetry of sensual experience, his carnal subject matter and verbal pyrotechnics revel in the corporeality of poetry, so much so that he was accused in one famous review of "fleshliness" to the exclusion of "meditation" and "thought." Swinburne's verse was important to the development of aestheticism, influencing later poets such as Wilde and Symonds, whose poetry tended to emphasize formal beauty, sonic effects, and the momentary over the timeless. Like the Spasmodic poets of the 1840s and 1850s, like Arthur Hugh Clough in the late 1850s and early 1860s, and, at the century's end, like Gerard Manley Hopkins, Swinburne also engaged in many challenging experiments with poetic form and meter, thereby anticipating some of the innovations and deliberate difficulties of modernist writing.

DRAMA

The Victorian period is not remembered for great stage dramas or for penetrating comedies, at least until the last decades of the century. Although Victorian audiences were avid theater-goers, they tended to prefer light-hearted entertainment to more serious fare. Comedies,

pantomimes, farces, and musicals attracted audiences from across the social spectrum, but it was the melodrama that became the most popular dramatic genre. For most literary critics, melodrama has little or no literary value, and is thus easy to dismiss as an aesthetically vacant genre. Yet popular texts can reveal much about a culture because they are so intimately connected with everyday assumptions and values. The melodrama of the Victorian period opens a window onto the nature of power relations within modern market culture and the patriarchal family; sometimes it seemed to support, and at other times to contest, these relations. With its sensational plots, stock characters, unadorned language, and a moral economy that unambiguously separates good from evil, melodrama exploited an audience's emotions, and invariably ended on a happy note. (We need look no further than the mass appeal of Hollywood films to begin to understand why stage melodrama was so popular.) Early in the century, melodramas often featured Gothic plots, settings, and characters, but the vogue for such subject matter gave way in the Victorian period to storylines centered on workaday conflicts in familiar settings, such as factories, cottages, and manor houses.

The most prolific and successful writer and adapter of melodramas was Dion Boucicault; his 1852 play *The Corsican Brothers* was such a hit with Queen Victoria that she saw it five times. Tom Taylor's popular *The Ticket-of-Leave Man* (1863) was set in recognizable London locations, and featured a sleuth named Jack Hawksure who became a prototype for later stage detectives. Many popular novels, including works by Dickens, Collins, and Braddon, were adapted or pirated for the stage soon after they had been published. Ellen Price Wood's *East Lynne*, a novel with a fallen woman theme, was adapted into several stage versions on the basis of its enormous success as one of the earliest sensation novels.

In 1881, theater impresario Richard D'Oyly Carte opened the Savoy Theatre in London for the express purpose of staging the comic operettas of W. S. Gilbert and Arthur Sullivan, whose collaboration had begun in 1875. Their most popular plays, such as *H.M.S. Pinafore*, *The Mikado*, and *Patience*, are still regularly staged today. Gilbert's storylines and lyrics combined frivolous romance with witty and genial mockery of certain contemporary values, as well as of the formulaic nature of most London stage fare; Sullivan's alternately lilting and bouncy melodies proved irresistible, and "Gilbert and Sullivan" rapidly became a popular phenomenon. The Savoy Operas, as they came to be known, anticipated the new directions in British theater of the 1890s, epitomized in the comic plays of Oscar Wilde and the "problem plays" of George Bernard Shaw; both Wilde and Shaw offered serious critiques of their society while dazzling their audiences with their audacious wit, brilliant dialogue, and shocking candor.

Prose Non-Fiction and Print Culture

Victorian writers of essays, criticism, history, and biography fully embraced the role of the public intellectual, whose particular mission was to instruct and edify readers on the day's key issues. Virtually no subject remained untouched: writers of non-fiction prose, also known as "sages," probed everything from the latest scientific developments, to religious controversies, to political and economic questions, to gender issues, to aesthetic developments, to social values and mores. In an age of growing religious skepticism, readers looked to their "sages" as latter-day prophets and interpreters who were uniquely qualified to offer an almost divinely inspired wisdom. This role of the secular cleric emerged along with the rise of the professional writer, or "man of letters," who could earn a comfortable living by the pen and maintain a level of gentlemanly respectability. Carlyle, Arnold, Ruskin, Mill, Newman, Pater, and Wilde produced some of the most influential cultural criticism of the age, using a variety of rhetorical techniques, verbal styles, and literary forms. For women writers, the decision to offer social and cultural critique often came at a price, since women were discouraged from involvement in—and even knowledge of—political issues. Writers such as Frances Power Cobbe, Florence Nightingale, Harriet Martineau, Caroline Norton, George Eliot, and Harriet Taylor Mill exploited a variety of "voices"—some gendered "male"—in their critiques of the role of women in Victorian

"A Gaiety Girl," music hall poster, 1893.

society, and in their writing on a variety of other topics, from political commentary to literary criticism. What united most of these writers, male and female, was their simultaneous position as societal outsiders and insiders: in a range of rhetorical styles, from prophetic to disinterested, prose writers typically argued from a marginal position under the assumption that their particular viewpoint had been abandoned or would be resisted by their readers. Yet it was precisely this outsider perspective that guaranteed the sage's unique authority within a society hungry for moral guidance by a voice from "beyond."

The opening of the Manchester Free Library, 1852. In 1845, local governments were given the authority to raise tax revenues to support the establishment of public libraries and museums. Free public libraries were distinguished from fee-charging circulating libraries such as Mudie's and W.H. Smith's.

For every writer or sage celebrated by his or her reading public as a visionary, there were countless, often nameless "hack" writers who also contributed nonfiction prose, or, more properly, journalism, to newspapers and periodicals. Indeed, the periodical and newspaper press afforded both the sages and the hacks, novelists and poets a space to disseminate their work and reach ever-expanding audiences. In Wilkie Collins's words, it was "the age of periodicals." Early in the century, prominent literary journals such as the *Edinburgh Review*, *Blackwood's Magazine*, the *Quarterly Review*, *Fraser's Magazine* and the *Athenaeum* attracted the most

eminent writers. In the early Victorian era, writers in these journals generally published anonymously or under a pseudonym, however, no matter how distinguished they were; not until the latter half of the century did signature gradually begin to replace anonymity in many of the periodicals. Throughout the period, the number of periodicals steadily increased, until there was a magazine for every taste, every income level, every hobby group, every political and religious organization. Domestic magazines aimed at women readers, children's magazines, satirical or humor magazines, and monthly and quarterly miscellanies publishing fiction, poetry, criticism, and news all competed with each other for readers' interest, loyalty, and purchasing power in an increasingly diverse literary marketplace. Nearly all of the best-known literary writers across the genres saw their work published in magazines and newspapers: Barrett Browning's "The Cry of the Children" in *Blackwood's*, Dickens's *Oliver Twist* in *Bentley's Miscellany*, Arnold's *Culture and Anarchy* in the *Cornhill Magazine*, Yonge's *The Clever Woman of the Family* in the *Churchman's Family Magazine*. In addition, the periodical press was key to the development of modern literary criticism. Book reviews in influential periodicals such as the *Athenaeum* could make or break a writer's reputation; prominent literary reviewers (some of whom, such as Henry James, were also celebrated authors in their own right), both forged a professional identity for themselves as literary critics and formulated principles of literary analysis that are today's tools of the trade.

Victorians were, in general, fascinated with characterizing their "age": Carlyle's "Signs of the Times," Mill's "Spirit of the Age," and Eliza Lynn Linton's "Girl of the Period" became popular catchphrases that signaled a self-conscious awareness of a society in transition. It was "the age of steam," the "age of doubt," and, perhaps most notably for students of literature, the "age of reading." Reading, like many other social institutions and cultural practices, gradually became democratized during Victoria's reign. The 1870 Education Act instituted compulsory elementary education in England and Wales for the first time; adult literacy was nearly universal by century's end. Readers were everywhere: in pubs, on trains, around the family hearth, at gentlemen's clubs, and in reading rooms (these were private libraries where readers could pay an annual fee for access to current newspapers and the latest books and periodicals). The single reader—particularly the woman reader—was a common subject for Victorian painters. Reading aloud was also a popular pastime; it was common for middle-class fathers to gather together their dependents, including the servants, at the end of the day or week to read edifying family literature, such as sermons, tracts, and didactic fiction. Drawing on his background in the London theater, Dickens delivered public readings of his novels that attracted huge crowds and increased sales of his books. His performance of Little Nell's death scene left audiences weeping.

The explosion of reading and reading cultures in Victorian England went hand in hand with new print technologies, the removal of prohibitive taxes on reading material, the ease of distribution made possible through the rail system, the rise of cheap, mass-produced print, and those political, economic, and social reforms that affected people at all levels of their existence. At the beginning of the century, mass literacy was regarded as a recipe for political revolution. From at least the middle of the century onwards, some worried that reading was becoming too popular, that it was a kind of "mania" or "disease" that "consumed" people. Critics such as Matthew Arnold argued that the newly literate but untutored masses lacked the necessary skills to distinguish between the timeless and the trashy, signaling the demise of English Culture. Yet there were also those who argued that literacy was a human right, and it was ultimately this viewpoint that prevailed. In 1840, Carlyle wrote, "Books are written by martyr-men, not for rich men alone but for all men. If we consider it, every human being has, by the nature of the case, a *right* to hear what other wise human beings have spoken to him. It is one of the Rights of Men; a very cruel injustice if you deny it to a man." The history of reading—the history of what and how different people read, the expectations that existed about what women and men should read, both in their leisure time and professionally—is inseparable from the history of the Victorian period.

The English Language in the Victorian Era

The vocabulary of English, of course, continued to expand throughout the period. New words entered the language to name aspects of the changing world of work (*trade-union* is recorded as first having entered the language in 1831, for example; *margin*, used with reference to profit to mean "amount of money available once certain costs are covered," in the 1850s). New words named aspects of human nature that were being seen in new ways or acknowledged for the first time (*personality*, used in the modern sense of "distinctive personal identity," in 1835; *sadism* in 1888; *homosexual* in 1892). New words were coined to name new religious movements (such as *evangelicanism*, *disestablishmentarianism*, and its famously long opposite *antidisestablishmentarianism*) and to name new developments in the culture of sports (*caddie* is first recorded in 1857). Less innocuously, new ways kept springing up to express old prejudices; *jew* is first recorded as being used derogatively as a transitive verb in 1845.

The Western Electric multiple telephone switchboard, the Royal Exchange, Manchester, 1888. The spread of English as the leading language of communication world-wide was aided by the invention of the telegraph in 1837, and of the telephone later in the century.

The coining of new words from Latin and Greek roots—especially new scientific terms—continued at a quickened pace, from *lithograph* and *locomotive*, to *photograph* and *phonograph*, to *telegraph*, *telephone* and *dictaphone*. Far fewer new words were entering English from French, however; the flow of new words from French into English, which had continued in the second half of the eighteenth century and the early years of the nineteenth at about the same pace as it had been a century earlier,[1] slowed to a trickle in the Victorian era; it was far more characteristic of the eighteenth-century English to turn to the French for *etiquette* (1750) than it was for Victorians to turn to the French for *élan* (1880).

The expansion of English in the nineteenth century was not restricted to new noun coinages. A lively feature of the growth of the language during this period was an expansion in the use of verb-adverb combinations (e.g., *bring up*, *hold up*, *let up*, *pass up*, *shut up*—to name only a few of those involving *up*). With the spread of such coinages (as well as of an ever-growing number of slang expressions) into the written language came a gradual reduction in the level of formality of standard English.

A reduction in dialect differences and in range of variation in English pronunciation had begun centuries earlier with the imposition of English authority over Wales, Scotland, and Ireland; no doubt it was influenced, too, by the inherently stabilizing effects of print culture following the introduction of the printing press to England in the late fifteenth century. This trend toward greater standardization of vocabulary and of pronunciation continued through the nineteenth century. The spread of standardized pronunciation in particular was assisted by the growing influence of the elite boarding schools (known as "public schools") as the preferred sites of education for the privileged classes and for those who aspired to join them. Increasingly in the late Victorian period, girls as well as boys were sent to such schools; the founding of boarding schools such as St. Andrews (1877) and Roedean (1885) were the first institutions for girls that were paralleled on centuries' old boys' schools such as Eton, Harrow, and Rugby.

Perhaps the greatest development relating to the history of the English language in the Victorian period was the initiation of a dictionary "on historical principles"—one that would record not only the various different meanings of words, but also how they had changed over time, and precisely when each meaning is first recorded in surviving written English. *The Oxford English Dictionary*, which was to be among the most ambitious of projects in an age of famously ambitious projects, had its origins in the work of the Philological Society, founded in 1842. In 1858, following the lead of a similar project initiated in Germany[2] and following years of discussion, the society issued a formal "Proposal for the Publication of a New Dictionary by the Philological Society." The society would invite volunteers to assist in sending in records they found of early or significant uses of words. (Eventually some six million slips with quotations written on them were submitted.) By 1879, the Philological Society concluded that the project was so vast that it would not be able to complete it on its own, and entered into an agreement with the Oxford University Press. Even with this assistance, it was not until 1884 that it proved possible to publish a volume covering one part of the letter *A*. By 1900 only four and one-half volumes had been published, and it was not until 1928 that a complete version of the full dictionary was available. (By then, of course, much of the early work was outdated; a second edition was published in 1989, and the *OED* is now continually being updated online.)

A less successful Victorian initiative was a multifaceted campaign to rationalize spelling—a campaign that extended in one form or another through almost the entire period; the prevalence of spellings that bear no relation to phonetic principles increasingly came to be criticised as antiquated and illogical.[3] In the early years

---

[1] The importation of French words into English, often thought of as beginning with the Norman conquest in 1066, in fact did not occur with any great frequency until roughly a century later; the flow reached its peak in the late fourteenth century.

[2] The *Deutsches Wöterbuch*, initiated by the classicist Franz Passow and the philologists (and compilers of fairy tales) Jacob and Wilhelm Grimm.

[3] As a late-Victorian spelling reformer pointed out, the ways in which English words are spelled often bear so little connection to pronunciation that it would be possible to spell *fish* as *ghoti*, with the *gh* pronounced as we do the *gh* in *cough*; the *o* pronounced as we do the *o* in *women*; and the *ti* pronounced as we do the *ti* in *nation*. This now-famous example is thought to have been first given common currency by Bernard Shaw (who later became a crusader for spelling reform).

of the Victorian era, interest in such matters was spurred by the introduction of Isaac Pitman's system of shorthand, with Pitman himself acting as a leading advocate for reform. By the 1850s, the Bible and a number of works were available in phonetic spelling versions, and by the end of the following decade, the Philological Society was taking an active role in airing all sides of the debate. Its American counterpart adopted a less impartial stance, calling in particular for the adoption of simplified phonetic spellings of words such as *tho*, *altho*, and *thruout*. Of their list only two—*program* and *catalog*—became generally adopted in the United States. In Britain resistance to such Americanisms carried the day—and in both countries, the campaign to rationalize spelling faltered by century's end in the face of a growing recognition of the degree to which English had become a written as well as a spoken language, with words comprehended very largely through the appearance on paper of the entire written word.

Resistance to Americanisms generally was felt not only in Britain herself, but also—indeed, perhaps even more strongly—in English Canada, in its unique position as staunchly British by history and by disposition but unavoidably "American" in the geographical sense. Complaints such as those of a contributor to the *Canadian Journal* in 1857 against words and expressions "imported by travellers, daily circulated by American newspapers, and eagerly incorporated into the language of our colour Provincial press," were far from uncommon. Words such as *travellers* (in its British spelling; *travelers* according to common practice in the United States) themselves became points of contention. As the American spellings of such words—introduced by Noah Webster in his dictionary in 1825—became entrenched in the United States, Canadians began to develop a hybrid somewhere in between British and American spellings.

Conventions for marking direct speech and quoted material finally stabilized in the Victorian period in something close to their current form (though with what are now established differences between American and British conventions of punctuation still unsettled). Quotation marks themselves are a relatively recent invention; they became widely used only in the eighteenth century. Even in the late eighteenth century a number of different indicators for quoted material were still being used, the most of common of which was to include quotation marks not only at the beginning of the quoted passage, but also at the beginning of each subsequent line for as long as the quotation extended. In the early Victorian period, it had become conventional to mark quotations with only an open quotation mark at the beginning of a passage and a closed quotation mark at the end—though it remained acceptable to use either single or double quotation marks.

The Victorian period also saw significant changes in the evolution of the paragraph as a primary means of signalling the shape of ideas in prose. The paragraph was originally simply a short horizontal marker added beneath a line in which a break in meaning occurred; in the sixteenth century it became conventional to mark such shifts by setting off blocks of text through indentation at the beginning of each block. Until the late eighteenth century, however, paragraphs of English prose were often extremely long by modern standards, and one paragraph of expository or argumentative prose might hold a large number of only loosely related ideas. Even in the Romantic era, a paragraph might often run to a page or more. Through the nineteenth century, however, paragraphs gradually but steadily became shorter, and the principle of restricting each paragraph to a set of closely related ideas became much more widely followed.

HISTORY OF THE LANGUAGE
AND OF PRINT CULTURE

In an effort to provide for readers a direct sense of the development of the language and of print culture, examples of texts in their original form (and of illustrations) have been provided in each volume. A list of these within the present volume appears below, arranged in chronological order. Overviews of "prose non-fiction and print culture" and of developments in the history of language during this period appear on pages lxix to lxxiii.

Poster, The Six Points of the People's Charter, p. xli.

A "Crossed" Letter (sample of the 1839 correspondence of Susanna Moodie), p. 76.

William Dodd, *A Narrative of the Experiences and Sufferings of William Dodd, A Factory Cripple*, title page, p. 53.

George Cruikshank, Illustrations from Charles Dickens, *Oliver Twist*, p. l.

Advertisements from the 1846 serial publication of Charles Dickens, *Oliver Twist*, p. lxv.

John Leech, illustrations to Charles Dickens, *A Christmas Carol*, pp. 313ff.

Charles Dickens, *A Christmas Carol*, passage in original spelling and punctuation, p. 325.

John Calcott Horsley, Christmas card commissioned by Sir Henry Cole, p. 360.

Notice to the Earl of Charlemont's Tenantry, p. xxxix.

Emily Brontë, [No coward soul is mine] and [The night is darkening round me], poems in original spelling and punctuation, pp. 371–73.

Illustration from *The Official Illustrated and Descriptive Catalogue*, the Great Exhibition of 1851, p. liv.

"The Lion of the Season," and "Man is But a Worm," cartoons from *Punch*, p. 260.

Christina Rossetti, *Goblin Market and Other Poems*, title page with illustration by Dante Gabriel Rossetti, p. 525; illustration by Laurence Housman from the 1893 edition, p. 526.

Gerard Manley Hopkins and Robert Bridges, manuscript versions of "The Windhover," pp. 642–43.

"The Angel in the House, or, The Result of Female Suffrage," illustration from *Punch*, p. 105.

Thomas Carlyle
1795 – 1881

Reviewing a book of selections from Thomas Carlyle's writings in 1855, George Eliot evaluated Carlyle's influence on his contemporaries: "There is hardly a superior or active mind of this generation that has not been modified by Carlyle's writings; there has hardly been an English book written for the last ten or twelve years that would not have been different if Carlyle had not lived. The character of his influence is best seen in the fact that many of the men who have the least agreement with his opinions are those to whom the reading of *Sartor Resartus* was an epoch in the history of their minds."

This evaluation stands as essentially correct. Whether it was Charles Dickens or John Ruskin, Robert Browning or William Morris, Matthew Arnold or George Eliot herself, Carlyle's thought and work affected the thinking and perspectives of those around him as few other writers did. This Victorian "sage" who was to become fluent in seven languages and count Johann Wolfgang von Goethe, J.S. Mill, Ralph Waldo Emerson, Alfred Lord Tennyson, Dickens, and Browning among his friends, had very humble beginnings in the village of Ecclefechan, Scotland. Born in 1795, the eldest child of a poor, strict, Calvinist stonemason and a working class, uneducated mother, the young Carlyle showed early promise, and his parents were determined to give their son an education befitting his bright mind. At the age of 14, having attended local schools since he was five, Carlyle walked the nearly 100 miles from his home to enroll in a program at the University of Edinburgh, where he studied mathematics and prepared to enter the ministry. During his years at the University, however, his faith in God was challenged by his studies of skeptics such as David Hume, François-Marie Arouet de Voltaire, and Edward Gibbon. He left Edinburgh at age 19 without attaining a degree, and for some years he taught mathematics at Annan Academy.

He also continued what he began at Edinburgh, his life-long reading and study of German writers, whose work he was to introduce to English readers. In 1823 Carlyle completed a biography of the German poet Schiller, which was published serially in *The London Magazine*; his second publication was a translation of Goethe's *Wilhelm Meister* (1824). In 1827 he published an essay on Jean Paul Richter in the influential *Edinburgh Review*. This sign of recognition was repeated in 1829, when he published his "Signs of the Times" in the *Review*, the first of his essays that focused on the social problems of nineteenth-century England and its "Age of Machinery." With "Signs" and "Characteristics" (1831), the voice of the great social prophet of England emerged.

It is in this period, as well, that Carlyle met and married Jane Baillie Welsh, the brilliant, articulate, talented daughter of a prosperous surgeon. She was well-placed to select from amongst many suitors; why she chose a coarse man from a working class background was a mystery to her friends and a source of sorrow for her mother. Although their arguments were legendary, their union in 1826 was a true meeting of minds, Carlyle's creative genius and ambition matching Welsh's intellect and drive. In 1834, they moved to London, to a home in Cheyne Row in Chelsea, where Carlyle began the long career of writing that was to make him the voice of his contemporaries, and where Jane Carlyle continued writing the letters that are amongst the most brilliant of all portraits of nineteenth-century London life.

Carlyle's work shows clearly and urgently the writer's confrontation with the age's dual heritage of religion and Romanticism, of tradition and the "march of mind." Born in a Scottish-Calvinist home in the same year as Keats, Carlyle discovered early in his reading of Gibbon and the Germans that the "old theorem" by which his own father had lived had "passed away," its "immaterialism, mysterious, divine though invisible character" banished by Locke and the mechanic world of the eighteenth century. For Carlyle, claiming that the Bible was factual truth "flatly contradicted all human science and experience." Yet he also believed that the Romantics' response to the passing of the "old beliefs"—the effort he saw in the early Goethe to form "his world out of himself"—led to despair and solipsism. Carlyle's celebration of Goethe's spiritual progress from narcissistic self-focus to a capacious view of man's role in a larger world became one of the main themes of his early work. This estimation was to become one of Carlyle's signature lines: "Close thy Byron, Open thy Goethe," commands Diogenes Teufelsdröckh, the book's questing protagonist.

Sartor Resartus appeared serially in *Fraser's Magazine* (1833–34). This semi-autobiographical book, whose Latin title translates as "The Tailor Retailored," owes a debt for its clothing metaphor to Jonathan Swift's *Tale of a Tub*. Its quirky, densely allusive, and multi-faceted style derive from Laurence Sterne's *The Life and Opinions of Tristram Shandy* and from the German writers whom Carlyle loved. Diogenes Teufelsdröckh (literally, "God-born devil's dung") is a German "Professor of Things-in-General" at the University of Weissnichtwo (literally "Don't know where"). Professor Teufelsdröckh has a theory of clothing, or symbol, by which the visible is read as a pathway to the invisible. From this symbolic reading of the world, Carlyle develops his idea of "natural supernaturalism"; nature and man become the physical manifestation, the "clothing," of the divine, "in this poor, miserable, hampered, despicable Actual, wherein thou even now standest." In presenting the quest of his German protagonist to say "Yes" to existence (within an English Editor's meditations on the strangeness of that quest and its language), Carlyle charted what was to be the Victorian response to the Enlightenment and Romanticism, and to Industrialism and the perceived withdrawal of God. For Carlyle, "Here or no where is thy Ideal: work it out therefrom; and working, believe, live, be free." Thus, when in the third volume, Teufelsdröckh goes to London and sees the worlds of wealth and poverty that constitute the "two sects" of England that were to be Carlyle's focus in *The French Revolution*, "Chartism" (1839), and *Past and Present* (1841), the connection of philosophical thinking to the real world is made clear; social prophecy and national health comes out of spiritual progress. The gospel is not "Know thyself," thundered Carlyle's protagonist, "till it be translated into this partially possible one, *Know what thou canst work at.*"

Carlyle began to achieve great fame with the publication of *The French Revolution* in 1836. His style resembled that of no other historian: highly metaphoric language, sentences that seemed "barbarous" because of their German-inflected structures and jarring syntax, the use of the present tense, representations of men and women so vivid that they seemed like characters from a novel. Carlyle used this style to articulate a sweeping view of history as a continual mingling of past and present and as the unfolding of a divine will.

In *The French Revolution*, Carlyle sees Revolutionary France as a warning to England in the 1830s. He structures the drama of France's Revolution as he had the drama of Teufelsdröckh's life, around the questions forced upon individuals or nations when they lose sight of moral and social accountability. Carlyle sees in France's materialism and its leaders' sense of the life as a "Thespian stage" an emptying of meaning out of all symbols; in this world, proclaiming ideas of Brotherhood—of liberty equality, fraternity—"will the sooner and the more surely lead to Cannibalism" and a "Brotherhood of Cain."

This exploration of the "Brotherhood of Cain" and how it comes to be the belief of a nation governs Carlyle's greatest social writing, *Past and Present*. By juxtaposing the medieval past of England, with its monks and serfs living in an organic community focused around a monastery, and the industrialism and *laissez-faire* economics of England's present that had produced poverty and starvation, Carlyle created a remarkable picture of the desperate social crises of the hungry forties. The book begins in prison and ends with a vision of a "green flowery world." The landscape between these points is equally polarized: the "formed" world of Abbot Samson and the "enchanted," demonic, "inorganic" world of the industrial present where no one will be his brother's keeper—or his brother's brother—because all have become Cains. This latter-day England is populated by a group of vividly realized demons escaped out of Bunyan and the daily newspapers: Pandarus Dogdraught, Bobus of Houndsditch, Plugson of Undershot (a captain of industry), Sir Jabesh Windbag, the amphibious Pope, and the Dead Sea Apes (who believe that soul and stomach are synonymous). Carlyle does not idealize the medieval world of Abbot Samson; he exonerates his hero from what he sees as the "spiritual rubbish" that characterizes religious exercises then and in Carlyle's own time. In Samson's work, Carlyle finds genuine redemption: "*Laborare est Orare* … true Work is Worship … a making of Madness Sane." *Past and Present* constitutes one of the century's great denunciations of the "Gospel of Enlightened Selfishness" that Carlyle and others saw as reducing the connections between human beings to those of a "cash nexus."

In 1840 Carlyle gave, and then published, a series of lectures, *On Heroes and Hero-Worship*. Here again he sets out his religious ideas, finding value in the Norse god Odin and in Mahomet because they understood the divine will at work in the universe (as did Martin Luther, Robert Burns, Samuel Johnson, Oliver Cromwell, and Napoleon). Each man in this unlikely collection of heroes apprehends the workings of the divine and can lead humankind out of darkness—if human beings will listen.

For many readers, Carlyle's exaltation of authority has represented a danger. Certainly this strong-man theme became predominant in his later work, in which he turned towards conservativism and authoritarianism. *The Letters and Speeches of Oliver Cromwell* (1845) and *The History of Friedrich II of Prussia, Called Frederick the Great*, published between 1858 and 1865, furthered Carlyle's doctrine of hero-worship and his principles of order. He strongly opposed the enfranchisement of women and just as vehemently supported the enslavement of black people in the West Indies. (Carlyle's 1849 essay on this topic ended his friendship with Mill, who wrote a spirited reply.) His 1850 publication of *Latter-Day Pamphlets*, with its corrosively satirical attacks on democracy and its representatives, is an extraordinarily splenetic outburst from a voice that had once challenged England to discover the godlike connections amongst all human beings.

Carlyle remained influential; Charles Dickens, John Ruskin, and Robert Browning all dedicated books to him. In 1874 he turned down a baronetcy offered by British Prime Minister Disraeli; he did, however, accept the Prussian Order of Merit in the same year. After his wife's death in 1866, he wrote little, though he did edit his wife's remarkable letters, *The Letters and Memorials of Jane Welsh Carlyle*, which were published after his death. Carlyle had earlier stated his aversion to the idea of being buried in Westminster Abbey; he was buried in 1881 beside his parents in Ecclefechan, Scotland. George Eliot's estimation of Carlyle is an apt epitaph: "When he is saying the opposite of what we think, he says it so finely, with so hearty conviction—he makes the object about which we differ stand out in such grand relief under the clear light of his strong and honest intellect—he appeals so constantly to our sense of the manly and the truthful—that we are obliged to say 'Hear! Hear!' to the writer before we can give the decorous 'Oh! Oh!' to his opinions."

⌘ ⌘ ⌘

from *Sartor Resartus*[1]

from BOOK 2
CHAPTER 6 — SORROWS OF TEUFELSDRÖCKH

We have long felt that, with a man like our Professor, matters must often be expected to take a course of their own; that in so multiplex, intricate a nature, there might be channels, both for admitting and emitting, such as the Psychologist had seldom noted; in short, that on no grand occasion and convulsion, neither in the joy-storm nor in the woe-storm, could you predict his demeanour.

To our less philosophical readers, for example, it is now clear that the so passionate Teufelsdröckh, precipitated through "a shivered Universe" in this extraordinary way, has only one of three things which he can next do: Establish himself in Bedlam;[2] begin writing Satanic Poetry; or blow out his brains. In the progress towards any of which consummations, do not such readers anticipate extravagance enough: breast-beating, brow-beating (against walls), lion-bellowings of blasphemy and the like, stampings, smitings, breakages of furniture, if not arson itself?

Nowise so does Teufelsdröckh deport him. He quietly lifts his *Pilgerstab* (Pilgrim-staff), "old business being soon wound-up"; and begins a perambulation and circumambulation of the terraqueous[3] Globe! Curious it is, indeed, how with such vivacity of conception, such intensity of feeling, above all, with these unconscionable habits of Exaggeration in speech, he combines that wonderful stillness of his, that stoicism in external procedure. Thus, if his sudden bereavement, in this matter of the Flower-goddess[4] is talked of as a real Doomsday and Dissolution of Nature, in which light doubtless it partly appeared to himself, his own nature is nowise dissolved thereby, but rather is compressed closer. For once, as we might say, a Blumine by magic appliances has unlocked that shut heart of his, and its hidden things rush out tumultuous, boundless, like genii enfranchised from their glass phial; but no sooner are your magic appliances withdrawn, than the strange casket of a heart springs to again; and perhaps there is now no key extant that will open it, for a Teufelsdröckh, as we remarked, will not love a second time. Singular Diogenes! No sooner has that heartrending occurrence fairly taken place, than he affects to regard it as a thing natural, of which there is nothing more to be said. "One highest hope, seemingly legible in the eyes of an Angel, had recalled him as out of Death-shadows into celestial Life: but a gleam of Tophet[5] passed over the face of his Angel; he was rapt away in whirlwinds, and heard the laughter of Demons. It was a Calenture,"[6] adds he, "whereby the Youth saw green Paradise-groves in the waste Ocean-waters: a lying vision, yet not wholly a lie, for *he* saw it." But what things soever passed in him, when he ceased to see it; what ragings and despairings soever Teufelsdröckh's soul was the scene of, he has the goodness to conceal under a quite opaque cover of Silence. We know it well: the first mad paroxysm past, our brave Gneschen[7] collected his dismembered philosophies, and buttoned himself together; he was meek, silent, or spoke of the weather and the Journals; only by a transient knitting of those shaggy brows, by some deep flash of those eyes, glancing one knew not whether with tear-dew or with fierce fire, might you have guessed what a Gehenna was within, that a whole Satanic School were spouting, though inaudibly, there. To consume your own choler,[8] as some chimneys consume their own

---

[1] *Sartor Resartus* Latin: "The Tailor Retailored." Carlyle writes about the fictional German philosopher Diogenes Teufelsdröckh, the author of *Clothes: Their Origin and Influence,* whose name literally means "God-born devil's dung." Teufelsdröckh details his philosophy of clothes and clothing's relationship to Transcendentalist theories. Popular for a twenty-five year span within the Victorian period, Transcendentalism was a philosophical and literary movement that sought to integrate spirit and matter by integrating the natural and the supernatural worlds as "one great Unity." Teufelsdröckh also comments on clothing as an analogy for government and other institutions that "wear out" and need to be replaced every so often. In this chapter and others, a fictional English editor comments on the professor's theories.

[2] *Bedlam* Common name for the Hospital of St. Mary of Bethlehem, an overcrowded and frenetic asylum for the emotionally disturbed.

[3] *terraqueous* Composed of land and water.

[4] *Flower-goddess* Blumine, the woman Teufelsdröckh loves, but who marries his friend Towgood.

[5] *Tophet* Gehenna, or hell.

[6] *Calenture* Feverish disease once suffered by sailors in the tropics, characterized by a tendency to mistake the ocean for green fields, which tempted some to jump overboard.

[7] *Gneschen* The young Diogenes.

[8] *choler* Bile.

smoke; to keep a whole Satanic School spouting, if it must spout, inaudibly, is a negative yet no slight virtue, nor one of the commonest in these times.

Nevertheless, we will not take upon us to say, that in the strange measure he fell upon, there was not a touch of latent Insanity; whereof indeed the actual condition of these Documents in *Capricornus* and *Aquarius* is no bad emblem. His so unlimited Wanderings, toilsome enough, are without assigned or perhaps assignable aim; internal Unrest seems his sole guidance; he wanders, wanders, as if that curse of the Prophet had fallen on him, and he were "made like unto a wheel." Doubtless, too, the chaotic nature of these Paper-bags aggravates our obscurity. Quite without note of preparation, for example, we come upon the following slip: "A peculiar feeling it is that will rise in the Traveller, when turning some hill range in his desert road, he descries lying far below, embosomed among its groves and green natural bulwarks, and all diminished to a toybox, the fair Town, where so many souls, as it were seen and yet unseen, axe driving their multifarious traffic. Its white steeple is then truly a starward-pointing finger; the canopy of blue smoke seems like a sort of Life-breath, for always, of its own unity, the soul gives unity to whatsoever it looks on with love; thus does the little Dwellingplace of men, in itself a congeries[1] of houses and huts, become for us an individual, almost a person. But what thousand other thoughts unite thereto, if the place has to ourselves been the arena of joyous or mournful experiences; if perhaps the cradle we were rocked in still stands there, if our Loving ones still dwell there, if our Buried ones there slumber!" Does Teufelsdröckh, as the wounded eagle is said to make for its own eyrie, and indeed military deserters, and all hunted outcast creatures, turn as if by instinct in the direction of their birth-land, fly first, in this extremity, towards his native Entepfuhl; but reflecting that there no help awaits him, take only one wistful look from the distance, and then wend elsewhither?

Little happier seems to be his next flight: into the wilds of Nature, as if in her mother-bosom he would seek healing. So at least we incline to interpret the following Notice, separated from the former by some considerable space, wherein, however, is nothing noteworthy:

"Mountains were not new to him; but rarely are Mountains seen in such combined majesty and grace as here. The rocks are of that sort called Primitive by the mineralogists, which always arrange themselves in masses of a rugged, gigantic character; which ruggedness, however, is here tempered by a singular airiness of form, and softness of environment; in a climate favourable to vegetation, the gray cliff, itself covered with lichens, shoots up through a garment of foliage or verdure; and white, bright cottages, tree-shaded, cluster round the everlasting granite. In fine vicissitude, Beauty alternates with Grandeur; you ride through stony hollows, along strait passes, traversed by torrents, overhung by high walls of rock; now winding amid broken shaggy chasms, and huge fragments; now suddenly emerging into some emerald valley, where the streamlet collects itself into a Lake, and man has again found a fair dwelling, and it seems as if Peace had established herself in the bosom of Strength.

"To Peace, however, in this vortex of existence, can the Son of Time not pretend: still less if some Spectre haunt him from the Past; and the Future is wholly a Stygian[2] Darkness, spectrebearing. Reasonably might the Wanderer exclaim to himself: Are not the gates of this world's Happiness inexorably shut against thee; hast thou a hope that is not mad? Nevertheless, one may still murmur audibly, or in the original Greek if that suit thee better: 'Whoso can look on Death will start at no shadows.'

"From such meditations is the Wanderer's attention called outwards; for now the Valley closes in abruptly, intersected by a huge mountain mass, the stony waterworn ascent of which is not to be accomplished on horseback. Arrived aloft, he finds himself again lifted into the evening sunset light and cannot but pause, and gaze round him, some moments there. An upland irregular expanse of wold,[3] where valleys in complex branchings are suddenly or slowly arranging their descent towards every quarter of the sky. The mountain ranges are beneath your feet, and folded together; only the loftier summits look down here and there as on a second plain; lakes also lie clear and earnest in their solitude. No trace of man now visible, unless indeed it were he who fashioned that little visible link of High-

---

[1] *congeries* Collection.

[2] *Stygian* Like the river Styx, which runs across the entrance to Hades (or hell).

[3] *wold* Open country.

way, here, as would seem, scaling the inaccessible, to unite Province with Province. But sunwards, lo you! how it towers sheer up, a world of Mountains, the diadem[1] and centre of the mountain region! A hundred and a hundred savage peaks, in the last light of Day, all glowing, of gold and amethyst, like giant spirits of the wilderness; there in their silence, in their solitude, even as on the night when Noah's Deluge first dried! Beautiful, nay solemn, was the sudden aspect to our Wanderer. He gazed over those stupendous masses with wonder, almost with longing desire; never till this hour had he known Nature, that she was One, that she was his Mother and divine. And as the ruddy glow was fading into clearness in the sky, and the Sun had now departed, a murmur of Eternity and Immensity, of Death and of Life, stole through his soul; and he felt as if Death and Life were one, as if the Earth were not dead, as if the Spirit of the Earth had its throne in that splendour, and his own spirit were therewith holding communion.

"The spell was broken by a sound of carriage wheels. Emerging from the hidden Northward, to sink soon into the hidden Southward, came a gay Barouche-and-four;[2] it was open; servants and postillions[3] wore wedding favours; that happy pair, then, had found each other, it was their marriage evening! Few moments brought them near: *Du Himmel!*[4] It was Herr Towgood and—Blumine! With slight unrecognising salutation they passed me, plunged down amid the neighbouring thickets, onwards, to Heaven, and to England; and I, in my friend Richter's words, *I remained alone, behind them, with the Night.*"

Were it not cruel in these circumstances, here might be the place to insert an observation, gleaned long ago from the great *Clothes-Volume,* where it stands with quite other intent: "Some time before Smallpox was extirpated," says the Professor, "there came a new malady of the same spiritual sort on Europe: I mean the epidemic, now endemical, of View-hunting. Poets of old date, being privileged with Senses, had also enjoyed external Nature; but chiefly as we enjoy the crystal cup which holds good or bad liquor for us, that is to say, in

silence, or with slight incidental commentary; never, as I compute, till after the *Sorrows of Werter,*[5] was there man found who would say: Come let us make a Description! Having drunk the liquor, come let us eat the glass! Of which endemic the Jenner[6] is unhappily still to seek." Too true!

We reckon it more important to remark that the Professor's Wanderings, so far as his stoical and cynical envelopment admits is to clear insight, here first take their permanent character, fatuous or not. That Basilisk-glance[7] of the Barouche-and-four seems to have withered up what little remnant of a purpose may have still lurked in him; Life has become wholly a dark labyrinth; wherein, through long years, our Friend, flying from spectres, has to stumble about at random, and naturally with more haste than progress.

Foolish were it in us to attempt following him, even from afar, in this extraordinary world-pilgrimage of his, the simplest record of which, were clear record possible, would fill volumes. Hopeless is the obscurity, unspeakable the confusion. He glides from country to country, from condition to condition, vanishing and reappearing, no man can calculate how or where. Through all quarters of the world he wanders, and apparently through all circles of society. If in any scene, perhaps difficult to fix geographically, he settles for a time, and forms connexions, be sure he will snap them abruptly asunder. Let him sink out of sight as Private Scholar (*Privatisirender*), living by the grace of God in some European capital, you may next find him as Hadjee[8] in the neighbourhood of Mecca. It is an inexplicable Phantasmagoria, capricious, quick-changing, as if our Traveller, instead of limbs and highways, had transported himself by some wishing-carpet, or Fortunatus' Hat.[9] The whole, too, imparted emblematically, in dim

---

[1] *diadem*   Crown.

[2] *Barouche-and-four*   Carriage for four passengers and driver.

[3] *postillions*   Messengers on horseback.

[4] *Du Himmel!*   German: Good heavens!

[5] *Sorrows of Werter*   *The Sorrows of Young Werther* (1774), a novel by German author Johann Wolfgang von Goethe about a young man who is rejected by his loved ones and who eventually decides to commit suicide.

[6] *Jenner*   Edward Jenner, the scientist who discovered the smallpox vaccine in 1796.

[7] *Basilisk-glance*   The glance of the basilisk, a serpent-like reptile, would kill.

[8] *Hadjee*   Muslim religious pilgrimage to Mecca.

[9] *Fortunatus' Hat*   Fortunatus was a hero of legend who was given an old hat that would transport him anywhere he wished to go.

multifarious tokens (as that collection of Street Advertisements), with only some touch of direct historical notice sparingly interspersed: little light-islets in the world of haze! So that, from this point, the Professor is more of an enigma than ever. In figurative language, we might say he becomes, not indeed a spirit, yet spiritualised, vaporised. Fact unparalleled in Biography: The river of his History, which we have traced from its tiniest fountains, and hoped to see flow onward, with increasing current, into the ocean, here dashes itself over that terrific Lover's Leap; and, as a mad-foaming cataract, flies wholly into tumultuous clouds of spray. Low down it indeed collects again into pools and plashes, yet only at a great distance, and with difficulty, if at all, into a general stream. To cast a glance into certain of those pools and plashes, and trace whither they run, must, for a chapter or two, form the limit of our endeavour.

For which end doubtless those direct historical Notices, where they can be met with, are the best. Nevertheless, of this sort too there occurs much, which, with our present light, it were questionable to emit. Teufelsdröckh, vibrating everywhere between the highest and the lowest levels, comes into contact with public History itself. For example, those conversations and relations with illustrious Persons, as Sultan Mahmoud, the Emperor Napoleon, and others, are they not as yet rather of a diplomatic character than of a biographic? The Editor, appreciating the sacredness of crowned heads, nay perhaps suspecting the possible trickeries of a Clothes-Philosopher, will eschew this province for the present; a new time may bring new insight and a different duty.

If we ask now, not indeed with what ulterior Purpose, for there was none, yet with what immediate outlooks, at all events, in what mood of mind, the Professor undertook and prosecuted this world pilgrimage, the answer is more distinct than favourable. "A nameless Unrest," says he, "urged me forward; to which the outward motion was some momentary lying solace. Whither should I go? My Loadstars were blotted out; in that canopy of grim fire shone no star. Yet forward must I; the ground burnt under me; there was no rest for the sole of my foot. I was alone, alone! Ever too the strong inward longing shaped Fantasms for itself; towards these, one after the other, must I fruitlessly wander. A feeling I had, that for my fever-thirst there was and must

be somewhere a healing Fountain. To many fondly imagined Fountains, the Saints' Wells of these days, did I pilgrim; to great Men, to great Cities, to great Events, but found there no healing. In strange countries, as in the well-known; in savage deserts, as in the press of corrupt civilisation, it was ever the same: how could your Wanderer escape from—*his own Shadow*? Nevertheless still Forward! I felt as if in great haste; to do I saw not what. From the depths of my own heart, it called to me, Forwards! The winds and the streams, and all Nature sounded to me, Forwards! *Ach Gott*,[1] I was even, once for all, a Son of Time."[2]

From which is it not clear that the internal Satanic School was till active enough? He says elsewhere: "The *Enchiridion of Epictetus*[3] I had ever with me, often as my sole rational companion, and regret to mention that the nourishment it yielded was trifling." Thou foolish Teufelsdröckh! How could it else? Hadst thou not Greek enough to understand thus much: *The end of Man is an Action, and not a Thought*, though it were the noblest? "How I lived?" writes he once: "Friend, hast thou considered the 'rugged all-nourishing Earth,' as Sophocles well names her; how she feeds the sparrow on the housetop, much more her darling, man? While thou stirrest and livest, thou hast a probability of victual. My breakfast of tea has been cooked by a Tartar[4] woman, with water of the Amur, who wiped her earthen kettle with a horse-tail. I have roasted wild eggs in the sand of Sahara; I have awakened in Paris *Estrapades* and Vienna *Malzleins*,[5] with no prospect of breakfast beyond elemental liquid. That I had my Living to seek saved me from Dying—by suicide. In our busy Europe, is there not an everlasting demand for Intellect, in the chemical, mechanical, political, religious, educational, commercial departments? In Pagan countries, cannot one write Fetishes? Living! Little knowest thou what alchemy[6] is

---

[1] *Ach Gott*   German: Oh, God.

[2] *Son of Time*   From Friedrich von Schiller's poem "The Artists" (1789).

[3] *Enchiridion of Epictetus*   Handbook or manual for living, purportedly written in 135 BCE by Epictetus, a Greek Stoic philosopher.

[4] *Tartar*   From the central Asian area formerly known as Tartary.

[5] *Paris Estrapades and Vienna Malzleins*   Streets in Paris and Vienna.

[6] *alchemy*   Here, magic power that transforms.

in an inventive Soul; how, as with its little finger, it can create provision enough for the body (of a Philosopher), and then, as with both hands, create quite other than provision, namely, spectres to torment itself withal."

Poor Teufelsdröckh! Flying with Hunger always parallel to him, and a whole Infernal Chase in his rear, so that the countenance of Hunger is comparatively a friend's! Thus must he, in the temper of ancient Cain,[1] or of the modern Wandering Jew, save only that he feels himself not guilty and but suffering the pains of guilt, wend to and fro with aimless speed. Thus must he, over the whole surface of the Earth (by foot-prints), write his *Sorrows of Teufelsdröckh*, even as the great Goethe, in passionate words, had to write his *Sorrows of Werter*, before the spirit freed herself, and he could become a Man. Vain truly is the hope of your swiftest Runner to escape "from his own Shadow"! Nevertheless, in these sick days, when the Born of Heaven first descries himself (about the age of twenty) in a world such as ours, richer than usual in two things, in Truths grown obsolete, and Trades grown obsolete—what can the fool think but that it is all a Den of Lies, wherein whoso will not speak Lies and act Lies, must stand idle and despair? Whereby it happens that, for your nobler minds, the publishing of some such Work of Art, in one or the other dialect, becomes almost a necessity. For what is it properly but an Altercation with the Devil, before you begin honestly Fighting him? Your Byron publishes his *Sorrows of Lord George*, in verse and in prose, and copiously otherwise; your Bonaparte represents his *Sorrows of Napoleon* Opera, in an all too stupendous style, with music of cannon volleys, and murder-shrieks of a world; his stage-lights are the fires of Conflagration; his rhyme and recitative are the tramp of embattled Hosts and the sound of falling Cities. Happier is he who, like our Clothes-Philosopher, can write such matter, since it must be written, on the insensible Earth, with his shoe-soles only, and also survive the writing thereof! ...

from BOOK 3
CHAPTER 8—NATURAL SUPERNATURALISM

It is in his stupendous Section, headed *Natural Supernaturalism*, that the Professor first becomes a Seer; and, after long effort, such as we have witnessed, finally subdues under his feet this refractory Clothes-Philosophy, and takes victorious possession thereof. Phantasms enough he has had to struggle with: "Cloth-webs and Cobwebs," of Imperial Mantles, Superannuated Symbols, and what not; yet still did he courageously pierce through. Nay, worst of all, two quite mysterious, world-embracing Phantasms, TIME and SPACE, have ever hovered round him, perplexing and bewildering; but with these also he now resolutely grapples, these also he victoriously rends asunder. In a word, he has looked fixedly on Existence, till, one after the other, its earthly hulls and garnitures[2] have all melted away; and now, to his rapt vision, the interior celestial Holy of Holies lies disclosed.

Here, therefore, properly it is that the Philosophy of Clothes attains to Transcendentalism;[3] this last leap, can we but clear it, takes us safe into the promised land, where *Palingenesis*,[4] in all senses, may be considered as beginning. "Courage, then!" may our Diogenes exclaim, with better right than Diogenes the First once did.[5] This stupendous Section we, after long painful meditation, have found not to be unintelligible, but, on the contrary, to grow clear, nay radiant, and all-illuminating. Let the reader, turning on it what utmost force of speculative intellect is in him, do his part, as we, by judicious selection and adjustment, shall study to do ours:

"Deep has been, and is, the significance of Miracles," thus quietly begins the Professor; "far deeper perhaps than we imagine. Meanwhile, the question of questions were: What specially is a Miracle? To that Dutch King of Siam, an icicle had been a miracle; whoso had carried

---

[1] *Cain* First son of Adam and Eve, who killed his brother Abel, and on whom God placed a mark of punishment (see Genesis 4).

[2] *garnitures* Ornaments.

[3] *Transcendentalism* In this case the professor refers to Transcendentalism's tendency to privilege the spiritual over the material. Nature, including human beings, has the powers, status, and authority traditionally attributed to an independent deity.

[4] *Palingenesis* Rebirth.

[5] *"Courage, then!" ... once did* Third-century philosopher Diogenes Laërtius once told his listeners to have faith that his dull lecture would soon be over.

with him an air-pump and vial of vitriolic ether, might have worked a miracle. To my Horse, again, who unhappily is still more unscientific, do not I work a miracle, and magical *Open sesame!*[1] every time I please to pay twopence and open for him an impassable *Schlagbaum*, or shut Turnpike?

"'But is not a real Miracle simply a violation of the Laws of Nature?' ask several. Whom I answer by this new question: What are the Laws of Nature? To me perhaps the rising of one from the dead were no violation of these Laws, but a confirmation, were some far deeper Law, now first penetrated into, and by Spiritual Force, even as the rest have all been, brought to bear on us with its Material Force.

"Here too may some inquire, not without astonishment: On what ground shall one, that can make Iron swim,[2] come and declare that therefore he can teach Religion? To us, truly, of the Nineteenth Century, such declaration were inept enough, which nevertheless to our fathers, of the First Century, was full of meaning.

"'But is it not the deepest Law of Nature that she be constant?' cries an illuminated class; 'Is not the Machine of the Universe fixed to move by unalterable rules?' Probable enough, good friends; nay I, too, must believe that the God, whom ancient inspired men assert to be 'without variableness or shadow of turning,'[3] does indeed never change; that Nature, that the Universe, which no one whom it so pleases can be prevented from calling a Machine, does move by the most unalterable rules. And now of you, too, I make the old inquiry: What those same unalterable rules, forming the complete Statute-Book of Nature, may possibly be?

"They stand written in our Works of Science, say you, in the accumulated records of Man's Experience?—Was Man with his Experience present at the Creation, then, to see how it all went on? Have any deepest scientific individuals yet dived down to the foundations of the Universe and gauged everything there? Did the Maker take them into His counsel; that they read His groundplan of the incomprehensible All; and can say, This stands marked therein, and no more

than this? Alas, not in anywise! These scientific individuals have been nowhere but where we also are, have seen some handbreadths deeper than we see into the Deep that is infinite, without bottom as without shore.

"Laplace's Book on the Stars,[4] wherein he exhibits that certain Planets, with their Satellites, gyrate round our worthy Sun, at a rate and in a course, which, by greatest good fortune, he and the like of him have succeeded in detecting, is to me as precious as to another. But is this what thou namest 'Mechanism of the Heavens,' and 'System of the World'; this, wherein Sirius[5] and the Pleiades, and all Herschel's[6] Fifteen-thousand Suns per minute, being left out, some paltry handful of Moons, and inert Balls, had been—looked at, nicknamed, and marked in the Zodiacal Way-bill,[7] so that we can now prate of their Whereabout; their How, their Why, their What, being hid from us, as in the signless Inane?

"System of Nature! To the wisest man, wide as is his vision, Nature remains of quite *infinite* depth, of quite infinite expansion; and all Experience thereof limits itself to some few computed centuries and measured square miles. The course of Nature's phases, on this our little fraction of a Planet, is partially known to us; but who knows what deeper courses these depend on; what infinitely larger Cycle (of causes) our little Epicycle[8] revolves on? To the Minnow every cranny and pebble, and quality and accident, of its little native Creek may have become familiar; but does the Minnow understand the Ocean Tides and periodic Currents, the Trade-winds, and Monsoons, and Moon's Eclipses, by all which the condition of its little Creek is regulated, and may, from time to time (*un*miraculously enough), be quite overset and reversed? Such a minnow is Man; his Creek this Planet Earth; his Ocean the immeasurable All; his Monsoons and periodic Currents the mysterious Course of Providence through Aeons of Aeons.

---

[1] *Open sesame!* Magical phrase used to open the cave in the story "Ali Baba and the Forty Thieves" in *The Arabian Nights*.

[2] *one … Iron swim* From 2 Kings 6.6, in which Elisha causes an iron axe head to swim.

[3] *without … turning* See James 1.17.

[4] *Laplace … stars Celestial Mechanics* (1799–1825), by French astronomer Pierre Simon, Marquis de Laplace.

[5] *Sirius* The so-called "dog star," the brightest star in the constellation Canis Major (Latin: big dog).

[6] *Herschel* English astronomer Sir William Herschel (1738–1822).

[7] *Way-bill* Inventory of goods.

[8] *Epicycle* The Ptolemaic description of the evolution of a planet in a small circle, the center of which is orbiting in the circumference of a larger circle.

"We speak of the Volume of Nature, and truly a Volume it is—whose Author and Writer is God. To read it! Dost thou, does man, so much as well know the Alphabet thereof? With its Words, Sentences, and grand descriptive Pages, poetical and philosophical, spread out through Solar Systems, and Thousands of Years, we shall not try thee. It is a Volume written in celestial hieroglyphs, in the true Sacred-writing, of which even Prophets are happy that they can read here a line and there a line. As for your Institutes, and Academies of Science, they strive bravely; and, from amid the thick-crowded, inextricably intertwisted hieroglyphic writing, pick out, by dexterous combination, some Letters in the vulgar Character, and therefrom put together this and the other economic Recipe, of high avail in Practice. That Nature is more than some boundless Volume of such Recipes, or huge, well-nigh inexhaustible Domestic Cookery Book, of which the whole secret will in this manner one day evolve itself, the fewest dream.

"Custom," continues the Professor, "doth make dotards of us all.[1] Consider well, thou wilt find that Custom is the greatest of Weavers; and weaves air-raiment[2] for all the Spirits of the Universe; whereby indeed these dwell with us visibly, as ministering servants, in our houses and workshops; but their spiritual nature becomes, to the most, forever hidden. Philosophy complains that Custom has hoodwinked us, from the first; that we do everything by Custom, even Believe by it; that our very Axioms, let us boast of Free-thinking as we may, are oftenest simply such Beliefs as we have never heard questioned. Nay, what is Philosophy throughout but a continual battle against Custom; an ever-renewed effort to *transcend* the sphere of blind Custom, and so become Transcendental?

"Innumerable are the illusions and legerdemain-tricks[3] of Custom; but of all these, perhaps the cleverest is her knack of persuading us that the Miraculous, by simple repetition, ceases to be Miraculous. True, it is by this means we live, for man must work as well as wonder; and herein is Custom so far a kind nurse, guiding him to his true benefit. But she is a fond foolish nurse, or rather we are false foolish nurselings, when, in our

resting and reflecting hours, we prolong the same deception. Am I to view the Stupendous with stupid indifference, because I have seen it twice, or two-hundred, or two-million times? There is no reason in Nature or in Art why I should; unless, indeed, I am a mere Work-Machine, for whom the divine gift of Thought were no other than the terrestrial gift of Steam is to the Steam-engine; a power whereby cotton might be spun, and money and money's worth realised.

"Notable enough too, here as elsewhere, wilt thou find the potency of Names, which indeed are but one kind of such custom-woven, wonder-hiding Garments. Witchcraft, and all manner of Spectre-work, and Demonology, we have now named Madness and Diseases of the Nerves. Seldom reflecting that still the new question comes upon us: What is Madness, what are Nerves? Ever, as before, does Madness remain a mysterious-terrific, altogether *infernal* boiling-up of the Nether Chaotic Deep, through this fair-painted Vision of Creation, which swims thereon, which we name the Real. Was Luther's Picture of the Devil[4] less a Reality, whether it were formed within the bodily eye, or without it? In even the wisest Soul lies a whole world of internal Madness, an authentic Demon-Empire, out of which, indeed, his world of Wisdom has been creatively built together, and now rests there, as on its dark foundations does a habitable flowery Earth-rind.

"But deepest of all illusory Appearances, for hiding Wonder, as for many other ends, are your two grand fundamental world-enveloping Appearances, SPACE and TIME. These, as spun and woven for us from before Birth itself, to clothe our celestial ME for dwelling here, and yet to blind it—lie all-embracing, as the universal canvas, or warp and woof, whereby all minor Illusions, in this Phantasm Existence, weave and paint themselves. In vain, while here on Earth, shall you endeavour to strip them off; you can, at best, but rend them asunder for moments, and look through.

"Fortunatus had a wishing Hat, which when he put on, and wished himself Anywhere, behold he was There. By this means had Fortunatus triumphed over Space, he had annihilated Space; for him there was no Where, but all was Here. Were a Hatter to establish himself, in the

---

[1] *Custom … us all* Cf. Shakespeare's *Hamlet* 3.1.91: "Thus conscience does make cowards of us all."

[2] *raiment* Clothing.

[3] *legerdemain tricks* Sleights of hand.

[4] *Luther's Picture of the Devil* While he was translating the Psalms, German leader of the Protestant Reformation Martin Luther (1483–1546) threw his inkpot at an apparition of the devil.

Wahngasse of Weissnichtwo, and make felts of this sort for all mankind, what a world we should have of it! Still stranger, should, on the opposite side of the street, another Hatter establish himself, and, as his fellow-craftsman made Space-annihilating Hats, make Time-annihilating! Of both would I purchase, were it with my last groschen,[1] but chiefly of this latter. To clap-on your felt, and, simply by wishing that you were Any*where*, straightway to be *There*! Next to clap-on your other felt, and, simply by wishing that you were Any*when*, straightway to be *Then*! This were indeed the grander; shooting at will from the Fire-Creation of the World to its Fire-Consummation; here historically present in the First Century, conversing face to face with Paul and Seneca;[2] there prophetically in the Thirty-first, conversing also face to face with other Pauls and Senecas, who as yet stand hidden in the depth of that late Time!

"Or thinkest thou it were impossible, unimaginable? Is the Past annihilated, then, or only past; is the Future non-extant, or only future? Those mystic faculties of thine, Memory and Hope, already answer; already through those mystic avenues, thou the Earth-blinded summonest both Past and Future, and communest with them, though as yet darkly, and with mute beckonings. The curtains of Yesterday drop down, the curtains of Tomorrow roll up; but Yesterday and Tomorrow both *are*. Pierce through the Time-element, glance into the Eternal. Believe what thou findest written in the sanctuaries of Man's Soul, even as all Thinkers, in all ages, have devoutly read it there: that Time and Space are not God, but creations of God; that with God as it is a universal HERE, so is it an everlasting Now.

"And seest thou therein any glimpse of IMMORTAL-ITY?—O Heaven! Is the white Tomb of our Loved One, who died from our arms, and had to be left behind us there, which rises in the distance, like a pale, mournfully receding Milestone, to tell how many toilsome un-cheered miles we have journeyed on alone,—but a pale spectral Illusion! Is the lost Friend still mysteriously Here, even as we are Here mysteriously, with God!—Know of a truth that only the Time-shadows have perished, or are perishable; that the real Being of what-

ever was, and whatever is, and whatever will be, *is* even now and forever. This, should it unhappily seem new, thou mayest ponder at thy leisure, for the next twenty years, or the next twenty centuries; believe it thou must; understand it thou canst not.

"That the Thought-forms, Space and Time,[3] where-in, once for all, we are sent into this Earth to live, should condition and determine our whole Practical reasonings, conceptions, and imagings or imaginings, seems altogether fit, just, and unavoidable. But that they should, furthermore, usurp such sway over pure spiritual Meditation, and blind us to the wonder everywhere lying close on us, seems nowise so. Admit Space and Time to their due rank as Forms of Thought, nay even, if thou wilt, to their quite undue rank of Realities; and consider, then, with thyself how their thin disguises hide from us the brightest God-effulgences! Thus, were it not miraculous, could I stretch forth my hand and clutch the Sun? Yet thou seest me daily stretch forth my hand and therewith clutch many a thing, and swing it hither and thither. Art thou a grown baby, then, to fancy that the Miracle lies in miles of distance, or in pounds avoirdupois[4] of weight; and not to see that the true inexplicable God-revealing Miracle lies in this, that I can stretch forth my hand at all; that I have free Force to clutch aught therewith? Innumerable other of this sort are the deceptions, and wonder-hiding stupefactions, which Space practises, on us.

"Still worse is it with regard to Time. Your grand anti-magician, and universal wonder-hider, is this same lying Time. Had we but the Time-annihilating Hat, to put on for once only, we should see ourselves in a World of Miracles, wherein all fabled or authentic Thauma-turgy,[5] and feats of Magic, were outdone. But unhappily we have not such a Hat; and man, poor fool that he is, can seldom and scantily help himself without one.

---

[1] *groschen*   German coin.

[2] *Paul and Seneca*   Roman philosopher Seneca (3 BCE to 65 CE) was said to have met and exchanged thoughts with his contemporary the apostle St. Paul.

[3] *Thought-forms, Space and Time*   Pertaining to philosopher Immanuel Kant's (1724–1804) view that space and time are not external realities, but rather what he called "categories," or modes of perception.

[4] *avoirdupois*   System of measurement of weight; one stone is fourteen pounds avoirdupois.

[5] *Thaumaturgy*   Working of miracles.

"Were it not wonderful, for instance, had Orpheus, or Amphion,[1] built the walls of Thebes by the mere sound of his Lyre? Yet tell me, Who built these walls of Weissnichtwo; summoning out all the sandstone rocks, to dance along from the *Steinbruch* (now a huge Troglodyte Chasm, with frightful green-mantled pools), and shape themselves into Doric and Ionic pillars, squared ashlar[2] houses and noble streets? Was it not the still higher Orpheus, or Orpheuses, who, in past centuries, by the divine Music of Wisdom, succeeded in civilising Man? Our highest Orpheus walked in Judea, eighteen-hundred years ago: his sphere-melody, flowing in wild native tones, took captive the ravished souls of men; and, being of a truth sphere-melody, still flows and sounds, though now with thousandfold accompaniments, and rich symphonies, through all our hearts; and modulates, and divinely leads them. Is that a wonder, which happens in two hours; and does it cease to be wonderful if happening in two million? Not only was Thebes built by the music of an Orpheus, but without the music of some inspired Orpheus was no city ever built, no work that man glories in ever done.

"Sweep away the Illusion of Time; glance, if thou have eyes, from the near moving-cause to its far-distant Mover. The stroke that came transmitted through a whole galaxy of elastic balls, was it less a stroke than if the last ball only had been struck, and sent flying? O, could I (with the Time-annihilating Hat) transport thee direct from the Beginnings to the Endings, how were thy eyesight unsealed, and thy heart set flaming in the Light-sea of celestial wonder! Then sawest thou that this fair Universe, were it in the meanest province thereof, is in very deed the star-domed City of God; that through every star, through every grass-blade, and most through every Living Soul, the glory of a present God still beams. But Nature, which is the Time-vesture of God, and reveals Him to the wise, hides Him from the foolish.

"Again, could anything be more miraculous than an actual authentic Ghost? The English Johnson longed, all his life, to see one, but could not, though he went to Cock Lane,[3] and thence to the church-vaults, and tapped on coffins. Foolish Doctor! Did he never, with the mind's eye as well as with the body's, look round him into that full tide of human Life he so loved; did he never so much as look into Himself? The good Doctor was a Ghost, as actual and authentic as heart could wish; well-nigh a million of Ghosts were travelling the streets by his side. Once more I say, sweep away the illusion of Time; compress the threescore years into three minutes; what else was he, what else are we? Are we not Spirits, that are shaped into a body, into an Appearance, and that fade away again into air and Invisibility? This is no metaphor, it is a simple scientific *fact*: we start out of Nothingness, take figure, and are Apparitions; round us, as round the veriest spectre, is Eternity; and to Eternity minutes are as years and aeons. Come there not tones of Love and Faith, as from celestial harp-strings, like the Song of beatified Souls? And again, do not we squeak and jibber (in our discordant, screech-owlish debatings and recriminatings); and glide bodeful, and feeble, and fearful; or uproar (*poltern*), and revel in our mad Dance of the Dead—till the scent of the morning air[4] summons us to our still Home; and dreamy Night becomes awake and Day? Where now is Alexander of Macedon; does the steel Host, that yelled in fierce battle-shouts at Issus and Arbela,[5] remain behind him; or have they all vanished utterly, even as perturbed Goblins must? Napoleon too, and his Moscow Retreats and Austerlitz Campaigns![6] Was it all other than the veriest Spectre-hunt, which has now, with its howling tumult that made Night hideous, flitted away?—Ghosts! There are nigh a thousand-million walking the Earth openly at noontide; some half-hundred have vanished from it, some half-hundred have arisen in it, ere thy watch ticks once.

"O Heaven, it is mysterious, it is awful to consider that we not only carry each a future Ghost within him, but are, in very deed, Ghosts! These Limbs, whence had we them; this stormy Force; this life-blood with its burning Passion? They are dust and shadow; a Shadow-

---

[1]   *Orpheus or Amphion*   Musicians of Greek myth whose music had marvelous powers.

[2]   *ashlar*   Stone block.

[3]   *The English ... Cock Lane*   Samuel Johnson investigated a ghost sighting, which turned out to be a hoax, on Cock Lane in London.

[4]   *scent of the morning air*   See Shakespeare's *Hamlet* 1.5.66.

[5]   *Alexander ... Arbela*   Alexander the Great (356–323 BCE), King of Macedon, fought and won battles in Issus and Arbela in his quest to defeat the Persian Empire.

[6]   *Napoleon ... Campaigns*   French Emperor Napoleon Bonaparte was successful in his Austerlitz campaign but was defeated when he invaded Russia.

system gathered round our ME, wherein, through some moments or years, the Divine Essence is to be revealed in the Flesh. That warrior on his strong war-horse, fire flashes through his eyes; force dwells in his arm and heart; but warrior and war-horse are a vision, a revealed Force, nothing more. Stately they tread the Earth, as if it were a firm substance; fool! the Earth is but a film; it cracks in twain, and warrior and war-horse sink beyond plummet's sounding.[1] Plummet's? Fantasy herself will not follow them. A little while ago, they were not; a little while, and they are not, their very ashes are not.

"So has it been from the beginning, so will it be to the end, Generation after generation takes to itself the Form of a Body; and forth-issuing from Cimmerian Night,[2] on Heaven's mission APPEARS. What Force and Fire is in each he expends; one grinding in the mill of Industry; one hunter-like climbing the giddy Alpine heights of Science; one madly dashed in pieces on the rocks of Strife, in war with his fellow—and then the Heaven-sent is recalled; his earthly Vesture falls away, and soon even to Sense becomes a vanished Shadow. Thus, like some wild-flaming, wild-thundering train of Heaven's Artillery, does this mysterious MANKIND thunder and flame, in long-drawn, quick-succeeding grandeur, through the unknown Deep. Thus, like a God-created, fire-breathing Spirit-host, we emerge from the Inane; haste stormfully across the astonished Earth; then plunge again into the Inane.[3] Earth's mountains are levelled, and her seas filled up, in our passage; can the Earth, which is but dead and a vision, resist Spirits which have reality and are alive? On the hardest adamant[4] some footprint of us is stamped in; the last Rear of the host will read traces of the earliest Van.[5] But whence?—O Heaven, whither? Sense knows not; Faith knows not; only that it is through Mystery to Mystery, from God and to God.

We *are such stuff*
As dreams are made of, and our little Life
Is rounded with a sleep![6]

—1830–31

from *Past and Present*[7]

from BOOK 1
CHAPTER I—MIDAS[8]

The condition of England, on which many pamphlets are now in the course of publication, and many thoughts unpublished are going on in every reflective head, is justly regarded as one of the most ominous, and withal one of the strangest, ever seen in this world. England is full of wealth, of multifarious produce, supply for human want in every kind; yet England is dying of inanition. With unabated bounty the land of England blooms and grows; waving with yellow harvests; thick-studded with workshops, industrial implements, with fifteen millions of workers, understood to be the strongest, the cunningest and the willingest our Earth ever had; these men are here; the work they have done, the fruit they have realised is here, abundant, exuberant on every hand of us: and behold, some baleful fiat as of Enchantment has gone forth, saying, "Touch it not, ye workers, ye master-workers, ye

---

[1] *plummet's sounding* See Shakespeare's *The Tempest* 5.1.61; a plummet is a plumb-bob, a line with a weight on the end, used to determine a straight vertical line.

[2] *Cimmerian Night* The Cimmerians of Homer's *Odyssey* (Book 11) lived in a land permanently enshrouded in darkness.

[3] *Inane* Here, void.

[4] *adamant* Hard rock or mineral.

[5] *Van* I.e., vanguard, the troops at the front of an army ("host").

[6] *We are ... sleep!* From Shakespeare's *The Tempest* 4.1.156–58; the original reads "dreams are made on."

[7] *Past and Present* Carlyle wrote this treatise in seven weeks, in response to the lack of order and leadership that he felt was contributing to the widespread social and economic difficulties England was experiencing at that time. Carlyle blamed both the complacent aristocracy, which sought to maintain the status quo, and the spread of democracy, which he felt did little to provide heroic leaders. In 1837, industry in England entered into a depression that lasted several years. Many factories closed and others were forced to cut wages, which led to rioting in the manufacturing districts. By 1845, approximately one-twelfth of the population was unemployed, and many people ended up in overcrowded poorhouses. When the Chartists organized peaceful protests for social and economic reform, many British citizens began to fear a full-scale revolution.

[8] *Midas* Fabled king of Phrygia who, in one myth, was granted his wish that everything he touched would turn to gold. As a result, he was unable to eat. In another myth, he judges the music of the woodland god Pan to be superior to that of Apollo, god of music. Apollo, offended, changes Midas's ears to those of a donkey.

master-idlers; none of you can touch it, no man of you shall be the better for it; this is enchanted fruit!" On the poor workers such fiat[1] falls first, in its rudest shape; but on the rich master-workers too it falls; neither can the rich master-idlers, nor any richest or highest man escape, but all are like to be brought low with it, and made "poor" enough, in the money sense or a far fataler one.

Of these successful skilful workers some two millions, it is now counted, sit in Workhouses, Poor-law Prisons; or have "out-door relief"[2] flung over the wall to them—the workhouse Bastille[3] being filled to bursting, and the strong Poor-law broken asunder by a stronger. They sit there, these many months now; their hope of deliverance as yet small. In workhouses, pleasantly so-named, because work cannot be done in them. Twelve-hundred-thousand workers in England alone; their cunning right-hand lamed, lying idle in their sorrowful bosom; their hopes, outlooks, share of this fair world, shut-in by narrow walls. They sit there, pent up, as in a kind of horrid enchantment; glad to be imprisoned and enchanted, that they may not perish starved. The picturesque Tourist, in a sunny autumn day, through this bounteous realm of England, descries the Union Workhouse on his path. "Passing by the Workhouse of St. Ives in Huntingdonshire, on a bright day last autumn," says the picturesque Tourist, "I saw sitting on wooden benches, in front of their Bastille and within their ring-wall and its railings, some half-hundred or more of these men. Tall robust figures, young mostly or of middle age; of honest countenance, many of them thoughtful and even intelligent-looking men. They sat there, near by one another; but in a kind of torpor, especially in a silence, which was very striking. In silence: for, alas, what word was to be said? An Earth all lying round, crying, Come and till me, come and reap me—yet we here sit enchanted! In the eyes and brows of these men hung the gloomiest expression, not of anger, but of grief and shame and manifold inarticulate distress and weariness; they returned my glance with a glance that seemed to say, 'Do not look at us. We sit enchanted here, we know not why. The Sun shines and the Earth calls; and, by the governing Powers and Impotences of this England, we are forbidden to obey. It is impossible, they tell us!' There was something that reminded me of Dante's Hell[4] in the look of all this; and I rode swiftly away."

So many hundred thousands sit in workhouses, and other hundred thousands have not yet got even workhouses; and in thrifty Scotland itself, in Glasgow or Edinburgh City, in their dark lanes, hidden from all but the eye of God, and of rare Benevolence, the minister of God, there are scenes of woe and destitution and desolation, such, as, one may hope, the Sun never saw before in the most barbarous regions where men dwelt. Competent witnesses, the brave and humane Dr. Alison,[5] who speaks what he knows, whose noble Healing Art in his charitable hands becomes once more a truly sacred one, report these things for us. These things are not of this year, or of last year, have no reference to our present state of commercial stagnation, but only to the common state. Not in sharp fever-fits, but in chronic gangrene of this kind is Scotland suffering. A Poor-law, any and every Poor-law, it may be observed, is but a temporary measure; an anodyne, not a remedy. Rich and Poor, when once the naked facts of their condition have come into collision, cannot long subsist together on a mere Poor-law. True enough—and yet, human beings cannot be left to die! Scotland too, till something better come, must have a Poor-law, if Scotland is not to be a byword among the nations. O what a waste is there; of noble and thrice-noble national virtues; peasant Stoicisms, Heroisms; valiant manful habits, soul of a Nation's worth, which all the metal of Potosi[6] cannot purchase back; to which the metal of Potosi, and all you can buy with it, is dross and dust!

Why dwell on this aspect of the matter? It is too

---

[1] *fiat* Order.

[2] *Workhouses* Established under the Poor Law Amendment Act of 1834 for the relief of the poor. They were designed to be as unpleasant as possible, in order to discourage people from entering them. Living conditions were poor, the work provided was equivalent to prison labor, and families were separated upon entering, with men and women lodged separately; *out-door relief* System, in place prior to the Poor Law Amendment Act, under which each parish would provide its poor with minimum allowances.

[3] *Bastille* Prison. (In reference to the Parisian prison of that name, the destruction of which by the mob in 1789 is commonly held to mark the beginning of the French Revolution.)

[4] *Dante's Hell* Reference to *The Divine Comedy* by thirteenth-century Italian poet Dante Alighieri.

[5] *Dr. Alison* Scottish physician and social reformer who wrote *Observations on the Management of the Poor in Scotland* (1840).

[6] *Potosi* Bolivian city fabled for its riches.

indisputable, not doubtful now to anyone. Descend where you will into the lower class, in Town or Country, by what avenue you will, by Factory Inquiries, Agricultural Inquiries, by Revenue Returns, by Mining-Labourer Committees, by opening your own eyes and looking, the same sorrowful result discloses itself: you have to admit that the working body of this rich English Nation has sunk or is fast sinking into a state, to which, all sides of it considered, there was literally never any parallel. At Stockport Assizes[1]—and this too has no reference to the present state of trade, being of date prior to that—a Mother and a Father are arraigned and found guilty of poisoning three of their children, to defraud a burial-society of some 3*l*.8*s*.[2] due on the death of each child. They are arraigned, found guilty; and the official authorities, it is whispered, hint that perhaps the case is not solitary, that perhaps you had better not probe farther into that department of things. This is in the autumn of 1841; the crime itself is of the previous year or season. "Brutal savages, degraded Irish,"[3] mutters the idle reader of Newspapers, hardly lingering on this incident. Yet it is an incident worth lingering on; the depravity, savagery, and degraded Irishism being never so well admitted. In the British land, a human Mother and Father, of white skin and professing the Christian religion, had done this thing; they, with their Irishism and necessity and savagery, had been driven to do it. Such instances are like the highest mountain apex emerged into view, under which lies a whole mountain region and land, not yet emerged. A human Mother and Father had said to themselves, What shall we do to escape starvation? We are deep sunk here, in our dark cellar; and help is far. Yes, in the Ugolino Hunger-tower[4] stern things happen; best-loved little Gaddo fallen dead on his Father's knees! The Stockport Mother

and Father think and hint: our poor little starveling Tom, who cries all day for victuals, who will see only evil and not good in this world; if he were out of misery at once; he well dead, and the rest of us perhaps kept alive? It is thought, and hinted; at last it is done. And now Tom being killed, and all spent and eaten, Is it poor little starveling Jack that must go, or poor little starveling Will? What a committee of ways and means!

In starved sieged cities, in the uttermost doomed ruin of old Jerusalem fallen under the wrath of God, it was prophesied and said, "The hands of the pitiful women have sodden their own children."[5] The stern Hebrew imagination could conceive no blacker gulf of wretchedness; that was the ultimatum of degraded god-punished man. And we here, in modern England, exuberant with supply of all kinds, besieged by nothing if it be not by invisible Enchantments, are we reaching that? How come these things? Wherefore are they, wherefore should they be?

Nor are they of the St. Ives workhouses, of the Glasgow lanes, and Stockport cellars, the only unblessed among us. This successful industry of England, with its plethoric wealth, has as yet made nobody rich; it is an enchanted wealth, and belongs yet to nobody. We might ask, Which of us has it enriched? We can spend thousands where we once spent hundreds, but can purchase nothing good with them. In Poor and Rich, instead of noble thrift and plenty, there is idle luxury alternating with mean scarcity and inability. We have sumptuous garnitures for our Life, but have forgotten to *live* in the middle of them. It is an enchanted wealth; no man of us can yet touch it. The class of men who feel that they are truly better off by means of it, let them give us their name!

Many men eat finer cookery, drink dearer liquors—with what advantage they can report, and their Doctors can; but in the heart of them, if we go out of the dyspeptic stomach, what increase of blessedness is there? Are they better, beautifuller, stronger, braver? Are they even what they call "happier"? Do they look with satisfaction on more things and human faces in this God's-Earth; do more things and human faces look with satisfaction on them? Not so. Human faces gloom discordantly, disloyally on one another. Things, if it be

---

[1] *Assizes* Court sessions held periodically in the various counties in England.

[2] *3l.8s.* Three pounds, eight shillings.

[3] *"Brutal … Irish"* This passage reflects the prejudice of many Englishmen and women against the native people of Ireland.

[4] *Ugolino Hunger-tower* In the thirteenth century, Count Ugolino of Pisa and his children and nephews were imprisoned and starved to death when Ugolino betrayed his political allies. According to Dante's *Inferno*, Ugolino ate his children's bodies after they died, in order to stave off starvation. The tower in Pisa's central piazza in which Ugolino was imprisoned has since been called the Tower of Hunger.

[5] *The hands … children* From Lamentations 4.10; *sodden* Boiled.

not mere cotton and iron things, are growing disobedient to man. The Master Worker is enchanted, for the present, like his Workhouse Workman; clamours, in vain hitherto, for a very simple sort of "Liberty"—the liberty "to buy where he finds it cheapest, to sell where he finds it dearest." With guineas jingling in every pocket, he was no whit richer; but now, the very guineas threatening to vanish, he feels that he is poor indeed. Poor Master Worker! And the Master Unworker,[1] is not he in a still fataler situation? Pausing amid his game-preserves, with awful eye—as he well may! Coercing fifty-pound tenants;[2] coercing, bribing, cajoling; "doing what he likes with his own." His mouth full of loud futilities, and arguments to prove the excellence of his Corn-law;[3] and in his heart the blackest misgiving, a desperate half-consciousness that his excellent Corn-law is *in*defensible, that his loud arguments for it are of a kind to strike men too literally *dumb*.

To whom, then, is this wealth of England wealth? Who is it that it blesses, makes happier, wiser, beautifuler, in any way better? Who has got hold of it, to make it fetch and carry for him, like a true servant, not like a false mock-servant, to do him any real service whatsoever? As yet no one. We have more riches than any Nation ever had before; we have less good of them than any Nation ever had before. Our successful industry is hitherto unsuccessful; a strange success, if we stop here! In the midst of plethoric plenty, the people perish; with gold walls, and full barns, no man feels himself safe or satisfied. Workers, Master Workers, Unworkers, all men, come to a pause; stand fixed, and cannot farther. Fatal paralysis spreading inwards, from the extremities, in St. Ives workhouses, in Stockport cellars, through all limbs, as if towards the heart itself. Have we actually got enchanted, then, accursed by some god?

Midas longed for gold, and insulted the Olympians. He got gold, so that whatsoever he touched became gold—and he, with his long ears, was little the better for it. Midas had misjudged the celestial music-tones; Midas

had insulted Apollo and the gods. The gods gave him his wish, and a pair of long ears, which also were a good appendage to it. What a truth in these old Fables! ...

CHAPTER 6—HERO-WORSHIP

To the present Editor, not less than to Bobus,[4] a Government of the Wisest, what Bobus calls an Aristocracy of Talent, seems the one healing remedy; but he is not so sanguine as Bobus with respect to the means of realising it. He thinks that we have at once missed realising it, and come to need it so pressingly, by departing far from the inner eternal Laws, and taking-up with the temporary outer semblances of Laws. He thinks that "enlightened Egoism,"[5] never so luminous, is not the rule by which man's life can be led. That "Laissez-faire," "Supply-and-demand," "Cash-payment for the sole nexus,"[6] and so forth, were not, are not and will never be, a practicable Law of Union for a Society of Men. The Poor and Rich, that Governed and Governing, cannot long live together on any such Law of Union. Alas, he thinks that man has a soul in him, *different* from the stomach in any sense of this word; that if said soul be asphyxied, and lie quietly forgotten, the man and his affairs are in a bad way. He thinks that said soul will have to be resuscitated from its asphyxia; that if it prove irresuscitable, the man is not long for this world. In brief, that Midas-eared Mammonism, double-barrelled Dilettantism,[7] and their thousand adjuncts and corollaries, are *not* the Law by which God Almighty has appointed this his Universe to go; that, once for all, these are not the Law; and then, further, that we shall

---

[1] *Unworker* I.e., person who does not work.

[2] *fifty-pound tenants* Tenants who paid fifty pounds or more in rent. Under the Reform Bill of 1832, these tenants were allowed to vote.

[3] *Corn-law* One of a series of laws passed in 1815 to regulate the import of grain and keep the price of grain artificially high.

[4] *Bobus* Carlyle creates this fictional character, whom he earlier refers to as "Bobus Higgins, Sausage-maker on the great scale," as a caricature of members of the middle class who take a narrow-minded view of social reform.

[5] *enlightened Egoism* I.e., rational egoism, according to which it is beneficial for society if individuals act in their own best interests.

[6] *Laissez-faire* Theory of economics, holding that the government should not interfere with business or trade, and that the market will regulate itself; *Cash ... nexus* I.e., cash is the only nexus (connection or bond) between people.

[7] *Mammonism* Worship of, or devotion to, Mammon, the personification of wealth. See Luke16.13:" "Ye cannot serve God and Mammon"; *Dilettantism* Pursuit of knowledge in an art or science as an idle pastime, without any serious interest or goal.

have to return to what *is* the Law—not by smooth flowery paths, it is like, and with "tremendous cheers" in our throat, but over steep untrodden places, through stormclad chasms, waste oceans, and the bosom of tornadoes; thank Heaven, if not through very Chaos and the Abyss! The resuscitating of a soul that has gone to asphyxia is no momentary or pleasant process, but a long and terrible one.

To the present Editor, Hero-worship, as he has else-where named it, means much more than an elected Parliament or stated Aristocracy of the Wisest; for in his dialect it is the summary, ultimate essence, and supreme practical perfection of all manner of worship, and true worthships and noblenesses whatsoever. Such blessed Parliament and, were it once in perfection, blessed Aristocracy of the Wisest, god-honoured and man-honoured, he does look for, more and more per-fected—as the topmost blessed practical apex of a whole world reformed from sham-worship, informed anew with worship, with truth and blessedness! He thinks that Hero-worship, done differently in every different epoch of the world, is the soul of all social business among men; that the doing of it well, or the doing of it ill, measures accurately what degree of well-being or of ill-being there is in the world's affairs. He thinks that we, on the whole, do our Hero-worship worse than any Nation in this world ever did it before; that the Burns an Exciseman, the Byron a Literary Lion,[1] are intrinsi-cally, all things considered, a baser and falser phenome-non than the Odin a God,[2] the Mahomet a Prophet of God. It is this Editor's clear opinion, accordingly, that we must learn to do our Hero-worship better; that to do it better and better means the awakening of the Nation's soul from its asphyxia, and the return of blessed life to us—Heaven's blessed life, not Mammon's galvanic[3] accursed one. To resuscitate the Asphyxied, apparently now moribund and in the last agony if not resuscitated, such and no other seems the consummation.

"Hero-worship," if you will—yes, friends; but, first of all, by being ourselves of heroic mind. A whole world of Heroes; a world not of Flunkies, where no Hero-King *can* reign: that is what we aim at! We, for our share, will put away all Flunkyism, Baseness, Unveracity from us; we shall then hope to have Noblenesses and Veracities set over us; never till then. Let Bobus and Company sneer, "That is your Reform!" Yes, Bobus, that is our Reform; and except in that, and what will follow out of that, we have no hope at all. Reform, like Charity, O Bobus, must begin at home. Once well at home, how will it radiate outwards, irrepressible, into all that we touch and handle, speak and work; kindling ever new light, by incalculable contagion, spreading in geometric ratio, far and wide—doing good only, wheresoever it spreads, and not evil.

By Reform Bills, Anti-Corn-Law Bills, and thousand other bills and methods, we will demand of our Gover-nors, with emphasis, and for the first time not without effect, that they cease to be quacks, or else depart; that they set no quackeries and block-headisms anywhere to rule over us, that they utter or act no cant to us—it will be better if they do not. For we shall now know quacks when we see them; cant, when we hear it, shall be horrible to us! We will say, with the poor Frenchman at the Bar of the Convention, though in wiser style than he, and "for the space" not "of an hour" but of a life-time: "*Je demands l'arrestation des coquins et des laches.*" "Arrestment of the knaves and dastards." Ah, we know what a work that is; how long it will be before *they* are all or mostly got "arrested"—but here is one; arrest him, in God's name; it is one fewer! We will, in all practicable ways, by word and silence, by act and refusal to act, energetically demand that arrestment—"*je demande cette arrestation-la!*"—and by degrees infallibly attain it. Infallibly, for light spreads; all human souls, never so bedarkened, love light; light once kindled spreads, till all is luminous, till the cry, "*Arrest* your knaves and das-tards" rises imperative from millions of hearts, and rings and reigns from sea to sea. Nay, how many of them may we not "arrest" with our own hands, even now, we! Do not countenance them, thou there: turn away from their lacquered sumptuosities, their belauded sophistries, their serpent graciosities, their spoken and acted cant, with a

---

[1] *Burns* Poet Robert Burns (1759–96), who worked as an excise officer. Burns came to be regarded as Scotland's national poet; *Byron* Romantic poet George Gordon, Lord Byron (1788–1824).

[2] *Odin* Norse god of war, art, and culture.

[3] *galvanic* Applying electricity; having the effect of an electric shock.

sacred horror, with an *Apage Satanas*.[1] Bobus and Company, and all men, will gradually join us. We demand arrestment of the knaves and dastards, and begin by arresting our own poor selves out of that fraternity. There is no other reform conceivable. Thou and I, my friend, can, in the most flunky world, make, each of us, *one* non-flunky, one hero, if we like. That will be two heroes to begin with—Courage! even that is a whole world of heroes to end with, or what we poor Two can do in furtherance thereof!

Yes, friends: Hero-kings, and a whole world not unheroic—there lies the port and happy haven, towards which, through all these stormtost seas, French Revolutions, Chartisms, Manchester Insurrections,[2] that make the heart sick in these bad days, the Supreme Powers are driving us. On the whole, blessed be the Supreme Powers, stern as they are! Towards that haven will we, O friends; let all true men, with what of faculty is in them, bend valiantly, incessantly, with thousandfold endeavour, thither, thither! There, or else in the Ocean-abysses, it is very clear to me, we shall arrive.

Well, here truly is no answer to the Sphinx-question[3]—not the answer a disconsolate public, inquiring at the College of Health, was in hopes of! A total change of regimen, change of constitution and existence from the very centre of it; a new body to be got, with resuscitated soul—not without convulsive travail-throes, as all birth and new-birth presupposes travail! This is sad news to a disconsolate discerning Public, hoping to have got off by some Morrison's Pill,[4] some Saint-John's corrosive mixture and perhaps a little blistery friction on the back! We were prepared to part with our Corn-Law, with various Laws and Unlaws, but this, what is this?

Nor has the Editor forgotten how it fares with your ill-boding Cassandras in Sieges of Troy.[5] Imminent perdition is not usually driven away by words of warning. Didactic Destiny has other methods in store, or these would fail always. Such words should, nevertheless, be uttered, when they dwell truly in the soul of any man. Words are hard, are importunate; but how much harder the importunate events they foreshadow! Here and there a human soul may listen to the words—who knows how many human souls?—whereby the importunate events, if not diverted and prevented, will be rendered *less* hard. The present Editor's purpose is to himself full of hope.

For though fierce travails, though wide seas and roaring gulfs lie before us, is it not something if a Loadstar, in the eternal sky, do once more disclose itself; an everlasting light, shining through all cloud-tempests and roaring billows, ever as we emerge from the trough of the sea; the blessed beacon, far off on the edge of far horizons, towards which we are to steer incessantly for life? Is it not something, O Heavens, is it not all? There lies the Heroic Promised Land; under that Heaven's-light, my brethren, bloom the Happy Isles—there, O there! Thither will we;

"There dwells the great Achilles whom we knew."[6] There dwell all Heroes, and will dwell: thither, all ye heroic-minded! The Heaven's Loadstar once clearly in our eye, how will each true man stand truly to *his* work in the ship; how, with undying hope, will all things be fronted, all be conquered. Nay, with the ship's prow once turned in that direction, is not all, as it were, already well? Sick wasting misery has become noble manful effort with a goal in our eye. The choking Nightmare chokes us no longer, for we *stir* under it; the Nightmare has already fled.

Certainly, could the present Editor instruct men how to know Wisdom, Heroism, when they see it, that they might do reverence to *it* only, and loyally make it ruler over them, yes, he were the living epitome of all

---

[1] *Apage Satanus* Latin: Begone, Satan.

[2] *Chartisms* Movements by the Chartists, peaceful democratic reformers whose principles were set out in the "People's Charter," published in 1838; *Manchester Insurrections* Rioting in Manchester in 1842 resulted from the reduction of wages in both the coal mines and the factories. Manchester was also the site of the famous 1819 Peterloo Massacre, at which cavalry charged on an outdoor political meeting, killing thirteen people and wounding several others.

[3] *Sphinx-question* Riddle, like those posed by the mythological sphinx, a winged half-woman, half-lion who would not allow travelers to pass unless they could correctly answer her riddle. If they answered incorrectly, they would be killed.

[4] *Morrison's Pill* I.e., a cure-all.

[5] *Cassandras … Troy* Cassandra, daughter of the King of Troy, was given the gift of prophecy, but cursed so that nobody would believe her.

[6] *There dwells … knew* Cf. lines 63–4 of Alfred Lord Tennyson's poem "Ulysses": "It may be we shall touch the Happy Isles, / And see the great Achilles, whom we knew." The Happy Isles were the Isles of the Blessed, supposedly (according to Greek myth) located in the Atlantic Ocean.

Editors, Teachers, Prophets, that now teach and prophesy; he were an *Apollo*-Morrison, a Trismegistus[1] and *effective* Cassandra! Let no Able Editor hope such things. It is to be expected the present laws of copyright, rate of reward per sheet, and other considerations will save him from that peril. Let no Editor hope such things; no—and yet let all Editors aim towards such things, and even towards such alone! One knows not what the meaning of editing and writing is, if even this be not it.

Enough, to the present Editor it has seemed possible some glimmering of light, for here and there a human soul might lie in these confused Paper-Masses now entrusted to him; wherefore he determines to edit the same. Out of old Books, new Writings, and much Meditation not of yesterday, he will endeavour to select a thing or two; and from the Past, in a circuitous way, illustrate the Present and the Future. The Past is a dim indubitable fact: the Future too is one, only dimmer; nay properly it is the *same* fact in new dress and development. For the Present holds it in both the whole Past and the whole Future—as the life-tree Igdrasil,[2] wide-waving, many-toned, has its roots down deep in the Death-kingdoms, among the oldest dead dust of men, and with its boughs reaches always beyond the stars, and in all times and places is one and the same Life-tree! …

from BOOK 3

CHAPTER I—PHENOMENA

But, it is said, our religion is gone: we no longer believe in St. Edmund,[3] no longer see the figure of him on the rim of the sky, minatory or confirmatory! God's absolute Laws, sanctioned by an eternal Heaven and an eternal Hell, have become Moral Philosophies, sanctioned by able computations of Profit and Loss, by weak considerations of Pleasures of Virtue and the Moral Sublime.

It is even so. To speak in the ancient dialect, we "have forgotten God"—in the most modern dialect and very truth of the matter, we have taken up the Fact of this Universe as it *is not*. We have quietly closed our eyes to the eternal Substance of things, and opened them only to the Shows and Shams of things. We quietly believe this Universe to be intrinsically a great unintelligible PERHAPS; extrinsically, clear enough, it is a great, most extensive Cattlefold and Workhouse, with most extensive Kitchen-ranges, Dining-tables—whereat he is wise who can find a place! All the Truth of this Universe is uncertain; only the profit and loss of it, the pudding and praise of it, are and remain very visible to the practical man.

There is no longer any God for us! God's Laws are become a Greatest-Happiness Principle, a Parliamentary Expediency. The Heavens overarch us only as an Astronomical Time-keeper, a butt for Herschel-telescopes[4] to shoot science at, to shoot sentimentalities at—in our and old Jonson's[5] dialect, man has lost the *soul* out of him, and now, after the due period, begins to find the want of it! This is verily the plague-spot, centre of the universal Social Gangrene, threatening all modern things with frightful death. To him that will consider it, here is the stem, with its roots and taproot, with its world-wide upas-boughs[6] and accursed poison-exudations, under which the world lies writhing in atrophy and agony. You touch the focal-centre of all our disease, of our frightful nosology[7] of diseases, when you lay your hand on this. There is no religion; there is no God; man has lost his soul, and vainly seeks antiseptic salt. Vainly: in killing Kings, in passing Reform Bills, in French Revolutions, Manchester Insurrections, is found no remedy. The foul elephantine leprosy, alleviated for an hour, reappears in new force and desperateness next hour.

For actually this is *not* the real fact of the world; the world is not made so, but otherwise! Truly, any Society

---

[1] *Apollo* Classical god of poetry, music, and prophecy; *Trismegistus* Greek: thrice great. This is an epithet of the classical god Hermes, the messenger and herald for the other gods.

[2] *Igdrasil* Great tree of Scandinavian mythology, the roots and branches of which stretched through the universe.

[3] *St. Edmund* King of East Anglia (c. 840–870), famous for the miracles attributed to him after his martyrdom.

[4] *Herschel-telescopes* Large telescopes of the sort designed by William Herschel (1738–1822), astronomer who studied the planets and stars with a telescope that had a 40-foot focal length and 48-inch mirror.

[5] *Jonson* Poet and dramatist Ben Jonson (1572–1637).

[6] *upas-boughs* Boughs of the upas tree, a fabled tree of Java said to be so poisonous that it destroyed all life within a fifteen-mile radius.

[7] *nosology* Catalogue.

setting out from this No-God hypothesis will arrive at a result or two. The *Un*veracities, escorted, each Unveracity of them by its corresponding Misery and Penalty; the Phantasms, and Fatuities, and ten-years Corn-Law Debatings, that shall walk the Earth at noonday, must needs be numerous! The Universe *being* intrinsically a Perhaps, being too probably an "infinite Humbug," why should any minor Humbug astonish us? It is all according to the order of Nature, and Phantasms riding with huge clatter along the streets, from end to end of our existence, astonish nobody. Enchanted St. Ives Workhouses and Joe-Manton[1] Aristocracies; giant Working Mammonism near strangled in the partridge-nets of giant-looking Idle Dilettantism—this, in all its branches, in its thousand-thousand modes and figures, is a sight familiar to us.

The Popish Religion,[2] we are told, flourishes extremely in these years; and is the most vivacious-looking religion to be met with at present. "*Elle a trois cents ans dans le ventre,*" counts Mr. Jouffroy; "*c'est pourquoi je la respecte!*"[3] The old Pope of Rome, finding it laborious to kneel so long while they cart him through the streets to bless the people on *Corpus Christi* Day,[4] complains of rheumatism; whereupon his Cardinals consult, construct him, after some study, a stuffed cloaked figure, of iron and wood, with wool or baked hair, and place it in a kneeling posture. Stuffed figure, or rump of a figure; to this stuffed rump he, sitting at his ease on a lower level, joins, by the aid of cloaks and drapery, his living head and outspread hands: the rump with its cloaks kneels, the Pope looks, and holds his hands spread; and so the two in concert bless the Roman population on *Corpus Christi* Day, as well as they can.

I have considered this amphibious Pope, with the wool-and-iron back, with the flesh head and hands, and endeavoured to calculate his horoscope. I reckon him the remarkablest Pontiff that has darkened God's daylight, or painted himself in the human retina, for these several thousand years. Nay, since Chaos first shivered, and "sneezed," as the Arabs say, with the first shaft of sunlight shot through it, "what stranger product was there of Nature and Art working together? Here is a Supreme Priest who believes God to be—What, in the name of God, *does* he believe God to be? —and discerns that all worship of God is a scenic phantasmagory of wax-candles, organ-blasts, Gregorian chants, mass-brayings, purple monsignori,[5] wool-and-iron rumps, artistically spread out—to save the ignorant from worse.

O reader, I say not who are Belial's[6] elect. This poor amphibious Pope too gives loaves to the Poor, has in him more good latent than he is himself aware of. His poor Jesuits, in the late Italian Cholera, were, with a few German Doctors, the only creatures whom dastard terror had not driven mad: they descended fearless into all gulfs and bedlams; watched over the pillow of the dying, with help, with counsel and hope; shone as luminous fixed stars, when all else had gone out in chaotic night: honour to them! This poor Pope—who knows what good is in him? In a Time otherwise too prone to forget, he keeps up the mournfulest ghastly memorial of the Highest, Blessedest, which once was; which, in new fit forms, will again partly have to be. Is he not as a perpetual death's-head and cross-bones, with their *Resurgam*,[7] on the grave of a Universal Heroism, grave of a Christianity? Such Noblenesses, purchased by the world's best heart's-blood, must not be lost; we cannot afford to lose them, in what confusions soever. To all of us the day will come, to a few of us it has already come, when no mortal, with his heart yearning for a "Divine Humility," or other "Highest form of Valour," will need to look for it in death's-heads, but will see it round him in here and there a beautiful living head.

Besides, there is in this poor Pope, and his practice of the Scenic Theory of Worship, a frankness which I rather honour. Not half and half, but with undivided heart does *he* set about worshipping by stage-machinery; as if there were now, and could again be, in Nature no

---

1 *Joe Manton*   Prestigious maker of high quality, expensive firearms (1766–1835).

2 *The Popish Religion*   Roman Catholicism.

3 *Elle a … respecte*   French: She [i.e., the Roman Catholic religion] has three hundred years in her stomach, that is why I respect her. Théodore Simon Jouffroy (1796–1842) was a French philosopher and translator.

4 *Corpus Christi Day*   Occasion of the Feast of the Blessed Sacrament, which occurs on the Thursday after Trinity Sunday.

5 *monsignori*   Roman Catholics of ecclesiastical rank. Bishops and lower monsignors wear robes of various shades of purple.

6 *Belial*   Name for the devil, or for evil personified.

7 *Resurgam*   Latin: I will rise again.

other. He will ask you, What other? Under this my Gregorian Chant, and beautiful waxlight Phantasmagory, kindly hidden from you is an Abyss of Black Doubt, Scepticism, nay Sansculottic[1] Jacobinism; an Orcus[2] that has no bottom. Think of that. "Groby Pool *is* thatched with pancakes," as Jeannie Deans's Innkeeper defied it to be![3] The Bottomless of Scepticism, Atheism, Jacobinism, behold, it is thatched over, hidden from your despair, by stage-properties judiciously arranged. This stuffed rump of mine saves not me only from rheumatism but you also from what other *isms*! In this your Life-pilgrimage Nowhither, a fine Squallacci marching-music, and Gregorian Chant, accompanies you, and the hollow Night of Orcus is well hid!

Yes truly, few men that worship by the rotatory Calabash of the Calmucks[4] do it in half so great, frank or effectual a way. Drury Lane,[5] it is said, and that is saying much, might learn from him in the dressing of parts, in the arrangement of lights and shadows. He is the greatest Play-actor that at present draws salary in this world. Poor Pope; and I am told he is fast growing bankrupt too, and will, in a measurable term of years (a great way *within* the "three hundred"), not have a penny to make his pot boil! His old rheumatic back will then get to rest, and himself and his stage-properties sleep well in Chaos forevermore.

Or, alas, why go to Rome for Phantasms walking the streets? Phantasms, ghosts, in this midnight hour, hold jubilee, and screech and jabber; and the question rather were, What high Reality anywhere is yet awake? Aristocracy has become Phantasm-Aristocracy, no longer able to *do* its work, not in the least conscious that it has any work longer to do. Unable, totally careless to *do* its work; careful only to clamour for the *wages* of doing its work—nay for higher, and *palpably* undue wages, and Corn Laws and *increase* of rents, the old rate of wages not being adequate now! In hydra[6]-wrestle, giant "*Millocracy*"[7] so-called, a real giant, though as yet a blind one and but half-awake, wrestles and wrings in choking nightmare, "like to be strangled in the partridge-nets of Phantasm-Aristocracy," as we said, which fancies itself still to be a giant. Wrestles, as under nightmare, till it do awaken, and gasps and struggles thousandfold, we may say, in a truly painful manner, through all fibres of our English Existence, in these hours and years! Is our poor English Existence wholly becoming a Nightmare, full of mere Phantasms?

The Champion of England, cased in iron or tin, rides into Westminster Hall, "being lifted into his saddle with little assistance," and there asks, If in the four quarters of the world, under the cope[8] of Heaven, is any man or demon that dare question the right of this King? Under the cope of Heaven no man makes intelligible answer—as several men ought already to have done. Does not this Champion too know the world; that it is a huge Imposture, and bottomless Inanity, thatched over with bright cloth and other ingenious tissues? Him let us leave there, questioning all men and demons.

Him we have left to his destiny; but whom else have we found? From this the highest apex of things, downwards through all strata and breadths, how many fully awakened Realities have we fallen in with—alas, on the contrary, what troops and populations of Phantasms, not God-Veracities but Devil-Falsities, down to the very lowest stratum, which now, by such superincumbent weight of Unveracities, lies enchanted in St. Ives' Workhouses, broad enough, helpless enough! You will walk in no public thoroughfare or remotest byway of English Existence but you will meet a man, an interest of men, that has given up hope in the Everlasting, True, and placed its hope in the Temporary, half or wholly False. The Honourable Member complains unmusically that there is "devil's-dust" in Yorkshire cloth.[9] Yorkshire cloth—why, the very Paper I now write on is made, it

---

[1] *Sansculottic* Revolutionary. "Sans-culottes" were radical members of the Republican party who refused to wear the short pants ("culottes") and stockings characteristic of the aristocracy, and instead donned the loose pants worn by the working classes.

[2] *Orcus* Underworld.

[3] *Groby Pool ... be* Reference to Sir Walter Scott's *The Heart of Midlothian* (1818), in which the heroine, Jeannie Deans, asks an innkeeper whether there is any bad company on the road. He replies, "Why, when it's clean without them I'll thatch Groby pool wi' pancakes."

[4] *Calabash* Vessel; *Calmucks* Kalmucks, Mongolian people who inhabit the north-west shores of the Caspian Sea.

[5] *Drury Lane* Location of London's Theatre Royal.

[6] *hydra* Many-headed snake of Greek mythology.

[7] *Millocracy* I.e., rule of mill owners.

[8] *cope* Canopy.

[9] *Yorkshire cloth* Thick, coarse cloth manufactured in Yorkshire.

seems, partly of plaster-lime well smoothed, and obstructs my writing! You are lucky if you can find now any good Paper, any work really *done*; search where you will, from highest Phantasm apex to lowest Enchanted basis.

Consider, for example, that great Hat seven-feet high, which now perambulates London Streets; which my Friend Sauerteig[1] regarded justly as one of our English notabilities. "The topmost point as yet," said he, "would it were your culminating and returning point, to which English Puffery has been observed to reach!" The Hatter in the Strand of London, instead of making better felt-hats than another, mounts a huge lath-and-plaster Hat, seven-feet high, upon wheels; sends a man to drive it through the streets, hoping to be saved *thereby*. He has not attempted to *make* better hats, as he was appointed by the Universe to do, and as with this ingenuity of his he could very probably have done; but his whole industry is turned to *persuade* us that he has made such! He too knows that the Quack has become God. Laugh not at him, O reader; or do not laugh only. He has ceased to be comic; he is fast becoming tragic. To me this all-deafening blast of Puffery, of poor Falsehood grown necessitous, of poor Heart-Atheism fallen now into Enchanted Workhouses, sounds too surely like a Doom's-blast! I have to say to myself in old dialect, "God's blessing is not written on all this; His curse is written on all this!" Unless perhaps the Universe *be* a chimera—some old totally deranged eightday clock, dead as brass, which the Maker, if there ever was any Maker, has long ceased to meddle with? To my Friend Sauerteig this poor seven-feet Hat-manufacturer, as the topstone of English Puffery, was very notable.

Alas, that we natives note him little, that we view him as a tiling of course, is the very burden of the misery. We take it for granted, the most rigorous of us, that all men who have made anything are expected and entitled to make the loudest possible proclamation of it, and call on a discerning public to reward them for it. Every man his own trumpeter—that is, to a really alarming extent, the accepted rule. Make loudest possible proclamation of your Hat: true proclamation if that will do; if that will not do, then false proclamation—to such extent of falsity as will serve your purpose,

as will not seem too false to be credible! I answer, once for all, that the fact is not so. Nature requires no man to make proclamation of his doings and hat-makings; Nature forbids all men to make such. There is not a man or hat-maker born into the world but feels, or has felt, that he is degrading himself if he speak of his excellencies and prowesses, and supremacy in his craft. His inmost heart says to him, "Leave thy friends to speak of these; if possible, thy enemies to speak of these; but at all events, thy friends!" He feels that he is already a poor braggart, fast hastening to be a falsity and speaker of the Untruth.

Nature's Laws, I must repeat, are eternal: her small still voice, speaking from the inmost heart of us, shall not, under terrible penalties, be disregarded. No one man can depart from the truth without damage to himself—no one million of men, no Twenty-seven Millions of men. Show me a Nation fallen everywhere into this course, so that each expects it, permits it to others and himself, I will show you a Nation travelling with one assent on the broad way. The broad way, however many Banks of England, Cotton Mills, and Duke's Palaces it may have. Not at happy Elysian fields,[2] and everlasting crowns of victory, earned by silent Valour, will this Nation arrive; but at precipices, devouring gulfs, if it pause not. Nature has appointed happy fields, victorious laurel-crowns,[3] but only to the brave and true. *Un*nature, what we call Chaos, holds nothing in it but vacuities, devouring gulfs. What are Twenty-seven Millions, and their unanimity? Believe them not: the Worlds and the Ages, God and Nature and All Men say otherwise.

"Rhetoric all this?" No, my brother, very singular to say, it is Fact all this. Cocker's Arithmetic[4] is not truer. Forgotten in these days, it is old as the foundations of the Universe, and will endure till the Universe cease. It is forgotten now, and the first mention of it puckers thy sweet countenance into a sneer, but it will be brought to mind again—unless indeed the Law of Gravitation

[1] *Sauerteig* Gottfried Sauerteig, the fictitious "Picturesque Tourist" who visits the St. Ives workhouse in Book 1, Chapter 1.

[2] *Elysian Fields* In Greek mythology, where the blessed reside after death.

[3] *laurel-crowns* Marks of honor conferred upon heroes, poets, and victorious athletes in ancient Greece and Rome.

[4] *Cocker's Arithmetic* Textbook by Edward Cocker (1631–75) that was so widely read and admired it gave rise to the phrase "according to Cocker," meaning "perfectly correct."

chance to cease, and men find that they *can* walk on vacancy. Unanimity of the Twenty-seven Millions will do nothing; walk not thou with them; fly from them as for thy life. Twenty-seven Millions travelling on such courses, with gold jingling in every pocket, with vivats[1] heaven-high, are incessantly advancing, let me again remind thee, towards the *firm-land's end*—towards the end and extinction of what Faithfulness, Veracity, real Worth, was in their way of life. Their noble ancestors have fashioned for them a "life-road"—in how many thousand senses, this! There is not an old wise Proverb on their tongue, an honest Principle articulated in their hearts into utterance, a wise true method of doing and dispatching any work or commerce of men, but helps yet to carry them forward. Life is still possible to them, because all is not yet Puffery, Falsity, Mammon-worship and Unnature; because somewhat is yet Faithfulness, Veracity, and Valour. With a certain very considerable finite quantity of Unveracity and Phantasm, social life is still possible; not with an infinite quantity! Exceed your certain quantity, the seven-feet Hat, and all things upwards to the very Champion cased in tin begin to reel and flounder—in Manchester Insurrections, Chartisms, Sliding-scales, the Law of Gravitation not forgetting to act. You advance incessantly towards the land's end; you are, literally enough, "consuming the way." Step after step, Twenty-seven Million unconscious men, till you are *at* the land's end, till there is not Faithfulness enough among you anymore, and the next step now is lifted *not* over land, but into air, over ocean-deeps and roaring abysses—unless perhaps the Law of Gravitation have forgotten to act?

Oh, it is frightful when a whole Nation, as our Fathers used to say, has "forgotten God," has remembered only Mammon, and what Mammon leads to! When your self-trumpeting Hatmaker is the emblem of almost all makers, and workers, and men, that make anything—from soul-overseerships, body-overseerships, epic poems, Acts of Parliament, to hats and shoe-blacking! Not one false man but does uncountable mischief: how much, in a generation or two, will Twenty-seven Millions, mostly false, manage to accumulate? The sum of it, visible in every street, market-place, senate-house, circulating-library, cathedral, cotton-mill, and union-workhouse, fills one *not* with a comic feeling!

Chapter 2—Gospel of Mammonism

Reader, even Christian Reader as thy title goes, hast thou any notion of Heaven and Hell? I rather apprehend, not. Often as the words are on our tongue, they have got a fabulous or semi-fabulous character for most of us, and pass on like a kind of transient similitude, like a sound signifying little.

Yet it is well worth while for us to know, once and always, that they are not a similitude, nor a fable nor semi-fable; that they are an everlasting highest fact! "No Lake of Sicilian or other sulphur[2] burns now anywhere in these ages," sayest thou? Well, and if there did not! Believe that there does not; believe it if thou wilt; nay, hold by it as a real increase, a rise to higher stages, to wider horizons and empires. All this has vanished, or has not vanished; believe as thou wilt as to all this. But that an Infinite of Practical Importance, speaking with strict arithmetical exactness, an *Infinite*, has vanished or can vanish from the Life of any Man, this thou shalt not believe! O brother, the Infinite of Terror, of Hope, of Pity, did it not at any moment disclose itself to thee, indubitable, unnameable? Came it never, like the gleam of eternal Oceans, like the voice of old Eternities, far-sounding through thy heart of hearts? Never? Alas, it was not thy Liberalism, then; it was thy Animalism! The Infinite is more sure than any other fact. But only men can discern it; mere building beavers, spinning arachnes, much more the predatory vulturous and vulpine species, do not discern it well!

"The word Hell," says Sauerteig, "is still frequently in use among the English people, but I could not without difficulty ascertain what they meant by it. Hell generally signifies the Infinite Terror, the thing a man *is* infinitely afraid of, and shudders and shrinks from, struggling with his whole soul to escape from it. There is a Hell, therefore, if you will consider, which accompanies man in all stages of his history and religious or other development. But the Hells of men and Peoples differ notably. With Christians it is the infinite terror of being found guilty before the Just Judge. With old

---

[1] *vivats* Expressions of acclamation or approval.

[2] *Lake ... sulphur* Sulphur, often found near volcanic rocks, was formerly known as "brimstone" (i.e., "burning stone") and was thought to feed the fires of hell. At this time, Sicily was the world's primary source of sulphur.

Romans, I conjecture, it was the terror not of Pluto,[1] for whom probably they cared little, but of doing unworthily, doing unvirtuously, which was their word for un*man*fully.[2] And now what is it, if you pierce through his Cants, his oft-repeated Hearsays, what he calls his Worships and so forth, what is it that the modern English soul does, in very truth, dread infinitely, and contemplate with entire despair? What *is* his Hell, after all these reputable, oft-repeated Hearsays, what is it? With hesitation, with astonishment, I pronounce it to be the terror of "Not succeeding"; of not making money, fame, or some other figure in the world—chiefly of not making money! Is not that a somewhat singular Hell?"

Yes, O Sauerteig, it is very singular. If we do not "succeed," where is the use of us? We had better never have been born. "Tremble intensely," as our friend the Emperor of China says: *there* is the black Bottomless of Terror, what Sauerteig calls the "Hell of the English!" But indeed this Hell belongs naturally to the Gospel of Mammonism, which also has its corresponding Heaven. For there *is* one Reality among so many Phantasms; about one thing we are entirely in earnest: the making of money. Working Mammonism does divide the world with idle game-preserving Dilettantism——thank Heaven that there is even a Mammonism, *anything* we are in earnest about! Idleness is worst, Idleness alone is without hope: work earnestly at anything, you will by degrees learn to work at almost all things. There is endless hope in work, were it even work at making money.

True, it must be owned, we for the present, with our Mammon-Gospel, have come to strange conclusions. We call it a Society; and go about professing openly the totalest separation, isolation. Our life is not a mutual helpfulness; but rather, cloaked under due laws-of-war, named "fair competition" and so forth, it is a mutual hostility. We have profoundly forgotten everywhere that *Cash payment* is not the sole relation of human beings; we think, nothing doubting, that *it* absolves and liquidates all engagements of man. "My starving workers?" answers the rich mill-owner: "Did not I hire them fairly in the market? Did I not pay them, to the last sixpence, the sum covenanted for? What have I to do with them more?" Verily Mammon-worship is a melancholy creed.

When Cain, for his own behoof, had killed Abel, and was questioned, "Where is thy brother?" he too made answer, "Am I my brother's keeper?" Did I not pay my brother *his* wages, the thing he had merited from me?[3]

O sumptuous Merchant Prince, illustrious game-preserving Duke, is there no way of "killing" thy brother but Cain's rude way! "A good man by the very look of him, by his very presence with us as a fellow wayfarer in this Life-pilgrimage, *promises* so much." Woe to him if he forget all such promises, if he never know that they were given! To a deadened soul, seared with the brute Idolatry of Sense, to whom going to Hell is equivalent to not making money, all "promises" and moral duties, that cannot be pleaded for in Courts of Requests,[4] address themselves in vain. Money he can be ordered to pay, but nothing more. I have not heard in all Past History, and expect not to hear in all Future History, of any Society anywhere under God's Heaven, supporting itself on such Philosophy. The Universe is not made so; it is made otherwise than so. The man or nation of men that thinks it is made so, marches forward nothing doubting, step after step, but marches—whither we know! In these last two centuries of Atheistic Government (near two centuries now, since the blessed restoration of his Sacred Majesty, and Defender of the Faith, Charles Second), I reckon that we have pretty well exhausted what of "firm earth" there was for us to march on—and are now, very ominously, shuddering, reeling, and let us hope trying to recoil, on the cliff's edge!

For out of this that we call Atheism come so many other *isms* and falsities, each falsity with its misery at its heels! A SOUL is not like wind (*spiritus*, or breath) contained within a capsule; the ALMIGHTY MAKER is not like a Clockmaker that once, in old immemorial ages, having *made* his Horologe of a Universe, sits ever since and sees it go! Not at all. Hence comes Atheism; come, as we say, many other *isms*, and, as the sum of all, comes Valetism,[5] the *reverse* of Heroism—sad root of all woes whatsoever. For indeed, as no man ever saw the above-said wind-element enclosed within its capsule, and finds it at bottom more deniable than conceivable;

---

[1]   *Pluto*   Roman god of the underworld.

[2]   *which was ... unmanfully*   The Latin word for man is *vir*.

[3]   *When Cain ... me*   See Genesis 4.9.

[4]   *Court of Requests*   Court that examined the petitions of the poor.

[5]   *Valetism*   I.e., the character of a valet. Carlyle defines valetism in Book 2 as "cloth-worship and quack-worship."

so too he finds, in spite of Bridgwater Bequests, your Clockmaker Almighty an entirely questionable affair, a deniable affair—and accordingly denies it, and along with it so much else. Alas, one knows not what and how much else! For the faith in an Invisible, Unnameable, Godlike, present everywhere in all that we see and work and suffer, is the essence of all faith whatsoever; and that once denied, or still worse, asserted with lips only, and out of bound prayerbooks only, what other thing remains believable? That Cant well-ordered is marketable Cant; that Heroism means gas-lighted Histrionism;[1] that seen with "clear eyes" (as they call Valet-eyes) no man is a Hero, or ever was a Hero, but all men are Valets and Varlets. The accursed practical quintessence of all sorts of Unbelief! For if there be now no Hero, and the Histrio himself begin to be seen into, what hope is there for the seed of Adam here below? We are the doomed everlasting prey of the Quack; who, now in this guise, now in that, is to filch us, to pluck and eat us, by such modes as are convenient for him. For the modes and guises I care little. The Quack once inevitable, let him come swiftly, let him pluck and eat me—swiftly, that I may at least have done with him, for in his Quack-world I can have no wish to linger. Though he slay me, yet will I *not* trust in him. Though he conquer nations, and have all the Flunkies of the Universe shouting at his heels, yet will I know well that *he* is an Inanity; that for him and his there is no continuance appointed, save only in Gehenna and the Pool.[2] Alas, the Atheist world, from its utmost summits of Heaven and Westminster Hall,[3] downwards through poor seven-feet Hats and "Unveracities fallen hungry," down to the lowest cellars and neglected hunger-dens of it, is very wretched.

One of Dr. Alison's Scotch facts struck us much. A poor Irish Widow, her husband having died in one of the Lanes of Edinburgh, went forth with her three children, bare of all resource, to solicit help from the Charitable Establishments of that City. At this Charitable Establishment and then at that she was refused, referred from one to the other, helped by none, till she had exhausted them all, till her strength and heart failed

her. She sank down in typhus-fever, died, and infected her Lane with fever, so that "seventeen other persons" died of fever there in consequence. The humane Physician asks thereupon, as with a heart too full for speaking, Would it not have been *economy* to help this poor Widow? She took typhus-fever, and killed seventeen of you! Very curious. The forlorn Irish Widow applies to her fellow-creatures, as if saying, "Behold I am sinking, bare of help. Ye must help me! I am your sister, bone of your bone; one God made us. Ye must help me!" They answer, "No, impossible; thou art no sister of ours." But she proves her sisterhood; her typhus-fever kills *them.* They actually were her brothers, though denying it! Had human creature ever to go lower for a proof?

For, as indeed was very natural in such case, all government of the Poor by the Rich has long ago been given over to Supply-and-demand, Laissez-faire and suchlike, and universally declared to be "impossible." "You are no sister of ours; what shadow of proof is there? Here are our parchments, our padlocks, proving indisputably our money-safes to be *ours,* and you to have no business with them. Depart! It is impossible!" Nay, what wouldst thou thyself have us do? cry indignant readers. Nothing, my friends—till you have got a soul for yourselves again. Till then all things are "impossible." Till then I cannot even bid you buy, as the old Spartans would have done, two-pence worth of powder and lead, and compendiously shoot to death this poor Irish Widow. Even that is "impossible" for you. Nothing is left but that she prove her sisterhood by dying, and infecting you with typhus. Seventeen of you lying dead will not deny such proof that she *was* flesh of your flesh; and perhaps some of the living may lay it to heart.

"Impossible": of a certain two-legged animal with feathers it is said, if you draw a distinct chalk-circle round him, he sits imprisoned, as if girt with the iron ring of Fate, and will die there, though within sight of victuals, or sit in sick misery there, and be fatted to death. The name of this poor two-legged animal is—Goose; and they make of him, when well fattened, *Pâté de foie gras,* much prized by some! …

CHAPTER II—LABOUR

For there is a perennial nobleness, and even sacredness, in Work. Were he never so benighted, forgetful of his

---

[1] *Histrionism* Acting.

[2] *Gehenna and the Pool* I.e., Hell.

[3] *Westminster Hall* Location of the British Houses of Parliament.

high calling, there is always hope in a man that actually and earnestly works: in Idleness alone is there perpetual despair. Work, never so Mammonish, mean, *is* in communication with Nature; the real desire to get Work done will itself lead one more and more to truth, to Nature's appointments and regulations, which are truth.

The latest Gospel in this world is, Know thy work and do it. "Know thyself": long enough has that poor "self" of thine tormented thee; thou wilt never get to "know" it, I believe! Think it not thy business, this of knowing thyself; thou art an unknowable individual. Know what thou canst work at, and work at it, like a Hercules![1] That will be thy better plan.

It has been written, "an endless significance lies in Work";[2] a man perfects himself by working. Foul jungles are cleared away, fair seedfields rise instead, and stately cities; and withal the man himself first ceases to be a jungle and foul unwholesome desert thereby. Consider how, even in the meanest sorts of Labour, the whole soul of a man is composed into a kind of real harmony the instant he sets himself to work! Doubt, Desire, Sorrow, Remorse, Indignation, Despair itself, all these like helldogs lie beleaguering the soul of the poor dayworker, as of every man; but he bends himself with free valour against his task, and all these are stilled, all these shrink murmuring far off into their caves. The man is now a man. The blessed glow of Labour in him is it not as purifying fire, wherein all poison is burnt up, and of sour smoke itself there is made bright blessed flame!

Destiny, on the whole, has no other way of cultivating us. A formless Chaos, once set it *revolving*, grows round and ever rounder; ranges itself, by mere force of gravity, into strata, spherical courses; is no longer a Chaos, but a round compacted World. What would become of the Earth, did she cease to revolve? In the poor old Earth, so long as she revolves, all inequalities, irregularities disperse themselves; all irregularities are incessantly becoming regular. Hast thou looked on the Potter's wheel, one of the venerablest objects, old as the

Prophet Ezechiel[3] and far older? Rude lumps of clay, how they spin themselves up, by mere quick whirling, into beautiful circular dishes. And fancy the most assiduous Potter, but without his wheel, reduced to make dishes, or rather amorphous botches, by mere kneading and baking! Even such a Potter were Destiny, with a human soul that would rest and lie at ease, that would not work and spin! Of an idle unrevolving man the kindest Destiny, like the most assiduous Potter without wheel, can bake and knead nothing other than a botch; let her spend on him what expensive colouring, what gilding and enamelling she will, he is but a botch. Not a dish; no, a bulging, kneaded, crooked, shambling, squint-cornered, amorphous botch—a mere enamelled vessel of dishonour! Let the idle think of this.

Blessed is he who has found his work; let him ask no other blessedness. He has a work, a life-purpose; he has found it, and will follow it! How, as a free-flowing channel, dug and torn by noble force through the sour mud-swamp of one's existence, like an ever-deepening river there, it runs and flows, draining off the sour festering water, gradually from the root of the remotest grassblade, making, instead of pestilential swamp, a green fruitful meadow with its clear-flowing stream. How blessed for the meadow itself, let the stream and *its* value be great or small! Labour is Life: from the inmost heart of the Worker rises his god-given Force, the sacred celestial Life-essence breathed into him by Almighty God; from his inmost heart awakens him to all nobleness, to all knowledge, "self-knowledge" and much else, so soon as Work fitly begins. Knowledge? The knowledge that will hold good in working, cleave thou to that; for Nature herself accredits that, says Yea to that. Properly thou hast no other knowledge but what thou hast got by working. The rest is yet all a hypothesis of knowledge, a thing to be argued of in schools, a thing floating in the clouds, in endless logic-vortices, till we try it and fix it. "Doubt, of whatever kind, can be ended by Action alone."

And again, hast thou valued Patience, Courage, Perseverance, Openness to light, readiness to own thyself mistaken, to do better next time? All these, all virtues, in wrestling with the dim brute Powers of Fact, in ordering of thy fellows in such wrestle, there and elsewhere not at

---

[1]   *Hercules*   In Greek mythology, Hercules had to complete twelve labors.

[2]   *an endless ... Work*   Probably a reference to German writer Johann Wolfgang von Goethe (1749–1832), who wrote on the value of work, and to whom Carlyle refers again later in this chapter.

[3]   *Ezechiel*   Hebrew prophet of the sixth century BCE.

all, thou wilt continually learn. Set down a brave Sir Christopher[1] in the middle of black ruined Stone-heaps, of foolish unarchitectural Bishops, redtape Officials, idle Nell-Gwyn Defenders[2] of the Faith, and see whether he will ever raise a Paul's Cathedral out of all that, yea or no! Rough, rude, contradictory are all things and persons, from the mutinous masons and Irish hodmen,[3] up to the idle Nell-Gwyn Defenders, to blustering redtape Officials, foolish unarchitectural Bishops. All these things and persons are there not for Christopher's sake and his Cathedral's; they are there for their own sake mainly! Christopher will have to conquer and constrain all these, if he be able. All these are against him. Equitable Nature herself, who carries her mathematics and architectonics not on the face of her, but deep in the hidden heart of her, Nature herself is but partially for him—will be wholly against him, if he constrain her not! His very money, where is it to come from? The pious munificence of England lies far-scattered, distant, unable to speak and say, "I am here," must be spoken to before it can speak. Pious munificence, and all help, is so silent, invisible like the gods; impediment, contradictions manifold are so loud and near! O brave Sir Christopher, trust thou in those notwithstanding, and front all these; understand all these; by valiant patience, noble effort, insight, by man's-strength, vanquish and compel all these, and, on the whole, strike down victoriously the last topstone of that Paul's Edifice, thy monument for certain centuries, the stamp "Great Man" impressed very legibly on Portland-stone[4] there!

Yes, all manner of help, and pious response from Men or Nature, is always what we call silent, cannot speak or come to light till it be seen, till it be spoken to. Every noble work is at first "impossible." In very truth,

for every noble work the possibilities will lie diffused through Immensity, inarticulate, undiscoverable except to faith. Like Gideon thou shalt spread out thy fleece at the door of thy tent,[5] see whether under the wide arch of Heaven there be any bounteous moisture, or none. Thy heart and life-purpose shall be as a miraculous Gideon's fleece, spread out in silent appeal to Heaven; and from the kind Immensities, what from the poor unkind Localities and town and country Parishes there never could, blessed dew-moisture to suffice thee shall have fallen!

Work is of a religious nature; work is of a *brave* nature, which it is the aim of all religion to be. All work of man is as the swimmer's: a waste ocean threatens to devour him; if he front it not bravely, it will keep its word. By incessant wise defiance of it, lusty rebuke and buffet of it, behold how it loyally supports him, bears him as its conqueror along. "It is so," says Goethe, "with all things that man undertakes in this world."[6]

Brave Sea-captain, Norse Sea-king—Columbus, my hero, royalest Sea king of all! It is no friendly environment this of thine, in the waste deep waters, around thee mutinous discouraged souls, behind thee disgrace and ruin, before thee the unpenetrated veil of Night. Brother, these wild water-mountains, bounding from their deep bases (ten miles deep, I am told), are not entirely there on thy behalf! Meseems *they* have other work than floating thee forward—and the huge Winds that sweep from Ursa Major to the Tropics and Equators, dancing their giant-waltz through the kingdoms of Chaos and Immensity, they care little about filling rightly or filling wrongly the small shoulder-of-mutton sails in this cockle-skiff of thine! Thou art not among articulate-speaking friends, my brother; thou art among immeasurable dumb monsters, tumbling, howling wide as the world here. Secret, far off, invisible to all hearts but thine, there lies a help in them: see how thou wilt get at that. Patiently thou wilt wait till the mad South-

[1] *Sir Christopher* Christopher Wren (1632–1723), renowned English architect who was in charge of restoring London's public buildings and churches after the Great Fire of 1666. Wren constructed St. Paul's Cathedral, in which he is buried.

[2] *Nell-Gwyn Defenders* Actress Nell Gwyn was a mistress of Charles II. This epithet is a play on the title "Defender of the Faith," given to Henry VIII by the Pope in 1521 (and still a part of the English monarch's title).

[3] *hodmen* Those who prepare and carry the mortar and bricks to the builders.

[4] *Portland-stone* Limestone mined on Portland Island, off the coast of Dorsetshire.

[5] *Gideon ... tent* See Judges 6.36–40, in which Gideon asks the Lord for proof that He will save Israel by Gideon's hand. First, Gideon puts a fleece of wool on the floor and asks that it be covered with dew in the morning, while the surrounding ground remains dry. When this occurs, Gideon asks that the following night the fleece be dry and the surrounding ground covered in dew. The Lord does this also.

[6] *It is ... world* Cf. Goethe's *Wilhelm Meister's Apprenticeship* (1796).

wester spend itself, saving thyself by dexterous science of defence, the while. Valiantly, with swift decision, wilt thou strike in, when the favouring East, the Possible, springs up. Mutiny of men thou wilt sternly repress; weakness, despondency, thou wilt cheerily encourage: thou wilt swallow down complaint, unreason, weariness, weakness of others and thyself—how much wilt thou swallow down! There shall be a depth of Silence in thee, deeper than this Sea, which is but ten miles deep, a Silence unsoundable, known to God only. Thou shalt be a Great Man. Yes, my World-Soldier, thou of the World Marine-service, thou wilt have to be *greater* than this tumultuous unmeasured World here round thee is. Thou, in thy strong soul, as with wrestler's arms, shalt embrace it, harness it down, and make it bear thee on—to new Americas, or whither God wills! ...

CHAPTER 13—DEMOCRACY

If the Serene Highnesses and Majesties do not take note of that,[1] then, as I perceive, *that* will take note of itself! The time for levity, insincerity, and idle babble and play-acting, in all kinds, is gone by; it is a serious, grave time. Old long-vexed questions, not yet solved in logical words or parliamentary laws, are fast solving themselves in facts, somewhat unblessed to behold! This largest of questions, this question of Work and Wages, which ought, had we heeded Heaven's voice, to have begun two generations ago or more, cannot be delayed longer without hearing Earth's voice. "Labour" will verily need to be somewhat "organised," as they say—God knows with what difficulty. Man will actually need to have his debts and earnings a little better paid by man; which, let Parliaments speak of them or be silent of them, are eternally his due from man, and cannot, without penalty and at length not without death penalty,[2] be withheld. How much ought to cease among us straightway, how much ought to begin straightway, while the hours yet are!

Truly they are strange results to which this of leaving all to "Cash," of quietly shutting-up the God's Temple, and gradually opening wide-open the Mammon's Temple, with "Lassez-faire, and Every man for himself," have led us in these days! We have Upper, speaking Classes, who indeed do "speak" as never man spake before; the withered flimsiness, the godless baseness and barrenness of whose Speech might of itself indicate what kind of Doing and practical Governing went on under it! For Speech is the gaseous element out of which most kinds of Practice and Performance, especially all kinds of moral Performance, condense themselves, and take shape; as the one is, so will the other be. Descending, accordingly, into the Dumb Class in its Stockport Cellars and Poor-Law Bastilles, have we not to announce that they also are hitherto unexampled in the History of Adam's Posterity?

Life was never a May-game[3] for men. In all times the lot of the dumb millions born to toil was defaced with manifold sufferings, injustices, heavy burdens, avoidable and unavoidable—not play at all, but hard work that made the sinews sore and the heart sore. As bond-slaves, *villani, bordarii, sochemanni,*[4] nay indeed as dukes, earls, and kings, men were oftentimes made weary of their life, and had to say, in the sweat of their brow and of their soul, Behold, it is not sport, it is grim earnest, and our back can bear no more! Who knows not what massacrings and harryings there have been—grinding, long-continuing, unbearable injustices—till the heart had to rise in madness, and some "*Eu Sachsen, nimith euer sachses*, You Saxons, out with your gully-knives,[5] then!" You Saxons, some "arrestment," partial "arrestment of the Knaves and Dastards" has become indispensable! The page of Dryasdust[6] is heavy with such details.

And yet I will venture to believe that in no time, since the beginnings of Society, was the lot of those same dumb millions of toilers so entirely unbearable as

---

[1] *that* At the end of the previous chapter, Carlyle urged that "the proper epic of this world" should be "Tools and the Man," rather than "Arms and the Man," a reference to the opening line of Virgil's *Aeneid*: "Arma virumque cano" (Latin: "Of arms and the man I sing").

[2] *death penalty* Reference to the deaths caused by violent revolutions, such as the French Revolution.

[3] *May-game* Entertainment or performance (such as those traditionally making up part of the celebration on the first day of May).

[4] *villani ... sochemanni* Classes of peasants in the feudal system.

[5] *gully-knives* Large household knives.

[6] *Dryasdust* Name given to a dull, pedantic historian, after the fictional antiquarian Dr. Jonas Dryasdust, to whom Walter Scott facetiously dedicated some of his novels.

it is even in the days now passing over us. It is not to die, or even to die of hunger, that makes a man wretched; many men have died; all men must die—the last exit of us all is in a Fire-Chariot of Pain.[1] But it is to live miserable we know not why; to work sore and yet gain nothing; to be heart-worn, weary, yet isolated, unrelated, girt-in with a cold universal Laissez-faire: it is to die slowly all our life long, imprisoned in a deaf, dead, Infinite Injustice, as in the accursed iron belly of a Phalaris' Bull![2] This is and remains forever intolerable to all men whom God has made. Do we wonder at French Revolutions, Chartisms, Revolts of Three Days? The times, if we will consider them, are really unexampled.

Never before did I hear of an Irish Widow reduced to "prove" her sisterhood by dying of typhus-fever and infecting seventeen "persons," saying in such undeniable way, "You *see* I was your sister!" Sisterhood, brotherhood, was often forgotten; but not till the rise of these ultimate Mammon and Shotbelt Gospels[3] did I ever see it so expressly denied. If no pious Lord or *Law-ward* would remember it, always some pious Lady ("*Hlaf-dig*,"[4] Benefactress, "*Loaf-giveress*," they say she is—blessings on her beautiful heart!) was there, with mild mother-voice and hand, to remember it; some pious thoughtful *Elder*, what we now call "Prester," *Presbyter* or "Priest," was there to put all men in mind of it, in the name of the God who had made all.

Not even in Black Dahomey[5] was it ever, I think, forgotten to the typhus-fever length. Mungo Park,[6] resourceless, had sunk down to die under the Negro Village-Tree, a horrible White object in the eyes of all. But in the poor Black Woman, and her daughter who stood aghast at him, whose earthly wealth and funded capital consisted of one small calabash of rice, there lived

a heart richer than *Laissez-faire*: they, with a royal munificence, boiled their rice for him; they sang all night to him, spinning assiduous on their cotton distaffs, as he lay to sleep: "Let us pity the poor white man; no mother has he to fetch him milk, no sister to grind him corn!" Thou poor black Noble One, thou *Lady* too. Did not a God make thee too; was there not in thee too something of a God!

Gurth, born thrall of Cedric the Saxon,[7] has been greatly pitied by Dryasdust and others. Gurth, with the brass collar round his neck, tending Cedric's pigs in the glades of the wood, is not what I call an exemplar of human felicity. But Gurth, with the sky above him, with the free air and tinted boscage and umbrage[8] round him, and in him at least the certainty of supper and social lodging when he came home, Gurth to me seems happy, in comparison with many a Lancashire and Buckinghamshire man of these days, not born thrall of anybody! Gurth's brass collar did not gall him; Cedric *deserved* to be his master. The pigs were Cedric's, but Gurth too would get his parings of them. Gurth had the inexpressible satisfaction of feeling himself related indissolubly, though in a rude brass-collar way, to his fellow-mortals in this Earth. He had superiors, inferiors, equals. Gurth is now "emancipated" long since, has what we call "Liberty." Liberty, I am told, is a divine thing. Liberty when it becomes the "Liberty to die by starvation" is not so divine!

Liberty? The true liberty of a man, you would say, consisted in his finding out, or being forced to find out, the right path, and to walk thereon. To learn, or to be taught, what work he actually was able for, and then by permission, persuasion, and even compulsion, to set about doing of the same! That is his true blessedness, honour, "liberty," and maximum of wellbeing: if liberty be not that, I for one have small care about liberty. You do not allow a palpable madman to leap over precipices; you violate his liberty, you that are wise, and keep him, were it in strait-waistcoats, away from the precipices! Every stupid, every cowardly and foolish man is but a less palpable madman: his true liberty were that a wiser man, that any and every wiser man, could, by brass

[1] *last exit ... Pain* See 2 Kings 2.11–12.

[2] *Phalaris' Bull* Phalaris, an ancient Sicilian tyrant, murdered wrong-doers by placing them in a brass bull that sat over a fire.

[3] *Shotbelt Gospels* I.e., principles of the landed aristocracy who sought to maintain their exclusive right to shoot game.

[4] *Hlaf-dig* I.e., loaf-giver.

[5] *Black Dahomey* Area of West Africa, formerly belonging to the French, in which human sacrifice and cannibalism were rumored to take place.

[6] *Mungo Park* Scottish explorer and author of *Travels in the Interior of Africa* (1799), who was killed by Africans in Bussa in 1806.

[7] *Gurth* In Walter Scott's *Ivanhoe* (1819), Gurth is a serf (thrall) of the wealthy farmer Cedric.

[8] *boscage and umbrage* Grove and shade.

collars, or in whatever milder or sharper way, lay hold of him when he was going wrong, and order and compel him to go a little righter. O, if thou really art my *Senior*, Seigneur, my *Elder*, Presbyter or Priest—if thou art in very deed my *Wiser*, may a beneficent instinct lead and impel thee to "conquer" me, to command me! If thou do know better than I what is good and right, I conjure thee in the name of God, force me to do it; were it by never such brass collars, whips and handcuffs, leave me not to walk over precipices! That I have been called, by all the Newspapers, a "free man" will avail me little, if my pilgrimage have ended in death and wreck. O that the Newspapers had called me slave, coward, fool, or what it pleased their *sweet* voices to name me, and I had attained not death, but life! Liberty requires new definitions.

A conscious abhorrence and intolerance of Folly, of Baseness, Stupidity, Poltroonery[1] and all that brood of things, dwells deep in some men; still deeper in others an *un*conscious abhorrence and intolerance, clotted moreover by the beneficent Supreme Powers in what stout appetites, energies, egoisms so-called, are suitable to it. These latter are your Conquerors, Romans, Normans, Russians, Indo-English; Founders of what we call Aristocracies. Which indeed have they not the most "divine right" to found—being themselves very truly Αριστοι[2] BRAVEST, BEST, and conquering generally a confused rabble of WORST, or at lowest, clearly enough, of WORSE? I think their divine right, tried, with affirmatory verdict, in the greatest Law-Court known to me, was good! A class of men who are dreadfully exclaimed against by Dryasdust, of whom nevertheless beneficent Nature has oftentimes had need, and may, alas, again have need.

When, across the hundredfold poor scepticisms, trivialisms and constitutional cobwebberies of Dryasdust, you catch any glimpse of a William the Conqueror, a Tancred of Hauteville[3] or suchlike, do you not discern veritably some rude outline of a true God-made King, whom not the Champion of England cased in tin,

but all Nature and the Universe were calling to the throne? It is absolutely necessary that he get thither. Nature does not mean her poor Saxon children to perish of obesity, stupor, or other malady, as yet. A stern Ruler and Line of Rulers therefore is called in—a stern but most beneficent *perpetual House-Surgeon* is by Nature herself called in, and even the appropriate *fees* are provided for him! Dryasdust talks lamentably about Hereward and the Fen Counties,[4] fate of Earl Waltheof,[5] Yorkshire and the North reduced to ashes—all which is undoubtedly lamentable. But even Dryasdust apprises me of one fact: "A child, in this William's reign, might have carried a purse of gold from end to end of England." My erudite friend, it is a fact which outweighs a thousand! Sweep away thy constitutional, sentimental, and other cobwebberies; look eye to eye, if thou still have any eye, in the face of this big burly William Bastard.[6] Thou wilt see a fellow of most flashing discernment, of most strong lion-heart, in whom, as it were, within a frame of oak and iron, the gods have planted the soul of "a man of genius"! Dost thou call that nothing? I call it an immense thing! Rage enough was in this Willelmus Conquaestor,[7] rage enough for his occasions—and yet the essential element of him, as of all such men, is not scorching *fire*, but shining illuminative *light*. Fire and light are strangely interchangeable; nay, at bottom, I have found them different forms of the same most godlike "elementary substance" in our world—a thing worth stating in these days. The essential element of this Conquaestor is, first of all, the most sun-eyed perception of what *is* really what on this God's-Earth—which, thou wilt find, does mean at bottom "Justice," and "Virtues" not a few—*Conformity* to what the Maker has seen good to make; that, I suppose, will mean Justice and a Virtue or two?

---

[1] *Poltroonery* Cowardliness; mean-spiritedness.

[2] Αριστοι Greek: aristocrats.

[3] *William the Conqueror* King William I of England (who ruled from 1066 to 1087) was named "the Conqueror" after he won the throne from King Harold at the Battle of Hastings in 1066; *Tancred of Hauteville* Norman Crusader (1076–1112).

[4] *Hereward ... Counties* Anglo-Saxon who rebelled against William I and organized uprisings in Lincolnshire and its surrounding counties (known collectively as the "Fen Counties" because of their marshland).

[5] *Earl Waltheof* Anglo-Saxon who was executed for treason by William I, but was later believed innocent and regarded as a martyr.

[6] *William Bastard* William I was an illegitimate son of Robert I, Duke of Normandy.

[7] *Willelmus Conquaestor* Latin: William the Conqueror.

Dost thou think Willelmus Conquaestor would have tolerated ten years' jargon, one hour's jargon, on the propriety of killing Cotton manufactures by partridge[1] Corn Laws? I fancy, this was not the man to knock out of his night's-rest with nothing but a noisy bedlamism[2] in your mouth! "Assist us still better to bush the partridges; strangle Plugson[3] who spins the shirts?"—"*Par la Splendeur de Dieu!*"[4]—Dost thou think Willelmus Conquaestor, in this new time, with Steamengine Captains of Industry on one hand of him, and Joe-Manton Captains of Idleness on the other, would have doubted which *was* really the BEST; which did deserve strangling, and which not?

I have a certain indestructible regard for Willelmus Conquaestor. A resident House-Surgeon, provided by Nature for her beloved English People, and even furnished with the requisite fees, as I said; for he by no means felt himself doing Nature's work, this Willelmus, but his own work exclusively! And his own work withal it was, informed "*par la Splendeur de Dieu!*" I say, it is necessary to get the work out of such a man, however harsh that be! When a world, not yet doomed for death, is rushing down to ever-deeper Baseness and Confusion, it is a dire necessity of Nature's to bring in her ARISTOCRACIES, her BEST, even by forcible methods. When their descendants or representatives cease entirely to *be* the Best, Nature's poor world will very soon rush down again to Baseness; and it becomes a dire necessity of Nature's to cast them out. Hence French Revolutions, Five-point Charters,[5] Democracies, and a mournful list of *Etceteras*, in these our afflicted times.

To what extent Democracy has now reached, how it advances irresistible with ominous, ever-increasing speed, he that will open his eyes on any province of human affairs may discern. Democracy is everywhere the inexorable demand of these ages, swiftly fulfilling itself. From the thunder of Napoleon battles, to the jabbering of Open-vestry in St. Mary Axe,[6] all things announce Democracy. A distinguished man, whom some of my readers will hear again with pleasure, thus writes to me what in these days he notes from the Wahngasse of Weissnichtwo,[7] where our London fashions seem to be in full vogue. Let us hear the Herr Teufelsdröckh[8] again, were it but the smallest word!

Democracy, which means despair of finding any Heroes to govern you, and contented putting-up with the want of them, alas, thou too, *mein Lieber*,[9] seest well how close it is of kin to *Atheism*, and other sad *Isms*: he who discovers no God whatever, how shall he discover Heroes, the visible Temples of God? Strange enough meanwhile it is to observe with what thoughtlessness, here in our rigidly Conservative Country, men rush into Democracy with full cry. Beyond doubt, his Excellenz the Titular Herr Ritter Kauderwalsch von Pferdefuss-Quacksalber,[10] he our distinguished Conservative Premier himself, and all but the thicker-headed of his Party discern Democracy to be inevitable as death, and are even desperate of delaying it much!

"You cannot walk the streets without beholding Democracy announce itself. The very Tailor has become, if not properly Sansculottic, which to him would be ruinous, yet a Tailor unconsciously symbolising, and prophesying with his scissors, the reign of Equality. What now is our fashionable coat? A thing of superfinest texture, of deeply meditated cut, with Malines-lace[11] cuffs, quilted with gold; so that a man can carry, without difficulty, an estate of land on his back? *Keines-*

---

[1] *partridge*   Reference to the aristocracy's attachment to hunting game.

[2] *bedlamism*   Something characteristic of madness—specifically, of the Hospital of St. Mary of Bethlehem (referred to as "Bedlam"), an overcrowded and frenetic London asylum.

[3] *Plugson*   Fictional industrial firm to which Carlyle refers several times throughout *Past and Present*.

[4] *Par la … Dieu*   French: By the splendor of God.

[5] *Five-point Charters*   The "People's Charter" (on which the Chartist movement was based) actually had six points, all concerning suffrage.

[6] *jabbering … Axe*   I.e., the bickering of the rate-paying parishioners, who were generally allowed to express their opinions on temporal affairs of the Church.

[7] *Wahngasse of Weissnichtwo*   German: Delusion alley of I-know-not-where.

[8] *Herr Teufelsdröckh*   Carlyle writes about this fictional German philosopher, Diogenes Teufelsdröckh, in *Sartor Resartus*. He is said to be the author of *Clothes: Their Origin and Influence*, and his name, in German, literally means "God-born devil's dung."

[9] *mein Lieber*   German: my dear.

[10] *Excellenz … Pferdefuss-Quacksalber*   German: Mr. Knight Gibberish Horsefoot-Mountebank. A reference to Sir Robert Peel, the Conservative Prime Minister.

[11] *Malines-lace*   Lace made in Malines, a town in Belgium.

wegs, By no manner of means! The Sumptuary Laws[1] have fallen into such a state of desuetude[2] as was never before seen. Our fashionable coat is an amphibium between barn-sack and drayman's doublet. The cloth of it is studiously coarse; the colour, a speckled soot-black or rust-brown gray, the nearest approach to a Peasant's. And for shape—thou shouldst see it! The last consummation of the year now passing over us is definable as Three Bags: a big bag for the body, two small bags for the arms, and by way of collar a hem! The first Antique Cheruscan[3] who, of felt-cloth or bear's-hide, with bone or metal needle, set about making himself a coat, before Tailors had yet awakened out of Nothing, did not he make it even so? A loose wide poke for body, with two holes to let out the arms, this was his original coat—to which holes it was soon visible that two small loose pokes, or sleeves, easily appended, would be an improvement.

"Thus has the Tailor-art, so to speak, overset itself, like most other things, changed its centre-of-gravity, whirled suddenly over from zenith to nadir. Your Stulz,[4] with huge somerset,[5] vaults from his high shopboard down to the depths of primal savagery, carrying much along with him! For I will invite thee to reflect that the Tailor, as topmost ultimate froth of Human Society, is indeed swift-passing, evanescent, slippery to decipher, yet significant of much, nay of all. Topmost evanescent froth, he is churned-up from the very lees, and from all intermediate regions of the liquor. The general outcome he, visible to the eye, of what men aimed to do, and were obliged and enabled to do, in this one public department of symbolising themselves to each other by covering of their skins. A smack of all Human Life lies in the Tailor: its wild struggles towards beauty, dignity, freedom, victory; and how, hemmed-in by Sedan and Huddersfield,[6] by Nescience,[7] Dullness, Prurience,[8] and

other sad necessities and laws of Nature, it has attained just to this: Gray savagery of Three Sacks with a hem!

"When the very Tailor verges towards Sansculottism, is it not ominous? The last Divinity of poor mankind dethroning himself, sinking *his* taper too, flame downmost, like the Genius of Sleep or of Death, admonitory that Tailor time shall be no more! For, little as one could advise Sumptuary Laws at the present epoch, yet nothing is clearer than that where ranks do actually exist, strict division of costumes will also be enforced; that if we ever have a new Hierarchy and Aristocracy, acknowledged veritably as such, for which I daily pray Heaven, the Tailor will reawaken, and be, by volunteering and appointment, consciously and unconsciously, a safeguard of that same." Certain farther observations, from the same invaluable pen, on our never-ending changes of mode, our perpetual nomadic and even ape-like appetite for change and mere change in all the equipments of our existence, and the "fatal revolutionary character" thereby manifested, we suppress for the present. It may be admitted that Democracy, in all meanings of the word, is in full career; irresistible by any Ritter Kauderwalsch or other Son of Adam, as times go. "Liberty" is a thing men are determined to have.

But truly, as I had to remark in the meanwhile, "the liberty of not being oppressed by your fellow man" is an indispensable, yet one of the most insignificant fractional, parts of Human Liberty. No man oppresses thee, can bid thee fetch or carry, come or go, without reason shown. True, from all men thou art emancipated; but from Thyself and from the Devil—? No man, wiser, unwiser, can make thee come or go; but thy own futilities, bewilderments, thy false appetites for Money, Windsor Georges[9] and suchlike? No man oppresses thee, O free and independent Franchiser; but does not this stupid Porter-pot[10] oppress thee? No Son of Adam can bid thee come or go; but this absurd Pot of Heavy-wet,[11] this can and does! Thou art the thrall not of Cedric the Saxon, but of thy own brutal appetites and this scoured dish of liquor. And thou pratest of thy "liberty"? Thou entire blockhead!

---

[1] *Sumptuary Laws*   Laws regulating expenditure on food, dress, etc.

[2] *desuetude*   Disuse.

[3] *Cheruscan*   Member of an ancient German tribe.

[4] *Stulz*   I.e., name of a high-class tailor.

[5] *somerset*   Somersault.

[6] *Sedan and Huddersfield*   Towns (the first French, the second English) where wool was woven.

[7] *Nescience*   Ignorance.

[8] *Prurience*   Tendency towards impure or lewd ideas.

[9] *Windsor Georges*   I.e., the pomp of royalty.

[10] *Porter-pot*   Vessel of porter, a dark beer.

[11] *Heavy-wet*   Malt liquor.

Heavy-wet and gin; alas, these are not the only kinds of thraldom. Thou who walkest in a vain show, looking out with ornamental dilettante sniff and serene supremacy at all Life and all Death; and amblest jauntily, perking up thy poor talk into crotchets,[1] thy poor conduct into fatuous somnambulisms; and *art* as an "enchanted Ape" under God's sky, where thou mightest have been a man, had proper Schoolmasters and Conquerors, and Constables with cat-o'-nine tails,[2] been vouchsafed thee—dost thou call that "liberty"? Or your unreposing Mammon-worshipper again, driven, as if by Galvanisms,[3] by Devils and Fixed Ideas, who rises early and sits late, chasing the impossible, straining every faculty to "fill himself with the east wind"[4]—how merciful were it, could you, by mild persuasion, or by the severest tyranny so-called, check him in his mad path, and turn him into a wiser one! All painful tyranny, in that case again, were but mild "surgery," the pain of it cheap, as health and life, instead of galvanism and fixed-idea, are cheap at any price.

Sure enough, of all paths a man could strike into, there *is*, at any given moment, a *best path* for every man; a thing which, here and now, it were of all things *wisest* for him to do—which, could he be but led or driven to do, he were then doing "like a man," as we phrase it, all men and gods agreeing with him, the whole Universe virtually exclaiming Well-done to him! His success, in such case, were complete; his felicity a maximum. This path, to find this path and walk in it, is the one thing needful for him. Whatsoever forwards him in that, let it come to him even in the shape of blows and spurnings, is liberty; whatsoever hinders him, were it wardmotes,[5] open-vestries, pollbooths, tremendous cheers, rivers of heavy-wet, is slavery.

The notion that a man's liberty consists in giving his vote at election-hustings,[6] and saying, "Behold, now I too have my twenty-thousandth part of a Talker in our National Palaver;[7] will not all the gods be good to me?" is one of the pleasantest! Nature nevertheless is kind at present, and puts it into the heads of many, almost of all. The liberty especially which has to purchase itself by social isolation, and each man standing separate from the other, having no business with him but a cash-account, this is such a liberty as the Earth seldom saw—as the Earth will not long put up with, recommend it how you may. This liberty turns out, before it have long continued in action, with all men flinging up their caps round it, to be, for the Working Millions, a liberty to die by want of food; for the Idle Thousands and Units, alas, a still more fatal liberty to live in want of work, to have no earnest duty to do in this God's-World anymore. What becomes of a man in such predicament? Earth's Laws are silent, and Heaven's speak in a voice which is not heard. No work, and the ineradicable need of work, give rise to new very wondrous life-philosophies, new very wondrous life-practices! Dilettantism, Pococurantism, Beau-Brummelism,[8] with perhaps an occasional, half-mad, protesting burst of Byronism, establish themselves; at the end of a certain period, if you go back to "the Dead Sea," there is, say our Moslem friends, a very strange "Sabbath day" transacting itself there![9] Brethren, we know but imperfectly yet, after ages of Constitutional Government, what Liberty and Slavery are.

Democracy, the chase of Liberty in that direction shall go its full course, unrestrainable by him of Pferdefuss-Quacksalber, or any of *his* household. The Toiling Millions of Mankind, in most vital need and passionate instinctive desire of Guidance, shall cast away False-Guidance and hope, for an hour, that No-Guid-

---

[1] *crotchets*   Odd notions; perverse conceits.

[2] *cat-o'-nine-tails*   Whip with nine lashes.

[3] *Galvanisms*   Applications of electricity.

[4] *east wind*   The east wind was proverbially harmful to one's health. In the Bible it is seen as destructive; the wind blowing from the east onto Palestine brings dry, hot air from the desert, and is harmful to crops.

[5] *wardmotes*   Meetings of the citizens of a ward, or area of the city.

[6] *election-hustings*   I.e., election proceedings. The husting was a temporary platform on which candidates for Parliament stood to address electors.

[7] *Palaver*   Rigamarole, prolonged and tedious discussion.

[8] *Pococurantism*   Attitude of indifference or unconcern, from an Italian expression describing an indifferent person; *Beau Brummelism*   Obsession with fashion. George Bryan Brummel (known as "Beau Brummel") was a leader of fashion in Regency England.

[9] *there is ... there*   According to an Islamic myth, a tribe living on the banks of the Dead Sea were turned into apes after refusing to acknowledge Moses's prophecies.

ance will suffice them; but it can be for an hour only. The smallest item of human Slavery is the oppression of man by his Mock Superiors; the palpablest, but I say at bottom the smallest. Let him shake off such oppression, trample it indignantly under his feet; I blame him not, I pity and commend him. But oppression by your Mock Superiors well shaken off, the grand problem yet remains to solve: that of finding government by your Real Superiors! Alas, how shall we ever learn the solution of that, benighted, bewildered, sniffing, sneering, god-forgetting unfortunates we are? It is a work for centuries, to be taught us by tribulations, confusions, insurrections, obstructions; who knows if not by conflagration and despair! It is a lesson inclusive of all other lessons; the hardest of all lessons to learn.

One thing I do know: those Apes, chattering on the branches by the Dead Sea, never got it learned, but chatter there to this day. To them no Moses need come a second time; a thousand Moseses would be but so many painted Phantasms, interesting Fellow-Apes of new strange aspect, whom they would "invite to dinner," be glad to meet with in lion-soirées. To them the voice of Prophecy, of heavenly monition, is quite ended. They chatter here, all Heaven shut to them, to the end of the world. The unfortunates! Oh, what is dying of hunger, with honest tools in your hand, with a manful purpose in your heart, and much real labour lying round you done, in comparison? You honestly quit your tools, quit a most muddy confused coil of sore work, short rations, of sorrow, dispiritments, and contradictions, having now honestly done with it all, and await, not entirely in a distracted manner, what the Supreme Powers, and the Silences and the Eternities may have to say to you.

A second thing I know: this lesson will have to be learned—under penalties! England will either learn it, or England also will cease to exist among Nations. England will either learn to reverence its Heroes, and discriminate them from its Sham-Heroes and Valets and gaslighted Histrios, and to prize them as the audible God's-voice, amid all inane jargons and temporary market-cries, and say to them with heart-loyalty, "Be ye King and Priest, and Gospel and Guidance for us," or else England will continue to worship new and ever-new forms of Quackhood—and so, with what resiliences and reboundings matters little, go down to the Father of

Quacks! Can I dread such things of England? Wretched, thickeyed, gross-hearted mortals, why will ye worship lies, and "Stuffed Clothes-suits created by the ninth-parts[1] of men"! It is not your purses that suffer, your farm-rents, your commerces, your mill-revenues, loud as ye lament over these; no, it is not these alone, but a far deeper than these: it is your souls that lie dead, crushed down under despicable Nightmares, Atheisms, Brain-fumes, and are not souls at all, but mere succedanea[2] for *salt* to keep your bodies and their appetites from putrefying! Your cotton-spinning and thrice-miraculous mechanism, what is this too, by itself, but a larger kind of Animalism? Spiders can spin, Beavers can build and show contrivance, the Ant lays-up accumulation of capital, and has, for aught I know, a Bank of Antland. If there is no soul in man higher than all that, did it reach to sailing on the cloud-rack and spinning sea-sand, then I say, man is but an animal, a more cunning kind of brute; he has no soul, but only a succedaneum for salt. Whereupon, seeing himself to be truly of the beasts that perish, he ought to admit it, I think—and also straightway universally to kill himself, and so, in a manlike manner at least *end*, and wave these brute-worlds *his* dignified farewell! …

from BOOK 4
CHAPTER 4—CAPTAINS OF INDUSTRY

If I believed that Mammonism with its adjuncts was to continue henceforth the one serious principle of our existence, I should reckon it idle to solicit remedial measures from any Government, the disease being insusceptible of remedy. Government can do much, but it can in no wise[3] do all. Government, as the most conspicuous object in Society, is called upon to give signal of what shall be done; and, in many ways, to preside over, further, and command the doing of it. But the Government cannot do, by all its signaling and commanding, what the Society is radically indisposed to do. In the long-run every Government is the exact symbol of its People, with their wisdom and unwisdom;

[1] *the ninth-parts of men* I.e., worthless men.
[2] *succedanea* Substitutes.
[3] *wise* Way.

we have to say, Like People like Government. The main substance of this immense Problem of Organising Labour, and first of all of Managing the Working Classes, will, it is very clear, have to be solved by those who stand practically in the middle of it, by those who themselves work and preside over work. Of all that can be enacted by any Parliament in regard to it, the germs must already lie potentially extant in those two Classes, who are to obey such enactment. A Human Chaos *in* which there is no light, you vainly attempt to irradiate by light shed *on* it; order never can arise there.

But it is my firm conviction that the "Hell of England" will *cease* to be that of "not making money," that we shall get a nobler Hell and a nobler Heaven! I anticipate light *in* the Human Chaos, glimmering, shining more and more, under manifold true signals from without That light shall shine. Our deity no longer being Mammon, O Heavens, each man will then say to himself, "Why such deadly haste to make money? I shall not go to Hell, even if I do not make money! There is another Hell, I am told!" Competition, at railway-speed, in all branches of commerce and work will then abate; good felt-hats for the head, in every sense, instead of seven-feet lath-and-plaster hats on wheels, will then be discoverable! Bubble-periods,[1] with their panics and commercial crises, will again become infrequent; steady modest industry will take the place of gambling speculation. To be a noble Master, among noble Workers, will again be the first ambition with some few; to be a rich Master only the second. How the Inventive Genius of England, with the whirr of its bobbins and billy-rollers[2] shoved somewhat into the backgrounds of the brain, will contrive and devise, not cheaper produce exclusively, but fairer distribution of the produce at its present cheapness! By degrees, we shall again have a Society with something of Heroism in it, something of Heaven's Blessing on it; we shall again have, as my German friend asserts, "instead of Mammon-Feudalism with unsold cotton-shirts and Preservation of the Game, noble just Industrialism and Government by the Wisest!"

It is with the hope of awakening here and there a British man to know himself for a man and divine soul, that a few words of parting admonition, to all persons to whom the Heavenly Powers have lent power of any kind in this land, may now be addressed. And first to those same Master-Workers, Leaders of Industry, who stand nearest and in fact powerfulest, though not most prominent, being as yet in too many senses a Virtuality rather than an Actuality.

The Leaders of Industry, if Industry is ever to be led, are virtually the Captains of the World; if there be no nobleness in them, there will never be an Aristocracy more. But let the Captains of Industry consider: once again, are they born of other clay than the old Captains of Slaughter, doomed forever to be no Chivalry, but a mere gold-plated *Doggery*—what the French well name *Canaille*, "Doggery" with more or less gold carrion at its disposal? Captains of Industry are the true Fighters, henceforth recognisable as the only true ones—Fighters against Chaos, Necessity, and the Devils and Jötuns[3]— and lead on Mankind in that great, and alone true and universal warfare; the stars in their courses fighting for them, and all Heaven and all Earth saying audibly, Well done! Let the Captains of Industry retire into their own hearts, and ask solemnly, If there is nothing but vulturous hunger for fine wines, valet reputation, and gilt carriages discoverable there? Of hearts made by the Almighty God I will not believe such a thing. Deep-hidden under wretchedest god-forgetting Cants, Epicurisms,[4] Dead-Sea Apisms, forgotten as under foulest fat Lethe[5] mud and weeds, there is yet, in all hearts born into this God's-World, a spark of the Godlike slumbering. Awake, O nightmare sleepers; awake, arise, or be forever fallen! This is not playhouse poetry, it is sober fact. Our England, our world, cannot live as it is. It will connect itself with a God again, or go down with nameless throes and fire-consummation to the Devils. Thou who feelest aught[6] of such a Godlike stirring in thee, any faintest intimation of it as through heavy-

---

1 *Bubble-periods* Violent fluctuations in the stock market.

2 *bobbins* Wooden spools or cylinders on which cotton or thread is wound; *billy-rollers* Machines for preparing cotton or wool for spinning.

3 *Jötuns* Members of a mythological Norse race of giants.

4 *Epicurisms* Pursuits of sensual pleasures, luxury, and ease, so named after the philosophical system of third-century BCE Greek thinker Epicurus.

5 *Lethe* River of forgetfulness in Hades, the classical underworld.

6 *aught* Anything.

laden dreams, follow *it*, I conjure thee. Arise, save thyself, be one of those that save thy country.

Buccaneers, Chactaw Indians,[1] whose supreme aim in fighting is that they may get the scalps, the money, that they may amass scalps and money—out of such came no Chivalry, and never will! Out of such came only gore and wreck, infernal rage and misery; desperation quenched in annihilation. Behold it, I bid thee; behold there, and consider! What is it that thou have a hundred thousand-pound bills laid-up in thy strong-room, a hundred scalps hung-up in thy wigwam? I value not them or thee. Thy scalps and thy thousand-pound bills are as yet nothing, if no nobleness from within irradiate them; if no Chivalry, in action, or in embryo ever struggling towards birth and action, be there.

Love of men cannot be bought by cash-payment, and without love men cannot endure to be together. You cannot lead a Fighting World without having it regimented, chivalried; the thing, in a day, becomes impossible. All men in it, the highest at first, the very lowest at last, discern consciously, or by a noble instinct, this necessity. And can you any more continue to lead a Working World unregimented, anarchic? I answer, and the Heavens and Earth are now answering, No! The thing becomes not "in a day" impossible; but in some two generations it does. Yes, when fathers and mothers, in Stockport hunger-cellars, begin to eat their children; and Irish widows have to prove their relationship by dying of typhus-fever; and amid Governing "Corporations of the Best and Bravest," busy to preserve their game by "bushing," dark millions of God's human creatures start up in mad Chartisms, impracticable Sacred-Months, and Manchester Insurrections; and there is a virtual Industrial Aristocracy as yet only half-alive, spell-bound amid money-bags and ledgers; and an actual Idle Aristocracy seemingly near dead in somnolent delusions, in trespasses[2] and double-barrels, "sliding," as on inclined planes, which every new year they

soap with new Hansard's-jargon[3] under God's sky, and so are "sliding," ever faster, towards a "scale" and balance-scale whereon is written *Thou art found Wanting*—in such days, after a generation or two, I say, it does become, even to the low and simple, very palpably impossible! No Working World, any more than a Fighting World, can be led on without a noble Chivalry of Work, and laws and fixed rules which follow out of that, far nobler than any Chivalry of Fighting was. As an anarchic multitude on mere Supply-and-demand, it is becoming inevitable that we dwindle in horrid suicidal convulsion and self-abrasion, frightful to the imagination, into *Chactaw* Workers. With wigwams and scalps, with palaces and thousand-pound bills, with savagery, depopulation, chaotic desolation! Good Heavens, will not one French Revolution and Reign of Terror suffice us, but must there be two? There will be two if needed; there will be twenty if needed; there will be precisely as many as are needed. The Laws of Nature will have themselves fulfilled. That is a thing certain to me.

Your gallant battle-hosts and work-hosts, as the others did, will need to be made loyally yours; they must and will be regulated, methodically secured in their just share of conquest under you—joined with you in veritable brotherhood, sonhood, by quite other and deeper ties than those of temporary day's wages! How would mere red-coated regiments, to say nothing of chivalries, fight for you, if you could discharge them on the evening of the battle, on payment of the stipulated shillings—and they discharge you on the morning of it! Chelsea Hospitals,[4] pensions, promotions, rigorous lasting covenant on the one side and on the other, are indispensable even for a hired fighter. The Feudal Baron, much more—how could he subsist with mere temporary mercenaries round him at sixpence a day, ready to go over to the other side, if sevenpence were offered? He could not have subsisted, and his noble instinct saved him from the necessity of even trying! The Feudal Baron had a Man's Soul in him, to which anarchy, mutiny, and the other fruits of temporary

---

[1]   *Chactaw Indians*   The Choctaw, who formerly inhabited central and southern Mississippi and southwest Alabama, and who were known to take as trophies the scalps of enemies killed in battle. The tribe had a friendly relationship with the American settlers; secessions of their eastern land to the settlers allowed Mississippi to become a state. In exchange, they were granted land in present-day Oklahoma, to which they were removed between 1831 and 1903.

[2]   *trespasses*   I.e., fear of trespassers encroaching on their game preserves.

[3]   *Hansard's-jargon*   Parliamentary debate (the official report of which is known as "Hansard," after the printer Luke Hansard, who compiled it for many years).

[4]   *Chelsea Hospitals*   Homes such as the Chelsea Royal Hospital, for elderly or disabled veterans.

mercenaries were intolerable; he had never been a Baron otherwise, but had continued a Chactaw and Buccaneer. He felt it precious, and at last it became habitual, and his fruitful enlarged existence included it as a necessity, to have men round him who in heart loved him; whose life he watched over with rigour yet with love; who were prepared to give their life for him, if need came. It was beautiful; it was human! Man lives not otherwise, nor can live contented, anywhere or anywhen. Isolation is the sum-total of wretchedness to man. To be cut off, to be left solitary; to have a world alien, not your world, all a hostile camp for you, not a home at all, of hearts and faces who are yours, whose you are! It is the frightfulest enchantment, too truly a work of the Evil One. To have neither superior, nor inferior, nor equal, united manlike to you. Without father, without child, without brother. Man knows no sadder destiny. "How is each of us," exclaims Jean Paul,[1] "so lonely in the wide bosom of the All!" Encased each as in his transparent "ice-palace," our brother visible in his, making signals and gesticulations to us—visible, but forever unattainable; on his bosom we shall never rest, nor he on ours. It was not a God that did this; no!

Awake, ye noble Workers, warriors in the one true war; all this must be remedied. It is you who are already half-alive, whom I will welcome into life, whom I will conjure, in God's name, to shake off your enchanted sleep, and live wholly! Cease to count scalps, gold-purses; not in these lies your or our salvation. Even these, if you count only these, will not long be left. Let buccaneering be put far from you; alter, speedily abrogate all laws of the buccaneers, if you would gain any victory that shall endure. Let God's justice, let pity, nobleness and manly valour, with more gold-purses or with fewer, testify themselves in this your brief Life-transit to all the Eternities, the Gods and Silences. It is to you I call; for ye are not dead, ye are already half-alive; there is in you a sleepless dauntless energy, the prime-matter of all nobleness in man. Honour to you in your kind. It is to you I call; ye know at least this, That the mandate of God to His creature man is Work! The future Epic of the World rests not with those that are near dead, but with those that are alive, and those that are coming into life.

Look around you. Your world-hosts are all in mutiny, in confusion, destitution; on the eve of fiery wreck and madness! They will not march farther for you, on the sixpence a day and supply-and-demand principle; they will not, nor ought they, nor can they. Ye shall reduce them to order, begin reducing them. To order, to just subordination; noble loyalty in return for noble guidance. Their souls are driven nigh mad; let yours be sane and ever saner. Not as a bewildered bewildering mob, but as a firm regimented mass, with real captains over them, will these men march any more. All human interests, combined human endeavours, and social growths in this world, have, at a certain stage of their development, required organising; and Work, the grandest of human interests, does now require it.

God knows, the task will be hard; but no noble task was ever easy. This task will wear away your lives, and the lives of your sons and grandsons; but for what purpose, if not for tasks like this, were lives given to men? Ye shall cease to count your thousand-pound scalps; the noble of you shall cease! Nay, the very scalps, as I say, will not long be left if you count only these. Ye shall cease wholly to be barbarous vulturous Chactaws, and become noble European Nineteenth-Century Men. Ye shall know that Mammon, in never such gigs[2] and flunky "respectabilities," is not the alone God, that of himself he is but a Devil, and even a Brute-god.

Difficult? Yes, it will be difficult. The short-fibre cotton, that too was difficult. The waste cotton-shrub, long useless, disobedient, as the thistle by the wayside—have ye not conquered it, made it into beautiful bandana webs, white woven shirts for men, bright-tinted air-garments wherein flit goddesses? Ye have shivered mountains asunder, made the hard iron pliant to you as soft putty; the Forest-giants, Marsh-jötuns bear sheaves of golden-grain; Aegir[3] the Sea-demon himself stretches his back for a sleek highway to you, and on Firehorses and Windhorses ye career. Ye are most strong. Thor[4] red-bearded, with his blue sun-eyes, with his cheery heart and strong thunder-hammer, he and you have prevailed. Ye are most strong, ye Sons of the icy North, of the far East—far marching from your rugged Eastern

1 *Jean Paul* German writer Jean Paul Richter (1763–1825).
2 *gigs* Two-wheeled carriages.
3 *Aegir* Norse god of the sea.
4 *Thor* Norse god of thunder and rain.

Wildernesses, hitherward from the gray Dawn of Time! Ye are Sons of the *Jötun-land*, the land of Difficulties Conquered. Difficult? You must try this thing. Once try it with the understanding that it will and shall have to be done. Try it as ye try the paltrier thing, making of

money! I will bet on you once more, against all Jötuns, Tailor-gods, Double-barrelled Law-wards, and Denizens of Chaos whatsoever!

—1843

THOMAS BABINGTON MACAULAY
1800 – 1859

Thomas Babington Macaulay enjoyed a stellar career as a politician, essayist, historian, and poet, moving from one dazzling success to another. A child prodigy, he later became a Member of Parliament and was one of the most eloquent rhetoricians ever to speak in the House of Commons. Macaulay's essays, written on such subjects as the benefits of industrialism and science, James Mill's Benthamism, Machiavelli, Milton, John Bunyan, and Samuel Johnson, were extremely popular as was his long, narrative ballad *Lays of Ancient Rome* (1842), which had sold 100,000 copies by 1875. He is mostly remembered today, however, for his five-volume *History of England*, biased in favor of Whig politics but an eloquent review of history from James I (1688) to the passing of the 1832 Reform Bill. Macaulay's *History* rivaled the Bible for sales records in Britain and the United States.

Born in Leicestershire to Selina Mills and Zachary Macaulay, an Evangelical and a staunch Tory who became well-known for his anti-slavery campaigns, Thomas Macaulay made an immediate impression on anyone whom he met. By the age of eight he had already shown extraordinary talent for writing, having penned hymns and heroic poetry that impressed the Evangelical philanthropist and author Hannah More. His impact upon his educators at Trinity College, Cambridge, where he attended university, was also considerable—Macaulay twice won Cambridge University's Chancellor's Medal for poetry. While at Cambridge, he was influenced by Utilitarianism (or Benthamite philosophy, as it was then known), but he did not advocate radicalism and distanced himself from the Tory politics of his family in favor of the Whigs.

At the age of 24, Macaulay began writing for the Whig *Edinburgh Review*, with an essay on Milton. During the next two decades he became the magazine's most popular writer. His brilliant essays and his Whig sympathies attracted the attention of Lord Lansdowne, who helped him get elected to Parliament in 1830, at which time Macaulay immediately began campaigning for the Reform Bill of 1832. His speech in support of the bill brought him fame as an orator; his closing argument attests to his rhetorical skills: "The danger is terrible. The time is short. If this bill should be rejected, I pray to God that none of those who concur in rejecting it may ever remember their votes with unavailing remorse, amidst the wreck of laws, the confusion of ranks, the spoilation of property, and the dissolution of social order."

In the wake of his success in Parliament, Macaulay became a commissioner on the Board of Control for India and soon afterward was awarded a lucrative position on the Supreme Council of the East India Company. While in India from 1834 to 1838, he worked to reform the education system and the penal code, even as he continued writing essays and poetry. Upon his return to Great Britain, he became Member of Parliament for Edinburgh and Secretary of War, and continued writing for the *Edinburgh Review*. An edition of his collected writings, *Critical and Historical Essays*, was published in 1843. After losing his seat in 1847, Macaulay concentrated on his *History of England*, publishing the first two volumes in 1848. These volumes became immediate and spectacular successes, with 13,000 copies selling in the first four months of their release.

Many honors followed: Macaulay became Rector of the University of Glasgow; was made a Knight of the Order of Merit of Prussia; was given a Doctorate of Civil Law from Oxford; and in 1857 became Baron Macaulay of Rothley. During these heady years, Macaulay returned to Parliament (1852) and published two more volumes of his *History* (1855), but was forced to resign his seat four years later due to ill health. Macaulay died in 1859 and is buried in the Poets' Corner of Westminster Abbey.

⌘ ⌘ ⌘

from *The History of England*

from CHAPTER 3: STATE OF ENGLAND IN 1685

I intend, in this chapter, to give a description of the state in which England was at the time when the crown passed from Charles the Second to his brother.[1] Such a description, composed from scanty and dispersed materials, must necessarily be very imperfect. Yet it may perhaps correct some false notions which would make the subsequent narrative unintelligible or uninstructive.

If we would study with profit the history of our ancestors, we must be constantly on our guard against that delusion which the well-known names of families, places, and offices naturally produce, and must never forget that the country of which we read was a very different country from that in which we live. In every experimental science there is a tendency toward perfection. In every human being there is a wish to ameliorate his own condition. These two principles have often sufficed, even when counteracted by great public calamities and by bad institutions, to carry civilization rapidly forward. No ordinary misfortune, no ordinary misgovernment, will do so much to make a nation wretched, as the constant progress of physical knowledge, and the constant effort of every man to better himself, will do to make a nation prosperous. It has often been found that profuse expenditure, heavy taxation, absurd commercial restrictions, corrupt tribunals, disastrous wars, seditions, persecutions, conflagrations, inundations, have not been able to destroy capital so fast as the exertions of private citizens have been able to create it. It can easily be proved that, in our own land, the national wealth has, during at least six centuries, been almost uninterruptedly increasing; that

it was greater under the Tudors than under the Plantagenets;[2] that it was greater under the Stuarts[3] than under the Tudors; that, in spite of battles, sieges, and confiscations, it was greater on the day of the Restoration than on the day when the Long Parliament met;[4] that, in spite of maladministration, of extravagance, of public bankruptcy, of two costly and unsuccessful wars,[5] of the pestilence,[6] and of the fire,[7] it was greater on the day of the death of Charles the Second than on the day of his restoration. This progress, having continued during many ages, became at length, about the middle of the eighteenth century, portentously rapid, and has proceeded, during the nineteenth, with accelerated velocity. In consequence partly of our geographical and partly of our moral position, we have, during several generations, been exempt from evils which have elsewhere impeded the efforts and destroyed the fruits of industry. While every part of the Continent, from Moscow to Lisbon, has been the theatre of bloody and devastating wars, no hostile standard has been seen here but as a trophy. While revolutions have taken place all around us, our government has never once been subverted by violence.

---

[1] *his brother*   James II.

[2] *Tudors*   Members of the family of monarchs that ruled England from 1485–1603 and that included Henry VII, Henry VIII, Edward VI, Mary I, and Elizabeth I; *Plantagenets*   Members of the line of kings that ruled England from Henry II to Richard III (1154–1485).

[3] *Stuarts*   Members of the family that ruled Scotland and England from 1603 to 1649 and from 1660 to 1714.

[4] *Restoration*   Re-establishment of the British monarchy with King Charles II in 1660; *Long Parliament*   Parliament which sat from 1640 until 1653, when it was dissolved by Oliver Cromwell, who led the Parliamentary victory in the English civil war.

[5] *two costly and unsuccessful wars*   With the Dutch.

[6] *pestilence*   The bubonic plague afflicted England for a year, beginning in the summer of 1665 and lasting into 1666.

[7] *the fire*   The Great Fire of 1666, which began in a bakery, burned for four days and destroyed approximately 80 per cent of London.

During more than a hundred years there has been in our island no tumult of sufficient importance to be called an insurrection; nor has the law been once borne down either by popular fury or by regal tyranny: public credit has been held sacred; the administration of justice has been pure; even in times which might by Englishmen be justly called evil times, we have enjoyed what almost every other nation in the world would have considered as an ample measure of civil and religious freedom. Every man has felt entire confidence that the state would protect him in the possession of what had been earned by his diligence and hoarded by his self-denial. Under the benignant influence of peace and liberty, science has flourished, and has been applied to practical purposes on a scale never before known. The consequence is that a change to which the history of the old world furnishes no parallel has taken place in our country. Could the England of 1685 be, by some magical process, set before our eyes, we should not know one landscape in a hundred or one building in ten thousand. The country gentleman would not recognize his own fields. The inhabitant of the town would not recognize his own street. Everything has been changed but the great features of nature, and a few massive and durable works of human art. We might find out Snowdon and Windermere, the Cheddar Cliffs and Beachy Head.[1] We might find out here and there a Norman minister,[2] or a castle which witnessed the wars of the Roses.[3] But, with such rare exceptions, everything would be strange to us. Many thousands of square miles which are now rich corn land and meadow, intersected by green hedgerows, and dotted with villages and pleasant country-seats, would appear as moors overgrown with furze,[4] or fens abandoned to wild ducks. We should see straggling huts built of wood and covered with thatch, where we now see manufacturing towns and seaports renowned to the farthest ends of the world. The capital itself would shrink to dimensions not much exceeding those of its present suburb on the south of the Thames. Not less strange to us would be the garb and manners of the people, the furniture and the equipages, the interior of the shops and dwellings. Such a change in the state of a nation seems to be at least as well entitled to the notice of a historian as any change of the dynasty or of the ministry.

One of the first objects of an inquirer who wishes to form a correct notion of the state of a community at a given time must be to ascertain of how many persons that community then consisted. Unfortunately the population of England in 1685 cannot be ascertained with perfect accuracy, for no great state had then adopted the wise course of periodically numbering the people. All men were left to conjecture for themselves; and, as they generally conjectured without examining facts, and under the influence of strong passions and prejudices, their guesses were often ludicrously absurd. Even intelligent Londoners ordinarily talked of London as containing several millions of souls. It was confidently asserted by many that, during the thirty-five years which elapsed between the accession of Charles the First and the Restoration, the population of the city had increased by two millions.[5] Even while the ravages of the plague and fire were recent, it was the fashion to say that the capital still had a million and a half of inhabitants.[6] Some persons, disgusted by these exaggerations, ran violently into the opposite extreme. Thus Isaac Vossius, a man of undoubted parts and learning, strenuously maintained that there were only two millions of human beings in England, Scotland, and Ireland taken together.[7]

We are not, however, left without the means of correcting the wild blunders into which some minds were hurried by national vanity and others by a morbid love of paradox. There are extant three computations which seem to be entitled to peculiar attention. They are entirely independent of each other: they proceed on

---

[1] *Snowdon* Mountain in northwest Wales which forms the highest point in that country; *Windermere* Largest lake in England, located in the Lake District of northwestern England; *Cheddar Cliffs* Limestone cliffs located near the town of Cheddar, in Somerset; *Beachy Head* Chalk cliffs on the southeast coast of England.

[2] *minister* I.e., minster, here the church of a monastery.

[3] *wars of the Roses* Fifteenth-century civil war between the rival Houses of York and Lancaster, whose emblems were white and red roses, respectively.

[4] *furze* Low-growing bush that covers uncultivated land.

[5] [Macaulay's note] *Observations on the Bills of Mortality*, by Captain John Graunt (Sir William Petty), Chap. 11.

[6] [Macaulay's note] "She doth comprehend / Full fifteen hundred thousand which do spend / Their days within."— *Great Britain's Beauty*, 1671.

[7] [Macaulay's note] Isaac Vossius, *De Magnitudine Urbium Sinarum*, 1685. Vossius, as we learn from Saint Evremond, talked on this subject oftener and longer than fashionable circles cared to listen.

different principles, and yet there is little difference in the results.

One of these computations was made in the year 1696 by Gregory King, Lancaster herald, a political arithmetician of great acuteness and judgment. The basis of his calculations was the number of houses returned in 1690 by the officers who made the last collection of the hearth-money.[1] The conclusion at which he arrived was that the population of England was nearly five millions and a half.[2]

About the same time, King William the Third was desirous to ascertain the comparative strength of the religious sects into which the community was divided. An inquiry was instituted, and reports were laid before him from all the dioceses of the realm. According to these reports, the number of his English subjects must have been about five million two hundred thousand.[3]

Lastly, in our own days, Mr. Finlaison, an actuary of eminent skill, subjected the ancient parochial registers of baptisms, marriages, and burials to all the tests which the modern improvements in statistical science enabled him to apply. His opinion was that at the close of the seventeenth century, the population of England was a little under five million, two hundred thousand souls.[4]

Of these three estimates, framed without concert by different persons from different sets of materials, the highest, which is that of King, does not exceed the lowest, which is that of Finlaison, by one-twelfth. We may, therefore, with confidence pronounce that, when James the Second reigned, England contained between five million and five million five hundred thousand inhabitants. On the very highest supposition she then had less than one-third of her present population, and less than three times the population which is now collected in her gigantic capital.

The increase of the people has been great in every part of the kingdom, but generally much greater in the northern than in the southern shires. In truth a large part of the country beyond Trent was, down to the eighteenth century, in a state of barbarism. Physical and moral causes had concurred to prevent civilization from spreading to that region. The air was inclement; the soil was generally such as required skilful and industrious cultivation; and there could be little skill or industry in a tract which was often the theatre of war, and which, even when there was nominal peace, was constantly desolated by bands of Scottish marauders. Before the union of the two British crowns,[5] and long after that union, there was as great a difference between Middlesex and Northumberland as there now is between Massachusetts and the settlements of those squatters who, far to the west of the Mississippi, administer a rude justice with the rifle and the dagger. In the reign of Charles the Second, the traces left by ages of slaughter and pillage were distinctly perceptible many miles south of the Tweed,[6] in the face of the country and in the lawless manners of the people. There was still a large class of moss-troopers,[7] whose calling was to plunder dwellings and to drive away whole herds of cattle. It was found necessary soon after the Restoration to enact laws of great severity for the prevention of these outrages. The magistrates of Northumberland and Cumberland were authorized to raise bands of armed men for the defence of property and order, and provision was made for meeting the expense of these levies by local taxation. The parishes were required to keep blood-hounds for the purpose of hunting the freebooters. Many old men who were living in the middle of the eighteenth century could well remember the time when those ferocious dogs were common.[8] Yet, even with such auxiliaries, it was often found impossible to track the robbers to their retreats among the hills and morasses. For the geography

---

[1] *hearth-money* Tax on hearths or fireplaces imposed by Charles II.

[2] [Macaulay's note] King's *Natural and Political Observations*, 1696. This valuable treatise, which ought to be read as the author wrote it, and not as garbled by Davenant, will be found in some editions of Chalmers's *Estimate*.

[3] [Macaulay's note] Dalrymple's Appendix to Part II, Book I. The practice of reckoning the population by sects was long fashionable. Gulliver [in Jonathan Swift's *Gulliver's Travels*] says of the King of Brobdingnag: "He laughed at my odd arithmetic, as he was pleased to call it, in reckoning the numbers of our people by a computation drawn from the several sects among us in religion and politics."

[4] [Macaulay's note] Preface to the Population Returns of 1831.

---

[5] *union of … crowns* On the accession of James VI of Scotland to the English throne in 1603, the new James I of England became king of both countries, uniting the crowns of England and Scotland.

[6] *Tweed* River forming part of the border between England and Scotland.

[7] *moss-troopers* Bands of marauders operating in the bogs that made up the border country between Scotland and England.

[8] [Macaulay's note] Nicholson and Bourne, *Discourse on the Ancient State of the Border*, 1777.

of that wild country was very imperfectly known. Even after the accession of George the Third, the path over the fells from Borrowdale to Ravenglas was still a secret carefully kept by the dalesmen, some of whom had probably in their youth escaped from the pursuit of justice by that road.[1] The seats of the gentry and the larger farm-houses were fortified. Oxen were penned at night beneath the overhanging battlements of the residence, which was known by the name of the Peel. The inmates slept with arms at their sides. Huge stones and boiling water were in readiness to crush and scald the plunderer who might venture to assail the little garrison. No traveller ventured into that country without making his will. The judges on circuit, with the whole body of barristers, attorneys, clerks, and serving-men, rode on horseback from Newcastle to Carlisle, armed and escorted by a strong guard under the command of the sheriffs. It was necessary to carry provisions, for the country was a wilderness which afforded no supplies. The spot where the cavalcade halted to dine, under an immense oak, is not yet forgotten. The irregular vigor with which criminal justice was administered shocked observers whose lives had been passed in more tranquil districts. Juries, animated by hatred and by a sense of common danger, convicted house-breakers and cattle-stealers with the promptitude of a court-martial in a mutiny; and the convicts were hurried by scores to the gallows.[2] Within the memory of some whom this generation has seen, the sportsman who wandered in pursuit of game to the sources of the Tyne found the heaths round Keeldar Castle peopled by a race scarcely less savage than the Indians of California, and heard with surprise the half-naked women chanting a wild measure, while the men with brandished dirks[3] danced a war-dance.[4]

Slowly and with difficulty peace was established on the border. In the train of peace came industry and all the arts of life. Meanwhile, it was discovered that the regions north of the Trent possessed in their coal-beds a source of wealth far more precious than the goldmines of Peru. It was found that, in the neighborhood of these beds, almost every manufacture might be most profitably carried on. A constant stream of emigrants began to roll northward. It appeared by the returns of 1841 that the ancient archiepiscopal[5] province of York contained two sevenths of the population of England. At the time of the Revolution[6] that province was believed to contain only one seventh of the population.[7] In Lancashire the number of inhabitants appears to have increased ninefold, while in Norfolk, Suffolk, and Northamptonshire it has hardly doubled.

Of the taxation we can speak with more confidence and precision than of the population. The revenue of England, when Charles the Second died, was small when compared with the resources which she even then possessed, or with the sums which were raised by the governments of the neighboring countries. It had, from the time of the Restoration, been almost constantly increasing; yet it was little more than three fourths of the revenue of the United Provinces,[8] and was hardly one fifth of the revenue of France.

… It seems clear … that the wages of labor, estimated in money, were, in 1685, not more than half of what they now are; and there were few articles important to the workingman of which the price was not, in 1685, more than half of what it now is. Beer was undoubtedly much cheaper in that age than at present. Meat was also cheaper, but was still so dear that hundreds of thousands of families scarcely knew the taste of it.[9] In the cost of wheat there has been very little change. The average price of the quarter,[10] during the last twelve

---

[1] [Macaulay's note] Gray's *Journal of a Tour in the Lakes*, Oct. 3, 1769.

[2] [Macaulay's note] North's *Life of Guildford*; Hutchinson's *History of Cumberland*, Parish of Brampton.

[3] *dirks* Highland daggers.

[4] [Macaulay's note] See Sir Walter Scott's Journal, Oct. 7, 1827, in his Life by Mr. Lockhart.

[5] *archiepiscopal* I.e., of or pertaining to an archbishop.

[6] *the time … Revolution* I.e., 1640.

[7] [Macaulay's note] Dalrymple, Appendix to Part 2, Book 1. The returns of the hearth-money lead to nearly the same conclusion. The hearths in the province of York were not a sixth of the hearths of England.

[8] *United Provinces* Seven northern provinces of the Netherlands, which later united to form Holland.

[9] [Macaulay's note] King, in his *Natural and Political Conclusions*, roughly estimated the common people of England at 880,000 families. Of these families 440,000, according to him, ate animal food twice a week. The remaining 440,000 ate it not at all, or at most not oftener than once a week.

[10] *quarter* I.e., a British imperial quarter, a measurement of grain equal to 8 bushels.

years of Charles the Second, was fifty shillings. Bread, therefore, such as is now given to the inmates of a workhouse, was then seldom seen, even on the trencher[1] of a yeoman or of a shopkeeper. The great majority of the nation lived almost entirely on rye, barley, and oats.

The produce of tropical countries, the produce of the mines, the produce of machinery, was positively dearer than at present. Among the commodities for which the laborer would have had to pay higher in 1685 than his posterity now pay were sugar, salt, coals, candles, soap, shoes, stockings, and generally all articles of clothing and all articles of bedding. It may be added that the old coats and blankets would have been, not only more costly, but less serviceable than the modern fabrics.

It must be remembered that those laborers who were able to maintain themselves and their families by means of wages were not the most necessitous members of the community. Beneath them lay a large class which could not subsist without some aid from the parish. There can hardly be a more important test of the condition of the common people than the ratio which this class bears to the whole society. At present the men, women, and children who receive relief appear from the official returns to be, in bad years, one tenth of the inhabitants of England, and, in good years, one thirteenth. Gregory King estimated them in his time at about a fourth; and this estimate, which all our respect for his authority will scarcely prevent us from calling extravagant, was pronounced by Davenant eminently judicious.

We are not quite without the means of forming an estimate for ourselves. The poor-rate[2] was undoubtedly the heaviest tax borne by our ancestors in those days. It was computed, in the reign of Charles the Second, at near seven hundred thousand pounds a year, much more than the produce either of the excise or of the customs, and little less than half the entire revenue of the crown. The poor-rate went on increasing rapidly, and appears to have risen in a short time to between eight and nine hundred thousand a year, that is to say, to one sixth of what it now is. The population was then less than a third of what it now is. The minimum of wages, estimated in money, was half of what it now is; and we can therefore hardly suppose that the average

allowance made to a pauper can have been more than half of what it now is. It seems to follow that the proportion of the English people which received parochial relief then must have been larger than the proportion which receives relief now. It is good to speak on such questions with diffidence; but it has certainly never yet been proved that pauperism was a less heavy burden or a less serious social evil during the last quarter of the seventeenth century than it is in our own time.

In one respect it must be admitted that the progress of civilization has diminished the physical comforts of a portion of the poorest class. It has already been mentioned that, before the Revolution, many thousands of square miles, now enclosed and cultivated, were marsh, forest, and heath. Of this wild land much was, by law, common, and much of what was not common by law was worth so little that the proprietors suffered it to be common in fact. In such a tract, squatters and trespassers were tolerated to an extent now unknown. The peasant who dwelt there could, at little or no charge, procure occasionally some palatable addition to his hard fare, and provide himself with fuel for the winter. He kept a flock of geese on what is now an orchard rich with apple-blossoms. He snared wild fowl on the fen which has long since been drained and divided into corn-fields and turnip-fields. He cut turf among the furze bushes on the moor which is now a meadow bright with clover and renowned for butter and cheese. The progress of agriculture and the increase of population necessarily deprived him of these privileges. But against this disadvantage a long list of advantages is to be set off. Of the blessings which civilization and philosophy bring with them, a large proportion is common to all ranks, and would, if withdrawn, be missed as painfully by the laborer as by the peer. The marketplace which the rustic can now reach with his cart in an hour was, a hundred and sixty years ago, a day's journey from him. The street which now affords to the artisan, during the whole night, a secure, a convenient, and a brilliantly lighted walk was, a hundred and sixty years ago, so dark after sunset that he would not have been able to see his hand, so ill paved that he would have run constant risk of breaking his neck, and so ill watched that he would have been in imminent danger of being knocked down and plundered of his small earnings. Every bricklayer who falls from a scaffold, every sweeper of a crossing who is

---

[1] *trencher* Plate.

[2] *poor-rate* Rate or sum demanded from the public for the relief of the poor.

run over by a carriage, may now have his wounds dressed and his limbs set with a skill such as, a hundred and sixty years ago, all the wealth of a great lord like Ormond, or of a merchant-prince like Clayton,[1] could not have purchased. Some frightful diseases have been extirpated by science; and some have been banished by police. The term of human life had been lengthened over the whole kingdom, and especially in the towns. The year 1685 was not accounted sickly; yet in the year 1685 more than one in twenty-three of the inhabitants of the capital died. At present only one inhabitant of the capital in forty dies annually. The difference in salubrity[2] between the London of the nineteenth century and the London of the seventeenth century is very far greater than the difference between London in an ordinary year and London in a year of cholera.

Still more important is the benefit which all orders of society, and especially the lower orders, have derived from the mollifying influence of civilization on the national character. The groundwork of that character has indeed been the same through many generations, in the sense in which the groundwork of the character of an individual may be said to be the same when he is a rude and thoughtless schoolboy and when he is a refined and accomplished man. It is pleasing to reflect that the public mind of England has softened while it has ripened, and that we have, in the course of ages, become not only a wiser, but also a kinder people. There is scarcely a page of the history or lighter literature of the seventeenth century which does not contain some proof that our ancestors were less humane than their posterity. The discipline of workshops, of schools, of private families, though not more efficient than at present, was infinitely harsher. Masters, well born and bred, were in the habit of beating their servants. Pedagogues knew no way of imparting knowledge but by beating their pupils. Husbands, of decent station, were not ashamed to beat their wives. The implacability of hostile factions was such as we can scarcely conceive. Whigs were disposed

to murmur because Stafford[3] was suffered to die without seeing his bowels burned before his face. Tories reviled and insulted Russell[4] as his coach passed from the Tower to the scaffold in Lincoln's Inn Fields.[5] As little mercy was shown by the populace to sufferers of a humbler rank. If an offender was put into the pillory,[6] it was well if he escaped with life from the shower of brickbats and paving-stones.[7] If he was tied to the cart's tail,[8] the crowd pressed round him, imploring the hangman to give it the fellow well, and make him howl.[9] Gentlemen arranged parties of pleasure to Bridewell[10] on court days, for the purpose of seeing the wretched women who beat hemp there whipped.[11] A man pressed to death for refusing to plead, a woman burned for coining, excited less sympathy than is now felt for a galled[12] horse or an overdriven ox. Fights compared with which a boxing-match is a refined and humane spectacle were among the favorite diversions of a large part of the town. Multitudes assembled to see gladiators hack each other to pieces with deadly weapons, and shouted with delight when one of the combatants lost a finger or an eye. The prisons were hells on earth, seminaries of every crime and of every disease. At the assizes[13] the lean and yellow culprits brought with them from their cells to the dock an atmosphere of stench and pestilence which some-

[3] *Stafford* William Howard, Viscount Stafford (1612–80). In 1673, Stafford, a Roman Catholic, was beheaded because of his supposed involvement in the "Popish Plot" to overthrow the King.

[4] *Russell* Lord William Russell (1639–83), Whig leader who was executed after being implicated in the Rye House Plot, a conspiracy to assassinate King Charles II and his brother James.

[5] [Macaulay's note] Burnet, i., 560.

[6] *pillory* Apparatus for punishment consisting of a wooden framework through which the criminal's head and arms were placed. The criminal would remain locked in this position while being exposed to public ridicule and harassment.

[7] [Macaulay's note] Muggleton's *Acts of the Witnesses of the Spirit.*

[8] *cart's tail* I.e., the back of the cart, to which offenders were tied to be whipped through the streets. The whipping was done by a hangman, who was responsible not only for the execution, but also the torturing, of prisoners.

[9] [Macaulay's note] Tom Brown describes such a scene in lines which I do not venture to quote.

[10] *Bridewell* I.e., Bridewell Prison.

[11] [Macaulay's note] Ward's *London Spy.*

[12] *galled* Sore from chafing (from a bridle, saddle, bit, etc.).

[13] *assizes* Trials.

[1] *Ormond* James Butler, First Duke of Ormond (1610–88), a Royalist leader in Ireland during the rebellion and Lord Lieutenant in Ireland from 1661 to 1669 and from 1677 to 1685; *Clayton* Sir Robert Clayton (1629–1707), founder of Clayton, Morris, & Co., law scriveners, merchant bankers, and estate agents. He went on to become a Member of Parliament and Lord Mayor of London.

[2] *salubrity* Air quality, with regard to its healthfulness.

times avenged them signally on bench, bar, and jury. But on all this misery society looked with profound indifference. Nowhere could be found that sensitive and restless compassion which has, in our time, extended a powerful protection to the factory child, to the Hindu widow, to the negro slave; which pries into the stores and water-casks of every immigrant ship; which winces at every lash laid on the back of a drunken soldier; which will not suffer the thief in the hulks to be ill fed or overworked; and which has repeatedly endeavored to save the life even of the murderer. It is true that compassion ought, like all other feelings, to be under the government of reason, and has, for want of such government, produced some ridiculous and some deplorable effects. But the more we study the annals of the past, the more shall we rejoice that we live in a merciful age, in an age in which cruelty is abhorred, and in which pain, even when deserved, is inflicted reluctantly and from a sense of duty. Every class doubtless has gained largely by this great moral change: but the class which has gained most is the poorest, the most dependent, and the most defenceless.

The general effect of the evidence which has been submitted to the reader seems hardly to admit of doubt. Yet, in spite of evidence, many will still image to themselves the England of the Stuarts as a more pleasant country than the England in which we live. It may at first sight seem strange that society, while constantly moving forward with eager speed, should be constantly looking backward with tender regret. But these two propensities, inconsistent as they may appear, can easily be resolved into the same principle. Both spring from our impatience of the state in which we actually are. That impatience, while it stimulates us to surpass preceding generations, disposes us to overrate their happiness. It is, in some sense, unreasonable and un-grateful in us to be constantly discontented with a condition which is constantly improving. But, in truth, there is constant improvement precisely because there is constant discontent. If we were perfectly satisfied with the present, we should cease to contrive, to labor, and to save with a view to the future. And it is natural that, being dissatisfied with the present, we should form a too favorable estimate of the past.

In truth, we are under a deception similar to that which misleads the traveller in the Arabian desert. Beneath the caravan all is dry and bare; but far in advance, and far in the rear, is the semblance of refresh-ing waters. The pilgrims hasten forward and find nothing but sand where, an hour before, they had seen a lake. They turn their eyes and see a lake where, an hour before, they were toiling through sand. A similar illusion seems to haunt nations through every stage of the long progress from poverty and barbarism to the highest degrees of opulence and civilization. But, if we resolutely chase the mirage backward, we shall find it recede before us into the regions of fabulous antiquity. It is now the fashion to place the Golden Age of Eng-land in times when noblemen were destitute of comforts the want of which would be intolerable to a modern footman; when farmers and shopkeepers breakfasted on loaves the very sight of which would raise a riot in a modern workhouse; when to have a clean shirt once a week was a privilege reserved for the higher class of gentry; when men died faster in the purest country air than they now die in the most pestilential lanes of our towns; and when men died faster in the lanes of our towns than they now die on the coast of Guiana. We too shall, in our turn, be outstripped, and in our turn be envied. It may well be, in the twentieth century, that the peasant of Dorsetshire may think himself miserably paid with twenty shillings a week; that the carpenter at Greenwich may receive ten shillings a day; that laboring men may be as little used to dine without meat as they now are to eat rye-bread; that sanitary police and medical discoveries may have added several more years to the average length of human life; that numerous comforts and luxuries which are now unknown, or confined to a few, may be within the reach of every diligent and thrifty workingman. And yet it may then be the mode to assert that the increase of wealth and the progress of science have benefited the few at the expense of the many, and to talk of the reign of Queen Victoria as the time when England was truly merry England, when all classes were bound together by brotherly sympathy, when the rich did not grind the faces of the poor, and when the poor did not envy the splendor of the rich.

—1849–61

WORK AND POVERTY
CONTEXTS

The Industrial Revolution brought rapid, pervasive, and frequently disorienting change to Britain. Manufacturing changed the face of the nation, from its physical appearance to the structure of family life. The Industrial Revolution had begun in the eighteenth century with the invention of new technology for spinning and weaving, and with the invention of the steam engine to power these machines, manufacturers established factories (originally called "mills") for centralized production. Mill towns, such as Manchester boomed as workers crowded into cities seeking employment. There they lived in crowded, unsanitary conditions that bred disease—resulting in frequent epidemics of cholera or typhoid. The second wave of the Industrial Revolution came with the spread of the railway in the 1840s, which allowed the iron and coal industries to flourish. Before legislation began to be passed in the 1840s, workers, including small children, worked long hours in dangerous, unhealthy conditions, without job security, insurance, or benefits. When occasional economic depressions caused factories and mines to close or cut down hours of operation, these workers often starved.

When workers moved from the countryside to the growing cities, they adapted many of their rural traditions to their new surroundings, including those of the bawdy ballad, which laborers often sang while they worked. "The Steam Loom Weaver" is an example from the 1830s. The daily reality for most mill workers, however, was far from amusing, despite the contrary implications of this light-hearted ballad. The next selection is from the testimony of Elizabeth Bentley, one of the few women to speak before the 1832 Sadler Committee on the Labour of Children in Factories. Social reformer Michael Sadler had argued in Parliament for the passing of a Ten Hours Bill (limiting factory work to ten hours a day) and had detailed the suffering of child laborers in order to move his fellow members of Parliament to action. When the government asked for a committee of enquiry into the conditions of child laborers, Sadler chaired it, and the resulting testimony was published in Samuel Kydd's 1857 *History of the Factory Movement*. Bentley was one of thirty-eight workers (only three of whom were female) to be interviewed.

Andrew Ure's *The Philosophy of Manufacturers* was one of the best-known works arguing in favor of the factory system. Ure viewed the factory system as a self-regulating organism that should be beyond government regulation, and into which workers should be introduced at a very young age, when they could be easily disciplined. While Ure speaks of the national wealth and prosperity that the factory system created, William Dodd, a child laborer, gives evidence in the excerpt following of the human costs of such "prosperity." Dodd's narrative of his life, which he published to expose the falsities of "eye-witness" accounts such as Ure's, details the lifetime of suffering and physical deformity that resulted from his early introduction to factory life.

Around the 1840s, Victorians began to take a greater interest in issues of public health, particularly the living conditions of the poor. The very worst of these conditions were being documented in newspapers, books, magazines, and journals by those who sought to arouse public concern and effect change. For many modern readers, it is strange to see the correspondent in Joseph Adshead's *Distress in Manchester* (excerpted here) insisting that the conditions of the poor did not result from any moral failings of their own. At the time, however, such ideas were not readily accepted. Poverty and disease in slums was often assumed to result from moral failings among the poor, and it was somewhat radical to suggest that change could best be effected if reformers focused on improving the environmental, rather than the moral, conditions of the slums. Adshead's text, which combines personal testimony given by those working for the relief of the poor with economic facts about the status of the poor—their numbers, earnings, expenditures, living conditions, etc.—showed that most poor people were not poor out of any fault of their own, but were hapless victims of the Industrial Revolution. The reality for many working-class people was that they would work until they could work no more, at which point they would likely perish—a fate the woman in Thomas Hood's poem "Song of the Shirt" (reprinted below) seems to anticipate eagerly—or live the remainder of their days in a workhouse.

Friedrich Engels, author of *The Condition of the Working Class in England*, excerpted below, sought to expose not only the degrading conditions of the poor, but also the deliberate ways in which the middle classes shielded themselves from the realities of working-class people's suffering. Having come from Germany to study the cotton trade, Engels was struck by the conditions in England's urban centers. In this excerpt, he examines the living conditions of the working-class areas of Manchester (he also examines those of England's other "Great Towns," such as London) and the ways in which these areas are systematically hidden from the view of wealthier citizens. Engels went on to collaborate with Karl Marx on *The Communist Manifesto* (1848), and together the two men laid the foundation of modern Communism.

The excerpt following, from Elizabeth Gaskell's novel *Mary Barton: A Tale of Manchester Life*, shows the opposing effects of industrialism on the rich and the poor, and the ways in which the factory system resulted in further alienation between classes. Gaskell contrasts the home lives of the rich and poor and details the private suffering of the latter during the economic depression known as the "hungry forties." *Mary Barton* was part of a developing genre known as the "social problem novel," which focused on the rampant poverty, unemployment, and disease that pervaded the Industrial Revolution. In his slightly later novel *Hard Times*, Charles Dickens details the dehumanizing effects of the factory system and factory managers' lack of recognition of the shared humanity of their employees. The fictional "Coketown" (so called because of the soot that blackens the city), in which his novel is set, is based on Dickens's observations of northern industrial towns such as Manchester and Preston.

One of the era's most influential depictions of working class and poor people was author and social reformer Henry Mayhew's *London Labour and the London Poor*, excerpted below. Asked by *The Morning Chronicle* to document, as metropolitan correspondent, the lives of the urban poor, Mayhew produced eighty-two articles that he later expanded into a four-volume collection of testimony of the lives of the lower class. He painted the underworld of Victorian society in unprecedented detail, shedding light on the specificities of economic exchange and the economic order that governed the poor. Perhaps more importantly, his work provided Victorians with a personal glimpse into the lives of the poor that helped to shape Victorian social theories. The serial newspaper publications were so popular that they resulted in the establishment of a Labour and the Poor Fund. Mayhew had an ear for individual dialects, slang, and other oddities of speech, and composed each subject's narrative in language that, as closely as possible, imitated the speaker's own words. His characters were so compelling that Mayhew's narratives influenced the depiction of such characters in fiction, and writers such as Charles Dickens drew upon his representations of the poor to bring life to their own characters.

⌘ ⌘ ⌘

Anonymous, "The Steam Loom Weaver" (c. 1830)

One morning in summer I did ramble,
   In the pleasant month of June,
The birds did sing the lambkins play,
Two lovers walking in their bloom,
5 The lassie was a steam loom weaver,
The lad an engine driver keen,
All their discourse was about weaving.
And the getting up of steam.

She said my loom is out of fettle,[1]
10 Can you right it yes or no,
You say you are an engine driver,
Which makes the steam so rapid flow;
My lambs and jacks[2] are out of order,
My laith[3] in motion has not been,
15 So work away without delay,
And quickly muster up the steam.

I said fair maid you seem determined,
No longer for to idle be,
Your healds[4] and laith I'll put in motion,
20 Then work you can without delay,
She said young man a pair of pickers,[5]
A shuttle too I want you ween,[6]
Without these three I cannot weave,
So useless would be the steam.

25 Dear lass these things I will provide,
But when to labour will you begin
As soon my lad as things are ready
My loom shop you can enter in.
A shuttle true and pickers too,
30 This young man did provide amain.[7]

And soon her loom was put in tune
So well it was supplied with steam.

Her loom worked well the shuttle flew,
His nickers[8] played the tune nick-nack,
35 Her laith did move with rapid motion,
Her temples, healds, long-lambs and jacks,
Her cloth beam rolled the cloth up tight,
The yarn beam emptied soon its seam,
The young man cried your loom works, light
40 And quickly then off shot the steam.

She said young man another web,
Upon the beam let's get don't strike,
But work away while yet it's day,
This steam loom weaving well I like.
45 He said good lass I cannot stay,
But if a fresh warp you will beam
If ready when I come this way,
I'd strive for to get up the steam.

from Elizabeth Bentley, *Testimony before the 1832 Committee on the Labour of Children in Factories* (1857)

"I am twenty-three years of age, and live at Leeds. I began to work at Mr. Busk's flax mill when I was six years old. I was then a little 'doffer.'[9] In that mill we worked from five in the morning till nine at night, when they were 'throng';[10] when they were not so 'throng,' the usual hours of labour were from six in the morning till seven at night. The time allowed for our meals was forty minutes at noon; not any time was allowed for breakfast or 'drinking': these we got as we could. When our work was bad, we had hardly any time to eat them at all: we were obliged to leave them or take them home. When we did not take our uneaten food home, the overlooker took it and gave it to his pigs. I consider 'doffing' to be a laborious employment. When the frames are full, the 'doffers' have to stop them, and

---

[1] *out of fettle* Out of order.

[2] *lambs and jacks* Lambs are foot pedals that operate the jacks, the oscillating levers that throw the yarn into two alternate sets.

[3] *laith* Loom; or (literally) the supporting stand of the loom.

[4] *healds* Small wires through which the warp passes.

[5] *pickers* Small instrument that moves back and forth in the shuttle-box, driving the shuttle through the warp (the threads that extend lengthwise in the loom).

[6] *ween* Consider; expect.

[7] *amain* At once.

---

[8] *nickers* Part of a center bit, which nicks a hole to be cut by a tool.

[9] *doffer* Worker who assists the spinner by removing the full spindles, or bobbins, from the carding machine (which combs the cotton or wool) and replacing them with empty ones.

[10] *throng* Busy.

take the 'flyers'[1] off, and take the full bobbins off, and carry them to the roller, and then put empty ones on, and set the frame going again. I was kept constantly on my feet; there were so many frames, and they run so quick, the labour was excessive, there was not time for anything. When the 'doffers' flagged[2] a little, or were too late, they were strapped. Those who were last in 'doffing' were constantly strapped—girls as well as boys. I have been strapped severely, and have been hurt by the strap excessively. The overlooker I was under was a very severe man. When I and others have been fatigued and worn out, and had not baskets enough to put the bobbins in, we used to put them in the window bottoms, and that broke the panes sometimes; and I broke one one time, and the overlooker strapped me on the arm, and it rose a blister, and I ran home to my mother. I worked at Mr. Busk's factory three or four years.

"When I left Mr. Busk's, I then went to Benyon's factory; I was about ten years of age, and was employed as a weigher in the card-room.[3] At Benyon's factory we worked from half-past five till eight at night; when they were 'throng,' until nine. The spinners at that mill were allowed forty minutes at noon for meals; no more time throughout the day was allowed. Those employed in the card-rooms had, in addition to the forty minutes at noon, a quarter of an hour allowed for their breakfast, and a quarter of an hour for their 'drinking.' The carding-room is more oppressive than the spinning department: those at work cannot see each other for dust. The 'cards' get so soon filled up with waste and dirt, they must be stopped or they would take fire: the stoppages are as much for the benefit of the employer as for the working people. The children at Benyon's factory were beat up to their labour with a strap.... The girls have many times had black marks upon their skins. Had the parents complained of this excessive ill-usage, the probable consequence would have been the loss of the employment of the child. Of this result the parents were afraid.

"I worked in the card-room; it was so dusty that the dust got upon my lungs, and the work was so hard. I was middling strong when I went there, but the work was so bad; I got so bad in health, that when I pulled the baskets down, I pulled my bones out of their places. The basket I pulled was a very large one; that was full of weights, upheaped, and pulling the basket, pulled my shoulder out of its place, and my ribs have grown over it. That hard work is generally done by women: it is not fit for children. There was no spinning for me, and I therefore did that work....

"I am considerably deformed in person in consequence of this labour. I was about thirteen years old when my deformity began to come on, and it has got worse since. It is five years since my mother died, and she was never able to get me a pair of good stays[4] to hold me up; and when my mother died I had to do for myself, and got me a pair. Before I worked at a mill I was as straight a little girl as ever went up and down town. I was straight until I was thirteen. I have been attended by a medical gentleman, Mr. Hare. He said it was owing to hard labour, and working in the factories. ...

"I have had the misfortune, from being a straight and healthful girl, to become very much otherwise in person. I do not know of any other girls that have become weak and deformed in like manner. I have known others who have been similarly injured in health. I am deformed in the shoulders; it is very common indeed to have weak ankles and crooked knees, that is brought on by stopping the spindle.

"I have had experience in wet spinning—it is very uncomfortable. I have stood before the frames till I have been wet through to my skin; and in winter-time, when myself and others have gone home, our clothes have been frozen, and we have nearly caught our death from cold. We have stopped at home one or two days, just as we were situated in our health; had we stopped away any length of time we should have found it difficult to keep our situation.

"I am now in the poor-house at Hunslet. Not any of my former employers come to see me. When I was at home, Mr. Walker made me a present of 1s. or 2s.,[5] but since I left my work and have gone to the poor-house, no one has come nigh me. I was very willing to have worked as long as I was able, and to have supported my

---

[1] *flyers* Part of the spinning machine that twists the thread and winds it upon the bobbin.

[2] *flagged* Slowed down.

[3] *card-room* Room that held the carding machines, which combed and cleaned the wool or cotton in preparation for spinning.

[4] *stays* Bodice stiffened with strips of whale-bone that gives support and shape to the figure; a corset.

[5] *s.* Shilling.

widowed mother. I am utterly incapable now of any exertion of that sort, and am supported by the parish."[1]

from Andrew Ure, *The Philosophy of Manufactures* (1835)

In its precise acceptation, the factory system is of recent origin, and may claim England for its birthplace. The mills for throwing silk, or making organzine,[2] which were mounted centuries ago in several of the Italian states, and furtively transferred to this country by Sir Thomas Lombe in 1718, contained indeed certain elements of a factory, and probably suggested some hints of those grander and more complex combinations of self-acting machines, which were first embodied half a century later in our cotton manufacture by Richard Arkwright, assisted by gentlemen of Derby, well acquainted with its celebrated silk establishment....

When the first water-frames for spinning cotton were erected at Cromford, in the romantic valley of the Derwent, about sixty years ago, mankind were little aware of the mighty revolution which the new system of labour was destined by Providence to achieve, not only in the structure of British society, but in the fortunes of the world at large. Arkwright alone had the sagacity to discern, and the boldness to predict in glowing language, how vastly productive human industry would become, when no longer proportioned in its results to muscular effort, which is by its nature fitful and capricious, but when made to consist in the task of guiding the work of mechanical fingers and arms, regularly impelled with great velocity by some indefatigable physical power. What his judgment so clearly led him to perceive, his energy of will enabled him to realize with such rapidity and success, as would have done honour to the most influential individuals, but were truly wonderful in that obscure and indigent artisan. The main difficulty did not, to my apprehension, lie so much in the invention of a proper self-acting mechanism for drawing out and twisting cotton into a continuous thread, as in the distribution of the different members of the apparatus into one cooperative body, in impelling each organ with its appropriate delicacy and speed, and,

above all, in training human beings to renounce their desultory[3] habits of work, and to identify themselves with the unvarying regularity of the complex automaton. To devise and administer a successful code of factory discipline, suited to the necessities of factory diligence, was the Herculean enterprise, the noble achievement of Arkwright. Even at the present day, when the system is perfectly organized, and its labour lightened to the utmost, it is found nearly impossible to convert persons past the age of puberty, whether drawn from rural or from handicraft occupations, into useful factory hands. After struggling for a while to conquer their listless or restive habits, they either renounce the employment spontaneously, or are dismissed by the overlookers on account of inattention....

It required, in fact, a man of a Napoleon nerve and ambition to subdue the refractory tempers of workpeople accustomed to irregular paroxysms of diligence, and to urge on his multifarious and intricate constructions in the face of prejudice, passion, and envy. Such was Arkwright, who, suffering nothing to stay or turn aside his progress, arrived gloriously at the goal, and has for ever affixed his name to a great era in the annals of mankind, an era which has laid open unbounded prospects of wealth and comfort to the industrious, however much they may have been occasionally clouded by ignorance and folly.

... In my recent tour, continued during several months, through the manufacturing districts, I have seen tens of thousands of old, young, and middle-aged of both sexes, many of them too feeble to get their daily bread by any of the former modes of industry, earning abundant food, raiment, and domestic accommodation, without perspiring at a single pore, screened meanwhile from the summer's sun and the winter's frost, in apartments more airy and salubrious[4] than those of the metropolis, in which our legislative and fashionable aristocracies assemble. In those spacious halls the benignant power of steam summons around him his myriads of willing menials, and assigns to each the regulated task, substituting for painful muscular effort on their part, the energies of his own gigantic arm, and demanding in return only attention and dexterity to correct such little aberrations as casually occur in his

---

[1] *supported by the parish*   I.e., with public funds.

[2] *organzine*   Silk yarn.

[3] *desultory*   Half-hearted, lacking enthusiasm.

[4] *salubrious*   Favorable to health.

workmanship. The gentle docility of this moving force qualifies it for impelling the tiny bobbins of the lace-machine with a precision and speed inimitable by the most dexterous hands, directed by the sharpest eyes. Hence, under its auspices, and in obedience to Ark-wright's polity,[1] magnificent edifices, surpassing far in number, value, usefulness, and ingenuity of construction, the boasted monuments of Asiatic, Egyptian, and Roman despotism, have, within the short period of fifty years, risen up in this kingdom, to show to what extent capital, industry, and science may augment the resources of a state, while they meliorate the condition of its citizens. Such is the factory system, replete with prodigies in mechanics and political economy, which promises, in its future growth, to become the great minister of civilization to the terraqueous[2] globe, enabling this country, as its heart, to diffuse along with its commerce the life-blood of science and religion to myriads of people still lying "in the region and shadow of death."[3] ...

No master would wish to have any wayward children to work within the walls of his factory who do not mind their business without beating, and he therefore usually fines or turns away any spinners who are known to maltreat their assistants. Hence, ill-usage of any kind is a very rare occurrence. I have visited many factories, both in Manchester and in the surrounding districts, during a period of several months, entering the spinning rooms, unexpectedly, and often alone, at different times of the day, and I never saw a single instance of corporal chastisement inflicted on a child, nor indeed did I ever see children in ill-humour. They seemed to be always cheerful and alert, taking pleasure in the light play of their muscles—enjoying the mobility natural to their age. The scene of industry, so far from exciting sad emotions in my mind, was always exhilarating. It was delightful to observe the nimbleness with which they pieced the broken ends, as the mule-carriage[4] began to

recede from the fixed roller beam, and to see them at leisure, after a few seconds' exercise of their tiny fingers, to amuse themselves in any attitude they chose, till the stretch and winding-on were once more completed. The work of these lively elves seemed to resemble a sport, in which habit gave them a pleasing dexterity. Conscious of their skill, they were delighted to show it off to any stranger. As to exhaustion by the day's work, they evinced no trace of it on emerging from the mill in the evening; for they immediately began to skip about any neighbouring playground, and to commence their little amusements with the same alacrity as boys issuing from a school. It is moreover my firm conviction that if children are not ill-used by bad parents or guardians, but receive in food and raiment the full benefit of what they earn, they would thrive better when employed in our modern factories than if left at home in apartments too often ill-aired, damp, and cold.

---

from William Dodd, *A Narrative of the Experience and Sufferings of William Dodd, Factory Cripple, Written by Himself* (1841)

Dear Reader,— I wish it to be distinctly and clearly understood, that, in laying before you the following sheets, I am not actuated by any motive of ill-feeling to any party with whom I have formerly been connected; on the contrary, I have a personal respect for some of my former masters, and am convinced that, had they been in any other line of life, they would have shone forth as ornaments to the age in which they lived; but having witnessed the efforts of some writers (who can know nothing of the factories by experience) to mislead the minds of the public upon a subject of so much importance, I feel it to be my duty to give to the world a fair and impartial account of the working of the factory system, as I have found it in twenty-five years' experience.

---

[1] *polity* Mode of administration.

[2] *terraqueous* Consisting of land and water.

[3] *in the ... death* From Matthew 4.16.

[4] *broken ends* I.e., of thread. This was the job of the "piecer," who ensured that the process of spinning could continue uninterrupted; *mule-carriage* The movable part of the mule, a kind of spinning machine, invented in 1779, that could spin yarn of varying thicknesses.

A

NARRATIVE

OF THE

EXPERIENCE AND SUFFERINGS

OF

WILLIAM DODD,

A FACTORY CRIPPLE.

WRITTEN BY HIMSELF.

GIVING AN ACCOUNT OF THE HARDSHIPS AND SUFFERINGS
HE ENDURED IN EARLY LIFE, UNDER WHAT DIFFICULTIES HE
ACQUIRED HIS EDUCATION, THE EFFECTS OF FACTORY LABOUR
ON HIS MIND AND PERSON, THE UNSUCCESSFUL EFFORTS MADE
BY HIM TO OBTAIN A LIVELIHOOD IN SOME OTHER LINE OF
LIFE, THE COMPARISON HE DRAWS BETWEEN AGRICULTURAL
AND MANUFACTURING LABOURERS, AND OTHER MATTERS
RELATING TO THE WORKING CLASSES.

SECOND EDITION.

LONDON:
PUBLISHED BY L. & G. SEELEY, 169, FLEET STREET,
AND HATCHARD & SON, 187, PICCADILLY.
1841.
PRICE ONE SHILLING.

Title page from William Dodd, *A Narrative of the
Experience and Sufferings of William Dodd, Factory Cripple,
Written by Himself* (1841).

… Of four children in our family, I was the only boy; and we were all, at different periods, as we could meet with employers, sent to work in the factories. My eldest sister was ten years of age before she went; consequently, she was, in a manner, out of harm's way, her bones having become firmer and stronger than ours, and capable of withstanding the hardships to which she was exposed much better than we could…. I was born on the 18th of June, 1804; and in the latter part of 1809, being then turned of five years of age, I was put to work at card-making,[1] and about a year after I was sent, with my sisters, to the factories. I was then a fine, strong, healthy, hardy boy, straight in every limb, and remark-

ably stout and active….

From six to fourteen years of age, I went through a series of uninterrupted, unmitigated suffering, such as very rarely falls to the lot of mortals so early in life, except to those situated as I was, and such as I could not have withstood, had I not been strong, and of a good constitution.

My first place in the factories was that of piecer, or the lowest situation: but as the term conveys only a vague idea of the duties to be performed, it will be necessary here to give such explanation as may enable those unacquainted with the business to form a just conception of what those duties are, and to judge of the inadequacy of the remuneration or reward for their performance, and the cruelty of the punishments inflicted for the neglect of those duties….

The position in which the piecer stands to his work is with his right foot forward, and his right side facing the frame: the motion he makes in going along in front of the frame, for the purpose of piecing, is neither forwards nor backwards, but in a sidling direction, constantly keeping his right side towards the frame. In this position he continues during the day, with his hands, feet, and eyes constantly in motion. It will be easily seen, that the chief weight of his body rests upon his right knee, which is almost always the first joint to give way. The number of cripples with the right knee in, greatly exceed those with the left knee in; a great many have both knees in such as my own from this cause.

Another evil resulting from the position in which the piecer stands, is what is termed "splay-foot," which may be explained thus: in a well-formed foot, there is a finely formed arch of bones immediately under the instep and ankle joint. The continual pressure of the body on this arch, before it is sufficiently strong to bear such pressure (as in the case of boys and girls in the factories) causes it to give way: the bones fall gradually down, the foot then becomes broad and flat, and the owner drags it after him with the broad side first. A great many factory cripples are in this state; this is very often attended with weak ankle and knee joints. I have a brother-in-law exactly thus, who has tried everything likely to do him good, but without success.

---

[1] *card-making*   Cards combed and cleansed fibers in preparation for spinning.

A wood engraving of a child mine-worker included in the *Report of the Commission of the Employment of Children and Young Persons in the Mines* (1842).

The spinner and the piecer are intimately connected together:[1] the spinner works by the piece, being paid by the stone[2] for the yarn spun; the piecer is hired by the week, and paid according to his abilities. The piecers are the servants of the spinners, and both are under an overlooker; and liable to be dismissed at a week's notice. Being thus circumstanced, it is clearly the advantage of the spinner to have good able piecers, who ought, in return, to be well paid....

In order to induce the piecer to do his work quick and well, the spinner has recourse to many expedients, such as offering rewards of a penny or two-pence for a good week's work inducing them to sing, which, like the music in the army, has a very powerful effect, and keeps them awake and active longer than any other thing; and, as a last resource, when nothing else will do, he takes the strap, or the billy-roller,[3] which are laid on most unmercifully, accompanied by a round volley of oaths; and I pity the poor wretch who has to submit to the infliction of either.

On one occasion, I remember being thrashed with the billy-roller till my back, arms, and legs were covered with ridges as thick as my finger. This was more than I could bear, and, seeing a favourable opportunity, I slipped out and stole off home along some by-ways, so as not to be seen. Mother stripped me, and was shocked at my appearance. The spinner, not meeting with any other to suit him, had the assurance to come and beg that mother would let me go again, and promised not to strike me with the billy-roller any more. He kept his promise, but instead of using the roller, he used his fist.

... A piecer, it will be seen, is an important person in the factories, inasmuch as it is impossible to do without them. Formerly, boys and girls were sent to work in the factories as piecers at the early age of five or six years—as in my own case—but now, owing to the introduction of some wise laws for the regulation of factories,[4] they cannot employ any as piecers before they have attained the age of 9 years; at which age their bones are comparatively strong, generally speaking, and more able to endure the hardships to which they will be exposed.

[1] *The spinner ... together* The spinner, who ran the "billy" (or "slubbing," the machine that spins yarn) was dependent on the piecer for the preparation of the wool.

[2] *stone* Unit of measurement equal to 14 pounds.

[3] *billy-roller* Uppermost of a series of wooden rollers through which the wool is moved to the spindles. It was very long and easily removed from the billy; as a result, it was a notorious instrument of punishment to factory children.

[4] *some wise ... factories* The 1833 Factory Act, which prevented children under nine from working in any factories except silk mills. It also decreed that children under 11 (and, eventually, under 13) could not work more than 9 hours a day or 48 hours a week, and that all working children had to be provided with eduction at the expense of the factory owners.

They now enjoy many privileges that we had not, such as attending schools, limited hours of labour, &c.; but still it is far from being a desirable place for a child. Formerly, it was nothing but work till we could work no longer. I have frequently worked at the frame till I could scarcely get home, and in this state have been stopped by people in the streets who noticed me shuffling along, and advised me to work no more in the factories: but I was not my own master. Thus year after year passed away, my afflictions and deformities increasing. I could not associate with anybody; on the contrary, I sought every opportunity to rest myself, and to shrink into any corner to screen myself from the prying eye of the curious and scornful! During the day, I frequently counted the clock, and calculated how many hours I had still to remain at work; my evenings were spent in preparing for the following day—in rubbing my knees, ankles, elbows, and wrists with oil, &c., and wrapping them in warm flannel! (for everything was tried to benefit me, except the right one—that of taking me from the work) after which, with a look at, rather than eating my supper (the bad smells of the factory having generally taken my appetite away) I went to bed, to cry myself to sleep, and pray that the Lord would take me to Himself before morning.

... A great many are made cripples by over-exertion. Among those who have been brought up from infancy with me in the factories, and whom death has spared, few have escaped without some injury. My brother-in-law and myself have been crippled by this cause, but in different ways; my sister partly by over-exertion and partly by machinery. On going home to breakfast one morning, I was much surprised at seeing several of the neighbours and two doctors in our house. On inquiring the cause, I found that my second sister had nearly lost her hand in the machinery. She had been working all night, and, fatigued and sleepy, had not been so watchful as she otherwise would have been; and consequently, her right hand became entangled in the machine which she was attending. Four iron teeth of a wheel, three-quarters of an inch broad, and one-quarter of an inch thick, had been forced through her hand, from the back part, among the leaders, &c.; and the fifth iron tooth fell upon the thumb, and crushed it to atoms. It was thought, for some time, that she would lose her hand. But it was saved; and, as you may be sure, it is stiff and contracted, and is but a very feeble apology for a hand. This accident might have been prevented, if the wheels above referred to had been boxed off,[1] which they might have been for a couple of shillings; and the very next week after this accident, a man had two fingers taken off his hand, by the very same wheels—and still they are not boxed off!

from Joseph Adshead, *Distress in Manchester. Evidence (Tabular and Otherwise) of the State of the Labouring Classes in 1840–42* (1842)

CHAPTER 3, NARRATIVES OF SUFFERING

The following painfully interesting report is furnished by a gentleman whose attention was directed to the social and moral condition of the labouring classes, with a view to its improvement. The inquiry was made in January last, and it will be seen that its details are, if possible, more harrowing than any yet given:

January, 1842.

Dear Sir,—An engagement I had made to oblige a friend rendered it necessary that I should visit the inhabitants of several streets in Ancoats and in the neighbourhood of Oldham Road. As this district is not selected as the most destitute, I believe a few cases I shall state will give a very faithful illustration of the condition of tens of thousands of the manufacturing poor.

Upon the first day of our visitation I called at a house occupied by a poor man, a widower with one child, a boy between seven and eight; they were in a state of extreme poverty; the man is about thirty-five years of age, and professed himself able and most anxious to work, but had not been able to obtain any employment for many months; both were living upon what the child could obtain by begging. Upon quitting this house the man called our attention to an adjoining cellar, occupied by a woman who had been deserted by

[1] *the wheels ... boxed off* The Factory Act of 1844 decreed that fly-wheels connected to mechanical parts, such as shafts, had to be boxed off or fenced until the Factory Act of 1844. However, such a project would cost a few shillings per wheel, which would add up to a considerable expense, and would make it difficult for workers to clean the machinery. As a result, many factory owners ignored the law when it came into effect.

her husband. This cellar was both very dark and very damp, the roof not more than seven feet high, and the area of the floor not more than twelve square yards; its occupants were this woman and her child, a boy six years old, a widow, a lodger with three children, and a second widow with two children, sister of the woman who tenanted the cellar; these nine individuals are all crowded in a place so dark and contracted as to be unfit for the residence of any human being. It was in this abode of wretchedness that we witnessed a remarkable illustration of the sympathy and compassion of the poor for those who are still less favourably circumstanced. On the day previous to our visit one of these poor women had observed a poor houseless wanderer with two children, ready to sink with hunger and fatigue; this poor creature's husband had left her three months before to seek employment, which she was sure he had not been able to procure, or, as she said, he would soon have found her and let her know. Her poor hostess had no better accommodation to offer than a dark unpaved closet adjoining their cellar, and here, without bed or bedding beyond a handful of dirty shavings which she used as a pillow, the mother and her famishing children were thankful to take shelter: during the night the younger of the children, an infant eleven months old, died, doubtless from long exposure to cold and the want of that support which the breast of the poor, starved, and perishing mother had failed to supply. When we entered the cellar we saw this victim of want laid out upon a board suspended from the roof, and the other children (some of whom were so poorly provided with clothing as to be unfit to quit the cellar without indecent exposure) standing around; the poor mother had left her remaining child and gone out to beg assistance to inter her infant.

In the next house we entered we found two men, one twenty-seven, the other twenty-five, both weavers, and out of work; they both appeared in delicate health, one, however, much worse than the other; neither of them had been able to earn a shilling for several weeks. To our inquiry how they lived, they replied, "We do indeed *exist*, we cannot say we live." One of them produced a dish with potato peelings, which one of their wives had been successful in begging; this they assured us was the only food they had or expected to taste that day. These men were members of a temperance society,

Thomas Annan, *Close No. 193, High Street, Glasgow* (1868). Thomas Annan was hired by the Glasgow City Improvement Trust to photograph the city's slums before they were demolished. Many of his pictures show the open sewers and narrow passageways that were features of slum life. (See also Annan's photographs on p. 395.)

were both remarkably intelligent, and we inferred from the kind and patient manner in which they spoke of their poverty and its causes, which they appear perfectly to comprehend, that their minds were considerably under the influence of moral and religious principles. These men were not victims of intemperance, nor improvidence, nor idleness, nor disease, nor anything else which they could have foreseen or provided against; but, reduced and broken-hearted by the impossibility of obtaining work, they and their families are sinking in the midst of misery which they can neither remove nor flee from.

This is a spectacle more calculated than almost any other we can conceive to distress a rightly constituted mind. Men, with physical strength, mental cultivation, and moral principle in active exercise, after having spent their time, and strength, and money, it may be, in learning a trade, starving in the largest manufacturing town in the world for the want of employment! And why? Let the supporters of corn laws[1] answer. ...

Many were the families we visited who assured us they had not tasted food that day. Misery and want, hunger and nakedness, are not confined to particular localities: they are widely spread, and are spreading more widely. The number of the destitute is daily increasing. The universal testimony is, that there never was any distress equal to that which exists at present—that all other seasons of distress were trifling in comparison. The intemperate and the improvident, indeed, are the first to suffer in all seasons of distress; but it is long since distress has reached the sober, the industrious, the provident, and the respected among the labouring class.

Thomas Hood, "Song of the Shirt" (1843)

With fingers weary and worn,
  With eyelids heavy and red,
A woman sat, in unwomanly rags,
Plying her needle and thread
5   Stitch—stitch—stitch!
In poverty, hunger, and dirt,
And still with a voice of dolorous pitch
She sang the "Song of the Shirt."

"Work—work—work
10 Till the brain begins to swim;
Work—work—work
Till the eyes are heavy and dim!
Seam, and gusset,[2] and band,
Band, and gusset, and seam;
15 Till over the buttons I fall asleep,
And sew them on in a dream!

"O! men, with sisters dear!
O! men, with mothers and wives!
It is not linen you're wearing out,
20 But human creatures' lives!

Stitch—stitch—stitch,
In poverty, hunger, and dirt,
Sewing at once, with a double thread,
A shroud[3] as well as a shirt.

25 "But why do I talk of Death?
That phantom of grisly bone;
I hardly fear his terrible shape,
It seems so like my own—
It seems so like my own,
30 Because of the fasts I keep:
Oh! God! that bread should be so dear,
And flesh and blood so cheap!

"Work—work—work!
My labour never flags;
35 And what are its wages? A bed of straw,
A crust of bread and rags,
That shatter'd roof, and this naked floor
A table—a broken chair—
40 A wall so blank, my shadow I thank
For sometimes falling there!

"Work—work—work!
From weary chime to chime,
Work—work—work
45 As prisoners work for crime!
Band, and gusset, and seam,
Seam, and gusset, and band,
Till the heart is sick, and the brain benumb'd,
As well as the weary hand.

50 "Work—work—work,
In the dull December light,
And work—work—work,
When the weather is warm and bright—
While underneath the eaves
55 The brooding swallows cling,
As if to show me their sunny backs
And twit me with the spring.

"Oh! but to breathe the breath
Of the cowslip and primrose[4] sweet—

---

[1] *corn laws* Laws that kept the prices of grain artificially high to prevent an agricultural depression after the Napoleonic Wars (1803–15). Sir Robert Peel, the Prime Minister, repealed the laws in 1846.

[2] *gusset* Triangular piece of material inserted into a piece of clothing to strengthen or enlarge some part.

[3] *shroud* Sheet in which a corpse is wrapped for burial.

[4] *cowslip ... primrose* Wildflowers.

60 With the sky above my head,
    And the grass beneath my feet,
    For only one short hour
    To feel as I used to feel,
    Before I knew the woes of want
65 And the walk that costs a meal:

    "Oh, but for one short hour!
    A respite, however brief!
    No blessed leisure for Love or Hope,
    But only time for grief!
70 A little weeping would ease my heart,
    But in their briny head
    My tears must stop, for every drop
    Hinders needle and thread!"

    With fingers weary and worn,
75 With eyelids heavy and red,
    A woman sat, in unwomanly rags,
    Plying her needle and thread—
    Stitch—stitch—stitch!
    In poverty, hunger, and dirt,
80 And still with a voice of dolorous pitch,
    Would that its tone could reach the rich!
    She sang this "Song of the Shirt!"

from Friedrich Engels, *The Condition of the Working Class in England in 1844* (1845; trans. Florence Wischnewetzky, 1887)

CHAPTER 3, THE GREAT TOWNS

Manchester lies at the foot of the southern slope of a range of hills, which stretch hither from Old-ham, their last peak, Kersallmoor, being at once the racecourse and the Mons Sacer[1] of Manchester. Manchester proper lies on the left bank of the Irwell, between that stream and the two smaller ones, the Irk and the Medlock, which here empty into the Irwell. On the right bank of the Irwell, bounded by a sharp curve of the river, lies Salford, and farther westward Pendleton; northward from the Irwell lie Upper and Lower Broughton; northward of the Irk, Cheetham Hill; south of the Medlock lies Hulme; farther east Chorlton on Medlock;

John Thomson's photograph of "The crawler" (1877). This photograph is taken from Thomson's famous project, *Street Life in London* (1877–78), one of the era's most influential pieces of social documentary. Thomson collaborated with Adolph Smith to create text to accompany the photographs. This picture, one of the best known, shows a destitute woman who told Thomson that she spent her nights on the steps of a workhouse and her days looking after a friend's baby, in exchange for a cup of tea and some bread.

still farther, pretty well to the east of Manchester, Ardwick. The whole assemblage of buildings is commonly called Manchester, and contains about four hundred thousand inhabitants, rather more than less. The town itself is peculiarly built, so that a person may live in it for years, and go in and out daily without coming into contact with a working people's quarter or even with workers, that is, so long as he confines himself to his business or to pleasure walks. This arises chiefly from the fact that by unconscious tacit agreement, as well as with outspoken conscious determination, the

---

[1] *Mons Sacer* Latin: sacred mountain.

working people's quarters are sharply separated from the sections of the city reserved for the middle class; or, if this does not succeed, they are concealed with the cloak of charity. Manchester contains, at its heart, a rather extended commercial district, perhaps half a mile long and about as broad, and consisting almost wholly of offices and warehouses. Nearly the whole district is abandoned by dwellers, and is lonely and deserted at night; only watchmen and policemen traverse its narrow lanes with their dark lanterns. This district is cut through by certain main thoroughfares upon which the vast traffic concentrates, and in which the ground level is lined with brilliant shops. In these streets the upper floors are occupied, here and there, and there is a good deal of life upon them until late at night. With the exception of this commercial district, all Manchester proper, all Salford and Hulme, a great part of Pendleton and Chorlton, two-thirds of Ardwick, and single stretches of Cheetham Hill and Broughton are all unmixed working people's quarters, stretching like a girdle, averaging a mile and a half in breadth, around the commercial district. Outside, beyond this girdle, lives the upper and middle bourgeoisie, the middle bourgeoisie in regularly laid out streets in the vicinity of the working quarters, especially in Chorlton and the lower lying portions of Cheetham Hill; the upper bourgeoisie in remoter villas with gardens in Chorlton and Ardwick, or on the breezy heights of Cheetham Hill, Broughton, and Pendleton, in free, wholesome country air, in fine, comfortable homes, passed once every half or quarter hour by omnibuses going into the city. And the finest part of the arrangements is this, that the members of this money aristocracy can take the shortest road through the middle of all the labouring districts to their places of business, without ever seeing that they are in the midst of the grimy misery that lurks to the right and the left. For the thoroughfares leading from the Exchange in all directions out of the city are lined, on both sides, with an almost unbroken series of shops, and are so kept in the hands of the middle and lower bourgeoisie, which, out of self-interest, cares for a decent and cleanly external appearance and can *care* for it. True, these shops bear some relation to the districts which lie behind them, and are more elegant in the commercial and residential quarters than when they hide grimy working men's dwellings; but they suffice to conceal from the eyes of the wealthy men and women of strong stomachs and weak nerves the misery and grime which form the complement to their wealth. So, for instance, Deansgate, which leads from the Old Church directly southward, is lined first with mills and warehouses, then with second-rate shops and alehouses; farther south, when it leaves the commercial district, with less inviting shops, which grow dirtier and more interrupted by beer houses and gin palaces the farther one goes, until at the southern end the appearance of the shops leaves no doubt that workers and workers only are their customers. So Market Street running south-east from the Exchange; at first brilliant shops of the best sort, with counting-houses or warehouses above; in the continuation, Piccadilly, immense hotels and warehouses; in the farther continuation, London Road, in the neighbourhood of the Medlock, factories, beerhouses, shops for the humbler bourgeoisie and the working population; and from this point onward, large gardens and villas of the wealthier merchants and manufacturers. In this way anyone who knows Manchester can infer the adjoining districts, from the appearance of the thoroughfare, but one is seldom in a position to catch from the street a glimpse of the real labouring districts. I know very well that this hypocritical plan is more or less common to all great cities; I know, too, that the retail dealers are forced by the nature of their business to take possession of the great highways; I know that there are more good buildings than bad ones upon such streets everywhere, and that the value of land is greater near them than in remoter districts; but at the same time I have never seen so systematic a shutting out of the working class from the thoroughfares, so tender a concealment of everything which might affront the eye and the nerves of the bourgeoisie, as in Manchester. And yet, in other respects, Manchester is less built according to a plan, after official regulations, is more an outgrowth of accident, than any other city; and when I consider in this connection the eager assurances of the middle class that the working class is doing famously, I cannot help feeling that the liberal manufacturers, the "Big Wigs" of Manchester, are not so innocent after all, in the matter of this sensitive method of construction.

I may mention just here that the mills almost all adjoin the rivers or the different canals that ramify throughout the city, before I proceed at once to describe the labouring quarters. First of all, there is the Old Town of Manchester, which lies between the northern boundary of the commercial district and the Irk. Here the streets, even the better ones, are narrow and winding, like Todd Street, Long Millgate, Withy Grove, and Shude Hill, the houses dirty, old, and tumble-down, and the construction of the side streets utterly horrible. Going from the Old Church to Long Millgate, the stroller has at once a row of old-fashioned houses on the right, of which not one has kept its original level; these are remnants of the old pre-manufacturing Manchester, whose former inhabitants have removed with their descendants into better-built districts, and have left the houses, which were not good enough for them, to a working-class population strongly mixed with Irish blood. Here one is in an almost undisguised working men's quarter, for even the shops and beerhouses hardly take the trouble to exhibit a trifing degree of cleanliness. But all this is nothing in comparison with the courts and lanes which lie behind, to which access can be gained only through covered passages, in which no two human beings can pass at the same time. Of the irregular cramming together of dwellings in ways which defy all rational plan, of the tangle in which they are crowded literally one upon the other, it is impossible to convey an idea. And it is not the buildings surviving from the old times of Manchester which are to blame for this; the confusion has only recently reached its height when every scrap of space left by the old way of building has been filled up and patched over until not a foot of land is left to be further occupied....

The south bank of the Irk is here very steep and between fifteen and thirty feet high. On this abrupt slope there are planted three rows of houses, of which the lowest rise directly out of the river, while the front walls of the highest stand on the crest of the rise in Long Millgate. Among them are mills on the river; in short, the method of construction is as crowded and disorderly here as in the lower part of Long Millgate. Right and left a multitude of covered passages lead from the main street into numerous courts, and he who turns in thither gets into filth and disgusting grime, the equal of which is not to be found—especially in the courts which lead down to the Irk, and which contain unqualifiedly the most horrible dwellings which I have yet beheld. In one of these courts there stands directly at the entrance, at the end of the covered passage, a privy without a door, so dirty that the inhabitants can pass into and out of the court only by passing through foul pools of stagnant urine and excrement. This is the first court on the Irk above Ducie Bridge—in case anyone should care to look into it. Below it on the river there are several tanneries which fill the whole neighbourhood with the stench of animal putrefaction. Below Ducie Bridge the only entrance to most of the houses is by means of narrow, dirty stairs and over heaps of refuse and filth. The first court below Ducie Bridge, known as Allen's Court, was in such a state at the time of the cholera[1] that the sanitary police ordered it evacuated, swept, and disinfected with chloride of lime.... Since then, it seems to have been partially torn down and rebuilt; at least, looking down from Ducie Bridge, the passer-by sees several ruined walls and heaps of debris with some newer houses. The view from this bridge, mercifully concealed from mortals of small stature by a parapet as high as a man, is characteristic for the whole district. At the bottom flows, or rather stagnates, the Irk, a narrow, coal-black, foul-smelling stream, full of debris and refuse, which it deposits on the lower right bank. In dry weather, a lone string of the most disgusting blackish-green slime pools are left standing on this bank, from the depths of which bubbles of miasmatic[2] gas constantly arise and give forth a stench unendurable even on the bridge forty or fifty feet above the surface of the stream. But besides this, the stream itself is checked every few paces by high weirs, behind which slime and refuse accumulate and rot in thick masses. Above the bridge are tanneries, bone mills, and gasworks, from which all drains and refuse find their way into the Irk, which receives further the contents of all the neighbouring sewers and privies. It may be easily imagined, therefore, what sort of residue the stream deposits. Below the bridge you look upon the piles of debris, the refuse, filth, and offal from the courts on the steep left bank; here each house is packed close behind its neighbour and a bit of each is visible, all black, smoky, crumbling, ancient, with broken panes and window-frames. The background is furnished by old barrack-like factory buildings. On the lower right bank stands a long row of houses and mills, the second row being a ruin

---

[1]   *the time of cholera* I.e., 1832.

[2]   *miasmatic* Consisting of noxious vapor.

without a roof, piled with debris; the third stands so low that the lowest floor is uninhabitable, and therefore without windows or doors. Here the background embraces the pauper burial-ground, the station of the Liverpool and Leeds railway, and, in the rear of this, the workhouse, the "Poor-Law Bastille"[1] of Manchester, which, like a citadel, looks threateningly down from behind its high walls and parapets on the hilltop, upon the working people's quarter below. ...

Such is the Old Town of Manchester, and, on re-reading my description, I am forced to admit that instead of being exaggerated, it is far from black enough to convey a true impression of the filth, ruin, and uninhabitableness, the defiance of all considerations of cleanliness, ventilation, and health which characterize the construction of this single district, containing at least twenty to thirty thousand inhabitants. And such a district exists in the heart of the second city of England, the first manufacturing city of the world. If anyone wishes to see in how little space a human being can move, how little air—and *such* air—he can breathe, how little of civilization he may share and yet live, it is only necessary to travel hither. True, this is the *Old* Town, and the people of Manchester emphasize the fact whenever anyone mentions to them the frightful condition of this Hell upon Earth; but what does that prove? Everything which here arouses horror and indignation is of recent origin, belongs to the *industrial epoch*. The couple of hundred houses which belong to Old Manchester have been long since abandoned by their original inhabitants; the industrial epoch alone has crammed into them the swarms of workers whom they now shelter; the industrial epoch alone has built up every spot between these old houses to make a covering for the masses whom it has conjured hither from the agricultural districts and from Ireland; the industrial epoch alone enables the owners of these cattle sheds to rent them for high prices to human beings, to plunder the poverty of the workers, to undermine the health of thousands, in order that they only, the owners, may grow rich. In the industrial epoch alone has it become possible that the worker scarcely freed from feudal servitude can be used as mere material, a mere chattel; that he must let himself be crowded into a dwelling too bad for every other, which he for his hard-earned wages buys the right to let go utterly to ruin. This is what manufacture has achieved, and, without these workers and their poverty, this slavery would have been impossible. True, the original construction of this quarter was bad, little good could have been made out of it; but, have the land-owners, has the municipality done any thing to improve it when rebuilding? On the contrary, wherever a nook or corner was free, a house has been run up; where a superfluous passage remained, it has been built on; the value of land rose with the blossoming out of manufacture, and the more it rose, the more madly was the work of building carried on, without reference to the health or comfort of the inhabitants, with sole reference to the highest possible profit, on the principle that *no hole is so bad but that some poor creature must take it who can pay for nothing better.* However, it is the Old Town, and with this reflection the bourgeoisie is comforted.

---

[1] *Poor-Law Bastille* Because of the terrible conditions in the workhouses (established by the Poor Laws in the 1830s), including poor food, monotonous make-work, and the separation of families, workhouses were often compared to prisons such as the famous Bastille in Paris.

A cross-section of working-class low-lodgings. The crowded rooms and open sewer running beneath the building provide examples of the sort of deplorable living conditions described by Engels in his examination of Manchester.

from Elizabeth Gaskell, *Mary Barton* (1848), Chapter 6

John Barton was not far wrong in his idea that the Messrs. Carson would not be over-much grieved for the consequences of the fire in their mill. They were well insured; the machinery lacked the improvements of late years, and worked but poorly in comparison with that which might now be procured. Above all, trade was very slack; cottons could find no market, and goods lay packed and piled in many a warehouse. The mills were merely worked to keep the machinery, human and metal, in some kind of order and readiness for better

times. So this was an excellent opportunity, Messrs. Carson thought, for refitting their factory with first-rate improvements, for which the insurance-money would amply pay. They were in no hurry about the business, however. The weekly drain of wages given for labour, useless in the present state of the market, was stopped. The partners had more leisure than they had known for years, and promised wives and daughters all manner of pleasant excursions, as soon as the weather should become more genial. It was a pleasant thing to be able to lounge over breakfast with a review or newspaper in hand; to have time for becoming acquainted with agreeable and accomplished daughters, on whose education no money had been spared, but whose fathers, shut up during a long day with calicoes[1] and accounts, had so seldom had leisure to enjoy their daughters' talents. There were happy family evenings, now that the men of business had time for domestic enjoyments. There is another side to the picture. There were homes over which Carsons' fire threw a deep, terrible gloom; the homes of those who would fain work, and no man gave unto them—the homes of those to whom leisure was a curse. There, the family music was angry wails, when week after week passed by, and there was no work to be had, and consequently no wages to pay for the bread the children cried aloud for in their young impatience of suffering. There was no breakfast to lounge over; their lounge was taken in bed, to try and keep warmth in them that bitter March weather, and, by being quiet, to deaden the gnawing wolf within. Many a penny that would have gone little way enough in oatmeal or potatoes bought opium to still the hungry little ones,[2] and make them forget their uneasiness in heavy troubled sleep. It was mother's mercy. The evil and the good of our nature came out strongly then. There were desperate fathers; there were bitter-tongued mothers (Oh God! what wonder!); there were reckless children; the very closest bonds of nature were snapped in that time of trial and distress. There was Faith such as the rich can never imagine on earth; there was "Love strong as death"; and, self-denial, among rude, coarse men, akin to that of Sir Philip Sidney's most glorious deed.[3] The vices of the poor sometimes astound us *here*; but when the secrets of all hearts shall be made known, their virtues will astound us in far greater degree. Of this I am certain.

As the cold, bleak spring came on (spring, in name alone), and consequently as trade continued dead, other mills shortened hours, turned off hands,[4] and finally stopped work altogether.

Barton worked short hours; Wilson, of course, being a hand in Carsons' factory, had no work at all. But his son, working at an engineer's, and a steady man, obtained wages enough to maintain all the family in a careful way. Still it preyed on Wilson's mind to be so long indebted to his son. He was out of spirits and depressed. Barton was morose, and soured towards mankind as a body, and the rich in particular. One evening, when the clear light at six o'clock contrasted strangely with the Christmas cold, and when the bitter wind piped down every entry, and through every cranny, Barton sat brooding over his stinted fire, and listening for Mary's step, in unacknowledged trust that her presence would cheer him. The door was opened, and Wilson came breathless in.

"You've not got a bit o' money by you, Barton?" asked he.

"Not I; who has now, I'd like to know. Whatten you want it for?"

"I donnot want it for mysel', tho' we've none to spare. But don[5] you know Ben Davenport as worked at Carsons'? He's down wi' the fever, and ne'er a stick o' fire nor a cowd[6] potato in the house."

"I han got no money, I tell ye," said Barton. Wilson looked disappointed. Barton tried not to be interested, but he could not help it in spite of his gruffness. He rose, and went to the cupboard (his wife's pride long ago). There lay the remains of his dinner, hastily put by ready for supper. Bread, and a slice of cold fat boiled bacon. He wrapped them in his handkerchief, put them in the crown of his hat and said—"Come, let's be going."

from Henry Mayhew, *London Labour and the London Poor*, "Boy Crossing-Sweepers and Tumblers" (written 1859–60, published 1861–65)

A remarkably intelligent lad, who, on being spoken to, at once consented to give all the information in his power, told me the following story of his life.

It will be seen from this boy's account, and the one or two following, that a kind of partnership exists among some of these young sweepers. They have

---

[1] *calicoes* Cotton cloths.

[2] *opium … hungry ones* The apparently common practice among working-class families of giving sick or hungry infants opium or laudanum to help them sleep was frequently discussed at the time.

[3] *Sir Philip … deed* Poet and courtier Sir Philip Sidney (1554–86), who served in many diplomatic missions on the Continent, is said to have refused a glass of water offered to him when he lay dying on the battlefield at Zutphen, in the Netherlands. He instead gave the glass to a less seriously wounded soldier, saying "Thy necessity is greater than mine."

[4] *turned off hands* I.e., laid off workers.

[5] *don* Do.

[6] *cowd* I.e., cold.

associated themselves together, appropriated several crossings to their use, and appointed a captain over them. They have their forms of trial, and "jury-house" for the settlement of disputes; laws have been framed, which govern their commercial proceedings, and a kind of language adopted by the society for its better protection from the arch-enemy, the policeman.

I found the lad who first gave me an insight into the proceedings of the associated crossing-sweepers crouched on the stone steps of a door in Adelaide Street, Strand; and when I spoke to him he was preparing to settle down in a corner and go to sleep—his legs and body being curled round almost as closely as those of a cat on a hearth. The moment he heard my voice he was upon his feet, asking me to "give a halfpenny to poor little Jack."

He was a good-looking lad, with a pair of large mild eyes, which he took good care to turn up with an expression of supplication as he moaned for a halfpenny.

A cap, or more properly a stuff bag, covered a crop of hair which had matted itself into the form of so many paint-brushes, while his face, from its roundness of feature and the complexion of dirt, had an almost Indian look about it; the colour of his hands, too, was such that you could imagine he had been shelling walnuts.

He ran before me, treading cautiously with his naked feet, until I reached a convenient spot to take down his statement, which was as follows:

"I've got no mother or father; mother has been dead for two years, and father's been gone for more than that—more nigh five years—he died at Ipswich, in Suffolk. He was a perfumer by trade, and used to make hair-dye, and scent, and pomatum,[1] and all kinds of scents. He didn't keep a shop himself, but he used to serve them as did; he didn't hawk his goods about, neether, but had regular customers, what used to send him a letter, and then he'd take them what they wanted. Yes, he used to serve some good shops: there was H—'s, of London Bridge, what's a large chemist's. He used to make a good deal of money, but he lost it betting; and so his brother, my uncle, did all his....

"After mother died, sister still kept on making nets,[2] and I lived with her for some time. But she was keeping

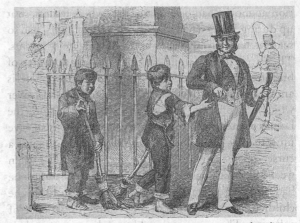

The Boy Crossing Sweepers, from Henry Mayhew's *London Labour and the London Poor* (1851).

company with a young man, and one day they went out, and came back and said they'd been and got married. It was him as got rid of me.

"He was kind to me for the first two or three months, while he was keeping her company; but before he was married he got a little cross, and after he was married he begun to get more cross, and used to send me to play in the streets, and tell me not to come home again till night. One day he hit me, and I said I wouldn't be hit about by him, and then at tea that night sister gave me three shillings, and told me I must go and get my own living. So I bought a box and brushes (they cost me just the money) and went cleaning boots, and I done pretty well with them, till my box was stole from me by a boy where I was lodging. He's in prison now—got six calendar[3] for picking pockets....

"I was fifteen the 24th of last May, sir, and I've been sweeping crossings now near upon two years. There's a party of six of us, and we have the crossings from St. Martin's Church as far as Pall Mall. I always go along with them as lodges in the same place as I do. In the daytime, if it's dry, we do anythink what we can—open cabs, or anythink; but if it's wet, we separate, and I an' another gets a crossing—those who gets on it first, keeps it—and we stand on each side and take our chance.

"We do it this way: if I was to see two gentlemen coming, I should cry out, 'Two toffs!' and then they are mine; and whether they give me anythink or not they

---

[1]   *pomatum* Scented ointment for the hair.

[2]   *nets* Meshwork or network, used for various purposes.

[3]   *six calendar* I.e., six months.

are mine, and my mate is bound not to follow them; for if he did he would get a hiding from the whole lot of us. If we both cry out together, then we share. If it's a lady and a gentleman, then we cries, 'A toff and a doll!' Sometimes we are caught out in this way. Perhaps it is a lady and gentleman and a child; and if I was to see them, and only say, 'A toff and a doll,' and leave out the child, then my mate can add the child; and as he is right and I wrong, then it's his party.

"If there's a policeman coming we musn't ask for money; but we are always on the look-out for policemen, and if we see one, then we calls out 'Phillup!' for that's our signal. One of the policemen at St. Martin's Church—Bandy, we calls him—knows what Phillup means, for he's up to us; so we had to change the word. (At the request of the young crossing-sweeper the present signal is omitted.)…

"When we see the rain we say together, 'Oh! there's a jolly good rain! we'll have a good day tomorrow.' If a shower comes on, and we are at our room, which we general are about three o'clock, to get somethink to eat—besides, we general go there to see how much each other's taken in the day—why, out we run with our brooms.

"At night-time we tumbles[1]—that is, if the policeman ain't nigh. We goes general to Waterloo Place when the opera's on. We sends on one of us ahead, as a looker-out, to look for the policeman, and then we follows. It's no good tumbling to gentlemen *going* to the opera; it's when they're coming back they gives us money. When they've got a young lady on their arm they laugh at us tumbling; some will give us a penny, others threepence, sometimes a sixpence or a shilling, and sometimes a halfpenny. We either do the cat'unwheel, or else we keep before the gentleman and lady, turning head-over-heels, putting our broom on the ground and then turning over it.…

"When we are talking together we always talk in a kind of slang. Each policeman we gives a regular name— there's 'Bull's Head,' 'Bandy Shanks,' and 'Old Cherry Legs,' and 'Dot-and-carry-one'; they all knows their names as well as us. We never talks of crossings, but 'fakes.' We don't make no slang of our own, but uses the regular one."

A group of homeless boys just after being admitted to a shelter. (Photograph by John Thomson, c. 1880.)

from Charles Dickens, *Hard Times*, Chapter 5, "The Key-Note" (1854)

Coketown, to which Messrs. Bounderby and Grad-grind now walked, was a triumph of fact; it had no greater taint of fancy in it than Mrs. Gradgrind herself. Let us strike the key-note, Coketown, before pursuing our tune.

It was a town of red brick, or of brick that would have been red if the smoke and ashes had allowed it; but as matters stood it was a town of unnatural red and black like the painted face of a savage. It was a town of machinery and tall chimneys, out of which interminable serpents of smoke trailed themselves forever and ever, and never got uncoiled. It had a black canal in it, and a river that ran purple with ill-smelling dye, and vast piles of building full of windows where there was a rattling and trembling all day long, and where the piston of the

[1] *tumbles* Perform leaps, somersaults, etc., like acrobats.

steam-engine worked monotonously up and down, like the head of an elephant in a state of melancholy madness. It contained several large streets all very like one another, and many small streets still more like one another, inhabited by people equally like one another, who all went in and out at the same hours, with the same sound upon the same pavements, to do the same work, and to whom every day was the same as yesterday and tomorrow, and every year the counterpart of the last and the next.

These attributes of Coketown were in the main inseparable from the work by which it was sustained; against them were to be set off, comforts of life which found their way all over the world, and elegancies of life which made, we will not ask how much of the fine lady, who could scarcely bear to hear the place mentioned. The rest of its features were voluntary, and they were these.

You saw nothing in Coketown but what was severely workful. If the members of a religious persuasion built a chapel there—as the members of eighteen religious persuasions had done—they made it a pious warehouse of red brick, with sometimes (but this is only in highly ornamental examples) a bell in a birdcage on the top of it. The solitary exception was the New Church; a stuccoed edifice with a square steeple over the door, terminating in four short pinnacles like florid wooden legs. All the public inscriptions in the town were painted alike, in severe characteristics of black and white. The jail might have been the infirmary, the infirmary might have been the jail, the town hall might have been either, or both, or anything else, for anything that appeared to the contrary in the graces of their construction. Fact, fact, fact, everywhere in the immaterial. The M'Choakumchild school was all fact, and the school of design was all fact, and the relations between master and man were all fact, and everything was fact between the lying-in hospital and the cemetery, and what you couldn't state in figures, or show to be purchaseable in the cheapest market and saleable in the dearest, was not, and never should be, world without end, Amen.[1]

A town so sacred to fact, and so triumphant in its assertion, of course got on well? Why no, not quite well. No? Dear me!

No. Coketown did not come out of its own furnaces, in all respects like gold that had stood the fire. First, the perplexing mystery of the place was, Who belonged to the eighteen denominations? Because, whoever did, the labouring people did not. It was very strange to walk through the streets on a Sunday morning, and note how few of *them* the barbarous jangling of bells that was driving the sick and nervous mad, called away from their own quarter, from their own close rooms, from the corners of their own streets, where they lounged listlessly, gazing at all the church and chapel going, as at a thing with which they had no manner of concern. Nor was it merely the stranger who noticed this, because there was a native organization in Coketown itself, whose members were to be heard of in the House of Commons every session, indignantly petitioning for Acts of Parliament that should make these people religious by main force.[2] Then came the Teetotal Society, who complained that these same people *would* get drunk, and showed their tabular statements that they did get drunk, and proved at tea parties that no inducement, human or divine (except a medal), would induce them to forego their custom of getting drunk. Then came the chemist and druggist, with other tabular statements, showing that when they didn't get drunk, they took opium. Then came the experienced chaplain of the jail, with more tabular statements, outdoing all the previous tabular statements, and showing that the same people *would* resort to low haunts, hidden from the public eye, where they heard low singing and saw low dancing, and mayhap joined in it; and where A. B., aged twenty-four next birthday, and committed for eighteen months' solitary, had himself said (not that he had ever shown himself particularly worthy of belief) his ruin began, as he was perfectly sure and confident that otherwise he would have been a tip-top moral specimen. Then came Mr. Gradgrind and Mr. Bounderby, the two gentlemen at this present

---

[1] *never should be ... Amen* From the Anglican Book of Common Prayer: "Glory be to the Father, and to the Son, and to the Holy Ghost; as it was in the beginning, is now, and ever shall be, world without end. Amen."

[2] *members ... main force* See Dickens's pamphlet *Sunday Under Three Heads* (written under the pseudonym "Timothy Sparks"), in which he vehemently opposes the "Sunday Observance Bill." Sir Andrew Agnew and his Evangelical group recommended to Parliament a series of moral reforms focusing on curtailing activities on Sunday, which Dickens contended would severely restrict the ability of the poor to enjoy their one day in the week that was free of labor.

moment walking through Coketown, and both eminently practical, who could, on occasion, furnish more tabular statements derived from their own personal experience, and illustrated by cases they had known and seen, from which it clearly appeared—in short, it was the only clear thing in the case—that these same people were a bad lot altogether, gentlemen; that do what you would for them they were never thankful for it, gentlemen; that they were restless, gentlemen; that they never knew what they wanted; that they lived upon the best, and bought fresh butter; and insisted on Mocha coffee, and rejected all but prime parts of meat, and yet were eternally dissatisfied and unmanageable. In short, it was the moral of the old nursery fable:

> There was an old woman, and what do you think
> She lived upon nothing but victuals and drink;
> Victuals and drink were the whole of her diet,
> And yet this old woman would NEVER be quiet.

London Nomads by John Thomson, from *Street Life in London* (1877).

SUSANNA MOODIE
1803 – 1885

Susanna Moodie once said about herself: "There is something in my character which always leads me to extremes." It was in writing about these extremes that she achieved her fame. The author of numerous books of verse and fiction, she is remembered primarily for her journal of her pioneering days in Upper Canada, *Roughing It in the Bush*, and its sequel, *Life in the Clearing*. Some, however, know of Moodie only through the version of her life that Margaret Atwood created more than a century later in a series of poems called *The Journals of Susanna Moodie* (1970), in which she explored the consciousness behind Moodie's writing—and by extension that of many immigrant and pioneering women.

Susanna Strickland was the youngest of six daughters in a family of eight children born to Elizabeth and Thomas Strickland, a middle-class family that moved from London to rural Suffolk County when Susanna was small. Her sister Catharine called Susanna a child of "excited imagination" with a temperament that was either "full of spirits or easily depressed." The children were educated by their father, about whom they would write with reverence decades after his death, as he instilled in them the values, independence, and skills necessary for the pioneering life many of them would lead.

Five of the six daughters became authors, among them Agnes Strickland, chiefly remembered for her biographies in *The Lives of the Queens of England* (written in 12 volumes in collaboration with her sister Elizabeth and published between 1840 and 1848), and Catharine Parr Traill, author of *The Backwoods of Canada* (1836). Both Moodie and Parr Traill had published essays, novels, and volumes of poetry before they immigrated to Canada with their Scottish husbands in 1832. In "Sketches from the Country" (1827–29), a series of essays about various people and customs in Suffolk County, Moodie displayed the humor, ear for realistic dialogue, and attention to detail that would appear in her later Canadian work. Her 1831 transcription of the slave narratives of Mary Prince and Ashton Warner also contributed to her ability to portray honestly and realistically the travails she endured.

By her own account, Catherine Parr Traill set out to inform her readers of the joys of the pioneering life, but Moodie wrote in a much more conflicted fashion, at one moment extolling the joys, at the next describing with candid honesty the adversity and suffering of an early British settler. Her ear for idiomatic and eccentric dialogue distinguishes her accounts of the bush fires, poverty, deaths, and other hardships she endured.

Roughing It in the Bush or Life in Canada (1852), Moodie's first and most famous account of bush life, was very popular in Britain and the United States, but it did not sell well in Canada, where Moodie became more infamous than famous. Critics and readers accused her of being an "ape of the [British] aristocracy," a colonial mouthpiece, and she was castigated for being critical of both the Canadians and the Irish. Noting that her reputation seemed to rest entirely on this one book, she wrote to her publisher complaining of the reception certain to meet her attempts to write fiction after *Roughing It*: "It is difficult to write a work of fiction, placing the scene in Canada, without rousing up the whole country against me. ... You don't know the touchy nature of the people. Vindictive, treacherous and dishonest, they always impute to your words and actions the worst motives, and no abuse is too coarse to express in their public journals, their hatred and defiance … Will they ever forgive me for writing *Roughing It*?" Canadians did eventually forgive Moodie—indeed, they turned her into an icon of pioneering life in Upper Canada.

Moodie lived the life of a pioneer for only a few years. By 1839 her husband had obtained a position in the town of Belleville as sheriff, and the family lived there for over thirty years. After her husband died in 1869, Moodie lived mainly with her children in Toronto. In her later years, she reached back to her painting, primarily producing beautifully detailed watercolors of flowers. She lived in Canada from 1832 to 1885, the year of her death from a stroke; on her passing her sister remarked that "the toil and mental strife were over."

⌘ ⌘ ⌘

from *Roughing It in the Bush*

INTRODUCTION

In most instances, emigration is a matter of necessity, not of choice; and this is more especially true of the emigration of persons of respectable connections, or of any station or position in the world. Few educated persons, accustomed to the refinements and luxuries of European society, ever willingly relinquish those advantages, and place themselves beyond the protective influence of the wise and revered institutions of their native land, without the pressure of some urgent cause. Emigration may, indeed, generally be regarded as an act of severe duty, performed at the expense of personal enjoyment, and accompanied by the sacrifice of those local attachments which stamp the scenes amid which our childhood grew, in imperishable characters upon the heart. Nor is it until adversity has pressed sorely upon the proud and wounded spirit of the well-educated sons and daughters of old but impoverished families, that they gird up the loins of the mind, and arm themselves with fortitude to meet and dare the heartbreaking conflict.

The ordinary motives for the emigration of such persons may be summed up in a few brief words—the emigrant's hope of bettering his condition, and of escaping from the vulgar sarcasms too often hurled at the less wealthy by the purse proud, commonplace people of the world. But there is a higher motive still, which has its origin in that love of independence which springs up spontaneously in the breasts of the high-souled children of a glorious land. They cannot labour in a menial capacity in the country where they were born and educated to command. They can trace no difference between themselves and the more fortunate individuals of a race whose blood warms their veins, and whose name they bear. The want of wealth alone places an impassable barrier between them and the more favoured offspring of the same parent stock; and they go forth to make for themselves a new name and to find another country, to forget the past and to live in the future, to exult in the prospect of their children being free and the land of their adoption great.

The choice of the country to which they devote their talents and energies depends less upon their pecuniary means than upon the fancy of the emigrant or the popularity of a name. From the year 1826 to 1829, Australia and the Swan River[1] were all the rage. No other portions of the habitable globe were deemed worthy of notice. These were the El Dorados and lands of Goshen[2] to which all respectable emigrants eagerly flocked. Disappointment, as a matter of course, followed their high-raised expectations. Many of the most sanguine of these adventurers returned to their native shores in a worse condition than when they left them. In 1830, the great tide of emigration flowed westward. Canada became the great landmark for the rich in hope and poor in purse. Public newspapers and private letters teemed with the unheard of advantages to be derived from a settlement in this highly-favoured region.

[1] *Swan River* In 1829 British emigrants formed the Swan River colony in Western Australia and called the settlement "Fremantle"; they chose a nearby location for the capital city and called it "Perth."

[2] *El Dorados* Sir Walter Raleigh searched the northern part of South America for the mythical "El Dorado," said to be a land of gold; *lands of Goshen* Area in the Nile delta near Palestine where Abraham is said to have led his people.

Its salubrious climate, its fertile soil, commercial advantages, great water privileges, its proximity to the mother country, and last, not least, its almost total exemption from taxation—that bugbear[1] which keeps honest John Bull[2] in a state of constant ferment—were the theme of every tongue, and lauded beyond all praise. The general interest, once excited, was industriously kept alive by pamphlets, published by interested parties, which prominently set forth all the *good* to be derived from a settlement in the backwoods of Canada, while they carefully concealed the toil and hardship to be endured in order to secure these advantages. They told of lands yielding forty bushels to the acre, but they said nothing of the years when these lands, with the most careful cultivation, would barely return fifteen; when rust and smut, engendered by the vicinity of damp overhanging woods, would blast the fruits of the poor emigrant's labour, and almost deprive him of bread. They talked of log houses to be raised in a single day, by the generous exertions of friends and neighbours, but they never ventured upon a picture of the disgusting scenes of riot and low debauchery exhibited during the raising, or upon a description of the dwellings when raised—dens of dirt and misery, which would, in many instances, be shamed by an English pigsty. The necessaries of life were described as inestimably cheap; but they forgot to add that in remote bush settlements, often twenty miles from a market town, and some of them even that distance from the nearest dwelling, the necessaries of life, which would be deemed indispensable to the European, could not be procured at all, or, if obtained, could only be so by sending a man and team through a blazed forest road—a process far too expensive for frequent repetition.

Oh, ye dealers in wild lands—ye speculators in the folly and credulity of your fellow men—what a mass of misery, and of misrepresentation productive of that misery, have ye not to answer for! You had your acres to sell, and what to you were the worn down frames and broken hearts of the infatuated purchasers? The public believed the plausible statements you made with such earnestness, and men of all grades rushed to hear your hired orators declaim upon the blessings to be obtained by the clearers of the wilderness.

… What the Backwoods of Canada are to the industrious and ever-to-be-honoured sons of honest poverty, and what they are to the refined and accomplished gentleman, these simple sketches will endeavour to portray. They are drawn principally from my own experience, during a sojourn of nineteen years in the colony.

Chapter 15: The Wilderness, and our Indian Friends

Man of strange race! stern dweller of the wild!
Nature's freeborn, untamed, and daring child![3]

The clouds of the preceding night, instead of dissolving in snow, brought on a rapid thaw. A thaw in the middle of winter is the most disagreeable change that can be imagined. After several weeks of clear, bright, bracing, frosty weather, with a serene atmosphere and cloudless sky, you awake one morning surprised at the change in the temperature, and, upon looking out of the window, behold the woods obscured by a murky haze—not so dense as an English November fog, but more black and lowering—and the heavens shrouded in a uniform covering of leaden-coloured clouds, deepening into a livid indigo at the edge of the horizon. The snow, no longer hard and glittering, has become soft and spongy, and the foot slips into a wet and insidiously yielding mass at every step. From the roof pours down a continuous stream of water, and the branches of the trees, collecting the moisture of the reeking atmosphere, shower it upon the earth from every dripping twig. The cheerless and uncomfortable aspect of things without never fails to produce a corresponding effect upon the minds of those within, and casts such a damp upon the spirits that it appears to destroy for a time all sense of enjoyment. Many persons (and myself among the number) are made aware of the approach of a thunderstorm by an intense pain and weight about the head; and I have heard numbers of Canadians complain that a thaw always made them feel bilious and heavy, and greatly depressed their animal spirits.

I had a great desire to visit our new location, but when I looked out upon the cheerless waste, I gave up

---

[1] *bugbear* Imaginary being.

[2] *John Bull* Personification of England or the typical Englishman.

[3] *Man … child* By Susanna Moodie.

the idea, and contented myself with hoping for a better day on the morrow; but many morrows came and went before a frost again hardened the road sufficiently for me to make the attempt.

The prospect from the windows of my sister's[1] log hut was not very prepossessing. The small lake in front, which formed such a pretty object in summer, now looked like an extensive field covered with snow, hemmed in from the rest of the world by a dark belt of sombre pine woods. The clearing round the house was very small, and only just reclaimed from the wilderness, and the greater part of it covered with piles of brush-wood, to be burnt the first dry days of spring. The charred and blackened stumps on the few acres that had been cleared during the preceding year were everything but picturesque, and I concluded, as I turned, disgusted, from the prospect before me, that there was very little beauty to be found in the backwoods. But I came to this decision during a Canadian thaw, be it remembered, when one is wont to view every object with jaundiced eyes.

Moodie[2] had only been able to secure sixty-six acres of his government grant upon the Upper Katchawanook Lake, which, being interpreted, means in English, the "Lake of the Waterfalls," a very poetical meaning, which most Indian names have. He had, however, secured a clergy reserve of two hundred acres adjoining; and he afterwards purchased a fine lot, which likewise formed part of the same block, one hundred acres, for £150.[3] This was an enormously high price for wild land, but the prospect of opening the Trent and Otonabee[4] for the navigation of steamboats and other small craft, was at that period a favourite speculation, and its practicability, and the great advantages to be derived from it, were so widely believed as to raise the value of the wild lands along these remote waters to an enormous price; and settlers in the vicinity were eager to secure lots, at any sacrifice, along their shores.

Our government grant was upon the lakeshore, and Moodie had chosen for the site of his log house a bank that sloped gradually from the edge of the water, until it attained to the dignity of a hill. Along the top of this ridge the forest road ran, and midway down the hill our humble home, already nearly completed, stood, sur-rounded by the eternal forest. A few trees had been cleared in its immediate vicinity, just sufficient to allow the workmen to proceed, and to prevent the fall of any tree injuring the building, or the danger of its taking fire during the process of burning the fallow.

A neighbour had undertaken to build this rude dwelling by contract, and was to have it ready for us by the first week in the new year. The want of boards to make the divisions in the apartments alone hindered him from fulfilling his contract. These had lately been procured, and the house was to be ready for our recep-tion in the course of a week. Our trunks and baggage had already been conveyed thither by Mr. D——; and in spite of my sister's kindness and hospitality, I longed to find myself once more settled in a home of my own.

… The first spring we spent in comparative ease and idleness. Our cows had been left upon our old place during the winter. The ground had to be cleared before it could receive a crop of any kind, and I had little to do but to wander by the lakeshore, or among the woods, and amuse myself.

These were the halcyon[5] days of the bush. My husband had purchased a very light cedar canoe, to which he attached a keel and a sail; and most of our leisure hours, directly the snows melted, were spent upon the water.

These fishing and shooting excursions were delight-ful. The pure beauty of the Canadian water, the sombre but august grandeur of the vast forest that hemmed us in on every side and shut us out from the rest of the world, soon cast a magic spell upon our spirits, and we began to feel charmed with the freedom and solitude around us. Every object was new to us. We felt as if we were the first discoverers of every beautiful flower and stately tree that attracted our attention, and we gave names to fantastic rocks and fairy isles, and raised imaginary houses and bridges on every picturesque spot which we floated past during our aquatic excursions. I

---

[1] *my sister* Catherine Parr Trail, also an author, wrote *The Backwoods of Canada* (1836).

[2] *Moodie* Susanna Moodie refers here to her husband, John Wedderburn Dunbar Moodie.

[3] [Moodie's note] After a lapse of fifteen years, we have been glad to sell these lots of land, after considerable clearings had been made upon them, for less than they originally cost us.

[4] *Trent and Otonabee* Rivers in Ontario.

[5] *halcyon* Peaceful.

learned the use of the paddle, and became quite a proficient in the gentle craft.

It was not long before we received visits from the Indians,[1] a people whose beauty, talents, and good qualities have been somewhat overrated, and invested with a poetical interest which they scarcely deserve. Their honesty and love of truth are the finest traits in characters otherwise dark and unlovely. But these are two God-like attributes, and from them spring all that is generous and ennobling about them.

There never was a people more sensible of kindness, or more grateful for any little act of benevolence exercised towards them. We met them with confidence; our dealings with them were conducted with the strictest integrity; and they became attached to our persons, and in no single instance ever destroyed the good opinion we entertained of them.

The tribes that occupy the shores of all these inland waters, back of the great lakes, belong to the Chippewa or Missasagua Indians, perhaps the least attractive of all these wild people, both with regard to their physical and mental endowments.

The men of this tribe are generally small of stature, with very coarse and repulsive features. The forehead is low and retreating, the observing faculties large, the intellectual ones scarcely developed; the ears large, and standing off from the face, the eyes looking towards the temples, keen, snakelike, and far apart; the cheekbones prominent; the nose long and flat, the nostrils very round; the jawbone projecting, massy, and brutal; the mouth expressing ferocity and sullen determination; the teeth large, even, and dazzlingly white. The mouth of the female differs widely in expression from that of the male; the lips are fuller, the jaw less projecting, and the smile is simple and agreeable. The women are a merry, lighthearted set, and their constant laugh and incessant prattle form a strange contrast to the iron taciturnity of their grim lords.

Now I am upon the subject, I will recapitulate a few traits and sketches of these people, as they came under my own immediate observation.

A dry cedar swamp, not far from the house, by the lakeshore, had been their usual place of encampment for many years. The whole block of land was almost entirely covered with maple trees, and had originally been an Indian sugar-bush.[2] Although the favourite spot had now passed into the hands of strangers, they still frequented the place, to make canoes and baskets, to fish and shoot, and occasionally to follow their old occupation.

Scarcely a week passed away without my being visited by the dark strangers; and as my husband never allowed them to eat with the servants (who viewed them with the same horror that Mrs. D—— did black Mollineux), but brought them to his own table they soon grew friendly and communicative, and would point to every object that attracted their attention, asking a thousand questions as to its use, the material of which it was made, and if we were inclined to exchange it for their commodities?

With a large map of Canada, they were infinitely delighted. In a moment they recognised every bay and headland in Ontario, and almost screamed with delight when, following the course of the Trent with their fingers, they came to their own lake.

How eagerly each pointed out the spot to his fellows; how intently their black heads were bent down, and their dark eyes fixed upon the map! What strange, uncouth exclamations of surprise burst from their lips as they rapidly repeated the Indian names for every lake and river on this wonderful piece of paper!

The old chief, Peter Nogan, begged hard for the coveted treasure. He would give "Canoe, venison, duck, fish, for it; and more by and by."

I felt sorry that I was unable to gratify his wishes; but the map had cost upwards of six dollars, and was daily consulted by my husband, in reference to the names and situations of localities in the neighbourhood.

… The affection of Indian parents to their children, and the deference which they pay to the aged, is another beautiful and touching trait in their character.

One extremely cold, wintry day, as I was huddled with my little ones over the stove, the door softly unclosed, and the moccasined foot of an Indian crossed the floor. I raised my head, for I was too much accustomed to their sudden appearance at any hour to feel

[1] *Indians* The use of this term to refer to Native North Americans is now out of favor in many quarters—though it remains common among many aboriginal peoples.

[2] *sugar-bush* Grove of maple trees from which syrup is extracted.

alarmed, and perceived a tall woman standing silently and respectfully before me, wrapped in a large blanket. The moment she caught my eye she dropped the folds of her covering from around her, and laid at my feet the attenuated figure of a boy, about twelve years of age, who was in the last stage of consumption.

"Papouse[1] die," she said, mournfully clasping her hands against her breast, and looking down upon the suffering lad with the most heartfelt expression of maternal love, while large tears tricked down her dark face. "Moodie's squaw save papouse—poor Indian woman much glad."

Her child was beyond all human aid. I looked anxiously upon him, and knew, by the pinched-up features and purple hue of his wasted cheek, that he had not many hours to live. I could only answer with tears her agonising appeal to my skill.

"Try and save him! All die but him." (She held up five of her fingers.) "Brought him all the way from Mutta Lake[2] upon my back, for white squaw to cure."

"I cannot cure him, my poor friend. He is in God's care; in a few hours he will be with Him."

The child was seized with a dreadful fit of coughing, which I expected every moment would terminate his frail existence. I gave him a teaspoonful of currant jelly, which he took with avidity, but could not retain a moment on his stomach.

"Papouse die," murmured the poor woman; "alone—alone! No papouse; the mother all alone."

She began readjusting the poor sufferer in her blanket. I got her some food, and begged her to stay and rest herself; but she was too much distressed to eat, and too restless to remain. She said little, but her face expressed the keenest anguish; she took up her mournful load, pressed for a moment his wasted, burning hand in hers, and left the room.

My heart followed her a long way on her melancholy journey. Think what this woman's love must have been for that dying son, when she had carried a lad of his age six miles, through the deep snow, upon her back, on such a day, in the hope of my being able to do him some good. Poor heartbroken mother! I learned from Joe Muskrat's squaw some days after that the boy died a few minutes after Elizabeth Iron, his mother, got home.

They never forget any little act of kindness. One cold night, late in the fall, my hospitality was demanded by six squaws, and puzzled I was how to accommodate them all. I at last determined to give them the use of the parlour floor during the night. Among these women there was one very old, whose hair was as white as snow. She was the only grey-haired Indian I ever saw, and on that account I regarded her with peculiar interest. I knew that she was the wife of a chief, by the scarlet embroidered leggings which only the wives and daughters of chiefs are allowed to wear. The old squaw had a very pleasing countenance, but I tried in vain to draw her into conversation. She evidently did not understand me; and the Muskrat squaw, and Betty Cow, were laughing at my attempts to draw her out. I administered supper to them with my own hands, and after I had satisfied their wants (which is no very easy task, for they have great appetites), I told our servant to bring in several spare mattresses and blankets for their use. "Now mind, Jenny, and give the old squaw the best bed," I said; "the others are young, and can put up with a little inconvenience."

The old Indian glanced at me with her keen, bright eye, but I had no idea that she comprehended what I said.

Some weeks after this, as I was sweeping over my parlour floor, a slight tap drew me to the door. On opening it I perceived the old squaw, who immediately slipped into my hand a set of beautifully embroidered bark trays, fitting one within the other, and exhibiting the very best sample of the porcupine quill work. While I stood wondering what this might mean, the good old creature fell upon my neck, and kissing me, exclaimed, "You remember old squaw—make her comfortable! Old squaw no forget you. Keep them for her sake," and before I could detain her she ran down the hill with a swiftness which seemed to bid defiance to years. I never saw this interesting Indian again, and I concluded that she died during the winter, for she must have been of a great age.

… The Indians, under their quiet exterior, possess a deal of humour. They have significant names for everything, and a nickname for everyone, and some of the latter are laughably appropriate. A fat, pompous,

---

[1] *Papouse* Young child.

[2] [Moodie's note]   Mud Lake, or Lake *Shemong*, in Indian.

ostentatious settler in our neighbourhood they called *Muckakee*, "the bullfrog." Another, rather a fine young man, but with a very red face, they named *Segoskee*, "the rising sun." Mr. Wood, who had a farm above ours, was a remarkably slender young man, and to him they gave the appellation of *Metiz*, "thin stick." A woman, that occasionally worked for me, had a disagreeable squint; she was known in Indian by the name of *Sachabo*, "crosseye." A gentleman with a very large nose was *Choojas*, "big or ugly nose." My little Addie, who was a fair, lovely creature, they viewed with great approbation, and called *Anoonk*, "a star," while the rosy Katie was *Nogesigook*, "the northern lights." As to me, I was *Nonocosiqui*, a "hummingbird," a ridiculous name for a tall woman, but it had reference to the delight I took in painting birds. My friend, Emilia, was "blue cloud," my little Donald, "frozen face," young C——, "the red-headed woodpecker," from the colour of his hair; my brother, *Chippewa*, and "the bald-headed eagle." He was an especial favourite among them.

The Indians are often made a prey of and cheated by the unprincipled settlers, who think it no crime to overreach a redskin. One anecdote will fully illustrate this fact. A young squaw, who was near becoming a mother, stopped at a Smithtown settler's house to rest herself. The woman of the house, who was Irish, was peeling for dinner some large white turnips, which her husband had grown in their garden. The Indian had never seen a turnip before, and the appearance of the firm, white, juicy root gave her such a keen craving to taste it that she very earnestly begged for a small piece to eat. She had purchased at Peterborough a large stone china bowl, of a very handsome pattern (or, perhaps, got it at the store in exchange for basket), the worth of which might be half a dollar. If the poor squaw longed for the turnip, the value of which could scarcely reach a copper, the covetous European had fixed as longing a glance upon the china bowl, and she was determined to gratify her avaricious desire and obtain it on the most easy terms. She told the squaw, with some disdain, that her man did not grow turnips to give away to "Injuns," but she would sell her one. The squaw offered her four coppers, all the change she had about her. This the woman refused with contempt. She then proffered a basket, but that was not sufficient; nothing would satisfy her but the bowl. The Indian demurred, but opposition

had only increased her craving for the turnip in a tenfold degree; and, after a short mental struggle, in which the animal propensity overcame the warnings of prudence, the squaw gave up the bowl, and received in return *one turnip*! The daughter of this woman told me this anecdote of her mother as a very clever thing. What ideas some people have of moral justice!

I have said before that the Indian never forgets a kindness. We had a thousand proofs of this, when overtaken by misfortune, and withering beneath the iron grasp of poverty, we could scarcely obtain bread for ourselves and our little ones; then it was that the truth of the Eastern proverb was brought home to our hearts, and the goodness of God fully manifested towards us, "Cast thy bread upon the waters, and thou shalt find it after many days."[1] During better times we had treated these poor savages with kindness and liberality, and when dearer friends looked coldly upon us they never forsook us. For many a good meal I have been indebted to them, when I had nothing to give in return, when the pantry was empty, and "the hearthstone growing cold," as they term the want of provisions to cook at it. And their delicacy in conferring these favours was not the least admirable part of their conduct. John Nogan, who was much attached to us, would bring a fine bunch of ducks, and drop them at my feet "for the papouse," or leave a large muskinonge[2] on the sill of the door, or place a quarter of venison just within it, and slip away without saying a word, thinking that receiving a present from a poor Indian might hurt our feelings, and he would spare us the mortification of returning thanks.

Often have I grieved that people with such generous impulses should be degraded and corrupted by civilised men, that a mysterious destiny involves and hangs over them, pressing them back into the wilderness, and slowly and surely sweeping them from the earth.

Their ideas of Christianity appeared to me vague and unsatisfactory. They will tell you that Christ died for men, and that He is the Saviour of the World, but they do not seem to comprehend the spiritual character of Christianity, nor the full extent of the requirements and application of the law of Christian love. These imperfect views may not be entertained by all Christian

---

[1]   *"Cast ... days"*   From Ecclesiastes 11.1.

[2]   *muskinonge*   Also called "muskellunge" or "muskie"; large fish of the same family as the pike.

Indians, but they were very common amongst those with whom I conversed. Their ignorance upon theological, as well as upon other subjects, is, of course, extreme. One Indian asked me very innocently if I came from the land where Christ was born, and if I had ever seen Jesus. They always mention the name of the Persons in the Trinity with great reverence.

They are a highly imaginative people. The practical meaning of their names, and their intense admiration for the beauties of nature, are proof of this. Nothing escapes their observing eyes.

There is not a flower that blooms in the wilderness, a bird that cuts the air with its wings, a beast that roams the wood, a fish that stems the water, or the most minute insect that sports in the sunbeams, but it has an Indian name to illustrate its peculiar habits and qualities. Some of their words convey the direct meaning of the thing implied—thus, *ché-charm*, "to sneeze," is the very sound of that act; *too-me-duh*, "to churn," gives the noise made by the dashing of the cream from side to side; and many others.

They believe in supernatural appearances—in spirits of the earth, the air, the waters. The latter they consider evil, and propitiate, before undertaking a long voyage, by throwing small portions of bread, meat, tobacco, and gunpowder into the water.

When an Indian loses one of his children, he must keep a strict fast for three days, abstaining from food of any kind. . . .

Their method of broiling fish, however, is excellent. They take a fish, just fresh out of the water, cut out the entrails, and, without removing the scales, wash it clean, dry it in a cloth, or in grease, and cover it all over with clear hot ashes. When the flesh will part from the bone, they draw it out of the ashes, strip off the skin, and it is fit for the table of the most fastidious epicure.

The deplorable want of chastity that exists among the Indian women of this tribe seems to have been more the result of their intercourse with the settlers in the country than from any previous disposition to this vice. The jealousy of their husbands has often been exercised in a terrible manner against the offending squaws; but this has not happened of late years. The men wink at these derelictions in their wives, and share with them the price of their shame.

The mixture of European blood adds greatly to the physical beauty of the half-race, but produces a sad falling off from the original integrity of the Indian character. The half-caste is generally a lying, vicious rogue, possessing the worst qualities of both parents in an eminent degree. We have many of these half-Indians in the penitentiary, for crimes of the blackest dye.

The skill of the Indian in procuring his game, either by land or water, has been too well described by better writers than I could ever hope to be to need any illustration from my pen, and I will close this long chapter with a droll anecdote which is told of a gentleman in this neighbourhood.

The early loss of his hair obliged Mr. —— to procure the substitute of a wig. This was such a good imitation of nature, that none but his intimate friends and neighbours were aware of the fact.

It happened that he had had some quarrel with an Indian, which had to be settled in one of the petty courts. The case was decided in favour of Mr. ——, which so aggrieved the savage, who considered himself the injured party, that he sprang upon him with a furious yell, tomahawk in hand, with the intention of depriving him of his scalp. He twisted his hand in the locks which adorned the cranium of his adversary, when—horror of horrors!—the treacherous wig came off in his hand, "Owgh! owgh!" exclaimed the affrighted savage, flinging it from him, and rushing from the court as if he had been bitten by a rattlesnake. His sudden exit was followed by peals of laughter from the crowd, while Mr. —— coolly picked up his wig, and dryly remarked that it had saved his head.

—1852

IN CONTEXT

Sample of Susanna Moodie's 1839 Correspondence: A "Crossed" Letter

In Upper Canada in the nineteenth century, as in Britain and America, letters were frequently "crossed" in order to save paper and postage.

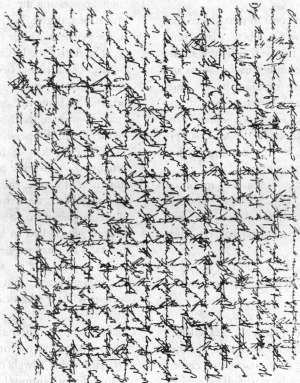

JOHN STUART MILL
1806 – 1873

Philosopher, social reformer, economist, and politician, John Stuart Mill was one of the most influential of Victorian thinkers. His breadth of knowledge and interests was staggering, as was his ability to apply his intellect to a wide range of subjects, including women's rights, civil liberties, economic theories, logic, and poetics. Mill's *Utilitarianism* and *On Liberty* are both still regarded as central works in the fields of moral and social philosophy and political science.

Mill seemed destined from an early age to become a polymath—his childhood was practically a monument to over-achievement. He was born in London in 1806, the first child of Harriet Burrow

and James Mill, a distinguished psychologist, philosopher, and historian. James was a disciple of Jeremy Bentham, who had founded the philosophical school of utilitarianism, an ethical doctrine whose main premise is that an action ought to be taken only if it produces happiness for all involved (later refined by J.S. Mill into the "greatest happiness principle," which suggests that people ought to act in ways that produce the greatest happiness for all involved). Participating in an experiment devised in part by Bentham, James decided that his eldest son would be a guinea pig for his educational theories, and at a very young age John began a rigorous education aimed at preparing him to become a future leader of the Benthamites.

In his autobiography, Mill described his formal instruction as beginning with Greek at age three; by the age of eight he could translate the works of Socrates and Plato. He then learned Latin well enough to translate such masters as Horace and Ovid, and also studied mathematics, the sciences, and English literature. Not being content to allow his son to learn simply by rote, James heavily emphasized rhetoric and debate, insisting that John make moral decisions about the principles he was learning. By the time he was 14, his father considered him to be ready for university study but felt that an institution would hold him back, and thus Mill began his career a full "quarter of a century before his contemporaries," as he would say in his autobiography.

James's experiment succeeded—John was a brilliant and erudite child, able to converse and debate with adults and to tutor all of his siblings from an early age. The daily ten-hour study regime, however, took a toll on him, and in his early twenties Mill experienced a period of deep depression that was relieved only when he discovered the poetry of William Wordsworth. During this time he pondered the virtues of Bentham's utilitarianism, which seemed to favor the good of the majority at the expense of the individual, who, Mill felt, is the best judge of his or her own happiness. Although he himself was an empiricist, he felt that Bentham's philosophy promoted the "science" of ethics at the expense of real life. Mill said of Bentham's utilitarianism: "It is wholly empirical and the empiricism of one who has had little experience." After reading the Romantic poets—Wordsworth in particular—Mill began to appreciate the therapeutic effects of poetry and the arts and the importance of an emotional life. The essay "What is Poetry?" (1833) speaks to his concerns about the necessity of individual pleasure.

After studying law for two years, Mill worked for decades in the East India Office, first as a clerk and then as head of his department, but he continued to be an outspoken advocate for individual rights and freedoms (he had been arrested as a teenager for disseminating literature in support of birth control). He published a modification of Bentham's philosophy, later reworked as *Utilitarianism* (1863); his most ambitious early work was *System of Logic*, published in 1843 and still highly regarded in philosophical circles today. The book that followed, *Principles of Political Economy* (1848), commands a similar level of respect in the field of economics. In 1859 Mill wrote another key work: *On Liberty*, a treatise that continued his theme of support for individual rights, deriding democratic majorities that conform to tradition and smother individuality.

In the planning and to some extent the writing of both these and subsequent works, Mill was assisted by Harriet Taylor, an aspiring author whom Mill had first met in 1831 and with whom he began to work closely. (The precise extent of Taylor's involvement remains the subject of debate among scholars.)

After serving as Member of Parliament from 1865 to 1868, Mill published *The Subjection of Women* (1869). He had worked on this book for years, and it had become a passionate subject for both Mill and Taylor. (The two were married in 1851 after her husband's death. Mill and Taylor never moved freely in society together, however; many of his friends, Carlyle and Tennyson included, viewed their relationship as inappropriate.) *The Subjection of Women* spoke to the rights of women, both legally and practically, arguing for government reforms of property and divorce laws, women's enfranchisement, and advocating the end of "slavery" in the home. Mill even argued in Parliament—well ahead of his time—for non-sexist language and the rewording of parliamentary bills to remove gender-specific terms.

Mill died in 1873 in Avignon, France, and was buried beside his wife, who had died prematurely in 1858. In his eloquent and insightful *Autobiography*, published shortly after his death, Mill wrote candidly about his childhood experiences with a demanding father and a thoroughly rational education; about his mental breakdown and his discovery of the value of works of the imagination; about his relationship with Harriet Taylor; and about his writing. The *Autobiography* is one of the great autobiographies in the English language.

⌘⌘⌘

What is Poetry?

It has often been asked, what is poetry? And many and various are the answers which have been returned. The vulgarest of all—one with which no person possessed of the faculties to which poetry addresses itself can ever have been satisfied—is that which confounds poetry with metrical composition: yet to this wretched mockery of a definition, many have been led back, by the failure of all their attempts to find any other that would distinguish what they have been accustomed to call poetry, from much which they have known only under other names.

That, however, the word *poetry* does import something quite peculiar in its nature, something which may exist in what is called prose as well as in verse, something which does not even require the instrument of words, but can speak, through those other audible symbols called musical sounds, and even through the visible ones, which are the language of sculpture, painting, and architecture; all this, as we believe, is and must be felt, though perhaps indistinctly, by all upon whom poetry in any of its shapes produces any impression beyond that of tickling the ear. To the mind, poetry is either nothing, or it is the better part of all art whatever, and of real life too; and the distinction between poetry and what is not poetry, whether explained or not, is felt to be fundamental.

Where everyone feels a difference, a difference there must be. All other appearance may be fallacious, but the appearance of a difference is itself a real difference. Appearances too, like other things, must have a cause, and that which can cause anything, even an illusion, must be a reality. And hence, while a half-philosophy disdains the classifications and distinctions indicated by popular language, philosophy carried to its highest point may frame new ones, but never sets aside the old, content with correcting and regularizing them. It cuts fresh channels for thought, but it does not fill up such as it finds ready-made, but traces, on the contrary, more deeply, broadly, and distinctly, those into which the current has spontaneously flowed.

Let us then attempt, in the way of modest inquiry, not to coerce and confine nature within the bounds of an arbitrary definition, but rather to find the boundaries which she herself has set, and erect a barrier round them; not calling mankind to account for having misapplied the word *poetry*, but attempting to clear up to them the conception which they already attach to it, and to bring before their minds as a distinct principle that which, as a vague feeling, has really guided them in their actual employment of the term.

The object of poetry is confessedly to act upon the emotions; and therein is poetry sufficiently distinguished from what Wordsworth affirms to be its logical opposite, namely, not prose, but matter of fact or science.[1] The one addresses itself to the belief, the other to the feelings. The one does its work by convincing or persuading, the other by moving. The one acts by presenting a proposition to the understanding, the other by offering interesting objects of contemplation to the sensibilities.

This, however, leaves us very far from a definition of poetry. We have distinguished it from one thing, but we are bound to distinguish it from everything. To present thoughts or images to the mind for the purpose of acting upon the emotions, does not belong to poetry alone. It is equally the province (for example) of the novelist: and yet the faculty of the poet and the faculty of the novelist are as distinct as any other two faculties; as the faculty of the novelist and of the orator, or of the poet and the metaphysician. The two characters may be united, as characters the most disparate may; but they have no natural connection.

Many of the finest poems are in the form of novels, and in almost all good novels there is true poetry. But there is a radical distinction between the interest felt in a novel as such, and the interest excited by poetry; for the one is derived from incident, the other from the representation of feeling. In one, the source of the emotion excited is the exhibition of a state or states of human sensibility; in the other, of a series of states of mere outward circumstances. Now, all minds are capable of being affected more or less by representations of the latter kind, and all, or almost all, by those of the former; yet the two sources of interest correspond to two distinct and (as respects their greatest development) mutually exclusive characters of mind. So much is the nature of poetry dissimilar to the nature of fictitious narrative, that to have a really strong passion for either of the two, seems to presuppose or to superinduce a comparative indifference to the other.

At what age is the passion for a story, for almost any kind of story, merely as a story, the most intense? In childhood. But that also is the age at which poetry, even of the simplest description, is least relished and least understood; because the feelings with which it is especially conversant are yet undeveloped, and not having been even in the slightest degree experienced, cannot be sympathized with. In what stage of the progress of society, again, is storytelling most valued, and the storyteller in greatest request and honor? In a rude state; like that of the Tartars and Arabs at this day, and of almost all nations in the earliest ages. But in this state of society there is little poetry except ballads, which are mostly narrative, that is, essentially stories, and derive their principal interest from the incidents. Considered as poetry, they are of the lowest and most elementary kind: the feelings depicted, or rather indicated, are the simplest our nature has; such joys and griefs as the immediate pressure of some outward event excites in rude minds, which live wholly immersed in outward things, and have never, either from choice or a force they could not resist, turned themselves to the contemplation of the world within. Passing now from childhood, and from the childhood of society, to the grown-up men and women of this most grown-up and unchild-like age—the minds and hearts of greatest depth and elevation are commonly those which take greatest delight in poetry; the shallowest and emptiest, on the contrary, are, by universal remark, the most addicted to novel reading. This accords, too, with all analogous experience of human nature. The sort of persons whom not merely in books but in their lives, we find perpetually engaged in hunting for excitement from without, are invariably those who do not possess, either in the

---

[1] *Wordsworth ... science* See William Wordsworth's "Note" in "Preface" to *Lyrical Ballads* (1800).

vigor of their intellectual powers or in the depth of their sensibilities, that which would enable them to find ample excitement nearer at home. The same persons whose time is divided between sightseeing, gossip, and fashionable dissipation, take a natural delight in fictitious narrative; the excitement it affords is of the kind which comes from without. Such persons are rarely lovers of poetry, though they may fancy themselves so, because they relish novels in verse. But poetry, which is the delineation of the deeper and more secret workings of the human heart, is interesting only to those to whom it recalls what they have felt, or whose imagination it stirs up to conceive what they could feel, or what they might have been able to feel, had their outward circumstances been different.

Poetry, when it is really such, is truth; and fiction also, if it is good for anything, is truth: but they are different truths. The truth of poetry is to paint the human soul truly: the truth of fiction is to give a true picture of life. The two kinds of knowledge are different, and come by different ways, come mostly to different persons. Great poets are often proverbially ignorant of life. What they know has come by observation of themselves; they have found there one highly delicate, and sensitive, and refined specimen of human nature, on which the laws of human emotion are written in large characters, such as can be read off without much study: and other knowledge of mankind, such as comes to men of the world by outward experience, is not indispensable to them as poets: but to the novelist such knowledge is all in all; he has to describe outward things, not the inward man; actions and events, not feelings; and it will not do for him to be numbered among those who, as Madame Roland said of Brissot,[1] know man but not men.

All this is no bar to the possibility of combining both elements, poetry and narrative or incident, in the same work, and calling it either a novel or a poem; but so may red and white combine on the same human features, or on the same canvas; and so may oil and vinegar, though opposite natures, blend together in the same composite taste. There is one order of composition which requires the union of poetry and incident, each in its highest kind—the dramatic. Even there the two elements are perfectly distinguishable, and may exist of unequal quality, and in the most various proportion. The incidents of a dramatic poem may be scant and ineffective, though the delineation of passion and character may be of the highest order; as in Goethe's glorious *Torquato Tasso*; or again, the story as a mere story may be well got up for effect, as is the case with some of the most trashy productions of the Minerva press:[2] it may even be, what those are not, a coherent and probable series of events, though there be scarcely a feeling exhibited which is not exhibited falsely, or in a manner absolutely commonplace. The combination of the two excellencies is what renders Shakespeare so generally acceptable, each sort of readers finding in him what is suitable to their faculties. To the many he is great as a storyteller, to the few as a poet.

In limiting poetry to the delineation of states of feeling, and denying the name where nothing is delineated but outward objects, we may be thought to have done what we promised to avoid—to have not found, but made a definition, in opposition to the usage of the English language, since it is established by common consent that there is a poetry called descriptive. We deny the charge. Description is not poetry because there is descriptive poetry, no more than science is poetry because there is such a thing as a didactic poem; no more, we might almost say, than Greek or Latin is poetry because there are Greek and Latin poems. But an object which admits of being described, or a truth which may fill a place in a scientific treatise, may also furnish an occasion for the generation of poetry, which we thereupon choose to call descriptive or didactic. The poetry is not in the object itself, nor in the scientific truth itself, but in the state of mind in which the one and the other may be contemplated. The mere delineation of the dimensions and colors of external objects is not poetry, no more than a geometrical ground plan of St. Peter's or Westminster Abbey is painting. Descriptive poetry consists, no doubt, in description, but in description of things as they appear, not as they are; and it paints them not in their bare and natural lineaments, but arranged in the colors and seen through the medium

---

[1] *Madame Roland* See Marie Jeanne Philipon Roland de la Platière's *Appeal to Impartial Posterity* (1796); *Brissot* Jacques-Pierre Brissot (1754–93), a French journalist and leader of the Girondists during the French Revolution, was executed by the Jacobins in 1793.

[2] *Minerva Press* Publishing company (1790–1820) that specialized in cheap, and many would say tasteless, novels.

of the imagination set in action by the feelings. If a poet is to describe a lion, he will not set about describing him as a naturalist would, nor even as a traveler would, who was intent upon stating the truth, the whole truth, and nothing but the truth. He will describe him by imagery, that is, by suggesting the most striking likenesses and contrasts which might occur to a mind contemplating the lion, in the state of awe, wonder, or terror, which the spectacle naturally excites, or is, on the occasion, supposed to excite. Now this is describing the lion professedly, but the state of excitement of the spectator really. The lion may be described falsely or in exaggerated colors, and the poetry be all the better; but if the human emotion be not painted with the most scrupulous truth, the poetry is bad poetry, i.e., is not poetry at all, but a failure.

Thus far our progress towards a clear view of the essentials of poetry has brought us very close to the last two attempts at a definition of poetry which we happen to have seen in print, both of them by poets and men of genius. The one is by Ebenezer Elliott, the author of *Corn-Law Rhymes*, and other poems of still greater merit. "Poetry," says he, "is impassioned truth."[1] The other is by a writer in *Blackwood's Magazine*, and comes, we think, still nearer the mark. We forget his exact words, but in substance he defined poetry as "man's thoughts tinged by his feelings." There is in either definition a near approximation to what we are in search of. Every truth which man can announce, every thought, even every outward impression, which can enter into his consciousness, may become poetry when shown through any impassioned medium, when invested with the coloring of joy, or grief, or pity, or affection, or admiration, or reverence, or awe, or even hatred or terror: and, unless so colored, nothing, be it as interesting as it may, is poetry. But both these definitions fail to discriminate between poetry and eloquence. Eloquence, as well as poetry, is impassioned truth; eloquence, as well as poetry, is thoughts colored by the feelings. Yet common apprehension and philosophic criticism alike recognize a distinction between the two: there is much that everyone would call eloquence, which no one would think of classing as poetry. A question will sometimes arise, whether some particular author is

a poet; and those who maintain the negative commonly allow, that though not a poet, he is a highly eloquent writer.

The distinction between poetry and eloquence appears to us to be equally fundamental with the distinction between poetry and narrative, or between poetry and description. It is still farther from having been satisfactorily cleared up than either of the others, unless, which is highly probable, the German artists and critics have thrown some light upon it which has not yet reached us. Without a perfect knowledge of what they have written, it is something like presumption to write upon such subjects at all, and we shall be the foremost to urge that, whatever we may be about to submit, may be received, subject to correction from them.

Poetry and eloquence are both alike the expression or uttering forth of feeling. But if we may be excused the seeming affectation of the antithesis, we should say that eloquence is *heard*, poetry is *over*heard. Eloquence supposes an audience; the peculiarity of poetry appears to us to lie in the poet's utter unconsciousness of a listener. Poetry is feeling confessing itself to itself, in moments of solitude, and bodying itself forth in symbols which are the nearest possible representations of the feeling in the exact shape in which it exists in the poet's mind. Eloquence is feeling pouring itself forth to other minds, courting their sympathy, or endeavoring to influence their belief, or move them to passion or to action.

All poetry is of the nature of soliloquy. It may be said that poetry, which is printed on hot-pressed paper, and sold at a bookseller's shop, is a soliloquy in full dress, and upon the stage. But there is nothing absurd in the idea of such a mode of soliloquizing. What we have said to ourselves, we may tell to others afterwards; what we have said or done in solitude, we may voluntarily reproduce when we know that other eyes are upon us. But no trace of consciousness that any eyes are upon us must be visible in the work itself. The actor knows that there is an audience present; but if he act as though he knew it, he acts ill. A poet may write poetry with the intention of publishing it; he may write it even for the express purpose of being paid for it; that it should be poetry, being written under any such influences, is far less probable; not, however, impossible; but not otherwise possible than if he can succeed in excluding from

---

[1] *"Poetry … truth"* See "Preface" to Elliot's *Corn-Law Rhymes* (1828).

his work every vestige of such lookings-forth into the outward and everyday world, and can express his feelings exactly as he has felt them in solitude, or as he feels that he should feel them, though they were to remain forever unuttered. But when he turns round and addresses himself to another person; when the act of utterance is not itself the end, but a means to an end—viz., by the feelings he himself expresses to work upon the feelings, or upon the belief, or the will of another—when the expression of his emotions, or of his thoughts, tinged by his emotions, is tinged also by that purpose, by that desire of making an impression upon another mind, then it ceases to be poetry, and becomes eloquence.

Poetry, accordingly, is the natural fruit of solitude and meditation; eloquence, of intercourse with the world. The persons who have most feeling of their own, if intellectual culture have given them a language in which to express it, have the highest faculty of poetry; those who best understand the feelings of others, are the most eloquent. The persons, and the nations, who commonly excel in poetry, are those whose character and tastes render them least dependent for their happiness upon the applause, or sympathy, or concurrence of the world in general. Those to whom that applause, that sympathy, that concurrence are most necessary, generally excel most in eloquence. And hence, perhaps, the French, who are the least poetical of all great and refined nations, are among the most eloquent: the French, also, being the most sociable, the vainest, and the least self-dependent.

If the above be, as we believe, the true theory of the distinction commonly admitted between eloquence and poetry; or though it be not that, yet if, as we cannot doubt, the distinction above stated be a real bona fide distinction, it will be found to hold, not merely in the language of words, but in all other language, and to intersect the whole domain of art.

Take, for example, music: we shall find in that art, so peculiarly the expression of passion, two perfectly distinct styles; one of which may be called the poetry, the other the oratory of music. This difference being seized would put an end to much musical sectarianism. There has been much contention whether the character of Rossini's music—the music, we mean, which is characteristic of that composer—is compatible with the

expression of passion. Without doubt, the passion it expresses is not the musing, meditative tenderness, or pathos, or grief of Mozart, the great poet of his art. Yet it is passion, but garrulous passion—the passion which pours itself into other ears; and therein the better calculated for dramatic effect, having a natural adaptation for dialogue. Mozart also is great in musical oratory; but his most touching compositions are in the opposite style—that of soliloquy. Who can imagine "*Dove sono*"[1] *heard?* We imagine it *over*-heard. The same is the case with many of the finest national airs. Who can hear those words, which speak so touchingly the sorrows of a mountaineer in exile:

> My heart's in the Highlands—my heart is not here;
> My heart's in the Highlands, a-chasing the deer,
> A-chasing the wild-deer, and following the roe—
> My heart's in the Highlands, wherever I go.[2]

Who can hear those affecting words, married to as affecting an air, and fancy that he sees the singer? That song has always seemed to us like the lament of a prisoner in a solitary cell, ourselves listening, unseen, in the next. As the direct opposite of this, take "Scots wha hae wi' Wallace bled,"[3] where the music is as oratorical as the poetry.

Purely pathetic music commonly partakes of soliloquy. The soul is absorbed in its distress, and though there may be bystanders, it is not thinking of them. When the mind is looking within and not without, its state does not often or rapidly vary; and hence the even, uninterrupted flow, approaching almost to monotony, which a good reader, or a good singer, will give to words or music of a pensive or melancholy cast. But grief, taking the form of a prayer, or of a complaint becomes oratorical; no longer low, and even, and subdued, it assumes a more emphatic rhythm, a more rapidly returning accent; instead of a few slow, equal notes, following one after another at regular intervals, it crowds note upon note, and oft-times assumes a hurry and bustle like joy. Those who are familiar with some of the best of Rossini's serious compositions, such as the air

---

[1] "*Dove sono*" From Mozart's *The Marriage of Figaro*, 1786.

[2] *My heart's ... Highlands* From a poem of the same name by Robert Burns (1798).

[3] "*Scots ... bled*" By Robert Burns (1793).

"*Tu che i miseri conforti*," in the opera of *Tancredi*, or the duet "*Ebben per mia memoria*," in *La Gazza Ladra*, will at once understand and feel our meaning. Both are highly tragic and passionate; the passion of both is that of oratory, not poetry. The like may be said of that most moving prayer in Beethoven's *Fidelio*, "*Komm, Hoffnung, lass das letzte Stern / Der Müde nicht erbleichen*";[1] in which Madame Devrient,[2] last summer, exhibited such consummate powers of pathetic expression. How different from Winter's beautiful "*Paga pii*,"[3] the very soul of melancholy exhaling itself in solitude; fuller of meaning, and, therefore, more profoundly poetical than the words for which it was composed—for it seems to express not simply melancholy, but the melancholy of remorse.

If, from vocal music, we now pass to instrumental, we may have a specimen of musical oratory in any fine military symphony or march: while the poetry of music seems to have attained its consummation in Beethoven's Overture to *Egmont*.[4] We question whether so deep an expression of mixed grandeur and melancholy was ever in any other instance produced by mere sounds.

In the arts which speak to the eye, the same distinctions will be found to hold, not only between poetry and oratory, but between poetry, oratory, narrative, and simple imitation or description.

Pure description is exemplified in a mere portrait or a mere landscape—productions of art, it is true, but of the mechanical rather than of the fine arts, being works of simple imitation, not creation. We say, a mere portrait, or a mere landscape, because it is possible for a portrait or a landscape, without ceasing to be such, to be also a picture. A portrait by Lawrence, or one of Turner's views,[5] is not a mere copy from nature: the one combines with the given features that particular expression (among all good and pleasing ones) which those features are most capable of wearing, and which, therefore, in combination with them, is capable of producing the greatest positive beauty. Turner, again, unites the objects of the given landscape with whatever sky, and whatever light and shade, enable those particular objects to impress the imagination most strongly. In both, there is creative art—not working after an actual model, but realizing an idea.

Whatever in painting or sculpture expresses human feeling, or character, which is only a certain state of feeling grown habitual, may be called, according to circumstances, the poetry or the eloquence of the painter's or the sculptor's art; the poetry, if the feeling declares itself by such signs as escape from us when we are unconscious of being seen; the oratory, if the signs are those we use for the purpose of voluntary communication.

The poetry of painting seems to be carried to its highest perfection in the *Peasant Girl* of Rembrandt,[6] or in any Madonna or Magdalen of Guido;[7] that of sculpture, in almost any of the Greek statues of the gods; not considering these in respect to the mere physical beauty, of which they are such perfect models, not undertaking either to vindicate or to contest the opinion of philosophers, that even physical beauty is ultimately resolvable into expression; we may safely affirm, that in no other of man's works did so much of soul ever shine through mere inanimate matter.

The narrative style answers to what is called historical painting, which it is the fashion among connoisseurs to treat as the climax of the pictorial art. That it is the most difficult branch of the art, we do not doubt, because, in its perfection, it includes, in a manner, the perfection of all the other branches. As an epic poem, though, insofar as it is epic (i.e., narrative), it is not poetry at all, is yet esteemed the greatest effort of poetic genius, because there is no kind whatever of poetry which may not appropriately find a place in it. But a historical picture, as such, that is, as the representation of an incident, must necessarily, as it seems to us, be poor and ineffective. The narrative powers of painting are extremely limited. Scarcely any picture, scarcely any series even of pictures, which we know of, tells its own story without the aid of an interpreter; you must know

---

[1] "*Komm ... erbleichen*" Beethoven's exact lines are "*Komm, Hoffnung, lass den letzten Stern / Der Müden nicht erbleichen*," which translate to "Come, Hope, do not let the last star of the weary fade away."

[2] *Madame Devrient* Famous opera singer Madame Wilhelmine Schröder-Devrient (1804–60).

[3] "*Paga pii*" Aria from Peter Winter's *Il ratto di Proserpina* (1804).

[4] *Egmont* Ludwig van Beethoven, Opus 84 (1809).

[5] *Lawrence* Sir Thomas Lawrence (1769–1830); *Turner* J.M.W. Turner (1755–1851).

[6] *Rembrandt* Rembrandt Harmenzoon Van Rijn (1606–69).

[7] *Guido* Guido Reni (1575–1642).

the story beforehand; then, indeed, you may see great beauty and appropriateness in the painting. But it is the single figures which, to us, are the great charm even of a historical picture. It is in these that the power of the art is really seen: in the attempt to narrate, visible and permanent signs are far behind the fugitive audible ones which follow so fast one after another, while the faces and figures in a narrative picture, even though they be Titian's,[1] stand still. Who would not prefer one *Virgin and Child* of Raphael,[2] to all the pictures which Rubens,[3] with his fat, frowzy Dutch Venuses, ever painted? Though Rubens, besides excelling almost everyone in his mastery over all the mechanical parts of his art, often shows real genius in grouping his figures, the peculiar problem of historical painting. But, then, who, except a mere student of drawing and coloring, ever cared to look twice at any of the figures themselves? The power of painting lies in poetry, of which Rubens had not the slightest tincture—not in narrative, where he might have excelled.

The single figures, however, in an historical picture, are rather the eloquence of painting than the poetry: they mostly (unless they are quite out of place in the picture) express the feelings of one person as modified by the presence of others. Accordingly the minds whose bent leads them rather to eloquence than to poetry, rush to historical painting. The French painters, for instance, seldom attempt, because they could make nothing of, single heads, like those glorious ones of the Italian masters, with which they might glut themselves day after day in their own Louvre. They must all be historical; and they are, almost to a man, attitudinizers. If we wished to give to any young artist the most impressive warning our imaginations could devise, against that kind of vice in the pictorial, which corresponds to rant in the histrionic art, we would advise him to walk once up and once down the gallery of the Luxembourg; even now when David,[4] the great corrupter of taste, has been translated from this world to the next, and from the Luxembourg, consequently, into the more elevated sphere of the Louvre. Every figure in French painting or statuary seems to be showing itself off before spectators: they are in the worst style of corrupted eloquence, but in no style of poetry at all. The best are stiff and unnatural; the worst resemble figures of cataleptic patients. The French artists fancy themselves imitators of the classics, yet they seem to have no understanding and no feeling of that repose which was the peculiar and pervading character of Grecian art, until it began to decline: a repose tenfold more indicative of strength than all their stretching and straining; for strength, as Thomas Carlyle says, does not manifest itself in spasms.

There are some productions of art which it seems at first difficult to arrange in any of the classes above illustrated. The direct aim of art as such, is the production of the beautiful; and as there are other things beautiful besides states of mind, there is much of art which may seem to have nothing to do with either poetry or eloquence as we have defined them. Take for instance a composition of Claude, or Salvator Rosa.[5] There is here creation of new beauty: by the grouping of natural scenery, conformably indeed to the laws of outward nature, but not after any actual model; the result being a beauty more perfect and faultless than is perhaps to be found in any actual landscape. Yet there is a character of poetry even in these, without which they could not be so beautiful. The unity, and wholeness, and aesthetic congruity of the picture still lies in singleness of expression; but it is expression in a different sense from that in which we have hitherto employed the term. The objects in an imaginary landscape cannot be said, like the words of a poem or the notes of a melody, to be the actual utterance of a feeling; but there must be some feeling with which they harmonize, and which they have a tendency to raise up in the spectator's mind. They must inspire a feeling of grandeur, a loveliness, a cheerfulness, a wildness, a melancholy, a terror. The painter must surround his principal objects with such imagery as would spontaneously arise in a highly imaginative mind, when contemplating those objects under the impression of the feelings which they are intended to inspire. This, if it be not poetry, is so nearly allied to it, as scarcely to require being distinguished.

In this sense we may speak of the poetry of architecture. All architecture, to be impressive, must be the expression or symbol of some interesting idea; some

---

[1] *Titian's*   Referring to the work of the Venetian painter Tiziano Vecellio (c. 1485–1576).

[2] *Raphael*   Raffaelo Sanzio (1483–1520).

[3] *Rubens*   Peter Paul Rubens (1577–1640).

[4] *David*   Jacques-Louis David (1748–1825).

[5] *Claude*   Claude Lorrain (c. 1600–82); *Salvator Rosa* (1615–73).

thought, which has power over the emotions. The reason why modern architecture is so paltry, is simply that it is not the expression of any idea; it is a mere parroting of the architectural tongue of the Greeks, or of our Teutonic ancestors, without any conception of a meaning.

To confine ourselves, for the present, to religious edifices: these partake of poetry, in proportion as they express, or harmonize with, the feelings of devotion. But those feelings are different according to the conception entertained of the beings, by whose supposed nature they are called forth. To the Greek, these beings were incarnations of the greatest conceivable physical beauty, combined with supernatural power: and the Greek temples express this, their predominant character being graceful strength; in other words, solidity, which is power, and lightness which is also power, accomplishing with small means what seemed to require great; to combine all in one word, *majesty*. To the Catholic, again, the Deity was something far less clear and definite; a being of still more resistless power than the heathen divinities; greatly to be loved; still more greatly to be feared; and wrapped up in vagueness, mystery, and incomprehensibility. A certain solemnity, a feeling of doubting and trembling hope, like that of one lost in a boundless forest who thinks he knows his way but is not sure, mixes in all the genuine expressions of Catholic devotion. This is eminently the expression of the pure Gothic cathedral; conspicuous equally in the mingled majesty and gloom of its vaulted roofs and stately aisles, and in the "dim religious light" which steals through its painted windows.

There is no generic distinction between the imagery which is the expression of feeling and the imagery which is felt to harmonize with feeling. They are identical. The imagery in which feeling utters itself forth from within, is also that in which it delights when presented to it from without. All art, therefore, in proportion as it produces its effects by an appeal to the emotions partakes of poetry, unless it partakes of oratory, or of narrative. And the distinction which these three words indicate, runs through the whole field of the fine arts.

The above hints have no pretension to the character of a theory. They are merely thrown out for the consideration of thinkers, in the hope that if they do not contain the truth, they may do somewhat to suggest it.

Nor would they, crude as they are, have been deemed worthy of publication, in any country but one in which the philosophy of art is so completely neglected, that whatever may serve to put any inquiring mind upon this kind of investigation, cannot well, however imperfect in itself, fail altogether to be of use.

—1833

from *The Subjection of Women*

CHAPTER I

If people are mostly so little aware how completely, during the greater part of the duration of our species, the law of force was the avowed rule of general conduct, any other being only a special and exceptional consequence of peculiar ties—and from how very recent a date it is that the affairs of society in general have been even pretended to be regulated according to any moral law; as little do people remember or consider, how institutions and customs which never had any ground but the law of force, last on into ages and states of general opinion which never would have permitted their first establishment. Less than forty years ago, Englishmen might still by law hold human beings in bondage as saleable property: within the present century they might kidnap them and carry them off, and work them literally to death. This absolutely extreme case of the law of force, condemned by those who can tolerate almost every other form of arbitrary power, and which, of all others, presents features the most revolting to the feelings of all who look at it from an impartial position, was the law of civilized and Christian England within the memory of persons now living: and in one half of Anglo-Saxon America three or four years ago, not only did slavery exist, but the slave trade, and the breeding of slaves expressly for it, was a general practice between slave states. Yet not only was there a greater strength of sentiment against it, but, in England at least, a less amount either of feeling or of interest in favour of it, than of any other of the customary abuses of force: for its motive was the love of gain, unmixed and undisguised; and those who profited by it were a very small numerical fraction of the country, while the natural feeling of all who were not personally interested in it, was unmitigated abhorrence. So extreme an instance makes it almost superfluous to refer to any other: but consider the long duration of absolute monarchy. In England at present it is the almost universal conviction that military despotism is a case of the law of force, having no other origin or justification. Yet in all the great nations of Europe except England it either still exists, or has only just ceased to exist, and has even now a strong party favourable to it in all ranks of the people, especially among persons of station and consequence. Such is the power of an established system, even when far from universal; when not only in almost every period of history there have been great and well-known examples of the contrary system, but these have almost invariably been afforded by the most illustrious and most prosperous communities. In this case, too, the possessor of the undue power, the person directly interested in it, is only one person, while those who are subject to it and suffer from it are literally all the rest. The yoke is naturally and necessarily humiliating to all persons, except the one who is on the throne, together with, at most, the one who expects to succeed to it. How different are these cases from that of the power of men over women! I am not now prejudging the question of its justifiableness. I am showing how vastly more permanent it could not but be, even if not justifiable, than these other dominations which have nevertheless lasted down to our own time. Whatever gratification of pride there is in the possession of power, and whatever personal interest in its exercise, is in this case not confined to a limited class, but common to the whole male sex. Instead of being, to most of its supporters, a thing desirable chiefly in the abstract, or, like the political ends usually contended for by factions, of little private importance to any but the leaders; it comes home to the person and hearth of every male head of a family, and of everyone who looks forward to being so. The clodhopper exercises, or is to exercise, his share of the power equally with the highest nobleman. And the case is that in which the desire of power is the strongest: for everyone who desires power, desires it most over those who are nearest to him, with whom his life is passed, with whom he has most concerns in common, and in whom any independence of his authority is oftenest likely to interfere with his individual preferences. If, in the other cases specified, powers manifestly grounded only on force, and having so much less to support them, are so slowly and with so much difficulty got rid of, much more must it be so with this, even if it rests on no better foundation than those. We must consider, too, that the possessors of the power have facilities in this case, greater than in any other, to prevent any uprising against it. Every one of the subjects lives under the very eye, and almost, it may be said, in the hands, of one of the masters—in closer intimacy with him than with any of her fellow-subjects; with no means of combining against him, no power of even locally overmastering him, and, on the other hand, with the strongest motives for seeking his favour and avoiding to give him offence. In struggles for political emancipation, everybody knows how often its champions are bought off by bribes, or daunted by terrors. In the case of women, each individual of the subject-class is in a chronic state of bribery and intimidation combined. In setting up the standard of resistance, a large number of the leaders, and still more of the followers, must make an almost complete sacrifice of the pleasures or the alleviations of their own individual lot. If ever any system of privilege and enforced subjection had its yoke tightly riveted on the necks of those who are kept down by it, this has. I have not yet shown that it is a wrong system: but everyone who is capable of thinking on the subject must see that even if it is, it was certain to outlast all other forms of unjust authority. And when some of the grossest of the other forms still exist in many civilized countries, and have only recently been got rid of in others, it would be strange if that which is so much the deepest rooted had yet been perceptibly shaken anywhere. There is more reason to wonder that the protests and testimonies against it should have been so numerous and so weighty as they are.

Some will object, that a comparison cannot fairly be made between the government of the male sex and the forms of unjust power which I have adduced in illustration of it, since these are arbitrary, and the effect of mere usurpation, while it on the contrary is natural. But was there ever any domination which did not appear natural to those who possessed it? There was a time when the division of mankind into two classes, a small one of masters and a numerous one of slaves, appeared, even to the most cultivated minds, to be a natural, and the only natural, condition of the human race. No less an intellect, and one which contributed no less to the progress of human thought, than Aristotle,[1] held this opinion without doubt or misgiving; and rested it on the same premises on which the same assertion in regard to the dominion of men over women is usually based, namely that there are different natures among mankind, free natures, and slave natures; that the Greeks were of a free nature, the barbarian races of Thracians[2] and Asiatics of a slave nature. But why need I go back to Aristotle? Did not the slaveowners of the Southern United States maintain the same doctrine, with all the fanaticism with which men cling to the theories that justify their passions and legitimate their personal interests? Did they not call heaven and earth to witness that the dominion of the white man over the black is natural, that the black race is by nature incapable of freedom, and marked out for slavery? some even going so far as to say that the freedom of manual labourers is an unnatural order of things anywhere. Again, the theorists of absolute monarchy have always affirmed it to be the only natural form of government; issuing from the patriarchal, which was the primitive and spontaneous form of society, framed on the model of the paternal, which is anterior to society itself, and, as they contend, the most natural authority of all. Nay, for that matter, the law of force itself, to those who could not plead any other, has always seemed the most natural of all grounds for the exercise of authority. Conquering races hold it to be Nature's own dictate that the conquered should obey the conquerors, or, as they euphoniously paraphrase it, that the feebler and more unwarlike races should submit to the braver and manlier. The smallest acquaintance with human life in the middle ages, shows how supremely natural the dominion of the feudal nobility over men of low condition appeared to the nobility themselves, and how unnatural the conception seemed, of a person of the inferior class claiming equality with them, or exercising authority over them. It hardly seemed less so to the class held in subjection. The emancipated serfs and burgesses, even in their most vigorous struggles, never made any pretension to a share of authority; they only demanded more or less of limitation to the power of tyrannizing over them. So true is it that unnatural generally means

only uncustomary, and that everything which is usual appears natural. The subjection of women to men being a universal custom, any departure from it quite naturally appears unnatural. But how entirely, even in this case, the feeling is dependent on custom, appears by ample experience. Nothing so much astonishes the people of distant parts of the world, when they first learn anything about England, as to be told that it is under a queen: the thing seems to them so unnatural as to be almost incredible. To Englishmen this does not seem in the least degree unnatural, because they are used to it; but they do feel it unnatural that women should be soldiers or members of parliament. In the feudal ages, on the contrary, war and politics were not thought unnatural to women, because not unusual; it seemed natural that women of the privileged classes should be of manly character, inferior in nothing but bodily strength to their husbands and fathers. The independence of women seemed rather less unnatural to the Greeks than to other ancients, on account of the fabulous Amazons[3] (whom they believed to be historical), and the partial example afforded by the Spartan women; who, though no less subordinate by law than in other Greek states, were more free in fact, and being trained to bodily exercises in the same manner with men, gave ample proof that they were not naturally disqualified for them. There can be little doubt that Spartan experience suggested to Plato,[4] among many other of his doctrines, that of the social and political equality of the two sexes.

But, it will be said, the rule of men over women differs from all these others in not being a rule of force: it is accepted voluntarily; women make no complaint, and are consenting parties to it. In the first place, a great number of women do not accept it. Ever since there have been women able to make their sentiments known by their writings (the only mode of publicity which society permits to them), an increasing number of them have recorded protests against their present social condition: and recently many thousands of them, headed by the most eminent women known to the public, have petitioned parliament for their admission to the Parliamentary Suffrage.[5] The claim of women to

[1] *Aristotle* See Aristotle's *Politics*.

[2] *Thracians* A warring group of tribes, the Thracians occupied the area north of Greece from 700 BCE to 4 CE.

[3] *Amazons* A race of women warriors.

[4] *Plato* See Plato's *The Republic*, 5.

[5] *petitioned ... Parliamentary Suffrage* Mill himself also introduced such a petition to the House of Commons in 1866.

be educated as solidly, and in the same branches of knowledge, as men, is urged with growing intensity, and with a great prospect of success; while the demand for their admission into professions and occupations hitherto closed against them, becomes every year more urgent. Though there are not in this country, as there are in the United States, periodical Conventions and an organized party to agitate for the Rights of Women, there is a numerous and active Society organized and managed by women, for the more limited object of obtaining the political franchise. Nor is it only in our own country and in America that women are beginning to protest, more or less collectively, against the disabilities under which they labour. France, and Italy, and Switzerland, and Russia now afford examples of the same thing. How many more women there are who silently cherish similar aspirations, no one can possibly know; but there are abundant tokens how many *would* cherish them, were they not so strenuously taught to repress them as contrary to the proprieties of their sex. It must be remembered, also, that no enslaved class ever asked for complete liberty at once. When Simon de Montfort[1] called the deputies of the commons to sit for the first time in parliament, did any of them dream of demanding that an assembly, elected by their constituents, should make and destroy ministries, and dictate to the king in affairs of state? No such thought entered into the imagination of the most ambitious of them. The nobility had already these pretensions; the commons pretended to nothing but to be exempt from arbitrary taxation, and from the gross individual oppression of the king's officers. It is a political law of nature that those who are under any power of ancient origin, never begin by complaining of the power itself, but only of its oppressive exercise. There is never any want of women who complain of ill usage by their husbands. There would be infinitely more, if complaint were not the greatest of all provocatives to a repetition and increase of the ill usage. It is this which frustrates all attempts to maintain the power but protect the woman against its abuses. In no other case (except that of a child) is the person who has been proved judicially to have suffered an injury, replaced under the physical power of the culprit who inflicted it. Accordingly wives, even in the most extreme and protracted cases of bodily ill usage, hardly ever dare avail themselves of the laws made for their protection: and if, in a moment of irrepressible indignation, or by the interference of neighbours, they are induced to do so, their whole effort afterwards is to disclose as little as they can, and to beg off their tyrant from his merited chastisement.

All causes, social and natural, combine to make it unlikely that women should be collectively rebellious to the power of men. They are so far in a position different from all other subject classes, that their masters require something more from them than actual service. Men do not want solely the obedience of women, they want their sentiments. All men, except the most brutish, desire to have, in the woman most nearly connected with them, not a forced slave but a willing one, not a slave merely, but a favourite. They have therefore put everything in practice to enslave their minds. The masters of all other slaves rely, for maintaining obedience, on fear; either fear of themselves, or religious fears. The masters of women wanted more than simple obedience, and they turned the whole force of education to effect their purpose. All women are brought up from the very earliest years in the belief that their ideal of character is the very opposite to that of men; not self-will, and government by self-control, but submission, and yielding to the control of others. All the moralities tell them that it is the duty of women, and all the current sentimentalities that it is their nature, to live for others; to make complete abnegation of themselves, and to have no life but in their affections. And by their affections are meant the only ones they are allowed to have—those to the men with whom they are connected, or to the children who constitute an additional and indefeasible tie between them and a man. When we put together three things—first, the natural attraction between opposite sexes; secondly, the wife's entire dependence on the husband, every privilege or pleasure she has being either his gift, or depending entirely on his will; and lastly, that the principal object of human pursuit, consideration, and all objects of social ambition, can in general be sought or obtained by her only through him, it would be a miracle if the object of being attractive to men had not become the polar star of feminine education and formation of character. And,

---

[1] *Simon de Montfort* The Earl of Leicester (c. 1208–65) led a baronial revolt against Henry III and subsequently established a newly representative Parliament.

this great means of influence over the minds of women having been acquired, an instinct of selfishness made men avail themselves of it to the utmost as a means of holding women in subjection, by representing to them meekness, submissiveness, and resignation of all individual will into the hands of a man, as an essential part of sexual attractiveness. Can it be doubted that any of the other yokes which mankind have succeeded in breaking, would have subsisted till now if the same means had existed, and had been so sedulously used, to bow down their minds to it? If it had been made the object of the life of every young plebeian to find personal favour in the eyes of some patrician, of every young serf with some seigneur;[1] if domestication with him, and a share of his personal affections, had been held out as the prize which they all should look out for, the most gifted and aspiring being able to reckon on the most desirable prizes; and if, when this prize had been obtained, they had been shut out by a wall of brass from all interests not centering in him, all feelings and desires but those which he shared or inculcated; would not serfs and seigneurs, plebeians and patricians, have been as broadly distinguished at this day as men and women are? and would not all but a thinker here and there, have believed the distinction to be a fundamental and unalterable fact in human nature?

The preceding considerations are amply sufficient to show that custom, however universal it may be, affords in this case no presumption, and ought not to create any prejudice, in favour of the arrangements which place women in social and political subjection to men. But I may go farther, and maintain that the course of history, and the tendencies of progressive human society, afford not only no presumption in favour of this system of inequality of rights, but a strong one against it; and that, so far as the whole course of human improvement up to this time, the whole stream of modern tendencies, warrants any inference on the subject, it is, that this relic of the past is discordant with the future, and must necessarily disappear.

For, what is the peculiar character of the modern world—the difference which chiefly distinguishes modern institutions, modern social ideas, modern life itself, from those of times long past? It is, that human beings are no longer born to their place in life, and chained down by an inexorable bond to the place they are born to, but are free to employ their faculties, and such favourable chances as offer, to achieve the lot which may appear to them most desirable. Human society of old was constituted on a very different principle. All were born to a fixed social position, and were mostly kept in it by law, or interdicted from any means by which they could emerge from it. As some men are born white and others black, so some were born slaves and others freemen and citizens; some were born patricians, others plebeians; some were born feudal nobles, others commoners and *roturiers*.[2] A slave or serf could never make himself free, nor, except by the will of his master, become so. In most European countries it was not till towards the close of the middle ages, and as a consequence of the growth of regal power, that commoners could be ennobled. Even among nobles, the eldest son was born the exclusive heir to the paternal possessions, and a long time elapsed before it was fully established that the father could disinherit him. Among the industrious classes, only those who were born members of a guild, or were admitted into it by its members, could lawfully practise their calling within its local limits; and nobody could practise any calling deemed important, in any but the legal manner—by processes authoritatively prescribed. Manufacturers have stood in the pillory[3] for presuming to carry on their business by new and improved methods. In modern Europe, and most in those parts of it which have participated most largely in all other modern improvements, diametrically opposite doctrines now prevail. Law and government do not undertake to prescribe by whom any social or industrial operation shall or shall not be conducted, or what modes of conducting them shall be lawful. These things are left to the unfettered choice of individuals. Even the laws which required that workmen should serve an apprenticeship, have in this country been repealed: there being ample assurance that in all cases in which an apprenticeship is necessary, its necessity will suffice to enforce it. The old theory was, that the least possible should be left to the choice of the individual agent; that all he had to do should, as far as

---

[1] *plebeian* Commoner; *patrician* Aristocrat; *serf* Laborer in a condition of servitude; *seigneur* Feudal lord.

[2] *roturiers* Commoners who owned land in feudal times.

[3] *pillory* Wooden framework in which wrongdoers were locked and exposed to public derision.

practicable, be laid down for him by superior wisdom. Left to himself he was sure to go wrong. The modern conviction, the fruit of a thousand years of experience, is, that things in which the individual is the person directly interested, never go right but as they are left to his own discretion; and that any regulation of them by authority, except to protect the rights of others, is sure to be mischievous. This conclusion, slowly arrived at, and not adopted until almost every possible application of the contrary theory had been made with disastrous result, now (in the industrial department) prevails universally in the most advanced countries, almost universally in all that have pretensions to any sort of advancement. It is not that all processes are supposed to be equally good, or all persons to be equally qualified for everything; but that freedom of individual choice is now known to be the only thing which procures the adoption of the best processes, and throws each operation into the hands of those who are best qualified for it. Nobody thinks it necessary to make a law that only a strong-armed man shall be a blacksmith. Freedom and competition suffice to make blacksmiths strong-armed men, because the weak-armed can earn more by engaging in occupations for which they are more fit. In consonance with this doctrine, it is felt to be an over-stepping of the proper bounds of authority to fix beforehand, on some general presumption, that certain persons are not fit to do certain things. It is now thoroughly known and admitted that if some such presumptions exist, no such presumption is infallible. Even if it be well grounded in a majority of cases, which it is very likely not to be, there will be a minority of exceptional cases in which it does not hold: and in those it is both an injustice to the individuals, and a detriment to society, to place barriers in the way of their using their faculties for their own benefit and for that of others. In the cases, on the other hand, in which the unfitness is real, the ordinary motives of human conduct will on the whole suffice to prevent the incompetent person from making, or from persisting in, the attempt.

If this general principle of social and economical science is not true; if individuals, with such help as they can derive from the opinion of those who know them, are not better judges than the law and the government, of their own capacities and vocation; the world cannot too soon abandon this principle, and return to the old system of regulations and disabilities. But if the principle is true, we ought to act as if we believed it, and not to ordain that to be born a girl instead of a boy, any more than to be born black instead of white, or a commoner instead of a nobleman, shall decide the person's position through all life—shall interdict people from all the more elevated social positions, and from all, except a few, respectable occupations. Even were we to admit the utmost that is ever pretended as to the superior fitness of men for all the functions now reserved to them, the same argument applies which forbids a legal qualification for members of parliament. If only once in a dozen years the conditions of eligibility exclude a fit person, there is a real loss, while the exclusion of thousands of unfit persons is no gain; for if the constitution of the electoral body disposes them to choose unfit persons, there are always plenty of such persons to choose from. In all things of any difficulty and importance, those who can do them well are fewer than the need, even with the most unrestricted latitude of choice: and any limitation of the field of selection deprives society of some chances of being served by the competent, without ever saving it from the incompetent.

At present, in the more improved countries, the disabilities of women are the only case, save one, in which laws and institutions take persons at their birth, and ordain that they shall never in all their lives be allowed to compete for certain things. The one exception is that of royalty. Persons still are born to the throne; no one, not of the reigning family, can ever occupy it, and no one even of that family can, by any means but the course of hereditary succession, attain it. All other dignities and social advantages are open to the whole male sex: many indeed are only attainable by wealth, but wealth may be striven for by anyone, and is actually obtained by many men of the very humblest origin. The difficulties, to the majority, are indeed insuperable without the aid of fortunate accidents; but no male human being is under any legal ban: neither law nor opinion superadd artificial obstacles to the natural ones. Royalty, as I have said, is excepted: but in this case everyone feels it to be an exception—an anomaly in the modern world, in marked opposition to its customs and principles, and to be justified only by extraordinary special expediencies, which, though individuals and nations differ in estimating their weight, unquestionably do in fact exist. But in this exceptional case, in which a high social function is, for important reasons, bestowed on birth instead of being put up to competition, all free nations contrive to adhere in substance to the principle from which they nominally derogate; for they circumscribe this high function by conditions avowedly intended to prevent the person to whom it ostensibly belongs from really performing it; while the person by whom it is performed, the responsible minister, does obtain the post by a competition from which no full-grown citizen of the male sex is legally excluded. The disabilities, therefore, to which women are subject from the mere fact of their birth, are the solitary examples of the kind in modern legislation. In no instance except this, which comprehends half the human race, are the higher social functions closed against anyone by a fatality of birth which no exertions, and no change of circumstances, can overcome; for even religious disabilities (besides that in England and in Europe they have practically almost ceased to exist) do not close any career to the disqualified person in case of conversion.

The social subordination of women thus stands out an isolated fact in modern social institutions; a solitary breach of what has become their fundamental law; a single relic of an old world of thought and practice exploded in everything else, but retained in the one thing of most universal interest; as if a gigantic dolmen,[1] or a vast temple of Jupiter Olympius, occupied the site of St. Paul's and received daily worship, while the surrounding Christian churches were only resorted to on fasts and festivals. This entire discrepancy between one social fact and all those which accompany it, and the radical opposition between its nature and the progressive movement which is the boast of the modern world, and which has successively swept away everything else of an analogous character, surely affords, to a conscientious observer of human tendencies, serious matter for reflection. It raises a *prima facie*[2] presumption on the unfavourable side, far outweighing any which custom and usage could in such circumstances create on the favourable; and should at least suffice to make this, like the choice between republicanism and royalty, a balanced question.

The least that can be demanded is, that the question should not be considered as prejudged by existing fact and existing opinion, but open to discussion on its merits, as a question of justice and expediency: the decision on this, as on any of the other social arrangements of mankind, depending on what an enlightened estimate of tendencies and consequences may show to be most advantageous to humanity in general, without distinction of sex. And the discussion must be a real discussion, descending to foundations, and not resting satisfied with vague and general assertions. It will not do, for instance, to assert in general terms, that the experience of mankind has pronounced in favour of the existing system. Experience cannot possibly have decided between two courses, so long as there has only been experience of one. If it be said that the doctrine of the equality of the sexes rests only on theory, it must be remembered that the contrary doctrine also has only theory to rest upon. All that is proved in its favour by direct experience, is that mankind have been able to exist under it, and to attain the degree of improvement and prosperity which we now see; but whether that prosperity has been attained sooner, or is now greater, than it would have been under the other system, experience does not say. On the other hand, experience does say, that every step in improvement has been so invariably accompanied by a step made in raising the social position of women, that historians and philosophers have been led to adopt their elevation or debasement as on the whole the surest test and most correct measure of the civilization of a people or an age. Through all the progressive period of human history, the condition of women has been approaching nearer to equality with men. This does not of itself prove that the assimilation must go on to complete equality; but it assuredly affords some presumption that such is the case.

Neither does it avail anything to say that the *nature* of the two sexes adapts them to their present functions and position, and renders these appropriate to them. Standing on the ground of common sense and the constitution of the human mind, I deny that anyone knows, or can know, the nature of the two sexes, as long as they have only been seen in their present relation to one another. If men had ever been found in society without women, or women without men, or if there had been a society of men and women in which the women

---

[1] *dolmen* Celtic monument associated with pagan rituals.

[2] *prima facie* Latin: arising at first sight.

were not under the control of the men, something might have been positively known about the mental and moral differences which may be inherent in the nature of each. What is now called the nature of women is an eminently artificial thing—the result of forced repression in some directions, unnatural stimulation in others. It may be asserted without scruple, that no other class of dependents have had their character so entirely distorted from its natural proportions by their relation with their masters; for, if conquered and slave races have been, in some respects, more forcibly repressed, whatever in them has not been crushed down by an iron heel has generally been let alone, and if left with any liberty of development, it has developed itself according to its own laws; but in the case of women, a hot-house and stove cultivation has always been carried on of some of the capabilities of their nature, for the benefit and pleasure of their masters. Then, because certain products of the general vital force sprout luxuriantly and reach a great development in this heated atmosphere and under this active nurture and watering, while other shoots from the same root, which are left outside in the wintry air, with ice purposely heaped all round them, have a stunted growth, and some are burnt off with fire and disappear; men, with that inability to recognise their own work which distinguishes the unanalytic mind, indolently believe that the tree grows of itself in the way they have made it grow, and that it would die if one half of it were not kept in a vapour bath and the other half in the snow.

Of all difficulties which impede the progress of thought, and the formation of well-grounded opinions on life and social arrangements, the greatest is now the unspeakable ignorance and inattention of mankind in respect to the influences which form human character. Whatever any portion of the human species now are, or seem to be, such, it is supposed, they have a natural tendency to be: even when the most elementary knowledge of the circumstances in which they have been placed, clearly points out the causes that made them what they are. Because a cottier[1] deeply in arrears to his landlord is not industrious, there are people who think that the Irish are naturally idle. Because constitutions can be overthrown when the authorities appointed to execute them turn their arms against them, there are

people who think the French incapable of free government. Because the Greeks cheated the Turks, and the Turks only plundered the Greeks, there are persons who think that the Turks are naturally more sincere: and because women, as is often said, care nothing about politics except their personalities, it is supposed that the general good is naturally less interesting to women than to men. History, which is now so much better understood than formerly, teaches another lesson: if only by showing the extraordinary susceptibility of human nature to external influences, and the extreme variableness of those of its manifestations which are supposed to be most universal and uniform. But in history, as in travelling, men usually see only what they already had in their own minds; and few learn much from history, who do not bring much with them to its study.

Hence, in regard to that most difficult question, what are the natural differences between the two sexes—a subject on which it is impossible in the present state of society to obtain complete and correct knowledge—while almost everybody dogmatizes upon it, almost all neglect and make light of the only means by which any partial insight can be obtained into it. This is, an analytic study of the most important department of psychology, the laws of the influence of circumstances on character. For, however great and apparently ineradicable the moral and intellectual differences between men and women might be, the evidence of there being natural differences could only be negative. Those only could be inferred to be natural which could not possibly be artificial—the residuum, after deducting every characteristic of either sex which can admit of being explained from education or external circumstances. The profoundest knowledge of the laws of the formation of character is indispensable to entitle anyone to affirm even that there is any difference, much more what the difference is, between the two sexes considered as moral and rational beings; and since no one, as yet, has that knowledge (for there is hardly any subject which, in proportion to its importance, has been so little studied), no one is thus far entitled to any positive opinion on the subject. Conjectures are all that can at present be made; conjectures more or less probable, according as more or less authorized by such knowledge as we yet have of the laws of psychology, as applied to the formation of character.

---

[1]   *cottier*   Tenant who rents a cottage and often works for a landlord in return.

Even the preliminary knowledge, what the differences between the sexes now are, apart from all question as to how they are made what they are, is still in the crudest and most incomplete state. Medical practitioners and physiologists have ascertained, to some extent, the differences in bodily constitution; and this is an important element to the psychologist: but hardly any medical practitioner is a psychologist. Respecting the mental characteristics of women; their observations are of no more worth than those of common men. It is a subject on which nothing final can be known, so long as those who alone can really know it, women themselves, have given but little testimony, and that little, mostly suborned. It is easy to know stupid women. Stupidity is much the same all the world over. A stupid person's notions and feelings may confidently be inferred from those which prevail in the circle by which the person is surrounded. Not so with those whose opinions and feelings are an emanation from their own nature and faculties. It is only a man here and there who has any tolerable knowledge of the character even of the women of his own family. I do not mean, of their capabilities; these nobody knows, not even themselves, because most of them have never been called out. I mean their actually existing thoughts and feelings. Many a man thinks he perfectly understands women, because he has had amatory relations with several, perhaps with many of them. If he is a good observer, and his experience extends to quality as well as quantity, he may have learnt something of one narrow department of their nature—an important department, no doubt. But of all the rest of it, few persons are generally more ignorant, because there are few from whom it is so carefully hidden. The most favourable case which a man can generally have for studying the character of a woman, is that of his own wife: for the opportunities are greater, and the cases of complete sympathy not so unspeakably rare. And in fact, this is the source from which any knowledge worth having on the subject has, I believe, generally come. But most men have not had the opportunity of studying in this way more than a single case: accordingly one can, to an almost laughable degree, infer what a man's wife is like, from his opinions about women in general. To make even this one case yield any result, the woman must be worth knowing, and the man not only a competent judge, but of a character so sympathetic in itself, and so well adapted to hers, that he can either read her mind by sympathetic intuition, or has nothing in himself which makes her shy of disclosing it. Hardly anything, I believe, can be more rare than this conjunction. It often happens that there is the most complete unity of feeling and community of interests as to all external things, yet the one has as little admission into the internal life of the other as if they were common acquaintance. Even with true affection, authority on the one side and subordination on the other prevent perfect confidence. Though nothing may be intentionally withheld, much is not shown. In the analogous relation of parent and child, the corresponding phenomenon must have been in the observation of everyone. As between father and son, how many are the cases in which the father, in spite of real affection on both sides, obviously to all the world does not know, nor suspect, parts of the son's character familiar to his companions and equals. The truth is, that the position of looking up to another is extremely unpropitious to complete sincerity and openness with him. The fear of losing ground in his opinion or in his feelings is so strong, that even in an upright character, there is an unconscious tendency to show only the best side, or the side which, though not the best, is that which he most likes to see: and it may be confidently said that thorough knowledge of one another hardly ever exists, but between persons who, besides being intimates, are equals. How much more true, then, must all this be, when the one is not only under the authority of the other, but has it inculcated on her as a duty to reckon everything else subordinate to his comfort and pleasure, and to let him neither see nor feel anything coming from her, except what is agreeable to him. All these difficulties stand in the way of a man's obtaining any thorough knowledge even of the one woman whom alone, in general, he has sufficient opportunity of studying. When we further consider that to understand one woman is not necessarily to understand any other woman; that even if he could study many women of one rank, or of one country, he would not thereby understand women of other ranks or countries; and even if he did, they are still only the women of a single period of history; we may safely assert that the knowledge which men can acquire of women, even as they have been and are, without reference to what they might be, is wretchedly imperfect and superficial, and always will be so, until women themselves have told all that they have to tell.

And this time has not come; nor will it come otherwise than gradually. It is but of yesterday that women have either been qualified by literary accomplishments or permitted by society, to tell anything to the general public. As yet very few of them dare tell anything, which men, on whom their literary success depends, are unwilling to hear. Let us remember in what manner, up to a very recent time, the expression, even by a male author, of uncustomary opinions, or what are deemed eccentric feelings, usually was, and in some degree still is, received; and we may form some faint conception under what impediments a woman, who is brought up to think custom and opinion her sovereign rule, attempts to express in books anything drawn from the depths of her own nature. The greatest woman who has left writings behind her sufficient to give her an eminent rank in the literature of her country, thought it necessary to prefix as a motto to her boldest work, "Un homme peut braver l'opinion; une femme doit s'y soumettre."[1] The greater part of what women write about women is mere sycophancy to men. In the case of unmarried women, much of it seems only intended to increase their chance of a husband. Many, both married and unmarried, overstep the mark, and inculcate a servility beyond what is desired or relished by any man, except the very vulgarest. But this is not so often the case as, even at a quite late period, it still was. Literary women are becoming more freespoken, and more willing to express their real sentiments. Unfortunately, in this country especially, they are themselves such artificial products, that their sentiments are compounded of a small element of individual observation and consciousness, and a very large one of acquired associations. This will be less and less the case, but it will remain true to a great extent, as long as social institutions do not admit the same free development of originality in women which is possible to men. When that time comes, and not before, we shall see, and not merely hear, as much as it is necessary to know of the nature of women, and the adaptation of other things to it.

I have dwelt so much on the difficulties which at present obstruct any real knowledge by men of the true nature of women, because in this as in so many other things "opinio copiæ inter maximas causas inopiæ est;"[2] and there is little chance of reasonable thinking on the matter, while people flatter themselves that they perfectly understand a subject of which most men know absolutely nothing, and of which it is at present impossible that any man, or all men taken together, should have knowledge which can qualify them to lay down the law to women as to what is, or is not, their vocation. Happily, no such knowledge is necessary for any practical purpose connected with the position of women in relation to society and life. For, according to all the principles involved in modern society, the question rests with women themselves—to be decided by their own experience, and by the use of their own faculties. There are no means of finding what either one person or many can do, but by trying—and no means by which anyone else can discover for them what it is for their happiness to do or leave undone.

One thing we may be certain of—that what is contrary to women's nature to do, they never will be made to do by simply giving their nature free play. The anxiety of mankind to interfere in behalf of nature, for fear lest nature should not succeed in effecting its purpose, is an altogether unnecessary solicitude. What women by nature cannot do, it is quite superfluous to forbid them from doing. What they can do, but not so well as the men who are their competitors, competition suffices to exclude them from; since nobody asks for protective duties and bounties in favour of women; it is only asked that the present bounties and protective duties in favour of men should be recalled. If women have a greater natural inclination for some things than for others, there is no need of laws or social inculcation to make the majority of them do the former in preference to the latter. Whatever women's services are most wanted for, the free play of competition will hold out the strongest inducements to them to undertake. And, as the words imply, they are most wanted for the things for which they are most fit; by the apportionment of which to them, the collective faculties of the two sexes

---

[1] [Mill's note] Title-page of Mme. de Staël's *Delphine*. [The French novelist's (1766–1817) words translate as: "A man can brave (public) opinion; a woman must submit to it."]

[2] *"opinio copiæ … inopiæ est"* Latin: "The belief in sufficiency is one of the greatest causes of insufficiency."

can be applied on the whole with the greatest sum of valuable result.

The general opinion of men is supposed to be, that the natural vocation of a woman is that of a wife and mother. I say, is supposed to be, because, judging from acts—from the whole of the present constitution of society—one might infer that their opinion was the direct contrary. They might be supposed to think that the alleged natural vocation of women was of all things the most repugnant to their nature; insomuch that if they are free to do anything else—if any other means of living, or occupation of their time and faculties, is open, which has any chance of appearing desirable to them—there will not be enough of them who will be willing to accept the condition said to be natural to them. If this is the real opinion of men in general, it would be well that it should be spoken out. I should like to hear somebody openly enunciating the doctrine (it is already implied in much that is written on the subject)—"It is necessary to society that women should marry and produce children. They will not do so unless they are compelled. Therefore it is necessary to compel them." The merits of the case would then be clearly defined. It would be exactly that of the slaveholders of South Carolina and Louisiana. "It is necessary that cotton and sugar should be grown. White men cannot produce them. Negroes will not, for any wages which we choose to give. *Ergo* they must be compelled." An illustration still closer to the point is that of impressment.[1] Sailors must absolutely be had to defend the country. It often happens that they will not voluntarily enlist. Therefore there must be the power of forcing them. How often has this logic been used! and, but for one flaw in it, without doubt it would have been successful up to this day. But it is open to the retort—First pay the sailors the honest value of their labour. When you have made it as well worth their while to serve you, as to work for other employers, you will have no more difficulty than others have in obtaining their services. To this there is no logical answer except "I will not:" and as people are now not only ashamed, but are not desirous, to rob the labourer of his hire, impressment is no longer advocated. Those who attempt to force women into marriage by closing all other doors against them, lay themselves open to a similar retort. If they mean what they say, their opinion must evidently be, that men do not render the married condition so desirable to women, as to induce them to accept it for its own recommendations. It is not a sign of one's thinking the boon one offers very attractive, when one allows only Hobson's choice,[2] "that or none." And here, I believe, is the clue to the feelings of those men, who have a real antipathy to the equal freedom of women. I believe they are afraid, not lest women should be unwilling to marry, for I do not think that anyone in reality has that apprehension; but lest they should insist that marriage should be on equal conditions; lest all women of spirit and capacity should prefer doing almost anything else, not in their own eyes degrading, rather than marry, when marrying is giving themselves a master, and a master too of all their earthly possessions. And truly, if this consequence were necessarily incident to marriage, I think that the apprehension would be very well founded. I agree in thinking it probable that few women, capable of anything else, would, unless under an irresistible *entrainement*,[3] rendering them for the time insensible to anything but itself, choose such a lot, when any other means were open to them of filling a conventionally honourable place in life: and if men are determined that the law of marriage shall be a law of despotism, they are quite right, in point of mere policy, in leaving to women only Hobson's choice. But, in that case, all that has been done in the modern world to relax the chain on the minds of women, has been a mistake. They never should have been allowed to receive a literary education. Women who read, much more women who write, are, in the existing constitution of things, a contradiction and a disturbing element: and it was wrong to bring women up with any acquirements but those of an odalisque,[4] or of a domestic servant.

—1869

---

[1] *impressment* Policy that pressed men into public service, even against their will; this practice was discontinued after 1835.

[2] *Hobson's choice* Expression originating from a Cambridge-London carrier, Thomas Hobson (1544–1630), who refused, when hiring out his horses, to allow any to leave the stable out of turn.

[3] *entrainement* Enchantment or charm.

[4] *odalisque* Concubine.

THE PLACE OF WOMEN IN SOCIETY
CONTEXTS

Throughout the nineteenth century, there was much debate concerning the proper place of women and the proper characteristics of femininity. The traditional roles of wives, mothers, and daughters, the structure of the family, and the nature of marriage—these were all open for examination by both men and women. In a nation ruled by a female queen who supported education for women but not female suffrage, the lines between traditional masculine and feminine realms were often blurred, and many writers and thinkers voiced their opinions on how such tensions and inconsistencies should best be reconciled.

Sarah Stickney Ellis, the author of the first excerpt here, from *The Women of England*, ran a school for girls but did not support intellectual advancement for women. Instead, she educated her pupils to become capable managers of their homes, from which they could best facilitate the advancement of their husbands and sons. Her numerous guides to female conduct, including *The Daughters of England* (1842), *The Wives of England* (1843), and *The Mothers of England* (1845) were extremely popular.

As the next excerpt (from *Fraser's Magazine*) shows, the growing role of the governess in Victorian society posed problems for traditional conception of gender and class roles. The role of the governess grew in importance along with the increasing emphasis on female education and the growing prosperity of the middle classes. In Victorian social hierarchy, the governess was a "lady"; as a result, this was *socially* a desirable occupation for many women, especially those daughters of tradespeople who sought to better themselves. Nevertheless, as a paid employee, the governess was part of the work force and, therefore, of the public sphere (although she worked within the private realm of the home), two qualities that would normally disqualify a woman from being considered a "lady." Consequently, the status of the governess was rife with tensions that often resulted in difficult conditions (Charlotte Brontë complained of the "wretched bondage" of being a governess).

The female suffrage campaign, which began in the 1850s, heightened the debate over women's proper role in society. There were a variety of arguments used in the effort to justify the subordination of women to men; these included the scientific argument, which presented evidence for women's supposed intellectual and physical inferiority, and the "divine will" argument, which portrayed female inferiority as part of the natural order established by God in Genesis. In her argument for female suffrage in *The Enfranchisement of Women* (excerpted below), Harriet Taylor presents (and attacks) some additional arguments used to protest women's entrance into politics. In a slightly later article, "Criminals, Idiots, Women, and Children," Frances Power Cobbe criticizes similar arguments (which she refers to as those of "Justice," "Expediency," and "Sentiment") used to deprive women of the legal rights that even convicted felons were afforded.

Coventry Patmore's long poem *The Angel in the House*, which became a best-seller in both Britain and the United States, is a sentimental depiction of the ideal female as conceived by many Victorian men of the upper and middle classes. The poem, which celebrated Patmore's first wife (he remarried twice after her death) details their courtship and marriage and epitomizes the view of women held by many men at the time. In the twentieth century the poem became the object of attacks by many feminist critics, particularly Virginia Woolf, and the phrase "angel in the house" was commonly used as a sort of shorthand to refer to an oppressive Victorian attitude towards gender roles.

The traditional social order that Patmore idealizes and celebrates also came under attack in the course of debates over "the woman question" in the late nineteenth century. At the center of this "woman question" was the issue of female equality and suffrage. As the satirical *Punch* cartoon reproduced below demonstrates, female suffragettes were often viewed as the antithesis of the ideal woman, epitomizing instead traditionally "masculine" characteristics. In the excerpt following, Eliza Lynn Linton, perhaps the most vocal anti-feminist of the period, criticizes what she sees as the unnatural, masculine boldness of the "modern girl," whose unwillingness to serve and support her husband and nurture her children, Linton argues, makes her not only unsuitable for marriage, but a disgrace to England's national character. In a slightly later article excerpted below, "The New Aspect of the Woman Question," Sarah Grand portrays the modern woman in a very different light. Grand (whose real name was Frances Elizabeth Clarke McFall) was a novelist, lecturer, and women's rights advocate who coined the phrase "the new woman" in this *North American Review* essay to express the values—principally social, political, and educational equality with men, as well as economic independence—of many women of her generation.

Within Victorian society's complex network of genders and class distinction, many citizens relied upon printed material for guidance in matters of conduct and etiquette, as well as for more practical advice on household management and professional opportunities. *The Girl's Own Paper*, a weekly paper founded in 1880 as a companion to the very successful *Boy's Own Paper*, provided such information to many female readers, as the two articles excerpted here (giving advice on the proper treatment of servants and the opportunities for self-improvement between school and marriage) demonstrate. According to its editor, the paper, which was published by the Religious Tract Society, aimed to provide female readers with instruction "in the moral and domestic virtues, preparing them for the responsibility of womanhood and for a heavenly home."

As the debates concerning women's political rights, their education, and their need for economic independence grew more heated, many realized that "the Woman Question is the Marriage Question," as Sarah Grand comments in her essay. The final excerpt printed below is Mona Caird's somewhat humorous response to the *Daily Telegraph*'s question "Does Marriage Hinder a Woman's Self-Development?" Her hypothetical reversal of men's and women's roles demonstrates how arbitrary—and confining—definitions of "masculine" and "feminine" characteristics could be.

⌘⌘⌘

from Sarah Stickney Ellis, *The Daughters of England: Their Position in Society, Character and Responsibilities* (1842)

… The sphere upon which a young woman enters on first leaving school, or, to use a popular phrase, on "completing her education," is so entirely new to her, her mind is so often the subject of new impressions, and her attention so frequently absorbed by new motives for exertion, that, if at all accustomed to reflect, we cannot doubt but she will make these, or similar questions, the subject of serious inquiry—"What is my position in society? What do I aim at? And what means do I intend to employ for the accomplishment of my purpose?" …

As women, then, the first thing of importance is to be content to be inferior to men—inferior in mental power, in the same proportion that you are inferior in bodily strength. Facility of movement, aptitude, and grace, the bodily frame of woman may possess in a higher degree than that of man; just as in the softer touches of mental and spiritual beauty her character may present a lovelier page than his. Yet, as the great attribute of power must still be wanting there, it becomes more immediately her business to inquire how this want may be supplied.

An able and eloquent writer on "Woman's Mission"[1] has justly observed that woman's strength is in her influence. And, in order to render this influence more complete, you will find on examination that you are by nature endowed with peculiar faculties—with a quickness of perception, facility of adaptation, and acuteness of feeling, which fit you especially for the part you have to act in life; and which, at the same time, render you, in a higher degree than men, susceptible both of pain and pleasure. ...

*   *   *

I have already stated that women, in their position in life, must be content to be inferior to men; but as their inferiority consists chiefly in their want of power, this deficiency is abundantly made up to them by their capability of exercising influence; it is made up to them also in other ways, incalculable in their number and extent; but in none so effectually as by that order of Divine Providence which places them, in a moral and religious point of view, on the same level with man; nor can it be a subject of regret to any right-minded woman that they are not only exempt from the most laborious occupations both of mind and body, but also from the necessity of engaging in those eager pecuniary speculations, and in that fierce conflict of worldly interests by which men are so deeply occupied as to be in a manner compelled to stifle their best feelings, until they become in reality the characters they at first only assumed. Can it be a subject of regret to any kind and feeling woman that her sphere of action is one adapted to the exercise of the affections, where she may love, and trust, and hope, and serve, to the utmost of her wishes? Can it be a subject of regret that she is not called upon, so much as man, to calculate, to compete, to struggle, but rather to occupy a sphere in which the elements of discord cannot with propriety be admitted—in which beauty and order are expected to denote her presence, and where the exercise of benevolence is the duty she is most frequently called upon to perform.

Women almost universally consider themselves, and wish to be considered by others, as extremely affectionate; scarcely can a more severe libel be pronounced upon

a woman than to say that she is not so. Now the whole law of woman's life is a law of love. I propose, therefore, to treat the subject in this light—to try whether the neglect of their peculiar duties does not imply an absence of love, and whether the principle of love, thoroughly carried out, would not so influence their conduct and feelings as to render them all which their best friends could desire.

Let us, however, clearly understand each other at the outset. To love, is a very different thing from a desire to be beloved. To love, is woman's nature—to be beloved is the consequence of her having properly exercised and controlled that nature. To love, is a woman's duty—to be beloved, is her reward.

*   *   *

... There is yet another flight of female ambition, another course which the love of distinction is apt to make, more product of folly, and of disappointment, perhaps, than all the rest. It is the ambition of the female author who writes for fame. Could those young aspirants know how little real dignity there is connected with the *trade* of authorship, their harps would be exchanged for distaffs,[2] their rose-tinted paper would be converted into ashes, and their Parnassus[3] would dwindle to a molehill. ... The same want of sympathy which so often inspires the first effort of female authorship, might often find a sweet and abundant interchange of kindness in many a faithful heart beside the homely hearth. And after all, there is more true poetry in the fire-side affections of early life than in all those sympathetic associations with unknown and untried developments of mind which ever have existed either amongst the sons or the daughters of men.

Taking a more sober view of the case, there are, unquestionably, subjects of deep interest with which women have opportunities peculiar to themselves of becoming acquainted, and thus of benefiting their fellow creatures through the medium of their writings. But, after all, literature is not the natural channel for a woman's feelings; and pity, not envy, ought to be the

---

[1] *An able ... Mission* Sarah Lewis, whose *Woman's Mission*, a popular book on female conduct, was published in 1839.

[2] *distaff* Staff on which wool or flax was wound when spinning.

[3] *Parnassus* Mountain in Greece sacred to the Muses, the nine daughters of Zeus and Mnemosyne, each of whom presided over, and provided inspiration for, a different aspect of the arts and sciences.

meed[1] of her who writes for the public. How much of what with other women is reserved for the select and chosen intercourse of affection, with her must be laid bare to the coarse cavillings,[2] and coarser commendations, of amateur or professional critics. How much of what no woman loves to say, except to the listening ear of domestic affection, by her must be told—nay, blazoned—to the world. And then, in her season of depression, or of wounded feeling, when her spirit yearns to sit in solitude, or even in darkness, so that it may be still; to know and feel that the very essence of that spirit, now embodied in a palpable form, has become an article of sale and bargain, tossed over from the hands of one workman to another, free alike to the touch of the prince and the peasant, and no longer to be reclaimed at will by the original possessor, let the world receive it as it may.

Is such, I ask, an enviable distinction?

from Anonymous, "Hints on the Modern Governess System," *Fraser's Magazine*, November 1844

… To trace the growth of woman's desire after knowledge would be the task of a philosopher; for us, it suffices to see that it is, that is has been from all ages. The barter of Paradise for the means of knowledge is the first recorded act of woman's life; she tempted man to forego all tried blessings, for the untried boon of "knowing good and evil." Thenceforth, man wreaked his vengeance upon woman, for the loss of ease and plenty, by keeping her ignorant, and, consequently, helpless. But since the day that Christianity dawned on the world, an emancipation of the weak out of the power of the strong has been silently progressing. The faint cry, uplifted at intervals, swelled into a chorus; there was a sudden rush; all the world clamoured for a better education for women; no wonder, in such a struggle, that the greater number mistook chaff and husks[3] for bread. The movement was all too sudden. Education, in as far as it implies intellectual and moral growth, is the work of life; its operations are as secret and as self-derived as the gradual shooting of the green blade into the wheat-ear.

Now, when that cry of women after knowledge pierced the air, a thousand sprang up, mushroomwise, in a night, to answer it. Mothers who had only read their Bibles and receipt-books[4] found themselves unprepared for the emergency—we have so little patience, so little foresight. Then, teaching, that holy vocation of a woman, became a trade. An universal demand creates its own supply. Here was a tempting opening to all aspiring women, who were free to try a new field; the unmarried daughters of the gentry left with scanty portions had, till now, been content to eke out their small incomes in trade; many were the gentlewomen, in our great-grandmothers' days, who lived in honoured independence, though they kept small shops, to which their old friends resorted. They did not lose caste[5] because they sat for part of the day behind the counter. However, this refuge grew insecure from the outward pressure of public opinion in favour of refinement…. Many left their quiet homes for the school-rooms of halls and castles. As they mounted the stair, others came from a lower rank, and filled the vacant steps. The restless rage to push on had stirred all classes. Those who, disappointed in their new stand, looked wistfully back to the old, found that when they would return they could not. There was no place left for them but that which they had chosen. Like much else, it looked best from a distance. Here, then, was a whole class of women driven into a new line, for which they had received no fitting preparation…. The new generation, thirsting to be taught, found teachers at their mercy, hanging between two ranks. Do the weak desire to learn what they may expect from the strong? Let them ponder deeply the governess system of the present day. This was the watch-word, "Teach us on our own terms, or work, and cease to be gentlewomen." To the newly risen race of governesses, even such equivocal gentility was preferable to a second change, though it was to be gained at the price of isolation….

---

[1] *meed* Recompense; reward.

[2] *cavillings* Unfair or petty fault-finding.

[3] *chaff and husks* Material separated out from grains when threshing cereal crops.

[4] *receipt-books* I.e., recipe books.

[5] *lose caste* I.e., lose their position in society.

The policy of the world is to take advantage of want. It became apparent that a whole family of daughters might be taught by one of these single women, struggling for bread, for less than it formerly cost to send one girl to school. Where competition was so great, there was no difficulty in driving a bargain. The means of instruction might be had so cheaply that the grocer's daughters could be taught to read *Paul and Virginia* in the original tongue, and to strum *The Fall of Paris*.[1] In process of time, therefore, a governess became a necessary appanage[2] in every family.

Whether it be right or wrong, as a general rule, for mothers to delegate their most sacred trust to hired strangers, we are not here to discuss. The fact exists. Is the system carried out fairly for all parties? Is there any question astir as to its abuse? Philanthropic eyes are scanning many social evils. Is it yet considered how far a whole race of women are dragging out weary lives under a mass of trials, the detail of which would fill a "blue book"[3] by themselves? True, if the case were known, "a thousand voices" would be "uplifted."[4] The miseries of the governess may even swell that sickening clamour about the "rights of women," which would never have been raised had women been true to themselves. But that trite saying in this case has its point. The modern governess system is a case between woman and woman. Before one sex demands its due from the other, let it be just to itself.

Punch has ably pleaded in the cause of salaries and qualifications.[5] The statistics touching lunatic asylums give a frightful proportion of governesses in the list of the insane.[6] But has the whole life in home schoolrooms ever been investigated? We ask this with a real wish to be informed, with a hope of directing eyes to this unknown page of human life. Have kind, ladylike, cultivated women ever reflected on the relation which subsists between themselves and others of like minds, and, perhaps, formerly in similar circumstances? Have they ever tried to put themselves in the position of the young women devoting themselves to the education of their children, who yet live as strangers in the midst of homes? …

… When the lesson-books are closed, and the little ones have capered out of the school-room, what becomes of the teacher, who has not exchanged a thought or a word with any one of congenial mind all day? Hour after hour she has *bent down* her mind, and *raised* the children's to given points, which, however interesting, are exhausting. A young thing, perhaps, still herself, ready to spring up again at one kindly touch. Do not even fond mothers, who teach their own children, feel that after the labours of the day they need some interchange of *mind*? They have often felt refreshed when husband or friend has given them a new thought, or understood an articulated feeling, after the repression of the day, necessary in fulfilling the duty of teaching. Who is there that has not known the dryness of spending time with people of more limited capacities and interests than one's own? … Let mothers ask if they would not expect their own daughters to languish in spirits and energy, if they had no intercourse with older companions. Whilst the children are with their parents and their guests, the governess, quite as often as not, is expected to remain in the school-room, unless specially invited to join the circle. This is peculiarly the case in large establishments, where the school-room arrangements are distinct from the rest of the family. We believe that most young

---

[1] *Paul and Virginia* The sentimental French novel *Paul et Virginie* (1787), by Jacques-Henri Bernadin de St. Pierre; *strum* Play poorly on the piano; *The Fall of Paris* Popular song of the period.

[2] *appanage* Possession, perquisite.

[3] *blue book* Parliamentary report.

[4] *a thousand … uplifted* A reference to the epigraph of this article, from French novelist George Sand's collection of fictional letters, *Lettres à Marcie* (1837): "Society is full of abuses. Women complain of being brutally enslaved, badly brought up, badly educated, badly treated, and badly defended. All this is, unfortunately, true. These complaints are just, and do not doubt but that before long a thousand voices will be uplifted to remedy the evil."

[5] *Punch has … qualifications* The satirical weekly magazine *Punch* had recently printed numerous articles advocating the improvement of conditions for governesses.

[6] *The statistics … insane* During the early and mid nineteenth century it was a commonplace that governesses tended toward mental instability as a result of the stressful nature of their employment. While some statistics did show that there was a high percentage of governesses in asylums, this may have been due in part to the fact that private asylums sometimes provided the cheapest respectable accommodation for women without family or employment.

women of delicate perceptions would prefer their desolate apartment to feeling themselves clogs[1] upon the family party. But do people know what they are about when they leave young creatures alone, long evening after evening, following days of seclusion and exhaustion? Factory-girls, shop-women, teachers of accomplishments, return to their homes at night. The servants gather round the work-table or the hall-fire. Prisoners in gaol[2] may collect together in knots in their yards, look in each other's faces, hear the sound of human voices, tell their troubles and joys, and listen to their neighbours. Solitary confinement, even for felons, is reserved to punish some special offence. It is only the governess, and a certain class of private tutors, who must hear the echoes from the drawing-room and the offices, feeling that, in a house full of people, they dwell alone. Nervous irritability, dejection, loss of energy, are the inevitable results which follow a too solitary life in youth. Yet, without elasticity in her own frame, how can the governess be a fitting companion and teacher of such gay, volatile creatures as children—so easily cowed and spirit-broken by harshness or settled sadness in those who live with them? Would not querulous temper of depression of spirits in the governess be complained of by the parents? Do they consider, when they expect cheerfulness and an even composure of spirits from one fretted with children's restless waywardness, and chilled by the frosty indifference and neglect of the grown-up members of the family, that they ask an impossible thing?

from Harriet Taylor, *The Enfranchisement of Women* (1851)

When a prejudice, which has any hold on the feeling, finds itself reduced to the unpleasant necessity of assigning reasons, it thinks it has done enough when it has re-asserted the very point in the dispute, in phrases which appeal to the pre-existing feelings. Thus, many persons think they have sufficiently justified the restrictions on women's field of action when they have said that the pursuits from which

women are excluded are *unfeminine*, and that the *proper sphere* of women is not politics or publicity, but private and domestic life.

We deny the right of any portion of the species to decide for another portion, or any individual for another individual, what is and what is not their "proper sphere." The proper sphere for all human beings is the largest and highest which they are able to attain to....

We shall follow the very proper convention, in not entering into the question of the alleged differences in physical or mental qualities between the sexes; not because we have nothing to say, but because we have too much.... But if those who assert that the "proper sphere" for women is the domestic, mean by this that they have not shown themselves qualified for any other, the assertion evinces great ignorance of life and of history. Women have shown fitness for the highest social functions, exactly in proportion as they have been admitted to them. By a curious anomaly, though ineligible to even the lowest offices of state, they are in some countries admitted to the highest of all, the regal; and if there is any one function for which they have shown a decided vocation, it is that of reigning....

Concerning the fitness, then, of women for politics, there can be no question: but the dispute is more likely to turn upon the fitness of politics for women. When the reasons alleged for excluding women from active life in all its higher departments are stripped of their garb of declamatory phrases, and reduced to the simple expression of a meaning, they seem to be mainly three: the incompatibility of active life with maternity and with the cares of a household; secondly, its alleged hardening effect on the character; and thirdly, the inexpediency of making an addition to the already excessive pressure of competition in every kind of professional or lucrative employment.

The first, the maternity argument, is usually laid most stress upon: although (it needs hardly be said) this reason, if it be one, can apply only to mothers. It is neither necessary nor just to make imperative on women that they shall be either mothers or nothing; or that if they have been mothers once, they shall be nothing else during the whole remainder of their lives. Neither women nor men need any law to exclude them from an

---

[1] *clogs* Encumbrances. Literally, blocks of wood attached to the leg or neck of a person or animal to prevent escape.

[2] *gaol* I.e., jail.

occupation if they have undertaken another which is incompatible with it. No one proposes to exclude the male sex from Parliament because a man may be a soldier or sailor in active service, or a merchant whose business requires all his time and energies. Nine-tenths of the occupations of men exclude them *de facto*[1] from public life, as effectually as if they were excluded by law; but that is no reason for making laws to exclude even the nine-tenths, much less the remaining tenth. The reason of the case is the same for women as for men. There is no need to make provision by law that a woman shall not carry on the active details of a household, or of the education of children, and at the same time practise a profession or be elected to Parliament. Where incompatibility is real, it will take care of itself: but there is gross injustice in making the incompatibility a pretence for the exclusion of those in whose case it does not exist. And these, if they were free to choose, would be a very large proportion. The maternity argument deserts its supporters in the case of single women, a large and increasing class of the population; a fact which, it is not irrelevant to remark, by tending to diminish the excessive competition of numbers, is calculated to assist greatly the prosperity of all. There is no inherent reason or necessity that all women should voluntarily choose to devote their lives to one animal function and its consequences. Numbers of women are wives and mothers only because there is no other career open to them, no other occupation for their feelings or their activities. Every improvement in their education, and enlargement of their faculties—everything which renders them more qualified for any other mode of life, increases the number of those to whom it is an injury and an oppression to be denied the choice. To say that women must be excluded from active life because maternity disqualifies them for it, is in fact to say that every other career should be forbidden them in order that maternity may be their only resource.

But secondly, it is urged that to give the same freedom of occupation to women as to men would be an injurious addition to the crowd of competitors, by whom the avenues to almost all kinds of employment are choked up, and its remuneration depressed. This argument, it is to be observed, does not reach the political question. It gives no excuse for withholding from women the rights of citizenship. The suffrage, the jury-box, admission to the legislature and to office, it does not touch. It bears only on the industrial branch of the subject. Allowing it, then, in an economical point of view, its full force; assuming that to lay open to women the employments now monopolized by men, would tend, like the breaking down of other monopolies, to lower the rate of remuneration in those employments; let us consider what is the amount of this evil consequence, and what the compensation for it. The worst ever asserted, much worse than is at all likely to be realized, is that if women competed with men, a man and a woman could not together earn more than is now earned by the man alone. Let us make this supposition, the most favourable supposition possible: the joint income of the two would be the same as before, while the woman would be raised from the position of a servant to that of a partner. Even if every woman, as matters now stand, had a claim on some man for support, how infinitely preferable is it that part of the income should be of the woman's earning, even if the aggregate sum were but little increased by it, rather than that she should be compelled to stand aside in order that men may be the sole earners, and the sole dispensers of what is earned. Even under the present laws respecting the property of women, a woman who contributes materially to the support of the family cannot be treated in the same contemptuously tyrannical manner as one who, however she may toil as a domestic drudge, is a dependent on the man for subsistence. As for the depression of wages by increase of competition, remedies will be found for it in time. Palliatives might be applied immediately; for instance, a more rigid exclusion of children from industrial employment, during the years in which they ought to be working only to strengthen their bodies and minds for after life. Children are necessarily dependent, and under the power of others; and their labour, being not for themselves but for the gain of their parents, is a proper subject for legislative regulation. With respect to the future, we neither believe that improvident multiplication, and the consequent excessive difficulty of gaining a subsistence, will always continue, nor that the division of mankind into capitalists and hired labourers, and the regulation

---

[1]   *de facto*   Latin: in reality; as a matter of fact.

of the reward of labourers mainly by demand and supply, will be for ever, or even much longer, the rule of the world. But so long as competition is the general law of human life, it is tyranny to shut out one half of the competitors. All who have attained the age of self-government have an equal claim to be permitted to sell whatever kind of useful labour they are capable of, for the price which it will bring.

The third objection to the admission of women to political or professional life, its alleged hardening tendency, belongs to an age now past, and is scarcely to be comprehended by people of the present time. There are still, however, persons who say that the world and its avocations render men selfish and unfeeling; that the struggles, rivalries, and collisions of business and of politics make them harsh and unamiable; that if half the species must unavoidably be given up to these things, it is the more necessary that the other half should be kept free from them; that to preserve women from the bad influences of the world is the only chance of preventing men from being wholly given up to them.

There would have been plausibility in this argument when the world was still in the age of violence; when life was full of physical conflict, and every man had to redress his injuries or those of others, by the sword or by the strength of his arm. Women, like priests, by being exempted from such responsibilities, and from some part of the accompanying dangers, may have been enabled to exercise a beneficial influence. But in the present condition of human life, we do not know where those hardening influences are to be found, to which men are subject and from which women are at present exempt. Individuals now-a-days are seldom called upon to fight hand to hand, even with peaceful weapons; personal enmities and rivalries count for little in worldly transactions; the general pressure of circumstances, not the adverse will of individuals, is the obstacle men now have to make head against. That pressure, when excessive, breaks the spirit, and cramps and sours the feelings, but not less of women than of men, since they suffer certainly not less from its evils. There are still quarrels and dislikes, but the sources of them are changed. The feudal chief once found his bitterest enemy in his powerful neighbour, the minister or courtier in his rival

for place: but opposition of interest in active life, as a cause of personal animosity, is out of date; the enmities of the present day arise not from great things but small, from what people say of one another, more than from what they do; and if there are hatred, malice, and all uncharitableness, they are to be found among women fully as much as among men. In the present state of civilization, the notion of guarding women from the hardening influences of the world could only be realized by secluding them from society altogether. The common duties of common life, as at present constituted, are incompatible with any other softness in women than weakness. Surely weak minds in weak bodies must ere long cease to be even supposed to be either attractive or amiable.

But, in truth, none of these arguments and considerations touch the foundations of the subject. The real question is, whether it is right and expedient that one half of the human race should pass through life in a state of forced subordination to the other half. If the best state of human society is that of being divided into two parts, one consisting of persons with a will and a substantive existence, the other of humble companions to these persons, attached, each of them to one, for the purpose of bringing up *his* children, and making *his* home pleasant to him; if this is the place assigned to women, it is but kindness to educate them for this; to make them believe that the greatest good fortune which can befall them is to be chosen by some man for this purpose; and that every other career which the world deems happy or honourable is closed to them by the law, not of social institutions, but of nature and destiny.

When, however, we ask why the existence of one-half the species should be merely ancillary to that of the other—why each woman should be a mere appendage to a man, allowed to have no interests of her own, that there may be nothing to compete in her mind with his interests and his pleasure; the only reason which can be given is, that men like it. It is agreeable to them that men should live for their own sake, women for the sake of men: and the qualities and conduct in subjects which are agreeable to rulers, they succeed for a long time in making the subjects themselves consider as their appropriate virtues.

from Coventry Patmore, *The Angel in the House* (1854–56)

THE WIFE'S TRAGEDY

Man must be pleased; but him to please
Is woman's pleasure; down the gulf
Of his condoled necessities
     She casts her best, she flings herself.
5 How often flings for nought! and yokes
     Her heart to an icicle or whim,
Whose each impatient word provokes
     Another, not from her, but him;
While she, too gentle even to force
10   His penitence by kind replies,
Waits by, expecting his remorse,
     With pardon in her pitying eyes;
And if he once, by shame oppressed,
     A comfortable word confers,
15 She leans and weeps against his breast,
     And seems to think the sin was hers;
And whilst his love has any life,
     Or any eye to see her charms,
At any time, she's still his wife,
20   Dearly devoted to his arms;
She loves with love that cannot tire;
     And when, ah woe, she loves alone,
Through passionate duty love flames higher,
     As grass grows taller round a stone....

THE FOREIGN LAND

A woman is a foreign land,
     Of which, though there he settle young
A man will ne'er quite understand
     The customs, politics, and tongue.
5 The foolish hie° them post-haste through,   hasten
     See fashions odd, and prospects fair,
Learn of the language, "How-d'ye do,"
     And go and brag that they've been there.
The most for leave to trade apply,
10   For once, at Empire's seat her heart,
Then get what knowledge ear and eye
     Glean chancewise in the life-long mart.°   market

And certain others few and fit,
     Attach them to the Court, and see
15 The country's best, its accent hit,
     And partly sound its polity.

from Eliza Lynn Linton, "The Girl of the Period," *Saturday Review*, March 1868

Time was when the stereotyped phrase "a fair young English girl" meant the ideal of womanhood, to us, at least, of home birth and breeding. It meant a creature generous, capable, and modest; something franker than a Frenchwoman, more to be trusted than an Italian, as brave as an American but more refined, as domestic as a German and more graceful. It meant a girl who could be trusted alone if need be, because of the innate purity and dignity of her nature, but who was neither bold in bearing nor masculine in mind; a girl who, when she married, would be her husband's friend and companion, but never his rival; one who would consider their interests identical, and not hold him as just so much fair game for spoil; who would make his house his true home and place of rest, not a mere passage-place for vanity and ostentation to go through; a tender mother, an industrious housekeeper, a judicious mistress. We prided ourselves as a nation on our women. We thought we had the pick of creation in this fair young English girl of ours, and envied no other men their own.... This was in the old time, and when English girls were content to be what God and nature had made them. Of late years we have changed the pattern, and have given to the world a race of women as utterly unlike the old insular ideal as if we had created another nation altogether. The girl of the period and the fair young English girl of the past have nothing in common save ancestry and their mother-tongue; and even of this last the modern version makes almost a new language, through the copious additions it has received from the current slang of the day.

   The girl of the period is a creature who dyes her hair and paints her face, as the first articles of her personal religion; whose sole idea of life is plenty of fun and luxury; and whose dress is the object of such thought

[JUNE 14, 1884.]   PUNCH, OR THE LONDON CHARIVARI.   270

"THE ANGEL IN 'THE HOUSE;'" OR, THE RESULT OF FEMALE SUFFRAGE.
(A Troubled Dream of the Future.)

A satirical representation of the female suffragette, here having gained the vote and a position of political power, speaking in the House of Commons. She is knitting a "blue stocking," an allusion to the term "bluestocking," a derogatory term that began to be applied to free-thinking women in the eighteenth century.

and intellect as she possesses. Her main endeavour in this is to outvie her neighbours in the extravagance of fashion. No matter whether, as in the time of crinolines, she sacrificed decency, or, as now, in the time of trains, she sacrifices cleanliness; no matter either, whether she makes herself a nuisance and an inconvenience to every one she meets. The girl of the period has done away with such moral muffishness[1] as consideration for others, or regard for counsel and rebuke. It was all very well in old-fashioned times, when fathers and mothers

had some authority and were treated with respect, to be tutored and made to obey, but she is far too fast and flourishing to be stopped in mid-career by these slow old morals; and as she dresses to please herself, she does not care if she displeases everyone else. Nothing is too extraordinary and nothing too exaggerated for her vitiated[2] taste; and things which in themselves would be useful reforms if let alone become monstrosities worse than those which they have displaced so soon as she begins to manipulate and improve. If a sensible fashion

---

[1] *muffishness* Foolishness, often describing someone or something seen as old-fashioned.

[2] *vitiated* Corrupted.

lifts the gown out of the mud, she raises hers midway to her knee. If the absurd structure of wire and buckram, once called a bonnet, is modified to something that shall protect the wearer's face without putting out the eyes of her companion, she cuts hers down to four straws and a rosebud, or a tag of lace and a bunch of glass beads! ... She has blunted the fine edges of feeling so much that she cannot understand why she should be condemned for an imitation of form which does not include imitation of fact; she cannot be made to see that modesty of appearance and virtue ought to be inseparable, and that no good girl can afford to appear bad, under penalty of receiving the contempt awarded to the bad.

This imitation of the *demi-monde*[1] in dress leads to something in manner and feeling, not quite so pronounced perhaps, but far too like to be honourable to herself or satisfactory to her friends. It leads to slang, bold talk, and fastness; to the love of pleasure and indifference to duty; to the desire of money before either love or happiness; to uselessness at home, dissatisfaction with the monotony of ordinary life, and horror of all useful work; in a word, to the worst forms of luxury and selfishness, to the most fatal effects arising from want of high principle and absence of tender feeling.... No one can say of the modern English girl that she is tender, loving, retiring, or domestic. The old fault so often found by keen-sighted Frenchwomen, that she was so fatally *romanesque*,[2] so prone to sacrifice appearances and social advantages for love, will never be set down to the girl of the period. Love indeed is the last thing she thinks of, and the least of the dangers besetting her. Love in a cottage, that seductive dream which used to vex the heart and disturb the calculations of prudent mothers, is now a myth of past ages. The legal barter of herself for so much money, representing so much dash, so much luxury and pleasure—that is her idea of marriage; the only idea worth entertaining. For all seriousness of thought respecting the duties or the consequences of marriage, she has not a trace. If children come, they find but a stepmother's cold welcome

from her; and if her husband thinks that he has married anything that is to belong to him—a *tacens et placens uxor*[3] pledged to make him happy—the sooner he wakes from his hallucination and understands that he has simply married someone who will condescend to spend his money on herself, and who will shelter her indiscretions behind the shield of his name, the less severe will be his disappointment. She has married his house, his carriage, his balance at the bankers, his title; and he himself is just the inevitable condition clogging the wheel of her fortune; at best an adjunct, to be tolerated with more or less patience as may chance. For it is only the old-fashioned sort, not girls of the period *pur sang*,[4] that marry for love, or put the husband before the banker. But she does not marry easily. Men are afraid of her; and with reason. They may amuse themselves with her of an evening, but they do not take her readily for life....

The marvel, in the present fashion of life among women, is how it holds its ground in spite of the disapprobation of men. It used to be an old-time notion that the sexes were made for each other, and that it was only natural for them to please each other, and to set themselves out for that end. But the girl of the period does not please men. She pleases them as little as she elevates them; and how little she does that, the class of women she has taken as her models of itself testifies. All men whose opinion is worth having prefer the simple and genuine girl of the past, with her tender little ways and pretty bashful modesties, to this loud and rampant modernization, with her false red hair and painted skin, talking slang as glibly as a man, and by preference leading the conversation to doubtful subjects. She thinks she is *piquante*[5] and exciting when she thus makes herself the bad copy of a worse original; and she will not see that though men laugh with her they do not respect her, though they flirt with her they do not marry her; she will not believe that she is not the kind of thing they want, and that she is acting against nature and her own interests when she disregards their advice and offends their taste. We do not see how she makes out her

---

[1]   *demi-monde* French: literally, "half world"; figuratively, the world existing below the level of respectable society. The term was often used to denote the world of the courtesan.

[2]   *romanesque* French: romantic.

[3]   *tacens ... uxor* Latin: silent and pleasing wife.

[4]   *pur sang* French: pure-blooded.

[5]   *piquante* Stimulating.

account, viewing her life from any side; but all we can do is to wait patiently until the national madness has passed, and our women have come back again to the old English ideal, once the most beautiful, the most modest, the most essentially womanly in the world.

from Frances Power Cobbe, "Criminals, Idiots, Women, and Minors," *Fraser's Magazine*, December 1868

There was an allegory rather popular about thirty years ago, whose manifest purpose was to impress on the juvenile mind that tendency which Mr. Matthew Arnold has ingeniously designated "Hebraism."[1] The hero of the tale descends upon earth from some distant planet, and is conducted by a mundane cicerone[2] through one of our great cities, where he beholds the docks and arsenals, the streets and marts, the galleries of art, and the palaces of royalty. The visitor admires everything till he happens to pass a graveyard. "What is that gloomy spot?" he asks of his companion. "It is a cemetery," replies the guide.

"A—what did you say? " inquires the son of the star.

"A graveyard; a place of public interment; where we bury our dead," reiterates the cicerone.

The visitor, pale with awe and terror, learns at last that there is in this world such a thing as *Death*, and (as he is forbidden to return to his own planet) he resolves to dedicate every moment left to him to prepare himself for that fearful event and all that may follow it.

Had that visitor heard for the first time upon his arrival on earth of another incident of human existence—namely, *Marriage*, it may be surmised that his astonishment and awe would also have been considerable. To his eager inquiry whether men and women earnestly strove to prepare themselves for so momentous an occurrence, he would have received the puzzling reply that women frequently devoted themselves with perfectly Hebraistic singleness of aim to that special

purpose; but that men, on the contrary, very rarely included any preparation for the married state among the items of their widest Hellenistic culture. But this anomaly would be trifling compared to others which would be revealed to him. "Ah," we can hear him say to his guide as they pass into a village church. "What a pretty sight is this! What is happening to that sweet young woman in white who is giving her hand to the good-looking fellow beside her, all the company decked in holiday attire, and the joy-bells shaking the old tower overhead? She is receiving some great honour, is she not? The Prize of Virtue, perhaps?"

"Oh, yes," would reply the friend; "an honour certainly. She is being Married." After a little further explanation the visitor would pursue his inquiry:

"Of course, having entered this honourable state of matrimony, she has some privilege above the women who are not chosen by anybody? I notice her husband has just said, 'With all my worldly goods I thee endow.' Does that mean that she will henceforth have the control of his money altogether, or only that he takes her into partnership?"

"*Pas précisément*,[3] my dear sir. By our law it is *her* goods and earnings, present and future, which belong to him from this moment."

"You don't say so? But then, of course, his goods are hers also?"

"Oh dear, no! not at all. He is only bound to find her food; and truth to tell, not very strictly or efficaciously bound to do that."

"How! do I understand you? Is it possible that here in the most solemn religious act, which I perceive your prayer book calls 'The Solemnisation of Holy Matrimony,' every husband makes a generous promise, which promise is not only a mockery, but the actual reverse and parody of the real state of the case: the man who promises giving nothing, and the woman who is silent giving all?"

"Well, yes; I suppose that is something like it, as to the letter of the law. But then, of course, practically—"

"Practically, I suppose few men can really be so unmanly and selfish as the law warrants them in being. Yet some, I fear, may avail themselves of such authority. May I ask another question? As you subject women who enter the marriage state to such very severe penalties as

---

[1] *Hebraism* Originally denoting an attribute of the Hebrew people, the term was used by Arnold to describe a moral (rather than intellectual) theory of life. Arnold used the term "Hellenistic," in contrast, to denote the intellectual culture or way of life typified by the ancient Greeks.

[2] *cicerone* Guide.

[3] *Pas précisément* French: not exactly.

this, what worse have you in store for women who lead a dissolute life, to the moral injury of the community?"

"Oh, the law takes nothing from them. Whatever they earn or inherit is their own. They are able, also, to sue the fathers of their children for their maintenance, which a wife, of course, is not allowed to do on behalf of *her* little ones, because she and her husband are one in the eye of the law."

"One question still further—your criminals? Do they always forfeit their entire property on conviction?"

"Only for the most heinous crimes; felony and murder, for example."

"Pardon me; I must seem to you so stupid! Why is the property of the woman who commits Murder, and the property of the woman who commits Matrimony, dealt with alike by your law?"

Leaving our little allegory and in sober seriousness, we must all admit that the just and expedient treatment of women by men is one of the most obscure problems, alike of equity and of policy. Nor of women only, but of all classes and races of human beings whose condition is temporarily or permanently one of comparative weakness and dependence....

By the common law of England a married woman has no legal existence, so far as property is concerned, independently of her husband. The husband and wife are assumed to be one person, and that person is the husband. The wife can make no contract, and can neither sue nor be sued. Whatever she possess of personal property at the time of her marriage, or whatever she may afterwards earn or inherit, belongs to her husband, without control on her part.... If she possess real estate, so long as her husband lives he receives and spends the income derived from it, being only forbidden to sell it without her consent. From none of her property is he bound to reserve anything, or make any provision for her maintenance or that of her children. This is the law for all, but practically it affects only two classes of women, *viz.*[1] those who marry hurriedly or without proper advisers, and those whose property at the time of marriage is too small to permit of the expense of a settlement; in other words, the whole middle and

lower ranks of women, and a certain portion of the upper ranks. Women of the richer class, with proper advisers, never come under the provisions of the Common Law, being carefully protected therefrom by an intricate system elaborated for the purpose by the courts of Equity, to which the victims of the Common Law have for years applied for redress. That system always involves considerable legal expenses, and an arrangement with trustees which is often extremely inconvenient and injurious to the interests of the married couple; nevertheless it is understood to be so great a boon that none who can afford to avail themselves of it fail to do so.

What then is the principle on which the Common Law mulcts[2] the poorer class of women of their property and earnings, and entails on the rich, if they wish to evade it, the costs and embarrassment of a marriage settlement? There is, of course, a principle in it, and one capable of clear statement. There are grounds for the law; first of Justice, then of Expediency, lastly (and as we believe) most influential of all, of Sentiment.

First, the grounds of Justice.

Man is the natural bread-winner. Woman lives by the bread which man has earned. Ergo, it is fit and right that the man who wins should have absolute disposal, not only of his winnings, but of every other small morsel or fraction of earning or property she may possess. It is a fair return to him for his labour in the joint interests of both.... The woman's case is that of a pauper who enters a workhouse. The ratepayers are bound to support him; but if he have any savings they must be given up to the board. HE cannot claim support and keep independent property.

Then for Expediency. "How can two walk together except they be agreed?" says the Bible. "How can they walk together except one of them have it all his own way?" says the voice of rough and ready practicality. Somebody must rule in a household, or everything will go to rack and ruin; and disputes will be endless. If somebody is to rule it can only be the husband, who is wiser, stronger, knows more of the world, and in any case has not the slightest intention of yielding his predominance. But to give a man such rule he must be allowed to keep the purse. Nothing but the power of the

---

[1] *viz.* Latin: namely; that is to say (an abbreviation of *videlicet*).

[2] *mulcts* Swindles.

purse—in default of the stick—can permanently and thoroughly secure authority....

Lastly, for the sentimental view. How painful is the notion of a wife holding back her money from him who is every day toiling for her support! How fair is the ideal picture of absolute concession on her part of all she possesses of this world's dross to the man to whom she gives her heart and life!... The young man and maiden, after years of affection, and carefully laying by of provision for the event, take each other at last, to be henceforth no more twain, but one flesh. Both have saved a little money, but it now belongs to the husband alone. He lays it out in the purchase of a cottage where they are henceforth to dwell. Day by day he goes forth to his labour, and weekly he brings home his earnings and places them in his wife's lap, bidding her spend them as she knows best for the supply of their homely board, their clothing which her deft fingers will make and many a time repair, and last for their common treasures, the little children who gather around them. Thus they grow old in unbroken peace and love, the man's will having never once been disputed, the wide yielding alike from choice and from necessity to his superior sense and his legal authority.

Surely this idea of life, for which the Common Law of England has done its utmost to provide, is well worth the pondering before we attempt to meddle with any of its safeguards? Who will suggest anything better in its room?

Alas, there are other scenes besides idylls of domestic peace and obedience promoted by the laws we are considering....

The existing Common Law is not *Just*, because it neither can secure nor actually even attempts to secure for the woman the equivalent support for whose sake she is forced to relinquish her property.

It is not *Expedient*, because while in happy marriages it is superfluous and useless, in unhappy ones it becomes highly injurious; often causing the final ruin of a family which the mother (if upheld by law) might have supported single-handed. It is also shown not to be considered expedient by the conduct of the entire upper class of the country, and even of the legislature itself in the system of the Court of Chancery. Where no one who can afford to evade the law fails to evade it, the pretence

that it is believed to be generally expedient is absurd. Further, the classes which actually evade it, and the countries where it is non-existing, show in no degree less connubial harmony than those wherein it is enforced.

Lastly, it does not tend to fulfil, but to counteract, the *Sentiment* regarding the marriage union, to which it aims to add the pressure of force. Real unanimity is not produced between two parties by forbidding one of them to have any voice at all. The hard mechanical contrivance of the law for making husband and wife of one heart and mind is calculated to produce a precisely opposite result.

from "Between School and Marriage," *The Girl's Own Paper*, Vol. 7 (4 September 1886)

This time in a girl's life corresponds to that in a man's which is passed in a university, or in learning the work of his profession. Too many girls look on it as a *mauvais quart d'heure*,[1] which may be dawdled through in an irresponsible way until they have a house of their own. Marriage represents a home, a position; sometimes even less than that—a trousseau,[2] or a wedding tour. So they hasten through the years of adolescence as well as may be in order to reach the end of a wearisome task.

And yet if the girl is mother to the woman—that is to say, if the woman will be what the girl now is, this time, which is essentially one for settling habits, cannot be anything less than the most important in life. If the girl spend it in thoughtless idleness and discontented trifling, the result will be seen in the character of the woman. It is well for any of us when our work is cut out for us, so to speak, and we have not to look about for a profitable way of passing the time; but this last is the miserable condition of many girls belonging to daughter-full houses in easy circumstances. What can they do between school and marriage?

When the financial resources of her father are slender, a girl is quite right to seek for some employment by which she may earn her own living, and

[1] *mauvais quart d'heure* French: an unpleasant time (literally, an unpleasant quarter of an hour), from the French expression "*passer un mauvais quart d'heure*," meaning "to have a bad time of it."

[2] *trousseau* A bride's collection of clothing and linens.

The Girl's Own Paper, sold weekly for a penny, was mainly marketed to working- and middle-class women, but it was read by women from all classes and age groups and soon after its founding reached a circulation of over 250,000.

perhaps help her brothers and sisters; but when this is not the case, let no feeling of quixotic restlessness induce her to rashly leave home. It may be her plain duty to remain at home, and she may be independent and pay her way quite as much as one who earns and pays current coin. She can pay her way by filling in the little spaces in home life as only a dear daughter can, by lifting the weight of care from her mother, and by slipping in a soft word or a smile where it is like oil on the troubled waters of a father's spirit. What better remuneration can a father have for his expenditure upon his daughters than their laughter, good humour, and sympathy?…

from Emma Brewer, "Our Friends the Servants," *The Girl's Own Paper*, Vol. 14 (25 March 1893)

Among mistresses who earnestly desire the welfare of their servants there is no question which causes more trouble and anxiety than that of allowing visitors in the kitchen, men visitors especially. It is indeed a difficult question, and cannot be solved for every one alike.

I know several ladies who have thought it right that such of their maids as were engaged should be permitted to receive their sweethearts from time to time in the kitchen; but in every case where this has been granted that has come under my notice, the results have been so disastrous as to necessitate the withdrawal of the privilege. It was found utterly destructive of harmony in the kitchen, and gave no real pleasure to anyone. In some cases the fickle men forsook their old love in favour of some younger and more attractive of the fellow-servants, and it is not difficult to imagine the bitterness, anger, and sharp words which became the fashion after such faithlessness.

In others the sweethearts borrowed money of all the foolish girls in order to lay it upon horses in which they were interested; in others, where more stimulant had been taken than was good for them, they have boasted among other men of the beautiful silver, etc., in the houses where their young women lived, with what results may be guessed.

In simple fairness the privilege cannot be granted to one without extending it to all; this, in many houses, would fill the kitchens of an evening; for no maid would acknowledge that she had no young man, and would get one on the spot without considering his character, and such a one would scarcely add to the safety or morality of the kitchen.…

There are a few things in the relationship between mistress and maid which distress me greatly, because I know they are utterly destructive of home-peace and comfort; one is a mistress reproving her servant in public, another is a maid answering her mistress rudely, and a third is a mistress finding fault with servants out of the room to one who is waiting in the room.

No good servant would endure the first nor be guilty of the second, but one and all are evil in their result, and it is easy to see that, let the fault be what it may, it cannot be remedied in this fashion.

Servants have feelings to be wounded and rights to be respected, and when these are ignored they feel that their occupation is compromising to their respectability and freedom.

We lose many good servants in this way, and get in their place large importations of very inferior ones from the Continent. It gives one a feeling of sadness that while the mother country stands in increased need of good and trustworthy servants, she cannot retain them or make friends of them, but has to look on while her colonies attract those she herself would so gladly keep.

I do not know if all are aware that every month ships leave England with a number of servants on board; indeed, as many as fourteen vessels go over to Queensland alone, carrying, on an average, two hundred servants on each ship. Any young woman with good health and good character can get a free passage to Queensland if she is under thirty-five years of age. This colony, even above others, values highly our friends the servants, whose success is undoubted. They try to live up to the high opinion formed of them, but it is grievous to see them leaving the old country which wants them even more than the colonies.

from Sarah Grand, "The New Aspect of the Woman Question," *North American Review* 158 (March 1894)

… What [the new woman] perceived at the outset was the sudden and violent upheaval of the suffering sex in all parts of the world. Women were awakening from their long apathy, and, as they woke, like healthy hungry children unable to articulate, they began to whimper for they knew not what. They might have been easily satisfied at that time had not society, like an ill-conditioned and ignorant nurse, instead of finding out what they lacked, shaken them and beaten them and stormed at them until what was once a little wail became convulsive shrieks and roused up the whole human household. Then man, disturbed by the uproar, came upstairs all anger and irritation, and, without waiting to learn what was the matter, added his own old theories to the din, but, finding they did not act rapidly, formed new ones, and made an intolerable nuisance of himself with his opinions and advice. He was in the state of one who cannot comprehend because he has no faculty to perceive the thing in question, and that is why he was so positive. The dimmest perception that you may be mistaken will save you from making an ass of yourself.

We must look upon man's mistakes, however, with some leniency, because we are not blameless in the matter ourselves. We have allowed him to arrange the whole social system and manage or mismanage it all these ages without ever seriously examining his work with a view to considering whether his abilities or motives were sufficiently good to qualify him for the task. We have listened without a smile to his preachments, about our place in life and all we are good for, on the text that "there is no understanding a woman." We have endured most poignant misery for his sins, and screened him when we should have exposed him and had him punished. We have allowed him to exact all things of us, and have been content to accept the little he grudgingly gave us in return. We have meekly bowed our heads when he called us bad names instead of demanding proofs of the superiority which alone would give him a right to do so. We have listened much edified to man's sermons on the subject of virtue, and have acquiesced uncomplainingly in the convenient arrangement by which this quality has come to be altogether practised for him by us vicariously. We have seen him set up Christ as an example for all men to follow, which argues his belief in the possibility of doing so, and have not only allowed his weakness and hypocrisy in the matter to pass without comment, but, until lately, have not even seen the humor of his pretensions when contrasted with his practices, nor held him up to that wholesome ridicule which is a stimulating corrective. Man deprived us of all proper education, and then jeered at us because we had no knowledge. He narrowed our outlook on life so that our view of it should be all distorted, and then declared that our mistaken impression of it proved us to be senseless creatures. He cramped our minds so that there was no room for reason in them, and then made merry at our want of logic. Our divine intuition was not to be controlled by him, but he did his best to damage it by sneering at it as an inferior feminine method of arriving at conclusions; and finally, after having had his own way until he lost his head completely, he set himself up as a sort of god and required us to worship him, and to our eternal shame be it said, we did so. The truth has all along been in us, but we have cared more for man than for truth, and so the whole human race has suffered. We have failed of our effect by neglecting our duty here, and have deserved much of the obloquy that was cast upon us. All that is over now, however, and while on the one hand man has shrunk to his true proportions in our estimation, we, on the other, have been expanding to our own; and now we come confidently forward to maintain, not that this or that was "intended," but that there are in ourselves, in both sexes, possibilities hitherto suppressed or abused, which, when properly developed, will supply to either what is lacking in the other.

The man of the future will be better, while the woman will be stronger and wiser. To bring this about is the whole aim and object of the present struggle, and with the discovery of the means lies the solution of the Woman Question. Man, having no conception of himself as imperfect from the woman's point of view, will find this difficult to understand, but we know his weakness, and will be patient with him, and help him with his lesson. It is the woman's place and pride and pleasure to teach the child, and man morally is in his infancy. There have been times when there was a doubt as to whether he was to be raised or woman was to be lowered, but we have turned that corner at last; and now woman holds out a strong hand to the child-man, and insists, but with infinite tenderness and pity, upon helping him up....

from Mona Caird, "Does Marriage Hinder A Woman's Self-Development?" *Lady's Realm*, March 1899

Perhaps it might throw some light on the question whether marriage interferes with a woman's self-development and career, if we were to ask ourselves honestly how a man would fare in the position, say, of his own wife.

We will take a mild case, so as to avoid all risk of exaggeration.

Our hero's wife is very kind to him. Many of his friends have far sadder tales to tell. Mrs. Brown is fond of her home and family. She pats the children on the head when they come down to dessert, and plies them with chocolate creams, much to the detriment of their health; but it amuses Mrs. Brown. Mr. Brown superintends the bilous[1] attacks, which the lady attributes to other causes. As she never finds fault with the children, and generally remonstrates with their father, in a good-natured way, when *he* does so, they are devoted to the indulgent parent, and are inclined to regard the other as second-rate....

John's faded cheeks, the hollow lines under the eyes, and hair out of curl, speak of the struggle for existence as it penetrates to the fireside. If Sophia but knew what it meant to keep going the multitudinous details and departments of a household!...

If incessant vigilance, tact, firmness, foresight, initiative, courage and judgment—in short, all the qualities required for governing a kingdom, and more—have made things go smoothly, the wife takes it as a matter of course; if they go wrong, she naturally lays the blame on the husband. In the same way, if the children are a credit to their parents, that is only as it should be. But if they are naughty, and fretful, and stupid, and untidy, is it not clear that there must be some serious flaw in the system which could produce such results in the offspring of Mrs. Brown? What word in the English language is too severe to describe the man who neglects to watch with sufficient vigilance over his children's health and moral training, who fails to see that his little boys' sailor-suits and knickerbockers are in good repair, that their bootlace ends do not fly out from their ankles at every step, that their hair is not like a hearth-brush, that they do not come down to dinner every day with dirty hands?

To every true man, the cares of fatherhood and home are sacred and all-sufficing. He realizes, as he looks around at his little ones, that they are his crown and recompense.

John often finds that *his* crown-and-recompense gives him a racking headache by war-whoops and

---

[1] *bilous* Angry, peevish.

stampedes of infinite variety, and there are moments when he wonders in dismay if he is really a true man! He has had the privilege of rearing and training five small crowns and recompenses, and he feels that he could face the future if further privilege, of this sort, were denied him. Not but that he is devoted to his family. Nobody who understands the sacrifices he has made for them could doubt that. Only, he feels that those parts of his nature which are said to distinguish the human from the animal kingdom are getting rather effaced.

He remembers the days before his marriage, when he was so bold, in his ignorant youth, as to cherish a passion for scientific research. He even went so far as to make a chemical laboratory of the family box-room, till attention was drawn to the circumstance by a series of terrific explosions, which shaved off his eyebrows, blackened his scientific countenance, and caused him to be turned out, neck and crop, with his crucibles, and a sermon on the duty that lay nearest him.... His own bent, however, has always been so painfully strong that

he even yet tries to snatch spare moments for his researches; but the strain in so many directions has broken down his health. People always told him that a man's constitution was not fitted for severe brain-work. He supposes it is true....

John still hoped, after twenty years of experience, that presently, by some different arrangement, some better management on his part, he would achieve leisure and mental repose to do the work that his heart was in; but that time never came.

No doubt John was not infallible, and made mistakes in dealing with his various problems: do the best of us achieve consummate wisdom? No doubt, if he had followed the advice that we could all have supplied him with, in such large quantities, he might have done rather more than he did. But the question is: Did his marriage interfere with his self-development and career, and would many other Johns, in his circumstances, have succeeded much better?

ELIZABETH BARRETT BROWNING
1806 – 1861

Once considered for the position of poet laureate of England, Elizabeth Barrett Browning was a highly renowned poet in her day, admired by contemporaries such as Wordsworth and Dickinson, critics, and the general public alike. Her poetry fell out of fashion in the first half of the twentieth century, but Barrett Browning began to be lauded once again in the past generation, particularly for her long narrative poem *Aurora Leigh*. Best known among the general public for the romantic vision of her *Sonnets from the Portuguese* ("How do I love thee? Let me count the ways" from "Sonnet XLII" is one of the most famous lines in English literature), Barrett Browning also addressed significant moral and political issues in her work.

Elizabeth Barrett was the eldest of twelve children born to a wealthy plantation-owning family in Durham, England. Just prior to her birth her parents, Edward Barrett Moulton-Barrett and Mary Graham Clarke Moulton-Barrett, moved from their slave plantation in Jamaica to raise a family in England. The young Barrett grew up in the sheltered environment of a country manor called Hope End, learning languages and studying the classics, at a time when a young woman's education was typically restricted to the domestic sphere. An exceptional and intellectually voracious student, Barrett learned Latin, Greek, and French from her brothers' tutors and studied philosophical, historical, and religious works on her own. She had read Milton's *Paradise Lost* by the time she was 10 years old and, encouraged by her parents, anonymously published her first poem, an epic entitled *The Battle of Marathon*, a few years later. In 1826, she published *An Essay on Mind and Other Poems*. In 1833 she published her translation from the Greek of Aeschylus's *Prometheus Unbound*; she also included some of her own poems in the volume.

Due to the abolition of slavery, the Barretts' fortune began to wane, and in 1832 they were required to sell Hope End, eventually moving to Wimpole Street in London. Her father was overly protective of his children, however, and Barrett fell into semi-seclusion within the family home; her seclusion was compounded by illnesses that had begun to plague her when she was about 12 years old. Critics speculate as to the name of those illnesses, but there is evidence to suggest that Barrett may have suffered from tuberculosis and possibly from a spinal injury. Her maladies were no doubt exacerbated by the opiates prescribed by doctors and the depression that followed the accidental death of her beloved brother Edward, who had accompanied her while she recuperated in the south of England. This tragedy, and Barrett's subsequent feelings of anguish and guilt, inspired some of her best-known poems, including the elegiac sonnet "Grief."

Much has been written about Barrett's middle years, but the image of the bed-ridden recluse remains somewhat at odds with the prolific reader and writer who wrote poetry, essays, reviews, and criticism for magazines and journals and published *The Seraphim and Other Poems* in 1838. The two-volume collection of her *Poems* published in 1844 contains some of her most politically-charged poetry, including "The Cry of the Children," which condemned the employment of children in factories. During these years, Barrett kept up an active correspondence with many writers, critics, and artists and accepted occasional visitors in the confines of her family home. It was in this way that she met Robert Browning, who called upon her after the 1844 collection appeared. He visited her after first writing to express his admiration for work that had already made Barrett famous in England and was rapidly gaining recognition in the United States.

The subsequent exchange of 574 letters between Barrett and Browning, six years her junior, and their eventual elopement have received much attention, with some suggesting that Barrett Browning's best work was inspired by this passionate relationship. It is worth noting here that she had already begun to write love poetry, having translated Petrarch's sonnets and written her own before she met Browning. There is no doubt, however, that the force of their relationship inspired some of her most enduring work, notably her famous *Sonnets from the Portuguese*, written during her courtship with Browning and published in 1850. "My little Portuguese," an allusion to her dark skin, was Browning's pet name for his wife.

Her 1846 marriage to Browning and their ensuing life together in Italy were a boon to Barrett Browning's health and her work. Her beloved father, however, who had forbidden his children to marry, refused to speak to or see his daughter again, going so far as to return her letters unopened. In 1849 the Brownings' only child, Robert Wiedemann Barrett Browning (nicknamed "Pen"), was born in Casa Guidi, just outside Florence.

Not long after the publication of *Sonnets*, Barrett Browning published *Casa Guidi Windows*, which promoted the cause of *Risorgimento*, the Italian struggle for unification and independence from foreign domination (the subject also of many of the later *Poems before Congress*). In 1850, she published the abolition poem "The Runaway Slave at Pilgrim's Point," one of the great dramatic monologues and political-protest poems written in English in the nineteenth century. Barrett Browning's comment on Harriet Beecher Stowe's *Uncle Tom's Cabin* summarizes her consistent response to critics who questioned her choice of subjects: "… is it possible you think a woman has no business with questions like the question of slavery? Then she had better use a pen no more. She had better subside into slavery and concubinage herself, I think, as in the times of old, shut herself up with the Penelopes in the 'women's apartment,' and take no rank among thinkers and speakers." The 1856 work *Aurora Leigh* further cemented Barrett Browning's immense popularity, even though its subject matter was deemed scandalous by many at the time. Coventry Patmore, Victorian author of *The Angel in the House*, a book of poems lauding feminine domestic virtues, was among those who attacked Barrett Browning's candor and audacity in *Aurora Leigh*. An ambitious, epic poem, *Aurora Leigh* is narrated in nine books of blank verse and is the zenith of Barrett Browning's life work, encompassing her convictions on desire, power, art, love, romance, race, class structures, and the subjugation of women. The independent and progressive heroine of the books is named in part after Barrett Browning's idol, French writer Georges Sand (née Aurore Dupin), known for her liberal, feminist views and her penchant for wearing men's clothing. Like Sand, and also like Barrett Browning herself, Aurora Leigh is a writer, one who questions her identity as both artist and woman and struggles to achieve independence from subjugation by staid societal mores and manners and yet still preserve the ability to attain love and companionship.

Elizabeth Barrett Browning predeceased her husband by 28 years when she passed away in his arms in 1861; she is buried in the Protestant cemetery in Florence.

⌘ ⌘ ⌘

The Cry of the Children [1]

"Φεῦ, φεῦ, τί προσδέρκεσθέ μ' ὄμμασιν, τέκνα;" —Medea. [2]

1

Do ye hear the children weeping, O my brothers,
    Ere the sorrow comes with years?
They are leaning their young heads against their mothers,
    And *that* cannot stop their tears.
5 The young lambs are bleating in the meadows,
    The young birds are chirping in the nest,
The young fawns are playing with the shadows,
    The young flowers are blowing toward the west—
But the young, young children, O my brothers,
10   They are weeping bitterly!
They are weeping in the playtime of the others,
    In the country of the free.

2

Do you question the young children in the sorrow
    Why their tears are falling so?
15 The old man may weep for his tomorrow
    Which is lost in Long Ago;
The old tree is leafless in the forest,
    The old year is ending in the frost,
The old wound, if stricken, is the sorest,
20   The old hope is hardest to be lost.
But the young, young children, O my brothers,
    Do you ask them why they stand
Weeping sore before the bosoms of their mothers,
    In our happy Fatherland?

3

25 They look up with their pale and sunken faces,
    And their looks are sad to see,
For the man's hoary anguish draws and presses
    Down the cheeks of infancy.
"Your old earth," they say, "is very dreary;
30 Our young feet," they say, "are very weak!
Few paces have we taken, yet are weary—
    Our grave rest is very far to seek.
Ask the aged why they weep, and not the children;
    For the outside earth is cold;
35 And we young ones stand without, in our
      bewildering,
    And the graves are for the old."

4

"True," say the children, "it may happen
    That we die before our time;
Little Alice died last year—her grave is shapen
40   Like a snowball, in the rime.
We looked into the pit prepared to take her:
    Was no room for any work in the close clay!
From the sleep wherein she lieth none will wake her,
    Crying, 'Get up, little Alice! it is day.'
45 If you listen by that grave, in sun and shower,
    With your ear down, little Alice never cries;
Could we see her face, be sure we should not know her,
    For the smile has time for growing in her eyes:
And merry go her moments, lulled and stilled in
50   The shroud by the kirk° chime.   *church*
It is good when it happens," say the children,
    "That we die before our time."

5

Alas, alas, the children! they are seeking
    Death in life, as best to have;
55 They are binding up their hearts away from breaking,
    With a cerement° from the grave.   *shroud*
Go out, children, from the mine and from the city,
    Sing out, children, as the little thrushes do;
Pluck you handfuls of the meadow cowslips pretty,
60   Laugh aloud, to feel your fingers let them through!
But they answer, "Are your cowslips of the meadows
    Like our weeds anear the mine?
Leave us quiet in the dark of the coal shadows,
    From your pleasures fair and fine!

6

65 "For oh," say the children, "we are weary,
    And we cannot run or leap;

---

[1] *The Cry of the Children* This poem was written in response to
Richard Henry Horne's 1843 "Report of the Children's Employment Commission" regarding child labor in the mining and
manufacturing industries (see "In Context," below). Horne was the
author of the epic poem *Orion* and the play *Cosmo de' Medici*, as well
as *A New Spirit of the Age*, co-written with Elizabeth Barrett.

[2] Φεῦ … τέκνα From Euripides's *Medea* (431 BCE) 1.1040, in
which Medea says, upon killing her children: "Alas, why do you gaze
at me thus, my children?"

If we cared for any meadows, it were merely
      To drop down in them and sleep.
Our knees tremble sorely in the stooping,
70   We fall upon our faces, trying to go;
And, underneath our heavy eyelids drooping,
      The reddest flower would look as pale as snow;
For, all day, we drag our burden tiring
      Through the coal dark, underground;
75 Or, all day, we drive the wheels of iron
      In the factories, round and round.

7

"For all day, the wheels are droning, turning;
      Their wind comes in our faces,
Till our hearts turn, our heads with pulses burning,
80   And the walls turn in their places:
Turns the sky in the high window blank and reeling,
      Turns the long light that drops adown the wall,
Turn the black flies that crawl along the ceiling,
      All are turning, all the day, and we with all.
85 And all day, the iron wheels are droning,
      And sometimes we could pray,
'O ye wheels,' (breaking out in a mad moaning)
      'Stop! be silent for today!'"

8

Aye, be silent! Let them hear each other breathing
90   For a moment, mouth to mouth!
Let them touch each other's hands, in a fresh wreathing
      Of their tender human youth!
Let them feel that this cold metallic motion
      Is not all the life God fashions or reveals:
95 Let them prove their living souls against the notion
      That they live in you, or under you, O wheels!
Still, all day, the iron wheels go onward,
      Grinding life down from its mark;
And the children's souls, which God is calling sunward,
100   Spin on blindly in the dark.

9

Now tell the poor young children, O my brothers,
      To look up to Him and pray;
So the blessed One who blesseth all the others,
      Will bless them another day.
105 They answer, "Who is God that He should hear us,

While the rushing of the iron wheels is stirred?
When we sob aloud, the human creatures near us
      Pass by, hearing not, or answer not a word.
And *we* hear not (for the wheels in their resounding)
110   Strangers speaking at the door:
Is it likely God, with angels singing round him,
      Hears our weeping any more?

10

"Two words, indeed, of praying we remember,
      And at midnight's hour of harm,
115 'Our Father,' looking upward in the chamber,
      We say softly for a charm.[1]
We know no other words except 'Our Father,'
      And we think that, in some pause of angels' song,
God may pluck them with the silence sweet to gather,
120   And hold both within His right hand which is strong.
'Our Father!' If He heard us, He would surely
      (For they call Him good and mild)
Answer, smiling down the steep world very purely,
      'Come and rest with me, my child.'"

11

125 "But no!" say the children, weeping faster,
      "He is speechless as a stone:
And they tell us, of His image is the master
      Who commands us to work on.
Go to!" say the children,—"up in heaven,
130   Dark, wheel-like, turning clouds are all we find.
Do not mock us; grief has made us unbelieving:
      We look up for God, but tears have made us blind."
Do you hear the children weeping and disproving,
      O my brothers, what ye preach?
135 For God's possible is taught by His world's loving,
      And the children doubt of each.

12

And well may the children weep before you!
      They are weary ere they run;
They have never seen the sunshine, nor the glory

---

1 [Barrett Browning's note]   A fact rendered pathetically historical
by Mr. Horne's report of his commission. The name of the poet of
Orion and *Cosmo de' Medici* has, however, a change of associations,
and comes in time to remind me that we have some noble poetic
heat of literature still, however open to the reproach of being
somewhat gelid in our humanity. [*gelid*   Cold.]

140   Which is brighter than the sun.
They know the grief of man, without its wisdom;
    They sink in man's despair, without its calm;
Are slaves, without the liberty in Christdom,
    Are martyrs, by the pang without the palm;
145 Are worn as if with age, yet unretrievingly
      The harvest of its memories cannot reap,—
Are orphans of the earthly love and heavenly.
      Let them weep! let them weep!

13

They look up with their pale and sunken faces,
150   And their look is dread to see,
For they mind you of their angels in high places,
    With eyes turned on Deity!
"How long," they say, "how long, O cruel nation,
    Will you stand, to move the world, on a child's
      heart,—
155 Stifle down with a mailed° heel its palpitation,   *armored*
    And tread onward to your throne amid the mart?
Our blood splashes upward, O gold-heaper,
    And your purple shows your path!
But the child's sob in the silence curses deeper
160   Than the strong man in his wrath."
    —1844

To George Sand [1]
A Desire

Thou large-brained woman and large-hearted man,
  Self-called George Sand! whose soul, amid the lions
Of thy tumultuous senses, moans defiance
And answers roar for roar, as spirits can:
5 I would some mild miraculous thunder ran
Above the applauded circus, in appliance
Of thine own nobler nature's strength and science,
Drawing two pinions,° white as wings of swan,   *wings*
From thy strong shoulders, to amaze the place
10 With holier light! that thou to woman's claim

And man's, mightst join beside the angel's grace
Of a pure genius sanctified from blame,
Till child and maiden pressed to thine embrace
To kiss upon thy lips a stainless fame.
—1844

To George Sand
A Recognition

True genius, but true woman! dost deny
  The woman's nature with a manly scorn,
And break away the gauds° and armlets worn   *ornaments*
By weaker women in captivity?
5 Ah, vain denial! that revolted cry
Is sobbed in by a woman's voice forlorn,—
Thy woman's hair, my sister, all unshorn
Floats back dishevelled strength in agony,
Disproving thy man's name: and while before
10 The world thou burnest in a poet fire,
We see thy woman heart beat evermore
Through the large flame. Beat purer, heart, and higher,
Till God unsex thee on the heavenly shore
Where unincarnate spirits purely aspire!
—1844

A Year's Spinning

1

He listened at the porch that day,
  To hear the wheel go on, and on;
And then it stopped, ran back away,
  While through the door he brought the sun:
5   But now my spinning is all done.

2

He sat beside me, with an oath
  That love ne'er ended, once begun;
I smiled—believing for us both,
  What was the truth for only one:
10   And now my spinning is all done.

---

[1] *George Sand* Pseudonym of French author Amandine Aurore Lucie Dupin (1804–76), who was often condemned for her free-spirited ways, which included wearing men's clothing. For images of Sand see "In Context," below.

3

My mother cursed me that I heard
    A young man's wooing as I spun:
Thanks, cruel mother, for that word—
    For I have, since, a harder known!
15   And now my spinning is all done.

4

I thought—O God!—my firstborn's cry
    Both voices to mine ear would drown:
I listened in mine agony—
    It was the *silence* made me groan!
20   And now my spinning is all done.

5

Bury me 'twixt my mother's grave,
    (Who cursed me on her deathbed lone)
And my dead baby's (God it save!)
    Who, not to bless me, would not moan.
25   And now my spinning is all done.

6

A stone upon my heart and head,
    But no name written on the stone!
Sweet neighbours, whisper low instead,
    "This sinner was a loving one—
30   And now her spinning is all done."

7

And let the door ajar remain,
    In case he should pass by anon;
And leave the wheel out very plain,—
    That HE, when passing in the sun,
35   May see the spinning is all done.
—1850

The Runaway Slave at Pilgrim's Point

1

I stand on the mark beside the shore
    Of the first white pilgrim's bended knee,
Where exile turned to ancestor,
    And God was thanked for liberty.
5 I have run through the night, my skin is as dark,

I bend my knee down on this mark:
    I look on the sky and the sea.

2

O pilgrim-souls, I speak to you!
    I see you come proud and slow
10 From the land of the spirits pale as dew
    And round me and round me ye go.
O pilgrims, I have gasped and run
All night long from the whips of one
    Who in your names works sin and woe!

3

15 And thus I thought that I would come
    And kneel here where you knelt before,
And feel your souls around me hum
    In undertone to the ocean's roar;
And lift my black face, my black hand,
20 Here, in your names, to curse this land
    Ye blessed in freedom's, evermore.

4

I am black, I am black,
    And yet God made me, they say:
But if He did so, smiling back
25   He must have cast His work away
Under the feet of His white creatures,
With a look of scorn, that the dusky features
    Might be trodden again to clay.

5

And yet He has made dark things
30   To be glad and merry as light:
There's a little dark bird sits and sings,
    There's a dark stream ripples out of sight,
And the dark frogs chant in the safe morass,
And the sweetest stars are made to pass
35   O'er the face of the darkest night.

6

But *we* who are dark, we are dark!
    Ah God, we have no stars!
About our souls in care and cark°   *troubles*
    Our blackness shuts like prison bars:
40 The poor souls crouch so far behind

That never a comfort can they find
　　By reaching through the prison bars.

7

Indeed we live beneath the sky,
　　That great smooth Hand of God stretched out
45 On all his children fatherly,
　　To save them from the dread and doubt
Which would be if, from this low place,
All opened straight up to His face
　　Into the grand eternity.

8

50 And still God's sunshine and His frost,
　　They make us hot, they make us cold,
As if we were not black and lost;
　　And the beasts and birds, in wood and fold,
Do fear and take us for very men:
55 Could the whippoorwill or the cat of the glen
　　Look into my eyes and be bold?

9

I am black, I am black!
　　But, once, I laughed in girlish glee,
For one of my colour stood in the track
60 　　Where the drivers drove, and looked at me,
And tender and full was the look he gave—
Could a slave look *so* at another slave?—
　　I look at the sky and sea.

10

And from that hour our spirits grew
65 　　As free as if unsold, unbought:
Oh, strong enough, since we were two,
　　To conquer the world, we thought.
The drivers drove us day by day;
We did not mind, we went one way,
70 　　And no better a freedom sought.

11

In the sunny ground between the canes,
　　He said "I love you" as he passed;
When the shingle roof rang sharp with the rains,
　　I heard how he vowed it fast:
75 While others shook he smiled in the hut,

As he carved me a bowl of the coconut
　　Through the roar of the hurricanes.

12

I sang his name instead of a song,
　　Over and over I sang his name,
80 Upward and downward I drew it along
　　My various notes,—the same, the same!
I sang it low, that the slave girls near
Might never guess, from aught they could hear,
　　It was only a name—a name.

13

85 I look on the sky and the sea.
　　We were two to love, and two to pray:
Yes, two, O God, who cried to Thee,
　　Though nothing didst Thou say!
Coldly Thou sat'st behind the sun:
90 And now I cry who am but one,
　　Thou wilt not speak today.

14

We were black, we were black,
　　We had no claim to love and bliss,
What marvel if each went to wrack?
95 　　They wrung my cold hands out of his
They dragged him—where? I crawled to touch
His blood's mark in the dust … not much,
　　Ye pilgrim-souls, though plain as this!

15

Wrong, followed by a deeper wrong!
100 　　Mere grief's too good for such as I:
So the white men brought the shame ere long
　　To strangle the sob of my agony.
They would not leave me for my dull
Wet eyes!—it was too merciful
105 　　To let me weep pure tears and die.

16

I am black, I am black!
　　I wore a child upon my breast,
An amulet that hung too slack,
　　And, in my unrest, could not rest:
110 Thus we went moaning, child and mother,

One to another, one to another,
  Until all ended for the best.

17

For hark! I will tell you low, low,
  I am black, you see,—
115 And the babe who lay on my bosom so,
  Was far too white, too white for me;
As white as the ladies who scorned to pray
Beside me at church but yesterday,
  Though my tears had washed a place for my knee.

18

120 My own, own child! I could not bear
  To look in his face, it was so white;
I covered him up with a kerchief there,
  I covered his face in close and tight:
And he moaned and struggled, as well might be,
125 For the white child wanted his liberty—
  Ha, ha! he wanted the master right.

19

He moaned and beat with his head and feet,
  His little feet that never grew;
He struck them out, as it was meet,
130   Against my heart to break it through:
I might have sung and made him mild,
But I dared not sing to the white-faced child
  The only song I knew.

20

I pulled the kerchief very close:
135   He could not see the sun, I swear,
More, then, alive, than now he does
  From between the roots of the mango … where?
I know where. Close! A child and mother
Do wrong to look at one another
140   When one is black and one is fair.

21

Why, in that single glance I had
  Of my child's face, … I tell you all,
I saw a look that made me mad!
  The master's look, that used to fall
145 On my soul like his lash … or worse!
And so, to save it from my curse,
  I twisted it round in my shawl.

22

And he moaned and trembled from foot to head,
  He shivered from head to foot;
150 Till after a time, he lay instead
  Too suddenly still and mute.
I felt, beside, a stiffening cold:
I dared to lift up just a fold,
  As in lifting a leaf of the mango fruit.

23

155 But *my* fruit … ha, ha!—there, had been
  (I laugh to think on't at this hour!)
Your fine white angels (who have seen
  Nearest the secret of God's power)
And plucked my fruit to make them wine,
160 And sucked the soul of that child of mine
  As the hummingbird sucks the soul of the flower.

24

Ha, ha, the trick of the angels white!
  They freed the white child's spirit so.
I said not a word, but day and night
165   I carried the body to and fro,
And it lay on my heart like a stone, as chill.
—The sun may shine out as much as he will:
  I am cold, though it happened a month ago.

25

From the white man's house, and the black man's hut,
170   I carried the little body on;
The forest's arms did round us shut,
  And silence through the trees did run:
They asked no question as I went,
They stood too high for astonishment,
175   They could see God sit on His throne.

26

My little body, kerchiefed fast,
  I bore it on through the forest, on;
And when I felt it was tired at last,
  I scooped a hole beneath the moon:
180 Through the forest tops the angels far,
With a white sharp finger from every star,
  Did point and mock at what was done.

27

Yet when it was all done aright,—
    Earth, 'twixt me and my baby, strewed,—
185 All, changed to black earth,—nothing white,—
    A dark child in the dark!—ensued
Some comfort, and my heart grew young;
I sat down smiling there and sung
    The song I learnt in my maidenhood.

28

190 And thus we two were reconciled,
    The white child and black mother, thus;
For as I sang it soft and wild,
    The same song, more melodious,
Rose from the grave whereon I sat:
195 It was the dead child singing that,
    To join the souls of both of us.

29

I look on the sea and the sky.
    Where the pilgrims' ships first anchored lay
The free sun rideth gloriously,
200   But the pilgrim-ghosts have slid away
Through the earliest streaks of the morn:
My face is black, but it glares with a scorn
    Which they dare not meet by day.

30

Ha!—in their stead, their hunter sons!
205   Ha, ha! they are on me—they hunt in a ring!
Keep off! I brave you all at once,
    I throw off your eyes like snakes that sting!
You have killed the black eagle at nest, I think:
Did you ever stand still in your triumph, and shrink
210   From the stroke of her wounded wing?

31

(Man, drop that stone you dared to lift!—)
    I wish you who stand there five abreast,
Each, for his own wife's joy and gift,
    A little corpse as safely at rest
215 As mine in the mangoes! Yes, but she
May keep live babies on her knee,
    And sing the song she likes the best.

32

I am not mad: I am black.
    I see you staring in my face—
220 I know you staring, shrinking back,
    Ye are born of the Washington race,
And this land is the free America,
And this mark on my wrist—(I prove what I say)
    Ropes tied me up here to the flogging place.

33

225 You think I shrieked then? Not a sound!
    I hung, as a gourd hangs in the sun;
I only cursed them all around
    As softly as I might have done
My very own child: from these sands
230 Up to the mountains, lift your hands,
    O slaves, and end what I begun!

34

Whips, curses; these must answer those!
    For in this UNION you have set
Two kinds of men in adverse rows,
235   Each loathing each; and all forget
The seven wounds in Christ's body fair,
While HE sees gaping everywhere
    Our countless wounds that pay no debt.

35

Our wounds are different. Your white men
240   Are, after all, not gods indeed,
Nor able to make Christs again
    Do good with bleeding. We who bleed
(Stand off!) we help not in our loss!
We are too heavy for our cross,
245   And fall and crush you and your seed.

36

I fall, I swoon! I look at the sky.
    The clouds are breaking on my brain;
I am floated along, as if I should die
    Of liberty's exquisite pain.
250 In the name of the white child waiting for me
In the death dark where we may kiss and agree,
White men, I leave you all curse-free
    In my broken heart's disdain!

—1850

from *Sonnets from the Portuguese*

1

I thought once how Theocritus[1] had sung
Of the sweet years, the dear and wished-for years,
Who each one in a gracious hand appears
To bear a gift for mortals, old or young:
5 And, as I mused it in his antique tongue,[2]
I saw, in gradual vision through my tears,
The sweet, sad years, the melancholy years,
Those of my own life, who by turns had flung
A shadow across me. Straightway I was 'ware,
10 So weeping, how a mystic Shape did move
Behind me, and drew me backward by the hair;
And a voice said in mastery, while I strove—
"Guess now who holds thee?"—"Death," I said. But,
    there,
The silver answer rang—"Not Death, but Love."

7

The face of all the world is changed, I think,
Since first I heard the footsteps of thy soul
Move still, oh, still, beside me, as they stole
Betwixt me and the dreadful outer brink
5 Of obvious death, where I, who thought to sink,
Was caught up into love, and taught the whole
Of life in a new rhythm. The cup of dole
God gave for baptism, I am fain to drink,
And praise its sweetness, Sweet, with thee anear.
10 The names of country, heaven, are changed away
For where thou art or shalt be, there or here;
And this ... this lute and song ... loved yesterday,
(The singing angels know) are only dear
Because thy name moves right in what they say.

13

And wilt thou have me fasten into speech
The love I bear thee, finding words enough,
And hold the torch out, while the winds are rough,
Between our faces, to cast light on each?—
5 I drop it at thy feet. I cannot teach

My hand to hold my spirit so far off
From myself—me—that I should bring thee proof
In words, of love hid in me out of reach.
Nay, let the silence of my womanhood
10 Commend my woman-love to thy belief—
Seeing that I stand unwon, however wooed,
And rend the garment of my life, in brief,
By a most dauntless, voiceless fortitude,
Lest one touch of this heart convey its grief.

21

Say over again, and yet once over again,
That thou dost love me. Though the word repeated
Should seem "a cuckoo-song," as thou dost treat it,
Remember, never to the hill or plain,
5 Valley and wood, without her cuckoo-strain
Comes the fresh Spring in all her green completed.
Belovèd, I, amid the darkness greeted
By a doubtful spirit-voice, in that doubt's pain
Cry, "Speak once more—thou lovest!" Who can fear
10 Too many stars, though each in heaven shall roll,
Too many flowers, though each shall crown the year?
Say thou dost love me, love me, love me—toll
The silver iterance![3]—only minding, Dear,
To love me also in silence with thy soul.

22

When our two souls stand up erect and strong,
Face to face, silent, drawing nigh and nigher,
Until the lengthening wings break into fire
At either curvèd point—what bitter wrong
5 Can the earth do to us, that we should not long
Be here contented? Think. In mounting higher,
The angels would press on us and aspire
To drop some golden orb of perfect song
Into our deep, dear silence. Let us stay
10 Rather on earth, Belovèd—where the unfit
Contrarious moods of men recoil away
And isolate pure spirits, and permit
A place to stand and love in for a day,
With darkness and the death hour rounding it.

---

[1] *Theocritus* Greek poet of the third century BCE who created the
genre of the pastoral (characterized by idyllic country life and love
between shepherds and shepherdesses).

[2] *antique tongue* Greek language.

[3] *iterance* Repetition.

24

Let the world's sharpness, like a clasping knife,
Shut in upon itself and do no harm
In this close hand of Love, now soft and warm,
And let us hear no sound of human strife
5   After the click of the shutting. Life to life—
I lean upon thee, Dear, without alarm,
And feel as safe as guarded by a charm
Against the stab of worldlings, who if rife
Are weak to injure. Very whitely still
10   The lilies of our lives may reassure
Their blossoms from their roots, accessible
Alone to heavenly dews that drop not fewer,
Growing straight, out of man's reach, on the hill.
God only, who made us rich, can make us poor.

26

I lived with visions for my company
Instead of men and women, years ago,
And found them gentle mates, nor thought to know
A sweeter music than they played to me.
5   But soon their trailing purple was not free
Of this world's dust, their lutes did silent grow,
And I myself grew faint and blind below
Their vanishing eyes. Then *thou* didst come—to be,
Belovèd, what they seemed. Their shining fronts,
10   Their songs, their splendours (better, yet the same,
As river water hallowed into fonts),
Met in thee, and from out thee overcame
My soul with satisfaction of all wants:
Because God's gifts put man's best dreams to shame.

28

My letters! all dead paper, mute and white!
And yet they seem alive and quivering
Against my tremulous hands which loose the string
And let them drop down on my knee tonight.
5   This said—he wished to have me in his sight
Once, as a friend: this fixed a day in spring
To come and touch my hand … a simple thing,
Yet I wept for it!—this, … the paper's light …
Said, *Dear, I love thee;* and I sank and quailed
10   As if God's future thundered on my past.
This said, *I am thine*—and so its ink has paled
With lying at my heart that beat too fast.

And this … O Love, thy words have ill availed
If, what this said, I dared repeat at last!

43

How do I love thee? Let me count the ways.
I love thee to the depth and breadth and height
My soul can reach, when feeling out of sight
For the ends of Being and ideal Grace.
5   I love thee to the level of every day's
Most quiet need, by sun and candle-light.
I love thee freely, as men strive for Right;
I love thee purely, as they turn from Praise.
I love thee with the passion put to use
10   In my old griefs, and with my childhood's faith.
I love thee with a love I seemed to lose
With my lost saints—I love thee with the breath,
Smiles, tears, of all my life!—and, if God choose,
I shall but love thee better after death.
—1845–47

Aurora Leigh

BOOK 1

Of writing many books there is no end;[1]
And I who have written much in prose and verse
For others' uses, will write now for mine—
Will write my story for my better self,
5   As when you paint your portrait for a friend,
Who keeps it in a drawer and looks at it
Long after he has ceased to love you, just
To hold together what he was and is.

I, writing thus, am still what men call young;
10   I have not so far left the coasts of life
To travel inward, that I cannot hear
That murmur of the outer Infinite[2]
Which unweaned babies smile at in their sleep
When wondered at for smiling; not so far,
15   But still I catch my mother at her post

---

[1]   *Of writing … end*   See Ecclesiastes 12.12: "[O]f making many books there is no end; and much study is a weariness of the flesh."

[2]   *I have not so far … outer Infinite*   Cf. William Wordsworth's "Ode: Intimations of Immortality from Recollections of Early Childhood," 9.

Beside the nursery door, with finger up,
"Hush, hush—here's too much noise!" while her
     sweet eyes
Leap forward, taking part against her word
In the child's riot. Still I sit and feel
20 My father's slow hand, when she had left us both,
Stroke out my childish curls across his knee,
And hear Assunta's daily jest (she knew
He liked it better than a better jest)
Inquire how many golden scudi[1] went
25 To make such ringlets. O my father's hand,
Stroke heavily, heavily the poor hair down,
Draw, press the child's head closer to thy knee!
I'm still too young, too young, to sit alone.

I write. My mother was a Florentine,
30 Whose rare blue eyes were shut from seeing me
When scarcely I was four years old, my life
A poor spark snatched up from a failing lamp
Which went out therefore. She was weak and frail;
She could not bear the joy of giving life,
35 The mother's rapture slew her. If her kiss
Had left a longer weight upon my lips
It might have steadied the uneasy breath,
And reconciled and fraternised my soul
With the new order. As it was, indeed,
40 I felt a mother-want about the world,
And still went seeking, like a bleating lamb
Left out at night in shutting up the fold—
As restless as a nest-deserted bird
Grown chill through something being away, though
     what
45 It knows not. I, Aurora Leigh, was born
To make my father sadder, and myself
Not overjoyous, truly. Women know
The way to rear up children (to be just),
They know a simple, merry, tender knack
50 Of tying sashes, fitting baby shoes,
And stringing pretty words that make no sense,
And kissing full sense into empty words,
Which things are corals[2] to cut life upon,
Although such trifles: children learn by such,
55 Love's holy earnest in a pretty play

And get not over-early solemnised,
But seeing, as in a rose-bush, Love's Divine
Which burns and hurts not,[3]—not a single bloom—
Become aware and unafraid of Love.
60 Such good do mothers. Fathers love as well
—Mine did, I know—but still with heavier brains,
And wills more consciously responsible,
And not as wisely, since less foolishly;
So mothers have God's license to be missed.

65 My father was an austere Englishman,
Who, after a dry lifetime spent at home
In college learning, law, and parish talk,
Was flooded with a passion unaware,
His whole provisioned and complacent past
70 Drowned out from him that moment. As he stood
In Florence, where he had come to spend a month
And note the secret of da Vinci's drains,[4]
He musing somewhat absently perhaps
Some English question … whether men should pay
75 The unpopular but necessary tax
With left or right hand—in the alien sun
In that great square of the Santissima[5]
There drifted past him (scarcely marked enough
To move his comfortable island scorn)
80 A train of priestly banners, cross and psalm,
The white-veiled rose-crowned maidens holding up
Tall tapers, weighty for such wrists, aslant
To the blue luminous tremor of the air,
And letting drop the white wax as they went
85 To eat the bishop's wafer[6] at the church;
From which long trail of chanting priests and girls,
A face flashed like a cymbal on his face
And shook with silent clangour brain and heart,
Transfiguring him to music. Thus, even thus,
90 He too received his sacramental gift
With eucharistic meanings; for he loved.

1 *scudi*   Italian coins no longer in use.
2 *corals*   Babies' teething toys made of polished coral.

3 *rose-bush … hurts not*   See Exodus 3.2, in which God appears in a burning bush.
4 *da Vinci's drains*   Leonardo da Vinci (1452–1519), Renaissance painter, sculptor, architect, and engineer, invented a system of drainage canals.
5 *Santissima*   Florence's baroque church of Santissima Annunziata.
6 *Eat … wafer*   Receive Holy Communion.

And thus beloved, she died. I've heard it said
That but to see him in the first surprise
Of widower and father, nursing me,
95 Unmothered little child of four years old,
His large man's hands afraid to touch my curls,
As if the gold would tarnish—his grave lips
Contriving such a miserable smile
As if he knew needs must, or I should die,
100 And yet 'twas hard—would almost make the stones
Cry out for pity.[1] There's a verse he set
In Santa Croce[2] to her memory—
"Weep for an infant too young to weep much
When death removed this mother"—stops the mirth
105 Today on women's faces when they walk
With rosy children hanging on their gowns,
Under the cloister to escape the sun
That scorches in the piazza. After which
He left our Florence and made haste to hide
110 Himself, his prattling child, and silent grief,
Among the mountains above Pelago;[3]
Because unmothered babes, he thought, had need
Of mother nature more than others use,
And Pan's[4] white goats, with udders warm and full
115 Of mystic contemplations, come to feed
Poor milkless lips of orphans like his own—
Such scholar-scraps he talked, I've heard from friends,
For even prosaic men who wear grief long
Will get to wear it as a hat aside
120 With a flower stuck in't. Father, then, and child,
We lived among the mountains many years,
God's silence on the outside of the house,
And we who did not speak too loud within,
And old Assunta to make up the fire,
125 Crossing herself whene'er a sudden flame
Which lightened from the firewood, made alive
That picture of my mother on the wall.

The painter drew it after she was dead,
And when the face was finished, throat and hands,

130 Her cameriera[5] carried him, in hate
Of the English-fashioned shroud, the last brocade
She dressed in at the Pitti;[6] "he should paint
No sadder thing than that," she swore, "to wrong
Her poor signora." Therefore very strange
135 The effect was. I, a little child, would crouch
For hours upon the floor with knees drawn up,
And gaze across them, half in terror, half
In adoration, at the picture there—
That swan-like supernatural white life
140 Just sailing upward from the red stiff silk
Which seemed to have no part in it nor power
To keep it from quite breaking out of bounds.
For hours I sat and stared. Assunta's awe
And my poor father's melancholy eyes
145 Still pointed that way. That way went my thoughts
When wandering beyond sight. And as I grew
In years, I mixed, confused, unconsciously,
Whatever I last read or heard or dreamed,
Abhorrent, admirable, beautiful,
150 Pathetical, or ghastly, or grotesque,
With still that face ... which did not therefore change,
But kept the mystic level of all forms,
Hates, fears, and admirations, was by turns
Ghost, fiend, and angel, fairy, witch, and sprite,
155 A dauntless Muse who eyes a dreadful Fate,[7]
A loving Psyche[8] who loses sight of Love,
A still Medusa[9] with mild milky brows
All curdled and all clothed upon with snakes
Whose slime falls fast as sweat will; or anon
160 Our Lady of the Passion, stabbed with swords

---

[1] *make the stones cry out for pity* Cf. Jesus's speech to the Pharisees in Luke 19:40: "If these should hold their peace, the stones would immediately cry out."

[2] *Santa Croce* Gothic church in Florence.

[3] *Pelago* Village near Florence.

[4] *Pan* Greek god of Nature who was half goat and half man, and to whom white goats were sacred.

---

[5] *cameriera* Maid.

[6] *Pitti* Renaissance palace in Florence, former home of the Medicis and other royal families.

[7] *Muse* One of the nine goddesses of the arts and sciences in Greek and Roman mythology; *Fate* One of three goddesses of fate and destiny in Greek and Roman mythology.

[8] *Psyche* Mortal daughter of royalty in Greek mythology. Eros, the god of love, visited Psyche in the dark of night as her lover, but he abandoned her after she disobeyed his command not to look at him.

[9] *Medusa* One of the three Gorgons, who was made mortal after claiming she was more beautiful than Athena. Medusa was transformed into a monster with hair made of snakes, whose gaze would turn men to stone.

Where the Babe sucked; or Lamia[1] in her first
Moonlighted pallor, ere she shrunk and blinked
And shuddering wriggled down to the unclean;
Or my own mother, leaving her last smile
165 In her last kiss upon the baby-mouth
My father pushed down on the bed for that—
Or my dead mother, without smile or kiss,
Buried at Florence. All which images,
Concentred on the picture, glassed themselves
170 Before my meditative childhood, as
The incoherencies of change and death
Are represented fully, mixed and merged,
In the smooth fair mystery of perpetual Life.

And while I stared away my childish wits
175 Upon my mother's picture (ah, poor child!),
My father, who through love had suddenly
Thrown off the old conventions, broken loose
From chin-bands of the soul, like Lazarus,[2]
Yet had no time to learn to talk and walk
180 Or grow anew familiar with the sun—
Who had reached to freedom, not to action, lived,
But lived as one entranced, with thoughts, not aims—
Whom love had unmade from a common man
But not completed to an uncommon man—
185 My father taught me what he had learnt the best
Before he died and left me—grief and love.
And, seeing we had books among the hills,
Strong words of counselling souls confederate
With vocal pines and waters—out of books
190 He taught me all the ignorance of men,
And how God laughs in heaven when any man
Says "Here I'm learned; this, I understand;
In that, I am never caught at fault or doubt."
He sent the schools to school, demonstrating
195 A fool will pass for such through one mistake,
While a philosopher will pass for such,
Through said mistakes being ventured in the gross

And heaped up to a system.
                    I am like,
200 They tell me, my dear father. Broader brows
Howbeit, upon a slenderer undergrowth
Of delicate features—paler, near as grave;
But then my mother's smile breaks up the whole,
And makes it better sometimes than itself.

205 So, nine full years, our days were hid with God
Among his mountains: I was just thirteen,
Still growing like the plants from unseen roots
In tongue-tied Springs—and suddenly awoke
To full life and life's needs and agonies
210 With an intense, strong, struggling heart beside
A stone-dead father. Life, struck sharp on death,
Makes awful lightning. His last word was "Love—"
"Love, my child, love, love!"—(then he had done with grief)
"Love, my child." Ere I answered he was gone,
215 And none was left to love in all the world.

There, ended childhood. What succeeded next
I recollect as, after fevers, men
Thread back the passage of delirium,
Missing the turn still, baffled by the door;
220 Smooth endless days, notched here and there with knives,
A weary, wormy darkness, spurred i' the flank
With flame, that it should eat and end itself
Like some tormented scorpion.[3] Then at last
I do remember clearly how there came
225 A stranger with authority, not right
(I thought not), who commanded, caught me up
From old Assunta's neck; how, with a shriek,
She let me go—while I, with ears too full
Of my father's silence to shriek back a word,
230 In all a child's astonishment at grief
Stared at the wharf edge where she stood and moaned,
My poor Assunta, where she stood and moaned!
The white walls, the blue hills, my Italy,
Drawn backward from the shuddering steamer deck,
235 Like one in anger drawing back her skirts
Which suppliants catch at. Then the bitter sea
Inexorably pushed between us both

---

[1] *Lady … Babe sucked* Catholic iconology portrays the Virgin Mary stabbed through the heart with the seven swords of grief (the seven sorrows) upon the events leading up to and the crucifixion of Christ, her son; *Lamia* After the goddess Hera killed her children, the mortal Lamia turned to killing others' children out of revenge.

[2] *chin-bands … Lazarus* Cloth used to hold a corpse's mouth closed. John 11.44 speaks of Lazarus rising from the dead, "bound hand and foot with graveclothes: and his face was bound about with a napkin. Jesus saith unto them, Loose him, and let him go."

[3] *flame … scorpion* When surrounded by fire a scorpion will arch its back in protection; this habit is the source of the myth that it is stinging itself and committing suicide.

And, sweeping up the ship with my despair,
Threw us out as a pasture to the stars.

240 Ten nights and days we voyaged on the deep;
Ten nights and days without the common face
Of any day or night; the moon and sun
Cut off from the green reconciling earth,
To starve into a blind ferocity
245 And glare unnatural; the very sky
(Dropping its bell-net down upon the sea,
As if no human heart should 'scape alive)
Bedraggled with the desolating salt,
Until it seemed no more that holy heaven
250 To which my father went. All new and strange;
The universe turned stranger, for a child.

Then, land!—then, England! oh, the frosty cliffs
Looked cold upon me. Could I find a home
Among those mean red houses through the fog?
255 And when I heard my father's language first
From alien lips which had no kiss for mine
I wept aloud, then laughed, then wept, then wept,
And someone near me said the child was mad
Through much seasickness. The train swept us on:
260 Was this my father's England? the great isle?
The ground seemed cut up from the fellowship
Of verdure, field from field, as man from man;
The skies themselves looked low and positive,
As almost you could touch them with a hand,
265 And dared to do it they were so far off
From God's celestial crystals; all things blurred
And dull and vague. Did Shakespeare and his mates
Absorb the light here?—not a hill or stone
With heart to strike a radiant colour up
270 Or active outline on the indifferent air.

I think I see my father's sister stand
Upon the hall step of her country house
To give me welcome. She stood straight and calm,
Her somewhat narrow forehead braided tight
275 As if for taming accidental thoughts
From possible pulses; brown hair pricked with gray
By frigid use of life (she was not old,
Although my father's elder by a year),
A nose drawn sharply, yet in delicate lines;
280 A close mild mouth, a little soured about

The ends, through speaking unrequited loves
Or peradventure niggardly half-truths;
Eyes of no colour—once they might have smiled,
But never, never have forgot themselves
285 In smiling; cheeks, in which was yet a rose
Of perished summers, like a rose in a book,
Kept more for ruth° than pleasure—if past bloom,   *pity*
Past fading also.
                    She had lived, we'll say,
290 A harmless life, she called a virtuous life,
A quiet life, which was not life at all
(But that, she had not lived enough to know),
Between the vicar and the county squires,
The lord-lieutenant looking down sometimes
295 From the empyrean° to assure their souls   *heaven*
Against chance vulgarisms, and, in the abyss,
The apothecary,[1] looked on once a year
To prove their soundness of humility.
The poor-club exercised her Christian gifts
300 Of knitting stockings, stitching petticoats,
Because we are of one flesh, after all,
And need one flannel (with a proper sense
Of difference in the quality)—and still
The book-club, guarded from your modern trick
305 Of shaking dangerous questions from the crease,
Preserved her intellectual. She had lived
A sort of cage-bird life, born in a cage,
Accounting that to leap from perch to perch
Was act and joy enough for any bird.
310 Dear heaven, how silly are the things that live
In thickets, and eat berries!
                              I, alas,
A wild bird scarcely fledged, was brought to her cage,
And she was there to meet me. Very kind.
315 Bring the clean water, give out the fresh seed.

She stood upon the steps to welcome me,
Calm, in black garb. I clung about her neck—
Young babes, who catch at every shred of wool
To draw the new light closer, catch and cling
320 Less blindly. In my ears my father's word
Hummed ignorantly, as the sea in shells,
"Love, love, my child." She, black there with my grief,
Might feel my love—she was his sister once—
I clung to her. A moment she seemed moved,

---

[1]   *apothecary*   One who dispenses medicines (a low status profession).

325 Kissed me with cold lips, suffered me to cling,
And drew me feebly through the hall into
The room she sat in.
                                    There, with some strange spasm
Of pain and passion, she wrung loose my hands
330 Imperiously, and held me at arm's length,
And with two grey-steel naked-bladed eyes
Searched through my face—ay, stabbed it through
      and through,
Through brows and cheeks and chin, as if to find
A wicked murderer in my innocent face,
335 If not here, there perhaps. Then, drawing breath,
She struggled for her ordinary calm—
And missed it rather—told me not to shrink,
As if she had told me not to lie or swear—
"She loved my father and would love me too
340 As long as I deserved it." Very kind.

I understood her meaning afterward;
She thought to find my mother in my face,
And questioned it for that. For she, my aunt,
Had loved my father truly, as she could,
345 And hated, with the gall of gentle souls,
My Tuscan mother who had fooled away
A wise man from wise courses, a good man
From obvious duties, and, depriving her,
His sister, of the household precedence,
350 Had wronged his tenants, robbed his native land,
And made him mad, alike by life and death,
In love and sorrow. She had pored° for years   pondered
What sort of woman could be suitable
To her sort of hate, to entertain it with,
355 And so, her very curiosity
Became hate too, and all the idealism
She ever used in life was used for hate,
Till hate, so nourished, did exceed at last
The love from which it grew, in strength and heat,
360 And wrinkled her smooth conscience with a sense
Of disputable virtue (say not, sin)
When Christian doctrine was enforced at church.

And thus my father's sister was to me
My mother's hater. From that day she did
365 Her duty to me (I appreciate it
In her own word as spoken to herself),
Her duty, in large measure, well pressed out

But measured always. She was generous, bland,
More courteous than was tender, gave me still
370 The first place—as if fearful that God's saints
Would look down suddenly and say "Herein
You missed a point, I think, through lack of love."
Alas, a mother never is afraid
Of speaking angerly to any child,
375 Since love, she knows, is justified of love.

And I, I was a good child on the whole,
A meek and manageable child. Why not?
I did not live, to have the faults of life:
There seemed more true life in my father's grave
380 Than in all England. Since *that* threw me off
Who fain would cleave (his latest will, they say,
Consigned me to his land), I only thought
Of lying quiet there where I was thrown
Like seaweed on the rocks, and suffering her
385 To prick me to a pattern with her pin,
Fibre from fibre, delicate leaf from leaf,
And dry out from my drowned anatomy
The last sea-salt left in me.
                                            So it was.
390 I broke the copious curls upon my head
In braids, because she like smooth-ordered hair.
I left off saying my sweet Tuscan words
Which still at any stirring of the heart
Came up to float across the English phrase
395 As lilies (*Bene* or *Che che*),[1] because
She liked my father's child to speak his tongue.
I learnt the collects and the catechism,[2]
The creeds, from Athanasius back to Nice,[3]
The Articles, the Tracts *against* the times[4]
400 (By no means Buonaventure's "Prick of Love"),[5]

---

[1] *Bene or Che che* Common Italian sayings.

[2] *collects* Short prayers; *catechism* Questions and answers in the Anglican *Book of Common Prayer*.

[3] *Athanasius … Nice* Doctrines of Athanasia and the Nicene Council, creeds of the Church of England.

[4] *Articles* Thirty-nine articles in the Anglican doctrine; *the Tracts against the times* Referring to the *Tracts for the Times*. The first tract was composed by John Henry Newman in 1833 and called for a return to the Catholic roots of the Anglican Church.

[5] *Buonaventure's "Prick of Love"* Once incorrectly attributed to the thirteenth-century Franciscan theologian St. Bonaventure, *Stimulus Divini Amoris* ("God of Love") was actually written by Jacobus Mediolanensis in the fourteenth century. The devotional text

And various popular synopses of
Inhuman doctrines never taught by John,
Because she liked instructed piety.
I learnt my complement of classic French
405 (Kept pure of Balzac[1] and neologism)
And German also, since she liked a range
Of liberal education—tongues, not books.
I learnt a little algebra, a little
Of the mathematics—brushed with extreme flounce
410 The circle of the sciences, because
She misliked women who are frivolous.
I learnt the royal genealogies
Of Oviedo,[2] the internal laws
Of the Burmese empire—by how many feet
415 Mount Chimborazo outsoars Teneriffe.[3]
What navigable river joins itself
To Lara,[4] and what census of the year five
Was taken at Klagenfurt,[5]—because she liked
A general insight into useful facts.
420 I learnt much music—such as would have been
As quite impossible in Johnson's day[6]
As still it might be wished—fine sleights of hand
And unimagined fingering, shuffling off
The hearer's soul through hurricanes of notes
425 To a noisy Tophet;° and I drew ... costumes   Hell
From French engravings, nereids° neatly draped   sea nymphs
(With smirks of simmering godship): I washed in
Landscapes from nature (rather say, washed out).
I danced the polka and Cellarius,[7]
430 Spun glass, stuffed birds, and modelled flowers in wax,

Because she liked accomplishments in girls.
I read a score of books on womanhood
To prove, if women do not think at all,
They may teach thinking (to a maiden aunt
435 Or else the author)—books that boldly assert
Their right of comprehending husband's talk
When not too deep, and even of answering
With pretty "may it please you," or "so it is"—
Their rapid insight and fine aptitude,
440 Particular worth and general missionariness,
As long as they keep quiet by the fire
And never say "no" when the world says "ay,"
For that is fatal—their angelic reach
Of virtue, chiefly used to sit and darn,
445 And fatten household sinners—their, in brief,
Potential faculty in everything
Of abdicating power in it: she owned
She liked a woman to be womanly,
And English women, she thanked God and sighed
450 (Some people always sigh in thanking God)
Were models to the universe. And last
I learnt cross-stitch, because she did not like
To see me wear the night with empty hands
A-doing nothing. So, my shepherdess
455 Was something after all (the pastoral saints
Be praised for't), leaning lovelorn with pink eyes
To match her shoes, when I mistook the silks;
Her head uncrushed by that round weight of hat
So strangely similar to the tortoise-shell
460 Which slew the tragic poet.[8]
                              By the way,
The works of women are symbolical.
We sew, sew, prick our fingers, dull our sight,
Producing what? A pair of slippers, sir,
465 To put on when you're weary—or a stool
To stumble over and vex you ... "curse that stool!"
Or else at best, a cushion, where you lean
And sleep, and dream of something we are not
But would be for your sake. Alas, alas!
470 This hurts most, this—that, after all, we are paid
The worth of our work, perhaps.
                              In looking down
Those years of education (to return)

concentrates on the emotional aspect of spirituality.

[1] *Balzac* French novelist Honoré de Balzac (1799–1850).

[2] *Oviedo* Gonzalo Fernandez de Oviedo y Valdez (1478–1557), Spanish historian, wrote a posthumously published book on the natural history of the Americas.

[3] *Mount Chimborazo outsoars Teneriffe* One of Spain's Canary Islands, Tenerife has a peak just over half the height of Chimborazo, the highest mountain in the Andes of Ecuador.

[4] *Lara* Town in Spain.

[5] *Klagenfurt* Capital city of Carinthia (Kärnten) in Austria.

[6] *music ... Johnson's day* The Classical and Baroque music popular during "Johnson's day" was extraordinarily difficult to play. Samuel Johnson (1709–84) once famously said of a renowned violinist's musical choice: "Difficult do you call it, Sir? I would it had been impossible."

[7] *Cellarius* Waltz-Mazurka named after dance master Henri Cellarius in 1842.

[8] *tortoise-shell ... poet* Greek tragedian Aeschylus (c. 525–456 BCE) was said to have been killed when an eagle dropped a tortoise on his bald head in order to crack the tortoise's shell.

I wonder if Brinvilliers suffered more
475 In the water torture[1] ... flood succeeding flood
To drench the incapable throat and split the veins ...
Than I did. Certain of your feebler souls
Go out in such a process; many pine
To a sick, inodorous light; my own endured:
480 I had relations in the Unseen, and drew
The elemental nutriment and heat
From nature, as earth feels the sun at nights,
Or as a babe sucks surely in the dark.
I kept the life thrust on me, on the outside
485 Of the inner life with all its ample room
For heart and lungs, for will and intellect,
Inviolable by conventions. God,
I thank thee for that grace of thine!
                                   At first
490 I felt no life which was not patience—did
The thing she bade me, without heed to a thing
Beyond it, sat in just the chair she placed,
With back against the window, to exclude
The sight of the great lime-tree on the lawn,
495 Which seemed to have come on purpose from the woods
To bring the house a message—ay, and walked
Demurely in her carpeted low rooms,
As if I should not, hearkening my own steps,
Misdoubt I was alive. I read her books,
500 Was civil to her cousin, Romney Leigh,
Gave ear to her vicar, tea to her visitors,
And heard them whisper, when I changed a cup
(I blushed for joy at that)—"The Italian child,
For all her blue eyes and her quiet ways,
505 Thrives ill in England: she is paler yet
Than when we came the last time; she will die."

"Will die." My cousin, Romney Leigh, blushed too,
With sudden anger, and approaching me
Said low between his teeth, "You're wicked now?
510 You wish to die and leave the world a-dusk
For others, with your naughty light blown out?"
I looked into his face defyingly;
He might have know that, being what I was,
'Twas natural to like to get away
515 As far as dead folk can: and then indeed

Some people make no trouble when they die.
He turned and went abruptly, slammed the door,
And shut his dog out.
                          Romney, Romney Leigh.
520 I have not named my cousin hitherto,
And yet I used him as a sort of friend;
My elder by few years, but cold and shy
And absent ... tender, when he thought of it,
Which scarcely was imperative, grave betimes,
525 As well as early master of Leigh Hall,
Whereof the nightmare sat upon his youth,
Repressing all its seasonable delights,
And agonising with a ghastly sense
Of universal hideous want and wrong
530 To incriminate possession. When he came
From college to the country, very oft
He crossed the hill on visits to my aunt,
With gifts of blue grapes from the hothouses,
A book in one hand—mere statistics (if
535 I chanced to lift the cover), count of all
The goats whose beards grow sprouting down toward
       hell
Against God's separative judgment hour.[2]
And she, she almost loved him—even allowed
That sometimes he should seem to sigh my way;
540 It made him easier to be pitiful,
And sighing was his gift. So, undisturbed,
At whiles she let him shut my music up
And push my needles down, and lead me out
To see in that south angle of the house
545 The figs grow black as if by a Tuscan rock,
On some light pretext. She would turn her head
At other moments, go to fetch a thing,
And leave me breath enough to speak with him,
For his sake; it was simple.
550   Sometimes too
He would have saved me utterly, it seemed,
He stood and looked so.
                              Once, he stood so near,
He dropped a sudden hand upon my hand
555 Bent down on woman's work, as soft as rain—
But then I rose and shook it off as fire,
The stranger's touch that took my father's place
Yet dared seem soft.
                        I used him for a friend

---

1 *Brinvilliers ... water torture* The Parisian Marquise de Brinvilliers (1630–76) was tortured and eventually beheaded after being convicted of poisoning various members of her family.

2 *The goats ... judgment hour* See Matthew 25.32–33, 41.

560 Before I ever knew him for a friend.
'Twas better, 'twas worse also, afterward:
We came so close, we saw our differences
Too intimately. Always Romney Leigh
Was looking for the worms, I for the gods.
565 A godlike nature his; the gods look down,
Incurious of themselves; and certainly
'Tis well I should remember, how, those days,
I was a worm too, and he looked on me.

A little by his act perhaps, yet more
570 By something in me, surely not my will,
I did not die. But slowly, as one in swoon,
To whom life creeps back in the form of death,
With a sense of separation, a blind pain
Of blank obstruction, and a roar i' the ears
575 Of visionary chariots which retreat
As earth grows clearer … slowly, by degrees;
I woke, rose up … where was I? in the world;
For uses therefore I must count worthwhile.

I had a little chamber in the house,
580 As green as any privet hedge a bird
Might choose to build in, though the nest itself
Could show but dead-brown sticks and straws; the walls
Were green, the carpet was pure green, the straight
Small bed was curtained greenly, and the folds
585 Hung green about the window which let in
The outdoor world with all its greenery.
You could not push your head out and escape
A dash of dawn-dew from the honeysuckle,
But so you were baptized into the grace
590 And privilege of seeing …
                                    First, the lime
(I had enough there, of the lime, be sure—
My morning-dream was often hummed away
By the bees in it); past the lime, the lawn,
595 Which, after sweeping broadly round the house,
Went trickling through the shrubberies in a stream
Of tender turf, and wore and lost itself
Among the acacias, over which you saw
The irregular line of elms by the deep lane
600 Which stopped the grounds and dammed the overflow
Of arbutus and laurel. Out of sight
The lane was; sunk so deep, no foreign tramp
Nor drover of wild ponies out of Wales

Could guess if lady's hall or tenant's lodge
605 Dispensed such odours—though his stick well crooked
Might reach the lowest trail of blossoming briar
Which dipped upon the wall. Behind the elms,
And through their tops, you saw the folded hills
Striped up and down with hedges (burly oaks
610 Projecting from the line to show themselves),
Through which my cousin Romney's chimneys smoked
As still as when a silent mouth in frost
Breathes, showing where the woodlands hid Leigh Hall;
While, far above, a jut of tableland,
615 A promontory without water, stretched—
You could not catch it if the days were thick,
Or took it for a cloud; but, otherwise,
The vigorous sun would catch it up at eve
And use it for an anvil till he had filled
620 The shelves of heaven with burning thunderbolts,
Protesting against night and darkness:—then,
When all his setting trouble was resolved
To a trance of passive glory, you might see
In apparition on the golden sky
625 (Alas, my Giotto's background!)[1] the sheep run
Along the fine clear outline, small as mice
That run along a witch's scarlet thread.[2]

Not a grand nature. Not my chestnut woods
Of Vallombrosa,[3] cleaving by the spurs
630 To the precipices. Not my headlong leaps
Of waters, that cry out for joy or fear
In leaping through the palpitating pines,
Like a white soul tossed out to eternity
With thrills of time upon it. Not indeed
635 My multitudinous mountains, sitting in
The magic circle, with the mutual touch
Electric, panting from their full deep hearts
Beneath the influent[4] heavens, and waiting for
Communion and commission. Italy
640 Is one thing, England one.
                                    On English ground
You understand the letter—ere the fall
How Adam lived in a garden. All the fields

---

1   *golden sky … background*   Renaissance Florentine painter Giotto
(1267–1337) often used gold as a background color.

2   *small as mice … scarlet thread*   Meaning obscure.

3   *Vallombrosa*   Summer resort in the mountains near Florence.

4   *influent*   Exerting celestial, astral, or occult power.

Are tied up fast with hedges, nosegay-like;
645 The hills are crumpled plains, the plains parterres,[1]
The trees, round, woolly, ready to be clipped,
And if you seek for any wilderness
You find, at best, a park. A nature tamed
And grown domestic like a barn-door fowl,
650 Which does not awe you with its claws and beak,
Nor tempt you to an eyrie too high up,
But which, in cackling, sets you thinking of
Your eggs tomorrow at breakfast, in the pause
Of finer meditation.
655   Rather say,
A sweet familiar nature, stealing in
As a dog might, or child, to touch your hand
Or pluck your gown, and humbly mind you so
Of presence and affection, excellent
660 For inner uses, from the things without.

I could not be unthankful, I who was
Entreated thus and holpen.° In the room   *helped*
I speak of, ere the house was well awake,
And also after it was well asleep,
665 I sat alone, and drew the blessing in
Of all that nature. With a gradual step,
A stir among the leaves, a breath, a ray,
It came in softly, while the angels made
A place for it beside me. The moon came,
670 And swept my chamber clean of foolish thoughts.
The sun came, saying, "Shall I lift this light
Against the lime-tree, and you will not look?
I make the birds sing—listen! but, for you,
God never hears your voice, excepting when
675 You lie upon the bed at nights and weep."

Then, something moved me. Then, I wakened up
More slowly than I verily write now,
But wholly, at last, I wakened, opened wide
The window and my soul, and let the airs
680 And outdoor sights sweep gradual gospels in,
Regenerating what I was. O, Life,
How oft we throw it off and think—"Enough,
Enough of life in so much!—here's a cause
For rupture;—herein we must break with Life,
685 Or be ourselves unworthy; here we are wronged,
Maimed, spoiled for aspiration: farewell, Life!"

And so, as froward° babes, we hide our eyes   *obstinate*
And think all ended.—Then, Life calls to us
In some transformed, apocalyptic voice,
690 Above us, or below us, or around:
Perhaps we name it Nature's voice, or Love's,
Tricking ourselves, because we are more ashamed
To own our compensations than our griefs:
Still, Life's voice!—still, we make our peace with Life.

695 And I, so young then, was not sullen. Soon
I used to get up early, just to sit
And watch the morning quicken in the gray,
And hear the silence open like a flower
Leaf after leaf—and stroke with listless hand
700 The woodbine through the window, till at last
I came to do it with a sort of love,
At foolish unaware: whereat I smiled—
A melancholy smile, to catch myself
Smiling for joy.
705   Capacity for joy
Admits temptation. It seemed, next, worthwhile
To dodge the sharp sword set against my life;
To slip downstairs through all the sleepy house,
As mute as any dream there, and escape
710 As a soul from the body, out of doors,
Glide through the shrubberies, drop into the lane,
And wander on the hills an hour or two,
Then back again before the house should stir.

Or else I sat on in my chamber green,
715 And lived my life, and thought my thoughts, and prayed
My prayers without the vicar; read my books
Without considering whether they were fit
To do me good. Mark, there. We get no good
By being ungenerous, even to a book,
720 And calculating profits—so much help
By so much reading. It is rather when
We gloriously forget ourselves and plunge
Soul-forward, headlong, into a book's profound,
Impassioned for its beauty and salt of truth—
725 'Tis then we get the right good from a book.

I read much. What my father taught before
From many a volume, Love re-emphasised

---

[1] *parterres* Patterned ornamental gardens.

Upon the self-same pages: Theophrast[1]
Grew tender with the memory of his eyes,
730   And Ælian[2] made mine wet. The trick of Greek
And Latin he had taught me, as he would
Have taught me wrestling or the game of fives[3]
If such he had known—most like a shipwrecked man
Who heaps his single platter with goats' cheese
735   And scarlet berries; or like any man
Who loves but one, and so gives all at once,
Because he has it, rather than because
He counts it worthy. Thus, my father gave;
And thus, as did the women formerly
740   By young Achilles,[4] when they pinned a veil
Across the boy's audacious front, and swept
With tuneful laughs the silver-fretted rocks,
He wrapt his little daughter in his large
Man's doublet,° careless did it fit or no.   *jacket*

745   But, after I had read for memory,
I read for hope. The path my father's foot
Had trod me out (which suddenly broke off
What time he dropped the wallet of the flesh
And passed), alone I carried on, and set
750   My child-heart 'gainst the thorny underwood,
To reach the grassy shelter of the trees.
Ah babe i' the wood, without a brother-babe!
My own self-pity, like the red-breast bird,
Flies back to cover all that past with leaves.[5]

755   Sublimest danger, over which none weeps,
When any young wayfaring soul goes forth
Alone, unconscious of the perilous road,
The day-sun dazzling in his limpid eyes,
To thrust his own way, he an alien, through
760   The world of books! Ah, you!—you think it fine,

You clap hands—"A fair day!"—you cheer him on,
As if the worst, could happen, were to rest
Too long beside a fountain. Yet, behold,
Behold!—the world of books is still the world,
765   And worldlings° in it are less merciful   *worldly people*
And more puissant.° For the wicked there   *powerful*
Are winged like angels; every knife that strikes
Is edged from elemental fire to assail
A spiritual life; the beautiful seems right
770   By force of beauty, and the feeble wrong
Because of weakness; power is justified
Though armed against Saint Michael;[6] many a crown
Covers bald foreheads. In the book world, true,
There's no lack, neither, of God's saints and kings,
775   That shake the ashes of the grave aside
From their calm locks and undiscomfited
Look steadfast truths against Time's changing mask.
True, many a prophet teaches in the roads;
True, many a seer pulls down the flaming heavens
780   Upon his own head in strong martyrdom
In order to light men a moment's space.
But stay!—who judges?—who distinguishes
'Twixt Saul and Nahash[7] justly, at first sight,
And leaves king Saul precisely at the sin,
785   To serve king David?[8] who discerns at once
The sound of the trumpets, when the trumpets blow
For Alaric as well as Charlemagne?[9]
Who judges wizards, and can tell true seers
From conjurers? the child, there? Would you leave
790   That child to wander in a battlefield
And push his innocent smile against the guns;
Or even in a catacomb—his torch
Grown ragged in the fluttering air, and all
The dark a-mutter round him? not a child.

795   I read books bad and good—some bad and good
At once (good aims not always make good books:
Well-tempered spades turn up ill-smelling soils

---

[1]   *Theophrast*   Greek philosopher (c. 370–287 BCE), student and successor of Aristotle at the Lyceum, the Athenian philosophical school founded by Aristotle.

[2]   *Ælian*   Greek rhetorician (c. 170–c. 230) and author of Greek books on natural history.

[3]   *game of fives*   Handball game similar to the game of squash.

[4]   *as did the women … Achilles*   The Greek god Thetis disguised her son Achilles as a girl and hid him among the women of the court in order to prevent him from perishing in the Trojan War.

[5]   *babe i' the wood … leaves*   Cf. the British children's ballad "The Babes in the Woods," in which two children are abandoned in the wood. After they die, robins come to cover them with leaves.

---

[6]   *Saint Michael*   One of the principal archangels, known as a protector and figured with a sword.

[7]   *Saul and Nahash*   See 1 Samuel 11: Saul was named king of Israel over his rival Nahash.

[8]   *king David*   David succeeded Saul as king of Israel.

[9]   *Alaric*   Visigoth king (c. 370–410 CE) and conqueror of much of the Eastern and Roman empires; *Charlemagne*   Charles the Great (742?–814), emperor of the West and king of the Franks.

In digging vineyards even); books that prove
God's being so definitely, that man's doubt
800 Grows self-defined the other side the line,
Made atheist by suggestion; moral books,
Exasperating to license; genial books,
Discounting from the human dignity;
And merry books, which set you weeping when
805 The sun shines—ay, and melancholy books,
Which make you laugh that anyone should weep
In this disjointed life for one wrong more.

The world of books is still the world, I write,
And both worlds have God's providence, thank God,
810 To keep and hearten: with some struggle, indeed,
Among the breakers, some hard swimming through
The deeps—I lost breath in my soul sometimes
And cried "God save me if there's any God,"
But, even so, God saved me; and, being dashed
815 From error on to error, every turn
Still brought me nearer to the central truth.

I thought so. All this anguish in the thick
Of men's opinions … press and counter-press,
Now up, now down, now underfoot, and now
820 Emergent … all the best of it, perhaps,
But throws you back upon a noble trust
And use of your own instinct—merely proves
Pure reason stronger than bare inference
At strongest. Try it—fix against heaven's wall
825 The scaling-ladders of school logic—mount
Step by step!—sight goes faster; that still ray
Which strikes out from you, how, you cannot tell,
And why, you know not (did you eliminate,
That such as you indeed should analyse?)
830 Goes straight and fast as light, and high as God.

The cygnet° finds the water, but the man   *young swan*
Is born in ignorance of his element
And feels out blind at first, disorganised
By sin i' the blood—his spirit-insight dulled
835 And crossed by his sensations. Presently
He feels it quicken in the dark sometimes,
When, mark, be reverent, be obedient,
For such dumb motions of imperfect life
Are oracles of vital Deity
840 Attesting the Hereafter. Let who says

"The soul's a clean white paper," rather say,
A palimpsest,[1] a prophet's holograph[2]
Defiled, erased and covered by a monk's—
The apocalypse, by a Longus![3] poring on
845 Which obscene text, we may discern perhaps
Some fair, fine trace of what was written once,
Some upstroke of an alpha and omega[4]
Expressing the old scripture.
                              Books, books, books!
850 I had found the secret of a garret room
Piled high with cases in my father's name,
Piled high, packed large—where, creeping in and out
Against the giant fossils of my past,
Like some small nimble mouse between the ribs
855 Of a mastodon, I nibbled here and there
At this or that box, pulling through the gap,
In heats of terror, haste, victorious joy,
The first book first. And how I felt it beat
Under my pillow, in the morning's dark,
860 An hour before the sun would let me read!
My books! At last because the time was ripe,
I chanced upon the poets.
                              As the earth
Plunges in fury, when the internal fires
865 Have reached and pricked her heart, and, throwing flat
The marts and temples, the triumphal gates
And towers of observation, clears herself
To elemental freedom—thus, my soul,
At poetry's divine first finger-touch,
870 Let go conventions and sprang up surprised,
Convicted of the great eternities
Before two worlds.
                      What's this, Aurora Leigh,
You write so of the poets, and not laugh?
875 Those virtuous liars, dreamers after dark,
Exaggerators of the sun and moon,

---

[1] *palimpsest* Paper or manuscript that has been written upon, rubbed out and written upon again, either partially or wholly obliterating the original.

[2] *holograph* Document handwritten by its author.

[3] *Longus* Greek poet of the third or fourth century, author of *Daphnis and Chloë* and originator of the pastoral romance, which often articulates intense physical desire.

[4] *alpha and omega* First and last letters of the Greek alphabet; metaphorically, the be all and end all. See Revelation 1.11, in which God says: "I am Alpha and Omega, the first and the last: and, What thou seest, write in a book."

And soothsayers in a teacup?
                 I write so
Of the only truth-tellers now left to God,
880 The only speakers of essential truth,
Opposed to relative, comparative,
And temporal truths; the only holders by
His sun-skirts, through conventional gray glooms;
The only teachers who instruct mankind
885 From just a shadow on a charnel° wall   *mortuary*
To find man's veritable stature out
Erect, sublime—the measure of a man,
And that's the measure of an angel, says
The apostle.[1] Ay, and while your common men
890 Lay telegraphs, gauge railroads, reign, reap, dine,
And dust the flaunty carpets of the world
For kings to walk on, or our president,
The poet suddenly will catch them up
With his voice like a thunder—"This is soul,
895 This is life, this word is being said in heaven,
Here's God down on us! what are you about?"
How all those workers start amid their work,
Look round, look up, and feel, a moment's space,
That carpet dusting, though a pretty trade,
900 Is not the imperative labour after all.

My own best poets, am I one with you,
That thus I love you—or but one through love?
Does all this smell of thyme about my feet
Conclude my visit to your holy hill
905 In personal presence, or but testify
The rustling of your vesture° through my dreams *clothing*
With influent odours? When my joy and pain,
My thought and aspiration like the stops
Of pipe or flute, are absolutely dumb
910 Unless melodious, do you play on me
My pipers—and if, sooth, you did not blow,
Would no sound come? or is the music mine,
As a man's voice or breath is called his own,
Inbreathed by the Life-breather? There's a doubt
915 For cloudy seasons!
                But the sun was high
When first I felt my pulses set themselves
For concord; when the rhythmic turbulence
Of blood and brain swept outward upon words,
920 As wind upon the alders, blanching them

By turning up their under-natures till
They trembled in dilation. O delight
And triumphs of the poet, who would say
A man's mere "yes," a woman's common "no,"
925 A little human hope of that or this,
And says the word so that it burns you through
With a special revelation, shakes the heart
Of all the men and women in the world,
As if one came back from the dead and spoke,
930 With eyes too happy, a familiar thing
Become divine i' the utterance! while for him
The poet, speaker, he expands with joy;
The palpitating angel in his flesh
Thrills inly with consenting fellowship
935 To those innumerous spirits who sun themselves
Outside of time.
             O life, O poetry,
—Which means life in life! cognisant of life
Beyond this blood-beat, passionate for truth
940 Beyond these senses!—poetry, my life,
My eagle, with both grappling feet still hot
From Zeus's thunder, who hast ravished me
Away from all the shepherds, sheep, and dogs,
And set me in the Olympian roar and round
945 Of luminous faces for a cupbearer,[2]
To keep the mouths of all the godheads moist
For everlasting laughters—I myself
Half drunk across the beaker with their eyes!
How those gods look!
950   Enough so, Ganymede,
We shall not bear above a round or two.
We drop the golden cup at Heré's[3] foot
And swoon back to the earth—and find ourselves
Face down among the pinecones, cold with dew,
955 While the dogs bark, and many a shepherd scoffs,
"What's come now to the youth?" Such ups and downs
Have poets.
          Am I such indeed? The name
Is royal, and to sign it like a queen
960 Is what I dare not—though some royal blood
Would seem to tingle in me now and then,

---

[1] *measure of a man ... apostle* See Revelation 21.17.

[2] *Zeus's thunder ... cupbearer* Zeus, king of the Greek gods, unleashed a thunderstorm on earth to confuse mortals and steal away the beautiful shepherd boy Ganymede. Zeus made the boy immortal and brought him to Olympus to serve as cupbearer to the gods.

[3] *Heré* Hera, wife of Zeus.

With sense of power and ache—with imposthumes° *abscesses*
And manias usual to the race. Howbeit
I dare not: 'tis too easy to go mad
965 And ape a Bourbon in a crown of straws;[1]
The thing's too common.
                                        Many fervent souls
Strike rhyme on rhyme, who would strike steel on steel
If steel had offered, in a restless heat
970 Of doing something. Many tender souls
Have strung their losses on a rhyming thread,
As children cowslips:[2] the more pains they take,
The work more withers. Young men, ay, and maids,
Too often sow their wild oats in tame verse,
975 Before they sit down under their own vine[3]
And live for use. Alas, near all the birds
Will sing at dawn—and yet we do not take
The chaffering° swallow for the holy lark. *chattering*

In those days, though, I never analysed,
980 Not even myself. Analysis comes late.
You catch a sight of Nature, earliest,
In full front sun-face, and your eyelids wink
And drop before the wonder of 't; you miss
The form, through seeing the light. I lived, those days,
985 And wrote because I lived—unlicensed else;
My heart beat in my brain. Life's violent flood
Abolished bounds—and, which my neighbour's field,
Which mine, what mattered? it is thus in youth!
We play at leapfrog over the god Term;[4]
990 The love within us and the love without
Are mixed, confounded; if we are loved or love,
We scarce distinguish: thus, with other power;
Being acted on and acting seem the same:
In that first onrush of life's chariot-wheels,
995 We know not if the forests move or we.

And so, like most young poets, in a flush
Of individual life I poured myself
Along the veins of others, and achieved
Mere lifeless imitations of live verse,

1000 And made the living answer for the dead,
Profaning nature. "Touch not, do not taste,
Nor handle,"[5]—we're too legal, who write young:
We beat the phorminx° till we hurt our thumbs, *lyre*
As if still ignorant of counterpoint;° *interwoven melodies*
1005 We call the Muse—"O Muse, benignant Muse,"—
As if we had seen her purple-braided head,
With the eyes in it, start between the boughs
As often as a stag's. What make-believe,
With so much earnest! what effete° results *effeminate*
1010 From virile efforts! what cold wire-drawn° odes *detailed*
From such white heats!—bucolics,[6] where the cows
Would scare the writer if they splashed the mud
In lashing off the flies—didactics, driven
Against the heels of what the master said;
1015 And counterfeiting epics, shrill with trumps
A babe might blow between two straining cheeks
Of bubbled rose, to make his mother laugh;
And elegiac griefs, and songs of love,
Like cast-off nosegays° picked up on the road, *bouquets*
1020 The worse for being warm: all these things, writ
On happy mornings, with a morning heart,
That leaps for love, is active for resolve,
Weak for art only. Oft, the ancient forms
Will thrill, indeed, in carrying the young blood.
1025 The wine-skins, now and then, a little warped,
Will crack even, as the new wine gurgles in.
Spare the old bottles!—spill not the new wine.[7]

By Keats's[8] soul, the man who never stepped
In gradual progress like another man,
1030 But, turning grandly on his central self,
Ensphered himself in twenty perfect years
And died, not young (the life of a long life
Distilled to a mere drop, falling like a tear
Upon the world's cold cheek to make it burn
1035 Forever); by that strong excepted soul,
I count it strange and hard to understand

---

1 *Bourbon in a crown of straws* The Bourbon dynasty was founded by Napoleon, who of course had no real title to the Crown of France.

2 *cowslips* Fragrant pasture flowers, sometimes made into garlands.

3 *sit down under their own vine* See 1 Kings 4.25.

4 *Term* Terminus, Roman god of boundaries.

5 *"Touch not ... handle"* From Colossians 2.21–22: "Touch not; taste not; handle not; Which all are to perish with the using."

6 *bucolics* Pastoral poems.

7 *Spare ... wine* See Matthew 9.17: "Neither do men put new wine into old bottles: else the bottles break, and the wine runneth out, and the bottles perish: but they put new wine into new bottles, and both are preserved."

8 *Keats* Romantic poet John Keats (1795–1821).

That nearly all young poets should write old,
That Pope was sexagenary at sixteen,
And beardless Byron[1] academical,
1040 And so with others. It may be perhaps
Such have not settled long and deep enough
In trance, to attain to clairvoyance—and still
The memory mixes with the vision, spoils,
And works it turbid.
1045   Or perhaps, again,
In order to discover the Muse-Sphinx,[2]
The melancholy desert must sweep round,
Behind you as before.—
                              For me, I wrote
1050 False poems, like the rest, and thought them true
Because myself was true in writing them.
I peradventure have writ true ones since
With less complacence.
                              But I could not hide
1055 My quickening inner life from those at watch.
They saw a light at a window, now and then,
They had not set there: who had set it there?
My father's sister started when she caught
My soul agaze in my eyes. She could not say
1060 I had no business with a sort of soul,
But plainly she objected—and demurred
That souls were dangerous things to carry straight
Through all the spilt saltpetre[3] of the world.

She said sometimes "Aurora, have you done
1065 Your task this morning? have you read that book?
And are you ready for the crochet here?"—
As if she said "I know there's something wrong;
I know I have not ground you down enough
To flatten and bake you to a wholesome crust
1070 For household uses and proprieties,
Before the rain has got into my barn
And set the grains a-sprouting. What, you're green
With outdoor impudence? you almost grow?"
To which I answered, "Would she hear my task,

1075 And verify my abstract of the book?
Or should I sit down to the crochet work?
Was such her pleasure?" Then I sat and teased
The patient needle till it split the thread,
Which oozed off from it in meandering lace
1080 From hour to hour. I was not, therefore, sad;
My soul was singing at a work apart
Behind the wall of sense, as safe from harm
As sings the lark when sucked up out of sight
In vortices of glory and blue air.

1085 And so, through forced work and spontaneous work,
The inner life informed the outer life,
Reduced the irregular blood to a settled rhythm,
Made cool the forehead with fresh-sprinkling dreams,
And, rounding to the spheric soul the thin,
1090 Pined body, struck a colour up the cheeks
Though somewhat faint. I clenched my brows across
My blue eyes greatening in the looking-glass,
And said "We'll live, Aurora! we'll be strong.
The dogs are on us—but we will not die."

1095 Whoever lives true life will love true love.
I learnt to love that England. Very oft,
Before the day was born, or otherwise
Through secret windings of the afternoons,
I threw my hunters off and plunged myself
1100 Among the deep hills, as a hunted stag
Will take the waters, shivering with the fear
And passion of the course. And when at last
Escaped, so many a green slope built on slope
Betwixt me and the enemy's house behind,
1105 I dared to rest, or wander, in a rest
Made sweeter for the step upon the grass,
And view the ground's most gentle dimplement[4]
(As if God's finger touched but did not press
In making England), such an up and down
1110 Of verdure—nothing too much up or down,
A ripple of land; such little hills, the sky
Can stoop to tenderly and the wheatfields climb;
Such nooks of valleys lined with orchises,
Fed full of noises by invisible streams;
1115 And open pastures where you scarcely tell
White daisies from white dew—at intervals
The mythic oaks and elm trees standing out

---

[1] *Pope ... Byron* Both Alexander Pope (1688–1744) and Lord Byron (1788–1824) were precocious poets who published while still in their teens.

[2] *Sphinx* In Greek mythology the Sphinx is represented with the body of a lion and the head of a woman. The Sphinx would pose a riddle to passersby and destroy them if they could not solve it.

[3] *saltpetre* Potassium nitrate, a component in explosives.

[4] *dimplement* Dimple (Barrett Browning coined this word).

Self-poised upon their prodigy of shade—
I thought my father's land was worthy too
1120 Of being my Shakespeare's.
                                    Very oft alone,
Unlicensed; not unfrequently with leave
To walk the third with Romney and his friend
The rising painter, Vincent Carrington,
1125 Whom men judge hardly as bee-bonneted,
Because he holds that, paint a body well,
You paint a soul by implication,[1] like
The grand first Master. Pleasant walks! for if
He said "When I was last in Italy,"
1130 It sounded as an instrument that's played
Too far off for the tune—and yet it's fine
To listen.
                    Often we walked only two
If cousin Romney pleased to walk with me.
1135 We read, or talked, or quarrelled, as it chanced.
We were not lovers, nor even friends well-matched:
Say rather, scholars upon different tracks,
And thinkers disagreed: he, overfull
Of what is, and I, haply, overbold
1140 For what might be.
                              But then the thrushes sang,
And shook my pulses and the elms' new leaves:
At which I turned, and held my finger up,
And bade him mark that, howsoe'er the world
1145 Went ill, as he related, certainly
The thrushes still sang in it. At the word
His brow would soften—and he bore with me
In melancholy patience, not unkind,
While breaking into voluble ecstasy
1150 I flattered all the beauteous country round,
As poets use, the skies, the clouds, the fields,
The happy violets hiding from the roads
The primroses run down to, carrying gold;
The tangled hedgerows, where the cows push out
1155 Impatient horns and tolerant churning mouths
'Twixt dripping ash boughs—hedgerows all alive
With birds and gnats and large white butterflies
While look as if the mayflower had caught life

And palpitated forth upon the wind;
1160 Hills, vales, woods, netted in a silver mist,
Farms, granges, doubled up among the hills;
And cattle grazing in the watered vales,
And cottage chimneys smoking from the woods,
And cottage gardens smelling everywhere,
1165 Confused with smell of orchards. "See," I said,
"And see! is God not with us on the earth?
And shall we put Him down by aught we do?
Who says there's nothing for the poor and vile
Save poverty and wickedness? behold!"
1170 And ankle-deep in English grass I leaped
And clapped my hands, and called all very fair.

In the beginning when God called all good,
Even then was evil near us,[2] it is writ;
But we indeed who call things good and fair,
1175 The evil is upon us while we speak;
Deliver us from evil,[3] let us pray.

from BOOK 2

Times followed one another. Came a morn
I stood upon the brink of twenty years,
And looked before and after, as I stood
Woman and artist—either incomplete,
5 Both credulous of completion. There I held
The whole creation in my little cup,
And smiled with thirsty lips before I drank
"Good health to you and me, sweet neighbour mine,
And all these peoples."
10   I was glad, that day;
The June was in me, with its multitudes
Of nightingales all singing in the dark,
And rosebuds reddening where the calyx[4] split.
I felt so young, so strong, so sure of God!
15 So glad, I could not choose be very wise!
And, old at twenty, was inclined to pull
My childhood backward in a childish jest
To see the face of 't once more, and farewell!
In which fantastic mood I bounded forth
20 At early morning—would not wait so long

---

[1] *paint a body ... soul by implication* Cf. Robert Browning's "Fra Lippo Lippi" 179–83, in which the painter/narrator says: "Your business is not to catch men with show, / With homage to the perishable clay, / But lift them over it, ignore it all, / Make them forget there's such a thing as flesh. / Your business is to paint the souls of men."

---

[2] *In the beginning ... near us* See Genesis 1.1, 1.31, and 2.9.

[3] *Deliver us from evil* From Matthew 6.13.

[4] *calyx* Outer leaves of a bud.

As even to snatch my bonnet by the strings,
But, brushing a green trail across the lawn
With my gown in the dew, took will and away
Among the acacias of the shrubberies,
25   To fly my fancies in the open air
And keep my birthday, till my aunt awoke
To stop good dreams. Meanwhile I murmured on
As honeyed bees keep humming to themselves,
"The worthiest poets have remained uncrowned
30   Till death has bleached their foreheads to the bone;
And so with me it must be unless I prove
Unworthy of the grand adversity,
And certainly I would not fail so much.
What, therefore, if I crown myself today
35   In sport, not pride, to learn the feel of it,
Before my brows be numbed as Dante's[1] own
To all the tender pricking of such leaves?
Such leaves! what leaves?"
                          I pulled the branches down
40   To choose from.
                    "Not the bay![2] I choose no bay
(The fates deny us if we are overbold),
Nor myrtle[3]—which means chiefly love; and love
Is something awful which one dares not touch
45   So early o' mornings. This verbena strains
The point of passionate fragrance; and hard by,
This guelder rose, at far too slight a beck
Of the wind, will toss about her flower-apples.
Ah—there's my choice—that ivy on the wall,
50   That headlong ivy! not a leaf will grow
But thinking of a wreath. Large leaves, smooth leaves,
Serrated like my vines, and half as green.
I like such ivy, bold to leap a height
'Twas strong to climb; as good to grow on graves
55   As twist about a thyrsus;[4] pretty too
(And that's not ill) when twisted round a comb."

Thus speaking to myself, half singing it,
Because some thoughts are fashioned like a bell

To ring with once being touched, I drew a wreath
60   Drenched, blinding me with dew, across my brow,
And fastening it behind so, turning faced
… My public!—cousin Romney—with a mouth
Twice graver than his eyes.
                          I stood there fixed—
65   My arms up, like the caryatid,[5] sole
Of some abolished temple, helplessly
Persistent in a gesture which derides
A former purpose. Yet my blush was flame,
As if from flax, not stone.
70   "Aurora Leigh,
The earliest of Auroras!"[6]
                          Hand stretched out
I clasped, as shipwrecked men will clasp a hand,
Indifferent to the sort of palm. The tide
75   Had caught me at my pastime, writing down
My foolish name too near upon the sea
Which drowned me with a blush as foolish. "You,
My cousin!"
            The smile died out in his eyes
80   And dropped upon his lips, a cold dead weight,
For just a moment, "Here's a book I found!
No name writ on it—poems, by the form;
Some Greek upon the margin—lady's Greek
Without the accents. Read it? Not a word.
85   I saw at once the thing had witchcraft in't,
Whereof the reading calls up dangerous spirits:
I rather bring it to the witch."
                          "My book.
You found it"…
90   "In the hollow by the stream
That beech leans down into—of which you said
The Oread in it has a Naiad's[7] heart
And pines for waters."
                          "Thank you."
95   "Thanks to you
My cousin! that I have seen you not too much
Witch, scholar, poet, dreamer, and the rest,
To be a woman also."
                    With a glance
100   The smile rose in his eyes again and touched

---

1   *Dante*   Italian poet Dante Alighieri (1265–1321), author of *The Divine Comedy*.

2   *bay*   Sacred tree of the Greek god Apollo; famous poets in Greece were given laurel wreaths as a symbol of honor.

3   *myrtle*   Plant sacred to Venus, Roman goddess of love.

4   *thyrsus*   Spear or staff of the Greek god Dionysus, tipped with a pinecone and entwined with vines.

5   *caryatid*   Building column sculpted in the figure of a woman.

6   *Auroras*   Dawns; personification of Aurora, Roman goddess of the dawn.

7   *Oread*   Mountain nymph; *Naiad*   River nymph.

The ivy on my forehead, light as air.
I answered gravely "Poets needs must be
Or men or women—more's the pity."

                                "Ah,
105 But men, and still less women, happily,
Scarce need be poets. Keep to the green wreath,
Since even dreaming of the stone and bronze
Brings headaches, pretty cousin, and defiles
The clean white morning dresses."

110   "So you judge!
Because I love the beautiful I must
Love pleasure chiefly, and be overcharged
For ease and whiteness! well, you know the world,
And only miss your cousin, 'tis not much.
115 But learn this; I would rather take my part
With God's Dead, who afford to walk in white
Yet spread His glory, than keep quiet here
And gather up my feet from even a step
For fear to soil my gown in so much dust.
120 I choose to walk at all risks.—Here, if heads
That hold a rhythmic thought, much ache perforce,
For my part I choose headaches—and today's
My birthday."

               "Dear Aurora, choose instead
125 To cure them. You have balsams."°   *salves*

                            "I perceive.
The headache is too noble for my sex.
You think the heartache would sound decenter,
Since that's the woman's special, proper ache,
130 And altogether tolerable, except
To a woman."

                  Saying which, I loosed my wreath,
And swinging it beside me as I walked,
Half-petulant, half-playful, as we walked,
135 I sent a sidelong look to find his thought—
As falcon set on falconer's finger may,
With sidelong head, and startled, braving eye,
Which means, "You'll see—you'll see! I'll soon take flight,
You shall not hinder." He, as shaking out
140 His hand and answering "Fly then," did not speak,
Except by such a gesture. Silently
We paced, until, just coming into sight
Of the house windows, he abruptly caught
At one end of the swinging wreath, and said
145 "Aurora!" There I stopped short, breath and all.

"Aurora, let's be serious, and throw by
This game of head and heart. Life means, be sure,
Both heart and head—both active, both complete,
And both in earnest. Men and women make
150 The world, as head and heart make human life.
Work man, work woman, since there's work to do
In this beleaguered earth, for head and heart,
And thought can never do the work of love:
But work for ends, I mean for uses, not
155 For such sleek fringes (do you call them ends,
Still less God's glory?) as we sew ourselves
Upon the velvet of those baldaquins°   *canopies*
Held 'twixt us and the sun. That book of yours,
I have not read a page of; but I toss
160 A rose up—it falls calyx down, you see!
The chances are that, being a woman, young
And pure, with such a pair of large, calm eyes,
You write as well … and ill … upon the whole,
As other women. If as well, what then?
165 If even a little better, … still, what then?
We want the Best in art now, or no art.
The time is done for facile settings up
Of minnow gods, nymphs here and tritons[1] there;
The polytheists have gone out in God,
170 That unity of Bests. No best, no God!
And so with art, we say. Give art's divine,
Direct, indubitable, real as grief,
Or leave us to the grief we grow ourselves
Divine by overcoming with mere hope
175 And most prosaic patience. You, you are young
As Eve with nature's daybreak on her face,
But this same world you are come to, dearest coz,
Has done with keeping birthdays, saves her wreaths
To hang upon her ruins—and forgets
180 To rhyme the cry with which she still beats back
Those savage, hungry dogs that hunt her down
To the empty grave of Christ. The world's hard pressed;
The sweat of labour in the early curse
Has (turning acrid in six thousand years)[2]
185 Become the sweat of torture. Who has time,

---

[1] *minnow gods … tritons* Minor deities of Greek mythology.

[2] *six thousand years* The world was then widely thought to have been created in 4004 BCE.

An hour's time ... think!—to sit upon a bank
And hear the cymbals tinkle[1] in white hands?
When Egypt's slain, I say, let Miriam sing!—
Before—where's Moses?"[2]
190   "Ah, exactly that.
Where's Moses?—is a Moses to be found?
You'll seek him vainly in the bulrushes,[3]
While I in vain touch cymbals. Yet concede,
Such sounding brass[4] has done some actual good
195 (The application in a woman's hand,
If that were credible, being scarcely spoilt,)
In colonising beehives."
                          "There it is!—
You play beside a deathbed like a child,
200 Yet measure to yourself a prophet's place
To teach the living. None of all these things
Can women understand. You generalise
Oh, nothing—not even grief! Your quick-breathed
        hearts,
So sympathetic to the personal pang,
205 Close on each separate knife stroke, yielding up
A whole life at each wound, incapable
Of deepening, widening a large lap of life
To hold the world-full woe. The human race
To you means, such a child, or such a man,
210 You saw one morning waiting in the cold,
Beside that gate, perhaps. You gather up
A few such cases, and when strong sometimes
Will write of factories and of slaves, as if
Your father were a negro, and your son
215 A spinner in the mills. All's yours and you,
All, coloured with your blood, or otherwise
Just nothing to you. Why, I call you hard
To general suffering. Here's the world half-blind
With intellectual light, half-brutalised
220 With civilisation, having caught the plague

In silks from Tarsus,[5] shrieking east and west
Along a thousand railroads, mad with pain
And sin too!... does one woman of you all
(You who weep easily) grow pale to see
225 This tiger shake his cage?—does one of you
Stand still from dancing, stop from stringing pearls,
And pine and die because of the great sum
Of universal anguish?—Show me a tear
Wet as Cordelia's,[6] in eyes bright as yours,
230 Because the world is mad. You cannot count,
That you should weep for this account, not you!
You weep for what you know. A red-haired child
Sick in a fever, if you touch him once,
Though but so little as with a fingertip,
235 Will set you weeping; but a million sick ...
You could as soon weep for the rule of three[7]
Or compound fractions. Therefore, this same world,
Uncomprehended by you, must remain
Uninfluenced by you.—Women as you are,
240 Mere women, personal and passionate,
You give us doting mothers, and perfect wives,
Sublime Madonnas, and enduring saints!
We get no Christ from you—and verily
We shall not get a poet, in my mind."

245 "With which conclusion you conclude!"...
                                    "But this,
That you, Aurora, with the large live brow
And steady eyelids, cannot condescend
To play at art, as children play at swords,
250 To show a pretty spirit, chiefly admired
Because true action is impossible.
You never can be satisfied with praise
Which men give women when they judge a book
Not as mere work but as mere woman's work,
255 Expressing the comparative respect
Which means the absolute scorn. 'Oh, excellent,
What grace, what facile turns, what fluent sweeps,
What delicate discernment ... almost thought!
The book does honour to the sex, we hold.
260 Among our female authors we make room
For this fair writer, and congratulate

---

1 *cymbals tinkle* See 1 Corinthians 13.1.
2 *Egypt's slain ... Moses* According to Exodus 15.19–22, Miriam
sang and danced after the Pharaoh and his men drowned and Moses
led the Jewish people through the Red Sea.
3 *bulrushes* In Exodus 2.3 Moses's mother hides her son in an ark
made from bulrushes.
4 *sounding brass* From 1 Corinthians 13.1: "Though I speak with
the tongues of men and of angels, and have not charity, I am become
as sounding brass, or a tinkling cymbal."

5 *Tarsus* City in Turkey.
6 *tear ... Cordelia's* See Shakespeare's *King Lear* 4.7.80.
7 *rule of three* Also called the "golden rule" or "rule of proportion."

The country that produces in these times
Such women, competent to … spell.'"

                                 "Stop there,"

265 I answered, burning through his thread of talk
With a quick flame of emotion—"You have read
My soul, if not my book, and argue well
I would not condescend … we will not say
To such a kind of praise (a worthless end

270 Is praise of all kinds), but to such a use
Of holy art and golden life. I am young,
And peradventure° weak—you tell me so—   *perhaps*
Through being a woman. And, for all the rest,
Take thanks for justice. I would rather dance

275 At fairs on tightrope, till the babies dropped
Their gingerbread for joy—than shift the types[1]
For tolerable verse, intolerable
To men who act and suffer. Better far
Pursue a frivolous trade by serious means,

280 Than a sublime art frivolously."

                                 "You,
Choose nobler work than either, O moist eyes
And hurrying lips and heaving heart! We are young,
Aurora, you and I. The world—look round—

285 The world, we're come to late, is swollen hard
With perished generations and their sins:
The civiliser's spade grinds horribly
On dead men's bones, and cannot turn up soil
That's otherwise than fetid. All success

290 Proves partial failure; all advance implies
What's left behind; all triumph, something crushed
At the chariot wheels; all government, some wrong
And rich men make the poor, who curse the rich,
Who agonise together, rich and poor,

295 Under and over, in the social spasm
And crisis of the ages. Here's an age
That makes its own vocation! here we have stepped
Across the bounds of time! here's nought to see,
But just the rich man and just Lazarus,

300 And both in torments, with a mediate gulf,
Though not a hint of Abraham's bosom.[2] Who
Being man, Aurora, can stand calmly by
And view these things, and never tease his soul

For some great cure? No physic for this grief,
305 In all the earth and heavens too?"

                                 "You believe
In God, for your part?—ay? that He who makes
Can make good things from ill things, best from worst,
As men plant tulips upon dunghills when
310 They wish them finest?"

                                 "True. A death-heat is
The same as life-heat, to be accurate,
And in all nature is no death at all,
As men account of death, so long as God
315 Stands witnessing for life perpetually,
By being just God. That's abstract truth, I know,
Philosophy, or sympathy with God:
But I, I sympathise with man, not God
(I think I was a man for chiefly this),
320 And when I stand beside a dying bed,
'Tis death to me. Observe—it had not much
Consoled the race of mastodons to know,
Before they went to fossil, that anon
Their place would quicken with the elephant.
325 They were not elephants but mastodons;
And I, a man, as men are now and not
As men may be hereafter, feel with men
In the agonising present."

                                 "Is it so,"
330 I said, "my cousin? is the world so bad,
While I hear nothing of it through the trees?
The world was always evil—but so bad?"

"So bad, Aurora. Dear, my soul is grey
With poring over the long sum of ill;
335 So much for vice, so much for discontent,
So much for the necessities of power,
So much for the connivances of fear,
Coherent in statistical despairs
With such a total of distracted life, …
340 To see it down in figures on a page,
Plain, silent, clear, as God sees through the earth
The sense of all the graves—that's terrible
For one who is not God, and cannot right
The wrong he looks on. May I choose indeed,
345 But vow away my years, my means, my aims,
Among the helpers, if there's any help
In such a social strait? The common blood
That swings along my veins is strong enough

---

[1] *types* Moveable type, or letters, used in the printing process.

[2] *rich man … Abraham's bosom* From Luke 16.19–22: the rich man who denied food to the beggar Lazarus was sent to hell, while Lazarus was sent to join Abraham in heaven.

To draw me to this duty."
350   Then I spoke.
"I have not stood long on the strand of life,
And these salt waters have had scarcely time
To creep so high up as to wet my feet:
I cannot judge these tides—I shall, perhaps.
355   A woman's always younger than a man
At equal years, because she is disallowed
Maturing by the outdoor sun and air,
And kept in long-clothes past the age to walk.
Ah well, I know you men judge otherwise!
360   You think a woman ripens, as a peach,
In the cheeks chiefly. Pass it to me now;
I'm young in age, and younger still, I think,
As a woman. But a child may say amen
To a bishop's prayer and feel the way it goes,
365   And I, incapable to loose the knot
Of social questions, can approve, applaud
August compassion, Christian thoughts that shoot
Beyond the vulgar white° of personal aims.   archery target
Accept my reverence."
370   There he glowed on me
With all his face and eyes. "No other help?"
Said he—"no more than so?"
                          "What help?" I asked.
"You'd scorn my help—as Nature's self, you say,
375   Has scorned to put her music in my mouth
Because a woman's. Do you now turn round
And ask for what a woman cannot give?"

"For what she only can, I turn and ask,"
He answered, catching up my hands in his,
380   And dropping on me from his high-eaved brow
The full weight of his soul—"I ask for love,
And that, she can; for life in fellowship
Through bitter duties—that, I know she can;
For wifehood—will she?"
385   "Now," I said, "may God
Be witness 'twixt us two!" and with the word,
Meseemed[1] I floated into a sudden light
Above his stature—"am I proved too weak
To stand alone, yet strong enough to bear
390   Such leaners on my shoulder? poor to think,
Yet rich enough to sympathise with thought?
Incompetent to sing, as blackbirds can,

Yet competent to love, like HIM?"
                          I paused;
395   Perhaps I darkened, as the lighthouse will
That turns upon the sea. "It's always so.
Anything does for a wife."
                          "Aurora, dear,
And dearly honoured,"—he pressed in at once
400   With eager utterance—"you translate me ill.
I do not contradict my thought of you
Which is most reverent, with another thought
Found less so. If your sex is weak for art
(And I, who said so, did but honour you
405   By using truth in courtship), it is strong
For life and duty. Place your fecund heart
In mine, and let us blossom for the world
That wants love's colour in the grey of time.
My talk, meanwhile, is arid to you, ay,
410   Since all my talk can only set you where
You look down coldly on the arena-heaps
Of headless bodies, shapeless, indistinct!
The Judgment-Angel scarce would find his way
Through such a heap of generalised distress
415   To the individual man with lips and eyes,
Much less Aurora. Ah, my sweet, come down,
And hand in hand we'll go where yours shall touch
These victims, one by one! till, one by one,
The formless, nameless trunk of every man
420   Shall seem to wear a head with hair you know,
And every woman catch your mother's face
To melt you into passion."
                          "I am a girl,"
I answered slowly; "you do well to name
425   My mother's face. Though far too early, alas,
God's hand did interpose 'twixt it and me,
I know so much of love as used to shine
In that face and another. Just so much;
No more indeed at all. I have not seen
430   So much love since, I pray you pardon me,
As answers even to make a marriage with
In this cold land of England. What you love
Is not a woman, Romney, but a cause:
You want a helpmate, not a mistress, sir,
435   A wife to help your ends—in her no end.
Your cause is noble, your ends excellent,
But I, being most unworthy of these and that,
Do otherwise conceive of love. Farewell."

---

[1] *Meseemed*   It seemed to me.

"Farewell, Aurora? you reject me thus?"
440 He said.
            "Sir, you were married long ago.
You have a wife already whom you love,
Your social theory. Bless you both, I say.
For my part, I am scarcely meek enough
445 To be the handmaid of a lawful spouse.
Do I look a Hagar,[1] think you?"
                        "So you jest."

"Nay, so, I speak in earnest," I replied.
"You treat of marriage too much like, at least,
450 A chief apostle: you would bear with you
A wife … a sister[2] … shall we speak it out?
A sister of charity."
                    "Then, must it be
Indeed farewell? And was I so far wrong
455 In hope and in illusion, when I took
The woman to be nobler than the man,
Yourself the noblest woman, in the use
And comprehension of what love is—love,
That generates the likeness of itself
460 Through all heroic duties? so far wrong,
In saying bluntly, venturing truth on love,
'Come, human creature, love and work with me,'—
Instead of 'Lady, thou art wondrous fair,
And, where the Graces[3] walk before, the Muse
465 Will follow at the lightning of their eyes,
And where the Muse walks, lovers need to creep:
Turn round and love me, or I die of love.'"
With quiet indignation I broke in.
"You misconceive the question like a man,
470 Who sees a woman as the complement
Of his sex merely. You forget too much
That every creature, female as the male,
Stands single in responsible act and thought
As also in birth and death. Whoever says
475 To a loyal woman, 'Love and work with me,'
Will get fair answers if the work and love,
Being good themselves, are good for her—the best

She was born for. Women of a softer mood,
Surprised by men when scarcely awake to life,
480 Will sometimes only hear the first word, love,
And catch up with it any kind of work,
Indifferent, so that dear love go with it.
I do not blame such women, though, for love,
They pick much oakum;[4] earth's fanatics make
485 Too frequently heaven's saints. But *me* your work
Is not the best for—nor your love the best,
Nor able to commend the kind of work
For love's sake merely. Ah, you force me, sir,
To be overbold in speaking of myself:
490 I too have my vocation—work to do,
The heavens and earth have set me since I changed
My father's face for theirs, and, though your world
Were twice as wretched as you represent,
Most serious work, most necessary work
495 As any of the economists'. Reform,
Make trade a Christian possibility,
And individual right no general wrong;
Wipe out earth's furrows of the Thine and Mine,
And leave one green for men to play at bowls,
500 With innings for them all!… What then, indeed,
If mortals are not greater by the head
Than any of their prosperities? what then,
Unless the artist keep up open roads
Betwixt the seen and unseen—bursting through
505 The best of your conventions with his best,
The speakable, imaginable best
God bids him speak, to prove what lies beyond
Both speech and imagination? A starved man
Exceeds a fat beast: we'll not barter, sir,
510 The beautiful for barley.—And, even so,
I hold you will not compass your poor ends
Of barley-feeding and material ease,
Without a poet's individualism
To work your universal. It takes a soul,
515 To move a body: it takes a high-souled man,
To move the masses, even to a cleaner stye:
It takes the ideal, to blow a hair's-breadth off
The dust of the actual.—Ah, your Fouriers[5] failed,

---

[1] *Hagar* See Genesis 16 1–4: Hagar was handmaid to Sarah, Abraham's wife, and she also bore Abraham's child, as Sarah was unable to conceive.

[2] *chief apostle … sister* See 1 Corinthians 9.5.

[3] *Graces* In Greek mythology, three goddesses of beauty and charm.

[4] *oakum* Rope fibers acquired by untwisting and picking at old rope, a chore commonly assigned to prisoners or the workhouse poor.

[5] *Fourier* Charles Fourier (1772–1837), French socialist philosopher and utopian theorist.

Because not poets enough to understand
520 That life develops from within.—For me,
Perhaps I am not worthy, as you say,
Of work like this: perhaps a woman's soul
Aspires, and not creates: yet we aspire,
And yet I'll try out your perhapses, sir,
525 And if I fail … why, burn me up my straw
Like other false works—I'll not ask for grace;
Your scorn is better, cousin Romney. I
Who love my art, would never wish it lower
To suit my stature. I may love my art.
530 You'll grant that even a woman may love art,
Seeing that to waste true love on anything
Is womanly, past question."
                         I retain
The very last word which I said that day,
535 As you the creaking of the door, years past,
Which let upon you such disabling news
You ever after have been graver. He,
His eyes, the motions in his silent mouth,
Were fiery points on which my words were caught,
540 Transfixed for ever in my memory
For his sake, not their own. And yet I know
I did not love him … nor he me … that's sure …
And what I said is unrepented of,
As truth is always. Yet … a princely man!—
545 If hard to me, heroic for himself!
He bears down on me through the slanting years,
The stronger for the distance. If he had loved,
Ay, loved me, with that retributive face,…
I might have been a common woman now
550 And happier, less known and less left alone,
Perhaps a better woman after all,
With chubby children hanging on my neck
To keep me low and wise. Ah me, the vines
That bear such fruit are proud to stoop with it.
555 The palm stands upright in a realm of sand.

And I, who spoke the truth then, stand upright,
Still worthy of having spoken out the truth,
By being content I spoke it though it set
Him there, me here.—O woman's vile remorse,
560 To hanker after a mere name, a show,
A supposition, a potential love!
Does every man who names love in our lives
Become a power for that? is love's true thing

So much best to us, that what personates love
565 Is next best? A potential love, forsooth!
I'm not so vile. No, no—he cleaves, I think,
This man, this image—chiefly for the wrong
And shock he gave my life, in finding me
Precisely where the devil of my youth
570 Had set me, on those mountain-peaks of hope[1]
All glittering with the dawn-dew, all erect
And famished for the noon—exclaiming, while
I looked for empire and much tribute, "Come,
I have some worthy work for thee below.
575 Come, sweep my barns and keep my hospitals,
And I will pay thee with a current coin
Which men give women."
…

from BOOK 5

Aurora Leigh, be humble. Shall I hope
To speak my poems in mysterious tune
With man and nature?—with the lava-lymph
That trickles from successive galaxies
5 Still drop by drop adown the finger of God
In still new worlds?—with summer days in this
That scarce dare breathe they are so beautiful?
With spring's delicious trouble in the ground,
Tormented by the quickened blood of roots,
10 And softly pricked by golden crocus sheaves
In token of the harvest-time of flowers?
With winters and with autumns—and beyond
With the human heart's large seasons, when it hopes
And fears, joys, grieves, and loves?—with all that strain
15 Of sexual passion, which devours the flesh
In a sacrament of souls? with mother's breasts
Which, round the new-made creatures hanging there,
Throb luminous and harmonious like pure spheres?—
With multitudinous life, and finally
20 With the great escapings of ecstatic souls,
Who, in a rush of too long prisoned flame,
Their radiant faces upward, burn away
This dark of the body, issuing on a world
Beyond our mortal?—can I speak my verse
25 So plainly in tune to these things and the rest

---

[1] *devil … hope* See Luke 4.5: "And the devil, taking him [Jesus] up into an high mountain, showed unto him all the kingdoms of the world in a moment of time."

That men shall feel it catch them on the quick
As having the same warrant over them
To hold and move them if they will or no,
Alike imperious as the primal rhythm
30 Of that theurgic[1] nature?—I must fail,
Who fail at the beginning to hold and move
One man—and he my cousin, and he my friend,
And he born tender, made intelligent,
Inclined to ponder the precipitous sides
35 Of difficult questions; yet, obtuse to *me*,
Of *me*, incurious! likes me very well,
And wishes me a paradise of good,
Good looks, good means, and good digestion—ay,
But otherwise evades me, puts me off
40 With kindness, with a tolerant gentleness—
Too light a book for a grave man's reading! Go,
Aurora Leigh: be humble.
                                    There it is,
We women are too apt to look to one,
45 Which proves a certain impotence in art.
We strain our natures at doing something great,
Far less because it's something great to do,
Than haply that we, so, commend ourselves
As being not small, and more appreciable
50 To some one friend. We must have mediators
Betwixt our highest conscience and the judge;
Some sweet saint's blood must quicken in our palms,
Or all the like in heaven seems slow and cold:
Good only being perceived as the end of good,
55 And God alone pleased—that's too poor, we think,
And not enough for us by any means.
Ay—Romney, I remember, told me once
We miss the abstract when we comprehend.
We miss it most when we aspire—and fail.

60 Yet, so, I will not.—This vile woman's way
Of trailing garments shall not trip me up:
I'll have no traffic with the personal thought
In Art's pure temple. Must I work in vain,
Without the approbation of a man?
65 It cannot be; it shall not. Fame itself,
That approbation of the general race,
Presents a poor end (though the arrow speed
Shot straight with vigorous finger to the white),

And the highest fame was never reached except
70 By what was aimed above it. Art for art,
And good for God Himself, the essential Good!
We'll keep our aims sublime, our eyes erect,
Although our woman-hands should shake and fail;
And if we fail … But must we?—
75   Shall I fail?
The Greeks said grandly in their tragic phrase,
"Let no one be called happy till his death."[2]
To which I add—Let no one till his death
Be called unhappy. Measure not the work
80 Until the day's out and the labour done,
Then bring your gauges. If the day's work's scant,
Why, call it scant; affect no compromise;
And, in that we have nobly striven at least,
Deal with us nobly, women though we be,
85 And honour us with truth if not with praise.
…
The critics say that epics have died out
With Agamemnon[3] and the goat-nursed gods;[4]
I'll not believe it. I could never deem,
As Payne Knight[5] did (the mythic mountaineer
90 Who travelled higher than he was born to live,
And showed sometimes the goitre[6] in his throat
Discoursing of an image seen through fog),
That Homer's heroes measured twelve feet high.[7]
They were but men:—his Helen's hair turned grey
95 Like any plain Miss Smith's who wears a front;[8]

---

1 *theurgic* Pertaining to the operation of the gods or the supernatural in human affairs.

2 *"Let no one … death."* The final lines of Sophocles's *Oedipus Rex*: "From hence the lesson draw, / To reckon no man happy till ye see / The closing day; until he pass the bourn / Which severs life from death, unscathed by woe."

3 *Agamemnon* King of Mycenae and head of the Greek forces in the Trojan War; Agamemnon was murdered by his wife and her lover.

4 *goat-nursed gods* Zeus, the supreme god of Greek mythology, was nursed by a goat as a baby.

5 *Payne Knight* Radical historian and author of much commentary on Greek mythology; Richard Payne Knight (1750–1824) released an edition of *The Iliad* and *The Odyssey* that deleted many of Homer's passages.

6 *goitre* Thyroid swelling in the neck, occurring disproportionately in people who dwell in mountainous areas.

7 *Homer's … high* Payne Knight felt that Greek art and literature idealized humans.

8 *front* False hair that covers the forehead.

And Hector's infant whimpered at a plume[1]
As yours last Friday at a turkey-cock.
All actual heroes are essential men,
And all men possible heroes: every age,
100 Heroic in proportions, double-faced,
Looks backward and before, expects a morn
And claims an epos.°   *epic poem*
                       Ay, but every age
Appears to souls who live in't (ask Carlyle)
105 Most unheroic.[2] Ours, for instance, ours:
The thinkers scout° it, and the poets abound   *mock*
Who scorn to touch it with a fingertip:
A pewter age—mixed metal, silver-washed;
An age of scum, spooned off the richer past,
110 An age of patches for old gaberdines,°   *woolen cloths*
An age of mere transition,[3] meaning nought
Except that what succeeds must shame it quite
If God please. That's wrong thinking, to my mind,
And wrong thoughts make poor poems.
115   Every age,
Through being beheld too close, is ill-discerned
By those who have not lived past it. We'll suppose
Mount Athos carved, as Alexander schemed,
To some colossal statue of a man.[4]
120 The peasants, gathering brushwood in his ear,
Had guessed as little as the browsing goats
Of form or feature of humanity
Up there—in fact, had travelled five miles off
Or ere the giant image broke on them,
125 Full human profile, nose and chin distinct,
Mouth, muttering rhythms of silence up the sky
And fed at evening with the blood of suns;
Grand torso—hand, that flung perpetually

The largesse of a silver river down
130 To all the country pastures. 'Tis even thus
With times we live in—evermore too great
To be apprehended near.
                            But poets should
Exert a double vision; should have eyes
135 To see near things as comprehensively
As if afar they took their point of sight,
And distant things as intimately deep
As if they touched them. Let us strive for this.
I do distrust the poet who discerns
140 No character or glory in his times,
And trundles back his soul five hundred years,
Past moat and drawbridge, into a castle court,
To sing—oh, not of lizard or of toad
Alive i' the ditch there—'twere excusable,
145 But of some black chief, half knight, half sheep-lifter,
Some beauteous dame, half chattel and half queen,
As dead as must be, for the greater part,
The poems made on their chivalric bones;
And that's no wonder: death inherits death.

150 Nay, if there's room for poets in this world
A little overgrown (I think there is),
Their sole work is to represent the age,
Their age, not Charlemagne's,[5]—this live, throbbing
    age,
That brawls, cheats, maddens, calculates, aspires,
155 And spends more passion, more heroic heat,
Betwixt the mirrors of its drawing-rooms,
Than Roland with his knights at Roncesvalles.[6]
To flinch from modern varnish, coat or flounce,
Cry out for togas and the picturesque,
160 Is fatal—foolish too. King Arthur's self
Was commonplace to Lady Guenever;
And Camelot to minstrels seemed as flat
As Fleet Street[7] to our poets.
                            Never flinch,
165 But still, unscrupulously epic, catch

---

[1] *Hector's ... plume* In Homer's the *Iliad* 6.575–78, Hector's son recoils in fear upon seeing his warrior father's plumed helmet.

[2] *every age ... unheroic* Thomas Carlyle wrote in *On Heroes, Hero-Worship, and the Heroic in History* (1840) that the heroism of any given age is never recognized in its time.

[3] *An age of mere transition* In *The Spirit of the Age* (1831) John Stuart Mill wrote: "In the Present age of transition, everything must be subordinate to freedom of inquiry."

[4] *Mount Athos ... man* In Plutarch's *The Life of Alexander*, the sculptor Stasicrates proposed to Alexander that he carve out of Mount Athos "a most enduring and most conspicuous statue of the king, which in its left hand should hold a city of ten thousand inhabitants, and with its right should pour forth a river running with generous current into the sea."

[5] *Charlemagne* Charles the Great (742–814), ruler of much of Europe in the early years of the ninth century.

[6] *Roland ... Roncesvalles* Roland, Charlemagne's commander, was immortalized in *Chanson de Roland*, which relates his death in a battle at Roncesvalles.

[7] *Fleet Street* In London, then the hub of the news and publishing industries.

Upon the burning lava of a song
The full-veined, heaving, double-breasted Age:
That, when the next shall come, the men of that
May touch the impress with reverent hand, and say
170 "Behold—behold the paps° we have all sucked!   *nipples*
This bosom seems to beat still, or at least
It sets ours beating: this is living art,
Which thus presents and thus records true life."
—1857

A Curse For A Nation

PROLOGUE

I heard an angel speak last night,
        And he said "Write!
Write a nation's curse for me,
And send it over the Western Sea."

5 I faltered, taking up the word:
        "Not so, my lord!
If curses must be, choose another
To send thy curse against my brother.

"For I am bound by gratitude,
10   By love and blood,
To brothers of mine across the sea,
Who stretch out kindly hands to me."

"Therefore," the voice said, "shalt thou write
        My curse tonight.
15 From the summits of love a curse is driven,
As lightning is from the tops of heaven."

"Not so," I answered. "Evermore
        My heart is sore
For my own land's sins: for little feet
20 Of children bleeding along the street:

"For parked-up honors that gainsay
        The right of way:
For almsgiving through a door that is
Not open enough for two friends to kiss:

25 "For love of freedom which abates
        Beyond the straits:
For patriot virtue starved to vice on
Self-praise, self-interest, and suspicion:

"For an oligarchic[1] parliament,
30   And bribes well-meant.
What curse to another land assign,
When heavy-souled for the sins of mine?"

"Therefore," the voice said, "shalt thou write
        My curse tonight.
35 Because thou hast strength to see and hate
A foul thing done within thy gate."

"Not so," I answered once again.
        "To curse, choose men.
For I, a woman, have only known
40 How the heart melts and the tears run down."

"Therefore," the voice said, "shalt thou write
        My curse tonight.
Some women weep and curse, I say
(And no one marvels), night and day.

45 "And thou shalt take their part tonight,
        Weep and write.
A curse from the depths of womanhood
Is very salt, and bitter, and good."

So thus I wrote, and mourned indeed,
50   What all may read.
And thus, as was enjoined on me,
I send it over the Western Sea.

THE CURSE

I

Because ye have broken your own chain
        With the strain
55 Of brave men climbing a nation's height,
Yet thence bear down with brand and thong
On souls of others—for this wrong
        This is the curse. Write.

---

[1] *oligarchic* Governed by a small, elite group.

60 Because yourselves are standing straight
        In the state
Of Freedom's foremost acolyte,
Yet keep calm footing all the time
On writhing bond-slaves—for this crime
        This is the curse. Write.

65 Because ye prosper in God's name,
        With a claim
To honor in the old world's sight,
Yet do the fiend's work perfectly
In strangling martyrs—for this lie
70   This is the curse. Write.

2

Ye shall watch while kings conspire
Round the people's smouldering fire,
        And, warm for your part,
Shall never dare—O shame!
75 To utter the thought into flame
        Which burns at your heart.
        This is the curse. Write.

Ye shall watch while nations strive
With the bloodhounds, die or survive,
80   Drop faint from their jaws,
Or throttle them backward to death;
And only under your breath
        Shall favor the cause.
        This is the curse. Write.

85 Ye shall watch while strong men draw
The nets of feudal law
        To strangle the weak;
And, counting the sin for a sin,
Your soul shall be sadder within
90   Than the word ye shall speak.
        This is the curse. Write.

When good men are praying erect
That Christ may avenge His elect
        And deliver the earth,
95 The prayer in your ears, said low,
Shall sound like the tramp of a foe
        That's driving you forth.
        This is the curse. Write.

100 When wise men give you their praise,
They shall praise in the heat of the phrase,
        As if carried too far.
When ye boast your own charters kept true,
Ye shall blush; for the thing which ye do
        Derides what ye are.
105   This is the curse. Write.

When fools cast taunts at your gate,
Your scorn ye shall somewhat abate
        As ye look o'er the wall;
For your conscience, tradition, and name
110 Explode with a deadlier blame
        Than the worst of them all.
        This is the curse. Write.

Go, wherever ill deeds shall be done,
Go, plant your flag in the sun
115   Beside the ill-doers!
And recoil from clenching the curse
Of God's witnessing universe
        With a curse of yours.
        This is the curse. Write.
—1860

A Musical Instrument

1

What was he doing, the great god Pan,[1]
        Down in the reeds by the river?
Spreading ruin and scattering ban,
Splashing and paddling with hoofs of a goat,
5 And breaking the golden lilies afloat
        With the dragonfly on the river.

2

He tore out a reed, the great god Pan,
        From the deep cool bed of the river:
The limpid water turbidly ran,
10 And the broken lilies a-dying lay,

---

[1] *Pan* Greek god of nature who was half goat and half man. After the nymph Syrinx turned herself into a bed of reeds in order to escape him, Pan created an instrument (the panpipe) out of the reeds.

And the dragonfly had fled away,
    Ere he brought it out of the river.

3

High on the shore sat the great god Pan
    While turbidly flowed the river;
15 And hacked and hewed as a great god can,
With his hard bleak steel at the patient reed,
Till there was not a sign of the leaf indeed
    To prove it fresh from the river.

4

He cut it short, did the great god Pan,
20   (How tall it stood in the river!)
Then drew the pith, like the heart of a man,
    Steadily from the outside ring,
And notched the poor dry empty thing
    In holes, as he sat by the river.

5

25 "This is the way," laughed the great god Pan
    (Laughed while he sat by the river),

"The only way, since gods began
    To make sweet music, they could succeed."
Then, dropping his mouth to a hole in the reed,
30   He blew in power by the river.

6

Sweet, sweet, sweet, O Pan!
    Piercing sweet by the river!
Blinding sweet, O great god Pan!
The sun on the hill forgot to die,
35 And the lilies revived, and the dragonfly
    Came back to dream on the river.

7

Yet half a beast is the great god Pan,
    To laugh as he sits by the river,
Making a poet out of a man:
40 The true gods sigh for the cost and pain—
For the reed which grows nevermore again
    As a reed with the reeds in the river.
        —1862

ALFRED, LORD TENNYSON
1809 – 1892

In 1850, the novelist and critic Charles Kingsley praised Tennyson's dramatic monologue, "Locksley Hall," as the poem that "has had most influence on the minds of the young men of our day." Throughout his long career, Tennyson's poems continued to resonate with Victorian audiences. The self-reflective grief of *In Memoriam* (1850) touched a chord of genuine sympathy in nineteenth-century readers, including Queen Victoria herself, much as Tennyson's re-telling of Arthurian legend in *Idylls of the King* (1859–85) echoed the nationalistic zeal of the later Victorian period. Britain's Poet Laureate from 1850 to his death in 1892, Tennyson was the quintessential poet of his age.

He was born in 1809 in Somersby, Lincolnshire, to a privileged family, and his poetic gifts became apparent early on. At age eight, Tennyson was composing pages of blank verse in the style of James Thomson; by ten or eleven he had graduated to studying the work of Alexander Pope, imitating hundreds of lines of Pope's translation of Homer's *Iliad*. At twelve, Tennyson set to work on his first epic, a six-thousand-line experiment that mimicked Walter Scott's octo-syllabic extravaganzas of war and romance. "I wrote as much as seventy lines at one time," he later recalled, "and used to go shouting them about the fields in the dark." By age fourteen, with an Elizabethan-style drama entitled *The Devil and the Lady*, Tennyson's work was approaching the sonorous agility and understated pathos for which it would be known. His first publication, *Poems by Two Brothers* (1827), a collaborative effort by Tennyson and his two older brothers, Frederick and Charles, was completed just prior to Tennyson's entrance to Trinity College, Cambridge.

Tennyson distinguished himself at Cambridge, establishing his reputation as both a deep thinker and a poet. In June of 1829, he won the Chancellor's Gold Medal with a blank-verse poem, *Timbuctoo*. Some time in that year, Tennyson met Arthur Henry Hallam, who was to become the poet's closest friend and companion. It was also in 1829 that Tennyson joined the Cambridge Apostles, an undergraduate debating society of which Hallam and many of Tennyson's other Cambridge friends were a part. 1830 saw the publication of Tennyson's first important volume, *Poems, Chiefly Lyrical*, which Hallam reviewed for the *Englishman's Magazine* in an essay entitled "On Some of the Characteristics of Modern Poetry and on the Lyrical Poems of Alfred Tennyson." Hallam describes Tennyson as a poet of "sensation," one of a school of poets, including Shelley and Keats, whose "fine organs tremble into emotion at colors, and sounds, and movements" and who translate this physiological sensitivity into their verses. It was precisely such sensitivity that Christopher North (the pseudonym of John Wilson) later attacked in his 1832 *Blackwood's* review of the volume. Subsequently many critics have charted Tennyson's gradual movement away from a poetics of sensation and toward a more restrained poetic style.

The early 1830s were a difficult time for the young poet. Following the death of his father in 1831, Tennyson left Cambridge without taking his degree. Soon afterward, his brother Edward lost his sanity, succumbing to what was known as the "black blood" of the Tennyson family. Finally, and perhaps most devastatingly, Arthur Hallam died suddenly in 1833 of a hemorrhage to his brain. Having published one volume, *Poems*, in 1832, Tennyson would remain silent as a poet for the next ten years, refusing to publish his many works in progress until the *Poems* of 1842, the volume that brought him his reputation as both a remarkable poet and a great voice of his age. During the "ten years' silence," however, Tennyson composed much of what many consider his masterwork, *In Memoriam* (1850), in addition to the innovative dramatic monologues of the 1842 volume, including "Ulysses," "Locksley Hall," and "St. Simeon Stylites."

In 1847, Tennyson published *The Princess*, a poetic medley that explored, through a wildly improbable narrative, the relations between the sexes and the viability of education for women. Interspersed throughout the work are many of Tennyson's best-known lyrics: "Sweet and Low," "The Splendour Falls," and "Tears, Idle Tears," among others. In 1850, Tennyson ascended to the Laureateship and married Emily Sellwood, to whom he had been engaged for fourteen years. That same year, Tennyson also published *In Memoriam*, the elegy on which he had been at work since Arthur Hallam's death. The first of many of Tennyson's books to sell in large numbers, *In Memoriam* went into three editions in its first year alone. Amid a rising swell of scientific discovery and industrial transformation, the poem captured the mood of the era, alternating between faith in science and faith in religion, and reflecting the hopes, doubts, and beliefs of the Victorians.

Tennyson's life changed notably as a result of both his marriage and his suddenly public role as Poet Laureate. The Tennysons had two sons within the next four years, the elder of whom was named Hallam after Tennyson's deceased friend. (After his father's death, Hallam Tennyson wrote a biography entitled *Alfred Lord Tennyson: A Memoir*, and he penned a second volume in 1911, *Tennyson and His Friends*. Alfred Tennyson's grandson Charles also wrote a biography in 1949.)

Many critics have argued that Tennyson's style changed after his appointment as Poet Laureate. Certainly it is true that he assumed a different voice in the occasional poems composed in his role as Poet Laureate, most notably the "Ode on the Death of the Duke of Wellington" (1852); likewise "The Charge of the Light Brigade" (1854) projects an explicit political stance largely absent in his earlier works. But Tennyson continued to evolve as a poet, publishing an experimental "monodrama," *Maud*, in 1855 and the first four segments of his epic, *Idylls of the King*, in 1859. *Maud* was in many ways Tennyson's most controversial publication. Critics complained of the poem's irregular rhythms and of the "screed of bombast" that seemed to some like "the rasping of a blacksmith's file." *Idylls of the King*, on the other hand, was largely—though not universally—hailed as a *magnum opus*. Tennyson had contemplated writing an epic from his childhood; the finished *Idylls* reflects the poet's mature thoughts about Victorian life, politics, and culture through the world of Camelot and King Arthur.

Tennyson's later publications include the plays *Queen Mary* (1875), *The Falcon* (1879), and *The Promise of May* (1882), all of which were produced on the Victorian stage, and numerous volumes of poetry, including *Enoch Arden* (1864), *Tiresias, and Other Poems* (1885), *Locksley Hall Sixty Years After* (1886), and *Demeter and Other Poems* (1889). In 1883, Tennyson accepted a baronetcy from the Queen and took a seat in the House of Lords. He died in 1892 at his second home, Aldworth, and is buried beside Robert Browning in the Poets' Corner of Westminster Abbey.

⌘ ⌘ ⌘

Julia Margaret Cameron, *Mariana*, 1875.

Mariana

Mariana in the moated grange
(Measure for Measure)[1]

With blackest moss the flower-plots
   Were thickly crusted, one and all:
The rusted nails fell from the knots
   That held the pear to the gable-wall.[2]
5 The broken sheds looked sad and strange:
   Unlifted was the clinking latch;
   Weeded and worn the ancient thatch
Upon the lonely moated grange.
     She only said, "My life is dreary,

10   He cometh not," she said;
     She said, "I am aweary, aweary,
      I would that I were dead!"

Her tears fell with the dews at even;°   *evening*
   Her tears fell ere° the dews were dried;   *before*
15 She could not look on the sweet heaven,
   Either at morn or eventide.
After the flitting of the bats,
   When thickest dark did trance° the sky,   *entrance*
   She drew her casement-curtain by,
20 And glanced athwart the glooming flats.[3]
     She only said, "The night is dreary,
      He cometh not," she said;
     She said, "I am aweary, aweary,
      I would that I were dead!"

25 Upon the middle of the night,
   Waking she heard the night-fowl crow:
The cock sung out an hour ere light:
   From the dark fen° the oxen's low   *lowlands*
Came to her: without hope of change,
30 In sleep she seemed to walk forlorn,
   Till cold winds woke the gray-eyed morn
About the lonely moated grange.
     She only said, "The day is dreary,
      He cometh not," she said;
35   She said, "I am aweary, aweary,
      I would that I were dead!"

About a stone-cast from the wall
   A sluice with blackened waters slept,
And o'er it many, round and small,
40 The clustered marish-mosses[4] crept.
Hard by a poplar shook alway,
   All silver-green with gnarlèd bark:
   For leagues no other tree did mark
The level waste, the rounding gray.
45   She only said, "My life is dreary,
      He cometh not," she said;
     She said, "I am aweary, aweary,
      I would that I were dead!"

---

[1] *Mariana ... Measure* Tennyson's epigraph is adapted from the words of the Duke in Shakespeare's *Measure for Measure*, 3.1.277: "There, at the moated grange, lies this dejected Mariana." Earlier in the scene, the Duke has recounted how Mariana, having lost her dowry (and her brother) in a shipwreck, has been deserted by her betrothed; *moated grange* Cottage or small farmhouse surrounded by a moat, or water-filled ditch.

[2] *The rusted ... wall* The pear has been espaliered, or trained to grow against a wall on a lattice or framework of stakes.

[3] *flats* Flatlands or lowlands.

[4] [Tennyson's note] *Marish-mosses*, the little marsh-moss lumps that float on the surface of the water.

And ever when the moon was low,
    And the shrill winds were up and away,
In the white curtain, to and fro,
    She saw the gusty shadow sway.
But when the moon was very low,
    And wild winds bound within their cell,[1]
    The shadow of the poplar fell
Upon her bed, across her brow.
        She only said, "The night is dreary,
           He cometh not," she said;
        She said, "I am aweary, aweary,
           I would that I were dead!"

All day within the dreamy house,
    The doors upon their hinges creaked;
The blue fly° sung in the pane; the mouse   *bluebottle*
    Behind the mouldering wainscot shrieked,
Or from the crevice peered about.
    Old faces glimmered through the doors,
    Old footsteps trod the upper floors,
Old voices called her from without.
        She only said, "My life is dreary,
           He cometh not," she said;
        She said, "I am aweary, aweary,
           I would that I were dead!"

The sparrow's chirrup on the roof,
    The slow clock ticking, and the sound
Which to the wooing wind aloof
    The poplar made, did all confound
Her sense; but most she loathed the hour
    When the thick-moted[2] sunbeam lay
    Athwart the chambers, and the day
Was sloping toward his western bower.
        Then, said she, "I am very dreary,
           He will not come," she said;
        She wept, "I am aweary, aweary,
           Oh God, that I were dead!"

—1830

50, 55, 60, 65, 70, 75, 80

---

1 *wild … cell* A reference to Virgil's *Aeneid*, 1.52, in which Aeolus, god of winds, keeps the winds imprisoned in a cavern.

2 *thick-moted* I.e., thick with motes of dust.

The Palace of Art

I built my soul a lordly pleasure-house,
    Wherein at ease for aye° to dwell.   *ever*
I said, "O Soul, make merry and carouse,
    Dear soul, for all is well."

A huge crag-platform, smooth as burnished brass
    I chose. The rangèd ramparts bright
From level meadow-bases of deep grass
    Suddenly scaled the light.

Thereon I built it firm. Of ledge or shelf
    The rock rose clear, or winding stair.
My soul would live alone unto herself
    In her high palace there.

And "while the world runs round and round," I said,
    "Reign thou apart, a quiet king,
Still as, while Saturn whirls, his steadfast shade
    Sleeps on his luminous ring."

To which my soul made answer readily:
    "Trust me, in bliss I shall abide
In this great mansion, that is built for me,
    So royal-rich and wide."

Four courts I made, East, West and South and North,
    In each a squared lawn, wherefrom
The golden gorge of dragons spouted forth
    A flood of fountain-foam.

And round the cool green courts there ran a row
    Of cloisters, branched like mighty woods,
Echoing all night to that sonorous flow
    Of spouted fountain-floods.

And round the roofs a gilded gallery
    That lent broad verge° to distant lands,   *view*
Far as the wild swan wings, to where the sky
    Dipped down to sea and sands.

5, 10, 15, 20, 25, 30

From those four jets four currents in one swell
    Across the mountain streamed below
35 In misty folds, that floating as they fell
      Lit up a torrent-bow.[1]

And high on every peak a statue seemed
    To hang on tiptoe, tossing up
A cloud of incense of all odour steamed
40   From out a golden cup.

So that she thought, "And who shall gaze upon
    My palace with unblinded eyes,
While this great bow will waver in the sun,
      And that sweet incense rise?"

45 For that sweet incense rose and never failed,
    And, while day sank or mounted higher,
The light aerial gallery, golden-railed,
      Burnt like a fringe of fire.

Likewise the deep-set windows, stained and traced,
50   Would seem slow-flaming crimson fires
From shadowed grots° of arches interlaced,   *grottoes*
      And tipped with frost-like spires.

Full of long-sounding corridors it was,
    That over-vaulted grateful° gloom,   *pleasing*
55 Through which the livelong day my soul did pass,
      Well-pleased, from room to room.

Full of great rooms and small the palace stood,
    All various, each a perfect whole
From living Nature, fit for every mood
60   And change of my still soul.

For some were hung with arras° green and blue,   *tapestries*
    Showing a gaudy summer-morn,
Where with puffed cheek the belted hunter blew
      His wreathèd bugle-horn.

65 One seemed all dark and red—a tract of sand,
    And someone pacing there alone,
Who paced forever in a glimmering land,
      Lit with a low large moon.

One showed an iron coast and angry waves.
70   You seemed to hear them climb and fall
And roar rock-thwarted under bellowing caves,
      Beneath the windy wall.

And one, a full-fed river winding slow
    By herds upon an endless plain,
75 The ragged rims of thunder brooding low,
      With shadow-streaks of rain.

And one, the reapers at their sultry toil.
    In front they bound the sheaves. Behind
Were realms of upland, prodigal in oil,
80   And hoary to the wind.[2]

And one a foreground black with stones and slags,
    Beyond, a line of heights, and higher
All barred with long white cloud the scornful crags,
      And highest, snow and fire.

85 And one, an English home—gray twilight poured
    On dewy pastures, dewy trees,
Softer than sleep—all things in order stored,
      A haunt of ancient Peace.

Nor these alone, but every landscape fair,
90   As fit for every mood of mind,
Or gay, or grave, or sweet, or stern, was there
      Not less than truth designed.

Or the maid-mother by a crucifix,
    In tracts of pasture sunny-warm,
95 Beneath branch-work of costly sardonyx[3]
      Sat smiling, babe in arm.

Or in a clear-walled city on the sea,
    Near gilded organ-pipes, her hair
Wound with white roses, slept St. Cecily;[4]
100   An angel looked at her.

---

[1] *torrent-bow* Rainbow formed in the spray of a torrent.

[2] *hoary … wind* The white underside of the olive leaves are exposed by the wind.

[3] *sardonyx* Onyx striped with sard, a yellow or orange quartz.

[4] *St. Cecily* St. Cecilia, patron saint of music.

Or thronging all one porch of Paradise
    A group of Houris[1] bowed to see
The dying Islamite, with hands and eyes
      That said, We wait for thee.

105 Or mythic Uther's deeply-wounded son[2]
    In some fair space of sloping greens
Lay, dozing in the vale of Avalon,
      And watched by weeping queens.

Or hollowing one hand against his ear,
110   To list° a foot-fall, ere he saw   *hear*
The wood-nymph, stayed the Ausonian king[3] to hear
      Of wisdom and of law.

Or over hills with peaky tops engrailed,°   *serrated*
    And many a tract of palm and rice.
115 The throne of Indian Cama[4] slowly sailed
      A summer fanned with spice.

Or sweet Europa's[5] mantle blew unclasped,
    From off her shoulder backward borne:
From one hand drooped a crocus: one hand grasped
120   The mild bull's golden horn.

Or else flushed Ganymede,[6] his rosy thigh
    Half-buried in the Eagle's down,
Sole as a flying star shot through the sky
      Above the pillared town.

125 Nor these alone: but every legend fair
    Which the supreme Caucasian mind
Carved out of Nature for itself, was there,
      Not less than life, designed.

Then in the towers I placed great bells that swung,
130   Moved of themselves, with silver sound;
And with choice paintings of wise men I hung
      The royal dais round.

For there was Milton like a seraph° strong,   *angel*
    Beside him Shakespeare bland and mild;
135 And there the world-worn Dante grasped his song,
      And somewhat grimly smiled.

And there the Ionian father[7] of the rest;
    A million wrinkles carved his skin;
A hundred winters snowed upon his breast,
140   From cheek and throat and chin.

Above, the fair hall-ceiling stately-set
    Many an arch high up did lift,
And angels rising and descending met
      With interchange of gift.

145 Below was all mosaic choicely planned
    With cycles of the human tale
Of this wide world, the times of every land
      So wrought, they will not fail.

The people here, a beast of burden slow,
150   Toiled onward, pricked with goads and stings;
Here played, a tiger, rolling to and fro
      The heads and crowns of kings;

Here rose, an athlete, strong to break or bind
    All force in bonds that might endure,
155 And here once more like some sick man declined,
      And trusted any cure.

But over these she trod: and those great bells
    Began to chime. She took her throne:
She sat betwixt the shining Oriels,°   *windows*
160   To sing her songs alone.

---

[1] *Houris* Nymphs of Muslim paradise.

[2] *Uther's ... son* King Arthur, son of Uther Pendragon, badly wounded in his last battle and carried to the mystic island of Avalon to heal.

[3] *Ausonian king* Numa, the legendary second king of Rome, who was said to have received the laws of the kingdom from the nymph Egeria; *Ausonia* was an ancient name for Italy often used by poets.

[4] [Tennyson's note] The Hindu God of young love, son of Brahma.

[5] *Europa* In Greek legend, the beautiful daughter of the king of Phoenicia. Zeus fell in love with her and assumed the shape of a bull in order to carry her off.

[6] *Ganymede* In Greek legend, a beautiful youth who was carried up to heaven at the command of Zeus, who made him cup-bearer to the gods.

[7] *Ionian father* Homer.

And through the topmost Oriels' coloured flame
　　Two godlike faces gazed below;
Plato the wise, and large-browed Verulam,[1]
　　The first of those who know.

165　And all those names, that in their motion were
　　Full-welling fountainheads of change,
Betwixt the slender shafts were blazoned fair
　　In diverse raiment° strange:　　　　　　*clothing*

Through which the lights, rose, amber, emerald, blue,
170　Flushed in her temples and her eyes,
And from her lips, as morn from Memnon, drew
　　Rivers of melodies.[2]

No nightingale delighteth to prolong
　　Her low preamble all alone,
175　More than my soul to hear her echoed song
　　Throb through the ribbèd stone;

Singing and murmuring in her feastful mirth,
　　Joying to feel herself alive,
Lord over Nature, Lord of the visible earth,
180　Lord of the senses five;

Communing with herself: "All these are mine,
　　And let the world have peace or wars,
'Tis one to me." She—when young night divine
　　Crowned dying day with stars,

185　Making sweet close of his delicious toils—
　　Lit light in wreaths and anadems,°　　*garlands*
And pure quintessences of precious oils
　　In hollowed moons of gems,

To mimic heaven; and clapped her hands and cried,
190　"I marvel if my still° delight　　　*constant*
In this great house so royal-rich, and wide,
　　Be flattered to the height.

"O all things fair to sate my various eyes!
　　O shapes and hues that please me well!
195　O silent faces of the Great and Wise,
　　My Gods, with whom I dwell!

"O God-like isolation which art mine,
　　I can but count thee perfect gain,
What time I watch the darkening droves of swine
200　That range on yonder plain.

"In filthy sloughs they roll a prurient skin,
　　They graze and wallow, breed and sleep;
And oft some brainless devil enters in,
　　And drives them to the deep."[3]

205　Then of the moral instinct would she prate
　　And of the rising from the dead,
As hers by right of full-accomplished Fate;
　　And at the last she said:

"I take possession of man's mind and deed.
210　I care not what the sects may brawl.
I sit as God holding no form of creed,
　　But contemplating all."

Full oft the riddle of the painful earth
　　Flashed through her as she sat alone,
215　Yet not the less held she her solemn mirth,
　　And intellectual throne.

And so she throve and prospered: so three years
　　She prospered: on the fourth she fell,
Like Herod, when the shout was in his ears,
220　Struck through with pangs of hell.[4]

Lest she should fail and perish utterly,
　　God, before whom ever lie bare
The abysmal deeps of Personality,
　　Plagued her with sore despair.

1　*Oriels' … Verulam*　Recessed windows decorated with colored stained glass in images of Plato and Francis Bacon, one of whose titles was Baron Verulam.

2　*Morn … melodies*　The statue of the legendary Ethiopian king Memnon at Thebes was said by the ancient Greeks to produce beautiful music when touched by the rays of the dawning sun.

3　*oft … deep*　A reference to Matthew 8.28–32, in which Jesus casts devils out of two men and into a herd of swine, whereupon the herd stampedes off a cliff into the sea.

4　*Herod … hell*　A reference to Acts 12.21–23, in which King Herod is struck dead as a crowd of his subjects shout that he is a god and not a man.

225   When she would think, where'er she turned her sight
      The airy hand confusion wrought,
  Wrote, "Mene, mene,"[1] and divided quite
      The kingdom of her thought.

  Deep dread and loathing of her solitude
230   Fell on her, from which mood was born
  Scorn of herself; again, from out that mood
      Laughter at her self-scorn.

  "What! is not this my place of strength," she said,
      "My spacious mansion built for me,
235   Whereof the strong foundation-stones were laid
      Since my first memory?"

  But in dark corners of her palace stood
      Uncertain shapes; and unawares
  On white-eyed phantasms weeping tears of blood,
240   And horrible nightmares,

  And hollow shades enclosing hearts of flame,
      And, with dim fretted foreheads all,
  On corpses three-months-old at noon she came,
      That stood against the wall.

245   A spot of dull stagnation, without light
      Or power of movement, seemed my soul,
  'Mid onward-sloping motions infinite
      Making for one sure goal.

  A still salt pool, locked in with bars of sand,
250   Left on the shore; that hears all night
  The plunging seas draw backward from the land
      Their moon-led waters white.

  A star that with the choral starry dance
      Joined not, but stood, and standing saw
255   The hollow orb of moving Circumstance
      Rolled round by one fixed law.

  Back on herself her serpent pride had curled.
      "No voice," she shrieked in that lone hall,
  "No voice breaks through the stillness of this world:
260   One deep, deep silence all!"

  She, mouldering with the dull earth's mouldering sod,
      Inwrapt tenfold in slothful shame,
  Lay there exilèd from eternal God,
      Lost to her place and name;

265   And death and life she hated equally,
      And nothing saw, for her despair,
  But dreadful time, dreadful eternity,
      No comfort anywhere;

  Remaining utterly confused with fears,
270   And ever worse with growing time,
  And ever unrelieved by dismal tears,
      And all alone in crime:

  Shut up as in a crumbling tomb, girt round
      With blackness as a solid wall,
275   Far off she seemed to hear the dully° sound   *faint*
      Of human footsteps fall.

  As in strange lands a traveller walking slow,
      In doubt and great perplexity,
  A little before moon-rise hears the low
280   Moan of an unknown sea;

  And knows not if it be thunder, or a sound
      Of rocks thrown down, or one deep cry
  Of great wild beasts; then thinketh, "I have found
      A new land, but I die."

285   She howled aloud, "I am on fire within.
      There comes no murmur of reply.
  What is it that will take away my sin,
      And save me lest I die?"

  So when four years were wholly finished,
290   She threw her royal robes away.
  "Make me a cottage in the vale," she said,
      "Where I may mourn and pray.

---

[1] *"Mene, mene"* The first of the words, seen by the Babylonian king Belshazzar, that are mysteriously written on the wall by a disembodied hand in Daniel 5.25–26. Daniel's interpretation of the words for the frightened king concludes with the phrase "Thy kingdom is divided."

"Yet pull not down my palace towers, that are
　　So lightly, beautifully built:
295 Perchance I may return with others there
　　　When I have purged my guilt."
　—1832 (REVISED 1842)

The Lady of Shalott [1]

PART I

On either side the river lie
Long fields of barley and of rye,
That clothe the wold° and meet the sky;　　　　*plain*
And through the field the road runs by
5　　To many-towered Camelot;
And up and down the people go,
Gazing where the lilies blow
Round an island there below,
　　The island of Shalott.

10 Willows whiten,[2] aspens quiver,
Little breezes dusk° and shiver　　　　*darken*
Through the wave that runs for ever
By the island in the river
　　Flowing down to Camelot.
15 Four gray walls, and four gray towers,
Overlook a space of flowers,
And the silent isle imbowers°　　　　*encloses*
　　The Lady of Shalott.

By the margin, willow-veiled,
20 Slide the heavy barges trailed
By slow horses; and unhailed
The shallop[3] flitteth silken-sailed
　　Skimming down to Camelot:
But who hath seen her wave her hand?

Or at the casement seen her stand?
Or is she known in all the land,
　　The Lady of Shalott?

Only reapers, reaping early
In among the bearded barley,
30 Hear a song that echoes cheerly
From the river winding clearly,
　　Down to towered Camelot:
And by the moon the reaper weary,
Piling sheaves in uplands airy,
35 Listening, whispers "'Tis the fairy
　　Lady of Shalott."

PART 2

There she weaves by night and day
A magic web with colours gay.
She has heard a whisper say,
40 A curse is on her if she stay
　　To look down to Camelot.
She knows not what the curse may be,
And so she weaveth steadily,
And little other care hath she,
45　　The Lady of Shalott.

And moving through a mirror clear
That hangs before her all the year,
Shadows of the world appear.
There she sees the highway near
50　　Winding down to Camelot:
There the river eddy whirls,
And there the surly village-churls,
And the red cloaks of market girls,
　　Pass onward from Shalott.

55 Sometimes a troop of damsels glad,
An abbot on an ambling pad,°　　　　*horse*
Sometimes a curly shepherd-lad,
Or long-haired page in crimson clad,
　　Goes by to towered Camelot;
60 And sometimes through the mirror blue
The knights come riding two and two:
She hath no loyal knight and true,
　　The Lady of Shalott.

---

[1] *The Lady of Shalott* Elaine of the Arthurian romances, who dies of love for Lancelot; she is called "the lily maid of Astolat" in Malory's *Morte dArthur.* Tennyson first encountered the story, however, in a medieval Italian romance called "La Donna di Scalotta" and changed the name to Shalott for a softer sound.

[2] *Willows whiten* I.e., the wind exposes the white undersides of the leaves.

[3] *shallop* Light open boat for use in shallow water.

But in her web she still delights
65　To weave the mirror's magic sights,
For often through the silent nights
A funeral, with plumes and lights
　　And music, went to Camelot:
Or when the moon was overhead,
70　Came two young lovers lately wed;
"I am half sick of shadows," said
　　The Lady of Shalott.

PART 3

A bow-shot from her bower-eaves,
He rode between the barley-sheaves,
75　The sun came dazzling through the leaves,
And flamed upon the brazen greaves[1]
　　Of bold Sir Lancelot.
A red-cross knight for ever kneeled
　　To a lady in his shield,
80　That sparkled on the yellow field,
　　Beside remote Shalott.

The gemmy° bridle glittered free,　　　　　*brilliant*
Like to some branch of stars we see
Hung in the golden Galaxy.
85　The bridle bells rang merrily
　　As he rode down to Camelot:
And from his blazoned baldric° slung　　*shoulder-strap*
A mighty silver bugle hung,
And as he rode his armour rung,
90　　Beside remote Shalott.

All in the blue unclouded weather
Thick-jewelled shone the saddle-leather,
The helmet and the helmet-feather
Burned like one burning flame together,
95　　As he rode down to Camelot.
As often through the purple night,
Below the starry clusters bright,
Some bearded meteor, trailing light,
　　Moves over still Shalott.

100　His broad clear brow in sunlight glowed;
On burnished hooves his war-horse trode;
From underneath his helmet flowed
His coal-black curls as on he rode,
　　As he rode down to Camelot.
105　From the bank and from the river
He flashed into the crystal mirror,
"Tirra lirra," by the river
　　Sang Sir Lancelot.

She left the web, she left the loom,
110　She made three paces through the room,
She saw the water-lily bloom,
She saw the helmet and the plume,
　　She looked down to Camelot.
Out flew the web and floated wide;
115　The mirror cracked from side to side;
"The curse is come upon me," cried
　　The Lady of Shalott.

PART 4

In the stormy east-wind straining,
The pale yellow woods were waning,
120　The broad stream in his banks complaining,
Heavily the low sky raining
　　Over towered Camelot;
Down she came and found a boat
Beneath a willow left afloat,
125　And round about the prow she wrote
　　The Lady of Shalott.

And down the river's dim expanse
Like some bold seer in a trance,
Seeing all his own mischance—
130　With a glassy countenance
　　Did she look to Camelot.
And at the closing of the day
She loosed the chain, and down she lay;
The broad stream bore her far away,
135　　The Lady of Shalott.

---

[1] *greaves* Armor worn below the knee.

Lying, robed in snowy white
That loosely flew to left and right—
The leaves upon her falling light—
Through the noises of the night
140   She floated down to Camelot:
And as the boat-head wound along
The willowy hills and fields among,
They heard her singing her last song,
    The Lady of Shalott.

145 Heard a carol, mournful, holy,
Chanted loudly, chanted lowly,
Till her blood was frozen slowly,
And her eyes were darkened wholly,
    Turned to towered Camelot.
150 For ere she reached upon the tide
The first house by the water-side,
Singing in her song she died,
    The Lady of Shalott.

Under tower and balcony,
155 By garden-wall and gallery,
A gleaming shape she floated by,
Dead-pale between the houses high,
    Silent into Camelot.
Out upon the wharfs they came,
160 Knight and burgher, lord and dame,
And round the prow they read her name,
    The Lady of Shalott.

Who is this? and what is here?
And in the lighted palace near
165 Died the sound of royal cheer;
And they crossed themselves for fear,
    All the knights at Camelot:
But Lancelot mused a little space;
He said, "She has a lovely face;
170 God in his mercy lend her grace,
    The Lady of Shalott."
    —1832 (REVISED 1842)

The Lotos-Eaters[1]

"Courage!" he said, and pointed toward the land,
    "This mounting wave will roll us shoreward
        soon."
In the afternoon they came unto a land
In which it seemed always afternoon.
5 All round the coast the languid air did swoon,
Breathing like one that hath a weary dream.
Full-faced above the valley stood the moon;
And like a downward smoke, the slender stream
Along the cliff to fall and pause and fall did seem.

10 A land of streams! some, like a downward smoke,
Slow-dropping veils of thinnest lawn,[2] did go;
And some through wavering lights and shadows broke,
Rolling a slumbrous sheet of foam below.
They saw the gleaming river seaward flow
15 From the inner land: far off, three mountain-tops,
Three silent pinnacles of agèd snow,
Stood sunset-flushed: and, dewed with showery drops,
Up-clomb the shadowy pine above the woven
        copse.°   *thicket*

The charmèd sunset lingered low adown
20 In the red West: through mountain clefts the dale
Was seen far inland, and the yellow down
Bordered with palm, and many a winding vale
And meadow, set with slender galingale;[3]
A land where all things always seemed the same!
25 And round about the keel with faces pale,
Dark faces pale against that rosy flame,
The mild-eyed melancholy Lotos-eaters came.

Branches they bore of that enchanted stem,
Laden with flower and fruit, whereof they gave
30 To each, but whoso did receive of them,

---

[1] *Lotos-Eaters* In Greek mythology, the Lotus Eaters (or Loto-phagi) were a race of people who inhabited an island near north Africa. They existed in peaceful apathy because of the narcotic effects of the lotus plants they ate. When Odysseus landed on the island, some of his men ate the lotus plants and wanted to stay on the island, rather than return home to their families. The incident is documented in Homer's *Odyssey* 9.2.

[2] *lawn* Fine fabric.

[3] *galingale* Species of sedge.

And taste, to him the gushing of the wave
Far far away did seem to mourn and rave
On alien shores; and if his fellow spake,
His voice was thin, as voices from the grave;
35 And deep-asleep he seemed, yet all awake,
And music in his ears his beating heart did make.

They sat them down upon the yellow sand,
Between the sun and moon upon the shore;
And sweet it was to dream of Fatherland,
40 Of child, and wife, and slave; but evermore
Most weary seemed the sea, weary the oar,
Weary the wandering fields of barren foam.
Then some one said, "We will return no more";
And all at once they sang, "Our island home
45 Is far beyond the wave; we will no longer roam."

CHORIC SONG[1]

1

There is sweet music here that softer falls
Than petals from blown roses on the grass,
Or night-dews on still waters between walls
Of shadowy granite, in a gleaming pass;
50 Music that gentlier on the spirit lies,
Than tired eyelids upon tired eyes;
Music that brings sweet sleep down from the blissful
      skies.
Here are cool mosses deep,
And through the moss the ivies creep,
55 And in the stream the long-leaved flowers weep,
And from the craggy ledge the poppy hangs in sleep.

2

Why are we weighed upon with heaviness,
And utterly consumed with sharp distress,
While all things else have rest from weariness?
60 All things have rest: why should we toil alone,
We only toil, who are the first of things,
And make perpetual moan,
Still from one sorrow to another thrown:
Nor ever fold our wings,
65 And cease from wanderings,
Nor steep our brows in slumber's holy balm;
Nor harken what the inner spirit sings,

"There is no joy but calm!"
Why should we only toil, the roof and crown of things?

3

70 Lo! in the middle of the wood,
The folded leaf is wooed from out the bud
With winds upon the branch, and there
Grows green and broad, and takes no care,
Sun-steeped at noon, and in the moon
75 Nightly dew-fed; and turning yellow
Falls, and floats adown the air.
Lo! sweetened with the summer light,
The full-juiced apple, waxing over-mellow,
Drops in a silent autumn night.
80 All its allotted length of days,
The flower ripens in its place,
Ripens and fades, and falls, and hath no toil,
Fast-rooted in the fruitful soil.

4

Hateful is the dark-blue sky,
85 Vaulted o'er the dark-blue sea.
Death is the end of life; ah, why
Should life all labour be?
Let us alone. Time driveth onward fast,
And in a little while our lips are dumb.
90 Let us alone. What is it that will last?
All things are taken from us, and become
Portions and parcels of the dreadful Past.
Let us alone. What pleasure can we have
To war with evil? Is there any peace
95 In ever climbing up the climbing wave?
All things have rest, and ripen toward the grave
In silence; ripen, fall and cease:
Give us long rest or death, dark death, or dreamful ease.

5

100 How sweet it were, hearing the downward stream,
With half-shut eyes ever to seem
Falling asleep in a half-dream!
To dream and dream, like yonder amber light,
Which will not leave the myrrh-bush on the height;
105 To hear each other's whispered speech;
Eating the Lotos day by day,
To watch the crisping ripples on the beach,

---

[1] *Choric Song*   As performed by the Chorus in an ancient Greek play.

And tender curving lines of creamy spray;
To lend our hearts and spirits wholly
110   To the influence of mild-minded melancholy;
To muse and brood and live again in memory,
With those old faces of our infancy
Heaped over with a mound of grass,
Two handfuls of white dust,[1] shut in an urn of brass!

6

Dear is the memory of our wedded lives,
115   And dear the last embraces of our wives
And their warm tears: but all hath suffered change:
For surely now our household hearths are cold:
Our sons inherit us: our looks are strange:
And we should come like ghosts to trouble joy.
120   Or else the island princes over-bold
Have eat our substance, and the minstrel sings
Before them of the ten years' war in Troy,
And our great deeds, as half-forgotten things.
Is there confusion in the little isle?
125   Let what is broken so remain.
The Gods are hard to reconcile:
'Tis hard to settle order once again.
There is confusion worse than death,
Trouble on trouble, pain on pain,
130   Long labour unto agèd breath,
Sore task to hearts worn out by many wars
And eyes grown dim with gazing on the pilot-stars.

7

But, propped on beds of amaranth[2] and moly,[3]
How sweet (while warm airs lull us, blowing lowly)
135   With half-dropped eyelid still,
Beneath a heaven dark and holy,
To watch the long bright river drawing slowly
His waters from the purple hill—
To hear the dewy echoes calling
140   From cave to cave through the thick-twinèd vine—
To watch the emerald-coloured water falling
Through many a woven acanthus[4]-wreath divine!

---

[1] white dust   I.e., cremated remains.

[2] amaranth   Mythical flowers that never wilted.

[3] moly   Herb with magical protective powers.

[4] acanthus   Plant native to Mediterranean shores. The Greeks and
Romans esteemed the plant for the elegance of its leaves.

Only to hear and see the far-off sparkling brine,
Only to hear were sweet, stretched out beneath the pine.

8

145   The Lotos blooms below the barren peak:
The Lotos blows by every winding creek:
All day the wind breathes low with mellower tone:
Through every hollow cave and alley lone
Round and round the spicy downs the yellow
        Lotos-dust is blown.
150   We have had enough of action, and of motion we,
Rolled to starboard, rolled to larboard,° when the
        surge was seething free,   port
Where the wallowing monster spouted his foam-
        fountains in the sea.
Let us swear an oath, and keep it with an equal mind,
In the hollow Lotos-land to live and lie reclined
155   On the hills like Gods together, careless of mankind.
For they lie beside their nectar, and the bolts are
        hurled
Far below them in the valleys, and the clouds are
        lightly curled
Round their golden houses, girdled with the gleaming
        world:
Where they smile in secret, looking over wasted lands,
160   Blight and famine, plague and earthquake, roaring
        deeps and fiery sands,
Clanging fights, and flaming towns, and sinking
        ships, and praying hands.
But they smile, they find a music centred in a doleful
        song
Steaming up, a lamentation and an ancient tale of
        wrong,
Like a tale of little meaning though the words are strong;
165   Chanted from an ill-used race of men that cleave the
        soil,
Sow the seed, and reap the harvest with enduring toil,
Storing yearly little dues of wheat, and wine and oil;
Till they perish and they suffer—some, 'tis whispered
        —down in hell
Suffer endless anguish, others in Elysian[5] valleys
        dwell,

---

[5] Elysian   Heavenly. According to the ancient Greeks, Elysium was
the dwelling place of the blessed after death.

170 Resting weary limbs at last on beds of asphodel.[1]
Surely, surely, slumber is more sweet than toil, the shore
Than labour in the deep mid-ocean, wind and wave
    and oar;
Oh rest ye, brother mariners, we will not wander more.
—1832 (REVISED 1842)

Ulysses[2]

It little profits that an idle king,
By this still hearth, among these barren crags,
Matched with an agèd wife, I mete and dole
Unequal laws unto a savage race,
5 That hoard, and sleep, and feed, and know not me.

I cannot rest from travel: I will drink
Life to the lees:° all times I have enjoyed   *dregs*
Greatly, have suffered greatly, both with those
That loved me, and alone; on shore, and when
10 Thro' scudding drifts the rainy Hyades[3]
Vexed the dim sea: I am become a name;
For always roaming with a hungry heart
Much have I seen and known; cities of men
And manners, climates, councils, governments,
15 Myself not least, but honoured of them all;
And drunk delight of battle with my peers,
Far on the ringing plains of windy Troy.
I am a part of all that I have met;
Yet all experience is an arch wherethrough
20 Gleams that untravelled world, whose margin°   *horizon*
    fades
For ever and for ever when I move.
How dull it is to pause, to make an end,
To rust unburnished, not to shine in use!
As though to breathe were life. Life piled on life
25 Were all too little, and of one to me
Little remains: but every hour is saved
From that eternal silence, something more,

A bringer of new things; and vile it were
For some three suns to store and hoard myself,
30 And this gray spirit yearning in desire
To follow knowledge like a sinking star,
Beyond the utmost bound of human thought.

This is my son, mine own Telemachus,
To whom I leave the sceptre and the isle—
35 Well-loved of me, discerning to fulfil
This labour, by slow prudence to make mild
A rugged people, and through soft degrees
Subdue them to the useful and the good.
Most blameless is he, centred in the sphere
40 Of common duties, decent not to fail
In offices of tenderness, and pay
Meet adoration to my household gods,
When I am gone. He works his work, I mine.

There lies the port; the vessel puffs her sail:
45 There gloom the dark broad seas. My mariners,
Souls that have toiled, and wrought, and thought
    with me—
That ever with a frolic welcome took
The thunder and the sunshine, and opposed
Free hearts, free foreheads—you and I are old;
50 Old age hath yet his honour and his toil;
Death closes all: but something ere the end,
Some work of noble note, may yet be done,
Not unbecoming men that strove with Gods.

The lights begin to twinkle from the rocks:
55 The long day wanes: the slow moon climbs: the deep
Moans round with many voices. Come, my friends,
'Tis not too late to seek a newer world.
Push off, and sitting well in order smite
The sounding furrows; for my purpose holds
60 To sail beyond the sunset, and the baths
Of all the western stars, until I die.
It may be that the gulfs will wash us down:
It may be we shall touch the Happy Isles,[4]
And see the great Achilles,[5] whom we knew.

---

[1] *asphodel*   Plant said to cover the Elysian fields.

[2] *Ulysses*   Latin name for Odysseus, the protagonist of Homer's *Odyssey*. Here, long after the adventures recounted in that book, the aged, yet restless, Ulysses prepares to embark on one last voyage of discovery.

[3] *Hyades*   Group of stars near the constellation Taurus and associated with rainstorms.

[4] *Happy Isles*   Elysium, or Isles of the Blessed, where heroes enjoyed the afterlife.

[5] *Achilles*   Hero from Greek mythology, also the central character of Homer's *Iliad*.

65 Though much is taken, much abides; and though
We are not now that strength which in old days
Moved earth and heaven; that which we are, we are;
One equal temper of heroic hearts,
Made weak by time and fate, but strong in will
70 To strive, to seek, to find, and not to yield.
—1842 (WRITTEN 1833)

The Epic [Morte d'Arthur]

At Francis Allen's on the Christmas-eve,—
The game of forfeits done—the girls all kissed
Beneath the sacred bush[1] and past away—
The parson Holmes, the poet Everard Hall,
5 The host, and I sat round the wassail-bowl,[2]
Then half-way ebbed: and there we held a talk,
How all the old honour had from Christmas gone,
Or gone, or dwindled down to some odd games
In some odd nooks like this; till I, tired out
10 With cutting eights[3] that day upon the pond,
Where, three times slipping from the outer edge,
I bumped the ice into three several stars,
Fell in a doze; and half-awake I heard
The parson taking wide and wider sweeps,
15 Now harping on the church-commissioners,
Now hawking at Geology and schism;
Until I woke, and found him settled down
Upon the general decay of faith
Right through the world, "at home was little left,
20 And none abroad: there was no anchor, none,
To hold by." Francis, laughing, clapped his hand
On Everard's shoulder, with "I hold by him."
"And I," quoth Everard, "by the wassail-bowl."
"Why yes," I said, "we knew your gift that way
25 At college: but another which you had,
I mean of verse (for so we held it then),
What came of that?" "You know," said Frank, "he
    burnt
His epic, his King Arthur, some twelve books"—
And then to me demanding why? "Oh, sir,
30 He thought that nothing new was said, or else

Something so said 'twas nothing—that a truth
Looks freshest in the fashion of the day:
God knows: he has a mint of reasons: ask.
It pleased me well enough." "Nay, nay," said Hall,
35 "Why take the style of those heroic times?
For nature brings not back the Mastodon,
Nor we those times; and why should any man
Remodel models? these twelve books of mine
Were faint Homeric echoes, nothing-worth,
40 Mere chaff and draff,[4] much better burnt." "But I,"
Said Francis, "picked the eleventh from this hearth
And have it: keep a thing, its use will come.
I hoard it as a sugar-plum for Holmes."
He laughed, and I, though sleepy, like a horse
45 That hears the corn-bin open, pricked my ears;
For I remembered Everard's college fame
When we were freshmen: then at my request
He brought it; and the poet little urged,
But with some prelude of disparagement,
50 Read, mouthing out his hollow oes and aes,
Deep-chested music, and to this result.

Morte d'Arthur[5]

So all day long the noise of battle rolled
Among the mountains by the winter sea;
Until King Arthur's table, man by man,
Had fallen in Lyonnesse[6] about their Lord,
5 King Arthur: then, because his wound was deep,
The bold Sir Bedivere uplifted him,
Sir Bedivere, the last of all his knights,
And bore him to a chapel nigh the field,
A broken chancel[7] with a broken cross,
10 That stood on a dark strait of barren land.
On one side lay the ocean, and on one
Lay a great water, and the moon was full.

Then spake King Arthur to Sir Bedivere:
"The sequel of today unsolders all

---

1 sacred bush   Mistletoe.

2 wassail-bowl   Punch bowl containing spiced ale.

3 cutting eights   Skating figure-eights.

4 chaff and draff   Here, refuse, material of little worth.

5 Morte d'Arthur   French: the death of [King] Arthur.

6 [Tennyson's note]   The country of legend that lay between
Cornwall and the Scilly Islands.

7 chancel   Area around the altar.

15 The goodliest fellowship of famous knights
Whereof this world holds record. Such a sleep
They sleep—the men I loved. I think that we
Shall never more, at any future time,
Delight our souls with talk of knightly deeds,
20 Walking about the gardens and the halls
Of Camelot, as in the days that were.
I perish by this people which I made,—
Though Merlin sware that I should come again
To rule once more—but let what will be, be,
25 I am so deeply smitten through the helm
That without help I cannot last till morn.
Thou therefore take my brand° Excalibur,   *sword*
Which was my pride: for thou rememberest how
In those old days, one summer noon, an arm
30 Rose up from out the bosom of the lake,
Clothed in white samite,° mystic, wonderful,   *silk*
Holding the sword—and how I rowed across
And took it, and have worn it, like a king:
And, wheresoever I am sung or told
35 In aftertime, this also shall be known:
But now delay not: take Excalibur,
And fling him far into the middle mere:[1]
Watch what thou seest, and lightly bring me word."

      To him replied the bold Sir Bedivere:
40 "It is not meet,° Sir King, to leave thee thus,   *appropriate*
Aidless, alone, and smitten through the helm.
A little thing may harm a wounded man.
Yet I thy hest° will all perform at full,   *command*
Watch what I see, and lightly bring thee word."

45   So saying, from the ruined shrine he stepped
And in the moon athwart the place of tombs,
Where lay the mighty bones of ancient men,
Old knights, and over them the sea-wind sang
Shrill, chill, with flakes of foam. He, stepping down
50 By zig-zag paths, and juts of pointed rock,
Came on the shining levels of the lake.

      There drew he forth the brand Excalibur,
And o'er him, drawing it, the winter moon,
Brightening the skirts of a long cloud, ran forth
55 And sparkled keen with frost against the hilt:

For all the haft° twinkled with diamond sparks,   *handle*
Myriads of topaz-lights, and jacinth[2]-work
Of subtlest jewellery. He gazed so long
That both his eyes were dazzled, as he stood,
60 This way and that dividing the swift mind,
In act to throw: but at the last it seemed
Better to leave Excalibur concealed
There in the many-knotted waterflags,°   *iris*
That whistled stiff and dry about the marge.°   *shore*
65 So strode he back slow to the wounded King.

      Then spake King Arthur to Sir Bedivere:
"Hast thou performed my mission which I gave?
What is it thou hast seen? or what hast heard?"

      And answer made the bold Sir Bedivere:
70 "I heard the ripple washing in the reeds,
And the wild water lapping on the crag."

      To whom replied King Arthur, faint and pale:
"Thou hast betrayed thy nature and thy name,
Not rendering true answer, as beseemed
75 Thy fealty,° nor like a noble knight: *sworn allegiance*
For surer sign had followed, either hand,
Or voice, or else a motion of the mere.
This is a shameful thing for men to lie.
Yet now, I charge thee, quickly go again
80 As thou art lief° and dear, and do the thing   *beloved*
I bad[3] thee, watch, and lightly bring me word."

      Then went Sir Bedivere the second time
Across the ridge, and paced beside the mere,
Counting the dewy pebbles, fix'd in thought;
85 But when he saw the wonder of the hilt,
How curiously and strangely chased,° he smote   *engraved*
His palms together, and he cried aloud,

      "And if indeed I cast the brand away,
Surely a precious thing, one worthy note,
90 Should thus be lost for ever from the earth,
Which might have pleased the eyes of many men.
What good should follow this, if this were done?
What harm, undone? deep harm to disobey,

---

[1] *middle mere* Middle of the lake.

[2] *jacinth* Reddish-orange gem.

[3] *bad* I.e., bade, commanded.

Seeing obedience is the bond of rule.
95 Were it well to obey then, if a king demand
An act unprofitable, against himself?
The King is sick, and knows not what he does.
What record, or what relic of my lord
Should be to aftertime, but empty breath
100 And rumours of a doubt? but were this kept,
Stored in some treasure-house of mighty kings,
Some one might show it at a joust of arms,
Saying, "King Arthur's sword, Excalibur,
Wrought by the lonely maiden of the Lake.
105 Nine years she wrought it, sitting in the deeps
Upon the hidden bases of the hills."
So might some old man speak in the aftertime
To all the people, winning reverence.
But now much honour and much fame were lost."

110   So spake he, clouded with his own conceit,
And hid Excalibur the second time,
And so strode back slow to the wounded King.

Then spoke King Arthur, breathing heavily:
"What is it thou hast seen? or what hast heard?"
115   And answer made the bold Sir Bedivere:
"I heard the water lapping on the crag,
And the long ripple washing in the reeds."

To whom replied King Arthur, much in wrath:
"Ah, miserable and unkind, untrue,
120 Unknightly, traitor-hearted! Woe is me!
Authority forgets a dying king,
Laid widowed of the power in his eye
That bowed the will. I see thee what thou art,
For thou, the latest-left of all my knights,
125 In whom should meet the offices of all,
Thou wouldst betray me for the precious hilt;
Either from lust of gold, or like a girl
Valuing the giddy pleasure of the eyes.
Yet, for a man may fail in duty twice,
130 And the third time may prosper, get thee hence:
But, if thou spare to fling Excalibur,
I will arise and slay thee with my hands."

Then quickly rose Sir Bedivere, and ran,
And, leaping down the ridges lightly, plunged
135 Among the bulrush-beds, and clutched the sword,
And strongly wheeled and threw it. The great brand
Made lightnings in the splendour of the moon,
And flashing round and round, and whirled in an arch,
Shot like a streamer of the northern morn,
140 Seen where the moving isles of winter shock
By night, with noises of the northern sea.
So flashed and fell the brand Excalibur:
But ere he dipped the surface, rose an arm
Clothed in white samite, mystic, wonderful,
145 And caught him by the hilt, and brandished him
Three times, and drew him under in the mere.
And lightly went the other to the King.

Then spoke King Arthur, drawing thicker breath:
"Now see I by thine eyes that this is done.
150 Speak out: what is it thou hast heard, or seen?"

And answer made the bold Sir Bedivere:
"Sir King, I closed mine eyelids, lest the gems
Should blind my purpose, for I never saw,
Nor shall see, here or elsewhere, till I die,
155 Not though I live three lives of mortal men,
So great a miracle as yonder hilt.
Then with both hands I flung him, wheeling him;
But when I looked again, behold an arm,
Clothed in white samite, mystic, wonderful,
160 That caught him by the hilt, and brandished him
Three times, and drew him under in the mere."

And answer made King Arthur, breathing hard:
"My end draws nigh; 'tis time that I were gone.
Make broad thy shoulders to receive my weight,
165 And bear me to the margin; yet I fear
My wound hath taken cold, and I shall die."

So saying, from the pavement he half rose,
Slowly, with pain, reclining on his arm,
And looking wistfully with wide blue eyes
170 As in a picture. Him Sir Bedivere
Remorsefully regarded through his tears,
And would have spoken, but he found not words,
Then took with care, and kneeling on one knee,
O'er both his shoulders drew the languid hands,
175 And rising bore him through the place of tombs.

But, as he walked, King Arthur panted hard,
Like one that feels a nightmare on his bed
When all the house is mute. So sighed the King,
Muttering and murmuring at his ear, "Quick, quick!
180 I fear it is too late, and I shall die."
But the other swiftly strode from ridge to ridge,
Clothed with his breath, and looking, as he walked,
Larger than human on the frozen hills.
He heard the deep behind him, and a cry
185 Before. His own thought drove him, like a goad.
Dry clashed his harness in the icy caves
And barren chasms, and all to left and right
The bare black cliff clanged round him, as he based
His feet on juts of slippery crag that rang
190 Sharp-smitten with the dint of armèd heels—
And on a sudden, lo! the level lake,
And the long glories of the winter moon.

    Then saw they how there hove a dusky barge,
Dark as a funeral scarf from stem to stern,
195 Beneath them; and descending they were ware°   *aware*
That all the decks were dense with stately forms
Black-stoled, black-hooded, like a dream—by these
Three Queens with crowns of gold—and from them
    rose
A cry that shivered to the tingling stars,
200 And, as it were one voice, an agony
Of lamentation, like a wind, that shrills
All night in a waste land, where no one comes,
Or hath come, since the making of the world.

    Then murmured Arthur, "Place me in the barge,"
205 And to the barge they came. There those three Queens
Put forth their hands, and took the King, and wept.
But she, that rose the tallest of them all
And fairest, laid his head upon her lap,
And loosed the shattered casque,° and chafed   *helmet*
    his hands,
210 And called him by his name, complaining loud,
And dropping bitter tears against his brow
Striped with dark blood: for all his face was white
And colourless, and like the withered moon
Smote by the fresh beam of the springing east;
215 And all his greaves and cuisses[1] dashed with drops
Of onset; and the light and lustrous curls—

That made his forehead like a rising sun
High from the dais-throne—were parched with dust;
Or, clotted into points and hanging loose,
220 Mix'd with the knightly growth that fringed his lips.
So like a shattered column lay the King;
Not like that Arthur who, with lance in rest,
From spur to plume a star of tournament,
Shot through the lists[2] at Camelot, and charged
225 Before the eyes of ladies and of kings.

    Then loudly cried the bold Sir Bedivere,
"Ah! my Lord Arthur, whither shall I go?
Where shall I hide my forehead and my eyes?
For now I see the true old times are dead,
230 When every morning brought a noble chance,
And every chance brought out a noble knight.
Such times have been not since the light that led
The holy Elders with the gift of myrrh.
But now the whole Round Table is dissolved
235 Which was an image of the mighty world;
And I, the last, go forth companionless,
And the days darken round me, and the years,
Among new men, strange faces, other minds."

    And slowly answered Arthur from the barge:
240 "The old order changeth, yielding place to new,
And God fulfils Himself in many ways,
Lest one good custom should corrupt the world.
Comfort thyself: what comfort is in me?
I have lived my life, and that which I have done
245 May He within Himself make pure! but thou,
If thou shouldst never see my face again,
Pray for my soul. More things are wrought by prayer
Than this world dreams of. Wherefore, let thy voice
Rise like a fountain for me night and day.
250 For what are men better than sheep or goats
That nourish a blind life within the brain,
If, knowing God, they lift not hands of prayer
Both for themselves and those who call them friend?
For so the whole round earth is every way
255 Bound by gold chains about the feet of God.
But now farewell. I am going a long way
With these thou seest—if indeed I go—
(For all my mind is clouded with a doubt)

---

[1] *greaves and cuisses* Armor for shins and thighs.

[2] *lists* Arenas in which jousting and tilting tournaments were held.

To the island-valley of Avilion;°   *i.e., Avalon*
260 Where falls not hail, or rain, or any snow,
Nor ever wind blows loudly; but it lies
Deep-meadowed, happy, fair with orchard-lawns
And bowery hollows crown'd with summer sea,
Where I will heal me of my grievous wound."

265   So said he, and the barge with oar and sail
Moved from the brink, like some full-breasted swan
That, fluting a wild carol ere her death,[1]
Ruffles her pure cold plume, and takes the flood
With swarthy webs.[2] Long stood Sir Bedivere
270 Revolving many memories, till the hull
Looked one black dot against the verge of dawn,
And on the mere the wailing died away.
—1842 (WRITTEN 1833–34)

[*Break, break, break*]

Break, break, break,
    On thy cold gray stones, O Sea!
And I would that my tongue could utter
    The thoughts that arise in me.

5   O well for the fisherman's boy,
    That he shouts with his sister at play!
O well for the sailor lad,
    That he sings in his boat on the bay!

And the stately ships go on
10   To their haven under the hill;
But O for the touch of a vanished hand,
    And the sound of a voice that is still![3]

Break, break, break,
    At the foot of thy crags, O Sea!
15 But the tender grace of a day that is dead
    Will never come back to me.
—1842 (WRITTEN 1834?)

---

[1] *swan … death* Swans were said to sing only once, at their deaths.

[2] *webs* I.e., webbed feet.

[3] *But … still* Probably a reference to Tennyson's closest friend, Arthur Hallam, who had died in 1833.

Locksley Hall

Comrades, leave me here a little, while as yet 'tis early morn:
Leave me here, and when you want me, sound upon the bugle-horn.

'Tis the place, and all around it, as of old, the curlews[4] call,
Dreary gleams about the moorland flying over Locksley Hall;

5 Locksley Hall, that in the distance overlooks the sandy tracts,
And the hollow ocean-ridges roaring into cataracts.

Many a night from yonder ivied casement, ere I went to rest,
Did I look on great Orion[5] sloping slowly to the West.

Many a night I saw the Pleiads,[6] rising through the mellow shade,
10 Glitter like a swarm of fire-flies tangled in a silver braid.

Here about the beach I wandered, nourishing a youth sublime
With the fairy tales of science, and the long result of Time;

When the centuries behind me like a fruitful land reposed;
When I clung to all the present for the promise that it closed:

15 When I dipped into the future far as human eye could see;

---

[4] *curlews* Species of shore-dwelling birds.

[5] *Orion* The constellation named after the hunter of Greek legend. It sets in November and so was associated with rains and storms.

[6] *Pleiads* The constellation commonly known as the Pleiades (named after the seven daughters of Atlas), which rises in May and sets in November.

Saw the Vision of the world, and all the wonder that
    would be.—

In the Spring a fuller crimson comes upon the robin's
    breast;
In the Spring the wanton lapwing gets himself
    another crest;

In the Spring a livelier iris changes on the burnished
    dove;
20 In the Spring a young man's fancy lightly turns to
    thoughts of love.

Then her cheek was pale and thinner than should be
    for one so young,
And her eyes on all my motions with a mute
    observance hung.

And I said, "My cousin Amy, speak, and speak the
    truth to me,
Trust me, cousin, all the current of my being sets to
    thee."

25 On her pallid cheek and forehead came a colour and a
    light,
As I have seen the rosy red flushing in the northern
    night.

And she turned—her bosom shaken with a sudden
    storm of sighs—
All the spirit deeply dawning in the dark of hazel eyes—

Saying, "I have hid my feelings, fearing they should
    do me wrong;"
30 Saying, "Dost thou love me, cousin?" weeping, "I
    have loved thee long."

Love took up the glass of Time,[1] and turned it in
    his glowing hands;
Every moment, lightly shaken, ran itself in golden
    sands.

Love took up the harp of Life, and smote on all the
    chords with might;

Smote the chord of Self, that, trembling, passed in
    music out of sight.

35 Many a morning on the moorland did we hear the
    copses ring,
And her whisper thronged my pulses with the fullness
    of the Spring.

Many an evening by the waters did we watch the
    stately ships,
And our spirits rushed together at the touching of
    the lips.

O my cousin, shallow-hearted! O my Amy, mine no
    more!
40 O the dreary, dreary moorland! O the barren, barren
    shore!

Falser than all fancy fathoms,° falser than all   *apprehends*
    songs have sung,
Puppet to a father's threat, and servile to a shrewish
    tongue!

Is it well to wish thee happy?—having known me—to
    decline
On a range of lower feelings and a narrower heart
    than mine!

45 Yet it shall be: thou shalt lower to his level day by day,
What is fine within thee growing coarse to sympathise
    with clay.

As the husband is, the wife is: thou art mated with a
    clown,[2]
And the grossness of his nature will have weight to
    drag thee down.

He will hold thee, when his passion shall have spent
    its novel force,
50 Something better than his dog, a little dearer than his
    horse.

What is this? his eyes are heavy: think not they are
    glazed with wine.

---

[1] *glass of Time* Hourglass.

[2] *Clown* Rustic, boorish fellow.

Go to him: it is thy duty: kiss him: take his hand in
    thine.

It may be my lord is weary, that his brain is
    overwrought:
Soothe him with thy finer fancies,° touch him with
    thy lighter thought.   *interests*

55 He will answer to the purpose, easy things to
    understand—
Better thou wert dead before me, though I slew thee
    with my hand!

Better thou and I were lying, hidden from the heart's
    disgrace,
Rolled in one another's arms, and silent in a last
    embrace.

Cursèd be the social wants that sin against the
    strength of youth!
60 Cursèd be the social lies that warp us from the
    living truth!

Cursèd be the sickly forms that err from honest
    Nature's rule!
Cursèd be the gold that gilds the straitened forehead
    of the fool![1]

Well—'tis well that I should bluster!—Hadst thou
    less unworthy proved—
Would to God—for I had loved thee more than ever
    wife was loved.

65 Am I mad, that I should cherish that which bears but
    bitter fruit?
I will pluck it from my bosom, though my heart be at
    the root.

Never, though my mortal summers to such length
    of years should come
As the many-wintered crow that leads the clanging
    rookery home.

Where is comfort? in division of the records of the
    mind?
70 Can I part her from herself, and love her, as I knew
    her, kind?

I remember one that perished: sweetly did she speak
    and move:
Such a one do I remember, whom to look at was to
    love.

Can I think of her as dead, and love her for the love
    she bore?
No—she never loved me truly: love is love for
    evermore.

75 Comfort? comfort scorned of devils! this is truth the
    poet sings,
That a sorrow's crown of sorrow is remembering
    happier things.[2]

Drug thy memories, lest thou learn it, lest thy heart be
    put to proof,
In the dead unhappy night, and when the rain is on
    the roof.

Like a dog, he hunts in dreams, and thou art staring at
    the wall,
80 Where the dying night-lamp flickers, and the
    shadows rise and fall.

Then a hand shall pass before thee, pointing to his
    drunken sleep,
To thy widowed[3] marriage-pillows, to the tears that
    thou wilt weep.

Thou shalt hear the "Never, never," whispered by the
    phantom years,
And a song from out the distance in the ringing of
    thine ears;

85 And an eye shall vex thee, looking ancient kindness on
    thy pain.

---

[1] *straitened ... fool* Narrow or low foreheads were thought to
indicate stupidity.

[2] *this ... things* Cf. Dante, *Inferno* v. 121–23: "No greater grief
than to remember joy, when misery is at hand."

[3] *widowed* In that she is no longer the poet's lover.

Turn thee, turn thee on thy pillow: get thee to thy
    rest again.

Nay, but Nature brings thee solace; for a tender
    voice will cry.
'Tis a purer life than thine; a lip to drain thy trouble dry.

Baby lips will laugh me down: my latest rival brings
    thee rest.
90 Baby fingers, waxen touches, press me from the
    mother's breast.

O, the child too clothes the father with a dearness not
    his due.
Half is thine and half is his: it will be worthy of the two.

O, I see thee old and formal, fitted to thy petty part,
With a little hoard of maxims preaching down a
    daughter's heart.

95 "They were dangerous guides the feelings—she[1]
    herself was not exempt—
Truly, she herself had suffered"—Perish in thy self-
    contempt!

Overlive it—lower yet—be happy! wherefore should I
    care?
I myself must mix with action, lest I wither by despair.

What is that which I should turn to, lighting upon
    days like these?
100 Every door is barred with gold, and opens but to
    golden keys.

Every gate is thronged with suitors, all the markets
    overflow.
I have but an angry fancy: what is that which I should
    do?

I had been content to perish, falling on the foeman's
    ground,
When the ranks are rolled in vapour, and the winds
    are laid with sound.

105 But the jingling of the guinea° helps the hurt   *coin*
    that Honour feels,
And the nations do but murmur, snarling at each
    other's heels.

Can I but relive in sadness? I will turn that earlier page.
Hide me from my deep emotion, O thou wondrous
    Mother-Age!

Make me feel the wild pulsation that I felt before the
    strife,
110 When I heard my days before me, and the tumult of
    my life;

Yearning for the large excitement that the coming
    years would yield,
Eager-hearted as a boy when first he leaves his father's
    field,

And at night along the dusky highway near and
    nearer drawn,
Sees in heaven the light of London flaring like a
    dreary dawn;

115 And his spirit leaps within him to be gone before him
    then,
Underneath the light he looks at, in among the
    throngs of men:

Men, my brothers, men the workers, ever reaping
    something new:
That which they have done but earnest of the things
    that they shall do:

For I dipped into the future, far as human eye could
    see,
120 Saw the Vision of the world, and all the wonder that
    would be;

Saw the heavens fill with commerce, argosies[2] of
    magic sails,
Pilots of the purple twilight, dropping down with
    costly bales;

---

[1] *she* The poet's cousin, pictured in the future speaking in the
third person of herself to her daughter.

[2] *argosies* Large merchant ships.

Heard the heavens fill with shouting, and there rained
    a ghastly dew
From the nations' airy navies grappling in the central
    blue;

125 Far along the world-wide whisper of the south-wind
    rushing warm,
With the standards of the peoples plunging through
    the thunder-storm;

Till the war-drum throbbed no longer, and the
    battle-flags were furled
In the Parliament of man, the Federation of the world.

There the common sense of most shall hold a fretful
    realm in awe,
130 And the kindly earth shall slumber, lapped in
    universal law.

So I triumphed ere my passion sweeping through me
    left me dry,
Left me with the palsied heart, and left me with the
    jaundiced eye;

Eye, to which all order festers, all things here are out
    of joint:
Science moves, but slowly slowly, creeping on from
    point to point:

135 Slowly comes a hungry people, as a lion creeping
    nigher,
Glares at one that nods and winks behind a slowly-
    dying fire.

Yet I doubt not through the ages one increasing
    purpose runs,
And the thoughts of men are widened with the
    process of the suns.

What is that to him that reaps not harvest of his
    youthful joys,
140 Though the deep heart of existence beat forever like a
    boy's?

Knowledge comes, but wisdom lingers, and I linger
    on the shore,
And the individual withers, and the world is more
    and more.

Knowledge comes, but wisdom lingers, and he bears a
    laden breast,
Full of sad experience, moving toward the stillness of
    his rest.

145 Hark, my merry comrades call me, sounding on the
    bugle-horn,
They to whom my foolish passion were a target for
    their scorn:

Shall it not be scorn to me to harp on such a
    mouldered string?
I am shamed through all my nature to have loved so
    slight a thing.

Weakness to be wroth° with weakness!   *angry*
    woman's pleasure, woman's pain—
150 Nature made them blinder motions bounded in a
    shallower brain:

Woman is the lesser man, and all thy passions,
    matched with mine,
Are as moonlight unto sunlight, and as water unto
    wine—

Here at least, where nature sickens, nothing. Ah, for
    some retreat
Deep in yonder shining Orient, where my life began
    to beat;

155 Where in wild Mahratta-battle[1] fell my father evil-
    starred;—[2]
I was left a trampled orphan, and a selfish uncle's
    ward.

Or to burst all links of habit—there to wander far away,
On from island unto island at the gateways of the day.

---

[1] *Mahratta-battle* Conflict between the British and the Mahratta
soldiers from Bombay in 1818.

[2] *evil-starred* Cursed with bad luck.

Larger constellations burning, mellow moons and
    happy skies,
160 Breadths of tropic shade and palms in cluster, knots of
    Paradise.

Never comes the trader, never floats an European flag,
Slides the bird o'er lustrous woodland, swings the
    trailer[1] from the crag;

Droops the heavy-blossomed bower, hangs the heavy-
    fruited tree—
Summer isles of Eden lying in dark-purple spheres
    of sea.

165 There methinks would be enjoyment more than in
    this march of mind,
In the steamship, in the railway, in the thoughts
    that shake mankind.

There the passions cramped no longer shall have
    scope and breathing space;
I will take some savage woman, she shall rear my
    dusky race.

Iron jointed, supple-sinewed, they shall dive, and they
    shall run,
170 Catch the wild goat by the hair, and hurl their lances
    in the sun;

Whistle back the parrot's call, and leap the rainbows
    of the brooks,
Not with blinded eyesight poring over miserable
    books—

Fool, again the dream, the fancy! but I *know* my
    words are wild,
But I count the gray barbarian lower than the
    Christian child.

175 I, to herd with narrow foreheads, vacant of our
    glorious gains,
Like a beast with lower pleasures, like a beast with
    lower pains!

Mated with a squalid savage—what to me were sun or
    clime?
I the heir of all the ages, in the foremost files[2] of
    time—

I that rather held it better men should perish one
    by one,
180 Than that earth should stand at gaze like Joshua's
    moon in Ajalon![3]

Not in vain the distance beacons. Forward,
    forward let us range,
Let the great world spin forever down the ringing
    grooves of change.

Through the shadow of the globe we sweep into
    the younger day:
Better fifty years of Europe than a cycle of
    Cathay.°   *China*

185 Mother-Age (for mine I knew not) help me as
    when life begun:
Rift° the hills, and roll the waters, flash the   *split open*
    lightnings, weigh the Sun.
O, I see the crescent promise of my spirit hath not set.
Ancient founts of inspiration well through all my
    fancy yet.

Howsoever these things be, a long farewell to Locksley
    Hall!
190 Now for me the woods may wither, now for me the
    roof-tree fall.

Comes a vapour from the margin, blackening over
    heath and holt,°   *wood*
Cramming all the blast before it, in its breast a
    thunderbolt.

Let it fall on Locksley Hall, with rain or hail, or fire or
    snow;
For the mighty wind arises, roaring seaward, and I go.
—1842

---

[1] *trailer* Vine or hanging branch.

[2] *files* The ages of time pictured as men marching in file.

[3] *Joshua's ... Ajalon* In Joshua 10.12–13, Joshua makes the moon
and sun stand still during a battle in the valley of Ajalon.

from *The Princess*

[*Sweet and Low*]

Sweet and low, sweet and low,
    Wind of the western sea,
Low, low, breathe and blow,
    Wind of the western sea!
5 Over the rolling waters go,
Come from the dying moon, and blow,
    Blow him again to me;
While my little one, while my pretty one, sleeps.

Sleep and rest, sleep and rest,
10   Father will come to thee soon;
Rest, rest, on mother's breast,
    Father will come to thee soon;
Father will come to his babe in the nest,
Silver sails all out of the west
15   Under the silver moon:
Sleep, my little one, sleep, my pretty one, sleep.

[*The Splendour Falls*]

The splendour falls on castle walls
    And snowy summits old in story:
The long light shakes across the lakes,
    And the wild cataract° leaps in glory.   *waterfall*
5 Blow, bugle, blow, set the wild echoes flying,
Blow, bugle; answer, echoes, dying, dying, dying.

O hark, O hear! how thin and clear,
    And thinner, clearer, farther going!
O sweet and far from cliff and scar[1]
10   The horns of Elfland faintly blowing!
Blow, let us hear the purple glens replying:
Blow, bugle; answer, echoes, dying, dying, dying.

O love, they die in yon rich sky,
    They faint on hill or field or river:
15 Our echoes roll from soul to soul,

And grow for ever and for ever.
Blow, bugle, blow, set the wild echoes flying,
And answer, echoes, answer, dying, dying, dying.

[*Tears, Idle Tears*]

Tears, idle tears, I know not what they mean,
    Tears from the depth of some divine despair
Rise in the heart, and gather to the eyes,
In looking on the happy Autumn-fields,
5 And thinking of the days that are no more.

Fresh as the first beam glittering on a sail,
That brings our friends up from the underworld,
Sad as the last which reddens over one
That sinks with all we love below the verge;°   *horizon*
10 So sad, so fresh, the days that are no more.

Ah, sad and strange as in dark summer dawns
The earliest pipe of half-awakened birds
To dying ears, when unto dying eyes
The casement° slowly grows a glimmering   *window frame*
    square;
15 So sad, so strange, the days that are no more.

Dear as remembered kisses after death,
And sweet as those by hopeless fancy feigned
On lips that are for others; deep as love,
Deep as first love, and wild with all regret;
20 O Death in Life, the days that are no more."

[*Now Sleeps the Crimson Petal*]

Now sleeps the crimson petal, now the white;
    Nor waves the cypress in the palace walk;
Nor winks the gold fin in the porphyry[2] font:
The fire-fly wakens: waken thou with me.

5 Now droops the milkwhite peacock like a ghost,
And like a ghost she glimmers on to me.

---

[1] *scar* Steep, craggy portion of mountainside.

[2] *porphyry* Beautiful, polished purple stone.

Now lies the Earth all Danaë[1] to the stars,
And all thy heart lies open unto me.

Now slides the silent meteor on, and leaves
10 A shining furrow, as thy thoughts in me.

Now folds the lily all her sweetness up,
And slips into the bosom of the lake:
So fold thyself, my dearest, thou, and slip
Into my bosom and be lost in me.

[Come Down, O Maid]

Come down, O maid, from yonder
mountain height:
What pleasure lives in height (the shepherd sang)
In height and cold, the splendour of the hills?
But cease to move so near the Heavens, and cease
5 To glide a sunbeam by the blasted Pine,
To sit a star upon the sparkling spire;
And come, for Love is of the valley, come,
For Love is of the valley, come thou down
And find him; by the happy threshold, he,
10 Or hand in hand with Plenty in the maize,
Or red with spurted purple of the vats,
Or foxlike in the vine;[2] nor cares to walk
With Death and Morning on the silver horns,
Nor wilt thou snare him in the white ravine,
15 Nor find him dropped upon the firths° of ice,   *juttings*
That huddling slant in furrow-cloven falls
To roll the torrent out of dusky doors:
But follow; let the torrent dance thee down
To find him in the valley; let the wild
20 Lean-headed Eagles yelp alone, and leave
The monstrous ledges there to slope, and spill
Their thousand wreaths of dangling water-smoke,
That like a broken purpose waste in air:
So waste not thou; but come; for all the vales

25 Await thee; azure pillars of the hearth
Arise to thee; the children call, and I
Thy shepherd pipe, and sweet is every sound,
Sweeter thy voice, but every sound is sweet;
Myriads of rivulets hurrying through the lawn,
30 The moan of doves in immemorial elms,
And murmuring of innumerable bees.

[The Woman's Cause is Man's]

"Blame not thyself too much," I said, "nor
blame
Too much the sons of men and barbarous laws;
These were the rough ways of the world till now.
Henceforth thou hast a helper, me, that know
5 The woman's cause is man's: they rise or sink
Together, dwarfed or godlike, bond or free:
For she that out of Lethe[3] scales with man
The shining steps of Nature, shares with man
His nights, his days, moves with him to one goal,
10 Stays° all the fair young planet in her hands—   *sustains*
If she be small, slight-natured, miserable,
How shall men grow? but work no more alone!
Our place is much: as far as in us lies
We two will serve them both in aiding her—
15 Will clear away the parasitic forms
That seem to keep her up but drag her down—
Will leave her space to burgeon out of all
Within her—let her make herself her own
To give or keep, to live and learn and be
20 All that not harms distinctive womanhood.
For woman is not undeveloped man,
But diverse: could we make her as the man,
Sweet Love were slain: his dearest bond is this,
Not like to like, but like in difference.
25 Yet in the long years liker must they grow;
The man be more of woman, she of man;
He gain in sweetness and in moral height,
Nor lose the wrestling thews° that throw   *muscles*
    the world;

---

1 *Danaë* In Greek mythology, a princess visited by Zeus in the
form of a shower of gold.

2 *foxlike ... vine* See *Song of Solomon* 2.15: "Take us the foxes, the
little foxes, that spoil the vines ...."

3 *Lethe* In Greek myth, one of the rivers of Hades. Drinking its
waters caused the souls of the dead to forget their past lives.

30 She mental breadth, nor fail in childward care,
Nor lose the childlike in the larger mind;
Till at the last she set herself to man,
Like perfect music unto noble words;
And so these twain, upon the skirts° of Time,   *borders*
Sit side by side, full-summed in all their powers,
35 Dispensing harvest, sowing the To-be,
Self-reverent each and reverencing each,
Distinct in individualities,
But like each other even as those who love.
Then comes the statelier Eden back to men:
40 Then reign the world's great bridals, chaste and calm:
Then springs the crowning race of humankind.
May these things be!
          Sighing she spoke "I fear
They will not."
45   "Dear, but let us type them now
In our own lives, and this proud watchword rest
Of equal; seeing either sex alone
Is half itself, and in true marriage lies
Nor equal, nor unequal: each fulfils
50 Defect in each, and always thought in thought,
Purpose in purpose, will in will, they grow,
The single pure and perfect animal,
The two-celled heart beating, with one full stroke, Life."
          And again sighing she spoke: "A dream
55 That once was mine! what woman taught you this?"
—1847

In Memoriam A.H.H.[1]

[PROLOGUE]

Strong Son of God, immortal Love,
    Whom we, that have not seen Thy face,
    By faith, and faith alone, embrace,
Believing where we cannot prove;

5 Thine are these orbs of light and shade;
    Thou madest Life in man and brute;

Thou madest Death; and lo, Thy foot
Is on the skull which Thou hast made.

Thou wilt not leave us in the dust:
10   Thou madest man, he knows not why,
    He thinks he was not made to die;
And Thou hast made him: Thou art just.

Thou seemest human and divine,
    The highest, holiest manhood, Thou:
15   Our wills are ours, we know not how;
Our wills are ours, to make them Thine.

Our little systems have their day;
    They have their day and cease to be:
    They are but broken lights of Thee,
20 And Thou, O Lord, art more than they.

We have but faith: we cannot know;
    For knowledge is of things we see;
    And yet we trust it comes from Thee,
A beam in darkness: let it grow.

25 Let knowledge grow from more to more,
    But more of reverence in us dwell;
    That mind and soul, according well,
May make one music as before,[2]

But vaster. We are fools and slight;
30   We mock Thee when we do not fear:
    But help Thy foolish ones to bear;
Help Thy vain worlds to bear Thy light.

Forgive what seemed my sin in me;
    What seemed my worth since I began;
35   For merit lives from man to man,
And not from man, O Lord, to Thee.

Forgive my grief for one removed,
    Thy creature, whom I found so fair.
    I trust he lives in Thee, and there
40 I find him worthier to be loved.

[1] *In Memoriam* Latin: in memory of; *A.H.H.* Arthur Henry Hallam (1811–1833), English poet, and one of Tennyson's closest friends. Hallam died suddenly of a brain hemorrhage while on vacation in Vienna.

[2] [Tennyson's note] As in the ages of faith.

Forgive these wild and wandering cries,
    Confusions of a wasted youth;
    Forgive them where they fail in truth,
And in Thy wisdom make me wise.
—1849

1

I held it truth, with him who sings
    To one clear harp in divers tones,
    That men may rise on stepping-stones
Of their dead selves to higher things.[1]

5 But who shall so forecast the years
        And find in loss a gain to match?
        Or reach a hand through time to catch
    The far-off interest of tears?

    Let Love clasp Grief lest both be drowned,
10   Let darkness keep her raven gloss:
        Ah, sweeter to be drunk with loss,
    To dance with death, to beat the ground,

    Than that the victor Hours[2] should scorn
        The long result of love, and boast,
15   "Behold the man that loved and lost,
    But all he was is overworn."

2

Old Yew,[3] which graspest at the stones
    That name the under-lying dead,
    Thy fibres net the dreamless head,
Thy roots are wrapped about the bones.

5 The seasons bring the flower again,
        And bring the firstling[4] to the flock;
        And in the dusk of thee, the clock
    Beats out the little lives of men.

---

[1] *him … things* The reference here is unclear. Tennyson said that he was alluding to a work by the German poet Goethe; however, the passage does not appear to correspond to any of Goethe's works.

[2] *Hours* Horai, Greek goddesses of time and of the changing of seasons.

[3] *Yew* Species of tree, often planted in graveyards and thus associated poetically with mourning.

[4] *firstling* Offspring born first in the season.

O not for thee the glow, the bloom,
10   Who changest not in any gale,
        Nor branding summer suns avail
    To touch thy thousand years of gloom:

    And gazing on thee, sullen tree,
        Sick[5] for thy stubborn hardihood,
15   I seem to fail from out my blood
    And grow incorporate into thee.

3

O Sorrow, cruel fellowship,
    O Priestess in the vaults of Death,
    O sweet and bitter in a breath,
What whispers from thy lying lip?

5 "The stars," she whispers, "blindly run;
        A web is woven across the sky;
        From out waste places comes a cry,
    And murmurs from the dying sun:

    "And all the phantom, Nature, stands—
10   With all the music in her tone,
        A hollow echo of my own,—
    A hollow form with empty hands."

    And shall I take a thing so blind,
        Embrace her as my natural good;
15   Or crush her, like a vice of blood,
    Upon the threshold of the mind?

4

To Sleep I give my powers away;
    My will is bondsman° to the dark;   *slave*
    I sit within a helmless bark,°   *ship*
And with my heart I muse and say:

5 O heart, how fares it with thee now,
        That thou should'st fail from thy desire,
        Who scarcely darest to inquire,
    "What is it makes me beat so low?"

    Something it is which thou hast lost,
10   Some pleasure from thine early years.

---

[5] *Sick* I.e., with envy.

Break, thou deep vase of chilling tears,
That grief hath shaken into frost!

Such clouds of nameless trouble cross
   All night below the darkened eyes;
15   With morning wakes the will, and cries,
"Thou shalt not be the fool of loss."

5

I sometimes hold it half a sin
   To put in words the grief I feel;
   For words, like Nature, half reveal
And half conceal the Soul within.

5 But, for the unquiet heart and brain,
   A use in measured language lies;
   The sad mechanic exercise,
Like dull narcotics, numbing pain.

In words, like weeds,[1] I'll wrap me o'er,
10   Like coarsest clothes against the cold:
   But that large grief which these enfold
Is given in outline and no more.

6

One writes, that "Other friends remain,"
   That "Loss is common to the race"—
   And common is the commonplace,
And vacant chaff well meant for grain.

5 That loss is common would not make
   My own less bitter, rather more:
   Too common! Never morning wore
To evening, but some heart did break.

O father, wheresoe'er thou be,
10   Who pledgest now thy gallant son;
   A shot, ere half thy draught be done,
Hath stilled the life that beat from thee.

O mother, praying God will save
   Thy sailor,—while thy head is bowed,

15 His heavy-shotted° hammock-shroud   *weighted*
Drops in his vast and wandering grave.

Ye know no more than I who wrought
   At that last hour to please him well;
   Who mused on all I had to tell,
20 And something written, something thought;

Expecting still his advent home;
   And ever met him on his way
   With wishes, thinking, "here today,"
Or "here tomorrow will he come."

25 O somewhere, meek, unconscious dove,[2]
   That sittest ranging° golden hair;   *arranging*
   And glad to find thyself so fair,
Poor child, that waitest for thy love!

For now her father's chimney glows
30   In expectation of a guest;
   And thinking "this will please him best,"
She takes a riband° or a rose;   *ribbon*

For he will see them on tonight;
   And with the thought her colour burns;
35   And, having left the glass, she turns
Once more to set a ringlet right;

And, even when she turned, the curse
   Had fallen, and her future Lord
   Was drowned in passing through the ford,
40 Or killed in falling from his horse.

O what to her shall be the end?
   And what to me remains of good?
   To her, perpetual maidenhood,
And unto me no second friend.

7

Dark house,[3] by which once more I stand
   Here in the long unlovely street,
   Doors, where my heart was used to beat
So quickly, waiting for a hand,

---

1 *weeds* Mourning clothes.

2 *dove* Here, pure young girl.

3 *Dark house* I.e., Hallam's house.

5   A hand that can be clasped no more—
        Behold me, for I cannot sleep,
        And like a guilty thing I creep
    At earliest morning to the door.

    He is not here; but far away
10   The noise of life begins again,
        And ghastly through the drizzling rain
    On the bald street breaks the blank day.

8

    A happy lover who has come
        To look on her that loves him well,
        Who 'lights[1] and rings the gateway bell,
    And learns her gone and far from home;

5   He saddens, all the magic light
        Dies off at once from bower and hall,
        And all the place is dark, and all
    The chambers emptied of delight:

    So find I every pleasant spot
10   In which we two were wont to meet,
        The field, the chamber and the street,
    For all is dark where thou art not.

    Yet as that other, wandering there
        In those deserted walks, may find
15   A flower beat with rain and wind,
    Which once she fostered up with care;

    So seems it in my deep regret,
        O my forsaken heart, with thee
        And this poor flower of poesy
20 Which little cared for fades not yet.

    But since it pleased a vanished eye,
        I go to plant it on his tomb,
        That if it can it there may bloom,
    Or dying, there at least may die.

9

    Fair ship, that from the Italian shore
        Sailest the placid ocean-plains

    With my lost Arthur's loved remains,
    Spread thy full wings, and waft him o'er.

5   So draw him home to those that mourn
        In vain; a favourable speed
        Ruffle thy mirrored mast, and lead
    Through prosperous floods his holy urn.

    All night no ruder° air perplex   *turbulent*
10   Thy sliding keel, till Phosphor,[2] bright
        As our pure love, through early light
    Shall glimmer on the dewy decks.

    Sphere all your lights around, above;
        Sleep, gentle heavens, before the prow;
15   Sleep, gentle winds, as he sleeps now,
    My friend, the brother of my love;

    My Arthur, whom I shall not see
        Till all my widowed race be run;
        Dear as the mother to the son,
20 More than my brothers are to me.

10

    I hear the noise about thy keel;
        I hear the bell struck in the night:
        I see the cabin-window bright;
    I see the sailor at the wheel.

5   Thou bring'st the sailor to his wife,
        And travelled men from foreign lands;
        And letters unto trembling hands;
    And, thy dark freight, a vanished life.

    So bring him: we have idle dreams:
10   This look of quiet flatters thus
        Our home-bred fancies: O to us,
    The fools of habit, sweeter seems

    To rest beneath the clover sod,
        That takes the sunshine and the rains,

---

[1]   *'lights*   Alights from a horse.

[2]   *Phosphor*   The planet Venus, also called the morning star.

15   Or where the kneeling hamlet[1] drains
      The chalice of the grapes of God;[2]

      Than if with thee the roaring wells
          Should gulf him fathom-deep in brine;
          And hands so often clasped in mine,
20   Should toss with tangle and with shells.

                    11

      Calm is the morn without a sound,
          Calm as to suit a calmer grief,
          And only through the faded leaf
      The chestnut pattering to the ground:

5   Calm and deep peace on this high wold,°   plain
          And on these dews that drench the furze,[3]
          And all the silvery gossamers°   cobwebs
      That twinkle into green and gold:

      Calm and still light on yon great plain
10   That sweeps with all its autumn bowers,
          And crowded farms and lessening towers,
      To mingle with the bounding main:

      Calm and deep peace in this wide air,
          These leaves that redden to the fall;
15   And in my heart, if calm at all,
      If any calm, a calm despair:

      Calm on the seas, and silver sleep,
          And waves that sway themselves in rest,
          And dead calm in that noble breast
20   Which heaves but with the heaving deep.

                    12

      Lo, as a dove when up she springs
          To bear through Heaven a tale of woe,
          Some dolorous message knit below
      The wild pulsation of her wings;

5   Like her I go; I cannot stay;
          I leave this mortal ark behind,

      A weight of nerves without a mind,
      And leave the cliffs, and haste away

      O'er ocean-mirrors rounded large,
10   And reach the glow of southern skies,
          And see the sails at distance rise,
      And linger weeping on the marge,°   shore

      And saying; "Comes he thus, my friend?
          Is this the end of all my care?"
15   And circle moaning in the air:
      "Is this the end? Is this the end?"

      And forward dart again, and play
          About the prow, and back return
          To where the body sits, and learn
20   That I have been an hour away.

                    13

      Tears of the widower, when he sees
          A late-lost form that sleep reveals,
          And moves his doubtful arms, and feels
      Her place is empty, fall like these;

5   Which weep a loss forever new,
          A void where heart on heart reposed;
          And, where warm hands have pressed and closed,
      Silence, till I be silent too.

      Which weep the comrade of my choice,
10   An awful thought, a life removed,
          The human-hearted man I loved,
      A Spirit, not a breathing voice.

      Come Time, and teach me, many years,
          I do not suffer in a dream;
15   For now so strange do these things seem,
      Mine eyes have leisure for their tears;

      My fancies time to rise on wing,
          And glance about the approaching sails,
          As though they brought but merchants' bales,[4]
20   And not the burden that they bring.

---

[1] *hamlet* I.e., the citizens of a hamlet.

[2] *drains ... God* I.e., partakes in communion.

[3] *furze* Evergreen shrubs.

---

[4] *bales* I.e., of cotton or other trade goods.

14

If one should bring me this report,
 That thou hadst touched the land today,
 And I went down unto the quay,
And found thee lying in the port;

5 And standing, muffled round with woe,
 Should see thy passengers in rank
 Come stepping lightly down the plank,
And beckoning unto those they know;

And if along with these should come
10 The man I held as half-divine;
 Should strike a sudden hand in mine,
And ask a thousand things of home;

And I should tell him all my pain,
 And how my life had drooped of late,
15 And he should sorrow o'er my state
And marvel what possessed my brain;

And I perceived no touch of change,
 No hint of death in all his frame,
 But found him all in all the same,
20 I should not feel it to be strange.

15

Tonight the winds begin to rise
 And roar from yonder dropping day:
 The last red leaf is whirled away,
The rooks° are blown about the skies;   *crows*

5 The forest cracked, the waters curled,
 The cattle huddled on the lea;°   *pasture*
 And wildly dashed on tower and tree
The sunbeam strikes along the world:

And but for fancies, which aver°   *declare*
10 That all thy motions gently pass
 Athwart a plane of molten glass,
I scarce could brook the strain and stir

That makes the barren branches loud;
 And but for fear it is not so,

The wild unrest that lives in woe
Would dote and pore on yonder cloud

That rises upward always higher,
 And onward drags a labouring breast,
 And topples round the dreary west,
20 A looming bastion° fringed with fire. *fortress*

16

What words are these have fallen from me?
 Can calm despair and wild unrest
 Be tenants of a single breast,
Or sorrow such a changeling be?

5 Or doth she only seem to take
 The touch of change in calm or storm;
 But knows no more of transient form
In her deep self, than some dead lake

That holds the shadow of a lark
10 Hung in the shadow of a heaven?
 Or has the shock, so harshly given,
Confused me like the unhappy bark

That strikes by night a craggy shelf,
 And staggers blindly ere she sink?
15 And stunned me from my power to think
And all my knowledge of myself;

And made me that delirious man
 Whose fancy fuses old and new,
 And flashes into false and true,
20 And mingles all without a plan?

17

Thou comest, much wept for: such a breeze
 Compelled thy canvas, and my prayer
 Was as the whisper of an air
To breathe thee over lonely seas.

5 For I in spirit saw thee move
 Through circles of the bounding sky,
 Week after week: the days go by:
Come quick, thou bringest all I love.

Henceforth, wherever thou mayst roam,
       My blessing, like a line of light,
       Is on the waters day and night,
And like a beacon guards thee home.

So may whatever tempest mars
       Mid-ocean, spare thee, sacred bark;
       And balmy drops in summer dark
Slide from the bosom of the stars.

So kind an office hath been done,
       Such precious relics brought by thee;
       The dust of him I shall not see
Till all my widowed race be run.

18

'Tis well; 'Tis something; we may stand
       Where he in English earth is laid,
       And from his ashes may be made
The violet of his native land.

"'Tis little; but it looks in truth"
       As if the quiet bones were blest
       Among familiar names to rest
And in the places of his youth.

Come then, pure hands, and bear the head
       That sleeps or wears the mask of sleep,
       And come, whatever loves to weep,
And hear the ritual of the dead.

Ah yet, even yet, if this might be,
       I, falling on his faithful heart,
       Would breathing through his lips impart
The life that almost dies in me;

That dies not, but endures with pain,
       And slowly forms the firmer mind,
       Treasuring the look it cannot find,
The words that are not heard again.

19

The Danube[1] to the Severn[2] gave

The darkened heart that beat no more;
       They laid him by the pleasant shore,
And in the hearing of the wave.

There twice a day the Severn fills;
       The salt sea-water passes by,
       And hushes half the babbling Wye,[3]
And makes a silence in the hills.

The Wye is hushed nor moved along,
       And hushed my deepest grief of all,
       When filled with tears that cannot fall,
I brim with sorrow drowning song.

The tide flows down, the wave again
       Is vocal in its wooded walls;
       My deeper anguish also falls,
And I can speak a little then.

20

The lesser griefs that may be said,
       That breathe a thousand tender vows,
       Are but as servants in a house
Where lies the master newly dead;

Who speak their feeling as it is,
       And weep the fullness from the mind:
       "It will be hard," they say, "to find
Another service such as this."[4]

My lighter moods are like to these,
       That out of words a comfort win;
       But there are other griefs within,
And tears that at their fountain freeze;

For by the hearth the children sit
       Cold in that atmosphere of Death,
       And scarce endure to draw the breath,
Or like to noiseless phantoms flit:

But open converse is there none,
       So much the vital spirits sink

---

1   *Danube*   River that flows through Vienna.

2   *Severn*   River in England. Hallam is buried at Clevedon, in Somerset, overlooking the Severn estuary.

3   *Wye*   The River Wye forms part of the border between England and Wales.

4   *"It will … this"*   I.e., it will be difficult to find employment with a master as good as this one.

To see the vacant chair, and think,
20 "How good! how kind! and he is gone."

21

I sing to him that rests below,
    And, since the grasses round me wave,
    I take the grasses of the grave,
And make them pipes whereon to blow.

5 The traveller hears me now and then,
    And sometimes harshly will he speak:
    "This fellow would make weakness weak,
And melt the waxen hearts of men."

Another answers, "Let him be,
10   He loves to make parade of pain,
    That with his piping he may gain
The praise that comes to constancy."

A third is wroth:° "Is this an hour   *indignant*
    For private sorrow's barren song,
15   When more and more the people throng°   *crowd*
The chairs and thrones of civil power?

"A time to sicken and to swoon,
    When Science reaches forth her arms
    To feel from world to world, and charms
20 Her secret from the latest moon?"

Behold, ye speak an idle thing:
    Ye never knew the sacred dust:
    I do but sing because I must,
And pipe but as the linnets[1] sing:

25 And one is glad; her note is gay,
    For now her little ones have ranged;
    And one is sad: her note is changed,
Because her brood is stolen away.

22

The path by which we twain did go,
    Which led by tracts that pleased us well,
    Through four sweet years arose and fell,
From flower to flower, from snow to snow:

5 And we with singing cheered the way,
    And, crowned with all the season lent,
    From April on to April went,
And glad at heart from May to May:

But where the path we walked began
10   To slant the fifth autumnal slope,[2]
    As we descended following Hope,
There sat the Shadow feared of man;

Who broke our fair companionship,
    And spread his mantle dark and cold,
15   And wrapped thee formless in the fold,
And dulled the murmur on thy lip,

And bore thee where I could not see
    Nor follow, though I walk in haste,
    And think, that somewhere in the waste
20 The Shadow sits and waits for me.

23

Now, sometimes in my sorrow shut,
    Or breaking into song by fits,
    Alone, alone, to where he sits,
The Shadow cloaked from head to foot,

5 Who keeps the keys of all the creeds,
    I wander, often falling lame,
    And looking back to whence I came,
Or on to where the pathway leads;

And crying, How changed from where it ran
10   Through lands where not a leaf was dumb;
    But all the lavish hills would hum
The murmur of a happy Pan:[3]

When each by turns was guide to each,
    And Fancy light from Fancy caught,
15   And Thought leapt out to wed with Thought
Ere Thought could wed itself with Speech;

---

[1] *linnets* Species of songbirds.

[2] *fifth ... slope* I.e., in the autumn of their fifth year of friendship.

[3] *Pan* Greek god of flocks and sheep, a common presence in English pastoral poetry. To the Romans, he was a universal god, the god of Nature.

And all we met was fair and good,
   And all was good that Time could bring,
   And all the secret of the Spring
20 Moved in the chambers of the blood;

And many an old philosophy
   On Argive° heights divinely sang,   *Greek*
   And round us all the thicket rang
To many a flute of Arcady.[1]

24

And was the day of my delight
   As pure and perfect as I say?
   The very source and fount of Day
Is dashed with wandering isles of night.[2]

5 If all was good and fair we met,
   This earth had been the Paradise
   It never looked to human eyes
Since our first Sun arose and set.

And is it that the haze of grief
10   Makes former gladness loom so great?
   The lowness of the present state,
That sets the past in this relief?

Or that the past will always win
   A glory from its being far;
15   And orb into the perfect star
We saw not, when we moved therein?

25

I know that this was Life,—the track
   Whereon with equal feet we fared;
   And then, as now, the day prepared
The daily burden for the back.

5 But this it was that made me move
   As light as carrier-birds in air;
   I loved the weight I had to bear,
Because it needed help of Love:

Nor could I weary, heart or limb,
10   When mighty Love would cleave in twain
   The lading° of a single pain,   *burden*
And part it, giving half to him.

26

Still onward winds the dreary way;
   I with it; for I long to prove
   No lapse of moons[3] can canker° Love,   *tarnish*
Whatever fickle tongues may say.

5 And if that eye which watches guilt
   And goodness, and hath power to see
   Within the green the mouldered tree,
And towers fallen as soon as built—

Oh, if indeed that eye foresee
10   Or see (in Him is no before)
   In more of life true life no more
And Love the indifference to be,

Then might I find, ere yet the morn
   Breaks hither over Indian seas,
15   That Shadow waiting with the keys,
To shroud me from my proper° scorn.   *own*

27

I envy not in any moods
   The captive void of noble rage,
   The linnet born within the cage,
That never knew the summer woods:

5 I envy not the beast that takes
   His license in the field of time,
   Unfettered by the sense of crime,
To whom a conscience never wakes;

Nor, what may count itself as blest,
10   The heart that never plighted troth[4]
   But stagnates in the weeds of sloth;
Nor any want-begotten rest.

---

1 *Arcady* Arcadia, a hilly area of central Greece, said to be the home of Pan.

2 *source ... night* The Sun, dotted with sunspots.

3 *lapse ... moons* Span of time.

4 *plighted troth* Vowed faithfulness.

I hold it true, whate'er befall;
    I feel it, when I sorrow most;
15   'Tis better to have loved and lost
Than never to have loved at all.

28

The time draws near the birth of Christ:
    The moon is hid; the night is still;
    The Christmas bells from hill to hill
Answer each other in the mist.

5 Four voices of four hamlets round,
    From far and near, on mead° and moor,   *meadow*
    Swell out and fail, as if a door
Were shut between me and the sound:

Each voice four changes on the wind,
10   That now dilate, and now decrease,
    Peace and goodwill, goodwill and peace,
Peace and goodwill, to all mankind.

This year I slept and woke with pain,
    I almost wished no more to wake,
15   And that my hold on life would break
Before I heard those bells again:

But they my troubled spirit rule,
    For they controlled me when a boy;
    They bring me sorrow touched with joy,
20 The merry merry bells of Yule.

29

With such compelling cause to grieve
    As daily vexes household peace,
    And chains regret to his decease,
How dare we keep our Christmas-eve;

5 Which brings no more a welcome guest
    To enrich the threshold of the night
    With showered largess of delight
In dance and song and game and jest?

Yet go, and while the holly boughs
10   Entwine the cold baptismal font,

Make one wreath more for Use and Wont,[1]
    That guard the portals of the house;

Old sisters of a day gone by,
    Gray nurses, loving nothing new;
15   Why should they miss their yearly due
Before their time? They too will die.

30

With trembling fingers did we weave
    The holly round the Christmas hearth;
    A rainy cloud possessed the earth,
And sadly fell our Christmas-eve.

5 At our old pastimes in the hall
    We gambolled,° making vain pretence   *danced*
    Of gladness, with an awful sense
Of one mute Shadow watching all.

We paused: the winds were in the beech:
10   We heard them sweep the winter land;
    And in a circle hand-in-hand
Sat silent, looking each at each.

Then echo-like our voices rang;
    We sung, though every eye was dim,
15   A merry song we sang with him
Last year: impetuously we sang:

We ceased: a gentler feeling crept
    Upon us: surely rest is meet:°   *appropriate*
    "They rest," we said, "their sleep is sweet,"
20 And silence followed, and we wept.

Our voices took a higher range;
    Once more we sang: "They do not die
    Nor lose their mortal sympathy,
Nor change to us, although they change;

25 "'Rapt from the fickle and the frail
    With gathered power, yet the same,

---

1 *Use ... Wont* I.e., habit and custom.

Pierces the keen seraphic flame[1]
From orb to orb, from veil to veil."

Rise, happy morn, rise, holy morn,
30   Draw forth the cheerful day from night:
      O Father, touch the east, and light
The light that shone when Hope was born,

31

When Lazarus left his charnel-cave,
      And home to Mary's house returned,[2]
      Was this demanded—if he yearned
To hear her weeping by his grave?

5   "Where wert thou, brother, those four days?"
      There lives no record of reply,
      Which telling what it is to die
Had surely added praise to praise.

From every house the neighbours met,
10   The streets were filled with joyful sound,
      A solemn gladness even crowned
The purple brows of Olivet.[3]

Behold a man raised up by Christ!
      The rest remaineth unrevealed;
15   He told it not; or something sealed
The lips of that Evangelist.[4]

32

Her eyes are homes of silent prayer,
      Nor other thought her mind admits
      But, he was dead, and there he sits,
And He that brought him back is there.

5   Then one deep love doth supersede
      All other, when her ardent gaze

Roves from the living brother's face,
And rests upon the Life[5] indeed.

All subtle thought, all curious fears,
10   Borne down by gladness so complete,
      She bows, she bathes the Saviour's feet
With costly spikenard[6] and with tears.[7]

Thrice blest whose lives are faithful prayers,
      Whose loves in higher love endure;
15   What souls possess themselves so pure,
Or is there blessedness like theirs?

33

O thou that after toil and storm
      Mayst seem to have reached a purer air,
      Whose faith has centre everywhere,
Nor cares to fix itself to form,

5   Leave thou thy sister when she prays,
      Her early Heaven, her happy views;
      Nor thou with shadowed hint confuse
A life that leads melodious days.

Her faith through form is pure as thine,
10   Her hands are quicker unto good:
      Oh, sacred be the flesh and blood
To which she links a truth divine!

See thou, that countest reason ripe
      In holding by the law within,
15   Thou fail not in a world of sin,
And even for want of such a type.

34

My own dim life should teach me this,
      That life shall live for evermore,
      Else earth is darkness at the core,
And dust and ashes all that is;

---

[1]   *seraphic flame*   Intense, purifying fire, associated with the angel-like Seraphim.

[2]   *Lazarus … returned*   See John 11.1–44, in which Jesus raises Lazarus from the dead. The Biblical account does not include any mention of Lazarus returning home to his sister Mary.

[3]   *Olivet*   Mount of Olives, in Jerusalem.

[4]   *Evangelist*   John the Apostle, who recorded the event in his Gospel.

[5]   *Life*   I.e., Christ. See John 11.25: "I am the Resurrection and the Life."

[6]   *spikenard*   Expensive aromatic oil.

[7]   *bathes … tears*   See Luke 7.37–50. Unlike the Biblical passage, Tennyson appears to identify the woman as Mary, sister of the resurrected Lazarus.

5　This round of green, this orb of flame,[1]
　　　Fantastic beauty; such as lurks
　　　In some wild Poet, when he works
　　Without a conscience or an aim.

　　What then were God to such as I?
10　　　'Twere hardly worth my while to choose
　　　Of things all mortal, or to use
　　A little patience ere I die;

　　'Twere best at once to sink to peace,
　　　Like birds the charming serpent draws,
15　　　To drop head-foremost in the jaws
　　Of vacant darkness and to cease.

                    35

　　Yet if some voice that man could trust
　　　Should murmur from the narrow house,
　　　"The cheeks drop in; the body bows;
　　Man dies: nor is there hope in dust:"

5　Might I not say? "Yet even here,
　　　But for one hour, O Love, I strive
　　　To keep so sweet a thing alive:"
　　But I should turn mine ears and hear

　　The moanings of the homeless sea,
10　　　The sound of streams that swift or slow
　　　Draw down Æonian° hills, and sow   eternal
　　The dust of continents to be;

　　And Love would answer with a sigh,
　　　"The sound of that forgetful shore
15　　　Will change my sweetness more and more,
　　Half-dead to know that I shall die."

　　O me, what profits it to put
　　　An idle case? If Death were seen
　　　At first as Death, Love had not been,
20　Or been in narrowest working shut,

　　Mere fellowship of sluggish moods,
　　　Or in his coarsest Satyr-shape[2]

---

[1]　*round ... flame*　I.e., the earth and the sun.

[2]　*Satyr-shape*　In the shape of satyrs; half-human, half-beast. In Greek mythology, satyrs are a class of woodland gods.

　　Had bruised the herb and crushed the grape,
　　And basked and battened° in the woods.   thrived

                    36

　　Though truths in manhood darkly join,
　　　Deep-seated in our mystic frame,
　　　We yield all blessing to the name
　　Of Him that made them current coin;

5　For Wisdom dealt with mortal powers,
　　　Where truth in closest words shall fail,
　　　When truth embodied in a tale
　　Shall enter in at lowly doors.

　　And so the Word had breath,[3] and wrought
10　　　With human hands the creed of creeds
　　　In loveliness of perfect deeds,
　　More strong than all poetic thought;

　　Which he may read that binds the sheaf,
　　　Or builds the house, or digs the grave,
15　　　And those wild eyes that watch the wave
　　In roarings round the coral reef.

                    37

　　Urania[4] speaks with darkened brow:
　　　"Thou pratest° here where thou art least;   chatter
　　　This faith has many a purer priest,
　　And many an abler voice than thou.

5　"Go down beside thy native rill,°   stream
　　　On thy Parnassus[5] set thy feet,
　　　And hear thy laurel whisper sweet
　　About the ledges of the hill."

　　And my Melpomene[6] replies,
10　　　A touch of shame upon her cheek:
　　　"I am not worthy even to speak
　　Of thy prevailing mysteries;

---

[3]　*Word ... breath*　See John 1.14: "The Word became flesh and dwelt among us."

[4]　*Urania*　Greek Muse of astronomy.

[5]　*thy Parnassus*　I.e., your home. Mount Parnassus was the home of the Muses.

[6]　*Melpomene*　Greek Muse of tragedy.

"For I am but an earthly Muse,
      And owning but a little art
15   To lull with song an aching heart,
And render human love his dues;

"But brooding on the dear one dead,
      And all he said of things divine,
      (And dear to me as sacred wine
20   To dying lips is all he said),

"I murmured, as I came along,
      Of comfort clasped in truth revealed;
      And loitered in the master's field,
And darkened sanctities with song."

38

With weary steps I loiter on,
      Though always under altered skies
      The purple from the distance dies,
My prospect and horizon gone.

5   No joy the blowing season gives,
      The herald melodies of spring,
      But in the songs I love to sing
A doubtful gleam of solace lives.

If any care for what is here
10   Survive in spirits rendered free,
      Then are these songs I sing of thee
Not all ungrateful to thine ear.

39

Old warder of these buried bones,
      And answering now my random stroke
      With fruitful cloud and living smoke,
Dark yew, that graspest at the stones

5   And dippest toward the dreamless head,
      To thee too comes the golden hour
      When flower is feeling after flower;
But Sorrow—fixed upon the dead,

And darkening the dark graves of men,—
10   What whispered from her lying lips?

Thy gloom is kindled at the tips,
And passes into gloom again.

40

Could we forget the widowed hour
      And look on Spirits breathed away,
      As on a maiden in the day
When first she wears her orange-flower![1]

5   When crowned with blessing she doth rise
      To take her latest leave of home,
      And hopes and light regrets that come
Make April of her tender eyes;

And doubtful joys the father move,
10   And tears are on the mother's face,
      As parting with a long embrace
She enters other realms of love;

Her office there to rear, to teach,
      Becoming as is meet and fit
15   A link among the days, to knit
The generations each with each;

And, doubtless, unto thee is given
      A life that bears immortal fruit
      In those great offices that suit
20   The full-grown energies of heaven.

Ay me, the difference I discern!
      How often shall her old fireside
      Be cheered with tidings of the bride,
How often she herself return,

25   And tell them all they would have told,
      And bring her babe, and make her boast,
      Till even those that missed her most
Shall count new things as dear as old:

But thou and I have shaken hands,
30   Till growing winters lay me low;

---

[1] *orange-flower* Brides often wore wreaths of orange-flowers in
this period.

My paths are in the fields I know,
And thine in undiscovered lands.[1]

41

Thy spirit ere our fatal loss
   Did ever rise from high to higher;
   As mounts the heavenward altar-fire,
As flies the lighter through the gross.°   *heavier*

5 But thou art turned to something strange,
   And I have lost the links that bound
   Thy changes; here upon the ground,
No more partaker of thy change.

Deep folly! yet that this could be—
10   That I could wing my will with might
   To leap the grades of life and light,
And flash at once, my friend, to thee.

For though my nature rarely yields
   To that vague fear implied in death;
15   Nor shudders at the gulfs beneath,
The howlings from forgotten fields;

Yet oft when sundown skirts the moor
   An inner trouble I behold,
   A spectral° doubt which makes me cold,   *ghostly*
20 That I shall be thy mate no more,

Though following with an upward mind
   The wonders that have come to thee,
   Through all the secular to-be,
But evermore a life behind.

42

I vex my heart with fancies dim:
   He still outstripped me in the race;
   It was but unity of place
That made me dream I ranked with him.

5 And so may Place retain us still,
   And he the much-beloved again,

A lord of large experience, train
To riper growth the mind and will:

And what delights can equal those
10   That stir the spirit's inner deeps,
   When one that loves but knows not, reaps
A truth from one that loves and knows?

43

If Sleep and Death be truly one,
   And every spirit's folded bloom
   Through all its intervital[2] gloom
In some long trance should slumber on;

5 Unconscious of the sliding hour,
   Bare of the body, might it last,
   And silent traces of the past
Be all the colour of the flower:

So then were nothing lost to man;
10   So that still garden of the souls
   In many a figured leaf enrolls
The total world since life began;

And love will last as pure and whole
   As when he loved me here in Time,
15   And at the spiritual prime
Rewaken with the dawning soul.

44

How fares it with the happy dead?
   For here the man is more and more;
   But he forgets the days before
God shut the doorways of his head.

5 The days have vanished, tone and tint,
   And yet perhaps the hoarding sense
   Gives out at times (he knows not whence)
A little flash, a mystic hint;

And in the long harmonious years
10   (If Death so taste Lethean springs),[3]

---

[1] *undiscovered lands* See *Hamlet* 3.1.79–80, in which death is "the undiscovered country, from whose bourne / No traveller returns."

[2] *intervital* Between two stages of existence.

[3] *Lethean springs* According to Greek mythology, drinking from the River Lethe in Hades caused the dead to forget their previous existences.

May some dim touch of earthly things
Surprise thee ranging with thy peers.

If such a dreamy touch should fall,
        O turn thee round, resolve the doubt;
15   My guardian angel will speak out
In that high place, and tell thee all.

45

The baby new to earth and sky,
        What time his tender palm is pressed
        Against the circle of the breast,
Has never thought that "this is I":

5   But as he grows he gathers much,
        And learns the use of "I," and "me,"
        And finds "I am not what I see,
And other than the things I touch."

So rounds he to a separate mind
10   From whence clear memory may begin,
        As through the frame that binds him in
His isolation grows defined.

This use may lie in blood and breath,
        Which else were fruitless of their due,
15   Had man to learn himself anew
Beyond the second birth of Death.

46

We ranging down this lower track,
        The path we came by, thorn and flower,
        Is shadowed by the growing hour,
Lest life should fail in looking back.

5   So be it: there no shade can last
        In that deep dawn behind the tomb,
        But clear from marge° to marge shall bloom   shore
The eternal landscape of the past;

A lifelong tract of time revealed;
10   The fruitful hours of still increase;
        Days ordered in a wealthy peace,
And those five years its richest field.

O Love, thy province were not large,
        A bounded field, nor stretching far;
15   Look also, Love, a brooding star,
A rosy warmth from marge to marge.

47

That each, who seems a separate whole,
        Should move his rounds, and fusing all
        The skirts of self again, should fall
Remerging in the general Soul,

5   Is faith as vague as all unsweet:
        Eternal form shall still divide
        The eternal soul from all beside;
And I shall know him when we meet:

And we shall sit at endless feast,
10   Enjoying each the other's good:
        What vaster dream can hit the mood
Of Love on earth? He seeks at least

Upon the last and sharpest height,
        Before the spirits fade away,
15   Some landing-place, to clasp and say,
"Farewell! We lose ourselves in light."

48

If these brief lays, of Sorrow born,
        Were taken to be such as closed
        Grave doubts and answers here proposed,
Then these were such as men might scorn:

5   Her care is not to part and prove;
        She takes, when harsher moods remit,
        What slender shade of doubt may flit,
And makes it vassal unto love:

And hence, indeed, she sports with words,
10   But better serves a wholesome law,
        And holds it sin and shame to draw
The deepest measure from the chords:

Nor dare she trust a larger lay,°   song
        But rather loosens from the lip

15   Short swallow-flights of song, that dip
        Their wings in tears, and skim away.

49

From art, from nature, from the schools,
    Let random influences glance,
    Like light in many a shivered lance
That breaks about the dappled pools:

5   The lightest wave of thought shall lisp,
    The fancy's tenderest eddy wreathe,
    The slightest air of song shall breathe
To make the sullen surface crisp.

And look thy look, and go thy way,
10   But blame not thou the winds that make
    The seeming-wanton ripple break,
The tender-pencilled shadow play.

Beneath all fancied hopes and fears
    Ay me, the sorrow deepens down,
15   Whose muffled motions blindly drown
The bases of my life in tears.

50

Be near me when my light is low,
    When the blood creeps, and the nerves prick
    And tingle; and the heart is sick,
And all the wheels of Being slow.

5   Be near me when the sensuous frame
    Is racked with pangs that conquer trust;
    And Time, a maniac scattering dust,
And Life, a Fury slinging flame.

Be near me when my faith is dry,
10   And men the flies of latter spring,
    That lay their eggs, and sting and sing
And weave their petty cells and die.

Be near me when I fade away,
    To point the term of human strife,
15   And on the low dark verge of life
The twilight of eternal day.

51

Do we indeed desire the dead
    Should still be near us at our side?
    Is there no baseness we would hide?
No inner vileness that we dread?

5   Shall he for whose applause I strove,
    I had such reverence for his blame,
    See with clear eye some hidden shame
And I be lessened in his love?

I wrong the grave with fears untrue:
10   Shall love be blamed for want of faith?
    There must be wisdom with great Death:
The dead shall look me through and through.

Be near us when we climb or fall:
    Ye watch, like God, the rolling hours
15   With larger other eyes than ours,
To make allowance for us all.

52

I cannot love thee as I ought,
    For love reflects the thing beloved;
    My words are only words, and moved
Upon the topmost froth of thought.

5   "Yet blame not thou thy plaintive song,"
    The Spirit of true love replied;
    "Thou canst not move me from thy side,
Nor human frailty do me wrong.

"What keeps a spirit wholly true
10   To that ideal which he bears?
    What record? not the sinless years
That breathed beneath the Syrian blue:[1]

"So fret not, like an idle girl,
    That life is dashed with flecks of sin.
15   Abide: thy wealth is gathered in,
When Time hath sundered shell from pearl."

---

[1] *Syrian blue* Blue skies of Syria, commonly used as a term for the land in which Christ lived.

53

How many a father have I seen,
    A sober man, among his boys,
    Whose youth was full of foolish noise,
Who wears his manhood hale° and green: *robust*

5   And dare we to this fancy give,
        That had the wild oat not been sown,
        The soil, left barren, scarce had grown
    The grain by which a man may live?

    Or, if we held the doctrine sound
10   For life outliving heats of youth,
        Yet who would preach it as a truth
    To those that eddy round and round?

    Hold thou the good: define it well:
        For fear divine Philosophy
15   Should push beyond her mark, and be
    Procuress to the Lords of Hell.

54

Oh yet we trust that somehow good
    Will be the final goal of ill,
    To pangs of nature, sins of will,
Defects of doubt, and taints of blood;

5   That nothing walks with aimless feet;
        That not one life shall be destroyed,
        Or cast as rubbish to the void,
    When God hath made the pile complete;

    That not a worm is cloven in vain;
10   That not a moth with vain desire
        Is shrivelled in a fruitless fire,
    Or but subserves another's gain.

    Behold, we know not anything;
        I can but trust that good shall fall
15   At last—far off—at last, to all,
    And every winter change to spring.

    So runs my dream: but what am I?
        An infant crying in the night:

An infant crying for the light:
20   And with no language but a cry.

55

The wish, that of the living whole
    No life may fail beyond the grave,
    Derives it not from what we have
The likest God within the soul?

5   Are God and Nature then at strife,
        That Nature lends such evil dreams?
        So careful of the type° she seems,   *species*
    So careless of the single life;

    That I, considering everywhere
10   Her secret meaning in her deeds,
        And finding that of fifty seeds
    She often brings but one to bear,

    I falter where I firmly trod,
        And falling with my weight of cares
15   Upon the great world's altar-stairs
    That slope through darkness up to God,

    I stretch lame hands of faith, and grope,
        And gather dust and chaff, and call
        To what I feel is Lord of all,
20   And faintly trust the larger hope.

56

"So careful of the type?" but no.
    From scarpèd[1] cliff and quarried stone
    She cries, "A thousand types are gone:
I care for nothing, all shall go.

5   "Thou makest thine appeal to me:
        I bring to life, I bring to death:
        The spirit does but mean the breath:
    I know no more." And he, shall he,

    Man, her last work, who seemed so fair,
10   Such splendid purpose in his eyes,
        Who rolled the psalm to wintry skies,
    Who built him fanes° of fruitless prayer,   *temples*

---

[1] *scarpèd* Steeply cut.

Who trusted God was love indeed
  And love Creation's final law—
15 Though Nature, red in tooth and claw
With ravine,° shrieked against his creed—   *violence*

Who loved, who suffered countless ills,
  Who battled for the True, the Just,
  Be blown about the desert dust,
20 Or sealed within the iron hills?

No more? A monster then, a dream,
  A discord. Dragons° of the prime,   *dinosaurs*
  That tare° each other in their slime,   *tore*
Were mellow music matched with him.

25 O life as futile, then, as frail!
  O for thy voice to soothe and bless!
  What hope of answer, or redress?
Behind the veil, behind the veil.

    57

Peace; come away: the song of woe
  Is after all an earthly song:
  Peace; come away: we do him wrong
To sing so wildly: let us go.

5 Come; let us go: your cheeks are pale;
  But half my life I leave behind:
  Methinks my friend is richly shrined;
But I shall pass; my work will fail.

Yet in these ears, till hearing dies,
10 One set slow bell will seem to toll
  The passing of the sweetest soul
That ever looked with human eyes.

I hear it now, and o'er and o'er,
  Eternal greetings to the dead;
15 And "Ave,° Ave, Ave," said,   *farewell*
"Adieu, adieu" for evermore.

    58

In those sad words I took farewell:
  Like echoes in sepulchral halls,

As drop by drop the water falls
In vaults and catacombs, they fell;

5 And, falling, idly broke the peace
  Of hearts that beat from day to day,
  Half-conscious of their dying clay,
And those cold crypts where they shall cease.

The high Muse answered: "Wherefore grieve
10 Thy brethren with a fruitless tear?
  Abide a little longer here,
And thou shalt take a nobler leave."

    59

O Sorrow, wilt thou live with me
  No casual mistress, but a wife,
  My bosom-friend and half of life;
As I confess it needs must be;

5 O Sorrow, wilt thou rule my blood,
  Be sometimes lovely like a bride,
  And put thy harsher moods aside,
If thou wilt have me wise and good.

My centred passion cannot move,
10 Nor will it lessen from today;
  But I'll have leave at times to play
As with the creature of my love;

And set thee forth, for thou art mine,
  With so much hope for years to come,
15 That, howsoe'er I know thee, some
Could hardly tell what name were thine.

    60

He passed; a soul of nobler tone:
  My spirit loved and loves him yet,
  Like some poor girl whose heart is set
On one whose rank exceeds her own.

5 He mixing with his proper sphere,
  She finds the baseness of her lot,
  Half jealous of she knows not what,
And envying all that meet him there.

The little village looks forlorn;
10   She sighs amid her narrow days,
    Moving about the household ways,
In that dark house where she was born.

The foolish neighbours come and go,
    And tease her till the day draws by:
15   At night she weeps, "How vain am I!
How should he love a thing so low?"

61

If, in thy second state sublime,
    Thy ransomed reason change replies
    With all the circle of the wise,
The perfect flower of human time;

5   And if thou cast thine eyes below,
    How dimly charactered and slight,
    How dwarfed a growth of cold and night,
How blanched with darkness must I grow!

Yet turn thee to the doubtful shore,
10   Where thy first form was made a man;
    I loved thee, Spirit, and love, nor can
The soul of Shakespeare love thee more.

62

Though if an eye that's downward cast
    Could make thee somewhat blench° or fail,   *flinch*
    Then be my love an idle tale,
And fading legend of the past;

5   And thou, as one that once declined,
    When he was little more than boy,
    On some unworthy heart with joy,
But lives to wed an equal mind;

And breathes a novel world, the while
10   His other passion wholly dies,
    Or in the light of deeper eyes
Is matter for a flying smile.

63

Yet pity for a horse o'er-driven,
    And love in which my hound has part,

Can hang no weight upon my heart
In its assumptions up to heaven;

5   And I am so much more than these,
    As thou, perchance, art more than I,
    And yet I spare them sympathy,
And I would set their pains at ease.

So mayst thou watch me where I weep,
10   As, unto vaster motions bound,
    The circuits of thine orbit round
A higher height, a deeper deep.

64

Dost thou look back on what hath been,
    As some divinely gifted man,
    Whose life in low estate began
And on a simple village green;

5   Who breaks his birth's invidious° bar,   *hated*
    And grasps the skirts of happy chance,
    And breasts the blows of circumstance,
And grapples with his evil star;

Who makes by force his merit known
10   And lives to clutch the golden keys,
    To mould a mighty state's decrees,
And shape the whisper of the throne;

And moving up from high to higher,
    Becomes on Fortune's crowning slope
15   The pillar of a people's hope,
The centre of a world's desire;

Yet feels, as in a pensive dream,
    When all his active powers are still,
    A distant dearness in the hill,
20   A secret sweetness in the stream,

The limit of his narrower fate,
    While yet beside its vocal springs
    He played at counsellors and kings,
With one that was his earliest mate;

25 Who ploughs with pain his native lea°   land
       And reaps the labour of his hands,
       Or in the furrow musing stands;
  "Does my old friend remember me?"

65

  Sweet soul, do with me as thou wilt;
       I lull a fancy trouble-tossed
       With "Love's too precious to be lost,
  A little grain shall not be spilt."

5 And in that solace can I sing,
       Till out of painful phases wrought
       There flutters up a happy thought,
  Self-balanced on a lightsome wing:

  Since we deserved the name of friends,
10   And thine effect so lives in me,
       A part of mine may live in thee
  And move thee on to noble ends.

66

  You thought my heart too far diseased;
       You wonder when my fancies play
       To find me gay among the gay,
  Like one with any trifle pleased.

5 The shade by which my life was crossed,
       Which makes a desert in the mind,
       Has made me kindly with my kind,
  And like to him whose sight is lost;

  Whose feet are guided through the land,
10   Whose jest among his friends is free,
       Who takes the children on his knee,
  And winds their curls about his hand:

  He plays with threads, he beats his chair
       For pastime, dreaming of the sky;
15   His inner day can never die,
  His night of loss is always there.

67

  When on my bed the moonlight falls,
       I know that in thy place of rest

  By that broad water of the west,[1]
  There comes a glory on the walls;

5 Thy marble bright in dark appears,
       As slowly steals a silver flame
       Along the letters of thy name,
  And o'er the number of thy years.

  The mystic glory swims away;
10   From off my bed the moonlight dies;
       And closing eaves of wearied eyes
  I sleep till dusk is dipped in gray:

  And then I know the mist is drawn
       A lucid veil from coast to coast,
15   And in the dark church like a ghost
  Thy tablet glimmers to the dawn.

68

  When in the down I sink my head,
       Sleep, Death's twin-brother, times my breath;
       Sleep, Death's twin-brother, knows not Death,
  Nor can I dream of thee as dead:

5 I walk as ere I walked forlorn,
       When all our path was fresh with dew,
       And all the bugle breezes blew
  Reveillée[2] to the breaking morn.

  But what is this? I turn about,
10   I find a trouble in thine eye,
       Which makes me sad I know not why,
  Nor can my dream resolve the doubt:

  But ere the lark hath left the lea
       I wake, and I discern the truth;
15   It is the trouble of my youth
  That foolish sleep transfers to thee.

69

  I dreamed there would be Spring no more,
       That Nature's ancient power was lost:

---

1 *broad ... west* I.e., the Severn Estuary.

2 *Reveillée* Music played to awaken soldiers in the morning.

The streets were black with smoke and frost,
They chattered trifles at the door:

5   I wandered from the noisy town,
        I found a wood with thorny boughs:
        I took the thorns to bind my brows,
    I wore them like a civic crown:[1]

    I met with scoffs, I met with scorns
10   From youth and babe and hoary° hairs: gray
        They called me in the public squares
    The fool that wears a crown of thorns:

    They called me fool, they called me child:
        I found an angel of the night;
15   The voice was low, the look was bright;
    He looked upon my crown and smiled:

    He reached the glory of a hand,
        That seemed to touch it into leaf:
        The voice was not the voice of grief,
20 The words were hard to understand.

70

    I cannot see the features right,
        When on the gloom I strive to paint
        The face I know; the hues are faint
    And mix with hollow masks of night;

5   Cloud-towers by ghostly masons wrought,
        A gulf that ever shuts and gapes,
        A hand that points, and pallèd° shapes   veiled
    In shadowy thoroughfares of thought;

    And crowds that stream from yawning doors,
10   And shoals of puckered faces drive;
        Dark bulks that tumble half alive,
    And lazy lengths on boundless shores;

    Till all at once beyond the will
        I hear a wizard music roll,
15   And through a lattice on the soul
    Looks thy fair face and makes it still.

---

[1]   *civic crown*   Highly prized garland of oak leaves and acorns, bestowed upon one who has saved the life of another in war.

71

    Sleep, kinsman thou to death and trance
        And madness, thou hast forged at last
        A night-long Present of the Past
    In which we went through summer France.[2]

5   Hadst thou such credit with the soul?
        Then bring an opiate trebly° strong,   *triply*
        Drug down the blindfold sense of wrong
    That so my pleasure may be whole;

    While now we talk as once we talked
10   Of men and minds, the dust of change,
        The days that grow to something strange,
    In walking as of old we walked

    Beside the river's wooded reach,
        The fortress, and the mountain ridge,
15   The cataract[3] flashing from the bridge,
    The breaker breaking on the beach.

72

    Risest thou thus, dim dawn, again,
        And howlest, issuing out of night,
        With blasts that blow the poplar white,[4]
    And lash with storm the streaming pane?

5   Day, when my crowned estate begun
        To pine in that reverse of doom,
        Which sickened every living bloom,
    And blurred the splendour of the sun;

    Who usherest in the dolorous hour
10   With thy quick tears that make the rose
        Pull sideways, and the daisy close
    Her crimson fringes to the shower;

    Who might'st have heaved a windless flame
        Up the deep East, or, whispering, played
15   A chequer-work of beam and shade
    Along the hills, yet looked the same,

---

[2]   *France*   Tennyson and Hallam vacationed together in France in 1830.

[3]   *cataract*   Waterfall.

[4]   *blow … white*   I.e., reveal the white underside of poplar leaves.

As wan,° as chill, as wild as now;   *pale*
    Day, marked as with some hideous crime,
    When the dark hand struck down through time,
20 And cancelled nature's best: but thou,

Lift as thou mayst thy burdened brows
    Through clouds that drench the morning star,[1]
    And whirl the ungarnered sheaf afar,
And sow the sky with flying boughs,

25 And up thy vault[2] with roaring sound
    Climb thy thick noon, disastrous day;
    Touch thy dull goal of joyless gray,
And hide thy shame beneath the ground.

73

So many worlds, so much to do,
    So little done, such things to be,
    How know I what had need of thee,
For thou wert strong as thou wert true?

5 The fame is quenched that I foresaw,
    The head hath missed an earthly wreath:
    I curse not nature, no, nor death;
For nothing is that errs from law.

We pass; the path that each man trod
10   Is dim, or will be dim, with weeds:
    What fame is left for human deeds
In endless age? It rests with God.

O hollow wraith of dying fame,
    Fade wholly, while the soul exults,
15   And self-infolds the large results
Of force that would have forged a name.

74

As sometimes in a dead man's face,
    To those that watch it more and more,
    A likeness, hardly seen before,
Comes out—to some one of his race:

---

[1] *morning star* The planet Venus.

[2] *up thy vault* Fill the sky.

So, dearest, now thy brows are cold,
    I see thee what thou art, and know
    Thy likeness to the wise below,
Thy kindred with the great of old.

But there is more than I can see,
10   And what I see I leave unsaid,
    Nor speak it, knowing Death has made
His darkness beautiful with thee.

75

I leave thy praises unexpressed
    In verse that brings myself relief,
    And by the measure of my grief
I leave thy greatness to be guessed;

5 What practice howsoe'er expert
    In fitting aptest words to things,
    Or voice the richest-toned that sings,
Hath power to give thee as thou wert?

I care not in these fading days
10   To raise a cry that lasts not long,
    And round thee with the breeze of song
To stir a little dust of praise.

Thy leaf has perished in the green,
    And, while we breathe beneath the sun,
15   The world which credits what is done
Is cold to all that might have been.

So here shall silence guard thy fame;
    But somewhere, out of human view,
    Whate'er thy hands are set to do
20 Is wrought with tumult of acclaim.

76

Take wings of fancy, and ascend,
    And in a moment set thy face
    Where all the starry heavens of space
Are sharpened to a needle's end;

5 Take wings of foresight; lighten through
    The secular abyss to come,

And lo, thy deepest lays are dumb
Before the mouldering of a yew;

And if the matin songs,[1] that woke
10   The darkness of our planet, last,
    Thine own shall wither in the vast,
Ere half the lifetime of an oak.

Ere these have clothed their branchy bowers
    With fifty Mays, thy songs are vain;
15   And what are they when these remain
The ruined shells of hollow towers?

77

What hope is here for modern rhyme
    To him, who turns a musing eye
    On songs, and deeds, and lives, that lie
Foreshortened in the tract of time?

5   These mortal lullabies of pain
    May bind a book, may line a box,
    May serve to curl a maiden's locks;[2]
Or when a thousand moons shall wane

A man upon a stall may find,
10   And, passing, turn the page that tells
    A grief, then changed to something else,
Sung by a long-forgotten mind.

But what of that? My darkened ways
    Shall ring with music all the same;
15   To breathe my loss is more than fame,
To utter love more sweet than praise.

78

Again at Christmas did we weave
    The holly round the Christmas hearth;
    The silent snow possessed the earth,
And calmly fell our Christmas-eve:

5   The yule-clog[3] sparkled keen with frost,
    No wing of wind the region swept,
    But over all things brooding slept
The quiet sense of something lost.

As in the winters left behind,
10   Again our ancient games had place,
    The mimic picture's breathing grace,
And dance and song and hoodman-blind.[4]

Who showed a token of distress?
    No single tear, no mark of pain:
15   O sorrow, then can sorrow wane?
O grief, can grief be changed to less?

O last regret, regret can die!
    No—mixed with all this mystic frame,
    Her deep relations are the same,
20   But with long use her tears are dry.

79

"More than my brothers are to me,"—
    Let this not vex thee, noble heart!
    I know thee of what force thou art
To hold the costliest love in fee.

5   But thou and I are one in kind,
    As moulded like in Nature's mint;
    And hill and wood and field did print
The same sweet forms in either mind.

For us the same cold streamlet curled
10   Through all his eddying coves; the same
    All winds that roam the twilight came
In whispers of the beauteous world.

At one dear knee we proffered vows,
    One lesson from one book we learned,
15   Ere childhood's flaxen ringlet turned
To black and brown on kindred brows.

And so my wealth resembles thine,
    But he was rich where I was poor,

---

[1]   *matin songs* Morning songs. Matins is the service that precedes
the first Mass of the day.

[2]   *curl … locks* I.e., serve as scrap paper to protect a young woman's
hair when it is being burned by hot tongs.

[3]   *yule-clog* Large log of wood burnt at Christmas.

[4]   *hoodman-blind* Blind-man's-bluff.

And he supplied my want the more
20 As his unlikeness fitted mine.

80

If any vague desire should rise,
    That holy Death ere Arthur died
    Had moved me kindly from his side,
And dropped the dust on tearless eyes;

5 Then fancy shapes, as fancy can,
    The grief my loss in him had wrought,
    A grief as deep as life or thought,
But stayed in peace with God and man.

I make a picture in the brain;
10   I hear the sentence that he speaks;
    He bears the burden of the weeks
But turns his burden into gain.

His credit thus shall set me free;
    And, influence-rich to soothe and save,
15   Unused example from the grave
Reach out dead hands to comfort me.

81

Could I have said while he was here,
    "My love shall now no further range;
    There cannot come a mellower change,
For now is love mature in ear."[1]

5 Love, then, had hope of richer store:
    What end is here to my complaint?
    This haunting whisper makes me faint,
"More years had made me love thee more."

But Death returns an answer sweet:
10   "My sudden frost was sudden gain,
    And gave all ripeness to the grain,
It might have drawn from after-heat."

82

I wage not any feud with Death
    For changes wrought on form and face;

No lower life that earth's embrace
May breed with him, can fright my faith.

5 Eternal process moving on,
    From state to state the spirit walks;
    And these are but the shattered stalks,
Or ruined chrysalis of one.

Nor blame I Death, because he bare
10   The use of virtue out of earth:
    I know transplanted human worth
Will bloom to profit, otherwhere.

For this alone on Death I wreak
    The wrath that garners in my heart;
15   He put our lives so far apart
We cannot hear each other speak.

83

Dip down upon the northern shore,
    O sweet new year delaying long;
    Thou doest expectant nature wrong;
Delaying long, delay no more.

5 What stays thee from the clouded noons,
    Thy sweetness from its proper place?
    Can trouble live with April days,
Or sadness in the summer moons?

Bring orchis,° bring the foxglove spire,   *orchid*
10   The little speedwell's darling blue,
    Deep tulips dashed with fiery dew,
Laburnums,[2] dropping-wells of fire.

O thou, new-year, delaying long,
    Delayest the sorrow in my blood,
15   That longs to burst a frozen bud
And flood a fresher throat with song.

84

When I contemplate all alone
    The life that had been thine below,

---

[1] *ear* I.e., of grain.

[2] *Laburnums* Trees with hanging bunches of bright yellow flowers.

And fix my thoughts on all the glow
To which thy crescent would have grown;

5   I see thee sitting crowned with good,
     A central warmth diffusing bliss
     In glance and smile, and clasp and kiss,
On all the branches of thy blood;

Thy blood, my friend, and partly mine;
10   For now the day was drawing on,
     When thou shouldst link thy life with one
Of mine own house, and boys of thine

Had babbled "Uncle" on my knee;
     But that remorseless iron hour
15   Made cypress[1] of her orange flower,
Despair of Hope, and earth of thee.

I seem to meet their least desire,
     To clap their cheeks, to call them mine.
     I see their unborn faces shine
20   Beside the never-lighted fire.

I see myself an honoured guest,
     Thy partner in the flowery walk
     Of letters, genial table-talk,
Or deep dispute, and graceful jest;

25   While now thy prosperous labour fills
     The lips of men with honest praise,
     And sun by sun the happy days
Descend below the golden hills

With promise of a morn as fair;
30   And all the train of bounteous hours
     Conduct by paths of growing powers,
To reverence and the silver hair;

Till slowly worn her earthly robe,
     Her lavish mission richly wrought,
35   Leaving great legacies of thought,
Thy spirit should fail from off the globe;

What time mine own might also flee,
     As linked with thine in love and fate,
     And, hovering o'er the dolorous strait
40   To the other shore, involved in thee,

Arrive at last the blessèd goal,
     And He that died in Holy Land[2]
     Would reach us out the shining hand,
And take us as a single soul.

45   What reed was that on which I leant?
     Ah, backward fancy, wherefore wake
     The old bitterness again, and break
The low beginnings of content.

85

This truth came borne with bier[3] and pall,[4]
     I felt it, when I sorrowed most,
     'Tis better to have loved and lost,
Than never to have loved at all—

5   O true in word, and tried in deed,
     Demanding, so to bring relief
     To this which is our common grief,
What kind of life is that I lead;

And whether trust in things above
10   Be dimmed of sorrow, or sustained;
     And whether love for him have drained
My capabilities of love;

Your words have virtue such as draws
     A faithful answer from the breast,
15   Through light reproaches, half expressed,
And loyal unto kindly laws.

My blood an even tenor kept,
     Till on mine ear this message falls,
     That in Vienna's fatal wall
20   God's finger touched him, and he slept.

---

1   *cypress* Tree symbolic of mourning.

2   *He … Land* I.e., Christ.

3   *bier* Moveable stand on which a corpse is carried to the grave.

4   *pall* Cloth that covers a corpse or a coffin.

The great Intelligences° fair   *angels*
    That range above our mortal state,
    In circle round the blessèd gate,
Received and gave him welcome there;

25 And led him through the blissful climes,
    And showed him in the fountain fresh
    All knowledge that the sons of flesh
Shall gather in the cycled times.

But I remained, whose hopes were dim,
30   Whose life, whose thoughts were little worth,
    To wander on a darkened earth,
Where all things round me breathed of him.

O friendship, equal-poised control,
    O heart, with kindliest motion warm,
35   O sacred essence, other form,
O solemn ghost, O crownèd soul!

Yet none could better know than I,
    How much of act at human hands
    The sense of human will demands
40 By which we dare to live or die.

Whatever way my days decline,
    I felt and feel, though left alone,
    His being working in mine own,
The footsteps of his life in mine;

45 A life that all the Muses decked
    With gifts of grace, that might express
    All-comprehensive tenderness,
All-subtilising° intellect: *elevating*

And so my passion hath not swerved
50   To works of weakness, but I find
    An image comforting the mind,
And in my grief a strength reserved.

Likewise the imaginative woe,
    That loved to handle spiritual strife,
55   Diffused the shock through all my life,
But in the present broke the blow.

My pulses therefore beat again
    For other friends that once I met;
    Nor can it suit me to forget
60 The mighty hopes that make us men.

I woo your love: I count it crime
    To mourn for any overmuch;
    I, the divided half of such
A friendship as had mastered Time;

65 Which masters Time indeed, and is
    Eternal, separate from fears:
    The all-assuming months and years
Can take no part away from this:

But Summer on the steaming floods,
70   And Spring that swells the narrow brooks,
    And Autumn, with a noise of rooks,
That gather in the waning woods,

And every pulse of wind and wave
    Recalls, in change of light or gloom,
75   My old affection of the tomb,
And my prime passion in the grave:

My old affection of the tomb,
    A part of stillness, yearns to speak:
    "Arise, and get thee forth and seek
80 A friendship for the years to come.

"I watch thee from the quiet shore;
    Thy spirit up to mine can reach;
    But in dear words of human speech
We two communicate no more."

85 And I, "Can clouds of nature stain
    The starry clearness of the free?
    How is it? Canst thou feel for me
Some painless sympathy with pain?"

And lightly does the whisper fall;
90   "'Tis hard for thee to fathom this;
    I triumph in conclusive bliss,
And that serene result of all."

So hold I commerce° with the dead;   conversation
95   Or so methinks the dead would say;
   Or so shall grief with symbols play
And pining life be fancy-fed.

Now looking to some settled end,
   That these things pass, and I shall prove
   A meeting somewhere, love with love,
100 I crave your pardon, O my friend;

If not so fresh, with love as true,
   I, clasping brother-hands, aver
   I could not, if I would, transfer
The whole I felt for him to you.

105 For which be they that hold apart
   The promise of the golden hours?
   First love, first friendship, equal powers,
That marry with the virgin heart.

Still mine, that cannot but deplore,
110   That beats within a lonely place,
   That yet remembers his embrace,
But at his footstep leaps no more,

My heart, though widowed, may not rest
   Quite in the love of what is gone,
115   But seeks to beat in time with one
That warms another living breast.

Ah, take the imperfect gift I bring,
   Knowing the primrose yet is dear,
   The primrose of the later year,
120 As not unlike to that of Spring.

86
Sweet after showers, ambrosial air,
   That rollest from the gorgeous gloom
   Of evening over brake° and bloom   fern
And meadow, slowly breathing bare

5 The round of space, and rapt below
   Through all the dewy-tasselled wood,
   And shadowing down the hornèd flood
In ripples, fan my brows and blow

The fever from my cheek, and sigh
10   The full new life that feeds thy breath
   Throughout my frame, till Doubt and Death,
Ill brethren, let the fancy fly

From belt to belt of crimson seas
   On leagues of odour streaming far,
15   To where in yonder orient star
A hundred spirits whisper "Peace."

87
I passed beside the reverend walls[1]
   In which of old I wore the gown;
   I roved at random through the town,
And saw the tumult of the halls;

5 And heard once more in college fanes°   chapels
   The storm their high-built organs make,
   And thunder-music, rolling, shake
The prophet blazoned on the panes;

And caught once more the distant shout,
10   The measured pulse of racing oars
   Among the willows; paced the shores
And many a bridge, and all about

The same gray flats again, and felt
   The same, but not the same; and last
15   Up that long walk of limes I passed
To see the rooms in which he dwelt.

Another name was on the door:
   I lingered; all within was noise
   Of songs, and clapping hands, and boys
20 That crashed the glass and beat the floor;

Where once we held debate, a band
   Of youthful friends, on mind and art,
   And labour, and the changing mart,°   market
And all the framework of the land;

25 When one would aim an arrow fair,
   But send it slackly from the string;

---

[1] *reverend walls* Trinity College, Cambridge, where Tennyson and
Hallam had been students, and where they first met.

And one would pierce an outer ring,
And one an inner, here and there;

And last the master-bowman, he,
30   Would cleave the mark. A willing ear
      We lent him. Who but hung to hear
The rapt oration flowing free

From point to point, with power and grace
      And music in the bounds of law,
35   To those conclusions when we saw
The God within him light his face,

And seem to lift the form, and glow
      In azure orbits heavenly-wise;
      And over those ethereal eyes
40 The bar[1] of Michael Angelo.

88

Wild bird, whose warble, liquid sweet,
      Rings Eden through the budded quicks,°   *hedgerows*
      O tell me where the senses mix,
      O tell me where the passions meet,

5 Whence radiate: fierce extremes employ
      Thy spirits in the darkening leaf,
      And in the midmost heart of grief
Thy passion clasps a secret joy:

And I—my harp would prelude woe—
10   I cannot all command the strings;
      The glory of the sum of things
Will flash along the chords and go.

89

Witch-elms that counterchange° the floor   *checker*
      Of this flat lawn with dusk and bright;
      And thou, with all thy breadth and height
Of foliage, towering sycamore;

5 How often, hither wandering down,
      My Arthur found your shadows fair,

And shook to all the liberal air
The dust and din and steam of town:

He brought an eye for all he saw;
10   He mixed in all our simple sports;
      They pleased him, fresh from brawling courts
And dusty purlieus[2] of the law.

O joy to him in this retreat,
      Immantled in ambrosial dark,
15   To drink the cooler air, and mark
The landscape winking through the heat:

O sound to rout the brood of cares,
      The sweep of scythe in morning dew,
      The gust that round the garden flew,
20 And tumbled half the mellowing pears!

O bliss, when all in circle drawn
      About him, heart and ear were fed
      To hear him, as he lay and read
The Tuscan poets[3] on the lawn:

25 Or in the all-golden afternoon
      A guest, or happy sister, sung,
      Or here she brought the harp and flung
A ballad to the brightening moon:

Nor less it pleased in livelier moods,
30   Beyond the bounding hill to stray,
      And break the livelong summer day
With banquet in the distant woods;

Whereat we glanced from theme to theme,
      Discussed the books to love or hate,
35   Or touched the changes of the state,
Or threaded some Socratic[4] dream;

---

[1] *bar* Forehead ridge. According to Tennyson's *Memoir* (1.38), Hallam once told Tennyson "Alfred, look over my eyes; surely I have the bar of Michael Angelo."

[2] *purlieus* Physical bounds, limits.

[3] *Tuscan poets* Renaissance poets Dante and Petrarch.

[4] *Socratic* Relating to the Greek philosopher Socrates and/or his mode of philosophical inquiry through dialogue. Originally Tennyson wrote "Platonic"; he may have changed the word because "Platonic" was sometimes employed as a euphemism for "homosexual."

But if I praised the busy town,
    He loved to rail against it still,
    For "ground in yonder social mill
40 We rub each other's angles down,

"And merge," he said, "in form and gloss
    The picturesque of man and man."
    We talked: the stream beneath us ran,
The wine-flask lying couched in moss,

45 Or cooled within the glooming wave;
    And last, returning from afar,
    Before the crimson-circled star
Had fallen into her father's grave,

And brushing ankle-deep in flowers,
50   We heard behind the woodbine veil
    The milk that bubbled in the pail,
And buzzings of the honeyed hours.

90

He tasted love with half his mind,
    Nor ever drank the inviolate spring
    Where nighest heaven, who first could fling
This bitter seed among mankind;

5 That could the dead, whose dying eyes
    Were closed with wail, resume their life,
    They would but find in child and wife
An iron welcome when they rise:

'Twas well, indeed, when warm with wine,
10   To pledge them with a kindly tear,
    To talk them o'er, to wish them here,
To count their memories half divine;

But if they came who passed away,
    Behold their brides in other hands;
15   The hard heir strides about their lands,
And will not yield them for a day.

Yea, though their sons were none of these,
    Not less the yet-loved sire would make
    Confusion worse than death, and shake
20 The pillars of domestic peace.

Ah dear, but come thou back to me:
    Whatever change the years have wrought,
    I find not yet one lonely thought
That cries against my wish for thee.

91

When rosy plumelets tuft the larch,
    And rarely pipes the mounted thrush;
    Or underneath the barren bush
Flits by the sea-blue bird[1] of March;

5 Come, wear the form by which I know
    Thy spirit in time among thy peers;
    The hope of unaccomplished years
Be large and lucid round thy brow.

When summer's hourly-mellowing change
10   May breathe, with many roses sweet,
    Upon the thousand waves of wheat,
That ripple round the lonely grange;

Come: not in watches of the night,
    But where the sunbeam broodeth warm,
15   Come, beauteous in thine after form,
And like a finer light in light.

92

If any vision should reveal
    Thy likeness, I might count it vain
    As but the canker of the brain;
Yea, though it spake and made appeal

5 To chances where our lots were cast
    Together in the days behind,
    I might but say, I hear a wind
Of memory murmuring the past.

Yea, though it spake and bared to view
10   A fact within the coming year;
    And though the months, revolving near,
Should prove the phantom-warning true,

They might not seem thy prophecies,
    But spiritual presentiments,

---

[1] *sea-blue bird* Kingfisher.

15 And such refraction of events
     As often rises ere they rise.

93

I shall not see thee. Dare I say
     No spirit ever brake the band
     That stays him from the native land
Where first he walked when clasped in clay?

5 No visual shade of some one lost,
     But he, the Spirit himself, may come
     Where all the nerve of sense is numb;
Spirit to Spirit, Ghost to Ghost.

O, therefore from thy sightless range
10   With gods in unconjectured bliss,
     O, from the distance of the abyss
Of tenfold-complicated change,

Descend, and touch, and enter; hear
     The wish too strong for words to name;
15   That in this blindness of the frame
My Ghost may feel that thine is near.

94

How pure at heart and sound in head,
     With what divine affections bold
     Should be the man whose thought would hold
An hour's communion with the dead.

5 In vain shalt thou, or any, call
     The spirits from their golden day,
     Except, like them, thou too canst say,
My spirit is at peace with all.

They haunt the silence of the breast,
10   Imaginations calm and fair,
     The memory like a cloudless air,
The conscience as a sea at rest:

But when the heart is full of din,
     And doubt beside the portal waits,
15   They can but listen at the gates,
And hear the household jar° within.   *sound*

95

By night we lingered on the lawn,
     For underfoot the herb was dry;
     And genial warmth; and o'er the sky
The silvery haze of summer drawn;

5 And calm that let the tapers burn
     Unwavering: not a cricket chirred:
     The brook alone far-off was heard,
And on the board the fluttering urn:

And bats went round in fragrant skies,
10   And wheeled or lit the filmy shapes
     That haunt the dusk, with ermine capes
And woolly breasts and beaded eyes;

While now we sang old songs that pealed
     From knoll to knoll, where, couched at ease,
15   The white kine° glimmered, and the trees   *cattle*
Laid their dark arms about the field.

But when those others, one by one,
     Withdrew themselves from me and night,
     And in the house light after light
20 Went out, and I was all alone,

A hunger seized my heart; I read
     Of that glad year which once had been,
     In those fallen leaves which kept their green,
The noble letters of the dead:

25 And strangely on the silence broke
     The silent-speaking words, and strange
     Was love's dumb cry defying change
To test his worth; and strangely spoke

The faith, the vigour, bold to dwell
30   On doubts that drive the coward back,
     And keen through wordy snares to track
Suggestion to her inmost cell.

So word by word, and line by line,
     The dead man touched me from the past,
35   And all at once it seemed at last
The living soul was flashed on mine,

And mine in this was wound, and whirled
   About empyreal° heights of thought,   *heavenly*
   And came on that which is, and caught
40 The deep pulsations of the world,

Æonian music measuring out
   The steps of Time—the shocks of Chance—
   The blows of Death. At length my trance
Was cancelled, stricken through with doubt.

45 Vague words! but ah, how hard to frame
   In matter-moulded forms of speech,
   Or even for intellect to reach
Through memory that which I became:

Till now the doubtful dusk revealed
50   The knolls once more where, couched at ease,
   The white kine glimmered, and the trees
Laid their dark arms about the field:

And sucked from out the distant gloom
   A breeze began to tremble o'er
55   The large leaves of the sycamore,
And fluctuate all the still perfume,

And gathering freshlier overhead,
   Rocked the full-foliaged elms, and swung
   The heavy-folded rose, and flung
60 The lilies to and fro, and said

"The dawn, the dawn," and died away;
   And East and West, without a breath,
   Mixed their dim lights, like life and death,
To broaden into boundless day.

96

You say, but with no touch of scorn,
   Sweet-hearted, you, whose light-blue eyes
   Are tender over drowning flies,
You tell me, doubt is Devil-born.

5 I know not: one indeed I knew
   In many a subtle question versed,
   Who touched a jarring lyre at first,
But ever strove to make it true:

Perplexed in faith, but pure in deeds,
   At last he beat his music out.
10   There lives more faith in honest doubt,
Believe me, than in half the creeds.

He fought his doubts and gathered strength,
   He would not make his judgment blind,
15   He faced the spectres of the mind
And laid them: thus he came at length

To find a stronger faith his own;
   And Power was with him in the night,
   Which makes the darkness and the light,
20 And dwells not in the light alone,

But in the darkness and the cloud,
   As over Sinai's peaks of old,
   While Israel made their gods of gold,
Although the trumpet blew so loud.[1]

97

My love has talked with rocks and trees;
   He finds on misty mountain-ground
   His own vast shadow glory-crowned;
He sees himself in all he sees.

5 Two partners of a married life—
   I looked on these and thought of thee
   In vastness and in mystery,
And of my spirit as of a wife.

These two—they dwelt with eye on eye,
10   Their hearts of old have beat in tune,
   Their meetings made December June,
Their every parting was to die.

Their love has never passed away;
   The days she never can forget
15   Are earnest that he loves her yet,
Whate'er the faithless people say.

Her life is lone, he sits apart,
   He loves her yet, she will not weep,

---

1 *Sinai's … loud*   See Exodus 19.16–19, Exodus 32.1–5.

Though rapt in matters dark and deep
20   He seems to slight her simple heart.

He thrids° the labyrinth of the mind,   *threads*
        He reads the secret of the star,
        He seems so near and yet so far,
He looks so cold: she thinks him kind.

25 She keeps the gift of years before,
        A withered violet is her bliss:
        She knows not what his greatness is,
For that, for all, she loves him more.

For him she plays, to him she sings
30   Of early faith and plighted vows;
        She knows but matters of the house,
And he, he knows a thousand things.

Her faith is fixed and cannot move,
        She darkly feels him great and wise,
35   She dwells on him with faithful eyes,
"I cannot understand: I love."

98

You leave us: you will see the Rhine,
        And those fair hills I sailed below,
        When I was there with him; and go
By summer belts of wheat and vine

5   To where he breathed his latest breath,
        That City. All her splendour seems
        No livelier than the wisp that gleams
On Lethe in the eyes of Death.

Let her great Danube rolling fair
10   Enwind her isles, unmarked of me:
        I have not seen, I will not see
Vienna; rather dream that there,

A treble darkness, Evil haunts
        The birth, the bridal; friend from friend
15   Is oftener parted, fathers bend
Above more graves, a thousand wants

Gnarr° at the heels of men, and prey   *snarl*
        By each cold hearth, and sadness flings
        Her shadow on the blaze of kings:
20 And yet myself have heard him say,

That not in any mother town
        With statelier progress to and fro
        The double tides of chariots flow
By park and suburb under brown

25 Of lustier leaves; nor more content,
        He told me, lives in any crowd,
        When all is gay with lamps, and loud
With sport and song, in booth and tent,

Imperial halls, or open plain;
30   And wheels the circled dance, and breaks
        The rocket molten into flakes
Of crimson or in emerald rain.

99

Risest thou thus, dim dawn, again,
        So loud with voices of the birds,
        So thick with lowings of the herds,
Day, when I lost the flower of men;

5   Who tremblest through thy darkling red
        On yon swollen brook that bubbles fast
        By meadows breathing of the past,
And woodlands holy to the dead;

Who murmurest in the foliaged eaves
10   A song that slights the coming care,
        And Autumn laying here and there
A fiery finger on the leaves;

Who wakenest with thy balmy breath
        To myriads on the genial earth,
15   Memories of bridal, or of birth,
And unto myriads more, of death.

O wheresoever those may be,
        Betwixt the slumber of the poles,
        Today they count as kindred souls;
20 They know me not, but mourn with me.

100

I climb the hill: from end to end
   Of all the landscape underneath,
   I find no place that does not breathe
Some gracious memory of my friend;

5 No gray old grange, or lonely fold,
   Or low morass and whispering reed,
   Or simple stile from mead to mead,
Or sheepwalk up the windy wold;

Nor hoary knoll of ash and haw°   *hawthorn*
10 That hears the latest linnet trill,
   Nor quarry trenched along the hill
And haunted by the wrangling daw;°   *jackdaw*

Nor runlet tinkling from the rock;
   Nor pastoral rivulet that swerves
15 To left and right through meadowy curves,
That feed the mothers of the flock;

But each has pleased a kindred eye,
   And each reflects a kindlier day;
   And, leaving these, to pass away,
20 I think once more he seems to die.

101

Unwatched, the garden bough shall sway,
   The tender blossom flutter down,
   Unloved, that beech will gather brown,
This maple burn itself away;

5 Unloved, the sun-flower, shining fair,
   Ray round with flames her disk of seed,
   And many a rose-carnation feed
With summer spice the humming air;

Unloved, by many a sandy bar,
10 The brook shall babble down the plain,
   At noon or when the lesser wain[1]
Is twisting round the polar star;

---

[1] *lesser wain* Constellation of Ursa Minor. Ursa Major and Ursa
Minor (Latin: Great Bear and Little Bear) each contain seven stars.
These are known as Charles's Wain and Lesser Wain. A wain is a
wagon, with poles used for hitching a horse; the word "pole," or
"plow" gives rise to the common names for the stars, "Great Plough"
and "Little Plough."

Uncared for, gird the windy grove,
   And flood the haunts of hern° and crake;°   *heron / crow*
15 Or into silver arrows break
The sailing moon in creek and cove;

Till from the garden and the wild
   A fresh association blow,
   And year by year the landscape grow
20 Familiar to the stranger's child;

As year by year the labourer tills
   His wonted glebe,[2] or lops the glades;
   And year by year our memory fades
From all the circle of the hills.

102

We leave the well-belovèd place
   Where first we gazed upon the sky;
   The roofs, that heard our earliest cry,
Will shelter one of stranger race.

5 We go, but ere we go from home,
   As down the garden-walks I move,
   Two spirits of a diverse love
Contend for loving masterdom.

One whispers, "Here thy boyhood sung
10 Long since its matin song, and heard
   The low love-language of the bird
In native hazels tassel-hung."

The other answers, "Yea, but here
   Thy feet have strayed in after hours
15 With thy lost friend among the bowers,
And this hath made them trebly dear."

These two have striven half the day,
   And each prefers his separate claim,
   Poor rivals in a losing game,
20 That will not yield each other way.

I turn to go: my feet are set
   To leave the pleasant fields and farms;
   They mix in one another's arms
To one pure image of regret.

---

[2] *wonted glebe* Customary field.

103

On that last night before we went
  From out the doors where I was bred,
  I dreamed a vision of the dead,
Which left my after-morn content.

5 Methought I dwelt within a hall,
  And maidens[1] with me: distant hills
  From hidden summits fed with rills
A river sliding by the wall.

The hall with harp and carol rang.
10 They sang of what is wise and good
  And graceful. In the centre stood
A statue veiled, to which they sang;

And which, though veiled, was known to me,
  The shape of him I loved, and love
15 Forever: then flew in a dove
And brought a summons from the sea:

And when they learnt that I must go
  They wept and wailed, but led the way
  To where a little shallop° lay   *dinghy*
20 At anchor in the flood below;

And on by many a level mead,
  And shadowing bluff that made the banks,
  We glided winding under ranks
Of iris, and the golden reed;

25 And still as vaster grew the shore
  And rolled the floods in grander space,
  The maidens gathered strength and grace
And presence, lordlier than before;

And I myself, who sat apart
30 And watched them, waxed in every limb;
  I felt the thews of Anakim,[2]
The pulses of a Titan's heart;

---

[1] [Tennyson's note] They are the Muses, poetry, arts—all that made life beautiful here, which we hope will pass with us beyond the grave.

[2] *Anakim* Race of giants mentioned in the Biblical books of Deuteronomy and Joshua.

As one would sing the death of war,
  And one would chant the history
35 Of that great race, which is to be,
And one the shaping of a star;

Until the forward-creeping tides
  Began to foam, and we to draw
  From deep to deep, to where we saw
40 A great ship lift her shining sides.

The man we loved was there on deck,
  But thrice as large as man he bent
  To greet us. Up the side I went,
And fell in silence on his neck:

45 Whereat those maidens with one mind
  Bewailed their lot; I did them wrong:
  "We served thee here," they said, "so long,
And wilt thou leave us now behind?"

So rapt I was, they could not win
50 An answer from my lips, but he
  Replying, "Enter likewise ye
And go with us:" they entered in.

And while the wind began to sweep
  A music out of sheet and shroud,
55 We steered her toward a crimson cloud
That landlike slept along the deep.

104

The time draws near the birth of Christ;
  The moon is hid, the night is still;
  A single church below the hill
Is pealing, folded in the mist.

5 A single peal of bells below,
  That wakens at this hour of rest
  A single murmur in the breast,
That these are not the bells I know.

Like strangers' voices here they sound,
10 In lands where not a memory strays,
  Nor landmark breathes of other days,
But all is new unhallowed ground.

105

Tonight ungathered let us leave
    This laurel, let this holly stand:
    We live within the stranger's land,
And strangely falls our Christmas-eve.

5 Our father's dust is left alone
    And silent under other snows:
    There in due time the woodbine blows,
The violet comes, but we are gone.

No more shall wayward grief abuse
10   The genial hour with mask and mime;
    For change of place, like growth of time,
Has broke the bond of dying use.

Let cares that petty shadows cast,
    By which our lives are chiefly proved,
15   A little spare the night I loved,
And hold it solemn to the past.

But let no footstep beat the floor,
    Nor bowl of wassail mantle warm;
    For who would keep an ancient form
20 Through which the spirit breathes no more?

Be neither song, nor game, nor feast;
    Nor harp be touched, nor flute be blown;
    No dance, no motion, save alone
What lightens in the lucid east

25 Of rising worlds by yonder wood.
    Long sleeps the summer in the seed;
    Run out your measured arcs, and lead
The closing cycle rich in good.

106

Ring out, wild bells, to the wild sky,
    The flying cloud, the frosty light:
    The year is dying in the night;
Ring out, wild bells, and let him die.

5 Ring out the old, ring in the new,
    Ring, happy bells, across the snow:

The year is going, let him go;
Ring out the false, ring in the true.

Ring out the grief that saps the mind,
10   For those that here we see no more;
    Ring out the feud of rich and poor,
Ring in redress to all mankind.

Ring out a slowly dying cause,
    And ancient forms of party strife;
15   Ring in the nobler modes of life,
With sweeter manners, purer laws.

Ring out the want, the care, the sin,
    The faithless coldness of the times;
    Ring out, ring out my mournful rhymes,
20 But ring the fuller minstrel in.

Ring out false pride in place and blood,
    The civic slander and the spite;
    Ring in the love of truth and right,
Ring in the common love of good.

25 Ring out old shapes of foul disease;
    Ring out the narrowing lust of gold;
    Ring out the thousand wars of old,
Ring in the thousand years of peace.

Ring in the valiant man and free,
30   The larger heart, the kindlier hand;
    Ring out the darkness of the land,
Ring in the Christ that is to be.

107

It is the day when he was born,
    A bitter day that early sank
    Behind a purple-frosty bank
Of vapour, leaving night forlorn.

5 The time admits not flowers or leaves
    To deck the banquet. Fiercely flies
    The blast of North and East, and ice
Makes daggers at the sharpened eaves,

And bristles all the brakes and thorns
10 To yon hard crescent, as she hangs
  Above the wood which grides° and clangs *scrapes*
Its leafless ribs and iron horns

Together, in the drifts that pass
 To darken on the rolling brine
15 That breaks the coast. But fetch the wine,
Arrange the board and brim the glass;

Bring in great logs and let them lie,
 To make a solid core of heat;
  Be cheerful-minded, talk and treat
20 Of all things even as he were by;

We keep the day. With festal cheer,
 With books and music, surely we
  Will drink to him, whate'er he be,
And sing the songs he loved to hear.

108

I will not shut me from my kind,
 And, lest I stiffen into stone,
  I will not eat my heart alone,
Nor feed with sighs a passing wind:

5 What profit lies in barren faith,
 And vacant yearning, though with might
  To scale the heaven's highest height,
Or dive below the wells of Death?

What find I in the highest place,
10 But mine own phantom chanting hymns?
  And on the depths of death there swims
The reflex of a human face.

I'll rather take what fruit may be
 Of sorrow under human skies:
15 'Tis held that sorrow makes us wise,
Whatever wisdom sleep with thee.

109

Heart-affluence in discursive talk
 From household fountains never dry;

 The critic clearness of an eye,
That saw through all the Muses' walk;

5 Seraphic intellect and force
 To seize and throw the doubts of man;
  Impassioned logic, which outran
The hearer in its fiery course;

High nature amorous of the good,
10 But touched with no ascetic gloom;
  And passion pure in snowy bloom
Through all the years of April blood;

A love of freedom rarely felt,
 Of freedom in her regal seat
15 Of England; not the schoolboy heat,
The blind hysterics of the Celt;

And manhood fused with female grace
 In such a sort, the child would twine
  A trustful hand, unasked, in thine,
20 And find his comfort in thy face;

All these have been, and thee mine eyes
 Have looked on: if they looked in vain,
  My shame is greater who remain,
Nor let thy wisdom make me wise.

110

Thy converse drew us with delight,
 The men of rathe° and riper years: *counsel*
  The feeble soul, a haunt of fears,
Forgot his weakness in thy sight.

5 On thee the loyal-hearted hung,
 The proud was half disarmed of pride,
  Nor cared the serpent at thy side
To flicker with his double tongue.

The stern were mild when thou wert by,
10 The flippant put himself to school
  And heard thee, and the brazen fool
Was softened, and he knew not why;

While I, thy nearest, sat apart,
    And felt thy triumph was as mine;
15 And loved them more, that they were thine,
The graceful tact, the Christian art;

Nor mine the sweetness or the skill,
    But mine the love that will not tire,
    And, born of love, the vague desire
20 That spurs an imitative will.

III

The churl in spirit, up or down
    Along the scale of ranks, through all,
    To him who grasps a golden ball,[1]
By blood a king, at heart a clown;

5   The churl in spirit, howe'er he veil
    His want in forms for fashion's sake,
    Will let his coltish nature break
At seasons through the gilded pale:

For who can always act? but he,
10   To whom a thousand memories call,
    Not being less but more than all
The gentleness he seemed to be,

Best seemed the thing he was, and joined
    Each office of the social hour
15   To noble manners, as the flower
And native growth of noble mind;

Nor ever narrowness or spite,
    Or villain fancy fleeting by,
    Drew in the expression of an eye,
20 Where God and Nature met in light;

And thus he bore without abuse
    The grand old name of gentleman,
    Defamed by every charlatan,
And soiled with all ignoble use.

112

High wisdom holds my wisdom less,
    That I, who gaze with temperate eyes

On glorious insufficiencies,
Set light by narrower perfectness.

5   But thou, that fillest all the room
    Of all my love, art reason why
    I seem to cast a careless eye
On souls, the lesser lords of doom.

For what wert thou? some novel power
10   Sprang up forever at a touch,
    And hope could never hope too much,
In watching thee from hour to hour,

Large elements in order brought,
    And tracts of calm from tempest made,
15   And world-wide fluctuation swayed
In vassal tides that followed thought.

113

'Tis held that sorrow makes us wise;
    Yet how much wisdom sleeps with thee
    Which not alone had guided me,
But served the seasons that may rise;

5   For can I doubt, who knew thee keen
    In intellect, with force and skill
    To strive, to fashion, to fulfil—
I doubt not what thou wouldst have been:

A life in civic action warm,
10   A soul on highest mission sent,
    A potent voice of Parliament,
A pillar steadfast in the storm,

Should licensed boldness gather force,
    Becoming, when the time has birth,
15   A lever to uplift the earth
And roll it in another course,

With thousand shocks that come and go,
    With agonies, with energies,
    With overthrowings, and with cries,
20 And undulations to and fro.

---

[1] *golden ball* I.e., the orb of the monarch.

114

Who loves not Knowledge? Who shall rail
   Against her beauty? May she mix
   With men and prosper! Who shall fix
Her pillars? Let her work prevail.

5 But on her forehead sits a fire:
   She sets her forward countenance
   And leaps into the future chance,
Submitting all things to desire.

Half-grown as yet, a child, and vain—
10   She cannot fight the fear of death.
   What is she, cut from love and faith,
But some wild Pallas[1] from the brain

Of Demons? fiery-hot to burst
   All barriers in her onward race
15   For power. Let her know her place;
She is the second, not the first.

A higher hand must make her mild,
   If all be not in vain; and guide
   Her footsteps, moving side by side
20 With wisdom, like the younger child:

For she is earthly of the mind,
   But Wisdom heavenly of the soul.
   O, friend, who camest to thy goal
So early, leaving me behind,

25 I would the great world grew like thee,
   Who grewest not alone in power
   And knowledge, but by year and hour
In reverence and in charity.

115

Now fades the last long streak of snow,
   Now burgeons every maze of quick°   *vegetation*
   About the flowering squares, and thick
By ashen roots the violets blow.

---

[1] *Pallas* Pallas Athena, Greek goddess of wisdom, who was said to
have leapt out from the forehead of Zeus, rather than having been
born in the usual manner.

5 Now rings the woodland loud and long,
   The distance takes a lovelier hue,
   And drowned in yonder living blue
The lark becomes a sightless song.

Now dance the lights on lawn and lea,
10   The flocks are whiter down the vale,
   And milkier every milky sail
On winding stream or distant sea;

Where now the seamew° pipes, or dives   *seagull*
   In yonder greening gleam, and fly
15   The happy birds, that change their sky
To build and brood; that live their lives

From land to land; and in my breast
   Spring wakens too; and my regret
   Becomes an April violet,
20 And buds and blossoms like the rest.

116

Is it, then, regret for buried time
   That keenlier in sweet April wakes,
   And meets the year, and gives and takes
The colours of the crescent prime?

5 Not all: the songs, the stirring air,
   The life re-orient out of dust,
   Cry through the sense to hearten trust
In that which made the world so fair.

Not all regret: the face will shine
10   Upon me, while I muse alone;
   And that dear voice, I once have known,
Still speak to me of me and mine:

Yet less of sorrow lives in me
   For days of happy commune dead;
15   Less yearning for the friendship fled,
Than some strong bond which is to be.

117

O days and hours, your work is this
   To hold me from my proper place,

A little while from his embrace,
For fuller gain of after bliss:

5   That out of distance might ensue
Desire of nearness doubly sweet;
And unto meeting when we meet,
Delight a hundredfold accrue,

For every grain of sand that runs,
10   And every span of shade[1] that steals,
And every kiss of toothèd wheels,[2]
And all the courses of the suns.

118

Contemplate all this work of Time,
The giant labouring in his youth;
Nor dream of human love and truth,
As dying Nature's earth and lime;

5   But trust that those we call the dead
Are breathers of an ampler day
For ever nobler ends. They say,
The solid earth whereon we tread

In tracts of fluent heat began,
10   And grew to seeming-random forms,
The seeming prey of cyclic storms,
Till at the last arose the man;

Who throve and branched from clime to clime,
The herald of a higher race,
15   And of himself in higher place,
If so he type this work of time

Within himself, from more to more;
Or, crowned with attributes of woe
Like glories, move his course, and show
20   That life is not as idle ore,

But iron dug from central gloom,
And heated hot with burning fears,
And dipped in baths of hissing tears,
And battered with the shocks of doom

25   To shape and use. Arise and fly
The reeling Faun, the sensual feast;
Move upward, working out the beast,
And let the ape and tiger die.

119

Doors, where my heart was used to beat
So quickly, not as one that weeps
I come once more; the city sleeps;
I smell the meadow in the street;

5   I hear a chirp of birds; I see
Betwixt the black fronts long-withdrawn
A light-blue lane of early dawn,
And think of early days and thee,

And bless thee, for thy lips are bland,
10   And bright the friendship of thine eye;
And in my thoughts with scarce a sigh
I take the pressure of thine hand.

120

I trust I have not wasted breath:
I think we are not wholly brain,
Magnetic mockeries; not in vain,
Like Paul with beasts,[3] I fought with Death;

5   Not only cunning casts in clay:
Let Science prove we are, and then
What matters Science unto men,
At least to me? I would not stay.

Let him, the wiser man who springs
10   Hereafter, up from childhood shape
His action like the greater ape,
But I was *born* to other things.

121

Sad Hesper[4] o'er the buried sun
And ready, thou, to die with him,

---

1   [Tennyson's note]   The sun-dial.

2   *toothèd wheels*   Gears of a clock.

3   *Paul … beasts*   See 1 Corinthians 15.32: "If I fought wild beasts in Ephesus for merely human reasons, what have I gained? If the dead are not raised, 'Let us eat and drink, for tomorrow we die.'"

4   *Hesper*   Hesperus, the evening star.

Thou watchest all things ever dim
And dimmer, and a glory done:

5 The team[1] is loosened from the wain,
The boat is drawn upon the shore;
Thou listenest to the closing door,
And life is darkened in the brain.

Bright Phosphor, fresher for the night,
10 By thee the world's great work is heard
Beginning, and the wakeful bird;
Behind thee comes the greater light:

The market boat is on the stream,
And voices hail it from the brink;
15 Thou hear'st the village hammer clink,
And see'st the moving of the team.

Sweet Hesper-Phosphor, double name
For what is one, the first, the last,
Thou, like my present and my past,
20 Thy place is changed; thou art the same.

122

Oh, wast thou with me, dearest, then,
While I rose up against my doom,
And yearned to burst the folded gloom,
To bare the eternal Heavens again,

5 To feel once more, in placid awe,
The strong imagination roll
A sphere of stars about my soul,
In all her motion one with law;

If thou wert with me, and the grave
10 Divide us not, be with me now,
And enter in at breast and brow,
Till all my blood, a fuller wave,

Be quickened with a livelier breath,
And like an inconsiderate boy,
15 As in the former flash of joy,
I slip the thoughts of life and death;

And all the breeze of Fancy blows,
And every dew-drop paints a bow,°   *rainbow*
The wizard lightnings[2] deeply glow,
20 And every thought breaks out a rose.

123

There rolls the deep where grew the tree.
O earth, what changes hast thou seen!
There where the long street roars, hath been
The stillness of the central sea.

5 The hills are shadows, and they flow
From form to form, and nothing stands;
They melt like mist, the solid lands,
Like clouds they shape themselves and go.

But in my spirit will I dwell,
10 And dream my dream, and hold it true;
For though my lips may breathe adieu,
I cannot think the thing farewell.

124

That which we dare invoke to bless;
Our dearest faith; our ghastliest doubt;
He, They, One, All; within, without;
The Power in darkness whom we guess;

5 I found Him not in world or sun,
Or eagle's wing, or insect's eye;
Nor through the questions men may try,
The petty cobwebs we have spun:

If e'er when faith had fallen asleep,
10 I heard a voice "believe no more"
And heard an ever-breaking shore
That tumbled in the Godless deep;

A warmth within the breast would melt
The freezing reason's colder part,
15 And like a man in wrath the heart
Stood up and answered "I have felt."

No, like a child in doubt and fear:
But that blind clamour made me wise;

---

[1] *team* I.e., of horses or oxen.

[2] *wizard lightnings* Northern lights, or aurora borealis.

Then was I as a child that cries,
20 But, crying, knows his father near;

And what I am beheld again
What is, and no man understands;
And out of darkness came the hands
That reach through nature, moulding men.

125

Whatever I have said or sung,
Some bitter notes my harp would give,
Yea, though there often seemed to live
A contradiction on the tongue,

5 Yet Hope had never lost her youth;
She did but look through dimmer eyes;
Or Love but played with gracious lies,
Because he felt so fixed in truth:

And if the song were full of care,
10 He breathed the spirit of the song;
And if the words were sweet and strong
He set his royal signet there;

Abiding with me till I sail
To seek thee on the mystic deeps,
15 And this electric force, that keeps
A thousand pulses dancing, fail.

126

Love is and was my Lord and King,
And in his presence I attend
To hear the tidings of my friend,
Which every hour his couriers bring.

5 Love is and was my King and Lord,
And will be, though as yet I keep
Within his court on earth, and sleep
Encompassed by his faithful guard,

And hear at times a sentinel
10 Who moves about from place to place,
And whispers to the worlds of space,
In the deep night, that all is well.

127

And all is well, though faith and form
Be sundered in the night of fear;
Well roars the storm to those that hear
A deeper voice across the storm,

5 Proclaiming social truth shall spread,
And justice, even though thrice again
The red fool-fury of the Seine[1]
Should pile her barricades with dead.

But ill for him that wears a crown,
10 And him, the lazar,° in his rags: *leper*
They tremble, the sustaining crags;
The spires of ice are toppled down,

And molten up, and roar in flood;
The fortress crashes from on high,
15 The brute earth lightens to the sky,
And the great Æon° sinks in blood,   *eon*

And compassed by the fires of Hell;
While thou, dear spirit, happy star,
O'erlook'st the tumult from afar,
20 And smilest, knowing all is well.

128

The love that rose on stronger wings,
Unpalsied when he met with Death,
Is comrade of the lesser faith
That sees the course of human things.

5 No doubt vast eddies in the flood
Of onward time shall yet be made,
And thronèd races may degrade;
Yet O ye mysteries of good,

Wild Hours that fly with Hope and Fear,
10 If all your office had to do
With old results that look like new;
If this were all your mission here,

---

1 *red ... Seine* I.e., the slaughter during the French Revolution. The Seine is the river than runs through Paris.

To draw, to sheathe a useless sword,
　　To fool the crowd with glorious lies,
15　　To cleave a creed in sects and cries,
To change the bearing of a word,

To shift an arbitrary power,
　　To cramp the student at his desk,
　　To make old bareness picturesque
20 And tuft with grass a feudal tower;

Why then my scorn might well descend
　　On you and yours. I see in part
　　That all, as in some piece of art,
Is toil cöoperant to an end.

129

Dear friend, far off, my lost desire,
　　So far, so near in woe and weal;
　　O loved the most, when most I feel
There is a lower and a higher;

5　Known and unknown; human, divine;
　　Sweet human hand and lips and eye;
　　Dear heavenly friend that canst not die,
Mine, mine, for ever, ever mine;

Strange friend, past, present, and to be;
10　　Loved deeplier, darklier understood;
　　Behold, I dream a dream of good,
And mingle all the world with thee.

130

Thy voice is on the rolling air;
　　I hear thee where the waters run;
　　Thou standest in the rising sun,
And in the setting thou art fair.

5　What art thou then? I cannot guess;
　　But though I seem in star and flower
　　To feel thee some diffusive power,
I do not therefore love thee less:

My love involves the love before;
10　　My love is vaster passion now;
　　Though mixed with God and Nature thou,
I seem to love thee more and more.

Far off thou art, but ever nigh;
　　I have thee still, and I rejoice;
15　　I prosper, circled with thy voice;
I shall not lose thee though I die.

131

O living will that shalt endure
　　When all that seems shall suffer shock,
　　Rise in the spiritual rock,
Flow through our deeds and make them pure,

5　That we may lift from out of dust
　　A voice as unto him that hears,
　　A cry above the conquered years
To one that with us works, and trust,

With faith that comes of self-control,
10　　The truths that never can be proved
　　Until we close with all we loved,
And all we flow from, soul in soul.

[EPILOGUE]

O true and tried, so well and long,
　　Demand not thou a marriage lay;
　　In that it is thy marriage day
Is music more than any song.[1]

5　Nor have I felt so much of bliss
　　Since first he told me that he loved
　　A daughter of our house; nor proved
Since that dark day a day like this;

Though I since then have numbered o'er
10　　Some thrice three years: they went and came,
　　Remade the blood and changed the frame,
And yet is love not less, but more;

No longer caring to embalm
　　In dying songs a dead regret,
15　　But like a statue solid-set,
And moulded in colossal calm.

---

[1] *O true … song* The Epilogue is a marriage song for Edmund Cushington and Tennyson's sister Cecilia.

Regret is dead, but love is more
    Than in the summers that are flown,
    For I myself with these have grown
20 To something greater than before;

Which makes appear the songs I made
    As echoes out of weaker times,
    As half but idle brawling rhymes,
The sport of random sun and shade.

25 But where is she, the bridal flower,
    That must be made a wife ere noon?
    She enters, glowing like the moon
Of Eden on its bridal bower:

On me she bends her blissful eyes
30   And then on thee; they meet thy look
    And brighten like the star that shook
Betwixt the palms of paradise.

O when her life was yet in bud,
    He too foretold the perfect rose.
35   For thee she grew, for thee she grows
Forever, and as fair as good.

And thou art worthy; full of power;
    As gentle; liberal-minded, great,
    Consistent; wearing all that weight
40 Of learning lightly like a flower.

But now set out: the noon is near,
    And I must give away the bride;
    She fears not, or with thee beside
And me behind her, will not fear.

45 For I that danced her on my knee,
    That watched her on her nurse's arm,
    That shielded all her life from harm
At last must part with her to thee;

Now waiting to be made a wife,
50   Her feet, my darling, on the dead;
    Their pensive tablets° round her head,   *gravestones*
And the most living words of life

Breathed in her ear. The ring is on,
    The "wilt thou" answered, and again
55   The "wilt thou" asked, till out of twain
Her sweet "I will" has made you one.

Now sign your names, which shall be read,
    Mute symbols of a joyful morn,
    By village eyes as yet unborn;
60 The names are signed, and overhead

Begins the clash and clang that tells
    The joy to every wandering breeze;
    The blind wall rocks, and on the trees
The dead leaf trembles to the bells.

65 O happy hour, and happier hours
    Await them. Many a merry face
    Salutes them—maidens of the place,
That pelt us in the porch with flowers.

O happy hour, behold the bride
70   With him to whom her hand I gave.
    They leave the porch, they pass the grave
That has today its sunny side.

Today the grave is bright for me,
    For them the light of life increased,
75   Who stay to share the morning feast,
Who rest tonight beside the sea.

Let all my genial spirits advance
    To meet and greet a whiter sun;
    My drooping memory will not shun
80 The foaming grape of eastern France.

It circles round, and fancy plays,
    And hearts are warmed and faces bloom,
    As drinking health to bride and groom
We wish them store of happy days.

85 Nor count me all to blame if I
    Conjecture of a stiller guest,
    Perchance, perchance, among the rest,
And, though in silence, wishing joy.

But they must go, the time draws on,
90   And those white-favoured horses wait;
They rise, but linger; it is late;
Farewell, we kiss, and they are gone.

A shade falls on us like the dark
        From little cloudlets on the grass,
95   But sweeps away as out we pass
To range the woods, to roam the park,

Discussing how their courtship grew,
        And talk of others that are wed,
        And how she looked, and what he said,
100 And back we come at fall of dew.

Again the feast, the speech, the glee,
        The shade of passing thought, the wealth
        Of words and wit, the double health,
The crowning cup, the three-times-three,[1]

105 And last the dance;—till I retire:
        Dumb is that tower which spake so loud,
        And high in heaven the streaming cloud,
And on the downs a rising fire:

And rise, O moon, from yonder down,
110   Till over down and over dale
        All night the shining vapour sail
And pass the silent-lighted town,

The white-faced halls, the glancing rills,
        And catch at every mountain head,
115   And o'er the friths[2] that branch and spread
Their sleeping silver through the hills;

And touch with shade the bridal doors,
        With tender gloom the roof, the wall;
        And breaking let the splendour fall
120 To spangle all the happy shores

By which they rest, and ocean sounds,
        And, star and system rolling past,

A soul shall draw from out the vast
And strike his being into bounds,

125 And, moved through life of lower phase
        Result in man, be born and think,
        And act and love, a closer link
Betwixt us and the crowning race

Of those that, eye to eye, shall look
130   On knowledge; under whose command
        Is Earth and Earth's, and in their hand
Is Nature like an open book;

No longer half-akin to brute,
        For all we thought and loved and did,
135   And hoped, and suffered, is but seed
Of what in them is flower and fruit;

Whereof the man, that with me trod
        This planet, was a noble type
        Appearing ere the times were ripe,
140 That friend of mine who lives in God,

That God, which ever lives and loves,
        One God, one law, one element,
        And one far-off divine event,
To which the whole creation moves.
—1850

The Eagle
[Fragment]

He clasps the crag with crooked hands;
Close to the sun in lonely lands,
Ringed with the azure world, he stands.

The wrinkled sea beneath him crawls;
5   He watches from his mountain walls,
And like a thunderbolt he falls.
—1851 (WRITTEN 1833?)

---

[1] *three-times-three*   A toast: "Three-times-three cheers for the bride and groom!"

[2] *friths*   Wooded areas.

The Charge of the Light Brigade[1]

1

Half a league,[2] half a league,
Half a league onward,
All in the valley of Death
    Rode the six hundred.[3]
5 "Forward, the Light Brigade!
Charge for the guns!" he said:
Into the valley of Death
    Rode the six hundred.

2

"Forward, the Light Brigade!"
10 Was there a man dismayed?
Not though the soldier knew
    Some one had blundered:
Their's not to make reply,
Their's not to reason why,
15 Their's but to do and die:
Into the valley of Death
    Rode the six hundred.

3

Cannon to right of them,
Cannon to left of them,
20 Cannon in front of them
    Volleyed and thundered;
Stormed at with shot and shell,
Boldly they rode and well,
Into the jaws of Death,
25 Into the mouth of Hell
    Rode the six hundred.

4

Flashed all their sabres bare,
Flashed as they turned in air
Sabring the gunners there,
30 Charging an army, while
    All the world wondered:
Plunged in the battery-smoke
Right through the line they broke;
Cossack and Russian
35 Reeled from the sabre-stroke
    Shattered and sundered.
Then they rode back, but not
    Not the six hundred.

5

Cannon to right of them,
40 Cannon to left of them,
Cannon behind them
    Volleyed and thundered;
Stormed at with shot and shell,
While horse and hero fell,
45 They that had fought so well
Came through the jaws of Death,
Back from the mouth of Hell,
All that was left of them,[4]
    Left of six hundred.

6

50 When can their glory fade?
O the wild charge they made!
    All the world wondered.
Honour the charge they made!
Honour the Light Brigade,
55   Noble six hundred!
—1854

[Flower in the Crannied Wall]

Flower in the crannied wall,
I pluck you out of the crannies,
I hold you here, root and all, in my hand,
Little flower—but if I could understand
5 What you are, root and all, and all in all,
I should know what God and man is.
—1869

---

[1] *The Charge ... Brigade* Written some weeks after a disastrous engagement during the Crimean War. At the Battle of Balaclava on 25 October 1854, the 700 cavalrymen of the Light Brigade, acting on a misinterpreted order, directly charged the Russian artillery.

[2] *league* About three miles.

[3] *six hundred* The initial newspaper account read by Tennyson mentioned "607 sabres," and he retained the number even when the correct number was discovered to be considerably higher because "six is much better than seven hundred ... metrically" (*Letters* ii.101).

[4] *All ... them* Only 195 men survived the charge.

Vastness

1

Many a hearth upon our dark globe sighs after many
  a vanished face,
Many a planet by many a sun may roll with the dust
  of a vanished race.

2

Raving politics, never at rest—as this poor earth's
  pale history runs,—
What is it all but a trouble° of ants in the gleam   *agitation*
  of a million million of suns?

3

5   Lies upon this side, lies upon that side, truthless violence
  mourned by the Wise,
Thousands of voices drowning his own in a popular
  torrent of lies upon lies;

4

Stately purposes, valour in battle, glorious annals of army
  and fleet,
Death for the right cause, death for the wrong cause,
  trumpets of victory, groans of defeat;

5

Innocence seethed° in her mother's milk,[1] and   *boiled*
  Charity setting the martyr aflame;
10   Thraldom° who walks with the banner of   *bondage*
  Freedom, and recks not[2] to ruin a realm in her name.

6

Faith at her zenith, or all but lost in the gloom of doubts
  that darken the schools;
Craft with a bunch of all-heal[3] in her hand,
  followed up by her vassal° legion of fools;   *servile*

7

Trade flying over a thousand seas with her spice

and her vintage, her silk and her corn;
Desolate offing,[4] sailorless harbours, famishing
  populace, wharves forlorn;

8

15   Star of the morning, Hope in the sunrise;
  gloom of the evening, Life at a close;
Pleasure who flaunts on her wide down-way
  with her flying robe and her poisoned rose;

9

Pain, that has crawled from the corpse of Pleasure,
  a worm which writhes all day, and at night
Stirs up again in the heart of the sleeper, and stings
  him back to the curse of the light;

10

Wealth with his wines and his wedded harlots;
  honest Poverty, bare to the bone;
20   Opulent Avarice, lean as Poverty; Flattery gilding
  the rift in a throne;

11

Fame blowing out from her golden trumpet
  a jubilant challenge to Time and to Fate;
Slander, her shadow, sowing the nettle on all the
  laurelled graves of the Great;

12

Love for the maiden, crowned with marriage,
  no regrets for aught that has been,
Household happinesss, gracious children,
  debtless competence, golden mean;

13

25   National hatreds of whole generations, and
  pigmy° spites of the village spire;   *trivial*
Vows that will last to the last death-ruckle,°   *death-rattle*
  and vows that are snapped in a moment of fire;

14

He that has lived for the lust of the minute,
  and died in the doing it, flesh without mind;

---

[1] *Innocence ... milk*   See *Exodus* 34.26: "Thou shalt not seethe a kid in his mother's milk."

[2] *recks not*   Is not reluctant.

[3] *all-heal*   Name given to various plants believed to possess healing properties.

[4] *offing*   Most distant part of the sea visible from shore.

He that has nailed all flesh to the Cross,
    till Self died out in the love of his kind;

15

Spring and Summer and Autumn and Winter,
    and all these old revolutions of earth;
30 All new-old revolutions of Empire—change of the
       tide—what is all of it worth?

16

What the philosophies, all the sciences, poesy,
    varying voices of prayer?
All that is noblest, all that is basest, all that is filthy
    with all that is fair?

17

What is it all, if we all of us end but in being our own
    corpse-coffins at last,
Swallowed in Vastness, lost in Silence, drowned
    in the deeps of a meaningless Past?

18

35 What but a murmur of gnats in the gloom,
    or a moment's anger of bees in their hive?—

     *   *   *

Peace, let it be! for I loved him, and love him for ever:
    the dead are not dead but alive.
—1885; 1889

Crossing the Bar[1]

Sunset and evening star,
    And one clear call for me!
And may there be no moaning of the bar,
    When I put out to sea,

5 But such a tide as moving seems asleep,
    Too full for sound and foam,
When that which drew from out the boundless deep
    Turns again home.

Twilight and evening bell,
10   And after that the dark!
And may there be no sadness of farewell,
    When I embark;

For though from out our bourne° of Time and   *limit*
    Place
    The flood may bear me far,
15 I hope to see my Pilot face to face
    When I have crossed the bar.
—1889

---

1 *bar* Sandbank or shoal across the mouth of a harbor or estuary.

IN CONTEXT

Images of Tennyson

Particularly in his later years, Tennyson became an iconic figure in Victorian Britain. The best known photographic images of him are those taken by Julia Margaret Cameron, one of which is reproduced, below. (Another appears in the introduction to Tennyson, above.) Tennyson as a younger man is described below by Thomas Carlyle.

from Thomas Carlyle, Letter to Ralph Waldo Emerson, 5 August 1844

Alfred is one of the few British or Foreign Figures (a not increasing number I think!) who are and remain beautiful to me;—a true human soul, or some authentic approximation thereto, to whom your own soul can say, Brother!— However, I doubt he will not come; he often skips me, in these brief visits to Town; skips everybody indeed; being a man solitary and sad, as certain men are, dwelling in an element of gloom,—carrying a bit of Chaos about him, in short, which he is manufacturing into Cosmos!

Alfred is the son of a Lincolnshire Gentleman Farmer, I think; indeed, you see in his verses that he is a native of "moated granges," and green, fat pastures, not of mountains and their torrents and storms. He had his breeding at Cambridge, as if for the Law or Church; being master of a small annuity on his Father's decease, he preferred clubbing with his Mother and some Sisters, to live unpromoted and write Poems. In this way he lives still, now here, now there; the family always within reach of London, never in it; he himself making rare and brief visits, lodging in some old comrade's rooms. I think he must be under forty, not much under it. One of the finest-looking men in the world. A great shock of rough dusty-dark hair; bright-laughing hazel eyes; massive aquiline face, most massive yet most delicate; of sallow-brown complexion, almost Indian-looking; clothes cynically loose, free-and-easy;—smokes infinite tobacco. His voice is musical metallic,—fit for loud laughter and piercing wail, and all that may lie between; speech and speculation free and plenteous: I do not meet, in these late decades, such company over a pipe!—We shall see what he will grow to. He is often unwell; very chaotic,—his way is through Chaos and the Bottomless and Pathless; not handy for making out many miles upon.

Julia Margaret Cameron, *Alfred Tennyson*, 1865. Tennyson nicknamed this photograph "the dirty monk" and claimed that it was his favorite photograph of himself.

from Evert A. Duyckinck,
*Portrait Gallery of Eminent Men
and Women in Europe and America*,
1873. This portrait appears to be
from the 1850s.

IN CONTEXT
Victorian Images of Arthurian Legend

Arthurian romance was a frequent subject of Victorian painting and photography as well as
Victorian literature; a sampling is reproduced below.

Julia Margaret Cameron, *The Parting of
Lancelot and Guinevere*, 1847.

Julia Margaret Cameron, *Vivien and
Merlin*, 1874.

John William Waterhouse, *The Lady of Shalott*, 1888.

William Holman Hunt, *The Lady of Shalott*, 1857.

IN CONTEXT

Crimea and the Camera

The Crimean War was the first to be photographed extensively—most notably by Roger Fenton, who spent three months in Crimea in 1855. Both the technology of the time and the demands of Victorian taste militated against shooting scenes of battle directly; unlike Matthew Brady and other photographers of the American Civil War a few years later, Fenton took no pictures of bloody and mangled corpses.

Fenton's most famous photograph of the war, *Valley of the Shadow of Death*, came to be closely associated with Tennyson's famous 1854 poem, "The Charge of the Light Brigade." The connection is not entirely a direct one, however. It was not the valley where the charge occurred that Fenton photographed but another valley in the vicinity—one that had begun to be referred to by soldiers as "the valley of the shadow of death" (in an echo both of Tennyson's poem and of the Bible) because of the frequency with which the Russians shelled it.

Roger Fenton,
*General Bosquet Giving Orders
to His Staff*, 1855.

Roger Fenton, *Captain Dames*, 1855.

Roger Fenton, *Group of Croat Chiefs*, 1855.

Roger Fenton, *Cookhouse of the 8ᵗʰ Hussars*, 1855.

Roger Fenton, *Valley of the Shadow of Death*, 1855.

CHARLES DARWIN
1809 – 1882

The name Charles Darwin has become synonymous in many minds with the theory of evolution, but theories of evolution did not begin with Darwin. Long before the Victorian era the ancient Greek thinkers Anaximander (611–547 BCE), Empedocles (492–432 BCE), and Aristotle (384–322 BCE) all speculated that life as we know it evolved from sea creatures. In the year Darwin was born, the French biologist Lamarck suggested that species respond and adapt to their environments and then transmit these adaptive traits to their offspring. And in 1850, drawing on the theories of Charles Lyell and Robert Chambers, Tennyson speculated on the idea of evolution in his poetic elegy *In Memoriam*. But when the unassuming British naturalist Charles Darwin articulated his acceptance of the concept of evolution and published his theory of natural selection in 1859 in *On the Origin of Species*, his views provoked comment and controversy internationally. He had offered a detailed, cogent, and plausible theory that to many appeared to call into question the idea of divine creation, as well as assumptions about human beings' innate superiority to, and difference from, other creatures.

Charles Robert Darwin was born in 1809 in Shrewsbury, England, to Robert Waring Darwin, a successful doctor (and son of the famous physician, botanist, philosopher, and poet Erasmus Darwin), and Susannah Wedgwood Darwin, daughter of the pottery manufacturer Josiah Wedgwood. Charles distinguished himself neither at school nor at the University of Edinburgh, where his father sent him to study medicine. He often complained throughout his school years of being bored, although he always showed an active interest in and enthusiasm for the natural sciences and for specimen collection. When he left medical school without taking his degree, his father pushed him into a second career track; ironically, the man who would be reviled by religious fundamentalists next studied theology at Cambridge with a view to joining the clergy. Darwin again became bored with his studies, preferring to spend his time collecting and studying beetles. He did make an important friend at Cambridge; his botany professor, John Henslow, recognized Darwin's potential as a natural scientist and recommended him for a position on the H.M.S. Beagle, the ship that would take him around the world to collect biological specimens and data. On this pivotal five-year voyage, Darwin compiled meticulous records of his findings along with an engaging account of his travels and the cultures he encountered, which he subsequently published as *The Voyage of the Beagle* in 1839.

Influenced by James Hutton's geological theories and Charles Lyell's *Principles of Geology*, Darwin also collected fossils and noted the relationship between creatures and their environments, particularly among the unique fauna of the Galapagos Islands. These isolated islands contained species of birds completely unlike those on the mainland, as well as others that closely resembled species of South America. After completing the voyage, Darwin devoted the rest of his career to researching and attempting to explain the differences between such species and their ancestors. After reading Thomas Malthus's *An Essay on the Principle of Population*, he came up with his answer: individuals that are strong enough to survive environmental pressures pass their favorable traits on to successive generations, and thus species adapt and gradually form new species, a process Darwin called "natural selection." Moreover, according to Darwinian theory this process has persisted for millions of years, with all species having evolved from a single life form.

Although he wrote essays on his evolutionary ideas, Darwin did not publish his findings for 20 years, until another naturalist, Alfred Russel Wallace, sent him a paper that included similar conclusions about natural selection. The two agreed to present a joint paper in 1858 to the Linnaean Society in London, and the next year Darwin published *On the Origin of Species*. *Origin* sold out its entire print run amidst a storm of protest and indignation. In the decade following its publication, responses to the book abounded in the literary world, with authors such as Charles Kingsley and Samuel Butler opposing Darwin, while George Eliot, Thomas Hardy, and Joseph Conrad drew on his theories and modes of explanation.

For the rest of his life, Darwin lived in his country house with his wife, his cousin Emma Wedgwood, whom he had married in 1839, and his many children, studying flora and fauna and publishing his findings. Although the world around him struggled to absorb the impact of his evolutionary theory, Darwin refused to engage in debates about the questions that haunted so many: are humans really evolved from lower life forms, and where does this theory leave the Bible's teachings? In *The Descent of Man, and Selection in Relation to Sex* (1871) Darwin explicitly extended his evolutionary theory to human beings and put forward the notion of sexual selection.

In 1882, after suffering from ill health for many years, quite possibly from a disease acquired during his voyage on the H.M.S. Beagle, Darwin died and was buried next to Sir Isaac Newton in Westminster Abbey.

⌘ ⌘ ⌘

from *The Voyage of the Beagle*

from Chapter 10, Tierra del Fuego

December 17th, 1832.—Having now finished with Patagonia[1] and the Falkland Islands, I will describe our first arrival in Tierra del Fuego.[2] A little after noon we doubled Cape St. Diego, and entered the famous strait of Le Maire. We kept close to the Fuegian shore, but the outline of the rugged, inhospitable Staten-land was visible amidst the clouds. In the afternoon we anchored in the Bay of Good Success. While entering we were saluted in a manner becoming the inhabitants of this savage land. A group of Fuegians partly concealed by the entangled forest, were perched on a wild point overhanging the sea; and as we passed by, they sprang up and waving their tattered cloaks sent forth a loud and sonorous shout. The savages followed the ship, and just before dark we saw their fire, and again heard their wild

cry. The harbour consists of a fine piece of water half surrounded by low rounded mountains of clay-slate, which are covered to the water's edge by one dense gloomy forest. A single glance at the landscape was sufficient to show me how widely different it was from any thing I had ever beheld. At night it blew a gale of wind, and heavy squalls from the mountains swept past us. It would have been a bad time out at sea, and we, as well as others, may call this Good Success Bay.

In the morning the Captain sent a party to communicate with the Fuegians. When we came within hail, one of the four natives who were present advanced to receive us, and began to shout most vehemently, wishing to direct us where to land. When we were on shore the party looked rather alarmed, but continued talking and making gestures with great rapidity. It was without exception the most curious and interesting spectacle I ever beheld. I could not have believed how wide was the difference between savage and civilized man: it is greater than between a wild and domesticated animal, inasmuch as in man there is a greater power of improvement. The

---

[1]   *Patagonia*   Southern portion of South America.

[2]   *Tierra del Fuego*   Southernmost tip of South America.

chief spokesman was old, and appeared to be the head of the family; the three others were powerful young men, about six feet high. The women and children had been sent away. These Fuegians are a very different race from the stunted, miserable wretches farther westward; and they seem closely allied to the famous Patagonians of the Strait of Magellan. Their only garment consists of a mantle made of guanaco[1] skin, with the wool outside; this they wear just thrown over their shoulders, leaving their persons as often exposed as covered. Their skin is of a dirty coppery red colour.

The old man had a fillet of white feathers tied round his head, which partly confined his black, coarse, and entangled hair. His face was crossed by two broad transverse bars; one, painted bright red, reached from ear to ear and included the upper lip; the other, white like chalk, extended above and parallel to the first, so that even his eyelids were thus coloured. The other two men were ornamented by streaks of black powder, made of charcoal. The party altogether closely resembled the devils which come on the stage in plays like *Der Freischutz*.[2]

Their very attitudes were abject, and the expression of their countenances distrustful, surprised, and startled. After we had presented them with some scarlet cloth, which they immediately tied round their necks, they became good friends. This was shown by the old man patting our breasts, and making a chuckling kind of noise, as people do when feeding chickens. I walked with the old man, and this demonstration of friendship was repeated several times; it was concluded by three hard slaps, which were given me on the breast and back at the same time. He then bared his bosom for me to return the compliment, which being done, he seemed highly pleased. The language of these people, according to our notions, scarcely deserves to be called articulate. Captain Cook[3] has compared it to a man clearing his throat, but certainly no European ever cleared his throat with so many hoarse, guttural, and clicking sounds.

They are excellent mimics: as often as we coughed or yawned, or made any odd motion, they immediately imitated us. Some of our party began to squint and look awry; but one of the young Fuegians (whose whole face was painted black, excepting a white band across his eyes) succeeded in making far more hideous grimaces. They could repeat with perfect correctness each word in any sentence we addressed them, and they remembered such words for some time. Yet we Europeans all know how difficult it is to distinguish apart the sounds in a foreign language. Which of us, for instance, could follow an American Indian through a sentence of more than three words? All savages appear to possess, to an uncommon degree, this power of mimicry. I was told, almost in the same words, of the same ludicrous habit among the Caffres:[4] the Australians, likewise, have long been notorious for being able to imitate and describe the gait of any man, so that he may be recognized. How can this faculty be explained? Is it a consequence of the more practised habits of perception and keener senses, common to all men in a savage state, as compared with those long civilized?

When a song was struck up by our party, I thought the Fuegians would have fallen down with astonishment. With equal surprise they viewed our dancing; but one of the young men, when asked, had no objection to a little waltzing. Little accustomed to Europeans as they appeared to be, yet they knew and dreaded our firearms; nothing would tempt them to take a gun in their hands. They begged for knives, calling them by the Spanish word "cuchilla." They explained also what they wanted, by acting as if they had a piece of blubber in their mouth, and then pretending to cut instead of tear it.

I have not as yet noticed the Fuegians whom we had on board. During the former voyage of the *Adventure* and *Beagle* in 1826 to 1830, Captain Fitz Roy[5] seized on a party of natives, as hostages for the loss of a boat, which had been stolen, to the great jeopardy of a party employed on the survey; and some of these natives, as well as a child whom he bought for a pearl-button, he took with him to England, determining to educate them and instruct them in religion at his own expense. To settle these natives in their own country, was one chief inducement to Captain Fitz Roy to undertake our

---

[1] *guanaco* Wild llama, the coat of which is a red-brown wool.

[2] *Der Freischutz* 1820 opera by Carl Maria von Weber.

[3] *Captain Cook* James Cook (1728–79), English explorer.

[4] *Caffres* Kaffirs, a common term for native Africans (now considered to be derogatory).

[5] *Captain Fitz Roy* Robert Fitz Roy (1805–65).

present voyage; and before the Admiralty had resolved to send out this expedition, Captain Fitz Roy had generously chartered a vessel, and would himself have taken them back. The natives were accompanied by a missionary, R. Matthews; of whom and of the natives, Captain Fitz Roy has published a full and excellent account. Two men, one of whom died in England of the smallpox, a boy and a little girl, were originally taken; and we had now on board, York Minster, Jemmy Button (whose name expresses his purchase-money), and Fuegia Basket. York Minster was a full-grown, short, thick, powerful man: his disposition was reserved, taciturn, morose, and when excited violently passionate; his affections were very strong towards a few friends on board; his intellect good. Jemmy Button was a universal favourite, but likewise passionate; the expression of his face at once showed his nice disposition. He was merry and often laughed, and was remarkably sympathetic with any one in pain: when the water was rough, I was often a little seasick, and he used to come to me and say in a plaintive voice, "Poor, poor fellow!" but the notion, after his aquatic life, of a man being sea-sick, was too ludicrous, and he was generally obliged to turn on one side to hide a smile or laugh, and then he would repeat his "Poor, poor fellow!" He was of a patriotic disposition; and he liked to praise his own tribe and country, in which he truly said there were "plenty of trees," and he abused all the other tribes: he stoutly declared that there was no Devil in his land. Jemmy was short, thick, and fat, but vain of his personal appearance; he used to wear gloves, his hair was neatly cut, and he was distressed if his well-polished shoes were dirtied. He was fond of admiring himself in a looking-glass; and a merry-faced little Indian boy from the Rio Negro, whom we had for some months on board, soon perceived this, and used to mock him: Jemmy, who was always rather jealous of the attention paid to this little boy, did not at all like this, and used to say, with rather a contemptuous twist of his head, "Too much skylark." It seems yet wonderful to me, when I think over all his many good qualities, that he should have been of the same race, and doubtless partaken of the same character, with the miserable, degraded savages whom we first met here. Lastly, Fuegia Basket was a nice, modest, reserved young girl, with a rather pleasing but sometimes sullen expression, and

very quick in learning anything, especially languages. This she showed in picking up some Portuguese and Spanish, when left on shore for only a short time at Rio de Janeiro and Monte Video, and in her knowledge of English. York Minster was very jealous of any attention paid to her; for it was clear he determined to marry her as soon as they were settled on shore.

Although all three could both speak and understand a good deal of English, it was singularly difficult to obtain much information from them, concerning the habits of their countrymen: this was partly owing to their apparent difficulty in understanding the simplest alternative. Every one accustomed to very young children, knows how seldom one can get an answer even to so simple a question as whether a thing is black or white; the idea of black or white seems alternately to fill their minds. So it was with these Fuegians, and hence it was generally impossible to find out, by cross-questioning, whether one had rightly understood anything which they had asserted. Their sight was remarkably acute: it is well known that sailors, from long practice, can make out a distant object much better than a landsman; but both York and Jemmy were much superior to any sailor on board: several times they have declared what some distant object has been, and though doubted by every one, they have proved right, when it has been examined through a telescope. They were quite conscious of this power; and Jemmy, when he had any little quarrel with the officer on watch, would say, "Me see ship, me no tell."

It was interesting to watch the conduct of the savages, when we landed, towards Jemmy Button: they immediately perceived the difference between him and ourselves, and held much conversation one with another on the subject. The old man addressed a long harangue to Jemmy, which it seems was to invite him to stay with them. But Jemmy understood very little of their language, and was, moreover, thoroughly ashamed of his countrymen. When York Minster afterwards came on shore, they noticed him in the same way, and told him he ought to shave; yet he had not twenty dwarf hairs on his face, whilst we all wore our untrimmed beards. They examined the colour of his skin, and compared it with ours. One of our arms being bared, they expressed the liveliest surprise and admiration at its whiteness, just in the same way in which I have seen the ourang-outang do at the Zoological Gardens. We thought that they mistook two or three of the officers, who were rather shorter and fairer, though adorned with large beards, for the ladies of our party. The tallest among the Fuegians was evidently much pleased at his height being noticed. When placed back to back with the tallest of the boat's crew, he tried his best to edge on higher ground, and to stand on tiptoe. He opened his mouth to show his teeth, and turned his face for a side view; and all this was done with such alacrity, that I dare say he thought himself the handsomest man in Tierra del Fuego. After our first feeling of grave astonishment was over, nothing could be more ludicrous than the odd mixture of surprise and imitation which these savages every moment exhibited. ...

December 25th.—Close by the cove, a pointed hill, called Rater's Peak, rises to the height of 1700 feet. The surrounding islands all consist of conical masses of greenstone, associated sometimes with less regular hills of baked and altered clay-slate. This part of Tierra del Fuego may be considered as the extremity of the sub-merged chain of mountains already alluded to. The cove takes its name of "Wigwam" from some of the Fuegian habitations; but every bay in the neighbourhood might be so called with equal propriety. The inhabitants, living chiefly upon shell-fish, are obliged constantly to change their place of residence; but they return at intervals to the same spots, as is evident from the piles of old shells, which must often amount to many tons in weight. These heaps can be distinguished at a long distance by the bright green colour of certain plants, which invariably grow on them. Among these may be enumerated the wild celery and scurvy grass, two very serviceable plants, the use of which has not been discovered by the natives.

The Fuegian wigwam resembles, in size and dimensions, a haycock.[1] It merely consists of a few broken branches stuck in the ground, and very imperfectly thatched on one side with a few tufts of grass and rushes. The whole cannot be the work of an hour, and it is only used for a few days. At Goeree Roads I saw a place where one of these naked men had slept, which absolutely offered no more cover than the form of a hare. The man was evidently living by himself, and York Minster said he was "very bad man," and that probably he had stolen something. On the west coast, however, the wigwams are rather better, for they are covered with seal-skins. We were detained here several days by the bad weather. The climate is certainly wretched: the summer solstice was now passed, yet every day snow fell on the hills, and in the valleys there was rain, accompanied by sleet. The thermometer generally stood about 45°, but in the night fell to 38° or 40°. From the damp and boisterous state of the atmosphere, not cheered by a gleam of sunshine, one fancied the climate even worse than it really was.

While going one day on shore near Wollaston Island, we pulled alongside a canoe with six Fuegians. These were the most abject and miserable creatures I anywhere beheld. On the east coast the natives, as we have seen, have guanaco cloaks, and on the west, they possess seal-skins. Amongst these central tribes the men generally have an otter-skin, or some small scrap about as large as a pocket-handkerchief, which is barely sufficient to cover their backs as low down as their loins. It is laced across the breast by strings, and according as the wind blows, it is shifted from side to side. But these Fuegians in the canoe were quite naked, and even one full-grown woman was absolutely so. It was raining heavily, and the fresh water, together with the spray, trickled down her body. In another harbour not far distant, a woman, who was suckling a recently-born child, came one day alongside the vessel, and remained there out of mere curiosity, whilst the sleet fell and thawed on her naked bosom, and on the skin of her naked baby! These poor wretches were stunted in their growth, their hideous faces bedaubed with white paint, their skins filthy and greasy, their hair entangled, their voices discordant, and their gestures violent. Viewing such men, one can hardly make oneself believe that they are fellow-creatures, and inhabitants of the same world. It is a common subject of conjecture what pleasure in life some of the lower animals can enjoy: how much more reasonably the same question may be asked with respect to these barbarians! At night, five or six human beings, naked and scarcely protected from the wind and rain of this tempestuous climate, sleep on the wet ground coiled up like animals. Whenever it is low water, winter or summer, night or day, they must rise to pick shellfish from the rocks; and the women either dive to

---

[1]   *haycock*   Haystack.

collect sea-eggs, or sit patiently in their canoes, and with a baited hairline without any hook, jerk out little fish. If a seal is killed, or the floating carcass of a putrid whale discovered, it is a feast; and such miserable food is assisted by a few tasteless berries and fungi.

They often suffer from famine: I heard Mr. Low, a sealingmaster intimately acquainted with the natives of this country, give a curious account of the state of a party of one hundred and fifty natives on the west coast, who were very thin and in great distress. A succession of gales prevented the women from getting shell-fish on the rocks, and they could not go out in their canoes to catch seal. A small party of these men one morning set out, and the other Indians explained to him, that they were going a four days' journey for food: on their return, Low went to meet them, and he found them excessively tired, each man carrying a great square piece of putrid whales-blubber with a hole in the middle, through which they put their heads, like the Gauchos[1] do through their ponchos or cloaks. As soon as the blubber was brought into a wigwam, an old man cut off thin slices, and muttering over them, broiled them for a minute, and distributed them to the famished party, who during this time preserved a profound silence. Mr. Low believes that whenever a whale is cast on shore, the natives bury large pieces of it in the sand, as a resource in time of famine; and a native boy, whom he had on board, once found a stock thus buried. ...

The different tribes have no government or chief; yet each is surrounded by other hostile tribes, speaking different dialects, and separated from each other only by a deserted border or neutral territory: the cause of their warfare appears to be the means of subsistence. Their country is a broken mass of wild rocks, lofty hills, and useless forests: and these are viewed through mists and endless storms. The habitable land is reduced to the stones on the beach; in search of food they are compelled unceasingly to wander from spot to spot, and so steep is the coast, that they can only move about in their wretched canoes. They cannot know the feeling of having a home, and still less that of domestic affection; for the husband is to the wife a brutal master to a laborious slave. Was a more horrid deed ever perpe-

trated, than that witnessed on the west coast by Byron,[2] who saw a wretched mother pick up her bleeding dying infant-boy, whom her husband had mercilessly dashed on the stones for dropping a basket of sea-eggs! How little can the higher powers of the mind be brought into play: what is there for imagination to picture, for reason to compare, for judgment to decide upon? To knock a limpet from the rock does not require even cunning, that lowest power of the mind. Their skill in some respects may be compared to the instinct of animals; for it is not improved by experience: the canoe, their most ingenious work, poor as it is, has remained the same, as we know from Drake,[3] for the last two hundred and fifty years. Whilst beholding these savages, one asks, whence have they come? What could have tempted, or what change compelled a tribe of men, to leave the fine regions of the north, to travel down the Cordillera or backbone of America, to invent and build canoes, which are not used by the tribes of Chile, Peru, and Brazil, and then to enter on one of the most inhospitable countries within the limits of the globe? Although such reflections must at first seize on the mind, yet we may feel sure that they are partly erroneous. There is no reason to believe that the Fuegians decrease in number; therefore we must suppose that they enjoy a sufficient share of happiness, of whatever kind it may be, to render life worth having. Nature by making habit omnipotent, and its effects hereditary, has fitted the Fuegian to the climate and the productions of his miserable country. ...

January 19th, 1833—Three whale-boats and the yawl,[4] with a party of twenty-eight, started under the command of Captain Fitz Roy. In the afternoon we entered the eastern mouth of the channel, and shortly afterwards found a snug little cove concealed by some surrounding islets. Here we pitched our tents and lighted our fires. Nothing could look more comfortable than this scene. The glassy water of the little harbour, with the branches of the trees hanging over the rocky beach, the boats at anchor, the tents supported by the

---

[1] *Gauchos* South American horsemen of mixed Native American and European descent.

[2] *Byron* John Byron (1723–86), British vice-admiral and explorer, and grandfather of the poet George Gordon, Lord Byron. See his *Narrative of Great Distresses on the Shores of Patagonia* (1768).

[3] *Drake* Sir Francis Drake (c. 1540–96), English explorer. In 1577 his travels took him past Tierra del Fuego.

[4] *yawl* Small boat.

crossed oars, and the smoke curling up the wooded valley, formed a picture of quiet retirement. The next day (20th) we smoothly glided onwards in our little fleet, and came to a more inhabited district. Few if any of these natives could ever have seen a white man; certainly nothing could exceed their astonishment at the apparition of the four boats. Fires were lighted on every point (hence the name of Tierra del Fuego, or the land of fire), both to attract our attention and to spread far and wide the news. Some of the men ran for miles along the shore. I shall never forget how wild and savage one group appeared: suddenly four or five men came to the edge of an overhanging cliff; they were absolutely naked, and their long hair streamed about their faces; they held rugged staffs in their hands, and, springing from the ground, they waved their arms round their heads, and sent forth the most hideous yells.

At dinner-time we landed among a party of Fuegians. At first they were not inclined to be friendly; for until the Captain pulled in ahead of the other boats, they kept their slings in their hands. We soon, however, delighted them by trifling presents, such as tying red tape round their heads. They liked our biscuit: but one of the savages touched with his finger some of the meat preserved in tin cases which I was eating, and feeling it soft and cold, showed as much disgust at it, as I should have done at putrid blubber. ...

On the last day of February in the succeeding year (1834), the *Beagle* anchored in a beautiful little cove at the eastern entrance of the Beagle Channel. Captain Fitz Roy determined on the bold, and as it proved successful, attempt to beat against the westerly winds by the same route, which we had followed in the boats to the settlement at Woollya. We did not see many natives until we were near Ponsonby Sound, where we were followed by ten or twelve canoes. The natives did not at all understand the reason of our tacking, and, instead of meeting us at each tack, vainly strove to follow us in our zig-zag course. I was amused at finding what a difference the circumstance of being quite superior in force made, in the interest of beholding these savages. While in the boats I got to hate the very sound of their voices, so much trouble did they give us. The first and last word was "yammerschooner." When, entering some quiet little cove, we have looked round and thought to pass a quiet night, the odious word "yammerschooner" has shrilly sounded from some gloomy nook, and then the little signal-smoke has curled up to spread the news far and wide. On leaving some place we have said to each other, "Thank Heaven, we have at last fairly left these wretches!" when one more faint halloo from an all-powerful voice, heard at a prodigious distance, would reach our ears, and clearly could we distinguish— "yammerschooner." But now, the more Fuegians the merrier; and very merry work it was. Both parties laughing, wondering, gaping at each other; we pitying them, for giving us good fish and crabs for rags, *et cetera*; they grasping at the chance of finding people so foolish as to exchange such splendid ornaments for a good supper. It was most amusing to see the undisguised smile of satisfaction with which one young woman with her face painted black, tied several bits of scarlet cloth round her head with rushes. Her husband, who enjoyed the very universal privilege in this country of possessing two wives, evidently became jealous of all the attention paid to his young wife; and, after a consultation with his naked beauties, was paddled away by them.

Some of the Fuegians plainly showed that they had a fair notion of barter. I gave one man a large nail (a most valuable present) without making any signs for a return; but he immediately picked out two fish, and handed them up on the point of his spear. If any present was designed for one canoe, and it fell near another, it was invariably given to the right owner. The Fuegian boy, whom Mr. Low had on board, showed, by going into the most violent passion, that he quite understood the reproach of being called a liar, which in truth he was. We were this time, as on all former occasions, much surprised at the little notice, or rather none whatever, which was taken of many things, the use of which must have been evident to the natives. Simple circumstances—such as the beauty of scarlet cloth or blue beads, the absence of women, our care in washing ourselves—excited their admiration far more than any grand or complicated object, such as our ship. Bougainville[1] has well remarked concerning these people, that they treat the "chefd'oeuvres de l'industrie humaine, comme ils

---

[1] *Bougainville* Louis de Bougainville (1729–1811), French navigator.

traitent les loix de la nature et ses phenomenes."[1]

On the 5th of March, we anchored in the cove at Woollya, but we saw not a soul there. We were alarmed at this, for the natives in Ponsonby Sound showed by gestures, that there had been fighting; and we afterwards heard that the dreaded Oens men had made a descent. Soon a canoe, with a little flag flying, was seen approaching, with one of the men in it washing the paint off his face. This man was poor Jemmy—now a thin haggard savage, with long disordered hair, and naked, except a bit of a blanket round his waist. We did not recognize him till he was close to us; for he was ashamed of himself, and turned his back to the ship. We had left him plump, fat, clean, and well dressed—I never saw so complete and grievous a change. As soon however as he was clothed, and the first flurry was over, things wore a good appearance. He dined with Captain Fitz Roy, and ate his dinner as tidily as formerly. He told us he had "too much" (meaning enough) to eat, that he was not cold, that his relations were very good people, and that he did not wish to go back to England: in the evening we found out the cause of this great change in Jemmy's feelings, in the arrival of his young and nice-looking wife. With his usual good feeling, he brought two beautiful otter-skins for two of his best friends, and some spear-heads and arrows made with his own hands for the Captain. He said he had built a canoe for himself, and he boasted that he could talk a little of his own language! But it is a most singular fact, that he appears to have taught all his tribe some English: an old man spontaneously announced "Jemmy Button's wife." Jemmy had lost all his property. He told us that York Minster had built a large canoe, and with his wife Fuegia, had several months since gone to his own country, and had taken farewell by an act of consummate villainy; he persuaded Jemmy and his mother to come with him, and then on the way deserted them by night, stealing every article of their property.

Jemmy went to sleep on shore, and in the morning returned, and remained on board till the ship got under weigh, which frightened his wife, who continued crying violently till he got into his canoe. He returned loaded with valuable property. Every soul on board was heartily sorry to shake hands with him for the last time. I do not now doubt that he will be as happy as, perhaps happier than, if he had never left his own country. Every one must sincerely hope that Captain Fitz Roy's noble hope may be fulfilled, of being rewarded for the many generous sacrifices which he made for these Fuegians, by some shipwrecked sailor being protected by the descendants of Jemmy Button and his tribe! When Jemmy reached the shore, he lighted a signal fire, and the smoke curled up, bidding us a last and long farewell, as the ship stood on her course into the open sea.

The perfect equality among the individuals composing the Fuegian tribes, must for a long time retard their civilization. As we see those animals, whose instinct compels them to live in society and obey a chief, are most capable of improvement, so is it with the races of mankind. Whether we look at it as a cause or a consequence, the more civilized always have the most artificial governments. For instance, the inhabitants of Otaheite,[2] who, when first discovered, were governed by hereditary kings, had arrived at a far higher grade than another branch of the same people, the New Zealanders—who, although benefited by being compelled to turn their attention to agriculture, were republicans in the most absolute sense. In Tierra del Fuego, until some chief shall arise with power sufficient to secure any acquired advantage, such as the domesticated animals, it seems scarcely possible that the political state of the country can be improved. At present, even a piece of cloth given to one is torn into shreds and distributed; and no one individual becomes richer than another. On the other hand, it is difficult to understand how a chief can arise till there is property of some sort by which he might manifest his superiority and increase his power.

I believe, in this extreme part of South America, man exists in a lower state of improvement than in any other part of the world. The South Sea islanders of the two races inhabiting the Pacific, are comparatively civilized. The Esquimaux,[3] in his subterranean hut, enjoys some of the comforts of life, and in his canoe, when fully equipped, manifests much skill. Some of the tribes of southern Africa, prowling about in search of

---

[1] *chef-d'oeuvres … phenomenes* French: "Masterworks of human industry as they treat the laws of nature and its phenomena."

[2] *Otaheite* Tahiti.

[3] *Esquimaux* Inuk, or Inuit person.

roots, and living concealed on the wild and arid plains, are sufficiently wretched. The Australian, in the simplicity of the arts of life, comes nearest the Fuegian: he can, however, boast of his boomerang, his spear and throwing-stick, his method of climbing trees, of tracking animals, and of hunting. Although the Australian may be superior in acquirements, it by no means follows that he is likewise superior in mental capacity: indeed, from what I saw of the Fuegians when on board, and from what I have read of the Australians, I should think the case was exactly the reverse.

from CHAPTER 17, GALAPAGOS ARCHIPELAGO[1]

… The natural history of these islands is eminently curious, and well deserves attention. Most of the organic productions are aboriginal creations, found nowhere else; there is even a difference between the inhabitants of the different islands; yet all show a marked relationship with those of America, though separated from that continent by an open space of ocean, between 500 and 600 miles in width. The archipelago is a little world within itself, or rather a satellite attached to America, whence it has derived a few stray colonists, and has received the general character of its indigenous productions. Considering the small size of these islands, we feel the more astonished at the number of their aboriginal beings, and at their confined range. Seeing every height crowned with its crater, and the boundaries of most of the lava-streams still distinct, we are led to believe that within a period, geologically recent, the unbroken ocean was here spread out. Hence, both in space and time, we seem to be brought somewhat near to that great fact—that mystery of mysteries—the first appearance of new beings on this earth. …

The tortoises, when purposely moving towards any point, travel by night and day, and arrive at their journey's end much sooner than would be expected. The inhabitants, from observing marked individuals, consider that they travel a distance of about eight miles in two or three days. One large tortoise, which I watched, walked at the rate of sixty yards in ten minutes, that is 360 yards in the hour, or four miles a day—allowing a

little time for it to eat on the road. During the breeding season, when the male and female are together, the male utters a hoarse roar or bellowing, which, it is said, can be heard at the distance of more than a hundred yards. The female never uses her voice, and the male only at these times; so that when the people hear this noise, they know that the two are together. They were at this time (October) laying their eggs. The female, where the soil is sandy, deposits them together, and covers them up with sand; but where the ground is rocky she drops them indiscriminately in any hole: Mr. Bynoe found seven placed in a fissure. The egg is white and spherical; one which I measured was seven inches and three-eighths in circumference, and therefore larger than a hen's egg. The young tortoises, as soon as they are hatched, fall a prey in great numbers to the carrion-feeding buzzard. The old ones seem generally to die from accidents, as from falling down precipices: at least, several of the inhabitants told me, that they had never found one dead without some evident cause. The inhabitants believe that these animals are absolutely deaf; certainly they do not overhear a person walking close behind them. I was always amused when overtaking one of these great monsters, as it was quietly pacing along, to see how suddenly, the instant I passed, it would draw in its head and legs, and uttering a deep hiss fall to the ground with a heavy sound, as if struck dead. I frequently got on their backs, and then giving a few raps on the hinder part of their shells, they would rise up and walk away—but I found it very difficult to keep my balance. The flesh of this animal is largely employed, both fresh and salted; and a beautifully clear oil is prepared from the fat. When a tortoise is caught, the man makes a slit in the skin near its tail, so as to see inside its body, whether the fat under the dorsal plate is thick. If it is not, the animal is liberated; and it is said to recover soon from this strange operation. In order to secure the tortoises, it is not sufficient to turn them like turtle, for they are often able to get on their legs again.

There can be little doubt that this tortoise is an aboriginal inhabitant of the Galapagos; for it is found on all, or nearly all, the islands, even on some of the smaller ones where there is no water; had it been an imported species, this would hardly have been the case in a group which has been so little frequented. …

[1] *Galapagos Archipelago* Series of islands off the coast of Ecuador, named after the Spanish word for tortoise.

... [T]his archipelago, though standing in the Pacific Ocean, is zoologically part of America.

If this character were owing merely to immigrants from America, there would be little remarkable in it; but we see that a vast majority of all the land animals, and that more than half of the flowering plants, are aboriginal productions. It was most striking to be surrounded by new birds, new reptiles, new shells, new insects, new plants, and yet by innumerable trifling details of structure, and even by the tones of voice and plumage of the birds, to have the temperate plains of Patagonia, or the hot dry deserts of northern Chile, vividly brought before my eyes. Why, on these small points of land, which within a late geological period must have been covered by the ocean, which are formed of basaltic lava, and therefore differ in geological character from the American continent, and which are placed under a peculiar climate—why were their aboriginal inhabitants, associated, I may add, in different proportions both in kind and number from those on the continent, and therefore acting on each other in a different manner—why were they created on American types of organization? It is probable that the islands of the Cape de Verd[1] group resemble, in all their physical conditions, far more closely the Galapagos Islands than these latter physically resemble the coast of America; yet the aboriginal inhabitants of the two groups are totally unlike; those of the Cape de Verd Islands bearing the impress of Africa, as the inhabitants of the Galapagos Archipelago are stamped with that of America.

I have not as yet noticed by far the most remarkable feature in the natural history of this archipelago; it is, that the different islands to a considerable extent are inhabited by a different set of beings. My attention was first called to this fact by the Vice-Governor, Mr. Lawson, declaring that the tortoises differed from the different islands, and that he could with certainty tell from which island any one was brought. I did not for some time pay sufficient attention to this statement, and I had already partially mingled together the collections from two of the islands. I never dreamed that islands, about fifty or sixty miles apart, and most of them in sight of each other, formed of precisely the same rocks, placed under a quite similar climate, rising to a nearly equal height, would have been differently tenanted; but we shall soon see that this is the case. It is the fate of most voyagers, no sooner to discover what is most interesting in any locality, than they are hurried from it; but I ought, perhaps, to be thankful that I obtained sufficient material to establish this most remarkable fact in the distribution of organic beings.

The inhabitants, as I have said, state that they can distinguish the tortoises from the different islands; and that they differ not only in size, but in other characters. Captain Porter[2] has described those from Charles and from the nearest island to it, namely, Hood Island, as having their shells in front thick and turned up like a Spanish saddle, whilst the tortoises from James Island are rounder, blacker, and have a better taste when cooked. M. Bibron,[3] moreover, informs me that he has seen what he considers two distinct species of tortoise from the Galapagos, but he does not know from which islands. The specimens that I brought from three islands were young ones; and probably owing to this cause, neither Mr. Gray[4] nor myself could find in them any specific differences. I have remarked that the marine Amblyrhynchus[5] was larger at Albemarle Island than elsewhere; and M. Bibron informs me that he has seen two distinct aquatic species of this genus; so that the different islands probably have their representative species or races of the Amblyrhynchus, as well as of the tortoise.

—1839

---

[1] *Cape de Verd* Cape Verde, a group of islands off the northwest coast of Africa, due west of Senegal.

[2] *Captain Porter* David Porter (1780–1843), captain of the *Essex*, who recorded his travels in *Journal of a Cruise* (1812).

[3] *M. Bibron* (Monsieur) Gabriel Bibron (1806–48), French zoologist.

[4] *Mr. Gray* Asa Gray (1810–88), a Harvard botanist and one of Darwin's strongest supporters.

[5] *marine Amblyrhynchus* Galapagos marine iguana (*Amblyrhynchus cristatus*).

IN CONTEXT

Images from *The Beagle*

There are extensive visual records of Darwin's voyages—perhaps most notably, the watercolor drawings of Conrad Martens, who was for nine months official artist on the *Beagle*. Several of these drawings were widely circulated in Victorian times in the form of engravings by Thomas Landseer that were based on original sketches by Martens and others sailing with Darwin.

Charles Darwin, 1840 (sketch by George Richmond).

Crossing the Line, 1832 (engraving by T. Landseer after a sketch by A. Earle).
It was a sailors' tradition to celebrate upon crossing the equator with mummery,
roughhousing and practical jokes.

Fuegian of the Yapoo Tekeenica tribe,
1832 (watercolor by Conrad Martens).

Fuegians at the Entrance to the Beagle Channel, 1832 (watercolor by Conrad Martens).

The Beagle in Murray Narrow, Tierra del Fuego, 1833 (watercolor by Conrad Martens).

Charles Island, Galapagos, 1835 (watercolor by Conrad Martens).

from *On the Origin of Species*

INTRODUCTION

When on board H.M.S. "Beagle," as naturalist,[1] I was much struck with certain facts in the distribution of the inhabitants of South America, and in the geological relations of the present to the past inhabitants of that continent. These facts seemed to me to throw some light on the origin of species—that mystery of mysteries, as it has been called by one of our greatest philosophers. On my return home, it occurred to me, in 1837, that something might perhaps be made out on this question by patiently accumulating and reflecting on all sorts of facts which could possibly have any bearing on it. After five years' work I allowed myself to speculate on the subject, and drew up some short notes; these I enlarged in 1844 into a sketch of the conclusions, which then seemed to me probable: from that period to the present day I have steadily pursued the same object. I hope that I may be excused for entering on these personal details, as I give them to show that I have not been hasty in coming to a decision.

My work is now nearly finished; but as it will take me two or three more years to complete it, and as my health is far from strong, I have been urged to publish this abstract. I have more especially been induced to do this, as Mr. Wallace,[2] who is now studying the natural history of the Malay archipelago, has arrived at almost exactly the same general conclusions that I have on the origin of species. Last year he sent to me a memoir on this subject, with a request that I would forward it to Sir Charles Lyell,[3] who sent it to the Linnean Society,[4] and it is published in the third volume of the Journal of that Society. Sir C. Lyell and Dr. Hooker,[5] who both knew of my work—the latter having read my sketch of 1844—honoured me by thinking it advisable to publish,

---

[1] *When on board ... naturalist* Darwin traveled on the *Beagle* between 1831 and 1836.

[2] *Mr. Wallace* Alfred Russel Wallace (1823–1913), English naturalist and social critic.

[3] *Sir Charles Lyell* British geologist (1797–1875).

[4] *Linnean Society* Prominent London scientific society.

[5] *Dr. Hooker* Joseph Dalton Hooker (1817–1911), botanist and friend of Darwin.

with Mr. Wallace's excellent memoir, some brief extracts from my manuscripts.

This abstract, which I now publish, must necessarily be imperfect. I cannot here give references and authorities for my several statements; and I must trust to the reader reposing some confidence in my accuracy. No doubt errors will have crept in, though I hope I have always been cautious in trusting to good authorities alone. I can here give only the general conclusions at which I have arrived, with a few facts in illustration, but which, I hope, in most cases will suffice. No one can feel more sensible than I do of the necessity of hereafter publishing in detail all the facts, with references, on which my conclusions have been grounded; and I hope in a future work to do this. For I am well aware that scarcely a single point is discussed in this volume on which facts cannot be adduced,[1] often apparently leading to conclusions directly opposite to those at which I have arrived. A fair result can be obtained only by fully stating and balancing the facts and arguments on both sides of each question; and this cannot possibly be here done.

I much regret that want of space prevents my having the satisfaction of acknowledging the generous assistance which I have received from very many naturalists, some of them personally unknown to me. I cannot, however, let this opportunity pass without expressing my deep obligations to Dr. Hooker, who for the last fifteen years has aided me in every possible way by his large stores of knowledge and his excellent judgment.

In considering the origin of species, it is quite conceivable that a naturalist, reflecting on the mutual affinities of organic beings, on their embryological relations, their geographical distribution, geological succession, and other such facts, might come to the conclusion that each species had not been independently created, but had descended, like varieties, from other species. Nevertheless, such a conclusion, even if well founded, would be unsatisfactory, until it could be shown how the innumerable species inhabiting this world have been modified, so as to acquire that perfection of structure and coadaptation which most justly excites our admiration. Naturalists continually refer to external conditions, such as climate, food, *et cetera*, as the only possible cause of variation. In one very limited sense, as we shall hereafter see, this may be true; but it is preposterous to attribute to mere external conditions, the structure, for instance, of the woodpecker, with its feet, tail, beak, and tongue, so admirably adapted to catch insects under the bark of trees. In the case of the mistletoe, which draws its nourishment from certain trees, which has seeds that must be transported by certain birds, and which has flowers with separate sexes absolutely requiring the agency of certain insects to bring pollen from one flower to the other, it is equally preposterous to account for the structure of this parasite, with its relations to several distinct organic beings, by the effects of external conditions, or of habit, or of the volition of the plant itself.

The author of the "Vestiges of Creation"[2] would, I presume, say that, after a certain unknown number of generations, some bird had given birth to a woodpecker, and some plant to the mistletoe, and that these had been produced perfect as we now see them; but this assumption seems to me to be no explanation, for it leaves the case of the coadaptations of organic beings to each other and to their physical conditions of life, untouched and unexplained.

It is, therefore, of the highest importance to gain a clear insight into the means of modification and coadaptation. At the commencement of my observations it seemed to me probable that a careful study of domesticated animals and of cultivated plants would offer the best chance of making out this obscure problem. Nor have I been disappointed; in this and in all other perplexing cases I have invariably found that our knowledge, imperfect though it be, of variation under domestication, afforded the best and safest clue. I may venture to express my conviction of the high value of such studies, although they have been very commonly neglected by naturalists.

From these considerations, I shall devote the first chapter of this abstract to variation under domestication. We shall thus see that a large amount of hereditary modification is at least possible, and, what is equally or more important, we shall see how great is the power of

---

[1] *adduced* Brought forth.

[2] "*Vestiges of Creation*" 1844 book, published anonymously but written by Robert Chambers, which suggests that progressive evolution is God's act of creation through geological time.

man in accumulating by his selection successive slight variations. I will then pass on to the variability of species in a state of nature; but I shall, unfortunately, be compelled to treat this subject far too briefly, as it can be treated properly only by giving long catalogues of facts. We shall, however, be enabled to discuss what circumstances are most favourable to variation. In the next chapter the struggle for existence amongst all organic beings throughout the world, which inevitably follows from their high geometrical ratio of increase, will be treated of. This is the doctrine of Malthus,[1] applied to the whole animal and vegetable kingdoms. As many more individuals of each species are born than can possibly survive; and as, consequently, there is a frequently recurring struggle for existence, it follows that any being, if it vary however slightly in any manner profitable to itself, under the complex and sometimes varying conditions of life, will have a better chance of surviving, and thus be *naturally selected*. From the strong principle of inheritance, any selected variety will tend to propagate its new and modified form.

This fundamental subject of natural selection will be treated at some length in the fourth chapter; and we shall then see how natural selection almost inevitably causes much extinction of the less improved forms of life and induces what I have called divergence of character. In the next chapter I shall discuss the complex and little known laws of variation and of correlation of growth. In the four succeeding chapters, the most apparent and gravest difficulties on the theory will be given: namely, first, the difficulties of transitions, or in understanding how a simple being or a simple organ can be changed and perfected into a highly developed being or elaborately constructed organ; secondly the subject of instinct, or the mental powers of animals, thirdly, hybridism, or the infertility of species and the fertility of varieties when intercrossed; and fourthly, the imperfection of the geological record. In the next chapter I shall consider the geological succession of organic beings throughout time; in the eleventh and twelfth, their geographical distribution throughout space; in the thirteenth, their classification or mutual affinities, both

when mature and in an embryonic condition. In the last chapter I shall give a brief recapitulation of the whole work, and a few concluding remarks.

No one ought to feel surprise at much remaining as yet unexplained in regard to the origin of species and varieties, if he makes due allowance for our profound ignorance in regard to the mutual relations of all the beings which live around us. Who can explain why one species ranges widely and is very numerous, and why another allied species has a narrow range and is rare? Yet these relations are of the highest importance, for they determine the present welfare, and, as I believe, the future success and modification of every inhabitant of this world. Still less do we know of the mutual relations of the innumerable inhabitants of the world during the many past geological epochs in its history. Although much remains obscure, and will long remain obscure, I can entertain no doubt, after the most deliberate study and dispassionate judgment of which I am capable, that the view which most naturalists entertain, and which I formerly entertained—namely, that each species has been independently created—is erroneous. I am fully convinced that species are not immutable; but that those belonging to what are called the same genera[2] are lineal descendants of some other and generally extinct species, in the same manner as the acknowledged varieties of any one species are the descendants of that species. Furthermore, I am convinced that natural selection has been the main but not exclusive means of modification.

from CHAPTER 3, STRUGGLE FOR EXISTENCE

Before entering on the subject of this chapter, I must make a few preliminary remarks, to show how the struggle for existence bears on natural selection. It has been seen in the last chapter that amongst organic beings in a state of nature there is some individual variability; indeed I am not aware that this has ever been disputed. It is immaterial for us whether a multitude of doubtful forms be called species or sub-species or varieties; what rank, for instance, the two or three hundred doubtful forms of British plants are entitled to hold, if the existence of any well-marked varieties be

[1] *Malthus* Thomas Robert Malthus (1766–1834), who theorized in his 1798 work *An Essay on the Principle of Population* that the human population would eventually outstrip its food resources.

[2] *genera* Latin: Groupings of species. Plural of "genus."

admitted. But the mere existence of individual variability and of some few well-marked varieties, though necessary as the foundation for the work, helps us but little in understanding how species arise in nature. How have all those exquisite adaptations of one part of the organisation to another part, and to the conditions of life, and of one distinct organic being to another being, been perfected? We see these beautiful co-adaptations most plainly in the woodpecker and mistletoe; and only a little less plainly in the humblest parasite which clings to the hairs of a quadruped or feathers of a bird; in the structure of the beetle which dives through the water; in the plumed seed which is wafted by the gentlest breeze; in short, we see beautiful adaptations everywhere and in every part of the organic world.

Again, it may be asked, how is it that varieties, which I have called incipient species, become ultimately converted into good and distinct species, which in most cases obviously differ from each other far more than do the varieties of the same species? How do those groups of species, which constitute what are called distinct genera, and which differ from each other more than do the species of the same genus, arise? All these results, as we shall more fully see in the next chapter, follow inevitably from the struggle for life. Owing to this struggle for life, any variation, however slight and from whatever cause proceeding, if it be in any degree profitable to an individual of any species, in its infinitely complex relations to other organic beings and to external nature, will tend to the preservation of that individual, and will generally be inherited by its offspring. The offspring, also, will thus have a better chance of surviving, for, of the many individuals of any species which are periodically born, but a small number can survive. I have called this principle, by which each slight variation, if useful, is preserved, by the term of natural selection, in order to mark its relation to man's power of selection. We have seen that man by selection can certainly produce great results, and can adapt organic beings to his own uses, through the accumulation of slight but useful variations, given to him by the hand of nature. But natural selection, as we shall hereafter see, is a power incessantly ready for action, and is as immeasurably superior to man's feeble efforts, as the works of nature are to those of art.

We will now discuss in a little more detail the struggle for existence. In my future work this subject shall be treated, as it well deserves, at much greater length. The elder De Candolle[1] and Lyell have largely and philosophically shown that all organic beings are exposed to severe competition. In regard to plants, no one has treated this subject with more spirit and ability than W. Herbert,[2] Dean of Manchester, evidently the result of his great horticultural knowledge. Nothing is easier than to admit in words the truth of the universal struggle for life, or more difficult—at least I have found it so—than constantly to bear this conclusion in mind. Yet unless it be thoroughly engrained in the mind, I am convinced that the whole economy of nature, with every fact on distribution, rarity, abundance, extinction, and variation, will be dimly seen or quite misunderstood. We behold the face of nature bright with gladness, we often see superabundance of food; we do not see, or we forget, that the birds which are idly singing round us mostly live on insects or seeds, and are thus constantly destroying life; or we forget how largely these songsters, or their eggs, or their nestlings, are destroyed by birds and beasts of prey; we do not always bear in mind, that though food may be now superabundant, it is not so at all seasons of each recurring year.

I should premise that I use the term struggle for existence in a large and metaphorical sense, including dependence of one being on another, and including (which is more important) not only the life of the individual, but success in leaving progeny. Two canine animals in a time of dearth, may be truly said to struggle with each other which shall get food and live. But a plant on the edge of a desert is said to struggle for life against the drought, though more properly it should be said to be dependent on the moisture. A plant which annually produces a thousand seeds, of which on an average only one comes to maturity, may be more truly said to struggle with the plants of the same and other kinds which already clothe the ground. The mistletoe is dependent on the apple and a few other trees, but can only in a far-fetched sense be said to struggle with these trees, for if too many of these parasites grow on the same

[1] *The elder De Candolle* Augustin-Pyramus de Candolle (1778–1841), Swiss botanist.

[2] *W. Herbert* William Herbert (1778–1847).

tree, it will languish and die. But several seedling mistletoes, growing close together on the same branch, may more truly be said to struggle with each other. As the mistletoe is disseminated by birds, its existence depends on birds; and it may metaphorically be said to struggle with other fruit-bearing plants, in order to tempt birds to devour and thus disseminate its seeds rather than those of other plants. In these several senses, which pass into each other, I use for convenience' sake the general term of struggle for existence.

A struggle for existence inevitably follows from the high rate at which all organic beings tend to increase. Every being, which during its natural lifetime produces several eggs or seeds, must suffer destruction during some period of its life, and during some season or occasional year, otherwise, on the principle of geometrical increase, its numbers would quickly become so inordinately great that no country could support the product. Hence, as more individuals are produced than can possibly survive, there must in every case be a struggle for existence, either one individual with another of the same species, or with the individuals of distinct species, or with the physical conditions of life. It is the doctrine of Malthus applied with manifold force to the whole animal and vegetable kingdoms; for in this case there can be no artificial increase of food, and no prudential restraint from marriage. Although some species may be now increasing, more or less rapidly, in numbers, all cannot do so, for the world would not hold them.

There is no exception to the rule that every organic being naturally increases at so high a rate, that if not destroyed, the earth would soon be covered by the progeny of a single pair. Even slow-breeding man has doubled in twenty-five years, and at this rate, in a few thousand years, there would literally not be standing room for his progeny. Linnaeus[1] has calculated that if an annual plant produced only two seeds—and there is no plant so unproductive as this—and their seedlings next year produced two, and so on, then in twenty years there would be a million plants. The elephant is reckoned to be the slowest breeder of all known animals, and I have taken some pains to estimate its probable

minimum rate of natural increase: it will be under the mark to assume that it breeds when thirty years old, and goes on breeding till ninety years old, bringing forth three pair of young in this interval; if this be so, at the end of the fifth century there would be alive fifteen million elephants, descended from the first pair.

But we have better evidence on this subject than mere theoretical calculations, namely, the numerous recorded cases of the astonishingly rapid increase of various animals in a state of nature, when circumstances have been favourable to them during two or three following seasons. Still more striking is the evidence from our domestic animals of many kinds which have run wild in several parts of the world: if the statements of the rate of increase of slow-breeding cattle and horses in South America, and latterly in Australia, had not been well authenticated, they would have been quite incredible. So it is with plants: cases could be given of introduced plants which have become common throughout whole islands in a period of less than ten years. Several of the plants now most numerous over the wide plains of La Plata,[2] clothing square leagues of surface almost to the exclusion of all other plants, have been introduced from Europe; and there are plants which now range in India, as I hear from Dr. Falconer,[3] from Cape Comorin[4] to the Himalaya, which have been imported from America since its discovery. In such cases, and endless instances could be given, no one supposes that the fertility of these animals or plants has been suddenly and temporarily increased in any sensible degree. The obvious explanation is that the conditions of life have been very favourable, and that there has consequently been less destruction of the old and young, and that nearly all the young have been enabled to breed. In such cases the geometrical ratio of increase, the result of which never fails to be surprising, simply explains the extraordinarily rapid increase and wide diffusion of naturalised productions in their new homes. ...

Many cases are on record showing how complex and unexpected are the checks and relations between organic

---

[1] *Linnaeus*   Carolus Linnaeus (1707–78), Swedish scientist who laid the foundations of modern taxonomy.

[2] *La Plata*   Region of Argentina.

[3] *Dr. Falconer*   Hugh Falconer (1808–65), one of the pre-eminent British palaeontologists of the time.

[4] *Cape Comorin*   Southernmost point of the Indian subcontinent.

beings, which have to struggle together in the same country. I will give only a single instance, which, though a simple one, has interested me. In Staffordshire, on the estate of a relation where I had ample means of investigation, there was a large and extremely barren heath, which had never been touched by the hand of man; but several hundred acres of exactly the same nature had been enclosed twenty-five years previously and planted with Scotch fir. The change in the native vegetation of the planted part of the heath was most remarkable, more than is generally seen in passing from one quite different soil to another: not only the proportional numbers of the heath-plants were wholly changed, but twelve species of plants (not counting grasses and carices[1]) flourished in the plantations, which could not be found on the heath. The effect on the insects must have been still greater, for six insectivorous birds were very common in the plantations, which were not to be seen on the heath; and the heath was frequented by two or three distinct insectivorous birds. Here we see how potent has been the effect of the introduction of a single tree, nothing whatever else having been done, with the exception that the land had been enclosed, so that cattle could not enter. But how important an element enclosure is, I plainly saw near Farnham, in Surrey. Here there are extensive heaths, with a few clumps of old Scotch firs on the distant hill-tops: within the last ten years large spaces have been enclosed, and self-sown firs are now springing up in multitudes, so close together that all cannot live. When I ascertained that these young trees had not been sown or planted, I was so much surprised at their numbers that I went to several points of view, whence I could examine hundreds of acres of the unenclosed heath, and literally I could not see a single Scotch fir, except the old planted clumps. But on looking closely between the stems of the heath, I found a multitude of seedlings and little trees, which had been perpetually browsed down by the cattle. In one square yard, at a point some hundreds yards distant from one of the old clumps, I counted thirty-two little trees; and one of them, judging from the rings of growth, had during twenty-six years tried to raise its head above the stems of the heath, and had failed. No wonder that, as soon as the land was enclosed, it became thickly clothed

with vigorously growing young firs. Yet the heath was so extremely barren and so extensive that no one would ever have imagined that cattle would have so closely and effectually searched it for food.

Here we see that cattle absolutely determine the existence of the Scotch fir; but in several parts of the world insects determine the existence of cattle. Perhaps Paraguay offers the most curious instance of this; for here neither cattle nor horses nor dogs have ever run wild, though they swarm southward and northward in a feral state; and Azara and Rengger[2] have shown that this is caused by the greater number in Paraguay of a certain fly, which lays its eggs in the navels of these animals when first born. The increase of these flies, numerous as they are, must be habitually checked by some means, probably by birds. Hence, if certain insectivorous birds (whose numbers are probably regulated by hawks or beasts of prey) were to increase in Paraguay, the flies would decrease—then cattle and horses would become feral, and this would certainly greatly alter (as indeed I have observed in parts of South America) the vegetation: this again would largely affect the insects; and this, as we just have seen in Staffordshire, the insectivorous birds, and so onwards in ever-increasing circles of complexity. We began this series by insectivorous birds, and we have ended with them. Not that in nature the relations can ever be as simple as this. Battle within battle must ever be recurring with varying success; and yet in the long-run the forces are so nicely balanced, that the face of nature remains uniform for long periods of time, though assuredly the merest trifle would often give the victory to one organic being over another. Nevertheless so profound is our ignorance, and so high our presumption, that we marvel when we hear of the extinction of an organic being; and as we do not see the cause, we invoke cataclysms to desolate the world, or invent laws on the duration of the forms of life!

I am tempted to give one more instance showing how plants and animals, most remote in the scale of nature, are bound together by a web of complex rela-

---

[1] *carices* Sedges.

[2] *Azara and Rengger* Félix de Azara (1746–1821), Spanish explorer and naturalist, and Johann Rudolph Rengger (1795–1832), German naturalist. In the early part of the nineteenth century, both published influential studies on Paraguayan fauna.

tions. I shall hereafter have occasion to show that the exotic *Lobelia fulgens*,[1] in this part of England, is never visited by insects, and consequently, from its peculiar structure, never can set a seed. Many of our orchidaceous plants absolutely require the visits of moths to remove their pollen-masses and thus to fertilise them. I have, also, reason to believe that humble-bees are indispensable to the fertilisation of the heartsease (*Viola tricolor*), for other bees do not visit this flower. From experiments which I have tried, I have found that the visits of bees, if not indispensable, are at least highly beneficial to the fertilisation of our clovers; but humble-bees alone visit the common red clover (*Trifolium pratense*), as other bees cannot reach the nectar. Hence I have very little doubt, that if the whole genus of humble-bees became extinct or very rare in England, the heartsease and red clover would become very rare, or wholly disappear. The number of humble-bees in any district depends in a great degree on the number of field-mice, which destroy their combs and nests; and Mr. H. Newman,[2] who has long attended to the habits of humble-bees, believes that "more than two thirds of them are thus destroyed all over England." Now the number of mice is largely dependent, as every one knows, on the number of cats; and Mr. Newman says, "Near villages and small towns I have found the nests of humble-bees more numerous than elsewhere, which I attribute to the number of cats that destroy the mice." Hence it is quite credible that the presence of a feline animal in large numbers in a district might determine, through the intervention first of mice and then of bees, the frequency of certain flowers in that district!

from CHAPTER 14, RECAPITULATION AND CONCLUSION

… I have now recapitulated the chief facts and considerations which have thoroughly convinced me that species have changed, and are still slowly changing by the preservation and accumulation of successive slight favourable variations. Why, it may be asked, have all the most eminent living naturalists and geologists rejected this view of the mutability of species? It cannot be

asserted that organic beings in a state of nature are subject to no variation; it cannot be proved that the amount of variation in the course of long ages is a limited quantity; no clear distinction has been, or can be, drawn between species and well-marked varieties. It cannot be maintained that species when intercrossed are invariably sterile, and varieties invariably fertile; or that sterility is a special endowment and sign of creation. The belief that species were immutable productions was almost unavoidable as long as the history of the world was thought to be of short duration; and now that we have acquired some idea of the lapse of time, we are too apt to assume, without proof, that the geological record is so perfect that it would have afforded us plain evidence of the mutation of species, if they had undergone mutation.

But the chief cause of our natural unwillingness to admit that one species has given birth to other and distinct species, is that we are always slow in admitting any great change of which we do not see the intermediate steps. The difficulty is the same as that felt by so many geologists, when Lyell first insisted that long lines of inland cliffs had been formed, and great valleys excavated, by the slow action of the coast-waves. The mind cannot possibly grasp the full meaning of the term of a hundred million years; it cannot add up and perceive the full effects of many slight variations, accumulated during an almost infinite number of generations.

Although I am fully convinced of the truth of the views given in this volume under the form of an abstract, I by no means expect to convince experienced naturalists whose minds are stocked with a multitude of facts all viewed, during a long course of years, from a point of view directly opposite to mine. It is so easy to hide our ignorance under such expressions as the "plan of creation," "unity of design," *et cetera*, and to think that we give an explanation when we only restate a fact. Any one whose disposition leads him to attach more weight to unexplained difficulties than to the explanation of a certain number of facts will certainly reject my theory. A few naturalists, endowed with much flexibility of mind, and who have already begun to doubt on the immutability of species, may be influenced by this volume; but I look with confidence to the future, to young and rising naturalists, who will be able to view

---

[1] *Lobelia fulgens* Queen Victoria Cardinal flower.

[2] *Mr. H. Newman* Unidentified.

both sides of the question with impartiality. Whoever is led to believe that species are mutable will do good service by conscientiously expressing his conviction; for only thus can the load of prejudice by which this subject is overwhelmed be removed. ...

When the views entertained in this volume on the origin of species, or when analogous views are generally admitted, we can dimly foresee that there will be a considerable revolution in natural history. Systematists will be able to pursue their labours as at present; but they will not be incessantly haunted by the shadowy doubt whether this or that form be in essence a species. This I feel sure, and I speak after experience, will be no slight relief. The endless disputes whether or not some fifty species of British brambles are true species will cease. Systematists will have only to decide (not that this will be easy) whether any form be sufficiently constant and distinct from other forms, to be capable of definition; and if definable, whether the differences be sufficiently important to deserve a specific name. This latter point will become a far more essential consideration than it is at present; for differences, however slight, between any two forms, if not blended by intermediate gradations, are looked at by most naturalists as sufficient to raise both forms to the rank of species. Hereafter we shall be compelled to acknowledge that the only distinction between species and well-marked varieties is, that the latter are known, or believed, to be connected at the present day by intermediate gradations, whereas species were formerly thus connected. Hence, without quite rejecting the consideration of the present existence of intermediate gradations between any two forms, we shall be led to weigh more carefully and to value higher the actual amount of difference between them. It is quite possible that forms now generally acknowledged to be merely varieties may hereafter be thought worthy of specific names, as with the primrose and cowslip; and in this case scientific and common language will come into accordance. In short, we shall have to treat species in the same manner as those naturalists treat genera, who admit that genera are merely artificial combinations made for convenience. This may not be a cheering prospect; but we shall at least be freed from the vain search for the undiscovered and undiscoverable essence of the term species.

The other and more general departments of natural history will rise greatly in interest. The terms used by naturalists of affinity, relationship, community of type, paternity, morphology, adaptive characters, rudimentary and aborted organs, et cetera, will cease to be metaphorical, and will have a plain signification. When we no longer look at an organic being as a savage looks at a ship, as at something wholly beyond his comprehension; when we regard every production of nature as one which has had a history; when we contemplate every complex structure and instinct as the summing up of many contrivances, each useful to the possessor, nearly in the same way as when we look at any great mechanical invention as the summing up of the labour, the experience, the reason, and even the blunders of numerous workmen; when we thus view each organic being, how far more interesting, I speak from experience, will the study of natural history become!

A grand and almost untrodden field of inquiry will be opened, on the causes and laws of variation, on correlation of growth, on the effects of use and disuse, on the direct action of external conditions, and so forth. The study of domestic productions will rise immensely in value. A new variety raised by man will be a far more important and interesting subject for study than one more species added to the infinitude of already recorded species. Our classifications will come to be, as far as they can be so made, genealogies; and will then truly give what may be called the plan of creation. The rules for classifying will no doubt become simpler when we have a definite object in view. We possess no pedigrees or armorial bearings; and we have to discover and trace the many diverging lines of descent in our natural genealogies, by characters of any kind which have long been inherited. Rudimentary organs will speak infallibly with respect to the nature of long-lost structures. Species and groups of species, which are called aberrant, and which may fancifully be called living fossils, will aid us in forming a picture of the ancient forms of life. Embryology will reveal to us the structure, in some degree obscured, of the prototypes of each great class.

When we can feel assured that all the individuals of the same species, and all the closely allied species of most genera, have within a not very remote period descended from one parent, and have migrated from some one birthplace; and when we better know the many means of migration, then, by the light which geology now throws, and will continue to throw, on former changes of climate and of the level of the land, we shall surely be enabled to trace in an admirable manner the former migrations of the inhabitants of the whole world. Even at present, by comparing the differences of the inhabitants of the sea on the opposite sides of a continent, and the nature of the various inhabitants of that continent in relation to their apparent means of immigration, some light can be thrown on ancient geography.

The noble science of geology loses glory from the extreme imperfection of the record. The crust of the earth with its embedded remains must not be looked at as a well-filled museum, but as a poor collection made at hazard and at rare intervals. The accumulation of each great fossiliferous formation will be recognised as having depended on an unusual concurrence of circumstances, and the blank intervals between the successive stages as having been of vast duration. But we shall be able to gauge with some security the duration of these intervals by a comparison of the preceding and succeeding organic forms. We must be cautious in attempting to correlate as strictly contemporaneous two formations, which include few identical species, by the general succession of their forms of life. As species are produced and exterminated by slowly acting and still existing causes, and not by miraculous acts of creation and by catastrophes; and as the most important of all causes of organic change is one which is almost independent of altered and perhaps suddenly altered physical conditions, namely, the mutual relation of organism to organism—the improvement of one being entailing the improvement or the extermination of others; it follows, that the amount of organic change in the fossils of consecutive formations probably serves as a fair measure of the lapse of actual time. A number of species, however, keeping in a body might remain for a long period unchanged, whilst within this same period, several of these species, by migrating into new countries and coming into competition with foreign associates, might become modified; so that we must not overrate the accuracy of organic change as a measure of time. During early periods of the earth's history, when the forms of life were probably fewer and simpler, the rate of change

was probably slower; and at the first dawn of life, when very few forms of the simplest structure existed, the rate of change may have been slow in an extreme degree. The whole history of the world, as at present known, although of a length quite incomprehensible by us, will hereafter be recognised as a mere fragment of time, compared with the ages which have elapsed since the first creature, the progenitor of innumerable extinct and living descendants, was created.

In the distant future I see open fields for far more important researches. Psychology will be based on a new foundation, that of the necessary acquirement of each mental power and capacity by gradation. Light will be thrown on the origin of man and his history.

Authors of the highest eminence seem to be fully satisfied with the view that each species has been independently created. To my mind it accords better with what we know of the laws impressed on matter by the Creator, that the production and extinction of the past and present inhabitants of the world should have been due to secondary causes, like those determining the birth and death of the individual. When I view all beings not as special creations, but as the lineal descendants of some few beings which lived long before the first bed of the Silurian[1] system was deposited, they seem to me to become ennobled. Judging from the past, we may safely infer that not one living species will transmit its unaltered likeness to a distant futurity. And of the species now living very few will transmit progeny of any kind to a far distant futurity; for the manner in which all organic beings are grouped, shows that the greater number of species of each genus, and all the species of many genera, have left no descendants, but have become utterly extinct. We can so far take a prophetic glance into futurity as to foretell that it will be the common and widely-spread species, belonging to the larger and dominant groups, which will ultimately prevail and procreate new and dominant species. As all the living forms of life are the lineal descendants of those which lived long before the Silurian epoch, we may feel certain that the ordinary succession by generation has never once been broken, and that no cataclysm has desolated the whole world. Hence we may look with

[1] *Silurian* Geological time period approximately 440 million to 410 million years ago.

some confidence to a secure future of equally inappreciable length. And as natural selection works solely by and for the good of each being, all corporeal and mental endowments will tend to progress towards perfection.

It is interesting to contemplate an entangled bank, clothed with many plants of many kinds, with birds singing on the bushes, with various insects flitting about, and with worms crawling through the damp earth, and to reflect that these elaborately constructed forms, so different from each other, and dependent on each other in so complex a manner, have all been produced by laws acting around us. These laws, taken in the largest sense, being growth with reproduction; inheritance which is almost implied by reproduction; variability from the indirect and direct action of the external conditions of life, and from use and disuse; a ratio of increase so high as to lead to a struggle for life, and as a consequence to natural selection, entailing divergence of character and the extinction of less-improved forms. Thus, from the war of nature, from famine and death, the most exalted object which we are capable of conceiving, namely, the production of the higher animals, directly follows. There is grandeur in this view of life, with its several powers, having been originally breathed into a few forms or into one; and that, whilst this planet has gone cycling on according to the fixed law of gravity, from so simple a beginning endless forms most beautiful and most wonderful have been, and are being, evolved.
—1859

from *The Descent of Man*

from CHAPTER 21
GENERAL SUMMARY AND CONCLUSION

A brief summary will be sufficient to recall to the reader's mind the more salient points in this work. Many of the views which have been advanced are highly speculative, and some no doubt will prove erroneous; but I have in every case given the reasons which have led me to one view rather than to another. It seemed worthwhile to try how far the principle of evolution would throw light on some or the more complex problems in the natural history of man. False facts are highly injurious to the progress of science, for they often endure long; but false views, if supported by some evidence, do little harm, for every one takes a salutary pleasure in proving their falseness: and when this is done, one path towards error is closed and the road to truth is often at the same time opened.

The main conclusion here arrived at, and now held by many naturalists who are well competent to form a sound judgment is that man is descended from some less highly organised form. The grounds upon which this conclusion rests will never be shaken, for the close similarity between man and the lower animals in embryonic development, as well as in innumerable points of structure and constitution both of high and of the most trifling importance—the rudiments which he retains, and the abnormal reversions to which he is occasionally liable—are facts which cannot be disputed. They have long been known, but until recently they told us nothing with respect to the origin of man. Now when viewed by the light of our knowledge of the whole organic world, their meaning is unmistakable. The great principle of evolution stands up clear and firm, when these groups or facts are considered in connection with others, such as the mutual affinities of the members of the same group, their geographical distribution in past and present times, and their geological succession. It is incredible that all these facts should speak falsely. He who is not content to look, like a savage, at the phenomena of nature as disconnected, cannot any longer believe that man is the work of a separate act of creation. He will be forced to admit that the close resemblance of the embryo of man to that, for instance, of a dog—the construction of his skull, limbs and whole frame on the same plan with that of other mammals, independently of the uses to which the parts may be put—the occasional re-appearance of various structures, for instance of several muscles, which man does not normally possess, but which are common to the Quadrumana[1]—and a crowd of analogous facts—all point in the plainest manner to the conclusion that man is the co-descendant with other mammals of a common progenitor.

---

[1] *Quadrumana* Order of mammals, including monkeys, apes, and baboons, in which both the hind and the forefeet have an opposable digit.

We have seen that man incessantly presents individual differences in all parts of his body and in his mental faculties. These differences or variations seem to be induced by the same general causes, and to obey the same laws as with the lower animals. In both cases similar laws of inheritance prevail. Man tends to increase at a greater rate than his means of subsistence; consequently he is occasionally subjected to a severe struggle for existence, and natural selection will have effected whatever lies within its scope. A succession of strongly-marked variations of a similar nature is by no means requisite; slight fluctuating differences in the individual suffice for the work of natural selection; not that we have any reason to suppose that in the same species, all parts of the organization tend to vary to the same degree. We may feel assured that the inherited effects of the long-continued use or disuse of parts will have done much in the same direction with natural selection. Modifications formerly of importance, though no longer of any special use, are long-inherited. When one part is modified, other parts change through the principle of correlation, of which we have instances in many curious cases of correlated monstrosities. Something may be attributed to the direct and definite action of the surrounding conditions of life, such as abundant food, heat or moisture; and lastly, many characters of slight physiological importance, some indeed of considerable importance, have been gained through sexual selection.

No doubt man, as well as every other animal, presents structures, which seem to our limited knowledge, not to be now of any service to him, nor to have been so formerly, either for the general conditions of life, or in the relations of one sex to the other. Such structures cannot be accounted for by any form of selection, or by the inherited effects of the use and disuse of parts. We know, however, that many strange and strongly-marked peculiarities of structure occasionally appear in our domesticated productions, and if their unknown causes were to act more uniformly, they would probably become common to all the individuals of the species. We may hope hereafter to understand something about the causes of such occasional modifications, especially through the study of monstrosities: hence the labours of experimentalists such as those of

M. Camille Dareste,[1] are full of promise for the future. In general we can only say that the cause of each slight variation and of each monstrosity lies much more in the constitution of the organism, than in the nature of the surrounding conditions; though new and changed conditions certainly play an important part in exciting organic changes of many kinds. Through the means just specified, aided perhaps by others as yet undiscovered, man has been raised to his present state. But since he attained to the rank of manhood, he has diverged into distinct races, or as they may be more fitly called sub-species. Some of these, such as the Negro and European, are so distinct that, if specimens had been brought to a naturalist without any further information, they would undoubtedly have been considered by him as good and true species. Nevertheless all the races agree in so many unimportant details of structure and in so many mental peculiarities that these can be accounted for only by inheritance from a common progenitor; and a progenitor thus characterised would probably deserve to rank as man.

It must not be supposed that the divergence of each race from the other races, and of all from a common stock, can be traced back to any one pair of progenitors. On the contrary, at every stage in the process of modification, all the individuals which were in any way better fitted for their conditions of life, though in different degrees, would have survived in greater numbers than the less well-fitted. The process would have been like that followed by man, when he does not intentionally select particular individuals, but breeds from all the superior individuals, and neglects the inferior. He thus slowly but surely modifies his stock, and unconsciously forms a new strain. So with respect to modifications acquired independently of selection, and due to variations arising from the nature of the organism and the action of the surrounding conditions, or from changed habits of life, no single pair will have been modified much more than the other pairs inhabiting the same country, for all will have been continually blended through free intercrossing.

---

[1] *M. Camille Dareste* (Monsieur) Camille Dareste, French zoologist (1822–99), founder of experimental teratology, the study of abnormalities in plants and animals.

By considering the embryological structure of man—the homologies[1] which he presents with the lower animals—the rudiments which he retains—and the reversions to which he is liable, we can partly recall in imagination the former condition of our early progenitors; and can approximately place them in their proper place in the zoological series. We thus learn that man is descended from a hairy, tailed quadruped, probably arboreal in its habits, and an inhabitant of the Old World. This creature, if its whole structure had been examined by a naturalist, would have been classed amongst the Quadrumana, as surely as the still more ancient progenitor of the Old and New World monkeys. The Quadrumana and all the higher mammals are probably derived from an ancient marsupial animal, and this through a long series of diversified forms, from some amphibian-like creature, and this again from some fish-like animal. In the dim obscurity of the past we can see that the early progenitor of all the Vertebrata must have been an aquatic animal provided with branchiae,[2] with the two sexes united in the same individual, and with the most important organs of the body (such as the brain and heart) imperfectly or not at all developed. This animal seems to have been more like the larvae of the existing marine Ascidians[3] than any other known form. ...

The belief in God has often been advanced as not only the greatest, but the most complete of all the distinctions between man and the lower animals. It is however impossible, as we have seen, to maintain that this belief is innate or instinctive in man. On the other hand a belief in all-pervading spiritual agencies seems to be universal; and apparently follows from a considerable advance in man's reason, and from a still greater advance in his faculties of imagination, curiosity and wonder. I am aware that the assumed instinctive belief in God has been used by many persons as an argument for His existence. But this is a rash argument, as we should thus be compelled to believe in the existence of many cruel and malignant spirits, only a little more powerful than man; for the belief in them is far more general than in a beneficent Deity. The idea of a universal and benefi-

cent Creator does not seem to arise in the mind of man, until he has been elevated by long-continued culture.

He who believes in the advancement of man from some low organised form, will naturally ask how does this bear on the belief in the immortality of the soul. The barbarous races of man, as Sir J. Lubbock[4] has shown, possess no clear belief of this kind; but arguments derived from the primeval beliefs of savages are, as we have just seen, of little or no avail. Few persons feel any anxiety from the impossibility of determining at what precise period in the development of the individual, from the first trace of a minute germinal vesicle,[5] man becomes an immortal being; and there is no greater cause for anxiety because the period cannot possibly be determined in the gradually ascending organic scale.

I am aware that the conclusions arrived at in this work will be denounced by some as highly irreligious; but he who denounces them is bound to show why it is more irreligious to explain the origin of man as a distinct species by descent from some lower form, through the laws of variation and natural selection, than to explain the birth of the individual through the laws of ordinary reproduction. The birth both of the species and of the individual are equally parts of that grand sequence of events, which our minds refuse to accept as the result of blind chance. The understanding revolts at such a conclusion, whether or not we are able to believe that every slight variation of structure—the union of each pair in marriage—the dissemination of each seed—and other such events, have all been ordained for some special purpose.

Sexual selection has been treated at great length in this work; for, as I have attempted to show, it has played an important part in the history of the organic world. I am aware that much remains doubtful, but I have endeavoured to give a fair view of the whole case. In the lower divisions of the animal kingdom, sexual selection seems to have done nothing: such animals are often affixed for life to the same spot, or have the sexes combined in the same individual, or what is still more important, their perceptive and intellectual faculties are not sufficiently advanced to allow of the feelings of love

---

[1] *homologies*   Similarities of structure due to common descent.

[2] *branchiae*   Breathing apparatus, gills.

[3] *Ascidians*   Molluscs.

[4] *Sir J. Lubbock*   John Lubbock, Lord Avebury (1834–1913), in his book *Prehistoric Times* (1865).

[5] *germinal vesicle*   Nucleus of animals' permanent ovum.

and jealousy, or of the exertion of choice. When, however, we come to the Arthropoda[1] and Vertebrata, even to the lowest classes in these two great sub-kingdoms, sexual selection has effected much.

In the several great classes of the animal kingdom—in mammals, birds, reptiles, fishes, insects, and even crustaceans—the differences between the sexes follow nearly the same rules. The males are almost always the wooers; and they alone are armed with special weapons for fighting with their rivals. They are generally stronger and larger than the females, and are endowed with the requisite qualities of courage and pugnacity. They are provided, either exclusively or in a much higher degree than the females, with organs for vocal or instrumental music, and with odoriferous glands. They are ornamental with infinitely diversified appendages, and with the most brilliant or conspicuous colours, often arranged in elegant patterns, whilst the females are unadorned. When the sexes differ in more important structures, it is the male which is provided with special sense-organs for discovering the female, with locomotive organs for reaching her, and often with prehensile organs for holding her. These various structures for charming or securing the female are often developed in the male during only part of the year, namely the breeding-season. They have in many cases been more or less transferred to the females; and in the latter case they often appear in her as mere rudiments. They are lost or never gained by the males after emasculation. Generally they are not developed in the male during early youth, but appear a short time before the age for reproduction. Hence in most cases the young of both sexes resemble each other; and the female somewhat resembles her young offspring throughout life. In almost every great class a few anomalous cases occur, where there has been an almost complete transposition of the characters proper to the two sexes; the females assuming characters which properly belong to the males. This surprising uniformity in the laws regulating the differences between the sexes in so many and such widely separated classes, is intelligible if we admit the action of one common cause, namely sexual selection.

Sexual selection depends on the success of certain individuals over others of the same sex, in relation to the propagation of the species; whilst natural selection depends on the success of both sexes, at all ages, in relation to the general conditions of life. The sexual struggle is of two kinds; in the one it is between individuals of the same sex, generally the males, in order to drive away or kill their rivals, the females remaining passive; whilst in the other, the struggle is likewise between the individuals of the same sex, in order to excite or charm those of the opposite sex, generally the females, which no longer remain passive, but select the more agreeable partners. This latter kind of selection is closely analogous to that which man unintentionally, yet effectually, brings to bear on his domesticated productions, when he preserves during a long period the most pleasing or useful individuals, without any wish to modify the breed.

The laws of inheritance determine whether characters gained through sexual selection by either sex shall be transmitted to the same sex, or to both; as well as the age at which they shall be developed. It appears that variations arising late in life are commonly transmitted to one and the same sex. Variability is the necessary basis for the action of selection, and is wholly independent of it. It follows from this, that variations of the same general nature have often been taken advantage of and accumulated through sexual selection in relation to the propagation of the species, as well as through natural selection in relation to the general purposes of life. Hence secondary sexual characters, when equally transmitted to both sexes can be distinguished from ordinary specific characters only by the light of analogy. The modifications acquired through sexual selection are often so strongly pronounced that the two sexes have frequently been ranked as distinct species, or even as distinct genera.[2] Such strongly-marked differences must be in some manner highly important; and we know that they have been acquired in some instances at the cost not only of inconvenience, but of exposure to actual danger.

The belief in the power of sexual selection rests chiefly on the following considerations. Certain characters are confined to one sex; and this alone renders it probable that in most cases they are connected with the

[1] *Arthropoda* Sub-kingdom which includes insects, spiders, crustaceans, etc.

[2] *genera* Latin: groups of species. Plural of genus.

act of reproduction. In innumerable instances these characters are fully developed only at maturity, and often during only a part of the year, which is always the breeding-season. The males (passing over a few exceptional cases) are the more active in courtship; they are the better armed, and are rendered the more attractive in various ways. It is to be especially observed that the males display their attractions with elaborate care in the presence of the females; and that they rarely or never display them excepting during the season of love. It is incredible that all this should be purposeless. Lastly we have distinct evidence with some quadrupeds and birds, that the individuals of one sex are capable of feeling a strong antipathy or preference for certain individuals of the other sex.

Bearing in mind these facts, and the marked results of man's unconscious selection, when applied to domesticated animals and cultivated plants, it seems to me almost certain that if the individuals of one sex were during a long series of generations to prefer pairing with certain individuals of the other sex, characterised in some peculiar manner, the offspring would slowly but surely become modified in this same manner. I have not attempted to conceal that, excepting when the males are more numerous than the females, or when polygamy prevails, it is doubtful how the more attractive males succeed in leaving a large number of offspring to inherit their superiority in ornaments or other charms than the less attractive males; but I have shown that this would probably follow from the females—especially the more vigorous ones, which would be the first to breed—preferring not only the more attractive but at the same time the more vigorous and victorious males.

Although we have some positive evidence that birds appreciate bright and beautiful objects, as with the bower-birds of Australia, and although they certainly appreciate the power of song, yet I fully admit that it is astonishing that the females of many birds and some mammals should be endowed with sufficient taste to appreciate ornaments, which we have reason to attribute to sexual selection; and this is even more astonishing in the case of reptiles, fish, and insects. But we really know little about the minds of the lower animals. It cannot be supposed, for instance, that male birds of paradise or peacocks should take such pains in erecting, spreading, and vibrating their beautiful plumes before the females for no purpose. We should remember the fact given on excellent authority in a former chapter, that several peahens, when debarred from an admired male, remained widows during a whole season rather than pair with another bird.

Nevertheless I know of no fact in natural history more wonderful than that of the female Argus pheasant should appreciate the exquisite shading of the ball-and-socket ornaments and the elegant patterns on the wing-feathers of the male. He who thinks that the male was created as he now exists must admit that the great plumes, which prevent the wings from being used for flight, and which are displayed during courtship and at no other time in a manner quite peculiar to this one species, were given to him as an ornament. If so, he must likewise admit that the female was created and endowed with the capacity of appreciating such ornaments. I differ only in the conviction that the male Argus pheasant acquired his beauty gradually, through the preference of the females during many generations for the more highly ornamented males; the aesthetic capacity of the females having been advanced through exercise or habit, just as our own taste is gradually improved. In the male through the fortunate chance of a few feathers, being left, unchanged, we can distinctly trace how simple spots with a little fulvous shading on one side may have been developed by small steps into the wonderful ball-and-socket ornaments; and it is probable that they were actually thus developed.

Everyone who admits the principle of evolution, and yet feels great difficulty in admitting that female mammals, birds, reptiles, and fish, could have acquired the high taste implied by the beauty of the males, and which generally coincides with our own standard, should reflect that the nerve-cells of the brain in the highest as well as in the lowest members of the Vertebrate series, are derived from those of the common progenitor of this great kingdom. For we can thus see how it has come to pass that certain mental faculties, in various and widely distinct groups of animals, have been developed in nearly the same manner and to nearly the same degree.

The reader who has taken the trouble to go through the several chapters devoted to sexual selection, will be able to judge how far the conclusions at which I have arrived are supported by sufficient evidence. If he accepts these conclusions he may, I think, safely extend them to mankind; but it would be superfluous here to repeat what I have so lately said on the manner in which sexual selection apparently has acted on man, both on the male and female side, causing the two sexes to differ in body and mind, and the several races to differ from each other in various characters, as well as from their ancient and lowly-organised progenitors. He who admits the principle of sexual selection will be led to the remarkable conclusion that the nervous system not only regulates most of the existing functions of the body, but has indirectly influenced the progressive development of various bodily structures and of certain mental qualities. Courage, pugnacity, perseverance, strength and size of body, weapons of all kinds, musical organs, both vocal and instrumental, bright colours and ornamental appendages, have all been indirectly gained by the one sex or the other, through the exertion of choice, the influence of love and jealousy, and the appreciation of the beautiful in sound, colour or form; and these powers of the mind manifestly depend on the development of the brain.

Man scans with scrupulous care the character and pedigree of his horses, cattle, and dogs before he matches them; but when he comes to his own marriage he rarely, or never, takes any such care. He is impelled by nearly the same motives as the lower animals, when they are left to their own free choice, though he is in so far superior to them that he highly values mental charms and virtues. On the other hand he is strongly attracted by mere wealth or rank. Yet he might by selection do something not only for the bodily constitution and frame of his offspring, but for their intellectual and moral qualities. Both sexes ought to refrain from marriage if they are in any marked degree inferior in body or mind; but such hopes are Utopian and will never be even partially realised until the laws of inheritance are thoroughly known. Everyone does good service who aids towards this end. When the principles of breeding and inheritance are better understood, we shall not hear ignorant members of our legislature rejecting with scorn a plan for ascertaining whether or not consanguineous marriages[1] are injurious to man.

The advancement of the welfare of mankind is a most intricate problem: all ought to refrain from marriage who cannot avoid abject poverty for their children; for poverty is not only a great evil, but tends to its own increase by leading to recklessness in marriage. On the other hand as Mr. Galton[2] has remarked, if the prudent avoid marriage, whilst the reckless marry, the inferior members tend to supplant the better members of society. Man, like every other animal, has no doubt advanced to his present high condition through a struggle for existence consequent on his rapid multiplication; and if he is to advance still higher, it is to be feared that he must remain subject to a severe struggle. Otherwise he would sink into indolence, and the more gifted men would not be more successful in the battle of life than the less gifted. Hence our natural rate of increase, though leading to many and obvious evils, must not be greatly diminished by any means. There should be open competition for all men; and the most able should not be prevented by laws or customs from succeeding best and rearing the largest number of offspring. Important as the struggle for existence has been and even still is, yet as far as the highest part of man's nature is concerned there are other agencies more important. For the moral qualities are advanced, either directly or indirectly, much more through the effects of habit, the reasoning powers, instruction, religion, *et cetera*, than through natural selection; though to this latter agency may be safely attributed the social instincts, which afforded the basis for the development of the moral sense.

The main conclusion arrived at in this work, namely, that man is descended from some lowly organised form, will, I regret to think, be highly distasteful to many. But there can hardly be a doubt that we are descended from barbarians. The astonishment which I felt on first seeing a party of Fuegians on a wild and broken shore will never be forgotten by me, for the reflection at once rushed into my mind—such were our ancestors. These men were absolutely naked and bedaubed with paint, their long hair was tangled, their mouths frothed with excitement, and their expression

---

[1] *consanguineous marriages* Marriages between blood relatives.

[2] *Mr. Galton* Sir Francis Galton (1822–94), Darwin's half cousin, one of the founders of eugenics, the "science" that aimed to improve the human species through selective breeding.

was wild, startled, and distrustful. They possessed hardly any arts, and like wild animals lived on what they could catch; they had no government, and were merciless to every one not of their own small tribe. He who has seen a savage in his native land will not feel much shame, if forced to acknowledge that the blood of some more humble creature flows in his veins. For my own part I would as soon be descended from that heroic little monkey, who braved his dreaded enemy in order to save the life of his keeper, or from that old baboon, who descending from the mountains, carried away in triumph his young comrade from a crowd of astonished dogs—as from a savage who delights to torture his enemies, offers up bloody sacrifices, practises infanticide without remorse, treats his wives like slaves, knows no decency, and is haunted by the grossest superstitions.

Man may be excused for feeling some pride at having risen, though not through his own exertions, to the very summit of the organic scale; and the fact of his having thus risen, instead of having been aboriginally placed there, may give him hope for a still higher destiny in the distant future. But we are not here concerned with hopes or fears, only with the truth as far as our reason permits us to discover it; and I have given the evidence to the best of my ability. We must, however, acknowledge, as it seems to me, that man with all his noble qualities, with sympathy which feels for the most debased, with benevolence which extends not only to other men but to the humblest living creature, with his god-like intellect which has penetrated into the movements and constitution of the solar system—with all these exalted powers—Man still bears in his bodily frame the indelible stamp of his lowly origin.

—1871

In Context

Defending and Attacking Darwin

One of Darwin's most important defenders was Thomas Henry Huxley (1825–95), a naturalist and essayist who in the 1870s developed the concept of agnosticism. In 1860 he became known as "Darwin's Bulldog" for his aggressive and persuasive efforts to popularize the theory of natural selection—and counter the backlash against it. He continued to write about evolutionary theory throughout the rest of his life.

from Thomas Huxley, "Criticisms on The Origin of Species" (1864)

It is singular how differently one and the same book will impress different minds. That which struck the present writer most forcibly on his first perusal of the "Origin of Species" was the conviction that teleology,[1] as commonly understood, had received its deathblow at Mr. Darwin's hands. For the teleological argument runs thus: an organ or organism (A) is precisely fitted to perform a function or purpose (B); therefore it was specially constructed to perform that function. In Paley's[2] famous illustration, the adaptation of all the parts of the watch to the function, or purpose, of showing the time, is held to be evidence that the watch was specially contrived to that end; on the ground, that the only cause we know of, competent to produce such an effect as a watch which shall keep time, is a contriving intelligence adapting the means directly to that end.

---

[1]   *teleology*   Study of intelligent design or purpose in nature.

[2]   *Paley*   William Paley (1743–1805), English philosopher. Huxley refers to Paley's 1802 book, *Natural Theology, or Evidences of the Existence and Attributes of the Deity collected from the Appearances of Nature.*

Suppose, however, that any one had been able to show that the watch had not been made directly by any person, but that it was the result of the modification of another watch which kept time but poorly; and that this again had proceeded from a structure which could hardly be called a watch at all—seeing that it had no figures on the dial and the hands were rudimentary; and that going back and back in time we came at last to a revolving barrel as the earliest traceable rudiment of the whole fabric. And imagine that it had been possible to show that all these changes had resulted, first, from a tendency of the structure to vary indefinitely; and secondly, from something in the surrounding world which helped all variations in the direction of an accurate time-keeper, and checked all those in other directions; then it is obvious that the force of Paley's argument would be gone. For it would be demonstrated that an apparatus thoroughly well adapted to a particular purpose might be the result of a method of trial and error worked by unintelligent agents, as well as of the direct application of the means appropriate to that end, by an intelligent agent.

Now it appears to us that what we have here, for illustration's sake, supposed to be done with the watch, is exactly what the establishment of Darwin's theory will do for the organic world. For the notion that every organism has been created as it is and launched straight at a purpose, Mr. Darwin substitutes the conception of something which may fairly be termed a method of trial and error. Organisms vary incessantly; of these variations the few meet with surrounding conditions which suit them and thrive; the many are unsuited and become extinguished.

from Thomas Huxley, "Mr. Darwin's Critics" (1871)

The gradual lapse of time has now separated us by more than a decade from the date of the publication of the "Origin of Species"—and whatever may be thought or said about Mr. Darwin's doctrines, or the manner in which he has propounded them, this much is certain, that, in a dozen years, the "Origin of Species" has worked as complete a revolution in biological science as the "Principia"[1] did in astronomy—and it has done so, because, in the words of Helmholtz,[2] it contains "an essentially new creative thought."

And as time has slipped by, a happy change has come over Mr. Darwin's critics. The mixture of ignorance and insolence which, at first, characterised a large proportion of the attacks with which he was assailed, is no longer the sad distinction of anti-Darwinian criticism. Instead of abusive nonsense, which merely discredited its writers, we read essays, which are, at worst, more or less intelligent and appreciative; while, sometimes, like that which appeared in the "North British Review" for 1867, they have a real and permanent value.

The several publications of Mr. Wallace and Mr. Mivart[3] contain discussions of some of Mr. Darwin's views, which are worthy of particular attention, not only on account of the acknowledged scientific competence of these writers, but because they exhibit an attention to those philosophical questions which underlie all physical science, which is as rare as it is needful.

---

[1] *Principia*   Sir Isaac Newton's *Philosophiae Naturalis Principia Mathematica* (1687).

[2] *Helmholtz*   Hermann Ludwig Ferdinand von Helmholtz (1821–94), German professor of physiology and physics.

[3] *Mr. Wallace*   Alfred Russel Wallace (1823–1913), English naturalist and social critic; *Mr. Mivart*   St. George Jackson Mivart (1827–1900), British biologist. His *Genesis of Species* (1871) established him as a leading opponent of Darwin's theory.

from *Punch*

The humor magazine *Punch* continued to lampoon Darwin's theories in its cartoons even after they had become widely accepted in the community at large. The first of the cartoons below (depicting a gorilla as a social "lion"), was published in 1861, the second (a response to Darwin's 1881 *The Formation of Vegetable Mould Through the Action of Worms*) in 1882.

THE LION OF THE SEASON.

MAN·IS·BVT·A·WORM.

IN CONTEXT

Social Darwinism

The term "Social Darwinism" is used to refer to ideas that attempt to apply certain evolutionary notions to social issues. Chief among the Victorian "Social Darwinists" was Herbert Spencer, a wide-ranging thinker who coined the term "survival of the fittest" in an 1852 essay, "A Theory of Population." Like that work, his 1851 book *Social Statics* (from which excerpts are reprinted below) pre-dates Darwin's *On the Origin of the Species* by several years; in fact the tenets of Social Darwinism were quite independent of Darwin's biological theories.

from Herbert Spencer, *Social Statics: or, the Conditions Essential to Human Happiness Specified, and the First of Them Developed* (1851)

Pervading all nature we may see at work a stern discipline, which is a little cruel that it may be very kind. That state of universal warfare maintained throughout the lower creation, to the great perplexity of many worthy people, is at bottom the most merciful provision which the circumstances admit of. It is much better that the ruminant animal, when deprived by age of the vigour which made its existence a pleasure, should be killed by some beast of prey, than that it should linger out a life made painful by infirmities, and eventually die of starvation. By the destruction of all such, not only is existence ended before it becomes burdensome, but room is made for a younger generation capable of the fullest enjoyment; and, moreover, out of the very act of substitution happiness is derived for a tribe of predatory creatures. Note further, that their carnivorous enemies not only remove from herbivorous herds individuals past their prime, but also weed out the sickly, the malformed, and the least fleet or powerful. By the aid of which purifying process, as well as by the fighting, so universal in the pairing season, all vitiation[1] of the race through the multiplication of its inferior samples is prevented; and the maintenance of a constitution completely adapted to surrounding conditions, and therefore most productive of happiness, is ensured.

The development of the higher creation is a progress towards a form of being capable of a happiness undiminished by these drawbacks. It is in the human race that the consummation is to be accomplished. Civilization is the last stage of its accomplishment. And the ideal man is the man in whom all the conditions of that accomplishment are fulfilled. Meanwhile the well-being of existing humanity, and the unfolding of it into this ultimate perfection, are both secured by that same beneficent, though severe discipline, to which the animate creation at large is subject: a discipline which is pitiless in the working out of good: a felicity-pursuing law which never swerves for the avoidance of partial and temporary suffering. The poverty of the incapable, the distresses that come upon the imprudent, the starvation of the idle, and those shoulderings aside of the weak by the strong, which leave so many "in shallows and in miseries,"[2] are the decrees of a large, far-seeing benevolence. It seems hard that an unskilfulness which with all his efforts he cannot overcome, should entail hunger upon the artisan. It seems hard that a labourer incapacitated by sickness from competing with

---

[1] *vitiation* Impairment.

[2] *in … miseries* From Shakespeare's *Julius Caesar* 4.2.70–73: "There is a tide in the affairs of men, / Which taken at the flood leads on to fortune; / Omitted, all the voyage of that life / Is bound in shallows and in miseries."

his stronger fellows, should have to bear the resulting privations. It seems hard that widows and orphans should be left to struggle for life or death. Nevertheless, when regarded not separately, but in connection with the interests of universal humanity, these harsh fatalities are seen to be full of the highest beneficence—the same beneficence which brings to early graves the children of diseased parents, and singles out the low-spirited,[1] the intemperate,[2] and the debilitated as the victims of an epidemic.

There are many very amiable people—people over whom in so far as their feelings are concerned we may fitly rejoice—who have not the nerve to look this matter fairly in the face. Disabled as they are by their sympathies with present suffering, from duly regarding ultimate consequences, they pursue a course which is very injudicious, and in the end even cruel. We do not consider it true kindness in a mother to gratify her child with sweetmeats that are certain to make it ill. We should think it a very foolish sort of benevolence which led a surgeon to let his patient's disease progress to a fatal issue, rather than inflict pain by an operation. Similarly, we must call those spurious philanthropists, who, to prevent present misery, would entail greater misery upon future generations. All defenders of a poor-law[3] must, however, be classed amongst such. That rigorous necessity which, when allowed to act on them, becomes so sharp a spur to the lazy, and so strong a bridle to the random, these paupers' friends would repeal, because of the wailings it here and there produces. Blind to the fact, that under the natural order of things society is constantly excreting its unhealthy, imbecile, slow, vacillating, faithless members, these unthinking, though well-meaning, men advocate an interference which not only stops the purifying process, but even increases the vitiation—absolutely encourages the multiplication of the reckless and incompetent by offering them an unfailing provision, and discourages the multiplication of the competent and provident by heightening the prospective difficulty of maintaining a family. And thus, in their eagerness to prevent the really salutary sufferings that surround us, these sigh-wise and groan-foolish people bequeath to posterity a continually increasing curse.

At first sight these considerations seem conclusive against *all* relief to the poor—voluntary as well as compulsory; and it is no doubt true that they imply a condemnation of whatever private charity enables the recipients to elude the necessities of our social existence. With this condemnation, however, no rational man will quarrel. That careless squandering of pence which has fostered into perfection a system of organized begging—which has made skilful mendicancy more profitable than ordinary manual labour—which induces the simulation of palsy, epilepsy, cholera, and no end of diseases and deformities—which has called into existence warehouses for the sale and hire of impostor's dresses—which has given to pity-inspiring babes a market value of *9d.* per day—the unthinking benevolence which has generated all this, cannot but be disapproved by every one. Now it is only against this injudicious charity that the foregoing argument tells. To that charity which may be described as helping men to help themselves, it makes no objection—countenances[4] it rather. And in helping men to help themselves, there remains abundant scope for the exercise of a people's sympathies. Accidents will still supply victims on whom generosity may be legitimately expended. Men thrown upon their backs by unforeseen events, men who have failed for want of knowledge inaccessible to them, men ruined by the dishonesty of others, and men in whom hope long delayed has made the heart sick, may, with advantage to all parties, be assisted. Even the prodigal, after severe hardship has branded his memory with the unbending conditions of social life to which he must submit, may properly have another trial afforded him. And, although by these ameliorations the

---

[1]   *low-spirited*   Depressed.

[2]   *intemperate*   Heavy drinkers.

[3]   *poor-law*   Law providing for the support of the poor at public expense.

[4]   *countenances*   Approves.

process of adaptation must be remotely interfered with, yet in the majority of cases, it will not be so much retarded in one direction as it will be advanced in another. ...

Progress ... is not accident, but a necessity. Instead of civilisation being artificial, it is part of nature; all of a piece with the development of the embryo or the unfolding of a flower. The modifications mankind have undergone, and are still undergoing, result from a law underlying the whole organic creation; and provided the human race continues, and the constitution of things remains the same, those modifications must end in completeness. As surely as the trees become bulky when it stands alone, and slender if one of a group ... so surely must things be called evil and immoral disappear; so surely must man become perfect.

ELIZABETH GASKELL
1810 – 1865

Mrs. Gaskell, as she was known to nineteenth-century readers, was one of the first authors of the Victorian era to write "social protest" novels dealing with contemporary issues of poverty, industrialization, and life in both rural and urban England. Gaskell presents brutally honest portrayals of very different sorts of Victorian reality—conditions of poor factory workers in *Mary Barton* and *North and South*, for example, and of the plight of an unwed mother in *Ruth*.

Elizabeth Cleghorn Stevenson was born in 1810 near London to William Stevenson, a Unitarian preacher and civil servant, and Elizabeth Holland, who died soon after childbirth. From the age of one, Elizabeth was raised by a beloved aunt in the village of Knutsford (the model for Gaskell's novel *Cranford*), near Manchester in northern England. She received a liberal, modern education at a boarding school in Warwick, in central England, and when she came of age went to visit a distant relative in Manchester, where she met her future husband, William Gaskell, a Unitarian minister.

According to Unitarian practices, the two lived a fulfilling life together as equals, with Gaskell free to pursue her own interests. For the first twelve years of their marriage, however, she devoted herself to the upbringing and education of her five children and performed many of the duties of her role as a minister's wife, which entailed teaching at a charity school and visiting poor parishioners. By listening to these people's tales of hardship and observing the conditions in factories and homes, Gaskell acquired much of the fodder for her books. She wrote a small number of short stories and co-authored a poem with her husband while raising her children, but it was not until her infant son died of scarlet fever in 1845 that she began to write novels and stories in earnest, an activity her husband recommended as a partial remedy for the depression brought on by her loss.

Mary Barton, Gaskell's first novel, was published in 1848. In it, she exposed the desperation and hopelessness of poverty-stricken millworkers who toiled in miserable, unhealthy conditions in the industrial city of Manchester. Although the book was originally published under the pseudonym "Cotton Mather Mills, Esq.," it was not long before the public's and critics' curiosity unmasked Gaskell. Even though many society people found her portrayal of factory owners to be harsh and unfair, she became an esteemed guest at literary gatherings and social events. Charles Dickens was so impressed with her writing that he asked her to contribute to his magazine, *Household Words* (and subsequently to *All the Year Round*). Gaskell agreed and contributed such short stories as "The Old Nurse's Story," as well as a series of humorous tales about upper and middle-class women and their milieu in a peaceful country village, later to be published as the novel *Cranford* (1853).

Gaskell's next novel was not received as enthusiastically as *Cranford* had been. *Ruth*, also published in 1853, tells the story of a woman who has a child out of wedlock. The subject would have been criticized in any event, but Gaskell's sympathetic portrayal of the woman and her exposure of the hypocrisy of Victorian society deeply angered many people. The book was so controversial that some parishioners burned their copies, and it was banned in many homes, including, ironically, Gaskell's own—even she felt that the subject matter was unsuitable for children. On the other hand, Victorian women writers Elizabeth Barrett Browning, George Eliot, and Charlotte Brontë spoke out in praise of the book. In her next novel, *North and South* (1855), also published in *Household Words* (1854–55), Gaskell returned to issues of factory workers, comparing life in both the rural and urban south with the harsh lives of the working poor in the north. Like *Mary Barton*, *North and South* addressed the need for factory owners to reform workplace conditions and for workers to fight for their rights.

After Charlotte Brontë's death in 1855, Gaskell wrote her biography at the behest of Charlotte's father, Patrick Brontë. Influenced by her close friendship with Charlotte, Gaskell created a very sympathetic portrait of the Brontës, echoing what they had written about various friends and acquaintances. Unfortunately, Gaskell's loyalty to her subject landed her in trouble when one of those maligned by the Brontës threatened legal action. Under pressure from her publisher, Gaskell was forced to apologize publicly, and the questionable material was removed from the book's subsequent editions. *The Life of Charlotte Brontë* (1857) remains, however, a highly readable biography and a masterpiece of characterization.

Gaskell had almost completed her final novel, *Wives and Daughters*, when she collapsed and died suddenly in 1865. Often compared with the novels of Jane Austen and George Eliot, *Wives and Daughters* exposes the social workings of various classes in a small country town, expressing social critique with delicate wit and sly humor for which the author was known. Gaskell was buried beside the Unitarian chapel in Knutsford, the town of her childhood that she had so loved and had immortalized in her stories.

⌘ ⌘ ⌘

The Old Nurse's Story

You know, my dears, that your mother was an orphan, and an only child; and I dare say you have heard that your grandfather was a clergyman up in Westmoreland, where I come from. I was just a girl in the village school, when, one day, your grandmother came in to ask the mistress if there was any scholar there who would do for a nurse-maid; and mighty proud I was, I can tell ye, when the mistress called me up, and spoke to my being a good girl at my needle, and a steady honest girl, and one whose parents were very respectable, though they might be poor. I thought I should like nothing better than to serve the pretty young lady, who was blushing as deep as I was, as she spoke of the coming baby, and what I should have to do with it. However, I see you don't care so much for this part of

my story, as for what you think is to come, so I'll tell you at once. I was engaged and settled at the parsonage before Miss Rosamond (that was the baby, who is now your mother) was born. To be sure, I had little enough to do with her when she came, for she was never out of her mother's arms, and slept by her all night long; and proud enough was I sometimes when missis trusted her to me. There never was such a baby before or since, though you've all of you been fine enough in your turns; but for sweet, winning ways, you've none of you come up to your mother. She took after her mother, who was a real lady born; a Miss Furnivall, a granddaughter of Lord Furnivall's, in Northumberland. I believe she had neither brother nor sister, and had been brought up in my lord's family till she had married your grandfather, who was just a curate, son to a shopkeeper in Carlisle—but a clever, fine gentleman as ever was—and one who was a right-down hard worker in his parish, which was very wide, and scattered all abroad over the Westmoreland Fells. When your mother, little Miss Rosamond, was about four or five years old, both her parents died in a fortnight—one after the other. Ah! that was a sad time. My pretty young mistress and me was looking for another baby, when my master came home from one of his long rides, wet, and tired, and took the fever he died of; and then she never held up her head again, but just lived to see her dead baby, and have it laid on her breast before she sighed away her life. My mistress had asked me, on her death-bed, never to leave Miss Rosamond; but if she had never spoken a word, I would have gone with the little child to the end of the world.

The next thing, and before we had well stilled our sobs, the executors and guardians came to settle the affairs. They were my poor young mistress's own cousin, Lord Furnivall, and Mr. Esthwaite, my master's brother, a shopkeeper in Manchester; not so well-to-do then as he was afterwards, and with a large family rising about him. Well! I don't know if it were their settling, or because of a letter my mistress wrote on her death-bed to her cousin, my lord; but somehow it was settled that Miss Rosamond and me were to go to Furnivall Manor House, in Northumberland, and my lord spoke as if it had been her mother's wish that she should live with his family, and as if he had no objections, for that one or two more or less could make no difference in so grand a household. So, though that was not the way in which I should have wished the coming of my bright and pretty pet to have been looked at—who was like a sunbeam in any family, be it never so grand—I was well pleased that all the folks in the Dale should stare and admire, when they heard I was going to be young lady's maid at my Lord Furnivall's at Furnivall Manor.

But I made a mistake in thinking we were to go and live where my lord did. It turned out that the family had left Furnivall Manor House fifty years or more. I could not hear that my poor young mistress had ever been there, though she had been brought up in the family; and I was sorry for that, for I should have liked Miss Rosamond's youth to have passed where her mother's had been.

My lord's gentleman,[1] from whom I asked as many questions as I durst, said that the Manor House was at the foot of the Cumberland Fells, and a very grand place; that an old Miss Furnivall, a great-aunt of my lord's, lived there, with only a few servants; but that it was a very healthy place, and my lord had thought that it would suit Miss Rosamond very well for a few years, and that her being there might perhaps amuse his old aunt.

I was bidden by my lord to have Miss Rosamond's things ready by a certain day. He was a stern proud man, as they say all the Lords Furnivall were; and he never spoke a word more than was necessary. Folk did say he had loved my young mistress; but that, because she knew that his father would object, she would never listen to him, and married Mr. Esthwaite; but I don't know. He never married at any rate. But he never took much notice of Miss Rosamond; which I thought he might have done if he had cared for her dead mother. He sent his gentleman with us to the Manor House, telling him to join him at Newcastle that same evening; so there was no great length of time for him to make us known to all the strangers before he, too, shook us off; and we were left, two lonely young things (I was not eighteen), in the great old Manor House. It seems like yesterday that we drove there. We had left our own dear parsonage very early, and we had both cried as if our hearts would break, though we were travelling in my lord's carriage, which I thought so much of once. And now it was long past noon on a September day, and we stopped to change horses for the last time at a little smoky town, all full of colliers[2] and miners. Miss Rosamond had fallen asleep, but Mr. Henry told me to waken her, that she might see the park and the Manor House as we drove up. I thought it rather a pity; but I did what he bade me, for fear he should complain of me to my lord. We had left all signs of a town, or even a village, and were then inside the gates of a large wild park—not like the parks here in the south, but with rocks, and the noise of running water, and gnarled thorn-trees, and old oaks, all white and peeled with age.

The road went up about two miles, and then we saw a great and stately house, with many trees close around it, so close that in some places their branches dragged against the walls when the wind blew; and some hung

---

[1]   *My lord's gentleman*   Personal attendant to Lord Furnivall.

[2]   *colliers*   Coal miners.

broken down; for no one seemed to take much charge of the place;—to lop the wood, or to keep the moss-covered carriage-way in order. Only in front of the house all was clear. The great oval drive was without a weed; and neither tree nor creeper was allowed to grow over the long, many-windowed front; at both sides of which a wing projected, which were each the ends of other side fronts; for the house, although it was so desolate, was even grander than I expected. Behind it rose the Fells, which seemed unenclosed and bare enough; and on the left hand of the house, as you stood facing it, was a little, old-fashioned flower-garden, as I found out afterwards. A door opened out upon it from the west front; it had been scooped out of the thick dark wood for some old Lady Furnivall; but the branches of the great forest trees had grown and overshadowed it again, and there were very few flowers that would live there at that time.

When we drove up to the great front entrance, and went into the hall I thought we should be lost—it was so large, and vast, and grand. There was a chandelier all of bronze, hung down from the middle of the ceiling; and I had never seen one before, and looked at it all in amaze. Then, at one end of the hall, was a great fire-place, as large as the sides of the houses in my country, with massy andirons and dogs[1] to hold the wood; and by it were heavy old-fashioned sofas. At the opposite end of the hall, to the left as you went in—on the western side—was an organ built into the wall, and so large that it filled up the best part of that end. Beyond it, on the same side, was a door; and opposite, on each side of the fire-place, were also doors leading to the east front; but those I never went through as long as I stayed in the house, so I can't tell you what lay beyond.

The afternoon was closing in, and the hall, which had no fire lighted in it, looked dark and gloomy, but we did not stay there a moment. The old servant, who had opened the door for us, bowed to Mr. Henry, and took us in through the door at the further side of the great organ, and led us through several smaller halls and passages into the west drawing-room, where he said that Miss Furnivall was sitting. Poor little Miss Rosamond held very tight to me, as if she were scared and lost in that great place, and as for myself, I was not much

better. The west drawing-room was very cheerful-looking, with a warm fire in it, and plenty of good, comfortable furniture about. Miss Furnivall was an old lady not far from eighty, I should think, but I do not know. She was thin and tall, and had a face as full of fine wrinkles as if they had been drawn all over it with a needle's point. Her eyes were very watchful, to make up, I suppose, for her being so deaf as to be obliged to use a trumpet. Sitting with her, working at the same great piece of tapestry, was Mrs. Stark, her maid and companion, and almost as old as she was. She had lived with Miss Furnivall ever since they both were young, and now she seemed more like a friend than a servant; she looked so cold and grey, and stony, as if she had never loved or cared for any one; and I don't suppose she did care for any one, except her mistress; and, owing to the great deafness of the latter, Mrs. Stark treated her very much as if she were a child. Mr. Henry gave some message from my lord, and then he bowed good-bye to us all—taking no notice of my sweet little Miss Rosamond's outstretched hand—and left us standing there, being looked at by the two old ladies through their spectacles.

I was right glad when they rung for the old footman who had shown us in at first, and told him to take us to our rooms. So we went out of that great drawing-room, and into another sitting-room, and out of that, and then up a great flight of stairs, and along a broad gallery—which was something like a library, having books all down one side, and windows and writing-tables all down the other—till we came to our rooms, which I was not sorry to hear were just over the kitchens; for I began to think I should be lost in that wilderness of a house. There was an old nursery, that had been used for all the little lords and ladies long ago, with a pleasant fire burning in the grate, and the kettle boiling on the hob,[2] and tea things spread out on the table; and out of that room was the night-nursery, with a little crib for Miss Rosamond close to my bed. And old James called up Dorothy, his wife, to bid us welcome; and both he and she were so hospitable and kind, that by and by Miss Rosamond and me felt quite at home; and by the time tea was over, she was sitting on Dorothy's knee, and chattering away as fast as her little tongue could go. I

---

[1] *dogs* Supports for logs.

[2] *hob* Warming shelf at the back or side of a fireplace.

soon found out that Dorothy was from Westmoreland, and that bound her and me together, as it were; and I would never wish to meet with kinder people than were old James and his wife. James had lived pretty nearly all his life in my lord's family, and thought there was no one so grand as they. He even looked down a little on his wife; because, till he had married her, she had never lived in any but a farmer's household. But he was very fond of her, as well he might be. They had one servant under them, to do all the rough work. Agnes they called her; and she and me, and James and Dorothy, with Miss Furnivall and Mrs. Stark, made up the family; always remembering my sweet little Miss Rosamond! I used to wonder what they had done before she came, they thought so much of her now. Kitchen and drawing-room, it was all the same. The hard, sad Miss Furnivall, and the cold Mrs. Stark, looked pleased when she came fluttering in like a bird, playing and pranking hither and thither, with a continual murmur, and pretty prattle of gladness. I am sure, they were sorry many a time when she flitted away into the kitchen, though they were too proud to ask her to stay with them, and were a little surprised at her taste; though to be sure, as Mrs. Stark said, it was not to be wondered at, remembering what stock her father had come of. The great, old rambling house was a famous place for little Miss Rosamond. She made expeditions all over it, with me at her heels; all, except the east wing, which was never opened, and whither we never thought of going. But in the western and northern part was many a pleasant room; full of things that were curiosities to us, though they might not have been to people who had seen more. The windows were darkened by the sweeping boughs of the trees, and the ivy which had overgrown them: but, in the green gloom, we could manage to see old China jars and carved ivory boxes, and great heavy books, and, above all, the old pictures!

Once, I remember, my darling would have Dorothy go with us to tell us who they all were; for they were all portraits of some of my lord's family, though Dorothy could not tell us the names of every one. We had gone through most of the rooms, when we came to the old state drawing-room over the hall, and there was a picture of Miss Furnivall; or, as she was called in those days, Miss Grace, for she was the younger sister. Such a beauty she must have been! but with such a set, proud look, and such scorn looking out of her handsome eyes, with her eyebrows just a little raised, as if she wondered how any one could have the impertinence to look at her; and her lip curled at us, as we stood there gazing. She had a dress on, the like of which I had never seen before, but it was all the fashion when she was young: a hat of some soft white stuff like beaver,[1] pulled a little over her brows, and a beautiful plume of feathers sweeping round it on one side; and her gown of blue satin was open in front to a quilted white stomacher.[2]

"Well, to be sure!" said I, when I had gazed my fill. "Flesh is grass,[3] they do say; but who would have thought that Miss Furnivall had been such an out-and-out beauty, to see her now?"

"Yes," said Dorothy. "Folks change sadly. But if what my master's father used to say was true, Miss Furnivall, the elder sister, was handsomer than Miss Grace. Her picture is here somewhere; but, if I show it you, you must never let on, even to James, that you have seen it. Can the little lady hold her tongue, think you?" asked she.

I was not so sure, for she was such a little sweet, bold, open-spoken child, so I set her to hide herself; and then I helped Dorothy to turn a great picture, that leaned with its face towards the wall, and was not hung up as the others were. To be sure, it beat Miss Grace for beauty; and, I think, for scornful pride, too, though in that matter it might be hard to choose. I could have looked at it an hour, but Dorothy seemed half frightened at having shown it to me, and hurried it back again, and bade me run and find Miss Rosamond, for that there were some ugly places about the house, where she should like ill for the child to go. I was a brave, high-spirited girl, and thought little of what the old woman said, for I liked hide-and-seek as well as any child in the parish; so off I ran to find my little one.

As winter drew on, and the days grew shorter, I was sometimes almost certain that I heard a noise as if some

---

[1]   *beaver* Cloth manufactured to resemble beaver felt, made from the fine, thick underhair of the animal, rather than the long-haired pelt.

[2]   *stomacher* Ornamental panel worn over the breast.

[3]   *Flesh is grass* Cf. Isaiah 40.6; 1 Peter 1.24.

one was playing on the great organ in the hall. I did not hear it every evening; but, certainly, I did very often; usually when I was sitting with Miss Rosamond, after I had put her to bed, and keeping quite still and silent in the bedroom. Then I used to hear it booming and swelling away in the distance. The first night, when I went down to my supper, I asked Dorothy who had been playing music, and James said very shortly that I was a gowk to take the wind soughing[1] among the trees for music: but I saw Dorothy look at him very fearfully, and Bessy, the kitchen-maid, said something beneath her breath, and went quite white. I saw they did not like my question, so I held my peace till I was with Dorothy alone, when I knew I could get a good deal out of her. So, the next day, I watched my time, and I coaxed and asked her who it was that played the organ; for I knew that it was the organ and not the wind well enough, for all I had kept silence before James. But Dorothy had had her lesson, I'll warrant, and never a word could I get from her. So then I tried Bessy, though I had always held my head rather above her, as I was evened to James and Dorothy, and she was little better than their servant. So she said I must never, never tell; and if I ever told, I was never to say *she* had told me; but it was a very strange noise, and she had heard it many a time, but most of all on winter nights, and before storms; and folks did say, it was the old lord playing on the great organ in the hall, just as he used to do when he was alive; but who the old lord was, or why he played, and why he played on stormy winter evenings in particular, she either could not or would not tell me. Well! I told you I had a brave heart; and I thought it was rather pleasant to have that grand music rolling about the house, let who would be the player; for now it rose above the great gusts of wind, and wailed and triumphed just like a living creature, and then it fell to a softness most complete; only it was always music, and tunes, so it was nonsense to call it the wind. I thought at first that it might be Miss Furnivall who played, unknown to Bessy; but, one day when I was in the hall by myself, I opened the organ and peeped all about it and around it, as I had done to the organ in Crosthwaite Church once before, and I saw it was all broken and

destroyed inside, though it looked so brave and fine; and then, though it was noonday, my flesh began to creep a little, and I shut it up, and run away pretty quickly to my own bright nursery; and I did not like hearing the music for some time after that, any more than James and Dorothy did. All this time Miss Rosamond was making herself more and more beloved. The old ladies liked her to dine with them at their early dinner; James stood behind Miss Furnivall's chair, and I behind Miss Rosamond's all in state; and, after dinner, she would play about in a corner of the great drawing-room, as still as any mouse, while Miss Furnivall slept, and I had my dinner in the kitchen. But she was glad enough to come to me in the nursery afterwards; for, as she said, Miss Furnivall was so sad, and Mrs. Stark so dull; but she and I were merry enough; and, by and by, I got not to care for that weird rolling music, which did one no harm, if we did not know where it came from.

That winter was very cold. In the middle of October the frosts began, and lasted many, many weeks. I remember, one day at dinner, Miss Furnivall lifted up her sad, heavy eyes, and said to Mrs. Stark, "I am afraid we shall have a terrible winter," in a strange kind of meaning way. But Mrs. Stark pretended not to hear, and talked very loud of something else. My little lady and I did not care for the frost; not we! As long as it was dry we climbed up the steep brows, behind the house, and went up on the Fells, which were bleak, and bare enough, and there we ran races in the fresh, sharp air; and once we came down by a new path that took us past the two old gnarled holly-trees, which grew about half-way down by the east side of the house. But the days grew shorter and shorter; and the old lord, if it was he, played away more and more stormily and sadly on the great organ. One Sunday afternoon—it must have been towards the end of November—I asked Dorothy to take charge of little Missey when she came out of the drawing-room, after Miss Furnivall had had her nap; for it was too cold to take her with me to church, and yet I wanted to go. And Dorothy was glad enough to promise, and was so fond of the child that all seemed well; and Bessy and I set off very briskly, though the sky hung heavy and black over the white earth, as if the night had never fully gone away; and the air, though still, was very biting and keen.

1 *gowk* Simpleton; *soughing* Making a soft moaning or rustling sound.

"We shall have a fall of snow," said Bessy to me. And sure enough, even while we were in church, it came down thick, in great large flakes, so thick it almost darkened the windows. It had stopped snowing before we came out, but it lay soft, thick, and deep beneath our feet, as we tramped home. Before we got to the hall the moon rose, and I think it was lighter then—what with the moon, and what with the white dazzling snow—than it had been when we went to church, between two and three o'clock. I have not told you that Miss Furnivall and Mrs. Stark never went to church: they used to read the prayers together, in their quiet gloomy way; they seemed to feel the Sunday very long without their tapestry-work to be busy at. So when I went to Dorothy in the kitchen, to fetch Miss Rosamond and take her upstairs with me, I did not much wonder when the old woman told me that the ladies had kept the child with them, and that she had never come to the kitchen, as I had bidden her, when she was tired of behaving pretty in the drawing-room. So I took off my things and went to find her, and bring her to her supper in the nursery. But when I went into the best drawing-room, there sat the two old ladies, very still and quiet, dropping out a word now and then, but looking as if nothing so bright and merry as Miss Rosamond had ever been near them. Still I thought she might be hiding from me; it was one of her pretty ways; and that she had persuaded them to look as if they knew nothing about her; so I went softly peeping under this sofa, and behind that chair, making believe I was sadly frightened at not finding her.

"What's the matter, Hester?" said Mrs. Stark, sharply. I don't know if Miss Furnivall had seen me, for, as I told you, she was very deaf, and she sat quite still, idly staring into the fire, with her hopeless face. "I'm only looking for my little Rosy-Posy," replied I, still thinking that the child was there, and near me, though I could not see her.

"Miss Rosamond is not here," said Mrs. Stark. "She went away more than an hour ago to find Dorothy." And she too turned and went on looking into the fire.

My heart sank at this, and I began to wish I had never left my darling. I went back to Dorothy and told her. James was gone out for the day, but she and me and Bessy took lights and went up into the nursery first, and then we roamed over the great large house, calling and entreating Miss Rosamond to come out of her hiding-place, and not frighten us to death in that way. But there was no answer; no sound.

"Oh!" said I at last, "Can she have got into the east wing and hidden there?"

But Dorothy said it was not possible, for that she herself had never been in there; that the doors were always locked, and my lord's steward had the keys, she believed; at any rate, neither she nor James had ever seen them: so I said I would go back, and see if, after all, she was not hidden in the drawing-room, unknown to the old ladies; and if I found her there, I said, I would whip her well for the fright she had given me; but I never meant to do it. Well, I went back to the west drawing-room, and I told Mrs. Stark we could not find her anywhere, and asked for leave to look all about the furniture there, for I thought now, that she might have fallen asleep in some warm hidden corner; but no! we looked, Miss Furnivall got up and looked, trembling all over, and she was nowhere there; then we set off again, every one in the house, and looked in all the places we had searched before, but we could not find her. Miss Furnivall shivered and shook so much, that Mrs. Stark took her back into the warm drawing-room; but not before they had made me promise to bring her to them when she was found. Well-a-day! I began to think she never would be found, when I bethought me to look out into the great front court, all covered with snow. I was upstairs when I looked out; but, it was such clear moonlight, I could see, quite plain, two little footprints, which might be traced from the hall door, and round the corner of the east wing. I don't know how I got down, but I tugged open the great, stiff hall door; and, throwing the skirt of my gown over my head for a cloak, I ran out. I turned the east corner, and there a black shadow fell on the snow; but when I came again into the moonlight, there were the little footmarks going up—up to the Fells. It was bitter cold; so cold that the air almost took the skin off my face as I ran, but I ran on, crying to think how my poor little darling must be perished, and frightened. I was within sight of the holly-trees when I saw a shepherd coming down the hill, bearing something in his arms wrapped in his maud.[1] He shouted to

---

[1] *maud* Gray plaid shawl worn by Scottish shepherds.

me, and asked me if I had lost a bairn;[1] and, when I could not speak for crying, he bore towards me, and I saw my wee bairnie lying still, and white, and stiff, in his arms, as if she had been dead. He told me he had been up the Fells to gather in his sheep, before the deep cold of night came on, and that under the holly-trees (black marks on the hill-side, where no other bush was for miles around) he had found my little lady—my lamb—my queen—my darling—stiff and cold, in the terrible sleep which is frost-begotten. Oh! the joy, and the tears of having her in my arms once again! for I would not let him carry her; but took her, maud and all, into my own arms, and held her near my own warm neck and heart, and felt the life stealing slowly back again into her little gentle limbs. But she was still insensible when we reached the hall, and I had no breath for speech. We went in by the kitchen door.

"Bring the warming-pan," said I; and I carried her upstairs and began undressing her by the nursery fire, which Bessy had kept up. I called my little lammie all the sweet and playful names I could think of—even while my eyes were blinded by my tears; and at last, oh! at length she opened her large blue eyes. Then I put her into her warm bed, and sent Dorothy down to tell Miss Furnivall that all was well; and I made up my mind to sit by my darling's bedside the live-long night. She fell away into a soft sleep as soon as her pretty head had touched the pillow, and I watched by her till morning light; when she wakened up bright and clear—or so I thought at first—and, my dears, so I think now.

She said that she had fancied that she should like to go to Dorothy, for that both the old ladies were asleep, and it was very dull in the drawing-room; and that, as she was going through the west lobby, she saw the snow through the high window falling—falling—soft and steady; but she wanted to see it lying pretty and white on the ground; so she made her way into the great hall; and then, going to the window, she saw it bright and soft upon the drive; but while she stood there, she saw a little girl, not so old as she was, "but so pretty," said my darling, "and this little girl beckoned to me to come out; and oh, she was so pretty and so sweet, I could not choose but go." And then this other little girl had taken her by the hand, and side by side the two had gone round the east corner.

"Now, you are a naughty little girl, and telling stories," said I. "What would your good mamma, that is in heaven, and never told a story in her life, say to her little Rosamond, if she heard her—and I dare say she does—telling stories!"

"Indeed, Hester," sobbed out my child, "I'm telling you true. Indeed I am."

"Don't tell me!" said I, very stern. "I tracked you by your footmarks through the snow; there were only yours to be seen: and if you had had a little girl to go hand-in-hand with you up the hill, don't you think the footprints would have gone along with yours?"

"I can't help it, dear, dear Hester," said she, crying, "if they did not; I never looked at her feet, but she held my hand fast and tight in her little one, and it was very, very cold. She took me up the Fell-path, up to the holly trees; and there I saw a lady weeping and crying; but when she saw me, she hushed her weeping, and smiled very proud and grand, and took me on her knee, and began to lull me to sleep; and that's all, Hester—but that is true; and my dear mamma knows it is," said she, crying. So I thought the child was in a fever, and pretended to believe her, as she went over her story—over and over again, and always the same. At last Dorothy knocked at the door with Miss Rosamond's breakfast; and she told me the old ladies were down in the eating parlour, and that they wanted to speak to me. They had both been into the night-nursery the evening before, but it was after Miss Rosamond was asleep; so they had only looked at her—not asked me any questions.

"I shall catch it," thought I to myself, as I went along the north gallery. "And yet," I thought, taking courage, "it was in their charge I left her; and it's they that's to blame for letting her steal away unknown and unwatched." So I went in boldly, and told my story. I told it all to Miss Furnivall, shouting it close to her ear; but when I came to the mention of the other little girl out in the snow, coaxing and tempting her out, and willing her up to the grand and beautiful lady by the holly-tree, she threw her arms up—her old and withered arms—and cried aloud, "Oh! Heaven, forgive! Have mercy!"

Mrs. Stark took hold of her; roughly enough, I thought; but she was past Mrs. Stark's management, and spoke to me, in a kind of wild warning and authority.

[1] bairn Child.

"Hester! keep her from that child! It will lure her to her death! That evil child! Tell her it is a wicked, naughty child." Then Mrs. Stark hurried me out of the room; where, indeed, I was glad enough to go; but Miss Furnivall kept shrieking out, "Oh! have mercy! Wilt Thou never forgive! It is many a long year ago"—

I was very uneasy in my mind after that. I durst never leave Miss Rosamond, night or day, for fear lest she might slip off again, after some fancy or other; and all the more, because I thought I could make out that Miss Furnivall was crazy, from their odd ways about her; and I was afraid lest something of the same kind (which might be in the family, you know) hung over my darling. And the great frost never ceased all this time; and, whenever it was a more stormy night than usual, between the gusts, and through the wind, we heard the old lord playing on the great organ. But, old lord, or not, wherever Miss Rosamond went, there I followed; for my love for her, pretty helpless orphan, was stronger than my fear for the grand and terrible sound. Besides, it rested with me to keep her cheerful and merry, as beseemed her age. So we played together, and wandered together, here and there, and everywhere; for I never dared to lose sight of her again in that large and rambling house. And so it happened, that one afternoon, not long before Christmas Day, we were playing together on the billiard-table in the great hall (not that we knew the right way of playing, but she liked to roll the smooth ivory balls with her pretty hands, and I liked to do whatever she did); and, by and by, without our noticing it, it grew dusk indoors, though it was still light in the open air, and I was thinking of taking her back into the nursery, when, all of a sudden, she cried out:

"Look, Hester! look! there is my poor little girl out in the snow!"

I turned towards the long narrow windows, and there, sure enough, I saw a little girl, less than my Miss Rosamond—dressed all unfit to be out-of-doors such a bitter night—crying, and beating against the window-panes, as if she wanted to be let in. She seemed to sob and wail, till Miss Rosamond could bear it no longer, and was flying to the door to open it, when, all of a sudden, and close upon us, the great organ pealed out so loud and thundering, it fairly made me tremble; and all the more, when I remembered me that, even in the

stillness of that dead-cold weather, I had heard no sound of little battering hands upon the window-glass, although the Phantom Child had seemed to put forth all its force; and, although I had seen it wail and cry, no faintest touch of sound had fallen upon my ears. Whether I remembered all this at the very moment, I do not know; the great organ sound had so stunned me into terror; but this I know, I caught up Miss Rosamond before she got the hall-door opened, and clutched her, and carried her away, kicking and screaming, into the large bright kitchen, where Dorothy and Agnes were busy with their mince-pies.

"What is the matter with my sweet one?" cried Dorothy, as I bore in Miss Rosamond, who was sobbing as if her heart would break.

"She won't let me open the door for my little girl to come in; and she'll die if she is out on the Fells all night. Cruel, naughty Hester," she said, slapping me; but she might have struck harder, for I had seen a look of ghastly terror on Dorothy's face, which made my very blood run cold.

"Shut the back-kitchen door fast, and bolt it well," said she to Agnes. She said no more; she gave me raisins and almonds to quiet Miss Rosamond: but she sobbed about the little girl in the snow, and would not touch any of the good things. I was thankful when she cried herself to sleep in bed. Then I stole down to the kitchen, and told Dorothy I had made up my mind. I would carry my darling back to my father's house in Applethwaite; where, if we lived humbly, we lived at peace. I said I had been frightened enough with the old lord's organ-playing; but now, that I had seen for myself this little moaning child, all decked out as no child in the neighbourhood could be, beating and battering to get in, yet always without any sound or noise—with the dark wound on its right shoulder; and that Miss Rosamond had known it again for the phantom that had nearly lured her to her death (which Dorothy knew was true); I would stand it no longer.

I saw Dorothy change colour once or twice. When I had done, she told me she did not think I could take Miss Rosamond with me, for that she was my lord's ward, and I had no right over her; and she asked me, would I leave the child that I was so fond of, just for sounds and sights that could do me no harm; and that they had all had to get used to in their turns? I was all in a hot, trembling passion; and I said it was very well for her to talk, that knew what these sights and noises betokened, and that had, perhaps, had something to do with the Spectre-Child while it was alive. And I taunted her so, that she told me all she knew, at last; and then I wished I had never been told, for it only made me more afraid than ever.

She said she had heard the tale from old neighbours, that were alive when she was first married; when folks used to come to the hall sometimes, before it had got such a bad name on the country side; it might not be true, or it might, what she had been told.

The old lord was Miss Furnivall's father—Miss Grace, as Dorothy called her, for Miss Maude was the elder, and Miss Furnivall by rights. The old lord was eaten up with pride. Such a proud man was never seen or heard of; and his daughters were like him. No one was good enough to wed them, although they had choice enough; for they were the great beauties of their day, as I had seen by their portraits, where they hung in the state drawing-room. But, as the old saying is, "Pride will have a fall"; and these two haughty beauties fell in love with the same man, and he no better than a foreign musician, whom their father had down from London to play music with him at the Manor House. For, above all things, next to his pride, the old lord loved music. He could play on nearly every instrument that ever was heard of: and it was a strange thing it did not soften him; but he was a fierce dour old man, and had broken his poor wife's heart with his cruelty, they said. He was mad after music, and would pay any money for it. So he got this foreigner to come; who made such beautiful music, that they said the very birds on the trees stopped their singing to listen. And, by degrees, this foreign gentleman got such a hold over the old lord, that nothing would serve him but that he must come every year; and it was he that had the great organ brought from Holland, and built up in the hall, where it stood now. He taught the old lord to play on it; but many and many a time, when Lord Furnivall was thinking of nothing but his fine organ, and his finer music, the dark foreigner was walking abroad in the woods with one of the young ladies; now Miss Maude, and then Miss Grace.

Miss Maude won the day and carried off the prize, such as it was; and he and she were married, all unknown to any one; and before he made his next yearly visit, she had been confined of a little girl at a farmhouse on the Moors, while her father and Miss Grace thought she was away at Doncaster Races. But though she was a wife and a mother, she was not a bit softened, but as haughty and as passionate as ever; and perhaps more so, for she was jealous of Miss Grace, to whom her foreign husband paid a deal of court—by way of blinding her—as he told his wife. But Miss Grace triumphed over Miss Maude, and Miss Maude grew fiercer and fiercer, both with her husband and with her sister; and the former—who could easily shake off what was disagreeable, and hide himself in foreign countries—went away a month before his usual time that summer, and half-threatened that he would never come back again. Meanwhile, the little girl was left at the farm-house, and her mother used to have her horse saddled and gallop wildly over the hills to see her once every week, at the very least—for where she loved, she loved; and where she hated, she hated. And the old lord went on playing—playing on his organ; and the servants thought the sweet music he made had soothed down his awful temper, of which (Dorothy said) some terrible tales could be told. He grew infirm too, and had to walk with a crutch; and his son—that was the present Lord Furnivall's father—was with the army in America, and the other son at sea; so Miss Maude had it pretty much her own way, and she and Miss Grace grew colder and bitterer to each other every day; till at last they hardly ever spoke, except when the old lord was by. The foreign musician came again the next summer, but it was for the last time; for they led him such a life with their jealousy and their passions, that he grew weary, and went away, and never was heard of again. And Miss Maude, who had always meant to have her marriage acknowledged when her father should be dead, was left now a deserted wife—whom nobody knew to have been married—with a child that she dared not own, although she loved it to distraction; living with a father whom she feared, and a sister whom she hated. When the next summer passed over and the dark foreigner never came, both Miss Maude and Miss Grace grew gloomy and sad; they had a haggard look about them, though they looked handsome as ever. But by and by Miss Maude brightened; for her father grew more and more infirm, and more than ever carried away by his music; and she and Miss Grace lived almost entirely apart, having separate rooms, the one on the west side, Miss Maude on the east—those very rooms which were now shut up. So she thought she might have her little girl with her, and no one need ever know except those who dared not speak about it, and were bound to believe that it was, as she said, a cottager's child she had taken a fancy to. All this, Dorothy said, was pretty well known; but what came afterwards no one knew, except Miss Grace, and Mrs. Stark, who was even then her maid, and much more of a friend to her than ever her sister had been. But the servants supposed, from words that were dropped, that Miss Maude had triumphed over Miss Grace, and told her that all the time the dark foreigner had been mocking her with pretended love—he was her own husband; the colour left Miss Grace's cheek and lips that very day for ever, and she was heard to say many a time that sooner or later she would have her revenge; and Mrs. Stark was for ever spying about the east rooms.

One fearful night, just after the New Year had come in, when the snow was lying thick and deep, and the flakes were still falling—fast enough to blind any one who might be out and abroad—there was a great and violent noise heard, and the old lord's voice above all, cursing and swearing awfully—and the cries of a little child—and the proud defiance of a fierce woman—and the sound of a blow—and a dead stillness—and moans and wailings dying away on the hill-side! Then the old lord summoned all his servants, and told them, with terrible oaths, and words more terrible, that his daughter had disgraced herself, and that he had turned her out of doors—her, and her child—and that if ever they gave her help—or food—or shelter—he prayed that they might never enter Heaven. And, all the while, Miss Grace stood by him, white and still as any stone; and when he had ended she heaved a great sigh, as much as to say her work was done, and her end was accomplished. But the old lord never touched his organ again, and died within the year; and no wonder! for, on the morrow of that wild and fearful night, the shepherds, coming down the Fell side, found Miss Maude sitting,

all crazy and smiling, under the holly-trees, nursing a dead child—with a terrible mark on its right shoulder. "But that was not what killed it," said Dorothy; "it was the frost and the cold;—every wild creature was in its hole, and every beast in its fold—while the child and its mother were turned out to wander on the Fells! And now you know all! and I wonder if you are less frightened now?"

I was more frightened than ever; but I said I was not. I wished Miss Rosamond and myself well out of that dreadful house for ever; but I would not leave her, and I dared not take her away. But oh! how I watched her, and guarded her! We bolted the doors, and shut the window-shutters fast, an hour or more before dark, rather than leave them open five minutes too late. But my little lady still heard the weird child crying and mourning; and not all we could do or say could keep her from wanting to go to her, and let her in from the cruel wind and the snow. All this time, I kept away from Miss Furnivall and Mrs. Stark, as much as ever I could; for I feared them—I knew no good could be about them, with their grey hard faces, and their dreamy eyes, looking back into the ghastly years that were gone. But, even in my fear, I had a kind of pity—for Miss Furnivall, at least. Those gone down to the pit can hardly have a more hopeless look than that which was ever on her face. At last I even got so sorry for her—who never said a word but what was quite forced from her—that I prayed for her; and I taught Miss Rosamond to pray for one who had done a deadly sin; but often when she came to those words, she would listen, and start up from her knees, and say, "I hear my little girl plaining and crying very sad—Oh! let her in, or she will die!"

One night—just after New Year's Day had come at last, and the long winter had taken a turn, as I hoped—I heard the west drawing-room bell ring three times, which was the signal for me. I would not leave Miss Rosamond alone, for all she was asleep—for the old lord had been playing wilder than ever—and I feared lest my darling should waken to hear the spectre child; see her I knew she could not. I had fastened the windows too well for that. So I took her out of her bed and wrapped her up in such outer clothes as were most handy, and carried her down to the drawing-room, where the old ladies sat at their tapestry work as usual. They looked up when I came in, and Mrs. Stark asked, quite astounded, "Why did I bring Miss Rosamond there, out of her warm bed?" I had begun to whisper, "Because I was afraid of her being tempted out while I was away, by the wild child in the snow," when she stopped me short (with a glance at Miss Furnivall), and said Miss Furnivall wanted me to undo some work she had done wrong, and which neither of them could see to unpick. So I laid my pretty dear on the sofa, and sat down on a stool by them, and hardened my heart against them, as I heard the wind rising and howling.

Miss Rosamond slept on sound, for all the wind blew so; and Miss Furnivall said never a word, nor looked round when the gusts shook the windows. All at once she started up to her full height, and put up one hand, as if to bid us listen.

"I hear voices!" said she. "I hear terrible screams—I hear my father's voice!"

Just at that moment my darling wakened with a sudden start: "My little girl is crying, oh, how she is crying!" and she tried to get up and go to her, but she got her feet entangled in the blanket, and I caught her up; for my flesh had begun to creep at these noises, which they heard while we could catch no sound. In a minute or two the noises came, and gathered fast, and filled our ears; we, too, heard voices and screams, and no longer heard the winter's wind that raged abroad. Mrs. Stark looked at me, and I at her, but we dared not speak. Suddenly Miss Furnivall went towards the door, out into the ante-room, through the west lobby, and opened the door into the great hall. Mrs. Stark followed, and I durst not be left, though my heart almost stopped beating for fear. I wrapped my darling tight in my arms, and went out with them. In the hall the screams were louder than ever; they sounded to come from the east wing—nearer and nearer—close on the other side of the locked-up doors—close behind them. Then I noticed that the great bronze chandelier seemed all alight, though the hall was dim, and that a fire was blazing in the vast hearth-place, though it gave no heat; and I shuddered up with terror, and folded my darling closer to me. But as I did so, the east door shook, and she, suddenly struggling to get free from me, cried, "Hester! I must go! My little girl is there; I hear her; she is coming! Hester, I must go!"

I held her tight with all my strength; with a set will, I held her. If I had died, my hands would have grasped her still, I was so resolved in my mind. Miss Furnivall stood listening, and paid no regard to my darling, who had got down to the ground, and whom I, upon my knees now, was holding with both my arms clasped round her neck; she still striving and crying to get free.

All at once the east door gave way with a thundering crash, as if torn open in a violent passion, and there came into that broad and mysterious light, the figure of a tall old man, with grey hair and gleaming eyes. He drove before him, with many a relentless gesture of abhorrence, a stern and beautiful woman, with a little child clinging to her dress.

"O Hester! Hester!" cried Miss Rosamond. "It's the lady! the lady below the holly-trees; and my little girl is with her. Hester! Hester! let me go to her; they are drawing me to them. I feel them—I feel them. I must go!"

Again she was almost convulsed by her efforts to get away; but I held her tighter and tighter, till I feared I should do her a hurt; but rather that than let her go towards those terrible phantoms. They passed along towards the great hall-door, where the winds howled and ravened for their prey; but before they reached that, the lady turned; and I could see that she defied the old man with a fierce and proud defiance; but then she quailed—and then she threw up her arms wildly and piteously to save her child—her little child—from a blow from his uplifted crutch.

And Miss Rosamond was torn as by a power stronger than mine, and writhed in my arms, and sobbed (for by this time the poor darling was growing faint).

"They want me to go with them on to the Fells—they are drawing me to them. Oh, my little girl! I would come, but cruel, wicked Hester holds me very tight." But when she saw the uplifted crutch she swooned away, and I thanked God for it. Just at this moment—when the tall old man, his hair streaming as in the blast of a furnace, was going to strike the little shrinking child—Miss Furnivall, the old woman by my side, cried out, "Oh, father! father! spare the little innocent child!" But just then I saw—we all saw— another phantom shape itself, and grow clear out of the blue and misty light that filled the hall; we had not seen her till now, for it was another lady who stood by the old man, with a look of relentless hate and triumphant scorn. That figure was very beautiful to look upon, with a soft white hat drawn down over the proud brows, and a red and curling lip. It was dressed in an open robe of blue satin. I had seen that figure before. It was the likeness of Miss Furnivall in her youth; and the terrible phantoms moved on, regardless of old Miss Furnivall's wild entreaty—and the uplifted crutch fell on the right shoulder of the little child, and the younger sister looked on, stony and

deadly serene. But at that moment, the dim lights, and the fire that gave no heat, went out of themselves, and Miss Furnivall lay at our feet stricken down by the palsy—death-stricken.

Yes! she was carried to her bed that night never to rise again. She lay with her face to the wall, muttering low but muttering alway: "Alas! alas! what is done in youth can never be undone in age! What is done in youth can never be undone in age!"
—1852

ROBERT BROWNING
1812 — 1889

"The spirit of passionate and imaginative poetry is not dead among us," wrote an exultant R.H. Horne in 1844, while reviewing the poems of the young Robert Browning. But Browning, for all his passion and imagination, was not a popular poet for much of his lifetime. Indeed, until the 1860s, Browning was better known as the husband of Elizabeth Barrett. His own poetry, in the eyes of many of his contemporaries, was far too obscure, littered as it was with recondite historical and literary references and with dubious subject matter—husbands murdering their wives, artists frolicking with prostitutes. Fame did come, however, and scholars now credit Browning for having realized new

possibilities in the dramatic monologue, a form of poetry that, like a monologue in a dramatic production, showcases the speech of a character to an implied or imaginary audience. The poems are, in Browning's own words, "so many utterances of so many imaginary persons, not mine." As Browning's dramatic monologues unfold, their speakers reveal levels of psychological complexity that have inspired generations of poets, from the Pre-Raphaelites who were coming of age in the 1840s to Modernists such as Ezra Pound and T.S. Eliot.

Browning was the eldest of two children born in an upper middle-class suburb of London to a scholarly father and a devout, Protestant mother, Sarah Anna Wiedemann. An opponent of slavery, Robert Browning Sr. rejected employment on his family's plantation in St. Kitts in favor of less lucrative but more morally-acceptable work as a clerk for the Bank of England. Both parents helped to shape Browning's religious, social, and intellectual tastes and values, with Browning Sr. in particular feeding his son's voracious appetite for knowledge. The young Browning composed his first poem at the age of six. He attended Peckham School between the ages of ten and twelve and later some classes at University College in London. But the great majority of his schooling took place at home with tutors, and he spent many hours studying the books in his family's voluminous library. Despite his relative lack of formal schooling, then, Browning had an exceptionally bookish education—which may help to explain the intellectual cast of Browning's poetic vision.

Browning first arrived on the literary scene with the publication in 1833 of *Pauline: A Fragment of a Confession*, a long poem in the style of Shelley's *Alastor* (1816), which John Stuart Mill credited with "considerable poetic powers" that yet revealed "a more intense and morbid self-consciousness than I ever knew in any sane human being." The volume, published with family funds, apparently sold not even a single copy. It was followed in 1835 by *Paracelsus*, which, though similarly obscure, at least made Browning known to a few important critics and ultimately brought him into contact with Carlyle, Dickens, and Wordsworth, among others. With *Sordello* (1840), Browning secured his reputation for writing poetry of bewildering difficulty. Browning claimed that his "stress [in *Sordello*] lay on the incidents in the development of a soul: little else is worth study," and yet few could make sense of such incidents as Browning had chosen to portray them.

In 1842 Browning published a volume of shorter poems, *Dramatic Lyrics*, which marked an important break from his earlier productions. Included were many of the poems on which his reputation came to be based: "My Last Duchess," "Soliloquy of the Spanish Cloister," "Johannes Agricola in Meditation," and "Porphyria's Lover," the last two of which had been published in the

Monthly Repository of 1836 under the heading "Madhouse Cells." With *Dramatic Romances and Lyrics* (1845) and *Men and Women* (1855), Browning confirmed his literary reputation as the foremost innovator of the dramatic monologue; he remained, however, little known among contemporary Victorians. *Men and Women* contained now-canonical poems such as "Fra Lippo Lippi" and "Andrea del Sarto." "Here," wrote George Eliot in the *Westminster Review,* the reader will find "no conventionality, no melodious commonplace, but freshness, originality, sometimes eccentricity of expression; no didactic laying-out of a subject, but dramatic indication, which requires the reader to trace by his own mental activity the underground stream of thought that jets out in elliptical and pithy verse." Eliot's commentary draws attention not only to Browning's unconventional subject matter and dramatic presentation, but also to the range of his accomplishment in poetic form, his lack of "melodious commonplace." Victorian critics noted with varying degrees of wonder and consternation the degree to which Browning experimented with rhythm and meter, an experimentation that in the early twentieth century earned him the nickname "Old Hippety-Hop o' the accents" from Ezra Pound.

In January of 1845 Browning began what became a celebrated correspondence with the already-famous poet Elizabeth Barrett. Even before meeting her personally (an event that took place after four months of writing), Browning praised Barrett's 1844 volume *Poems* with the words, "I do, as I say, love these books with all my heart—and I love you too." Barrett fell in love with Browning after meeting him, and in 1846, despite her semi-invalid state and her father's command never to marry, the two eloped in London and moved to Italy, where they remained for the rest of her life. Their only child, Robert Wiedemann Barrett Browning (nicknamed "Pen"), was born in 1849 in their Florence home, Casa Guidi.

Browning returned to London and society life after his wife's death in 1861. 1864 brought the publication of *Dramatis Personae,* the first of his volumes to be popular among British readers. This was followed in 1868–69 by his twelve-part epic "murder-poem" (as Browning called it), *The Ring and the Book.* Browning conceived the idea of writing this epic in 1860, when in a Florence market he chanced upon a book of documents concerning a 1698 murder trial. He organized the story so that each book in the epic gives voice to a different participant in the event: the murderer, various onlookers, the victim, and even the Pope. In juxtaposing these varying testimonies, Browning suggests the impossibility of ever finding a coherent or truthful narrative and the importance of recognizing the relativity of points of view—something enacted in his dramatic monologues. These "filthy rags of speech," says the Pope, are "tatters all too contaminate for use."

The 1879–80 volumes of *Dramatic Idyls* brought the poet even greater fame, both in England and internationally; the public in the United States flocked to buy his books, and wearing brown articles of clothing in his honor became fashionable. In 1889, on the day his final volume of poems, *Asolando,* was published, Robert Browning died at his son's home in Venice. He is buried next to Alfred, Lord Tennyson, in the Poets' Corner of Westminster Abbey.

⌘ ⌘ ⌘

Porphyria's Lover

The rain set early in tonight,
  The sullen wind was soon awake,
It tore the elm tops down for spite,
  And did its worst to vex the lake:

5   I listened with heart fit to break.
When glided in Porphyria; straight
She shut the cold out and the storm,
And kneeled and made the cheerless grate
Blaze up, and all the cottage warm;
10   Which done, she rose, and from her form

Withdrew the dripping cloak and shawl,
    And laid her soiled gloves by, untied
Her hat and let the damp hair fall,
    And, last, she sat down by my side
15   And called me. When no voice replied,
She put my arm about her waist,
    And made her smooth white shoulder bare,
And all her yellow hair displaced,
    And, stooping, made my cheek lie there,
20   And spread, o'er all, her yellow hair,
Murmuring how she loved me—she
    Too weak, for all her heart's endeavour,
To set its struggling passion free
    From pride, and vainer ties dissever,
25   And give herself to me forever.
But passion sometimes would prevail,
    Nor could tonight's gay feast restrain
A sudden thought of one so pale
    For love of her, and all in vain:
30   So, she was come through wind and rain.
Be sure I looked up at her eyes
    Happy and proud; at last I knew
Porphyria worshipped me; surprise
    Made my heart swell, and still it grew
35   While I debated what to do.
That moment she was mine, mine, fair,
    Perfectly pure and good: I found
A thing to do, and all her hair
    In one long yellow string I wound
40   Three times her little throat around,
And strangled her. No pain felt she;
    I am quite sure she felt no pain.
As a shut bud that holds a bee,
    I warily oped her lids: again
45   Laughed the blue eyes without a stain.
And I untightened next the tress
    About her neck; her cheek once more
Blushed bright beneath my burning kiss:
    I propped her head up as before,
50   Only, this time my shoulder bore
Her head, which droops upon it still:
    The smiling rosy little head,
So glad it has its utmost will,
    That all it scorned at once is fled,
55   And I, its love, am gained instead!

Porphyria's love: she guessed not how
    Her darling one wish would be heard.
And thus we sit together now,
    And all night long we have not stirred,
60   And yet God has not said a word!
—1836

Soliloquy of the Spanish Cloister

1

Gr-r-r—there go, my heart's abhorrence!
    Water your damned flowerpots, do!
If hate killed men, Brother Lawrence,
    God's blood, would not mine kill you!
5   What? your myrtle bush wants trimming?
    Oh, that rose has prior claims—
Needs its leaden vase filled brimming?
    Hell dry you up with its flames!

2

At the meal we sit together:
10   *Salve tibi!* [1] I must hear
Wise talk of the kind of weather,
    Sort of season, time of year:
Not a plenteous cork crop: scarcely
    Dare we hope oak galls, [2] *I doubt:*
15   *What's the Latin name for "parsley"?*
    What's the Greek name for Swine's Snout?[3]

3

Whew! We'll have our platter burnished,
    Laid with care on our own shelf!
With a fire-new spoon we're furnished,
20   And a goblet for ourself,
Rinsed like something sacrificial
    Ere 'tis fit to touch our chaps°—   *jaws*
Marked with L. for our initial!
    (He-he! There his lily snaps!)

---

[1] *Salve tibi* Hail to thee.

[2] *oak galls* Growths on oak trees that are used to produce certain inks and tannins.

[3] *Swine's Snout* Dandelion.

25 *Saint*, forsooth! While brown Dolores
    Squats outside the Convent bank
With Sanchicha, telling stories,
    Steeping tresses in the tank,
Blue-black, lustrous, thick like horsehairs,
30   —Can't I see his dead eye glow,
Bright as 'twere a Barbary corsair's?[1]
    (That is, if he'd let it show!)

5

When he finishes refection,°   *a meal*
    Knife and fork he never lays
35 Crosswise, to my recollection,
    As do I, in Jesu's praise.
I the Trinity illustrate,
    Drinking watered orange pulp—
In three sips the Arian[2] frustrate;
40   While he drains his at one gulp.

6

Oh, those melons? If he's able
    We're to have a feast! so nice!
One goes to the Abbot's table,
    All of us get each a slice.
45 How go on your flowers? None double?
    Not one fruit-sort can you spy?
Strange!—And I, too, at such trouble,
    Keep them close-nipped on the sly!

7

There's a great text in Galatians,
50   Once you trip on it, entails
Twenty-nine distinct damnations,[3]
    One sure, if another fails:
If I trip him just a-dying,
    Sure of heaven as sure can be,

55 Spin him round and send him flying
    Off to hell, a Manichee?[4]

8

Or, my scrofulous° French novel   *morally corrupt*
    On grey paper with blunt type!
Simply glance at it, you grovel
60   Hand and foot in Belial's° gripe: *the devil's*
If I double down its pages
    At the woeful sixteenth print,
When he gathers his greengages,°   *plums*
    Ope a sieve and slip it in't?

9

65 Or, there's Satan!—one might venture
    Pledge one's soul to him, yet leave
Such a flaw in the indenture
    As he'd miss till, past retrieve,
Blasted lay that rose acacia
70   We're so proud of! *Hy, Zy, Hine* …
'St, there's Vespers![5] Plena gratiâ
    Ave, Virgo![6] Gr-r-r—you swine!

—1842

My Last Duchess[7]

Ferrara

That's my last Duchess painted on the wall,
  Looking as if she were alive. I call
That piece a wonder, now: Frà° Pandolf's hands   *Brother*

---

[1] *Barbary corsair* Pirate of the Barbary Coast (former name of the Mediterranean coastal region of North Africa).

[2] *Arian* Follower of Arius (256–336), considered a heretic in his day for his disavowal of the notion (inherent in the concept of the Trinity) that Jesus Christ was of the same essence or substance as God.

[3] *Galatians … damnations* See Galatians 5.19–21 for a list of 17, not 29, sins.

[4] *Manichee* Heretic; follower of the Persian theologian Mani's third-century beliefs in dualism.

[5] *Hy, Zy, Hine … Vespers* Sound of the bell that rings for Vespers, or evening prayers.

[6] *Plena … Virgo* Version of the Latin prayer "Ave Maria": "Full of grace / Hail, Virgin."

[7] *My Last Duchess* According to Louis S. Friedland, Browning likely modeled the speaker of this poem on Alfonso II (1533–1598), Duke of Ferrara. His first wife, a member of the wealthy Medici family, was only fourteen years old when they married. Only three days after the wedding, Alfonso left his wife for two years, and she died of suspicious causes a year after he returned. Four years later the duke negotiated with a servant to marry the daughter of the Count of Tyrol.

Worked busily a day, and there she stands.
5   Will't please you sit and look at her? I said
"Frà Pandolf" by design, for never read
Strangers like you that pictured countenance,
The depth and passion of its earnest glance,
But to myself they turned (since none puts by
10 The curtain I have drawn for you, but I)
And seemed as they would ask me, if they durst,
How such a glance came there; so, not the first
Are you to turn and ask thus. Sir, 'twas not
Her husband's presence only, called that spot
15 Of joy into the Duchess' cheek: perhaps
Frà Pandolf chanced to say "Her mantle laps
Over my lady's wrist too much," or "Paint
Must never hope to reproduce the faint
Half-flush that dies along her throat": such stuff
20 Was courtesy, she thought, and cause enough
For calling up that spot of joy. She had
A heart—how shall I say?—too soon made glad,
Too easily impressed; she liked whate'er
She looked on, and her looks went everywhere.
25 Sir, 'twas all one! My favour° at her breast,   gift
The dropping of the daylight in the West,
The bough of cherries some officious fool
Broke in the orchard for her, the white mule
She rode with round the terrace—all and each
30 Would draw from her alike the approving speech,
Or blush, at least. She thanked men—good! but
     thanked
Somehow—I know not how—as if she ranked
My gift of a nine-hundred-years-old name
With anybody's gift. Who'd stoop to blame
35 This sort of trifling? Even had you skill
In speech—(which I have not)—to make your will
Quite clear to such an one, and say, "Just this
Or that in you disgusts me; here you miss,
Or there exceed the mark"—and if she let
40 Herself be lessoned so, nor plainly set
Her wits to yours, forsooth, and made excuse,
—E'en then would be some stooping; and I choose
Never to stoop. Oh sir, she smiled, no doubt,
Whene'er I passed her; but who passed without

45 Much the same smile? This grew; I gave commands;
Then all smiles stopped together. There she stands
As if alive. Will't please you rise? We'll meet
The company below, then. I repeat,
The Count your master's known munificence
50 Is ample warrant that no just pretence
Of mine for dowry will be disallowed;
Though his fair daughter's self, as I avowed
At starting, is my object. Nay, we'll go
Together down, sir. Notice Neptune,[1] though,
55 Taming a seahorse, thought a rarity,
Which Claus of Innsbruck cast in bronze for me!
—1842

Home-Thoughts, from Abroad

1

Oh, to be in England
Now that April's there,
And whoever wakes in England
Sees, some morning, unaware,
5   That the lowest boughs and the brushwood sheaf
Round the elm-tree bole° are in tiny leaf,   trunk
While the chaffinch sings on the orchard bough
In England—now!

2

And after April, when May follows,
10 And the whitethroat builds, and all the swallows!
Hark, where my blossomed pear tree in the hedge
Leans to the field and scatters on the clover
Blossoms and dewdrops—at the bent spray's edge—
That's the wise thrush; he sings each song twice over,
15 Lest you should think he never could recapture
The first fine careless rapture!
And though the fields look rough with hoary dew
All will be gay when noontide wakes anew
The buttercups, the little children's dower—
20 Far brighter than this gaudy melon flower!
—1845

1   *Neptune* Roman god of the sea, who rides in a chariot pulled by seahorses.

The Bishop Orders His Tomb at Saint Praxed's Church

Rome, 15—

Vanity, saith the preacher, vanity![1]
     Draw round my bed: is Anselm keeping back?
Nephews—sons mine ... ah God, I know not! Well—
She, men would have to be your mother once,
5   Old Gandolf envied me, so fair she was!
What's done is done, and she is dead beside,
Dead long ago, and I am Bishop since,
And as she died so must we die ourselves,
And thence ye may perceive the world's a dream.
10 Life, how and what is it? As here I lie
In this state-chamber, dying by degrees,
Hours and long hours in the dead night, I ask
"Do I live, am I dead?" Peace, peace seems all.
Saint Praxed's ever was the church for peace;
15 And so, about this tomb of mine. I fought
With tooth and nail to save my niche, ye know:
—Old Gandolf cozened me,° despite my care;   cheated
Shrewd was that snatch from out the corner south
He graced his carrion with, God curse the same!
20 Yet still my niche is not so cramped but thence
One sees the pulpit o' the epistle side,[2]
And somewhat of the choir, those silent seats,
And up into the aery dome where live
The angels, and a sunbeam's sure to lurk.
25 And I shall fill my slab of basalt there,
And 'neath my tabernacle take my rest,
With those nine columns round me, two and two,
The odd one at my feet where Anselm stands:
Peach-blossom marble all, the rare, the ripe
30 As fresh-poured red wine of a mighty pulse.
—Old Gandolf with his paltry onion-stone,[3]
Put me where I may look at him! True peach,
Rosy and flawless: how I earned the prize!
Draw close: that conflagration of my church

35 —What then? So much was saved if aught were
        missed!
My sons, ye would not be my death? Go dig
The white-grape vineyard where the oil-press stood,
Drop water gently till the surface sink,
And if ye find ... Ah God, I know not, I! ...
40 Bedded in store of rotten fig leaves soft,
And corded up in a tight olive-frail,°   basket
Some lump, ah God, of *lapis lazuli*,[4]
Big as a Jew's head cut off at the nape,
Blue as a vein o'er the Madonna's breast ...
45 Sons, all have I bequeathed you, villas, all,
That brave Frascati[5] villa with its bath,
So, let the blue lump poise between my knees,
Like God the Father's globe on both his hands
Ye worship in the Jesu Church[6] so gay,
50 For Gandolf shall not choose but see and burst!
Swift as a weaver's shuttle[7] fleet our years:
Man goeth to the grave, and where is he?[8]
Did I say basalt for my slab, sons? Black—
'Twas ever antique-black° I meant! How else   black marble
55 Shall ye contrast my frieze[9] to come beneath?
The bas-relief in bronze ye promised me,
Those Pans and Nymphs[10] ye wot of, and perchance
Some tripod, thyrsus,[11] with a vase or so,
The Saviour at his sermon on the mount,

---

[1] *Vanity, saith the preacher* From Ecclesiastes 1.2: "Vanity of vanities, saith the Preacher, vanity of vanities; all is vanity."

[2] *epistle side* Right-hand side, where the pulpit is and from which the epistles are read.

[3] *onion stone* Variety of less expensive marble that is named for its tendency to peel into layers.

[4] *lapis lazuli* Semi-precious blue stone; the altar-tomb of St. Ignatius at Il Gesù (Church of the Holy Name of Jesus) in Rome is decorated with huge columns made from lapis lazuli.

[5] *Frascati* Summer resort near Rome.

[6] *Jesu Church* Il Gesù.

[7] *Swift ... years* From Job 7.6: "My days are swifter than a weaver's shuttle, and are spent without hope."

[8] *Man goeth ... where is he?* From Job 7.9: "As the cloud is consumed and vanisheth away: so he that goeth down to the grave shall come up no more."

[9] *frieze* Painted or sculpted band on a wall or column.

[10] *bas-relief ... Pans and Nymphs* Shallow carvings that depict Greek mythological figures alongside Biblical figures.

[11] *tripod* Vessel on which sat the Oracle at Delphi, where she delivered her prophecies; *thyrsus* Staff adorned with a pine cone and ivy, carried by Dionysus, the Greek god of wine, and his followers.

60 Saint Praxed[1] in a glory,° and one Pan[2]   *halo; lightbeam*
   Ready to twitch the Nymph's last garment off,
   And Moses with the tables°… but I know   *Ten Commandments*
   Ye mark me not! What do they whisper thee,
   Child of my bowels, Anselm? Ah, ye hope
65 To revel down my villas while I gasp
   Bricked o'er with beggar's mouldy travertine°   *limestone*
   Which Gandolf from his tomb top chuckles at!
   Nay, boys, ye love me—all of jasper,° then!   *precious stone*
   'Tis jasper ye stand pledged to, lest I grieve
70 My bath must needs be left behind, alas!
   One block, pure green as a pistachio nut,
   There's plenty jasper somewhere in the world—
   And have I not Saint Praxed's ear to pray
   Horses for ye, and brown Greek manuscripts,
75 And mistresses with great smooth marbly limbs?
   —That's if ye carve my epitaph aright,
   Choice Latin, picked phrase, Tully's[3] every word,
   No gaudy ware like Gandolf's second line—
   Tully, my masters? Ulpian[4] serves his need!
80 And then how I shall lie through centuries,
   And hear the blessed mutter of the mass,
   And see God made and eaten all day long,
   And feel the steady candle flame, and taste
   Good strong thick stupefying incense smoke!
85 For as I lie here, hours of the dead night,
   Dying in state and by such slow degrees,
   I fold my arms as if they clasped a crook,°   *bishop's staff*
   And stretch my feet forth straight as stone can point,
   And let the bedclothes, for a mortcloth,[5] drop
90 Into great laps and folds of sculptor's work:
   And as yon tapers dwindle, and strange thoughts
   Grow, with a certain humming in my ears,
   About the life before I lived this life,
   And this life too, popes, cardinals and priests,
95 Saint Praxed at his sermon on the mount,

   Your tall pale mother with her talking eyes,
   And newfound agate urns as fresh as day,
   And marble's language, Latin pure, discreet,
   —Aha, *ELUCESCEBAT*[6] quoth our friend?
100 No Tully, said I, Ulpian at the best!
   Evil and brief hath been my pilgrimage.[7]
   All *lapis*, all, sons! Else I give the Pope
   My villas! Will ye ever eat my heart?
   Ever your eyes were as a lizard's quick,
105 They glitter like your mother's for my soul,
   Or ye would heighten my impoverished frieze,
   Piece out its starved design, and fill my vase
   With grapes, and add a vizor and a Term,[8]
   And to the tripod ye would tie a lynx
110 That in his struggle throws the thyrsus down,
   To comfort me on my entablature°   *column*
   Whereon I am to lie till I must ask
   "Do I live, am I dead?" There, leave me, there!
   For ye have stabbed me with ingratitude
115 To death—ye wish it—God, ye wish it! Stone—
   Gritstone, a-crumble! Clammy squares which sweat
   As if the corpse they keep were oozing through—
   And no more lapis to delight the world!
   Well go! I bless ye. Fewer tapers° there,   *candles*
120 But in a row: and, going, turn your backs
   —Ay, like departing altar ministrants,
   And leave me in my church, the church for peace,
   That I may watch at leisure if he leers—
   Old Gandolf, at me, from his onion-stone,
125 As still he envied me, so fair she was!
   —1845

Meeting at Night

I

The grey sea and the long black land;
   And the yellow half moon large and low;

---

[1]   *Saint Praxed*   Roman virgin of the second century who gave away all of her wealth to the poor.

[2]   *Pan*   Greek shepherd god of nature, who chased the nymph Syrinx until she turned herself into a bed of reeds.

[3]   *Tully*   Commonly known as Cicero, Roman orator, philosopher, and statesman of the first century BCE.

[4]   *Ulpian*   Roman jurist (?–228), whose writings were acknowledged to be of a lower standard than Cicero's.

[5]   *mortcloth*   Funeral cloth draped over the dead.

[6]   *ELUCESCEBAT*   Latin: "He was illustrious." *Elucescebat* is a later Latin verb form; Cicero would have written *elucebat*.

[7]   *Evil… pilgrimage*   Cf. Genesis 47.9: "Jacob said unto Pharaoh… few and evil have the days of the years of my life been, and have not attained unto the days of the years of the life of my fathers in the days of their pilgrimage."

[8]   *vizor*   Helmet piece represented in Roman sculpture;   *Term* Statue of Terminus, Roman god of boundaries.

And the startled little waves that leap
In fiery ringlets from their sleep,
5   As I gain the cove with pushing prow,
And quench its speed i' the slushy sand.

2

Then a mile of warm sea-scented beach;
Three fields to cross till a farm appears;
A tap at the pane, the quick sharp scratch
10   And blue spurt of a lighted match,
And a voice less loud, thro' its joys and fears,
Than the two hearts beating each to each!
—1845

Parting at Morning

Round the cape of a sudden came the sea,
   And the sun looked over the mountain's rim:
And straight was a path of gold for him,
And the need of a world of men for me.
—1845

How It Strikes a Contemporary

I only knew one poet in my life:
   And this, or something like it, was his way.

You saw go up and down Valladolid,[1]
A man of mark, to know next time you saw.
5   His very serviceable suit of black
Was courtly once and conscientious still,
And many might have worn it, though none did:
The cloak, that somewhat shone and showed the
      threads,
Had purpose, and the ruff, significance.
10   He walked and tapped the pavement with his cane,
Scenting the world, looking it full in face,
An old dog, bald and blindish, at his heels.
They turned up, now, the alley by the church,
That leads nowhither; now, they breathed themselves
15   On the main promenade just at the wrong time:

_____
[1]   *Valladolid*   City in Spain north of Madrid.

You'd come upon his scrutinizing hat,
Making a peaked shade blacker than itself
Against the single window spared some house
Intact yet with its mouldered Moorish work—
20   Or else surprise the ferrel° of his stick   *metal cap*
Trying the mortar's temper 'tween the chinks
Of some new shop a-building, French and fine.
He stood and watched the cobbler at his trade,
The man who slices lemons into drink,
25   The coffee roaster's brazier, and the boys
That volunteer to help him turn its winch.
He glanced o'er books on stalls with half an eye,
And fly-leaf ballads on the vendor's string,
And broad-edge bold-print posters by the wall.
30   He took such cognizance of men and things,
If any beat a horse, you felt he saw;
If any cursed a woman, he took note;
Yet stared at nobody—you stared at him,
And found, less to your pleasure than surprise,
35   He seemed to know you and expect as much.
So, next time that a neighbour's tongue was loosed,
It marked the shameful and notorious fact,
We had among us, not so much a spy,
As a recording chief inquisitor,
40   The town's true master if the town but knew!
We merely kept a governor for form,
While this man walked about and took account
Of all thought, said and acted, then went home,
And wrote it fully to our Lord the King
45   Who has an itch to know things, he knows why,
And reads them in his bedroom of a night.
Oh, you might smile! there wanted not a touch,
A tang of … well, it was not wholly ease
As back into your mind the man's look came.
50   Stricken in years a little—such a brow
His eyes had to live under!—clear as flint
On either side the formidable nose
Curved, cut and coloured like an eagle's claw.
Had he to do with A.'s surprising fate?
55   When altogether old B. disappeared
And young C. got his mistress—was't our friend,
His letter to the King, that did it all?
What paid the bloodless man for so much pains?
Our Lord the King has favourites manifold,
60   And shifts his ministry some once a month;

Our city gets new governors at whiles—
But never word or sign, that I could hear,
Notified to this man about the streets
The King's approval of those letters conned°   studied
65   The last thing duly at the dead of night.
Did the man love his office? Frowned our Lord,
Exhorting when none heard—"Beseech me not!
Too far above my people—beneath me!
I set the watch—how should the people know?
70   Forget them, keep me all the more in mind!"
Was some such understanding 'twixt the two?

        I found no truth in one report at least—
That if you tracked him to his home, down lanes
Beyond the Jewry,[1] and as clean to pace,
75   You found he ate his supper in a room
Blazing with lights, four Titians[2] on the wall,
And twenty naked girls to change his plate!
Poor man, he lived another kind of life
In that new stuccoed third house by the bridge,
80   Fresh-painted, rather smart than otherwise!
The whole street might o'erlook him as he sat,
Leg crossing leg, one foot on the dog's back,
Playing a decent cribbage with his maid
(Jacynth, you're sure her name was) o'er the cheese
85   And fruit, three red halves of starved winter pears,
Or treat of radishes in April. Nine,
Ten, struck the church clock, straight to bed went he.

        My father, like the man of sense he was,
Would point him out to me a dozen times;
90   "'St—'St," he'd whisper, "the Corregidor!"°   magistrate
I had been used to think that personage
Was one with lacquered breeches, lustrous belt,
And feathers like a forest in his hat,
Who blew a trumpet and proclaimed the news,
95   Announced the bullfights, gave each church its turn,
And memorized the miracle in vogue!
He had a great observance from us boys;
We were in error; that was not the man.

        I'd like now, yet had haply been afraid,
100   To have just looked, when this man came to die,

And seen who lined the clean gay garret sides
And stood about the neat low truckle-bed,[3]
With the heavenly manner of relieving guard.
Here had been, mark, the general-in-chief,
105   Thro' a whole campaign of the world's life and death,
Doing the King's work all the dim day long,
In his old coat and up to knees in mud,
Smoked like a herring, dining on a crust—
And, now the day was won, relieved at once!
110   No further show or need for that old coat,
You are sure, for one thing! Bless us, all the while
How sprucely we are dressed out, you and I!
A second, and the angels alter that.
Well, I could never write a verse—could you?
115   Let's to the Prado[4] and make the most of time.
—1855

Memorabilia[5]

1

Ah, did you once see Shelley plain,
    And did he stop and speak to you
And did you speak to him again?
    How strange it seems and new!

2

5   But you were living before that,
    And also you are living after;
And the memory I started at—
    My starting moves your laughter.

3

I crossed a moor, with a name of its own
10   And a certain use in the world no doubt,

---

[1] *Jewry*   Area of the city in which Jews were required to live.

[2] *Titians*   Paintings by the Venetian artist Titian (c. 1490–1576).

[3] *truckle-bed*   Trundle bed (one that can be pushed under a bed of regular height).

[4] *Prado*   Museum in Madrid.

[5] [Browning's note] I was one day in the bookshop of Hodgson, the well-known London bookseller, when a stranger came in, who, in the course of conversation with the bookseller, spoke of something that Shelley had once said to him. Suddenly, the stranger paused, and burst into laughter as he observed me staring at him with blanched face; and … I still vividly remember how strangely the presence of a man who had seen and spoken with Shelley affected me.

Yet a hand's-breath of it shines alone
    'Mid the blank miles round about:

4

For there I picked up on the heather
    And there I put inside my breast
15 A moulted feather, an eagle feather!
      Well, I forget the rest.
—1855

Love Among the Ruins

1

Where the quiet-coloured end of evening smiles,
    Miles and miles
On the solitary pastures where our sheep
    Half-asleep
5 Tinkle homeward thro' the twilight, stray or stop
    As they crop—
Was the site once of a city great and gay,
    (So they say)
Of our country's very capital, its prince
10   Ages since
Held his court in, gathered councils, wielding far
    Peace or war.

2

Now—the country does not even boast a tree,
    As you see,
15 To distinguish slopes of verdure, certain rills°   *brooks*
    From the hills
Intersect and give a name to, (else they run
    Into one)
Where the domed and daring palace shot its spires
20   Up like fires
O'er the hundred-gated circuit of a wall
    Bounding all,
Made of marble, men might march on nor be pressed,
    Twelve abreast.

3

25 And such plenty and perfection, see, of grass
    Never was!

Such a carpet as, this summertime, o'erspreads
    And embeds
Every vestige of the city, guessed alone,
30   Stock or stone—
Where a multitude of men breathed joy and woe
    Long ago;
Lust of glory pricked their hearts up, dread of shame
    Struck them tame;
35 And that glory and that shame alike, the gold
    Bought and sold.

4

Now—the single little turret that remains
    On the plains,
By the caper° overrooted, by the gourd   *shrub*
40   Overscored,
While the patching houseleek's° head of blossom
    winks   *herb's*
    Through the chinks—
Marks the basement whence a tower in ancient time
    Sprang sublime,
45 And a burning ring, all round, the chariots traced
    As they raced,
And the monarch and his minions and his dames
    Viewed the games.

5

And I know, while thus the quiet-coloured eve
50   Smiles to leave
To their folding, all our many-tinkling fleece
    In such peace,
And the slopes and rills in undistinguished grey
    Melt away—
55 That a girl with eager eyes and yellow hair
    Waits me there
In the turret whence the charioteers caught soul
    For the goal,
When the king looked, where she looks now,
    breathless, dumb
60   Till I come.

6

But he looked upon the city, every side,
    Far and wide,

All the mountains topped with temples, all the glades'
    Colonnades,
65 All the causeys,° bridges, aqueducts—and then, *embankments*
    All the men!
When I do come, she will speak not, she will stand,
    Either hand
On my shoulder, give her eyes the first embrace
70   Of my face,
Ere we rush, ere we extinguish sight and speech
    Each on each.

7

In one year they sent a million fighters forth
    South and north,
75 And they built their gods a brazen pillar high
    As the sky,
Yet reserved a thousand chariots in full force—
    Gold, of course.
Oh heart! oh blood that freezes, blood that burns!
80   Earth's returns
For whole centuries of folly, noise and sin!
    Shut them in,
With their triumphs and their glories and the rest!
    Love is best.
—1855

"Childe Roland to the Dark Tower Came"
(*See Edgar's song in* Lear)[1]

1

My first thought was, he lied in every word,
  That hoary°cripple, with malicious eye   *wizened*
Askance to watch the working of his lie
On mine, and mouth scarce able to afford
5 Suppression of the glee, that pursed and scored
    Its edge, at one more victim gained thereby.

2

What else should he be set for, with his staff?
  What, save to waylay with his lies, ensnare
  All travellers who might find him posted there,
10 And ask the road? I guessed what skull-like laugh
Would break, what crutch 'gin° write my epitaph   *begin*
    For pastime in the dusty thoroughfare,

3

If at his counsel I should turn aside
  Into that ominous tract which, all agree,
15   Hides the Dark Tower. Yet acquiescingly
I did turn as he pointed: neither pride
Nor hope rekindling at the end descried,
    So much as gladness that some end might be.

4

For, what with my whole world-wide wandering,
20   What with my search drawn out thro' years, my hope
  Dwindled into a ghost not fit to cope
With that obstreperous joy success would bring—
I hardly tried now to rebuke the spring
    My heart made, finding failure in its scope.

5

25 As when a sick man very near to death
  Seems dead indeed, and feels begin and end
  The tears and takes the farewell of each friend,
And hears one bid the other go, draw breath
Freelier outside ("since all is o'er," he saith,
30   "And the blow fallen no grieving can amend");

6

While some discuss if near the other graves
  Be room enough for this, and when a day
  Suits best for carrying the corpse away,
With care about the banners, scarves and staves:
35 And still the man hears all, and only craves
    He may not shame such tender love and stay.

7

Thus, I had so long suffered in this quest,
  Heard failure prophesied so oft, been writ
  So many times among "The Band"—to wit,

[1] *Edgar ... Lear* From Shakespeare's *King Lear* 3.4.130–32, in which the character Edgar, disguised as the beggar Poor Tom, sings about the French hero Rowland, nephew of Charlemagne: "Child Rowland to the dark tower came, / His word was still, Fie, foh, and fum, / I smell the blood of a British man." "Childe" refers to a youth born of noble stock, who would usually become a candidate for knighthood.

40 The knights who to the Dark Tower's search addressed
    Their steps—that just to fail as they, seemed best,
        And all the doubt was now—should I be fit?

8

    So, quiet as despair, I turned from him,
        That hateful cripple, out of his highway
45   Into the path he pointed. All the day
    Had been a dreary one at best, and dim
    Was settling to its close, yet shot one grim
        Red leer to see the plain catch its estray.°   *stray animal*

9

    For mark! no sooner was I fairly found
50   Pledged to the plain, after a pace or two,
        Than, pausing to throw backward a last view
    O'er the safe road, 'twas gone; grey plain all round:
    Nothing but plain to the horizon's bound.
        I might go on; nought else remained to do.

10

55 So, on I went. I think I never saw
        Such starved ignoble nature; nothing throve:
        For flowers—as well expect a cedar grove!
    But cockle, spurge,[1] according to their law
    Might propagate their kind, with none to awe,
60   You'd think; a burr had been a treasure trove.

11

    No! penury, inertness and grimace,
        In some strange sort, were the land's portion. "See
        Or shut your eyes," said Nature peevishly,
    "It nothing skills: I cannot help my case:
65   'Tis the Last Judgment's fire must cure this place,
        Calcine° its clods and set my prisoners
            free."   *burn completely*

12

    If there pushed any ragged thistle-stalk
        Above its mates, the head was chopped; the
            bents°   *reed-like grasses*
        Were jealous else. What made those holes and rents
70 In the dock's° harsh swarth leaves, bruised as to
        baulk   *weed's*

_____
[1] *cockle, spurge* Types of weeds.

All hope of greenness? 'tis a brute must walk
    Pashing° their life out, with a brute's intents.   *smashing*

13

    As for the grass, it grew as scant as hair
        In leprosy; thin dry blades pricked the mud
75   Which underneath looked kneaded up with blood.
    One stiff blind horse, his every bone a-stare,
    Stood stupefied, however he came there:
        Thrust out past service from the devil's stud!

14

    Alive? he might be dead for aught I know,
80   With that red gaunt and colloped[2] neck a-strain,
        And shut eyes underneath the rusty mane;
    Seldom went such grotesqueness with such woe;
    I never saw a brute I hated so;
        He must be wicked to deserve such pain.

15

85 I shut my eyes and turned them on my heart.
        As a man calls for wine before he fights,
        I asked one draught of earlier, happier sights,
    Ere fitly I could hope to play my part.
    Think first, fight afterwards—the soldier's art:
90   One taste of the old time sets all to rights.

16

    Not it! I fancied Cuthbert's reddening face
        Beneath its garniture of curly gold,
        Dear fellow, till I almost felt him fold
    An arm in mine to fix me to the place,
95 That way he used. Alas, one night's disgrace!
        Out went my heart's new fire and left it cold.

17

    Giles then, the soul of honour—there he stands
        Frank as ten years ago when knighted first.
        What honest man should dare (he said) he durst.
100 Good—but the scene shifts—faugh! what hangman
        hands
    Pin to his breast a parchment? His own bands
        Read it. Poor traitor, spit upon and curst!

_____
[2] *colloped* Having folds of fat.

18

Better this present than a past like that;
　　Back therefore to my darkening path again!
105　　No sound, no sight as far as eye could strain.
Will the night send a howlet° or a bat?　　　　　　*owl*
I asked: when something on the dismal flat
　　Came to arrest my thoughts and change their train.

19

A sudden little river crossed my path
110　　As unexpected as a serpent comes.
　　No sluggish tide congenial to the glooms;
This, as it frothed by, might have been a bath
For the fiend's glowing hoof—to see the wrath
　　Of its black eddy bespate° with flakes and　　*flooded*
　　　spumes.

20

115 So petty yet so spiteful! All along,
　　Low scrubby alders kneeled down over it;
　　Drenched willows flung them headlong in a fit
Of mute despair, a suicidal throng:
The river which had done them all the wrong,
120　　Whate'er that was, rolled by, deterred no whit.

21

Which, while I forded—good saints, how I feared
　　To set my foot upon a dead man's cheek,
　　Each step, or feel the spear I thrust to seek
For hollows, tangled in his hair or beard!
125　—It may have been a water-rat I speared,
　　But, ugh! it sounded like a baby's shriek.

22

Glad was I when I reached the other bank.
　　Now for a better country. Vain presage!
　　Who were the strugglers, what war did they wage,
130 Whose savage trample thus could pad the dank
Soil to a plash?° Toads in a poisoned tank,　　*pool*
　　Or wild cats in a red-hot iron cage—

23

The fight must so have seemed in that fell cirque.[1]
　　What penned them there, with all the plain to
　　　choose?

[1] *fell cirque* Dreadful arena.

135　No footprint leading to that horrid mews,
None out of it. Mad brewage set to work
Their brains, no doubt, like galley slaves the Turk
　　Pits for his pastime, Christians against Jews.

24

And more than that—a furlong on—why, there!
140　　What bad use was that engine for, that wheel,
　　Or brake, not wheel—that harrow fit to reel
Men's bodies out like silk? with all the air
Of Tophet's° tool, on earth left unaware,　　　*hell's*
　　Or brought to sharpen its rusty teeth of steel.

25

145 Then came a bit of stubbed ground, once a wood,
　　Next a marsh, it would seem, and now mere earth
　　Desperate and done with; (so a fool finds mirth,
Makes a thing and then mars it, till his mood
Changes and off he goes!) within a rood°　　*quarter acre*
150　　Bog, clay and rubble, sand and stark black dearth.

26

Now blotches rankling, coloured gay and grim,
　　Now patches where some leanness of the soil's
　　Broke into moss or substances like boils;
Then came some palsied oak, a cleft in him
155 Like a distorted mouth that splits its rim
　　Gaping at death, and dies while it recoils.

27

And just as far as ever from the end!
　　Nought in the distance but the evening, nought
　　To point my footstep further! At the thought,
160 A great black bird, Apollyon's[2] bosom-friend,
Sailed past, nor beat his wide wing dragon-
　　　penned°　　　　　　　　　　　　　　　*winged*
　　That brushed my cap—perchance the guide I sought.

28

For, looking up, aware I somehow grew,
　　'Spite of the dusk, the plain had given place
165　　All round to mountains—with such name to grace
Mere ugly heights and heaps now stolen in view.

[2] *Apollyon* Devil, or winged "angel of the bottomless pit," in
Revelations 9.11.

How thus they had surprised me,—solve it, you!
    How to get from them was no clearer case.

29

Yet half I seemed to recognize some trick
170   Of mischief happened to me, God knows when—
    In a bad dream perhaps. Here ended, then,
Progress this way. When, in the very nick
Of giving up, one time more, came a click
    As when a trap shuts—you're inside the den!

30

175 Burningly it came on me all at once,
    This was the place! those two hills on the right,
    Crouched like two bulls locked horn in horn in
        fight;
While to the left, a tall scalped mountain … Dunce,
Dotard, a-dozing at the very nonce,°   *moment*
180   After a life spent training for the sight!

31

What in the midst lay but the Tower itself?
    The round squat turret, blind as the fool's heart,
    Built of brown stone, without a counterpart
In the whole world. The tempest's mocking elf
185 Points to the shipman° thus the unseen shelf   *sailor*
    He strikes on, only when the timbers start.

32

Not see? because of night perhaps?—why, day
    Came back again for that! before it left,
    The dying sunset kindled through a cleft:
190 The hills, like giants at a hunting, lay,
Chin upon hand, to see the game at bay,—
    "Now stab and end the creature—to the
        heft!"°   *sword handle*

33

Not hear? when noise was everywhere! it tolled
    Increasing like a bell. Names in my ears
195   Of all the lost adventurers my peers—
How such a one was strong, and such was bold,
And such was fortunate, yet each of old
    Lost, lost! one moment knelled the woe of years.

34

200 There they stood, ranged along the hillsides, met
    To view the last of me, a living frame
    For one more picture! in a sheet of flame
I saw them and I knew them all. And yet
Dauntless the slug-horn° to my lips I set,   *trumpet*
    And blew. "*Childe Roland to the Dark Tower came.*"
—1855

Fra Lippo Lippi [1]

I am poor brother Lippo, by your leave!
  You need not clap your torches to my face.
Zooks,[2] what's to blame? you think you see a monk!
What, 'tis past midnight, and you go the rounds,
5 And here you catch me at an alley's end
Where sportive ladies leave their doors ajar?
The Carmine's[3] my cloister: hunt it up,
Do—harry out, if you must show your zeal,
Whatever rat, there, haps on his wrong hole,
10 And nip each softling of a wee white mouse,
Weke, weke, that's crept to keep him company!
Aha, you know your betters! Then, you'll take
Your hand away that's fiddling on my throat,
And please to know me likewise. Who am I?
15 Why, one, sir, who is lodging with a friend
Three streets off—he's a certain … how d'ye call?
Master—a … Cosimo of the Medici,[4]
I' the house that caps the corner. Boh! you were best!
Remember and tell me, the day you're hanged,
20 How you affected such a gullet's-gripe!°   *stranglehold*
But you, sir, it concerns you that your knaves
Pick up a manner nor discredit you:

---

[1] *Fra Lippo Lippi* Browning extracted details of the life of Florentine painter and Carmelite monk Fra (Brother) Filippo Lippi
(1406–69) from Giorgio Vasari's *The Lives of the Painters* (1550);
the art theory Lippi propounds, however, is envisioned by Browning.

[2] *Zooks* Exclamation of surprise.

[3] *Carmine* Lippi was raised an orphan and eventually took his vows
in Santa Maria del Carmine, a Carmelite monastery.

[4] *Cosimo of the Medici* The wealthy Medici family, headed up by
Lippi's patron, Cosimo dé Medici (1389–1464), ruled Florence for
many years.

Zooks, are we pilchards,[1] that they sweep the streets
And count fair prize what comes into their net?
25 He's Judas to a tittle,[2] that man is!
Just such a face! Why, sir, you make amends.
Lord, I'm not angry! Bid your hangdogs go
Drink out this quarter-florin[3] to the health
Of the munificent House that harbours me
30 (And many more beside, lads! more beside!)
And all's come square again. I'd like his face—
His, elbowing on his comrade in the door
With the pike and lantern—for the slave that holds
John Baptist's head a-dangle by the hair
35 With one hand ("Look you, now," as who should say)
And his weapon in the other, yet unwiped!
It's not your chance to have a bit of chalk,
A wood-coal or the like? or you should see!
Yes, I'm the painter, since you style me so.
40 What, brother Lippo's doings, up and down,
You know them and they take you? like enough!
I saw the proper twinkle in your eye—
'Tell you, I liked your looks at very first.
Let's sit and set things straight now, hip to haunch.
45 Here's spring come, and the nights one makes up bands
To roam the town and sing out carnival,[4]
And I've been three weeks shut within my
        mew,°   *confined space*
A-painting for the great man, saints and saints
And saints again. I could not paint all night—
50 Ouf! I leaned out of window for fresh air.
There came a hurry of feet and little feet,
A sweep of lute strings, laughs, and whifts of song—
Flower o' the broom,
Take away love, and our earth is a tomb![5]
55 *Flower o' the quince,*
I let Lisa go, and what good in life since?
Flower o' the thyme—and so on. Round they went.
Scarce had they turned the corner when a titter

Like the skipping of rabbits by moonlight—three slim
        shapes,
60 And a face that looked up … zooks, sir, flesh and blood,
That's all I'm made of! Into shreds it went,
Curtain and counterpane and coverlet,
All the bed furniture—a dozen knots,
There was a ladder! Down I let myself,
65 Hands and feet, scrambling somehow, and so dropped,
And after them. I came up with the fun
Hard by Saint Laurence,[6] hail fellow, well met—
Flower o' the rose,
If I've been merry, what matter who knows?
70 And so as I was stealing back again
To get to bed and have a bit of sleep
Ere I rise up tomorrow and go work
On Jerome[7] knocking at his poor old breast
With his great round stone to subdue the flesh,
75 You snap me of the sudden. Ah, I see!
Though your eye twinkles still, you shake your head—
Mine's shaved—a monk, you say—the sting's in that!
If Master Cosimo announced himself,
Mum's the word naturally; but a monk!
80 Come, what am I a beast for? tell us, now!
I was a baby when my mother died
And father died and left me in the street.
I starved there, God knows how, a year or two
On fig skins, melon parings, rinds and shucks,
85 Refuse and rubbish. One fine frosty day,
My stomach being empty as your hat,
The wind doubled me up and down I went.
Old Aunt Lapaccia trussed me with one hand,
(Its fellow was a stinger as I knew)
90 And so along the wall, over the bridge,
By the straight cut to the convent. Six words there,
While I stood munching my first bread that month:
"So, boy, you're minded," quoth the good fat father
Wiping his own mouth, 'twas refection°-time—   *meal*
95 "To quit this very miserable world?
Will you renounce"… "the mouthful of bread?"
        thought I;
By no means! Brief, they made a monk of me;
I did renounce the world, its pride and greed,

---

[1] *pilchards*   Herring-like fish.

[2] *to a tittle*   Exactly (a "tittle" is a letter stroke or punctuation mark).

[3] *florin*   Florentine currency.

[4] *carnival*   Celebrations before Lent.

[5] *Flower … tomb*   This song takes the form of a *stornelli*, a three-line Italian folk song about a flower.

---

[6] *Saint Laurence*   Church of San Lorenzo in Florence.

[7] *Jerome*   The ascetic St. Jerome, who lived many years as a hermit in the Syrian desert.

Palace, farm, villa, shop and banking-house,
100 Trash, such as these poor devils of Medici
Have given their hearts to—all at eight years old.
Well, sir, I found in time, you may be sure,
'Twas not for nothing—the good bellyful,
The warm serge and the rope that goes all round,[1]
105 And day-long blessed idleness beside!
"Let's see what the urchin's fit for"—that came next.
Not overmuch their way, I must confess.
Such a to-do! They tried me with their books:
Lord, they'd have taught me Latin in pure waste!
110 *Flower o' the clove,*
All the Latin I construe is, "amo," I love!
But, mind you, when a boy starves in the streets
Eight years together, as my fortune was,
Watching folk's faces to know who will fling
115 The bit of half-stripped grape bunch he desires,
And who will curse or kick him for his pains—
Which gentleman processional and fine,
Holding a candle to the Sacrament,
Will wink and let him lift a plate and catch
120 The droppings of the wax to sell again,
Or holla for the Eight[2] and have him whipped—
How say I?—nay, which dog bites, which lets drop
His bone from the heap of offal in the street—
Why, soul and sense of him grow sharp alike,
125 He learns the look of things, and none the less
For admonition from the hunger pinch.
I had a store of such remarks, be sure,
Which, after I found leisure, turned to use.
I drew men's faces on my copy books,
130 Scrawled them within the antiphonary's marge,[3]
Joined legs and arms to the long music notes,
Found eyes and nose and chin for A's and B's,
And made a string of pictures of the world
Betwixt the ins and outs of verb and noun,
135 On the wall, the bench, the door. The monks looked
       black.
"Nay," quoth the Prior, "turn him out, d'ye say?
In no wise. Lose a crow and catch a lark.

What if at last we get our man of parts,[4]
We Carmelites, like those Camaldolese
140 And Preaching Friars,[5] to do our church up fine
And put the front on it that ought to be!"
And hereupon he bade me daub away.
Thank you! my head being crammed, the walls a blank,
Never was such prompt disemburdening.
145 First, every sort of monk, the black and white,
I drew them, fat and lean: then, folk at church,
From good old gossips waiting to confess
Their cribs° of barrel droppings, candle ends—   *pilferings*
To the breathless fellow at the altar foot,
150 Fresh from his murder, safe[6] and sitting there
With the little children round him in a row
Of admiration, half for his beard and half
For that white anger of his victim's son
Shaking a fist at him with one fierce arm,
155 Signing himself[7] with the other because of Christ
(Whose sad face on the cross sees only this
After the passion of a thousand years)
Till some poor girl, her apron o'er her head,
(Which the intense eyes looked through) came at eve
160 On tiptoe, said a word, dropped in a loaf,
Her pair of earrings and a bunch of flowers
(The brute took growling), prayed, and so was gone.
I painted all, then cried "'Tis ask and have;
Choose, for more's ready!"—laid the ladder flat,
165 And showed my covered bit of cloister wall.
The monks closed in a circle and praised loud
Till checked, taught what to see and not to see,
Being simple bodies—"That's the very man!
Look at the boy who stoops to pat the dog!
170 That woman's like the Prior's niece who comes
To care about his asthma: it's the life!"
But there my triumph's straw-fire flared and
       funked;°   *smoked*
Their betters took their turn to see and say:
The Prior and the learned pulled a face
175 And stopped all that in no time. "How? what's here?
Quite from the mark of painting, bless us all!

---

1 *rope ... round* I.e., rope belt.

2 *Eight* The eight magistrates who governed Florence.

3 *antiphonary's marge* Margin of a book of choral—or antipho-
nal—music, normally sung in harmony by two choirs.

4 *man of parts* Man of intellect, ability.

5 *Preaching Friars* Dominican monks.

6 *fellow ... safe* Safe from prosecution within the church.

7 *Signing himself* Making the sign of the cross.

Faces, arms, legs and bodies like the true
As much as pea and pea! it's devil's game!
Your business is not to catch men with show,
180 With homage to the perishable clay,
But lift them over it, ignore it all,
Make them forget there's such a thing as flesh.
Your business is to paint the souls of men—
Man's soul, and it's a fire, smoke … no, it's not …
185 It's vapour done up like a newborn babe—
(In that shape when you die it leaves your mouth)
It's … well, what matters talking, it's the soul!
Give us no more of body than shows soul!
Here's Giotto,[1] with his Saint a-praising God,
190 That sets us praising—why not stop with him?
Why put all thoughts of praise out of our head
With wonder at lines, colours, and what not?
Paint the soul, never mind the legs and arms!
Rub all out, try at it a second time.
195 Oh, that white smallish female with the breasts,
She's just my niece … Herodias, I would say—
Who went and danced and got men's heads cut off![2]
Have it all out!' Now, is this sense, I ask?
A fine way to paint soul, by painting body
200 So ill, the eye can't stop there, must go further
And can't fare worse! Thus, yellow does for white
When what you put for yellow's simply black,
And any sort of meaning looks intense
When all beside itself means and looks nought.
205 Why can't a painter lift each foot in turn,
Left foot and right foot, go a double step,
Make his flesh liker and his soul more like,
Both in their order? Take the prettiest face,
The Prior's niece … patron saint—is it so pretty
210 You can't discover if it means hope, fear,
Sorrow or joy? won't beauty go with these?
Suppose I've made her eyes all right and blue,
Can't I take breath and try to add life's flash,
And then add soul and heighten them threefold?
215 Or say there's beauty with no soul at all—

(I never saw it—put the case the same—)
If you get simple beauty and nought else,
You get about the best thing God invents:
That's somewhat: and you'll find the soul you have
        missed,
220 Within yourself, when you return him thanks.
"Rub all out!" Well, well, there's my life, in short,
And so the thing has gone on ever since.
I'm grown a man no doubt, I've broken bounds:
You should not take a fellow eight years old
225 And make him swear to never kiss the girls.
I'm my own master, paint now as I please—
Having a friend, you see, in the Corner-house!
Lord, it's fast holding by the rings in front—
Those great rings serve more purposes than just
230 To plant a flag in, or tie up a horse!
And yet the old schooling sticks, the old grave eyes
Are peeping o'er my shoulder as I work,
The heads shake still—"It's art's decline, my son!
You're not of the true painters, great and old;
235 Brother Angelico's the man, you'll find;
Brother Lorenzo[3] stands his single peer:
Fag on at flesh, you'll never make the third!"
Flower o' the pine,
You keep your mistr … manners, and I'll stick to mine!
240 I'm not the third, then: bless us, they must know!
Don't you think they're the likeliest to know,
They with their Latin? So, I swallow my rage,
Clench my teeth, suck my lips in tight, and paint
To please them—sometimes do and sometimes don't;
245 For, doing most, there's pretty sure to come
A turn, some warm eve finds me at my saints—
A laugh, a cry, the business of the world—
(*Flower o' the peach,*
Death for us all, and his own life for each!)
250 And my whole soul revolves, the cup runs over,
The world and life's too big to pass for a dream,
And I do these wild things in sheer despite,
And play the fooleries you catch me at,
In pure rage! The old mill-horse, out at grass
255 After hard years, throws up his stiff heels so,
Although the miller does not preach to him

---

[1] *Giotto* Renowned Florentine artist (1267–1337), whose works consist mainly of religious paintings and frescoes.

[2] *Herodias … heads cut off* According to Matthew 14.6–10, King Herod's niece Salomé (the daughter of his sister Herodias) danced for the king and then requested that he bring her the head of John the Baptist, now the patron saint of Florence.

[3] *Brother Angelico … Brother Lorenzo* Italian Renaissance artists who painted in in the early 1400s in the conventional style, as opposed to Lippi's naturalist style.

The only good of grass is to make chaff.
What would men have? Do they like grass or no—
May they or mayn't they? all I want's the thing
260 Settled forever one way. As it is,
You tell too many lies and hurt yourself:
You don't like what you only like too much,
You do like what, if given you at your word,
You find abundantly detestable.
265 For me, I think I speak as I was taught;
I always see the garden and God there
A-making man's wife: and, my lesson learned,
The value and significance of flesh,
I can't unlearn ten minutes afterwards.

270   You understand me: I'm a beast, I know.
But see, now—why, I see as certainly
As that the morning star's about to shine,
What will hap some day. We've a youngster here
Comes to our convent, studies what I do,
275 Slouches and stares and lets no atom drop:
His name is Guidi[1]—he'll not mind the monks—
They call him Hulking Tom, he lets them talk—
He picks my practice up—he'll paint apace,
I hope so—though I never live so long,
280 I know what's sure to follow. You be judge!
You speak no Latin more than I, belike;
However, you're my man, you've seen the world
—The beauty and the wonder and the power,
The shapes of things, their colours, lights and shades,
285 Changes, surprises—and God made it all!
—For what? Do you feel thankful, ay or no,
For this fair town's face, yonder river's line,
The mountain round it and the sky above,
Much more the figures of man, woman, child,
290 These are the frame to? What's it all about?
To be passed over, despised? or dwelt upon,
Wondered at? oh, this last of course!—you say.
But why not do as well as say—paint these
Just as they are, careless what comes of it?
295 God's works—paint anyone, and count it crime
To let a truth slip. Don't object, "His works
Are here already; nature is complete:

Suppose you reproduce her—(which you can't)
There's no advantage! you must beat her, then."
300 For, don't you mark? we're made so that we love
First when we see them painted, things we have passed
Perhaps a hundred times nor cared to see;
And so they are better, painted—better to us,
Which is the same thing. Art was given for that;
305 God uses us to help each other so,
Lending our minds out. Have you noticed, now,
Your cullion's° hanging face? A bit of chalk,   scoundrel's
And trust me but you should, though! How much
     more,
If I drew higher things with the same truth!
310 That were to take the Prior's pulpit place,
Interpret God to all of you! Oh, oh,
It makes me mad to see what men shall do
And we in our graves! This world's no blot for us,
Nor blank; it means intensely, and means good:
315 To find its meaning is my meat and drink.
"Ay, but you don't so instigate to prayer!"
Strikes in the Prior: "when your meaning's plain
It does not say to folk—remember matins,[2]
Or, mind you fast next Friday!" Why, for this
320 What need of art at all? A skull and bones,
Two bits of stick nailed crosswise, or, what's best,
A bell to chime the hour with, does as well.
I painted a Saint Laurence[3] six months since
At Prato,[4] splashed the fresco in fine style:
325 "How looks my painting, now the scaffold's down?"
I ask a brother: "Hugely," he returns—
"Already not one phiz° of your three slaves   face
Who turn the Deacon off his toasted side,
But's scratched and prodded to our heart's content,
330 The pious people have so eased their own
With coming to say prayers there in a rage:
We get on fast to see the bricks beneath.
Expect another job this time next year,
For pity and religion grow i' the crowd—
335 Your painting serves its purpose!" Hang the fools!

---

[1] *Guidi* Tommaso Guidi (1401–28), who became known as Masaccio, was highly skilled at creating naturalistic portrayals of human figures; he was likely Lippi's teacher, not his student.

[2] *matins* Morning prayer services.

[3] *Saint Laurence* Roman deacon (?–258) who was martyred by being burnt on a gridiron, an instrument of torture.

[4] *Prato* Town west of Florence.

—That is—you'll not mistake an idle word
Spoke in a huff by a poor monk, God wot,
Tasting the air this spicy night which turns
The unaccustomed head like Chianti wine!
340 Oh, the church knows! don't misreport me, now!
It's natural a poor monk out of bounds
Should have his apt word to excuse himself:
And hearken how I plot to make amends.
I have bethought me: I shall paint a piece
345 … There's for you! Give me six months, then go, see
Something in Sant' Ambrogio's![1] Bless the nuns!
They want a cast o' my office. I shall paint
God in the midst, Madonna and her babe,
Ringed by a bowery flowery angel brood,
350 Lilies and vestments and white faces, sweet
As puff on puff of grated orris-root[2]
When ladies crowd to Church at midsummer.
And then i' the front, of course a saint or two—
Saint John, because he saves the Florentines,
355 Saint Ambrose, who puts down in black and white
The convent's friends and gives them a long day,
And Job, I must have him there past mistake,
The man of Uz[3] (and Us without the z,
Painters who need his patience). Well, all these
360 Secured at their devotion, up shall come
Out of a corner when you least expect,
As one by a dark stair into a great light,
Music and talking, who but Lippo! I!—
Mazed, motionless and moonstruck—I'm the man!
365 Back I shrink—what is this I see and hear?
I, caught up with my monk's things by mistake,
My old serge gown and rope that goes all round,
I, in this presence, this pure company!
Where's a hole, where's a corner for escape?
370 Then steps a sweet angelic slip of a thing
Forward, puts out a soft palm—"Not so fast!"
—Addresses the celestial presence, "nay—
He made you and devised you, after all,

Though he's none of you! Could Saint John there draw—
375 His camel hair[4] make up a painting brush?
We come to brother Lippo for all that,
Iste perfecit opus!"[5] So, all smile—
I shuffle sideways with my blushing face
Under the cover of a hundred wings
380 Thrown like a spread of kirtles° when you're gay   *skirts*
And play hot cockles,[6] all the doors being shut,
Till, wholly unexpected, in there pops
The hothead husband! Thus I scuttle off
To some safe bench behind, not letting go
385 The palm of her, the little lily thing
That spoke the good word for me in the nick,
Like the Prior's niece … Saint Lucy,[7] I would say.
And so all's saved for me, and for the church
A pretty picture gained. Go, six months hence!
390 Your hand, sir, and goodbye: no lights, no lights!
The street's hushed, and I know my own way back,
Don't fear me! There's the grey beginning. Zooks!
—1855

The Last Ride Together

I

I said—Then, dearest, since 'tis so,
Since now at length my fate I know,
Since nothing all my love avails,
Since all, my life seemed meant for, fails,
5   Since this was written and needs must be—
My whole heart rises up to bless
Your name in pride and thankfulness!
Take back the hope you gave—I claim
Only a memory of the same,
10   —And this beside, if you will not blame,
     Your leave for one more last ride with me.

---

1 *Sant' Ambrogio's* Lippi painted *Coronation of the Virgin* for the main altar of Florence's Sant' Ambrogio convent.

2 *orris-root* Roots of the iris flower, used as a fragrant cosmetic powder.

3 *man of Uz* See Job 1.1: Job was a righteous man who lost everything when God allowed Satan to challenge his faith.

---

4 *Saint John … camel hair* St. John the Baptist "was clothed in camel hair," according to Mark 1.6.

5 *Iste perfecit opus* Latin: he caused the work to be created; inscription on the *Coronation*, placed beside a portrait that Browning (following Vasari) mistakenly took to be Lippi's.

6 *hot cockles* Christmas game played blindfolded.

7 *Saint Lucy* Virgin martyr of Sicily (? –304?).

2

My mistress bent that brow of hers;
Those deep dark eyes where pride demurs
When pity would be softening through,
15 Fixed me a breathing-while or two
    With life or death in the balance: right!
The blood replenished me again;
My last thought was at least not vain:
I and my mistress, side by side
20 Shall be together, breathe and ride,
So, one day more am I deified.
    Who knows but the world may end tonight?

3

Hush! if you saw some western cloud
All billowy-bosomed, over-bowed
25 By many benedictions—sun's
And moon's and evening-star's at once—
    And so, you, looking and loving best,
Conscious grew, your passion drew
Cloud, sunset, moonrise, star-shine too,
30 Down on you, near and yet more near,
Till flesh must fade for heaven was here!—
Thus leant she and lingered—joy and fear!
    Thus lay she a moment on my breast.

4

Then we began to ride. My soul
35 Smoothed itself out, a long-cramped scroll
Freshening and fluttering in the wind.
Past hopes already lay behind.
    What need to strive with a life awry?
Had I said that, had I done this,
40 So might I gain, so might I miss.
Might she have loved me? just as well
She might have hated, who can tell!
Where had I been now if the worst befell?
    And here we are riding, she and I.

5

45 Fail I alone, in words and deeds?
Why, all men strive and who succeeds?
We rode; it seemed my spirit flew,
Saw other regions, cities new,
    As the world rushed by on either side.

50 I thought—All labour, yet no less
Bear up beneath their unsuccess.
Look at the end of work, contrast
The petty done, the undone vast,
This present of theirs with the hopeful past!
55   I hoped she would love me; here we ride.

6

What hand and brain went ever paired?
What heart alike conceived and dared?
What act proved all its thought had been?
What will but felt the fleshly screen?
60   We ride and I see her bosom heave.
There's many a crown for who can reach.
Ten lines, a statesman's life in each!
The flag stuck on a heap of bones,
A soldier's doing! what atones?
65 They scratch his name on the Abbey[1] stones.
    My riding is better, by their leave.

7

What does it all mean, poet? Well,
Your brains beat into rhythm, you tell
What we felt only; you expressed
70 You hold things beautiful the best,
    And pace them in rhyme so, side by side.
'Tis something, nay 'tis much: but then,
Have you yourself what's best for men?
Are you—poor, sick, old ere your time—
75 Nearer one whit your own sublime
Than we who never have turned a rhyme?
    Sing, riding's a joy! For me, I ride.

8

And you, great sculptor—so, you gave
A score of years to Art, her slave,
80 And that's your Venus,[2] whence we turn
To yonder girl that fords the burn!°   *stream*
    You acquiesce, and shall I repine?°   *complain*
What, man of music, you grown grey
With notes and nothing else to say,
85 Is this your sole praise from a friend,
"Greatly his opera's strains intend,

---

[1] *Abbey* Westminster Abbey.

[2] *Venus* Roman goddess of love.

But in music we know how fashions end!"
    I gave my youth; but we ride, *in fine*.[1]

9

Who knows what's fit for us? Had fate
90 Proposed bliss here should sublimate
My being—had I signed the bond—
Still one must lead some life beyond,
    Have a bliss to die with, dim-descried.
This foot once planted on the goal,
95 This glory-garland round my soul,
Could I descry such? Try and test!
I sink back shuddering from the quest.
Earth being so good, would heaven seem best?
    Now, heaven and she are beyond this ride.

10

100 And yet—she has not spoke so long!
What if heaven be that, fair and strong
At life's best, with our eyes upturned
Whither life's flower is first discerned,
    We, fixed so, ever should so abide?
105 What if we still ride on, we two
With life forever old yet new,
Changed not in kind but in degree,
The instant made eternity—
And heaven just prove that I and she
110   Ride, ride together, forever ride?
—1855

Andrea del Sarto[2]
(*Called "The Faultless Painter"*)

But do not let us quarrel any more,
No, my Lucrezia;[3] bear with me for once:
Sit down and all shall happen as you wish.
You turn your face, but does it bring your heart?

5 I'll work then for your friend's friend, never fear,
Treat his own subject after his own way,
Fix his own time, accept too his own price,
And shut the money into this small hand
When next it takes mine. Will it? tenderly?
10 Oh, I'll content him—but tomorrow, Love!
I often am much wearier than you think,
This evening more than usual, and it seems
As if—forgive now—should you let me sit
Here by the window with your hand in mine
15 And look a half-hour forth on Fiesole,[4]
Both of one mind, as married people use,
Quietly, quietly the evening through,
I might get up tomorrow to my work
Cheerful and fresh as ever. Let us try.
20 Tomorrow, how you shall be glad for this!
Your soft hand is a woman of itself,
And mine the man's bared breast she curls inside.
Don't count the time lost, neither; you must serve
For each of the five pictures we require:
25 It saves a model. So! keep looking so—
My serpentining beauty, rounds on rounds!
—How could you ever prick those perfect ears,
Even to put the pearl there! oh, so sweet—
My face, my moon, my everybody's moon,
30 Which everybody looks on and calls his,
And, I suppose, is looked on by in turn,
While she looks—no one's: very dear, no less.
You smile? why, there's my picture ready made,
There's what we painters call our harmony!
35 A common greyness silvers everything—
All in a twilight, you and I alike
—You, at the point of your first pride in me
(That's gone you know)—but I, at every point;
My youth, my hope, my art, being all toned down
40 To yonder sober pleasant Fiesole.
There's the bell clinking from the chapel top;
That length of convent wall across the way
Holds the trees safer, huddled more inside;
The last monk leaves the garden; days decrease,
45 And autumn grows, autumn in everything.
Eh? the whole seems to fall into a shape
As if I saw alike my work and self
And all that I was born to be and do,

---

1 *in fine* In the end.

2 *Andrea del Sarto* Browning's poem explores the life of the painter Andrea del Sarto (1486–1531), as narrated by Giorgio Vasari (once del Sarto's pupil) in *The Lives of the Painters*. In this biography, Vasari speculates as to why del Sarto (translated, this name means "son of a tailor") failed to fulfill the promise of his early paintings.

3 *Lucrezia* Lucrezia del Fede, del Sarto's wife and model.

4 *Fiesole* Hill town near Florence.

A twilight piece. Love, we are in God's hand.
50 How strange now, looks the life he makes us lead;
So free we seem, so fettered° fast we are!   *shackled*
I feel he laid the fetter: let it lie!
This chamber for example—turn your head—
All that's behind us! You don't understand
55 Nor care to understand about my art,
But you can hear at least when people speak:
And that cartoon,° the second from the door   *sketch*
—It is the thing, Love! so such things should be—
Behold Madonna!—I am bold to say.
60 I can do with my pencil what I know,
What I see, what at bottom of my heart
I wish for, if I ever wish so deep—
Do easily, too—when I say, perfectly,
I do not boast, perhaps: yourself are judge,
65 Who listened to the Legate's[1] talk last week,
And just as much they used to say in France.
At any rate 'tis easy, all of it!
No sketches first, no studies, that's long past:
I do what many dream of, all their lives,
70 —Dream? strive to do, and agonize to do,
And fail in doing. I could count twenty such
On twice your fingers, and not leave this town,
Who strive—you don't know how the others strive
To paint a little thing like that you smeared
75 Carelessly passing with your robes afloat—
Yet do much less, so much less, Someone says,
(I know his name, no matter)—so much less!
Well, less is more, Lucrezia: I am judged.
There burns a truer light of God in them,
80 In their vexed beating stuffed and stopped-up brain,
Heart, or whate'er else, than goes on to prompt
This low-pulsed forthright craftsman's hand of mine.
Their works drop groundward, but themselves, I know,
Reach many a time a heaven that's shut to me,
85 Enter and take their place there sure enough,
Though they come back and cannot tell the world.
My works are nearer heaven, but I sit here.
The sudden blood of these men! at a word—
Praise them, it boils, or blame them, it boils too.
90 I, painting from myself and to myself,
Know what I do, am unmoved by men's blame
Or their praise either. Somebody remarks

Morello's[2] outline there is wrongly traced,
His hue mistaken; what of that? or else,
95 Rightly traced and well ordered; what of that?
Speak as they please, what does the mountain care?
Ah, but a man's reach should exceed his grasp,
Or what's a heaven for? All is silver-grey
Placid and perfect with my art: the worse!
100 I know both what I want and what might gain,
And yet how profitless to know, to sigh
"Had I been two, another and myself,
Our head would have o'erlooked the world!" No doubt.
Yonder's a work now, of that famous youth
105 The Urbinate[3] who died five years ago.
('Tis copied, George Vasari sent it me.)
Well, I can fancy how he did it all,
Pouring his soul, with kings and popes to see,
Reaching, that heaven might so replenish him,
110 Above and through his art—for it gives way;
That arm is wrongly put—and there again—
A fault to pardon in the drawing's lines,
Its body, so to speak: its soul is right,
He means right—that, a child may understand.
115 Still, what an arm! and I could alter it:
But all the play, the insight and the stretch—
Out of me, out of me! And wherefore out?
Had you enjoined them on me, given me soul,
We might have risen to Rafael, I and you!
120 Nay, Love, you did give all I asked, I think—
More than I merit, yes, by many times.
But had you—oh, with the same perfect brow,
And perfect eyes, and more than perfect mouth,
And the low voice my soul hears, as a bird
125 The fowler's pipe,[4] and follows to the snare—
Had you, with these the same, but brought a mind!
Some women do so. Had the mouth there urged
"God and the glory! never care for gain.
The present by the future, what is that?
130 Live for fame, side by side with Agnolo![5]
Rafael is waiting: up to God, all three!"

---

[1] *Legate*   Representative of the Pope.

[2] *Morello*   Monte Morello, a mountain near Florence.

[3] *Urbinate*   The painter Raphael (1483–1520), who was born in Urbino.

[4] *fowler's pipe*   Call used by hunters to lure fowl.

[5] *Agnolo*   I.e., Michelangelo Buonarroti (1475–1564), sculptor and painter.

I might have done it for you. So it seems:
Perhaps not. All is as God over-rules.
Beside, incentives come from the soul's self;
135 The rest avail not. Why do I need you?
What wife had Rafael, or has Agnolo?
In this world, who can do a thing, will not;
And who would do it, cannot, I perceive:
Yet the will's somewhat—somewhat, too, the power—
140 And thus we half-men struggle. At the end,
God, I conclude, compensates, punishes.
'Tis safer for me, if the award be strict,
That I am something underrated here,
Poor this long while, despised, to speak the truth.
145 I dared not, do you know, leave home all day,
For fear of chancing on the Paris lords.[1]
The best is when they pass and look aside;
But they speak sometimes; I must bear it all.
Well may they speak! That Francis, that first time,
150 And that long festal year at Fontainebleau!
I surely then could sometimes leave the ground,
Put on the glory, Rafael's daily wear,
In that humane great monarch's golden look—
One finger in his beard or twisted curl
155 Over his mouth's good mark that made the smile,
One arm about my shoulder, round my neck,
The jingle of his gold chain in my ear,
I painting proudly with his breath on me,
All his court round him, seeing with his eyes,
160 Such frank French eyes, and such a fire of souls
Profuse, my hand kept plying by those hearts—
And, best of all, this, this, this face beyond,
This in the background, waiting on my work,
To crown the issue with a last reward!
165 A good time, was it not, my kingly days?
And had you not grown restless ... but I know—
'Tis done and past; 'twas right, my instinct said;
Too live the life grew, golden and not grey,
And I'm the weak-eyed bat no sun should tempt
170 Out of the grange whose four walls make his world.
How could it end in any other way?
You called me, and I came home to your heart.
The triumph was—to reach and stay there; since

I reached it ere the triumph, what is lost?
175 Let my hands frame your face in your hair's gold,
You beautiful Lucrezia that are mine!
"Rafael did this, Andrea painted that;
The Roman's is the better when you pray,
But still the other's Virgin was his wife—"
180 Men will excuse me. I am glad to judge
Both pictures in your presence; clearer grows
My better fortune, I resolve to think.
For, do you know, Lucrezia, as God lives,
Said one day Agnolo, his very self,
185 To Rafael ... I have known it all these years ...
(When the young man was flaming out his thoughts
Upon a palace wall for Rome to see,
Too lifted up in heart because of it)
"Friend, there's a certain sorry little scrub
190 Goes up and down our Florence, none cares how,
Who, were he set to plan and execute
As you are, pricked on by your popes and kings,
Would bring the sweat into that brow of yours!"
To Rafael's!—And indeed the arm is wrong.
195 I hardly dare ... yet, only you to see,
Give the chalk here—quick, thus the line should go!
Ay, but the soul! he's Rafael! rub it out!
Still, all I care for, if he spoke the truth,
(What he? why, who but Michel Agnolo?
200 Do you forget already words like those?)
If really there was such a chance, so lost—
Is, whether you're—not grateful—but more pleased.
Well, let me think so. And you smile indeed!
This hour has been an hour! Another smile?
205 If you would sit thus by me every night
I should work better, do you comprehend?
I mean that I should earn more, give you more.
See, it is settled dusk now; there's a star;
Morello's gone, the watch-lights show the wall,
210 The cue-owls[2] speak the name we call them by.
Come from the window, love—come in, at last,
Inside the melancholy little house
We built to be so gay with. God is just.
King Francis may forgive me: oft at nights
215 When I look up from painting, eyes tired out,
The walls become illumined, brick from brick

---

[1] *For fear ... lords* According to Vasari, del Sarto absconded with funds given to him at Fontainebleau by his patron, King Francis I of France.

[2] *cue-owls* Also known as scops-owls, whose cries sounds like "cue."

Distinct, instead of mortar, fierce bright gold,
That gold of his I did cement them with!
Let us but love each other. Must you go?
220 That cousin here again? he waits outside?
Must see you—you, and not with me? Those loans?
More gaming debts to pay? you smiled for that?
Well, let smiles buy me! have you more to spend?
While hand and eye and something of a heart
225 Are left me, work's my ware, and what's it worth?
I'll pay my fancy. Only let me sit
The grey remainder of the evening out,
Idle, you call it, and muse perfectly
How I could paint, were I but back in France,
230 One picture, just one more—the Virgin's face,
Not yours this time! I want you at my side
To hear them—that is, Michel Agnolo—
Judge all I do and tell you of its worth.
Will you? Tomorrow, satisfy your friend.
235 I take the subjects for his corridor,
Finish the portrait out of hand—there, there,
And throw him in another thing or two
If he demurs; the whole should prove enough
To pay for this same cousin's freak. Beside,
240 What's better and what's all I care about,
Get you the thirteen scudi° for the ruff!   *Italian currency*
Love, does that please you? Ah, but what does he,
The cousin! what does he to please you more?

I am grown peaceful as old age tonight.
245 I regret little, I would change still less.
Since there my past life lies, why alter it?
The very wrong to Francis!—it is true
I took his coin, was tempted and complied,
And built this house and sinned, and all is said.
250 My father and my mother died of want.
Well, had I riches of my own? you see
How one gets rich! Let each one bear his lot.
They were born poor, lived poor, and poor they died:
And I have laboured somewhat in my time
255 And not been paid profusely. Some good son
Paint my two hundred pictures—let him try!
No doubt, there's something strikes a balance. Yes,
You loved me quite enough, it seems tonight.
This must suffice me here. What would one have?
260 In heaven, perhaps, new chances, one more chance—

Four great walls in the New Jerusalem,[1]
Meted on each side by the angel's reed,
For Leonard,[2] Rafael, Agnolo and me
To cover—the three first without a wife,
265 While I have mine! So—still they overcome
Because there's still Lucrezia—as I choose.

Again the cousin's whistle! Go, my Love.
—1855

A Woman's Last Word

1

Let's contend no more, Love,
    Strive nor weep:
All be as before, Love,
    —Only sleep!

2

5 What so wild as words are?
    I and thou
In debate, as birds are,
    Hawk on bough!

3

See the creature stalking
10   While we speak!
Hush and hide the talking,
    Cheek on cheek!

4

What so false as truth is,
    False to thee?
15 Where the serpent's tooth is
    Shun the tree—

5

Where the apple reddens
    Never pry—
Lest we lose our Edens,
20   Eve and I.

6

Be a god and hold me

---

1   *Four … Jerusalem* See Revelations 21.10.
2   *Leonard* Artist Leonardo da Vinci (1452–1519).

With a charm!
Be a man and fold me
    With thine arm!

7

25 Teach me, only teach, Love!
        As I ought
    I will speak thy speech, Love,
        Think thy thought—

8

    Meet, if thou require it,
30   Both demands,
    Laying flesh and spirit
        In thy hands.

9

    That shall be tomorrow
        Not tonight:
35 I must bury sorrow
        Out of sight:

10

    —Must a little weep, Love,
        (Foolish me!)
    And so fall asleep, Love,
40   Loved by thee.
        —1855

Essay on Shelley[1]

An opportunity having presented itself for the acquisition of a series of unedited letters by Shelley, all more or less directly supplementary to and illustrative of the collection already published by Mr. Moxon,[2] that gentleman has decided on securing them. They will prove an acceptable addition to a body of correspondence, the value of which towards a right understanding of its author's purpose and work, may be said to exceed

that of any similar contribution exhibiting the worldly relations of a poet whose genius has operated by a different law.

Doubtless we accept gladly the biography of an objective poet, as the phrase now goes; one whose endeavour has been to reproduce things external (whether the phenomena of the scenic universe, or the manifested action of the human heart and brain) with an immediate reference, in every case, to the common eye and apprehension of his fellow men, assumed capable of receiving and profiting by this reproduction. It has been obtained through the poet's double faculty of seeing external objects more clearly, widely, and deeply, than is possible to the average mind, at the same time that he is so acquainted and in sympathy with its narrow comprehension as to be careful to supply it with no other materials than it can combine into an intelligible whole. The auditory of such a poet will include, not only the intelligences which, save for such assistance, would have missed the deeper meaning and enjoyment of the original objects, but also the spirits of a like endowment with his own, who, by means of his abstract, can forthwith pass to the reality it was made from, and either corroborate their impressions of things known already, or supply themselves with new from whatever shows in the inexhaustible variety of existence may have hitherto escaped their knowledge. Such a poet is properly the ποιητής, the fashioner; and the thing fashioned, his poetry, will of necessity be substantive, projected from himself and distinct. We are ignorant what the inventor of *Othello*[3] conceived of that fact as he beheld it in completeness, how he accounted for it, under what known law he registered its nature, or to what unknown law he traced its coincidence. We learn only what he intended we should learn by that particular exercise of his power—the fact itself—which, with its infinite significances, each of us receives for the first time as a creation, and is hereafter left to deal with, as, in proportion to his own intelligence, he best may. We are ignorant, and would fain be otherwise.

Doubtless, with respect to such a poet, we covet his biography. We desire to look back upon the process of gathering together in a lifetime the materials of the work we behold entire; of elaborating, perhaps under diffi-

---

[1] *Shelley*   English poet Percy Bysshe Shelley (1792–1822).

[2] *unedited letters … Mr. Moxon*   In 1840, Mary Shelley edited Percy Shelley's two-volume *Essays, Letters from Abroad, Translations and Fragments*, published by Edward Moxon. A second edition was released the year Browning wrote this essay.

[3] *inventor of Othello*   I.e., William Shakespeare.

culty and with hindrance, all that is familiar to our admiration in the apparent facility of success. And the inner impulse of this effort and operation, what induced it? Did a soul's delight in its own extended sphere of vision set it, for the gratification of an insuppressible power, on labour, as other men are set on rest? Or did a sense of duty or of love lead it to communicate its own sensations to mankind? Did an irresistible sympathy with men compel it to bring down and suit its own provision of knowledge and beauty to their narrow scope? Did the personality of such a one stand like an open watchtower in the midst of the territory it is erected to gaze on, and were the storms and calms, the stars and meteors, its watchman was wont to report of, the habitual variegation of his everyday life, as they glanced across its open roof or lay reflected on its four-square parapet? Or did some sunken and darkened chamber of imagery witness, in the artificial illumination of every storied compartment we are permitted to contemplate, how rare and precious were the outlooks through here and there an embrasure upon a world beyond, and how blankly would have pressed on the artificer the boundary of his daily life, except for the amorous diligence with which he had rendered permanent by art whatever came to diversify the gloom? Still, fraught with instruction and interest as such details undoubtedly are, we can, if needs be, dispense with them. The man passes, the work remains. The work speaks for itself, as we say; and the biography of the worker is no more necessary to an understanding or enjoyment of it, than is a model or anatomy of some tropical tree, to the right tasting of the fruit we are familiar with on the market stall—or a geologist's map and stratification, to the prompt recognition of the hilltop, our landmark of every day.

We turn with stronger needs to the genius of an opposite tendency—the subjective poet of modern classification. He, gifted like the objective poet with the fuller perception of nature and man, is impelled to embody the thing he perceives, not so much with reference to the many below, as to the One above him, the supreme Intelligence which apprehends all things in their absolute truth—an ultimate view ever aspired to, if but partially attained, by the poet's own soul. Not what man sees, but what God sees—the *Ideas* of Plato,

seeds of creation lying burningly on the Divine Hand—it is toward these that he struggles. Not with the combination of humanity in action, but with the primal elements of humanity he has to do; and he digs where he stands—preferring to seek them in his own soul as the nearest reflex of that absolute Mind, according to the intuitions of which he desires to perceive and speak. Such a poet does not deal habitually with the picturesque groupings and tempestuous tossings of the forest trees, but with their roots and fibres naked to the chalk and stone. He does not paint pictures and hang them on the walls, but rather carries them on the retina of his own eyes: we must look deep into his human eyes, to see those pictures on them. He is rather a seer, accordingly, than a fashioner, and what he produces will be less a work than an effluence. That effluence cannot be easily considered in abstraction from his personality—being indeed the very radiance and aroma of his personality, projected from it but not separated. Therefore, in our approach to the poetry, we necessarily approach the personality of the poet; in apprehending it we apprehend him, and certainly we cannot love it without loving him. Both for love's and for understanding's sake we desire to know him, and as readers of his poetry must be readers of his biography also.

I shall observe, in passing, that it seems not so much from any essential distinction in the faculty of the two poets or in the nature of the objects contemplated by either, as in the more immediate adaptability of these objects to the distinct purpose of each, that the objective poet, in his appeal to the aggregate human mind, chooses to deal with the doings of men, (the result of which dealing, in its pure form, when even description, as suggesting a describer, is dispensed with, is what we call dramatic poetry), while the subjective poet, whose study has been himself, appealing through himself to the absolute Divine mind, prefers to dwell upon those external scenic appearances which strike out most abundantly and uninterruptedly his inner light and power, selects that silence of the earth and sea in which he can best hear the beating of his individual heart, and leaves the noisy, complex, yet imperfect exhibitions of nature in the manifold experience of man around him, which serve only to distract and suppress the working of his brain. These opposite tendencies of genius will be more readily descried in their artistic effect than in their moral spring and cause. Pushed to an extreme and manifested as a deformity, they will be seen plainest of all in the fault of either artist, when subsidiarily to the human interest of his work his occasional illustrations from scenic nature are introduced as in the earlier works of the originative painters—men and women filling the foreground with consummate mastery, while mountain, grove and rivulet show like an anticipatory revenge on that succeeding race of landscape painters whose "figures" disturb the perfection of their earth and sky. It would be idle to inquire, of these two kinds of poetic faculty in operation, which is the higher or even rarer endowment. If the subjective might seem to be the ultimate requirement of every age, the objective, in the strictest state, must still retain its original value. For it is with this world, as starting point and basis alike, that we shall always have to concern ourselves; the world is not to be learned and thrown aside, but reverted to and relearned. The spiritual comprehension may be infinitely subtilised,[1] but the raw material it operates upon, must remain. There may be no end of the poets who communicate to us what they see in an object with reference to their own individuality; what it was before they saw it, in reference to the aggregate human mind, will be as desirable to know as ever. Nor is there any reason why these two modes of poetic faculty may not issue hereafter from the same poet in successive perfect works, examples of which, according to what are now considered the exigencies of art, we have hitherto possessed in distinct individuals only. A mere running-in of the one faculty upon the other, is, of course, the ordinary circumstance. Far more rarely it happens that either is found so decidedly prominent and superior, as to be pronounced comparatively pure; while of the perfect shield, with the gold and the silver side set up for all comers to challenge, there has yet been no instance. Either faculty in its eminent state is doubtless conceded by Providence as a best gift to men, according to their especial want. There is a time when the general eye has, so to speak, absorbed its fill of the phenomena around it, whether spiritual or material, and desires rather to learn the exacter significance of what it possesses, than to receive any augmentation of what is possessed. Then

is the opportunity for the poet of loftier vision, to lift his fellows, with their half-apprehensions, up to his own sphere, by intensifying the import of details and rounding the universal meaning. The influence of such an achievement will not soon die out. A tribe of successors (Homerides[2]) working more or less in the same spirit, dwell on his discoveries and reinforce his doctrine; till, at unawares, the world is found to be subsisting wholly on the shadow of a reality, on sentiments diluted from passions, on the tradition of a fact, the convention of a moral, the straw of last year's harvest. Then is the imperative call for the appearance of another sort of poet, who shall at once replace this intellectual rumination of food swallowed long ago, by a supply of the fresh and living swathe;[3] getting at new substance by breaking up the assumed wholes into parts of independent and unclassed value, careless of the unknown laws for recombining them (it will be the business of yet another poet to suggest those hereafter), prodigal of objects for men's outer and not inner sight, shaping for their uses a new and different creation from the last, which it displaces by the right of life over death—to endure until, in the inevitable process, its very sufficiency to itself shall require, at length, an exposition of its affinity to something higher—when the positive yet conflicting facts shall again precipitate themselves under a harmonising law, and one more degree will be apparent for a poet to climb in that mighty ladder, of which, however cloud-involved and undefined may glimmer the topmost step, the world dares no longer doubt that its gradations ascend.

Such being the two kinds of artists, it is naturally, as I have shown, with the biography of the subjective poet that we have the deeper concern. Apart from his recorded life altogether, we might fail to determine with satisfactory precision to what class his productions belong, and what amount of praise is assignable to the producer. Certainly, in the face of any conspicuous achievement of genius, philosophy, no less than sympathetic instinct, warrants our belief in a great moral purpose having mainly inspired even where it does not visibly look out of the same. Greatness in a work sug-

---

[1]   *subtilised* Thinned down.

[2]   *Homerides* Successors of ancient Greek poet Homer, author of the *Iliad* and the *Odyssey*.

[3]   *swathe* Row of fresh grass or corn.

gests an adequate instrumentality; and none of the lower incitements, however they may avail to initiate or even effect many considerable displays of power, simulating the nobler inspiration to which they are mistakenly referred, have been found able, under the ordinary conditions of humanity, to task themselves to the end of so exacting a performance as a poet's complete work. As soon will the galvanism, that provokes to violent action the muscles of a corpse, induce it to cross the chamber steadily: sooner. The love of displaying power for the display's sake, the love of riches, of distinction, of notoriety—the desire of a triumph over rivals, and the vanity in the applause of friends—each and all of such whetted appetites grow intenser by exercise and increasingly sagacious as to the best and readiest means of self-appeasement—while for any of their ends, whether the money or the pointed finger of the crowd, or the flattery and hate to heart's content, there are cheaper prices to pay, they will all find soon enough, than the bestowment of a life upon a labour, hard, slow, and not sure. Also, assuming the proper moral aim to have produced a work, there are many and various states of an aim: it may be more intense than clear-sighted, or too easily satisfied with a lower field of activity than a steadier aspiration would reach. All the bad poetry in the world (accounted poetry, that is, by its affinities) will be found to result from some one of the infinite degrees of discrepancy between the attributes of the poet's soul, occasioning a want of correspondency between his work and the verities of nature—issuing in poetry, false under whatever form, which shows a thing not as it is to mankind generally, nor as it is to the particular describer, but as it is supposed to be for some unreal neutral mood, midway between both and of value to neither, and living its brief minute simply through the indolence of whoever accepts it, or his incapacity to denounce a cheat. Although of such depths of failure there can be no question here, we must in every case betake ourselves to the review of a poet's life ere we determine some of the nicer questions concerning his poetry—more especially if the performance we seek to estimate aright, has been obstructed and cut short of completion by circumstances—a disastrous youth or a premature death. We may learn from the biography whether his spirit invariably saw and spoke from the last

height to which it had attained. An absolute vision is not for this world, but we are permitted a continual approximation to it, every degree of which in the individual, provided it exceed the attainment of the masses, must procure him a clear advantage. Did the poet ever attain to a higher platform than where he rested and exhibited a result? Did he know more than he spoke of?

I concede however, in respect to the subject of our study as well as some few other illustrious examples, that the unmistakeable quality of the verse would be evidence enough, under usual circumstances, not only of the kind and degree of the intellectual but of the moral constitution of Shelley, the whole personality of the poet shining forward from the poems, without much need of going further to seek it. The "Remains"[1]—produced within a period of ten years, and at a season of life when other men of at all comparable genius have hardly done more than prepare the eye for future sight and the tongue for speech—present us with the complete enginery of a poet, as signal in the excellence of its several adaptitudes as transcendent in the combination of effects—examples, in fact, of the whole poet's function of beholding with an understanding keenness the universe, nature and man, in their actual state of perfection in imperfection—of the whole poet's virtue of being untempted by the manifold partial developments of beauty and good on every side, into leaving them the ultimates he found them—induced by the facility of the gratification of his own sense of those qualities, or by the pleasure of acquiescence in the shortcomings of his predecessors in art, and the pain of disturbing their conventionalisms—the whole poet's virtue, I repeat, of looking higher than any manifestation yet made of both beauty and good, in order to suggest from the utmost actual realisation of the one a corresponding capability in the other, and out of the calm, purity and energy of nature, to reconstitute and store up for the forthcoming stage of man's being, a gift in repayment of that former gift, in which man's own thought and passion had been lavished by the poet on the else-incompleted magnificence of the sunrise, the else-uninterpreted mystery of

---

[1] *The "Remains"* I.e., poetic remains, a phrase that refers to those works, especially those that are unpublished, that are left at the time of an author's death.

the lake—so drawing out, lifting up, and assimilating this ideal of a future man, thus described as possible, to the present reality of the poet's soul already arrived at the higher state of development, and still aspirant to elevate and extend itself in conformity with its still-improving perceptions of, no longer the eventual Human, but the actual Divine. In conjunction with which noble and rare powers, came the subordinate power of delivering these attained results to the world in an embodiment of verse more closely answering to and indicative of the process of the informing spirit, (failing as it occasionally does, in art, only to succeed in highest art)—with a diction more adequate to the task in its natural and acquired richness, its material colour and spiritual transparency—the whole being moved by and suffused with a music at once of the soul and the sense, expressive both of an external might of sincere passion and an internal fitness and consonancy—than can be attributed to any other writer whose record is among us. Such was the spheric poetical faculty of Shelley, as its own self-sufficing central light, radiating equally through immaturity and accomplishment, through many fragments and occasional completion, reveals it to a competent judgment.

But the acceptance of this truth by the public, has been retarded by certain objections which cast us back on the evidence of biography, even with Shelley's poetry in our hands. Except for the particular character of these objections, indeed, the non-appreciation of his contemporaries would simply class, now that it is over, with a series of experiences which have necessarily happened and needlessly been wondered at, ever since the world began, and concerning which any present anger may well be moderated, no less in justice to our forerunners than in policy to ourselves. For the misapprehensiveness of his age is exactly what a poet is sent to remedy; and the interval between his operation and the generally perceptible effect of it, is no greater, less indeed, than in many other departments of the great human effort. The "*E pur si muove*" of the astronomer[1] was as bitter a word as any uttered before or since by a poet over his rejected

living work, in that depth of conviction which is so like despair.

But in this respect was the experience of Shelley peculiarly unfortunate—that the disbelief in him as a man, even preceded the disbelief in him as a writer; the misconstruction of his moral nature preparing the way for the misappreciation of his intellectual labours. There existed from the beginning—simultaneous with, indeed anterior to his earliest noticeable works, and not brought forward to counteract any impression they had succeeded in making—certain charges against his private character and life,[2] which, if substantiated to their whole breadth, would materially disturb, I do not attempt to deny, our reception and enjoyment of his works, however wonderful the artistic qualities of these. For we are not sufficiently supplied with instances of genius of his order, to be able to pronounce certainly how many of its constituent parts have been tasked and strained to the production of a given lie, and how high and pure a mood of the creative mind may be dramatically simulated as the poet's habitual and exclusive one. The doubts, therefore, arising from such a question, required to be set at rest, as they were effectually, by those early authentic notices of Shelley's career and the corroborative accompaniment of his letters, in which not only the main tenor and principal result of his life, but the purity and beauty of many of the processes which had conducted to them, were made apparent enough for the general reader's purpose—whoever lightly condemned Shelley first, on the evidence of reviews and gossip, as lightly acquitting him now, on that of memoirs and correspondence. Still, it is advisable to lose no opportunity of strengthening and completing the chain of biographical testimony; much more, of course, for the sake of the poet's original lovers, whose volunteered sacrifice of particular principle in favour of absorbing sympathy we might desire to dispense with, than for the sake of his foolish haters, who have long since diverted upon other objects their obtuseness or malignancy. A full life of Shelley should be written at once, while the

---

[1] "*E pur si muove*" *of the astronomer* Italian: and yet it moves. This was Galileo's purported response after being forced by the Catholic Church during the Inquisition of 1633 to recant his theory that the earth revolves around the sun.

[2] *charges against his private character and life* Shelley had been attacked for his radical politics, his atheism, and for his relationship with the young Mary Godwin, with whom he fled to the Continent while still married to Harriet Shelley (who eventually committed suicide).

materials for it continue in reach; not to minister to the curiosity of the public, but to obliterate the last stain of that false life which was forced on the public's attention before it had any curiosity on the matter—a biography, composed in harmony with the present general disposition to have faith in him, yet not shrinking from a candid statement of all ambiguous passages, through a reasonable confidence that the most doubtful of them will be found; consistent with a belief in the eventual perfection of his character, according to the poor limits of our humanity. Nor will men persist in confounding, any more than God confounds, with genuine infidelity and an atheism of the heart, those passionate, impatient struggles of a boy towards distant truth and love, made in the dark, and ended by one sweep of the natural seas before the full moral sunrise could shine out on him. Crude convictions of boyhood, conveyed in imperfect and inapt forms of speech—for such things all boys have been pardoned. There are growing pains, accompanied by temporary distortion, of the soul also. And it would be hard indeed upon this young Titan of genius, murmuring in divine music his human ignorances, through his very thirst for knowledge, and his rebellion, in mere aspiration to law, if the melody itself substantiated the error, and the tragic cutting short of life perpetuated into sins, such faults as, under happier circumstances, would have been left behind by the consent of the most arrogant moralist, forgotten on the lowest steps of youth.

The responsibility of presenting to the public a biography of Shelley, does not, however lie with me: I have only to make it a little easier by arranging these few supplementary letters, with a recognition of the value of the whole collection. This value I take to consist in a most truthful conformity of the Correspondence, in its limited degree, with the moral and intellectual character of the writer as displayed in the highest manifestations of his genius. Letters and poems are obviously an act of the same mind, produced by the same law, only differing in the application to the individual or collective understanding. Letters and poems may be used indifferently as the basement of our opinion upon the writer's character; the finished expression of a sentiment in the poems, giving light and significance to the rudiments of the same in the letters, and these, again, in their incipiency and unripeness, authenticating the exalted mood

and reattaching it to the personality of the writer. The musician speaks on the note he sings with; there is no change in the scale, as he diminishes the volume into familiar intercourse. There is nothing of that jarring between the man and the author, which has been found so amusing or so melancholy; no dropping of the tragic mask, as the crowd melts away; no mean discovery of the real motives of a life's achievement, often, in other lives, laid bare as pitifully as when, at the close of a holiday, we catch sight of the internal lead pipes and wood valves, to which, and not to the ostensible conch and dominant Triton of the fountain,[1] we have owed our admired waterwork. No breaking out, in household privacy, of hatred anger and scorn, incongruous with the higher mood and suppressed artistically in the book: no brutal return to self-delighting, when the audience of philanthropic schemes is out of hearing: no indecent stripping off the grander feeling and rule of life as too costly and cumbrous for everyday wear. Whatever Shelley was, he was with an admirable sincerity. It was not always truth that he thought and spoke; but in the purity of truth he spoke and thought always. Everywhere is apparent his belief in the existence of Good, to which Evil is an accident; his faithful holding by what he assumed to be the former, going everywhere in company with the tenderest pity for those acting or suffering on the opposite hypothesis. For he was tender, though tenderness is not always the characteristic of very sincere natures; he was eminently both tender and sincere. And not only do the same affection and yearning after the well-being of his kind, appear in the letters as in the poems, but they express themselves by the same theories and plans, however crude and unsound. There is no reservation of a subtler, less costly, more serviceable remedy for his own ill, than he has proposed for the general one; nor does he ever contemplate an object on his own account, from a less elevation than he uses in exhibiting it to the world. How shall we help believing Shelley to have been, in his ultimate attainment, the splendid spirit of his own best poetry, when we find even his carnal speech to agree faithfully, at faintest as at

---

[1]   *Triton of the fountain*   The *Fontana del Tritone* in Rome, sculpted by Gian Lorenzo Bernini, depicts Triton, the half-man half-fish son of Poseidon in Greek mythology, blowing into a trumpet-like conch shell.

strongest, with the tone and rhythm of his most oracular utterances?

For the rest, these new letters are not offered as presenting any new feature of the poet's character. Regarded in themselves, and as the substantive productions of a man, their importance would be slight. But they possess interest beyond their limits, in confirming the evidence just dwelt on, of the poetical mood of Shelley being only the intensification of his habitual mood; the same tongue only speaking, for want of the special excitement to sing. The very first letter, as one instance for all, strikes the keynote of the predominating sentiment of Shelley throughout his whole life—his sympathy with the oppressed. And when we see him at so early an age, casting out, under the influence of such a sympathy, letters and pamphlets on every side, we accept it as the simple exemplification of the sincerity, with which, at the close of his life, he spoke of himself, as—

> One whose heart a stranger's tear might wear
> As water-drops the sandy fountain stone;
> Who loved and pitied all things, and could moan
> For woes which others hear not, and could see
> The absent with the glass of phantasy,
> And near the poor and trampled sit and weep,
> Following the captive to his dungeon deep—
> One who was as a nerve o'er which do creep
> The else-unfelt oppressions of this earth.[1]

Such sympathy with his kind was evidently developed in him to an extraordinary and even morbid degree, at a period when the general intellectual powers it was impatient to put in motion, were immature or deficient.

I conjecture, from a review of the various publications of Shelley's youth, that one of the causes of his failure at the outset, was the peculiar *practicalness* of his mind, which was not without a determinate effect on his progress in theorising. An ordinary youth, who turns his attention to similar subjects, discovers falsities, incongruities, and various points for amendment, and, in the natural advance of the purely critical spirit

unchecked by considerations of remedy, keeps up before his young eyes so many instances of the same error and wrong, that he finds himself unawares arrived at the startling conclusion, that all must be changed—or nothing: in the face of which plainly impossible achievement, he is apt (looking perhaps a little more serious by the time he touches at the decisive issue), to feel, either carelessly or considerately, that his own attempting a single piece of service would be worse than useless even, and to refer the whole task to another age and person—safe in proportion to his incapacity. Wanting words to speak, he has never made a fool of himself by speaking. But, in Shelley's case, the early fervour and power to *see*, was accompanied by as precocious a fertility to *contrive*: he endeavoured to realise as he went on idealising; every wrong had simultaneously its remedy, and, out of the strength of his hatred for the former, he took the strength of his confidence in the latter—till suddenly he stood pledged to the defence of a set of miserable little expedients, just as if they represented great principles, and to an attack upon various great principles, really so, without leaving himself time to examine whether, because they were antagonistical to the remedy he had suggested, they must therefore be identical or even essentially connected with the wrong he sought to cure—playing with blind passion into the hands of his enemies, and dashing at whatever red cloak was held forth to him, as the cause of the fireball he had last been stung with—mistaking Churchdom for Christianity, and for marriage, "the sale of love"[2] and the law of sexual oppression.

Gradually, however, he was leaving behind him this low practical dexterity, unable to keep up with his widening intellectual perception; and, in exact proportion as he did so, his true power strengthened and proved itself. Gradually he was raised above the contemplation of spots and the attempt at effacing them, to the great Abstract Light, and, through the discrepancy of the creation, to the sufficiency of the First Cause. Gradually he was learning that the best way of removing abuses is to stand fast by truth. Truth is one, as they are manifold; and innumerable negative effects are pro-

---

[1] *One whose heart ... earth* From "Julian and Maddalo" (1824) 442–50, based on conversations in Italy between Shelley (Julian) and Lord Byron (Maddalo).

[2] *"sale of love"* See Tibullus's (c. 55–19 BCE) *Elegies* 1.4.57: "Whoever thou art that first didst teach the sale of love, may an unhallowed stone weigh heavy on thy bones."

duced by the upholding of one positive principle. I shall say what I think—had Shelley lived he would have finally ranged himself with the Christians; his very instinct for helping the weaker side (if numbers make strength), his very "hate of hate,"[1] which at first mistranslated itself into delirious Queen Mab[2] notes and the like, would have got clearer-sighted by exercise. The preliminary step to following Christ, is the leaving the dead to bury their dead[3]—not clamouring on his doctrine for an especial solution of difficulties which are referable to the general problem of the universe. Already he had attained to a profession of "a worship to the Spirit of good within, which requires (before it sends that inspiration forth, which impresses its likeness upon all it creates) devoted and disinterested homage, *as Coleridge says*"[4]—and Paul likewise. And we find in one of his last exquisite fragments, avowedly a record of one of his own mornings and its experience, as it dawned on him at his soul and body's best in his boat on the Serchio—that as surely as

> The stars burnt out in the pale blue air,
> And the thin white moon lay withering there—
> Day had kindled the dewy woods,
> And the rocks above, and the stream below,
> And the vapours in their multitudes,
> And the Apennine's shroud of summer snow—
> Day had awakened all things that be;

just so surely, he tells us (stepping forward from this delicious dance-music, choragus-like, into the grander measure befitting the final enunciation),

> All rose to do the task He set to each,
> Who shaped us to his ends and not our own;
> The million rose to learn, and One to teach
> What none yet ever knew or can be known.[5]

No more difference than this, from David's pregnant conclusion[6] so long ago!

Meantime, as I call Shelley a moral man, because he was true, simple-hearted, and brave, and because what he acted corresponded to what he knew, so I call him a man of religious mind, because every audacious negative cast up by him against the Divine, was interpenetrated with a mood of reverence and adoration—and because I find him everywhere taking for granted some of the capital dogmas of Christianity, while most vehemently denying their historical basement. There is such a thing as an efficacious knowledge of and belief in the politics of Junius,[7] or the poetry of Rowley, though a man should at the same time dispute the title of Chatterton[8] to the one, and consider the author of the other, as Byron wittily did, "really, truly, nobody at all."[9] There is even such a thing, we come to learn wonderingly in these very letters, as a profound sensibility and adaptitude for art, while the science of the percipient is so little advanced as to admit of his stronger admiration for

---

[1] *"hate of hate"* See Alfred Lord Tennyson's "The Poet" 1–3: "The poet in a golden clime was born, / With golden stars above; / Dowered with the hate of hate, the scorn of scorn."

[2] *Queen Mab* See Shelley's poem of this name.

[3] *leaving … dead* See Luke 6.60.

[4] *"a worship … Coleridge says"* From Shelley's Letter 24 to Mrs. Gisborne (1819).

[5] *The stars … known* From Shelley's "The Boat on the Serchio" (1824) 7–8, 11–14, 17, 30–33.

[6] *David's pregnant conclusion* King David in the Psalms.

[7] *Junius* Pseudonym of an unidentified English political author, whose letters were first published in 1772.

[8] *poetry of Rowley … Chatterton* In the late 1760s, Thomas Chatterton sent "The Rowley Poems" to Horace Walpole, claiming that they were written by a fifteenth-century monk. The poems were discovered to be imitations, but are thought to be brilliant and innovative in their own right.

[9] *really … all* Browning quotes Byron from "The Vision of Judgment" (1822) 80.7–8: "what Junius we are wont to call / Was really, truly, nobody at all." [Browning's note] Or, to take our illustrations from the writings of Shelley himself, there is such a thing as admirably appreciating a work by Andrea Verrocchio—and fancifully characterising the Pisan Torre Guelfa by the Ponte a Mare, black against the sunsets—and consummately painting the islet of San Clemente with its penitentiary for rebellious priests, to the west between Venice and the Lido—while you believe the first to be a fragment of an antique sarcophagus—the second, Ugolino's Tower of Famine (the vestiges of which should be sought for in the Piazza de' Cavalieri)—and the third (as I convinced myself last summer at Venice), San Servolo with its madhouse—which, far from being "windowless," is as full of windows as a barrack. [*Andrea Verrocchio* Italian painter and sculptor (1435–88); *Pisan Torre Guelfa* Guelph Tower in Pisa; *Ugolino's Tower of Famine* As told by Dante in Canto 33 of the *Inferno*, Count Ugolino Gherardesca was left to starve to death in a Pisan tower after attempting to overthrow the ruling party; *San Servolo … "windowless"* In Shelley's "Julian and Maddalo," Julian describes the madhouse of San Servolo as "a windowless, deformed and dreary pile."]

Guido (and Carlo Dolci!) than for Michelangelo.[1] A Divine Being has Himself said, that "a word against the Son of man shall be forgiven to a man," while "a word against the Spirit of God" (implying a general deliberate preference of perceived evil to perceived good) "shall not be forgiven to a man."[2] Also, in religion, one earnest and unextorted assertion of belief should outweigh, as a matter of testimony, many assertions of unbelief. The fact that there is a gold region is established by the finding of one lump, though you miss the vein never so often.

Shelley died before his youth ended. In taking the measure of him as a man, he must be considered on the whole and at his ultimate spiritual stature, and not be judged of at the immaturity and by the mistakes of ten years before: that, indeed, would be to judge of the author of "Julian and Maddalo" by *Zastrozzi*.[3] Let the whole truth be told of his worst mistake. I believe, for my own part, that if anything could now shame or grieve Shelley, it would be an attempt to vindicate him at the expense of another. In forming a judgment, I would, however, press on the reader the simple justice of considering tenderly his constitution of body as well as mind, and how unfavourable it was to the steady symmetries of conventional life; the body, in the torture of incurable disease, refusing to give repose to the bewildered soul, tossing in its hot fever of the fancy—and the laudanum[4] bottle making but a perilous and pitiful truce between these two. He was constantly subject to "that state of mind" (I quote his own note to *Hellas*[5]) "in which ideas may be supposed to assume the force of sensation, through the confusion of thought with the objects of thought, and excess of passion animating the creations of the imagination"; in other words, he was liable to remarkable delusions and hallucinations. The nocturnal attack in Wales, for instance, was assuredly a delusion; and I venture to express my own conviction, derived from a little attention to the circumstances of either story, that the idea of the enamoured lady following him to Naples, and of the "man in the cloak" who struck him at the Pisan post office, were equally illusory—the mere projection, in fact, from himself, of the image of his own love and hate.

> To thirst and find no fill—to wail and wander
> With short unsteady steps—to pause and ponder—
> To feel the blood run through the veins and tingle
> What busy thought and blind sensation mingle—
> To nurse the image of unfelt caresses
> Till dim imagination just possesses
> The half-created shadow—[6]

of unfelt caresses—and of unfelt blows as well: to such conditions was his genius subject. It was not at Rome only (where he heard a mystic voice exclaiming, "Cenci, Cenci," in reference to the tragic theme which occupied him at the time[7])—it was not at Rome only that he mistook the cry of "old rags." The habit of somnambulism is said to have extended to the very last days of his life.

Let me conclude with a thought of Shelley as a poet. In the hierarchy of creative minds, it is the presence of the highest faculty that gives first rank, in virtue of its kind, not degree; no pretension of a lower nature, whatever the completeness of development or variety of effect, impeding the precedency of the rarer endowment though only in the germ. The contrary is sometimes maintained; it is attempted to make the lower gifts (which are potentially included in the higher faculty) of independent value, and equal to some exercise of the special function. For instance, should not a poet possess common sense? Then the possession of abundant common sense implies a step towards becoming a poet. Yes; such a step as the lapidary's,[8] when, strong in the fact of carbon entering largely into the composition of the diamond, he heaps up a sack of charcoal in order to compete with the Koh-i-noor.[9] I pass at once, therefore, from Shelley's minor excellencies to his noblest and

---

[1]   *Guido (Carlo Dolci!)*   Shelley was said to have preferred the art of Italian artists Guido Reni (1575–1642) and Carlo Dolci (1616–86) to that of Michelangelo.

[2]   *"a word ... to a man"*   From Luke 12.10.

[3]   *Zastrozzi*   Shelley's first publication, a Gothic novel (1810).

[4]   *laudanum*   Liquid form of opium.

[5]   *Hellas*   Shelley's *Hellas: A Lyrical Drama* (1822).

[6]   *To thirst ... shadow*   From Shelley's "Fragment: 'Igniculus Desiderii'" (1839).

[7]   *Cenci ... time*   In 1819 Shelley published *The Cenci*, a tragedy based on a true story about a sixteenth-century Roman family.

[8]   *lapidary*   One who works with precious stones.

[9]   *Koh-i-noor*   Large and precious diamond of India that became one of the British Crown jewels.

predominating characteristic.

This I call his simultaneous perception of Power and Love in the absolute, and of Beauty and Good in the concrete, while he throws, from his poet's station between both, swifter, subtler, and more numerous films for the connexion of each with each, than have been thrown by any modern artificer of whom I have knowledge; proving how, as he says,

> The spirit of the worm within the sod,
> In love and worship blends itself with God.[1]

I would rather consider Shelley's poetry as a sublime fragmentary essay towards a presentment of the correspondency of the universe to Deity, of the natural to the spiritual, and of the actual to the ideal, than I would isolate and separately appraise the worth of many detachable portions which might be acknowledged as utterly perfect in a lower moral point of view, under the mere conditions of art. It would be easy to take my stand on successful instances of objectivity in Shelley: there is the unrivalled *Cenci*; there is the "Julian and Maddalo" too; there is the magnificent "Ode to Naples"; why not regard, it may be said, the less organised

matter as the radiant elemental foam and solution, out of which would have been evolved, eventually, creations as perfect even as those? But I prefer to look for the highest attainment, not simply the high—and, seeing it, I hold by it. There is surely enough of the work "Shelley" to be known enduringly among men, and, I believe, to be accepted of God, as human work may; and around the imperfect proportions of such, the most elaborated productions of ordinary art must arrange themselves as inferior illustrations.

It is because I have long held these opinions in assurance and gratitude, that I catch at the opportunity offered to me of expressing them here; knowing that the alacrity to fulfil an humble office conveys more love than the acceptance of the honour of a higher one, and that better, therefore, than the signal service it was the dream of my boyhood to render to his fame and memory, may be the saying of a few, inadequate words upon these scarcely more important supplementary letters of SHELLEY.

—1852

---

[1]   *The spirit ... god*   From Shelley's "Epipsychidion" (1821), 128–29.

CHARLES DICKENS
1812 – 1870

Few English novelists have attracted the huge audiences and lasting fame of Charles Dickens. People the world over are familiar with the moral transformation of *A Christmas Carol*'s Ebenezer Scrooge and the life of the orphan Oliver Twist, immortalized in his piteous request for a second bowl of water gruel: "Please, sir, I want some more." From Pickwick and Sam Weller in *The Pickwick Papers* to Mr. Micawber in *David Copperfield* to Pip in *Great Expectations*, from Mr. Guppy and Mrs. Jellyby in *Bleak House* to Mr. Gradgrind in *Hard Times* and Flora Finching in *Little Dorrit*, Dickens created a panoply of memorable characters. Combining his comic genius with astute criticisms of the laws, institutions, and the social order of Victorian society, he created novels that continue to command the attention of critics and the general public alike. His novels still stand as a testament to his stature both as a popular writer and as a social critic.

Dickens's early childhood was signally important as source material for the concerns and themes of his novels. His father worked as a naval office clerk in Portsmouth when Charles was born in 1812, the second of 10 children (two died in infancy). John and Elizabeth Dickens aspired to a middle-class life, but had unending difficulties controlling their spending and were always on the brink of penury. At one time, they served a four-month stint in the Marshalsea debtors' prison. Charles was able to attend school in Chatham, near London, after the family was transferred to the dockyards there, but in 1823 his education was halted, and he joined his parents in Camden Town, London. The young Dickens worked at odd jobs for his parents and was eventually sent off to work at Warren's Boot Blacking Factory at the age of 12. The psychological impact of this environment on Dickens was permanent. He never forgot the humiliation he had suffered or the dismay he had felt at the relatively harsh working conditions under which he and other children were forced to toil.

After the family came into a modest inheritance, Dickens returned to school, but in 1827, at just 15 years of age, he left school again because his father was unable to pay the fees. Working as a clerk in a law firm, he studied shorthand in his spare time, eventually becoming a parliamentary reporter. In 1833, *Monthly Magazine* published Dickens's first story, "Dinner at Poplar Walk." While working as a newspaper reporter the next year, he launched a highly popular series of articles that were eventually collected and published as *Sketches by Boz* (his journalistic pseudonym) in 1836. The success of this book allowed Dickens to marry Catherine Hogarth and to begin another series that cemented his fame and secured his financial stability. A monthly illustrated serial about the Pickwick Club was commissioned by publishers Chapman and Hall, and the absurd characters of Mr. Pickwick, Mr. Winkle, Mr. Tupman, Mr. Snodgrass, and Sam Weller soon had people all over England clamoring for the latest installment of *The Pickwick Papers*. Dickens consolidated this success by beginning *Oliver Twist* (1837–38) in *Bentley's Miscellany*, which he had begun editing, and then launching *Nicholas Nickleby* (1838–39) as a monthly serial.

In 1837, Dickens and his wife began to raise a family (they eventually had 10 children). In this same year, he lost his beloved sister-in-law, Mary Hogarth, who would become the inspiration for

Little Nell in *The Old Curiosity Shop* (1840–41) and for many of the childlike women that constitute the "good angels" of his novels. By the time this book was published, Dickens's fame had spread throughout North America; eager fans would line the piers in New York waiting for the latest installment of a Dickens story to arrive from England.

In 1842, Dickens journeyed to the United States to take advantage of his fame, but the trip turned out to be a disappointment. The hordes that crowded around him relentlessly, trying to speak to, touch, or even just glimpse the famous author were only part of the problem. He scorned, publicly and at any opportunity, the lack of international copyright laws, which meant that Americans could pirate editions of his books without any of the proceeds going to him. Dickens set out his disdain for American habits (such as chewing and spitting tobacco) and for American institutions, such as slavery, and what he thought was a ruthless prison system in a book about his travels, *American Notes* (1842), and made Americans the object of derision in his novel *Martin Chuzzlewit* (1843–44). Americans were incensed and reacted with an outpouring of vindictive editorials in the press. As it happened, *Martin Chuzzlewit* did not sell well on either side of the Atlantic. Americans began to forgive Dickens after the appearance of the overwhelmingly successful *A Christmas Carol* (1843), the first in his Christmas book series and a novel that is all about forgiveness and redemption.

Dickens was an astonishingly energetic and prolific writer, becoming the editor of *Household Words* in 1850, while writing and acting in theatrical works, traveling widely, and working in various social causes. Throughout the 1840s and 1850s, he published at an unprecedented rate: *Dombey and Son* (1846–48), *David Copperfield* (his most autobiographical work, 1849–50), *Bleak House* (1852–53), *Hard Times* (1854), *Little Dorrit* (1855–57), and *A Tale of Two Cities* (1859). Dickens published all of his novels in serial form. The episodic structure of his novels prompted Dickens to develop methods of characterizations that allowed immediate identification of characters by readers waiting for weekly or monthly installments. The Dickens "character" is invariably recognizable as a type that speaks in a marvelously individualized dialect and often more closely resembles a caricature from the popular press than a fully rounded character. (George Eliot complained that Dickens's characters had little psychology.) He also wove numerous peripheral stories and characters into the main plotlines, and used coincidence—in which, for example, characters discover long-lost parents and siblings by accident—with Victorian abandon. Yet for Dickens and his readers, coincidence did not undermine reality so much as suggest that divinity shapes our ends.

In 1858 Dickens separated from Catherine, an event complicated by his relationship with the actress Ellen Ternan and by the degree of publicity that (partly at Dickens's instigation) attended his change in marital status. In that same year, Dickens began an extensive tour of public readings, a most lucrative but exhausting enterprise that severely compromised his health. He continued touring throughout the 1860s while editing his new journal, *All the Year Round* (begun in 1859), in which he serialized both *A Tale of Two Cities* (1859) and *Great Expectations* (1860–61). During this decade Dickens completed only one other novel, *Our Mutual Friend* (1864–65). He was at work on *The Mystery of Edwin Drood* when he died in 1870 during a grueling schedule of readings. In his will Dickens requested an "unostentatious, and strictly private" burial attended only by a few close friends and family, but throngs gathered later around his grave in Westminster Abbey to mourn his death.

A Christmas Carol: in Prose, Being a Ghost Story of Christmas

PREFACE

I have endeavoured in this ghostly little book, to raise the ghost of an idea, which shall not put my readers out of humour with themselves, with each other, with the season, or with me. May it haunt their houses pleasantly, and no one wish to lay it.

Their faithful friend and servant,

C.D.

December, 1843

STAVE[1] I: MARLEY'S GHOST

Marley was dead: to begin with. There is no doubt whatever about that. The register of his burial was signed by the clergyman, the clerk, the undertaker, and the chief mourner. Scrooge signed it: and Scrooge's name was good upon 'Change,[2] for anything he chose to put his hand to. Old Marley was as dead as a doornail.

Mind! I don't mean to say that I know, of my own knowledge, what there is particularly dead about a doornail. I might have been inclined, myself, to regard a coffin-nail as the deadest piece of ironmongery in the trade. But the wisdom of our ancestors is in the simile; and my unhallowed hands shall not disturb it, or the country's done for. You will therefore permit me to repeat, emphatically, that Marley was as dead as a doornail.

Scrooge knew he was dead? Of course he did. How could it be otherwise? Scrooge and he were partners for I don't know how many years. Scrooge was his sole executor, his sole administrator, his sole assign,[3] his sole residuary legatee, his sole friend and sole mourner. And even Scrooge was not so dreadfully cut up by the sad event, but that he was an excellent man of business on the very day of the funeral, and solemnised it with an undoubted bargain.

This illustration of Mr. Fezziwig's Ball appeared as the frontispiece of the 1843 first edition.[4]

The mention of Marley's funeral brings me back to the point I started from. There is no doubt that Marley was dead. This must be distinctly understood, or nothing wonderful can come of the story I am going to relate. If we were not perfectly convinced that Hamlet's father died before the play began, there would be nothing more remarkable in his taking a stroll at night, in an easterly wind, upon his own ramparts, than there would be in any other middle-aged gentleman rashly turning out after dark in a breezy spot—say Saint Paul's churchyard for instance—literally to astonish his son's weak mind.

Scrooge never painted out old Marley's name. There it stood, years afterwards, above the warehouse door: Scrooge and Marley. The firm was known as Scrooge and Marley. Sometimes people new to the business called Scrooge Scrooge, and sometimes Marley, but he

---

1   *Stave*   Verse.

2   *'Change*   The Royal Exchange, center of commerce and trade in London.

3   *assign*   Inheritor of property.

---

4   The illustrations reprinted here and that follow were executed by John Leech (1817–64).

answered to both names: it was all the same to him.

Oh! But he was a tightfisted hand at the grindstone, Scrooge! a squeezing, wrenching, grasping, scraping, clutching, covetous old sinner! Hard and sharp as flint, from which no steel had ever struck out generous fire; secret, and self-contained, and solitary as an oyster. The cold within him froze his old features, nipped his pointed nose, shrivelled his cheek, stiffened his gait; made his eyes red, his thin lips blue; and spoke out shrewdly in his grating voice. A frosty rime was on his head, and on his eyebrows, and his wiry chin. He carried his own low temperature always about with him; he iced his office in the dog-days;[1] and didn't thaw it one degree at Christmas.

External heat and cold had little influence on Scrooge. No warmth could warm, nor wintry weather chill him. No wind that blew was bitterer than he, no falling snow was more intent upon its purpose, no pelting rain less open to entreaty. Foul weather didn't know where to have him. The heaviest rain, and snow, and hail, and sleet, could boast of the advantage over him in only one respect. They often "came down"[2] handsomely, and Scrooge never did.

Nobody ever stopped him in the street to say, with gladsome looks, "My dear Scrooge, how are you? when will you come to see me?" No beggars implored him to bestow a trifle, no children asked him what it was o'clock, no man or woman ever once in all his life inquired the way to such and such a place, of Scrooge. Even the blindmen's dogs appeared to know him; and when they saw him coming on, would tug their owners into doorways and up courts; and then would wag their tails as though they said "no eye at all is better than an evil eye, dark master!"

But what did Scrooge care? It was the very thing he liked. To edge his way along the crowded paths of life, warning all human sympathy to keep its distance, was what the knowing ones call "nuts"[3] to Scrooge.

Once upon a time—of all the good days in the year, on Christmas Eve—old Scrooge sat busy in his counting-house. It was cold, bleak, biting weather: foggy withal: and he could hear the people in the court outside go wheezing up and down, beating their hands upon their breasts, and stamping their feet upon the pavement-stones to warm them. The city clocks had only just gone three, but it was quite dark already: it had not been light all day: and candles were flaring in the windows of the neighbouring offices, like ruddy smears upon the palpable brown air. The fog came pouring in at every chink and keyhole, and was so dense without, that although the court was of the narrowest, the houses opposite were mere phantoms. To see the dingy cloud come drooping down, obscuring everything, one might have thought that Nature lived hard by, and was brewing on a large scale.

The door of Scrooge's counting-house was open that he might keep his eye upon his clerk, who in a dismal little cell beyond, a sort of tank, was copying letters. Scrooge had a very small fire, but the clerk's fire was so very much smaller that it looked like one coal. But he couldn't replenish it, for Scrooge kept the coal-box in his own room; and so surely as the clerk came in with the shovel, the master predicted that it would be necessary for them to part. Wherefore the clerk put on his white comforter,[4] and tried to warm himself at the candle; in which effort, not being a man of a strong imagination, he failed.

"A merry Christmas, uncle! God save you!" cried a cheerful voice. It was the voice of Scrooge's nephew, who came upon him so quickly that this was the first intimation he had of his approach.

"Bah!" said Scrooge, "Humbug!"[5]

He had so heated himself with rapid walking in the fog and frost, this nephew of Scrooge's, that he was all in a glow; his face was ruddy and handsome; his eyes sparkled, and his breath smoked again.

"Christmas a humbug, uncle!" said Scrooge's nephew. "You don't mean that, I am sure."

"I do," said Scrooge. "Merry Christmas! what right have you to be merry? what reason have you to be merry? You're poor enough."

"Come, then," returned the nephew gaily. "What right have you to be dismal? what reason have you to be morose? You're rich enough."

---

1   *dog-days*   Hot summer days.

2   *"came down"*   Pun on a phrase that also means "gave money."

3   *"nuts"*   Enjoyable.

4   *comforter*   Woolen scarf.

5   *Humbug*   Nonsense.

Scrooge having no better answer ready on the spur of the moment, said, "Bah!" again; and followed it up with "Humbug."

"Don't be cross, uncle," said the nephew.

"What else can I be," returned the uncle, "when I live in such a world of fools as this? Merry Christmas! Out upon merry Christmas! What's Christmas time to you but a time for paying bills without money; a time for finding yourself a year older, and not an hour richer; a time for balancing your books and having every item in 'em through a round dozen of months presented dead against you? If I could work my will," said Scrooge, indignantly, "every idiot who goes about with 'Merry Christmas' on his lips should be boiled with his own pudding, and buried with a stake of holly through his heart. He should!"

"Uncle!" pleaded the nephew.

"Nephew!" returned the uncle, sternly, "keep Christmas in your own way, and let me keep it in mine."

"Keep it!" repeated Scrooge's nephew. "But you don't keep it."

"Let me leave it alone, then," said Scrooge. "Much good may it do you! Much good it has ever done you!"

"There are many things from which I might have derived good, by which I have not profited, I dare say," returned the nephew: "Christmas among the rest. But I am sure I have always thought of Christmas time, when it has come round—apart from the veneration due to its sacred name and origin, if anything belonging to it can be apart from that—as a good time: a kind, forgiving, charitable, pleasant time: the only time I know of, in the long calendar of the year, when men and women seem by one consent to open their shut-up hearts freely, and to think of people below them as if they really were fellow-passengers to the grave, and not another race of creatures bound on other journeys. And therefore, uncle, though it has never put a scrap of gold or silver in my pocket, I believe that it *has* done me good, and *will* do me good; and I say, God bless it!"

The clerk in the tank involuntarily applauded: becoming immediately sensible of the impropriety, he poked the fire, and extinguished the last frail spark forever.

"Let me hear another sound from *you*," said Scrooge, "and you'll keep your Christmas by losing your situa-tion. You're quite a powerful speaker, sir," he added, turning to his nephew. "I wonder you don't go into Parliament."

"Don't be angry, uncle. Come! Dine with us tomorrow."

Scrooge said that he would see him—yes, indeed he did. He went the whole length of the expression, and said that he would see him in that extremity[1] first.

"But why?" cried Scrooge's nephew. "Why?"

"Why did you get married?" said Scrooge.

"Because I fell in love."

"Because you fell in love!" growled Scrooge, as if that were the only one thing in the world more ridiculous than a merry Christmas. "Good afternoon!"

"Nay, uncle, but you never came to see me before that happened. Why give it as a reason for not coming now?"

"Good afternoon," said Scrooge.

"I want nothing from you; I ask nothing of you; why cannot we be friends?"

"Good afternoon," said Scrooge.

"I am sorry, with all my heart, to find you so resolute. We have never had any quarrel, to which I have been a party. But I have made the trial in homage to Christmas, and I'll keep my Christmas humour to the last. So a merry Christmas, uncle!"

"Good afternoon!" said Scrooge.

"And A Happy New Year!"

"Good afternoon!" said Scrooge.

His nephew left the room without an angry word, notwithstanding. He stopped at the outer door to bestow the greetings of the season on the clerk, who, cold as he was, was warmer than Scrooge; for he returned them cordially.

"There's another fellow," muttered Scrooge; who overheard him: "my clerk, with fifteen shillings a week, and a wife and family, talking about a merry Christmas. I'll retire to Bedlam."[2]

This lunatic, in letting Scrooge's nephew out, had let two other people in. They were portly gentlemen, pleasant to behold, and now stood, with their hats off, in Scrooge's office. They had books and papers in their hands, and bowed to him.

---

[1] *in that extremity* Dead.

[2] *Bedlam* Hospital of St. Mary of Bethlehem, an asylum for the mentally ill in London.

"Scrooge and Marley's, I believe," said one of the gentlemen, referring to his list. "Have I the pleasure of addressing Mr. Scrooge, or Mr. Marley?"

"Mr. Marley has been dead these seven years," Scrooge replied. "He died seven years ago, this very night."

"We have no doubt his liberality is well represented by his surviving partner," said the gentleman, presenting his credentials.

It certainly was; for they had been two kindred spirits. At the ominous word "liberality," Scrooge frowned, and shook his head, and handed the credentials back.

"At this festive season of the year, Mr. Scrooge," said the gentleman, taking up a pen, "it is more than usually desirable that we should make some slight provision for the poor and destitute, who suffer greatly at the present time. Many thousands are in want of common necessaries; hundreds of thousands are in want of common comforts, sir."

"Are there no prisons?" asked Scrooge.

"Plenty of prisons," said the gentleman, laying down the pen again.

"And the union workhouses?" demanded Scrooge. "Are they still in operation?"

"They are. Still," returned the gentleman, "I wish I could say they were not."

"The treadmill and the Poor Law[1] are in full vigour, then?" said Scrooge.

"Both very busy, sir."

"Oh I was afraid, from what you said at first, that something had occurred to stop them in their useful course," said Scrooge. "I'm very glad to hear it."

"Under the impression that they scarcely furnish Christian cheer of mind or body to the multitude," returned the gentleman, "a few of us are endeavouring to raise a fund to buy the poor some meat and drink, and means of warmth. We choose this time, because it is a time, of all others, when Want is keenly felt, and Abundance rejoices. What shall I put you down for?"

"Nothing!" Scrooge replied.

"You wish to be anonymous?"

"I wish to be left alone," said Scrooge. "Since you ask me what I wish, gentlemen, that is my answer. I don't make merry myself at Christmas, and I can't afford to make idle people merry. I help to support the establishments I have mentioned; they cost enough: and those who are badly off must go there."

"Many can't go there; and many would rather die."

"If they would rather die," said Scrooge, "they had better do it, and decrease the surplus population.[2] Besides—excuse me—I don't know that."

"But you might know it," observed the gentleman.

"It's not my business," Scrooge returned. "It's enough for a man to understand his own business, and not to interfere with other people's. Mine occupies me constantly. Good afternoon, gentlemen!"

Seeing clearly that it would be useless to pursue their point, the gentlemen withdrew. Scrooge resumed his labours with an improved opinion of himself, and in a more facetious temper than was usual with him.

Meanwhile the fog and darkness thickened so, that people ran about with flaring links,[3] proffering their services to go before horses in carriages, and conduct them on their way. The ancient tower of a church, whose gruff old bell was always peeping slily down at Scrooge out of a gothic window in the wall, became invisible, and struck the hours and quarters in the clouds, with tremulous vibrations afterwards, as if its teeth were chattering in its frozen head up there. The cold became intense. In the main street, at the corner of the court, some labourers were repairing the gas-pipes, and had lighted a great fire in a brazier,[4] round which a party of ragged men and boys were gathered: warming their hands and winking their eyes before the blaze in rapture. The water-plug being left in solitude, its overflowings sullenly congealed, and turned to misanthropic ice. The brightness of the shops where holly sprigs and berries crackled in the lamp-heat of the windows, made pale faces ruddy as they passed. Poul-

---

[1]   *Treadmill and the Poor Law*   The Poor Law Amendment Act of 1834 was designed to grant employment to the poor in workhouses administered by separate parishes (or unions of parishes). The poor were deliberately provided with working conditions harsh enough to discourage them from choosing this lifestyle. If no other work was available, they would be assigned pointless and exhausting tasks, such as walking on treadmills.

[2]   *decrease the surplus population*   Cf. *An Essay on the Principle of Population* (1798), in which economist Thomas Malthus suggested that a population increase among the poor would lead to starvation.

[3]   *flaring links*   Tar-burning torches.

[4]   *brazier*   Metal container used for burning coal.

terers' and grocers' trades became a splendid joke: a glorious pageant, with which it was next to impossible to believe that such dull principles as bargain and sale had anything to do. The Lord Mayor, in the stronghold of the mighty Mansion House, gave orders to his fifty cooks and butlers to keep Christmas as a Lord Mayor's household should; and even the little tailor, whom he had fined five shillings on the previous Monday for being drunk and bloodthirsty in the streets, stirred up tomorrow's pudding in his garret, while his lean wife and the baby sallied out to buy the beef.

Foggier yet, and colder! Piercing, searching, biting cold. If the good Saint Dunstan had but nipped the Evil Spirit's nose[1] with a touch of such weather as that, instead of using his familiar weapons, then indeed he would have roared to lusty purpose. The owner of one scant young nose, gnawed and mumbled by the hungry cold as bones are gnawed by dogs, stooped down at Scrooge's keyhole to regale him with a Christmas carol: but at the first sound of—

"God bless you merry gentleman!
May nothing you dismay!"[2]

Scrooge seized the ruler with such energy of action, that the singer fled in terror, leaving the keyhole to the fog and even more congenial frost.

At length the hour of shutting up the counting-house arrived. With an ill will Scrooge dismounted from his stool, and tacitly admitted the fact to the expectant clerk in the Tank, who instantly snuffed his candle out, and put on his hat.

"You'll want all day tomorrow, I suppose?" said Scrooge.

"If quite convenient, Sir."

"It's not convenient," said Scrooge, "and it's not fair. If I was to stop half-a-crown for it; you'd think yourself ill used, I'll be bound?"

The clerk smiled faintly.

"And yet," said Scrooge, "you don't think me ill-used, when I pay a day's wages for no work."

The clerk observed that it was only once a year. "A poor excuse for picking a man's pocket every twenty-fifth of December!" said Scrooge, buttoning his great-coat to the chin. "But I suppose you must have the whole day. Be here all the earlier next morning!"

The clerk promised that he would; and Scrooge walked out with a growl. The office was closed in a twinkling, and the clerk, with the long ends of his white comforter dangling below his waist (for he boasted no greatcoat), went down a slide on Cornhill,[3] at the end of a lane of boys, twenty times, in honour of its being Christmas Eve, and then ran home to Camden Town[4] as hard as he could pelt, to play at blindman's buff.[5]

Scrooge took his melancholy dinner in his usual melancholy tavern; and having read all the newspapers, and beguiled the rest of the evening with his banker's-book, went home to bed. He lived in chambers which had once belonged to his deceased partner. They were a gloomy suite of rooms, in a lowering pile of building up a yard, where it had so little business to be, that one could scarcely help fancying it must have run there when it was a young house, playing at hide-and-seek with other houses, and have forgotten the way out again. It was old enough now, and dreary enough, for nobody lived in it but Scrooge, the other rooms being all let out as offices. The yard was so dark that even Scrooge, who knew its every stone, was fain to grope with his hands. The fog and frost so hung about the black old gateway of the house, that it seemed as if the Genius[6] of the Weather sat in mournful meditation on the threshold.

Now, it is a fact, that there was nothing at all particular about the knocker on the door, except that it was very large. It is also a fact, that Scrooge had seen it night and morning during his whole residence in that place; also that Scrooge had as little of what is called

---

1 *Saint Dunstan ... nose* English monk and blacksmith, about whom was written: "St. Dunstan, as the story goes, / Once pulled the devil by the nose / With red-hot tongs, which made him roar, / That he was heard three miles or more."

2 *God ... gentlemen* From the traditional English carol "God Rest Ye Merry Gentlemen."

3 *Cornhill* Neighborhood that lies to the south of the Royal Exchange and was named for the grain market that formerly occupied the area.

4 *Camden Town* Poor working-class neighborhood.

5 *blindman's buff* Game in which a blindfolded player attempts to catch any one of the other players.

6 *Genius* God or spirit.

fancy[1] about him as any man in the city of London, even including—which is a bold word—the corporation, aldermen, and livery. Let it also be borne in mind that Scrooge had not bestowed one thought on Marley, since his last mention of his seven-years' dead partner that afternoon. And then let any man explain to me, if he can, how it happened that Scrooge, having his key in the lock of the door, saw in the knocker, without its undergoing any intermediate process of change: not a knocker, but Marley's face.

Marley's face. It was not in impenetrable shadow as the other objects in the yard were, but had a dismal light about it, like a bad lobster in a dark cellar. It was not angry or ferocious, but looked at Scrooge as Marley used to look: with ghostly spectacles turned up upon its ghostly forehead. The hair was curiously stirred, as if by breath or hot air; and though the eyes were wide open, they were perfectly motionless. That, and its livid colour, made it horrible; but its horror seemed to be, in spite of the face and beyond its control, rather than a part of its own expression.

As Scrooge looked fixedly at this phenomenon, it was a knocker again.

To say that he was not startled, or that his blood was not conscious of a terrible sensation to which it had been a stranger from infancy, would be untrue. But he put his hand upon the key he had relinquished, turned it sturdily, walked in, and lighted his candle.

He *did* pause, with a moment's irresolution, before he shut the door; and he *did* look cautiously behind it first, as if he half expected to be terrified with the sight of Marley's pigtail sticking out into the hall. But there was nothing on the back of the door, except the screws and nuts that held the knocker on; so he said "Pooh, pooh!" and closed it with a bang.

The sound resounded through the house like thunder. Every room above, and every cask in the wine merchant's cellars below, appeared to have a separate peal of echoes of its own. Scrooge was not a man to be frightened by echoes. He fastened the door, and walked across the hall, and up the stairs, slowly too, trimming his candle as he went.

You may talk vaguely about driving a coach-and-six up a good old flight of stairs, or through a bad young Act of Parliament; but I mean to say you might have got a hearse up that staircase, and taken it broadwise, with the splinter-bar[2] towards the wall, and the door towards the balustrades: and done it easy. There was plenty of width for that, and room to spare; which is perhaps the reason why Scrooge thought he saw a locomotive hearse going on before him in the gloom. Half a dozen gas-lamps out of the street wouldn't have lighted the entry too well, so you may suppose that it was pretty dark with Scrooge's dip.[3]

Up Scrooge went, not caring a button for that: darkness is cheap, and Scrooge liked it. But before he shut his heavy door, he walked through his rooms to see that all was right. He had just enough recollection of the face to desire to do that.

Sitting room, bedroom, lumber-room.[4] All as they should be. Nobody under the table, nobody under the sofa; a small fire in the grate; spoon and basin ready; and the little saucepan of gruel (Scrooge had a cold in his head) upon the hob.[5] Nobody under the bed; nobody in the closet; nobody in his dressing-gown, which was hanging up in a suspicious attitude against the wall. Lumber-room as usual. Old fire-guard,[6] old shoes, two fish-baskets, washing-stand on three legs, and a poker.

Quite satisfied, he closed his door, and locked himself in: double-locked himself in, which was not his custom. Thus secured against surprise, he took off his cravat; put on his dressing-gown and slippers, and his night-cap, and sat down before the fire to take his gruel.

It was a very low fire indeed; nothing on such a bitter night. He was obliged to sit close to it, and brood over it, before he could extract the least sensation of warmth from such a handful of fuel. The fireplace was an old one, built by some Dutch merchant long ago, and paved all round with quaint Dutch tiles, designed to illustrate the Scriptures. There were Cains and Abels; Pharaoh's daughters, Queens of Sheba, angelic messengers descending through the air on clouds like feather-beds, Abrahams, Belshazzars, Apostles putting off to sea

---

1. *fancy* Imagination.
2. *splinter-bar* Supporting rail on a coach.
3. *dip* Candle.
4. *lumber-room* Storage room.
5. *hob* Warming shelf in a fireplace.
6. *fire-guard* Fireplace screen.

in butter-boats, hundreds of figures, to attract his thoughts; and yet that face of Marley, seven years dead, came like the ancient Prophet's rod, and swallowed up the whole.[1] If each smooth tile had been a blank at first, with power to shape some picture on its surface from the disjointed fragments of his thoughts, there would have been a copy of old Marley's head on every one.

"Humbug!" said Scrooge, and walked across the room.

After several turns, he sat down again. As he threw his head back in the chair, his glance happened to rest upon a bell, a disused bell, that hung in the room, and communicated for some purpose now forgotten with a chamber in the highest story of the building. It was with great astonishment, and with a strange, inexplicable dread, that as he looked, he saw this bell begin to swing. It swung so softly in the outset that it scarcely made a sound; but soon it rang out loudly, and so did every bell in the house.

This might have lasted half a minute, or a minute, but it seemed an hour. The bells ceased as they had begun, together. They were succeeded by a clanking noise, deep down below; as if some person were dragging a heavy chain over the casks in the wine-merchant's cellar. Scrooge then remembered to have heard that ghosts in haunted houses were described as dragging chains.

The cellar-door flew open with a booming sound, and then he heard the noise much louder, on the floors below; then coming up the stairs; then coming straight towards his door.

"It's humbug still!" said Scrooge. "I won't believe it."

His colour changed though, when, without a pause, it came on through the heavy door, and passed into the room before his eyes. Upon its coming in, the dying flame leaped up, as though it cried "I know him! Marley's ghost!" and fell again.

The same face: the very same. Marley in his pigtail, usual waistcoat, tights, and boots; the tassels on the latter bristling, like his pigtail, and his coat-skirts, and the hair upon his head. The chain he drew was clasped about his middle. It was long, and wound about him like a tail; and it was made (for Scrooge observed it

closely) of cash-boxes, keys, padlocks, ledgers, deeds, and heavy purses wrought in steel. His body was transparent: so that Scrooge, observing him, and looking through his waistcoat, could see the two buttons on his coat behind.

Scrooge had often heard it said that Marley had no bowels,[2] but he had never believed it until now.

No, nor did he believe it even now. Though he looked the phantom through and through, and saw it standing before him; though he felt the chilling influence of its death-cold eyes; and marked the very texture of the folded kerchief bound about its head and chin, which wrapper he had not observed before; he was still incredulous, and fought against his senses.

"How now!" said Scrooge, caustic and cold as ever. "What do you want with me?"

"Much!"—Marley's voice, no doubt about it.

"Who are you?"

"Ask me who I *was*."

"Who *were* you then?" said Scrooge, raising his voice. "You're particular—for a shade."[3] He was going to say "*to* a shade,"[4] but substituted this, as more appropriate.

"In life I was your partner, Jacob Marley."

"Can you—can you sit down?" asked Scrooge, looking doubtfully at him.

"I can."

"Do it then."

Scrooge asked the question, because he didn't know whether a ghost so transparent might find himself in a condition to take a chair; and felt that in the event of its being impossible, it might involve the necessity of an embarrassing explanation. But the ghost sat down on the opposite side of the fireplace, as if he were quite used to it.

"You don't believe in me," observed the Ghost.

"I don't," said Scrooge.

"What evidence would you have of my reality, beyond that of your senses?"

"I don't know," said Scrooge.

"Why do you doubt your senses?"

"Because," said Scrooge, "a little thing affects them. A slight disorder of the stomach makes them cheats. You

---

1 *ancient Prophet's ... whole* Cf. Exodus 7.12: "They cast down every man his rod, and they became serpents: but Aaron's rod swallowed up [the magicians of Egypt's] rods."

2 *bowels* Then considered the seat of emotion and compassion.

3 *shade* Ghost.

4 *to a shade* Figurative expression meaning "to a very small degree of difference."

may be an undigested bit of beef, a blot of mustard, a crumb of cheese, a fragment of an underdone potato. There's more of gravy than of grave about you, whatever you are!"

Scrooge was not much in the habit of cracking jokes, nor did he feel, in his heart, by any means waggish then. The truth is, that he tried to be smart, as a means of distracting his own attention, and keeping down his terror; for the spectre's voice disturbed the very marrow in his bones.

To sit, staring at those fixed, glazed eyes, in silence for a moment, would play, Scrooge felt, the very deuce[1] with him. There was something very awful, too, in the spectre's being provided with an infernal atmosphere of its own. Scrooge could not feel it himself, but this was clearly the case; for though the Ghost sat perfectly motionless, its hair, and skirts, and tassels, were still agitated as by the hot vapour from an oven.

"You see this toothpick?" said Scrooge, returning quickly to the charge, for the reason just assigned; and wishing, though it were only for a second, to divert the vision's stony gaze from himself.

"I do," replied the Ghost.

"You are not looking at it," said Scrooge.

"But I see it," said the Ghost, "notwithstanding."

"Well!" returned Scrooge. "I have but to swallow this, and be for the rest of my days persecuted by a legion of goblins, all of my own creation. Humbug, I tell you—humbug!"

At this, the spirit raised a frightful cry, and shook its chain with such a dismal and appalling noise, that Scrooge held on tight to his chair, to save himself from falling in a swoon. But how much greater was his horror, when the phantom taking off the bandage round its head, as if it were too warm to wear indoors, its lower jaw dropped down upon its breast!

Scrooge fell upon his knees, and clasped his hands before his face.

"Mercy!" he said. "Dreadful apparition, why do you trouble me?"

"Man of the worldly mind!" replied the Ghost, "do you believe in me or not?"

"I do," said Scrooge. "I must. But why do spirits walk the earth, and why do they come to me?"

"It is required of every man," the Ghost returned, "that the spirit within him should walk abroad among his fellow men, and travel far and wide; and if that spirit goes not forth in life, it is condemned to do so after death. It is doomed to wander through the world—oh, woe is me!—and witness what it cannot share, but might have shared on earth, and turned to happiness!"

Again the spectre raised a cry, and shook its chain, and wrung its shadowy hands.

"You are fettered," said Scrooge, trembling. "Tell me why?"

"I wear the chain I forged in life," replied the Ghost. "I made it link by link, and yard by yard; I girded it on of my own free will, and of my own free will I wore it. Is its pattern strange to you?"

Scrooge trembled more and more.

"Or would you know," pursued the Ghost, "the weight and length of the strong coil you bear yourself? It was full as heavy and as long as this, seven Christmas Eves ago. You have laboured on it, since. It is a ponderous chain!"

---

1 *deuce* Devil; "play the deuce with" meant "ruin."

Scrooge glanced about him on the floor, in the expectation of finding himself surrounded by some fifty or sixty fathoms of iron cable: but he could see nothing.

"Jacob," he said, imploringly. "Old Jacob Marley, tell me more. Speak comfort to me, Jacob."

"I have none to give," the Ghost replied. "It comes from other regions, Ebenezer Scrooge, and is conveyed by other ministers, to other kinds of men. Nor can I tell you what I would. A very little more, is all permitted to me. I cannot rest, I cannot stay, I cannot linger anywhere. My spirit never walked beyond our counting-house—mark me!—in life my spirit never roved beyond the narrow limits of our money-changing hole; and weary journeys lie before me!"

It was a habit with Scrooge, whenever he became thoughtful, to put his hands in his breeches pockets. Pondering on what the Ghost had said, he did so now, but without lifting up his eyes, or getting off his knees.

"You must have been very slow about it, Jacob," Scrooge observed, in a businesslike manner, though with humility and deference.

"Slow!" the Ghost repeated.

"Seven years dead," mused Scrooge. "And travelling all the time?"

"The whole time," said the Ghost. "No rest, no peace. Incessant torture of remorse."

"You travel fast?" said Scrooge.

"On the wings of the wind," replied the Ghost.

"You might have got over a great quantity of ground in seven years," said Scrooge.

The Ghost, on hearing this, set up another cry, and clanked its chain so hideously in the dead silence of the night, that the ward[1] would have been justified in indicting it for a nuisance.

"Oh! captive, bound, and double-ironed," cried the phantom, "not to know, that ages of incessant labour by immortal creatures, for this earth must pass into eternity before the good of which it is susceptible is all developed. Not to know that any Christian spirit working kindly in its little sphere, whatever it may be, will find its mortal life too short for its vast means of usefulness. Not to know that no space of regret can make amends for one life's opportunities misused! Yet such was I! Oh! such was I!"

"But you were always a good man of business, Jacob," faltered Scrooge, who now began to apply this to himself.

"Business!" cried the Ghost, wringing its hands again. "Mankind was my business. The common welfare was my business; charity, mercy, forbearance, and benevolence, were, all, my business. The dealings of my trade were but a drop of water in the comprehensive ocean of my business!"

It held up its chain at arm's length, as if that were the cause of all its unavailing grief, and flung it heavily upon the ground again.

"At this time of the rolling year," the spectre said, "I suffer most. Why did I walk through crowds of fellow beings with my eyes turned down, and never raise them to that blessed Star which led the wise men to a poor abode?[2] Were there no poor homes to which its light would have conducted *me*!"

Scrooge was very much dismayed to hear the spectre going on at this rate, and began to quake exceedingly.

"Hear me!" cried the Ghost. "My time is nearly gone."

"I will," said Scrooge. "But don't be hard upon me! Don't be flowery, Jacob! Pray!"

"How it is that I appear before you in a shape that you can see I may not tell. I have sat invisible beside you many and many a day."

It was not an agreeable idea. Scrooge shivered, and wiped the perspiration from his brow.

"That is no light part of my penance," pursued the Ghost. "I am here tonight to warn you, that you have yet a chance and hope of escaping my fate. A chance and hope of my procuring, Ebenezer."

"You were always a good friend to me," said Scrooge. "Thank'ee!"

"You will be haunted," resumed the Ghost, "by three spirits."

Scrooge's countenance fell almost as low as the Ghost's had done.

---

[1] *ward* Patrol officer.

[2] *blessed Star … abode* Cf. Matthew 2.1–3: "Now when Jesus was born in Bethlehem of Judaea in the days of Herod the king, behold, there came wise men from the east to Jerusalem, / Saying, Where is he that is born King of the Jews? for we have seen his star in the east, and are come to worship him."

"Is that the chance and hope you mentioned, Jacob?" he demanded, in a faltering voice.

"It is."

"I—I think I'd rather not," said Scrooge.

"Without their visits," said the Ghost, "you cannot hope to shun the path I tread. Expect the first tomorrow, when the bell tolls one."

"Couldn't I take 'em all at once, and have it over, Jacob?" hinted Scrooge.

"Expect the second on the next night at the same hour. The third upon the next night when the last stroke of twelve has ceased to vibrate. Look to see me no more; and look that, for your own sake, you remember what has passed between us!"

When it had said these words, the spectre took its wrapper from the table, and bound it round its head, as before. Scrooge knew this, by the smart sound its teeth made, when the jaws were brought together by the bandage. He ventured to raise his eyes again, and found his supernatural visitor confronting him in an erect attitude, with its chain wound over and about its arm.

The apparition walked backward from him; and at every step it took, the window raised itself a little, so that when the spectre reached it, it was wide open. It beckoned Scrooge to approach, which he did. When they were within two paces of each other, Marley's Ghost held up its hand, warning him to come no nearer. Scrooge stopped.

Not so much in obedience, as in surprise and fear: for on the raising of the hand, he became sensible of confused noises in the air; incoherent sounds of lamentation and regret; wailings inexpressibly sorrowful and self-accusatory. The spectre, after listening for a moment, joined in the mournful dirge; and floated out upon the bleak, dark night.

Scrooge followed to the window, desperate in his curiosity. He looked out.

The air was filled with phantoms, wandering hither and thither in restless haste, and moaning as they went. Every one of them wore chains like Marley's Ghost; some few (they might be guilty governments) were linked together; none were free. Many had been personally known to Scrooge in their lives. He had been quite familiar with one old ghost, in a white waistcoat, with a monstrous iron safe attached to its ankle, who cried

piteously at being unable to assist a wretched woman with an infant, whom it saw below, upon a doorstep. The misery with them all was, clearly, that they sought to interfere, for good, in human matters, and had lost the power forever.

Whether these creatures faded into mist, or mist enshrouded them, he could not tell. But they and their spirit voices faded together; and the night became as it had been when he walked home.

Scrooge closed the window, and examined the door by which the Ghost had entered. It was double-locked, as he had locked it with his own hands, and the bolts were undisturbed. He tried to say "Humbug!" but stopped at the first syllable. And being, from the emotion he had undergone, or the fatigues of the day, or his glimpse of the Invisible World, or the dull conversation of the Ghost, or the lateness of the hour, much in need of repose; went straight to bed, without undressing, and fell asleep upon the instant.

STAVE 2: THE FIRST OF THE THREE SPIRITS

When Scrooge awoke, it was so dark, that looking out of bed, he could scarcely distinguish the transparent window from the opaque walls of his chamber. He was endeavouring to pierce the darkness with his ferret eyes, when the chimes of a neighbouring church struck the four quarters. So he listened for the hour.

To his great astonishment the heavy bell went on from six to seven, and from seven to eight, and regularly up to twelve; then stopped. Twelve! It was past two when he went to bed. The clock was wrong. An icicle must have got into the works. Twelve!

He touched the spring of his repeater,[1] to correct this most preposterous clock. Its rapid little pulse beat twelve; and stopped.

"Why, it isn't possible," said Scrooge, "that I can have slept through a whole day and far into another night. It isn't possible that anything has happened to the sun, and this is twelve at noon!"

The idea being an alarming one, he scrambled out of bed, and groped his way to the window. He was obliged to rub the frost off with the sleeve of his dressing-gown before he could see anything; and could see very little then. All he could make out was, that it was still very foggy and extremely cold, and that there was no noise of people running to and fro, and making a great stir, as there unquestionably would have been if night had beaten off bright day, and taken possession of the world. This was a great relief, because "three days after sight of this First of Exchange[2] pay to Mr. Ebenezer Scrooge or his order," and so forth, would have become a mere United States' security[3] if there were no days to count by.

Scrooge went to bed again, and thought, and thought, and thought it over and over and over, and could make nothing of it. The more he thought, the more perplexed he was; and the more he endeavoured not to think, the more he thought. Marley's Ghost bothered him exceedingly. Every time he resolved

---

[1]   *repeater*   Watch.

[2]   *First of Exchange*   Original draft.

[3]   *United States' security*   Dickens is referring to the 1837 financial crisis, in which many American states defaulted on their foreign loans.

within himself, after mature inquiry, that it was all a dream, his mind flew back again, like a strong spring released, to its first position, and presented the same problem to be worked all through, "Was it a dream or not?"

Scrooge lay in this state until the chimes had gone three quarters more, when he remembered, on a sudden, that the Ghost had warned him of a visitation when the bell tolled one. He resolved to lie awake until the hour was past; and, considering that he could no more go to sleep than go to heaven, this was perhaps the wisest resolution in his power.

The quarter was so long, that he was more than once convinced he must have sunk into a doze unconsciously, and missed the clock. At length it broke upon his listening ear.

"Ding, dong!"

"A quarter past," said Scrooge, counting.

"Ding, dong!"

"Half past!" said Scrooge.

"Ding, dong!"

"A quarter to it," said Scrooge.

"Ding, dong!"

"The hour itself," said Scrooge, triumphantly, "and nothing else!"

He spoke before the hour bell sounded, which it now did with a deep, dull, hollow, melancholy ONE. Light flashed up in the room upon the instant, and the curtains of his bed were drawn.

The curtains of his bed were drawn aside, I tell you, by a hand. Not the curtains at his feet, nor the curtains at his back, but those to which his face was addressed. The curtains of his bed were drawn aside; and Scrooge, starting up into a half-recumbent attitude, found himself face to face with the unearthly visitor who drew them: as close to it as I am now to you, and I am standing in the spirit at your elbow.

It was a strange figure—like a child: yet not so like a child as like an old man, viewed through some supernatural medium, which gave him the appearance of having receded from the view, and being diminished to a child's proportions. Its hair, which hung about its neck and down its back, was white as if with age; and yet the face had not a wrinkle in it, and the tenderest bloom was on the skin. The arms were very long and muscular;

the hands the same, as if its hold were of uncommon strength. Its legs and feet, most delicately formed, were, like those upper members, bare. It wore a tunic of the purest white; and round its waist was bound a lustrous belt, the sheen of which was beautiful. It held a branch of fresh green holly in its hand; and, in singular contradiction of that wintry emblem, had its dress trimmed with summer flowers. But the strangest thing about it was, that from the crown of its head there sprung a bright clear jet of light, by which all this was visible; and which was doubtless the occasion of its using, in its duller moments, a great extinguisher for a cap, which it now held under its arm.

Even this, though, when Scrooge looked at it with increasing steadiness, was *not* its strangest quality. For as its belt sparkled and glittered now in one part and now in another, and what was light one instant, at another time was dark, so the figure itself fluctuated in its distinctness: being now a thing with one arm, now with one leg, now with twenty legs, now a pair of legs without a head, now a head without a body: of which dissolving parts, no outline would be visible in the dense gloom wherein they melted away. And in the very wonder of this, it would be itself again, distinct and clear as ever.

"Are you the Spirit, sir, whose coming was foretold to me?" asked Scrooge.

"I am!"

The voice was soft and gentle. Singularly low, as if instead of being so close beside him, it were at a distance.

"Who, and what are you?" Scrooge demanded.

"I am the Ghost of Christmas Past."

"Long past?" inquired Scrooge, observant of its dwarfish stature.

"No. Your past."

Perhaps, Scrooge could not have told anybody why, if anybody could have asked him; but he had a special desire to see the Spirit in his cap; and begged him to be covered.

"What!" exclaimed the Ghost, "would you so soon put out, with worldly hands, the light I give? Is it not enough that you are one of those whose passions made this cap, and force me through whole trains of years to wear it low upon my brow!"

Scrooge reverently disclaimed all intention to offend, or any knowledge of having wilfully "bonneted" the Spirit[1] at any period of his life. He then made bold to inquire what business brought him there.

"Your welfare!" said the Ghost.

Scrooge expressed himself much obliged, but could not help thinking that a night of unbroken rest would have been more conducive to that end. The Spirit must have heard him thinking, for it said immediately:

"Your reclamation, then. Take heed!"

It put out its strong hand as it spoke, and clasped him gently by the arm.

"Rise! and walk with me!"

It would have been in vain for Scrooge to plead that the weather and the hour were not adapted to pedestrian purposes; that bed was warm, and the thermometer a long way below freezing; that he was clad but lightly in his slippers, dressing-gown, and nightcap; and that he had a cold upon him at that time. The grasp, though gentle as a woman's hand, was not to be resisted. He rose: but finding that the Spirit made towards the window, clasped its robe in supplication.

"I am a mortal," Scrooge remonstrated, "and liable to fall."

"Bear but a touch of my hand *there*," said the Spirit, laying it upon his heart, "and you shall be upheld in more than this!"

As the words were spoken, they passed through the wall, and stood upon an open country road, with fields on either hand. The city had entirely vanished. Not a vestige of it was to be seen. The darkness and the mist had vanished with it, for it was a clear, cold, winter day, with snow upon the ground.

"Good heaven!" said Scrooge, clasping his hands together, as he looked about him. "I was bred in this place. I was a boy here!"

The Spirit gazed upon him mildly. Its gentle touch, though it had been light and instantaneous, appeared still present to the old man's sense of feeling. He was conscious of a thousand odours floating in the air, each one connected with a thousand thoughts, and hopes, and joys, and cares long, long, forgotten!

"Your lip is trembling," said the Ghost. "And what is that upon your cheek?"

---

[1] *"bonneted" the Spirit* Yanked a hat down over the Spirit's eyes.

Scrooge muttered, with an unusual catching in his voice, that it was a pimple; and begged the Ghost to lead him where he would.

"You recollect the way?" inquired the Spirit.

"Remember it!" cried Scrooge with fervour—"I could walk it blindfold."

"Strange to have forgotten it for so many years!" observed the Ghost. "Let us go on."

They walked along the road; Scrooge recognising every gate, and post, and tree; until a little market-town[1] appeared in the distance, with its bridge, its church, and winding river. Some shaggy ponies now were seen trotting towards them with boys upon their backs, who called to other boys in country gigs and carts, driven by farmers. All these boys were in great spirits, and shouted to each other, until the broad fields were so full of merry music, that the crisp air laughed to hear it.

"These are but shadows of the things that have been," said the Ghost. "They have no consciousness of us."

The jocund travellers came on; and as they came, Scrooge knew and named them every one. Why was he rejoiced beyond all bounds to see them! Why did his cold eye glisten, and his heart leap up as they went past! Why was he filled with gladness when he heard them give each other Merry Christmas, as they parted at cross-roads and bye-ways, for their several homes! What was merry Christmas to Scrooge? Out upon merry Christmas! What good had it ever done to him?

"The school is not quite deserted," said the Ghost. "A solitary child, neglected by his friends, is left there still."

Scrooge said he knew it. And he sobbed.

They left the high-road, by a well remembered lane, and soon approached a mansion of dull red brick, with a little weathercock-surmounted cupola, on the roof, and a bell hanging in it. It was a large house, but one of broken fortunes; for the spacious offices were little used, their walls were damp and mossy, their windows broken, and their gates decayed. Fowls clucked and strutted in the stables; and the coach-houses and sheds were overrun with grass. Nor was it more retentive of its

original spelling

ancient state, within; for entering the dreary hall, and glancing through the open doors of many rooms, they found them poorly furnished, cold, and vast.

original spelling

There was an earthy savour in the air, a chilly bareness in the place, which associated itself somehow with too much getting up by candle-light, and not too much to eat.

They went, the Ghost and Scrooge, across the hall, to a door at the back of the house. It opened before them, and disclosed a long, bare, melancholy room, made barer still by lines of plain deal forms[2] and desks. At one of these a lonely boy was reading near a feeble fire; and Scrooge sat down upon a form, and wept to see his poor forgotten self as he had used to be.

Not a latent echo in the house, not a squeak and scuffle from the mice behind the paneling, not a drip from the half-thawed water spout in the dull yard behind, not a sigh among the leafless boughs of one despondent poplar, not the idle swinging of an empty storehouse door, no, not a clicking in the fire, but fell upon the heart of Scrooge with softening influence, and gave a freer passage to his tears.

The Spirit touched him on the arm, and pointed to his younger self, intent upon his reading. Suddenly a man, in foreign garments: wonderfully real and distinct to look at: stood outside the window, with an axe stuck in his belt, and leading an ass laden with wood by the bridle.

"Why, it's Ali Baba!"[3] Scrooge exclaimed in ecstacy. "It's dear old honest Ali Baba! Yes, yes, I know! One Christmas time, when yonder solitary child was left here all alone, he *did* come, for the first time, just like that. Poor boy! And Valentine," said Scrooge, "and his wild brother, Orson;[4] there they go! And what's his name, who was put down in his drawers, asleep, at the Gate of Damascus; don't you see him! And the Sultan's groom turned upside-down by the genii; there he is upon his head! Serve him right. I'm glad of it. What business had

---

[1] *market-town* Victorian usage employed many more hyphens for compound formations than we do today. For a discussion of the English language in the Victorian period (both as reflected in this original spelling and punctuation section and elsewhere), see the general introduction to the Victorian era.

[2] *plain deal forms* Roughly hewn benches.

[3] *Ali Baba* Heroic character in one of the tales of *The Arabian Nights*.

[4] *Valentine … Orson* Protagonists in the folktale published in 1489 as *The Historye of the two Valyannte Brethren: Valentyne and Orson*.

he to be married to the princess!"[1]

To hear Scrooge expending all the earnestness of his nature on such subjects, in a most extraordinary voice between laughing and crying; and to see his heightened and excited face; would have been a surprise to his business friends in the city, indeed.

"There's the parrot!" cried Scrooge. "Green body and yellow tail, with a thing like a lettuce growing out of the top of his head; there he is! Poor Robin Crusoe, he called him, when he came home again after sailing round the island. 'Poor Robin Crusoe, where have you been, Robin Crusoe?' The man thought he was dreaming, but he wasn't. It was the Parrot, you know. There goes Friday,[2] running for his life to the little creek! Halloa! Hoop! Halloo!"

Then, with a rapidity of transition very foreign to his usual character, he said, in pity for his former self, "Poor boy!" and cried again.

"I wish," Scrooge muttered, putting his hand in his pocket, and looking about him, after drying his eyes with his cuff: "but it's too late now."

"What is the matter?" asked the Spirit.

"Nothing," said Scrooge. "Nothing. There was a boy singing a Christmas carol at my door last night. I should like to have given him something: that's all."

The Ghost smiled thoughtfully, and waved its hand, saying as it did so, "Let us see another Christmas!"

Scrooge's former self grew larger at the words, and the room became a little darker and more dirty. The panels shrunk, the windows cracked; fragments of plaster fell out of the ceiling, and the naked laths were shown instead; but how all this was brought about, Scrooge knew no more than you do. He only knew that it was quite correct; that everything had happened so; that there he was, alone again, when all the other boys had gone home for the jolly holidays.

He was not reading now, but walking up and down despairingly. Scrooge looked at the Ghost, and with a mournful shaking of his head, glanced anxiously towards the door.

It opened; and a little girl, much younger than the boy, came darting in, and putting her arms about his neck, and often kissing him, addressed him as her "Dear, dear brother."

"I have come to bring you home, dear brother!" said the child, clapping her tiny hands, and bending down to laugh. "To bring you home, home, home!"

"Home, little Fan?" returned the boy.

"Yes!" said the child, brimful of glee. "Home, for good and all. Home, forever and ever. Father is so much kinder than he used to be, that home's like heaven! He spoke so gently to me one dear night when I was going to bed, that I was not afraid to ask him once more if you might come home; and he said Yes, you should; and sent me in a coach to bring you. And you're to be a man!" said the child, opening her eyes, "and are never to come back here; but first, we're to be together all the Christmas long, and have the merriest time in all the world."

"You are quite a woman, little Fan!" exclaimed the boy.

She clapped her hands and laughed, and tried to touch his head; but being too little, laughed again, and stood on tiptoe to embrace him. Then she began to drag him, in her childish eagerness, towards the door; and he, nothing loth[3] to go, accompanied her.

A terrible voice in the hall cried, "Bring down Master Scrooge's box, there!" and in the hall appeared the schoolmaster himself, who glared on Master Scrooge with a ferocious condescension, and threw him into a dreadful state of mind by shaking hands with him. He then conveyed him and his sister into the veriest old well of a shivering best-parlour that ever was seen, where the maps upon the wall, and the celestial and terrestrial globes in the windows, were waxy with cold. Here he produced a decanter of curiously light wine, and a block of curiously heavy cake, and administered instalments of those dainties to the young people, at the same time, sending out a meagre servant to offer a glass of "something" to the postboy, who answered that he thanked the gentleman, but if it was the same tap as he had tasted before, he had rather not. Master Scrooge's trunk being by this time tied on to the top of the chaise, the children bade the schoolmaster goodbye right willingly, and getting into it, drove gaily down the garden-sweep,[4] the quick wheels dashing the hoar frost and snow from

1   *what's his name ... princess* Characters in *The Arabian Nights* tale "Noureddin Ali of Cairo and his Son Bedreddin Hassan."

2   *parrot ... Friday* Characters in Daniel Defoe's *The Life and Strange and Surprising Adventures of Robinson Crusoe* (1719).

3   *nothing loth* Not at all reluctant.

4   *garden-sweep* Carriage driveway.

off the dark leaves of the evergreens like spray.

"Always a delicate creature, whom a breath might have withered," said the Ghost. "But she had a large heart!"

"So she had," cried Scrooge. "You're right. I'll not gainsay it, Spirit. God forbid!"

"She died a woman," said the Ghost, "and had, as I think, children."

"One child," Scrooge returned.

"True," said the Ghost. "Your nephew!"

Scrooge seemed uneasy in his mind, and answered briefly, "Yes."

Although they had but that moment left the school behind them, they were now in the busy thoroughfares of a city, where shadowy passengers passed and repassed; where shadowy carts and coaches battled for the way, and all the strife and tumult of a real city were. It was made plain enough, by the dressing of the shops, that here too it was Christmas time again; but it was evening, and the streets were lighted up.

The Ghost stopped at a certain warehouse door, and asked Scrooge if he knew it.

"Know it!" said Scrooge. "Was I apprenticed here?"

They went in. At sight of an old gentleman in a Welch wig,[1] sitting behind such a high desk, that if he had been two inches taller he must have knocked his head against the ceiling, Scrooge cried in great excitement:

"Why, it's old Fezziwig! Bless his heart; it's Fezziwig alive again!"

Old Fezziwig laid down his pen, and looked up at the clock, which pointed to the hour of seven. He rubbed his hands; adjusted his capacious waistcoat; laughed all over himself, from his shoes to his organ of benevolence;[2] and called out in a comfortable, oily, rich, fat, jovial voice:

"Yo ho, there! Ebenezer! Dick!"

Scrooge's former self, now grown a young man, came briskly in, accompanied by his fellow-'prentice.

"Dick Wilkins, to be sure!" said Scrooge to the Ghost. "Bless me, yes. There he is. He was very much attached to me, was Dick. Poor Dick! Dear, dear!"

"Yo ho, my boys!" said Fezziwig. "No more work tonight. Christmas Eve, Dick. Christmas, Ebenezer! Let's have the shutters up," cried old Fezziwig, with a sharp clap of his hands, "before a man can say, Jack Robinson!"[3]

You wouldn't believe how those two fellows went at it! They charged into the street with the shutters—one, two, three—had 'em up in their places—four, five, six—barred 'em and pinned 'em—seven, eight, nine—and came back before you could have got to twelve, panting like racehorses.

"Hilli-ho!" cried old Fezziwig, skipping down from the high desk, with wonderful agility. "Clear away, my lads, and let's have lots of room here! Hilli-ho, Dick! Chirrup, Ebenezer!"

Clear away! There was nothing they wouldn't have cleared away, or couldn't have cleared away, with old Fezziwig looking on. It was done in a minute. Every movable was packed off, as if it were dismissed from public life forevermore; the floor was swept and watered, the lamps were trimmed, fuel was heaped upon the fire; and the warehouse was as snug, and warm, and dry, and bright a ballroom, as you would desire to see upon a winter's night.

In came a fiddler with a music-book, and went up to the lofty desk, and made an orchestra of it, and tuned like fifty stomach-aches. In came Mrs. Fezziwig, one vast substantial smile. In came the three Miss Fezziwigs, beaming and loveable. In came the six young followers[4] whose hearts they broke. In came all the young men and women employed in the business. In came the house-maid, with her cousin, the baker. In came the cook, with her brother's particular friend, the milkman. In came the boy from over the way, who was suspected of not having board enough from his master; trying to hide himself behind the girl from next door but one, who was proved to have had her ears pulled by her mistress. In they all came, one after another; some shyly, some boldly, some gracefully, some awkwardly, some pushing, some pulling; in they all came, anyhow and everyhow. Away they all went, twenty couple at once, hands half round and back again the other way; down the middle and up again; round and round in various stages of

---

[1] *Welch wig* Woolen cap.

[2] *organ of benevolence* I.e., head. According to phrenology, the teachings of which proposed that character traits can be linked to various shapes of and specific areas on the skull, benevolence stemmed from an organ located at the top of the head.

[3] *before … Robinson* Before you know it.

[4] *followers* Admirers.

affectionate grouping; old top couple always turning up in the wrong place; new top couple starting off again, as soon as they got there; all top couples at last, and not a bottom one to help them. When this result was brought about, old Fezziwig, clapping his hands to stop the dance, cried out, "Well done!" and the fiddler plunged his hot face into a pot of porter, especially provided for that purpose. But scorning rest upon his reappearance, he instantly began again, though there were no dancers yet, as if the other fiddler had been carried home, exhausted, on a shutter; and he were a brand-new man resolved to beat him out of sight, or perish.

There were more dances, and there were forfeits, and more dances, and there was cake, and there was negus,[1] and there was a great piece of cold roast, and there was a great piece of cold boiled, and there were mince-pies, and plenty of beer. But the great effect of the evening came after the roast and boiled, when the fiddler (an artful dog, mind! The sort of man who knew his business better than you or I could have told it him!) struck up "Sir Roger de Coverley."[2] Then old Fezziwig stood out to dance with Mrs. Fezziwig. Top couple too; with a good stiff piece of work cut out for them; three or four and twenty pair of partners; people who were not to be trifled with; people who *would* dance, and had no notion of walking.

But if they had been twice as many: ah, four times: old Fezziwig would have been a match for them, and so would Mrs. Fezziwig. As to *her*, she was worthy to be his partner in every sense of the term. If that's not high praise, tell me higher, and I'll use it. A positive light appeared to issue from Fezziwig's calves. They shone in every part of the dance like moons. You couldn't have predicted, at any given time, what would become of 'em next. And when old Fezziwig and Mrs. Fezziwig had gone all through the dance; advance and retire, hold hands with your partner; bow and curtsey; corkscrew; thread-the-needle, and back again to your place; Fezziwig "cut"[3]—cut so deftly, that he appeared to wink with his legs, and came upon his feet again without a stagger.

When the clock struck eleven, this domestic ball broke up. Mr. and Mrs. Fezziwig took their stations, one on either side the door, and shaking hands with every person individually as he or she went out, wished him or her a merry Christmas. When everybody had retired but the two 'prentices, they did the same to them; and thus the cheerful voices died away, and the lads were left to their beds; which were under a counter in the back shop.

During the whole of this time, Scrooge had acted like a man out of his wits. His heart and soul were in the scene, and with his former self. He corroborated everything, remembered everything, enjoyed everything, and underwent the strangest agitation. It was not until now, when the bright faces of his former self and Dick were turned from them, that he remembered the Ghost, and became conscious that it was looking full upon him, while the light upon its head burnt very clear.

"A small matter," said the Ghost, "to make these silly folks so full of gratitude."

"Small!" echoed Scrooge.

The Spirit signed to him to listen to the two apprentices, who were pouring out their hearts in praise of Fezziwig: and when he had done so, said,

"Why! Is it not? He has spent but a few pounds of your mortal money: three or four, perhaps. Is that so much that he deserves this praise?"

"It isn't that," said Scrooge, heated by the remark, and speaking unconsciously like his former, not his latter, self. "It isn't that, Spirit. He has the power to render us happy or unhappy; to make our service light or burdensome, a pleasure or a toil. Say that his power lies in words and looks; in things so slight and insignificant that it is impossible to add and count 'em up: what then? The happiness he gives, is quite as great as if it cost a fortune."

He felt the Spirit's glance, and stopped. "What is the matter?" asked the Ghost.

"Nothing particular," said Scrooge.

"Something, I think?" the Ghost insisted.

"No," said Scrooge, "No. I should like to be able to say a word or two to my clerk just now! That's all."

His former self turned down the lamps as he gave utterance to the wish; and Scrooge and the Ghost again stood side by side in the open air.

---

[1]   *negus* Drink made from sweetened wine, lemon, and spices.

[2]   *"Sir Roger de Coverley"* English country dance.

[3]   *"cut"* Leapt in the air and moved his feet back and forth rapidly before descending.

"My time grows short," observed the Spirit. "Quick!"

This was not addressed to Scrooge, or to any one whom he could see, but it produced an immediate effect. For again Scrooge saw himself. He was older now; a man in the prime of life. His face had not the harsh and rigid lines of later years, but it had begun to wear the signs of care and avarice. There was an eager, greedy, restless motion in the eye, which showed the passion that had taken root, and where the shadow of the growing tree would fall.

He was not alone, but sat by the side of a fair young girl in a mourning-dress: in whose eyes there were tears, which sparkled in the light that shone out of the Ghost of Christmas Past.

"It matters little," she said, softly. "To you, very little. Another idol has displaced me; and if it can cheer and comfort you in time to come, as I would have tried to do, I have no just cause to grieve."

"What idol has displaced you?" he rejoined.

"A golden one."

"This is the seaweeded dealing of the world!" he said. "There is nothing on which it is so hard as poverty; and there is nothing it professes to condemn with such severity as the pursuit of wealth!"

"You fear the world too much," she answered, gently. "All your other hopes have merged into the hope of being beyond the chance of its sordid reproach. I have seen your nobler aspirations fall off one by one, until the master passion, gain, engrosses you. Have I not?"

"What then?" he retorted. "Even if I have grown so much wiser, what then? I am not changed towards you."

She shook her head.

"Am I?"

"Our contract is an old one. It was made when we were both poor and content to be so, until, in good season, we could improve our worldly fortune by our patient industry. You are changed. When it was made, you were another man."

"I was a boy," he said impatiently.

"Your own feeling tells you that you were not what you are," she returned. "I am. That which promised happiness when we were one in heart, is fraught with misery now that we are two. How often and how keenly I have thought of this, I will not say. It is enough that I have thought of it, and can release you."

"Have I ever sought release?"

"In words. No. Never."

"In what, then?"

"In a changed nature; in an altered spirit; in another atmosphere of life; another hope as its great end. In everything that made my love of any worth or value in your sight. If this had never been between us," said the girl, looking mildly, but with steadiness, upon him; "tell me, would you seek me out and try to win me now? Ah, no!"

He seemed to yield to the justice of this supposition, in spite of himself. But he said, with a struggle, "You think not."

"I would gladly think otherwise if I could," she answered, "Heaven knows! When I have learned a truth like this, I know how strong and irresistible it must be. But if you were free today, tomorrow, yesterday, can even I believe that you would choose a dowerless girl—you who, in your very confidence with her, weigh everything by gain: or, choosing her, if for a moment you were false enough to your one guiding principle to do so, do I not know that your repentance and regret would surely follow? I do; and I release you. With a full heart, for the love of him you once were."

He was about to speak; but with her head turned from him, she resumed.

"You may—the memory of what is past half makes me hope you will—have pain in this. A very, very brief time, and you will dismiss the recollection of it, gladly, as an unprofitable dream, from which it happened well that you awoke. May you be happy in the life you have chosen!"

She left him, and they parted.

"Spirit!" said Scrooge, "show me no more! Conduct me home. Why do you delight to torture me?"

"One shadow more!" exclaimed the Ghost.

"No more!" cried Scrooge. "No more. I don't wish to see it. Show me no more!"

But the relentless Ghost pinioned him in both his arms, and forced him to observe what happened next.

They were in another scene and place: a room, not very large or handsome, but full of comfort. Near to the winter fire sat a beautiful young girl, so like the last that

Scrooge believed it was the same, until he saw her, now a comely matron, sitting opposite her daughter. The noise in this room was perfectly tumultuous, for there were more children there, than Scrooge in his agitated state of mind could count; and, unlike the celebrated herd in the poem, they were not forty children conducting themselves like one,[1] but every child was conducting itself like forty. The consequences were uproarious beyond belief, but no one seemed to care; on the contrary, the mother and daughter laughed heartily, and enjoyed it very much; and the latter, soon beginning to mingle in the sports, got pillaged by the young brigands most ruthlessly. What would I not have given to be one of them! Though I never could have been so rude, no, no! I wouldn't for the wealth of all the world have crushed that braided hair, and torn it down; and for the precious little shoe, I wouldn't have plucked it off, God bless my soul! to save my life. As to measuring her waist in sport, as they did, bold young brood, I couldn't have done it; I should have expected my arm to have grown round it for a punishment, and never come straight again. And yet I should have dearly liked, I own, to have touched her lips; to have questioned her, that she might have opened them; to have looked upon the lashes of her downcast eyes, and never raised a blush; to have let loose waves of hair, an inch of which would be a keepsake beyond price: in short, I should have liked, I do confess, to have had the lightest licence of a child, and yet been man enough to know its value.

But now a knocking at the door was heard, and such a rush immediately ensued that she with laughing face and plundered dress was borne towards it the centre of a flushed and boisterous group, just in time to greet the father, who came home attended by a man laden with Christmas toys and presents. Then the shouting and the struggling, and the onslaught that was made on the defenceless porter! The scaling him, with chairs for ladders, to dive into his pockets, despoil him of brown paper parcels, hold on tight by his cravat, hug him round the neck, pommel his back, and kick his legs in irrepressible affection! The shouts of wonder and delight with which the development of every package was received! The terrible announcement that the baby had been taken in the act of putting a doll's frying pan into his mouth, and was more than suspected of having swallowed a fictitious turkey, glued on a wooden platter! The immense relief of finding this a false alarm! The joy, and gratitude, and ecstacy! They are all indescribable alike. It is enough that by degrees the children and their emotions got out of the parlour and by one stair at a time, up to the top of the house; where they went to bed, and so subsided.

And now Scrooge looked on more attentively than ever, when the master of the house, having his daughter leaning fondly on him, sat down with her and her mother at his own fireside; and when he thought that such another creature, quite as graceful and as full of promise, might have called him father, and been a springtime in the haggard winter of his life, his sight grew very dim indeed.

"Belle," said the husband, turning to his wife with a smile, "I saw an old friend of yours this afternoon."

"Who was it?"

"Guess!"

"How can I? Tut, don't I know," she added in the same breath, laughing as he laughed. "Mr. Scrooge."

"Mr. Scrooge it was. I passed his office window; and as it was not shut up, and he had a candle inside, I could scarcely help seeing him. His partner lies upon the point of death, I hear; and there he sat alone. Quite alone in the world, I do believe."

"Spirit!" said Scrooge in a broken voice, "remove me from this place."

"I told you these were shadows of the things that have been," said the Ghost. "That they are what they are; do not blame me!"

"Remove me!" Scrooge exclaimed. "I cannot bear it!"

He turned upon the Ghost, and seeing that it looked upon him with a face, in which in some strange way there were fragments of all the faces it had shown him, wrestled with it.

"Leave me! Take me back. Haunt me no longer!"

In the struggle, if that can be called a struggle in which the Ghost with no visible resistance on its own part was undisturbed by any effort of its adversary, Scrooge observed that its light was burning high and bright; and dimly connecting that with its influence

---

[1]   *celebrated … like one*   Reference to William Wordsworth's poem "Written in March": "The cattle are grazing, / Their heads never raising; / There are forty feeding like one!"

over him, he seized the extinguisher-cap, and by a sudden action pressed it down upon its head.

The Spirit dropped beneath it, so that the extinguisher covered its whole form; but though Scrooge pressed it down with all his force, he could not hide the light, which streamed from under it, in an unbroken flood upon the ground.

He was conscious of being exhausted, and overcome by an irresistible drowsiness; and, further, of being in his own bedroom. He gave the cap a parting squeeze, in which his hand relaxed; and had barely time to reel to bed, before he sank into a heavy sleep.

STAVE 3: THE SECOND OF THE THREE SPIRITS

Awaking in the middle of a prodigiously tough snore, and sitting up in bed to get his thoughts together, Scrooge had no occasion to be told that the bell was again upon the stroke of one. He felt that he was restored to consciousness in the right nick of time, for the especial purpose of holding a conference with the second messenger despatched to him through Jacob

Marley's intervention. But finding that he turned uncomfortably cold when he began to wonder which of his curtains this new spectre would draw back, he put them every one aside with his own hands; and lying down again, established a sharp lookout all round the bed. For he wished to challenge the Spirit on the moment of its appearance, and did not wish to be taken by surprise and made nervous.

Gentlemen of the free-and-easy sort, who plume themselves on being acquainted with a move or two, and being usually equal to the time of day, express the wide range of their capacity for adventure by observing that they are good for anything from pitch-and-toss[1] to manslaughter; between which opposite extremes, no doubt, there lies a tolerably wide and comprehensive range of subjects. Without venturing for Scrooge quite as hardily as this, I don't mind calling on you to believe that he was ready for a good broad field of strange appearances, and that nothing between a baby and a rhinoceros would have astonished him very much.

Now, being prepared for almost anything, he was not by any means prepared for nothing; and, consequently, when the bell struck one, and no shape appeared, he was taken with a violent fit of trembling. Five minutes, ten minutes, a quarter of an hour went by, yet nothing came. All this time, he lay upon his bed, the very core and centre of a blaze of ruddy light, which streamed upon it when the clock proclaimed the hour; and which being only light, was more alarming than a dozen ghosts, as he was powerless to make out what it meant, or would be at; and was sometimes apprehensive that he might be at that very moment an interesting case of spontaneous combustion,[2] without having the consolation of knowing it. At last, however, he began to think—as you or I would have thought at first; for it is

---

1   *pitch-and-toss* Game of heads and tails played with coins.

2   *spontaneous combustion* In his preface to *Bleak House*, Dickens defended the belief that, if sufficiently corrupted, the human body can spontaneously take fire: "The possibility of what is called spontaneous combustion has been denied ... and my good friend Mr. Lewes ... published some ingenious letters to me at the time when that event was chronicled, arguing that spontaneous combustion could not possibly be. I have no need to observe that I do not wilfully or negligently mislead my readers and that before I wrote that description I took pains to investigate the subject. There are about thirty cases on record."

always the person not in the predicament who knows what ought to have been done in it, and would unquestionably have done it too—at last, I say, he began to think that the source and secret of this ghostly light might be in the adjoining room: from whence, on further tracing it, it seemed to shine. This idea taking full possession of his mind, he got up softly and shuffled in his slippers to the door.

The moment Scrooge's hand was on the lock, a strange voice called him by his name, and bade him enter. He obeyed.

It was his own room. There was no doubt about that. But it had undergone a surprising transformation. The walls and ceiling were so hung with living green, that it looked a perfect grove, from every part of which, bright gleaming berries glistened. The crisp leaves of holly, mistletoe, and ivy reflected back the light, as if so many little mirrors had been scattered there; and such a mighty blaze went roaring up the chimney, as that dull petrifaction of a hearth had never known in Scrooge's time, or Marley's, or for many and many a winter season gone. Heaped up upon the floor, to form a kind of throne, were turkeys, geese, game, poultry, brawn, great joints of meat, sucking pigs, long wreaths of sausages, mince-pies, plum-puddings, barrels of oysters, red-hot chestnuts, cherry-cheeked apples, juicy oranges, luscious pears, immense twelfth-cakes,[1] and seething bowls of punch, that made the chamber dim with their delicious steam. In easy state upon this couch, there sat a jolly giant, glorious to see; who bore a glowing torch, in shape not unlike Plenty's horn, and held it up, high up, to shed its light on Scrooge, as he came peeping round the door.

"Come in!" exclaimed the Ghost. "Come in! and know me better, man!"

Scrooge entered timidly, and hung his head before this Spirit. He was not the dogged Scrooge he had been; and though its eyes were clear and kind, he did not like to meet them.

"I am the Ghost of Christmas Present," said the Spirit. "Look upon me!"

Scrooge reverently did so. It was clothed in one simple deep green robe, or mantle, bordered with white fur. This garment hung so loosely on the figure, that its capacious breast was bare, as if disdaining to be warded or concealed by any artifice. Its feet, observable beneath the ample folds of the garment, were also bare; and on its head it wore no other covering than a holly wreath set here and there with shining icicles. Its dark brown curls were long and free: free as its genial face, its sparkling eye, its open hand, its cheery voice, its unconstrained demeanour, and its joyful air. Girded round its middle was an antique scabbard; but no sword was in it, and the ancient sheath was eaten up with rust.

"You have never seen the like of me before!" exclaimed the Spirit.

"Never," Scrooge made answer to it.

"Have never walked forth with the younger members of my family; meaning (for I am very young) my elder brothers born in these later years?" pursued the Phantom.

---

[1]   *twelfth-cakes*   Rich cakes served during the festival of Twelfth Night, twelve days after Christmas.

"I don't think I have," said Scrooge. "I am afraid I have not. Have you had many brothers, Spirit?"

"More than eighteen hundred," said the Ghost.

"A tremendous family to provide for!" muttered Scrooge.

The Ghost of Christmas Present rose.

"Spirit," said Scrooge submissively, "conduct me where you will. I went forth last night on compulsion, and I learnt a lesson which is working now. Tonight, if you have aught to teach me, let me profit by it."

"Touch my robe!"

Scrooge did as he was told, and held it fast. Holly, mistletoe, red berries, ivy, turkeys, geese, game, poultry, brawn, meat, pigs, sausages, oysters, pies, puddings, fruit, and punch, all vanished instantly. So did the room, the fire, the ruddy glow, the hour of night, and they stood in the city streets on Christmas morning, where (for the weather was severe) the people made a rough, but brisk and not unpleasant kind of music, in scraping the snow from the pavement in front of their dwellings, and from the tops of their houses: whence it was mad delight to the boys to see it come plumping down into the road below, and splitting into artificial little snowstorms.

The house fronts looked black enough, and the windows blacker, contrasting with the smooth white sheet of snow upon the roofs, and with the dirtier snow upon the ground; which last deposit had been ploughed up in deep furrows by the heavy wheels of carts and wagons; furrows that crossed and re-crossed each other hundreds of times where the great streets branched off, and made intricate channels, hard to trace, in the thick yellow mud and icy water. The sky was gloomy, and the shortest streets were choked up with a dingy mist, half thawed half frozen, whose heavier particles descended in a shower of sooty atoms, as if all the chimneys in Great Britain had, by one consent, caught fire, and were blazing away to their dear hearts' content. There was nothing very cheerful in the climate or the town, and yet was there an air of cheerfulness abroad that the clearest summer air and brightest summer sun might have endeavoured to diffuse in vain.

For the people who were shovelling away on the house-tops were jovial and full of glee; calling out to one another from the parapets, and now and then exchang-

ing a facetious snowball—better-natured missile far than many a wordy jest—laughing heartily if it went right, and not less heartily if it went wrong. The poulterers' shops were still half open, and the fruiterers' were radiant in their glory. There were great, round, pot-bellied baskets of chestnuts, shaped like the waistcoats of jolly old gentlemen, lolling at the doors, and tumbling out into the street in their apoplectic opulence. There were ruddy, brown-faced, broad-girthed Spanish onions, shining in the fatness of their growth like Spanish friars; and winking from their shelves in wanton slyness at the girls as they went by, and glanced demurely at the hung-up mistletoe. There were pears and apples, clustered high in blooming pyramids; there were bunches of grapes, made, in the shopkeepers' benevolence, to dangle from conspicuous hooks, that people's mouths might water gratis as they passed; there were piles of filberts, mossy and brown, recalling, in their fragrance, ancient walks among the woods, and pleasant shufflings ankle deep through withered leaves; there were Norfolk biffins,[1] squab and swarthy, setting off the yellow of the oranges and lemons, and, in the great compactness of their juicy persons, urgently entreating and beseeching to be carried home in paper bags and eaten after dinner. The very gold and silver fish, set forth among these choice fruits in a bowl, though members of a dull and stagnant-blooded race, appeared to know that there was something going on; and, to a fish, went gasping round and round their little world in slow and passionless excitement.

The grocers'! oh the grocers'! nearly closed, with perhaps two shutters down, or one; but through those gaps such glimpses! It was not alone that the scales descending on the counter made a merry sound, or that the twine and roller parted company so briskly, or that the canisters were rattled up and down like juggling tricks, or even that the blended scents of tea and coffee were so grateful to the nose, or even that the raisins were so plentiful and rare, the almonds so extremely white, the sticks of cinnamon so long and straight, the other spices so delicious, the candied fruits so caked and spotted with molten sugar as to make the coldest lookers-on feel faint and subsequently bilious. Nor was it that the figs were moist and pulpy, or that the French

---

[1] *Norfolk biffins* Apples.

plums blushed in modest tartness from their highly-decorated boxes, or that everything was good to eat and in its Christmas dress: but the customers were all so hurried and so eager in the hopeful promise of the day, that they tumbled up against each other at the door, clashing their wicker baskets wildly, and left their purchases upon the counter, and came running back to fetch them, and committed hundreds of the like mistakes in the best humour possible; while the grocer and his people were so frank and fresh that the polished hearts with which they fastened their aprons behind might have been their own, worn outside for general inspection, and for Christmas daws to peck at[1] if they chose.

But soon the steeples called good people all, to church and chapel, and away they came, flocking through the streets in their best clothes, and with their gayest faces. And at the same time there emerged from scores of by-streets, lanes, and nameless turnings, innumerable people, carrying their dinners to the bakers' shops.[2] The sight of these poor revellers appeared to interest the Spirit very much, for he stood with Scrooge beside him in a baker's doorway, and taking off the covers as their bearers passed, sprinkled incense on their dinners from his torch. And it was a very uncommon kind of torch, for once or twice when there were angry words between some dinner-carriers who had jostled with each other, he shed a few drops of water on them from it, and their good humour was restored directly. For they said, it was a shame to quarrel upon Christmas Day. And so it was! God love it, so it was!

In time the bells ceased, and the bakers' were shut up; and yet there was a genial shadowing forth of all these dinners and the progress of their cooking, in the thawed blotch of wet above each baker's oven; where the pavement smoked as if its stones were cooking too.

"Is there a peculiar flavour in what you sprinkle from your torch?" asked Scrooge.

"There is. My own."

"Would it apply to any kind of dinner on this day?" asked Scrooge.

"To any kindly given. To a poor one most."

"Why to a poor one most?" asked Scrooge.

"Because it needs it most."

"Spirit," said Scrooge, after a moment's thought, "I wonder you, of all the beings in the many worlds about us, should desire to cramp these people's opportunities of innocent enjoyment."

"I!" cried the Spirit.

"You would deprive them of their means of dining every seventh day, often the only day on which they can be said to dine at all," said Scrooge. "Wouldn't you?"

"I!" cried the Spirit.

"You seek to close these places on the seventh day?"[3] said Scrooge. "And it comes to the same thing."

"_I_ seek!" exclaimed the Spirit.

"Forgive me if I am wrong. It has been done in your name, or at least in that of your family," said Scrooge.

"There are some upon this earth of yours," returned the Spirit, "who lay claim to know us, and who do their deeds of passion, pride, ill will, hatred, envy, bigotry, and selfishness in our name; who are as strange to us and all our kith and kin, as if they had never lived. Remember that, and charge their doings on themselves, not us."

Scrooge promised that he would; and they went on, invisible, as they had been before, into the suburbs of the town. It was a remarkable quality of the Ghost (which Scrooge had observed at the baker's) that notwithstanding his gigantic size, he could accommodate himself to any place with ease; and that he stood beneath a low roof quite as gracefully and like a supernatural creature, as it was possible he could have done in any lofty hall.

---

[1]   _polished hearts ... peck at_   Cf. Shakespeare's _Othello_ 1.1.65–66: "I will wear my heart upon my sleeve / For daws to peck at: I am not what I am."

[2]   _carrying ... bakers' shops_   On Sundays and holidays bakers could use their ovens and could charge for cooking their customers' dinners, but they were forbidden to bake bread on those days.

[3]   _You seek ... seventh day_   Writing under the pseudonym "Timothy Sparks," Dickens wrote a pamphlet called _Sunday Under Three Heads_ in fervent opposition to moral reforms proposed by Evangelicals headed by Sir Andrew Agnew. Agnew recommended to Parliament a "Sunday Observance Bill," which would have limited people's freedom to partake in leisure activities and to purchase bread on Sundays. Dickens wrote: "[I]t is by no means the worst characteristic of this bill, that it is a bill of blunders: it is, from beginning to end, a piece of deliberate cruelty, and crafty injustice. If the rich composed the whole population of this country, not a single comfort of one single man would be affected by it. It is directed exclusively, and without the exception of a solitary instance, against the amusements and recreations of the poor."

And perhaps it was the pleasure the good Spirit had in showing off this power of his, or else it was his own kind, generous, hearty nature, and his sympathy with all poor men, that led him straight to Scrooge's clerk's; for there he went, and took Scrooge with him, holding to his robe; and on the threshold of the door the Spirit smiled, and stopped to bless Bob Cratchit's dwelling with the sprinklings of his torch. Think of that! Bob had but fifteen "Bob"[1] a week himself; he pocketed on Saturdays but fifteen copies of his Christian name; and yet the Ghost of Christmas Present blessed his four-roomed house!

Then up rose Mrs. Cratchit, Cratchit's wife, dressed out but poorly in a twice-turned gown, but brave in ribbons, which are cheap and make a goodly show for sixpence; and she laid the cloth, assisted by Belinda Cratchit, second of her daughters, also brave in ribbons; while Master Peter Cratchit plunged a fork into the saucepan of potatoes, and getting the corners of his monstrous shirt collar (Bob's private property, conferred upon his son and heir in honour of the day) into his mouth, rejoiced to find himself so gallantly attired, and yearned to show his linen in the fashionable parks. And now two smaller Cratchits, boy and girl, came tearing in, screaming that outside the baker's they had smelt the goose, and known it for their own; and basking in luxurious thoughts of sage and onion, these young Cratchits danced about the table, and exalted Master Peter Cratchit to the skies, while he (not proud, although his collars nearly choked him) blew the fire, until the slow potatoes, bubbling up, knocked loudly at the saucepan lid to be let out and peeled.

"What has ever got your precious father then," said Mrs. Cratchit. "And your brother, Tiny Tim; and Martha warn't as late last Christmas Day by half an hour!"

"Here's Martha, mother!" said a girl, appearing as she spoke.

"Here's Martha, mother!" cried the two young Cratchits. "Hurrah! There's *such* a goose, Martha!"

"Why, bless your heart alive, my dear, how late you are!" said Mrs. Cratchit, kissing her a dozen times, and taking off her shawl and bonnet for her, with officious zeal.

"We'd a deal of work to finish up last night," replied the girl, "and had to clear away this morning, mother!"

"Well! Never mind so long as you are come," said Mrs. Cratchit. "Sit ye down before the fire, my dear, and have a warm, Lord bless ye!"

"No no! There's father coming," cried the two young Cratchits, who were everywhere at once. "Hide Martha, hide!"

So Martha hid herself, and in came little Bob, the father, with at least three feet of comforter exclusive of the fringe, hanging down before him; and his threadbare clothes darned up and brushed, to look seasonable; and Tiny Tim upon his shoulder. Alas for Tiny Tim, he bore a little crutch, and had his limbs supported by an iron frame!

"Why, where's our Martha?" cried Bob Cratchit looking round.

"Not coming," said Mrs. Cratchit.

"Not coming!" said Bob, with a sudden declension in his high spirits; for he had been Tim's blood horse[2] all the way from church, and had come home rampant. "Not coming upon Christmas Day!"

Martha didn't like to see him disappointed, if it were only in joke; so she came out prematurely from behind the closet door, and ran into his arms, while the two young Cratchits hustled Tiny Tim, and bore him off into the wash-house, that he might hear the pudding singing in the copper.[3]

"And how did little Tim behave?" asked Mrs. Cratchit, when she had rallied Bob on his credulity and Bob had hugged his daughter to his heart's content.

"As good as gold," said Bob, "and better. Somehow he gets thoughtful sitting by himself so much, and thinks the strangest things you ever heard. He told me, coming home, that he hoped the people saw him in the church, because he was a cripple, and it might be pleasant to them to remember upon Christmas Day, who made lame beggars walk and blind men see."

Bob's voice was tremulous when he told them this, and trembled more when he said that Tiny Tim was growing strong and hearty.

His active little crutch was heard upon the floor, and back came Tiny Tim before another word was spoken,

---

1 "*Bob*" Shillings.

2 *blood horse* Thoroughbred.

3 *copper* Washing or cooking vessel.

escorted by his brother and sister to his stool beside the fire; and while Bob, turning up his cuffs—as if, poor fellow, they were capable of being made more shabby—compounded some hot mixture in a jug with gin and lemons, and stirred it round and round and put it on the hob to simmer; Master Peter and the two ubiquitous young Cratchits went to fetch the goose, with which they soon returned in high procession.

Such a bustle ensued that you might have thought a goose the rarest of all birds; a feathered phenomenon, to which a black swan was a matter of course: and in truth it was something very like it in that house. Mrs. Cratchit made the gravy (ready beforehand in a little saucepan) hissing hot; Master Peter mashed the potatoes with incredible vigour; Miss Belinda sweetened up the applesauce; Martha dusted the hot plates; Bob took Tiny Tim beside him in a tiny corner at the table; the two young Cratchits set chairs for everybody, not forgetting themselves, and mounting guard upon their posts, crammed spoons into their mouths, lest they should shriek for goose before their turn came to be helped. At last the dishes were set on, and grace was said. It was succeeded by a breathless pause, as Mrs. Cratchit, looking slowly all along the carving knife, prepared to plunge it in the breast; but when she did, and when the long expected gush of stuffing issued forth, one murmur of delight arose all round the board, and even Tiny Tim, excited by the two young Cratchits, beat on the table with the handle of his knife, and feebly cried Hurrah!

There never was such a goose. Bob said he didn't believe there ever was such a goose cooked. Its tenderness and flavour, size and cheapness, were the themes of universal admiration. Eked out by the applesauce and mashed potatoes, it was a sufficient dinner for the whole family; indeed, as Mrs. Cratchit said with great delight (surveying one small atom of a bone upon the dish), they hadn't ate it all at last! Yet everyone had had enough, and the youngest Cratchits in particular, were steeped in sage and onion to the eyebrows! But now, the plates being changed by Miss Belinda, Mrs. Cratchit left the room alone—too nervous to bear witnesses—to take the pudding up, and bring it in.

Suppose it should not be done enough! Suppose it should break in turning out! Suppose somebody should have got over the wall of the back-yard, and stolen it, while they were merry with the goose: a supposition at which the two young Cratchits became livid! All sorts of horrors were supposed.

Hallo! A great deal of steam! The pudding was out of the copper. A smell like a washing day! That was the cloth. A smell like an eating house, and a pastry cook's next door to each other, with a laundress's next door to that! That was the pudding. In half a minute Mrs. Cratchit entered, flushed, but smiling proudly, with the pudding, like a speckled cannonball, so hard and firm, blazing in half of half-a-quartern[1] of ignited brandy, and bedight[2] with Christmas holly stuck into the top.

Oh, a wonderful pudding! Bob Cratchit said, and calmly too, that he regarded it as the greatest success achieved by Mrs. Cratchit since their marriage. Mrs. Cratchit said that now the weight was off her mind, she would confess she had had her doubts about the quantity of flour. Everybody had something to say about it, but nobody said or thought it was at all a small pudding for a large family. It would have been flat heresy to do so. Any Cratchit would have blushed to hint at such a thing.

At last the dinner was all done, the cloth was cleared, the hearth swept, and the fire made up. The compound in the jug being tasted and considered perfect, apples and oranges were put upon the table, and a shovel-full of chestnuts on the fire. Then all the Cratchit family drew round the hearth, in what Bob Cratchit called a circle, meaning half a one, and at Bob Cratchit's elbow stood the family display of glass; two tumblers, and a custard-cup without a handle.

These held the hot stuff from the jug, however, as well as golden goblets would have done; and Bob served it out with beaming looks, while the chestnuts on the fire sputtered and crackled noisily. Then Bob proposed:

"A merry Christmas to us all, my dears. God bless us!"

Which all the family re-echoed.

"God bless us every one!" said Tiny Tim, the last of all.

He sat very close to his father's side, upon his little stool. Bob held his withered little hand in his, as if he

---

1   *half of half-a-quartern*   1¼ fluid ounces.

2   *bedight*   Decorated.

loved the child, and wished to keep him by his side, and dreaded that he might be taken from him.

"Spirit," said Scrooge, with an interest he had never felt before, "tell me if Tiny Tim will live."

"I see a vacant seat," replied the Ghost, "in the poor chimney corner, and a crutch without an owner, carefully preserved. If these shadows remain unaltered by the future, the child will die."

"No, no," said Scrooge. "Oh no, kind Spirit say he will be spared."

"If these shadows remain unaltered by the future, none other of my race," returned the Ghost, "will find him here. What then? If he be like to die, he had better do it, and decrease the surplus population."

Scrooge hung his head to hear his own words quoted by the Spirit, and was overcome with penitence and grief.

"Man," said the Ghost, "if man you be in heart, not adamant, forbear that wicked cant until you have discovered what the surplus is, and where it is. Will you decide what men shall live, what men shall die? It may be, that in the sight of heaven, you are more worthless and less fit to live than millions like this poor man's child. Oh God! to hear the insect on the leaf pronouncing on the too much life among his hungry brothers in the dust!"

Scrooge bent before the Ghost's rebuke, and trembling cast his eyes upon the ground. But he raised them speedily, on hearing his own name.

"Mr. Scrooge!" said Bob; "I'll give you Mr. Scrooge, the founder of the feast!"

"The founder of the feast indeed!" cried Mrs. Cratchit, reddening. "I wish I had him here. I'd give him a piece of my mind to feast upon, and I hope he'd have a good appetite for it."

"My dear," said Bob, "the children; Christmas Day."

"It should be Christmas Day, I am sure," said she, "on which one drinks the health of such an odious, stingy, hard, unfeeling man as Mr. Scrooge. You know he is, Robert! Nobody knows it better than you do, poor fellow!"

"My dear," was Bob's mild answer, "Christmas Day."

"I'll drink his health for your sake and the day's," said Mrs. Cratchit, "not for his. Long life to him! A merry Christmas and a happy new year!—he'll be very merry and very happy, I have no doubt!"

The children drank the toast after her. It was the first of their proceedings which had no heartiness in it. Tiny Tim drank it last of all, but he didn't care twopence for it. Scrooge was the ogre of the family. The mention of his name cast a dark shadow on the party, which was not dispelled for full five minutes.

After it had passed away, they were ten times merrier than before, from the mere relief of Scrooge the Baleful being done with. Bob Cratchit told them how he had a situation in his eye for Master Peter, which would bring in, if obtained, full five-and-sixpence weekly. The two young Cratchits laughed tremendously at the idea of Peter's being a man of business; and Peter himself looked thoughtfully at the fire from between his collars, as if he were deliberating what particular investments he should favour when he came into the receipt of that bewildering income. Martha, who was a poor apprentice at a milliner's, then told them what kind of work she had to do, and how many hours she worked at a stretch, and how she meant to lie abed tomorrow morning for a good long rest; tomorrow being a holiday she passed at home. Also how she had seen a countess and a lord some days before, and how the lord "was much about as tall as Peter"; at which Peter pulled up his collars so high that you couldn't have seen his head if you had been there. All this time the chestnuts and the jug went round and round; and by and by they had a song, about a lost child travelling in the snow, from Tiny Tim, who had a plaintive little voice, and sang it very well indeed.

There was nothing of high mark in this. They were not a handsome family; they were not well dressed; their shoes were far from being waterproof; their clothes were scanty; and Peter might have known, and very likely did, the inside of a pawnbroker's. But they were happy, grateful, pleased with one another, and contented with the time; and when they faded, and looked happier yet in the bright sprinklings of the Spirit's torch at parting, Scrooge had his eye upon them, and especially on Tiny Tim, until the last.

By this time it was getting dark, and snowing pretty heavily; and as Scrooge and the Spirit went along the streets, the brightness of the roaring fires in kitchens, parlours, and all sorts of rooms, was wonderful. Here, the flickering of the blaze showed preparations for a cosy dinner, with hot plates baking through and through before the fire, and deep red curtains, ready to be drawn, to shut out cold and darkness. There, all the children of the house were running out into the snow to meet their married sisters, brothers, cousins, uncles, aunts, and be the first to greet them. Here, again, were shadows on the windowblind of guests assembling; and there a group of handsome girls, all hooded and fur-booted, and all chattering at once, tripped lightly off to some near neighbour's house; where, woe upon the single man who saw them enter—artful witches: well they knew it—in a glow!

But if you had judged from the numbers of people on their way to friendly gatherings, you might have thought that no one was at home to give them welcome when they got there, instead of every house expecting company, and piling up its fires half-chimney high. Blessings on it, how the Ghost exulted! How it bared its breadth of breast, and opened its capacious palm, and floated on, outpouring, with a generous hand, its bright and harmless mirth on everything within its reach! The very lamplighter, who ran on before dotting the dusky street with specks of light, and who was dressed to spend the evening somewhere, laughed out loudly as the Spirit passed: though little kenned the lamplighter that he had any company but Christmas!

And now, without a word of warning from the Ghost, they stood upon a bleak and desert moor, where monstrous masses of rude stone were cast about, as though it were the burial-place of giants; and water spread itself wheresoever it listed—or would have done so, but for the frost that held it prisoner—and nothing grew but moss and furze,[1] and coarse, rank grass. Down in the west the setting sun had left a streak of fiery red, which glared upon the desolation for an instant, like a sullen eye, and frowning lower, lower, lower yet, was lost in the thick gloom of darkest night.

"What place is this?" asked Scrooge.

"A place where miners live, who labour in the bowels of the earth," returned the Spirit. "But they know me. See!"

A light shone from the window of a hut, and swiftly they advanced towards it. Passing through the wall of

mud and stone, they found a cheerful company assembled round a glowing fire. An old, old man and woman, with their children and their children's children, and another generation beyond that, all decked out gaily in their holiday attire. The old man, in a voice that seldom rose above the howling of the wind upon the barren waste, was singing them a Christmas song; it had been a very old song when he was a boy; and from time to time they all joined in the chorus. So surely as they raised their voices, the old man got quite blithe and loud; and so surely as they stopped, his vigour sank again.

The Spirit did not tarry here, but bade Scrooge hold his robe, and passing on above the moor, sped whither? Not to sea? To sea. To Scrooge's horror, looking back, he saw the last of the land, a frightful range of rocks, behind them; and his ears were deafened by the thundering of water, as it rolled, and roared, and raged among the dreadful caverns it had worn, and fiercely tried to undermine the earth.

Built upon a dismal reef of sunken rocks, some league or so from shore, on which the waters chafed and dashed, the wild year through, there stood a solitary lighthouse. Great heaps of seaweed clung to its base, and storm birds—born of the wind one might suppose, as seaweed of the water—rose and fell about it, like the waves they skimmed.

But even here, two men who watched the light had made a fire, that through the loophole in the thick stone wall shed out a ray of brightness on the awful sea. Joining their horny hands over the rough table at which they sat, they wished each other merry Christmas in their can of grog; and one of them, the elder, too, with his face all damaged and scarred with hard weather, as the figurehead of an old ship might be: struck up a sturdy song that was like a gale in itself.

Again the Ghost sped on, above the black and heaving sea—on, on—until, being far away, as he told Scrooge, from any shore, they lighted on a ship. They stood beside the helmsman at the wheel, the lookout in the bow, the officers who had the watch, dark, ghostly figures in their several stations; but every man among them hummed a Christmas tune, or had a Christmas thought, or spoke below his breath to his companion of some bygone Christmas Day, with homeward hopes

---

[1]   *furze*   Gorse; spiny shrubs found on waste land.

belonging to it. And every man on board, waking or sleeping, good or bad, had had a kinder word for another on that day than on any day in the year; and had shared to some extent in its festivities; and had remembered those he cared for at a distance, and had known that they delighted to remember him.

It was a great surprise to Scrooge, while listening to the moaning of the wind, and thinking what a solemn thing it was to move on through the lonely darkness over an unknown abyss, whose depths were secrets as profound as death: it was a great surprise to Scrooge, while thus engaged, to hear a hearty laugh. It was a much greater surprise to Scrooge to recognise it as his own nephew's, and to find himself in a bright, dry, gleaming room, with the Spirit standing smiling by his side, and looking at that same nephew with approving affability!

"Ha, ha!" laughed Scrooge's nephew. "Ha, ha, ha!"

If you should happen, by any unlikely chance, to know a man more blest in a laugh than Scrooge's nephew, all I can say is, I should like to know him too. Introduce him to me, and I'll cultivate his acquaintance.

It is a fair, evenhanded, noble adjustment of things, that while there is infection in disease and sorrow, there is nothing in the world so irresistibly contagious as laughter and good humour. When Scrooge's nephew laughed in this way: holding his sides, rolling his head, and twisting his face into the most extravagant contortions: Scrooge's niece, by marriage, laughed as heartily as he. And their assembled friends being not a bit behindhand, roared out, lustily.

"Ha, ha! Ha, ha, ha, ha!"

"He said that Christmas was a humbug, as I live!" cried Scrooge's nephew. "He believed it too!"

"More shame for him, Fred!" said Scrooge's niece, indignantly. Bless those women; they never do anything by halves. They are always in earnest.

She was very pretty: exceedingly pretty. With a dimpled, surprised-looking, capital face; a ripe little mouth, that seemed made to be kissed—as no doubt it was; all kinds of good little dots about her chin, that melted into one another when she laughed; and the sunniest pair of eyes you ever saw in any little creature's head. Altogether she was what you would have called provoking, you know; but satisfactory, too. Oh, per-

fectly satisfactory!

"He's a comical old fellow," said Scrooge's nephew, "that's the truth; and not so pleasant as he might be. However, his offences carry their own punishment, and I have nothing to say against him."

"I'm sure he is very rich, Fred," hinted Scrooge's niece. "At least you always tell *me* so."

"What of that, my dear!" said Scrooge's nephew. "His wealth is of no use to him. He don't do any good with it. He don't make himself comfortable with it. He hasn't the satisfaction of thinking—ha, ha, ha!—that he is ever going to benefit us with it."

"I have no patience with him," observed Scrooge's niece. Scrooge's niece's sisters, and all the other ladies, expressed the same opinion.

"Oh, I have!" said Scrooge's nephew. "I am sorry for him; I couldn't be angry with him if I tried. Who suffers by his ill whims? Himself, always. Here, he takes it into his head to dislike us, and he won't come and dine with us. What's the consequence? He don't lose much of a dinner."

"Indeed, I think he loses a very good dinner," interrupted Scrooge's niece. Everybody else said the same, and they must be allowed to have been competent judges, because they had just had dinner; and, with the dessert upon the table, were clustered round the fire, by lamplight.

"Well! I am very glad to hear it," said Scrooge's nephew, "because I haven't any great faith in these young housekeepers. What do you say, Topper?"

Topper had clearly got his eye upon one of Scrooge's niece's sisters, for he answered that a bachelor was a wretched outcast, who had no right to express an opinion on the subject. Whereat Scrooge's niece's sister—the plump one with the lace tucker:[1] not the one with the roses—blushed.

"Do go on, Fred," said Scrooge's niece, clapping her hands. "He never finishes what he begins to say! He is such a ridiculous fellow!"

Scrooge's nephew revelled in another laugh, and as it was impossible to keep the infection off, though the plump sister tried hard to do it with aromatic vinegar, his example was unanimously followed.

---

[1] *tucker* Frill or piece of material, usually lace, worn around or inside the bodice of a dress.

"I was only going to say," said Scrooge's nephew, "that the consequence of his taking a dislike to us, and not making merry with us, is, as I think, that he loses some pleasant moments, which could do him no harm. I am sure he loses pleasanter companions than he can find in his own thoughts, either in his mouldy old office, or his dusty chambers. I mean to give him the same chance every year, whether he likes it or not, for I pity him. He may rail at Christmas till he dies, but he can't help thinking better of it—I defy him—if he finds me going there, in good temper, year after year, and saying Uncle Scrooge, how are you? If it only puts him in the vein to leave his poor clerk fifty pounds, that's something; and I think I shook him, yesterday."

It was their turn to laugh now, at the notion of his shaking Scrooge. But being thoroughly good natured, and not much caring what they laughed at, so that they laughed at any rate, he encouraged them in their merriment, and passed the bottle, joyously.

After tea, they had some music. For they were a musical family, and knew what they were about, when they sung a glee or catch,[1] I can assure you: especially Topper, who could growl away in the bass like a good one, and never swell the large veins in his forehead, or get red in the face over it. Scrooge's niece played well upon the harp; and played among other tunes a simple little air (a mere nothing: you might learn to whistle it in two minutes), which had been familiar to the child who fetched Scrooge from the boarding school, as he had been reminded by the Ghost of Christmas Past. When this strain of music sounded, all the things that Ghost had shown him came upon his mind; he softened more and more, and thought that if he could have listened to it often, years ago, he might have cultivated the kindnesses of life for his own happiness with his own hands, without resorting to the sexton's spade that buried Jacob Marley.

But they didn't devote the whole evening to music. After a while they played at forfeits;[2] for it is good to be children sometimes, and never better than at Christmas, when its mighty founder was a child himself. Stop! There was first a game at blindman's buff. Of course there was. And I no more believe Topper was really blind than I believe he had eyes in his boots. My opinion is, that it was a done thing between him and Scrooge's nephew, and that the Ghost of Christmas Present knew it. The way he went after that plump sister in the lace tucker, was an outrage on the credulity of human nature. Knocking down the fire irons, tumbling over the chairs, bumping up against the piano, smothering himself among the curtains, wherever she went, there went he. He always knew where the plump sister was. He wouldn't catch anybody else. If you had fallen up against him, as some of them did, and stood there, he would have made a feint of endeavouring to seize you, which would have been an affront to your understanding; and would instantly have sidled off in the direction of the plump sister. She often cried out that it wasn't fair, and it really was not. But when at last, he caught her; when, in spite of all her silken rustlings, and her rapid flutterings past him, he got her into a corner whence there was no escape; then his conduct was the most execrable. For his pretending not to know her; his pretending that it was necessary to touch her head-dress, and further to assure himself of her identity by pressing a certain ring upon her finger, and a certain chain about her neck, was vile, monstrous! No doubt she told him her opinion of it, when, another blindman being in office, they were so very confidential together, behind the curtains.

Scrooge's niece was not one of the blindman's buff party, but was made comfortable with a large chair and a footstool,[3] in a snug corner, where the Ghost and Scrooge were close behind her. But she joined in the forfeits, and loved her love to admiration with all the letters of the alphabet. Likewise at the game of How, When, and Where, she was very great, and to the secret joy of Scrooge's nephew, beat her sisters hollow: though they were sharp girls too, as Topper could have told you. There might have been twenty people there, young and old, but they all played, and so did Scrooge; for, wholly forgetting in the interest he had in what was going on, that his voice made no sound in their ears, he sometimes came out with his guess quite loud, and very often guessed right, too; for the sharpest needle, best White-

---

[1] *glee or catch* Songs sung by three or more singers.

[2] *forfeits* Game in which losers must forfeit, or give up, their possessions, which they can redeem by performing silly tasks.

[3] *Scrooge's niece ... a footstool* Scrooge's niece is pregnant.

chapel,[1] warranted not to cut in the eye, was not sharper than Scrooge, blunt as he took it in his head to be.

The Ghost was greatly pleased to find him in this mood, and looked upon him with such favour that he begged like a boy to be allowed to stay until the guests departed. But this the Spirit said could not be done.

"Here's a new game," said Scrooge. "One half hour, Spirit, only one!" It was a game called Yes and No, where Scrooge's nephew had to think of something, and the rest must find out what, he only answering to their questions yes or no as the case was. The brisk fire of questioning to which he was exposed, elicited from him that he was thinking of an animal, a live animal, rather a disagreeable animal, a savage animal, an animal that growled and grunted sometimes, and talked sometimes, and lived in London, and walked about the streets, and wasn't made a show of, and wasn't led by anybody, and didn't live in a menagerie, and was never killed in a market, and was not a horse, or an ass, or a cow, or a bull, or a tiger, or a dog, or a pig, or a cat, or a bear. At every fresh question that was put to him, this nephew burst into a fresh roar of laughter; and was so inexpressibly tickled, that he was obliged to get up off the sofa and stamp. At last the plump sister, falling into a similar state, cried out:

"I have found it out! I know what it is, Fred! I know what it is!"

"What is it?" cried Fred.

"It's your Uncle Scro-o-o-o-oge!"

Which it certainly was. Admiration was the universal sentiment, though some objected that the reply to "Is it a bear?" ought to have been "Yes"; inasmuch as an answer in the negative was sufficient to have diverted their thoughts from Mr. Scrooge, supposing they had ever had any tendency that way.

"He has given us plenty of merriment, I am sure," said Fred, "and it would be ungrateful not to drink his health. Here is a glass of mulled wine ready to our hand at the moment; and I say 'Uncle Scrooge!'"

"Well! Uncle Scrooge!" they cried.

"A merry Christmas and a happy New Year to the old man, whatever he is!" said Scrooge's nephew. "He wouldn't take it from me, but may he have it, nevertheless. Uncle Scrooge!"

Uncle Scrooge had imperceptibly become so gay and light of heart, that he would have pledged the unconscious company in return, and thanked them in an inaudible speech, if the Ghost had given him time. But the whole scene passed off in the breath of the last word spoken by his nephew; and he and the Spirit were again upon their travels.

Much they saw, and far they went, and many homes they visited, but always with a happy end. The Spirit stood beside sickbeds, and they were cheerful; on foreign lands, and they were close at home; by struggling men, and they were patient in their greater hope; by poverty, and it was rich. In almshouse, hospital, and jail, in misery's every refuge, where vain man in his little brief authority[2] had not made fast the door, and barred the Spirit out, he left his blessing, and taught Scrooge his precepts.

It was a long night, if it were only a night; but Scrooge had his doubts of this, because the Christmas holidays appeared to be condensed into the space of time they passed together. It was strange, too, that while Scrooge remained unaltered in his outward form, the Ghost grew older, clearly older. Scrooge had observed this change, but never spoke of it, until they left a children's Twelfth Night party, when, looking at the Spirit as they stood together in an open place, he noticed that its hair was gray.

"Are Spirits' lives so short?" asked Scrooge.

"My life upon this globe is very brief," replied the Ghost. "It ends tonight."

"Tonight!" cried Scrooge.

"Tonight at midnight. Hark! The time is drawing near."

The chimes were ringing the three quarters past eleven at that moment.

"Forgive me if I am not justified in what I ask," said Scrooge, looking intently at the Spirit's robe, "but I see something strange, and not belonging to yourself, protruding from your skirts. Is it a foot or a claw?"

"It might be a claw, for the flesh there is upon it," was the Spirit's sorrowful reply. "Look here."

From the foldings of its robe, it brought two children; wretched, abject, frightful, hideous, miserable.

---

1   *Whitechapel*   Make of sewing needle.

2   *vain man ... authority*   Cf. Shakespeare's *Measure for Measure* 2.2.144–46: "man, proud man, / Drest in a little brief authority, / Most ignorant of what he's most assured."

They knelt down at its feet, and clung upon the outside of its garment.

"Oh, man! look here. Look, look, down here!" exclaimed the Ghost.

They were a boy and girl. Yellow, meagre, ragged, scowling, wolfish; but prostrate, too, in their humility. Where graceful youth should have filled their features out, and touched them with its freshest tints, a stale and shrivelled hand, like that of age, had pinched, and twisted them, and pulled them into shreds. Where angels might have sat enthroned, devils lurked, and glared out menacing. No change, no degradation, no perversion of humanity, in any grade, through all the mysteries of wonderful creation, has monsters half so horrible and dread.

Scrooge started back, appalled. Having them shown to him in this way, he tried to say they were fine children, but the words choked themselves, rather than be parties to a lie of such enormous magnitude.

"Spirit! are they yours?" Scrooge could say no more.

"They are man's," said the Spirit, looking down upon them. "And they cling to me, appealing from their fathers. This boy is Ignorance. This girl is Want. Beware them both, and all of their degree, but most of all beware this boy, for on his brow I see that written which is doom, unless the writing be erased. Deny it!" cried the Spirit, stretching out its hand towards the city. "Slander those who tell it ye! Admit it for your factious purposes, and make it worse! And bide the end!"

"Have they no refuge or resource?" cried Scrooge.

"Are there no prisons?" said the Spirit, turning on him for the last time with his own words. "Are there no workhouses?"

The bell struck twelve.

Scrooge looked about him for the Ghost, and saw it not. As the last stroke ceased to vibrate, he remembered the prediction of old Jacob Marley, and lifting up his eyes, beheld a solemn Phantom, draped and hooded, coming, like a mist along the ground, towards him.

STAVE 4: THE LAST OF THE SPIRITS

The Phantom slowly, gravely, silently, approached. When it came near him, Scrooge bent down upon his knee; for in the very air through which this Spirit moved it seemed to scatter gloom and mystery.

It was shrouded in a deep black garment, which concealed its head, its face, its form, and left nothing of it visible save one outstretched hand. But for this it would have been difficult to detach its figure from the night, and separate it from the darkness by which it was surrounded.

He felt that it was tall and stately when it came beside him, and that its mysterious presence filled him with a solemn dread. He knew no more, for the Spirit neither spoke nor moved.

"I am in the presence of the Ghost of Christmas Yet To Come?" said Scrooge.

The Spirit answered not, but pointed onward with its hand.

"You are about to show me shadows of the things that have not happened, but will happen in the time before us," Scrooge pursued. "Is that so, Spirit?"

The upper portion of the garment was contracted for an instant in its folds, as if the Spirit had inclined its head. That was the only answer he received.

Although well used to ghostly company by this time, Scrooge feared the silent shape so much that his legs trembled beneath him, and he found that he could hardly stand when he prepared to follow it. The Spirit paused a moment, as observing his condition, and giving him time to recover.

But Scrooge was all the worse for this. It thrilled him with a vague uncertain horror, to know that behind the dusky shroud there were ghostly eyes intently fixed upon him, while he, though he stretched his own to the utmost, could see nothing but a spectral hand and one great heap of black.

"Ghost of the Future!" he exclaimed, "I fear you more than any spectre I have seen. But, as I know your purpose is to do me good, and as I hope to live to be another man from what I was, I am prepared to bear you company, and do it with a thankful heart. Will you not speak to me?"

It gave him no reply. The hand was pointed straight before them.

"Lead on!" said Scrooge. "Lead on! The night is waning fast, and it is precious time to me, I know. Lead on, Spirit!"

The Phantom moved away as it had come towards him. Scrooge followed in the shadow of its dress, which bore him up, he thought, and carried him along.

They scarcely seemed to enter the city; for the city rather seemed to spring up about them, and encompass them of its own act. But there they were, in the heart of it; on 'Change, amongst the merchants; who hurried up and down, and chinked the money in their pockets, and conversed in groups, and looked at their watches, and trifled thoughtfully with their great gold seals; and so forth, as Scrooge had seen them often.

The Spirit stopped beside one little knot of business-men. Observing that the hand was pointed to them, Scrooge advanced to listen to their talk.

"No," said a great fat man with a monstrous chin, "I don't know much about it, either way. I only know he's dead."

"When did he die?" inquired another.

"Last night, I believe."

"Why, what was the matter with him?" asked a third, taking a vast quantity of snuff out of a very large snuffbox. "I thought he'd never die."

"God knows," said the first, with a yawn.

"What has he done with his money?" asked a red-faced gentleman with a pendulous excrescence on the end of his nose, that shook like the gills of a turkey-cock.

"I haven't heard," said the man with the large chin, yawning again. "Left it to his company, perhaps. He hasn't left it to *me*. That's all I know."

This pleasantry was received with a general laugh.

"It's likely to be a very cheap funeral," said the same speaker; "for upon my life I don't know of anybody to go to it. Suppose we make up a party and volunteer?"

"I don't mind going if a lunch is provided," observed the gentleman with the excrescence on his nose. "But I must be fed, if I make one."

Another laugh.

"Well, I am the most disinterested among you, after all," said the first speaker, "for I never wear black gloves, and I never eat lunch. But I'll offer to go, if anybody else will. When I come to think of it, I'm not at all sure that I wasn't his most particular friend; for we used to stop and speak whenever we met. Bye, bye!"

Speakers and listeners strolled away, and mixed with other groups. Scrooge knew the men, and looked towards the Spirit for an explanation.

The Phantom glided on into a street. Its finger pointed to two persons meeting. Scrooge listened again, thinking that the explanation might lie here.

He knew these men, also, perfectly. They were men of business: very wealthy, and of great importance. He had made a point always of standing well in their esteem: in a business point of view, that is, strictly in a business point of view.

"How are you?" said one.

"How are you?" returned the other.

"Well!" said the first. "Old Scratch[1] has got his own at last, hey?"

"So I am told," returned the second. "Cold, isn't it?"

"Seasonable for Christmas time. You're not a skater, I suppose?"

"No. No. Something else to think of. Good morning!"

Not another word. That was their meeting, their conversation, and their parting.

---

[1] *Old Scratch* Satan.

Scrooge was at first inclined to be surprised that the Spirit should attach importance to conversations apparently so trivial; but feeling assured that they must have some hidden purpose, he set himself to consider what it was likely to be. They could scarcely be supposed to have any bearing on the death of Jacob, his old partner, for that was past, and this Ghost's province was the future. Nor could he think of any one immediately connected with himself, to whom he could apply them. But nothing doubting that to whomsoever they applied they had some latent moral for his own improvement, he resolved to treasure up every word he heard, and everything he saw; and especially to observe the shadow of himself when it appeared. For he had an expectation that the conduct of his future self would give him the clue he missed, and would render the solution of these riddles easy.

He looked about in that very place for his own image; but another man stood in his accustomed corner, and though the clock pointed to his usual time of day for being there, he saw no likeness of himself among the multitudes that poured in through the porch. It gave him little surprise, however; for he had been revolving in his mind a change of life, and thought and hoped he saw his newborn resolutions carried out in this.

Quiet and dark, beside him stood the Phantom, with its outstretched hand. When he roused himself from his thoughtful quest, he fancied from the turn of the hand, and its situation in reference to himself, that the unseen eyes were looking at him keenly. It made him shudder, and feel very cold.

They left the busy scene, and went into an obscure part of the town, where Scrooge had never penetrated before, although he recognised its situation, and its bad repute. The ways were foul and narrow; the shops and houses wretched; the people half-naked, drunken, slipshod, ugly. Alleys and archways, like so many cesspools, disgorged their offences of smell, and dirt, and life, upon the straggling streets; and the whole quarter reeked with crime, with filth, and misery.

Far in this den of infamous resort, there was a low-browed, beetling shop, below a pent-house roof, where iron, old rags, bottles, bones, and greasy offal, were bought.[1] Upon the floor within, were piled up heaps of rusty keys, nails, chains, hinges, files, scales, weights, and refuse iron of all kinds. Secrets that few would like to scrutinise were bred and hidden in mountains of unseemly rags, masses of corrupted fat, and sepulchres of bones. Sitting in among the wares he dealt in, by a charcoal stove, made of old bricks, was a gray-haired rascal, nearly seventy years of age; who had screened himself from the cold air without, by a frousy curtaining of miscellaneous tatters, hung upon a line; and smoked his pipe in all the luxury of calm retirement.

Scrooge and the Phantom came into the presence of this man, just as a woman with a heavy bundle slunk into the shop. But she had scarcely entered when another woman, similarly laden, came in too; and she was closely followed by a man in faded black, who was no less startled by the sight of them than they had been upon the recognition of each other. After a short period of blank astonishment, in which the old man with the pipe had joined them, they all three burst into a laugh.

"Let the charwoman alone to be the first!" cried she who had entered first. "Let the laundress alone to be the second; and let the undertaker's man alone to be the third. Look here, old Joe, here's a chance! If we haven't all three met here without meaning it!"

"You couldn't have met in a better place," said old Joe, removing his pipe from his mouth. "Come into the parlour. You were made free of it long ago, you know; and the other two an't strangers. Stop till I shut the door of the shop. Ah! How it skreeks! There an't such a rusty bit of metal in the place as its own hinges, I believe; and I'm sure there's no such old bones here, as mine. Ha, ha! We're all suitable to our calling, we're well matched. Come into the parlour. Come into the parlour."

The parlour was the space behind the screen of rags. The old man raked the fire together with an old stair rod, and having trimmed his smoky lamp (for it was night), with the stem of his pipe, put it in his mouth again.

While he did this, the woman who had already spoken threw her bundle on the floor and sat down in a flaunting manner on a stool; crossing her elbows on her knees, and looking with a bold defiance at the other two.

[1]   *lowbrowed ... were bought* Second-hand shop with a sloping roof.

"What odds then! What odds, Mrs. Dilber?" said the woman. "Every person has a right to take care of themselves. *He* always did!"

"That's true, indeed!" said the laundress. "No man more so."

"Why, then, don't stand staring as if you was afraid, woman; who's the wiser? We're not going to pick holes in each other's coats, I suppose?"

"No, indeed!" said Mrs. Dilber and the man together. "We should hope not."

"Very well, then!" cried the woman. "That's enough. Who's the worse for the loss of a few things like these? Not a dead man, I suppose."

"No, indeed," said Mrs. Dilber, laughing.

"If he wanted to keep 'em after he was dead, a wicked old screw," pursued the woman, "why wasn't he natural in his lifetime? If he had been, he'd have had somebody to look after him when he was struck with death, instead of lying gasping out his last there, alone by himself."

"It's the truest word that ever was spoke," said Mrs. Dilber. "It's a judgment on him."

"I wish it was a little heavier one," replied the woman; "and it should have been, you may depend upon it, if I could have laid my hands on anything else. Open that bundle, old Joe, and let me know the value of it. Speak out plain. I'm not afraid to be the first, nor afraid for them to see it. We knew pretty well that we were helping ourselves, before we met here, I believe. It's no sin. Open the bundle, Joe."

But the gallantry of her friends would not allow of this; and the man in faded black, mounting the breach first, produced his plunder. It was not extensive. A seal or two, a pencil-case, a pair of sleeve buttons, and a brooch of no great value, were all. They were severally examined and appraised by old Joe, who chalked the sums he was disposed to give for each upon the wall, and added them up into a total when he found that there was nothing more to come.

"That's your account," said Joe, "and I wouldn't give another sixpence, if I was to be boiled for not doing it. Who's next?"

Mrs. Dilber was next. Sheets and towels, a little wearing apparel, two old-fashioned silver teaspoons, a pair of sugar-tongs, and a few boots. Her account was stated on the wall in the same manner.

"I always give too much to ladies. It's a weakness of mine, and that's the way I ruin myself," said old Joe. "That's your account. If you asked me for another penny, and made it an open question, I'd repent of being so liberal, and knock off half-a-crown."

"And now undo my bundle, Joe," said the first woman.

Joe went down on his knees for the greater convenience of opening it, and having unfastened a great many knots, dragged out a large and heavy roll of some dark stuff.

"What do you call this?" said Joe. "Bed-curtains!"

"Ah!" returned the woman, laughing and leaning forward on her crossed arms. "Bed-curtains!"

"You don't mean to say you took 'em down, rings and all, with him lying there?" said Joe.

"Yes I do," replied the woman. "Why not?"

"You were born to make your fortune," said Joe, "and you'll certainly do it."

"I certainly shan't hold my hand, when I can get anything in it by reaching it out, for the sake of such a man as he was, I promise you, Joe," returned the woman coolly. "Don't drop that oil upon the blankets, now."

"His blankets?" asked Joe.

"Whose else's do you think?" replied the woman. "He isn't likely to take cold without 'em, I dare say."

"I hope he didn't die of anything catching? Eh?" said old Joe, stopping in his work, and looking up.

"Don't you be afraid of that," returned the woman. "I an't so fond of his company that I'd loiter about him for such things, if he did. Ah! You may look through that shirt till your eyes ache; but you won't find a hole in it, nor a threadbare place. It's the best he had, and a fine one too. They'd have wasted it, if it hadn't been for me."

"What do you call wasting of it?" asked old Joe.

"Putting it on him to be buried in, to be sure," replied the woman with a laugh. "Somebody was fool enough to do it, but I took it off again. If calico an't good enough for such a purpose, it isn't good enough for anything. It's quite as becoming to the body. He can't look uglier than he did in that one."

Scrooge listened to this dialogue in horror. As they sat grouped about their spoil, in the scanty light afforded by the old man's lamp, he viewed them with a detestation and disgust, which could hardly have been greater, though they had been obscene demons, marketing the corpse itself.

"Ha, ha!" laughed the same woman, when old Joe, producing a flannel bag with money in it, told out their several gains upon the ground. "This is the end of it, you see! He frightened everyone away from him when he was alive, to profit us when he was dead! Ha, ha, ha!"

"Spirit!" said Scrooge, shuddering from head to foot. "I see, I see. The case of this unhappy man might be my own. My life tends that way, now. Merciful heaven, what is this!"

He recoiled in terror, for the scene had changed, and now he almost touched a bed: a bare, uncurtained bed: on which, beneath a ragged sheet, there lay a something covered up, which, though it was dumb, announced itself in awful language.

The room was very dark, too dark to be observed with any accuracy, though Scrooge glanced round it in obedience to a secret impulse, anxious to know what kind of room it was. A pale light, rising in the outer air, fell straight upon the bed; and on it, plundered and bereft, unwatched, unwept, uncared for, was the body of this man.

Scrooge glanced towards the Phantom. Its steady hand was pointed to the head. The cover was so carelessly adjusted that the slightest raising of it, the motion of a finger upon Scrooge's part, would have disclosed the face. He thought of it, felt how easy it would be to do, and longed to do it; but had no more power to withdraw the veil than to dismiss the spectre at his side.

Oh cold, cold, rigid, dreadful Death, set up thine altar here, and dress it with such terrors as thou hast at thy command: for this is thy dominion! But of the loved, revered, and honoured head, thou canst not turn one hair to thy dread purposes, or make one feature odious. It is not that the hand is heavy and will fall down when released; it is not that the heart and pulse are still; but that the hand was open, generous, and true; the heart brave, warm, and tender; and the pulse a man's. Strike, Shadow, strike! And see his good deeds springing from the wound, to sow the world with life immortal!

No voice pronounced these words in Scrooge's ears, and yet he heard them when he looked upon the bed. He thought, if this man could be raised up now, what would be his foremost thoughts? Avarice, hard dealing, griping cares? They have brought him to a rich end, truly!

He lay, in the dark empty house, with not a man, a woman, or a child, to say he was kind to me in this or that, and for the memory of one kind word I will be kind to him. A cat was tearing at the door, and there was a sound of gnawing rats beneath the hearthstone. What they wanted in the room of death, and why they were so restless and disturbed, Scrooge did not dare to think.

"Spirit!" he said, "this is a fearful place. In leaving it, I shall not leave its lesson, trust me. Let us go!"

Still the Ghost pointed with an unmoved finger to the head.

"I understand you," Scrooge returned, "and I would do it, if I could. But I have not the power, Spirit. I have not the power."

Again it seemed to look upon him.

"If there is any person in the town, who feels emotion caused by this man's death," said Scrooge quite agonized, "show that person to me, Spirit, I beseech you!"

The phantom spread its dark robe before him for a moment, like a wing; and withdrawing it, revealed a room by daylight, where a mother and her children were.

She was expecting someone, and with anxious eagerness; for she walked up and down the room; started at every sound; looked out from the window; glanced at the clock; tried, but in vain, to work with her needle; and could hardly bear the voices of the children in their play.

At length the long-expected knock was heard. She hurried to the door, and met her husband; a man whose face was careworn and depressed, though he was young. There was a remarkable expression in it now; a kind of serious delight of which he felt ashamed, and which he struggled to repress.

He sat down to the dinner that had been hoarding[1] for him by the fire; and when she asked him faintly what news (which was not until after a long silence), he appeared embarrassed how to answer.

"Is it good," she said, "or bad?"—to help him. "Bad," he answered.

"We are quite ruined?"

---

[1]   *hoarding* Saved.

"No. There is hope yet, Caroline."

"If *he* relents," she said, amazed, "there is! Nothing is past hope, if such a miracle has happened."

"He is past relenting," said her husband. "He is dead."

She was a mild and patient creature if her face spoke truth; but she was thankful in her soul to hear it, and she said so, with clasped hands. She prayed forgiveness the next moment, and was sorry; but the first was the emotion of her heart.

"What the half-drunken woman whom I told you of last night said to me, when I tried to see him and obtain a week's delay; and what I thought was a mere excuse to avoid me; turns out to have been quite true. He was not only very ill, but dying, then."

"To whom will our debt be transferred?"

"I don't know. But before that time we shall be ready with the money; and even though we were not, it would be bad fortune indeed to find so merciless a creditor in his successor. We may sleep tonight with light hearts, Caroline!"

Yes. Soften it as they would, their hearts were lighter. The children's faces hushed, and clustered round to hear what they so little understood, were brighter; and it was a happier house for this man's death! The only emotion that the Ghost could show him, caused by the event, was one of pleasure.

"Let me see some tenderness connected with a death," said Scrooge; "or that dark chamber, Spirit, which we left just now, will be forever present to me."

The Ghost conducted him through several streets familiar to his feet; and as they went along, Scrooge looked here and there to find himself, but nowhere was he to be seen. They entered poor Bob Cratchit's house, the dwelling he had visited before, and found the mother and the children seated round the fire.

Quiet. Very quiet. The noisy little Cratchits were as still as statues in one corner, and sat looking up at Peter, who had a book before him. The mother and her daughters were engaged in sewing. But surely they were very quiet!

"'And He took a child, and set him in the midst of them.'"[1]

Where had Scrooge heard those words? He had not dreamed them. The boy must have read them out, as he and the Spirit crossed the threshold. Why did he not go on?

The mother laid her work upon the table, and put her hand up to her face.

"The colour hurts my eyes," she said.

The colour? Ah, poor Tiny Tim!

"They're better now again," said Cratchit's wife. "It makes them weak by candlelight; and I wouldn't show weak eyes to your father when he comes home, for the world. It must be near his time."

"Past it rather," Peter answered, shutting up his book. "But I think he's walked a little slower than he used, these few last evenings, mother."

They were very quiet again. At last she said, and in a steady cheerful voice, that only faltered once:

"I have known him walk with—I have known him walk with Tiny Tim upon his shoulder, very fast indeed."

"And so have I," cried Peter. "Often."

"And so have I!" exclaimed another. So had all.

"But he was very light to carry," she resumed, intent upon her work, "and his father loved him so, that it was no trouble—no trouble. And there is your father at the door!"

She hurried out to meet him; and little Bob in his comforter—he had need of it, poor fellow—came in. His tea was ready for him on the hob, and they all tried who should help him to it most. Then the two young Cratchits got upon his knees and laid, each child a little cheek, against his face, as if they said, "Don't mind it, father. Don't be grieved!"

Bob was very cheerful with them, and spoke pleasantly to all the family. He looked at the work upon the table, and praised the industry and speed of Mrs. Cratchit and the girls. They would be done long before Sunday he said.

"Sunday! You went today then, Robert?" said his wife.

"Yes, my dear," returned Bob. "I wish you could have gone. It would have done you good to see how green a place it is. But you'll see it often. I promised him that I would walk there on a Sunday. My little, little child!" cried Bob. "My little child!"

---

[1]   *And he took ... of them*   From Mark 9.36.

He broke down all at once. He couldn't help it. If he could have helped it, he and his child would have been farther apart perhaps than they were.

He left the room, and went upstairs into the room above, which was lighted cheerfully, and hung with Christmas. There was a chair set close beside the child, and there were signs of someone having been there, lately. Poor Bob sat down in it, and when he had thought a little and composed himself, he kissed the little face. He was reconciled to what had happened, and went down again quite happy.

They drew about the fire, and talked; the girls and mother working still. Bob told them of the extraordinary kindness of Mr. Scrooge's nephew, whom he had scarcely seen but once, and who, meeting him in the street that day, and seeing that he looked a little—"just a little down you know" said Bob, enquired what had happened to distress him. "On which," said Bob, "for he is the pleasantest-spoken gentleman you ever heard, I told him. 'I am heartily sorry for it, Mr. Cratchit,' he said, 'and heartily sorry for your good wife.' By the by, how he ever knew *that*, I don't know."

"Knew what, my dear?"

"Why, that you were a good wife," replied Bob.

"Everybody knows that!" said Peter.

"Very well observed, my boy!" cried Bob. "I hope they do. 'Heartily sorry,' he said, 'for your good wife. If I can be of service to you in any way,' he said, giving me his card, 'that's where I live. Pray come to me.' Now, it wasn't," cried Bob, "for the sake of anything he might be able to do for us, so much as for his kind way, that this was quite delightful. It really seemed as if he had known our Tiny Tim, and felt with us."

"I'm sure he's a good soul!" said Mrs. Cratchit.

"You would be surer of it, my dear," returned Bob, "if you saw and spoke to him. I shouldn't be at all surprised, mark what I say, if he got Peter a better situation."

"Only hear that, Peter," said Mrs. Cratchit.

"And then," cried one of the girls, "Peter will be keeping company with someone, and setting up for himself."

"Get along with you!" retorted Peter, grinning.

"It's just as likely as not," said Bob, "one of these days; though there's plenty of time for that, my dear.

But however and whenever we part from one another, I am sure we shall none of us forget poor Tiny Tim—shall we—or this first parting that there was among us?"

"Never, father!" cried they all.

"And I know," said Bob, "I know, my dears, that when we recollect how patient and how mild he was; although he was a little, little child; we shall not quarrel easily among ourselves, and forget poor Tiny Tim in doing it."

"No, never, father!" they all cried again.

"I am very happy," said little Bob, "I am very happy!"

Mrs. Cratchit kissed him, his daughters kissed him, the two young Cratchits kissed him, and Peter and himself shook hands. Spirit of Tiny Tim, thy childish essence was from God!

"Spectre," said Scrooge, "something informs me that our parting moment is at hand. I know it, but I know not how. Tell me what man that was whom we saw lying dead?"

The Ghost of Christmas Yet To Come conveyed him, as before—though at a different time, he thought: indeed, there seemed no order in these latter visions, save that they were in the Future—into the resorts of businessmen, but showed him not himself. Indeed, the Spirit did not stay for anything, but went straight on, as to the end just now desired, until besought by Scrooge to tarry for a moment.

"This court," said Scrooge, "through which we hurry now, is where my place of occupation is, and has been for a length of time. I see the house. Let me behold what I shall be, in days to come."

The Spirit stopped; the hand was pointed elsewhere.

"The house is yonder," Scrooge exclaimed. "Why do you point away?"

The inexorable finger underwent no change. Scrooge hastened to the window of his office, and looked in. It was an office still, but not his. The furniture was not the same, and the figure in the chair was not himself. The Phantom pointed as before.

He joined it once again, and wondering why and whither he had gone, accompanied it until they reached an iron gate. He paused to look round before entering.

A churchyard. Here, then, the wretched man whose name he had now to learn, lay underneath the ground.

It was a worthy place. Walled in by houses; overrun by grass and weeds, the growth of vegetation's death, not life; choked up with too much burying; fat with repleted appetite. A worthy place!

The Spirit stood among the graves, and pointed down to one. He advanced towards it trembling. The Phantom was exactly as it had been, but he dreaded that he saw new meaning in its solemn shape.

"Before I draw nearer to that stone to which you point," said Scrooge, "answer me one question. Are these the shadows of the things that will be, or are they shadows of the things that may be, only?"

Still the Ghost pointed downward to the grave by which it stood.

"Men's courses will foreshadow certain ends, to which, if persevered in, they must lead," said Scrooge. "But if the courses be departed from, the ends will change. Say it is thus with what you show me!"

The Spirit was immovable as ever.

Scrooge crept towards it, trembling as he went; and following the finger, read upon the stone of the ne-

glected grave his own name, EBENEZER SCROOGE.

"Am *I* that man who lay upon the bed?" he cried, upon his knees.

The finger pointed from the grave to him, and back again.

"No, Spirit! Oh no, no!"

The finger still was there.

"Spirit!" he cried, tight clutching at its robe, "hear me! I am not the man I was. I will not be the man I must have been but for this intercourse. Why show me this, if I am past all hope?" For the first time the hand appeared to shake.

"Good Spirit," he pursued, as down upon the ground he fell before it: "Your nature intercedes for me, and pities me. Assure me that I yet may change these shadows you have shown me, by an altered life!"

The kind hand trembled.

"I will honour Christmas in my heart, and try to keep it all the year. I will live in the past, the present, and the future. The spirits of all three shall strive within me. I will not shut out the lessons that they teach. Oh, tell me I may sponge away the writing on this stone!"

In his agony, he caught the spectral hand. It sought to free itself, but he was strong in his entreaty, and detained it. The Spirit, stronger yet, repulsed him.

Holding up his hands in one last prayer to have his fate reversed, he saw an alteration in the Phantom's hood and dress. It shrunk, collapsed, and dwindled down into a bedpost.

STAVE 5: THE END OF IT

Yes! and the bedpost was his own. The bed was his own, the room was his own. Best and happiest of all, the time before him was his own, to make amends in!

"I will live in the past, the present, and the future!" Scrooge repeated, as he scrambled out of bed. "The Spirits of all three shall strive within me. Oh Jacob Marley! Heaven, and the Christmas time be praised for this! I say it on my knees, old Jacob; on my knees!"

He was so fluttered and so glowing with his good intentions, that his broken voice would scarcely answer to his call. He had been sobbing violently in his conflict with the Spirit, and his face was wet with tears.

"They are not torn down," cried Scrooge, folding one of his bed-curtains in his arms, "they are not torn down, rings and all. They are here: I am here: the shadows of the things that would have been, may be dispelled. They will be. I know they will!"

His hands were busy with his garments all this time: turning them inside out, putting them on upside down, tearing them, mislaying them, making them parties to every kind of extravagance.

"I don't know what to do!" cried Scrooge, laughing and crying in the same breath; and making a perfect Laocoön[1] of himself with his stockings. "I am as light as a feather, I am as happy as an angel. I am as merry as a schoolboy. I am as giddy as a drunken man. A merry Christmas to everybody! A happy New Year to all the world. Hallo here! Whoop! Hallo!"

He had frisked into the sitting-room, and was now standing there, perfectly winded.

"There's the saucepan that the gruel was in!" cried Scrooge, starting off again, and frisking round the fireplace. "There's the door, by which the ghost of Jacob Marley entered! There's the corner where the Ghost of Christmas Present sat! There's the window where I saw the wandering spirits! It's all right, it's all true, it all happened. Ha ha ha!"

Really, for a man who had been out of practice for so many years, it was a splendid laugh, a most illustrious laugh. The father of a long, long, line of brilliant laughs!

"I don't know what day of the month it is!" said Scrooge. "I don't know how long I've been among the spirits. I don't know anything. I'm quite a baby. Never mind. I don't care. I'd rather be a baby. Hallo! Whoop! Hallo here!"

He was checked in his transports by the churches ringing out the lustiest peals he had ever heard. Clash, clang, hammer, ding, dong, bell. Bell, dong, ding, hammer, clang, clash! Oh, glorious, glorious!

Running to the window, he opened it, and put out his head. No fog, no mist; clear, bright, jovial, stirring, cold; cold, piping for the blood to dance to; golden sunlight; heavenly sky; sweet fresh air; merry bells. Oh, glorious. Glorious!

"What's today?" cried Scrooge, calling downward to a boy in Sunday clothes, who perhaps had loitered in to look about him.

"EH?" returned the boy, with all his might of wonder.

"What's today, my fine fellow?" said Scrooge.

"Today!" replied the boy. "Why, CHRISTMAS DAY."

"It's Christmas Day!" said Scrooge to himself. "I haven't missed it. The spirits have done it all in one night. They can do anything they like. Of course they can. Of course they can. Hallo, my fine fellow!"

"Hallo!" returned the boy.

"Do you know the poulterer's, in the next street but one, at the corner?" Scrooge inquired.

"I should hope I did," replied the lad.

"An intelligent boy!" said Scrooge. "A remarkable boy! Do you know whether they've sold the prize turkey that was hanging up there? Not the little prize turkey: the big one?"

"What, the one as big as me?" returned the boy.

"What a delightful boy!" said Scrooge. "It's a pleasure to talk to him. Yes, my buck!"

"It's hanging there now," replied the boy.

"Is it?" said Scrooge. "Go and buy it."

"Walk-ER!"[2] exclaimed the boy.

"No, no," said Scrooge, "I am in earnest. Go and buy it, and tell 'em to bring it here, that I may give them the direction where to take it. Come back with the man, and I'll give you a shilling. Come back with him in less than five minutes, and I'll give you half-a-crown!"

The boy was off like a shot. He must have had a steady hand at a trigger who could have got a shot off half so fast.

"I'll send it to Bob Cratchit's!" whispered Scrooge, rubbing his hands, and splitting with a laugh. "He sha'n't know who sends it. It's twice the size of Tiny Tim. Joe Miller[3] never made such a joke as sending it to Bob's will be!"

The hand in which he wrote the address was not a steady one, but write it he did, somehow, and went downstairs to open the street door, ready for the coming of the poulterer's man. As he stood there, waiting his arrival, the knocker caught his eye.

---

1   *Laocoön*   In Greek mythology, a Trojan priest who was viciously attacked and strangled by sea serpents.

2   *Walk-ER!*   Cockney expression of incredulity.

3   *Joe Miller*   Comic actor, whose name came to be synonymous with a tired joke; after Miller's death John Mottley published *Joe Miller's Jests* (1739).

"I shall love it, as long as I live!" cried Scrooge, patting it with his hand. "I scarcely ever looked at it before. What an honest expression it has in its face! It's a wonderful knocker!—Here's the turkey. Hallo! Whoop! How are you! Merry Christmas!"

It *was* a turkey! He never could have stood upon his legs, that bird. He would have snapped 'em short off in a minute, like sticks of sealing wax.

"Why, it's impossible to carry that to Camden Town," said Scrooge. "You must have a cab."

The chuckle with which he said this, and the chuckle with which he paid for the turkey, and the chuckle with which he paid for the cab, and the chuckle with which he recompensed the boy, were only to be exceeded by the chuckle with which he sat down breathless in his chair again, and chuckled till he cried.

Shaving was not an easy task, for his hand continued to shake very much; and shaving requires attention, even when you don't dance while you are at it. But if he had cut the end of his nose off, he would have put a piece of sticking-plaster over it, and been quite satisfied.

He dressed himself "all in his best," and at last got out into the streets. The people were by this time pouring forth, as he had seen them with the Ghost of Christmas Present; and walking with his hands behind him, Scrooge regarded everyone with a delighted smile. He looked so irresistibly pleasant, in a word, that three or four good-humoured fellows said, "Good morning, sir! A merry Christmas to you!" And Scrooge said often afterwards, that of all the blithe sounds he had ever heard, those were the blithest in his ears.

He had not gone far, when coming on towards him he beheld the portly gentleman, who had walked into his counting-house the day before and said, "Scrooge and Marley's, I believe?" It sent a pang across his heart to think how this old gentleman would look upon him when they met; but he knew what path lay straight before him, and he took it.

"My dear sir," said Scrooge, quickening his pace, and taking the old gentleman by both his hands. "How do you do? I hope you succeeded yesterday. It was very kind of you. A merry Christmas to you, sir!"

"Mr. Scrooge?"

"Yes," said Scrooge. "That is my name, and I fear it may not be pleasant to you. Allow me to ask your pardon. And will you have the goodness"—here Scrooge whispered in his ear.

"Lord bless me!" cried the gentleman, as if his breath were gone. "My dear Mr. Scrooge, are you serious?"

"If you please," said Scrooge. "Not a farthing less. A great many back-payments are included in it, I assure you. Will you do me that favour?"

"My dear sir," said the other, shaking hands with him. "I don't know what to say to such munifi—"

"Don't say anything, please," retorted Scrooge. "Come and see me. Will you come and see me?"

"I will!" cried the old gentleman. And it was clear he meant to do it.

"Thank 'ee," said Scrooge. "I am much obliged to you. I thank you fifty times. Bless you!"

He went to church, and walked about the streets, and watched the people hurrying to and fro, and patted children on the head, and questioned beggars, and looked down into the kitchens of houses, and up to the windows; and found that everything could yield him pleasure. He had never dreamed that any walk—that anything—could give him so much happiness. In the afternoon, he turned his steps towards his nephew's house.

He passed the door a dozen times, before he had the courage to go up and knock. But he made a dash, and did it:

"Is your master at home, my dear?" said Scrooge to the girl. Nice girl! Very.

"Yes, sir."

"Where is he, my love?" said Scrooge.

"He's in the dining room, sir, along with mistress. I'll show you upstairs, if you please."

"Thank'ee. He knows me," said Scrooge, with his hand already on the dining room lock. "I'll go in here, my dear."

He turned it gently, and sidled his face in, round the door. They were looking at the table (which was spread out in great array); for these young housekeepers are always nervous on such points, and like to see that everything is right.

"Fred!" said Scrooge.

Dear heart alive, how his niece by marriage started! Scrooge had forgotten, for the moment, about her sitting in the corner with the footstool, or he wouldn't have done it, on any account.

"Why bless my soul!" cried Fred, "who's that?"

"It's I. Your uncle Scrooge. I have come to dinner. Will you let me in, Fred?"

Let him in! It is a mercy he didn't shake his arm off. He was at home in five minutes. Nothing could be heartier. His niece looked just the same. So did Topper when *he* came. So did the plump sister, when *she* came. So did everyone when *they* came. Wonderful party, wonderful games, wonderful unanimity, won-der-ful happiness!

But he was early at the office next morning. Oh he was early there. If he could only be there first, and catch Bob Cratchit coming late! That was the thing he had set his heart upon.

And he did it; yes he did! The clock struck nine. No Bob. A quarter past. No Bob. He was full eighteen minutes and a half, behind his time. Scrooge sat with his door wide open, that he might see him come into the tank.

His hat was off, before he opened the door; his comforter too. He was on his stool in a jiffy; driving away with his pen, as if he were trying to overtake nine o'clock.

"Hallo!" growled Scrooge, in his accustomed voice as near as he could feign it. "What do you mean by coming here at this time of day?"

"I'm very sorry, sir," said Bob. "I am behind my time."

"You are?" repeated Scrooge. "Yes. I think you are. Step this way, if you please."

"It's only once a year, sir," pleaded Bob, appearing from the Tank. "It shall not be repeated. I was making rather merry yesterday, sir."

"Now, I'll tell you what, my friend," said Scrooge, "I am not going to stand this sort of thing any longer. And therefore," he continued, leaping from his stool, and giving Bob such a dig in the waistcoat that he staggered back into the tank again: "and therefore I am about to raise your salary!"

Bob trembled, and got a little nearer to the ruler. He had a momentary idea of knocking Scrooge down with it; holding him; and calling to the people in the court for help and a strait-waistcoat.

"A merry Christmas, Bob!" said Scrooge, with an earnestness that could not be mistaken, as he clapped him on the back. "A merrier Christmas, Bob, my good fellow, than I have given you, for many a year! I'll raise our salary, and endeavour to assist your struggling family, and we will discuss your affairs this very afternoon, over a Christmas bowl of smoking bishop,[1] Bob! Make up the fires, and buy another coal scuttle before you dot another i, Bob Cratchit!"

Scrooge was better than his word. He did it all, and infinitely more; and to Tiny Tim, who did NOT die, he was a second father. He became as good a friend, as good a master, and as good a man, as the good old city knew, or any other good old city, town, or borough, in the good old world. Some people laughed to see the alteration in him, but he let them laugh, and little heeded them; for he was wise enough to know that nothing ever happened on this globe, for good, at which some people did not have their fill of laughter in the outset; and knowing that such as these would be blind anyway, he thought it quite as well that they should

[1] *smoking bishop* Hot punch made from wine, oranges, sugar, and cloves.

wrinkle up their eyes in grins, as have the malady in less attractive forms. His own heart laughed: and that was quite enough for him.

He had no further intercourse with spirits, but lived upon the Total Abstinence Principle, ever afterwards; and it was always said of him, that he knew how to keep Christmas well, if any man alive possessed the knowledge. May that be truly said of us, and all of us! And so, as Tiny Tim observed, God Bless Us, Every One!

THE END

—1843

In Context

A Victorian Christmas

Several of the rituals of Christmas as it is now observed in Western societies were still taking shape in 1843 when Dickens published *A Christmas Carol*; the first Christmas card was designed by a London illustrator that same year, while the Christmas tree had been introduced into England only two years earlier by Prince Albert. Christmas as an occasion for family get-togethers, mistletoe, and turkey dinners, however, was already well established, as the following sentimental piece from *Sketches by Boz* illustrates.

from Charles Dickens, *Sketches by Boz* (1843)

CHAPTER 2: A CHRISTMAS DINNER

Christmas time! That man must be a misanthrope indeed, in whose breast something like a jovial feeling is not roused—in whose mind some pleasant associations are not awakened—by the recurrence of Christmas. There are people who will tell you that Christmas is not to them what it used to be; that each succeeding Christmas has found some cherished hope, or happy prospect, of the year before, dimmed or passed away; that the present only serves to remind them of reduced circumstances and straitened[1] incomes—of the feasts they once bestowed on hollow friends, and of the cold looks that meet them now, in adversity and misfortune. Never heed such dismal reminiscences. There are few men who have lived long enough in the world, who cannot call up such thoughts any day in the year. Then do not select the merriest of the three hundred and sixty-five for your doleful recollections, but draw your chair nearer the blazing fire—fill the glass and send round the song—and if your room be smaller than it was a dozen years ago, or if your glass be filled with reeking punch, instead of sparkling wine, put a good face on the matter, and empty it offhand, and fill another, and troll off the old ditty you used to sing, and thank God it's no worse. Look on the merry faces of your children (if you have any) as they sit round the fire. One little seat may be empty; one slight form that gladdened the father's heart, and roused the mother's pride to look upon, may not be there. Dwell not upon the past; think not that one short year ago, the fair child now resolving into dust, sat before you, with the bloom of health upon its cheek and the gaiety of infancy in its joyous eye. Reflect upon your present blessings—of which every man has many—not your misfortunes, of which all men have some. Fill your glass again, with a merry face and contented heart. Our life on it, but your Christmas shall be merry, and your new year a happy one!

---

[1] *straitened* Insufficient.

Who can be insensible to the outpourings of good feeling, and the honest interchange of affectionate attachment, which abound at this season of the year? A Christmas family party! We know nothing in nature more delightful! There seems a magic in the very name of Christmas. Petty jealousies and discords are forgotten; social feelings are awakened, in bosoms to which they have long been strangers; father and son, or brother and sister, who have met and passed with averted gaze, or a look of cold recognition, for months before, proffer and return the cordial embrace, and bury their past animosities in their present happiness. Kindly hearts that have yearned towards each other, but have been withheld by false notions of pride and self-dignity, are again reunited, and all is kindness and benevolence! Would that Christmas lasted the whole year through (as it ought), and that the prejudices and passions which deform our better nature were never called into action among those to whom they should ever be strangers!

The Christmas family party that we mean, is not a mere assemblage of relations got up at a week or two's notice, originating this year, having no family precedent in the last, and not likely to be repeated in the next. No. It is an annual gathering of all the accessible members of the family, young or old, rich or poor; and all the children look forward to it, for two months beforehand, in a fever of anticipation. Formerly it was held at grandpapa's; but grandpapa getting old, and grandmamma getting old too, and rather infirm, they have given up housekeeping, and domesticated themselves with Uncle George; so, the party always takes place at Uncle George's house, but grandmamma sends in most of the good things, and grandpapa always *will* toddle down, all the way to Newgate market, to buy the turkey, which he engages a porter to bring home behind him in triumph, always insisting on the man's being rewarded with a glass of spirits, over and above his hire, to drink "a merry Christmas and a happy new year" to Aunt George. As to grandmamma, she is very secret and mysterious for two or three days beforehand, but not sufficiently so to prevent rumours getting afloat that she has purchased a beautiful new cap with pink ribbons for each of the servants, together with sundry books, and pen-knives, and pencil-cases, for the younger branches; to say nothing of diverse secret additions to the order originally given by Aunt George at the pastry cook's, such as another dozen of mince pies for the dinner, and a large plum cake for the children.

On Christmas Eve, grandmamma is always in excellent spirits, and after employing all the children during the day, in stoning the plums, and all that, insists, regularly every year, on Uncle George coming down into the kitchen, taking off his coat, and stirring the pudding for half an hour or so, which Uncle George good humouredly does to the vociferous delight of the children and servants. The evening concludes with a glorious game of blindman's buff, in an early stage of which grandpapa takes great care to be caught, in order that he may have an opportunity of displaying his dexterity.

On the following morning, the old couple, with as many of the children as the pew will hold, go to church in great state: leaving Aunt George at home dusting decanters and filling castors, and Uncle George carrying bottles into the dining parlour, and calling for corkscrews, and getting into everybody's way.

When the church party return to lunch, grandpapa produces a small sprig of mistletoe from his pocket, and tempts the boys to kiss their little cousins under it—a proceeding which affords both the boys and the old gentleman unlimited satisfaction, but which rather outrages grandmamma's ideas of decorum, until grandpapa says that when he was just thirteen years and three months old *he* kissed grandmamma under a mistletoe too, on which the children clap their hands, and laugh very heartily, as do Aunt George and Uncle George; and grandmamma looks pleased, and says, with a benevolent smile, that grandpapa was an impudent young dog, on which the children laugh very heartily again, and grandpapa more heartily than any of them.

But all these diversions are nothing to the subsequent excitement when grandmamma in a high cap, and slate-coloured silk gown; and grandpapa with a beautifully plaited shirt frill, and white neckerchief; seat themselves on one side of the drawing room fire, with Uncle George's children and little cousins innumerable seated in the front, waiting the arrival of the expected visitors. Suddenly a hackney coach is heard to stop, and Uncle George, who has been looking out of the window, exclaims, "Here's Jane!" on which the children rush to the door, and helter skelter downstairs; and Uncle Robert and Aunt Jane, and the dear little baby, and the nurse, and the whole party, are ushered upstairs amidst tumultuous shouts of "Oh, my!" from the children, and frequently repeated warnings not to hurt baby from the nurse. And grandpapa takes the child, and grandmamma kisses her daughter, and the confusion of this first entry has scarcely subsided, when some other aunts and uncles with more cousins arrive, and the grown-up cousins flirt with each other, and so do the little cousins too, for that matter, and nothing is to be heard but a confused din of talking, laughing, and merriment.

A hesitating double knock at the street door, heard during a momentary pause in the conversation, excites a general inquiry of "Who's that?" and two or three children, who have been standing at the window, announce in a low voice, that it's "poor Aunt Margaret." Upon which, Aunt George leaves the room to welcome the newcomer; and grandmamma draws herself up, rather stiff and stately; for Margaret married a poor man without her consent, and poverty not being a sufficient weighty punishment for her offence, has been discarded by her friends, and debarred the society of her dearest relatives. But Christmas has come round, and the unkind feelings that have struggled against better dispositions during the year, have melted away before its genial influence, like half-formed ice beneath the morning sun. It is not difficult in a moment of angry feeling for a parent to denounce a disobedient child; but, to banish her at a period of general good will and hilarity from the hearth, round which she has sat on so many anniversaries of the same day, expanding by slow degrees from infancy to girlhood, and then bursting, almost imperceptibly, into a woman, is widely different. The air of conscious rectitude, and cold forgiveness, which the old lady has assumed, sits ill upon her; and when the poor girl is led in by her sister, pale in looks and broken in hope—not from poverty, for that she could bear, but from the consciousness of undeserved neglect, and unmerited unkindness—it is easy to see how much of it is assumed. A momentary pause succeeds; the girl breaks suddenly from her sister and throws herself, sobbing, on her mother's neck. The father steps hastily forward, and takes her husband's hand. Friends crowd round to offer their hearty congratulations, and happiness and harmony again prevail.

As to the dinner, it's perfectly delightful—nothing goes wrong, and everybody is in the very best of spirits, and disposed to please and be pleased. Grandpapa relates a circumstantial account of the purchase of the turkey, with a slight digression relative to the purchase of previous turkeys, on former Christmas Days, which grandmamma corroborates in the minutest particular. Uncle George tells stories, and carves poultry, and takes wine, and jokes with the children at the side table, and winks at the cousins that are making love,[1] or being made love to, and exhilarates everybody with his good humour and hospitality; and when, at last, a stout servant staggers in with a gigantic pudding, with a sprig of holly in the top, there is such a laughing, and shouting, and clapping of little chubby hands, and kicking up of fat dumpy legs, as can only be equalled by the applause with which the astonishing feat of pouring lighted brandy into mince pies, is received by the younger visitors. Then the dessert!—and the wine!—and the fun! Such beautiful speeches, and *such* songs, from Aunt Margaret's husband, who turns out to be such a nice man, and *so* attentive to grandmamma! Even grandpapa not only sings his annual song with unprecedented vigour, but on being honoured with an unanimous *encore*, according to annual custom, actually comes out with a new one which nobody but grandmamma ever heard before; and a young scapegrace[2] of a cousin, who has been in some disgrace

[1]   *making love*   Wooing; flirting.

[2]   *scapegrace*   Rascal.

with the old people, for certain heinous sins of omission and commission—neglecting to call, and persisting in drinking Burton ale—astonishes everybody into convulsions of laughter by volunteering the most extraordinary comic songs that ever were heard. And thus the evening passes, in a strain of rational goodwill and cheerfulness, doing more to awaken the sympathies of every member of the party in behalf of his neighbour, and to perpetuate their good feeling, during the ensuing year, than half the homilies that have ever been written, by half the Divines that have ever lived.

IN CONTEXT

The Workhouse

The condition of the poor—and in particular the condition of poor children—was always of great concern to Dickens. Perhaps most notably among his previous work, *Oliver Twist* (1838) portrays the hardships for children of life in the workhouse. The workhouse as an institution is also referred to in *A Christmas Carol*, and Dickens continued to write on the subject in later years; the following essay appeared in 1850 in Dickens's magazine *Household Words*.

Charles Dickens, "A Walk in the Workhouse," from *Household Words* (1850)

On a certain Sunday I formed one of the congregation assembled in the chapel of a large metropolitan Workhouse. With the exception of the clergyman and clerk, and a very few officials, there were none but paupers present. The children sat in the galleries; the women in the body of the chapel, and in one of the side aisles; the men in the remaining aisle. The service was decorously performed, though the sermon might have been much better adapted to the comprehension and to the circumstances of the hearers. The usual supplications were offered, with more than the usual significancy in such a place, for the fatherless children and widows, for all sick persons and young children, for all that were desolate and oppressed, for the comforting and helping of the weak-hearted, for the raising up of them that had fallen; for all that were in danger, necessity, and tribulation. The prayers of the congregation were desired "for several persons in the various wards dangerously ill"; and others who were recovering returned their thanks to Heaven.

Among this congregation were some evil-looking young women, and beetle-browed young men; but not many—perhaps that kind of characters kept away. Generally, the faces (those of the children excepted) were depressed and subdued, and wanted colour. Aged people were there in every variety. Mumbling, blear-eyed, spectacled, stupid, deaf, lame; vacantly winking in the gleams of sun that now and then crept in through the open doors, from the paved yard; shading their listening ears, or blinking eyes, with their withered hands; poring over their books, leering at nothing, going to sleep, crouching and drooping in corners. There were weird old women, all skeleton within, all bonnet and cloak without, continually wiping their eyes with dirty dusters of pocket handkerchiefs; and there were ugly old crones, both male and female, with a ghastly kind of contentment upon them which was not at all comforting to see. Upon the whole, it was the dragon, Pauperism, in a very weak and impotent condition: toothless, fangless, drawing his breath heavily enough, and hardly worth chaining up.

When the service was over, I walked with the humane and conscientious gentleman whose duty it was to take that walk, that Sunday morning, through the little world of poverty enclosed within the workhouse walls. It was inhabited by a population of some fifteen hundred or two thousand paupers, ranging from the infant newly born or not yet come into the pauper world, to the old man dying on his bed.

In a room opening from a squalid yard, where a number of listless women were lounging to and fro, trying to get warm in the ineffectual sunshine of the tardy May morning—in the "Itch Ward," not to compromise the truth—a woman such as HOGARTH[1] has often drawn, was hurriedly getting on her gown before a dusty fire. She was the nurse, or wardswoman, of that insalubrious department—herself a pauper—flabby, raw-boned, untidy—unpromising and coarse of aspect as need be. But, on being spoken to about the patients whom she had in charge, she turned round, with her shabby gown half on, half off, and fell a crying with all her might. Not for show, not querulously, not in any mawkish sentiment, but in the deep grief and affliction of her heart; turning away her dishevelled head: sobbing most bitterly, wringing her hands, and letting fall abundance of great tears, that choked her utterance. What was the matter with the nurse of the itch ward? Oh, "the dropped child" was dead! Oh, the child that was found in the street, and she had brought up ever since, had died an hour ago, and see where the little creature lay, beneath this cloth! The dear, the pretty dear!

The dropped child seemed too small and poor a thing for Death to be in earnest with, but Death had taken it; and already its diminutive form was neatly washed, composed, and stretched as if in sleep upon a box. I thought I heard a voice from Heaven saying, It shall be well for thee, O nurse of the itch ward, when some less gentle pauper does those offices to thy cold form, that such as the dropped child are the angels who behold my Father's face!

In another room were several ugly old women crouching, witch-like, round a hearth, and chattering and nodding, after the manner of the monkeys. "All well here? And enough to eat?" A general chattering and chuckling; at last an answer from a volunteer. "Oh yes, gentleman! Bless you, gentleman! Lord bless the Parish of St. So-and-So! It feed the hungry, sir, and give drink to the thusty, and it warm them which is cold, so it do, and good luck to the parish of St. So-and-So, and thankee, gentleman!" Elsewhere, a party of pauper nurses were at dinner. "How do YOU get on?" "Oh pretty well, sir! We works hard, and we lives hard—like the sodgers!"[2]

In another room, a kind of purgatory or place of transition, six or eight noisy madwomen were gathered together, under the superintendence of one sane attendant. Among them was a girl of two or three and twenty, very prettily dressed, of most respectable appearance and good manners, who had been brought in from the house where she had lived as domestic servant (having, I suppose, no friends), on account of being subject to epileptic fits, and requiring to be removed under the influence of a very bad one. She was by no means of the same stuff, or the same breeding, or the same experience, or in the same state of mind, as those by whom she was surrounded; and she pathetically complained that the daily association and the nightly noise made her worse, and was driving her mad—which was perfectly evident. The case was noted for inquiry and redress, but she said she had already been there for some weeks.

If this girl had stolen her mistress's watch, I do not hesitate to say she would have been infinitely better off. We have come to this absurd, this dangerous, this monstrous pass, that the dishonest felon is, in respect of cleanliness, order, diet, and accommodation, better provided for, and taken care of, than the honest pauper.

And this conveys no special imputation on the workhouse of the parish of St. So-and-So, where, on the contrary, I saw many things to commend. It was very agreeable, recollecting that most infamous and atrocious enormity committed at Tooting[3]—an enormity which, a hundred years

---

[1]   *Hogarth*   Artist and printmaker William Hogarth (1697–1764), was greatly admired by Dickens for his satirical paintings and prints of eighteenth-century London life.

[2]   *sodgers*   I.e., soldiers.

[3]   *Tooting*   In 1849, after four half-starved children had died of cholera in a Tooting workhouse, the proprietor was found guilty of manslaughter.

hence, will still be vividly remembered in the byways of English life, and which has done more to engender a gloomy discontent and suspicion among many thousands of the people than all the Chartist leaders[1] could have done in all their lives—to find the pauper children in this workhouse looking robust and well, and apparently the objects of very great care. In the Infant School—a large, light, airy room at the top of the building—the little creatures, being at dinner, and eating their potatoes heartily, were not cowed by the presence of strange visitors, but stretched out their small hands to be shaken, with a very pleasant confidence. And it was comfortable to see two mangy pauper rocking-horses rampant in a corner. In the girls' school, where the dinner was also in progress, everything bore a cheerful and healthy aspect. The meal was over in the boys' school by the time of our arrival there, and the room was not yet quite rearranged; but the boys were roaming unrestrained about a large and airy yard, as any other schoolboys might have done. Some of them had been drawing large ships upon the schoolroom wall; and if they had a mast with shrouds and stays set up for practice (as they have in the Middlesex House of Correction), it would be so much the better. At present, if a boy should feel a strong impulse upon him to learn the art of going aloft, he could only gratify it, I presume, as the men and women paupers gratify their aspirations after better board and lodging, by smashing as many workhouse windows as possible, and being promoted to prison.

In one place, the Newgate[2] of the workhouse, a company of boys and youths were locked up in a yard alone; their dayroom being a kind of kennel where the casual poor used formerly to be littered down at night. Diverse of them had been there some long time. "Are they never going away?" was the natural inquiry. "Most of them are crippled, in some form or other," said the wardsman, "and not fit for anything." They slunk about, like dispirited wolves or hyenas; and made a pounce at their food when it was served out, much as those animals do. The big-headed idiot shuffling his feet along the pavement, in the sunlight outside, was a more agreeable object everyway.

Groves of babies in arms; groves of mothers and other sick women in bed; groves of lunatics; jungles of men in stone-paved downstairs dayrooms, waiting for their dinners; longer and longer groves of old people, in upstairs infirmary wards, wearing out life, God knows how—this was the scenery through which the walk lay, for two hours. In some of these latter chambers, there were pictures stuck against the wall, and a neat display of crockery and pewter on a kind of sideboard; now and then it was a treat to see a plant or two; in almost every ward there was a cat.

In all of these long walks of aged and infirm, some old people were bedridden, and had been for a long time; some were sitting on their beds half naked; some dying in their beds; some out of bed, and sitting at a table near the fire. A sullen or lethargic indifference to what was asked, a blunted sensibility to everything but warmth and food, a moody absence of complaint as being of no use, a dogged silence and resentful desire to be left alone again, I thought were generally apparent. On our walking into the midst of one of these dreary perspectives of old men, nearly the following little dialogue took place, the nurse not being immediately at hand:

"All well here?"

No answer. An old man in a Scotch cap[3] sitting among others on a form at the table, eating out of a tin porringer,[4] pushes back his cap a little to look at us, claps it down on his forehead again with the palm of his hand, and goes on eating.

"All well here?" (repeated).

No answer. Another old man sitting on his bed, paralytically peeling a boiled potato, lifts his head

[1]   *Chartist leaders*   The Chartist movement pressed for political (and by implication, social and economic) reform from 1836 onwards.

[2]   *Newgate*   Newgate was London's main prison.

[3]   *Scotch cap*   Woolen hat worn in the Highlands.

[4]   *porringer*   Bowl for porridge, soups, and other runny foods.

and stares.

"Enough to eat?"

No answer. Another old man, in bed, turns himself and coughs.

"How are YOU today?" To the last old man.

That old man says nothing; but another old man, a tall old man of very good address, speaking with perfect correctness, comes forward from somewhere, and volunteers an answer. The reply almost always proceeds from a volunteer, and not from the person looked at or spoken to.

"We are very old, sir," in a mild, distinct voice. "We can't expect to be well, most of us."

"Are you comfortable?"

"I have no complaint to make, sir." With a half shake of his head, a half shrug of his shoulders, and a kind of apologetic smile.

"Enough to eat?"

"Why, sir, I have but a poor appetite," with the same air as before; "and yet I get through my allowance very easily."

"But," showing a porringer with a Sunday dinner in it; "here is a portion of mutton, and three potatoes. You can't starve on that?"

"Oh dear no, sir," with the same apologetic air. "Not starve."

"What do you want?"

"We have very little bread, sir. It's an exceedingly small quantity of bread."

The nurse, who is now rubbing her hands at the questioner's elbow, interferes with, "It ain't much raly, sir. You see they've only six ounces a day, and when they've took their breakfast, there CAN only be a little left for night, sir." Another old man, hitherto invisible, rises out of his bedclothes, as out of a grave, and looks on.

"You have tea at night?" The questioner is still addressing the well-spoken old man.

"Yes, sir, we have tea at night."

"And you save what bread you can from the morning, to eat with it?"

"Yes, sir—if we can save any."

"And you want more to eat with it?"

"Yes, sir." With a very anxious face.

The questioner, in the kindness of his heart, appears a little discomposed, and changes the subject.

"What has become of the old man who used to lie in that bed in the corner?"

The nurse don't remember what old man is referred to. There has been such a many old men. The well-spoken old man is doubtful. The spectral old man who has come to life in bed says "Billy Stevens." Another old man who has previously had his head in the fireplace, pipes out, "Charley Walters."

Something like a feeble interest is awakened. I suppose Charley Walters had conversation in him.

"He's dead," says the piping old man.

Another old man, with one eye screwed up, hastily displaces the piping old man, and says.

"Yes! Charley Walters died in that bed, and—and—"

"Billy Stevens," persists the spectral old man.

"No, no! and Johnny Rogers died in that bed, and—and—they're both on 'em dead—and Sam'l Bowyer"; this seems very extraordinary to him; "he went out!"

With this he subsides, and all the old men (having had quite enough of it) subside, and the spectral old man goes into his grave again, and takes the shade of Billy Stevens with him.

As we turn to go out at the door, another previously invisible old man, a hoarse old man in a flannel gown, is standing there, as if he had just come up through the floor.

"I beg your pardon, sir, could I take the liberty of saying a word?"

"Yes, what is it?"

"I am greatly better in my health, sir; but what I want, to get me quite round," with his hand on his throat, "is a little fresh air, sir. It has always done my complaint so much good, sir. The regular leave for going out, comes round so seldom, that if the gentlemen, next Friday, would give me leave to go out walking, now and then—for only an hour or so, sir!—"

Who could wonder, looking through those weary vistas of bed and infirmity, that it should do him good to meet with some other scenes, and assure himself that there was something else on earth? Who could help wondering why the old men lived on as they did; what grasp they had on life; what crumbs of interest or occupation they could pick up from its bare board; whether Charley Walters had ever described to them the days when he kept company with some old pauper woman in the bud, or Billy Stevens ever told them of the time when he was a dweller in the far off foreign land called Home!

The morsel of burnt child, lying in another room, so patiently, in bed, wrapped in lint, and looking steadfastly at us with his bright quiet eyes when we spoke to him kindly, looked as if the knowledge of these things, and of all the tender things there are to think about, might have been in his mind as if he thought, with us, that there was a fellow-feeling in the pauper nurses which appeared to make them more kind to their charges than the race of common nurses in the hospitals—as if he mused upon the future of some older children lying around him in the same place, and thought it best, perhaps, all things considered, that he should die—as if he knew, without fear, of those many coffins, made and unmade, piled up in the store below—and of his unknown friend, "the dropped child," calm upon the box lid covered with a cloth. But there was something wistful and appealing, too, in his tiny face, as if, in the midst of all the hard necessities and incongruities he pondered on, he pleaded, in behalf of the helpless and the aged poor, for a little more liberty—and a little more bread.

The first Christmas card, 1843. The card was commissioned by man of business Sir Henry Cole to save time in sending greetings, and designed by illustrator John Callcott Horsley.

GRACE AGUILAR
1816 – 1847

Although she began her writing career as a poet and published many essays on theology, Grace Aguilar is known chiefly as a novelist. Her novels are mainly historical and focus on the domestic, but she was also one of the first Victorian women writers to stretch beyond topics of a domestic nature and deal with the political, concentrating on issues of exile, piety, morality, assimilation, and religious tolerance, with particular reference to Judaism and Zionism. Both her novels and her essays became well known in England and America, particularly among Jews. In a tribute, a group of Jewish women wrote that until Aguilar began writing, it had "in modern times never been the case that a woman … should stand forth the public advocate of the faith of Israel."

Aguilar was born in London to Sarah Dias Fernandes and Emanuel Aguilar, both of Portuguese-Jewish descent; they had come to England in order to avoid the Spanish Inquisition. Although Aguilar lived in the city for much of her early childhood, she was regularly sent to the south coast of England, a location thought to be more salubrious for a child of delicate health. Mainly educated by her parents, she spent much time in isolation, reading books from a precocious age and writing in her journals, which she continued to keep throughout her life. She began writing poems and completed a play before reaching her teens. Her early poems were eventually published in her first collection of poetry, *The Magic Wreath* (1835). Even in these early writings Aguilar displays an abiding concern for Jewish people and their traditions.

Aguilar published many of her poems and essays in major Jewish periodicals, such as *The Occident* (she was one of the American magazine's highest paid writers), but she also published in Christian women's magazines, and she earned a good living by her pen. In her popular poem "The Wanderers," Aguilar brought together her concerns about the rights of Jews and of women by re-imagining the Biblical story of Hagar, who was sent into exile by Abraham's wife, Sarah, for conceiving a child by Abraham. It was a period in which women of all faiths were beginning to speak out strongly and in which Jews in general were trying to obtain full civil rights—although there was increasing pressure on British Jews to assimilate or convert to Christianity.

As Michael Galchinsky has observed, much of Aguilar's work demonstrates an attempt to bargain with both Christian and Jewish men in order to obtain tolerance from both: "If Christians would tolerate Jews, Aguilar agreed that Jews would keep their different practices within the domestic sphere. Similarly, if Jewish men would provide women in the community with the education they lacked, women would agree to restrict their use of this education to training children in the home." Novels such as *Home Influence: A Tale for Mothers and Daughters* (1847) and its sequels concentrate on the concerns of women, while *The Vale of Cedars* (1850) brings together both of Aguilar's interests. Her *Women of Israel* series (1844)—biographical studies of Biblical, historical, and modern women—shows Aguilar at the height of both her passion and her talent.

Aguilar, always of delicate health, was considerably weakened by a bout of measles that she contracted in 1938, at the age of 21. She became increasingly frail, and in 1847 her brother Emanuel persuaded her to visit Frankfurt to consult a German physician. It was there that Aguilar died and was buried in a Jewish cemetery. Her mother later edited and compiled several volumes of her work, and her readership increased after her death.

⌘⌘⌘

Past, Present, and Future: A Sketch

It was a place of graves, and still and lone,
As all of life's strange history were flown,
And nothing left but the cold stones, that lay
Thick-crested o'er with emblems of decay—
5 High wavy grass, where never flowers had rest,
And the dull clinging moss, that lay caressed
E'en by the pale cold marble. There was one,
A mother's last low resting; and her child
Stood gazing round bewildered. There was none
10 Like that her soul trail pictured, undefiled
By Time's too with'ring hand. She sought a stone,
Pure in its spotless marble—standing lone,
With its brief record of a loved one gone,
And all untouched by shadow of decay;
15 For, oh! that full heart, but yesterday
It felt, since they had laid her there, alas!
Through bloomless weeds, and melancholy grass.
They led her where a lowly grave reposed,
Whose marble shrine thick clustering weeds enclosed,
20 There! lay she there! her tomb by Time's cold hand
Touched as all others, in that grave-girt sand,
When scarcely seemed it that a week had passed
Since those fond eyes had looked and smiled their last;
Since that loved voice its last low whisper said,
25 And breathed its blessing on that mourner's head.
Were these but memories now? and could it be
Long months had passed into eternity?
That time had flung his mantle o'er the grave,
And when the long grass in dark masses wave,
30 Low wailing accents filled the breezy blast;
"The loved, the mourned, the cherished, all are past."
Shrine of the past! that solitude—around,
Beneath, that word of woe hath impress found—
Impress and echo; but on that lone heart
35 The past was present, sweeter joys t'impart
In shadow than in being. From the cup

Of mem'ry, life in such sweet hues gleamed up,
And brought forth bliss which had been with such
    power,
How might she deem them phantoms of the hour,
40 To shine a while and pass? Too soon she felt
They were but shadows, in her heart that dwelt
And mingled with her being. Oh! the woe
Of such awak'ning! Fled the sunny glow,
The cherished dream—the past once more was past,
45 And the dim present all its misery cast
One little moment; then, by Mercy sent,
The future to the present radiance lent,
And o'er that mourning spirit softly stole
Sweet visions of the freed, the heaven-born soul,
50 Awaiting hers in those fair realms of love,
Which smiled in beauty, life's last home, above.
The past, the present, merged in Faith's fond thought,
Which such bright glimpses of the future brought,
And softened that deep woe—and she hath bowed,
55 Believing and adoring, while the cloud
Folding that spirit, melted into tears,
Which grief assuaging, e'en its pang endears—
She knew her heart must wear a while its chain,
But earth in Faith's effulgence smiled again.
—1842

The Hebrew's Appeal

On Occasion of the Late Fearful Ukase Promoted by the Emperor of Russia[1]

Awake! arise! ye friends of Israel's race,
The wail of thousands lingers on the air,

---

[1] [Aguilar's note] The above poem was written nearly six months ago, when the Russian ukase [decree] was first made public, and sent to the only paper in England devoted to Jewish interests—the Voice of Jacob—the writer wishing to prove that at least one female Jewish

By heavy pinions borne, through realms of space,
'Til Israel shudd'ring, Israel's woe must bear;
5 The voice of suff'ring echoes to the skies,
And oh, not yet! one pitying heart replies.

List to the groan from manly bosoms rent,
The wilder sob from weaker spirits wrung,
The deep woe that hath in voice no vent,
10 Yet round the heart her deathly robe has flung,
And childish tears flow thick and fast like rain,
From eyes that never wept, and ne'er shall weep again.

Vain, vain, the mother's piteous shriek of woe,
Her dying infants clinging to her breast;
15 And age infirm, and youth, whose high hearts glow;
Vain, vain their cry for mercy on the oppressed.
The Ukase has gone forth—a word, a breath,
And thousands are cast out, to exile and to death.

Ay, death! for such is exile—fearful doom,
20 From homes expelled—yet still to Poland chained;
'Til want and famine mind and life consume,
And sorrow's poisoned chalice, all is drained.
Oh God, that this should be! that one frail man
Hath power to crush a nation 'neath his ban.

25 Will none arise! with outstretched hand to save!
No prayer for pity, and for aid awake?
Will She° who gave to Liberty the slave,   *England*
For God's own people not one effort make?
Will She not rise once more, in mercy clad,
30 And heal the bleeding heart, and Sorrow's sons make
    glad?

Will England sleep, when Justice bids her wake,
And send her voice all thrillingly afar?
Will England sleep, when her rebuke might shake
With shame and terror, e'en the tyrant Czar,
35 And 'neath the magic of her mild appeal,
Move Russia's frozen soul for Israel to feel?

Oh England! thou hast called us to thy breast,
And done to orphans all a mother's part,
And given them peace, and liberty, and rest,
40 And healing poured into the homeless heart;
Then, oh once more, let Israel mercy claim,
And suff'ring thousands bless our England's honoured
    name.

And let one prayer from Hebrew hearths ascend
To Israel's God, that He may deign reply,
45 And yet again His chosen race defend,
And "have respect"[1] once more "unto their cry,"[2]
And e'en from depths of darkness and despair,
Give freedom to His own, and "all their burden bear."[3]

For shall we sink, though dark our way and drear,
50 And Hope hath found in misery a tomb?
Though man be silent, Mercy hath no tear,
And Love and Joy are withered 'neath the gloom?
No! God is near to hear us while we crave,
And He will "bare His holy arm, to shield us and to
    save."[4]
—1844

heart and voice were raised in an appeal for her afflicted brethren. The editor of the V. of J. did not insert it, on the plea of having so much press of matter as to prevent giving it the required space. The Christian Lady's Magazine not only accepted and inserted it, but in bold and spirited prose appealed to her countrymen on the same subject. Still a Jewish paper is the natural channel for the public appearance of the poem, and therefore the writer sends it to the Occident, believing that though somewhat late, it will not there be disregarded. [Aguilar's poem responds to an 1844 proclamation by Emperor Nicolas I restricting Russian Jews' activities and ordering them to resettle on the Russian/Polish border.]

[1] *"have respect"* From Leviticus 26.9, in which God says to the Jewish people: "I will have respect unto you, and make you fruitful, and multiply you, and establish my covenant with you."

[2] *"unto their cry"* From Psalms 34.15: "The eyes of the Lord are upon the righteous, and his ears are open unto their cry."

[3] *"all their burden bear"* See Psalms 55.22: "Cast thy burden upon the Lord, and he shall sustain thee: he shall never suffer the righteous to be moved."

[4] *"bare ... save"* See Isaiah 52.10: "The Lord hath made bare His holy arm in the eyes of all the nations; and all the ends of the earth shall see the salvation of our God."

The Wanderers
Genesis 21, 14–20[1]

With saddened heart and tearful eye the mother went her way,
The Patriarch's[2] mandate had gone forth, and Hagar must not stay.
Oh! who can tell the emotions deep that pressed on Abra'am's heart—
As thus, obedient to his God, from Ismael called to part!

5 But God had spoken, and he knew His word was changeless truth,
He could not doubt His blessing would protect the friendless youth;
He bade him go, nor would he heed the anguish of his soul;
He turned aside—a father's woe in silence to control.

Now hand in hand they wend their way, o'er hills and vale and wild;
10 The mother's heart was full of grief, but smiled in glee her child:
Fearless and free, he felt restraint would never gall him now—
And hailed with joy the fresh'ning breeze that fanned his fair young brow.

His mother's heart was desolate, and tears swelled in her eye;
Scarce to his artless words of love her quiv'ring lips reply.
15 *She* only saw the *future* as a lone and dreary wild:
The *present* stood before the lad in joyance undefiled.

She knew, alas! his boyish strength too soon would droop and fade;
And who was, in that lonely scene, to give them food and aid?
With trembling gaze she oft would mark the flushing of his cheek,
20 And list in terror, lest he should 'gin falteringly to speak!

Fatigue she felt not for herself, not heeded care nor pain—
But nearer, nearer to her breast her boy at times she'd strain;
Beersheba's wilderness they see before them dark and wide;
Oh, who across its scorching sand their wandering steps will guide?

25 The flush departed from the cheek which she so oft has kissed;
To his glad tones of childish glee no longer may she list;
A pallor as of death is spread o'er those sweet features now—
She sees him droop before the blast that fanned his aching brow.

"Oh, mother lay me down," he cried, "I know not what I feel,
30 But something cold and rushing seems thro' all my limbs to steal—
Oh kiss me, mother dear, and then ah, lay me down to sleep—
Nay, do not look upon me thus—kiss me and do not weep!"

Scarce could her feeble arms support her child, and lay him where
Some clustering shrubs might shield him from the heavy scorching air;
35 His drooping eyelids closed; his breath came painfully and slow—
She bent her head on his a while in wild yet speechless woe.

Then from his side she hurried, as impelled she knew not why,

---

[1] *Genesis 21, 14–20* In which God orders Abraham to cast out his mistress, Hagar, and their illegitimate son, Ishmael, upon the birth of a son by his wife, Sarah. Hagar wanders the parched desert and has just given up hope for Ishmael's life, when God sees her sorrow, leads her to water, and promises her that Ishmael will begin "a great nation."

[2] *Patriarch* I.e., Abraham.

Save that she could not linger there—she could not
    see him die—
She lifted up her voice and wept—and o'er the lonely
    wild
40 "Let me not see his death!" was borne, "my Ismael,
    my child!"

And silence came upon her then, her stricken soul to
    calm;
And suddenly and strange there fell a soft and
    soothing balm—
And then a voice came stealing, on the still and
    fragrant air—
A still small voice[1] that would be heard, tho' solitude
    was there.

45 "What aileth thee, oh Hagar?" thus it spoke: "fear not,
    for God hath heard
The lad's voice where he is—and thou, trust in thy
    Maker's word!
Awake! arise! lift up the lad and hold him in thine
    hand—
I will of him a nation make, before Me, he shall
    stand."[2]

It ceased, that voice; and silence now, as strangely soft
    and still,

50 The boundless desert once again with eloquence
    would fill—
And strength returned to Hagar's frame, for God hath
    oped her eyes—
And lo! amid the arid sands a well of water lies!

Quick to her boy, with beating heart, the anxious
    mother flies,
And to his lips, and hands, and brow, the cooling
    draught applies—
55 He wakes! he breathes! the flush of life is mantling on
    his cheek—
He smiles! he speaks! oh those quick tears his mother's
    joy shall speak!

She held him to her throbbing breast, she gazed upon
    his face—
The beaming features, one by one, in silent love to
    trace.
She bade him kneel to bless the Hand that saved him
    in the wild—
60 But oh! few words her lips could speak, save these
    —"My child, my child!"
    —1845

---

[1]   A still small voice   See 1 Kings 19.12.

[2]   "What aileth ... stand."   From Genesis 21.17.

EMILY BRONTË

1818 – 1848

It would seem that there were two Emily Brontës: one a shy, introverted, and unremarkable young woman, and the other the strong-willed, brilliant, and legendary woman who became almost a mythic figure after her death at the age of thirty. Both versions develop from the portrait her sister Charlotte gave of her in the second edition of *Wuthering Heights*, published shortly after her death. It is by this novel that most people now know her, although she also published a relatively small number of poems, often enigmatic and mystical in their tone. She was at work on a second, lost novel at the time of her death. While many Victorians were suspicious of *Wuthering Heights* on account of its expressions of passion and of violence, it became a classic text in the twentieth century. Its reputation has been enhanced by film adaptations, particularly by the 1939 version starring Laurence Olivier, which helped make it into a by-word for romantic tragedy.

Emily Brontë's literary talent flourished in a house of creative writers that included her sisters Charlotte (*Jane Eyre*) and Anne (*The Tenant of Wildfell Hall*). Emily was the fifth child of Patrick Brontë and Maria Branwell, born in 1818 into poor circumstances in Thornton, Yorkshire. Maria died just two years later, not long after Patrick, an Anglican clergyman, had taken a post in nearby Haworth, where he and the children remained for practically all their lives. The six children were cared for by Maria's sister, Elizabeth Branwell, and educated primarily by Patrick (who had graduated from Cambridge). For the most part the children had the run of the stone parsonage that sat next to a graveyard in the desolate West Yorkshire moors. At the same time, industrial Yorkshire was close at hand.

When she was just five years old, Emily followed her three elder sisters to a charity school for the daughters of poor clergy. The conditions there were wretched, and all the sisters returned home when the two eldest, Maria and Elizabeth, contracted tuberculosis; they died soon afterward. The remaining children were left mainly to their own devices, performing household chores, reading literary classics and current affairs periodicals, walking on the moors, and writing elaborate plays and stories together. The two oldest children, Charlotte and Branwell, created an imaginary kingdom called "Angria"; the two younger children, Emily and Anne, fashioned the island of "Gondal," inspired by their father's colorful descriptions of political and historical events. Although the children's transcripts of Gondal no longer exist, Brontë continued its themes in her later, published poems.

Brontë again went off to school when she was 16, to the harsh institution that Charlotte subsequently depicted in *Jane Eyre*; she returned home after only six months due to illness. Two years later she left home for another brief sojourn—this time to teach—but her homesickness and what she called her life of slavery brought her back again soon afterward. Her last stint away from home was in 1842, when she joined Charlotte at a teaching institution in Brussels. The two had planned to open their own school in Yorkshire, hoping they could turn around the family's desperate financial circumstances.

Charlotte eventually persuaded her sisters to publish a volume of their poems using pseudonyms. Unfortunately, *The Poems of Currer, Ellis, and Acton Bell* (1846), which was published with their own funds, sold only two copies and was ignored by most reviewers, although one did say that Ellis

(Emily) showed the most promise. Within a year, however, all three Brontë sisters had completed novels: Charlotte, *The Professor*; Emily, *Wuthering Heights*; and Anne, *Agnes Grey*. When Charlotte's subsequently published novel, *Jane Eyre*, became a bestseller, Emily's and Anne's books were also published together in three volumes (*Agnes Grey* being the third). All three sisters used their pseudonyms.

Wuthering Heights is a book so full of passion and violence that the Victorian public assumed it had been written by a man (some even speculated that Branwell Brontë penned it), and some conjectured that the author of *Jane Eyre* had written it. Its dark and brooding story is set against the wild and bleak landscape of the Yorkshire moors. Highly charged with sexuality and with powerful moral ambiguities, the novel broke many conventions of the time. The marriage plot is at once respected (the "good characters," Cathy Linton and Hareton Earnshaw, inherit their rightful property and a happy ending) and damned (the "lovers" Catherine and Heathcliff finally exist only in story, and in their graves, even if they are rumored to still roam the moors). The idea of love, so central to Victorian realism, exists in *Wuthering Heights* as at once "normal" and frightening. It is no wonder that some reviewers found the novel chaotically written, gloomy, too unrelenting in its violence, and morally suspect. Even Charlotte Brontë, who always championed the novel as a work of genius, questioned its meaning.

Much of Brontë's poetry shares the bleakness of *Wuthering Heights* and its preoccupation with passion, loss, and death. Many of the poems display a desire for transcendence reminiscent of Catherine and Heathcliff's yearnings and yet a tenderness that is not evident in them or in the narrators of the novel. There is often in the poems a view of an existence free of the restraints of everyday life, even though this existence is often realized only through the realm of the imagination—perspectives that connect Brontë to her Romantic predecessors much more than to her Victorian contemporaries.

In 1848 Emily Brontë caught a cold at the funeral of the only Brontë son, Branwell, a failed painter and writer and the sibling on whom the family had pinned its biggest hopes, who had died of complications from chronic alcohol and drug use. The cold soon afterward developed into tuberculosis, and, having refused all medical treatment, Emily Brontë died in December of 1848, only one year after the publication of *Wuthering Heights*.

⌘⌘⌘

Remembrance

Cold in the earth—and the deep snow piled above thee,
　Far, far removed, cold in the dreary grave!
Have I forgot, my only Love, to love thee,
　Severed at last by Time's all-severing wave?

5　Now, when alone, do my thoughts no longer hover
　　Over the mountains, on that northern shore,
Resting their wings where heath and fern-leaves cover
　　Thy noble heart for ever, ever more?

10　Cold in the earth—and fifteen wild Decembers,
　　From those brown hills, have melted into spring:
Faithful, indeed, is the spirit that remembers
　　After such years of change and suffering!

Sweet Love of youth, forgive, if I forget thee,
　While the world's tide is bearing me along;
15　Other desires and other hopes beset me,
　　Hopes which obscure, but cannot do thee wrong!

No later light has lightened up my heaven,
　No second morn has ever shone for me;

All my life's bliss from thy dear life was given,
20   All my life's bliss is in the grave with thee.

But when the days of golden dreams had perished,
      And even Despair was powerless to destroy;
Then did I learn how existence could be cherished,
      Strengthened, and fed without the aid of joy.

25 Then did I check the tears of useless passion,
      Weaned my young soul from yearning after thine;
Sternly denied its burning wish to hasten
      Down to that tomb already more than mine.

And, even yet, I dare not let it languish,
30   Dare not indulge in memory's rapturous pain;
Once drinking deep of that divinest anguish,
      How could I seek the empty world again?
      —1846

Plead for Me

Oh, thy bright eyes must answer now,
      When Reason, with a scornful brow,
Is mocking at my overthrow!
Oh, thy sweet tongue must plead for me
5 And tell, why I have chosen thee!

Stern Reason is to judgment come,
Arrayed in all her forms of gloom:
Wilt thou, my advocate, be dumb?
No, radiant angel, speak and say,
10 Why I did cast the world away.

Why I have persevered to shun
The common paths that others run,
And on a strange road journeyed on,
Heedless, alike, of wealth and power—
15 Of glory's wreath and pleasure's flower.

These, once, indeed, seemed Beings Divine,
And they, perchance, heard vows of mine,
And saw my offerings on their shrine;
But, careless gifts are seldom prized,
20 And mine were worthily despised.

So, with a ready heart I swore
To seek their altar-stone no more;
And gave my spirit to adore
Thee, ever-present, phantom thing;
25 My slave, my comrade, and my king,

A slave, because I rule thee still;
Incline thee to my changeful will,
And make thy influence good or ill:
A comrade, for by day and night
30 Thou art my intimate delight,—

My darling pain that wounds and sears
And wrings a blessing out from tears
By deadening me to earthly cares;
And yet, a king, though prudence well
35 Have taught thy subject to rebel.

And am I wrong to worship, where
Faith cannot doubt, nor hope despair,
Since my own soul can grant my prayer?
Speak, God of visions, plead for me,
40 And tell why I have chosen thee!
      —1846

The Old Stoic

Riches I hold in light esteem;
      And love I laugh to scorn;
And lust of fame was but a dream
      That vanished with the morn:

5 And if I pray, the only prayer
      That moves my lips for me
Is, "Leave the heart that now I bear,
      And give me liberty!"[1]

Yes, as my swift days near their goal,
10   'Tis all that I implore;

---

[1] *give me liberty!* Cf. Patrick Henry's 1775 speech, in which he recommended that his fellow Virginians rise in arms against British rule: "I know not what course others may take; but as for me, give me liberty or give me death!"

In life and death, a chainless soul,
    With courage to endure.
—1846 (WRITTEN 1841)

My Comforter

Well hast thou spoken, and yet, not taught
    A feeling strange or new;
Thou hast but roused a latent thought,
A cloud-closed beam of sunshine, brought
5   To gleam in open view.

Deep down, concealed within my soul,
    That light lies hid from men;
Yet, glows unquenched—though shadows roll,
Its gentle ray cannot control,
10   About the sullen den.

Was I not vexed, in these gloomy ways
    To walk alone so long?
Around me, wretches uttering praise,
Or howling o'er their hopeless days,
15   And each with Frenzy's tongue;—

A brotherhood of misery,
    Their smiles as sad as sighs;
Whose madness daily maddened me,
Distorting into agony
20   The bliss before my eyes!

So stood I, in Heaven's glorious sun,
    And in the glare of Hell;
My spirit drank a mingled tone,
Of seraph's° song, and demon's moan;   *angel's*
25 What my soul bore, my soul alone
    Within itself may tell!

Like a soft air, above a sea,
    Tossed by the tempest's stir;
A thaw-wind, melting quietly
30 The snow-drift, on some wintry lea;
No: what sweet thing resembles thee,
    My thoughtful Comforter?

And yet a little longer speak,
    Calm this resentful mood;
35 And while the savage heart grows meek,
For other token do not seek,
But let the tear upon my cheek
    Evince my gratitude!
—1846

[*Loud without the wind was roaring*]

Loud without the wind was roaring
    Through the waned autumnal sky,
Drenching wet, the cold rain pouring
    Spoke of stormy winters nigh.

5   All too like that dreary eve
    Sighed within repining grief—
    Sighed at first—but sighed not long
    Sweet—How softly sweet it came!
    Wild words of an ancient song—
10   Undefined, without a name—

"It was spring, for the skylark was singing."
Those words they awakened a spell—
They unlocked a deep fountain whose springing
Nor absence nor distance can quell.

15   In the gloom of a cloudy November
    They uttered the music of May—
    They kindled the perishing ember
    Into fervour that could not decay

Awaken on all my dear moorlands
20 The wind in its glory and pride!
O call me from valleys and highlands
To walk by the hill-river's side!

It is swelled with the first snowy weather;
The rocks they are icy and hoar
25 And darker waves round the long heather
And the fern-leaves are sunny no more

There are no yellow-stars on the mountain,
The bluebells have long died away

From the brink of the moss-bedded fountain,
30   From the side of the wintery brae°—   *hillside*

But lovelier than cornfields all waving
In emerald and scarlet and gold
Are the slopes where the north wind is raving
And the glens where I wandered of old—

35   "It was morning; the bright sun was beaming."
How sweetly that brought back to me
The time when nor labour nor dreaming
Broke the sleep of the happy and free

But blithely we rose as the dusk heaven
40   Was melting to amber and blue—
And swift were the wings to our feet given
While we traversed the meadows of dew.

For the moors, for the moors where the short grass
Like velvet beneath us should lie!
45   For the moors, for the moors where each high pass
Rose sunny against the clear sky!

For the moors, where the linnet° was trilling   *songbird*
Its song on the old granite stone—
Where the lark—the wild skylark was filling
50   Every breast with delight like its own.

What language can utter the feeling
That rose when, in exile afar,
On the brow of a lonely hill kneeling
I saw the brown heath growing there.

55   It was scattered and stunted, and told me
That soon even that would be gone
It whispered, "The grim walls enfold me
I have bloomed in my last summer's sun."

But not the loved music whose waking
60   Makes the soul of the Swiss die away
Has a spell more adored and heartbreaking
Than in its half-blighted bells lay—

The spirit that bent 'neath its power
How it longed, how it burned to be free!

65   If I could have wept in that hour
Those tears had been heaven to me—

Well, well the sad minutes are moving
Though loaded with trouble and pain—
And sometime the loved and the loving
70   Shall meet on the mountains again—
—1850 (WRITTEN 1835)

[A little while, a little while]

A little while, a little while
The noisy crowd are barred away;
And I can sing and I can smile—
A little while I've holiday!

5   Where wilt thou go my harassed heart?
Full many a land invites thee now;
And places near, and far apart
Have rest for thee, my weary brow—

There is a spot 'mid barren hills
10   Where winter howls and driving rain
But if the dreary tempest chills
There is a light that warms again

The house is old, the trees are bare
And moonless bends the misty dome
15   But what on earth is half so dear—
So longed for as the hearth of home?

The mute bird sitting on the stone,
The dank moss dripping from the wall,
The garden-walk with weeds o'ergrown
20   I love them—how I love them all!

Shall I go there? Or shall I seek
Another clime, another sky.
Where tongues familiar music speak
In accents dear to memory?

25   Yes, as I mused, the naked room,
The flickering firelight died away

And from the midst of cheerless gloom
I passed to bright, unclouded day—

A little and a lone green lane
30 That opened on a common wide
A distant, dreamy, dim blue chain
Of mountains circling every side—

A heaven so clear, an earth so calm,
So sweet, so soft, so hushed an air
35 And, deepening still the dreamlike charm,
Wild moor-sheep feeding everywhere—

That was the scene—I knew it well
I knew the pathways far and near
That winding o'er each billowy swell
40 Marked out the tracks of wandering deer

Could I have lingered but an hour
It well had paid a week of toil
But truth has banished fancy's power
I hear my dungeon bars recoil—

45 Even as I stood with raptured eye
Absorbed in bliss so deep and dear
My hour of rest had fleeted by
And given me back to weary care—
—1850 (WRITTEN 1838)

[Shall Earth no more inspire thee]

Shall Earth no more inspire thee,
Thou lonely dreamer now?
Since passion may not fire thee
Shall nature cease to bow?

5 Thy mind is ever moving
In regions dark to thee;
Recall its useless roving—
Come back and dwell with me.

I know my mountain breezes
10 Enchant and soothe thee still—

I know my sunshine pleases
Despite thy wayward will.

When day with evening blending
Sinks from the summer sky,
15 I've seen thy spirit bending
In fond idolatry.

I've watched thee every hour;
I know my mighty sway,
I know my magic power
20 To drive thy griefs away.

Few hearts to mortals given
On earth so wildly pine;
Yet none would ask a heaven
More like this earth than thine.

25 Then let my winds caress thee;
Thy comrade let me be—
Since nought beside can bless thee,
Return and dwell with me.
—1850 (WRITTEN 1841)

[No coward soul is mine] [1]

No coward soul is mine
No trembler in the world's storm-troubled sphere
I see Heaven's glories shine
And Faith shines equal arming me from Fear

5 O God within my breast
Almighty ever-present Deity
Life, that in me hast rest
As I Undying Life, have power in Thee

Vain are the thousand creeds
10 That move men's hearts, unutterably vain,
Worthless as withered weeds
Or idlest froth amid the boundless main

---

[1] *No coward soul is mine* Like much of Brontë's poetry, this poem was not published until after her death. In preparing the poems for publication in 1850, Charlotte Brontë made some alterations in punctuation and syntax. The copy printed here is from the original 1846 manuscript, which is largely unpunctuated.

original spelling

To waken doubt in one
Holding so fast by thy infinity
15   So surely anchored on
The steadfast rock of Immortality.

With wide-embracing love
Thy spirit animates eternal years
Pervades and broods above,
20   Changes, sustains, dissolves, creates and rears

Though Earth and moon were gone
And suns and universes ceased to be
And thou wert left alone
Every Existence would exist in thee

25   There is not room for Death
Nor atom that his might could render void
Since thou art Being and Breath
And what thou art may never be destroyed.
　　—1850 (WRITTEN 1846)

Stanzas[1]

Often rebuked, yet always back returning
　　To those first feelings that were born with me,
And leaving busy chase of wealth and learning
　　For idle dreams of things which cannot be:

5   Today, I will seek not the shadowy region;
　　Its unsustaining vastness waxes drear;
And visions rising, legion after legion,
　　Bring the unreal world too strangely near.

I'll walk, but not in old heroic traces,
10   And not in paths of high morality,
And not among the half-distinguished faces,
　　The clouded forms of long-past history.

I'll walk where my own nature would be leading:
　　It vexes me to choose another guide:

15   Where the gray flocks in ferny glens are feeding;
　　Where the wild wind blows on the mountain side.

What have those lonely mountains worth revealing?
　　More glory and more grief than I can tell:
The earth that wakes *one* human heart to feeling
20   Can centre both the worlds of heaven and hell.
　　—1850[2]

[*The night is darkening round me*][3]

The night is darkening round me
　　The wild winds coldly blow
But a tyrant spell has bound me
And I cannot cannot go

5   The giant trees are bending
Their bare boughs weighed with snow
And the storm is fast descending
And yet I cannot go

Clouds beyond clouds above me
10   Wastes beyond wastes below
But nothing drear can move me
I will not cannot go

I'll come when thou art saddest
Laid alone in the darkened room
When the mad day's mirth has vanished
And the smile of joy is banished
5   From evening's chilly gloom

I'll come when the heart's real feeling
Has entire unbiased sway
And my influence o'er thee stealing

---

1   *Stanzas*   This authorship of "Often rebuked" has been variously credited to Emily, Charlotte, and Anne Brontë; when the poem was first printed it was recorded as having been written by Emily.

2   *1850*   Brontë did not record the date on which she composed this poem.

3   *The night … me*   Sometimes considered three separate poems, "The Night" is unfinished. Brontë tended even in her published work to punctuate less heavily than most Victorian poets. As this poem demonstrates, the tendency was far more pronounced in her written drafts.

Grief deepening joy congealing
10 Shall bear thy soul away

Listen 'tis just the hour
The awful time for thee
Dost thou not feel upon thy soul
A flood of strange sensations roll
15 Forerunners of a sterner power
Heralds of me

_____

I would have touched the heavenly key
That spoke alike of bliss and thee
I would have woke the entrancing song
But its words died upon my tongue
5   And then I knew that entheal° strain   *hallowed*
Could never speak of joy again
And then I felt
—1902 (WRITTEN 1837)

original spelling

[I'm happiest when most away]

I'm happiest when most away
I can bear my soul from its home of clay
On a windy night when the moon is bright
And the eye can wander through worlds of light—

5   When I am not and none beside—
Nor earth nor sea nor cloudless sky—
But only spirit wandering wide
Through infinite immensity.
—1910 (WRITTEN 1838)

[If grief for grief can touch thee]

If grief for grief can touch thee,
If answering woe for woe,
If any ruth° can melt thee   *compassion*
Come to me now!

5   I cannot be more lonely,
More drear I cannot be!
My worn heart throbs so wildly
'Twill break for thee—

And when the world despises—
10 When heaven repels my prayer—
Will not mine angel comfort?
Mine idol hear?

Yes by the tears I've poured,
By all my hours of pain
15 O I shall surely win thee
Beloved, again!
—1902 (WRITTEN 1840)

The New Art of Photography

CONTEXTS

If the Victorian era was in many ways an "age of realism" in literature, it was also an age in which the "real" was given new definition through the medium of photography. Photography was developed virtually simultaneously by Louis Daguerre and Henry Fox Talbot, with the Frenchman and the Englishman making announcements of their discoveries within three weeks of each other in 1839. As Charles Dickens describes in his essay on "Photography" (excerpted in this section), the technologies developed by the two were quite distinct; the "daguerreotype" resulted in a single image, while the calotype technology developed by Talbot involved paper negatives from which multiple images could be created. Later in the century a variety of other techniques were developed, including glass plate technology, which provided levels of photographic detail that remain virtually unrivaled, even in the twenty-first century. By the 1890s, the advent of the portable "Kodak" camera had put photography into the reach of the middle classes. Not only was it possible for one to obtain a few images of one's loved ones from a professional; one could also take up the activity of photography as an amateur. But even in the 1840s, the new science and art of photography was helping to transform a number of aspects of Victorian culture.

One aspect of culture on which photography had a particularly strong impact was print culture. Engraving had for centuries made possible the reproduction of illustrations, and wood engraving, one of the first methods used to produce illustrations in books, enjoyed a renaissance in the period, as did all things medieval. Metal engravings, a slightly later invention, enjoyed a short revival in popularity during the nineteenth century—particularly steel engravings, which could be used to produce a large number of proofs. This practice was soon superceded, however, by photo-engraving, a photomechanical process by which a photographic image was recorded on a sensitized metal plate, which was then etched in an acid bath and used to reproduce the photograph. The widespread reproduction of actual photographs in newspapers and magazines did not come until the early twentieth century, but these engraving techniques, pioneered in such publications as the satirical magazine *Punch* (founded in 1841), and, especially, in *The Illustrated London News* (founded 14 May 1842), allowed engravings based on photographic images to be reproduced—and to give readers a sense of the world being shown to them as it really was.

The connections between photography and print were not restricted to newspapers and magazines, of course; new technologies such as the engraving machine (created in the 1830s) enabled an unprecedented expansion of book illustration in the Victorian period. And sometimes the connections between literature and photography were entirely direct; Tennyson, for example, commissioned the photographer Julia Margaret Cameron to illustrate his *Idylls of the King*.

Photography interacted just as powerfully with other arts. The connection between photography and painting was an obvious one, and certainly many artists began to use photographs in their work, sometimes merely as an *aide memoire*, sometimes as a "copy text," sometimes as something in-between. For his famous panorama of *Derby Day* (1856–58), for example, the painter William Powell Frith commissioned the photographer Robert Howlett to take photographs not of the entire scene in which Frith was interested (for which Frith relied on his own sketches from life) but of a range of different individuals within it, so that he could fill in human details with greater accuracy and completeness.

Some expressed an outright preference for the newer art over the arts of painting and drawing. In an essay that appeared in the 21 January 1857 issue of the *Journal of the Photographic Society*, for example, "Theta" argued that "what in painting is a tiresome pedantry of observation, becomes in photography an inexhaustible delight, a study, and a piece of instruction. What we cared not for in nature, becomes a joy and wonder in the photographic picture." But when practitioners of the new art began to stake claims for an artistic status that went beyond fidelity to nature and aspired to the condition of "High Art," they met with considerable resistance. A landmark was the exhibition in 1857 at the Art Treasures Exhibition in Manchester (the first major exhibition to showcase photography alongside painting and other traditional visual arts). The most controversial work exhibited was Oscar Rejlander's vast photographic tableau, *The Two Ways of Life*, in which a montage of photographic images of allegorical figures are brought together against an artificial backdrop. To many, the artistic presumption of the work crossed a line; reviewing the exhibition in *The Art-Journal*, Robert Hunt allowed that "the pose of each figure is good and the grouping of the whole as nearly perfect as possible," but nevertheless concluded that "we do not … desire to see many advances in this direction. Works of High Art are not to be executed by a mechanical contrivance. The hand of man, guided by the heaven-born mind, can alone achieve greatness in this direction."

Rejlander was not alone in his desire to create photographs that would be recognized as "High Art," that is, in the same sorts of ways as oil paintings were received. Henry Peach Robinson argued unabashedly in "Pictorial Effect in Photography" (1867) for the use of the photographer's artifice to contrive a pleasing result: "any dodge, trick, and conjuration of any kind is open to the photographer's use. His imperative duty is to avoid the mean, the base, and the ugly, and to aim to elevate his subject, … to correct the unpicturesque. … A great deal can be done and very beautiful pictures made, by a mixture of the real and the artificial in a picture." Robinson's most controversial work of precisely this sort was *Fading Away* (1858), a composition combining images from five negatives, with the full image depicting a girl dying of consumption. Some saw the result of Robinson's artistry as a tasteless exploitation of grief, but the image was extremely popular (Prince Albert was prompted by his admiration of *Fading Away* to place a standing order for a copy of any composite photograph Robinson produced).

A very different approach to the art of photography was taken by Henry Emerson, who strongly criticized the approaches of photographers such as Rejlander, Robinson, and Julia Margaret Cameron. "Photograph people as they really are," he advised in *Naturalistic Photography* (1886). "Do not dress them up. … The photographic technique is perfect." Emerson's recommended photographic techniques, however, were themselves highly original—and in their own way as consciously artistic as those of Robinson or Cameron. In Emerson's view, one should emulate the natural, and "nothing in nature has a hard outline, but everything is seen against something else, and its outlines fade gently into something else, often so subtly that you cannot distinguish clearly where one ends and the other begins." To represent nature as the eye perceives it, then, Emerson recommended shooting photographs slightly out of focus. Emerson's impressionistic approach was popular for a time (and continued to influence some important photographers well into the twentieth century), but by the 1890s it was in painting rather than in photography that impressionism was putting down deep roots. Emerson himself came to recant his earlier views; in "The Death of Naturalistic Photography" (1890), he wrote that he had given up hope of photography being able to compete with painting; and regretting that he had compared "photographs to great works of art, and photographers to great artists … I throw in my lot with those who say Photography is a very limited Art."

But "limited" was by then precisely what photography had proven it was *not*. Within Britain and its colonies alone, the medium had produced the war photographs, nature photographs and still-lifes of Roger Fenton; the social realism of John Thomson and Thomas Annan; the memorably idealized expressions of female beauty of Julia Margaret Cameron and Lady Clementia Hawarden; suggestive representations of the exotic by Fenton, Thomson, Cameron, Francis Frith, and others; powerful representations by Howlett and others of the vitality of industrial Britain, and Annan's and Thomson's equally powerful images of its brutality; Frank Sutcliffe's and Henry Taunt's evocative images of village and rural life; and the compelling portraiture of Cameron, Lewis Carroll, William Notman, and many others.

The practice of photography was diverse, too. Early on it had become established as a professional pursuit—in the 1851 census there were already 51 British citizens who listed "photographer" as their occupation. But aristocratic amateurs such as Cameron, Hawarden, and Talbot continued to make their marks. With the notable exception of Lady Elizabeth Butler, women remained excluded from the ranks of accepted artists in the medium of painting; in photography, however, Cameron, Hawarden—and, later in the century, Anna Atkins and others—were leading figures.

More generally, it was also true that the sorts of individuals who were attracted to photography formed a diverse group. The barriers that today divide photography as an artistic pursuit from its commercial and scientific applications had for the most part not yet been erected in the Victorian era. Even those who saw photography as an art simultaneously appreciated it as science; Roger Fenton, for example, in his 1852 "Proposal for the Formation of a Royal Photographic Society" (reprinted in this section), refers to photography both as an art and as a "branch of natural science," and proposes to open the society to opticians and chemists as well as artists and "practical photographers, both professional and amateur."

Such breadth was to a large extent characteristic of the age—and should seem less surprising to us in this instance if we remember not only the degree to which photography represented a new technology, but also the degree to which it was initially a severely limited one. No means existed, for example, to enlarge photographic images, and the very long exposure times required in photography's early years meant that it remained impossible for a photograph to "capture a moment"; figures passing quickly in front of the camera would remain entirely unrecorded. (That Fenton's most famous photograph of the Crimean War showed cannon balls in an empty valley was a reflection of Victorian sensibilities, but also a reflection of the limits of technology: he could have depicted dead bodies, but to photograph the action of battle was still impossible.) The diversity and the depth of the achievement of practitioners of the photographic arts in the Victorian era is all the more impressive for the technical obstacles that they faced.

⌘ ⌘ ⌘

Roger Fenton, "Proposal for the Formation of a Photographic Society" (1852)

Roger Fenton, a 32-year-old painter and sometime law student, was among the many in whom the displays at the Great Exhibition of 1851 sparked an interest in the new art of photography. Much of the finest work displayed at the Exhibition was by French photographers (prominent among them Hippolyte Bayard and Gustave Le Gray), and in October of 1851, Fenton traveled to Paris to meet members of the Societé Héliographique, the world's first photographic society. By the summer of 1852, Fenton was becoming prominent in English photographic circles, and later that year he put forward the proposal reprinted here, for the formation of a new society. The Photographic Society came into existence in 1853, with the Queen and Prince Albert as patrons; in 1894 the name was changed to The Royal Photographic Society.

The science of Photography gradually progressing for several years, seems to have advanced at a more rapid pace during and since the Exhibition of 1851. Its lovers and students in all parts of Europe were brought into more immediate and frequent communication.

Ideas of theory and methods of practice were interchanged, the pleasure and the instruction were mutual. In order that this temporary may become the normal condition of the art and of its professors, it is proposed to unite in a common society, with a fixed place of meeting, and a regular official organization, all those gentlemen whose tastes have led them to the cultivation of this branch of natural science.

As the object proposed is not only to form a pleasant and convenient Photographic Club, but a society that shall be as advantageous for the art as is the Geographic Society to the advancement of knowledge in its department, it follows necessarily that it shall include among its members men of all ranks of life; that while men of eminence, from their fortune, social position, or scientific reputation, are welcomed, no photographer of respectability in his particular sphere of life be rejected.

The society then will consist of those eminent in the study of natural philosophy, of opticians, chemists, artists, and practical photographers, professional and amateur. It will admit both town and country members. It is proposed:—

That, after the society has been once organized, persons who may in future wish to become members will have to be proposed and seconded, a majority of votes deciding their election.

That the entrance fee and subscription shall be as small as possible, in order that none may be excluded by the narrowness of their means.

That there shall be an entrance fee of £2.2s.—a subscription of £1.1s.

That the society should have appropriate premises fitted up with laboratory, glass operating room, and salon, in which to hold its meetings.

That such meetings should be periodically held, for the purpose of hearing and discussing written or verbal communications on the subject of Photography, receiving and verifying claims as to priority of invention, exhibiting and comparing pictures produced by different applications of photographic principles; making known improvements in construction of cameras and lenses; and, in fine, promoting by emulation and comparison the progress of the art.

That the proceedings of the society shall be published regularly in some acknowledged organ, which shall be sent to all subscribing members.

That a library of works bearing upon the history or tending to the elucidation of the principles of the science be formed upon the premises, and at the expense of the society, to be used by the members, subject to such rules as may hereafter be agreed upon.

That the society should publish an annual album, of which each member should receive a copy, who had contributed a good negative photograph to its formation, other members having to pay (and the public being charged at the rate of   )?[1]

The heaviest expense attendant upon this plan would be leasing or construction of convenient premises, and this expense might be lessened by the letting off the lower part as a shop for the sale of photographic chemicals, and the upper part to some person who would form a commercial establishment for the printing of positives.

Before any progress can be made in the organization of such a society as the foregoing, it is necessary first to ascertain the amount of support which it would be likely to obtain. If those gentlemen, therefore, who feel inclined to become members of such a society will send in their names and addresses to R. FENTON, Esq., 2, Albert Terrace, and 50, King William Street, City,[2] together with any suggestion which may occur to them individually on the perusal of this outline of a plan, arrangements will be made as soon as a sufficient number of persons have sent in their names, to hold a meeting in some central situation, to which they will be invited to discuss the matter and to elect a committee for the organization of a society.

from Charles Dickens, "Photography," *Household Words*, Volume 7 (1853)

Among Dickens's many contributions to *Household Words* (a widely-circulated miscellany of articles and literary pieces) were installments of his fiction, essays on political issues, and articles on various cultural topics—such as the selection excerpted below.

… Light from the sky is, in fact, the chief part of the stock-in-trade of a photographer. Other light than the

---

[1] *rate of   )?* The space left here, together with the question mark, suggest that the specific amount was an issue left for later discussion.

[2] *City* I.e., the City of London.

sun's can be employed; but, while the sun continues to pour down to us a daily flow of light of the best quality, as cheap as health (we will not say as cheap as dirt, for dirt is a dear article), sunlight will be consumed by the photographers in preference to any other. A diffused, mellow light from the sky, which moderates the darkness of all shadows, is much better suited to the purpose of photography than a direct sunbeam; which creates hard contrasts of light and shade. For in the picture formed by light, whether on metal, glass, or paper, such hard contrasts will be made still harder. Lumpy shadows haunt the chambers of all bad photographers.

He who would not be vexed by them and would produce a portrait in which the features shall be represented with the necessary softness, finds it generally advantageous not only to let the shades be cast upon the face in a room full of diffused rays—that is to say, under a skylight—but also by the waving of large black velvet screens over the head to moderate and stint the quantity of light that falls on features not thrown into shadow. For this reason few very good photographic pictures can be taken from objects illuminated only by a side light, as in a room with ordinary windows. The diffused light of cloudy weather, if the air be free from fog, hinders the process of photography only by lengthening the time occupied in taking impressions. Light, when it is jaundiced by a fog, is quite as liable as jaundiced men to give erroneous views of mankind.

Photography, out of England, has made its most rapid advances, and produced its best results in the United States and in France; but, although both the French and the Americans have the advantage of a much purer and more certain supply of sunlight, it is satisfactory to know that the English photographers have thrown as much light of their own on the new science as any of their neighbours. ...

The den of the photographer, in which he goes through those mysterious operations which are not submitted to the observation of the sitter, is a small room lighted by a window, and communicating into a dark closet, veiled with heavy curtains. Our sense of the supernatural, always associated with dark closets, was excited strongly in this chamber, by the sound of a loud rumbling in the bowels of the house, and the visible departure of a portion of the wall to lower regions. "We

thought instinctively of bandits who wind victims up and down in moveable rooms or turn them up in treacherous screw bedsteads. But, of course; there was no danger to be apprehended. What we saw was, of course, only a contrivance to save labour in conveying pictures up or down for colouring or framing. Our consciences having been satisfied on this point, the expert magician took a plate of the prescribed size, made ready to his hand. Such plates consist of a thin layer of silver fixed upon copper, and are provided to the artist highly polished; but a final and superlative polish is given to each plate, with a "buff" or pad like a double handled razor strop, tinged with a fine mineral powder. Simple as it appears, the final polishing of the plate is an operation that can only succeed well under a practised pair of hands, that regulate their pressure by a refined sense of touch. The plate thus polished was brushed over finally and very lightly, as with the touch of a cat's paw, with a warm pad of black velvet freshly taken from an oven.

To witness the next process we went into the dark closet itself, the very head quarters of spectredom. There, having carefully excluded daylight, the operator lifted up the lid of a small bin, rapidly fixed the plate, silver side downwards, in a place made underneath for its reception, shut down the lid, and began to measure seconds by counting, talking between whiles, thus:—"One—that box—two contains—three—chloride of iodine—four—strewn—five—six—at the bottom. Now!" (Presto, out came the plate in a twinkling, and was held against a sheet of white paper, upon which it reflected a ghastly straw colour by the light of a small jet of gas.) "Ah, tint not deep enough!" The plate was popped into its vapour bath again with magic quickness. "Seven—the action of the iodine" (continued the operator, counting seconds, and teaching us our lesson in the same breath) "rising in vapour upon the surface—eleven—of the plate—twelve—causes it to take in succession—thirteen—fourteen—fifteen—all the colours of the spectrum—sixteen—seventeen; and deposits upon it a film." As he went on solemnly counting, we asked how long he exposed the plate to the visitation of that potent vapour. "A very short time," he replied; "but it varies—thirty—thirty-one—according to the light in the next room—thirty-five—thirty-six—

thirty-seven. Adjusting the plate to the weather, thirty-eight—is the result of an acquired instinct—thirty-nine—forty. Now it is ready." The plate was out, and its change to a deeper straw colour was shown. The lid of an adjoining bin was lifted, and the iodized plate was hung in the same way over another vapour; that of the chloride of bromine, that the wraiths of the two vapours might mingle, mingle, mingle as black spirits with white, blue spirits with gray. In this position it remained but a very short time, while we stood watching by in the dark cupboard. The plate having had its temper worked upon by these mysterious agencies was rendered so extremely sensitive, that it was requisite to confine it at once, in a dark hole or solitary cell, made ready for it in a wooden frame; a wooden slide was let down over it, and it was ready to be carried to the camera.

Before quitting this part of the subject, we must add to the preceding description two or three external facts. We have been discussing hitherto the kernel without touching the nutshell in which these, like all other reasonable matters in this country, may be (and usually are) said to lie. The nutshell is in fact as important to a discussion in this country as the small end of the wedge or the British Lion:—In the action of light upon surfaces prepared in a certain manner lies the whole idea of photography. The camera-obscura is an old friend; how to fix chemically the illuminated images formed in the camera by light, was a problem at which Sir Humphrey Davy,[1] half a century ago, was one of the first men who worked. Sir Humphrey succeeded no farther than in the imprinting of a faint image, but as he could not discover how to fix it, the whole subject was laid aside. Between the years 1814 and 1828, two Frenchmen, M. Daguerre and M. Nièpce,[2] were at work upon the problem. In 1827 M. Nièpce produced before the Royal Society what he then called heliographs, sun-pictures, formed and fixed upon glass, copper plated with silver, and well-polished tin. But, as he kept the

secret of his processes, no scientific use was made of his discovery. M. Daguerre, working at the same problem, succeeded about the same time in fixing sun-pictures on paper impregnated with nitrate of silver. M. Daguerre and M. Niepce having combined their knowledge to increase the value of their art, the French government—in the year 1839—acting nobly, as it has often acted in the interests of science, bought for the free use of the world the details of the new discovery. For the full disclosure of their secrets there was granted to M. Daguerre a life pension of two hundred and forty pounds (he died not many months ago), and a pension of one hundred and sixty pounds to the son of M. Nièpce, with the reversion of one half to their widows.

Six months before the disclosure of the processes in France, Mr. Fox Talbot[3] in England had discovered a process leading to a like result—the fixing of sun-pictures upon paper. As the English parliament buys little for science, nothing unfortunately hindered the patenting of Mr. Talbot's method. That patent in certain respects very much obstructed the advance of photography in this country, and great credit is due to Mr. Talbot for having recently and voluntarily abandoned his exclusive rights, and given his process to the public for all purposes and uses, except that of the portrait-taker. By so doing he acted in the spirit of a liberal art born in our own days, and peculiarly marked with the character of our own time. It does one good to think how photographers, even while exercising the new art for money, have pursued it with a generous ardour for its own sake, and emulate each other in the magnanimity with which they throw their own discoveries into the common heap, and scorn to check the progress of their art for any selfish motive. After the completion of the French discovery two daguerreotype establishments were formed in London armed with patent rights, and their proprietors, Messrs. Claudet and Beard, do in fact still hold those rights, of which they have long cheerfully permitted the infringement. Mr. Beard tried to enforce them only once, we believe; and M. Claudet, with distinguished liberality, never. . . .

And we may observe here that another illustration of our vanities was furnished to us on a different occasion.

---

[1] *Sir Humphrey Davy* English scientist. The discoverer of several chemical elements, Davy (1778–1829) also invented a safety lamp for use in mines.

[2] *two Frenchman … Niépce* Louis-Jacques-Mandé Daguerre (1787–1851), now more commonly referred to as "Louis Daguerre," inventor of the daguerreotype process of photography, and Nicéphore Niépce, said by many to have produced the world's first photograph.

[3] *Mr. Fox Talbot* Henry Fox Talbot (1800–77), English scientist and mathematician, inventor of the calotype photographic process.

Daguerreotype plates commonly present faces as they would be seen in a looking-glass, that is to say, reversed: the left side of the face, in nature, appearing upon the right side of the miniature. That is the ordinary aspect in which every one sees his own face, for it is only possible for him to behold it reflected in a mirror. This reversing, of course, alters in the slightest degree the similitude.... and it is a curious fact that few of us are content to have even our faces shown to us as others see them. The non-inverted daguerreotypes differ too much from the dear images of self that we are used to learn by heart out of our looking-glasses. They invariably please the friend to whom they are to be given, but they frequently displease the sitter ... A daguerreotype, formed in the usual way and inverted, if held before a looking-glass, becomes again inverted, and shows therefore a non-inverted picture of the person whom it represents.

... There are many processes by which photographic impressions may be taken upon paper and glass; a book full of them lies at this moment before us: we have ourselves seen two, and shall confine ourselves to the telling of a part of our experience. We rang the artist's bell of Mr. Henneman in Regent-street, who takes very good portraits upon paper by a process cousin to the Talbotype. By that gentleman we were introduced into a neat little chamber lighted by gas, with a few pans and chemicals upon a counter. His process was excessively simple: he would show it to us. He took a square of glass, cleaned it very perfectly, then holding it up by one corner with the left hand, he poured over the centre of the glass some collodion, which is, as most people know, gun-cotton dissolved in ether. By a few movements of the left hand, which appear easy, but are acquired with trouble, the collodion was caused to flow into an even coat over the surface of the glass, and the excess was poured off at another corner. To do this by a few left-handed movements without causing any ripple upon the collodion adhering to the glass is really very difficult. This done, the plate was left till the ether had almost evaporated, and deposited a film of gun-cotton—which is in fact a delicate paper—spread evenly over the surface of the glass. The glass covered with this delicate paper, before it was yet quite dry, was plunged carefully into a pan or bath, containing a solution of nitrate of

silver, about eight grains of it to every hundred of distilled water. In about two minutes it was taken out, and ready for the camera. It was a sheet of glass covered with a fine film of cotton-paper impregnated with nitrate of silver, a colourless salt blackened by light.

It was removed in a dark frame to the camera. Then an assistant, opening a book, assumed an attitude and sat for his picture. In a few seconds it was taken in the usual way, and the glass carried again into the operator's room. There it was dipped into another bath—a bath of pyrogallic acid—and the impression soon became apparent. To bring it out with greater force it was then dipped into a second and much weaker bath of nitrate of silver. The image was then made perfect; but, as the light parts were all depicted by the blackest shades, and the black parts were left white, the courteous assistant was there represented as a negro.

That negro stage was not of course the finished portrait, it was "the negative"—or stereotype plate, as it were—from which, after it had been fixed with a solution of the sulphate of the peroxyde of iron, any number of impressions could be taken. For it is obvious that if a plate like this be placed on sensitive paper, and exposed to daylight, the whole process will be reversed. The black face will obstruct the passage of the light and leave a white face underneath, the white hair will allow the light to pass, making black hair below, and so on. Impressions thus taken on paper, and afterwards fixed, may either serve for portraits, as they are, or, like the silver plates, they may be coloured.

... Photography already has been found available by the astronomer; the moon has sat for a full-face picture,[1] and there is hope that in a short time photographic paper will become a common auxiliary to the telescope. History will be indebted to photography for facsimiles of documents and volumes that have perished; travellers may bring home incontestible transcripts of inscriptions upon monuments, or foreign scenery. The artist will no longer be delayed in travelling to execute his sketches on the spot. He can now wander at his ease, and bring

---

[1] *moon has sat for a full-face picture* Amateur photographer John Dillwyn Llewelyn (1810–82) and his daughter Thereza Llewelyn were pioneers in astronomical photography, taking pictures of the moon through the telescope Llewelyn had constructed in 1851 at his estate in Wales.

home photographic views, from which to work, as. sculptors from the model. Photography is a young art, but from its present aspect we can judge what power it will have in its maturity. The mind may readily become bewildered among expectations, but one thing will suggest many. We understand that a catalogue of the national library of Paris has been commenced, in which each work is designated by a photographic miniature of its title-page.

Photography and Immortality

The following brief extracts are from a letter of poet Elizabeth Barrett (later Elizabeth Barrett Browning) to a friend, and from a speech by one of the first presidents of the photographic society. Pollard's belief was that photography was first and foremost "a *practical science*," but his enthusiasm for it was no less than that of those who valued it more as an art.

from Elizabeth Barrett, Letter to Mary Russell Mitford (1843)

Do you know anything about that wonderful invention of the day, called the Daguerrotype? Think of a man sitting down in the sun and leaving his facsimile in all its full completion of outline and shadow, steadfast on a plate, at the end of a minute and a half! The Mesmeric[1] disembodiment of spirits strikes one as a degree less marvelous ... It is not merely the likeness which is precious in such cases—but the association and the sense of nearness involved in the thing ... the fact of the very shadow of the person lying there fixed for ever! It is the very sanctification of portraits.

from Sir Frederick Pollock, "Presidential Address," Photographic Society (1855)

The varied objects to which Photography can address itself, its power of rendering permanent that which appears to be as fleeting as he shadows that go across the dial, the power that it possesses of giving fixedness to instantaneous objects, are for the purposes of history ... a matter of the greatest importance. It is not too much to say that no individual—not merely individual man, but no individual substance, no individual matter, nothing that is extraordinary in art, that is celebrated in architecture, that is calculated to excite the imagination of those who behold it, need now perish; but may be rendered immortal by the assistance of Photography.

---

[1] *Mesmeric* Franz Mesmer (1734–1835) claimed to have discovered a mysterious force he termed "animal magnetism"; it was termed *mermerism* by others.

Henry Fox Talbot, *Nelson's Column in Trafalgar Square*, 1843.

Roger Fenton, *The British Museum*, 1857.

Roger Fenton, *Fruit and Flowers*, 1860.

Roger Fenton, *The Long Walk*, 1860.

Oscar Gustav Rejlander, *The Two Ways of Life* (detail), 1857.

Robert Howlett, *The Great Eastern: Isambard Kingdom Brunel Inspecting Construction Work* (detail), 1857.

Oscar Gustav Rejlander, *Homeless*, c. 1860. (This well-known and widely-praised photograph was also sometimes referred to as *A Night in Town* or *Poor Joe*.)

Henry Peach Robinson, *Fading Away*, 1858.

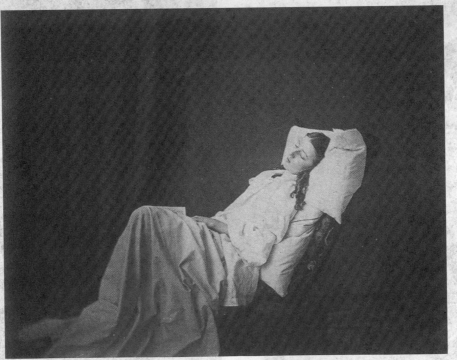

Henry Peach Robinson, *She Never Told Her Love*, 1858.

Francis Frith, *The Pyramids of Dahshoor, From the East*, c. 1858.

Francis Frith, *Crocodile on a Bank of the Nile* (detail), 1857.

Lady Clementina Hawarden, *The Toilette*, c. 1864.

Lady Clementina Hawarden, *Lady Isabella Grace and
Clementina Maude, 5 Princes Gardens*, c. 1862–63.

Lewis Carroll, *Ellen Watts* (Ellen Terry), 1865.

Lewis Carroll, *Tuning*, 1876.

Lewis Carroll, *John Everett Millais, His wife, and Two of Their Daughters,* 1865.

Francis Bedford, *A Peaceful Village*, 1859.

Julia Margaret Cameron, *Annie—My First Success*, 1864. Cameron maintained that this image was her first successful photograph.

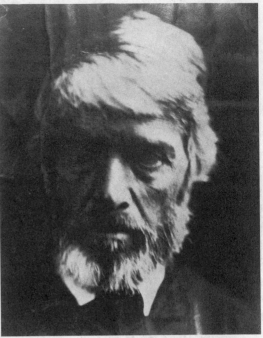

Julia Margaret Cameron, *Thomas Carlyle*, 1867. Carlyle wrote of the photo, "it is as if it suddenly began to speak, terrifically ugly and woebegone!"

Julia Margaret Cameron, *Ophelia*, 1867.

Julia Margaret Cameron, *The Angel at the Sepulchre*, 1869.

Julia Margaret Cameron, *Cingalese Girl*, 1875.

Julia Margaret Cameron, *The Passing of Arthur*, 1875.

Samuel Bourne, *The Rajah of Drangadra*, c. 1868.

Thomas Annan, *Close No. 46, Saltmarket, Glasgow*, 1868.

John Thomson, *Physic Street, Canton*, c. 1869.

William Notman, *Blackfoot Brave, near Calgary, Alberta*, 1889.

William Notman, *Miss Thomas*, 1876.

Peter Henry Emerson, *Gathering Water-lilies*, 1886.

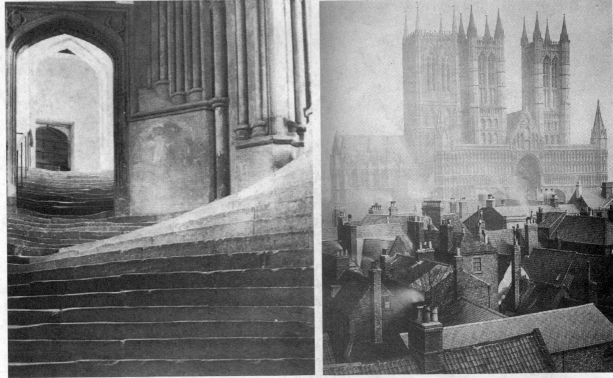

Frederick Evans, *A Sea of Steps*, 1898.   Frederick Evans, *Lincoln Cathedral from the Castle*, 1898.

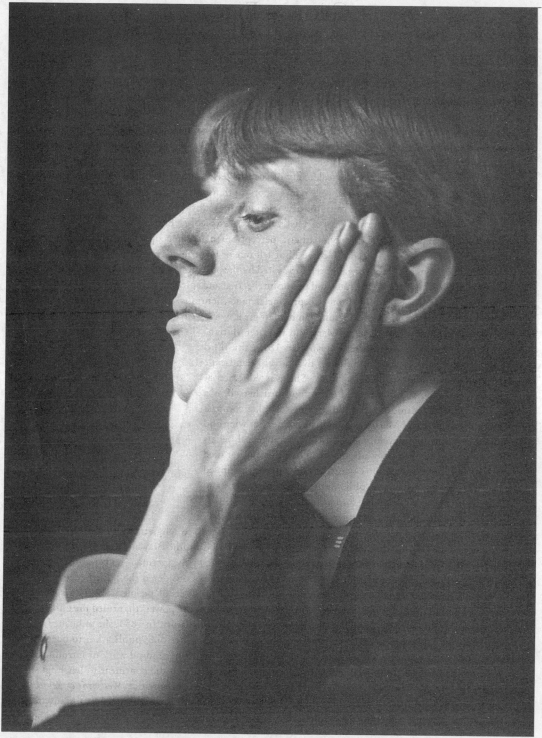

Frederick Evans, *Portrait of Aubrey Beardsley*, 1893.

GEORGE ELIOT
1819 – 1880

George Eliot chose her masculine pen name with good reason: she did not wish to be received by the public as a woman writer and judged by terms thought to be appropriate to women's work. Eliot was a writer who valued sympathy above all other qualities, and one who constructed memorable domestic and romantic scenes; hers was a notable intellectual and philosophical voice that produced perhaps the most remarkable novels of the Victorian period. She was hailed for the extraordinary writing and psychological acuity of such novels as *Adam Bede*, *The Mill on the Floss*, *Middlemarch*, and *Daniel Deronda*, as well as for important translations, criticism, and essays. She was also notorious in her time for her common-law relationship with the biographer, novelist, botanist, and literary and theatrical critic George Henry Lewes. Yet George Eliot's evocations of English provincial life and her acute and sympathetic perceptions of rural people remained immensely popular. As with many Victorians, George Eliot fell out of favor in the modernist period, but for many decades now readers have again been captivated by the portrayal of life in the English Midlands in such works as *The Mill on the Floss*, and by the intellectual and spiritual struggles of characters like Dorothea Brooke, the heroine from the provincial (and fictitious) town of Middlemarch, and Gewndolen Harleth and Daniel Deronda in her last great work.

Mary Anne Evans (she also used Mary Ann and later Marian) was born in rural Warwickshire, England, in 1819, the third child of Christiana Pearson and Robert Evans. This landscape was to figure in almost all her fiction. She was educated at various boarding schools where she distinguished herself as a studious, shy and introspective child. At one school, a compassionate teacher named Maria Lewis took her under her wing and molded her spiritual development, instilling evangelical beliefs that would persist into early adulthood. When her mother died in 1836, her formal education came to an end, but she continued to study theology, languages, philosophy, Romantic poetry, and German literature while caring for her father.

Her close relationship with her father was tested in 1842 when she announced her loss of faith in Christianity and organized religion, after falling under the influence of the freethinking, radical intellectuals Charles and Caroline Bray and Caroline's brother, Charles Hennell. Hennell urged her to translate *The Life of Jesus*, by the German "higher critic" David Friedrich Strauss,; the translation appeared in 1846. This study considered the Bible's texts not as factual histories ordained by God, but rather as myths, the products of people living in a specific historical period trying to find language to articulate their sense of the powers that ruled the universe; essentially, Strauss wrote as a cultural anthropologist of early Christianity. In 1854, she published her translation of Ludwig Feuerbach's *Essence of Christianity* (1854), her only publication to bear the name of Marian Evans on its title page. Here again she continued her radical work of introducing ideas that challenged traditional religious beliefs that were current on the continent to her English readers. Before this work, in 1851, she had become assistant editor of the radical *Westminster Review*, a position she held for two years, helping to restore the magazine to the high intellectual standards it had attained while under the editorship of the philosopher John Stuart Mill. Even after leaving her position at the *Review*, George Eliot continued to contribute many important essays to the magazine, among them "Silly Novels by Lady Novelists" and "The Natural History of German Life" (1856).

In 1851 she met George Henry Lewes, and in 1854 they began to live together (though he was married). The decision to live in a common-law "marriage," as they called it (indeed, George Eliot called herself and became known to many as "Mrs. Lewes"), came at great personal expense; the brother to whom she had once been very close persuaded the entire family to shun her, which they did for the duration of her quarter-century relationship with Lewes. The relationship also constricted her involvement in the literary and intellectual world of London, especially in the early years of her writing career.

George Eliot's novels and shorter fiction (three novellas were published in *Blackwood's Magazine* under her pseudonym and collected in *Scenes of Clerical Life* in 1858) mostly harken back to the early part of the century in pre-industrial England and concentrate on the lives of ordinary people at a time when great changes were on the horizon; indeed, she draws our attention to how tragedy, as well as sublime comedy, may form part of the lives of common people. In a passage in *The Mill on the Floss*, George Eliot explained the appeal of the Midland landscape and its Wordsworthian influence upon her imagination: "These familiar flowers, these well-remembered bird-notes, this sky, with its fitful brightness, these furrowed and grassy fields ... such things as these are the mother tongue of our imagination, the language that is laden with all the subtle inextricable associations the fleeting hours of our childhood left behind them. Our delight in the sunshine on the deep-bladed grass to-day, might be no more than the faint perception of wearied souls, if it were not for the sunshine and the grass in the far-off years which still live in us, and transform our perception into love." These scenes become the sources of the moral imagination, "with its deep immoveable roots in memory." They are also the sources of George Eliot's moral realism. As she wrote in Chapter 17 of *Adam Bede*, her focus was not heroes or sublimely beautiful women, but people who do "the rough work of the world" because human beings need to reverence "that other beauty ... which lies in no secret of proportion, but in the secret of deep human sympathy."

Even though George Eliot was almost forty when she began writing fiction, once she began she was prolific. *Adam Bede* appeared in 1859 to great critical acclaim (Queen Victoria was among its admirers); *The Mill on the Floss* was published in 1860 and *Silas Marner* in 1861; her Renaissance historical novel, *Romola*, in 1863; *Felix Holt, the Radical*, a book about the First Reform Bill, in 1866; a collection of poetry, *The Spanish Gypsy*, in 1868; *Middlemarch* in 1871–72; and another collection of poetry, *The Legend of Jubal and Other Poems*, in 1874. *Daniel Deronda* (1876) was George Eliot's final novel. Her interest in Judaism and in the Hebrew language informed this epic story, set in contemporary England, of a woman who is forced into an oppressive marriage with an aristocrat and of an idealistic young man, the eponymous Daniel, who discovers his Jewish roots and works toward a renewal of the Jewish nation. For the agnostic George Eliot, the appeal of Judaism lay in its role as the foundation of the images and texts that inform a morality divinely human; Judaism was the source of western culture's moral imagination. She may not have been a believer, but her fiction finds much of its life in the tropes and images of the religious imagination as she found them in the King James Bible, Milton, Bunyan, and the English hymns. This most intellectually sophisticated of all Victorian novelists was also one of its most deeply traditional.

In 1878, George Eliot's beloved "husband," as she called Lewes, died. In May of 1880, she married John Walter Cross, a man 20 years her junior. She died in December 1880, and was buried beside Lewes in Highgate Cemetery. Before her death she reconciled with her brother Isaac, who welcomed the "legitimacy" of her marriage to Cross. Five years after her death, Cross published a reverent biography of Mary Anne Evans, entitled *George Eliot's Life as Related in her Letters and Journals*.

⌘ ⌘ ⌘

O, May I Join the Choir Invisible

Longum illud tempus, quum non ero, magis me movet,
quam hoc exiguum.[1]

—CICERO, ad Att., 12.18.

O, may I join the choir invisible
  Of those immortal dead who live again
In minds made better by their presence: live
In pulses stirred to generosity,
5 In deeds of daring rectitude, in scorn
For miserable aims that end with self,
In thoughts sublime that pierce the night like stars,
And with their mild persistence urge man's search
To vaster issues.
10   So to live is heaven:
To make undying music in the world,
Breathing as beauteous order that controls
With growing sway the growing life of man.
So we inherit that sweet purity
15 For which we struggled, failed, and agonised
With widening retrospect that bred despair.
Rebellious flesh that would not be subdued,
A vicious parent shaming still its child,
Poor anxious penitence, is quick dissolved;
20 Its discords, quenched by meeting harmonies,
Die in the large and charitable air.
And all our rarer, better, truer self,
That sobbed religiously in yearning song,
That watched to ease the burthen of the world,
25 Laboriously tracing what must be,
And what may yet be better—saw within
A worthier image for the sanctuary,
And shaped it forth before the multitude
Divinely human, raising worship so
30 To higher reverence more mixed with love—
That better self shall live till human Time
Shall fold its eyelids, and the human sky

Be gathered like a scroll within the tomb
Unread forever.
35   This is life to come,
Which martyred men have made more glorious
For us who strive to follow. May I reach
That purest heaven, be to other souls
The cup of strength in some great agony,
40 Enkindle generous ardour, feed pure love,
Beget the smiles that have no cruelty—
Be the sweet presence of a good diffused,
And in diffusion ever more intense.
So shall I join the choir invisible,
45 Whose music is the gladness of the world.
—1867

from *Brother and Sister Sonnets*

SONNET II

School parted us; we never found again
  That childish world where our two spirits mingled
Like scents from varying roses that remain
One sweetness, nor can evermore be singled.

5 Yet the twin habit of that early time
Lingered for long about the heart and tongue:
We had been natives of one happy clime,
And its dear accent to our utterance clung.

Till the dire years whose awful name is Change
10 Had grasped our souls still yearning in divorce,
And pitiless shaped them in two forms that range
Two elements which sever their life's course.

But were another childhood world my share,
I would be born a little sister there.
—1874

---

[1] *Longum ... exiguum* Latin: "And the great length of time after
I shall cease to be matters more to me than the short time I have
here."

from *Adam Bede*

CHAPTER 17: IN WHICH THE STORY PAUSES A LITTLE

"This Rector of Broxton is little better than a pagan!" I hear one of my readers exclaim. "How much more edifying it would have been if you had made him give Arthur some truly spiritual advice. You might have put into his mouth the most beautiful things—quite as good as reading a sermon."

Certainly I could, if I held it the highest vocation of the novelist to represent things as they never have been and never will be. Then, of course, I might refashion life and character entirely after my own liking; I might select the most unexceptionable type of clergyman, and put my own admirable opinions into his mouth on all occasions. But it happens, on the contrary, that my strongest effort is to avoid any such arbitrary picture, and to give a faithful account of men and things as they have mirrored themselves in my mind. The mirror is doubtless defective; the outlines will sometimes be disturbed, the reflection faint or confused; but I feel as much bound to tell you as precisely as I can what that reflection is, as if I were in the witness-box narrating my experience on oath.

Sixty years ago—it is a long time, so no wonder things have changed—all clergymen were not zealous; indeed there is reason to believe that the number of zealous clergymen was small, and it is probable that if one among the small minority had owned the livings of Broxton and Hayslope in the year 1799, you would have liked him no better than you like Mr. Irwine. Ten to one, you would have thought him a tasteless, indiscreet, methodistical[1] man. It is so very rarely that facts hit that nice medium required by our own enlightened opinions and refined taste! Perhaps you will say, "Do improve the facts a little, then; make them more accordant with those correct views which it is our privilege to possess. The world is just what we like; do touch it up with a tasteful pencil, and make believe it is not quite such a mixed entangled affair. Let all people who hold unexceptionable opinions act unexceptionally. Let your most faulty characters always be on the wrong side, and your virtuous ones on the right. Then we shall see at a glance whom we are to condemn, and whom we are to approve. Then we shall be able to admire, without the slightest disturbance of our prepossessions: we shall hate and despise with that true ruminant relish which belongs to undoubting confidence."

But, my good friend, what will you do then with your fellow parishioner who opposes your husband in the vestry?—with your newly-appointed vicar, whose style of preaching you find painfully below that of his regretted predecessor?—with the honest servant who worries your soul with her one failing?—with your neighbour, Mrs. Green, who was really kind to you in your last illness, but has said several ill-natured things about you since your convalescence?—nay, with your excellent husband himself, who has other irritating habits besides that of not wiping his shoes? These fellow mortals, every one, must be accepted as they are: you can neither straighten their noses, nor brighten their wit, nor rectify their dispositions; and it is these people—amongst whom your life is passed—that it is needful you should tolerate, pity, and love: it is these more or less ugly, stupid, inconsistent people, whose movements of goodness you should be able to admire—for whom you should cherish all possible hopes, all possible patience. And I would not, even if I had the choice, be the clever novelist who could create a world so much better than this, in which we get up in the morning to do our daily work, that you would be likely to turn a harder, colder eye on the dusty streets and the common green fields—on the real breathing men and women, who can be chilled by your indifference or injured by your prejudice, who can be cheered and helped onward by your fellow feeling, your forbearance, your outspoken, brave justice.

So I am content to tell my simple story, without trying to make things seem better than they were; dreading nothing, indeed, but falsity, which, in spite of one's best efforts, there is reason to dread. Falsehood is so easy, truth so difficult. The pencil is conscious of a delightful facility in drawing a griffin[2]—the longer the claws, and the larger the wings, the better; but that marvellous facility which we mistook for genius is apt to forsake us when we want to draw a real unexaggerated

---

[1] *methodistical* Rigidly adhering to systems and methods.

[2] *griffin* Mythological creature with features of both an eagle and a lion.

lion. Examine your words well, and you will find that even when you have no motive to be false, it is a very hard thing to say the exact truth, even about your own immediate feelings—much harder than to say something fine about them which is *not* the exact truth.

It is for this rare, precious quality of truthfulness that I delight in many Dutch paintings, which lofty-minded people despise. I find a source of delicious sympathy in these faithful pictures of a monotonous homely existence, which has been the fate of so many more among my fellow mortals than a life of pomp or of absolute indigence, of tragic suffering or of world-stirring actions. I turn, without shrinking, from cloud-borne angels, from prophets, sibyls, and heroic warriors, to an old woman bending over her flowerpot, or eating her solitary dinner, while the noonday light, softened perhaps by a screen of leaves, falls on her mob cap,[1] and just touches the rim of her spinning-wheel, and her stone jug, and all those cheap common things which are the precious necessaries of life to her—or I turn to that village wedding, kept between four brown walls, where an awkward bridegroom opens the dance with a high-shouldered, broad-faced bride, while elderly and middle-aged friends look on, with very irregular noses and lips, and probably with quart-pots in their hands, but with an expression of unmistakeable contentment and goodwill. "Foh!" says my idealistic friend, "what vulgar details! What good is there in taking all these pains to give an exact likeness of old women and clowns? What a low phase of life!—what clumsy, ugly people!"

But bless us, things may be lovable that are not altogether handsome, I hope? I am not at all sure that the majority of the human race have not been ugly, and even among those "lords of their kind," the British, squat figures, ill-shapen nostrils, and dingy complexions are not startling exceptions. Yet there is a great deal of family love amongst us. I have a friend or two whose class of features is such that the Apollo curl[2] on the summit of their brows would be decidedly trying; yet to my certain knowledge tender hearts have beaten for them, and their miniatures—flattering, but still not lovely—are kissed in secret by motherly lips. I have seen many an excellent matron, who could never in her best days have been handsome, and yet she had a packet of yellow love-letters in a private drawer, and sweet children showered kisses on her sallow cheeks. And I believe there have been plenty of young heroes, of middle stature and feeble beards, who have felt quite sure they could never love anything more insignificant than a Diana,[3] and yet have found themselves in middle life happily settled with a wife who waddles. Yes! thank God; human feeling is like the mighty rivers that bless the earth: it does not wait for beauty—it flows with resistless force and brings beauty with it.

All honour and reverence to the divine beauty of form! Let us cultivate it to the utmost in men, women, and children—in our gardens and in our houses. But let us love that other beauty too, which lies in no secret of proportion, but in the secret of deep human sympathy. Paint us an angel, if you can, with a floating violet robe, and a face paled by the celestial light; paint us yet oftener a Madonna, turning her mild face upward and opening her arms to welcome the divine glory; but do not impose on us any aesthetic rules which shall banish from the region of Art those old women scraping carrots with their work-worn hands, those heavy clowns taking holiday in a dingy pot-house,[4] those rounded backs and stupid weather-beaten faces that have bent over the spade and done the rough work of the world—those homes with their tin pans, their brown pitchers, their rough curs, and their clusters of onions. In this world there are so many of these common coarse people, who have no picturesque sentimental wretchedness! It is so needful we should remember their existence, else we may happen to leave them quite out of our religion and philosophy, and frame lofty theories which only fit a world of extremes. Therefore let Art always remind us of them; therefore let us always have men ready to give the loving pains of a life to the faithful representing of commonplace things—men who see beauty in these commonplace things, and delight in showing how kindly the light of heaven falls on them. There are few prophets in the world; few sublimely beautiful women; few heroes. I can't afford to give all my love and reverence to such rarities; I want a great deal of those

---

[1]   *mob cap*   Women's cotton bonnet with a ruffled edge that ties under the chin.

[2]   *Apollo curl*   I.e., curl like that of the Greek god Apollo.

[3]   *Diana*   Roman goddess of the hunt.

[4]   *pot-house*   Tavern.

feelings for my everyday fellow men, especially for the few in the foreground of the great multitude, whose faces I know, whose hands I touch, for whom I have to make way with kindly courtesy. Neither are picturesque lazzaroni[1] or romantic criminals half so frequent as your common labourer, who gets his own bread, and eats it vulgarly but creditably with his own pocketknife. It is more needful that I should have a fibre of sympathy connecting me with that vulgar citizen who weighs out my sugar in a vilely assorted cravat[2] and waistcoat, than with the handsomest rascal in red scarf and green feathers—more needful that my heart should swell with loving admiration at some trait of gentle goodness in the faulty people who sit at the same hearth with me, or in the clergyman of my own parish, who is perhaps rather too corpulent, and in other respects is not an Oberlin[3] or a Tillotson, than at the deeds of heroes whom I shall never know except by hearsay, or at the sublimest abstract of all clerical graces that was ever conceived by an able novelist.

And so I come back to Mr. Irwine, with whom I desire you to be in perfect charity, far as he may be from satisfying your demands on the clerical character. Perhaps you think he was not—as he ought to have been—a living demonstration of the benefits attached to a national church? But I am not sure of that; at least I know that the people in Broxton and Hayslope would have been very sorry to part with their clergyman, and that most faces brightened at his approach; and until it can be proved that hatred is a better thing for the soul than love, I must believe that Mr. Irwine's influence in his parish was a more wholesome one than that of the zealous Mr. Ryde, who came there twenty years afterwards, when Mr. Irwine had been gathered to his fathers. It is true, Mr. Ryde insisted strongly on the doctrines of the Reformation,[4] visited his flock a great deal in their own homes, and was severe in rebuking the aberrations of the flesh—put a stop, indeed, to the Christmas rounds of the church singers, as promoting drunkenness, and too light a handling of sacred things. But I gathered from Adam Bede, to whom I talked of these matters in his old age, that few clergymen could be less successful in winning the hearts of their parishioners than Mr. Ryde. They learned a great many notions about doctrine from him, so that almost every churchgoer under fifty began to distinguish as well between the genuine gospel and what did not come precisely up to that standard, as if he had been born and bred a Dissenter;[5] and for some time after his arrival there seemed to be quite a religious movement in that quiet rural district. "But," said Adam, "I've seen pretty clear, ever since I was a young un, as religion's something else besides notions. It isn't notions sets people doing the right thing—it's feelings. It's the same with the notions in religion as it is with mathematics—a man may be able to work problems straight off in's head as he sits by the fire and smokes his pipe; but if he has to make a machine or a building, he must have a will and a resolution, and love something else better than his own ease. Somehow, the congregation began to fall off, and people began to speak light o' Mr. Ryde. I believe he meant right at bottom; but, you see, he was sourish-tempered, and was for beating down prices with the people as worked for him; and his preaching wouldn't go down well with that sauce. And he wanted to be like my lord judge i' the parish, punishing folks for doing wrong; and he scolded 'em from the pulpit as if he'd been a Ranter,[6] and yet he couldn't abide the Dissenters, and was a deal more set against 'em than Mr. Irwine was. And then he didn't keep within his income, for he seemed to think at first go-off that six hundred a year was to make him as big a man as Mr. Donnithorne; that's a sore mischief I've often seen with the poor curates jumping into a bit of a living all of a sudden. Mr. Ryde was a deal thought on at a distance, I believe, and he wrote books, but as for mathematics and the natur o' things, he was as ignorant as a woman. He was

---

[1] *lazzaroni* Vagabonds or beggars.

[2] *cravat* Neck scarf.

[3] *Oberlin* German pastor J.F. Oberlin (1740–1826), who cared for Livonian author J.M.R. Lenz, and about whom Eliot might have read in Georg Büchner's novella *Lenz* (1850); *Tillotson* John Tillotson (1630–94), Archbishop of Canterbury.

[4] *Reformation* Sixteenth-century religious movement that sought to reform the Catholic Church and eventually established the Protestant religion.

[5] *Dissenter* Member of a Protestant sect that rebelled against and eventually broke with the Church of England.

[6] *Ranter* Member of a religious sect called "Primitive Methodist," whose name arose from a tradition of singing in the streets.

very knowing about doctrines, and used to call 'em the bulwarks of the Reformation, but I've always mistrusted that sort o' learning as leaves folks foolish and unreasonable about business. Now Mester Irwine was as different as could be, as quick!—he understood what you meant in a minute; and he knew all about building, and could see when you'd made a good job. And he behaved as much like a gentleman to the farmers, and th' old women and the labourers, as he did to the gentry. You never saw *him* interfering and scolding, and trying to play th' emperor. Ah! he was a fine man as ever you set eyes on, and so kind to's mother and sisters. That poor sickly Miss Anne—he seemed to think more of her than of anybody else in the world. There wasn't a soul in the parish had a word to say against him; and his servants stayed with him till they were so old and pottering, he had to hire other folks to do their work."

"Well," I said, "that was an excellent way of preaching in the weekdays; but I daresay, if your old friend Mr. Irwine were to come to life again, and get into the pulpit next Sunday, you would be rather ashamed that he didn't preach better after all your praise of him."

"Nay, nay," said Adam, broadening his chest and throwing himself back in his chair, as if he were ready to meet all inferences, "nobody has ever heard me say Mr. Irwine was much of a preacher. He didn't go into deep speritial experience; and I know there's a deal in a man's inward life as you can't measure by the square, and say, 'Do this and that'll follow,' and, 'Do that and this'll follow.' There's things go on in the soul, and times when feelings come into you like a rushing mighty wind, as the Scripture says, and part your life in two a'most, so as you look back on yourself as if you was somebody else. Those are things as you can't bottle up in a 'do this' and 'do that'; and I'll go so far with the strongest Methodist ever you'll find. That shows me there's deep speritial things in religion. You can't make much out wi' talking about it, but you feel it. Mr. Irwine didn't go into those things; he preached short moral sermons, and that was all. But then he acted pretty much up to what he said; he didn't set up for being so different from other folks one day, and then be as like 'em as two peas the next. And he made folks love him and respect him, and that was better nor stirring up

their gall wi' being over busy. Mrs. Poyser used to say—you know she would have her word about everything—she said, Mr. Irwine was like a good meal o' victual, you were the better for him without thinking on it, and Mr. Ryde was like a dose o' physic, he gripped you and worreted[1] you, and after all he left you much the same."

"But didn't Mr. Ryde preach a great deal more about that spiritual part of religion that you talk of, Adam? Couldn't you get more out of his sermons than out of Mr. Irwine's?"

"Eh, I knowna. He preached a deal about doctrines. But I've seen pretty clear ever since I was a young un, as religion's something else besides doctrines and notions. I look at it as if the doctrines was like finding names for your feelings, so as you can talk of 'em when you've never known 'em, just as a man may talk o' tools when he knows their names, though he's never so much as seen 'em, still less handled 'em. I've heard a deal o' doctrine i' my time, for I used to go after the dissenting preachers along wi' Seth, when I was a lad o' seventeen, and got puzzling myself a deal about th' Arminians and the Calvinists. The Wesleyans,[2] you know, are strong Arminians; and Seth, who could never abide anything harsh, and was always for hoping the best, held fast by the Wesleyans from the very first; but I thought I could pick a hole or two in their notions, and I got disputing wi' one o' the class leaders down at Treddles'on, and harassed him so, first o' this side and then o' that, till at last he said, 'Young man, it's the devil making use o' your pride and conceit as a weapon to war against the simplicity o' the truth.' I couldn't help laughing then, but as I was going home, I thought the man wasn't far wrong. I began to see as all this weighing and sifting what this text means and that text means, and whether folks are saved all by God's grace, or whether there goes an ounce o' their own will to 't, was no part o' real religion at all. You may talk o' these things for hours on

---

[1]   *worreted* Annoyed.

[2]   *Arminians* Followers of Dutch Protestant theologian James Arminius (1560–1609), who opposed certain Calvinist doctrines, such as predestination, original sin, and the notion that God is the creator of both good and evil; *Calvinists* Also called "Reformed Protestants"; Christian followers of John Calvin (1509–64); *Wesleyans* Methodists; followers of John Wesley (1703–91), who embraced Arminian theology and founded Methodism.

end, and you'll only be all the more coxy[1] and conceited for 't. So I took to going nowhere but to church, and hearing nobody but Mr. Irwine, for he said nothing but what was good, and what you'd be the wiser for remembering. And I found it better for my soul to be humble before the mysteries o' God's dealings, and not be making a clatter about what I could never understand. And they're poor foolish questions after all; for what have we got either inside or outside of us but what comes from God? If we've got a resolution to do right, He gave it us, I reckon, first or last; but I see plain enough we shall never do it without a resolution, and that's enough for me."

Adam, you perceive, was a warm admirer, perhaps a partial judge, of Mr. Irwine, as, happily, some of us still are of the people we have known familiarly. Doubtless it will be despised as a weakness by that lofty order of minds who pant after the ideal, and are oppressed by a general sense that their emotions are of too exquisite a character to find fit objects among their everyday fellow men. I have often been favoured with the confidence of these select natures, and find them concur in the experience that great men are over-estimated and small men are insupportable; that if you would love a woman without ever looking back on your love as a folly, she must die while you are courting her; and if you would maintain the slightest belief in human heroism, you must never make a pilgrimage to see the hero. I confess I have often meanly shrunk from confessing to these accomplished and acute gentlemen what my own experience has been. I am afraid I have often smiled with hypocritical assent, and gratified them with an epigram on the fleeting nature of our illusions, which anyone moderately acquainted with French literature can command at a moment's notice. Human converse, I think some wise man has remarked, is not rigidly sincere. But I herewith discharge my conscience, and declare that I have had quite enthusiastic movements of admiration towards old gentlemen who spoke the worst English, who were occasionally fretful in their temper, and who had never moved in a higher sphere of influence than that of parish overseer; and that the way in which I have come to the conclusion that human nature is lovable—the way I have learnt something of its

deep pathos, its sublime mysteries—has been by living a great deal among people more or less commonplace and vulgar, of whom you would perhaps hear nothing very surprising if you were to inquire about them in the neighbourhoods where they dwelt. Ten to one most of the small shopkeepers in their vicinity saw nothing at all in them. For I have observed this remarkable coincidence, that the select natures who pant after the ideal, and find nothing in pantaloons or petticoats great enough to command their reverence and love, are curiously in unison with the narrowest and pettiest. For example, I have often heard Mr. Gedge, the landlord of the Royal Oak, who used to turn a bloodshot eye on his neighbours in the village of Shepperton, sum up his opinion of the people in his own parish—and they were all the people he knew—in these emphatic words: "Ay, sir, I've said it often, and I'll say it again, they're a poor lot i' this parish—a poor lot, sir, big and little." I think he had a dim idea that if he could migrate to a distant parish, he might find neighbours worthy of him; and indeed he did subsequently transfer himself to the Saracen's Head, which was doing a thriving business in the back street of a neighbouring market-town. But, oddly enough, he has found the people up that back street of precisely the same stamp as the inhabitants of Shepperton—"a poor lot, sir, big and little, and them as comes for a go o' gin are no better than them as comes for a pint o' twopenny[2]—a poor lot."
—1859

Silly Novels By Lady Novelists

Silly novels by Lady Novelists are a genus with many species, determined by the particular quality of silliness that predominates in them—the frothy, the prosy, the pious, or the pedantic. But it is a mixture of all these—a composite order of feminine fatuity, that produces the largest class of such novels, which we shall distinguish as the *mind-and-millinery* species. The heroine is usually an heiress, probably a peeress in her own right, with perhaps a vicious baronet, an amiable duke, and an irresistible younger son of a marquis as

---

[1]   *coxy* Cocky.

[2]   *twopenny* Ale.

lovers in the foreground, a clergyman and a poet sighing for her in the middle distance, and a crowd of undefined adorers dimly indicated beyond. Her eyes and her wit are both dazzling; her nose and her morals are alike free from any tendency to irregularity; she has a superb *contralto* and a superb intellect; she is perfectly well-dressed and perfectly religious; she dances like a sylph,[1] and reads the Bible in the original tongues. Or it may be that the heroine is not an heiress—that rank and wealth are the only things in which she is deficient; but she infallibly gets into high society, she has the triumph of refusing many matches and securing the best, and she wears some family jewels or other as a sort of crown of righteousness at the end. Rakish[2] men either bite their lips in impotent confusion at her repartees, or are touched to penitence by her reproofs, which, on appropriate occasions, rise to a lofty strain of rhetoric; indeed, there is a general propensity in her to make speeches, and to rhapsodize at some length when she retires to her bedroom. In her recorded conversations she is amazingly eloquent, and in her unrecorded conversations, amazingly witty. She is understood to have a depth of insight that looks through and through the shallow theories of philosophers, and her superior instincts are a sort of dial by which men have only to set their clocks and watches, and all will go well. The men play a very subordinate part by her side. You are consoled now and then by a hint that they have affairs, which keeps you in mind that the working-day business of the world is somehow being carried on, but ostensibly the final cause of their existence is that they may accompany the heroine on her "starring" expedition through life. They see her at a ball, and are dazzled; at a flower show, and they are fascinated; on a riding excursion, and they are witched by her noble horsemanship; at church, and they are awed by the sweet solemnity of her demeanour. She is the ideal woman in feelings, faculties, and flounces. For all this, she as often as not marries the wrong person to begin with, and she suffers terribly from the plots and intrigues of the vicious baronet; but even death has a soft place in his heart for such a paragon, and remedies all mistakes for her just at the right moment. The

vicious baronet is sure to be killed in a duel, and the tedious husband dies in his bed requesting his wife, as a particular favour to him, to marry the man she loves best, and having already dispatched a note to the lover informing him of the comfortable arrangement. Before matters arrive at this desirable issue our feelings are tried by seeing the noble, lovely, and gifted heroine pass through many *mauvais*[3] moments, but we have the satisfaction of knowing that her sorrows are wept into embroidered pocket handkerchiefs, that her fainting form reclines on the very best upholstery, and that whatever vicissitudes she may undergo, from being dashed out of her carriage to having her head shaved in a fever, she comes out of them all with a complexion more blooming and locks more redundant than ever.

We may remark, by the way, that we have been relieved from a serious scruple by discovering that silly novels by lady novelists rarely introduce us into any other than very lofty and fashionable society. We had imagined that destitute women turned novelists, as they turned governesses, because they had no other "ladylike" means of getting their bread. On this supposition, vacillating syntax and improbable incident had a certain pathos for us, like the extremely supererogatory[4] pincushions and ill-devised nightcaps that are offered for sale by a blind man. We felt the commodity to be a nuisance, but we were glad to think that the money went to relieve the necessitous, and we pictured to ourselves lonely women struggling for a maintenance, or wives and daughters devoting themselves to the production of "copy" out of pure heroism— perhaps to pay their husband's debts, or to purchase luxuries for a sick father. Under these impressions we shrank from criticising a lady's novel; her English might be faulty, but, we said to ourselves, her motives are irreproachable; her imagination may be uninventive, but her patience is untiring. Empty writing was excused by an empty stomach, and twaddle was consecrated by tears. But no! This theory of ours, like many other pretty theories, has had to give way before observation. Women's silly novels, we are now convinced, are written under totally different circumstances. The fair writers have evidently never talked to a tradesman except from a carriage

---

[1]   *sylph* Mythical being whose element is air.

[2]   *rakish* Fashionable; slightly suggestive of immorality.

[3]   *mauvais* French: bad.

[4]   *supererogatory* Unnecessary.

window; they have no notion of the working classes except as "dependents"; they think five hundred a year a miserable pittance; Belgravia[1] and "baronial halls" are their primary truths; and they have no idea of feeling interest in any man who is not at least a great landed proprietor, if not a prime minister. It is clear that they write in elegant boudoirs, with violet-coloured ink and a ruby pen; that they must be entirely indifferent to publishers' accounts, and inexperienced in every form of poverty except poverty of brains. It is true that we are constantly struck with the want of verisimilitude in their representations of the high society in which they seem to live; but then they betray no closer acquaintance with any other form of life. If their peers and peeresses are improbable, their literary men, tradespeople, and cottagers are impossible; and their intellect seems to have the peculiar impartiality of reproducing both what they *have* seen and heard, and what they have *not* seen and heard, with equal unfaithfulness.

There are few women, we suppose, who have not seen something of children under five years of age, yet in "Compensation,"[2] a recent novel of the mind-and-millinery species, which calls itself a "story of real life," we have a child of four and a half years old talking in this Ossianic[3] fashion—

"Oh, I am so happy, dear gran'mamma—I have seen—I have seen such a delightful person; he is like everything beautiful—like the smell of sweet flowers, and the view from Ben Lomond—or no, *better than that*—he is like what I think of and see when I am very, very happy; and he is really like mamma, too, when she sings; and his forehead is like *that distant sea*," she continued, pointing to the blue Mediterranean; "there seems no end—no end; or like the clusters of stars I like best to look at on a warm fine night ... Don't look so ... your forehead is like Loch Lomond, when the wind is blowing and the sun is gone in; I like the sunshine best when the

lake is smooth.... So now—I like it better than ever ... it is more beautiful still from the dark cloud that has gone over it, *when the sun suddenly lights up all the colours of the forests and shining purple rocks, and it is all reflected in the waters below.*"

We are not surprised to learn that the mother of this infant phenomenon, who exhibits symptoms so alarmingly like those of adolescence repressed by gin, is herself a phoenix.[4] We are assured, again and again, that she had a remarkably original mind, that she was a genius, and "conscious of her originality," and she was fortunate enough to have a lover who was also a genius, and a man of "most original mind."

This lover, we read, though "wonderfully similar" to her "in powers and capacity," was "infinitely superior to her in faith and development," and she saw in him the "'Agape'[5]—so rare to find—of which she had read and admired the meaning in her Greek Testament; having, *from her great facility in learning languages,* read the Scriptures in their original *tongues.*" Of course! Greek and Hebrew are mere play to a heroine; Sanskrit is no more than *a b c* to her; and she can talk with perfect correctness in any language except English. She is a polking polyglot,[6] a Creuzer[7] in crinoline. Poor men! There are so few of you who know even Hebrew; you think it something to boast of if, like Bolingbroke,[8] you only "understand that sort of learning, and what is writ about it"; and you are perhaps adoring women who can think slightingly of you in all the Semitic languages successively. But, then, as we are almost invariably told, that a heroine has a "beautifully small head," and as her intellect has probably been early invigorated by an attention to costume and deportment, we may conclude that she can pick up the Oriental tongues, to say nothing of their dialects, with the same aerial facility that the butterfly sips nectar. Besides, there can be no

---

[1] *Belgravia* Fashionable district in London.

[2] *"Compensation"* Subtitled "A Story of Real Life Thirty Years Ago," by Georgiana, Lady Chatterton; published in the *Athenaeum* in 1856.

[3] *Ossianic* Resembling the poetry of the supposed ancient Gaelic poet Ossian, which were later discovered to have been written by the eighteenth-century Scottish poet James Macpherson.

[4] *phoenix* Figuratively, from the mythical bird of which there was said to be only one, a unique person.

[5] *Agape* Greek: spiritual (as opposed to sexual) love.

[6] *polking polyglot* Dancing master of languages.

[7] *Creuzer* German philologist Georg Friedrich Creuzer (1771–1858).

[8] *Bolingbroke* English statesman and humanist Henry St. John, Viscount Bolingbroke (1678–1751).

difficulty in conceiving the depth of the heroine's erudition, when that of the authoress is so evident.

In "Laura Gay,"[1] another novel of the same school, the heroine seems less at home in Greek and Hebrew, but she makes up for the deficiency by a quite playful familiarity with the Latin classics—with the "dear old Virgil," "the graceful Horace, the humane Cicero, and the pleasant Livy";[2] indeed, it is such a matter of course with her to quote Latin, that she does it at a picnic in a very mixed company of ladies and gentlemen, having, we are told, "no conception that the nobler sex were capable of jealousy on this subject. And if, indeed," continues the biographer of Laura Gay, "the wisest and noblest portion of that sex were in the majority, no such sentiment would exist; but while Miss Wyndhams and Mr. Redfords abound, great sacrifices must be made to their existence." Such sacrifices, we presume, as abstaining from Latin quotations, of extremely moderate interest and applicability, which the wise and noble minority of the other sex would be quite as willing to dispense with as the foolish and ignoble majority. It is as little the custom of well-bred men as of well-bred women to quote Latin in mixed parties; they can contain their familiarity with "the humane Cicero" without allowing it to boil over in ordinary conversation, and even references to "the pleasant Livy" are not absolutely irrepressible. But Ciceronian Latin is the mildest form of Miss Gay's conversational power. Being on the Palatine[3] with a party of sightseers, she falls into the following vein of well-rounded remark: "Truth can only be pure objectively, for even in the creeds where it predominates, being subjective, and parcelled out into portions, each of these necessarily receives a hue of idiosyncrasy, that is, a taint of superstition more or less strong; while in such creeds as the Roman Catholic, ignorance, interest, the bias of ancient idolatries, and the force of authority, have gradually accumulated on the pure truth, and transformed it, at last, into a mass of superstition for the majority of its votaries; and how few are there, alas! whose zeal, courage, and intellectual energy are equal to the analysis of this accumulation, and to the discovery of the pearl of great price which lies hidden beneath this heap of rubbish." We have often met with women much more novel and profound in their observations than Laura Gay, but rarely with any so inopportunely long winded. A clerical lord, who is half in love with her, is alarmed by the daring remarks just quoted, and begins to suspect that she is inclined to free thinking. But he is mistaken; when in a moment of sorrow he delicately begs leave to "recall to her memory, a *depot* of strength and consolation under affliction, which, until we are hard pressed by the trials of life, we are too apt to forget," we learn that she really has "recurrence to that sacred depot," together with the teapot. There is a certain flavour of orthodoxy mixed with the parade of fortunes and fine carriages in "Laura Gay," but it is an orthodoxy mitigated by study of the humane Cicero, and by an "intellectual disposition to analyse."

"Compensation" is much more heavily dosed with doctrine, but then it has a treble amount of snobbish worldliness and absurd incident to tickle the palate of pious frivolity. Linda, the heroine, is still more speculative and spiritual than Laura Gay, but she has been "presented," and has more, and far grander, lovers; very wicked and fascinating women are introduced —even a French *lionne*;[4] and no expense is spared to get up as exciting a story as you will find in the most immoral novels. In fact, it is a wonderful *potpourri* of Almack's,[5] Scotch second sight, Mr. Rogers's breakfasts,[6] Italian brigands, deathbed conversions, superior authoresses, Italian mistresses, and attempts at poisoning old ladies, the whole served up with a garnish of talk about "faith and development," and "most original minds." Even Miss Susan Barton, the superior authoress, whose pen moves in a "quick decided manner when she is composing," declines the finest opportunities of marriage, and though old enough to be

---

[1]   *"Laura Gay"* Author anonymous; published 1856 in the *Athenaeum*.

[2]   *Virgil* Latin poet of the first century BCE, author of *The Aeneid*; *Horace* Latin lyric poet of the first century BCE; *Cicero* Roman orator, philosopher, and statesman of the first century BCE; *Livy* First century BCE historian and author of *The History of Rome*.

[3]   *Palatine* One of the seven hills of the ancient city of Rome.

[4]   *lionne* Literary celebrity.

[5]   *Almack's* Almack's Assembly Rooms, where fashionable subscription dances were held.

[6]   *Mr. Rogers's breakfasts* English poet Samuel Rogers (1763–1855) was known for holding breakfasts for the literary elite.

Linda's mother (since we are told that she refused Linda's father), has her hand sought by a young earl, the heroine's rejected lover. Of course, genius and morality must be backed by eligible offers, or they would seem rather a dull affair; and piety, like other things, in order to be *comme il faut*,[1] must be in "society," and have admittance to the best circles.

"Rank and Beauty"[2] is a more frothy and less religious variety of the mind-and-millinery species. The heroine, we are told, "if she inherited her father's pride of birth and her mother's beauty of person, had in herself a tone of enthusiastic feeling that perhaps belongs to her age even in the lowly born, but which is refined into the high spirit of wild romance only in the far descended, who feel that it is their best inheritance." This enthusiastic young lady, by dint of reading the newspaper to her father, falls in love with the *prime minister*, who, through the medium of leading articles and "the *resumé* of the debates," shines upon her imagination as a bright particular star, which has no parallax for her, living in the country as simple Miss Wyndham. But she forthwith becomes Baroness Umfraville in her own right, astonishes the world with her beauty and accomplishments when she bursts upon it from her mansion in Spring Gardens, and, as you foresee, will presently come into contact with the unseen *objet aimé*.[3] Perhaps the words "prime minister" suggest to you a wrinkled or obese sexagenarian; but pray dismiss the image. Lord Rupert Conway has been "called while still almost a youth to the first situation which a subject can hold in the *universe*," and even leading articles and a *resumé* of the debates have not conjured up a dream that surpasses the fact.

> The door opened again, and Lord Rupert Conway entered. Evelyn gave one glance. It was enough; she was not disappointed. It seemed as if a picture on which she had long gazed was suddenly instinct with life, and had stepped from its frame before her. His tall figure, the distinguished

simplicity of his air—it was a living Vandyke,[4] a cavalier, one of his noble cavalier ancestors, or one to whom her fancy had always likened him, who long of yore had, with an Umfraville, fought the Paynim[5] far beyond sea. Was this reality?

Very little like it, certainly.

By and by, it becomes evident that the ministerial heart is touched. Lady Umfraville is on a visit to the Queen at Windsor, and,

> The last evening of her stay, when they returned from riding, Mr. Wyndham took her and a large party to the top of the Keep,[6] to see the view. She was leaning on the battlements, gazing from that "stately height" at the prospect beneath her, when Lord Rupert was by her side. "What an unrivalled view!" exclaimed she.
>
> "Yes, it would have been wrong to go without having been up here. You are pleased with your visit?"
>
> "Enchanted! A Queen to live and die under, to live and die for!"
>
> "Ha!" cried he, with sudden emotion, and with a *eureka* expression of countenance, as if he had *indeed found a heart in unison with his own*.

The "*eureka* expression of countenance," you see at once to be prophetic of marriage at the end of the third volume; but before that desirable consummation, there are very complicated misunderstandings, arising chiefly from the vindictive plotting of Sir Luttrell Wycherley, who is a genius, a poet, and in every way a most remarkable character indeed. He is not only a romantic poet, but a hardened rake[7] and a cynical wit; yet his deep passion for Lady Umfraville has so impoverished his epigrammatic[8] talent, that he cuts an extremely poor figure in conversation. When she rejects him, he rushes into the shrubbery, and rolls himself in the dirt, and on recovering, devotes himself to the most diabolical and

---

[1] *comme il faut* Proper; correct (from the French: "as it must be").

[2] *"Rank and Beauty"* Subtitled "The Young Baroness," published 1856; author anonymous.

[3] *objet aimé* French: object of affection.

[4] *Vandyke* I.e., like a portrait by seventeenth-century Flemish artist Anthony Van Dyke, elegant, noble, and aristocratic.

[5] *Paynim* Non-Christians, generally Muslims.

[6] *Keep* Castle tower.

[7] *rake* Fashionable man of loose character.

[8] *epigrammatic* Witty.

laborious schemes of vengeance, in the course of which he disguises himself as a quack physician, and enters into general practice, foreseeing that Evelyn will fall ill, and that he shall be called in to attend her. At last, when all his schemes are frustrated, he takes leave of her in a long letter, written, as you will perceive from the following passage, entirely in the style of an eminent literary man:

"Oh, lady, nursed in pomp and pleasure, will you ever cast one thought upon the miserable being who addresses you? Will you ever, as your gilded galley is floating down the unruffled stream of prosperity, will you ever, while lulled by the sweetest music—thine own praises,—hear the far off sigh from that world to which I am going?"

On the whole, however, frothy as it is, we rather prefer "Rank and Beauty" to the other two novels we have mentioned. The dialogue is more natural and spirited; there is some frank ignorance, and no pedantry; and you are allowed to take the heroine's astounding intellect upon trust, without being called on to read her conversational refutations of sceptics and philosophers, or her rhetorical solutions of the mysteries of the universe.

Writers of the mind-and-millinery school are remarkably unanimous in their choice of diction. In their novels, there is usually a lady or gentleman who is more or less of a upas tree:[1] the lover has a manly breast; minds are redolent of various things; hearts are hollow; events are utilized; friends are consigned to the tomb; infancy is an engaging period; the sun is a luminary that goes to his western couch, or gathers the raindrops into his refulgent bosom; life is a melancholy boon; Albion and Scotia[2] are conversational epithets. There is a striking resemblance, too, in the character of their moral comments, such, for instance, as that "It is a fact, no less true than melancholy, that all people, more or less, richer or poorer, are swayed by bad example"; that "Books, however trivial, contain some subjects from which useful information may be drawn"; that "Vice can too often borrow the language of virtue"; that "Merit and nobility of nature must exist, to be accepted,

for clamour and pretension cannot impose upon those too well read in human nature to be easily deceived"; and that, "In order to forgive, we must have been injured." There is, doubtless, a class of readers to whom these remarks appear peculiarly pointed and pungent, for we often find them doubly and trebly scored with the pencil, and delicate hands giving in their determined adhesion to these hardy novelties by a distinct *très vrai*,[3] emphasized by many notes of exclamation. The colloquial style of these novels is often marked by much ingenious inversion, and a careful avoidance of such cheap phraseology as can be heard every day. Angry young gentlemen exclaim—"'Tis ever thus, methinks"; and in the half hour before dinner a young lady informs her next neighbour that the first day she read Shakespeare she "stole away into the park, and beneath the shadow of the greenwood tree, devoured with rapture the inspired page of the great magician." But the most remarkable efforts of the mind-and-millinery writers lie in their philosophic reflections. The authoress of "Laura Gay," for example, having married her hero and heroine, improves the event by observing that "if those sceptics, whose eyes have so long gazed on matter that they can no longer see aught else in man, could once enter with heart and soul into such bliss as this, they would come to say that the soul of man and the polypus[4] are not of common origin, or of the same texture." Lady novelists, it appears, can see something else besides matter; they are not limited to phenomena, but can relieve their eyesight by occasional glimpses of the *noumenon*,[5] and are, therefore, naturally better able than anyone else to confound sceptics, even of that remarkable, but to us unknown school, which maintains that the soul of man is of the same texture as the polypus.

The most pitiable of all silly novels by lady novelists are what we may call the *oracular* species—novels intended to expound the writer's religious, philosophical, or moral theories. There seems to be a notion abroad among women, rather akin to the superstition that the speech and actions of idiots are inspired, and

---

[1]   *upas tree*   Notoriously poisonous tree.

[2]   *Albion and Scotia*   Archaic names for England and Scotland, their use here signifying pretension.

[3]   *très vrai*   French: very true.

[4]   *polypus*   Octopus.

[5]   *noumenon*   Greek: intangible article that is known only through the intellect.

that the human being most entirely exhausted of common sense is the fittest vehicle of revelation. To judge from their writings, there are certain ladies who think that an amazing ignorance, both of science and of life, is the best possible qualification for forming an opinion on the knottiest moral and speculative questions. Apparently, their recipe for solving all such difficulties is something like this: Take a woman's head, stuff it with a smattering of philosophy and literature chopped small, and with false notions of society baked hard, let it hang over a desk a few hours every day, and serve up hot in feeble English, when not required. You will rarely meet with a lady novelist of the oracular class who is diffident of her ability to decide on theological questions—who has any suspicion that she is not capable of discriminating with the nicest accuracy between the good and evil in all church parties—who does not see precisely how it is that men have gone wrong hitherto—and pity philosophers in general that they have not had the opportunity of consulting her. Great writers, who have modestly contented themselves with putting their experience into fiction, and have thought it quite a sufficient task to exhibit men and things as they are, she sighs over as deplorably deficient in the application of their powers. "They have solved no great questions"—and she is ready to remedy their omission by setting before you a complete theory of life and manual of divinity, in a love story, where ladies and gentlemen of good family go through genteel vicissitudes, to the utter confusion of Deists, Puseyites,[1] and ultra-Protestants, and to the perfect establishment of that particular view of Christianity which either condenses itself into a sentence of small caps, or explodes into a cluster of stars on the three hundred and thirtieth page. It is true, the ladies and gentlemen will probably seem to you remarkably little like any you have had the fortune or misfortune to meet with, for, as a general rule, the ability of a lady novelist to describe actual life and her fellow men, is in inverse proportion to her confident eloquence about God and the other world, and the means by which she usually chooses to conduct you to true ideas of the invisible is a totally false

picture of the visible.

As typical a novel of the oracular kind as we can hope to meet with, is "The Enigma: a Leaf from the Chronicles of the Wolchorley House."[2] The "enigma" which this novel is to solve, is certainly one that demands powers no less gigantic than those of a lady novelist, being neither more nor less than the existence of evil. The problem is stated, and the answer dimly foreshadowed on the very first page. The spirited young lady, with raven hair, says, "All life is an inextricable confusion"; and the meek young lady, with auburn hair, looks at the picture of the Madonna which she is copying, and—"*There* seemed the solution of that mighty enigma." The style of this novel is quite as lofty as its purpose; indeed, some passages on which we have spent much patient study are quite beyond our reach, in spite of the illustrative aid of italics and small caps; and we must await further "development" in order to understand them. Of Ernest, the model young clergyman, who sets everyone right on all occasions, we read, that "he held not of marriage in the marketable kind, after a social desecration"; that, on one eventful night, "sleep had not visited his divided heart, where tumultuated, in varied type and combination, the aggregate feelings of grief and joy"; and that, "for the *marketable* human article he had no toleration, be it of what sort, or set for what value it might, whether for worship or class, his upright soul abhorred it, whose ultimatum, the self-deceiver, was to him THE *great spiritual lie*, 'living in a vain show, deceiving and being deceived'; since he did not suppose the phylactery and enlarged border on the garment to be *merely* a social trick." (The italics and small caps are the author's, and we hope they assist the reader's comprehension.) Of Sir Lionel, the model old gentleman, we are told that "the simple ideal of the middle age, apart from its anarchy and decadence, in him most truly seemed to live again, when the ties which knit men together were of heroic cast. The first-born colours of pristine faith and truth engraven on the common soul of man, and blent into the wide arch of brotherhood, where the primeval law of *order* grew and multiplied, each perfect after his kind, and mutually interdependent." You see clearly, of course, how colours

---

[1]   *Puseyites* Followers of Edward Bouverie Pusey (1800–82), English clergyman, leader of the Oxford Movement, and supporter of the Anglican church.

[2]   *"The Enigma ... House"* Published 1856 in the *Athenaeum*; author anonymous.

are first engraven on a soul, and then blent into a wide arch, on which arch of colours—apparently a rainbow —the law of order grew and multiplied, each— apparently the arch and the law—perfect after his kind? If, after this, you can possibly want any further aid towards knowing what Sir Lionel was, we can tell you, that in his soul "the scientific combinations of thought could educe no fuller harmonies of the good and the true, than lay in the primeval pulses which floated as an atmosphere around it!" and that, when he was sealing a letter, "Lo! the responsive throb in that good man's bosom echoed back in simple truth the honest witness of a heart that condemned him not, as his eye, bedewed with love, rested, too, with something of ancestral pride, on the undimmed motto of the family—'LOIAUTÉ.'"[1]

The slightest matters have their vulgarity fumigated out of them by the same elevated style. Commonplace people would say that a copy of Shakespeare lay on a drawing-room table; but the authoress of "The Enigma," bent on edifying periphrasis,[2] tells you that there lay on the table, "that fund of human thought and feeling, which teaches the heart through the little name, 'Shakespeare.'" A watchman sees a light burning in an upper window rather longer than usual, and thinks that people are foolish to sit up late when they have an opportunity of going to bed; but, lest this fact should seem too low and common, it is presented to us in the following striking and metaphysical manner: "He marvelled—as man *will* think for others in a necessarily separate personality, consequently (though disallowing it) in false mental premise—how differently *he* should act, how gladly *he* should prize the rest so lightly held of within." A footman—an ordinary Jeames, with large calves and aspirated vowels—answers the doorbell, and the opportunity is seized to tell you that he was a "type of the large class of pampered menials, who follow the curse of Cain[3]—'vagabonds' on the face of the earth, and whose estimate of the human class varies in the graduated scale of money and expenditure…. These,

and such as these, O England, be the false lights of thy morbid civilization!" We have heard of various "false lights," from Dr. Cumming to Robert Owen,[4] from Dr. Pusey to the Spirit-rappers,[5] but we never before heard of the false light that emanates from plush and powder.

In the same way very ordinary events of civilized life are exalted into the most awful crises, and ladies in full skirts and *manches à la Chinoise*,[6] conduct themselves not unlike the heroines of sanguinary melodramas. Mrs. Percy, a shallow woman of the world, wishes her son Horace to marry the auburn-haired Grace, she being an heiress; but he, after the manner of sons, falls in love with the raven-haired Kate, the heiress's portionless cousin; and, moreover, Grace herself shows every symptom of perfect indifference to Horace. In such cases, sons are often sulky or fiery, mothers are alternately manoeuvering and waspish, and the portionless young lady often lies awake at night and cries a good deal. We are getting used to these things now, just as we are used to eclipses of the moon, which no longer set us howling and beating tin kettles. We never heard of a lady in a fashionable "front"[7] behaving like Mrs. Percy under these circumstances. Happening one day to see Horace talking to Grace at a window, without in the least knowing what they are talking about, or having the least reason to believe that Grace, who is mistress of the house and a person of dignity, would accept her son if he were to offer himself, she suddenly rushes up to them and clasps them both, saying, "with a flushed countenance and in an excited manner"—"This is indeed happiness; for, may I not call you so, Grace?—my Grace—my Horace's Grace!—my dear children!" Her son tells her she is mistaken, and that he is engaged to Kate, whereupon we have the following scene and tableau:

> Gathering herself up to an unprecedented height, (!) her eyes lightning forth the fire of her

[1] *LOIAUTÉ* Old French: loyalty.

[2] *periphrasis* Figure of speech by which a meaning is expressed by many words rather than few or one.

[3] *curse of Cain* First son of Adam and Eve, who killed his brother Abel, and was banished from the country where his parents lived (see Genesis 4).

[4] *Dr. Cumming* The Reverend John Cumming (1807–81), Calvinist preacher; *Robert Owen* Social reformer (1771–1858).

[5] *Spirit-rappers* Mediums who performed séances and claimed to communicate with the dead, interpreting the knocking sounds allegedly made by their spirits.

[6] *manches à la Chinoise* French: Chinese sleeves.

[7] *front* False curls worn on the forehead.

anger—

"Wretched boy!" she said, hoarsely and scornfully, and clenching her hand, "Take then the doom of your own choice! Bow down your miserable head and let a mother's—"

"Curse not!" spake a deep low voice from behind, and Mrs. Percy started, scared, as though she had seen a heavenly visitant appear, to break upon her in the midst of her sin.

Meantime, Horace had fallen on his knees at her feet, and hid his face in his hands.

Who, then, is she—who! Truly his "guardian spirit" hath stepped between him and the fearful words, which, however unmerited, must have hung as a pall over his future existence—a spell which could not be unbound—which could not be unsaid.

Of an earthly paleness, but calm with the still, iron-bound calmness of death—the only calm one there—Katherine stood; and her words smote on the ear in tones whose appallingly slow and separate intonation rung on the heart like the chill, isolated tolling of some fatal knell.

"He would have plighted me his faith, but I did not accept it; you cannot, therefore—you *dare* not curse him. And here," she continued, raising her hand to heaven, whither her large dark eyes also rose with a chastened glow, which, for the first time, *suffering* had lighted in those passionate orbs,— "here I promise, come weal, come woe, that Horace Wolchorley and I do never interchange vows without his mother's sanction—without his mother's blessing!"

Here, and throughout the story, we see that confusion of purpose which is so characteristic of silly novels written by women. It is a story of quite modern drawing-room society—a society in which polkas are played and Puseyism discussed; yet we have characters, and incidents, and traits of manner introduced, which are mere shreds from the most heterogeneous romances. We have a blind Irish harper, "relic of the picturesque bards of yore," startling us at a Sunday-school festival of tea and cake in an English village; we have a crazy gipsy, in a scarlet cloak, singing snatches of romantic song, and revealing a secret on her deathbed which, with the testimony of a dwarfish miserly merchant, who salutes strangers with a curse and a devilish laugh, goes to prove

that Ernest, the model young clergyman, is Kate's brother; and we have an ultra-virtuous Irish Barney, discovering that a document is forged, by comparing the date of the paper with the date of the alleged signature, although the same document has passed through a court of law, and occasioned a fatal decision. The "Hall" in which Sir Lionel lives is the venerable country seat of an old family, and this, we suppose, sets the imagination of the authoress flying to donjons[1] and battlements, where "lo! the warder blows his horn"; for, as the inhabitants are in their bedrooms on a night certainly within the recollection of Pleaceman X., and a breeze springs up, which we are at first told was faint, and then that it made the old cedars bow their branches to the greensward, she falls into this mediaeval vein of description (the italics are ours): "The banner *unfurled it* at the sound, and shook its guardian wing above, while the startled owl *flapped her* in the ivy; the firmament looking down through her 'argus eyes,'"—

"Ministers of heaven's mute melodies."
And lo! two strokes tolled from out the warder tower, and 'Two o'clock' re-echoed its interpreter below."

Such stories as this of "The Enigma" remind us of the pictures clever children sometimes draw "out of their own head," where you will see a modern villa on the right, two knights in helmets fighting in the foreground, and a tiger grinning in a jungle on the left, the several objects being brought together because the artist thinks each pretty, and perhaps still more because he remembers seeing them in other pictures.

But we like the authoress much better on her mediaeval stilts than on her oracular ones—when she talks of the *Ich*[2] and of "subjective" and "objective," and lays down the exact line of Christian verity, between "right-hand excesses and left-hand declensions." Persons who deviate from this line are introduced with a patronizing air of charity. Of a certain Miss Inshquine she informs us, with all the lucidity of italics and small caps, that *"function,* not *form,* AS *the inevitable outer expression of the spirit in this tabernacled age,* weakly engrossed her." And *à propos* of Miss Mayjar, an evangelical lady who is a little too apt to talk of her visits to sick women and the state of their souls, we are told that the

---

[1] *donjon* The main tower within a walled castle or fortress.

[2] *Ich* German: I.

model clergyman is "not one to disallow, through the *super* crust, the undercurrent towards good in the *subject,* or the positive benefits, nevertheless, to the *object.*" We imagine the double-refined accent and protrusion of chin which are feebly represented by the italics in this lady's sentences! We abstain from quoting any of her oracular doctrinal passages, because they refer to matters too serious for our pages just now.

The epithet "silly" may seem impertinent, applied to a novel which indicates so much reading and intellectual activity as "The Enigma"; but we use this epithet advisedly. If, as the world has long agreed, a very great amount of instruction will not make a wise man, still less will a very mediocre amount of instruction make a wise woman. And the most mischievous form of feminine silliness is the literary form, because it tends to confirm the popular prejudice against the more solid education of women. When men see girls wasting their time in consultations about bonnets and ball dresses, and in giggling or sentimental love confidences, or middle-aged women mismanaging their children, and solacing themselves with acrid gossip, they can hardly help saying, "For Heaven's sake, let girls be better educated; let them have some better objects of thought —some more solid occupations." But after a few hours' conversation with an oracular literary woman, or a few hours' reading of her books, they are likely enough to say, "After all, when a woman gets some knowledge, see what use she makes of it! Her knowledge remains acquisition, instead of passing into culture; instead of being subdued into modesty and simplicity by a larger acquaintance with thought and fact, she has a feverish consciousness of her attainments; she keeps a sort of mental pocket mirror, and is continually looking in it at her own 'intellectuality'; she spoils the taste of one's muffin by questions of metaphysics; 'puts down' men at a dinner table with her superior information; and seizes the opportunity of a *soirée* to catechise us on the vital question of the relation between mind and matter. And then, look at her writings! She mistakes vagueness for depth, bombast for eloquence, and affectation for originality; she struts on one page, rolls her eyes on another, grimaces in a third, and is hysterical in a fourth. She may have read many writings of great men, and a few writings of great women; but she is as unable to discern the difference between her own style and theirs as a Yorkshireman is to discern the difference between his own English and a Londoner's: rhodomontade[1] is the native accent of her intellect. No—the average nature of women is too shallow and feeble a soil to bear much tillage; it is only fit for the very lightest crops."

It is true that the men who come to such a decision on such very superficial and imperfect observation may not be among the wisest in the world; but we have not now to contest their opinion—we are only pointing out how it is unconsciously encouraged by many women who have volunteered themselves as representatives of the feminine intellect. We do not believe that a man was ever strengthened in such an opinion by associating with a woman of true culture, whose mind had absorbed her knowledge instead of being absorbed by it. A really cultured woman, like a really cultured man, is all the simpler and the less obtrusive for her knowledge; it has made her see herself and her opinions in something like just proportions; she does not make it a pedestal from which she flatters herself that she commands a complete view of men and things, but makes it a point of observation from which to form a right estimate of herself. She neither spouts poetry nor quotes Cicero on slight provocation; not because she thinks that a sacrifice must be made to the prejudices of men, but because that mode of exhibiting her memory and Latinity does not present itself to her as edifying or graceful. She does not write books to confound philosophers, perhaps because she is able to write books that delight them. In conversation she is the least formidable of women, because she understands you, without wanting to make you aware that you *can't* understand her. She does not give you information, which is the raw material of culture—she gives you sympathy, which is it subtlest essence.

A more numerous class of silly novels than the oracular, (which are generally inspired by some form of High Church, or transcendental Christianity) is what we may call the *white neck-cloth* species, which represent the tone of thought and feeling in the Evangelical party.[2]

---

[1] *rhodomontade* Pretentious, inflated style of speaking.

[2] *High Church ... Evangelical party* The Anglican Church (the Church of England) split into factions, with the High Church practicing the more formal rituals and ceremonies of Catholicism

This species is a kind of genteel tract on a large scale, intended as a sort of medicinal sweetmeat for Low Church young ladies; an Evangelical substitute for the fashionable novel, as the May Meetings[1] are a substitute for the Opera. Even Quaker children, one would think, can hardly have been denied the indulgence of a doll; but it must be a doll dressed in a drab gown and a coal-scuttle bonnet—not a wordly doll, in gauze and spangles. And there are no young ladies, we imagine —unless they belong to the Church of the United Brethren, in which people are married without any love-making—who can dispense with love stories. Thus, for Evangelical young ladies there are Evangelical love stories, in which the vicissitudes of the tender passion are sanctified by saving views of Regeneration and the Atonement. These novels differ from the oracular ones, as a Low Churchwoman often differs from a High Churchwoman: they are a little less supercilious, and a great deal more ignorant, a little less correct in their syntax, and a great deal more vulgar.

The Orlando[2] of Evangelical literature is the young curate, looked at from the point of view of the middle class, where cambric bands are understood to have as thrilling an effect on the hearts of young ladies as epaulettes[3] have in the classes above and below it. In the ordinary type of these novels, the hero is almost sure to be a young curate,[4] frowned upon, perhaps, by worldly mammas, but carrying captive the hearts of their daughters, who can "never forget *that* sermon"; tender glances are seized from the pulpit stairs instead of the opera box; *tête-à-têtes*[5] are seasoned with quotations from Scripture, instead of quotations from the poets; and questions as to the state of the heroine's affections are mingled with anxieties as to the state of her soul. The young curate always has a background of well-dressed

and wealthy, if not fashionable society—for Evangelical silliness is as snobbish as any other kind of silliness; and the Evangelical lady novelist, while she explains to you the type of the scapegoat on one page, is ambitious on another to represent the manners and conversation of aristocratic people. Her pictures of fashionable society are often curious studies considered as efforts of the Evangelical imagination; but in one particular the novels of the White Neck-cloth School are meritoriously realistic—their favourite hero, the Evangelical young curate, is always rather an insipid personage.

The most recent novel of this species that we happen to have before us, is "The Old Grey Church."[6] It is utterly tame and feeble; there is no one set of objects on which the writer seems to have a stronger grasp than on any other; and we should be entirely at a loss to conjecture among what phases of life her experience has been gained, but for certain vulgarisms of style which sufficiently indicate that she has had the advantage, though she has been unable to use it, of mingling chiefly with men and women whose manners and characters have not had all their bosses[7] and angles rubbed down by refined conventionalism. It is less excusable in an Evangelical novelist, than in any other, gratuitously to seek her subjects among titles and carriages. The real drama of Evangelicalism—and it has abundance of fine drama for anyone who has genius enough to discern and reproduce it—lies among the middle and lower classes; and are not Evangelical opinions understood to give an especial interest in the weak things of the earth, rather than in the mighty? Why then, cannot our Evangelical lady novelists show us the operation of their religious views among people (there really are many such in the world) who keep no carriage, "not so much as a brass-bound gig," who even manage to eat their dinner without a silver fork, and in whose mouths the author-ess's questionable English would be strictly consistent? Why can we not have pictures of religious life among the industrial classes in England, as interesting as Mrs. Stowe's pictures of religious life among the negroes?[8]

and the Low Church, or Evangelical branch, rejecting them.

[1]   *May Meetings*   Yearly Missionary Society meetings for the Church of England were held in May.

[2]   *Orlando*   Hero of medieval romance.

[3]   *cambric bands*   Strips of fine linen that hang from the neck of clerics' dress; *epaulettes* Worn on the shoulders of officers' uniforms.

[4]   *curate*   Pastor.

[5]   *tête-à-têtes*   French: literally, "head to heads," private conversations among two people.

[6]   *"The Old Grey Church"*   By Lady Caroline Scott, published 1856 in the *Athenaeum*.

[7]   *bosses*   Protuberances; bumps.

[8]   *Mrs. Stowe's … negroes*   In Harriet Beecher Stowe's novels *Uncle Tom's Cabin* (1852), and *Dred* (1856).

Instead of this, pious ladies nauseate us with novels which remind us of what we sometimes see in a worldly woman recently "converted" —she is as fond of a fine dinner table as before, but she invites clergymen instead of beaux; she thinks as much of her dress as before, but she adopts a more sober choice of colours and patterns; her conversation is as trivial as before, but the triviality is flavoured with gospel instead of gossip. In "The Old Grey Church," we have the same sort of Evangelical travesty of the fashionable novel, and of course the vicious, intriguing baronet is not wanting. It is worthwhile to give a sample of the style of conversation attributed to this high-born rake—a style that in its profuse italics and palpable innuendoes, is worthy of Miss Squeers.[1] In an evening visit to the ruins of the Colosseum, Eustace, the young clergyman, has been withdrawing the heroine, Miss Lushington, from the rest of the party, for the sake of a *tête-à-tête*. The baronet is jealous, and vents his pique in this way:

> There they are, and Miss Lushington, no doubt, quite safe; for she is under the holy guidance of Pope Eustace the First, who has, of course, been delivering to her an edifying homily on the wickedness of the heathens of yore, who, as tradition tells us, in this very place let loose the wild *beastises* on poor St. Paul!—Oh, no! by the bye, I believe I am wrong, and betraying my want of clergy, and that it was not at all St. Paul, nor was it here. But no matter, it would equally serve as a text to preach from, and from which to diverge to the degenerate *heathen* Christians of the present day, and all their naughty practices, and so end with an exhortation to "come out from among them, and be separate" —and I am sure, Miss Lushington, you have most scrupulously conformed to that injunction this evening, for we have seen nothing of you since our arrival. But everyone seems agreed it has been a *charming party of pleasure,* and I am sure we all feel *much indebted* to Mr. Grey for having *suggested* it; and as he seems so capital a cicerone,[2] I hope he will think of something else equally agreeable to *all.*

This drivelling kind of dialogue, and equally drivelling narrative, which, like a bad drawing, represents nothing, and barely indicates what is meant to be represented, runs through the book; and we have no doubt is considered by the amiable authoress to constitute an improving novel, which Christian mothers will do well to put into the hands of their daughters. But everything is relative; we have met with American vegetarians whose normal diet was dry meal, and who, when their appetite wanted stimulating, tickled it with *wet* meal; and so, we can imagine that there are Evangelical circles in which "The Old Grey Church" is devoured as a powerful and interesting fiction.

But, perhaps, the least readable of silly women's novels, are the *modern-antique* species, which unfold to us the domestic life of Jannes and Jambres, the private love affairs of Sennacherib, or the mental struggles and ultimate conversion of Demetrius the silversmith.[3] From most silly novels we can at least extract a laugh; but those of the modern antique school have a ponderous, a leaden kind of fatuity, under which we groan. What can be more demonstrative of the inability of literary women to measure their own powers, than their frequent assumption of a task which can only be justified by the rarest concurrence of acquirement with genius? The finest effort to reanimate the past is of course only approximative—is always more or less an infusion of the modern spirit into the ancient form—

> Was ihr den Geist der Zeiten heisst,
> Das ist im Grund der Herren eigner Geist,
> In dem die Zeiten sich bespiegeln.[4]

Admitting that genius which has familiarized itself with all the relics of an ancient period can sometimes, by the force of its sympathetic divination, restore the missing notes in the "music of humanity,"[5] and reconstruct the fragments into a whole which will really bring

---

[1] *Miss Squeers* Pathetic character in Charles Dickens's *Nicholas Nickleby* (1838).

[2] *cicerone* Guide to antiquities.

[3] *Jannes and Jambres* Egyptian magicians in 2 Timothy 3.8; *Sennacherib* Biblical king of Assyria; see 2 Kings 18.13; *Demetrius the silversmith* See Acts 19.24.

[4] *Was ihr ... bespiegeln* German, from Johann Wolfgang von Goethe's *Faust*: "That which people call the spirit of the times is actually their own spirit reflecting the past."

[5] *"music of humanity"* From William Wordsworth's "Tintern Abbey," line 91.

the remote past nearer to us, and interpret it to our duller apprehension—this form of imaginative power must always be among the very rarest, because it demands as much accurate and minute knowledge as creative vigour. Yet we find ladies constantly choosing to make their mental mediocrity more conspicuous, by clothing it in a masquerade of ancient names; by putting their feeble sentimentality into the mouths of Roman vestals or Egyptian princesses, and attributing their rhetorical arguments to Jewish high priests and Greek philosophers. A recent example of this heavy imbecility is "Adonijah, a Tale of the Jewish Dispersion,"[1] which forms part of a series, "uniting," we are told, "taste, humour, and sound principles." "Adonijah," we presume, exemplifies the tale of "sound principles"; the taste and humour are to be found in other members of the series. We are told on the cover, that the incidents of this tale are "fraught with unusual interest," and the preface winds up thus: "To those who feel interested in the dispersed of Israel and Judea, these pages may afford, perhaps, information on an important subject, as well as amusement." Since the "important subject" on which this book is to afford information is not specified, it may possibly lie in some esoteric meaning to which we have no key; but if it has relation to the dispersed of Israel and Judea at any period of their history, we believe a tolerably well-informed schoolgirl already knows much more of it than she will find in this "Tale of the Jewish Dispersion." "Adonijah" is simply the feeblest kind of love story, supposed to be instructive, we presume, because the hero is a Jewish captive, and the heroine a Roman vestal; because they and their friends are converted to Christianity after the shortest and easiest method approved by the "Society for Promoting the Conversion of the Jews"; and because, instead of being written in plain language, it is adorned with that peculiar style of grandiloquence which is held by some lady novelists to give an antique colouring, and which we recognise at once in such phrases as these: "the splendid regnal talents undoubtedly possessed by the Emperor Nero"—"the expiring scion of a lofty stem"— "the virtuous partner of his couch"—"ah, by Vesta!"— and "I tell thee, Roman." Among the quotations which serve at once for instruction and ornament on the cover of

this volume, there is one from Miss Sinclair,[2] which informs us that "Works of imagination are *avowedly* read by men of science, wisdom, and piety"; from which we suppose the reader is to gather the cheering inference that Dr. Daubeny, Mr. Mill, or Mr. Maurice,[3] may openly indulge himself with the perusal of "Adonijah," without being obliged to secrete it among the sofa cushions, or read it by snatches under the dinner table.

"Be not a baker if your head be made of butter," says a homely proverb, which, being interpreted, may mean, let no woman rush into print who is not prepared for the consequences. We are aware that our remarks are in a very different tone from that of the reviewers who, with a perennial recurrence of precisely similar emotions, only paralleled, we imagine, in the experience of monthly nurses, tell one lady novelist after another that they "hail" her productions "with delight." We are aware that the ladies at whom our criticism is pointed are accustomed to be told, in the choicest phraseology of puffery, that their pictures of life are brilliant, their characters well drawn, their style fascinating, and their sentiments lofty. But if they are inclined to resent our plainness of speech, we ask them to reflect for a moment on the chary praise, and often captious blame, which their panegyrists[4] give to writers whose works are on the way to become classics. No sooner does a woman show that she has genius or effective talent, than she receives the tribute of being moderately praised and severely criticised. By a peculiar thermometric adjustment, when a woman's talent is at zero, journalistic approbation is at the boiling pitch; when she attains mediocrity, it is already at no more than summer heat; and if ever she reaches excellence, critical enthusiasm drops to the freezing point. Harriet Martineau, Currer Bell, and Mrs. Gaskell[5] have been treated as cavalierly as if they had

---

[1] *Adonijah … Dispersion* 1856, by Jane Margaret Strickland.

[2] *Miss Sinclair* Scottish novelist Catherine Sinclair (1800–64).

[3] *Dr. Daubeny* English chemist and botanist Charles Giles Bridle Daubeny (1795–1867); *Mr. Mill* English philosopher John Stuart Mill (1806–73); *Mr. Maurice* English theologian Rev. Frederick D. Maurice (1805–72).

[4] *chary* Careful; *captious* Crafty; *panegyrists* Those who deliver praise.

[5] *Harriet Martineau* British journalist (1802–76); *Currer Bell* Pseudonym of British novelist Charlotte Brontë (1816–55); *Mrs. Gaskell* British novelist Elizabeth Gaskell (1810–65).

been men. And every critic who forms a high estimate of the share women may ultimately take in literature, will, on principle, abstain from any exceptional indulgence towards the productions of literary women. For it must be plain to everyone who looks impartially and extensively into feminine literature, that its greatest deficiencies are due hardly more to the want of intellectual power than to the want of those moral qualities that contribute to literary excellence—patient diligence, a sense of the responsibility involved in publication, and an appreciation of the sacredness of the writer's art. In the majority of women's books you see that kind of facility which springs from the absence of any high standard; that fertility in imbecile combination or feeble imitation which a little self-criticism would check and reduce to barrenness, just as with a total want of musical ear people will sing out of tune, while a degree more melodic sensibility would suffice to render them silent. The foolish vanity of wishing to appear in print, instead of being counter-balanced by any consciousness of the intellectual or moral derogation implied in futile authorship, seems to be encouraged by the extremely false impression that to write *at all* is a proof of superiority in a woman. On this ground, we believe that the average intellect of women is unfairly represented by the mass of feminine literature, and that while the few women who write well are very far above the ordinary intellectual level of their sex, the many women who write ill are very far below it. So that, after all, the severer critics are fulfilling a chivalrous duty in depriving the mere fact of feminine authorship of any false prestige which may give it a delusive attraction, and in recommending women of mediocre faculties—as at least a negative service they can render their sex—to abstain from writing.

The standing apology for women who become writers without any special qualification is that society shuts them out from other spheres of occupation. Society is a very culpable entity, and has to answer for the manufacture of many unwholesome commodities, from bad pickles to bad poetry. But society, like "matter," and Her Majesty's Government, and other lofty abstractions, has its share of excessive blame as well as excessive praise. Where there is one woman who writes from necessity, we believe there are three women who write from vanity; and, besides, there is something so

antiseptic in the mere healthy fact of working for one's bread, that the most trashy and rotten kind of feminine literature is not likely to have been produced under such circumstances. "In all labour there is profit";[1] but ladies' silly novels, we imagine, are less the result of labour than of busy idleness.

Happily, we are not dependent on argument to prove that Fiction is a department of literature in which women can, after their kind, fully equal men. A cluster of great names, both living and dead, rush to our memories in evidence that women can produce novels not only fine, but among the very finest—novels, too, that have a precious speciality, lying quite apart from masculine aptitudes and experience. No educational restrictions can shut women out from the materials of fiction, and there is no species of art which is so free from rigid requirements. Like crystalline masses, it may take any form, and yet be beautiful; we have only to pour in the right elements—genuine observation, humour, and passion. But it is precisely this absence of rigid requirement which constitutes the fatal seduction of novel writing to incompetent women. Ladies are not wont to be very grossly deceived as to their power of playing on the piano; here certain positive difficulties of execution have to be conquered, and incompetence inevitably breaks down. Every art which has its absolute *technique* is, to a certain extent, guarded from the intrusions of mere left-handed imbecility. But in novel writing there are no barriers for incapacity to stumble against, no external criteria to prevent a writer from mistaking foolish facility for mastery. And so we have again and again the old story of La Fontaine's ass,[2] who puts his nose to the flute, and, finding that he elicits some sound, exclaims, "Moi, aussi, je joue de la flute"[3]—a fable which we commend, at parting, to the consideration of any feminine reader who is in danger of adding to the number of "silly novels by lady novelists." —1856

---

[1]   "*In all labour there is profit*"   From Proverbs 14.23.

[2]   *La Fontaine's ass*   French poet Jean de la Fontaine (1621–95) wrote many fables, but "The Ass and the Flute" was written by Tomás de Iriarte (1750–91).

[3]   *Moi aussi … flute*   French: I too play the flute.

JOHN RUSKIN
1819 – 1900

John Ruskin was a painter and a poet, author of dozens of books on the arts and sciences, and a dedicated believer in fundamental links between all disciplines. Famous as an art, cultural, and social critic, Ruskin synthesized subjects in fluid and poetic ways, and he exerted an enormous influence on the aesthetic, philosophical, and political sensibilities of his day. This influence bore heavily on the work of the Pre-Raphaelite painters, notably Dante Gabriel Rossetti, John Everett Millais, and William Holman Hunt. In addition, Ruskin's opposition to industrialization and his ideas about the sacredness of human work inspired William Morris and the Arts and Crafts Movement. Mahatma Gandhi, who translated Ruskin's *Unto the Last* into Gujarati, said about the work's effect on him: "I believe that I discovered some of my deepest convictions reflecting on this great book of Ruskin's, [… which] captured me and made me transform my life."

Ruskin was born in London in 1819 to Margaret Cox and John James Ruskin, a successful wine merchant. Possibly because the couple bore John in midlife and had no other children, the Evangelical Ruskins raised their child in an overprotective and cloistered manner, allowing him neither friends nor toys. The young John's schooling, administered by his mother, was strict and included hours of Bible study every day (the two would read the entire Bible and then resume from the beginning), while his father, also a stern Evangelical, procured tutors for the arts and languages. When Ruskin came of age, he attended Oxford (where he won the Newdigate Prize for poetry), but even then his mother accompanied him, living in rooms nearby, and his father joined the two every weekend.

Even though he had a talent for both poetry and painting, Ruskin realized after graduation that he did not wish to pursue either as a career. His admiration for the British painter J.M.W. Turner, however, led to his first work of art criticism, which evolved into the five-volume *Modern Painters*, published over a period of more than a decade. The first volume of *Modern Painters* was a defense of Turner's "fidelity" to his landscapes and his ability to see and express "truth" in nature. It was not only Ruskin's aesthetic analyses that attracted attention, however, but also his elegant and engaging prose style.

In 1848, Ruskin entered into a disastrous marriage with Euphemia ("Effie") Chalmers, which ended six years later in an annulment on the grounds that the marriage had never been consummated. The following year Effie married the painter John Everett Millais. Throughout his life, Ruskin's relationships with women were fraught, most notably his relationship with Rose La Touche, whom he met (and with whom he apparently fell in love) in 1858 when she was only nine years old. Ruskin proposed marriage to Rose in 1866, but because he had lost his religious faith (he said he had been "unconverted" while attending church in Turin) and she was a strict Evangelical, she ultimately rejected his offer. Not long after her death in 1875, Ruskin suffered an attack of madness, the first of many such episodes he experienced throughout his life.

Although there were times when Ruskin could not function due to mental illness, he was astonishingly prolific: his *Collected Works* fill thirty-nine volumes, and he wrote thousands of letters. His books on architecture, *The Seven Lamps of Architecture* (1849) and the three-volume *Stones of Venice* (1851–53), were so influential that they provoked a revival of Gothic architecture that in some ways ran counter to his philosophies. Ruskin felt that the hand of God was present in those who labored on the stone buildings of the Middle Ages, and that the magnificent Gothic architecture of Venice was a manifestation of a virtuous and honorable people. His writing inspired many to support the preservation and restoration of architectural treasures. Ruskin himself, however, promoted a social, rather than simply an architectural, restoration.

Ruskin's attacks on society became increasingly focused on the effects of modern production, and he became an outspoken challenger of the Industrial Age. His views on economic and social reform, radical at the time, have affected social thinking to this day. Ruskin was strongly opposed to *laissez faire* economics and advocated the organization of labor (the founders of the Labour Party in Britain attributed their ideas to Ruskin), cooperative business ventures, an old-age pension, a minimum wage, public libraries and art galleries, a national health service, equal education opportunities, and pollution control, among many other initiatives. In 1878, Ruskin founded the Guild of St. George, an organization that still exists today, in order to educate the public and to preserve and support small businesses and the production of local crafts.

After writing and lecturing throughout the 1860s, Ruskin was offered the first Slade Professorship of Fine Arts at Oxford, where he delivered (and subsequently published) many famous lectures and speeches to awestruck students, including the young Oscar Wilde. During this decade he also began a series of letters addressed to English laborers, published as *Fors Clavigera*. Ruskin was forced to resign his position at Oxford in 1880 due to mental illness, and although he resumed his professorship for a brief period and published two final books of lectures, *The Pleasures of England* and *The Art of England*, these years were not good to him. He managed to write many installments of his brilliant autobiography, *Praeterita*, but it remained unfinished. After a long illness he died in 1900. Although Westminster Abbey offered a resting place, Ruskin's last wishes were honored, and he was buried near his home in the Coniston graveyard. For the great Russian writer Leo Tolstóy, and for many others, Ruskin's legacy remained alive: "Ruskin was one of the most remarkable of men, not only of England and our time but of all countries and all times. He was one of those rare men who think with their hearts, and so he thought and said not only what he himself had seen and felt, but what everyone will think and say in the future."

⌘ ⌘ ⌘

from *Modern Painters*

A DEFINITION OF GREATNESS IN ART

Painting, or art generally, as such, with all its technicalities, difficulties, and particular ends, is nothing but a noble and expressive language, invaluable as the vehicle of thought, but by itself nothing. He who has learned what is commonly considered the whole art of painting, that is, the art of representing any natural object faithfully, has as yet only learned the language by which his thoughts are to be expressed. He has done just as much towards being that which we ought to respect as a great painter, as a man who has learned how to express himself grammatically and melodiously has towards being a great poet. The language is, indeed, more difficult of acquirement in the one case than in the other, and possesses more power of delighting the sense, while it speaks to the intellect; but it is, nevertheless, nothing more than language, and all those excellences which are peculiar to the painter as such, are merely what rhythm, melody, precision, and force are in the words of the orator and the poet, necessary to their greatness, but not the tests of their greatness. It is not by the mode of representing and saying, but by what is represented and said, that the respective greatness either of the painter or the writer is to be finally determined. ...

So that, if I say that the greatest picture is that which conveys to the mind of the spectator the greatest number of the greatest ideas, I have a definition which will include as subjects of comparison every pleasure which art is capable of conveying. If I were to say, on the contrary, that the best picture was that which most closely imitated nature, I should assume that art could only please by imitating nature; and I should cast out of the pale of criticism those parts of works of art which are not imitative, that is to say, intrinsic beauties of colour and form, and those works of art wholly, which, like the Arabesques of Raffaelle[1] in the Loggias,[2] are not imitative at all. Now, I want a definition of art wide enough to include all its varieties of aim. I do not say, therefore, that the art is greatest which gives most pleasure, because perhaps there is some art whose end is to teach, and not to please. I do not say that the art is greatest which teaches us most, because perhaps there is some art whose end is to please, and not to teach. I do not say that the art is greatest which imitates best, because perhaps there is some art whose end is to create and not to imitate. But I say that the art is greatest which conveys to the mind of the spectator, by any means whatsoever, the greatest number of the greatest ideas; and I call an idea great in proportion as it is received by a higher faculty of the mind, and as it more fully occupies, and in occupying, exercises and exalts, the faculty by which it is received.

If this, then, be the definition of great art, that of a great artist naturally follows. He is the greatest artist who has embodied, in the sum of his works, the greatest number of the greatest ideas. ...

[1] *Raffaelle* I.e., Raphael (1483–1520), Italian Renaissance painter.
[2] *Loggias* Open-air galleries.

Of Truth of Water

I believe it is a result of the experience of all artists, that it is the easiest thing in the world to give a certain degree of depth and transparency to water; but that it is next to impossible, to give a full impression of surface. If no reflection be given, a ripple being supposed, the water looks like lead: if reflection be given, it, in nine cases out of ten, looks *morbidly* clear and deep, so that we always go down *into* it, even when the artist most wishes us to glide *over* it. Now, this difficulty arises from the very same circumstance which occasions the frequent failure in effect of the best-drawn foregrounds ... the change, namely, of focus necessary in the eye in order to receive rays of light coming from different distances. Go to the edge of a pond in a perfectly calm day, at some place where there is duckweed floating on the surface, not thick, but a leaf here and there. Now, you may either see in the water the reflection of the sky, or you may see the duckweed; but you cannot, by any effort, see both together. If you look for the reflection, you will be sensible of a sudden change or effort in the eye, by which it adapts itself to the reception of the rays which have come all the way from the clouds, have struck on the water, and so been sent up again to the eye. The focus you adopt is one fit for great distance; and, accordingly, you will feel that you are looking down a great way under the water, while the leaves of the duckweed, though they lie upon the water at the very spot on which you are gazing so intently, are felt only as a vague uncertain interruption, causing a little confusion in the image below, but entirely undistinguishable as leaves, and even their colour unknown and unperceived. Unless you think of them, you will not even feel that anything interrupts your sight, so excessively slight is their effect. If, on the other hand, you make up your mind to look for the leaves of the duckweed, you will perceive an instantaneous change in the effort of the eye, by which it becomes adapted to receive near rays, those which have only come from the surface of the pond. You will then see the delicate leaves of the duckweed with perfect clearness, and in vivid green; but, while you do so, you will be able to perceive nothing of the reflections in the very water on which they float, nothing but a vague flashing and melting of light and dark hues, without form or meaning, which to investigate, or find out what they mean or are, you must quit your hold of the duckweed, and plunge down.

Hence it appears, that whenever we see plain reflections of comparatively distant objects, in near water, we cannot possibly see the surface, and *vice versa;* so that when in a painting we give the reflections with the same clearness with which they are visible in nature, we presuppose the effort of the eye to look under the surface, and, of course, destroy the surface, and induce an effect of clearness which, perhaps, the artist has not particularly wished to attain, but which he has found himself forced into, by his reflections, in spite of himself. And the reason of this effect of clearness appearing preternatural is, that people are not in the habit of looking at water with the distant focus adapted to the reflections, unless by particular effort. We invariably, under ordinary circumstances, use the surface focus; and, in consequence, receive nothing more than a vague and confused impression of the reflected colours and lines, however clearly, calmly, and vigorously all may be defined underneath, if we choose to look for them. We do not look for them, but glide along over the surface, catching only playing light and capricious colour for evidence of reflection, except where we come to images of objects close to the surface, which the surface focus is of course adapted to receive; and these we see clearly, as of the weeds on the shore, or of sticks rising out of the water, etc. Hence, the ordinary effect of water is only to be rendered by giving the reflections of the *margin* clear and distinct (so clear they usually are in nature, that it is impossible to tell where the water begins); but the moment we touch the reflection of distant objects, as of high trees or clouds, that instant we must become vague and uncertain in drawing, and, though vivid in colour and light as the object itself, quite indistinct in form and feature. If we take such a piece of water as that in the foreground of Turner's[1] Château of Prince Albert, the first impression from it is, "What a wide *surface!*" We glide over it a quarter of a mile into the picture before we know where we are, and yet the water is as calm and crystalline as a mirror; but we are not allowed to tumble into it, and gasp for breath as we go down, we are kept upon the surface, though

that surface is flashing and radiant with every hue of cloud, and sun, and sky, and foliage. But the secret is in the drawing of these reflections. We cannot tell, when we look *at* them and *for* them, what they mean. They have all character, and are evidently reflections of something definite and determined; but yet they are all uncertain and inexplicable; playing colour and palpitating shade, which, though we recognize them in an instant for images of something, and feel that the water is bright, and lovely, and calm, we cannot penetrate nor interpret; we are not allowed to go down to them, and we repose, as we should in nature, upon the lustre of the level surface. It is in this power of saying everything, and yet saying nothing too plainly, that the perfection of art here, as in all other cases, consists.

—1843

from *The Stones of Venice*

THE NATURE OF GOTHIC

… In the definition proposed, I shall only endeavour to analyze the idea which I suppose already to exist in the reader's mind. We all have some notion, most of us a very determined one, of the meaning of the term Gothic, but I know that many persons have this idea in their minds without being able to define it: that is to say, understanding generally that Westminster Abbey is Gothic, and St. Paul's is not, that Strasburg Cathedral is Gothic, and St. Peter's is not, they have, nevertheless, no clear notion of what it is that they recognize in the one or miss in the other, such as would enable them to say how far the work at Westminster or Strasburg is good and pure of its kind; still less to say of any nondescript building, like St. James's Palace or Windsor Castle, how much right Gothic element there is in it, and how much wanting. And I believe this inquiry to be a pleasant and profitable one; and that there will be found something more than usually interesting in tracing out this grey, shadowy, many-pinnacled image of the Gothic spirit within us; and discerning what fellowship there is between it and our Northern hearts. And if, at any point of the inquiry, I should interfere with any of the reader's

---

[1]   *Turner* J.M.W. Turner (1775–1851), English landscape artist.

previously formed conceptions, and use the term Gothic in any sense which he would not willingly attach to it, I do not ask him to accept, but only to examine and understand, my interpretation, as necessary to the intelligibility of what follows in the rest of the work. …

I believe, then, that the characteristic or moral elements of Gothic are the following, placed in the order of their importance:

1. Savageness.
2. Changefulness.
3. Naturalism.
4. Grotesqueness.
5. Rigidity.
6. Redundance.

These characters are here expressed as belonging to the building; as belonging to the builder, they would be expressed thus: —1. Savageness or Rudeness. 2. Love of Change. 3. Love of Nature. 4. Disturbed Imagination. 5. Obstinacy. 6. Generosity. And I repeat, that the withdrawal of any one, or any two, will not at once destroy the Gothic character of a building, but the removal of a majority of them will. I shall proceed to examine them in their order.

(1.) Savageness. I am not sure when the word "Gothic" was first generically applied to the architecture of the North; but I presume that, whatever the date of its original usage, it was intended to imply reproach, and express the barbaric character of the nations among whom that architecture arose. It never implied that they were literally of Gothic lineage, far less that their architecture had been originally invented by the Goths themselves; but it did imply that they and their buildings together exhibited a degree of sternness and rudeness, which, in contradistinction to the character of Southern and Eastern nations, appeared like a perpetual reflection of the contrast between the Goth and the Roman in their first encounter. And when that fallen Roman, in the utmost impotence of his luxury, and insolence of his guilt, became the model for the imitation of civilized Europe, at the close of the so-called Dark ages, the word Gothic became a term of unmitigated contempt, not unmixed with aversion. From that contempt, by the exertion of the antiquaries

and architects of this century, Gothic architecture has been sufficiently vindicated; and perhaps some among us, in our admiration of the magnificent science of its structure, and sacredness of its expression, might desire that the term of ancient reproach should be withdrawn, and some other, of more apparent honourableness, adopted in its place. There is no chance, as there is no need, of such a substitution. As far as the epithet was used scornfully, it was used falsely; but there is no reproach in the word, rightly understood; on the contrary, there is a profound truth, which the instinct of mankind almost unconsciously recognizes. It is true, greatly and deeply true, that the architecture of the North is rude and wild; but it is not true, that, for this reason, we are to condemn it, or despise. Far otherwise: I believe it is in this very character that it deserves our profoundest reverence.

The charts of the world which have been drawn up by modern science have thrown into a narrow space the expression of a vast amount of knowledge, but I have never yet seen any one pictorial enough to enable the spectator to imagine the kind of contrast in physical character which exists between Northern and Southern countries. We know the differences in detail, but we have not that broad glance and grasp which would enable us to feel them in their fulness. We know that gentians[1] grow on the Alps, and olives on the Apennines; but we do not enough conceive for ourselves that variegated mosaic of the world's surface which a bird sees in its migration, that difference between the district of the gentian and of the olive which the stork and the swallow see far off, as they lean upon the sirocco wind.[2] Let us, for a moment, try to raise ourselves even above the level of their flight, and imagine the Mediterranean lying beneath us like an irregular lake, and all its ancient promontories sleeping in the sun: here and there an angry spot of thunder, a grey stain of storm, moving upon the burning field; and here and there a fixed wreath of white volcano smoke, surrounded by its circle of ashes; but for the most part a great peacefulness of light, Syria and Greece, Italy and Spain, laid like pieces of a golden pavement into the sea-blue, chased, as we stoop nearer to them, with bossy beaten work of

[1] *gentians* Flowers.

[2] *sirocco wind* Hot, moist wind from North Africa.

mountain chains, and glowing softly with terraced gardens, and flowers heavy with frankincense, mixed among masses of laurel, and orange, and plumy palm, that abate with their grey-green shadows the burning of the marble rocks, and of the ledges of porphyry[1] sloping under lucent sand. Then let us pass farther towards the north, until we see the orient colours change gradually into a vast belt of rainy green, where the pastures of Switzerland, and poplar valleys of France, and dark forests of the Danube and Carpathians stretch from the mouths of the Loire to those of the Volga, seen through clefts in grey swirls of rain-cloud and flaky veils of the mist of the brooks, spreading low along the pasture lands: and then, farther north still, to see the earth heave into mighty masses of leaden rock and heathy moor, bordering with a broad waste of gloomy purple that belt of field and wood, and splintering into irregular and grisly islands amidst the northern seas, beaten by storm, and chilled by ice-drift, and tormented by furious pulses of contending tide, until the roots of the last forests fail from among the hill ravines, and the hunger of the north wind bites their peaks into barrenness; and, at last, the wall of ice, durable like iron, sets, deathlike, its white teeth against us out of the polar twilight. And, having once traversed in thought this gradation of the zoned iris of the earth in all its material vastness, let us go down nearer to it, and watch the parallel change in the belt of animal life; the multitudes of swift and brilliant creatures that glance in the air and sea, or tread the sands of the southern zone; striped zebras and spotted leopards, glistening serpents, and birds arrayed in purple and scarlet. Let us contrast their delicacy and brilliancy of colour, and swiftness of motion, with the frost-cramped strength, and shaggy covering, and dusky plumage of the northern tribes; contrast the Arabian horse with the Shetland, the tiger and leopard with the wolf and bear, the antelope with the elk, the bird of paradise with the osprey; and then, submissively acknowledging the great laws by which the earth and all that it bears are ruled throughout their being, let us not condemn, but rejoice in the expression by man of his own rest in the statutes of the lands that gave him birth. Let us watch him with reverence as he sets side by side the burning gems, and smoothes with soft sculpture the

jasper pillars, that are to reflect a ceaseless sunshine, and rise into a cloudless sky: but not with less reverence let us stand by him, when, with rough strength and hurried stroke, he smites an uncouth animation out of the rocks which he has torn from among the moss of the moorland, and heaves into the darkened air the pile of iron buttress and rugged wall, instinct with work of an imagination as wild and wayward as the northern sea; creatures of ungainly shape and rigid limb, but full of wolfish life; fierce as the winds that beat, and changeful as the clouds that shade them....

In ... the first volume of this work, it was noticed that the systems of architectural ornament, properly so called, might be divided into three:—i. Servile ornament, in which the execution or power of the inferior workman is entirely subjected to the intellect of the higher;—2. Constitutional ornament, in which the executive inferior power is, to a certain point, emancipated and independent, having a will of its own, yet confessing its inferiority and rendering obedience to higher powers;—and 3. Revolutionary ornament, in which no executive inferiority is admitted at all. I must here explain the nature of these divisions at somewhat greater length.

Of Servile ornament, the principal schools are the Greek, Ninevite, and Egyptian; but their servility is of different kinds. The Greek master-workman was far advanced in knowledge and power above the Assyrian or Egyptian. Neither he nor those for whom he worked could endure the appearance of imperfection in anything; and, therefore, what ornament he appointed to be done by those beneath him was composed of mere geometrical forms—balls, ridges, and perfectly symmetrical foliage—which could be executed with absolute precision by line and rule, and were as perfect in their way, when completed, as his own figure sculpture. The Assyrian and Egyptian, on the contrary, less cognizant of accurate form in anything, were content to allow their figure sculpture to be executed by inferior workmen, but lowered the method of its treatment to a standard which every workman could reach, and then trained him by discipline so rigid, that there was no chance of his falling beneath the standard appointed. The Greek gave to the lower workman no subject which he could not perfectly execute. The

[1]   *porphyry*   Red crystalline rock.

Assyrian gave him subjects which he could only execute imperfectly, but fixed a legal standard for his imperfection. The workman was, in both systems, a slave.

But in the mediaeval, or especially Christian, system of ornament, this slavery is done away with altogether; Christianity having recognized, in small things as well as great, the individual value of every soul. But it not only recognizes its value; it confesses its imperfection, in only bestowing dignity upon the acknowledgment of unworthiness. That admission of lost power and fallen nature, which the Greek or Ninevite felt to be intensely painful, and, as far as might be, altogether refused, the Christian makes daily and hourly, contemplating the fact of it without fear, as tending, in the end, to God's greater glory. Therefore, to every spirit which Christianity summons to her service, her exhortation is: Do what you can, and confess frankly what you are unable to do; neither let your effort be shortened for fear of failure, nor your confession silenced for fear of shame. And it is, perhaps, the principal admirableness of the Gothic schools of architecture, that they thus receive the results of the labour of inferior minds; and out of fragments full of imperfection, and betraying that imperfection in every touch, indulgently raise up a stately and unaccusable whole. …

And now, reader, look round this English room of yours, about which you have been proud so often, because the work of it was so good and strong, and the ornaments of it so finished. Examine again all those accurate mouldings, and perfect polishings, and unerring adjustments of the seasoned wood and tempered steel. Many a time you have exulted over them, and thought how great England was, because her slightest work was done so thoroughly. Alas! if read rightly, these perfectnesses are signs of a slavery in our England a thousand times more bitter and more degrading than that of the scourged African, or helot[1] Greek. Men may be beaten, chained, tormented, yoked like cattle, slaughtered like summer flies, and yet remain in one sense, and the best sense, free. But to smother their souls with them, to blight and hew into rotting

pollards[2] the suckling branches of their human intelligence, to make the flesh and skin which, after the worm's work on it, is to see God, into leathern thongs to yoke machinery with—this is to be slave-masters indeed; and there might be more freedom in England, though her feudal lords' lightest words were worth men's lives, and though the blood of the vexed husbandman dropped in the furrows of her fields, than there is while the animation of her multitudes is sent like fuel to feed the factory smoke, and the strength of them is given daily to be wasted into the fineness of a web, or racked into the exactness of a line.

And, on the other hand, go forth again to gaze upon the old cathedral front, where you have smiled so often at the fantastic ignorance of the old sculptors: examine once more those ugly goblins, and formless monsters, and stern statues, anatomiless and rigid; but do not mock at them, for they are signs of the life and liberty of every workman who struck the stone; a freedom of thought, and rank in scale of being, such as no laws, no charters, no charities can secure; but which it must be the first aim of all Europe at this day to regain for her children. …

We have much studied and much perfected, of late, the great civilized invention of the division of labour; only we give it a false name. It is not, truly speaking, the labour that is divided; but the men: divided into mere segments of men—broken into small fragments and crumbs of life; so that all the little piece of intelligence that is left in a man is not enough to make a pin, or a nail, but exhausts itself in making the point of a pin or the head of a nail. Now it is a good and desirable thing, truly, to make many pins in a day; but if we could only see with what crystal sand their points were polished—sand of human soul, much to be magnified before it can be discerned for what it is—we should think there might be some loss in it also. And the great cry that rises from all our manufacturing cities, louder than their furnace blast, is all in very deed for this— that we manufacture everything there except men; we blanch cotton, and strengthen steel, and refine sugar, and shape pottery; but to brighten, to strengthen, to refine, or to form a single living spirit, never enters into

---

[1] *helot* Of a class of serfs, falling between slave and citizen in the Spartan social hierarchy.

[2] *pollards* Trees whose branches have been lopped off to shape them.

our estimate of advantages. And all the evil to which that cry is urging our myriads can be met only in one way: not by teaching nor preaching, for to teach them is but to show them their misery, and to preach to them, if we do nothing more than preach, is to mock at it. It can be met only by a right understanding, on the part of all classes, of what kinds of labour are good for men, raising them, and making them happy; by a determined sacrifice of such convenience, or beauty, or cheapness as is to be got only by the degradation of the workman; and by equally determined demand for the products and results of healthy and ennobling labour.

And how, it will be asked, are these products to be recognized, and this demand to be regulated? Easily: by the observance of three broad and simple rules:

1. Never encourage the manufacture of any article not absolutely necessary, in the production of which *Invention* has no share.

2. Never demand an exact finish for its own sake, but only for some practical or noble end.

3. Never encourage imitation or copying of any kind, except for the sake of preserving records of great works.

The second of these principles is the only one which directly rises out of the consideration of our immediate subject; but I shall briefly explain the meaning and extent of the first also, reserving the enforcement of the third for another place.

1. Never encourage the manufacture of anything not necessary, in the production of which invention has no share.

For instance. Glass beads are utterly unnecessary, and there is no design or thought employed in their manufacture. They are formed by first drawing out the glass into rods; these rods are chopped up into fragments of the size of beads by the human hand, and the fragments are then rounded in the furnace. The men who chop up the rods sit at their work all day, their hands vibrating with a perpetual and exquisitely timed palsy, and the beads dropping beneath their vibration like hail. Neither they, nor the men who draw out the rods or fuse the fragments, have the smallest occasion for the use of any single human faculty; and every young lady, therefore, who buys glass beads is engaged in the slave-trade, and in a much more cruel one than that which we have so long been endeavouring to put down. ...

[One example to] show the reader what I mean [comes] from the manufacture already alluded to, that of glass. Our modern glass is exquisitely clear in its substance, true in its form, accurate in its cutting. We are proud of this. We ought to be ashamed of it. The old Venice glass was muddy, inaccurate in all its forms, and clumsily cut, if at all. And the old Venetian was justly proud of it. For there is this difference between the English and Venetian workman, that the former thinks only of accurately matching his patterns, and getting his curves perfectly true and his edges perfectly sharp, and becomes a mere machine for rounding curves and sharpening edges; while the old Venetian cared not a whit whether his edges were sharp or not, but he invented a new design for every glass that he made, and never moulded a handle or a lip without a new fancy in it. And therefore, though some Venetian glass is ugly and clumsy enough when made by clumsy and uninventive workmen, other Venetian glass is so lovely in its forms that no price is too great for it; and we never see the same form in it twice. Now you cannot have the finish and the varied form too. If the workman is thinking about his edges, he cannot be thinking of his design; if of his design, he cannot think of his edges. Choose whether you will pay for the lovely form or the perfect finish, and choose at the same moment whether you will make the worker a man or a grindstone.

Nay, but the reader interrupts me—"If the workman can design beautifully, I would not have him kept at the furnace. Let him be taken away and made a gentleman, and have a studio, and design his glass there, and I will have it blown and cut for him by common workmen, and so I will have my design and my finish too."

All ideas of this kind are founded upon two mistaken suppositions: the first, that one man's thoughts can be, or ought to be, executed by another man's hands; the second, that manual labour is a degradation, when it is governed by intellect.

On a large scale, and in work determinable by line and rule, it is indeed both possible and necessary that the thoughts of one man should be carried out by the labour of others; in this sense I have already defined the best architecture to be the expression of the mind of manhood by the hands of childhood. But on a smaller scale, and in a design which cannot be mathematically defined, one man's thoughts can never be expressed by another: and the difference between the spirit of touch of the man who is inventing, and of the man who is obeying directions, is often all the difference between a great and a common work of art. How wide the separation is between original and second-hand execution, I shall endeavour to show elsewhere; it is not so much to our purpose here as to mark the other and more fatal error of despising manual labour when governed by intellect; for it is no less fatal an error to despise it when thus regulated by intellect, than to value it for its own sake. We are always in these days endeavouring to separate the two; we want one man to be always thinking, and another to be always working, and we call one a gentleman, and the other an operative; whereas the workman ought often to be thinking, and the thinker often to be working, and both should be gentlemen, in the best sense. As it is, we make both ungentle, the one envying, the other despising, his brother; and the mass of society is made up of morbid thinkers, and miserable workers. Now it is only by labour that thought can be made healthy, and only by thought that labour can be made happy, and the two cannot be separated with impunity. It would be well if all of us were good handicraftsmen in some kind, and the dishonour of manual labour done away with altogether; so that though there should still be a trenchant distinction of race between nobles and commoners, there should not, among the latter, be a trenchant distinction of employment, as between idle and working men, or between men of liberal and illiberal professions. All professions should be liberal, and there should be less pride felt in peculiarity of employment, and more in excellence of achievement. And yet more, in each several profession, no master should be too proud to do its hardest work. The painter should grind his own colours; the architect work in the mason's yard with his men.... Hitherto I have used the words imperfect and perfect merely to distinguish between work grossly unskilful, and work executed with average precision and science; and I have been pleading that any degree of unskilfulness should be admitted, so only that the labourer's mind had room for expression.

But, accurately speaking, no good work whatever can be perfect, and *the demand for perfection is always a sign of a misunderstanding of the ends of art.*

This for two reasons, both based on everlasting laws. The first, that no great man ever stops working till he has reached his point of failure: that is to say, his mind is always far in advance of his powers of execution, and the latter will now and then give way in trying to follow it; ... And therefore, if we are to have great men working at all, or less men doing their best, the work will be imperfect, however beautiful. Of human work none but what is bad can be perfect, in its own bad way.

The second reason is, that imperfection is in some sort essential to all that we know of life. It is the sign of life in a mortal body, that is to say, of a state of progress and change. Nothing that lives is, or can be, rigidly perfect; part of it is decaying, part nascent. The foxglove blossom—a third part bud, a third part past, a third part in full bloom—is a type of the life of this world. And in all things that live there are certain irregularities and deficiencies which are not only signs of life, but sources of beauty. No human face is exactly the same in its lines on each side, no leaf perfect in its lobes, no branch in its symmetry. All admit irregularity as they imply change; and to banish imperfection is to destroy expression, to check exertion, to paralyze vitality. All things are literally better, lovelier, and more beloved for the imperfections which have been divinely appointed, that the law of human life may be Effort, and the law of human judgment, Mercy.

Accept this then for a universal law, that neither architecture nor any other noble work of man can be good unless it be imperfect; and let us be prepared for the otherwise strange fact, which we shall discern clearly as we approach the period of the Renaissance, that the first cause of the fall of the arts of Europe was a relentless requirement of perfection, incapable alike either of being silenced by veneration for greatness, or softened into forgiveness of simplicity.

Thus far then of the Rudeness or Savageness, which is the first mental element of Gothic architecture. It is an element in many other healthy architectures also, as the Byzantine and Romanesque; but true Gothic cannot exist without it.

The second mental element above named was

Changefulness, or Variety.

I have already enforced the allowing independent operation to the inferior workman, simply as a duty *to him,* and as ennobling the architecture by rendering it more Christian. We have now to consider what reward we obtain for the performance of this duty, namely, the perpetual variety of every feature of the building.

Wherever the workman is utterly enslaved, the parts of the building must of course be absolutely like each other; for the perfection of his execution can only be reached by exercising him in doing one thing, and giving him nothing else to do. The degree in which the workman is degraded may be thus known at a glance, by observing whether the several parts of the building are similar or not; and if, as in Greek work, all the capitals are alike, and all the mouldings unvaried, then the degradation is complete; if, as in Egyptian or Ninevite work, though the manner of executing certain figures is always the same, the order of design is perpetually varied, the degradation is less total; if, as in Gothic work, there is perpetual change both in design and execution, the workman must have been altogether set free.

How much the beholder gains from the liberty of the labourer may perhaps be questioned in England, where one of the strongest instincts in nearly every mind is that love of order which makes us desire that our house windows should pair like our carriage horses, and allows us to yield our faith unhesitatingly to architectural theories which fix a form for everything, and forbid variation from it. I would not impeach love of order: it is one of the most useful elements of the English mind; it helps us in our commerce and in all purely practical matters; and it is in many cases one of the foundation stones of morality. Only do not let us suppose that love of order is love of art. It is true that order, in its highest sense, is one of the necessities of art, just as time is a necessity of music; but love of order has no more to do with our right enjoyment of architecture or painting, than love of punctuality with the appreciation of an opera. ...

From these general uses of variety in the economy of the world, we may at once understand its use and abuse in architecture. The variety of the Gothic schools is the more healthy and beautiful, because in many cases it is entirely unstudied, and results, not from mere love of change, but from practical necessities. For in one point of view Gothic is not only the best, but the *only rational* architecture, as being that which can fit itself most easily to all services, vulgar or noble. Undefined in its slope of roof, height of shaft, breadth of arch, or disposition of ground plan, it can shrink into a turret, expand into a hall, coil into a staircase, or spring into a spire, with undegraded grace and unexhausted energy; and whenever it finds occasion for change in its form or purpose, it submits to it without the slightest sense of loss either to its unity or majesty,—subtle and flexible like a fiery serpent, but ever attentive to the voice of the charmer. And it is one of the chief virtues of the Gothic builders, that they never suffered ideas of outside symmetries and consistencies to interfere with the real use and value of what they did. If they wanted a window, they opened one; a room, they added one; a buttress, they built one; utterly regardless of any established conventionalities of external appearance, knowing (as indeed it always happened) that such daring interruptions of the formal plan would rather give additional interest to its symmetry than injure it. ...

The third constituent element of the Gothic mind was stated to be Naturalism; that is to say, the love of natural objects for their own sake, and the effort to represent them frankly, unconstrained by artistical laws.

This characteristic of the style partly follows in necessary connection with those named above. For, so soon as the workman is left free to represent what subjects he chooses, he must look to the nature that is round him for material, and will endeavour to represent it as he sees it, with more or less accuracy according to the skill he possesses, and with much play of fancy, but with small respect for law. There is, however, a marked distinction between the imaginations of the Western and Eastern races, even when both are left free; the Western, or Gothic, delighting most in the representation of facts, and the Eastern (Arabian, Persian, and Chinese) in the harmony of colours and forms. ...

Now the noblest art is an exact unison of the abstract value, with the imitative power, of forms and colours. It is the noblest composition, used to express the noblest facts. But the human mind cannot in general unite the two perfections: it either pursues the fact to the neglect of the composition, or pursues the composition to the neglect of the fact.

And it is intended by the Deity that it *should* do this: the best art is not always wanted. Facts are often wanted without art, as in a geological diagram; and art often without facts, as in a Turkey carpet. And most men have been made capable of giving either one or the other, but not both; only one or two, the very highest, can give both....

We have now, I believe, obtained a sufficiently accurate knowledge both of the spirit and form of Gothic architecture; but it may, perhaps, be useful to the general reader, if, in conclusion, I set down a few plain and practical rules for determining, in every instance, whether a given building be good Gothic or not, and, if not Gothic, whether its architecture is of a kind which will probably reward the pains of careful examination.

First, look if the roof rises in a steep gable, high above the walls. If it does not do this, there is something wrong: the building is not quite pure Gothic, or has been altered.

Secondly, look if the principal windows and doors have pointed arches with gables over them. If not pointed arches, the building is not Gothic; if they have not any gables over them, it is either not pure, or not first-rate.

If, however, it has the steep roof, the pointed arch, and gable all united, it is nearly certain to be a Gothic building of a very fine time....

... See if it looks as if it had been built by strong men; if it has the sort of roughness, and largeness, and nonchalance, mixed in places with the exquisite tenderness which seems always to be the sign-manual of the broad vision, and massy[1] power of men, who can see *past* the work they are doing, and betray here and there

The Ducal Palace—Bird's Eye View.

something like disdain for it....

Secondly, observe if it be irregular, its different parts fitting themselves to different purposes, no one caring what becomes of them, so that they do their work. If one part always answers accurately to another part, it is sure to be a bad building; and the greater and more conspicuous the irregularities, the greater the chances are that it is a good one. For instance, in the Ducal Palace,[2] of which a rough woodcut [appears here], the general idea is sternly symmetrical; but two windows are lower than the rest of the six; and if the reader will count the arches of the small arcade as far as to the great balcony, he will find it is not in the centre, but set to the right-hand side by the whole width of one of those arches. We may be pretty sure that the building is a good one; none but a master of his craft would have ventured to do this.

—1853

---

[1] *massy* Heavy.

[2] *Ducal Palace* Gothic palace in Venice.

Matthew Arnold
1822 – 1888

Nicknamed "the Emperor" by his friends and family, Matthew Arnold was an ardent and, in the view of some Victorians, arrogant critic of modernity. Arnold embodied both the idealist expectations and the apocalyptic anxieties of the approaching *fin-de-siécle* in his poetry and prose. In the face of an increasingly materialistic mass culture, dominated by the vacuity of what he called "the average man" or "Philistine" of the democratized middle classes, Arnold sought to revive culture in

the image of liberal humanism. Only an education in the ostensibly timeless and universal works of masters like Marcus Aurelius, Tolstoy, Homer and Wordsworth, Arnold believed, could cure the *malaise* of modern life.

"For the creation of a masterwork of literature, two powers must concur," Arnold wrote in 1865, "The power of the man and the power of the moment, and the man is not enough without the moment." Arnold believed that modern industrial life and the materialism it had made possible were radically indisposed towards artistic genius and indeed had created a climate of psychological and moral enervation that poetry was powerless to heal. The *Zeitgeist* (one of his terms for the powerful work of modern popular culture) was profoundly "unpoetical," and was best anatomized through prose. His own career shows symptoms of the fragmentation he analyzed. Arnold incisively broke with the often melancholic poetry of his early years in order to pursue prose criticism, for him the best possible literary work, he believed, in an era that he saw as spiritually bankrupt. Modern society was in no condition to produce great poets; the best that modern life could muster, according to Arnold, were powerful critics—*if* they stayed away from the politics of the passing moment.

The River Thames ran past the village of Laleham where Matthew Arnold was born in 1822. Arnold was the eldest son of Mary Penrose Arnold and Dr. Thomas Arnold. His father, a clergyman and headmaster of Rugby School, was celebrated for reforming the school's curriculum to foreground Christian values, classical languages, and competitive games. Ironically, Arnold, who in later life would come to resemble his father by valuing above all else great humanist texts and a classical education, was lazy, laconic and flippant as a student. Upon meeting the young dilettante, Charlotte Brontë wrote that "his manner displeases, from its seeming foppery." Yet, in spite of a flamboyant indifference to academia and a studied attempt to dissociate himself from all that his father represented, he amazed family and friends by winning a scholarship to Oxford's Balliol College in 1840, the prodigious Newdigate Prize for poetry in 1843, and a Fellowship at Oriel College in 1845.

Wordsworth, a friend of the family, was one of the most tangible influences on Arnold's poetry. When Wordsworth died, Arnold wondered sadly, "Who will teach us how to feel?" He frequently fled from classes to wander the countryside around the Lake District or to hike in the Alps, landscapes memorialized by Wordsworth and Coleridge. Many critics claim that Arnold was most accomplished as a poet of nature. The "simple joy the country yields," rendered in poems like "Thyrsis," reveals a surprising affinity with the quiet style of Thomas Gray; his "Resignation" speaks to Wordsworth's "Tintern Abbey." Arnold's personal manner, reminiscent of his idols Lord Byron and Goethe, did not cancel out a heartfelt relation to nature, whose unadorned expression modelled the "high seriousness" he admired in Sophocles and Aeschylus.

In 1847, Arnold obtained employment in London as a private secretary to the liberal politician Lord Lansdowne, a period during which he produced most of his poetry. 1849 saw the publication of *The Strayed Reveller, and Other Poems*, by "A," followed by *Empedocles on Etna, and Other Poems* (1852). The controversial preface to *Poems* (1853) provoked heated debate. Here Arnold focused on the ponderous force of the "unpoetical" nineteenth century writ large over his earlier work and damned the "dialogue of the mind with itself" that his *Empedocles on Etna* exhibited. Great poetry, Arnold claimed, must be distinguished from verse produced by a restless intellect fragmented by attempts to address the problems of contemporary life. Poetry should create works of beauty and unity that rise above the historical moment to "inspirit and rejoice" readers.

Letters to his best friend and fellow poet Arthur Hugh Clough, who did address the intellectual issues of the current moment, provide valuable insight into the demanding standards Arnold set for poetry. "I am glad you like the *Gypsy Scholar*," he wrote, "—but what does it *do* for you? Homer *animates*—Shakespeare *animates*— in its poor way I think *Sohrab and Rustum animates*—the *Gypsy Scholar* at best awakens a pleasing melancholy." Considered an often biting critic of the work of his contemporaries, including Clough, Arnold's harshest criticisms were first addressed to his own work. His poem "Dover Beach," probably written in 1851, but published in 1867, is one of English literature's profound expressions of modernity's disaffection with itself. Yet perceiving that his own poetry seemed passively ensnared in the "continual state of mental distress" that he took to task in the preface to *Poems*, he largely ceased writing poetry from the mid-1850s onward. After *New Poems* (1867), Arnold would refashion himself as a prose writer. According to Lionel Trilling, Arnold "perceived in himself the poetic power, but knew that his genius was not of the greatest, that the poetic force was not irresistible in him," not enough, at any rate, to act as a transformative agent in an age of disillusionment.

In 1851, Arnold married Frances Lucy Wightman and to support his family accepted a position as a public school inspector. Initially thinking the job would suffice "for the next three or four years," Arnold continued to be employed in the public service for thirty-five years. In contrast to writers like Tennyson or Carlyle, Arnold had to work for a living, writing only in his spare time. He believed that his inspections of schools in Britain and across Europe gave him first-hand experience to support his conviction that educating the public in a classical humanist tradition was key to "civilizing the next generation of the lower classes."

Arnold was elected Professor of Poetry at Oxford University in 1857, where he delivered public lectures for the following ten years. Though a proponent of an exacting standard of classical scholarship, Arnold was the first to lecture in English rather than Latin, altering an elitist institutional practice that acted as a barrier to the kind of education that the nineteenth century urgently needed, in his opinion. Arnold turned many of his lectures into essays and books, including *On Translating Homer* (1861) and *Friendship's Garland* (1871).

Though by his own standards of greatness Arnold could not *transform* society as a poet, as a critic he was determined to *reform* it. In his famous essay "The Function of Criticism at the Present Time," published in *Essays in Criticism* (1865), Arnold helped raise the value of criticism from its status as a "baneful and injurious employment" to a creative activity in its own right. Deftly juxtaposing snatches from tabloids alongside texts of high culture, Arnold's critical methodology foreshadowed the kind of work pursued in cultural studies today. While few have unanimously agreed with Arnold's pronouncements on literature and society, he has influenced almost every significant English-speaking critic since his time, including T.S. Eliot, F.R. Leavis, Lionel Trilling, and Raymond Williams.

In *Culture and Anarchy* (1869), arguably his most important work of social criticism, Arnold proposed that antagonistic factions of British society could learn to overcome their differences through an education in "disinterested" and universal human values. The differences allowed expression in democratic societies would disintegrate into anarchic disorder, thought Arnold, unless tethered to the "higher" ideals of the humanist tradition. His witty veneer and Apollonian appeal to transcendent virtues of "sweetness and light" sometimes enamored, and sometimes exasperated, a public whose prominent figures he often singled out by name for critical interrogation. Leslie Stephen, Virginia Woolf's father, remarked drily: "I often wished … that I too had a little sweetness and light that I might be able to say such nasty things of my enemies."

During the 1870s, Arnold published a series of attacks on orthodox religion: *St. Paul and Protestantism* (1870), *Literature and Dogma* (1873) and *God and the Bible* (1875). Even in a period that witnessed the challenges to traditional religious belief posed by Darwin's theories, the work of geologists, and the "higher criticism" of the Bible that came from Germany and elsewhere, Arnold's religious critiques scandalized many Victorians. He recommended that Victorians exchange their faith in a religion founded on the assumption of the truth of the Bible for faith in a transcendent, secular humanism. When he returned to literary criticism in "The Study of Poetry" (1880), he claimed, as Thomas Carlyle had before him in the 1830s, that "most of what now passes for religion and philosophy will be replaced by poetry."

Like Dickens and Thackeray before him, Arnold embarked on a lecture tour of the United States, in 1883. Tired and burdened by debts, Arnold saw the trip as a money-making venture that would also allow him to visit a daughter who had married an American. He was loved in Washington but received with mixed success in other cities. He compiled his lectures in *Discourses in America* (1885), which contains his discussion of Emerson as well as the essay "Literature and Science." Here Arnold responds to Thomas Huxley's claim in "Science and Culture" (1881) that "for the purpose of attaining real culture, an exclusively scientific education is at least as effectual as an exclusively literary education." Especially in America, Arnold argued, where the democratic impulse to glorify "the average man" was particularly enthusiastic, education must safeguard the guiding ideals of the Western tradition, "the best that is known and thought."

Arnold died suddenly of a heart attack in 1888, leaving behind him a remarkable body of cultural criticism and a few poems familiar to all readers of English poetry. His statement about Oxford and modernity in *Culture and Anarchy* may well be taken as fitting epitaph: "We in Oxford … have not failed to seize one truth,—the truth that beauty and sweetness are essential characters of a complete human perfection. … We have not won our political battles, we have not carried our main points, we have not stopped our adversaries' advance, we have not marched victoriously with the modern world; but we have told silently upon the mind of the century, we have prepared currents of feeling which sap our adversaries' position when it seems gained, we have kept up our communications with the future."

⌘ ⌘ ⌘

The Forsaken Merman

Come, dear children, let us away;
Down and away below!
Now my brothers call from the bay,
Now the great winds shoreward blow,
5 Now the salt tides seaward flow;

Now the wild white horses play,
Champ and chafe and toss in the spray.
Children dear, let us away!
This way, this way!
10 Call her once before you go—
Call once yet!

In a voice that she will know:
"Margaret! Margaret!"
Children's voices should be dear
15 (Call once more) to a mother's ear;
Children's voices, wild with pain—
Surely she will come again!
Call her once and come away;
This way, this way!
20 "Mother dear, we cannot stay!
The wild white horses foam and fret."
Margaret! Margaret!

Come, dear children, come away down;
Call no more!
25 One last look at the white-walled town,
And the little grey church on the windy shore,
Then come down!
She will not come though you call all day;
Come away, come away!

30 Children dear, was it yesterday
We heard the sweet bells over the bay?
In the caverns where we lay,
Through the surf and through the swell,
The far-off sound of a silver bell?
35 Sand-strewn caverns, cool and deep,
Where the winds are all asleep;
Where the spent lights quiver and gleam,
Where the salt weed sways in the stream,
Where the sea-beasts, ranged all round,
40 Feed in the ooze of their pasture-ground;
Where the sea-snakes coil and twine,
Dry their mail and bask in the brine;
Where great whales come sailing by,
Sail and sail, with unshut eye,
45 Round the world for ever and aye?
When did music come this way?
Children dear, was it yesterday?

Children dear, was it yesterday
(Call yet once) that she went away?
50 Once she sat with you and me,
On a red gold throne in the heart of the sea,

And the youngest sat on her knee.
She combed its bright hair, and she tended it well,
When down swung the sound of a far-off bell.
55 She sighed, she looked up through the clear green sea;
She said: "I must go, for my kinsfolk pray
In the little grey church on the shore today.
'Twill be Easter-time in the world—ah me!
And I lose my poor soul, Merman! here with thee."[1]
60 I said: "Go up, dear heart, through the waves;
Say thy prayer, and come back to the kind sea-caves!"
She smiled, she went up through the surf in the bay.
Children dear, was it yesterday?

Children dear, were we long alone?
65 The sea grows stormy, the little ones moan;
"Long prayers," I said, "in the world they say;
Come!" I said; and we rose through the surf in the bay.
We went up the beach, by the sandy down
Where the sea-stocks bloom, to the white-walled town;
70 Through the narrow paved streets, where all was still,
To the little grey church on the windy hill.
From the church came a murmur of folk at their
        prayers,
But we stood without in the cold blowing airs.
We climbed on the graves, on the stones worn with
        rains,
75 And we gazed up the aisle through the small leaded
        panes.
She sat by the pillar; we saw her clear:
"Margaret, hist! come quick, we are here!
Dear heart," I said, "we are long alone;
The sea grows stormy, the little ones moan."
80 But, ah, she gave me never a look,
For her eyes were seal'd to the holy book!
Loud prays the priest; shut stands the door.
Come away, children, call no more!
Come away, come down, call no more!

85 Down, down, down!
Down to the depths of the sea!
She sits at her wheel in the humming town,
Singing most joyfully.

---

[1] *I lose … thee* According to popular folk belief, mermaids and
mermen had no souls, and humans who went to live with them
would lose theirs as well.

Hark what she sings: "O joy, O joy,
90 For the humming street, and the child with its toy!
For the priest, and the bell, and the holy well;
For the wheel where I spun,
And the blessed light of the sun!"
And so she sings her fill,
95 Singing most joyfully,
Till the spindle drops from her hand,
And the whizzing wheel stands still.
She steals to the window, and looks at the sand,
And over the sand at the sea;
100 And her eyes are set in a stare;
And anon there breaks a sigh,
And anon there drops a tear,
From a sorrow-clouded eye,
And a heart sorrow-laden,
105 A long, long sigh;
For the cold strange eyes of a little Mermaiden
And the gleam of her golden hair.

Come away, away children;
Come children, come down!
110 The hoarse wind blows coldly;
Lights shine in the town.
She will start from her slumber
When gusts shake the door;
She will hear the winds howling,
115 Will hear the waves roar.
We shall see, while above us
The waves roar and whirl,
A ceiling of amber,
A pavement of pearl.
120 Singing: "Here came a mortal,
But faithless was she!
And alone dwell for ever
The kings of the sea."

But, children, at midnight,
125 When soft the winds blow,
When clear falls the moonlight,
When spring-tides are low;

When sweet airs come seaward
From heaths starred with broom,[1]
130 And high rocks throw mildly
On the blanched sands a gloom;
Up the still, glistening beaches,
Up the creeks we will hie,° _hasten_
Over banks of bright seaweed
135 The ebb-tide leaves dry.
We will gaze, from the sand-hills,
At the white, sleeping town;
At the church on the hill-side—
And then come back down.
140 Singing: "There dwells a loved one,
But cruel is she!
She left lonely for ever
The kings of the sea."
—1849

Isolation. To Marguerite [2]

We were apart; yet, day by day,
    I bade my heart more constant be.
I bade it keep the world away,
    And grow a home for only thee;
5 Nor feared but thy love likewise grew,
    Like mine, each day, more tried, more true.

The fault was grave! I might have known,
    What far too soon, alas! I learned—
The heart can bind itself alone,
10 And faith may oft be unreturned.
Self-swayed our feelings ebb and swell—
Thou lov'st no more—Farewell! Farewell!

Farewell!—and thou, thou lonely heart,
    Which never yet without remorse
15 Even for a moment didst depart
    From thy remote and sphered course

---

[1]   _broom_   Type of shrub bearing yellow flowers, common in England.

[2]   _Marguerite_   An unidentified woman, perhaps someone Arnold met in Switzerland in the 1840s, or Mary Claude, an Englishwoman Arnold knew during that same time.

To haunt the place where passions reign—
Back to thy solitude again!

Back! with the conscious thrill of shame
20 Which Luna felt, that summer-night,
Flash through her pure immortal frame,
When she forsook the starry height
To hang over Endymion's sleep
Upon the pine-grown Latmian steep.[1]

25 Yet she, chaste queen, had never proved
How vain a thing is mortal love,
Wandering in Heaven, far removed.
But thou hast long had place to prove
This truth—to prove, and make thine own:
30 "Thou hast been, shalt be, art, alone."

Or, if not quite alone, yet they
Which touch thee are unmating things—
Ocean and clouds and night and day;
Lorn autumns and triumphant springs;
35 And life, and others' joy and pain,
And love, if love, of happier men.

Of happier men—for they, at least,
Have *dream'd* two human hearts might blend
In one, and were through faith released
40 From isolation without end
Prolong'd; nor knew, although not less
Alone than thou, their loneliness.
—1857 (1849)

To Marguerite—Continued

Yes! in the sea of life enisled,
With echoing straits between us thrown,
Dotting the shoreless watery wild,
We mortal millions live *alone*.
5 The islands feel the enclasping flow,
And then their endless bounds they know.

But when the moon their hollows lights,
And they are swept by balms of spring,
And in their glens, on starry nights,
10 The nightingales divinely sing;
And lovely notes, from shore to shore,
Across the sounds and channels pour—

Oh! then a longing like despair
Is to their farthest caverns sent;
15 For surely once, they feel, we were
Parts of a single continent!
Now round us spreads the watery plain—
Oh might our marges° meet again!   borders

Who ordered, that their longing's fire
20 Should be, as soon as kindled, cooled?
Who renders vain their deep desire?—
A God, a God their severance ruled!
And bade betwixt their shores to be
The unplumbed, salt, estranging sea.
—1852 (1849)

The Buried Life

Light flows our war of mocking words, and yet,
Behold, with tears mine eyes are wet!
I feel a nameless sadness o'er me roll.
Yes, yes, we know that we can jest,
5 We know, we know that we can smile!
But there's a something in this breast,
To which thy light words bring no rest,
And thy gay smiles no anodyne.°   remedy
Give me thy hand, and hush awhile,
10 And turn those limpid eyes on mine,
And let me read there, love! thy inmost soul.

Alas! is even love too weak
To unlock the heart, and let it speak?
Are even lovers powerless to reveal
15 To one another what indeed they feel?
I knew the mass of men concealed
Their thoughts, for fear that if revealed
They would by other men be met
With blank indifference, or with blame reproved;

1 *Which Luna ... steep* Luna (or Diana), goddess of chastity and the moon, fell in love with the shepherd boy Endymion when she found him sleeping on Mount Latmos.

20   I knew they lived and moved
     Tricked in disguises, alien to the rest
     Of men, and alien to themselves—and yet
     The same heart beats in every human breast!

     But we, my love!—doth a like spell benumb
25   Our hearts, our voices?—must we too be dumb?

     Ah! well for us, if even we,
     Even for a moment, can get free
     Our heart, and have our lips unchained;
     For that which seals them hath been deep-ordained!
30   Fate, which foresaw
     How frivolous a baby man would be—
     By what distractions he would be possessed,
     How he would pour himself in every strife,
     And well-nigh change his own identity—
35   That it might keep from his capricious play
     His genuine self, and force him to obey
     Even in his own despite his being's law,
     Bade through the deep recesses of our breast
     The unregarded river of our life
40   Pursue with indiscernible flow its way;
     And that we should not see
     The buried stream, and seem to be
     Eddying at large in blind uncertainty,
     Though driving on with it eternally.

45   But often, in the world's most crowded streets,
     But often, in the din of strife,
     There rises an unspeakable desire
     After the knowledge of our buried life;
     A thirst to spend our fire and restless force
50   In tracking out our true, original course;
     A longing to inquire
     Into the mystery of this heart which beats
     So wild, so deep in us—to know
     Whence our lives come and where they go.
55   And many a man in his own breast then delves,
     But deep enough, alas! none ever mines.
     And we have been on many thousand lines,
     And we have shown, on each, spirit and power;
     But hardly have we, for one little hour,
60   Been on our own line, have we been ourselves—

     Hardly had skill to utter one of all
     The nameless feelings that course through our breast,
     But they course on for ever unexpressed.
     And long we try in vain to speak and act
65   Our hidden self, and what we say and do
     Is eloquent, is well—but 'tis not true!
     And then we will no more be racked
     With inward striving, and demand
     Of all the thousand nothings of the hour
70   Their stupefying power;
     Ah yes, and they benumb us at our call!
     Yet still, from time to time, vague and forlorn,
     From the soul's subterranean depth upborne
     As from an infinitely distant land,
75   Come airs, and floating echoes, and convey
     A melancholy into all our day.

     Only—but this is rare—
     When a beloved hand is laid in ours,
     When, jaded with the rush and glare
80   Of the interminable hours,
     Our eyes can in another's eyes read clear,
     When our world-deafened ear
     Is by the tones of a loved voice caressed—
     A bolt is shot back somewhere in our breast,
85   And a lost pulse of feeling stirs again.
     The eye sinks inward, and the heart lies plain,
     And what we mean, we say, and what we would, we
        know.
     A man becomes aware of his life's flow,
     And hears its winding murmur; and he sees
90   The meadows where it glides, the sun, the breeze.

     And there arrives a lull in the hot race
     Wherein he doth for ever chase
     That flying and elusive shadow, rest.
     An air of coolness plays upon his face,
95   And an unwonted calm pervades his breast.
     And then he thinks he knows
     The hills where his life rose,
     And the sea where it goes.
     —1852

The Scholar-Gipsy [1]

Go, for they call you, shepherd, from the hill;
   Go, shepherd, and untie the wattled cotes! [2]
     No longer leave thy wistful flock unfed,
   Nor let thy bawling fellows rack their throats,
5   Nor the cropped herbage shoot another head.
        But when the fields are still,
   And the tired men and dogs all gone to rest,
     And only the white sheep are sometimes seen
     Cross and recross the strips of moon-blanched green,
10   Come, shepherd, and again begin the quest!

Here, where the reaper was at work of late—
   In this high field's dark corner, where he leaves
     His coat, his basket, and his earthen cruse,°   *jug*
   And in the sun all morning binds the sheaves,
15   Then here, at noon, comes back his stores to use—
       Here will I sit and wait,
   While to my ear from uplands far away
     The bleating of the folded° flocks is borne, *enclosed*
     With distant cries of reapers in the corn—
20   All the live murmur of a summer's day.

Screened is this nook o'er the high, half-reaped field,
   And here till sun-down, shepherd! will I be.
     Through the thick corn the scarlet poppies peep,
   And round green roots and yellowing stalks I see
25   Pale pink convolvulus [3] in tendrils creep;
       And air-swept lindens yield
   Their scent, and rustle down their perfumed showers
     Of bloom on the bent grass where I am laid,
     And bower me from the August sun with shade;
30   And the eye travels down to Oxford's towers.

And near me on the grass lies Glanvil's book—
   Come, let me read the oft-read tale again!
     The story of the Oxford scholar poor,
   Of pregnant [4] parts and quick inventive brain,
35   Who, tired of knocking at preferment's door,
       One summer-morn forsook
   His friends, and went to learn the gipsy-lore,
     And roamed the world with that wild brotherhood,
     And came, as most men deemed, to little good,
40   But came to Oxford and his friends no more.

But once, years after, in the country-lanes,
   Two scholars, whom at college erst he knew,
     Met him, and of his way of life enquired;
   Whereat he answered, that the gipsy-crew,
45   His mates, had arts to rule as they desired
       The workings of men's brains,
   And they can bind them to what thoughts they will.
     "And I," he said, "the secret of their art,
     When fully learned, will to the world impart;
50   But it needs heaven-sent moments for this skill."

This said, he left them, and returned no more.
   But rumours hung about the country-side,
     That the lost Scholar long was seen to stray,
   Seen by rare glimpses, pensive and tongue-tied,
55   In hat of antique shape, and cloak of grey,
       The same the gypsies wore.

---

[1] *The Scholar-Gipsy*   Arnold said this poem was inspired by the following passage in Joseph Glanville's *Vanity of Dogmatizing* (1661): "There was very lately a lad in the University of Oxford, who was by his poverty forced to leave his studies there; and at last to join himself to a company of vagabond gypsies. Among these extravagant people, by the insinuating subtilty of his carriage, he quickly got so much of their love and esteem as that they discovered to him their mystery. After he had been a pretty while exercised in the trade, there chanced to ride by a couple of scholars, who had formerly been of his acquaintance. They quickly spied out their old friend among the gypsies; and he gave them an account of the necessity which drove him to that kind of life, and told them that the people he went with were not such imposters as they were taken for, but that they had a traditional kind of learning among them, and could do wonders by the power of imagination, their fancy binding that of others; that he himself had learned much of their art, and when he had compassed the whole secret, he intended, he said, to leave their company, and give the world an account of what he had learned." Arnold imagines this student still roaming the area surrounding Oxford, where Arnold spent "the freest and most delightful part, perhaps, of my life."

[2] *wattled cotes*   Sheepfolds made of woven sticks.

[3] *convolvulus*   Morning-glory.

[4] *pregnant*   Full of ideas.

Shepherds had met him on the Hurst[1] in spring;
　　At some lone alehouse in the Berkshire moors,
　　　　On the warm ingle-bench,[2] the smock-frocked
　　　　　　boors°　　　　　　　　　　　　　　　　　*rustics*
60　Had found him seated at their entering,

But, 'mid their drink and clatter, he would fly.
　　And I myself seem half to know thy looks,
　　　　And put the shepherds, wanderer! on thy trace;
　　And boys who in lone wheatfields scare the rooks
65　　　　I ask if thou hast passed their quiet place;
　　　　　　Or in my boat I lie
　　Moored to the cool bank in the summer-heats,
　　　　'Mid wide grass meadows which the sunshine
　　　　　　fills,
　　　　And watch the warm, green-muffled Cumner
　　　　　　hills,
70　And wonder if thou haunt'st their shy retreats.

For most, I know, thou lov'st retired ground!
　　Thee at the ferry Oxford riders blithe,
　　　　Returning home on summer-nights, have met
　　Crossing the stripling Thames at Bab-lock-hithe,
75　　　　Trailing in the cool stream thy fingers wet,
　　　　　　As the punt's[3] rope chops round;
　　And leaning backward in a pensive dream,
　　　　And fostering in thy lap a heap of flowers
　　　　Plucked in shy fields and distant Wychwood
　　　　　　bowers,
80　And thine eyes resting on the moonlit stream.

And then they land, and thou art seen no more!
　　Maidens, who from the distant hamlets come
　　　　To dance around the Fyfield elm in May,
　　Oft through the darkening fields have seen thee
　　　　roam,
85　　　　Or cross a stile into the public way.
　　　　　　Oft thou hast given them store
　　Of flowers—the frail-leafed, white anemone,
　　　　Dark bluebells drenched with dews of summer
　　　　　　eves,

And purple orchises with spotted leaves—
90　But none hath words she can report of thee.

And, above Godstow Bridge, when hay-time's here
　　In June, and many a scythe in sunshine flames,
　　　　Men who through those wide fields of breezy
　　　　　　grass
　　Where black-winged swallows haunt the glittering
　　　　　　Thames,
95　　　　To bathe in the abandoned lasher pass,[4]
　　　　　　Have often passed thee near
　　Sitting upon the river bank o'ergrown;
　　　　Marked thine outlandish garb, thy figure
　　　　　　spare,
　　　　Thy dark vague eyes, and soft abstracted air—
100　But, when they came from bathing, thou wast gone!

At some lone homestead in the Cumner hills,
　　Where at her open door the housewife darns,
　　　　Thou hast been seen, or hanging on a gate
　　To watch the threshers in the mossy barns.
105　　　　Children, who early range these slopes and late
　　　　　　For cresses from the rills,
　　Have known thee eyeing, all an April-day,
　　　　The springing pastures and the feeding kine;°　　*cows*
　　　　And marked thee, when the stars come out
　　　　　　and shine,
110　Through the long dewy grass move slow away.

In autumn, on the skirts of Bagley Wood—
　　Where most the gypsies by the turf-edged way
　　　　Pitch their smoked tents, and every bush you
　　　　　　see
　　With scarlet patches tagged and shreds of grey,[5]
115　　　　Above the forest-ground called Thessaly —
　　　　　　The blackbird, picking food,
　　Sees thee, nor stops his meal, nor fears at all;
　　　　So often has he known thee past him stray,
　　　　Rapt, twirling in thy hand a withered spray,
120　And waiting for the spark from heaven to fall.

---

[1] *the Hurst* Hill outside Oxford. All the places mentioned in the stanzas following are located in the area surrounding Oxford.

[2] *ingle-bench* Fireside bench.

[3] *punt* Small, shallow boat propelled with a long pole pushed against the river bottom.

---

[4] *lasher pass* Place where water collects after spilling over a dam.

[5] *With scarlet … grey* Reference to the clothes of the gypsies, which they hang on the bushes to dry.

And once, in winter, on the causeway chill
    Where home through flooded fields foot-travellers go,
        Have I not passed thee on the wooden bridge,
    Wrapt in thy cloak and battling with the snow,
125   Thy face toward Hinksey and its wintry ridge?
        And thou hast climbed the hill,
    And gained the white brow of the Cumner range;
        Turned once to watch, while thick the snowflakes fall,
        The line of festal light in Christ-Church hall[1]—
130 Then sought thy straw in some sequestered grange.

But what—I dream! Two hundred years are flown
    Since first thy story ran through Oxford halls,
        And the grave Glanvil did the tale inscribe
    That thou wert wandered from the studious walls
135   To learn strange arts, and join a gipsy-tribe;
        And thou from earth art gone
    Long since, and in some quiet churchyard laid—
        Some country-nook, where o'er thy unknown grave
        Tall grasses and white flowering nettles wave,
140 Under a dark, red-fruited yew-tree's shade.

—No, no, thou hast not felt the lapse of hours!
    For what wears out the life of mortal men?
        'Tis that from change to change their being rolls;
    'Tis that repeated shocks, again, again,
145   Exhaust the energy of strongest souls
        And numb the elastic powers.
    Till having used our nerves with bliss and teen,°   *vexation*
        And tired upon a thousand schemes our wit,
    To the just-pausing Genius[2] we remit
150 Our worn-out life, and are—what we have been.

Thou hast not lived, why should'st thou perish, so?
    Thou hadst *one* aim, *one* business, *one* desire;

Else wert thou long since numbered with the dead!
    Else hadst thou spent, like other men, thy fire!
155   The generations of thy peers are fled,
        And we ourselves shall go;
    But thou possessest an immortal lot,
        And we imagine thee exempt from age
        And living as thou liv'st on Glanvil's page,
160 Because thou hadst—what we, alas! have not.

For early didst thou leave the world, with powers
    Fresh, undiverted to the world without,
        Firm to their mark, not spent on other things;
    Free from the sick fatigue, the languid doubt,
165   Which much to have tried, in much been baffled, brings.
        O life unlike to ours!
    Who fluctuate idly without term or scope,
        Of whom each strives, nor knows for what he strives,
        And each half lives a hundred different lives;
170 Who wait like thee, but not, like thee, in hope.

Thou waitest for the spark from heaven! and we,
    Light half-believers of our casual creeds,
        Who never deeply felt, nor clearly willed,
    Whose insight never has borne fruit in deeds,
175   Whose vague resolves never have been fulfilled;
        For whom each year we see
    Breeds new beginnings, disappointments new;
        Who hesitate and falter life away,
        And lose tomorrow the ground won today—
180 Ah! do not we, wanderer! await it too?

Yes, we await it!—but it still delays,
    And then we suffer! and amongst us one,
        Who most has suffered,[3] takes dejectedly
    His seat upon the intellectual throne;
185   And all his store of sad experience he
        Lays bare of wretched days;
    Tells us his misery's birth and growth and signs,

---

[1] *Christ-Church hall* Dining hall of Christ Church, an Oxford College.

[2] *Genius* Attendant spirit that accompanies a soul from birth to death and shapes his or her character.

[3] *one ... suffered* Reference probably either to Tennyson—whose *In Memoriam* appeared in 1850, the year he succeeded Wordsworth as Poet Laureate—or to German philosopher Johann Wolfgang von Goethe (1749–1832).

And how the dying spark of hope was fed,
And how the breast was soothed, and how the
head,
190   And all his hourly varied anodynes.

This for our wisest! and we others pine,
And wish the long unhappy dream would end,
And waive all claim to bliss, and try to bear;
With close-lipped patience for our only friend,
195   Sad patience, too near neighbour to despair—
But none has hope like thine!
Thou through the fields and through the woods
dost stray,
Roaming the country-side, a truant boy,
Nursing thy project in unclouded joy,
200   And every doubt long blown by time away.

O born in days when wits were fresh and clear,
And life ran gaily as the sparkling Thames;
Before this strange disease of modern life,
With its sick hurry, its divided aims,
205   Its heads o'ertaxed, its palsied hearts, was rife—
Fly hence, our contact fear!
Still fly, plunge deeper in the bowering wood!
Averse, as Dido did with gesture stern
From her false friend's approach in Hades turn,[1]
210   Wave us away, and keep thy solitude!

Still nursing the unconquerable hope,
Still clutching the inviolable shade,
With a free, onward impulse brushing through,
By night, the silvered branches of the glade—
215   Far on the forest-skirts, where none pursue.
On some mild pastoral slope
Emerge, and resting on the moonlit pales
Freshen thy flowers as in former years
With dew, or listen with enchanted ears,
220   From the dark dingles,[2] to the nightingales!

But fly our paths, our feverish contact fly!
For strong the infection of our mental strife,

Which, though it gives no bliss, yet spoils for rest;
And we should win thee from thy own fair life,
225   Like us distracted, and like us unblest.
Soon, soon thy cheer would die,
Thy hopes grow timorous, and unfixed thy powers,
And thy clear aims be cross and shifting made;
And then thy glad perennial youth would fade,
230   Fade, and grow old at last, and die like ours.

Then fly our greetings, fly our speech and smiles!
—As some grave Tyrian[3] trader, from the sea,
Descried at sunrise an emerging prow
Lifting the cool-haired creepers stealthily,
235   The fringes of a southward-facing brow
Among the Aegean isles;
And saw the merry Grecian coaster come,
Freighted with amber grapes, and Chian wine,
Green, bursting figs, and tunnies°   *tuna fish*
steeped in brine—
240   And knew the intruders on his ancient home,

The young light-hearted masters of the waves—
And snatched his rudder, and shook out more sail;
And day and night held on indignantly
O'er the blue Midland waters with the gale,
245   Betwixt the Syrtes[4] and soft Sicily,
To where the Atlantic raves
Outside the western straits; and unbent sails
There, where down cloudy cliffs, through
sheets of foam,
Shy traffickers, the dark Iberians[5] come;
250   And on the beach undid his corded bales.
—1853

---

1   *as Dido … turn*   In Virgil's *Aeneid*, Dido, Queen of Carthage, commits suicide when her lover, Aeneas, deserts her. When he encounters her in Hades, she turns away from him.

2   *dingles*   Wooded dales.

3   *Tyrian*   From Tyre, ancient capital of Phoenicia.

4   *Syrtes*   Two treacherous gulfs off the coast of northern Africa.

5   *dark Iberians*   Inhabitants of Spain or Portugal. The story of these "shy traffickers" comes from fifth-century BCE Greek historian Herodotus's *History*, in which he explains that the Carthaginians would sail through the Strait of Gibraltar to trade with the West Africans. In a unique trading process, these Carthaginians would leave their goods on the beach, withdrawing to their ships. The Africans would come out of their hiding places and leave gold beside the goods they wished to purchase. After they had retreated, the Carthaginians would return and decide if this was adequate payment. The process would be repeated until the two sides reached an agreement.

Stanzas from The Grande Chartreuse[1]

Through Alpine meadows soft-suffused
  With rain, where thick the crocus blows,
Past the dark forges long disused,
  The mule-track from Saint Laurent goes.
5 The bridge is crossed, and slow we ride,
  Through forest, up the mountain-side.

The autumnal evening darkens round,
  The wind is up, and drives the rain;
While, hark! far down, with strangled sound
10 Doth the Dead Guier's[2] stream complain,
  Where that wet smoke, among the woods,
  Over his boiling cauldron broods.

Swift rush the spectral vapours white
  Past limestone scars with ragged pines,
15 Showing—then blotting from our sight!—
  Halt—through the cloud-drift something shines!
  High in the valley, wet and drear,
  The huts of Courrerie appear.

Strike leftward! cries our guide; and higher
20 Mounts up the stony forest-way.
At last the encircling trees retire;
  Look! through the showery twilight grey
  What pointed roofs are these advance?
  A palace of the Kings of France?

25 Approach, for what we seek is here!
  Alight, and sparely sup, and wait
For rest in this outbuilding near;
  Then cross the sward[3] and reach that gate.
  Knock; pass the wicket! Thou art come
30 To the Carthusians' world-famed home.

The silent courts, where night and day
  Into their stone-carved basins cold
The splashing icy fountains play—
  The humid corridors behold!
35 Where, ghostlike in the deepening night,
  Cowled forms brush by in gleaming white.

The chapel, where no organ's peal
  Invests the stern and naked prayer—
With penitential cries they kneel
40 And wrestle; rising then, with bare
  And white uplifted faces stand,
  Passing the Host from hand to hand;

Each takes, and then his visage wan
  Is buried in his cowl once more.
45 The cells!—the suffering Son of Man
  Upon the wall—the knee-worn floor—
  And where they sleep, that wooden bed,
  Which shall their coffin be, when dead![4]

The library, where tract and tome
50 Not to feed priestly pride are there,
To hymn the conquering march of Rome,
  Nor yet to amuse, as ours are!
  They paint of souls the inner strife,
  Their drops of blood, their death in life.

55 The garden, overgrown—yet mild,
  See, fragrant herbs[5] are flowering there!
Strong children of the Alpine wild
  Whose culture is the brethren's care;
  Of human tasks their only one,
60 And cheerful works beneath the sun.

Those halls, too, destined to contain
  Each its own pilgrim-host of old,
From England, Germany, or Spain—

---

[1] *Grande Chartreuse* Carthusian monastery in a nearly inaccessible valley in the French Alps, established by Saint Bruno in 1804. Arnold visited the monastery on his honeymoon in 1851. The Carthusians are known for their austerity, and devote their time to fasting, solitary contemplation, and prayer.

[2] *Dead Guier* Guiers Mort, a river that flows down past the monastery and into the Guiers Vif (French: "Living Guiers").

[3] *sward* Stretch of grass.

[4] *that wooden … dead* Carthusians are buried on wooden planks. They are sometimes (incorrectly) thought to sleep in their coffins.

[5] *fragrant herbs* From which the Carthusians make the liqueur Chartreuse, the sales of which provide their primary source of income.

All are before me! I behold
65   The House, the Brotherhood austere!
—And what am I, that I am here?

For rigorous teachers seized my youth,
And purged its faith, and trimmed its fire,
Showed me the high, white star of Truth,
70   There bade me gaze, and there aspire.
Even now their whispers pierce the gloom:
What dost thou in this living tomb?

Forgive me, masters of the mind!
At whose behest I long ago
75   So much unlearnt, so much resigned—
I come not here to be your foe!
I seek these anchorites, not in ruth,°   remorse
To curse and to deny your truth;

Not as their friend, or child, I speak!
80   But as, on some far northern strand,
Thinking of his own Gods, a Greek
In pity and mournful awe might stand
Before some fallen Runic[1] stone—
For both were faiths, and both are gone.

85   Wandering between two worlds, one dead,
The other powerless to be born,
With nowhere yet to rest my head,
Like these, on earth I wait forlorn.
Their faith, my tears, the world deride—
90   I come to shed them at their side.

Oh, hide me in your gloom profound,
Ye solemn seats of holy pain!
Take me, cowled forms, and fence me round,
Till I possess my soul again;
95   Till free my thoughts before me roll,
Not chafed by hourly false control!

For the world cries your faith is now
But a dead time's exploded dream;
My melancholy, sciolists[2] say,
100   Is a passed mode, an outworn theme—

As if the world had ever had
A faith, or sciolists been sad!

Ah, if it *be* passed, take away,
At least, the restlessness, the pain;
105   Be man henceforth no more a prey
To these out-dated stings again!
The nobleness of grief is gone—
Ah, leave us not the fret alone!

But—if you cannot give us ease—
110   Last of the race of them who grieve
Here leave us to die out with these
Last of the people who believe!
Silent, while years engrave the brow;
Silent—the best are silent now.

115   Achilles[3] ponders in his tent,
The kings of modern thought are dumb;
Silent they are, though not content,
And wait to see the future come.
They have the grief men had of yore,
120   But they contend and cry no more.

Our fathers[4] watered with their tears
This sea of time whereon we sail,
Their voices were in all men's ears
Who passed within their puissant° hail.   powerful
125   Still the same ocean round us raves,
But we stand mute, and watch the waves.

For what availed it, all the noise
And outcry of the former men?
Say, have their sons achieved more joys,
130   Say, is life lighter now than then?
The sufferers died, they left their pain—
The pangs which tortured them remain.

What helps it now, that Byron bore,
With haughty scorn which mocked the smart,

---

1   *Runic*   Carved with runes (early Norse letters).

2   *sciolists*   Pretenders to knowledge.

3   *Achilles*   Greek warrior who, during the Trojan War, stayed in
his tent, refusing to participate, until the death of his best friend,
Patrocles, in battle, moved him to action.

4   *Our fathers*   I.e., the previous generation of writers.

135 Through Europe to the Aetolian shore[1]
The pageant of his bleeding heart?
That thousands counted every groan,
And Europe made his woe her own?

What boots it, Shelley! that the breeze
140 Carried thy lovely wail away,
Musical through Italian trees
Which fringe thy soft blue Spezzian bay?[2]
Inheritors of thy distress
Have restless hearts one throb the less?

145 Or are we easier, to have read,
O Obermann![3] the sad, stern page,
Which tells us how thou hidd'st thy head
From the fierce tempest of thine age
In the lone brakes of Fontainebleau,
150 Or chalets near the Alpine snow?

Ye slumber in your silent grave!
The world, which for an idle day
Grace to your mood of sadness gave,
Long since hath flung her weeds[4] away.
155 The eternal trifler breaks your spell;
But we—we learnt your lore too well!

Years hence, perhaps, may dawn an age,
More fortunate, alas! than we,
Which without hardness will be sage,
160 And gay without frivolity.
Sons of the world, oh, speed those years;
But, while we wait, allow our tears!

Allow them! We admire with awe
The exulting thunder of your race;
165 You give the universe your law,
You triumph over time and space!

Your pride of life, your tireless powers,
We laud them, but they are not ours.

We are like children reared in shade
170 Beneath some old-world abbey wall,
Forgotten in a forest-glade,
And secret from the eyes of all.
Deep, deep the greenwood round them waves,
Their abbey, and its close° of graves!   *enclosure*

175 But, where the road runs near the stream,
Oft through the trees they catch a glance
Of passing troops in the sun's beam—
Pennon,[5] and plume, and flashing lance!
Forth to the world those soldiers fare,
180 To life, to cities, and to war!

And through the wood, another way,
Faint bugle-notes from far are borne,
Where hunters gather, staghounds bay,
Round some fair forest-lodge at morn.
185 Gay dames are there, in sylvan green;
Laughter and cries—those notes between!

The banners flashing through the trees
Make their blood dance and chain their eyes;
That bugle-music on the breeze
190 Arrests them with a charmed surprise.
Banner by turns and bugle woo:
Ye shy recluses, follow too!

O children, what do ye reply?
"Action and pleasure, will ye roam
195 Through these secluded dells to cry
And call us?—but too late ye come!
Too late for us your call ye blow,
Whose bent was taken long ago.

"Long since we pace this shadowed nave;
200 We watch those yellow tapers shine,
Emblems of hope over the grave,
In the high altar's depth divine;

[1] *Aetolian shore* In Greece, where the English poet George Gordon, Lord Byron, died.

[2] *Spezzian bay* Where English poet Percy Bysshe Shelley drowned, in Italy.

[3] *Obermann* Protagonist of the 1804 novel of that name by Etienne Pivert de Senancour (1770–1846).

[4] *weeds* Mourning garments.

[5] *Pennon* Narrow triangular flag, usually borne on the head of a lance.

The organ carries to our ear
Its accents of another sphere.

205 "Fenced early in this cloistral round
Of reverie, of shade, of prayer,
How should we grow in other ground?
How should we flower in foreign air?
—Pass, banners, pass, and bugles, cease;
210 And leave our desert to its peace!"
—1855

Dover Beach

The sea is calm tonight.
The tide is full, the moon lies fair
Upon the straits—on the French coast the light
Gleams and is gone; the cliffs of England stand,
5 Glimmering and vast, out in the tranquil bay.
Come to the window, sweet is the night-air!
Only, from the long line of spray
Where the sea meets the moon-blanched land,
Listen! you hear the grating roar
10 Of pebbles which the waves draw back, and fling,
At their return, up the high strand,°   shore
Begin, and cease, and then again begin,
With tremulous cadence slow, and bring
The eternal note of sadness in.

15 Sophocles long ago
Heard it on the Aegean, and it brought
Into his mind the turbid ebb and flow
Of human misery;[1] we
Find also in the sound a thought,
20 Hearing it by this distant northern sea.

The Sea of Faith
Was once, too, at the full, and round earth's shore

Lay like the folds of a bright girdle furled.
But now I only hear
25 Its melancholy, long, withdrawing roar.
Retreating, to the breath
Of the night-wind, down the vast edges drear
And naked shingles[2] of the world.

Ah, love, let us be true
30 To one another! for the world, which seems
To lie before us like a land of dreams,
So various, so beautiful, so new,
Hath really neither joy, nor love, nor light,
Nor certitude, nor peace, nor help for pain;
35 And we are here as on a darkling plain
Swept with confused alarms of struggle and flight,
Where ignorant armies clash by night.[3]
—1867

Obermann Once More[4]

Savez-vous quelque bien qui console du regret d'un monde?[5]
OBERMANN.

Glion?—Ah, twenty years, it cuts
All meaning from a name!
White houses prank where once were huts.
Glion, but not the same!

---

[2]   *shingles* Water-worn pebbles.

[3]   *as on … night* Reference to Thucydides's *History of the Pelopon-nesian War*, in which the invading Athenians became confused as night fell on the battle at Epipolae. Combatants could not tell friend from foe in the moonlight.

[4]   *Obermann* 1804 novel by French writer Etienne Pivert de Senancour, one of Arnold's major influences. The book's protago-nist, Obermann, retreats to a remote valley in the Swiss Alps (Glion), and writes letters describing his life of solitude in nature. In a note to his poem *Stanzas in Memory of the Author of Obermann*, Arnold says, "The stir of all the main forces by which modern life is and has been impelled lives in the letters of Obermann; the dissolv-ing agencies of the eighteenth century, the fiery storm of the French Revolution, the first faint promise and dawn of that new world which our own time is but now fully bringing to light—all these are to be felt, almost to be touched there."

[5]   *Savez-vous … monde?* French: "Do you know of some good that soothes the regrets of a world?"

---

[1]   *Sophocles … misery* Cf. Sophocles's *Antigone* 583–91: "Blest are those whose days have not tasted of evil. For when a house has once been shaken by the gods, no form of ruin is lacking, but it spreads over the bulk of the race, just as, when the surge is driven over the darkness of the deep by the fierce breath of Thracian sea-winds, it rolls up the black sand from the depths, and the wind-beaten headlands that front the blows of the storm give out a mournful roar."

5 And yet I know not! All unchanged
The turf, the pines, the sky!
The hills in their old order ranged;
The lake, with Chillon[1] by!

And, 'neath those chestnut-trees, where stiff
10 And stony mounts the way,
The crackling husk-heaps burn, as if
I left them yesterday!

Across the valley, on that slope,
The huts of Avant shine!
15 Its pines, under their branches, ope
Ways for the pasturing kine.°   *cows*

Full-foaming milk-pails, Alpine fare,
Sweet heaps of fresh-cut grass,
Invite to rest the traveller there
20 Before he climb the pass—

The gentian-flowered pass, its crown
With yellow spires aflame;
Whence drops the path to Allière down,
And walls where Byron came,[2]

25 By their green river, who doth change
His birth-name just below;
Orchard, and croft, and full-stored grange
Nursed by his pastoral flow.

But stop!—to fetch back thoughts that stray
30 Beyond this gracious bound,
The cone of Jaman,[3] pale and grey,
See, in the blue profound!

Ah, Jaman! delicately tall
Above his sun-warmed firs—

---

1 *Chillon* Famous castle that dates back to the medieval period, located on Lake Geneva.

2 *And walls ... came* Byron toured the area surrounding Lake Geneva in 1816 and was inspired by the Castle of Chillon to compose his poem *The Prisoner of Chillon*.

3 *Jaman* Dent du Jaman, a rock summit located northeast of Montreaux.

35 What thoughts to me his rocks recall,
What memories he stirs!

And who but thou must be, in truth,
Obermann! with me here?
Thou master of my wandering youth,
40 But left this many a year!

Yes, I forget the world's work wrought,
Its warfare waged with pain;
An eremite° with thee, in thought   *hermit*
Once more I slip my chain,

45 And to thy mountain-chalet come,
And lie beside its door,
And hear the wild bee's Alpine hum,
And thy sad, tranquil lore!

Again I feel the words inspire
50 Their mournful calm; serene,
Yet tinged with infinite desire
For all that *might* have been—

The harmony from which man swerved
Made his life's rule once more!
55 The universal order served,
Earth happier than before!

—While thus I mused, night gently ran
Down over hill and wood.
Then, still and sudden, Obermann
60 On the grass near me stood.

Those pensive features well I knew,
On my mind, years before,
Imaged so oft! imaged so true!
—A shepherd's garb he wore,

65 A mountain-flower was in his hand,
A book was in his breast.
Bent on my face, with gaze which scanned
My soul, his eyes did rest.

"And is it thou," he cried, "so long
70 Held by the world which we

Loved not, who turnest from the throng
Back to thy youth and me?

"And from thy world, with heart opprest,
Choosest thou *now* to turn?—
75   Ah me! we anchorites° read things best,   recluses
Clearest their course discern!

"Thou fledst me when the ungenial[1] earth,
Man's work-place, lay in gloom.
Return'st thou in her hour of birth,
80   Of hopes and hearts in bloom?

"Perceiv'st thou not the change of day?
Ah! Carry back thy ken,°   gaze
What, some two thousand years! Survey
The world as it was then!

85   "Like ours it looked in outward air.
Its head was clear and true,
Sumptuous its clothing, rich its fare,
No pause its action knew;

"Stout was its arm, each thew° and bone   muscle
90   Seemed puissant and alive—
But, ah! its heart, its heart was stone,
And so it could not thrive!

"On that hard Pagan world disgust
And secret loathing fell.
95   Deep weariness and sated lust
Made human life a hell.

"In his cool hall, with haggard eyes,
The Roman noble lay;
He drove abroad, in furious guise,
100 Along the Appian way.

"He made a feast, drank fierce and fast,
And crowned his hair with flowers—
No easier nor no quicker passed
The impracticable hours.

105 "The brooding East with awe beheld
Her impious younger world.
The Roman tempest swelled and swelled,
And on her head was hurled.

"The East bowed low before the blast
110 In patient, deep disdain;
She let the legions thunder past,
And plunged in thought again.

"So well she mused, a morning broke
Across her spirit grey;
115 A conquering, new-born joy awoke,
And filled her life with day.

" 'Poor world,' she cried, 'so deep accurst,
That runn'st from pole to pole
To seek a draught to slake thy thirst—
120 Go, seek it in thy soul!'

"She heard it, the victorious West,
In crown and sword arrayed!
She felt the void which mined her breast,
She shivered and obeyed.

125 "She veiled her eagles, snapped her sword,
And laid her sceptre down;
Her stately purple she abhorred,
And her imperial crown.

"She broke her flutes, she stopped her sports,
130 Her artists could not please;
She tore her books, she shut her courts,
She fled her palaces;

"Lust of the eye and pride of life
She left it all behind,
135 And hurried, torn with inward strife,
The wilderness to find.

"Tears washed the trouble from her face!
She changed into a child!
'Mid weeds and wrecks she stood—a place
140 Of ruin—but she smiled!

---

[1]   *ungenial*   Unfavorable for growth.

"Oh, had I lived in that great day,
How had its glory new
Filled earth and heaven, and caught away
My ravished spirit too!

145 "No thoughts that to the world belong
Had stood against the wave
Of love which set so deep and strong
From Christ's then open grave.

"No cloister-floor of humid stone
150 Had been too cold for me.
For me no Eastern desert lone
Had been too far to flee.

"No lonely life had passed too slow,
When I could hourly scan
155 Upon his Cross, with head sunk low,
That nailed, thorn-crowned Man!

"Could see the Mother with her Child
Whose tender winning arts
Have to his little arms beguiled
160 So many wounded hearts!

"And centuries came and ran their course,
And unspent all that time
Still, still went forth that Child's dear force,
And still was at its prime.

165 "Ay, ages long endured his span
Of life—'tis true received—
That gracious Child, that thorn-crowned Man!
—He lived while we believed.

"While we believed, on earth he went,
170 And open stood his grave.
Men called from chamber, church, and tent;
And Christ was by to save.

"Now he is dead! Far hence he lies
In the lorn Syrian town;
175 And on his grave, with shining eyes,
The Syrian stars look down.

"In vain men still, with hoping new,
Regard his death-place dumb,
And say the stone is not yet to,
180 And wait for words to come.

"Ah, o'er that silent sacred land,
Of sun, and arid stone,
And crumbling wall, and sultry sand,
Sounds now one word alone!

185 "*Unduped of fancy, henceforth man*
Must labour!—must resign
His all too human creeds, and scan
Simply the way divine!

"But slow that tide of common thought,
190 Which bathed our life, retired;
Slow, slow the old world wore to nought,
And pulse by pulse expired.

"Its frame yet stood without a breach
When blood and warmth were fled;
195 And still it spake its wonted speech—
But every word was dead.

"And oh, we cried, that on this corse°   corpse
Might fall a freshening storm!
Rive its dry bones, and with new force
200 A new-sprung world inform!

"—Down came the storm! O'er France it passed
In sheets of scathing fire;
All Europe felt that fiery blast,
And shook as it rushed by her.

205 "Down came the storm! In ruins fell
The worn-out world we knew.
It passed, that elemental swell!
Again appeared the blue;

"The sun shone in the new-washed sky,
210 And what from heaven saw he?
Blocks of the past, like icebergs high,
Float on a rolling sea!

"Upon them plies the race of man
All it before endeavoured;
215 'Ye live,' I cried, 'ye work and plan,
And know not ye are severed!

"'Poor fragments of a broken world
Whereon men pitch their tent!
Why were ye too to death not hurled
220 When your world's day was spent?

"'That glow of central fire is done
Which with its fusing flame
Knit all your parts, and kept you one—
But ye, ye are the same!

225 "'The past, its mask of union on,
Had ceased to live and thrive.
The past, its mask of union gone,
Say, is it more alive?

"'Your creeds are dead, your rites are dead,
230 Your social order too!
Where tarries he, the Power who said:
See, I make all things new?[1]

"'The millions suffer still, and grieve,
And what can helpers heal
235 With old-world cures men half believe
For woes they wholly feel?

"'And yet men have such need of joy!
But joy whose grounds are true;
And joy that should all hearts employ
240 As when the past was new.

"'Ah, not the emotion of that past,
Its common hope, were vain!
Some new such hope must dawn at last,
Or man must toss in pain.

245 "'But now the old is out of date,
The new is not yet born,
And who can be alone elate,
While the world lies forlorn?'

---

[1] he the ... new See Revelation 21.5.

"Then to the wilderness I fled—
250 There among Alpine snows
And pastoral huts I hid my head,
And sought and found repose.

"It was not yet the appointed hour.
Sad, patient, and resigned,
255 I watched the crocus fade and flower,
I felt the sun and wind.

"The day I lived in was not mine,
Man gets no second day.
In dreams I saw the future shine—
260 But ah! I could not stay!

"Action I had not, followers, fame;
I passed obscure, alone.
The after-world forgets my name,
Nor do I wish it known.

265 "Composed to bear, I lived and died,
And knew my life was vain,
With fate I murmur not, nor chide,
At Sèvres by the Seine

"(If Paris that brief flight allow)
270 My humble tomb explore!
It bears: Eternity, be thou
My refuge! and no more.

"But thou, whom fellowship of mood
Did make from haunts of strife
275 Come to my mountain-solitude,
And learn my frustrate life;

"O thou, who, ere thy flying span
Was past of cheerful youth,
Didst find the solitary man
280 And love his cheerless truth—

"Despair not thou as I despaired,
Nor be cold gloom thy prison!

Forward the gracious hours have fared,
And see! the sun is risen!

285　"He breaks the winter of the past;
A green, new earth appears.
Millions, whose life in ice lay fast,
Have thoughts, and smiles, and tears.

"What though there still need effort, strife?
290　Though much be still unwon?
Yet warm it mounts, the hour of life!
Death's frozen hour is done!

"The world's great order dawns in sheen,
After long darkness rude,
295　Divinelier imaged, clearer seen,
With happier zeal pursued.

"With hope extinct and brow composed
I marked the present die;
Its term of life was nearly closed,
300　Yet it had more than I.

"But thou, though to the world's new hour
Thou come with aspect marred,
Shorn of the joy, the bloom, the power
Which best befits its bard—

305　"Though more than half thy years be past,
And spent thy youthful prime;
Though, round thy firmer manhood cast,
Hang weeds of our sad time

"Whereof thy youth felt all the spell,
310　And traversed all the shade—
Though late, though dimmed, though weak, yet tell
Hope to a world new-made!

"Help it to fill that deep desire,
The want which racked our brain,
315　Consumed our heart with thirst like fire,
Immedicable pain;

"Which to the wilderness drove out
Our life, to Alpine snow,

And palsied all our word with doubt,
320　And all our work with woe—

"What still of strength is left, employ
That end to help attain:
*One common wave of thought and joy
Lifting mankind again!*"

325　—The vision ended. I awoke
As out of sleep, and no
Voice moved—only the torrent broke
The silence, far below.

Soft darkness on the turf did lie.
330　Solemn, o'er hut and wood,
In the yet star-sown nightly sky,
The peak of Jaman stood.

Still in my soul the voice I heard
Of Obermann!—away
335　I turned; by some vague impulse stirred,
Along the rocks of Naye[1]

Past Sonchaud's piny flanks I gaze
And the blanched summit bare
Of Malatrait, to where in haze
340　The Valais opens fair,

And the domed Velan, with his snows,
Behind the upcrowding hills,
Doth all the heavenly opening close
Which the Rhone's murmur fills;

345　And glorious there, without a sound,
Across the glimmering lake,
High in the Valais-depth profound,
I saw the morning break.
—1867

---

[1]　*rocks of Naye*　Les Rochers de Naye, a mountain above Montreaux. All the landmarks Arnold describes in the following stanzas are located in the Valais region of southern Switzerland, which stretches from the Italian border to the heart of the Alps, and contains part of the Rhone river as well as several of Switzerland's most spectacular mountain peaks.

East London[1]

'Twas August, and the fierce sun overhead
Smote on the squalid streets of Bethnal Green,
And the pale weaver, through his windows seen
In Spitalfields, looked thrice dispirited.

5   I met a preacher there I knew, and said:
"Ill and o'erworked, how fare you in this scene?"
"Bravely!" said he; "for I of late have been
Much cheered with thoughts of Christ, *the living
    bread.*"

O human soul! as long as thou canst so
10   Set up a mark of everlasting light,
Above the howling senses' ebb and flow,

To cheer thee, and to right thee if thou roam—
Not with lost toil thou labourest through the night!
Thou mak'st the heaven thou hop'st indeed thy
    home.
—1867

West London[2]

Crouched on the pavement, close by Belgrave
    Square,
A tramp I saw, ill, moody, and tongue-tied.
A babe was in her arms, and at her side
A girl; their clothes were rags, their feet were bare.

5   Some labouring men, whose work lay somewhere
    there,
Passed opposite ; she touched her girl, who hied°   *hastened*
Across, and begged, and came back satisfied.
The rich she had let pass with frozen stare.

Thought I: "Above her state this spirit towers;
10   She will not ask of aliens, but of friends,
Of sharers in a common human fate.

"She turns from that cold succour, which attends
The unknown little from the unknowing great,
And points us to a better time than ours."
—1867

Preface to the First Edition of Poems

In two small volumes of poems, published anonymously, one in 1849, the other in 1852, many of the poems which compose the present volume have already appeared. The rest are now published for the first time.

I have, in the present collection, omitted the poem from which the volume published in 1852 took its title.[3] I have done so, not because the subject of it was a Sicilian Greek born between two and three thousand years ago, although many persons would think this a sufficient reason. Neither have I done so because I had, in my own opinion, failed in the delineation which I intended to effect. I intended to delineate the feelings of one of the last of the Greek religious philosophers, one of the family of Orpheus and Musaeus,[4] having survived his fellows, living on into a time when the habits of Greek thought and feeling had begun fast to change, character to dwindle, the influence of the Sophists to prevail. Into the feelings of a man so situated there entered much that we are accustomed to consider as exclusively modern; how much, the fragments of Empedocles[5] himself which remain to us are sufficient at least to indicate. What those who are familiar only with the great monuments of early Greek genius suppose to be its exclusive characteristics, have disappeared; the calm, the cheerfulness, the disinterested objectivity have disappeared; the dialogue of the mind with itself has commenced; modern problems have presented themselves; we hear already the doubts, we witness the discouragement, of Hamlet and of Faust.[6]

---

[1]   *East London*   Working-class area of the city. Bethnal Green and Spitalfields are districts in East London.

[2]   *West London*   Wealthy end of the city. Belgrave Square was (and is) a particularly affluent district.

[3]   *the Poem ... title*   Arnold's *Empedocles on Etna.*

[4]   *Orpheus*   Legendary   Thracian   poet   and   musician; *Musaeus*   Pupil of Orpheus.

[5]   *fragments of Empedocles*   Fragments of Empedocles's scientific treatises survive.

[6]   *Faust*   Sixteenth-century German doctor who performed many supposedly miraculous feats. He is the subject of several legends, folk tales, dramas and poems, including Christopher Marlowe's play

The representations of such a man's feelings must be interesting, if consistently drawn. We all naturally take pleasure, says Aristotle, in any imitation or representation whatever: this is the basis of our love of Poetry: and we take pleasure in them, he adds, because all knowledge is naturally agreeable to us; not to the philosopher only, but to mankind at large. Every representation therefore which is consistently drawn may be supposed to be interesting, inasmuch as it gratifies this natural interest in knowledge of all kinds. What is not interesting, is that which does not add to our knowledge of any kind; that which is vaguely conceived and loosely drawn; a representation which is general, indeterminate, and faint, instead of being particular, precise, and firm.

Any accurate representation may therefore be expected to be interesting; but, if the representation be a poetical one, more than this is demanded. It is demanded, not only that it shall interest, but also that it shall inspirit and rejoice the reader: that it shall convey a charm, and infuse delight. For the Muses, as Hesiod says, were born that they might be "a forgetfulness of evils, and a truce from cares":[1] and it is not enough that the Poet should add to the knowledge of men, it is required of him also that he should add to their happiness. "All art," says Schiller, "is dedicated to Joy, and there is no higher and no more serious problem, than how to make men happy. The right art is that alone, which creates the highest enjoyment."[2]

A poetical work, therefore, is not yet justified when it has been shown to be an accurate, and therefore interesting representation; it has to be shown also that it is a representation from which men can derive enjoyment. In presence of the most tragic circumstances, represented in a work of Art, the feeling of enjoyment, as is well known, may still subsist: the representation of the most utter calamity, of the liveliest anguish, is not sufficient to destroy it: the more tragic the situation, the deeper becomes the enjoyment; and the situation is more tragic in proportion as it becomes more terrible.

What then are the situations, from the representation of which, though accurate, no poetical enjoyment can be derived? They are those in which the suffering finds no vent in action; in which a continuous state of mental distress is prolonged, unrelieved by incident, hope, or resistance; in which there is everything to be endured, nothing to be done. In such situations there is inevitably something morbid, in the description of them something monotonous. When they occur in actual life, they are painful, not tragic; the representation of them in poetry is painful also.

To this class of situations, poetically faulty as it appears to me, that of Empedocles, as I have endeavoured to represent him, belongs; and I have therefore excluded the poem from the present collection.

And why, it may be asked, have I entered into this explanation respecting a matter so unimportant as the admission or exclusion of the poem in question? I have done so, because I was anxious to avow that the sole reason for its exclusion was that which has been stated above; and that it has not been excluded in deference to the opinion which many critics of the present day appear to entertain against subjects chosen from distant times and countries: against the choice, in short, of any subjects but modern ones.

"The poet," it is said, and by an intelligent critic, "the poet who would really fix the public attention must leave the exhausted past, and draw his subjects from matters of present import, and therefore both of interest and novelty."[3]

Now this view I believe to be completely false. It is worth examining, inasmuch as it is a fair sample of a class of critical dicta everywhere current at the present day, having a philosophical form and air, but no real basis in fact; and which are calculated to vitiate the judgement of readers of poetry, while they exert, so far as they are adopted, a misleading influence on the practice of those who make it.

What are the eternal objects of poetry, among all

Doctor Faustus (c. 1588), and Goethe's tragedy *Faust* (1808).

[1] *Muses* In Greek mythology, the nine daughters of Zeus and Mnemosyne, each of whom presided over and provided inspiration for an aspect of the arts and sciences; *a forgetfulness … cares* From early Greek poet Hesiod's *Theogony*.

[2] *"All art … enjoyment"* From celebrated German dramatist and poet Friedrich von Schiller's *On the Use of the Chorus in Tragedy* (1803).

[3] [Arnold's note] In the *Spectator* of April 2nd, 1853. The words quoted were not used with reference to poems of mine.

nations and at all times? They are actions; human actions; possessing an inherent interest in themselves, and which are to be communicated in an interesting manner by the art of the poet. Vainly will the latter imagine that he has everything in his own power; that he can make an intrinsically inferior action equally delightful with a more excellent one by his treatment of it; he may indeed compel us to admire his skill, but his work will possess, within itself, an incurable defect.

The poet, then, has in the first place to select an excellent action; and what actions are the most excellent? Those, certainly, which most powerfully appeal to the great primary human affections: to those elementary feelings which subsist permanently in the race, and which are independent of time. These feelings are permanent and the same; that which interests them is permanent and the same also. The modernness or antiquity of an action, therefore, has nothing to do with its fitness for poetical representation; this depends upon its inherent qualities. To the elementary part of our nature, to our passions, that which is great and passionate is eternally interesting; and interesting solely in proportion to its greatness and to its passion. A great human action of a thousand years ago is more interesting to it than a smaller human action of today, even though upon the representation of this last the most consummate skill may have been expended, and though it has the advantage of appealing by its modern language, familiar manners, and contemporary allusions, to all our transient feelings and interests. These, however, have no right to demand of a poetical work that it shall satisfy them; their claims are to be directed elsewhere. Poetical works belong to the domain of our permanent passions: let them interest these, and the voice of all subordinate claims upon them is at once silenced.

Achilles, Prometheus, Clytemnestra, Dido—what modern poem presents personages as interesting, even to us moderns, as these personages of an "exhausted past"? We have the domestic epic dealing with the details of modern life which pass daily under our eyes; we have poems representing modern personages in contact with the problems of modern life, moral, intellectual, and social; these works have been produced by poets the most distinguished of their nation and time; yet I fearlessly assert that *Hermann and Dorothea*, *Childe Harold*, *Jocelyn*, *The Excursion*,[1] leave the reader cold in comparison with the effect produced upon him by the later books of the *Iliad*, by the *Oresteia*, or by the episode of Dido.[2] And why is this? Simply because in the three last-named cases the action is greater, the personages nobler, the situations more intense: and this is the true basis of the interest in a poetical work, and this alone.

It may be urged, however, that past actions may be interesting in themselves, but that they are not to be adopted by the modern poet, because it is impossible for him to have them clearly present to his own mind, and he cannot therefore feel them deeply, nor represent them forcibly. But this is not necessarily the case. The externals of a past action, indeed, he cannot know with the precision of a contemporary; but his business is with its essentials. The outward man of Oedipus or of Macbeth, the houses in which they lived, the ceremonies of their courts, he cannot accurately figure to himself; but neither do they essentially concern him. His business is with their inward man; with their feelings and behaviour in certain tragic situations, which engage their passions as men; these have in them nothing local and casual; they are as accessible to the modern poet as to a contemporary.

The date of an action, then, signifies nothing: the action itself, its selection and construction, this is what is all-important. This the Greeks understood far more clearly than we do. The radical difference between their poetical theory and ours consists, as it appears to me, in this: that, with them, the poetical character of the action in itself, and the conduct of it, was the first consideration; with us, attention is fixed mainly on the value of the separate thoughts and images which occur in the treatment of an action. They regarded the whole; we regard the parts. With them, the action predominated over the expression of it; with us, the

---

[1]   *Hermann ... Excursion*   Poems by Johann Wolfgang von Goethe (1797), Lord Byron (1818), Alphonse de Lamartine (1836), and William Wordsworth (1814).

[2]   *Oresteia*   Dramatic trilogy by Greek playwright Aeschylus concerning King Agamemnon, his wife Clytemnestra, and their son Orestes; *episode of Dido*   Queen Dido is the subject of Book 4 of Virgil's *Aeneid*.

expression predominates over the action. Not that they failed in expression or were inattentive to it; on the contrary, they are the highest models of expression, the unapproached masters of the grand style: but their expression is so excellent because it is so admirably kept in its right degree of prominence; because it is so simple and so well subordinated; because it draws its force directly from the pregnancy of the matter which it conveys. For what reason was the Greek tragic poet confined to so limited a range of subjects? Because there are so few actions which unite in themselves, in the highest degree, the conditions of excellence: and it was not thought that on any but an excellent subject could an excellent poem be constructed. A few actions, therefore, eminently adapted for tragedy, maintained almost exclusive possession of the Greek tragic stage; their significance appeared inexhaustible; they were as permanent problems, perpetually offered to the genius of every fresh poet. This too is the reason of what appears to us moderns a certain baldness of expression in Greek tragedy; of the triviality with which we often reproach the remarks of the chorus, where it takes part in the dialogue: that the action itself, the situation of Orestes, or Merope, or Alcmaeon,[1] was to stand the central point of interest, unforgotten, absorbing, principal; that no accessories were for a moment to distract the spectator's attention from this; that the tone of the parts was to be perpetually kept down, in order not to impair the grandiose effect of the whole. The terrible old mythic story on which the drama was founded stood, before he entered the theatre, traced in its bare outlines upon the spectator's mind; it stood in his memory, as a group of statuary, faintly seen, at the end of a long and dark vista: then came the poet, embodying outlines, developing situations, not a word wasted, not a sentiment capriciously thrown in: stroke upon stroke, the drama proceeded: the light deepened upon the group; more and more it revealed itself to the rivetted gaze of the spectator: until at last, when the final words were spoken, it stood before him in broad sunlight, a model of immortal beauty.

This was what a Greek critic demanded; this was what a Greek poet endeavoured to effect. It signified

nothing to what time an action belonged; we do not find that the *Persae*[2] occupied a particularly high rank among the dramas of Aeschylus because it represented a matter of contemporary interest: this was not what a cultivated Athenian required; he required that the permanent elements of his nature should be moved; and dramas of which the action, though taken from a long-distant mythic time, yet was calculated to accomplish this in a higher degree than that of the *Persae*, stood higher in his estimation accordingly. The Greeks felt, no doubt, with their exquisite sagacity of taste, that an action of present times was too near them, too much mixed up with what was accidental and passing, to form a sufficiently grand, detached, and self-subsistent object for a tragic poem: such objects belonged to the domain of the comic poet, and of the lighter kinds of poetry. For the more serious kinds, for pragmatic poetry, to use an excellent expression of Polybius,[3] they were more difficult and severe in the range of subjects which they permitted. Their theory and practice alike, the admirable treatise of Aristotle, and the unrivalled works of their poets, exclaim with a thousand tongues—"All depends upon the subject; choose a fitting action, penetrate yourself with the feeling of its situations; this done, everything else will follow."

But for all kinds of poetry alike there was one point on which they were rigidly exacting; the adaptability of the subject to the kind of poetry selected, and the careful construction of the poem.

How different a way of thinking from this is ours! We can hardly at the present day understand what Menander[4] meant, when he told a man who inquired as to the progress of his comedy that he had finished it, not having yet written a single line, because he had constructed the action of it in his mind. A modern critic would have assured him that the merit of his piece depended on the brilliant things which arose under his pen as he went along. We have poems which seem to exist merely for the sake of single lines and passages; not for the sake of producing any total-impression. We have

1   *Merope* Greek queen of Messene; *Alcmaeon* Greek hero who killed his mother to avenge his father's death.

2   *Persae* Play by Aeschylus, set during a Greek victory over the invading Persians, one that had occurred a few years before.

3   *Polybius* Second-century BCE Greek historian; author of a forty-volume history of Rome, of which only five volumes survive.

4   *Menander* Fourth-century BCE comic dramatist.

critics who seem to direct their attention merely to detached expressions, to the language about the action, not to the action itself. I verily think that the majority of them do not in their hearts believe that there is such a thing as a total-impression to be derived from a poem at all, or to be demanded from a poet; they think the term a common-place of metaphysical criticism. They will permit the poet to select any action he pleases, and to suffer that action to go as it will, provided he gratifies them with occasional bursts of fine writing, and with a shower of isolated thoughts and images. That is, they permit him to leave their poetical sense ungratified, provided that he gratifies their rhetorical sense and their curiosity. Of his neglecting to gratify these, there is little danger; he needs rather to be warned against the danger of attempting to gratify these alone; he needs rather to be perpetually reminded to prefer his action to everything else; so to treat this, as to permit its inherent excellences to develop themselves, without interruption from the intrusion of his personal peculiarities: most fortunate, when he most entirely succeeds in effacing himself, and in enabling a noble action to subsist as it did in nature.

But the modern critic not only permits a false practice; he absolutely prescribes false aims.—"A true allegory of the state of one's own mind in a representative history," the poet is told, "is perhaps the highest thing that one can attempt in the way of po-etry."[1]—And accordingly he attempts it. An allegory of the state of one's own mind, the highest problem of an art which imitates actions! No assuredly, it is not, it never can be so: no great poetical work has ever been produced with such an aim. *Faust* itself, in which something of the kind is attempted, wonderful passages as it contains, and in spite of the unsurpassed beauty of the scenes which relate to Margaret,[2] *Faust* itself, judged as a whole, and judged strictly as a poetical work, is defective: its illustrious author, the greatest poet of modern times, the greatest critic of all times, would have been the first to acknowledge it; he only defended his work, indeed, by asserting it to be "something incommensurable."

The confusion of the present times is great, the multitude of voices counselling different things bewildering, the number of existing works capable of attracting a young writer's attention and of becoming his models, immense: what he wants is a hand to guide him through the confusion, a voice to prescribe to him the aim which he should keep in view, and to explain to him that the value of the literary works which offer themselves to his attention is relative to their power of helping him forward on his road towards this aim. Such a guide the English writer at the present day will nowhere find. Failing this, all that can be looked for, all indeed that can be desired, is, that his attention should be fixed on excellent models; that he may reproduce, at any rate, something of their excellence, by penetrating himself with their works and by catching their spirit, if he cannot be taught to produce what is excellent independently.

Foremost among these models for the English writer stands Shakespeare: a name the greatest perhaps of all poetical names; a name never to be mentioned without reverence. I will venture, however, to express a doubt whether the influence of his works, excellent and fruitful for the readers of poetry, for the great majority, has been of unmixed advantage to the writers of it. Shakespeare indeed chose excellent subjects—the world could afford no better than Macbeth, or Romeo and Juliet, or Othello: he had no theory respecting the necessity of choosing subjects of present import, or the paramount interest attaching to allegories of the state of one's own mind; like all great poets, he knew well what constituted a poetical action; like them, wherever he found such an action, he took it; like them, too, he found his best in past times. But to these general characteristics of all great poets he added a special one of his own; a gift, namely, of happy, abundant, and ingenious expression, eminent and unrivalled: so eminent as irresistibly to strike the attention first in him, and even to throw into comparative shade his other excellences as a poet. Here has been the mischief. These other excellences were his fundamental excellences as a poet; what distinguishes the artist from the mere amateur, says Goethe, is *Architectonicè* in the highest sense; that power of execution, which creates, forms, and constitutes: not the profoundness of single thoughts, not the richness of imagery, not the abundance of illustration. But these

---

1   *"A true … poetry"* From *North British Review* 19 (August 1853).

2   *Margaret* Faust's lover in Goethe's tragedy.

attractive accessories of a poetical work being more easily seized than the spirit of the whole, and these accessories being possessed by Shakespeare in an unequalled degree, a young writer having recourse to Shakespeare as his model runs great risk of being vanquished and absorbed by them, and, in consequence, of reproducing, according to the measure of his power, these, and these alone. Of this preponderating quality of Shakespeare's genius, accordingly, almost the whole of modern English poetry has, it appears to me, felt the influence. To the exclusive attention on the part of his imitators to this it is in a great degree owing, that of the majority of modern poetical works the details alone are valuable, the composition worthless. In reading them one is perpetually reminded of that terrible sentence on a modern French poet—*Il dit tout ce qu'il veut, mais malheureusement il n'a rien à dire.*[1]

Let me give an instance of what I mean. I will take it from the works of the very chief among those who seem to have been formed in the school of Shakespeare: of one whose exquisite genius and pathetic death render him for ever interesting. I will take the poem of *Isabella, or the Pot of Basil*, by Keats. I choose this rather than the *Endymion*, because the latter work (which a modern critic has classed with the *Fairy Queen*!),[2] although undoubtedly there blows through it the breath of genius, is yet as a whole so utterly incoherent, as not strictly to merit the name of a poem at all. The poem of *Isabella*, then, is a perfect treasure-house of graceful and felicitous words and images: almost in every stanza there occurs one of those vivid and picturesque turns of expression, by which the object is made to flash upon the eye of the mind, and which thrill the reader with a sudden delight. This one short poem contains, perhaps, a greater number of happy single expressions which one could quote than all the extant tragedies of Sophocles. But the action, the story? The action in itself is an excellent one; but so feebly is it conceived by the poet, so loosely constructed, that the effect produced by it, in and for itself, is absolutely null. Let the reader, after he has finished the poem of Keats, turn to the same story in

the Decameron:[3] he will then feel how pregnant and interesting the same action has become in the hands of a great artist, who above all things delineates his object; who subordinates expression to that which it is designed to express.

I have said that the imitators of Shakespeare, fixing their attention on his wonderful gift of expression, have directed their imitation to this, neglecting his other excellences. These excellences, the fundamental excellences of poetical art, Shakespeare no doubt possessed them—possessed many of them in a splendid degree; but it may perhaps be doubted whether even he himself did not sometimes give scope to his faculty of expression to the prejudice of a higher poetical duty. For we must never forget that Shakespeare is the great poet he is from his skill in discerning and firmly conceiving an excellent action, from his power of intensely feeling a situation, of intimately associating himself with a character; not from his gift of expression, which rather even leads him astray, degenerating sometimes into a fondness for curiosity of expression, into an irritability of fancy, which seems to make it impossible for him to say a thing plainly, even when the press of the action demands the very directest language, or its level character the very simplest. Mr. Hallam,[4] than whom it is impossible to find a saner and more judicious critic, has had the courage (for at the present day it needs courage) to remark, how extremely and faultily difficult Shakespeare's language often is. It is so: you may find main scenes in some of his greatest tragedies, *King Lear* for instance, where the language is so artificial, so curiously tortured, and so difficult, that every speech has to be read two or three times before its meaning can be comprehended. This over-curiousness of expression is indeed but the excessive employment of a wonderful gift—of the power of saying a thing in a happier way than any other man; nevertheless, it is carried so far that one understands what M. Guizot[5] meant, when he said that Shakespeare appears in his language to have tried all

[3] *the Decameron* Collection of tales written in the fourteenth century by the Italian writer Boccaccio.

[4] *Mr. Hallam* Henry Hallam, author of *Introduction to the Literature of Europe* (1838–9).

[5] *M. Guizot* French historian (1787–1874). His discussion of Shakespeare is found in his *Shakespeare et son temps* (1852).

[1] *Il dit ... dire* French: "He says everything he wishes to, but unfortunately he has nothing to say."

[2] *Fairy Queen* I.e., Edmund Spenser's *The Faerie Queene*.

styles except that of simplicity. He has not the severe and scrupulous self-restraint of the ancients, partly no doubt, because he had a far less cultivated and exacting audience: he has indeed a far wider range than they had, a far richer fertility of thought; in this respect he rises above them: in his strong conception of his subject, in the genuine way in which he is penetrated with it, he resembles them, and is unlike the moderns: but in the accurate limitation of it, the conscientious rejection of superfluities, the simple and rigorous development of it from the first line of his work to the last, he falls below them, and comes nearer to the moderns. In his chief works, besides what he has of his own, he has the elementary soundness of the ancients; he has their important action and their large and broad manner: but he has not their purity of method. He is therefore a less safe model; for what he has of his own is personal, and inseparable from his own rich nature; it may be imitated and exaggerated, it cannot be learned or applied as an art; he is above all suggestive; more valuable, therefore, to young writers as men than as artists. But clearness of arrangement, rigour of development, simplicity of style—these may to a certain extent be learned: and these may, I am convinced, be learned best from the ancients, who although infinitely less suggestive than Shakespeare, are thus, to the artist, more instructive.

What then, it will be asked, are the ancients to be our sole models? the ancients with their comparatively narrow range of experience, and their widely different circumstances? Not, certainly, that which is narrow in the ancients, nor that in which we can no longer sympathize. An action like the action of the *Antigone* of Sophocles, which turns upon the conflict between the heroine's duty to her brother's corpse and that to the laws of her country, is no longer one in which it is possible that we should feel a deep interest. I am speaking too, it will be remembered, not of the best sources of intellectual stimulus for the general reader, but of the best models of instruction for the individual writer. This last may certainly learn of the ancients, better than anywhere else, three things which it is vitally important for him to know: the all-importance of the choice of a subject; the necessity of accurate construction; and the subordinate character of expression. He will learn from them how unspeakably

superior is the effect of the one moral impression left by a great action treated as a whole, to the effect produced by the most striking single thought or by the happiest image. As he penetrates into the spirit of the great classical works, as he becomes gradually aware of their intense significance, their noble simplicity, and their calm pathos, he will be convinced that it is this effect, unity and profoundness of moral impression, at which the ancient poets aimed; that it is this which constitutes the grandeur of their works, and which makes them immortal. He will desire to direct his own efforts towards producing the same effect. Above all, he will deliver himself from the jargon of modern criticism, and escape the danger of producing poetical works conceived in the spirit of the passing time, and which partake of its transitoriness.

The present age makes great claims upon us: we owe it service, it will not be satisfied without our admiration. I know not how it is, but their commerce with the ancients appears to me to produce, in those who constantly practise it, a steadying and composing effect upon their judgement, not of literary works only, but of men and events in general. They are like persons who have had a very weighty and impressive experience; they are more truly than others under the empire of facts, and more independent of the language current among those with whom they live. They wish neither to applaud nor to revile their age: they wish to know what it is, what it can give them, and whether this is what they want. What they want, they know very well; they want to educe and cultivate what is best and noblest in themselves: they know, too, that this is no easy task— χαλεπὸν as Pittacus said, χαλεπὸν ἐσθλὸν ἔμμεναι[1] —and they ask themselves sincerely whether their age and its literature can assist them in the attempt. If they are endeavouring to practise any art, they remember the plain and simple proceedings of the old artists, who attained their grand results by penetrating themselves with some noble and significant action, not by inflating themselves with a belief in the pre-eminent importance and greatness of their own times. They do not talk of their mission, nor of interpreting their age, nor of the coming poet; all this, they know, is the mere delirium of

---

[1] χαλεπὸν ἐσθλὸν ἔμμεναι Greek: It is hard to be good. Pittacus was a seventh-century BCE Greek statesman.

vanity; their business is not to praise their age, but to afford to the men who live in it the highest pleasure which they are capable of feeling. If asked to afford this by means of subjects drawn from the age itself, they ask what special fitness the present age has for supplying them: they are told that it is an era of progress, an age commissioned to carry out the great ideas of industrial development and social amelioration. They reply that with all this they can do nothing; that the elements they need for the exercise of their art are great actions, calculated powerfully and delightfully to affect what is permanent in the human soul; that so far as the present age can supply such actions, they will gladly make use of them; but that an age wanting in moral grandeur can with difficulty supply such, and an age of spiritual discomfort with difficulty be powerfully and delightfully affected by them.

A host of voices will indignantly rejoin that the present age is inferior to the past neither in moral grandeur nor in spiritual health. He who possesses the discipline I speak of will content himself with remembering the judgements passed upon the present age, in this respect, by the two men, the one of strongest head, the other of widest culture, whom it has produced; by Goethe and by Niebuhr.[1] It will be sufficient for him that he knows the opinions held by these two great men respecting the present age and its literature; and that he feels assured in his own mind that their aims and demands upon life were such as he would wish, at any rate, his own to be; and their judgement as to what is impeding and disabling such as he may safely follow. He will not, however, maintain a hostile attitude towards the false pretensions of his age; he will content himself with not being overwhelmed by them. He will esteem himself fortunate if he can succeed in banishing from his mind all feelings of contradiction, and irritation, and impatience; in order to delight himself with the contemplation of some noble action of a heroic time, and to enable others, through his representation of it, to delight in it also.

I am far indeed from making any claim, for myself, that I possess this discipline; or for the following poems, that they breathe its spirit. But I say, that in the sincere

endeavour to learn and practise, amid the bewildering confusion of our times, what is sound and true in poetical art, I seemed to myself to find the only sure guidance, the only solid footing, among the ancients. They, at any rate, knew what they wanted in art, and we do not. It is this uncertainty which is disheartening, and not hostile criticism. How often have I felt this when reading words of disparagement or of cavil: that it is the uncertainty as to what is really to be aimed at which makes our difficulty, not the dissatisfaction of the critic, who himself suffers from the same uncertainty. *Non me tua fervida terrent Dicta: Dii me terrent, et Jupiter hostis.*[2]

Two kinds of *dilettanti*, says Goethe, there are in poetry: he who neglects the indispensable mechanical part, and thinks he has done enough if he shows spirituality and feeling; and he who seeks to arrive at poetry merely by mechanism, in which he can acquire an artisan's readiness, and is without soul and matter. And he adds, that the first does most harm to art, and the last to himself. If we must be *dilettanti*: if it is impossible for us, under the circumstances amidst which we live, to think clearly, to feel nobly, and to delineate firmly: if we cannot attain to the mastery of the great artists—let us, at least, have so much respect for our art as to prefer it to ourselves: let us not bewilder our successors: let us transmit to them the practice of poetry, with its boundaries and wholesome regulative laws, under which excellent works may again, perhaps, at some future time, be produced, not yet fallen into oblivion through our neglect, not yet condemned and cancelled by the influence of their eternal enemy, Caprice.

—1853

from *The Function of Criticism at the Present Time*

Many objections have been made to a proposition which, in some remarks of mine on translating

---

[1]   *Niebuhr* German historian Barthold Georg Niebuhr (1776–1831).

[2]   *Non me ... hostis* Latin: "Your fiery words do not frighten me; the gods frighten me, as does the enmity of Jupiter." From *Aeneid* 12.894-5, in which Turnus, a warrior forsaken by the gods, responds to Aeneas, who has mocked his fear.

Homer,[1] I ventured to put forth; a proposition about criticism, and its importance at the present day. I said: "Of the literature of France and Germany, as of the intellect of Europe in general, the main effort, for now many years, has been a critical effort; the endeavour, in all branches of knowledge, theology, philosophy, history, art, science, to see the object as in itself it really is." I added, that owing to the operation in English literature of certain causes, "almost the last thing for which one would come to English literature is just that very thing which now Europe most desires—criticism"; and that the power and value of English literature was thereby impaired. More than one rejoinder declared that the importance I here assigned to criticism was excessive, and asserted the inherent superiority of the creative effort of the human spirit over its critical effort. And the other day, having been led by a Mr. Shairp's excellent notice of Wordsworth[2] to turn again to his biography, I found, in the words of this great man, whom I, for one, must always listen to with the profoundest respect, a sentence passed on the critic's business, which seems to justify every possible disparagement of it. Wordsworth says in one of his letters:

> The writers in these publications [the reviews], while they prosecute their inglorious employment, can not be supposed to be in a state of mind very favourable for being affected by the finer influences of a thing so pure as genuine poetry.

And a trustworthy reporter of his conversation quotes a more elaborate judgement to the same effect:

Wordsworth holds the critical power very low, infinitely lower than the inventive; and he said today that if the quantity of time consumed in writing critiques on the works of others were given to original composition, of whatever kind it might be, it would be much better employed; it would make a man find out sooner his own level, and it would do infinitely less mischief. A false or malicious criticism may do much injury to the minds of others, a stupid invention, either in prose or verse, is quite harmless.

It is almost too much to expect of poor human nature, that a man capable of producing some effect in one line of literature, should, for the greater good of society, voluntarily doom himself to impotence and obscurity in another. Still less is this to be expected from men addicted to the composition of the "false or malicious criticism" of which Wordsworth speaks. However, everybody would admit that a false or malicious criticism had better never been written. Everybody, too, would be willing to admit, as a general proposition, that the critical faculty is lower than the inventive. But is it true that criticism is really, in itself, a baneful and injurious employment; is it true that all time given to writing critiques on the works of others would be much better employed if it were given to original composition of whatever kind this may be? Is it true Johnson had better have gone on producing more *Irenes* instead of writing his *Lives of the Poets*;[3] nay, is it certain that Wordsworth himself was better employed in making his Ecclesiastical Sonnets than when he made his celebrated Preface,[4] so full of criticism, and criticism of the works of others? Wordsworth was himself a great critic, and it is to be sincerely regretted that he has not left us more criticism; Goethe[5] was one of the greatest of critics, and we may sincerely congratulate ourselves that he has left us so much criticism. Without wasting time over the exaggeration which Wordsworth's judgement

[1]   *in some ... Homer* In Arnold's *On Translating Homer* (1861).

[2]   [Arnold's note] I cannot help thinking that a practice, common in England during the last century, and still followed in France, of printing a notice of this kind—a notice by competent critics—to serve as an introduction to an eminent author's works, might be revived among us with advantage. To introduce all succeeding editions of Wordsworth, Mr. Shairp's notice might, it seems it me, excellently serve; it is written from the point of view of an admirer, nay, or a disciple, and that is right; but then the disciple must also be, as in this case he is, a critic, a man of letters, not, as too often happens, some relation or friend with no qualification for his task except affection for his author. [Arnold refers to J.C. Shairp's essay *Wordsworth: The Man and the Poet* (1864).]

[3]   *Johnson ... Poets* Samuel Johnson is probably most celebrated today for his biographical and critical work *Lives of the English Poets* (1779–81), while his play *Irene* (1736) has never been highly regarded.

[4]   *Preface* To Wordsworth and Coleridge's *Lyrical Ballads* (1800). His *Ecclesiastical Sonnets* is not his best known work.

[5]   *Goethe* German poet and dramatist Johann Wolfgang von Goethe (1749–1832).

on criticism clearly contains, or over an attempt to trace the causes—not difficult, I think, to be traced—which may have led Wordsworth to this exaggeration, a critic may with advantage seize an occasion for trying his own conscience, and for asking himself of what real service at any given moment the practice of criticism either is or may be made to his own mind and spirit, and to the minds and spirits of others.

The critical power is of lower rank than the creative. True; but in assenting to this proposition, one or two things are to be kept in mind. It is undeniable that the exercise of a creative power, that a free creative activity, is the highest function of man; it is proved to be so by man's finding in it his true happiness. But it is undeniable, also, that men may have the sense of exercising this free creative activity in other ways than in producing great words of literature or art; if it were not so, all but a very few men would be shut out from the true happiness of all men. They may have it in well-doing, they may have it in learning, they may have it even in criticising. This is one thing to be kept in mind. Another is, that the exercise of the creative power in the production of great works of literature or art, however high this exercise of it may rank, is not at all epochs and under all conditions possible; and that therefore labour may be vainly spent in attempting it, which might with more fruit be used in preparing for it, in rendering it possible. This creative power works with elements, with materials; what if it has not those materials, those elements, ready for its use? In that case it must surely wait till they are ready. Now in literature—I will limit myself to literature, for it is about literature that the question arises—the elements with which the creative power works are ideas; the best ideas, on every matter which literature touches, current at the time. At any rate we may lay it down as certain that in modern literature no manifestation of the creative power not working with these can be very important or fruitful. And I say current at the time, not merely accessible at the time; for creative literary genius does not principally show itself in discovering new ideas; that is rather the business of the philosopher. The grand work of literary genius is a work of synthesis and exposition, not of analysis and discovery; its gift lies in the faculty of being happily inspired by a certain intellectual and spiritual atmosphere, by a certain order of ideas, when it finds itself in them; of dealing divinely with these ideas, presenting them in the most effective and attractive combinations—making beautiful works with them, in short. But it must have the atmosphere, it must find itself amidst the order of ideas, in order to work freely; and these it is not so easy to command. This is why great creative epochs in literature are so rare, this is why there is so much that is unsatisfactory in the productions of many men of real genius; because, for the creation of a masterwork of literature two powers must concur, the power of the man and the power of the moment, and the man is not enough without the moment; the creative power has, for its happy exercise, appointed elements, and those elements are not in its own control.

Nay, they are more within the control of the critical power. It is the business of the critical power, as I said in the words already quoted, "in all branches of knowledge, theology, philosophy, history, art, science, to see the object as in itself it really is." Thus it tends, at last, to make an intellectual situation of which the creative power can profitably avail itself. It tends to establish an order of ideas, if not absolutely true, yet true by comparison with that which it displaces; to make the best ideas prevail. Presently these new ideas reach society, the touch of truth is the touch of life, and there is a stir and growth everywhere; out of this stir and growth come the creative epochs of literature.

Or, to narrow our range, and quit these considerations of the general march of genius and of society—considerations which are apt to become too abstract and impalpable—every one can see that a poet, for instance, ought to know life and the world before dealing with them in poetry; and life and the world being in modern times very complex things, the creation of a modern poet, to be worth much, implies a great critical effort behind it; else it must be a comparatively poor, barren, and short-lived affair. This is why Byron's poetry had so little endurance in it, and Goethe's so much; both Byron and Goethe had a great productive power, but Goethe's was nourished by a great critical effort providing the true materials for it, and Byron's was not; Goethe knew life and the world, the poet's necessary subjects, much more comprehensively and thoroughly than Byron. He knew a great deal more of them, and he knew them much more as they really are.

It has long seemed to me that the burst of creative activity in our literature, through the first quarter of this century, had about it in fact something premature; and that from this cause its productions are doomed, most of them, in spite of the sanguine hopes which accompanied and do still accompany them, to prove hardly more lasting than the productions of far less splendid epochs. And this prematureness comes from its having proceeded without having its proper data, without sufficient materials to work with. In other words, the English poetry of the first quarter of this century, with plenty of energy, plenty of creative force, did not know enough. This makes Byron so empty of matter, Shelley so incoherent, Wordsworth even, profound as he is, yet so wanting in completeness and variety. Wordsworth cared little for books, and disparaged Goethe. I admire Wordsworth, as he is, so much that I cannot wish him different; and it is vain, no doubt, to imagine such a man different from what he is, to suppose that he could have been different. But surely the one thing wanting to make Wordsworth an even greater poet than he is—his thought richer, and his influence of wider application—was that he should have read more books, among them, no doubt, those of that Goethe whom he disparaged without reading him.

But to speak of books and reading may easily lead to a misunderstanding here. It was not really books and reading that lacked to our poetry at this epoch; Shelley had plenty of reading, Coleridge had immense reading. Pindar[1] and Sophocles—as we all say so glibly, and often with so little discernment of the real import of what we are saying—had not many books; Shakespeare was no deep reader. True; but in the Greece of Pindar and Sophocles, in the England of Shakespeare, the poet lived in a current of ideas in the highest degree animating and nourishing to the creative power; society was, in the fullest measure, permeated by fresh thought, intelligent and alive. And this state of things is the true basis for the creative power's exercise, in this it finds its data, its materials, truly ready for its hand; all the books and reading in the world are only valuable as they are helps to this. Even when this does not actually exist, books and reading may enable a man to construct a kind of

semblance of it in his own mind, a world of knowledge and intelligence in which he may live and work. This is by no means an equivalent to the artist for the nationally diffused life and thought of the epochs of Sophocles or Shakespeare; but, besides that it may be a means of preparation for such epochs, it does really constitute, if many share in it, a quickening and sustaining atmosphere of great value. Such an atmosphere the many-sided learning and the long and widely combined critical effort of Germany formed for Goethe, when he lived and worked. There was no national glow of life and thought there, as in the Athens of Pericles[2] or the England of Elizabeth. That was the poet's weakness. But there was a sort of equivalent for it in the complete culture and unfettered thinking of a large body of Germans. That was his strength. In the England of the first quarter of this century there was neither a national glow of life and thought, such as we had in the age of Elizabeth, nor yet a culture and a force of learning and criticism such as were to be found in Germany. Therefore the creative power of poetry wanted, for success in the highest sense, materials and a basis; a thorough interpretation of the world was necessarily denied to it.

… The Englishman has been called a political animal, and he values what is political and practical so much that ideas easily become objects of dislike in his eyes, and thinkers "miscreants," because ideas and thinkers have rashly meddled with politics and practice. This would be all very well if the dislike and neglect confined themselves to ideas transported out of their own sphere, and meddling rashly with practice; but they are inevitably extended to ideas as such, and to the whole life of intelligence; practice is everything, a free play of the mind is nothing. The notion of the free play of the mind upon all subjects being a pleasure in itself, being an object of desire, being an essential provider of elements without which a nation's spirit, whatever compensations it may have for them, must, in the long run, die of inanition, hardly enters into an Englishman's thoughts. It is noticeable that the word *curiosity*, which

---

[1]   *Pindar* Greek lyric poet of the fifth century BCE.

[2]   *Athens of Pericles* Pericles was a leading Athenian statesman of the early fifth century BCE and was responsible for the construction of the Parthenon.

in other languages is used in a good sense, to mean, as a high and fine quality of man's nature, just this disinterested love of a free play of the mind on all subjects, for its own sake—it is noticeable, I say, that this word has in our language no sense of the kind, no sense but a rather bad and disparaging one. But criticism, real criticism, is essentially the exercise of this very quality; it obeys an instinct prompting it to try to know the best that is known and thought in the world, irrespectively of practice, politics, and everything of the kind; and to value knowledge and thought as they approach this best, without the intrusion of any other considerations whatever. This is an instinct for which there is, I think, little original sympathy in the practical English nature, and what there was of it has undergone a long benumbing period of blight and suppression in the epoch of concentration which followed the French Revolution.

But epochs of concentration cannot well endure for ever; epochs of expansion, in the due course of things, follow them. Such an epoch of expansion seems to be opening in this country. In the first place all danger of a hostile forcible pressure of foreign ideas upon our practice has long disappeared; like the traveller in the fable, therefore, we begin to wear our cloak a little more loosely.[1] Then, with a long peace, the ideas of Europe steal gradually and amicably in, and mingle, though in infinitesimally small quantities at a time, with our own notions. Then, too, in spite of all that is said about the absorbing and brutalising influence of our passionate material progress, it seems to me indisputable that this progress is likely, though not certain, to lead in the end to an apparition of intellectual life; and that man, after he has made himself perfectly comfortable and has now to determine what to do with himself next, may begin to remember that he has a mind, and that the mind may be made the source of great pleasure. I grant it is mainly the privilege of faith, at present, to discern this end to our railways, our business, and our fortune-making; but we shall see if, here as elsewhere, faith is not in the end

the true prophet. Our ease, our travelling, and our unbounded liberty to hold just as hard and securely as we please to the practice to which our notions have given birth, all tend to beget an inclination to deal a little more freely with these notions themselves, to canvass them a little, to penetrate a little into their real nature. Flutterings of curiosity, in the foreign sense of the word, appear amongst us, and it is in these that criticism must look to find its account. Criticism first; a time of true creative activity, perhaps—which, as I have said, must inevitably be preceded amongst us by a time of criticism—hereafter, when criticism has done its work.

It is of the last importance that English criticism should clearly discern what rule for its course, in order to avail itself of the field now opening to it, and to produce fruit for the future, it ought to take. The rule may be summed up in one word—*disinterestedness*.[2] And how is criticism to show disinterestedness? By keeping aloof from what is called "the practical view of things"; by resolutely following the law of its own nature, which is to be a free play of the mind on all subjects which it touches. By steadily refusing to lend itself to any of those ulterior, political, practical considerations about ideas, which plenty of people will be sure to attach to them, which perhaps ought often to be attached to them, which in this country at any rate are certain to be attached to them quite sufficiently, but which criticism has really nothing to do with. Its business is, as I have said, simply to know the best that is known and thought in the world, and by in its turn making this known, to create a current of true and fresh ideas. Its business is to do this with inflexible honesty, with due ability; but its business is to do no more, and to leave alone all questions of practical consequences and applications, questions which will never fail to have due prominence given to them. Else criticism, besides being really false to its own nature, merely continues in the old rut which it has hitherto followed in this country, and will certainly miss the chance now given to it. For what is at present the bane of criticism in this country? It is that practical considerations cling to it and stifle it. It subserves interests not its own. Our organs of criticism are organs of men and parties having practical ends to serve, and

---

[1] *like the … loosely* In one of Aesop's fables, the wind and the sun compete to see who is more powerful, betting on which of them can cause a traveler to take his cloak off first. The wind attempts to use force, but the fierce gusts only cause the traveler to clutch his cloak more tightly. When the sun shines on him, however, the traveler is persuaded to take off his cloak.

[2] *disinterestedness* I.e., objectivity.

with them those practical ends are the first thing and the play of the mind the second; so much play of mind as is compatible with the prosecution of those practical ends is all that is wanted. An organ like the *Revue des Deux Mondes*,[1] having for its main function to understand and utter the best that is known and thought in the world, existing, it may be said, as just an organ for a free play of the mind, we have not. But we have the *Edinburgh Review*, existing as an organ of the old Whigs, and for as much play of the mind as may suit its being that; we have the *Quarterly Review*, existing as an organ of the Tories, and for as much play of mind as may suit its being that; we have the *British Quarterly Review*, existing as an organ of the political Dissenters, and for as much play of mind as may suit its being that; we have *The Times*, existing as an organ of the common, satisfied, well-to-do Englishman, and for as much play of mind as may suit its being that. And so on through all the various fractions, political and religious, of our society; every fraction has, as such, its organ of criticism, but the notion of combining all fractions in the common pleasure of a free disinterested play of mind meets with no favour. Directly this play of mind wants to have more scope, and to forget the pressure of practical considerations a little, it is checked, it is made to feel the chain. We saw this the other day in the extinction, so much to be regretted, of the *Home and Foreign Review*.[2] Perhaps in no organ of criticism in this country was there so much knowledge, so much play of mind; but these could not save it. The *Dublin Review* subordinates play of mind to the practical business of English and Irish Catholicism, and lives. It must needs be that men should act in sects and parties, that each of these sects and parties should have its organ, and should make this organ subserve the interests of its action; but it would be well, too, that there should be a criticism, not the minister of these interests, not their enemy, but absolutely and entirely independent of them. No other criticism will ever attain any real authority or make any real way towards its end—the creating a current of true and fresh ideas.

It is because criticism has so little kept in the pure intellectual sphere, has so little detached itself from practice, has been so directly polemical and controversial, that it has so ill accomplished, in this country, its best spiritual work; which is to keep man from a self-satisfaction which is retarding and vulgarizing, to lead him towards perfection, by making his mind dwell upon what is excellent in itself, and the absolute beauty and fitness of things. A polemical practical criticism makes men blind even to the ideal imperfection of their practice, makes them willingly assert its ideal perfection, in order the better to secure it against attack; and clearly this is narrowing and baneful for them. If they were reassured on the practical side, speculative considerations of ideal perfection they might be brought to entertain, and their spiritual horizon would thus gradually widen. Sir Charles Adderley[3] says to the Warwickshire farmers—

Talk of the improvement of breed! Why, the race we ourselves represent, the men and women, the old Anglo-Saxon race, are the best breed in the whole world...The absence of a too enervating climate, too unclouded skies, and a too luxurious nature, has produced so vigorous a race of people, and has rendered us so superior to all the world.

Mr. Roebuck says to the Sheffield cutlers—

I look around me and ask what is the state of England? Is not property safe? Is not every man able to say what he likes? Can you not walk from one end of England to the other in perfect security? I ask you whether, the world over or in past history, there in anything like it? Nothing. I pray that our unrivaled happiness may last.

Now obviously there is a peril for poor human nature in words and thoughts of such exuberant self-satisfaction, until we find ourselves safe in the streets of the Celestial City.

Das wenige verschwindet leicht dem Blicke

1   *Revue ... Mondes*   International magazine founded in Paris in 1829.

2   *Home ... Review*   Liberal, predominantly Catholic periodical (1862–64).

3   *Sir Charles Adderley*   Conservative member of Parliament and landowner (1814–1905).

Der vorwärts sieht, wie viel noch übrig bleibt[1]—

says Goethe; "the little that is done seems nothing when we look forward and see how much we have yet to do." Clearly this is a better line of reflection for weak humanity, so long as it remains on this earthly field of labour and trial.

But neither Sir Charles Adderley nor Mr. Roebuck is by nature inaccessible to considerations of this sort. They only lose sight of them owing to the controversial life we all lead, and the practical from which all speculation takes with us. They have in view opponents whose aim is not ideal, but practical; and in their zeal to uphold their own practice against these innovators, they go so far as even to attribute to this practice an ideal perfection. Somebody has been wanting to introduce a six-pound franchise, or to abolish church-rates, or to collect agricultural statistics by force, or to diminish local self-government. How natural, in reply to such proposals, very likely improper or ill-timed, to go a little beyond the mark and to say stoutly, "such a race of people as we stand, so superior to all the world! The Old Anglo-Saxon race, the best breed in the whole world! I pray that our unrivaled happiness may last! I ask you whether, the world over or in past history, there is anything like it?" And so long as criticism answers this dithyramb by insisting that the old Anglo-Saxon race would be still more superior to all others if it had no church-rates,[2] or that our unrivalled happiness would last yet longer with a six-pound franchise, so long will the strain, "The best breed in the whole world!" swell louder and louder, everything ideal and refining will be lost out of sight, and both the assailed and their critics will remain in a sphere, to say the truth, perfectly unvital, a sphere in which spiritual progression is impossible. But let criticism leave church-rates and the franchise alone, and in the most candid spirit, without a single lurking thought of practical innovation, confront with our dithyramb this paragraph on which I stumbled in a newspaper immediately after reading

Mr. Roebuck:

> A shocking child murder has just been committed at Nottingham. A girl named Wragg left the workhouse there on Saturday morning with her young illegitimate child. The child was soon afterwards found dead on Mapperly Hills, having been strangled. Wragg is in custody.

Nothing but that; but, in juxtaposition with the absolute eulogies of Sir Charles Adderley and Mr. Roebuck, how eloquent, how suggestive are those few lines! "Our old Anglo-Saxon breed, the best in the whole world!"—how much that is harsh and ill-favoured there is in this best! *Wragg*! If we are to talk of ideal perfection of "the best in the whole world," has any one reflected what a touch of grossness in our race, what an original shortcoming in the more delicate spiritual perceptions, is shown by the natural growth amongst us of such hideous names—Higginbottom, Stiggins, Bugg! In Ionia and Attica they were luckier in this respect than "the best race in the world"; by the Ilissus[3] there was no Wragg, poor thing! And "our unrivaled happiness"—what an element of grimness, bareness, and hideousness mixes with it and blurs it; the workhouse, the dismal Mapperly Hills[4]—how dismal those who have seen them will remember—the gloom, the smoke, the cold, the strangled illegitimate child! "I ask you whether, the world over or in past history, there is anything like it?" Perhaps not, one is inclined to answer; but at any rate, in that case, the world is very much to be pitied. And the final touch—short, bleak, and inhuman: *Wragg is in custody.* The sex lost in the confusion of our unrivalled happiness; or (shall I say?) the superfluous Christian name lopped off by the straightforward vigour of our old Anglo-Saxon breed! There is profit for the spirit in such contrasts as this; criticism serves the cause of perfection by establishing them. By eluding sterile conflict, by refusing to remain in the sphere where alone narrow and relative conceptions have any worth and validity, criticism may diminish its momentary importance, but only in this

---

[1]   *Das wenige … bleibt* Goethe's *Iphigenie auf Tauris* 1.291–92.

[2]   *six-pound franchise* Proposal to extend voting rights to anyone whose property was worth six pounds or more annual rent—a radical idea at the time; *church-rates* Taxes paid to support the Church of England.

[3]   *Ilisus* River in Attica.

[4]   *Mapperly Hills* Located near the coal-mining, industrial area of Nottingham.

way has it a chance of gaining admittance for those wider and more perfect conceptions to which all its duty is really owed. Mr. Roebuck will have a poor opinion of an adversary who replies to his defiant songs of triumph only by murmuring under his breath, *Wragg is in custody*; but in no other way will these songs of triumph be induced gradually to moderate themselves, to get rid of what in them is excessive and offensive, and to fall into a softer and truer key.

It will be said that it is a very subtle and indirect action which I am thus prescribing for criticism, and that, by embracing in this manner the Indian virtue of detachment and abandoning the sphere of practical life, it condemns itself to a slow and obscure work. Slow and obscure it may be, but it is the only proper work of criticism. The mass of mankind will never have any ardent zeal for seeing things as they are; very inadequate ideas will always satisfy them. On these inadequate ideas reposes, and must repose, the general practice of the world. That is as much as saying that whoever sets himself to see things as they are will find himself one of a very small circle; but it is only by this small circle resolutely doing its own work that adequate ideas will ever get current at all. The rush and roar of practical life will always have a dizzying and attracting effect upon the most collected spectator, and tend to draw him into its vortex; most of all will this be the case where that life is so powerful as it is in England. But it is only by remaining collected, and refusing to lend himself to the point of view of the practical man, that the critic can do the practical man any service; and it is only by the greatest sincerity in pursuing his own course, and by at last convincing even the practical man of his sincerity, that he can escape misunderstandings which perpetually threaten him.

For the practical man is not apt for fine distinctions, and yet in these distinctions truth and the highest culture greatly find their account. But it is not easy to lead a practical man—unless you reassure him as to your practical intentions, you have no chance of leading him—to see a thing which he has always been used to look at from one side only, which he greatly values, and which, looked at from that side, quite deserves, perhaps, all the prizing and admiring which he bestows upon it—that this thing, looked at from another side, may

appear much less beneficent and beautiful, and yet retain all its claims to our practical allegiance. Where shall we find language innocent enough, how shall we make the spotless purity of our intentions evident enough, to enable us to say to the political Englishman that the British Constitution itself, which, seen from the practical side, looks such a magnificent organ of progress and virtue, seen from the speculative side—with its compromises, its love of facts, its horror of theory, its studied avoidance of clear thoughts—that, seen from this side, our august Constitution sometimes looks—forgive me, shade of Lord Somers![1]—a colossal machine for the manufacture of Philistines?[2] How is Cobbett[3] to say this and not be misunderstood, blackened as he is with the smoke of a lifelong conflict in the field of political practice? How is Mr. Carlyle to say it and not be misunderstood, after his furious raid into this field with his Latter-day Pamphlets?[4] How is Mr. Ruskin, after his pugnacious political economy?[5] I say, the critic must keep out of the region of immediate practice in the political, social, humanitarian sphere, if he wants to make a beginning for that more free speculative treatment of things, which may perhaps one day make its benefits felt even in this sphere, but in a natural and thence irresistible manner. ...

If I have insisted so much on the course which criticism must take where politics and religion are concerned, it is because, where these burning matters are in question, it is most likely to go astray. I have wished, above all, to insist on the attitude which criticism should adopt towards things in general; on its right tone and temper of mind. But then comes another question as to the subject-matter which literary criticism should most

[1] *Lord Somers* Statesman who presided over the creation of the Declaration of Rights (1689).

[2] *Philistines* Members of the Biblical tribe that fought against the Israelites. Here Arnold uses the term humorously to denote the unenlightened middle classes; "the enemy."

[3] *Cobbett* William Cobbett (1762–1835), farmer and radical political writer.

[4] *Latter-day Pamphlets* Satirical pamphlets, published in 1850, in which Thomas Carlyle expressed vehement anti-democratic views.

[5] *Mr. Ruskin ... economy* In his *Unto the Last* (1862), John Ruskin moved away from art criticism and attacked laissez-faire economics.

seek. Here, in general, its course is determined for it by the idea which is the law of its being; the idea of a disinterested endeavour to learn and propagate the best that is known and thought in the world, and thus to establish a current of fresh and true ideas. By the very nature of things, as England is not all the world, much of the best that is known and thought in the world cannot be of English growth, must be foreign; by the nature of things, again, it is just this that we are least likely to know, while English thought is streaming in upon us from all sides, and takes excellent care that we shall not be ignorant of its existence. The English critic of literature, therefore, must dwell much on foreign thought, and with particular heed on any part of it, which, while significant and fruitful in itself, is for any reason specially likely to escape him. Again, judging is often spoken of as the critic's one business, and so in some sense it is; but the judgement which almost insensibly forms itself in a fair and clear mind, along with fresh knowledge, is the valuable one; and thus knowledge, and ever fresh knowledge, must be the critic's great concern for himself. And it is by communicating fresh knowledge, and letting his own judgement pass along with it—but insensibly, and in the second place, not the first, as a sort of companion and clue, not as an abstract lawgiver—that the critic will generally do most good to his readers. Sometimes, no doubt, for the sake of establishing an author's place in literature, and his relation to a central standard (and if this is not done, how are we to get at our best in the world?) criticism may have to deal with a subject-matter so familiar that fresh knowledge is out of the question, and then it must be all judgement; an enunciation and detailed application of principles. Here the great safeguard is never to let oneself become abstract, always to retain an intimate and lively consciousness of the truth of what one is saying, and, the moment this fails us, to be sure that something is wrong. Still, under all circumstances, this mere judgement and application of principles is, in itself, not the most satisfactory work to the critic; like mathematics, it is tautological, and cannot well give us, like fresh learning, the sense of creative activity.

But stop, someone will say; all this talk is of no practical use to us whatever; this criticism of yours is not what we have in our minds when we speak of criticism; when we speak of critics and criticism, we mean critics and criticism of the current English literature of the day; when you offer to tell criticism of its function, it is to this criticism that we expect you to address yourself. I am sorry for it, for I am afraid I must disappoint these expectations. I am bound by my own definition of criticism: a disinterested endeavour to learn and propagate the best that is known and thought in the world. How much of current English literature comes into this "best that is known and thought in the world"? Not very much, I fear; certainly less, at this moment, than of the current literature of France or Germany. Well, then, am I to alter my definition of criticism, in order to meet the requirements of a number of practising English critics, who, after all, are free in their choice of a business? That would be making criticism lend itself just to one of those alien practical considerations, which, I have said, are so fatal to it. One may say, indeed, to those who have to deal with the mass—so much better disregarded—of current English literature, that they may at all events endeavour, in dealing with this, to try it, so far as they can, by the standard of the best that is known and thought in the world; one may say, that to get anywhere near this standard, every critic should try and possess one great literature, at least, besides his own; and the more unlike his own, the better. But, after all, the criticism I am really concerned with—the criticism which alone can much help us for the future, the criticism which, throughout Europe, is at the present day meant, when so much stress is laid on the importance of criticism and the critical spirit—is a criticism which regards Europe as being, for intellectual and spiritual purposes, one great confederation, bound to a joint action and working to a common result; and whose members have, for their proper outfit, a knowledge of Greek, Roman, and Eastern antiquity, and of one another. Special, local, and temporary advantages being put out of account, that modern nation will in the intellectual and spiritual sphere make most progress, which most thoroughly carries out this programme. And what is that but saying that we too, all of us, as individuals, the more thoroughly we carry it out, shall make the more progress?

There is so much inviting us!—what are we to take? what will nourish us in growth towards perfection? That is the question which, with the immense field of life and of literature lying before him, the critic has to answer; for himself first, and afterwards for others. In this idea of the critic's business the essays brought together in the following pages have had their origin; in this idea, widely different as are their subjects, they have, perhaps, their unity.

I conclude with what I said at the beginning: to have the sense of creative activity is the great happiness and the great proof of being alive, and it is not denied to criticism to have it; but then criticism must be sincere, simple, flexible, ardent, ever widening its knowledge. Then it may have, in no contemptible measure, a joyful sense of creative activity; a sense which a man of insight and conscience will prefer to what he might derive from a poor, starved, fragmentary, inadequate creation. And at some epochs no other creation is possible.

Still, in full measure, the sense of creative activity belongs only to genuine creation; in literature we must never forget that. But what true man of letters ever can forget it? It is no such common matter for a gifted nature to come into possession of a current of true and living ideas, and to produce amidst the inspiration of them, that we are likely to underrate it. The epochs of Aeschylus and Shakespeare make us feel their pre-eminence. In an epoch like those is, no doubt, the true life of literature; there is the promised land, towards which criticism can only beckon. That promised land it will not be ours to enter, and we shall die in the wilderness: but to have desired to enter it, to have saluted it from afar, is already, perhaps, the best distinction among contemporaries; it will certainly be the best title to esteem with posterity.

—1864

from *Culture and Anarchy*[1]

from CHAPTER I: SWEETNESS AND LIGHT

The disparagers of culture make its motive curiosity; sometimes, indeed, they make its motive mere exclusiveness and vanity. The culture which is supposed to plume itself on a smattering of Greek and Latin is a culture which is begotten by nothing so intellectual as curiosity; it is valued either out of sheer vanity and ignorance or else as an engine of social and class distinction, separating its holder, like a badge or title, from other people who have not got it. No serious man would call this *culture*, or attach any value to it, as culture, at all. To find the real ground for the very different estimate which serious people will set upon culture, we must find some motive for culture in the terms of which may lie a real ambiguity; and such a motive the word *curiosity* gives us.

I have before now pointed out that we English do not, like the foreigners, use this word in a good sense as well as in a bad sense. With us the word is always used in a somewhat disapproving sense. A liberal and intelligent eagerness about the things of the mind may be meant by a foreigner when he speaks of curiosity, but with us the word always conveys a certain notion of frivolous and unedifying activity. In the *Quarterly Review*, some little time ago, was an estimate of the celebrated French critic, M. Sainte-Beuve,[2] and a very inadequate estimate it in my judgement was. And its inadequacy consisted chiefly in this: that in our English way it left out of sight the double sense really involved

---

[1] *Culture and Anarchy* This work grew out of Arnold's last Oxford lecture, in 1869, and responds to the political climate surrounding the passage of the Second Reform Bill in 1867. Arnold feared that the individualism, or self-serving attitude, that seemed to fuel much of laissez-faire capitalism would lead to a state of anarchy—a state in which no culture could flourish. "Sweetness and light" is taken from a fable in Jonathan Swift's *The Battle of the Books* (1704). In this fable, the bee (who represents ancient culture) travels far to fill its hive with honey and wax (which is used to make candles). The bee thus provides "the two noblest things, which are sweetness and light," while the spider (representing modern culture) stays at home and forms its own web, producing "nothing at all but flybane and cobweb."

[2] *M. Saint-Beuve* French critic Augustine Saint-Beuve (1804–69).

in the word *curiosity*, thinking enough was said to stamp M. Sainte-Beuve with blame if it was said that he was impelled in his operations as a critic by curiosity, and omitting either to perceive that M. Sainte-Beuve himself, and many other people with him, would consider that this was praiseworthy and not blameworthy, or to point out why it ought really to be accounted worthy of blame and not of praise. For as there is a curiosity about intellectual matters which is futile, and merely a disease, so there is certainly a curiosity—a desire after the things of the mind simply for their own sakes and for the pleasure of seeing them as they are—which is, in an intelligent being, natural and laudable. Nay, and the very desire to see things as they are implies a balance and regulation of mind which is not often attained without fruitful effort, and which is the very opposite of the blind and diseased impulse of mind which is what we mean to blame when we blame curiosity. Montesquieu[1] says: "The first motive which ought to impel us to study is the desire to augment the excellence of our nature, and to render an intelligent being yet more intelligent." This is the true ground to assign for the genuine scientific passion, however manifested, and for culture, viewed simply as a fruit of this passion; and it is a worthy ground, even though we let the term *curiosity* stand to describe it.

But there is of culture another view, in which not solely the scientific passion, the sheer desire to see things as they are, natural and proper in an intelligent being, appears as the ground of it. There is a view in which all the love of our neighbour, the impulses towards action, help, and beneficence, the desire for removing human error, clearing human confusion, and diminishing human misery, the noble aspiration to leave the world better and happier than we found it—motives eminently such as are called social—come in as part of the grounds of culture, and the main and pre-eminent part. Culture is then properly described not as having its origin in curiosity, but as having its origin in the love of perfection; it is *a study of perfection*. It moves by the force, not merely or primarily of the scientific passion for pure knowledge, but also of the moral and social passion for doing good. As, in the first view of it, we took for its worthy motto Montesquieu's words: "To

render an intelligent being yet more intelligent!" so, in the second view of it, there is no better motto which it can have than these words of Bishop Wilson:[2] "To make reason and the will of God prevail!"...

Nothing is more common than for people to confound the inward peace and satisfaction which follows the subduing of the obvious faults of our animality with what I may call absolute inward peace and satisfaction—the peace and satisfaction which are reached as we draw near to complete spiritual perfection, and not merely to moral perfection, or rather to relative moral perfection. No people in the world have done more and struggled more to attain this relative moral perfection than our English race has. For no people in the world has the command to *resist the devil, to overcome the wicked one*, in the nearest and most obvious sense of those words, had such a pressing force and reality. And we have had our reward, not only in the great worldly prosperity which our obedience to this command has brought us, but also, and far more, in great inward peace and satisfaction. But to me few things are more pathetic than to see people, on the strength of the inward peace and satisfaction which their rudimentary efforts towards perfection have brought them, employ, concerning their incomplete perfection and the religious organisations within which they have found it, language which properly applies only to complete perfection, and is a far-off echo of the human soul's prophecy of it. Religion itself, I need hardly say, supplies them in abundance with this grand language. And very freely do they use it; yet it is really the severest possible criticism of such an incomplete perfection as alone we have yet reached through our religious organisations.

The impulse of the English race towards moral development and self-conquest has nowhere so powerfully manifested itself as in Puritanism. Nowhere has Puritanism found so adequate an expression as in the religious organisation of the Independents.[3] The modern Independents have a newspaper, the *Nonconformist*, written with great sincerity and ability. The motto, the standard, the profession of faith which

---

[1]   *Montesquieu* French political philosopher (1689–1755).

[2]   *Bishop Wilson* Church of England clergyman (1601–53) whose *Maxims* Arnold admired.

[3]   *Independents* Members of a seventeenth-century Puritan sect.

this organ of theirs carries aloft, is: "The Dissidence of Dissent and the Protestantism of the Protestant religion." There is sweetness and light, and an ideal of complete harmonious human perfection! One need not go to culture and poetry to find language to judge it. Religion, with its instinct for perfection, supplies language to judge it, language, too, which is in our mouths every day. "Finally, be of one mind, united in feeling," says St. Peter.[1] There is an ideal which judges the Puritan ideal: "The Dissidence of Dissent and the Protestantism of the Protestant religion!" And religious organisations like this are what people believe in, rest in, would give their lives for! Such, I say, is the wonderful virtue of even the beginnings of perfection, of having conquered even the plain faults of our animality, that the religious organisation which has helped us to do it can seem to us something precious, salutary, and to be propagated, even when it wears such a brand of imperfection on its forehead as this. And men have got such a habit of giving to the language of religion a special application, of making it a mere jargon, that for the condemnation which religion itself passes on the shortcomings of their religious organisations they have no ear; they are sure to cheat themselves and to explain this condemnation away. They can only be reached by the criticism which culture, like poetry, speaking a language not to be sophisticated, and resolutely testing these organisations by the ideal of a human perfection complete on all sides, applies to them.

But men of culture and poetry, it will be said, are again and again failing, and failing conspicuously, in the necessary first stage to a harmonious perfection, in the subduing of the great obvious faults of our animality, which it is the glory of these religious organisations to have helped us to subdue. True, they do often so fail. They have often been without the virtues as well as the faults of the Puritan; it has been one of their dangers that they so felt the Puritan's faults that they too much neglected the practice of his virtues. I will not, however, exculpate them at the Puritan's expense. They have often failed in morality, and morality is indispensable. And they have been punished for their failure, as the Puritan has been rewarded for his performance. They have been punished wherein they erred; but their ideal

of beauty, of sweetness and light, and a human nature complete on all its sides, remains the true ideal of perfection still; just as the Puritan's ideal of perfection remains narrow and inadequate, although for what he did well he has been richly rewarded. Notwithstanding the mighty results of the Pilgrim Fathers' voyage, they and their standard of perfection are rightly judged when we figure to ourselves Shakespeare or Virgil—souls in whom sweetness and light, and all that in human nature is most humane, were eminent—accompanying them on their voyage, and think what intolerable company Shakespeare and Virgil would have found them! In the same way let us judge the religious organisations which we see all around us. Do not let us deny the good and the happiness which they have accomplished; but do not let us fail to see clearly that their idea of human perfection is narrow and inadequate, and that the Dissidence of Dissent and the Protestantism of the Protestant religion will never bring humanity to its true goal. As I said with regard to wealth: Let us look at the life of those who live in and for it—so I say with regard to the religious organisations. Look at the life imaged in such a newspaper as the *Nonconformist*—a life of jealousy of the Establishment,[2] disputes, tea-meetings, openings of chapels, sermons; and then think of it as an ideal of a human life completing itself on all sides, and aspiring with all its organs after sweetness, light, and perfection!

Another newspaper, representing, like the *Nonconformist*, one of the religious organisations of this country, was a short time ago giving an account of the crowd at Epsom on the Derby day,[3] and of all the vice and hideousness which was to be seen in that crowd; and then the writer turned suddenly round upon Professor Huxley,[4] and asked him how he proposed to cure all this vice and hideousness without religion. I confess I felt disposed to ask the asker this question: and how do you propose to cure it with such a religion as yours? How is the ideal of a life so unlovely, so

1   *Finally ... Peter*   From 1 Peter 3.8.

2   *Establishment*   I.e., the established Church, the Church of England.

3   *Epsom ... day*   The Derby Stakes, a thoroughbred horse race, is held every June in Epsom, Surrey.

4   *Professor Huxley*   Thomas Huxley (1825–95), biologist, educator, and vocal supporter of the theory of evolution.

unattractive, so incomplete, so narrow, so far removed from a true and satisfying ideal of human perfection, as is the life of your religious organisation as you yourself reflect it, to conquer and transform all this vice and hideousness? Indeed, the strongest plea for the study of perfection as pursued by culture, the clearest proof of the actual inadequacy of the idea of perfection held by the religious organisations—expressing, as I have said, the most widespread effort which the human race has yet made after perfection—is to be found in the state of our life and society with these in possession of it, and having been in possession of it I know not how many hundred years. We are all of us included in some religious organisation or other; we all call ourselves, in the sublime and aspiring language of religion which I have before noticed, children of God. Children of God—it is an immense pretension!—and how are we to justify it? By the works which we do, and the words which we speak. And the work which we collective children of God do, our grand centre of life, our city which we have builded for us to dwell in, is London! London, with its unutterable external hideousness, and with its internal canker of *publice egestas, privatim opulentia*—to use the words which Sallust puts into Cato's mouth about Rome[1]—unequalled in the world! The word, again, which we children of God speak, the voice which most hits our collective thought, the newspaper with the largest circulation in England, nay, with the largest circulation in the whole world, is the *Daily Telegraph*! I say that when our religious organisations—which I admit to express the most considerable effort after perfection that our race has yet made—land us in no better result than this, it is high time to examine carefully their idea of perfection, to see whether it does not leave out of account sides and forces of human nature which we might turn to great use; whether it would not be more operative if it were more complete. And I say that English reliance on our religious organisations and on their ideas of human perfection just as they stand, is like our reliance on freedom, on muscular Christianity, on population, on coal, on wealth—mere belief in machinery, and unfruitful; and that it is wholesomely counteracted by culture, bent on seeing things as they are, and on drawing the human race onwards to a more complete, a harmonious perfection.

Culture, however, shows its single-minded love of perfection, its desire simply to make reason and the will of God prevail, its freedom from fanaticism, by its attitude towards all this machinery, even while it insists that it is machinery. Fanatics, seeing the mischief men do themselves by their blind belief in some machinery or other—whether it is wealth and industrialism, or whether it is the cultivation of bodily strength and activity, or whether it is a political organisation—or whether it is a religious organisation—oppose with might and main the tendency to this or that political and religious organisation, or to games and athletic exercises, or to wealth and industrialism, and try violently to stop it. But the flexibility which sweetness and light give, and which is one of the rewards of culture pursued in good faith, enables a man to see that a tendency may be necessary, and even, as a preparation for something in the future, salutary, and yet that the generations or individuals who obey this tendency are sacrificed to it, that they fall short of the hope of perfection by following it; and that its mischiefs are to be criticised, lest it should take too firm a hold and last after it has served its purpose. . . .

—1868

---

[1] *publice ... opulentia* Latin: public poverty; private opulence; *Sallust* First-century BCE Roman historian; *Cato* Roman statesman Cato the Younger (95–46 BCE).

WILKIE COLLINS
1824 — 1889

Wilkie Collins is no longer the household name that he was a century ago, but the two books for which he is best known have never gone out of print. *The Woman in White* (1860) and *The Moonstone* (1868), often referred to as the first detective novels written in English, are also among the best. Collins was one of the most popular and highly-paid authors of his day, publishing many of his novels in serial form in widely circulating magazines such as *Household Words* and *All the Year Round* (both under the management of Charles Dickens). Collins's style in fiction was to "make 'em laugh, make 'em cry, make 'em wait" (as he put it himself in offering advice to other novelists), and for much of his career he had the public lining up for new installments, eager to find out how the story of his latest "sensation fiction" would be resolved. Collins wrote—and lived his life—at much the same pace as that of his plots. In all, he found time to write some 25 novels, 15 plays, and 50 short stories.

WILKIE COLLINS.

Readers today have become fascinated almost as much by the man and his unconventional lifestyle as Victorian readers were by his labyrinthine plots and sympathetic heroines. Collins was born in London in 1824, the first son of Harriet Geddes and the well-known landscape painter William Collins, a member of the Royal Academy. He was educated privately, but his schooling was interrupted by extended travels to the continent with his family, where he gained an appreciation of more liberal attitudes to religion, the arts, food, and sex; he often regaled his friends with tales of his teenage sexual adventures. Collins worked for five years in the tea trade for an enterprise that he referred to as a "prison"; he fared no better in law, which he studied but never practiced. As soon as he began writing, however, he found his niche and thereafter maintained a feverish writing pace, publishing first a biography of his 0father (after Collins Sr.'s death in 1847) and two years later an historical novel, *Antonina: or The Fall of Rome* (1850), which was a popular success. This was closely followed by *Basil: A Story of Modern Life* (1852), Collins's first experiment with sensation fiction.

In the early 1850s Collins met Dickens and soon joined the already successful author in his theatrical ventures and eventually his magazines. (A story co-written by Dickens and Collins appears elsewhere in this volume.) Collins began writing for *Bentley's Miscellany* then edited by Dickens. From 1856 to 1862 he was a staff journalist and fiction writer for Dickens's *Household Words* and his later journal *All the Year Round*. The two writers became fast friends, taking many trips to the continent together and occasionally collaborating on plays and short stories. These years of close friendship became Collins' most creative and successful period. He was thought to be the most accomplished writer in England of "sensation fiction," a genre that entailed developing complex and frequently sensational plots around controversial contemporary issues, with sexuality and criminality often going hand in hand with striking psychological states of mind, strong and sometimes unprincipled heroines, and intriguing, if often sinister, locales. *The Moonstone* (1868), for example, was based on a spectacular murder case of the early 1860s; the novel concerns a jewel stolen from a Hindu temple and sought not only by the temple's Brahmin priests, but also by Sergeant Cuff. *The Woman in White*

(1860) also features a range of striking characters, including the exceedingly fat villain, Count Fosco, who is accompanied by canary birds and white mice, and the amazing non-heroine, Marian Halcombe, one of the first female characters in English fiction to be assigned "masculine" intelligence and even characteristics (she is also plain). The story touched a chord so resonant with the public that it spawned "Woman in White" perfume, clothing, and even a "Woman in White" waltz.

Collins's unconventional life was in many ways more sensational than his fiction. Choosing never to marry, he lived with his mistress, Caroline Graves, for three decades. Not long into their relationship, however, Collins met Martha Rudd, and a few years later he was openly living with her as well, dividing his time between the two households. Collins fathered three children with Rudd, all the while maintaining his liaison with Graves. Graves left the relationship in 1868 when she married Joseph Clow (in a ceremony that Collins attended), but a few years later she returned to live out her life with Collins.

Collins continued to write dozens of novels, short stories, and plays, but as time went on he moved away from sensation fiction, as he was becoming increasingly concerned with social injustices. Subjects of his later novels include the rights of illegitimate children in the brilliant *No Name* (1862); vivisection in *Heart and Science* (1883); and attitudes towards divorce in *The Evil Genius* (1886). His championing of social causes did not increase sales. Critics attributed his dip in popularity after 1870 to his fondness for the laudanum, a narcotic to which he became increasingly addicted because of the pain of "rheumatic gout." Other writers suggested that his talent had been damaged by the shift in subject matter. The poet Swinburne famously asked: "What brought good Wilkie's genius nigh perdition? / Some demon whispered— 'Wilkie! have a mission.'" In 1889, sensing he was nearing death, Collins gave explicit instructions to his friend Walter Besant to finish his final novel, *Blind Love* (1890). After his death that same year from a stroke, a group of friends that included Thomas Hardy appealed to St. Paul's Cathedral to have a memorial erected for Collins, but their request was refused on moral grounds.

⌘ ⌘ ⌘

The Diary of Anne Rodway [1]

March 3rd, 1840. A long letter today from Robert, which surprised and vexed and fluttered me so, that I have been sadly behindhand with my work ever since. He writes in worse spirits than last time, and absolutely declares that he is poorer even than when he went to America, and that he has made up his mind to come home to London.

How happy I should be at this news, if he only returned to me a prosperous man! As it is, though I love him dearly, I cannot look forward to meeting him again, disappointed and broken down and poorer than ever, without a feeling almost of dread for both of us. I was

twenty-six last birthday and he was thirty-three, and there seems less chance now than ever of our being married. It is all I can do to keep myself by my needle;[2] and his prospects, since he failed in the small stationery business three years ago, are worse, if possible, than mine.

Not that I mind so much for myself; all women, in all ways of life, and especially in my dress-making way, learn, I think, to be more patient than men. What I dread is Robert's despondency, and the hard struggle he will have in this cruel city to get his bread, let alone making money enough to marry me. So little as poor people want to set up in housekeeping and be happy together, it seems hard that they can't get it when they are honest and hearty, and willing to work. The clergyman said in his sermon last Sunday evening that all

1 *The Diary of Anne Rodway* First published in *The Queen of Hearts* (1859) as "Brother Owen's Story of Anne Rodway (Taken from her Diary)."

2 *by my needle* I.e., as a seamstress.

things were ordered for the best, and we are all put into the stations in life that are properest for us. I suppose he was right, being a very clever gentleman who fills the church to crowding; but I think I should have understood him better if I had not been very hungry at the time, in consequence of my own station in life being nothing but plain needlewoman.

March 4th. Mary Mallinson came down to my room to take a cup of tea with me. I read her bits of Robert's letter, to show her that, if she has her troubles, I have mine too; but I could not succeed in cheering her. She says she is born to misfortune, and that, as long back as she can remember, she has never had the least morsel of luck to be thankful for. I told her to go and look in my glass, and to say if she had nothing to be thankful for then; for Mary is a very pretty girl, and would look still prettier if she could be more cheerful and dress neater. However, my compliment did no good. She rattled her spoon impatiently in her tea-cup, and said, "If I was only as good a hand at needlework as you are, Anne, I would change faces with the ugliest girl in London." "Not you!" says I, laughing. She looked at me for a moment, and shook her head, and was out of the room before I could get up and stop her. She always runs off in that way when she is going to cry, having a kind of pride about letting other people see her in tears.

March 5th. A fright about Mary. I had not seen her all day, as she does not work at the same place where I do; and in the evening she never came down to have tea with me, or sent me word to go to her; so, just before I went to bed, I ran upstairs to say good-night. She did not answer when I knocked; and when I stepped softly in the room I saw her in bed, asleep, with her work not half done, lying about the room in the untidiest way. There was nothing remarkable in that, and I was just going away on tiptoe, when a tiny bottle and wine-glass on the chair by her bedside caught my eye. I thought she was ill and had been taking physic, and looked at the bottle. It was marked in large letters, "Laudanum—Poison."

My heart gave a jump as if it was going to fly out of me. I laid hold of her with both hands, and shook her with all my might. She was sleeping heavily, and woke slowly, as it seemed to me—but still she did wake. I tried to pull her out of bed, having heard that people ought to be always walked up and down when they have taken laudanum; but she resisted, and pushed me away violently.

"Anne!" says she, in a fright. "For gracious sake, what's come to you! Are you out of your senses?"

"O, Mary! Mary!" says I, holding up the bottle before her, "if I hadn't come in when I did—" And I laid hold of her to shake her again.

She looked puzzled at me for a moment—then smiled (the first time I had seen her do so for many a long day)—then put her arms round my neck.

"Don't be frightened about me, Anne," she says; "I am not worth it, and there is no need."

"No need!" says I, out of breath—"no need, when the bottle has got poison marked on it!"

"Poison, dear, if you take it all," says Mary, looking at me very tenderly; "and a night's rest if you only take a little."

I watched her for a moment, doubtful whether I ought to believe what she said or to alarm the house. But there was no sleepiness now in her eyes, and nothing drowsy in her voice; and she sat up in bed quite easily without anything to support her.

"You have given me a dreadful fright, Mary," says I, sitting down by her in the chair, and beginning by this time to feel rather faint after being startled so.

She jumped out of bed to get me a drop of water, and kissed me, and said how sorry she was, and how undeserving of so much interest being taken in her. At the same time, she tried to possess herself of the laudanum-bottle which I still kept cuddled up tight in my own hands.

"No," says I. "You have got into a low-spirited despairing way. I won't trust you with it."

"I am afraid I can't do without it," says Mary, in her usual quiet, hopeless voice. "What with work that I can't get through as I ought, and troubles that I can't help thinking of, sleep won't come to me unless I take a few drops out of that bottle. Don't keep it away from me, Anne; it's the only thing in the world that makes me forget myself."

"Forget yourself!" says I. "You have no right to talk in that way, at your age. There's something horrible in the notion of a girl of eighteen sleeping with a bottle of laudanum by her bedside every night. We all of us have our troubles. Haven't I got mine?"

"You can do twice the work I can, twice as well as me," says Mary. "You are never scolded and rated[1] at for awkwardness with your needle, and I always am. You can pay for your room every week, and I am three weeks in debt for mine."

"A little more practice," says I, "and a little more courage, and you will soon do better. You have got all your life before you——"

"I wish I was at the end of it," says she, breaking in. "I am alone in the world, and my life's no good to me."

"You ought to be ashamed of yourself for saying so," says I. "Haven't you got me for a friend? Didn't I take a fancy to you when first you left your step-mother, and came to lodge in this house? And haven't I been sisters with you ever since? Suppose you are alone in the world, am I much better off? I'm an orphan like you. I've almost as many things in pawn as you; and, if your pockets are empty, mine have only got ninepence in them, to last me for all the rest of the week."

"Your father and mother were honest people," says Mary, obstinately. "My mother ran away from home, and died in a hospital. My father was always drunk, and always beating me. My step-mother is as good as dead, for all she cares about me. My only brother is thousands of miles away in foreign parts, and never writes to me, and never helps me with a farthing. My sweetheart—"

She stopped, and the red flew into her face. I knew, if she went on that way, she would only get to the saddest part of her sad story, and give both herself and me unnecessary pain.

"*My* sweetheart is too poor to marry me, Mary," I said. "So I'm not so much to be envied even there. But let's give over disputing which is worst off. Lie down in bed, and let me tuck you up. I'll put a stitch or two into that work of yours while you go to sleep."

Instead of doing what I told her, she burst out crying (being very like a child in some of her ways), and hugged me so tight round the neck that she quite hurt me. I let her go on till she had worn herself out, and was obliged to lie down. Even then, her last few words before she dropped off to sleep were such as I was half sorry, half frightened to hear.

"I won't plague you long, Anne," she said. "I haven't

courage to go out of the world as you seem to fear I shall; but I began my life wretchedly, and wretchedly I am sentenced to end it."

It was of no use lecturing her again, for she closed her eyes.

I tucked her up as neatly as I could, and put her petticoat over her, for the bedclothes were scanty, and her hands felt cold. She looked so pretty and delicate as she fell asleep that it quite made my heart ache to see her, after such talk as we had held together. I just waited long enough to be quite sure that she was in the land of dreams, then emptied the horrible laudanum-bottle into the grate, took up her half-done work, and, going out softly, left her for that night.

March 6th. Sent off a long letter to Robert, begging and entreating him not to be so down-hearted, and not to leave America without making another effort. I told him I could bear any trial except the wretchedness of seeing him come back a helpless, broken-down man, trying uselessly to begin life again when too old for a change.

It was not till after I had posted my own letter, and read over parts of Robert's again, that the suspicion suddenly floated across me, for the first time, that he might have sailed for England immediately after writing to me. There were expressions in the letter which seemed to indicate that he had some such headlong project in his mind. And yet, surely if it were so, I ought to have noticed them at the first reading. I can only hope I am wrong in my present interpretation of much of what he has written to me—hope it earnestly for both our sakes.

This has been a doleful day for me. I have been uneasy about Robert and uneasy about Mary. My mind is haunted by those last words of hers: "I began my life wretchedly, and wretchedly I am sentenced to end it." Her usual melancholy way of talking never produced the same impression on me that I feel now. Perhaps the discovery of the laudanum-bottle is the cause of this. I would give many a hard day's work to know what to do for Mary's good. My heart warmed to her when we first met in the same lodging-house, two years ago, and, although I am not one of the over-affectionate sort myself, I feel as if I could go to the world's end to serve that girl. Yet, strange to say, if I was asked why I was so

---

[1]   *rated* Harshly reprimanded.

fond of her, I don't think I should know how to answer the question.

March 7th. I am almost ashamed to write it down, even in this journal, which no eyes but mine ever look on; yet I must honestly confess to myself that here I am, at nearly one in the morning, sitting up in a state of serious uneasiness because Mary has not yet come home.

I walked with her this morning to the place where she works, and tried to lead her into talking of the relations she has got who are still alive. My motive in doing this was to see if she dropped anything in the course of conversation which might suggest a way of helping her interests with those who are bound to give her all reasonable assistance. But the little I could get her to say to me led to nothing. Instead of answering my questions about her step-mother and her brother, she persisted at first, in the strangest way, in talking of her father, who was dead and gone, and of one Noah Truscott, who had been the worst of all the bad friends he had, and had taught him to drink and game. When I did get her to speak of her brother, she only knew that he had gone out to a place called Assam, where they grew tea. How he was doing, or whether he was there still, she did not seem to know, never having heard a word from him for years and years past.

As for her step-mother, Mary not unnaturally flew into a passion the moment I spoke of her. She keeps an eating-house at Hammersmith, and could have given Mary good employment in it; but she seems always to have hated her, and to have made her life so wretched with abuse and ill usage that she had no refuge left but to go away from home, and do her best to make a living for herself. Her husband (Mary's father) appears to have behaved badly to her, and, after his death, she took the wicked course of revenging herself on her step-daughter. I felt, after this, that it was impossible Mary could go back, and that it was the hard necessity of her position, as it is of mine, that she should struggle on to make a decent livelihood without assistance from any of her relations. I confessed as much as this to her; but I added that I would try to get her employment with the persons for whom I work, who pay higher wages, and show a little more indulgence to those under them than the people to whom she is now obliged to look for support.

I spoke much more confidently than I felt, about being able to do this, and left her, as I thought, in better spirits than usual. She promised to be back tonight to tea, at nine o'clock, and now it is nearly one in the morning, and she is not home yet. If it was any other girl I should not feel uneasy, for I should make up my mind that there was extra work to be done in a hurry, and that they were keeping her late, and I should go to bed. But Mary is so unfortunate in everything that happens to her, and her own melancholy talk about herself keeps hanging on my mind so, that I have fears on her account which would not distress me about any one else. It seems inexcusably silly to think such a thing, much more to write it down; but I have a kind of nervous dread upon me that some accident—

What does that loud knocking at the street door mean? And those voices and heavy footsteps outside? Some lodger who has lost his key, I suppose. And yet, my heart— What a coward I have become all of a sudden!

More knocking and louder voices. I must run to the door and see what it is. Oh Mary! Mary! I hope I am not going to have another fright about you, but I feel sadly like it.

March 8th.
March 9th.
March 10th.

March 11th. Oh me! all the troubles I have ever had in my life are as nothing to the trouble I am in now. For three days I have not been able to write a single line in this journal, which I have kept so regularly ever since I was a girl. For three days I have not once thought of Robert—I, who am always thinking of him at other times.

My poor, dear, unhappy Mary! the worst I feared for you on that night when I sat up alone was far below the dreadful calamity that has really happened. How can I write about it, with my eyes full of tears and my hand all of a tremble? I don't even know why I am sitting down at my desk now, unless it is habit that keeps me to my old everyday task, in spite of all the grief and fear which seem to unfit me entirely for performing it.

The people of the house were asleep and lazy on that dreadful night, and I was the first to open the door.

Never, never, could I describe in writing, or even say in plain talk, though it is so much easier, what I felt when I saw two policemen come in, carrying between them what seemed to me to be a dead girl, and that girl Mary! I caught hold of her and gave a scream that must have alarmed the whole house, for frightened people came crowding downstairs in their night-dresses. There was a dreadful confusion and noise of loud talking, but I heard nothing, and saw nothing, till I had got her into my room and laid on my bed. I stooped down, frantic-like, to kiss her, and saw an awful mark of a blow on her left temple, and felt, at the same time, a feeble flutter of her breath on my cheek. The discovery that she was not dead seemed to give me back my senses again. I told one of the policemen where the nearest doctor was to be found, and sat down by the bedside while he was gone, and bathed her poor head with cold water. She never opened her eyes, or moved, or spoke; but she breathed, and that was enough for me, because it was enough for life.

The policeman left in the room was a big, thick-voiced, pompous man, with a horrible unfeeling pleasure in hearing himself talk before an assembly of frightened, silent people. He told us how he had found her, as if he had been telling a story in a tap-room,[1] and began with saying, "I don't think the young woman was drunk."

Drunk! My Mary, who might have been a born lady for all the spirits she ever touched—drunk! I could have struck the man for uttering the word, with her ly-ing—poor suffering angel—so white, and still, and helpless before him. As it was, I gave him a look, but he was too stupid to understand it, and went droning on, saying the same thing over and over again in the same words. And yet the story of how they found her was, like all the sad stories I have ever heard told in real life, so very, very short. They had just seen her lying along on the curb-stone a few streets off, and had taken her to the station-house. There she had been searched, and one of my cards, that I give to ladies who promise me employ-ment, had been found in her pocket, and so they had brought her to our house. This was all the man really had to tell. There was nobody near her when she was found, and no evidence to show how the blow on her

temple had been inflicted.

What a time it was before the doctor came, and how dreadful to hear him say, after he had looked at her, that he was afraid all the medical men in the world could be of no use here! He could not get her to swallow any-thing, and the more he tried to bring her back to her senses, the less chance there seemed of his succeeding. He examined the blow on her temple, and said he thought she must have fallen down in a fit of some sort, and struck her head against the pavement, and so have given her brain what he was afraid was a fatal shake. I asked what was to be done if she showed any return to sense in the night. He said, "Send for me directly;" and stopped for a little while afterwards stroking her head gently with his hand, and whispering to himself, "Poor girl, so young and so pretty!" I had felt, some minutes before, as if I could have struck the policeman, and I felt now as if I could have thrown my arms round the doctor's neck and kissed him. I did put out my hand when he took up his hat, and he shook it in the friendli-est way. "Don't hope, my dear," he said, and went out.

The rest of the lodgers followed him, all silent and shocked, except the inhuman wretch who owns the house, and lives in idleness on the high rents he wrings from poor people like us.

"She's three weeks in my debt," says he, with a frown and an oath. "Where the devil is my money to come from now?" Brute! brute!

I had a long cry alone with her that seemed to ease my heart a little. She was not the least changed for the better when I had wiped away the tears and could see her clearly again. I took up her right hand, which lay nearest to me. It was tight clenched. I tried to unclasp the fingers, and succeeded after a little time. Some-thing dark fell out of the palm of her hand as I straight-ened it.

I picked the thing up, and smoothed it out, and saw that it was an end of a man's cravat.[2]

A very old, rotten, dingy strip of black silk, with thin lilac lines, all blurred and deadened with dirt, running across and across the stuff in a sort of trellis-work pattern. The small end of the cravat was hemmed in the usual way, but the other end was all jagged, as if the morsel then in my hands had been torn off violently

---

[1]   *tap-room* Bar.

[2]   *cravat* Man's scarf used as a tie.

from the rest of the stuff. A chill ran all over me as I looked at it; for that poor, stained, crumpled end of a cravat seemed to be saying to me, as though it had been in plain words, "If she dies, she has come to her death by foul means, and I am the witness of it."

I had been frightened enough before, lest she should die suddenly and quietly without my knowing it, while we were alone together; but I got into a perfect agony now for fear this last worst affliction should take me by surprise. I don't suppose five minutes passed all that woeful night through without my getting up and putting my cheek close to her mouth, to feel if the faint breaths still fluttered out of it. They came and went just the same as at first, though the fright I was in often made me fancy they were stilled for ever.

Just as the church clocks were striking four, I was startled by seeing the room door open. It was only Dusty Sal (as they call her in the house) the maid-of-all-work. She was wrapped up in the blanket off her bed; her hair was all tumbled over her face, and her eyes were heavy with sleep, as she came up to the bedside where I was sitting.

"I've two hours good before I begin to work," says she, in her hoarse, drowsy voice, "and I've come to sit up and take my turn at watching her. You lay down and get some sleep on the rug. Here's my blanket for you. I don't mind the cold—it will keep me awake."

"You are very kind—very, very kind and thoughtful, Sally," says I, "but I am too wretched in my mind to want sleep, or rest, or to do anything but wait where I am, and try and hope for the best."

"Then I'll wait, too," says Sally. "I must do something; if there's nothing to do but waiting, I'll wait."

And she sat down opposite me at the foot of the bed, and drew the blanket close round her with a shiver.

"After working so hard as you do, I'm sure you must want all the little rest you can get," says I.

"Excepting only you," says Sally, putting her heavy arm very clumsily, but very gently at the same time, round Mary's feet, and looking hard at the pale, still face on the pillow. "Excepting you, she's the only soul in this house as never swore at me, or give me a hard word that I can remember. When you made puddings on Sundays, and gave her half, she always give me a bit. The rest of 'em calls me Dusty Sal. Excepting only you, again, she

always called me Sally, as if she knowed me in a friendly way. I ain't no good here, but I ain't no harm neither; and I shall take my turn at the sitting up—that's what I shall do!"

She nestled her head down close at Mary's feet as she spoke those words, and said no more. I once or twice thought she had fallen asleep, but whenever I looked at her, her heavy eyes were always wide open. She never changed her position an inch till the church clocks stuck six; then she gave one little squeeze to Mary's feet with her arm, and shuffled out of the room without a word. A minute or two after, I heard her down below, lighting the kitchen fire just as usual.

A little later, the doctor stepped over before his breakfast time, to see if there had been any change in the night. He only shook his head when he looked at her, as if there was no hope. Having nobody else to consult that I could put trust in, I showed him the end of the cravat, and told him of the dreadful suspicion that had arisen in my mind when I found it in her hand.

"You must keep it carefully, and produce it at the inquest," he said. "I don't know though, that it is likely to lead to anything. The bit of stuff may have been lying on the pavement near her, and her hand may have unconsciously clutched it when she fell. Was she subject to fainting-fits?"

"Not more so, sir, than other young girls who are hard-worked and anxious, and weakly from poor living," I answered.

"I can't say that she may not have got that blow from a fall," the doctor went on, looking at her temple again. "I can't say that it presents any positive appearance of having been inflicted by another person. It will be important, however, to ascertain what state of health she was in last night. Have you any idea where she was yesterday evening?"

I told him where she was employed at work, and said I imagined she must have been kept there later than usual.

"I shall pass the place this morning," said the doctor, "in going my rounds among my patients, and I'll just step in and make some inquiries."

I thanked him, and we parted. Just as he was closing the door he looked in again.

"Was she your sister?" he asked.

"No, sir, only my dear friend."

He said nothing more; but I heard him sigh, as he shut the door softly. Perhaps he once had a sister of his own, and lost her? Perhaps she was like Mary in the face?

The doctor was hours gone away. I began to feel unspeakably forlorn and helpless, so much so as even to wish selfishly that Robert might really have sailed from America and might get to London in time to assist and console me.

No living creature came into the room but Sally. The first time she brought me some tea; the second and third she only looked in to see if there was any change and glanced her eye toward the bed. I had never known her so silent before; it seemed almost as if this dreadful accident had struck her dumb. I ought to have spoken to her, perhaps, but there was something in her face that daunted me and, besides, the fever of anxiety I was in began to dry up my lips as if they would never be able to shape any words again. I was still tormented by that frightful apprehension of the past night, that she would die without my knowing it—die without saying one word to clear up the awful mystery of this blow, and set the suspicions at rest forever which I still felt whenever my eyes fell on the end of the old cravat.

At last the doctor came back.

"I think you may safely clear your mind of any doubts which that bit of stuff may have given rise," he said. "She was, as you supposed, detained late by her employers, and she fainted in the work-room. They most unwisely and unkindly let her go home alone, without giving her any stimulant, as soon as she came to her senses again. Nothing more probable, under these circumstances, than that she should faint a second time on her way here. A fall on the pavement, without any friendly arm to break it, might have produced even a worse injury than the injury we see. I believe that the only ill usage to which the poor girl was exposed was the neglect she met with in the work-room."

"You speak very reasonably, I own, sir," said I, not yet quite convinced. "Still, perhaps she may—"

"My poor girl, I told you not to hope," said the doctor, interrupting me. He went to Mary, and lifted up her eyelids, and looked at her eyes while he spoke, then added: "If you still doubt how she came by that blow,

do not encourage the idea that any words of hers will ever enlighten you. She will never speak again."

"Not dead! Oh sir, don't say she's dead!"

"She is dead to pain and sorrow—dead to speech and recognition. There is more animation in the life of the feeblest insect that flies than in the life that is left in her. When you look at her now, try to think that she is in heaven. That is the best comfort I can give you, after telling the hard truth."

I did not believe him. I could not believe him. So long as she breathed at all, so long I was resolved to hope. Soon after the doctor was gone, Sally came in again, and found me listening (if I may call it so) at Mary's lips. She went to where my little hand-glass hangs against the wall, took it down, and gave it to me. "See if the breath marks it," she said.

Yes; her breath did mark it, but very faintly. Sally cleaned the glass with her apron, and gave it back to me. As she did so, she half stretched out her hand to Mary's face, but drew it in again suddenly, as if she was afraid of soiling Mary's delicate skin with her hard, horny fingers. Going out, she stopped at the foot of the bed, and scraped away a little patch of mud that was on one of Mary's shoes.

"I always used to clean 'em for her," said Sally, "to save her hands from getting blacked. May I take 'em off now, and clean 'em again?"

I nodded my head, for my heart was too heavy to speak Sally took the shoes off with a slow, awkward tenderness, and went out.

An hour or more must have passed, when, putting glass over her lips again, I saw no mark on it. I held it closer and closer. I dulled it accidentally with my own breath, and cleaned it. I held it over her again. Oh, Mary, Mary, the doctor was right! I ought to have only thought of you in heaven!

Dead, without a word, without a sign—without even a look to tell the true story of the blow that killed her! I could not call to any body, I could not cry, I could not so much as put the glass down and give her a kiss for the last time. I don't know how long I had sat there with my eyes burning, and my hands deadly cold, when Sally came in with the shoes cleaned, and carried carefully in her apron for fear of a soil touching them. At the sight of that—

I can write no more. My tears drop so fast on the paper that I can see nothing.

March 12th. She died on the afternoon of the eighth. On the morning of the ninth, I wrote, as in duty bound, to her step-mother, at Hammersmith. There was no answer. I wrote again; my letter was returned to me this morning unopened. For all that woman cares, Mary might be buried with a pauper's funeral; but this shall never be, if I pawn everything about me, down to the very gown that is on my back.

The bare thought of Mary being buried by the workhouse[1] gave me the spirit to dry my eyes, and go to the undertaker's, and tell him how I was placed. I said, if he would get me an estimate of all that would have to be paid, from first to last, for the cheapest decent funeral that could be had, I would undertake to raise the money. He gave the estimate, written in this way, like a common bill:

A walking funeral complete	£1	13	8
Vestry	0	4	4
Rector	0	4	4
Clerk	0	1	0
Sexton	0	1	0
Beadle	0	1	0
Bell	0	1	0
Six feet of ground	0	2	0
Total	£	2	8	4

If I had the heart to give any thought to it, I should be inclined to wish that the Church could afford to do without so many small charges for burying poor people, to whose friends even shillings are of consequence. But it is useless to complain; the money must be raised at once. The charitable doctor—a poor man himself, or he would not be living in our neighborhood—has subscribed ten shillings toward the expenses; and the coroner, when the inquest was over, added five more. Perhaps others may assist me. If not, I have fortunately clothes and furniture of my own to pawn. And I must set about parting with them without delay, for the funeral is to be tomorrow, the thirteenth.

The funeral—Mary's funeral! It is well that the straits and difficulties I am in keep my mind on the stretch. If I had leisure to grieve, where should I find the courage to face tomorrow?

Thank God they did not want me at the inquest. The verdict given, with the doctor, the policeman, and two persons from the place where she worked, for witnesses, was Accidental Death. The end of the cravat was produced, and the coroner said that it was certainly enough to suggest suspicion; but the jury, in the absence of any positive evidence, held to the doctor's notion that she had fainted and fallen down, and so got the blow on her temple. They reproved the people where Mary worked for letting her go home alone, without so much as a drop of brandy to support her, after she had fallen into a swoon from exhaustion before their eyes. The coroner added, on his own account, that he thought the reproof was thoroughly deserved. After that, the cravat-end was given back to me, by my own desire, the police saying that they could make no investigations with such a slight clue to guide them. They may think so, and the coroner, and doctor, and jury may think so; but, in spite of all that has passed, I am now more firmly persuaded than ever that there is some dreadful mystery in connection with that blow on my poor lost Mary's temple which has yet to be revealed, and which may come to be discovered through this very fragment of a cravat found in her hand. I cannot give any good reason for why I think so, but I know that if I had been one of the jury at the inquest, nothing should have induced me to consent to such a verdict as Accidental Death.

After I had pawned my things, and had begged a small advance of wages at the place where I work, to make up what was still wanting to pay for Mary's funeral, I thought I might have had a little quiet time to prepare myself as I best could for tomorrow. But this was not to be. When I got home, the landlord met me in the passage. He was in liquor, and more brutal and pitiless in his way of looking and speaking than ever I saw him before.

"So you're going to be fool enough to pay for her funeral, are you?" were his first words to me.

I was too weary and heart-sick to answer; I only tried to get by him to my own door.

"If you can pay for burying her," he went on, putting himself in front of me, "you can pay her lawful debts. She owes me three weeks' rent. Suppose you raise the money for that next, and hand it over to me? I'm

---

[1]   *workhouse* Institution for the unemployed poor.

not joking, I can promise you. I mean to have my rent; and, if somebody don't pay it, I'll have her body seized and sent to the workhouse!"

Between terror and disgust, I thought I should have dropped to the floor at his feet. But I determined not to let him see how he had horrified me, if I could possibly control myself. So I mustered resolution enough to answer that I did not believe the law gave him any such wicked power over the dead.

"I'll teach you what the law is!" he broke in; "you'll raise money to bury her like a born lady, when she's died in my debt, will you! And you think I'll let my rights be trampled upon like that, do you? See if I do! I give you till tonight to think about it. If I don't have the three weeks before tomorrow, dead or alive, she shall go to the workhouse!"

This time I managed to push by him, and get to my own room, and lock the door in his face. As soon as I was alone I fell into a breathless, suffocating fit of crying that seemed to be shaking me to pieces. But there was no good and no help in tears; I did my best to calm myself after a little, and tried to think who I should run to for help and protection.

The doctor was the first friend I thought of; but I knew he was always out seeing his patients of an afternoon. The beadle[1] was the next person who came into my head. He had the look of being a very dignified, unapproachable kind of man when he came about the inquest; but he talked to me a little then, and said I was a good girl, and seemed, I really thought, to pity me. So to him I determined to apply in my great danger and distress.

Most fortunately I found him at home. When I told him of the landlord's infamous threats, and of the misery I was in in consequence of them, he rose up with a stamp of his foot, and sent for his gold-laced cocked hat that he wears on Sundays, and his long cane with the ivory top to it.

"I'll give it to him," said the beadle. "Come along with me, my dear. I think I told you you were a good girl at the inquest—if I didn't, I tell you so now. I'll give it to him! Come along with me."

And he went out, striding on with his cocked hat and his great cane, and I followed him.

"Landlord!" he cries the moment he gets into the passage, with a thump of his cane on the floor. "Landlord!" with a look all round him as if he was King of England calling to a beast, "come out!"

The moment the landlord came out and saw who it was, his eye fixed on the cocked hat, and he turned as pale as ashes.

"How dare you frighten this poor girl?" said the beadle. "How dare you bully her at this sorrowful time with threatening to do what you know you can't do? How dare you be a cowardly, bullying, braggadocio of an unmanly landlord? Don't talk to me: I won't hear you! I'll pull you up, sir! If you say another word to the young woman, I'll pull you up before the authorities of this metropolitan parish! I've had my eye on you, and the authorities have had their eye on you, and the rector has had his eye on you. We don't like the look of your small shop round the corner; we don't like the look of some of the customers who deal at it; we don't like disorderly characters; and we don't by any manner of means like *you*. Go away! Leave the young woman alone. Hold your tongue, or I'll pull you up. If he says another word, or interferes with you again, my dear, come and tell me; and, as sure as he's a bullying, unmanly braggadocio of a landlord, I'll pull him up!"

With those words the beadle gave a loud cough to clear his throat, and another thump of his cane on the floor, and so went striding out again before I could open my lips to thank him. The landlord slunk back into his room without a word. I was left alone and unmolested at last, to strengthen myself for the hard trial of my poor love's funeral tomorrow.

March 13th. It is all over. A week ago, her head rested on my bosom. It is laid in the church-yard now; the fresh earth lies heavy over her grave. I and my dearest friend, the sister of my love, are parted in this world forever.

I followed her funeral alone through the cruel, bustling streets. Sally, I thought, might have offered to go with me, but she never so much as came into my room. I did not like to think badly of her for this, and I am glad I restrained myself; for, when we got into the churchyard, among the two or three people who were standing by the open grave, I saw Sally, in her ragged grey shawl and her patched black bonnet. She did not

---

[1]   *beadle* Parish constable.

seem to notice me till the last words of the service had been read and the clergyman had gone away; then she came up and spoke to me.

"I couldn't follow along with you," she said, looking at her ragged shawl, "for I haven't a decent suit of clothes to walk in. I wish I could get vent in crying for her, like you, but I can't; all the crying's been drudged and starved out of me long ago. Don't you think about lighting your fire when you get home. I'll do that, and get you a drop of tea to comfort you."

She seemed on the point of saying a kind word or two more, when, seeing the beadle coming toward me, she drew back, as if she was afraid of him, and left the church-yard.

"Here's my subscription toward the funeral," said the beadle, giving me back his shilling fee. "Don't say anything about it, for it mightn't be approved of in a business point of view, if it came to some people's ears. Has the landlord said anything more to you? No, I thought not. He's too polite a man to give me the trouble of pulling him up. Don't stop crying here, my dear. Take the advice of a man familiar with funerals, and go home."

I tried to take his advice, but it seemed like deserting Mary to go away when all the rest forsook her.

I waited about till the earth was thrown in and the man had left the place, then I returned to the grave. Oh, how bare and cruel it was, without so much as a bit of green turf to soften it! Oh, how much harder it seemed to live than to die, when I stood alone looking at the heavy piled-up lumps of clay, and thinking of what was hidden beneath them!

I was driven home by my own despairing thoughts. The sight of Sally lighting the fire in my room eased my heart a little. When she was gone, I took up Robert's letter again to keep my mind employed on the only subject in the world that has any interest for it now.

This fresh reading increased the doubts I had already felt relative to his having remained in America after writing to me. My grief and forlornness have made a strange alteration in my former feelings about his coming back. I seem to have lost all my prudence and self-denial, and to care so little about his poverty, and so much about himself, that the prospect of his return is really the only comforting thought I have now to support me. I know this is weak in me, and that his coming back poor can lead to no good result for either of us; but he is the only living being left me to love; and—I can't explain it—but I want to put my arms round his neck and tell him about Mary.

March 14th. I locked up the end of the cravat in my writing-desk. No change in the dreadful suspicions that the bare sight of it rouses in me. I tremble if I so much as touch it.

March 15th, 16th, 17th. Work, work, work. If I don't knock up,[1] I shall be able to pay back the advance in another week; and then, with a little more pinching in my daily expenses, I may succeed in saving a shilling or two to get some turf to put over Mary's grave, and perhaps even a few flowers besides to grow round it.

March 18th. Thinking of Robert all day long. Does this mean that he is really coming back? If it does, reckoning the distance he is at from New York, and the time ships take to get to England, I might see him by the end of April or the beginning of May.

March 19th. I don't remember my mind running once on the end of the cravat yesterday, and I am certain I never looked at it; yet I had the strangest dream concerning it at night. I thought it was lengthened into a long clue, like the silken thread that led to Rosamond's Bower.[2] I thought I took hold of it, and followed it a little way, and then got frightened and tried to go back, but found that I was obliged, in spite of myself, to go on. It led me through a place like the Valley of the Shadow of Death, in an old print I remember in my mother's copy of the Pilgrim's Progress.[3] I seemed to be months and months following it, without any respite, till at last it brought me, on a sudden, face to face with an angel whose eyes were like Mary's. He said to me, "Go on, still; the truth is at the end, waiting for you to find it." I burst out crying, for the angel had Mary's voice as well as Mary's eyes, and woke with my heart throbbing and my cheeks all wet. What is the meaning of this? Is it always superstitious, I wonder, to

---

[1]   *knock up*   Become exhausted.

[2]   *silken thread that led to Rosamond's Bower*   An old tale of King Henry II relates how Henry's wife, Eleanor, discovered the whereabouts of the king's lover, fair Rosamond, by following a silken thread through a maze to Rosamond's hiding place.

[3]   *Pilgrim's Progress*   By John Bunyan (1675).

believe that dreams may come true?
....

April 30th. I have found it! God knows to what results it may lead; but it is as certain as that I am sitting here before my journal, that I have found the cravat from which the end in Mary's hand was torn. I discovered it last night; but the flutter I was in, and the nervousness and uncertainty I felt, prevented me from noting down this most extraordinary and most unexpected event at the time when it happened. Let me try if I can preserve the memory of it in writing now.

I was going home rather late from where I work, when I suddenly remembered that I had forgotten to buy myself any candles the evening before, and that I should be left in the dark if I did not manage to rectify this mistake in some way. The shop close to me, at which I usually deal, would be shut up, I knew, before I could get to it; so I determined to go into the first place I passed where candles were sold. This turned out to be a small shop with two counters, which did business on one side in the general grocery way, and on the other in the rag and bottle and old iron line.

There were several customers on the grocery side when I went in, so I waited on the empty rag side till I could be served. Glancing about me here at the worthless-looking things by which I was surrounded, my eye was caught by a bundle of rags lying on the counter, as if they had just been brought in and left there. From mere idle curiosity, I looked close at the rags, and saw among them something like an old cravat. I took it up directly and held it under a gaslight. The pattern was blurred lilac lines, running across and across the dingy black ground in a trellis-work form. I looked at the ends: one of them was torn off.

How I managed to hide the breathless surprise into which this discovery threw me, I cannot say, but I certainly contrived to steady my voice somehow, and to ask for my candles calmly when the man and woman serving in the shop, having disposed of their other customers, inquired of me what I wanted.

As the man took down the candles, my brain was all in a whirl with trying to think how I could get possession of the old cravat without exciting any suspicion. Chance, and a little quickness on my part in taking advantage of it, put the object within my reach in a

moment. The man, having counted out the candles, asked the woman for some paper to wrap them in. She produced a piece much too small and flimsy for the purpose, and declared, when he called for something better, that the day's supply of stout paper was all exhausted. He flew into a rage with her for managing so badly. Just as they were beginning to quarrel violently, I stepped back to the rag-counter, took the old cravat carelessly out of the bundle, and said, in as light a tone as I could possibly assume,

"Come, come! don't let my candles be the cause of hard words between you. Tie this ragged old thing round them with a bit of string, and I shall carry them home quite comfortably."

The man seemed disposed to insist on the stout paper being produced; but the woman, as if she was glad of an opportunity of spiting him, snatched the candles away, and tied them up in a moment in the torn old cravat. I was afraid he would have struck her before my face, he seemed in such a fury; but, fortunately, another customer came in, and obliged him to put his hands to peaceable and proper uses.

"Quite a bundle of all-sorts on the opposite counter there," I said to the woman, as I paid her for the candles.

"Yes, and all hoarded up for sale by a poor creature with a lazy brute of a husband, who lets his wife do all the work while he spends all the money," answered the woman, with a malicious look at the man by her side.

"He can't surely have much money to spend, if his wife has no better work to do than picking up rags," said I.

"It isn't her fault if she hasn't got no better," says the woman, rather angrily. "She's ready to turn her hand to anything. Charing,[1] washing, laying-out, keeping empty houses—nothing comes amiss to her. She's my half-sister, and I think I ought to know."

"Did you say she went out charing?" I asked, making believe as if I knew of somebody who might employ her.

"Yes, of course I did," answered the woman; "and if you can put a job into her hands, you'll be doing a good turn to a poor hard-working creature as wants it. She lives down the Mews here to the right—name of Horlick, and as honest a woman as ever stood in shoe-leather. Now then, ma'am, what for you?"

Another customer came in just then, and occupied

1   *Charing* Performing housework by the day.

her attention. I left the shop, passed the turning that led down to the Mews, looked up at the name of the street, so as to know how to find it again, and then ran home as fast as I could. Perhaps it was the remembrance of my strange dream striking me on a sudden, or perhaps it was the shock of the discovery I had just made, but I began to feel frightened without knowing why, and anxious to be under shelter in my own room.

If Robert should come back! Oh, what a relief and help it would be now if Robert should come back!

May 1st. On getting indoors last night, the first thing I did, after striking a light, was to take the ragged cravat off the candles and smooth it out on the table. I then took the end that had been in poor Mary's hand out of my writing-desk, and smoothed that out too. It matched the torn side of the cravat exactly. I put them together, and satisfied myself that there was not a doubt of it.

Not once did I close my eyes that night. A kind of fever got possession of me—a vehement yearning to go on from this first discovery and find out more, no matter what the risk might be. The cravat now really became, to my mind, the clue that I thought I saw in my dream—the clue that I was resolved to follow. I determined to go to Mrs. Horlick this evening on my return from work.

I found the Mews easily. A crook-backed dwarf of a man was lounging at the corner of it smoking his pipe. Not liking his looks, I did not enquire of him where Mrs. Horlick lived, but went down the Mews till I met with a woman, and asked her. She directed me to the right number. I knocked at the door, and Mrs. Horlick herself—a lean, ill-tempered, miserable-looking woman —answered it. I told her at once that I had come to ask what her terms were for charing. She stared at me for a moment, then answered my question civilly enough.

"You look surprised at a stranger like me finding you out," I said. "I first came to hear of you last night from a relation of yours, in rather an odd way."

And I told her all that had happened in the chandler's shop, bringing in the bundle of rags, and the circumstance of my carrying home the candles in the old torn cravat, as often as possible.

"It's the first time I've heard of anything belonging to him turning out any use," said Mrs. Horlick, bitterly.

"What, the spoiled old neck-handkerchief belonged to your husband, did it?" said I at a venture.

"Yes; I pitched his rotten rag of a neck'andkercher into the bundle along with the rest, and I wish 1 could have pitched him in after it," said Mrs. Horlick. "I'd sell him cheap at any rag-shop. There he stands, smoking his pipe at the end of the Mews, out of work for weeks past, the idlest hump-backed pig in all London!"

She pointed to the man whom I had passed on entering the Mews. My cheeks began to burn and my knees to tremble, for I knew that in tracing the cravat to its owner I was advancing a step toward a fresh discovery. I wished Mrs. Horlick good evening, and said I would write and mention the day on which I wanted her.

What I had just been told put a thought into my mind that I was afraid to follow out. I have heard people talk of being light-headed, and I felt as I have heard them say they felt, when I retraced my steps up the Mews. My head got giddy, and my eyes seemed able to see nothing but the figure of the little crook-back man, still smoking his pipe in his former place. I could see nothing but that; I could think of nothing but the mark of the blow on my poor lost Mary's temple. I know that I must have been light-headed, for as I came close to the crook-backed man, I stopped without meaning it. The minute before, there had been no idea in me of speaking to him. I did not know how to speak, or in what way it would be safest to begin; and yet, the moment I came face to face with him something out of myself seemed to stop me, and to make me speak, without considering beforehand, without thinking of consequences, without knowing, I may almost say, what words I was uttering till the instant when they rose to my lips.

"When your old neck-tie was torn, did you know that one end of it went to the rag-shop and the other fell into my hands?"

I said these bold words to him suddenly, and, as it seemed, without my own will taking any part in them. He started, stared, changed color. He was too much amazed by my sudden speaking to find an answer for me. When he did open his lips it was to say rather to himself than me:

"You're not the girl."

"No," I said, with a strange choking at my heart.

"I'm her friend."

By this time he had recovered his surprise, and he seemed to be aware that he had let out more than he ought.

"You may be anybody's friend you like," he said brutally," long as you don't come jabbering nonsense here. I don't know you, and I don't understand your jokes."

He turned quickly away from me when he had said the last words. He had never once looked fairly at me since I first spoke to him.

Was it his hand that had struck the blow?

I had only sixpence in my pocket, but I took it out and followed him. If it had been a five-pound note, I should have done the same in the state I was in then.

"Would a pot of beer help you to understand me?" I said, and offered him the sixpence.

"A pot ain't no great things," he answered, taking the sixpence doubtfully.

"It may lead to something better," I said.

His eyes began to twinkle, and he came close to me. Oh, how my legs trembled—how my head swam!

"This is all in a friendly way, is it?" he asked in a whisper. I nodded my head. At that moment, I could not have spoken for worlds.

"Friendly, of course," he went on to himself, "or there would have been a policeman in it. She told you, I suppose, that that wasn't the man?"

I nodded my head again. It was all I could do to keep myself standing upright.

"I suppose it's a case of threatening to have him up, and making him settle it quietly for a pound or two? How much for me if you lay hold of him?"

"Half."

I began to be afraid that he would suspect some thing if I was still silent. The wretch's eyes twinkled again, and he came yet closer.

"I drove him to the Red Lion, corner of Dodd Street and Rudgely Street. The house was shut up, but he was let in at the jug and bottle door, like a man who was known to the landlord. That's as much as I can tell you, and I'm certain I'm right. He was the last fare I took up at night. The next morning master gave me the sack—said I cribbed his corn[1] and his fares. I wish I

[1]   *cribbed his corn* Stole his liquor.

had!"

I gathered from this that the crook-backed man had been a cab-driver.

"Why don't you speak," he asked suspiciously. "Has she been telling you a pack of lies about me? What did she say when she came home?"

"What ought she to have said?"

"She ought to have said my fare was drunk, and she came in the way as he was going to get into the cab. That's what she ought to have said to begin with."

"But after?"

"Well, after, my fare by way of larking with her, puts out his leg for to trip her up, and she stumbles and catches at me for to save herself, and tears off one of the limp ends of my rotten old tie. 'What do you mean by that, you brute?' says she, turning round as soon as she was steady on her legs, to my fare. Says my fare to her, 'I means to teach you to keep a civil tongue in your head.' And he ups with his fist, and—what's come to you, now? What are you looking at me like that for? How do you think a man of my size was to take her part against a man big enough to have eaten me up? Look as much as you like, in my place you would have done what I done—drew off when he shook his fist at you, and swore he'd be the death of you if you didn't start your horse in no time."

I saw he was working himself into a rage; but I could not, if my life had depended on it, have stood near him, or looked at him any longer. I just managed to stammer out that I had been walking a long way, and that, not being used to much exercise, I felt faint and giddy with fatigue. He only changed from angry to sulky when I made that excuse. I got a little farther away from him, and then added that if he would be at the Mews entrance the next evening, I should have something more to say and something more to give him. He grumbled a few suspicious words in answer about doubting whether he should trust me to come back. Fortunately, at that moment, a policeman passed on the opposite side of the way, he slunk down the Mews immediately, and I was free to make my escape.

How I got home I can't say, except that I think I ran the greater part of the way. Sally opened the door, and asked if anything was the matter the moment she saw my face. I answered, "Nothing—nothing." She stopped me as I was going into my room, and said,

"Smooth your hair a bit, and put your collar straight. There's a gentleman in there waiting for you."

My heart gave one great bound: I knew who it was in an instant, and rushed into the room like a mad woman.

"Oh, Robert! Robert!"

All my heart went out to him in those two little words.

"Good God, Anne! has anything happened? Are you ill?"

"Mary! my poor, lost, murdered, dear, dear Mary!"

That was all I could say before I fell on his breast.

May 2nd. Misfortunes and disappointments have saddened him a little, but toward me he is unaltered. He is as good, as kind, as gently and truly affectionate as ever. I believe no other man in the world could have listened to the story of Mary's death with such tenderness and pity as he. Instead of cutting me short anywhere, he drew me on to tell more than I had intended; and his first generous words when I had done were to assure me that he would see himself to the grass being laid and the flowers planted on Mary's grave. I could have almost gone on my knees and worshipped him when he made me that promise.

Surely, this best, and kindest, and noblest of men cannot always be unfortunate! My cheeks burn when I think that he has come back with only a few pounds in his pocket, after all his hard and honest struggles to do well in America. They must be bad people there when such a man as Robert cannot get on among them. He now talks calmly and resignedly of trying for any one of the lowest employments by which a man can earn his bread honestly in this great city—he who knows French, who can write so beautifully! Oh, if the people who have places to give away only knew Robert as well as I do, what a salary he would have, what a post he would be chosen to occupy!

I am writing these lines alone, while he has gone to the Mews to treat with the dastardly, heartless wretch with whom I spoke yesterday.

Robert says the creature—I won't call him a man—must be humored and kept deceived about poor Mary's end, in order that we may discover and bring to justice the monster whose drunken blow was the death

of her. I shall know no ease of mind till her murderer is secured, and till I am certain that he will be made to suffer for his crimes. I wanted to go with Robert to the Mews, but he said it was best that he should carry out the rest of the investigation alone, for my strength and resolution had been too hardly taxed already. He said more words in praise of me for what I have been able to do up to this time, which I am almost ashamed to write down with my own pen. Besides, there is no need: praise from his lips is one of the things that I can trust my memory to preserve to the latest day of my life.

May 3rd. Robert was very long last night before he came back to tell me what he had done. He easily recognized the hunchback at the corner of the mews by my description of him; but he found it a hard matter, even with the help of money, to overcome the cowardly wretch's distrust of him as a stranger and a man. However, when this had been accomplished, the main difficulty was conquered. The hunchback, excited by the promise of more money, went at once to the Red Lion to enquire about the person whom he had driven there in his cab. Robert followed him, and waited at the corner of the street. The tidings brought by the cabman were of the most unexpected kind. The murderer—I can write of him by no other name—had fallen ill on the very night when he was driven to the Red Lion, had taken to his bed there and then, and was still confined to it at that very moment. His disease was of a kind that is brought on by excessive drinking, and that affects the mind as well as the body. The people at the public house called it the Horrors.

Hearing these things, Robert determined to see if he could not find out something more for himself by going and enquiring at the public house, in the character of one of the friends of the sick man in bed upstairs. He made two important discoveries. First, he found out the name and address of the doctor in attendance. Secondly, he entrapped the barman into mentioning the murderous wretch by his name. This last discovery adds an unspeakably fearful interest to the dreadful catastrophe of Mary's death. Noah Truscott, as she told me herself in the last conversation I ever had with her, was the name of the man whose drunken example ruined her father, and Noah Truscott is also the name of the man whose drunken fury killed her. There is something that makes one shudder, something fatal and supernatural in this awful fact. Robert agrees with me that the hand of Providence must have guided my steps to that shop from which all the discoveries since made took their rise. He says he believes we are the instruments of effecting a righteous retribution; and, if he spends his last farthing, he will have the investigation brought to its full end in a court of justice.

May 4th. Robert went today to consult a lawyer whom he knew in former times. The lawyer much interested, though not so seriously impressed as he ought to have been by the story of Mary's death and of the events that have followed it. He gave Robert a confidential letter to take to the doctor in attendance on the double-dyed villain at the Red Lion. Robert left the letter, and called again and saw the doctor, who said his patient was getting better, and would most likely be up again in ten days or a fortnight. This statement Robert communicated to the lawyer, and the lawyer has undertaken to have the public house properly watched, and the hunchback (who is the most important witness) sharply looked after for the next fortnight, or longer if necessary. Here, then, the progress of this dreadful business stops for awhile.

May 5th. Robert has got a little temporary employment in copying for his friend the lawyer. I am working harder than ever at my needle to make up for the time that has been lost lately.

May 6th. Today was Sunday, and Robert proposed that we should go and look at Mary's grave. He, who forgets nothing where a kindness is to be done, has found time to perform the promise he made to me on the night when we first met. The grave is already, by his orders, covered with turf, and planted round with shrubs. Some flowers, and a low headstone, are to be added to make the place look worthier of my poor lost darling who is beneath it. Oh, I hope I shall live long after I am married to Robert! I want so much time to show him all my gratitude!

May 20th. A hard trial to my courage today. I have given evidence at the police-office, and have seen the monster who murdered her.

I could only look at him once. I could just see that he was a giant in size, and that he kept his dull, lowering, bestial face turned toward the witness-box, and his bloodshot, vacant eyes staring on me. For an instant I tried to confront that look; for an instant I kept my attention fixed on him—on his blotched face—on the short grizzled hair above it—on his knotty, murderous right hand, hanging loose over the bar in front of him, like the paw of a wild beast over the edge of his den. Then the horror of him—the double horror of confronting him, in the first place, and afterwards of seeing that he was an old man—overcame me, and I turned away faint, sick, and shuddering. I never faced him again; and at the end of my evidence, Robert considerately took me out.

When we met once more at the end of the examination, Robert told me that the prisoner never spoke and never changed his position. He was either fortified by the cruel composure of the savage, or his faculties had not yet thoroughly recovered from the disease that had so lately shaken them. The magistrate seemed to doubt if he was in his right mind; but the evidence of the medical man relieved his uncertainty, and the prisoner was committed for trial on a charge of manslaughter.

Why not on a charge of murder? Robert explained the law to me when I asked that question. I accepted the explanation, but it did not satisfy me. Mary Mallinson was killed by a blow from the hand of Noah Truscott. That is murder in the sight of God. Why not murder in the sight of the law also?

June 18th. Tomorrow is the day appointed for the trial at the Old Bailey.[1]

Before sunset this evening I went to look at Mary's grave. The turf has grown so green since I saw it last, and the flowers are springing up so prettily. A bird was perched dressing his feathers on the low white headstone that bears the inscription of her name and age. I did not go near enough to disturb the little creature. He looked innocent and pretty on the grave, as Mary herself was in her lifetime. When he flew away, I went and sat for a little by the headstone, and read the mournful lines on it. Oh, my love, my love! what harm or wrong had you ever done in this world, that you should die at eighteen by a blow from a drunkard's hand?

June 19th. The trial. My experience of what happened at it is limited, like my experience of the exami-

---

[1] *Old Bailey* Central Criminal Court in London.

nation at the police-office, to the time occupied in giving my own evidence They made me say much more than I said before the magistrate. Between examination and cross-examination, I had to go into almost all the particulars about poor Mary and her funeral that I have written in this journal; the jury listening to every word I spoke with the most anxious attention. At the end, the judge said a few words to me approving of my conduct, and then there was a clapping of hands among the people in court. I was so agitated and excited that I trembled all over when they let me go out into the air again.

I looked at the prisoner both when I entered the witness-box and when I left it. The lowering brutality of his face was unchanged, but his faculties seemed to be more alive and observant than they were at the police-office. A frightful blue change passed over his face, and he drew his breath so heavily that the gasps were distinctly audible, while I mentioned Mary by name, and described the mark of the blow on her temple. When they asked me if I knew anything of the prisoner, and I answered that I only knew what Mary herself had told me about his having been her father's ruin, he gave a kind of groan, and struck both his hands heavily on the dock. And when I passed beneath him on my way out of the court, he leaned over suddenly, whether to speak to me or to strike me I can't say, for he was immediately made to stand upright again by the turnkeys[1] on either side of him. While the evidence proceeded (as Robert described it to me), the signs that he was suffering under superstitious terror became more and more apparent; until, at last, just as the lawyer appointed to defend him was rising to speak, he suddenly cried out, in a voice that startled every one, up to the very judge on the bench, "Stop!"

There was a pause, and all eyes looked at him. The perspiration was pouring over his face like water, and he made strange, uncouth signs with his hands to the judge opposite. "Stop all this!" he cried again; "I've been the ruin of the father and the death of the child. Hang me before I do more harm! Hang me, for God's sake, out of the way!" As soon as the shock produced by this extraordinary interruption had subsided, he was removed, and there followed a long discussion about whether he was

of sound mind or not. The point was left to the jury to decide by their verdict. They found him guilty of the charge of manslaughter, without the excuse of insanity. He was brought up again, and condemned to transportation for life. All he did on hearing the sentence was to reiterate his desperate words, "Hang me before I do more harm! Hang me, for God's sake, out of the way!"

June 20th. I made yesterday's entry in sadness of heart, and I have not been better in my spirits today. It is something to have brought the murderer to the punishment that he deserves. But the knowledge that this most righteous act of retribution is accomplished brings no consolation with it. The law does indeed punish Noah Truscott for his crime, but can it raise up Mary Mallinson from her last resting place in the churchyard?

While writing of the law, I ought to record that the heartless wretch who allowed Mary to be struck down in his presence without making any attempt to defend her is not likely to escape with perfect impunity. The policeman who looked after him to insure his attendance at the trial discovered that he had committed past offenses, for which the law can make him answer. A summons was executed upon him, and he was taken before the magistrate the moment he left the court after giving his evidence.

I had just written these few lines, and was closing my journal, when there came a knock at the door. I answered it, thinking that Robert had called in his way home to say good-night, and found myself face to face with a strange gentleman, who immediately asked for Anne Rodway. On hearing that I was the person inquired for, he requested five minutes conversation with me. I showed him into the little empty room at the back of the house, and waited, rather surprised and fluttered, to hear what he had to say.

He was a dark man, with a serious manner, and a short stern way of speaking. I was certain that he was a stranger, and yet there seemed something in his face not unfamiliar to me. He began by taking a newspaper from his pocket, and asking me if I was the person who had given evidence at the trial of Noah Truscott on a charge of manslaughter. I answered immediately that I was.

"I have been for nearly two years in London seeking Mary Mallinson, and always seeking her in vain," he

---

[1]   *turnkeys*   Warders or jailers.

said. "The first and only news I have had of her I found in the newspaper report of the trial yesterday."

He still spoke calmly, but there was something in the look of his eyes which showed me that he was suffering in spirit. A sudden nervousness overcame me, and I was obliged to sit down.

"You knew Mary Mallinson, sir?" I asked, as quietly as I could.

"I am her brother."

I clasped my hands and hid my face in despair. Oh, the bitterness of heart with which I heard him say those simple words!

"You were very kind to her," said the calm, tearless man. "In her name and for her sake, I thank you."

"Oh, sir," I said, "why did you never write to her when you were in foreign parts?"

"I wrote often," he answered, "but each of my letters contained a remittance of money. Did Mary tell you she had a step-mother? If she did, you may guess why none of my letters were allowed to reach her. I now know that this woman robbed my sister. Has she lied in telling me that she was never informed of Mary's place of abode?"

I remembered that Mary had never communicated with her step-mother after the separation, and could therefore assure him that the woman had spoken the truth.

He paused for a moment after that, and sighed. Then he took out a pocket-book, and said,

"I have already arranged for the payment of any legal expenses that may have been incurred by the trial, but I have still to reimburse you for the funeral charges which you so generously defrayed. Excuse my speaking bluntly on this subject; I am accustomed to look on all matters where money is concerned purely as matters of business."

I saw that he was taking several bank-notes out of the pocket-book, and stopped him.

"I will gratefully receive back the little money I actually paid, sir, because I am not well off, and it would be an ungracious act of pride in me to refuse it from you," I said. "But I see you handling bank-notes, any one of which is far beyond the amount you have to repay me. Pray put them back, sir. What I did for your poor lost sister I did from my love and fondness for her. You have thanked me for that; and your thanks are all

I can receive.

He had hitherto concealed his feelings, but I saw them now begin to get the better of him. His eyes softened, and he took my hand and squeezed it hard.

"I beg your pardon," he said. "I beg your pardon, with all my heart."

There was silence between us, for I was crying, and I believe, at heart, he was crying too. At last, he dropped my hand, and seemed to change back, by an effort, to his former calmness.

"Is there no one belonging to you to whom I can be of service?" he asked. "I see among the witnesses on the trial the name of a young man who appears to have assisted you in the enquiries which led to the prisoner's conviction. Is he a relation?"

"No, sir—at least, not now—but I hope—"

"What?"

"I hope that he may, one day, be the nearest and dearest relation to me that a woman can have." I said those words boldly, because I was afraid of his otherwise taking some wrong view of the connection between Robert and me.

"One day?" he repeated. "One day may be a long time hence."

"We are neither of us well off, sir," I said. "One day means the day when we are a little richer than we are now."

"Is the young man educated? Can he produce testimonials to his character? Oblige me by writing his name and address down on the back of that card." When I had obeyed, in a handwriting which I am afraid did me no credit, he took out another card and gave it to me.

"I shall leave England tomorrow," he said. "There is nothing now to keep me in my own country. If you are ever in any difficulty or distress (which, I pray God, you may never be), apply to my London agent, whose address you have there."

He stopped, and looked at me attentively, then took my hand again.

"Where is she buried?" he said suddenly, in a quick whisper, turning his head away.

I told him, and added that we had made the grave as beautiful as we could with grass and flowers.

I saw his lips whiten and tremble.

"God bless and reward you!" he said, and drew me toward him quickly and kissed my forehead. I was quite overcome, and sank down and hid my face on the table. When I looked up again he was gone.

*   *   *   *   *

June 25th, 1841. I write these lines on my wedding morning, when little more than a year has passed since Robert returned to England.

His salary was increased yesterday to one hundred and fifty pounds a year. If I only knew where Mr. Mallinson was, I would write and tell him of our present happiness. But for the situation which his kindness procured for Robert, we might still have been waiting vainly for the day that has now come.

I am to work at home for the future, and Sally is to help us in our new abode. If Mary could have lived to see this day! I am not ungrateful for my blessings; but oh, how I miss that sweet face on this morning of all others!

I got up today early enough to go alone to the grave, and to gather the nosegay that now lies before me from the flowers that grow round it. I shall put it in my bosom when Robert comes to fetch me to the church. Mary would have been my bridesmaid if she had lived; and I can't forget Mary, even on my wedding-day.

—1859

George Meredith
1828 – 1909

George Meredith occupies an uncertain status as a literary figure. Although he considered himself primarily a poet, he has always been better known as a novelist. He was praised by his contemporaries and respected by younger writers—including Oscar Wilde, Robert Louis Stevenson, Arthur Conan Doyle, and H.G. Wells—yet he never achieved great critical or commercial success. He was central to the literary society of his day, but is now often regarded as a minor Victorian figure. Further uncertainty is prompted by his writing style, which fits neither with that of his fellow Victorians, nor with that of the Modernists who followed. Like modernist works, his plots lack both the linear development and the highly dramatic moments favored by Victorian novelists. His didacticism, obtrusive philosophizing, ornate style, and elevated diction, however, are recognizably Victorian.

Meredith was born 12 February 1828, in Portsmouth, England. He was reticent about the details of his youth, preferring not even to reveal the location of his birth. Nevertheless, aspects of his experiences growing up as a lower middle class son of a tailor often made their way into his fiction, particularly in his novel *Evan Harrington* (1860). Meredith studied briefly to become a lawyer before turning instead to poetry. In 1849 he was struggling to realize the dream of becoming a poet when he married Mary Ellen Peacock Nicolls, daughter of novelist Thomas Love Peacock. The two were ill suited, and in 1858 Meredith's wife departed for Capri with the painter Henry Wallis. Although she returned to England alone a year later, she and her husband were never reconciled.

Meredith completed "Modern Love" (1862), his most famous poem, in the months following his wife's death in 1861. This series of sixteen-line sonnets (a stanzaic form Meredith invented) depicts isolated scenes in an unhappy marriage that disintegrates as both partners take lovers. Many readers, accustomed to poets of the day describing the emotional aspects of love but not the physical, thought Meredith's poem (and the others in his collection *Modern Love and Other Peoms*) low and vulgar. Critical reaction to "Modern Love" was generally unfavorable, but one significant letter of praise came from Algernon Swinburne, a fellow poet who later became a close friend and—along with William and Dante Gabriel Rossetti—a housemate of Meredith's.

Meredith did not publish another book of poems until 1883, focusing instead on writing novels. To supplement his income he worked as a journalist and as a manuscript reader for Chapman and Hall, his publishers until 1893. In this latter capacity he advised many soon-to-be famous young writers, including Thomas Hardy and George Gissing. Of Meredith's thirteen novels, three of the best known are *The Ordeal of Richard Feverel* (1859), the witty comedy *The Egoist* (1879), and his most successful work, *Diana of the Crossways* (1885). Grammatically and syntactically complex, his novels were labeled difficult and obscure. Nevertheless, he won the praise of many female readers for his atypical portrayal of women. Meredith's heroines are celebrated for their courage and strength of character, rather than their physical beauty, and are often shown fighting the limitations imposed upon them by convention and the flaws in their education.

Despite continual fluctuations in Meredith's popularity, one thing about him is certain: he was an extremely innovative and influential writer. By departing from the poetic and novelistic conventions of his time he created new methods of literary expression. He was able, as Virginia Woolf wrote, "to prepare the way for a new and an original sense of the human scene." Meredith died in 1909 at the age of 81.

⌘ ⌘ ⌘

Modern Love

1

By this he knew she wept with waking eyes:
That, at his hand's light quiver by her head,
The strange low sobs that shook their common bed,
Were called into her with a sharp surprise,
5   And strangled mute, like little gaping snakes,
Dreadfully venomous to him. She lay
Stone-still, and the long darkness flowed away
With muffled pulses. Then, as midnight makes
Her giant heart of Memory and Tears
10 Drink the pale drug of silence, and so beat
Sleep's heavy measure, they from head to feet
Were moveless, looking through their dead black years,
By vain regret scrawled over the blank wall.
Like sculptured effigies they might be seen
15 Upon their marriage-tomb, the sword between;
Each wishing for the sword that severs all.

2

It ended, and the morrow brought the task.
Her eyes were guilty gates, that let him in
By shutting all too zealous for their sin:
Each sucked a secret, and each wore a mask.
5   But, oh, the bitter taste her beauty had!
He sickened as at breath of poison-flowers:
A languid humour stole among the hours,
And if their smiles encountered, he went mad,
And raged deep inward, till the light was brown
10 Before his vision, and the world forgot,
Looked wicked as some old dull murder-spot.
A star with lurid beams, she seemed to crown
The pit of infamy: and then again
He fainted on his vengefulness, and strove
15 To ape° the magnanimity of love,   *imitate*
And smote himself, a shuddering heap of pain.

3

This was the woman; what now of the man?
But pass him. If he comes beneath a heel,
He shall be crushed until he cannot feel,
Or, being callous, haply till he can.
5   But he is nothing—nothing? Only mark
The rich light striking out from her on him!
Ha! what a sense it is when her eyes swim
Across the man she singles, leaving dark
All else! Lord God, who mad'st the thing so fair,
10 See that I am drawn to her even now!
It cannot be such harm on her cool brow
To put a kiss? Yet if I meet him there!
But she is mine! Ah, no! I know too well
I claim a star whose light is overcast:
15 I claim a phantom-woman in the Past.
The hour has struck, though I heard not the bell!

4

All other joys of life he strove to warm,
And magnify, and catch them to his lip:
But they had suffered shipwreck with the ship,
And gazed upon him sallow from the storm.
5   Or if Delusion came, 'twas but to show
The coming minute mock the one that went.
Cold as a mountain in its star-pitched tent,
Stood high Philosophy, less friend than foe:
Whom self-caged Passion, from its prison-bars,
10 Is always watching with a wondering hate.
Not till the fire is dying in the grate,
Look we for any kinship with the stars.
Oh, wisdom never comes when it is gold,
And the great price we pay for it full worth:
15 We have it only when we are half earth.
Little avails that coinage to the old!

5

A message from her set his brain aflame.
A world of household matters filled her mind,
Wherein he saw hypocrisy designed:
She treated him as something that is tame,
5 And but at other provocation bites.
Familiar was her shoulder in the glass,
Through that dark rain: yet it may come to pass
That a changed eye finds such familiar sights
More keenly tempting than new loveliness.
10 The "What has been" a moment seemed his own:
The splendours, mysteries, dearer because known,
Nor less divine: Love's inmost sacredness,
Called to him, "Come!"—In his restraining start,
Eyes nurtured to be looked at, scarce could see
15 A wave of the great waves of Destiny
Convulsed at a checked impulse of the heart.

6

It chanced his lips did meet her forehead cool.
She had no blush, but slanted down her eye.
Shamed nature, then, confesses love can die:
And most she punishes the tender fool
5 Who will believe what honours her the most!
Dead! is it dead? She has a pulse, and flow
Of tears, the price of blood-drops, as I know,
For whom the midnight sobs around Love's ghost,
Since then I heard her, and so will sob on.
10 The love is here; it has but changed its aim.
O bitter barren woman! what's the name?
The name, the name, the new name thou hast won?
Behold me striking the world's coward stroke!
That will I not do, though the sting is dire.
15 —Beneath the surface this, while by the fire
They sat, she laughing at a quiet joke.

7

She issues radiant from her dressing-room,
Like one prepared to scale an upper sphere:
—By stirring up a lower, much I fear!
How deftly that oiled barber lays his bloom!
5 That long-shanked dapper Cupid[1] with frisked curls,
Can make known women torturingly fair;

The gold-eyed serpent dwelling in rich hair,
Awakes beneath his magic whisks and twirls.
His art can take the eyes from out my head,
10 Until I see with eyes of other men;
While deeper knowledge crouches in its den,
And sends a spark up—is it true we are wed?
Yea! filthiness of body is most vile,
But faithlessness of heart I do hold worse.
15 The former, it were not so great a curse
To read on the steel-mirror of her smile.

8

Yet it was plain she struggled, and that salt
Of righteous feeling made her pitiful.
Poor twisting worm, so queenly beautiful!
Where came the cleft between us? whose the fault?
5 My tears are on thee, that have rarely dropped
As balm for any bitter wound of mine:
My breast will open for thee at a sign!
But, no: we are two reed-pipes, coarsely stopped:
The God once filled them with his mellow breath;
10 And they were music till he flung them down,
Used! used! Hear now the discord-loving clown
Puff his gross spirit in them, worse than death!
I do not know myself without thee more:
In this unholy battle I grow base:
15 If the same soul be under the same face,
Speak, and a taste of that old time restore!

9

He felt the wild beast in him between whiles
So masterfully rude, that he would grieve
To see the helpless delicate thing receive
His guardianship through certain dark defiles.
5 Had he not teeth to rend, and hunger too?
But still he spared her. Once: "Have you no fear?"
He said: 'twas dusk; she in his grasp; none near.
She laughed: "No, surely; am I not with you?"
And uttering that soft starry "you," she leaned
10 Her gentle body near him, looking up;
And from her eyes, as from a poison-cup,
He drank until the flittering eyelids screened.
Devilish malignant witch! and oh, young beam
Of heaven's circle-glory! Here thy shape

---

[1] *Cupid* Roman god of love.

15   To squeeze like an intoxicating grape—
      I might, and yet thou goest safe, supreme.

10

      But where began the change; and what's my crime?
      The wretch condemned, who has not been arraigned,
      Chafes at his sentence. Shall I, unsustained,
      Drag on Love's nerveless body through all time?
5   I must have slept, since now I wake. Prepare,
      You lovers, to know Love a thing of moods:
      Not like hard life, of laws. In Love's deep woods,
      I dreamt of loyal Life—the offence is there!
      Love's jealous woods about the sun are curled;
10   At least, the sun far brighter there did beam.—
      My crime is that, the puppet of a dream,
      I plotted to be worthy of the world.
      Oh, had I with my darling helped to mince
      The facts of life, you still had seen me go
15   With hindward feather and with forward toe,
      Her much-adored delightful Fairy Prince!

11

      Out in the yellow meadows, where the bee
      Hums by us with the honey of the Spring,
      And showers of sweet notes from the larks on wing,
      Are dropping like a noon-dew, wander we.
5   Or is it now? or was it then? for now,
      As then, the larks from running rings send showers:
      The golden foot of May is on the flowers,
      And friendly shadows dance upon her brow.
      What's this, when Nature swears there is no change
10   To challenge eyesight? Now, as then, the grace
      Of heaven seems holding earth in its embrace.
      Nor eyes, nor heart, has she to feel it strange?
      Look, woman, in the West. There wilt thou see
      An amber cradle near the sun's decline:
15   Within it, featured even in death divine,
      Is lying a dead infant, slain by thee.

12

      Not solely that the Future she destroys,
      And the fair life which in the distance lies
      For all men, beckoning out from dim rich skies:
      Nor that the passing hour's supporting joys
5   Have lost the keen-edged flavour, which begat

      Distinction in old times, and still should breed
      Sweet Memory, and Hope—earth's modest seed,
      And heaven's high-prompting: not that the world is flat
      Since that soft-luring creature I embraced,
10   Among the children of Illusion went:
      Methinks with all this loss I were content,
      If the mad Past, on which my foot is based,
      Were firm, or might be blotted: but the whole
      Of life is mixed: the mocking Past will stay:
15   And if I drink oblivion of a day,
      So shorten I the stature of my soul.

13

      "I play for Seasons; not Eternities!"
      Says Nature, laughing on her way. "So must
      All those whose stake is nothing more than dust!"
      And lo, she wins, and of her harmonies
5   She is full sure! Upon her dying rose,
      She drops a look of fondness, and goes by,
      Scarce any retrospection in her eye;
      For she the laws of growth most deeply knows,
      Whose hands bear, here, a seed-bag—there, an urn.
10   Pledged she herself to aught, 'twould mark her end!
      This lesson of our only visible friend,
      Can we not teach our foolish hearts to learn?
      Yes! yes!—but, oh, our human rose is fair
      Surpassingly! Lose calmly Love's great bliss,
15   When the renewed for ever of a kiss
      Whirls life within the shower of loosened hair!

14

      What soul would bargain for a cure that brings
      Contempt the nobler agony to kill?
      Rather let me bear on the bitter ill,
      And strike this rusty bosom with new stings!
5   It seems there is another veering fit,
      Since on a gold-haired lady's eyeballs pure,
      I looked with little prospect of a cure,
      The while her mouth's red bow loosed shafts of wit.
      Just heaven! can it be true that jealousy
10   Has decked the woman thus? and does her head
      Swim somewhat for possessions forfeited?
      Madam, you teach me many things that be.
      I open an old book, and there I find,
      That "Women still may love whom they deceive."

15 Such love I prize not, madam: by your leave,
The game you play at is not to my mind.

15

I think she sleeps: it must be sleep, when low
Hangs that abandoned arm toward the floor;
The face turned with it. Now make fast the door.
Sleep on: it is your husband, not your foe!
5 The Poet's black stage-lion of wronged love,
Frights not our modern dames:—well if he did!
Now will I pour new light upon that lid,
Full-sloping like the breasts beneath. "Sweet dove,
Your sleep is pure. Nay, pardon: I disturb.
10 I do not? good!" Her waking infant-stare
Grows woman to the burden my hands bear:
Her own handwriting to me when no curb
Was left on Passion's tongue. She trembles through;
A woman's tremble—the whole instrument—
15 I show another letter lately sent.
The words are very like: the name is new.

16

In our old shipwrecked days there was an hour,
When in the firelight steadily aglow,
Joined slackly, we beheld the red chasm grow
Among the clicking coals. Our library-bower
5 That eve was left to us: and hushed we sat
As lovers to whom Time is whispering.
From sudden-opened doors we heard them sing:
The nodding elders mixed good wine with chat.
Well knew we that Life's greatest treasure lay
10 With us, and of it was our talk. "Ah, yes!
Love dies!" I said: I never thought it less.
She yearned to me that sentence to unsay.
Then when the fire domed blackening, I found
Her cheek was salt against my kiss, and swift
15 Up the sharp scale of sobs her breast did lift:—
Now am I haunted by that taste! that sound!

17

At dinner, she is hostess, I am host.
Went the feast ever cheerfuller? She keeps
The Topic over intellectual deeps
In buoyancy afloat. They see no ghost.
5 With sparkling surface-eyes we play the ball:

It is in truth a most contagious game:
HIDING THE SKELETON, shall be its name.
Such play as this, the devils might appal!
But here's the greater wonder; in that we
10 Enamoured of an acting nought can tire,
Each other, like true hypocrites, admire;
Warm-lighted looks, Love's ephemerioe,[1]
Shoot gaily o'er the dishes and the wine.
We waken envy of our happy lot.
15 Fast, sweet, and golden, shows the marriage-knot.
Dear guests, you now have seen Love's corpse-light shine.

18

Here Jack and Tom are paired with Moll and Meg.
Curved open to the river-reach is seen
A country merry-making on the green.
Fair space for signal shakings of the leg.
5 That little screwy° fiddler from his booth,   *tipsy*
Whence flows one nut-brown stream, commands the joints
Of all who caper here at various points.
I have known rustic revels in my youth:
The May-fly[2] pleasures of a mind at ease.
10 An early goddess was a county lass:
A charmed Amphion-oak[3] she tripped the grass.
What life was that I lived? The life of these?
Heaven keep them happy! Nature they seem near.
They must, I think, be wiser than I am;
15 They have the secret of the bull and lamb.
'Tis true that when we trace its source, 'tis beer.

19

No state is enviable. To the luck alone
Of some few favoured men I would put claim.
I bleed, but her who wounds I will not blame.
Have I not felt her heart as 'twere my own
5 Beat thro' me? could I hurt her? heaven and hell!
But I could hurt her cruelly! Can I let
My Love's old time-piece to another set,
Swear it can't stop, and must for ever swell?

---

1 *ephemerioe* Short-lived or fleeting aspects; ephemera.

2 *May-fly* Insect that lives only for one day.

3 *Amphion-oak* In Roman myth, Amphion was the son of Zeus and Antiope. Given a lyre by the goddess Hermes, he played it with such magical beauty that the stones and trees danced.

Sure, that's one way Love drifts into the mart
10   Where goat-legged[1] buyers throng. I see not plain—
My meaning is, it must not be again.
Great God! the maddest gambler throws his heart.
If any state be enviable on earth,
'Tis yon born idiot's, who, as days go by,
15   Still rubs his hands before him, like a fly,
In a queer sort of meditative mirth.

20

I am not of those miserable males
Who sniff at vice and, daring not to snap,
Do therefore hope for heaven. I take the hap°   *result*
Of all my deeds. The wind that fills my sails,
5   Propels; but I am helmsman. Am I wrecked,
I know the devil has sufficient weight
To bear: I lay it not on him, or fate.
Besides, he's damned. That man I do suspect
A coward, who would burden the poor deuce
10   With what ensues from his own slipperiness.
I have just found a wanton-scented tress
In an old desk, dusty for lack of use.
Of days and nights it is demonstrative,
That, like some aged star, gleam luridly
15   If for those times I must ask charity,
Have I not any charity to give?

21

We three are on the cedar-shadowed lawn;
My friend being third. He who at love once laughed
Is in the weak rib by a fatal shaft
Struck through, and tells his passion's bashful dawn
5   And radiant culmination, glorious crown,
When "this" she said: went "thus": most wondrous she!
Our eyes grow white, encountering: that we are three,
Forgetful; then together we look down.
But he demands our blessing; is convinced
10   That words of wedded lovers must bring good.
We question; if we dare! or if we should!
And pat him, with light laugh. We have not winced.
Next, she has fallen. Fainting points the sign
To happy things in wedlock. When she wakes,

---
[1]   *goat-legged* Lustful.

15   She looks the star that through the cedar shakes:
Her lost moist hand clings mortally to mine.

22

What may the woman labour to confess?
There is about her mouth a nervous twitch.
'Tis something to be told, or hidden—which?
I get a glimpse of hell in this mild guess.
5   She has desires of touch, as if to feel
That all the household things are things she knew.
She stops before the glass. What sight in view?
A face that seems the latest to reveal!
For she turns from it hastily, and tossed
10   Irresolute, steals shadow-like to where
I stand; and wavering pale before me there,
Her tears fall still as oak-leaves after frost.
She will not speak. I will not ask. We are
League-sundered by the silent gulf between.
15   You burly lovers on the village green,
Yours is a lower, and a happier star!

23

'Tis Christmas weather, and a country house
Receives us: rooms are full: we can but get
An attic-crib. Such lovers will not fret
At that, it is half-said. The great carouse
5   Knocks hard upon the midnight's hollow door,
But when I knock at hers, I see the pit.
Why did I come here in that dullard° fit?   *stupid*
I enter, and lie couched upon the floor.
Passing, I caught the coverlet's quick beat:—
10   Come, Shame, burn to my soul! and Pride, and Pain—
Foul demons that have tortured me, enchain!
Out in the freezing darkness the lambs bleat.
The small bird stiffens in the low starlight.
I know not how, but shuddering as I slept,
15   I dreamed a banished angel to me crept:
My feet were nourished on her breasts all night.

24

The misery is greater, as I live!
To know her flesh so pure, so keen her sense,
That she does penance now for no offence,
Save against Love. The less can I forgive!

5 The less can I forgive, though I adore
That cruel lovely pallor which surrounds
Her footsteps; and the low vibrating sounds
That come on me, as from a magic shore.
Low are they, but most subtle to find out
10 The shrinking soul. Madam, 'tis understood
When women play upon their womanhood,
It means, a Season gone. And yet I doubt
But I am duped. That nun-like look waylays
My fancy. Oh! I do but wait a sign!
15 Pluck out the eyes of pride! thy mouth to mine!
Never! though I die thirsting. Go thy ways!

25

You like not that French novel? Tell me why.
You think it quite unnatural. Let us see.
The actors are, it seems, the usual three:
Husband, and wife, and lover. She—but fie!
5 In England we'll not hear of it. Edmond,
The lover, her devout chagrin doth share;
Blanc-mange[1] and absinthe are his penitent fare,
Till his pale aspect makes her over-fond:
So, to preclude fresh sin, he tries rosbif.[2]
10 Meantime the husband is no more abused:
Auguste forgives her ere the tear is used.
Then hangeth all on one tremendous IF—
If she will choose between them! She does choose;
And takes her husband, like a proper wife.
15 Unnatural? My dear, these things are life:
And life, some think, is worthy of the Muse.

26

Love ere he bleeds, an eagle in high skies,
Has earth beneath his wings: from reddened eve
He views the rosy dawn. In vain they weave
The fatal web below while far he flies.
5 But when the arrow strikes him, there's a change.
He moves but in the track of his spent pain,
Whose red drops are the links of a harsh chain,
Binding him to the ground, with narrow range.
A subtle serpent then has Love become.

---

1 *Blanc-mange* Milk jelly.
2 *rosbif* French: roast beef.

10 I had the eagle in my bosom erst:°   *at first*
Henceforward with the serpent I am cursed.
I can interpret where the mouth is dumb.
Speak, and I see the side-lie of a truth.
Perchance my heart may pardon you this deed:
15 But be no coward—you that made Love bleed,
You must bear all the venom of his tooth!

27

Distraction is the panacea, Sir!
I hear my oracle of Medicine say.
Doctor! that same specific yesterday
I tried, and the result will not deter
5 A second trial. Is the devil's line
Of golden hair, or raven black, composed?
And does a cheek, like any seashell rosed,
Or clear as widowed sky, seem most divine?
No matter, so I taste forgetfulness.
10 And if the devil snare me, body and mind,
Here gratefully I score—he seemèd kind,
When not a soul would comfort my distress!
O sweet new world, in which I rise new made!
O Lady, once I gave love: now I take!
15 Lady, I must be flattered. Shouldst thou wake
The passion of a demon, be not afraid.

28

I must be flattered. The imperious
Desire speaks out. Lady, I am content
To play with you the game of Sentiment,
And with you enter on paths perilous;
5 But if across your beauty I throw light,
To make it threefold, it must be all mine.
First secret; then avowed. For I must shine
Envied—I, lessened in my proper sight!
Be watchful of your beauty, Lady dear!
10 How much hangs on that lamp you cannot tell.
Most earnestly I pray you, tend it well:
And men shall see me as a burning sphere;
And men shall mark you eyeing me, and groan
To be the God of such a grand sunflower!
15 I feel the promptings of Satanic power,
While you do homage unto me alone.

29

Am I failing? For no longer can I cast
A glory round about this head of gold.
Glory she wears, but springing from the mould
Not like the consecration of the Past!
5 Is my soul beggared? Something more than earth
I cry for still: I cannot be at peace
In having Love upon a mortal lease.
I cannot take the woman at her worth!
Where is the ancient wealth wherewith I clothed
10 Our human nakedness, and could endow
With spiritual splendour a white brow
That else had grinned at me the fact I loathed?
A kiss is but a kiss now! and no wave
Of a great flood that whirls me to the sea.
15 But, as you will! we'll sit contentedly,
And eat our pot of honey on the grave.

30

What are we first? First, animals; and next
Intelligences at a leap; on whom
Pale lies the distant shadow of the tomb,
And all that draweth on the tomb for text,
5 Into which state comes Love, the crowning sun:
Beneath whose light the shadow loses form.
We are the lords of life, and life is warm.
Intelligence and instinct now are one.
But nature says: "My children most they seem
10 When they least know me: therefore I decree
That they shall suffer." Swift doth young Love flee,
And we stand wakened, shivering from our dream.
Then if we study Nature we are wise.
Thus do the few who live but with the day:
15 The scientific animals are they.—
Lady, this is my sonnet to your eyes.

31

This golden head has wit in it. I live
Again, and a far higher life, near her.
Some women like a young philosopher;
Perchance because he is diminutive.
5 For woman's manly god must not exceed
Proportions of the natural nursing size.
Great poets and great sages draw no prize
With women: but the little lap-dog breed,

Who can be hugged, or on a mantel-piece
10 Perched up for adoration, these obtain
Her homage. And of this we men are vain?
Of this! 'Tis ordered for the world's increase!
Small flattery! Yet she has that rare gift
To beauty, Common Sense. I am approved.
15 It is not half so nice as being loved,
And yet I do prefer it. What's my drift?

32

Full faith I have she holds that rarest gift
To beauty, Common Sense. To see her lie
With her fair visage an inverted sky
Bloom-covered, while the underlids uplift,
5 Would almost wreck the faith; but when her mouth
(Can it kiss sweetly? sweetly!) would address
The inner me that thirsts for her no less,
And has so long been languishing in drought,
I feel that I am matched; that I am man!
10 One restless corner of my heart or head,
That holds a dying something never dead,
Still frets, though Nature giveth all she can.
It means, that woman is not, I opine,[1]
Her sex's antidote. Who seeks the asp
15 For serpent's bites? 'Twould calm me could I clasp
Shrieking Bacchantes[2] with their souls of wine!

33

"In Paris, at the Louvre, there have I seen
The sumptuously-feathered angel pierce
Prone Lucifer, descending.[3] Looked he fierce,
Showing the fight a fair one? Too serene!
5 The young Pharsalians[4] did not disarray
Less willingly their locks of floating silk:
That suckling mouth of his, upon the milk

---

1 *I opine* I hold the opinion.

2 *Bacchantes* Female followers of Bacchus, Roman god of wine, whose revelries included wild, orgiastic dancing.

3 *"sumptuously-feathered … descending"* St. Michael and Satan, painting by Raphael (1483– 1520) depicting St. Michael forcing Satan into Hell. This painting is, however, housed at the Prado in Madrid.

4 *Pharsalians* Followers of Julius Caesar who won a decisive victory over Pompey in the Battle of Pharsalia in 48 BCE.

Of heaven might still be feasting through the fray.
Oh, Raphael! when men the Fiend do fight,
10 They conquer not upon such easy terms.
Half serpent in the struggle grow these worms.
And does he grow half human, all is right."
This to my Lady in a distant spot,
Upon the theme: *While mind is mastering clay,*
15 *Gross clay invades it.* If the spy you play,
My wife, read this! Strange love talk, is it not?

34

Madam would speak with me. So, now it comes:
The Deluge or else Fire! She's well; she thanks
My husbandship. Our chain on silence clanks.
Time leers between, above his twiddling thumbs.
5 Am I quite well? Most excellent in health!
The journals, too, I diligently peruse.
Vesuvius[1] is expected to give news:
Niagara[2] is no noisier. By stealth
Our eyes dart scrutinizing snakes.
10 She's glad I'm happy, says her quivering under-lip.
"And are not you?" "How can I be?" "Take ship!
For happiness is somewhere to be had."
"Nowhere for me!" Her voice is barely heard.
I am not melted, and make no pretence.
15 With commonplace I freeze her, tongue and sense.
Niagara, or Vesuvius, is deferred.

35

It is no vulgar nature I have wived,
Secretive, sensitive, she takes a wound
Deep to her soul, as if the sense had swooned,
And not a thought of vengeance had survived.
5 No confidences has she: but relief
Must come to one whose suffering is acute.
O have a care of natures that are mute!
They punish you in acts: their steps are brief.
What is she doing? What does she demand
10 From Providence, or me? She is not one
Long to endure this torpidly, and shun
The drugs that crowd about a woman's hand.

---

1 *Vesuvius* Mount Vesuvius, an active volcano on the Bay of Naples.

2 *Niagara* Niagara Falls, waterfalls on the Niagara River.

At Forfeits[3] during snow we played, and I
Must kiss her. "Well performed!" I said: then she:
15 "'Tis hardly worth the money, you agree?"
Save her? What for? To act this wedded lie!

36

My Lady unto Madam makes her bow.
The charm of women is, that even while
You're probed by them for tears, you yet may smile,
Nay, laugh outright, as I have done just now.
5 The interview was gracious: they anoint
(To me aside) each other with fine praise:
Discriminating compliments they raise,
That hit with wondrous aim on the weak point:
My Lady's nose of Nature might complain.
10 It is not fashioned aptly to express
Her character of large-browed steadfastness.
But Madam says: Thereof she may be vain!
Now, Madam's faulty feature is a glazed
And inaccessible eye, that has soft fires,
15 Wide gates, at love-time only. This admires
My Lady. At the two I stand amazed.

37

Along the garden terrace, under which
A purple valley (lighted at its edge
By smoky torch-flame on the long cloud-ledge
Whereunder dropped the chariot), glimmers rich,
5 A quiet company we pace, and wait
The dinner-bell in pre-digestive calm.
So sweet up violet banks the Southern balm
Breathes round, we care not if the bell be late:
Though here and there grey seniors question Time
10 In irritable coughings. With slow foot
The low rosed moon, the face of Music mute,
Begins among her silent bars to climb.
As in and out, in silvery dusk, we thread,
I hear the laugh of Madam, and discern
15 My Lady's heel before me at each turn.
Our tragedy, is it alive or dead?

---

3 *Forfeits* Game in which players give up articles as penalties for mistakes made and then redeem those articles by performing small tasks.

38

Give to imagination some pure light
In human form to fix it, or you shame
The devils with that hideous human game:—
Imagination urging appetite!
5   Thus fallen have earth's greatest Gogmagogs,[1]
Who dazzle us, whom we can not revere:
Imagination is the charioteer
That, in default of better, drives the hogs.
So, therefore, my dear Lady, let me love!
10 My soul is arrowy to the light in you.
You know me that I never can renew
The bond that woman broke: what would you have?
'Tis Love, or Vileness! not a choice between,
Save petrifaction! What does Pity here?
15 She killed a thing, and now it's dead, 'tis dear.
Oh, when you counsel me, think what you mean!

39

She yields: my Lady in her noblest mood
Has yielded: she, my golden-crownëd rose!
The bride of every sense! more sweet than those
Who breathe the violet breath of maidenhood.
5   O visage of still music in the sky!
Soft moon! I feel thy song, my fairest friend!
True harmony within can apprehend
Dumb harmony without. And hark! 'tis nigh!
Belief has struck the note of sound: a gleam
10 Of living silver shows me where she shook
Her long white fingers down the shadowy brook,
That sings her song, half waking, half in dream.
What two come here to mar this heavenly tune?
A man is one: the woman bears my name,
15 And honour. Their hands touch! Am I still tame?
God, what a dancing spectre seems the moon!

40

I bade my Lady think what she might mean.
Know I my meaning, I? Can I love one,
And yet be jealous of another? None
Commits such folly. Terrible Love, I ween,°   *think*
5   Has might, even dead, half sighing to upheave
The lightless seas of selfishness amain:[2]
Seas that in a man's heart have no rain
To fall and still them. Peace can I achieve,
By turning to this fountain-source of woe,
10 This woman, who's to Love as fire to wood?
She breathed the violet breath of maidenhood
Against my kisses once! but I say, No!
The thing is mocked at! Helplessly afloat,
I know not what I do, whereto I strive,
15 The dread that my old love may be alive,
Has seized my nursling new love by the throat.

41

How many a thing which we cast to the ground,
When others pick it up becomes a gem!
We grasp at all the wealth it is to them;
And by reflected light its worth is found.
5   Yet for us still 'tis nothing! and that zeal
Of false appreciation quickly fades.
This truth is little known to human shades,
How rare from their own instinct 'tis to feel!
They waste the soul with spurious desire,
10 That is not the ripe flame upon the bough:
We two have taken up a lifeless vow
To rob a living passion: dust for fire!
Madam is grave, and eyes the clock that tells
Approaching midnight. We have struck despair
15 Into two hearts. O, look we like a pair
Who for fresh nuptials joyfully yield all else?

42

I am to follow her. There is much grace
In woman when thus bent on martyrdom.
They think that dignity of soul may come,
Perchance, with dignity of body. Base!
5   But I was taken by that air of cold
And statuesque sedateness, when she said

---

[1]   *Gogmagogs*   Giants. Gogmagog was the greatest of British giants, according to the history of Britain by Geoffrey of Monmouth (c. 1100–54). In British legend, Gog and Magog were two giants who were taken prisoner and forced to serve as porters at the royal palace. In Revelation 20.8, Gog and Magog represent the superhuman adversaries of the Kingdom of God at the end of time.

[2]   *amain*   At full speed, in full force.

"I'm going"; lit a taper, bowed her head,
And went, as with the stride of Pallas[1] bold.
Fleshly indifference horrible! The hands
10 Of Time now signal: O, she's safe from me!
Within those secret walls what do I see?
Where first she set the taper down she stands:
Not Pallas: Hebe[2] shamed! Thoughts black as death,
Like a stirred pool in sunshine break. Her wrists
15 I catch: she faltering, as she half resists,
"You love …? love …? love …?" all in an indrawn breath.

43

Mark where the pressing wind shoots javelin-like,
Its skeleton shadow on the broad-backed wave!
Here is a fitting spot to dig Love's grave;
Here where the ponderous breakers plunge and strike,
5 And dart their hissing tongues high up the sand:
In hearing of the ocean, and in sight
Of those ribbed wind-streaks running into white.
If I the death of Love had deeply planned,
I never could have made it half so sure,
10 As by the unblest kisses which upbraid
The full-waked sense; or failing that, degrade!
'Tis morning: but no morning can restore
What we have forfeited. I see no sin:
The wrong is mixed. In tragic life, God wot,°   knows
15 No villain need be! Passions spin the plot:
We are betrayed by what is false within.

44

They say, that Pity in Love's service dwells,
A porter at the rosy temple's gate.
I missed him going: but it is my fate
To come upon him now beside his wells;
5 Whereby I know that I Love's temple leave,
And that the purple doors have closed behind.
Poor soul! if in those early days unkind,
Thy power to sting had been but power to grieve,
We now might with an equal spirit meet,
10 And not be matched like innocence and vice.

She for the Temple's worship has paid price,
And takes the coin of Pity as a cheat.
She sees through simulation to the bone:
What's best in her impels her to the worst:
15 Never, she cries, shall Pity soothe Love's thirst,
Or foul hypocrisy for truth atone!

45

It is the season of the sweet wild rose,
My Lady's emblem in the heart of me!
So golden-crownèd shines she gloriously,
And with that softest dream of blood she glows:
5 Mild as an evening heaven round Hesper[3] bright!
I pluck the flower, and smell it, and revive
The time when in her eyes I stood alive.
I seem to look upon it out of Night.
Here's Madam, stepping hastily. Her whims
10 Bid her demand the flower, which I let drop.
As I proceed, I feel her sharply stop,
And crush it under heel with trembling limbs.
She joins me in a cat-like way, and talks
Of company, and even condescends
15 To utter laughing scandal of old friends.
These are the summer days, and these our walks.

46

At last we parley: we so strangely dumb
In such a close communion! It befell
About the sounding of the Matin-bell,[4]
And lo! her place was vacant, and the hum
5 Of loneliness was round me. Then I rose,
And my disordered brain did guide my foot
To that old wood where our first love-salute
Was interchanged: the source of many throes![5]
There did I see her, not alone. I moved
10 Toward her, and made proffer of my arm.
She took it simply, with no rude alarm;
And that disturbing shadow passed reproved.
I felt the pained speech coming, and declared
My firm belief in her, ere she could speak.

---

1 *Pallas* Epithet of Athena, Roman goddess of wisdom, protectress of towns, and patroness of the arts.

2 *Hebe* Goddess of youth and spring, the cup-bearer of Olympus until accused of immodesty by Jupiter and dismissed.

3 *Hesper* I.e., Hesperus, the evening star.

4 *Matin-bell* Bell announcing the start of the service of matins, which precedes the first mass of the day.

5 *throes* Severe pangs or spasms, here of pain or longing.

15   A ghastly morning came into her cheek,
      While with a widening soul on me she stared.

47

      We saw the swallows gathering in the sky,
      And in the osier-isle[1] we heard their noise.
      We had not to look back on summer joys,
      Or forward to a summer of bright dye:
5   But in the largeness of the evening earth
      Our spirits grew as we went side by side.
      The hour became her husband and my bride.
      Love that had robbed us so, thus blessed our dearth!
      The pilgrims of the year waxed very loud
10   In multitudinous chatterings, as the flood
      Full brown came from the West, and like pale blood
      Expanded to the upper crimson cloud.
      Love that had robbed us of immortal things,
      This little moment mercifully gave
15   Where I have seen across the twilight wave,
      The swan sail with her young beneath her wings.

48

      Their sense is with their senses all mixed in,
      Destroyed by subtleties these women are!
      More brain, O Lord, more brain! or we shall mar
      Utterly this fair garden we might win.
5   Behold! I looked for peace, and thought it near.
      Our inmost hearts had opened, each to each.
      We drank the pure daylight of honest speech.
      Alas! that was the fatal draught, I fear.
      For when of my lost Lady came the word,
10   This woman, O this agony of flesh!
      Jealous devotion bade her break the mesh,
      That I might seek that other like a bird.
      I do adore the nobleness! despise
      The act! She has gone forth, I know not where.
15   Will the hard world my sentience of her share?
      I feel the truth; so let the world surmise.

---

1   *osier-isle* Island of willow trees.

49

      He found her by the ocean's moaning verge,
      Nor any wicked change in her discerned;
      And she believed his old love had returned,
      Which was her exultation, and her scourge.
5   She took his hand, and walked with him, and seemed
      The wife he sought, though shadow-like and dry.
      She had one terror, lest her heart should sigh,
      And tell her loudly she no longer dreamed.
      She dared not say, "This is my breast: look in."
10   But there's a strength to help the desperate weak.
      That night he learned how silence best can speak
      The awful things when Pity pleads for Sin.
      About the middle of the night her call
      Was heard, and he came wondering to the bed.
15   "Now kiss me, dear! it may be, now!" she said.
      Lethe[2] had passed those lips, and he knew all.

50

      Thus piteously Love closed what he begat:
      The union of this ever-diverse pair!
      These two were rapid falcons in a snare,
      Condemned to do the flitting of the bat.
5   Lovers beneath the singing sky of May,
      They wandered once; clear as the dew on flowers:
      But they fed not on the advancing hours:
      Their hearts held cravings for the buried day.
      Then each applied to each that fatal knife,
10   Deep questioning, which probes to endless dole.
      Ah, what a dusty answer gets the soul
      When hot for certainties in this our life!—
      In tragic hints here see what evermore
      Moves dark as yonder midnight ocean's force,
15   Thundering like ramping° hosts of warrior horse,   *rearing*
      To throw that faint thin line upon the shore!
      —1862

---

2   *Lethe* A river in Hades (the underworld in Greek mythology) the
waters of which produced forgetfulness of the past in those who drank
it.

DANTE GABRIEL ROSSETTI
1828 – 1882

Dante Gabriel Rossetti's best work in both poetry and painting resembles a kind of illuminated manuscript glimpsed in "a fragment of Venetian glass." Walter Pater used these words to describe the Aesthetic arts whose efflorescence at the end of the nineteenth-century owed so much to Rossetti.

Stylized and radiant scenes of knights, maidens, and lovers—soon synonymous with Rossetti's name—found their original inspiration in works of early Italian, Christian, and medieval iconography. The subject of "The Blessed Damozel," one of Rossetti's finest poems, glows with the spiritually luminous effects associated with the religious poetry of Dante (Rossetti's namesake). Yet Rossetti also endowed his damsel with an earthly voluptuousness. Borrowing from Dantesque and Arthurian mythology, Rossetti created fantasies whose "stained glass" quality reflects both the literary outlines of religious allegory and the sensual strokes of an artist enraptured by the female figure. It was an artistic approach that ran the risk of causing offence at a time when soul and body, love and sex, were separate compartments of Victorian life, and Rossetti's work was frequently attacked in the later half of his career for trying to solder spiritual to "fleshly" desires.

Born in 1828 into an erudite family, Rossetti was the third of four children. He was a competitive yet fiercely fond older brother to his sister, the future poet Christina. His mother, Frances Polidori Rossetti, was Anglo-Italian; his father, Gabriele Rossetti, an exiled Italian patriot, was a Professor at King's College, London. The Rossetti's childhood home, with its assortment of orthodox and unorthodox books, was a meeting place where politicized ex-patriots spent many an evening debating the past and future of Italy. From the stream of sketches and literary compositions issuing from the temperamental imaginations of Dante Gabriel and Christina, it was apparent early on that the two youngest Rossettis were extraordinarily gifted. Their parents held high hopes that Dante Gabriel would become a great painter, even though his schooling in painting and his knowledge of European painting were not extensive.

Rossetti was a moody student at the Royal Academy art school in 1848 when he co-founded the Pre-Raphaelite Brotherhood with fellow painters William Holman Hunt, John Everett Millais, James Collinson, Frederic George Stephens, Thomas Woolner, and Dante Gabriel's brother, critic William Michael Rossetti. In a letter to his sister Christina, Rossetti spoke of it the group as a "Round Table" whose knights shared a mutual love of Keats. (They also adored Malory's *Morte Darthur*, the novels of Walter Scott, and the work of Blake, Dante, Tennyson, and Browning.) By referencing early Florentine and Sienese schools (dubbed "the Italian Primitives" because they predated the High Renaissance), the Pre-Raphaelites sought to reform what they saw as the florid emptiness of Victorian art and its lack of truth to nature. "Sincerity" as a quality of near-devotional feeling communicated through purity of line and color was more important to the Pre-Raphaelites than mere technical virtuosity. As one critic put it, the Pre-Raphaelites favored "primitive but vital imperfection, as opposed to lifeless perfection." A movement in both literature and painting, Pre-Raphaelitism was identified with a vivid palette, formal patterning, and symbolic details woven into exotic scenes of religious or romantic love whose settings evoked a sumptuous "elsewhere." In Pre-Raphaelite poetry and painting, there was always a "definiteness of sensible imagery," as Pater said of "The Blessed Damozel."

When sixteen-year old Christina published *Verses* in 1847, Rossetti was compelled to try with meter what he was doing with color. "Colour and metre," Rossetti claimed, "are the true parents of nobility in painting and poetry." In 1850, the Pre-Raphaelite Brotherhood published a journal of poems and illustrations entitled *The Germ*, in which Rossetti's "The Blessed Damozel" first appeared. The publication gained Rossetti a small group of admirers that would steadily increase. Ruskin, who helped turn the tide in his favor by praising the art of the Pre-Raphaelites in *The Times* in 1851, became one of Rossetti's prominent patrons and closest friends. Rossetti cherished intellectual friendships with Robert Browning and William Morris, and socialized with the flamboyant Algernon Swinburne. He obtained stable employment teaching art at the Working Men's College. Stumbling across a book of William Blake's poems and paintings, Rossetti discovered another kindred spirit, albeit one who had died a year before he was born. Having secured his own reputation, Rossetti was able to rescue Blake from near oblivion, rediscovering him for a Victorian audience. In 1861, he also published *The Early Italian Poets*, which introduced, through his translations of the *Vita Nuova* and other poems by Dante and his predecessors and contemporaries, many poets whose work had been unknown in England.

Rossetti was also prone to what one biographer calls "rescue missions" of unknown beauties. Elizabeth Gaskell wrote that Rossetti was "hair-mad," with a penchant for the wavy tresses of women he and his friends called "stunners." On the one hand, Rossetti supported the equality and independence of working-class women like Elizabeth Siddal, whom he eventually married. On the other hand, his rescue of beautiful women from their class obscurity dramatized a sexual imbalance of power that was titillating; like many Victorian men, Rossetti enjoyed the license to "fall in love" with working class women without seriously compromising his reputation, a license prohibited women under the double standards of Victorian society.

Siddal, a model for the Pre-Raphaelites and an artist and poet in her own right, committed suicide in 1862, two years after her marriage to Rossetti. Invoking Dante's dead beloved, Beatrice, Rossetti memorialized Siddal in a painting entitled *Beata Beatrix* (c.1863). Seized with remorse at her funeral, he tucked a manuscript of poems into her coffin. He had them exhumed years later in order to publish his first collection of verse, *Poems* (1870). Though Rossetti afterwards lived with Fanny Cornforth, he fell in love with Jane Burden, the wife of William Morris. Both Fanny and "Janey" came from working class backgrounds and modeled for Rossetti, becoming sensuously stylized objects of desire in paintings such as *Proserpine* (1874).

Soon after the appearance of Rossetti's *The House of Life*, a sequence of 101 sonnets that appeared in his first volume of poetry, the poet Robert Buchanan denounced its "animalism" in a scalding critique entitled *The Fleshly School of Poetry* (1871). According to Buchanan, Rossetti's "house of life" was suggestive of a brothel and his sonnets bore the stamp of "the same sense of weary, wasting, yet exquisite sensuality." Rossetti counterattacked with *The Stealthy School of Criticism* (1872), but many readers since have felt that there was a germ of truth in Buchanan's criticisms: the spiritual impulse that strove to unite love and sexuality in Rossetti's art seems at times overshadowed by a carnal undergrowth verging upon the fetishistic.

Rossetti had always been temperamental, and Buchanan's attack temporarily deranged him. Though Yeats's youthful claim that he was "in all things Pre-Raphaelite" was proof of Rossetti's influence on the next generation of poets, Rossetti himself never fully recovered from being "stigmatized as a sensualist," in the words of one critic. He continued to paint and write, however, publishing *Ballads and Sonnets* in 1881. Bouts of nervous depression, made worse by the consumption of whiskey and narcotics, led to a decline in Rossetti's health; he died in 1882.

⌘ ⌘ ⌘

The Blessed Damozel [1]

The blessed damozel leaned out
　From the gold bar of Heaven;
Her eyes were deeper than the depth
　Of waters stilled at even;
5　She had three lilies in her hand,
　And the stars in her hair were seven.

Her robe, ungirt from clasp to hem,
　No wrought flowers did adorn,
But a white rose of Mary's gift,
10　For service meetly worn;
Her hair that lay along her back
　Was yellow like ripe corn.

Herseemed she scarce had been a day
　One of God's choristers;
15　The wonder was not yet quite gone
　From that still look of hers;
Albeit, to them she left, her day
　Had counted as ten years.

(To one, it is ten years of years.
20　… Yet now, and in this place,
Surely she leaned o'er me—her hair
　Fell all about my face….
Nothing: the autumn-fall of leaves.
　The whole year sets apace.)

25　It was the rampart of God's house
　That she was standing on;
By God built over the sheer depth
　The which is Space begun;
So high, that looking downward thence
30　She scarce could see the sun.

Dante Gabriel Rossetti, *The Blessed
Damozel* (1875–78).

It lies in Heaven, across the flood
　Of ether, as a bridge.
Beneath, the tides of day and night
　With flame and darkness ridge
35　The void, as low as where this earth
　Spins like a fretful midge.[2]

Around her, lovers, newly met
　'Mid deathless love's acclaims,
Spoke evermore among themselves
40　Their heart-remembered names;
And the souls mounting up to God
　Went by her like thin flames.

And still she bowed herself and stooped
　Out of the circling charm;

1　*The Blessed Damozel*　After the poem's publication, Rossetti told novelist Hall Caine that he had written it as something of a sequel to Edgar Allen Poe's poem "The Raven" (1845): "I saw that Poe had done the utmost it was possible to do with the grief of the lover on earth, and so determined to reverse the conditions, and give utterance to the yearning of the loved one in heaven." A "damozel" is a damsel, a young, unmarried woman.

2　*midge*　Small fly.

45 Until her bosom must have made
        The bar she leaned on warm,
And the lilies lay as if asleep
        Along her bended arm.

From the fixed place of Heaven she saw
50   Time like a pulse shake fierce
Through all the worlds. Her gaze still strove
        Within the gulf to pierce
Its path; and now she spoke as when
        The stars sang in their spheres.[1]

55 The sun was gone now; the curled moon
        Was like a little feather
Fluttering far down the gulf; and now
        She spoke through the still weather.
Her voice was like the voice the stars
60   Had when they sang together.

(Ah sweet! Even now, in that bird's song,
        Strove not her accents there,
Fain to be hearkened? When those bells
        Possessed the mid-day air,
65 Strove not her steps to reach my side
        Down all the echoing stair?)

"I wish that he were come to me,
        For he will come," she said.
"Have I not prayed in Heaven?—on earth,
70   Lord, Lord, has he not prayed?
Are not two prayers a perfect strength?
        And shall I feel afraid?

"When round his head the aureole° clings,   *halo*
        And he is clothed in white,
75 I'll take his hand and go with him
        To the deep wells of light;
As unto a stream we will step down,
        And bathe there in God's sight.

"We two will stand beside that shrine,
80   Occult,° withheld, untrod,   *secret*

Whose lamps are stirred continually
        With prayer sent up to God;
And see our old prayers, granted, melt
        Each like a little cloud.

85 "We two will lie i'the shadow of
        That living mystic tree[2]
Within whose secret growth the Dove[3]
        Is sometimes felt to be,
While every leaf that His plumes touch
90   Saith His Name audibly.

"And I myself will teach to him,
        I myself, lying so,
The songs I sing here; which his voice
        Shall pause in, hushed and slow,
95 And find some knowledge at each pause,
        Or some new thing to know."

(Alas! We two, we two, thou say'st!
        Yea, one wast thou with me
That once of old. But shall God lift
100   To endless unity
The soul whose likeness with thy soul
        Was but its love for thee?)

"We two," she said, "will seek the groves
        Where the lady Mary is,
105 With her five handmaidens, whose names
        Are five sweet symphonies,
Cecily, Gertrude, Magdalen,
        Margaret and Rosalys.

"Circlewise sit they, with bound locks
110   And foreheads garlanded;
Into the fine cloth white like flame
        Weaving the golden thread,
To fashion the birth-robes for them
        Who are just born, being dead.

115 "He shall fear, haply,° and be dumb: *perchance*
        Then will I lay my cheek
To his, and tell about our love,

---

1 *as when ... spheres* See Job 38.7, in which the morning stars sing on creation day. Rossetti probably also refers to the Pythagorean concept of the music of the spheres, inaudible to those on earth.

2 *living mystic tree* Tree of life (See Revelation 22.2).

3 *Dove* Holy Spirit.

Not once abashed or weak:
And the dear Mother will approve
120   My pride, and let me speak.

"Herself shall bring us, hand in hand,
    To him round whom all souls
Kneel, the clear-ranged unnumbered heads
    Bowed with their aureoles:°   *haloes*
125 And angels meeting us shall sing
    To their citherns and citoles.[1]

"There will I ask of Christ the Lord
    Thus much for him and me:
Only to live as once on earth
130   With Love—only to be,
As then awhile, for ever now
    Together, I and he."

She gazed and listened and then said,
    Less sad of speech than mild—
135 "All this is when he comes." She ceased.
    The light thrilled towards her, filled
With angels in strong level flight.
    Her eyes prayed, and she smiled.

(I saw her smile.) But soon their path
140   Was vague in distant spheres:
And then she cast her arms along
    The golden barriers,
And laid her face between her hands,
    And wept. (I heard her tears.)
—1850

The Woodspurge [2]

The wind flapped loose, the wind was still,
  Shaken out dead from tree and hill:

I had walked on at the wind's will—
I sat now, for the wind was still.

5 Between my knees my forehead was—
My lips, drawn in, said not Alas!
My hair was over in the grass,
My naked ears heard the day pass.

My eyes, wide open, had the run
10 Of some ten weeds to fix upon;
Among those few, out of the sun,
The woodspurge flowered, three cups in one.

From perfect grief there need not be
Wisdom or even memory:
15 One thing then learnt remains to me—
The woodspurge has a cup of three.
—1870

Jenny

"Vengeance of Jenny's case! Fie on her!
Never name her, child"

                 (Mrs. Quickly.)[3]

Lazy laughing languid Jenny,
  Fond of a kiss and fond of a guinea,[4]
Whose head upon my knee to-night
Rests for a while, as if grown light
5 With all our dances and the sound
To which the wild tunes spun you round:
Fair Jenny mine, the thoughtless queen
Of kisses which the blush between
Could hardly make much daintier;
10 Whose eyes are as blue skies, whose hair
Is countless gold incomparable;
Fresh flower, scarce touched with signs that tell
Of Love's exuberant hotbed—Nay,
Poor flower left torn since yesterday
15 Until to-morrow leave you bare;

---

[1] *citherns* Guitar-like instruments strung with wire and played with a quill, popular in the sixteenth and seventeenth centuries; *citoles* Stringed instruments common in the thirteenth to fifteenth centuries.

[2] *Woodspurge* Wildflower with cup-like, yellowish-green flowers that excrete a milky juice.

[3] *Vengeance ... Quickly* From Shakespeare's *The Merry Wives of Windsor* 1.1. The rest of Mistress Quickly's speech reads, "if she be a whore."

[4] *guinea* English gold coin.

Poor handful of bright spring-water
Flung in the whirlpool's shrieking face;
Poor shameful Jenny, full of grace
Thus with your head upon my knee—
20   Whose person or whose purse may be
The lodestar[1] of your reverie?

This room of yours, my Jenny, looks
A change from mine so full of books,
Whose serried[2] ranks hold fast, forsooth,
25   So many captive hours of youth—
The hours they thieve from day and night
To make one's cherished work come right,
And leave it wrong for all their theft,
Even as to-night my work was left:
30   Until I vowed that since my brain
And eyes of dancing seemed so fain,
My feet should have some dancing too—
And thus it was I met with you.
Well, I suppose 'twas hard to part,
35   For here I am. And now, sweetheart,
You seem too tired to get to bed.

It was a careless life I led
When rooms like this were scarce so strange
Not long ago. What breeds the change—
40   The many aims or the few years?
Because to-night it all appears
Something I do not know again.

The cloud's not danced out of my brain—
The cloud that made it turn and swim
45   While hour by hour the books grew dim.
Why, Jenny, as I watch you there,
For all your wealth of loosened hair,
Your silk ungirdled and unlaced
And warm sweets open to the waist,
50   All golden in the lamplight's gleam,
You know not what a book you seem,
Half-read by lightning in a dream!
How should you know, my Jenny? Nay,
And I should be ashamed to say—
55   Poor beauty, so well worth a kiss!

----

1   *lodestar*   Pole star; i.e., guiding star.

2   *serried*   Pressed close together.

But while my thought runs on like this
With wasteful whims more than enough,
I wonder what you're thinking of.

If of myself you think at all,
60   What is the thought?—conjectural
On sorry matters best unsolved?—
Or inly° is each grace revolved   *inwardly*
To fit me with a lure?—or (sad
To think!) perhaps you're merely glad
65   That I'm not drunk or ruffianly
And let you rest upon my knee.

For sometimes, were the truth confessed,
You're thankful for a little rest—
Glad from the crush to rest within,
70   From the heart-sickness and the din
Where envy's voice at virtue's pitch
Mocks you because your gown is rich;
And from the pale girl's dumb rebuke,
Whose ill-clad grace and toil-worn look
75   Proclaim the strength that keeps her weak
And other nights than yours bespeak;
And from the wise unchildish elf,
To schoolmate lesser than himself
Pointing you out, what thing you are—
80   Yes, from the daily jeer and jar,
From shame and shame's outbraving too,
Is rest not sometimes sweet to you?
But most from the hatefulness of man
Who spares not to end what he began,
85   Whose acts are ill and his speech ill,
Who, having used you at his will,
Thrusts you aside, as when I dine
I serve the dishes and the wine.

Well, handsome Jenny mine, sit up,
90   I've filled our glasses, let us sup,
And do not let me think of you,
Lest shame of yours suffice for two.
What, still so tired? Well, well then, keep
Your head there, so you do not sleep;
95   But that the weariness may pass
And leave you merry, take this glass.
Ah! lazy lily hand, more blessed

If ne'er in rings it had been dressed
Nor ever by a glove concealed!

100   Behold the lilies of the field,
They toil not neither do they spin;[1]
(So doth the ancient text begin—
Not of such rest as one of these
Can share.) Another rest and ease
105 Along each summer-sated path
From its new lord the garden hath,
Than that whose spring in blessings ran
Which praised the bounteous husbandman,
Ere yet, in days of hankering breath,
110 The lilies sickened unto death.

    What, Jenny, are your lilies dead?
Aye, and the snow-white leaves are spread
Like winter on the garden-bed.
But you had roses left in May—
115 They were not gone too. Jenny, nay,
But must your roses die, and those
Their purfled[2] buds that should unclose?
Even so; the leaves are curled apart,
Still red as from the broken heart,
120 And here's the naked stem of thorns.

    Nay, nay, mere words. Here nothing warns
As yet of winter. Sickness here
Or want alone could waken fear—
Nothing but passion wrings a tear.
125 Except when there may rise unsought
Haply° at times a passing thought   *perchance*
Of the old days which seem to be
Much older than any history
That is written in any book;
130 When she would lie in fields and look
Along the ground through the blown grass,
And wonder where the city was,
Far out of sight, whose broil° and bale°   *tumult / woe*
They told her then for a child's tale.

135   Jenny, you know the city now.
A child can tell the tale there, how
Some things which are not yet enrolled
In market-lists are bought and sold
Even till the early Sunday light,
140 When Saturday night is market-night
Everywhere, be it dry or wet,
And market-night in the Haymarket.
Our learned London children know,
Poor Jenny, all your pride and woe;
145 Have seen your lifted silken skirt
Advertise dainties through the dirt;
Have seen your coach-wheels splash rebuke
On virtue; and have learned your look
When, wealth and health slipped past, you stare
150 Along the streets alone, and there,
Round the long park, across the bridge,
The cold lamps at the pavement's edge
Wind on together and apart,
A fiery serpent for your heart.

155   Let the thoughts pass, an empty cloud!
Suppose I were to think aloud—
What if to her all this were said?
Why, as a volume seldom read
Being opened halfway shuts again,
160 So might the pages of her brain
Be parted at such words, and thence
Close back upon the dusty sense.
For is there hue or shape defined
In Jenny's desecrated mind,
165 Where all contagious currents meet,
A Lethe[3] of the middle street?
Nay, it reflects not any face,
Nor sound is in its sluggish pace,
But as they coil those eddies clot,
170 And night and day remember not.

    Why, Jenny, you're asleep at last!
Asleep, poor Jenny, hard and fast—
So young and soft and tired; so fair,
With chin thus nestled in your hair,

---

[1] *Behold … spin* Reference to Matthew 6.28: "And why take ye thought for raiment? Consider the lilies of the field, how they grow; they toil not, neither do they spin."

[2] *purfled* Edged with another color.

---

[3] *Lethe* River in Hades (the underworld of classical mythology) whose waters bring forgetfulness to those who drink from them.

175 Mouth quiet, eyelids almost blue
As if some sky of dreams shone through!

Just as another woman sleeps!
Enough to throw one's thoughts in heaps
Of doubt and horror—what to say
180 Or think—this awful secret sway,
The potter's power over the clay!
Of the same lump (it has been said)
For honour and dishonour made,
Two sister vessels.[1] Here is one.

185 My cousin Nell is fond of fun,
And fond of dress, and change, and praise,
So mere a woman in her ways:
And if her sweet eyes rich in youth
Are like her lips that tell the truth,
190 My cousin Nell is fond of love.
And she's the girl I'm proudest of.
Who does not prize her, guard her well?
The love of change, in cousin Nell,
Shall find the best and hold it dear:
195 The unconquered mirth turn quieter
Not through her own, through others' woe:
The conscious pride of beauty glow
Beside another's pride in her,
One little part of all they share.
200 For Love himself shall ripen these
In a kind soil to just increase
Through years of fertilizing peace.

Of the same lump (as it is said)
For honour and dishonour made,
205 Two sister vessels. Here is one.

It makes a goblin of the sun.

So pure—so fallen! How dare to think
Of the first common kindred link?
Yet, Jenny, till the world shall burn
210 It seems that all things take their turn;
And who shall say but this fair tree

May need, in changes that may be,
Your children's children's charity?
Scorned then, no doubt, as you are scorned!
215 Shall no man hold his pride forewarned
Till in the end, the Day of Days,
At Judgment, one of his own race,
As frail and lost as you, shall rise—
His daughter, with his mother's eyes?

220 How Jenny's clock ticks on the shelf!
Might not the dial scorn itself
That has such hours to register?
Yet as to me, even so to her
Are golden sun and silver moon,
225 In daily largesse of earth's boon,
Counted for life-coins to one tune.
And if, as blindfold fates are tossed,
Through some one man this life be lost,
Shall soul not somehow pay for soul?

230 Fair shines the gilded aureole°   *halo*
In which our highest painters place
Some living woman's simple face.
And the stilled features thus descried
As Jenny's long throat droops aside—
235 The shadows where the cheeks are thin,
And pure wide curve from ear to chin—
With Raffael's, Leonardo's[2] hand
To show them to men's souls, might stand,
Whole ages long, the whole world through,
240 For preachings of what God can do.
What has man done here? How atone,
Great God, for this which man has done?
And for the body and soul which by
Man's pitiless doom must now comply
245 With lifelong hell, what lullaby
Of sweet forgetful second birth
Remains? All dark. No sign on earth
What measure of God's rest endows
The many mansions of his house.

250 If but a woman's heart might see
Such erring heart unerringly

---

[1] *The potter's ... vessels* Reference to Romans 9.21: "Hath not the potter power over the clay, of the same lump to make one vessel unto honor, and another unto dishonor?"

[2] *Raffael's, Leonardo's* I.e., Italian painters Raphael (1483–1520) and Leonardo da Vinci (1452–1519).

For once! But that can never be.

    Like a rose shut in a book
In which pure women may not look,
255 For its base pages claim control
To crush the flower within the soul;
Where through each dead rose-leaf that clings,
Pale as transparent psyche-wings,
To the vile text, are traced such things
260 As might make lady's cheek indeed
More than a living rose to read;
So nought save foolish foulness may
Watch with hard eyes the sure decay;
And so the life-blood of this rose,
265 Puddled with shameful knowledge, flows
Through leaves no chaste hand may unclose:
Yet still it keeps such faded show
Of when 'twas gathered long ago,
That the crushed petals' lovely grain,
270 The sweetness of the sanguine stain,
Seen of a woman's eyes, must make
Her pitiful heart, so prone to ache,
Love roses better for its sake—
Only that this can never be:
275 Even so unto her sex is she.

    Yet, Jenny, looking long at you,
The woman almost fades from view.
A cipher of man's changeless sum
Of lust, past, present, and to come,
280 Is left. A riddle that one shrinks
To challenge from the scornful sphinx.[1]

    Like a toad within a stone
Seated while Time crumbles on;[2]

Which sits there since the earth was cursed
285 For Man's transgression at the first;
Which, living through all centuries,
Not once has seen the sun arise;
Whose life, to its cold circle charmed,
The earth's whole summers have not warmed;
290 Which always—whitherso the stone
Be flung—sits there, deaf, blind, alone;
Aye, and shall not be driven out
Till that which shuts him round about
Break at the very Master's stroke,
295 And the dust thereof vanish as smoke,
And the seed of Man vanish as dust—
Even so within this world is Lust.

    Come, come, what use in thoughts like this?
Poor little Jenny, good to kiss—
300 You'd not believe by what strange roads
Thought travels, when your beauty goads
A man to-night to think of toads!
Jenny, wake up … Why, there's the dawn!

    And there's an early wagon drawn
305 To market, and some sheep that jog
Bleating before a barking dog;
And the old streets come peering through
Another night that London knew;
And all as ghostlike as the lamps.

310   So on the wings of day decamps
My last night's frolic. Glooms begin
To shiver off as lights creep in
Past the gauze curtains half drawn-to,
And the lamp's doubled shade grows blue—
315 Your lamp, my Jenny, kept alight,
Like a wise virgin's, all one night!
And in the alcove coolly spread
Glimmers with dawn your empty bed;
And yonder your fair face I see
320 Reflected lying on my knee,
Where teems with first foreshadowings
Your pier-glass[3] scrawled with diamond rings:

---

[1] *sphinx* Winged creature of Greek mythology who killed those who could not answer its riddles.

[2] *Like a … on* The phenomenon of living toads, frogs, or other creatures trapped in stone or wood is one that has been occasionally reported. Once such instance occurred in 1865, when workers excavating in Hartlepool, England, split open a magnesium limestone rock found 25 feet underground to discover a living toad. The *Hartlepool Free Press* reported, "The cavity was no larger than its body, and presented the appearance of being cast for it." There was no evidence as to how the toad could have gotten into the stone or survived in it for any length of time. But, from its appearance and

---

the age of the rock in which it was found, the toad was estimated to be over 6000 years old.

[3] *pier-glass* Large, tall mirror.

And on your bosom all night worn
Yesterday's rose now droops forlorn
325   But dies not yet this summer morn.

And now without, as if some word
Had called upon them that they heard,
The London sparrows far and nigh
Clamour together suddenly;
330   And Jenny's cage-bird grown awake
Here in their song his part must take,
Because here too the day doth break.

And somehow in myself the dawn
Among stirred clouds and veils withdrawn
335   Strikes greyly on her. Let her sleep.
But will it wake her if I heap
These cushions thus beneath her head
Where my knee was? No—there's your bed,
My Jenny, while you dream. And there
340   I lay among your golden hair
Perhaps the subject of your dreams,
These golden coins.

For still one deems
That Jenny's flattering sleep confers
345   New magic on the magic purse—
Grim web, how clogged with shrivelled flies!
Between the threads fine fumes arise
And shape their pictures in the brain.
There roll no streets in glare and rain,
350   Nor flagrant man-swine whets his tusk;
But delicately sighs in musk
The homage of the dim boudoir;
Or like a palpitating star
Thrilled into song, the opera-night
355   Breathes faint in the quick pulse of light;
Or at the carriage-window shine
Rich wares for choice; or, free to dine,
Whirls through its hour of health (divine
For her) the concourse of the Park.
360   And though in the discounted dark
Her functions there and here are one,
Beneath the lamps and in the sun
There reigns at least the acknowledged belle

Apparelled beyond parallel.
365   Ah Jenny, yes, we know your dreams.

For even the Paphian Venus[1] seems
A goddess o'er the realms of love,
When silver-shrined in shadowy grove:
Aye, or let offerings nicely placed
370   But hide Priapus[2] to the waist,
And whoso looks on him shall see
An eligible deity.

Why, Jenny, waking here alone
May help you to remember one,
375   Though all the memory's long outworn
Of many a double-pillowed morn.
I think I see you when you wake,
And rub your eyes for me, and shake
My gold, in rising, from your hair,
380   A Danaë[3] for a moment there.

Jenny, my love rang true! for still
Love at first sight is vague, until
That tinkling makes him audible.

And must I mock you to the last,
385   Ashamed of my own shame—aghast
Because some thoughts not born amiss
Rose at a poor fair face like this?
Well, of such thoughts so much I know:
In my life, as in hers, they show,
390   By a far gleam which I may near,
A dark path I can strive to clear.

Only one kiss. Goodbye, my dear.
—1870

---

[1] *Paphian Venus*   Venus, goddess of love, was said to have been born of sea-form, but emerged on the island of Paphos, Cypress.

[2] *Priapus*   God of procreation, and a personification of an erect phallus.

[3] *Danaë*   According to Greek mythology, Acrisius imprisoned his daughter Danaë in a room of bronze to ensure she would never conceive a son. Zeus, however, fell in love with Danaë and came to her through the ceiling as a shower of gold that fell in her lap.

My Sister's Sleep

She fell asleep on Christmas Eve:
    At length the long-ungranted shade
    Of weary eyelids overweighed
The pain nought else might yet relieve.

5 Our mother, who had leaned all day
    Over the bed from chime to chime,
    Then raised herself for the first time,
And as she sat her down, did pray.

Her little work-table was spread
10   With work to finish. For the glare
    Made by her candle, she had care
To work some distance from the bed.

Without, there was a cold moon up,
    Of winter radiance sheer and thin;
15   The hollow halo it was in
Was like an icy crystal cup.

Through the small room, with subtle sound
    Of flame, by vents the fireshine drove
    And reddened. In its dim alcove
20 The mirror shed a clearness round.

I had been sitting up some nights,
    And my tired mind felt weak and blank;
    Like a sharp strengthening wine it drank
The stillness and the broken lights.

25 Twelve struck. That sound, by dwindling years
    Heard in each hour, crept off; and then
    The ruffled silence spread again,
Like water that a pebble stirs.

Our mother rose from where she sat:
30   Her needles, as she laid them down,

Met lightly, and her silken gown
Settled: no other noise than that.

"Glory unto the Newly Born!"
35   So, as said angels, she did say;
    Because we were in Christmas Day,
Though it would still be long till morn.

Just then in the room over us
    There was a pushing back of chairs,
    As some who had sat unawares
40 So late, now heard the hour, and rose.

With anxious softly-stepping haste
    Our mother went where Margaret lay,
    Fearing the sounds o'erhead—should they
Have broken her long watched-for rest!

45 She stopped an instant, calm, and turned;
    But suddenly turned back again;
    And all her features seemed in pain
With woe, and her eyes gazed and yearned.

For my part, I but hid my face,
50   And held my breath, and spoke no word:
    There was none spoken; but I heard
The silence for a little space.

Our mother bowed herself and wept:
    And both my arms fell, and I said,
55   "God knows I knew that she was dead."
And there, all white, my sister slept.

Then kneeling, upon Christmas morn
    A little after twelve o'clock
    We said, ere the first quarter struck,
60 "Christ's blessing on the newly born!"
—1850

Dante Gabriel Rossetti, *Mary Magdalene at the Door of Simon the Pharisee* (1858).

Mary Magdalene at the Door of Simon the Pharisee[1] *(For a Drawing)*[2]

"Why wilt thou cast the roses from thine hair?
    Nay, be thou all a rose—wreath, lips, and
        cheek.
    Nay, not this house—that banquet-house we seek;
See how they kiss and enter; come thou there.

5 This delicate day of love we two will share
    Till at our ear love's whispering night shall speak.
    What, sweet one—hold'st thou still the foolish
        freak?°   *whim*
Nay, when I kiss thy feet they'll leave the stair."

"Oh loose me! See'st thou not my Bridegroom's face
10   That draws me to Him? For His feet my kiss,
      My hair, my tears He craves to-day—and oh!
What words can tell what other day and place
    Shall see me clasp those blood-stained feet of His?
      He needs me, calls me, loves me: let me go!"
—1870

from *The House of Life*

The Sonnet

A Sonnet is a moment's monument—
  Memorial from the Soul's eternity
  To one dead deathless hour. Look that it be,
Whether for lustral° rite or dire portent,   *purification*
5 Of its own arduous fulness reverent:
    Carve it in ivory or in ebony,
    As Day or Night may rule; and let Time see
Its flowering crest impearled and orient.

A Sonnet is a coin: its face reveals
10   The soul—its converse, to what Power 'tis due—
Whether for tribute to the august appeals
    Of Life, or dower in Love's high retinue,
It serve; or, 'mid the dark wharf's cavernous breath,
In Charon's[3] palm it pay the toll to Death.
—1881

---

[1] *Mary ... Pharisee* See Luke 7.36–50, which tells how an anonymous penitent, often assumed to be Mary Magdalene, burst into the house of Simon, a Pharisee, where Jesus was dining. She prostrated herself at his feet, which she then washed with her tears and dried with her hair.

[2] [Rossetti's note] In the drawing Mary has left a procession of revellers, and is ascending by a sudden impulse the steps of the house where she sees Christ. Her lover has followed her and is trying to turn her back.

---

[3] *Charon* In Greek mythology, ferryman of the river Styx who, for a fee, transports dead souls into Hades.

6a. Nuptial Sleep[1]

At length their long kiss severed, with sweet smart:
  And as the last slow sudden drops are shed
  From sparkling eaves when all the storm has fled,
So singly flagged the pulses of each heart.
Their bosoms sundered, with the opening start
  Of married flowers to either side outspread
  From the knit stem; yet still their mouths, burnt red,
Fawned on each other where they lay apart.

Sleep sank them lower than the tide of dreams,
  And their dreams watched them sink, and slid away.
Slowly their souls swam up again, through gleams
  Of watered light and dull drowned waifs of day;
Till from some wonder of new woods and streams
  He woke, and wondered more: for there she lay.
—1870

10. The Portrait

O Lord of all compassionate control,
  O Love! let this my lady's picture glow
  Under my hand to praise her name, and show
Even of her inner self the perfect whole:
That he who seeks her beauty's furthest goal,
  Beyond the light that the sweet glances throw
  And refluent wave of the sweet smile, may know
The very sky and sea-line of her soul.

Lo! it is done. Above the enthroning throat
  The mouth's mould testifies of voice and kiss,
    The shadowed eyes remember and foresee.
Her face is made her shrine. Let all men note
  That in all years (O Love, thy gift is this!)
    They that would look on her must come to me.
—1870

Dante Gabriel Rossetti, *Sibylla Palmifera* (1868).

77. Soul's Beauty [2]

Under the arch of Life, where love and death,
  Terror and mystery, guard her shrine, I saw
  Beauty enthroned; and though her gaze struck awe,
I drew it in as simply as my breath.
Hers are the eyes which, over and beneath,
  The sky and sea bend on thee—which can draw,
  By sea or sky or woman, to one law,
The allotted bondman of her palm and wreath.

This is that Lady Beauty, in whose praise
  Thy voice and hand shake still—long known to thee
    By flying hair and fluttering hem—the beat
  Following her daily of thy heart and feet,
    How passionately and irretrievably,
In what fond flight, how many ways and days!
—1870

---

[1] *Nuptial Sleep* This sonnet was published in Rossetti's 1870 volume, *Poems*, but was omitted from the 1881 edition of *The House of Life* after Robert Buchanan, in his review *The Fleshly School of Poetry* (1871), attacked its depiction of "shameless nakedness."

[2] *Soul's Beauty* Originally titled "Sibylla Palmifera" ("palm-bearing sibyl"), this sonnet was composed to accompany the painting of that title, included above. The Sibyl (prophetess) of Cumae wrote her prophesies on palm leaves.

Dante Gabriel Rossetti, *Lady Lilith* (1868).

78. Body's Beauty[1]

O		f Adam's first wife, Lilith, it is told
    (The witch he loved before the gift of Eve,)
      That, ere the snake's, her sweet tongue could deceive,
And her enchanted hair was the first gold.
5 And still she sits, young while the earth is old,
    And, subtly of herself contemplative,
      Draws men to watch the bright web she can weave,
Till heart and body and life are in its hold.

The rose and poppy are her flowers; for where
10   Is he not found, O Lilith, whom shed scent
And soft-shed kisses and soft sleep shall snare?
    Lo! as that youth's eyes burned at thine, so went
      Thy spell through him, and left his straight neck
        bent

---

[1]   *Body's Beauty*   This sonnet, whose original title was "Lilith," was also composed to accompany a painting. Lilith was the first wife of Adam; according to Talmudic legend, she rejected Adam when she refused to accept a subservient position in sexual intercourse. She left the Garden of Eden and mated with various demons.

And round his heart one strangling golden hair.
—1870

97. A Superscription

L		ook in my face; my name is Might-have-been;
  I am also called No-more, Too-late, Farewell;
    Unto thine ear I hold the dead-sea shell
Cast up thy Life's foam-fretted feet between;
5 Unto thine eyes the glass where that is seen
    Which had Life's form and Love's, but by my spell
      Is now a shaken shadow intolerable,
Of ultimate things unuttered the frail screen.

Mark me, how still I am! But should there dart
10   One moment through thy soul the soft surprise
    Of that winged Peace which lulls the breath of
        sighs—
Then shalt thou see me smile, and turn apart
Thy visage to mine ambush at thy heart
    Sleepless with cold commemorative eyes.
—1870

101. The One Hope

W		hen vain desire at last and vain regret
  Go hand in hand to death, and all is vain,
    What shall assuage the unforgotten pain
And teach the unforgetful to forget?
5 Shall Peace be still a sunk stream long unmet—
    Or may the soul at once in a green plain
      Stoop through the spray of some sweet life- fountain
And cull the dew-drenched flowering amulet?[2]

Ah! when the wan soul in that golden air
10   Between the scriptured petals softly blown
    Peers breathless for the gift of grace unknown—
Ah! let none other alien spell soe'er
But only the one Hope's one name be there—
    Not less nor more, but even that word alone.
—1870

---

[2]   *amulet*   Charm against evil, sickness, harm, etc.

CHRISTINA ROSSETTI
1830 — 1894

To the late-Victorian critic Edmund Gosse, Christina Rossetti was "one of the most perfect poets of the age." Of her works, Rossetti's fellow-poet Algernon Charles Swinburne claimed that "nothing more glorious in poetry has ever been written." Rossetti may have been less popular than contemporaries such as Alfred Tennyson and Elizabeth Barrett Browning, melding of sensuous

imagery and stringent form earned her the admiration and devotion of many nineteenth-century readers. Her lyricism elicited praise for being, as one critic wrote in 1862, "remarkably fresh and free," as well as "true and most genuine." The ease of Rossetti's lyric voice remains apparent in works as diverse as the sensual *Goblin Market* and the subtle religious hymns she penned throughout her career.

She was born in London in 1830, the youngest of four children. Her father, Gabriel Rossetti, was a scholar and an Italian exile, and her mother, Frances Polidori, was the English-Italian daughter of another Italian exile. Italian revolutionaries-in-exile frequented the Rossetti home, creating a provocative and unconventional environment for the Rossetti children. Other influences included their mother's devotion to Christianity and visits to their maternal grandfather's rural home. "If any one thing schooled me in the direction of poetry," Rossetti was later to write, "it was perhaps the delightful idle liberty to prowl all alone about my grandfather's cottage-grounds some thirty miles from London."

Rossetti's grandfather Polidori printed her first volume of poems, *Verses: Dedicated to Her Mother*, in 1847. Though immature in light of the works that would follow, the poems of the sixteen-year-old Rossetti already exhibited many of the qualities for which her work would later be known: directness of expression and simplicity of narrative colored with vivid and often sensuous detail. In 1850 several of her poems were published in *The Germ*, the journal of the Pre-Raphaelite Brotherhood founded in part by her two brothers, Dante Gabriel and William Michael. Although Rossetti was not formally a member of the Brotherhood, Rossetti's aesthetic sense—and especially her attention to color and detail—link her to the movement. Other Pre-Raphaelite values were also central to Rossetti's poetic vision, including a devotion to the faithful representation of nature and, at the same time, a penchant for symbolic representation.

The 1850s were a difficult time for Rossetti. Early in the decade she rejected, most likely on religious grounds, a suitor to whom she had been engaged for two years, the Pre-Raphaelite painter James Collinson. Collinson had converted to Anglicanism to please Rossetti, but he ultimately returned to his original faith, Catholicism. (In 1866 Rossetti appears to have rejected a second suitor, Charles Bagot Cayley, perhaps because he was an agnostic.) In 1854 Rossetti volunteered to join Florence Nightingale's nursing efforts in the Crimean War, but she was rejected for being too young. She volunteered instead at the Highgate Penitentiary for "fallen women." Throughout this period, she lived with her mother, sister, and brother William in the family home.

Rossetti first gained attention in the literary world with her 1862 publication of *Goblin Market and Other Poems*. Before publication of the volume, the eminent critic John Ruskin had declared the poems irregular in both their rhyme schemes and meters. Ruskin advised Rossetti to "exercise herself in the severest commonplace of metre until she [could] write as the public like." Rossetti nevertheless went ahead with publication, and the vast majority of her Victorian critics praised the volume for what one reviewer called its "very decided character and originality, both in theme and treatment." "Here," notes the *Eclectic Review*, "is a volume of really true poetry." "Goblin Market" remains among her most discussed works. Few readers have believed William Michael Rossetti's insistence that his sister "did not mean anything profound" by "Goblin Market," but many have found the precise nature of its deep suggestiveness elusive.

More volumes followed, among the most important of which were *The Prince's Progress and Other Poems* (1866), *Sing-Song* (1872), *A Pageant and Other Poems* (1881), and *Verses* (1893). In *Sing-Song* Rossetti proved herself a talented writer of children's verses. With "Monna Innominata," the "sonnet of sonnets" published in *A Pageant and Other Poems*, Rossetti offered her own bold contribution to the sonnet-sequence tradition. In the prose preface to "Monna Innominata," Rossetti notes that women such as Dante's Beatrice and Petrarch's Laura were denied the opportunity to speak for themselves. If either had spoken in her own voice, Rossetti writes, "the portrait left us might have appeared more tender, if less dignified, than any drawn even by a devoted friend." According to Rossetti, even the *Sonnets from the Portuguese* of the "Great Poetess" Elizabeth Barrett Browning do not offer us a voice "drawn from feeling": her circumstances, that is, her happy love-story, precluded her from giving her speaker such a voice. Rossetti's sonnets, in contrast, speak of unfulfilled yearning and painful loss, bringing to the sonnet form the voice of a woman's suffering such as Rossetti believed had never before been written. Critics have often read the poem in biographical terms, following from William Michael Rossetti's suggestion that the "introductory prose-note … is a blind … interposed to draw off attention from the writer in her proper person." But such readings, however tempting, limit interpretation of the poems and fail to account for the deep complexities of Rossetti's work.

In 1871, Rossetti was stricken with exophthalmic bronchocele, or Graves's disease, a disease causing protrusion of the eyeballs, which led her to retreat even further into an already quiet life. Rossetti continued to live with and care for her mother and two aunts. She lived to see editions of her collected poems published in 1875 and then again in 1890, and in 1892 she was among those mentioned as a possible successor to Tennyson as England's Poet Laureate. She died in 1894 from cancer, having undergone surgery for breast cancer in 1892.

⌘ ⌘ ⌘

Goblin Market

Morning and evening
Maids heard the goblins cry:
"Come buy our orchard fruits,
Come buy, come buy:
5   Apples and quinces,
Lemons and oranges,
Plump unpecked cherries,
Melons and raspberries,
Bloom-down-cheeked peaches,
10 Swart°-headed mulberries,   *dark*

Wild free-born cranberries,
Crabapples, dewberries,
Pine-apples, blackberries,
Apricots, strawberries;—
15 All ripe together
In summer weather,—
Morns that pass by,
Fair eves that fly;
Come buy, come buy:
20 Our grapes fresh from the vine,
Pomegranates full and fine,
Dates and sharp bullaces,
Rare pears and greengages,

Damsons[1] and bilberries
25 Taste them and try:
Currants and gooseberries,
Bright-fire-like barberries,
Figs to fill your mouth,
Citrons from the South,
30 Sweet to tongue and sound to eye;
Come buy, come buy."

Evening by evening
Among the brookside rushes,
Laura bowed her head to hear,
35 Lizzie veiled her blushes:
Crouching close together
In the cooling weather,
With clasping arms and cautioning lips,
With tingling cheeks and finger tips.
40 "Lie close," Laura said,
Pricking up her golden head:
"We must not look at goblin men,
We must not buy their fruits:
Who knows upon what soil they fed
45 Their hungry thirsty roots?"
"Come buy," call the goblins
Hobbling down the glen.
"Oh," cried Lizzie, "Laura, Laura,
You should not peep at goblin men."
50 Lizzie covered up her eyes,
Covered close lest they should look;
Laura reared her glossy head,
And whispered like the restless brook:
"Look, Lizzie, look, Lizzie,
55 Down the glen tramp little men.
One hauls a basket,
One bears a plate,
One lugs a golden dish
Of many pounds weight.
60 How fair the vine must grow
Whose grapes are so luscious;
How warm the wind must blow
Through those fruit bushes."
"No," said Lizzie: "No, no, no;
65 Their offers should not charm us,

---

[1] *bullaces ... Damsons* Bullaces, greengages, and damsons are all varieties of plums.

Their evil gifts would harm us."
She thrust a dimpled finger
In each ear, shut eyes and ran:
Curious Laura chose to linger
70 Wondering at each merchant man.
One had a cat's face,
One whisked a tail,
One tramped at a rat's pace,
One crawled like a snail,
75 One like a wombat prowled obtuse and furry,
One like a ratel° tumbled hurry skurry.   *badger*
She heard a voice like voice of doves
Cooing all together:
They sounded kind and full of loves
80 In the pleasant weather.

Laura stretched her gleaming neck
Like a rush-imbedded swan,
Like a lily from the beck,°   *stream*
Like a moonlit poplar branch,
85 Like a vessel at the launch
When its last restraint is gone.

Backwards up the mossy glen
Turned and trooped the goblin men,
With their shrill repeated cry,
90 "Come buy, come buy."
When they reached where Laura was
They stood stock still upon the moss,
Leering at each other,
Brother with queer brother;
95 Signalling each other,
Brother with sly brother.
One set his basket down,
One reared his plate;
One began to weave a crown
100 Of tendrils, leaves, and rough nuts brown
(Men sell not such in any town);
One heaved the golden weight
Of dish and fruit to offer her:
"Come buy, come buy," was still their cry.
105 Laura stared but did not stir,
Longed but had no money:
The whisk-tailed merchant bade her taste
In tones as smooth as honey,

The cat-faced purr'd,
110 The rat-paced spoke a word
Of welcome, and the snail-paced even was heard;
One parrot-voiced and jolly
Cried "Pretty Goblin" still for "Pretty Polly";—
One whistled like a bird.

115 But sweet-tooth Laura spoke in haste:
"Good Folk, I have no coin;
To take were to purloin:
I have no copper in my purse,
I have no silver either,
120 And all my gold is on the furze°   *evergreen shrub*
That shakes in windy weather
Above the rusty heather."
"You have much gold upon your head,"
They answered all together:
125 "Buy from us with a golden curl."
She clipped a precious golden lock,
She dropped a tear more rare than pearl,
Then sucked their fruit globes fair or red.
Sweeter than honey from the rock,[1]
130 Stronger than man-rejoicing wine,
Clearer than water flowed that juice;
She never tasted such before,
How should it cloy with length of use?
She sucked and sucked and sucked the more
135 Fruits which that unknown orchard bore;
She sucked until her lips were sore;
Then flung the emptied rinds away
But gathered up one kernel-stone,
And knew not was it night or day
140 As she turned home alone.

Lizzie met her at the gate
Full of wise upbraidings:
"Dear, you should not stay so late,
Twilight is not good for maidens;
145 Should not loiter in the glen
In the haunts of goblin men.
Do you not remember Jeanie,
How she met them in the moonlight,
Took their gifts both choice and many,
150 Ate their fruits and wore their flowers

Plucked from bowers
Where summer ripens at all hours?
But ever in the noonlight
She pined and pined away;
155 Sought them by night and day,
Found them no more but dwindled and grew grey;
Then fell with the first snow,
While to this day no grass will grow
Where she lies low:
160 I planted daisies there a year ago
That never blow.
You should not loiter so."
"Nay, hush," said Laura:
"Nay, hush, my sister:
165 I ate and ate my fill,
Yet my mouth waters still;
Tomorrow night I will
Buy more": and kissed her:
"Have done with sorrow;
170 I'll bring you plums tomorrow
Fresh on their mother twigs,
Cherries worth getting;
You cannot think what figs
My teeth have met in,
175 What melons icy cold
Piled on a dish of gold
Too huge for me to hold,
What peaches with a velvet nap,
Pellucid° grapes without one seed: *translucent*
180 Odorous indeed must be the mead
Whereon they grow, and pure the wave they drink
With lilies at the brink,
And sugar-sweet their sap."

Golden head by golden head,
185 Like two pigeons in one nest
Folded in each other's wings,
They lay down in their curtained bed:
Like two blossoms on one stem,
Like two flakes of new-fall'n snow,
190 Like two wands of ivory
Tipped with gold for awful° kings.   *awe-inspiring*
Moon and stars gazed in at them,
Wind sang to them lullaby,

---

[1] *honey from the rock*   See Deuteronomy 32.13.

Lumbering owls forbore to fly,
195 Not a bat flapped to and fro
Round their rest:
Cheek to cheek and breast to breast
Locked together in one nest.

Early in the morning
200 When the first cock crowed his warning,
Neat like bees, as sweet and busy,
Laura rose with Lizzie:
Fetched in honey, milked the cows,
Aired and set to rights the house,
205 Kneaded cakes of whitest wheat,
Cakes for dainty mouths to eat,
Next churned butter, whipped up cream,
Fed their poultry, sat and sewed;
Talked as modest maidens should:
210 Lizzie with an open heart,
Laura in an absent dream,
One content, one sick in part;
One warbling for the mere bright day's delight,
One longing for the night.

215 At length slow evening came:
They went with pitchers to the reedy brooks;
Lizzie most placid in her look,
Laura most like a leaping flame.
They drew the gurgling water from its deep.
220 Lizzie plucked purple and rich golden flags,
Then turning homeward said: "The sunset flushes
Those furthest loftiest crags;
Come Laura, not another maiden lags.
No wilful squirrel wags,
225 The beasts and birds are fast asleep."
But Laura loitered still among the rushes,
And said the bank was steep.

And said the hour was early still,
The dew not fall'n, the wind not chill;
230 Listening ever, but not catching
The customary cry,
"Come buy, come buy,"
With its iterated jingle
Of sugar-baited words:
235 Not for all her watching

Once discerning even one goblin
Racing, whisking, tumbling, hobbling—
Let alone the herds
That used to tramp along the glen,
240 In groups or single,
Of brisk fruit-merchant men.
Till Lizzie urged, "O Laura, come;
I hear the fruit-call, but I dare not look:
You should not loiter longer at this brook:
245 Come with me home.
The stars rise, the moon bends her arc,
Each glowworm winks her spark,
Let us get home before the night grows dark:
For clouds may gather
250 Though this is summer weather,
Put out the lights and drench us thro';
Then if we lost our way what should we do?"

Laura turned cold as stone
To find her sister heard that cry alone,
255 That goblin cry,
"Come buy our fruits, come buy."
Must she then buy no more such dainty fruit?
Must she no more such succous° pasture find,   *juicy*
Gone deaf and blind?
260 Her tree of life drooped from the root:
She said not one word in her heart's sore ache;
But peering through the dimness, nought discerning,
Trudged home, her pitcher dripping all the way;
So crept to bed, and lay
265 Silent till Lizzie slept;
Then sat up in a passionate yearning,
And gnashed her teeth for baulked desire, and wept
As if her heart would break.

Day after day, night after night,
270 Laura kept watch in vain
In sullen silence of exceeding pain.
She never caught again the goblin cry,
"Come buy, come buy"—
She never spied the goblin men
275 Hawking their fruits along the glen:
But when the noon waxed bright
Her hair grew thin and grey;
She dwindled, as the fair full moon doth turn

To swift decay and burn
280   Her fire away.

One day remembering her kernel-stone
She set it by a wall that faced the south;
Dewed it with tears, hoped for a root,
Watched for a waxing shoot,
285   But there came none.
It never saw the sun,
It never felt the trickling moisture run:
While with sunk eyes and faded mouth
She dreamed of melons, as a traveller sees
290   False waves in desert drouth
With shade of leaf-crowned trees,
And burns the thirstier in the sandful breeze.

She no more swept the house,
Tended the fowl or cows,
295   Fetched honey, kneaded cakes of wheat,
Brought water from the brook:
But sat down listless in the chimney-nook
And would not eat.

Tender Lizzie could not bear
300   To watch her sister's cankerous care,
Yet not to share.
She night and morning
Caught the goblins' cry:
"Come buy our orchard fruits,
305   Come buy, come buy:"—
Beside the brook, along the glen,
She heard the tramp of goblin men,
The voice and stir
Poor Laura could not hear;
310   Longed to buy fruit to comfort her,
But feared to pay too dear.
She thought of Jeanie in her grave,
Who should have been a bride;
But who for joys brides hope to have
315   Fell sick and died
In her gay prime,
In earliest winter time,
With the first glazing rime,
With the first snow-fall of crisp Winter time.

320   Till Laura dwindling
Seemed knocking at Death's door.
Then Lizzie weighed no more
Better and worse;
But put a silver penny in her purse,
325   Kissed Laura, crossed the heath with clumps of furze
At twilight, halted by the brook:
And for the first time in her life
Began to listen and look.

Laughed every goblin
330   When they spied her peeping:
Came towards her hobbling,
Flying, running, leaping,
Puffing and blowing,
Chuckling, clapping, crowing.
335   Clucking and gobbling,
Mopping and mowing,
Full of airs and graces,
Pulling wry faces,
Demure grimaces,
340   Cat-like and rat-like,
Ratel- and wombat-like,
Snail-paced in a hurry,
Parrot-voiced and whistler,
Helter skelter, hurry skurry,
345   Chattering like magpies,
Fluttering like pigeons,
Gliding like fishes,—
Hugged her and kissed her:
Squeezed and caressed her:
350   Stretched up their dishes,
Panniers, and plates:
"Look at our apples
Russet and dun,
Bob at our cherries,
355   Bite at our peaches,
Citrons and dates,
Grapes for the asking,
Pears red with basking
Out in the sun,
360   Plums on their twigs;
Pluck them and suck them,—
Pomegranates, figs."

"Good folk," said Lizzie,
Mindful of Jeanie:
365 "Give me much and many"—
Held out her apron,
Tossed them her penny.
"Nay, take a seat with us,
Honour and eat with us,"
370 They answered grinning:
"Our feast is but beginning.
Night yet is early,
Warm and dew-pearly,
Wakeful and starry:
375 Such fruits as these
No man can carry;
Half their bloom would fly,
Half their dew would dry,
Half their flavour would pass by.
380 Sit down and feast with us,
Be welcome guest with us,
Cheer you and rest with us."—
"Thank you," said Lizzie: "But one waits
At home alone for me:
385 So without further parleying,°   *discussion*
If you will not sell me any
Of your fruits though much and many,
Give me back my silver penny
I tossed you for a fee."—
390 They began to scratch their pates,°   *heads*
No longer wagging, purring,
But visibly demurring,
Grunting and snarling.
One called her proud,
395 Cross-grained, uncivil;
Their tones waxed loud,
Their looks were evil.
Lashing their tails
They trod and hustled her,
400 Elbowed and jostled her,
Clawed with their nails,
Barking, mewing, hissing, mocking,
Tore her gown and soiled her stocking,
Twitched her hair out by the roots,
405 Stamped upon her tender feet,
Held her hands and squeezed their fruits
Against her mouth to make her eat.

White and golden Lizzie stood,
Like a lily in a flood,—
410 Like a rock of blue-veined stone
Lashed by tides obstreperously,—
Like a beacon left alone
In a hoary roaring sea,
Sending up a golden fire,—
415 Like a fruit-crowned orange tree
White with blossoms honey-sweet
Sore beset by wasp and bee,—
Like a royal virgin town
Topped with gilded dome and spire
420 Close beleaguered by a fleet
Mad to tug her standard down.

One may lead a horse to water,
Twenty cannot make him drink.
Though the goblins cuffed and caught her,
425 Coaxed and fought her,
Bullied and besought her,
Scratched her, pinched her black as ink,
Kicked and knocked her,
Mauled and mocked her,
430 Lizzie uttered not a word;
Would not open lip from lip
Lest they should cram a mouthful in:
But laughed in heart to feel the drip
Of juice that syruped all her face,
435 And lodged in dimples of her chin,
And streaked her neck which quaked like curd.
At last the evil people,
Worn out by her resistance,
Flung back her penny, kicked their fruit
440 Along whichever road they took,
Not leaving root or stone or shoot;
Some writhed into the ground,
Some dived into the brook
With ring and ripple,
445 Some scudded on the gale without a sound,
Some vanished in the distance.

In a smart, ache, tingle,
Lizzie went her way;
Knew not was it night or day;
450 Sprang up the bank, tore through the furze,

Threaded copse and dingle,°   dell
And heard her penny jingle
Bouncing in her purse,—
Its bounce was music to her ear.
455   She ran and ran
As if she feared some goblin man
Dogged her with gibe or curse
Or something worse:
But not one goblin skurried after,
460   Nor was she pricked by fear;
The kind heart made her windy-paced
That urged her home quite out of breath with haste
And inward laughter.

She cried, "Laura," up the garden,
465   "Did you miss me?
Come and kiss me.
Never mind my bruises,
Hug me, kiss me, suck my juices
Squeezed from goblin fruits for you,
470   Goblin pulp and goblin dew.
Eat me, drink me, love me;
Laura, make much of me;
For your sake I have braved the glen
And had to do with goblin merchant men."

475   Laura started from her chair,
Flung her arms up in the air,
Clutched her hair:
"Lizzie, Lizzie, have you tasted
For my sake the fruit forbidden?
480   Must your light like mine be hidden,
Your young life like mine be wasted,
Undone in mine undoing,
And ruined in my ruin,
Thirsty, cankered, goblin-ridden?"—
485   She clung about her sister,
Kissed and kissed and kissed her:
Tears once again
Refreshed her shrunken eyes,
Dropping like rain
490   After long sultry drouth;
Shaking with aguish[1] fear, and pain,
She kissed and kissed her with a hungry mouth.

---

[1]   *aguish* Feverish.

Her lips began to scorch,
That juice was wormwood to her tongue,
495   She loathed the feast:
Writhing as one possessed she leaped and sung,
Rent all her robe, and wrung
Her hands in lamentable haste,
And beat her breast.
500   Her locks streamed like the torch
Borne by a racer at full speed,
Or like the mane of horses in their flight,
Or like an eagle when she stems the light
Straight toward the sun,
505   Or like a caged thing freed,
Or like a flying flag when armies run.

Swift fire spread through her veins, knocked at her
        heart,
Met the fire smouldering there
And overbore its lesser flame;
510   She gorged on bitterness without a name:
Ah! fool, to choose such part
Of soul-consuming care!
Sense failed in the mortal strife:
Like the watchtower of a town
515   Which an earthquake shatters down,
Like a lightning-stricken mast,
Like a wind-uprooted tree
Spun about,
Like a foam-topped waterspout
520   Cast down headlong in the sea,
She fell at last;
Pleasure past and anguish past,
Is it death or is it life?

Life out of death.
525   That night long Lizzie watched by her,
Counted her pulse's flagging stir,
Felt for her breath,
Held water to her lips, and cooled her face
With tears and fanning leaves.
530   But when the first birds chirped about their eaves,
And early reapers plodded to the place
Of golden sheaves,
And dew-wet grass
Bowed in the morning winds so brisk to pass,

535 And new buds with new day
      Opened of cup-like lilies on the stream,
      Laura awoke as from a dream,
      Laughed in the innocent old way,
      Hugged Lizzie but not twice or thrice;
540 Her gleaming locks showed not one thread of grey,
      Her breath was sweet as May,
      And light danced in her eyes.

      Days, weeks, months, years
      Afterwards, when both were wives
545 With children of their own;
      Their mother-hearts beset with fears,
      Their lives bound up in tender lives;
      Laura would call the little ones
      And tell them of her early prime,
550 Those pleasant days long gone
      Of not-returning time:

      Would talk about the haunted glen,
      The wicked quaint fruit-merchant men,
      Their fruits like honey to the throat
555 But poison in the blood;
      (Men sell not such in any town):
      Would tell them how her sister stood
      In deadly peril to do her good,
      And win the fiery antidote:
560 Then joining hands to little hands
      Would bid them cling together,—
      "For there is no friend like a sister
      In calm or stormy weather;
      To cheer one on the tedious way,
565 To fetch one if one goes astray,
      To lift one if one totters down,
      To strengthen whilst one stands."
      —1862

In Context

Illustrating *Goblin Market*

The first edition of *Goblin Market* appeared in 1862 with a frontispiece by the author's brother, the Pre-Raphaelite painter and poet Dante Gabriel Rossetti. The round inset above the drawing of sisters Laura and Lizzie depicts the goblins carrying their fruits to market. Another notable edition was that of 1893, with art nouveau illustrations by artist and writer Laurence Housman (brother of poet A.E. Housman).

1862 Macmillan edition—illustration by
D.G. Rossetti.

Illustration by Laurence Housman from the 1893
Macmillan edition.

A Triad

Three sang of love together: one with lips
    Crimson, with cheeks and bosom in a glow,
Flushed to the yellow hair and finger tips;
    And one there sang who soft and smooth as snow
5   Bloomed like a tinted hyacinth at a show;

And one was blue with famine after love,
    Who like a harpstring snapped rang harsh and low
The burden of what those were singing of.
One shamed herself in love; one temperately
10   Grew gross in soulless love, a sluggish wife;
One famished died for love. Thus two of three
    Took death for love and won him after strife;
One droned in sweetness like a fattened bee:
    All on the threshold, yet all short of life.
—1862

Remember

Remember me when I am gone away,
    Gone far away into the silent land;
    When you can no more hold me by the hand,
Nor I half turn to go yet turning stay.
5   Remember me when no more day by day
    You tell me of our future that you planned:
    Only remember me; you understand
It will be late then to counsel or to pray.
Yet if you should forget me for a while
10   And afterwards remember, do not grieve:
    For if the darkness and corruption leave
    A vestige of the thoughts that once I had,
Better by far you should forget and smile
    Than that you should remember and be sad.
—1862

A Birthday

My heart is like a singing bird
    Whose nest is in a watered shoot;
My heart is like an apple tree
    Whose boughs are bent with thickset fruit;
5   My heart is like a rainbow shell
    That paddles in a halcyon° sea;   calm
My heart is gladder than all these
    Because my love is come to me.

Raise me a dais of silk and down;
10   Hang it with vair° and purple dyes;   squirrel fur
Carve it in doves and pomegranates,

And peacocks with a hundred eyes;
Work it in gold and silver grapes,
    In leaves, and silver fleurs-de-lys;
15 Because the birthday of my life
    Is come, my love is come to me.
      —1861

After Death

The curtains were half drawn, the floor was swept
    And strewn with rushes, rosemary and may
Lay thick upon the bed on which I lay,
Where thro' the lattice ivy-shadows crept.
5 He leaned above me, thinking that I slept
    And could not hear him; but I heard him say:
    "Poor child, poor child": and as he turned away
Came a deep silence, and I knew he wept.
He did not touch the shroud, or raise the fold
10   That hid my face, or take my hand in his,
      Or ruffle the smooth pillows for my head:
    He did not love me living; but once dead
He pitied me; and very sweet it is
To know he still is warm tho' I am cold.
      —1862

An Apple-Gathering

I plucked pink blossoms from mine apple tree
    And wore them all that evening in my hair:
Then in due season when I went to see
    I found no apples there.

5 With dangling basket all along the grass
    As I had come I went the selfsame track:
My neighbours mocked me while they saw me pass
    So empty-handed back.

Lilian and Lilias smiled in trudging by,
10   Their heaped-up basket teazed me like a jeer;
Sweet-voiced they sang beneath the sunset sky,
    Their mother's home was near.

Plump Gertrude passed me with her basket full,
    A stronger hand than hers helped it along;
15 A voice talked with her thro' the shadows cool
    More sweet to me than song.

Ah Willie, Willie, was my love less worth
    Than apples with their green leaves piled above?
I counted rosiest apples on the earth
20   Of far less worth than love.

So once it was with me you stooped to talk
    Laughing and listening in this very lane;
To think that by this way we used to walk
    We shall not walk again!

25 I let my neighbours pass me, ones and twos
    And groups; the latest said the night grew chill,
And hastened: but I loitered, while the dews
    Fell fast I loitered still.
      —1862

Echo

Come to me in the silence of the night;
    Come in the speaking silence of a dream;
Come with soft rounded cheeks and eyes as bright
    As sunlight on a stream;
5   Come back in tears,
O memory, hope, love of finished years.

O dream how sweet, too sweet, too bitter sweet,
    Whose wakening should have been in Paradise,
Where souls brimfull of love abide and meet;
10   Where thirsting longing eyes
    Watch the slow door
That opening, letting in, lets out no more.

Yet come to me in dreams, that I may live
    My very life again tho' cold in death:
15 Come back to me in dreams, that I may give
    Pulse for pulse, breath for breath:
    Speak low, lean low,
As long ago, my love, how long ago.
      —1862

Winter: My Secret

I tell my secret? No indeed, not I:
　　Perhaps some day, who knows?
But not today; it froze, and blows, and snows,
　　And you're too curious: fie!
5　You want to hear it? well:
　　Only, my secret's mine, and I won't tell.

Or, after all, perhaps there's none:
　　Suppose there is no secret after all,
　　But only just my fun.
10　Today's a nipping day, a biting day;
　　In which one wants a shawl,
　　A veil, a cloak, and other wraps:
I cannot ope to every one who taps,
And let the draughts come whistling thro' my hall;
15　Come bounding and surrounding me,
　　Come buffeting, astounding me,
Nipping and clipping thro' my wraps and all.
I wear my mask for warmth: who ever shows
　　His nose to Russian snows
20　To be pecked at by every wind that blows?
You would not peck? I thank you for good will,
Believe, but leave that truth untested still.

Spring's an expansive time: yet I don't trust
March with its peck of dust,
25　Nor April with its rainbow-crowned brief showers,
　　Nor even May, whose flowers
One frost may wither thro' the sunless hours.

Perhaps some languid summer day,
　　When drowsy birds sing less and less,
30　And golden fruit is ripening to excess,
　　If there's not too much sun nor too much cloud,
　　And the warm wind is neither still nor loud,
Perhaps my secret I may say,
　　Or you may guess.
—1862

"No, Thank You, John"

I never said I loved you, John:
　　Why will you teaze me day by day,
And wax a weariness to think upon
　　With always "do" and "pray"?

5　You know I never loved you, John;
　　No fault of mine made me your toast:[1]
Why will you haunt me with a face as wan
　　As shows an hour-old ghost?

I dare say Meg or Moll would take
10　Pity upon you, if you'd ask:
And pray don't remain single for my sake
　　Who can't perform that task.

I have no heart?—Perhaps I have not;
　　But then you're mad to take offence
15　That I don't give you what I have not got:
　　Use your own common sense.

Let bygones be bygones:
　　Don't call me false, who owed not to be true:
I'd rather answer "No" to fifty Johns
20　Than answer "Yes" to you.

Let's mar our pleasant days no more,
　　Songbirds of passage, days of youth:
Catch at today, forget the days before:
　　I'll wink at your untruth.

25　Let us strike hands as hearty friends;
　　No more, no less; and friendship's good:
Only don't keep in view ulterior ends,
　　And points not understood

In open treaty. Rise above
30　Quibbles and shuffling off and on:
Here's friendship for you if you like; but love,—
　　No, thank you, John.
—1862

---

[1] *your toast* I.e., the woman to whom John would raise a glass when toasting his lady.

A Pause Of Thought

I looked for that which is not, nor can be,
    And hope deferred made my heart sick in truth:
But years must pass before a hope of youth
    Is resigned utterly.

5 I watched and waited with a steadfast will:
    And though the object seemed to flee away
That I so longed for, ever day by day
    I watched and waited still.

Sometimes I said, "This thing shall be no more;
10   My expectation wearies and shall cease;
I will resign it now and be at peace:"
    Yet never gave it o'er.

Sometimes I said, "It is an empty name
    I long for; to a name why should I give
15 The peace of all the days I have to live?"—
    Yet gave it all the same.

Alas, thou foolish one! alike unfit
    For healthy joy and salutary pain:
Thou knowest the chase useless, and again
20   Turnest to follow it.
    —1848

Song

She sat and sang alway
    By the green margin of a stream,
Watching the fishes leap and play
    Beneath the glad sunbeam.

5 I sat and wept alway
    Beneath the moon's most shadowy beam,
Watching the blossoms of the May
    Weep leaves into the stream.

I wept for memory;
10   She sang for hope that is so fair:
My tears were swallowed by the sea;
    Her songs died on the air.
    —1862

Song

When I am dead, my dearest,
    Sing no sad songs for me;
Plant thou no roses at my head,
    Nor shady cypress tree.
5 Be the green grass above me
    With showers and dewdrops wet;
And if thou wilt, remember,
    And if thou wilt, forget.

I shall not see the shadows,
10   I shall not feel the rain;
I shall not hear the nightingale
    Sing on as if in pain.
And dreaming through the twilight
    That doth not rise nor set,
15 Haply° I may remember,   *by chance*
    And haply may forget.
    —1862

Dead Before Death

Ah! changed and cold, how changed and very cold!
    With stiffened smiling lips and cold calm eyes:
    Changed, yet the same; much knowing, little wise;
This was the promise of the days of old!
5 Grown hard and stubborn in the ancient mould,
    Grown rigid in the sham of lifelong lies:
    We hoped for better things as years would rise,
But it is over as a tale once told.
All fallen the blossom that no fruitage bore,
10   All lost the present and the future time,
All lost, all lost, the lapse that went before:
So lost till death shut-to the opened door,
    So lost from chime to everlasting chime,
So cold and lost for ever evermore.
    —1862

Monna Innominata [1]
A Sonnet of Sonnets

Beatrice, immortalized by "*altissimo poeta ... cotanto amante*";[2] Laura, celebrated by a great though an inferior bard[3]—have alike paid the exceptional penalty of exceptional honour, and have come down to us resplendent with charms, but (at least, to my apprehension) scant of attractiveness.

These heroines of worldwide fame were preceded by a bevy of unnamed ladies "*donne innominate*" sung by a school of less conspicuous poets; and in that land and that period which gave simultaneous birth to Catholics, to Albigenses, and to Troubadours,[4] one can imagine many a lady as sharing her lover's poetic aptitude, while the barrier between them might be one held sacred by both, yet not such as to render mutual love incompatible with mutual honour.

Had such a lady spoken for herself, the portrait left us might have appeared more tender, if less dignified, than any drawn even by a devoted friend. Or had the Great Poetess[5] of our own day and nation only been unhappy instead of happy, her circumstances would have invited her to bequeath to us, in lieu of the "Portuguese Sonnets," an inimitable "*donna innominata*" drawn not from fancy but from feeling, and worthy to occupy a niche beside Beatrice and Laura.

1

"Lo dì che han detto a' dolci amici addio."—DANTE
"Amor, con quanto sforzo oggi mi vinci!"—PETRARCA[6]

Come back to me, who wait and watch for you:—
    Or come not yet, for it is over then,
    And long it is before you come again,
So far between my pleasures are and few.
While, when you come not, what I do I do
    Thinking "Now when he comes," my sweetest "when":
    For one man is my world of all the men
This wide world holds; O love, my world is you.
Howbeit, to meet you grows almost a pang
    Because the pang of parting comes so soon;
    My hope hangs waning, waxing, like a moon
        Between the heavenly days on which we meet:
Ah me, but where are now the songs I sang
    When life was sweet because you called them sweet?

2

"Era già l'ora che volge il desio."—DANTE
"Ricorro al tempo ch' io vi vidi prima."—PETRARCA[7]

I wish I could remember that first day,
    First hour, first moment of your meeting me,
    If bright or dim the season, it might be
Summer or winter for aught I can say;
So unrecorded did it slip away,
    So blind was I to see and to foresee,
    So dull to mark the budding of my tree
That would not blossom yet for many a May.
If only I could recollect it, such
    A day of days! I let it come and go
    As traceless as a thaw of bygone snow;
It seemed to mean so little, meant so much;
If only now I could recall that touch,
    First touch of hand in hand—Did one but know!

3

"O ombre vane, fuor che ne l'aspetto!"—DANTE
"Immaginata guida la conduce."—PETRARCA[8]

I dream of you to wake: would that I might
    Dream of you and not wake but slumber on;
    Nor find with dreams the dear companion gone,
As summer ended summer birds take flight.
In happy dreams I hold you full in sight,
    I blush again who waking look so wan;

---

[1] *Monna Innominata* Italian: unnamed lady.

[2] *altissimo poeta ... cotanto amante* Italian: loftiest poet ... equally great lover (Italian). Rossetti refers to Italian poet Dante Alighieri (1265–1321), whose muse was Beatrice.

[3] *great ... bard* Italian poet Francesco Petrarca (1304–74) wrote many love songs to Laura.

[4] *Albigenses* Albigensians were members of a religious sect of the twelfth and thirteenth centuries; *Troubadours* Wandering lyric poets of the eleventh to thirteenth centuries.

[5] *Great Poetess* Elizabeth Barrett Browning.

[6] *Dante* From *Purgatorio* 8.3: "Who in the morn have bid sweet friends farewell"; *Petrarca* From *Canzone* 85.12: "Love, with what forces you conquer me now!"

[7] *Dante* From *Purgatorio* 8.1: "Now was the hour that wakens fond desire"; *Petrarca* From Sonnet 20.3: "I remember when I saw you for the first time."

[8] *Dante* From *Purgatorio* 2.79: "Oh vain shadows, except in outward aspect"; *Petrarca* From *Canzone* 277.9: "An imagined guide leads her."

Brighter than sunniest day that ever shone,
In happy dreams your smile makes day of night.
Thus only in a dream we are at one,
10   Thus only in a dream we give and take
        The faith that maketh rich who take or give;
    If thus to sleep is sweeter than to wake,
        To die were surely sweeter than to live,
    Tho' there be nothing new beneath the sun.

4

"Poca favilla gran fiamma seconda."—DANTE
"Ogni altra cosa, ogni pensier va fore,
E sol ivi con voi rimansi amore."—PETRARCA[1]

I loved you first: but afterwards your love,
    Outsoaring mine, sang such a loftier song
As drowned the friendly cooings of my dove.
    Which owes the other most? My love was long,
5   And yours one moment seemed to wax more strong;
I loved and guessed at you, you construed me
And loved me for what might or might not be—
    Nay, weights and measures do us both a wrong.
For verily love knows not "mine" or "thine";
10   With separate "I" and "thou" free love has done,
        For one is both and both are one in love:
Rich love knows nought of "thine that is not mine";
        Both have the strength and both the length
            thereof,
    Both of us, of the love which makes us one.

5

"Amor che a nullo amato amar perdona."—DANTE
"Amor m'addusse in sì gioiosa spene."—PETRARCA[2]

O my heart's heart, and you who are to me
    More than myself myself, God be with you,
    Keep you in strong obedience leal° and true   *loyal*
To Him whose noble service setteth free;
5   Give you all good we see or can foresee,
    Make your joys many and your sorrows few,

Bless you in what you bear and what you do,
Yea, perfect you as He would have you be.
So much for you; but what for me, dear friend?
10   To love you without stint and all I can
Today, tomorrow, world without an end;
        To love you much and yet to love you more,
        As Jordan at his flood sweeps either shore;
Since woman is the helpmeet made for man.

6

"Or puoi la quantitate
Comprender de l'amor che a te mi scalda."—DANTE
"Non vo' che da tal nodo amor mi sciolglia."—PETRARCA[3]

Trust me, I have not earned your dear rebuke,
    I love, as you would have me, God the most;
    Would lose not Him, but you, must one be lost,
Nor with Lot's wife cast back a faithless look,[4]
5   Unready to forego what I forsook;
    This say I, having counted up the cost,
    This, tho' I be the feeblest of God's host,
The sorriest sheep Christ shepherds with His crook.
Yet while I love my God the most, I deem
    That I can never love you overmuch;
        I love Him more, so let me love you too;
    Yea, as I apprehend it, love is such
I cannot love you if I love not Him,
    I cannot love Him if I love not you.

7

"Qui primavera sempre ed ogni frutto."—DANTE
"Ragionando con meco ed io con lui."—PETRARCA[5]

"Love me, for I love you"—and answer me,
    "Love me, for I love you": so shall we stand
    As happy equals in the flowering land
Of love, that knows not a dividing sea.
5   Love builds the house on rock and not on sand,
    Love laughs what while the winds rave desperately;

---

[1] *Dante* From *Paradiso* 1.34: "From a small spark a great flame rises"; *Petrarca* From *Canzone* 72.44–45: "All other hopes, all other thoughts are gone, and love with you remains there alone."

[2] *Dante* From *Inferno* 5.103: "Love, that denial takes from none beloved"; *Petrarca* From Sonnet 56.11: "Love urged me in this gladness to believe."

[3] *Dante* From *Purgatorio* 21.133–34: "Now has thou proved the force and ardor of the love I bear thee"; *Petrarca* From Canzone 59.17: "I do not wish love to release me from this knot."

[4] *Lot's wife ... look* See Genesis 19.26: "[Lot's] wife looked back from behind him, and she became a pillar of salt."

[5] *Dante* From *Purgatorio* 28.143: "Perpetual spring and every fruit"; *Petrarca* From Canzone 35.14: "Speaking with me and I with him."

And who hath found love's citadel unmanned?
    And who hath held in bonds love's liberty?—
My heart's a coward tho' my words are brave—
10   We meet so seldom, yet we surely part
    So often; there's a problem for your art!
    Still I find comfort in his Book, who saith,
Tho' jealousy be cruel as the grave,
    And death be strong, yet love is strong as death.[1]

8

    "Come dicesse a Dio, D'altro non calme." —DANTE
    "Spero trovar pietà non che perdono."—PETRARCA[2]

"I, if I perish, perish"—Esther spake:[3]
    And bride of life or death she made her fair
    In all the lustre of her perfumed hair
And smiles that kindle longing but to slake.
5 She put on pomp of loveliness, to take
    Her husband through his eyes at unaware;
    She spread abroad her beauty for a snare,
Harmless as doves and subtle as a snake.
She trapped him with one mesh of silken hair,
10   She vanquished him by wisdom of her wit,
    And built her people's house that it should
        stand:—
    If I might take my life so in my hand,
And for my love to Love put up my prayer,
    And for love's sake by Love be granted it!

9

    "O dignitosa coscienza e netta!"—DANTE
    "Spirto più acceso di virtuti ardenti."—PETRARCA[4]

Thinking of you, and all that was, and all
    That might have been and now can never be,
    I feel your honoured excellence, and see
Myself unworthy of the happier call:
5 For woe is me who walk so apt to fall,
    So apt to shrink afraid, so apt to flee,
    Apt to lie down and die (ah woe is me!)
Faithless and hopeless turning to the wall.
And yet not hopeless quite nor faithless quite,
10 Because not loveless; love may toil all night,
    But take at morning; wrestle till the break
        Of day, but then wield power with God and
        man:—
    So take I heart of grace as best I can,
    Ready to spend and be spent for your sake.

10

    "Con miglior corso e con migliore stella."—DANTE
    "La vita fugge e non s'arresta un' ora."—Petrarca[5]

Time flies, hope flags, life plies a wearied wing;
    Death following hard on life gains ground apace;
    Faith runs with each and rears an eager face,
Outruns the rest, makes light of everything,
5 Spurns earth, and still finds breath to pray and sing;
    While love ahead of all uplifts his praise,
    Still asks for grace and still gives thanks for grace,
Content with all day brings and night will bring.
Life wanes; and when love folds his wings above
10   Tired hope, and less we feel his conscious pulse,
        Let us go fall asleep, dear friend, in peace:
    A little while, and age and sorrow cease;
    A little while, and life reborn annuls
Loss and decay and death, and all is love.

---

[1] his Book ... death   See The Song of Solomon 6: "Set me as a seal upon your heart, as a seal upon your arm; for love is strong as death, passion fierce as the grave."

[2] *Dante* From *Purgatorio* 8.12: "As if telling God, "I care for nothing else"; *Petrarca* From *Canzone* 1.8: "I hope to find pity, not just forgiveness."

[3] *I ... spake* From Esther 4.16, in which Queen Esther says to Mordecai, before donning beautiful robes and appealing to her husband to cease his mission to kill her people, the Jews: "Go, gather together all the Jews ... and neither eat nor drink three days, night or day: I also and my maidens will fast likewise; and so will I go in unto the king, which is not according to the law: and if I perish, I perish."

[4] *Dante* From *Purgatorio* 3.8: "Oh conscience clear and upright!"; *Petrarca* From *Canzone* 283.3: "Spirit dazzling with blazing virtues."

[5] *Dante* From *Paradiso* 1.40: "In best course and in happiest constellation"; *Petrarca* From *Canzone* 272.1: "Life flies and doesn't stay for an hour."

11

"Vien dietro a me e lascia dir le genti."—DANTE
"Contando i casi della vita nostra."—PETRARCA[1]

Many in aftertimes will say of you
    "He loved her"—while of me what will they say?
    Not that I loved you more than just in play,
For fashion's sake as idle women do.
5 Even let them prate; who know not what we knew
    Of love and parting in exceeding pain,
    Of parting hopeless here to meet again,
Hopeless on earth, and heaven is out of view.
But by my heart of love laid bare to you,
10 My love that you can make not void nor vain,
Love that foregoes you but to claim anew
      Beyond this passage of the gate of death,
    I charge you at the Judgment make it plain
      My love of you was life and not a breath.

12

"Amor, che ne la mente mi ragiona."—DANTE
"Amor vien nel bel viso di costei."—PETRARCA[2]

If there be any one can take my place
    And make you happy whom I grieve to grieve,
    Think not that I can grudge it, but believe
I do commend you to that nobler grace,
5 That readier wit than mine, that sweeter face;
    Yea, since your riches make me rich, conceive
    I too am crowned, while bridal crowns I weave,
And thread the bridal dance with jocund° pace.   *merry*
For if I did not love you, it might be
10 That I should grudge you some one dear delight;
      But since the heart is yours that was mine own,
    Your pleasure is my pleasure, right my right,
Your honourable freedom makes me free,
      And you companioned I am not alone.

13

"E drizzeremo glí occhi al Primo Amore."—DANTE
"Ma trovo peso non de le mie braccia." —PETRARCA[3]

If I could trust mine own self with your fate,
    Shall I not rather trust it in God's hand?
    Without Whose Will one lily doth not stand,
Nor sparrow fall at His appointed date;
5 Who numbereth the innumerable sand,
Who weighs the wind and water with a weight,
To Whom the world is neither small nor great,
    Whose knowledge foreknew every plan we planned.
Searching my heart for all that touches you,
10 I find there only love and love's goodwill
Helpless to help and impotent to do,
      Of understanding dull, of sight most dim;
      And therefore I commend you back to Him
Whose love your love's capacity can fill.

14

"E la Sua Volontade è nostra pace."—DANTE
"Sol con questi pensier, con altre chiome."—PETRARCA[4]

Youth gone, and beauty gone if ever there
    Dwelt beauty in so poor a face as this;
    Youth gone and beauty, what remains of bliss?
I will not bind fresh roses in my hair,
5 To shame a cheek at best but little fair,—
    Leave youth his roses, who can bear a thorn,—
I will not seek for blossoms anywhere,
    Except such common flowers as blow with corn.[5]
Youth gone and beauty gone, what doth remain?
10 The longing of a heart pent up forlorn,
      A silent heart whose silence loves and longs;
      The silence of a heart which sang its songs
      While youth and beauty made a summer morn,
Silence of love that cannot sing again.
—1881

---

[1] *Dante* From *Purgatorio* 5.13: "Come after me, and leave behind the people's babblings"; *Petrarca* From *Canzone* 285.12: "Telling of the changes in our lives."

[2] *Dante* From *Purgatorio* 2.112: "Love that discourses in my thoughts"; *Petrarca* From *Canzone* 13.2: "Love appears in the beautiful face of this lady."

[3] *Dante* From *Paradiso* 32.142: "And our eyes will turn unto the first Love"; *Petrarca* From Sonnet 20.5: "The burden I find too great a weight for my arms."

[4] *Dante* From *Paradiso* 3.85: "And in his will is our tranquility"; *Petrarca* From *Canzone* 30.32: "Alone with these thoughts, with time-altered locks of hair."

[5] *corn* Grain.

Cobwebs

It is a land with neither night nor day,
Nor heat nor cold, nor any wind, nor rain,
    Nor hills nor valleys; but one even plain
Stretches thro' long unbroken miles away:
5 While thro' the sluggish air a twilight grey
    Broodeth; no moons or seasons wax and wane,
    No ebb and flow are there along the main,
No bud-time no leaf-falling there for aye,°   *any*
No ripple on the sea, no shifting sand,
10 No beat of wings to stir the stagnant space,
No pulse of life thro' all the loveless land:
And loveless sea; no trace of days before,
    No guarded home, no toil-won resting place
No future hope no fear for evermore.
—1896 (WRITTEN 1855)

In an Artist's Studio

One face[1] looks out from all his canvasses,
One selfsame figure sits or walks or leans:
    We found her hidden just behind those screens,
That mirror gave back all her loveliness.
5 A queen in opal or in ruby dress,
    A nameless girl in freshest summer-greens,
    A saint, an angel;—every canvass means
The same one meaning, neither more nor less.
He feeds upon her face by day and night,
10   And she with true kind eyes looks back on him,
Fair as the moon and joyful as the light:
    Not wan with waiting, nor with sorrow dim;
Not as she is, but was when hope shone bright;
    Not as she is, but as she fills his dream.
—1896

Dante Gabriel Rossetti's *Beata Beatrix* (1864–70).

Promises like Pie-crust[2]

Promise me no promises,
    So will I not promise you;
Keep we both our liberties,
    Never false and never true:
5 Let us hold the die uncast,
    Free to come as free to go;
For I cannot know your past,
    And of mine what can you know?

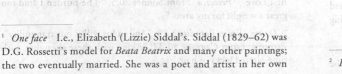

1 *One face* I.e., Elizabeth (Lizzie) Siddal's. Siddal (1829–62) was
D.G. Rossetti's model for *Beata Beatrix* and many other paintings;
the two eventually married. She was a poet and artist in her own
right.

2 *Promises like Pie-crust* See Jonathan Swift's comment: "Promises
and pie-crust are made to be broken."

You, so warm, may once have been
    Warmer towards another one;
10
I, so cold, may once have seen
    Sunlight, once have felt the sun:
Who shall show us if it was
    Thus indeed in time of old?
15 Fades the image from the glass
    And the fortune is not told.

If you promised, you might grieve
    For lost liberty again;
If I promised, I believe
20   I should fret to break the chain:
Let us be the friends we were,
    Nothing more but nothing less;
Many thrive on frugal fare
    Who would perish of excess.
—1896 (WRITTEN 1861)

In Progress

Ten years ago it seemed impossible
    That she should ever grow so calm as this,
    With self-remembrance in her warmest kiss
And dim dried eyes like an exhausted well.
5 Slow-speaking when she has some fact to tell,
    Silent with long-unbroken silences,
    Centred in self yet not unpleased to please,

Gravely monotonous like a passing bell.
Mindful of drudging daily common things,
10   Patient at pastime, patient at her work,
Wearied perhaps but strenuous certainly.
Sometimes I fancy we may one day see
    Her head shoot forth seven stars from where they
      lurk
And her eyes lightnings and her shoulders wings.
—1896

Sleeping at Last

Sleeping at last, the trouble & tumult over,
    Sleeping at last, the struggle & horror past,
Cold & white out of sight of friend & of lover
Sleeping at last.

5 No more a tired heart downcast or overcast,
No more pangs that wring or shifting fears that hover,
Sleeping at last in a dreamless sleep locked fast.

Fast asleep. Singing birds in their leafy cover
Cannot wake her, nor shake her gusty blast.
10 Under the purple thyme & the purple clover
Sleeping at last.
—1896

LEWIS CARROLL
1832 – 1898

Lewis Carroll (the pseudonym of Charles Dodgson) created some of the most beloved and enduring literature for children ever written in English. *Alice's Adventures in Wonderland* and *Through the Looking-Glass* have remained perennially popular since their first publication. His famously frustrated protagonist, who engages in bewildering exchanges with such memorable characters as the Mad Hatter, the Cheshire Cat, the March Hare, and the Mock Turtle, is as familiar a figure as any character in nineteenth-century fiction.

Charles Lutwidge Dodgson was the third of eleven children born to Frances Jane Lutwidge and the Reverend Charles Dodgson, who was a mathematician and later a curate in Daresbury, Cheshire. Because they lived in a remote village, the Dodgson children were largely schooled at home and relied on one another for amusement; Charles contributed many stories and drawings to their various family magazines. He became a fine student when he later entered boarding school, winning many awards and scholarships.

Dodgson continued to excel at Oxford University, where he followed in his father's footsteps and took first place honors in mathematics. He thereafter spent almost his entire life as a lecturer in mathematics at Oxford, where he was given a lifetime fellowship, with the stipulation that he enter the ministry and refrain from marrying. During his early years there, he took up the then-new art of photography as a hobby and devoted himself to taking exquisite photographs—primarily of children, although he later also became known for his portraits of famous literary figures, Alfred, Lord Tennyson and Dante Gabriel Rossetti among them.

Dodgson eventually became acquainted with the family of Henry Liddell, who was then Dean of Christ Church College. As he had done with many other children, Dodgson endeared himself to the three Liddell daughters by weaving elaborate tales for their amusement. On one occasion, Dodgson and a friend took advantage of a beautiful summer's day to go boating down the Thames with the Liddell girls. During the outing Carroll began making up the story of Alice's adventures underground, wherein Alice goes down a rabbit hole and meets various characters that both fascinate and confound her. He later often looked back upon this day wistfully, as when he wrote of the "birth" of the Alice of his tales: "I can call it up almost as clearly as if it were yesterday—the cloudless blue above, the watery mirror below, the boat drifting idly on its way, the tinkle of the drops that fell from the oars … the three eager faces, hungry for news of fairy-land, and who would not be said 'nay' to: from whose lips 'Tell us a story, please,' had all the stern immutability of Fate!" The poet W.H. Auden later called July 4, the day of this 1862 outing, "as memorable a day in the history of literature as it is in American history."

After Dodgson had complied with Alice Liddell's request to write up the story for her, Henry Kingsley (brother of novelist Charles Kingsley) saw the manuscript and persuaded him to publish it. Having already published several books on mathematics under his own name, he took the name Lewis, which he anglicized from "Ludovicus," the Latin word for "Lutwidge," and Carroll from "Carolus," Latin for "Charles." *Alice's Adventures in Wonderland* appeared in 1865 with illustrations by *Punch* cartoonist John Tenniel. From that point on, Lewis Carroll's fame far surpassed that of

Charles Dodgson. In 1872 he published the sequel *Through the Looking-Glass and what Alice Found There*, which continued the tale of Alice as she passes through a mirror and finds herself engaged as a pawn in a topsy-turvy game of chess. (By this time, sadly, he was entirely estranged from the Liddells.)

Carroll later wrote three books of nonsense poems including *The Hunting of the Snark* (1876). He also published *Sylvie and Bruno* and *Sylvie and Bruno Concluded* (1889 and 1893), but the novel and its sequel never achieved the fame of the Alice series. The author died of bronchitis in 1898; he is buried in a cemetery near the home he bought for his family in Surrey.

⌘ ⌘ ⌘

Verses Recited by Humpty Dumpty[1]

In winter when the fields are white,
I sing this song for your delight.

In spring, when woods are getting green,
I'll try and tell you what I mean.

5 In summer, when the days are long,
Perhaps you'll understand the song.

In autumn, when the leaves are brown,
Take pen and ink and write it down.

I sent a message to the fish:
10 I told them "This is what I wish."

The little fishes of the sea,
They sent an answer back to me.

The little fishes' answer was
"We cannot do it, sir, because."

15 I sent to them again to say
"It will be better to obey."

The fishes answered with a grin,
"Why, what a temper you are in!"

I told them once, I told them twice;
20 They would not listen to advice.

I took a kettle large and new,
Fit for the deed I had to do.

My heart went hop, my heart went thump;
I filled the kettle at the pump.

25 Then someone came to me and said,
"The little fishes are in bed."

I said to him, I said it plain,
"Then you must wake them up again."

I said it very loud and clear;
30 I went and shouted in his ear.

But he was very stiff and proud;
He said, "You needn't shout so loud!"

And he was very proud and stiff;
He said, "I'd go and wake them, if ——"

35 I took a corkscrew from the shelf;
I went to wake them up myself.

And when I found the door was locked,
I pulled and pushed and kicked and knocked.

And when I found the door was shut,
40 I tried to turn the handle, but ——
("That's all," said Humpty Dumpty.)
—1872

---

[1] *Verses … Dumpty* From *Through the Looking-Glass and What Alice Found There*, Ch. 6: "Humpty Dumpty."

Jabberwocky[1]

'Twas brillig and the slithy toves
   Did gyre and gimble in the wabe;
All mimsy were the borogroves,
   And the mome raths outgrabe.

5 "Beware the Jabberwock, my son!
   The jaws that bite, the claws that catch!
Beware the Jubjub bird, and shun
   The frumious Bandersnatch!"

He took his vorpal sword in hand:
10   Long time the manxome foe he sought—
So rested he by the Tumtum tree.
   And stood awhile in thought.

And as in uffish thought he stood,
   The Jabberwock, with eyes of flame,

15 Came whiffling through the tulgey wood,
   And burbled as it came!

One, two! One, two! And through and through
   The vorpal blade went snicker-snack!
He left it dead, and with its head
20   He went galumphing back.

"And hast thou slain the Jabberwock?
   Come to my arms, my beamish boy!
O frabjous day! Callooh! Callay!"
   He chortled in his joy.

25 'Twas brillig and the slithy toves
   Did gyre and gimble in the wabe;
All mimsy were the borogroves,
   And the mome raths outgrabe.

—1872

IN CONTEXT

"Jabberwocky"

The poem "Jabberwocky" appears in the first chapter of *Through the Looking-Glass and What Alice Found There*. The first of the following excerpts provides the surrounding context in that chapter; the second is an excerpt from later in the book, when the poem is again discussed.

from *Through the Looking-Glass and What Alice Found There* (1872)

from CHAPTER 1: LOOKING-GLASS HOUSE

There was a book lying near Alice on the table, and while she sat watching the White King (for she was still a little anxious about him, and had the ink all ready to throw over him, in case he fainted again), she turned over the leaves, to find some part that she could read, "—for it's all in some language I don't know," she said to herself.

It was like this.

YKCOWREBBAJ

sevot yhtils eht dna ,gillirb sawT'
ebaw eht ni elbmig dna eryg diD
,sevorgorob eht erew ysmim llA

---

[1] *Jabberwocky* From *Through the Looking-Glass and What Alice Found There*, Ch. 1: "Looking-Glass House."

.ebargtuo shtar emom eht dnA

She puzzled over this for some time, but at last a bright thought struck her. "Why, it's a looking-glass book, of course! And if I hold it up to a glass, the words will all go the right way again."

This was the poem that Alice read.

[Here the poem appears.]

"It seems very pretty," she said when she had finished it, "but it's rather hard to understand." (You see she didn't like to confess, even to herself, that she couldn't make it out at all.) "Somehow it seems to fill my head with ideas—only I don't exactly know what they are! However, somebody killed something: that's clear, at any rate—."

from CHAPTER 6: HUMPTY DUMPTY

"You seem very clever at explaining words, sir," said Alice. "Would you kindly tell me the meaning of the poem called 'Jabberwocky'?"

"Let's hear it," said Humpty Dumpty. "I can explain all the poems that ever were invented—and a good many that haven't been invented just yet."

This sounded very hopeful, so Alice repeated the first verse:

> " 'Twas brillig, and the slithy toves
> Did gyre and gimble in the wabe;
> All mimsy were the borogroves,
> And the mome raths outgrabe."

"That's enough to begin with," Humpty Dumpty interrupted: "there are plenty of hard words there. '*Brillig*' means four o'clock in the afternoon—the time when you begin *broiling* things for dinner."

"That'll do very well," said Alice: "and '*slithy*'?"

"Well, '*slithy*' means 'lithe and slimy.' 'Lithe' is the same as 'active.' You see it's like a portmanteau[1]— there are two meanings packed up into one word."

"I see it now," Alice remarked thoughtfully: "and what about '*toves*'?"

"Well, '*toves*' are something like badgers—they're something like lizards—and they're something like corkscrews."

"They must be very curious-looking creatures."

"They are that," said Humpty Dumpty: "also they made their nests under sundials—also they live on cheese."

"And what's to '*gyre*' and to '*gimble*'?"

"To '*gyre*' is to go round and round like a gyroscope. To '*gimble*' is to make holes like a gimlet.[2]"

"And 'the *wabe*' is the grass plot round a sundial, I suppose?" said Alice, surprised at her own ingenuity.

"Of course it is. It's called '*wabe*,' you know, because it goes a long way before it, and a long way behind it ——"

"And a long way beyond it on each side," Alice added.

"Exactly so. Well, then, '*mimsy*' is 'flimsy and miserable' (there's another portmanteau for you). And a '*borogrove*' is a thin, shabby-looking bird with its feathers sticking out all round—something like a live mop."

"And then '*mome raths*'?" said Alice. "If I'm not giving you too much trouble."

---

[1] *portmanteau* Leather carrying case; "portmanteau" has since entered the English language in the sense to which Humpty Dumpty refers, i.e., a blended word.

[2] *gimlet* Small tool used for boring holes.

"Well, a '*rath*' is a sort of green pig; but '*mome*' I'm not certain about. I think it's short for '*from home*'—meaning that they'd lost their way, you know."

"And what does '*outgrabe*' mean?"

"Well, '*outgribing*' is something between bellowing and whistling, with a kind of sneeze in the middle: however, you'll hear it done, maybe—down in the wood yonder—and when you've once heard it you'll be *quite* content. Who's been repeating all that hard stuff to you?"

"I read it in a book," said Alice.

IN CONTEXT

The Photographs of Lewis Carroll

Though as a photographer Carroll is best known for his images of children—and of Alice Liddell in particular—he was among the most accomplished of Victorian portrait photographers. Like many photographers of the time, he often portrayed his subjects in dramatic roles.

Alice, Lorina, Harry, and Edith Liddell, 1860.

Alice Liddell as "The Beggar Maid," 1858.

Alexander Munro, the sculptor,
with his wife, Mary, 1863.

George Macdonald and his
daughter Lily, 1863.

Ella Chlora Monier-William, 1866.   "Andromeda," 1865.   "Captive Princess," 1875.

William Morris
1834 – 1896

Morris applied his prodigious, pragmatic genius to a staggering array of artistic and social pursuits: poetry, translation, painting, woodcuts, furniture, wallpaper and textile design, illuminated manuscripts, stained glass windows, and commerce. He combined the qualities of a Renaissance man —an athletic, artistic aristocrat able to do all things well—with an acute political consciousness of his good fortune in "being born prosperous and rich." Fiercely committed to breaking down class distinctions between "intellectual" and "workman," Morris was an artist-activist who insisted on manually producing his own designs, At a time when crafts such as embroidery were regarded as lesser, feminine arts, Morris researched long-forgotten techniques to authenticate the organic integrity of his designs, and promptly took up the needle himself. In giving serious regard to crafts like embroidery and in teaching unusual techniques to the women who helped to produce his designs, Morris was what one critic calls "the prophet of the subversive stitch."

Born in 1834 to prosperous Evangelical parents, Morris was brought up in the Essex countryside. At four years old he was reading novels. By the time he was seven, he had devoured the works of Walter Scott, an author whose imaginative vision, especially in the Waverley novels, would never wear thin for Morris. Scott's work, Malory's *Morte Darthur*, and John Ruskin's *Modern Painters* and *Stones of Venice* provided the formulative influences for his life's work, whether in poetry or crafts or his socialist politics. Although Morris enjoyed a golden childhood and cherished his Welsh roots, he eventually rebelled against a stolid family dynasty which seemed to personify capitalism's more boorish traits. Morris saw little of a father who had secured the family fortune by investing in copper mines, an industry the exploitation of labor and of the environment of which was diametrically opposed to the principles of socialist utopia Morris would depict in the novel *News from Nowhere* (1890). Morris's mother, though in some ways a fond presence during his childhood, embodied to him an intellectual vacancy that he would increasingly associate with the bourgeoisie.

In 1848, Morris was sent to Marlborough College. At Marlborough, lessons were a daily grind of learning by rote; the crushing monotony surely contributed to Morris's later stand as an educational anarchist in the tradition of Godwin and Kropotkin. Acquaintances recall Morris sitting at his desk compulsively weaving nets for catching fish and birds, an image of manual dexterity and absorption in the making of objects simultaneously decorative and useful that would become a leitmotif: Morris at embroidery, Morris knotting rugs and tapestries, Morris stirring dyes mixed from original recipes in his quest for purity of color, Morris arranging exquisite type for his Kelmscott Press.

Morris met Edward Burne-Jones, an aspiring painter, as a student at Oxford. He was to prove a lifelong friend. They read Tennyson and Ruskin, and admired Ruskin's critique of Victorian industrialization and its de-valuation of the worker. Morris pursued a radical yet thorough study of Oxford's historic architecture; to his mind, Oxford was a precious remnant of medieval life threatened by the rising tide of mechanization and industrialization. In 1877, he would found the Society for the

Protection of Ancient Buildings, fighting off a species of commercial restoration that he saw as destructive of the original beauty of England's architecture.

Through Burne-Jones, Morris was introduced to poet and painter Dante Gabriel Rossetti and the Pre-Raphaelite Brotherhood. Morris's artistic gifts were immediately recognized by the fraternity, though he lacked charm with women, which made him the target of some of the members of the group. For years both Burne-Jones and Rossetti sketched caricatures of Morris, Rossetti cruelly exaggerating Morris as a skulking or hulking sexual buffoon. The antagonism that marked Rossetti's and Morris's friendship intensified when Morris proposed to Jane Burden, the beautiful laboring-class daughter of a stablehand, whom Rossetti had "discovered" and used as a model. An offer of marriage from a man of wealth was too good to be refused. Yet their marriage in 1859 initiated an unhappy life together, one aggravated by a long love affair between Jane Morris and Rossetti.

Morris, who had planned to become an architect, turned to painting and poetry because of his connections with the Pre-Raphaelites. In his first volume of poetry, *The Defence of Guenevere and Other Poems* (1858), Morris recreates a medieval world, and in the title poem gives a powerful, sensuous voice to King Arthur's Queen. In his recreation, he adheres to what he would later describe (in 1891) as the primary characteristics of the Pre-Raphaelite school: "Naturalism," "the conscientious presentment of incident," and "a definite, harmonious, conscious beauty." His popular poem *The Life and Death of Jason* (1867), about the search for the Golden Fleece, was followed by a masterful homage to Chaucer, *The Earthly Paradise* (1868-70). As a series of twenty-four stories related by different narrators, the multi-volume narrative poem echoed the structure of Chaucer's *The Canterbury Tales*. In place of English characters, however, Morris wrote of a band of fourteenth-century Norsemen fleeing the Black Death and searching for a rumored Earthly Paradise "where none grow old." Paradise never found, the band returns home, and on feast-days each of them take turns telling tales of their voyage. With *The Earthly Paradise*, Morris enjoyed tremendous popularity as a poet, nearly becoming Tennyson's successor as Poet Laureate.

In 1861 he opened Morris & Co., a design-manufacturing firm that would become the best-known decorating business in Victorian Britain, producing stained-glass windows, wallpapers, furniture, carpets, and tapestries. The vision of Morris & Co. was best expressed by Morris himself when he said, "Have nothing in your houses which you do not know to be useful or believe to be beautiful." Around this time, the bard in Morris began to gravitate northward, drawn to the bluntness and stoicism of Icelandic sagas. In 1871 Morris set sail on the first of two voyages to Iceland. His voyages inspired him to write *The Story of Sigurd the Volsung* (1876), described by one critic as "a Nordic cathedral, a strong and simple edifice of anapestic couplets in four colossal books." Upon co-translating the *Volsunga Saga*, Morris emerged as an authority on Icelandic lore.

Morris underwent what he called a "conversion" to socialism in 1883. If his life and work had been a steady accumulation of evidence against industrial capitalism, it finally found its full articulation in the socialist cause. Morris organized, lectured, and contributed regular articles to socialist journals. In 1884 he founded the Socialist League and its official journal, *The Commonweal*. In "How I Became A Socialist," published in *Justice* magazine in 1894, Morris declared: "Apart from the desire to produce beautiful things, the leading passion of my life has been and is hatred of modern civilization."

Politically disillusioned by growing rifts in the Socialist League, Morris eventually retreated to his favorite house, Kelmscott Manor, and set up a small press. Its finest work was the Kelmscott Chaucer, an edition of *The Canterbury Tales* complete with Edward Burne-Jones's illustrations and Morris's own designs. But age came upon Morris suddenly; his tremendous creative energies were finally spent and he died in 1896, aged sixty-two. His pastoral idealization of earlier times, and the futurist paradise envisioned in *News From Nowhere*, had challenged Victorian culture with the radical possibility of social equality and happiness. But as C.S. Lewis argued, "Morris may build a world in some ways happier than the real one, but happiness puts as stern a question as misery."

⌘ ⌘ ⌘

The Defence of Guenevere[1]

But, knowing now that they would have her speak,
She threw her wet hair backward from her brow,
Her hand close to her mouth touching her cheek,

As though she had had there a shameful blow,
5   And feeling it shameful to feel aught° but shame   *anything*
All through her heart, yet felt her cheek burned so,

She must a little touch it; like one lame
She walked away from Gauwaine,[2] with her head
Still lifted up; and on her cheek of flame

10 The tears dried quick; she stopped at last and said:
"O knights and lords, it seems but little skill°   *use*
To talk of well-known things past now and dead.

"God wot° I ought to say, I have done ill,   *knows*
And pray you all forgiveness heartily!
15 Because you must be right, such great lords—still

"Listen, suppose your time were come to die,
And you were quite alone and very weak;
Yea, laid a dying while very mightily

"The wind was ruffling up the narrow streak
20 Of river through your broad lands running well:
Suppose a hush should come, then some one speak:

"'One of these cloths is heaven, and one is hell,
Now choose one cloth for ever; which they be,
I will not tell you, you must somehow tell

25 "'Of your own strength and mightiness; here, see!'
Yea, yea, my lord, and you to ope° your eyes,   *open*
At foot of your familiar bed to see

"A great God's angel standing, with such dyes,°   *colors*
Not known on earth, on his great wings, and hands
30 Held out two ways, light from the inner skies

"Showing him well, and making his commands
Seem to be God's commands, moreover, too,
Holding within his hands the cloths on wands;

"And one of these strange choosing cloths was blue,
35 Wavy and long, and one cut short and red;
No man could tell the better of the two.

"After a shivering half-hour you said:
'God help! heaven's colour, the blue'; and he said, 'hell.'
Perhaps you then would roll upon your bed,

40 "And cry to all good men that loved you well,
'Ah Christ! if only I had known, known, known;'
Launcelot went away, then I could tell,

"Like wisest man how all things would be, moan,
And roll and hurt myself, and long to die,
45 And yet fear much to die for what was sown.

"Nevertheless you, O Sir Gauwaine, lie,
Whatever may have happened through these years,
God knows I speak truth, saying that you lie."

Her voice was low at first, being full of tears,
50 But as it cleared, it grew full loud and shrill,
Growing a windy shriek in all men's ears,

A ringing in their startled brains, until
She said that Gauwaine lied, then her voice sunk,
And her great eyes began again to fill,

---

[1]   *Guenevere*   Wife of King Arthur, Guenevere has a love affair with Lancelot, one of Arthur's Knights of the Round Table. Here, Morris envisions Guinevere defending herself against Gawain's accusation of adultery.

[2]   *Gauwaine*   Arthur's nephew and one of the chief knights of the Round Table.

55 Though still she stood right up, and never shrunk,
    But spoke on bravely, glorious lady fair!
    Whatever tears her full lips may have drunk,

    She stood, and seemed to think, and wrung her hair,
    Spoke out at last with no more trace of shame,
60 With passionate twisting of her body there:

    "It chanced upon a day that Launcelot came
    To dwell at Arthur's court: at Christmas-time
    This happened; when the heralds sung his name,

    " 'Son of King Ban of Benwick,'[1] seemed to chime
65 Along with all the bells that rang that day,
    O'er the white roofs, with little change of rhyme.

    "Christmas and whitened winter passed away,
    And over me the April sunshine came,
    Made very awful with black hail-clouds, yea

70 "And in the Summer I grew white with flame,
    And bowed my head down—Autumn, and the sick
    Sure knowledge things would never be the same,

    "However often Spring might be most thick
    Of blossoms and buds, smote° on me, and I grew   shone
75 Careless of most things, let the clock tick, tick,

    "To my unhappy pulse, that beat right through
    My eager body; while I laughed out loud,
    And let my lips curl up at false or true,

    "Seemed cold and shallow without any cloud.
80 Behold my judges, then the cloths were brought:
    While I was dizzied thus, old thoughts would crowd,

    "Belonging to the time ere° I was bought   before
    By Arthur's great name and his little love;
    Must I give up for ever then, I thought,

85 "That which I deemed would ever round me move
    Glorifying all things; for a little word,
    Scarce ever meant at all, must I now prove

    "Stone-cold for ever? Pray you, does the Lord
    Will that all folks should be quite happy and good?
90 I love God now a little, if this cord

    "Were broken, once for all what striving could
    Make me love anything in earth or heaven?
    So day by day it grew, as if one should

    "Slip slowly down some path worn smooth and even,
95 Down to a cool sea on a summer day;
    Yet still in slipping there was some small leaven[2]

    "Of stretched hands catching small stones by the way,
    Until one surely reached the sea at last,
    And felt strange new joy as the worn head lay

100 "Back, with the hair like sea-weed; yea all past
    Sweat of the forehead, dryness of the lips,
    Washed utterly out by the dear waves o'ercast

    "In the lone sea, far off from any ships!
    Do I not know now of a day in Spring?
105 No minute of that wild day ever slips

    "From out my memory; I hear thrushes sing,
    And wheresoever I may be, straightway°   immediately
    Thoughts of it all come up with the most fresh sting;

    "I was half mad with beauty on that day,
110 And went without my ladies all alone,
    In a quiet garden walled round every way;

    "I was right joyful of that wall of stone,
    That shut the flowers and trees up with the sky,
    And trebled all the beauty: to the bone,

115 "Yea right through to my heart, grown very shy
    With weary thoughts, it pierced, and made me glad;
    Exceedingly glad, and I knew verily,°   truly

    "A little thing just then had made me mad;
    I dared not think, as I was wont° to do,   accustomed
120 Sometimes, upon my beauty; if I had

    ---
    [1] *King ... Benwick* Lancelot's father, King of Brittany in France.

    [2] *leaven* Tempering element.

"Held out my long hand up against the blue,
And, looking on the tenderly darken'd fingers,
Thought that by rights one ought to see quite through,

"There, see you, where the soft still light yet lingers,
125   Round by the edges; what should I have done,
If this had joined with yellow spotted singers,

"And startling green drawn upward by the sun?
But shouting, loosed out, see now! all my hair,
And trancedly stood watching the west wind run

130   "With faintest half-heard breathing sound—why there
I lose my head e'en now in doing this;
But shortly listen—In that garden fair

"Came Launcelot walking; this is true, the kiss
Wherewith we kissed in meeting that spring day,
135   I scarce dare talk of the remember'd bliss,

"When both our mouths went wandering in one way,
And aching sorely, met among the leaves;
Our hands being left behind strained far away.

"Never within a yard of my bright sleeves
140   Had Launcelot come before—and now, so nigh!
After that day why is it Guenevere grieves?

"Nevertheless you, O Sir Gauwaine, lie,
Whatever happened on through all those years,
God knows I speak truth, saying that you lie.

145   "Being such a lady could I weep these tears
If this were true? A great queen such as I
Having sinn'd this way, straight her conscience sears;

"And afterwards she liveth hatefully,
Slaying and poisoning, certes never weeps,—
150   Gauwaine be friends now, speak° me lovingly.   *address*

"Do I not see how God's dear pity creeps
All through your frame, and trembles in your mouth?
Remember in what grave your mother sleeps,

"Buried in some place far down in the south,
155   Men are forgetting as I speak to you;
By her head sever'd in that awful drouth°   *drought*

"Of pity that drew Agravaine's fell blow,[1]
I pray your pity! let me not scream out
For ever after, when the shrill winds blow

160   "Through half your castle-locks![2] let me not shout
For ever after in the winter night
When you ride out alone! in battle-rout°   *battle formation*

"Let not my rusting tears make your sword light!
Ah! God of mercy, how he turns away!
165   So, ever must I dress me° to the fight;   *prepare myself*

"So—let God's justice work! Gauwaine, I say,
See me hew down your proofs:[3] yea, all men know
Even as you said how Mellyagraunce one day,

"One bitter day in *la Fausse Garde*,[4] for so
170   All good knights held it after, saw—
Yea, sirs, by cursed unknightly outrage; though

"You, Gauwaine, held his word without a flaw,
This Mellyagraunce saw blood upon my bed—[5]
Whose blood then pray you? is there any law

175   "To make a queen say why some spots of red
Lie on her coverlet? or will you say,
'Your hands are white, lady, as when you wed,

"'Where did you bleed?' and must I stammer out—'Nay,
I blush indeed, fair lord, only to rend
180   My sleeve up to my shoulder, where there lay

"'A knife-point last night': so must I defend
The honour of the lady Guenevere?

---

1   *By ... blow* Morgause (Arthur's half-sister) was murdered by her
sons Gawain, Gaheris, Mordred and Agravaine after they discovered
her having a love affair with a young knight, Sir Lamorak.

2   *castle-locks* Castle casements, hatches, wickets.

3   *hew* Cut; *proofs* Evidence.

4   *Mellyagraunce* Outlaw knight who captures Guinevere; *la Fausse
Garde* The False Keep, Mellyagraunce's castle.

5   *blood ... bed* Taken as evidence for Guinevere's infidelity.

Not so, fair lords, even if the world should end

"This very day, and you were judges here
185   Instead of God. Did you see Mellyagraunce
When Launcelot stood by him? what white fear

"Curdled his blood, and how his teeth did dance,
His side sink in? as my knight cried and said,
'Slayer of unarm'd men,[1] here is a chance!

190   "'Setter of traps, I pray you guard your head,
By God I am so glad to fight with you,
Stripper of ladies, that my hand feels lead

"'For driving weight; hurrah now! draw and do,
For all my wounds are moving in my breast,
195   And I am getting mad with waiting so.'

"He struck his hands together o'er the beast,
Who fell down flat, and grovell'd at his feet,
And groan'd at being slain so young—'at least.'

"My knight said: 'Rise you, sir, who are so fleet
200   At catching ladies, half-arm'd will I fight,
My left side all uncovered!' then I weet,[2]

"Up sprang Sir Mellyagraunce with great delight
Upon his knave's face; not until just then
Did I quite hate him, as I saw my knight

205   "Along the lists[3] look to my stake and pen
With such a joyous smile, it made me sigh
From agony beneath my waist-chain, when

"The fight began, and to me they drew nigh;
Ever Sir Launcelot kept him on the right,
210   And traversed warily, and ever high

"And fast leapt caitiff's° sword, until my knight   *villain's*
Sudden threw up his sword to his left hand,
Caught it, and swung it; that was all the fight.

---

[1]   *Slayer … men* Just after abducting Guinevere, Mellyagraunce
had his soldiers attack Lancelot, who was unarmed.

[2]   *uncovered* Unarmored; *weet* Know.

[3]   *lists* Place for combat.

"Except a spout of blood on the hot land;
215   For it was hottest summer; and I know
I wonder'd how the fire, while I should stand,

"And burn, against the heat, would quiver so,
Yards above my head; thus these matters went;
Which things were only warnings of the woe

220   "That fell on me. Yet Mellyagraunce was shent,°   *ruined*
For Mellyagraunce had fought against the Lord;
Therefore, my lords, take heed lest you be blent[4]

"With all this wickedness; say no rash word
Against me, being so beautiful; my eyes,
225   Wept all away to grey, may bring some sword

"To drown you in your blood; see my breast rise,
Like waves of purple sea, as here I stand;
And how my arms are moved in wonderful wise,

"Yea also at my full heart's strong command,
230   See through my long throat how the words go up
In ripples to my mouth; how in my hand

"The shadow lies like wine within a cup
Of marvellously colour'd gold; yea now
This little wind is rising, look you up,

235   "And wonder how the light is falling so
Within my moving tresses: will you dare,
When you have looked a little on my brow,

"To say this thing is vile? or will you care
For any plausible lies of cunning woof,°   *weave*
240   When you can see my face with no lie there

"For ever? am I not a gracious proof—
'But in your chamber Launcelot was found'—
Is there a good knight then would stand aloof,

"When a queen says with gentle queenly sound:
245   'O true as steel, come now and talk with me,
I love to see your step upon the ground

---

[4]   *blent* Mingled.

" 'Unwavering, also well I love to see
That gracious smile light up your face, and hear
Your wonderful words, that all mean verily

250 " 'The thing they seem to mean: good friend, so dear
To me in everything, come here to-night,
Or else the hours will pass most dull and drear;

" 'If you come not, I fear this time I might
Get thinking over much of times gone by,
255 When I was young, and green hope was in sight:

" 'For no man cares now to know why I sigh;
And no man comes to sing me pleasant songs,
Nor any brings me the sweet flowers that lie

" 'So thick in the gardens; therefore one so longs
260 To see you, Launcelot; that we may be
Like children once again, free from all wrongs

" 'Just for one night.' Did he not come to me?
What thing could keep true Launcelot away
If I said 'Come'? there was one less than three

265 "In my quiet room that night, and we were gay;
Till sudden I rose up, weak, pale, and sick,
Because a bawling broke our dream up, yea

"I looked at Launcelot's face and could not speak,
For he looked helpless too, for a little while;
270 Then I remember how I tried to shriek,

"And could not, but fell down; from tile to tile
The stones they threw up rattled o'er my head
And made me dizzier; till within a while

"My maids were all about me, and my head
275 On Launcelot's breast was being soothed away
From its white chattering, until Launcelot said—

"By God! I will not tell you more to-day,
Judge any way you will—what matters it?
You know quite well the story of that fray,°   *noisy quarrel*

280 "How Launcelot still'd their bawling, the mad fit
That caught up Gauwaine—all, all, verily,
But just that which would save me; these things flit.

"Nevertheless you, O Sir Gauwaine, lie,
Whatever may have happen'd these long years,
285 God knows I speak truth, saying that you lie!

"All I have said is truth, by Christ's dear tears."
She would not speak another word, but stood
Turn'd sideways; listening, like a man who hears

His brother's trumpet sounding through the wood
290 Of his foes' lances. She lean'd eagerly,
And gave a slight spring sometimes, as she could

At last hear something really; joyfully
Her cheek grew crimson, as the headlong speed
Of the roan charger[1] drew all men to see,
295 The knight who came was Launcelot at good need.[2]
   —1858

Queen Guenevere (1858) by William Morris.

[1] *roan charger* Horse with coat of mixed color.
[2] *at … need* Just in time.

The Haystack in the Floods

Had she come all the way for this,
To part at last without a kiss?
Yea, had she borne the dirt and rain
That her own eyes might see him slain
Beside the haystack in the floods?

Along the dripping leafless woods,
The stirrup touching either shoe,
She rode astride as troopers° do;   *horse soldiers*
With kirtle kilted[1] to her knee,
To which the mud splash'd wretchedly;
And the wet dripp'd from every tree
Upon her head and heavy hair,
And on her eyelids broad and fair;
The tears and rain ran down her face.
By fits and starts they rode apace,[2]
And very often was his place
Far off from her; he had to ride
Ahead, to see what might betide°   *happen*
When the roads cross'd; and sometimes, when
There rose a murmuring from his men,
Had to turn back with promises;
Ah me! she had but little ease;
And often for pure doubt and dread
She sobb'd, made giddy in the head
By the swift riding; while, for cold,
Her slender fingers scarce could hold
The wet reins; yea, and scarcely, too,
She felt the foot within her shoe
Against the stirrup: all for this,
To part at last without a kiss
Beside the haystack in the floods.

For when they near'd that old soak'd hay,
They saw across the only way
That Judas, Godmar, and the three
Red running lions dismally
Grinn'd from his pennon,° under which,   *flag*
In one straight line along the ditch,
They counted thirty heads.

So then,
While Robert turn'd round to his men,
She saw at once the wretched end,
And, stooping down, tried hard to rend
Her coif° the wrong way from her head,   *cap*
And hid her eyes; while Robert said:
"Nay, love, 'tis scarcely two to one,
At Poictiers[3] where we made them run
So fast—why, sweet my love, good cheer.
The Gascon frontier[4] is so near,
Nought° after this."   *nothing*

But, "O," she said,
"My God! my God! I have to tread
The long way back without you; then
The court at Paris; those six men;
The gratings of the Chatelet;[5]
The swift Seine[6] on some rainy day
Like this, and people standing by,
And laughing, while my weak hands try
To recollect how strong men swim.
All this, or else a life with him,
For which I should be damned at last,
Would God that this next hour were past!"

He answer'd not, but cried his cry,
"St. George for Marny!"[7] cheerily;
And laid his hand upon her rein.
Alas! no man of all his train°   *retinue*
Gave back that cheery cry again;
And, while for rage his thumb beat fast
Upon his sword-hilt, some one cast
About his neck a kerchief long,
And bound him.

---

[1] *kirtle* Long gown; *kilted* Fastened or tied up.

[2] *apace* At a good pace.

[3] *Poictiers* I.e., Poitiers, a city in west-central France where England won a decisive victory over French forces in 1356.

[4] *Gascon* Gascony, province of southern France that served as a major battlefield in the Hundred Years' War (1337–1453); *frontier* Border.

[5] *Chatelet* The Châtelet prison at Paris.

[6] *Seine* River flowing through Paris.

[7] *St. George* Patron saint of England; *St … Marny* Battle-cry asking St. George to help Sir Robert de Morny, the "Robert" of the poem.

Then they went along
To Godmar; who said: "Now, Jehane,
Your lover's life is on the wane
So fast, that, if this very hour
75 You yield not as my paramour,°   *mistress*
He will not see the rain leave off—
Nay, keep your tongue from gibe° and scoff,   *taunts*
Sir Robert, or I slay you now."

She laid her hand upon her brow,
80 Then gazed upon the palm, as though
She thought her forehead bled, and—"No!"
She said, and turn'd her head away,
As there were nothing else to say,
And everything were settled: red
85 Grew Godmar's face from chin to head:
"Jehane, on yonder hill there stands
My castle, guarding well my lands:
What hinders me from taking you,
And doing that I list° to do   *like*
90 To your fair wilful body, while
Your knight lies dead?"
                    A wicked smile
Wrinkled her face, her lips grew thin,
A long way out she thrust her chin:
"You know that I should strangle you
95 While you were sleeping; or bite through
Your throat, by God's help—ah!" she said,
"Lord Jesus, pity your poor maid!
For in such wise they hem me in,
I cannot choose but sin and sin,
100 Whatever happens: yet I think
They could not make me eat or drink,
And so should I just reach my rest."
"Nay, if you do not my behest,°   *bidding*
105 O Jehane! though I love you well,"
Said Godmar, "would I fail to tell
All that I know?" "Foul lies," she said.
"Eh? lies, my Jehane? by God's head,
At Paris folks would deem° them true!   *judge*
110 Do you know, Jehane, they cry for you,
'Jehane the brown! Jehane the brown!
Give us Jehane to burn or drown!'—
Eh—gag me Robert!—sweet my friend,
This were indeed a piteous end

115 For those long fingers, and long feet,
And long neck, and smooth shoulders sweet;
An end that few men would forget
That saw it—So, an hour yet:
Consider, Jehane, which to take
120 Of life or death!"
                    So, scarce awake,
Dismounting, did she leave that place,
And totter some yards: with her face
Turn'd upward to the sky she lay,
125 Her head on a wet heap of hay,
And fell asleep: and while she slept,
And did not dream, the minutes crept
Round to the twelve again; but she,
Being waked at last, sigh'd quietly,
130 And strangely childlike came, and said:
"I will not." Straightway Godmar's head,
As though it hung on strong wires, turn'd
Most sharply round, and his face burn'd.

For Robert—both his eyes were dry,
135 He could not weep, but gloomily
He seem'd to watch the rain; yea, too,
His lips were firm; he tried once more
To touch her lips, she reach'd out, sore
And vain desire so tortured them,
140 The poor grey lips, and now the hem
Of his sleeve brush'd them.
                    With a start
Up Godmar rose, thrust them apart;
From Robert's throat he loosed the bands
145 Of silk and mail; with empty hands
Held out, she stood and gazed, and saw,
The long bright blade without a flaw
Glide out from Godmar's sheath, his hand
In Robert's hair; she saw him bend
150 Back Robert's head; she saw him send
The thin steel down; the blow told well,[1]
Right backward the knight Robert fell,
And moan'd as dogs do, being half dead,
Unwitting,° as I deem: so then   *senseless*
155 Godmar turn'd grinning to his men,
Who ran, some five or six, and beat
His head to pieces at their feet.

---

[1] *told well* Landed accurately.

Then Godmar turn'd again and said
"So, Jehane, the first fitte[1] is read!
160 Take note, my lady, that your way
Lies backward to the Chatelet!"
She shook her head and gazed awhile
At her cold hands with a rueful smile,
As though this thing had made her mad.

165 This was the parting that they had
Beside the haystack in the floods.
    —1858

The Beauty of Life[2]
from Hopes and Fears for Art. Five Lectures

I stand before you this evening weighted with a disadvantage that I did not feel last year;—I have little fresh to tell you; I can somewhat enlarge on what I said then; here and there I may make bold to give you a practical suggestion, or I may put what I have to say in a way which will be clearer to some of you perhaps; but my message is really the same as it was when I first had the pleasure of meeting you.

It is true that if all were going smoothly with art, or at all events so smoothly that there were but a few malcontents in the world, you might listen with some pleasure, and perhaps advantage, to the talk of an old hand in the craft concerning ways of work, the snares that beset[3] success, and the shortest road to it, to a tale of workshop receipts and the like: that would be a pleasant talk surely between friends and fellow-workmen; but it seems to me as if it were not for us as yet; nay, maybe we may live long and find no time fit for such restful talk as the cheerful histories of the hopes and fears of our workshops: anyhow to-night I cannot do it, but must once again call the faithful of art to a battle wider and more distracting than that kindly struggle with nature, to which all true craftsmen are born; which is both the building-up and the wearing-away of their lives.

As I look round on this assemblage, and think of all that it represents, I cannot choose but be moved to the soul by the troubles of the life of civilised man, and the hope that thrusts itself through them; I cannot refrain from giving you once again the message with which, as it seems, some chance-hap has charged me: that message is, in short, to call on you to face the latest danger which civilisation is threatened with, a danger of her own breeding: that men in struggling towards the complete attainment of all the luxuries of life for the strongest portion of their race should deprive their whole race of all the beauty of life: a danger that the strongest and wisest of mankind, in striving to attain to a complete mastery over nature, should destroy her simplest and widest-spread gifts, and thereby enslave simple people to them, and themselves to themselves, and so at last drag the world into a second barbarism more ignoble, and a thousandfold more hopeless, than the first.

Now of you who are listening to me, there are some, I feel sure, who have received this message, and taken it to heart, and are day by day fighting the battle that it calls on you to fight: to you I can say nothing but that if any word I speak discourage you, I shall heartily wish I had never spoken at all: but to be shown the enemy, and the castle we have got to storm, is not to be bidden to run from him; nor am I telling you to sit down deedless in the desert because between you and the promised land lies many a trouble, and death itself maybe: the hope before you you know, and nothing that I can say can take it away from you; but friend may with advantage cry out to friend in the battle that a stroke is coming from this side or that: take my hasty words in that sense, I beg of you.

But I think there will be others of you in whom vague discontent is stirring: who are oppressed by the life that surrounds you; confused and troubled by that oppression, and not knowing on which side to seek a remedy, though you are fain[4] to do so: well, we, who have gone further into those troubles, believe that we can help you: true we cannot at once take your trouble from you; nay, we may at first rather add to it; but we can tell you what we think of the way out of it; and then amidst the many things you will have to do to set yourselves and others fairly on that way, you will many

---

[1] fitte Section of a poem or song.

[2] The Beauty of Life Delivered to the Birmingham Society of Arts and School of Design 19 February 1880.

[3] beset Surround.

[4] fain Obliged.

days, nay most days, forget your trouble in thinking of the good that lies beyond it, for which you are working. But, again, there are others amongst you (and to speak plainly, I daresay they are the majority), who are not by any means troubled by doubt of the road the world is going, nor excited by any hope of its bettering that road: to them the cause of civilisation is simple and even commonplace: wonder, hope, and fear no longer hang about it; it has become to us like the rising and setting of the sun; it cannot err, and we have no call to meddle with it, either to complain of its course, or to try to direct it.

There is a ground of reason and wisdom in that way of looking at the matter: surely the world will go on its ways, thrust forward by impulses which we cannot understand or sway: but as it grows in strength for the journey, its necessary food is the life and aspirations of *all* of us: and we discontented strugglers with what at times seems the hurrying blindness of civilisation, no less than those who see nothing but smooth, unvarying progress in it, are bred of civilisation also, and shall be used up to further it in some way or other, I doubt not: and it may be of some service to those who think themselves the only loyal subjects of progress to hear of our existence, since their not hearing of it would not make an end of it: it may set them a-thinking not unprofitably to hear of burdens that they do not help to bear, but which are nevertheless real and weighty enough to some of their fellow-men, who are helping, even as they are, to form the civilisation that is to be. The danger that the present course of civilisation will destroy the beauty of life—these are hard words, and I wish I could mend them, but I cannot, while I speak what I believe to be the truth.

That the beauty of life is a thing of no moment,[1] I suppose few people would venture to assert, and yet most civilised people act as if it were of none, and in so doing are wronging both themselves and those that are to come after them; for that beauty, which is what is meant by *art*, using the word in its widest sense, is, I contend, no mere accident to human life, which people can take or leave as they choose, but a positive necessity of life, if we are to live as nature meant us to; that is, unless we are content to be less than men.

Now I ask you, as I have been asking myself this long while, what proportion of the population in civilised countries has any share at all in that necessity of life?

I say that the answer which must be made to that question justifies my fear that modern civilisation is on the road to trample out all the beauty of life, and to make us less than men.

Now if there should be any here who will say: It was always so; there always was a mass of rough[2] ignorance that knew and cared nothing about art; I answer first, that if that be the case, then it was always wrong, and we, as soon as we have become conscious of that wrong, are bound to set it right if we can.

But moreover, strange to say, and in spite of all the suffering that the world has wantonly made for itself, and has in all ages so persistently clung to, as if it were a good and holy thing, this wrong of the mass of men being regardless[3] of art was *not* always so.

So much is now known of the periods of art that have left abundant examples of their work behind them, that we can judge of the art of all periods by comparing these with the remains of times of which less has been left us; and we cannot fail to come to the conclusion that down to very recent days everything that the hand of man touched was more or less beautiful: so that in those days all people who made anything shared in art, as well as all people who used the things so made: that is, *all* people shared in art.

But some people may say: And was that to be wished for? would not this universal spreading of art stop progress in other matters, hinder the work of the world? Would it not make us unmanly? or if not that, would it not be intrusive, and push out other things necessary also for men to study?

Well, I have claimed a necessary place for art, a natural place, and it would be in the very essence of it, that it would apply its own rules of order and fitness to the general ways of life: it seems to me, therefore, that people who are over-anxious of the outward expression of beauty becoming too great a force among the other forces of life, would, if they had had the making of the

---

[1]   *moment*   Significance.

[2]   *rough*   Lacking refinement.

[3]   *regardless*   Indifferent.

external world, have been afraid of making an ear of wheat beautiful, lest it should not have been good to eat.

But indeed there seems no chance of art becoming universal, unless on the terms that it shall have little self-consciousness, and for the most part be done with little effort; so that the rough work of the world would be as little hindered by it, as the work of external nature is by the beauty of all her forms and moods: this was the case in the times that I have been speaking of: of art which was made by conscious effort, the result of the individual striving towards perfect expression of their thoughts by men very specially gifted, there was perhaps no more than there is now, except in very wonderful and short periods; though I believe that even for such men the struggle to produce beauty was not so bitter as it now is. But if there were not more great thinkers than there are now, there was a countless multitude of happy workers whose work did express, and could not choose but express, some original thought, and was consequently both interesting and beautiful: now there is certainly no chance of the more individual art becoming common, and either wearying us by its over-abundance, or by noisy self-assertion preventing highly cultivated men taking their due part in the other work of the world; it is too difficult to do: it will be always but the blossom of all the half-conscious work below it, the fulfilment of the shortcomings of less complete minds: but it will waste much of its power, and have much less influence on men's minds, unless it be surrounded by abundance of that commoner work, in which all men once shared, and which, I say, will, when art has really awakened, be done so easily and constantly, that it will stand in no man's way to hinder him from doing what he will, good or evil. And as, on the one hand, I believe that art made by the people and for the people as a joy both to the maker and the user would further progress in other matters rather than hinder it, so also I firmly believe that that higher art produced only by great brains and miraculously gifted hands cannot exist without it: I believe that the present state of things in which it does exist, while popular art is, let us say, asleep or sick, is a transitional state, which must end at last either in utter defeat or utter victory for the arts.

"Strawberry Thief" chintz designed by William Morris in 1883.

For whereas all works of craftsmanship were once beautiful, unwittingly or not, they are now divided into two kinds, works of art and non-works of art: now nothing made by man's hand can be indifferent: it must be either beautiful and elevating, or ugly and degrading; and those things that are without art are so aggressively; they wound it by their existence, and they are now so much in the majority that the works of art we are obliged to set ourselves to seek for, whereas the other things are the ordinary companions of our everyday life; so that if those who cultivate art intellectually were inclined never so much to wrap themselves in their special gifts and their high cultivation, and so live happily, apart from other men, and despising them, they could not do so: they are as it were living in an enemy's country; at every turn there is something lying in wait to offend and vex their nicer sense and educated eyes: they must share in the general discomfort—and I am glad of it.

So the matter stands: from the first dawn of history till quite modern times, art, which nature meant to solace all, fulfilled its purpose; all men shared in it; that was what made life romantic, as people call it, in those days; that and not robber-barons[1] and inaccessible kings

---

[1] *robber-barons* Feudal leaders who prospered through plundering.

with their hierarchy of serving-nobles[1] and other such rubbish: but art grew and grew, saw empires sicken and sickened with them; grew hale[2] again, and haler, and grew so great at last, that she seemed in good truth to have conquered everything, and laid the material world under foot. Then came a change at a period of the greatest life and hope in many ways that Europe had known till then: a time of so much and such varied hope that people call it the time of the New Birth:[3] as far as the arts are concerned I deny it that title; rather it seems to me that the great men who lived and glorified the practice of art in those days, were the fruit of the old, not the seed of the new order of things: but a stirring and hopeful time it was, and many things were newborn then which have since brought forth fruit enough: and it is strange and perplexing that from those days forward the lapse of time, which, through plenteous confusion and failure, has on the whole been steadily destroying privilege and exclusiveness in other matters, has delivered up art to be the exclusive privilege of a few, and has taken from the people their birthright; while both wronged and wrongers have been wholly unconscious of what they were doing.

Wholly unconscious—yes, but we are no longer so: there lies the sting of it, and there also the hope.

When the brightness of the so-called Renaissance faded, and it faded very suddenly, a deadly chill fell upon the arts: that New-birth mostly meant looking back to past times, wherein the men of those days thought they saw a perfection of art, which to their minds was different in kind, and not in degree only, from the ruder suggestive art of their own fathers: this perfection they were ambitious to imitate, this alone seemed to be art to them, the rest was childishness: so wonderful was their energy, their success so great, that no doubt to commonplace minds among them, though surely not to the great masters, that perfection seemed to be gained: and, perfection being gained, what are you to do?—you can go no further, you must aim at standing still—which you cannot do.

Art by no means stood still in those latter days of the

Renaissance, but took the downward road with terrible swiftness, and tumbled down at the bottom of the hill, where as if bewitched it lay long in great content, believing itself to be the art of Michelangelo,[4] while it was the art of men whom nobody remembers but those who want to sell their pictures.

Thus it fared with the more individual forms of art. As to the art of the people; in countries and places where the greater art had flourished most, it went step by step on the downward path with that: in more out-of-the-way places, England for instance, it still felt the influence of the life of its earlier and happy days, and in a way lived on a while; but its life was so feeble, and, so to say, illogical, that it could not resist any change in external circumstances, still less could it give birth to anything new; and before this century began, its last flicker had died out. Still, while it was living, in whatever dotage,[5] it did imply something going on in those matters of daily use that we have been thinking of, and doubtless satisfied some cravings for beauty: and when it was dead, for a long time people did not know it, or what had taken its place, crept so to say into its dead body—that pretence of art, to wit, which is done with machines, though sometimes the machines are called men, and doubtless are so out of working hours: nevertheless long before it was quite dead it had fallen so low that the whole subject was usually treated with the utmost contempt by every one who had any pretence of being a sensible man, and in short the whole civilised world had forgotten that there had ever been an art *made by the people for the people as a joy for the maker and the user.*

But now it seems to me that the very suddenness of the change ought to comfort us, to make us look upon this break in the continuity of the golden chain as an accident only, that itself cannot last: for think how many thousand years it may be since that primeval man graved[6] with a flint splinter on a bone the story of the mammoth he had seen, or told us of the slow uplifting of the heavily-horned heads of the reindeer that he stalked: think I say of the space of time from then till

---

[1] *inaccessible ... serving-nobles* Noble courts typically depicted in medieval romance.

[2] *hale* Healthy.

[3] *New Birth* I.e., the Renaissance.

[4] *Michelangelo* Florentine sculptor and painter (1475–1564).

[5] *dotage* Senility.

[6] *graved* Engraved.

the dimming of the brightness of the Italian Renaissance! whereas from that time till popular art died unnoticed and despised among ourselves is just but two hundred years.

Strange too, that very death is contemporaneous with new-birth of something at all events; for out of all despair sprang a new time of hope lighted by the torch of the French Revolution: and things that have languished with the languishing of art, rose afresh and surely heralded its new birth: in good earnest poetry was born again, and the English Language, which under the hands of sycophantic verse-makers[1] had been reduced to a miserable jargon, whose meaning, if it have a meaning, cannot be made out without translation, flowed clear, pure, and simple, along with the music of Blake and Coleridge:[2] take those names, the earliest in date among ourselves, as a type of the change that has happened in literature since the time of George II.[3]

With that literature in which romance, that is to say humanity, was re-born, there sprang up also a feeling for the romance of external nature, which is surely strong in us now, joined with a longing to know something real of the lives of those who have gone before us; of these feelings united you will find the broadest expression in the pages of Walter Scott:[4] it is curious as showing how sometimes one art will lag behind another in a revival, that the man who wrote the exquisite and wholly unfettered naturalism of the Heart of Midlothian, for instance, thought himself continually bound to seem to feel ashamed of, and to excuse himself for, his love of Gothic Architecture:[5] he felt that it was romantic, and

he knew that it gave him pleasure, but somehow he had not found out that it was art, having been taught in many ways that nothing could be art that was not done by a named man under academical rules.

I need not perhaps dwell much on what of change has been since: you know well that one of the master-arts, the art of painting, has been revolutionised. I have a genuine difficulty in speaking to you of men who are my own personal friends, nay my masters: still, since I cannot quite say nothing of them I must say the plain truth, which is this; never in the whole history of art did any set of men come nearer to the feat of making something out of nothing than that little knot of painters[6] who have raised English art from what it was, when as a boy I used to go to the Royal Academy Exhibition,[7] to what it is now.

It would be ungracious indeed for me who have been so much taught by him, that I cannot help feeling continually as I speak that I am echoing his words, to leave out the name of John Ruskin[8] from an account of what has happened since the tide, as we hope, began to turn in the direction of art. True it is, that his unequalled style of English and his wonderful eloquence would, whatever its subject-matter, have gained him some sort of a hearing in a time that has not lost its relish for literature; but surely the influence that he has exercised over cultivated people must be the result of that style and that eloquence expressing what was already stirring in men's minds; he could not have written what he has done unless people were in some sort ready for it; any more than those painters could have begun their crusade against the dulness and incompetency that was the rule in their art thirty years ago unless they had some hope that they would one day move people to understand them.

---

[1] *sycophantic* Characterized by servile self-seeking; *sycophantic verse-makers* Here, poets writing for patrons.

[2] *Blake* William Blake (1757–1827), British poet and artist; *Coleridge* Samuel Taylor Coleridge (1772–1834), British poet and critic.

[3] *George II* British monarch (1683–1760) who reigned from 1727–60.

[4] *Walter Scott* I.e., Sir Walter Scott, Scots author noted for his ballads and for developing the historical novel (1771–1832).

[5] *Heart of Midlothian* Novel by Sir Walter Scott (1818) that follows a fictitious Scottish family during the mid-eighteenth century Anglo-Scottish hostilities; *Gothic Architecture* Medieval European architectural style dominant from the twelfth through the fifteenth centuries, characterized by pointed arches and ribbed vaulting.

[6] *little ... painters* Pre-Raphaelite Brotherhood, the school of painters and critics that demanded a return to the artistic conventions of fourteenth-century Italy. Their work is characterized by vibrant color, complex composition and a high level of detail. Notable artists associated with this movement are Dante Gabriel Rossetti (1828–82), John Everett Millais (1829–96), and William Holman Hunt (1827–1910);

[7] *Royal Academy* British arts institution founded in 1769; *Royal Academy Exhibition* Annual Royal Academy exhibition of new art, held each summer.

[8] *John Ruskin* British author and art critic (1819–1900).

Well, we find that the gains since the turning-point of the tide are these: that there are some few artists who have, as it were, caught up the golden chain dropped two hundred years ago, and that there are a few highly cultivated people who can understand them; and that beyond these there is a vague feeling abroad among people of the same degree,[1] of discontent at the ignoble ugliness that surrounds them.

That seems to me to mark the advance that we have made since the last of popular art came to an end amongst us, and I do not say, considering where we then were, that it is not a great advance, for it comes to this, that though the battle is still to win, there are those who are ready for the battle.

Indeed it would be a strange shame for this age if it were not so: for as every age of the world has its own troubles to confuse it, and its own follies to cumber[2] it, so has each its own work to do, pointed out to it by unfailing signs of the times; and it is unmanly and stupid for the children of any age to say: We will not set our hands to the work; we did not make the troubles, we will not weary ourselves seeking a remedy for them: so heaping up for their sons a heavier load than they can lift without such struggles as will wound and cripple them sorely. Not thus our fathers served us, who, working late and early, left us at last that seething mass of people so terribly alive and energetic, that we call modern Europe; not thus those served us, who have made for us these present days, so fruitful of change and wondering expectation.

The century that is now beginning to draw to an end, if people were to take to nicknaming centuries, would be called the Century of Commerce; and I do not think I undervalue the work that it has done: it has broken down many a prejudice and taught many a lesson that the world has been hitherto slow to learn: it has made it possible for many a man to live free, who would in other times have been a slave, body or soul, or both: if it has not quite spread peace and justice through the world, as at the end of its first half we fondly hoped it would, it has at least stirred up in many fresh cravings for peace and justice: its work has been good and plenteous, but much of it was roughly done, as needs was;[3] recklessness has commonly gone with its energy, blindness too often with its haste: so that perhaps it may be work enough for the next century to repair the blunders of that recklessness, to clear away the rubbish which that hurried work has piled up; nay even we in the second half of its last quarter may do something towards setting its house in order.

You, of this great and famous town, for instance, which has had so much to do with the Century of Commerce,[4] your gains are obvious to all men, but the price you have paid for them is obvious to many—surely to yourselves most of all: I do not say that they are not worth the price; I know that England and the world could very ill afford to exchange the Birmingham of to-day for the Birmingham of the year 1700: but surely if what you have gained be more than a mockery, you cannot stop at those gains, or even go on always piling up similar ones. Nothing can make me believe that the present condition of your Black Country yonder[5] is an unchangeable necessity of your life and position: such miseries as this were begun and carried on in pure thoughtlessness, and a hundredth part of the energy that was spent in creating them would get rid of them: I do think if we were not all of us too prone to acquiesce in the base byword "after me the deluge,"[6] it would soon be something more than an idle dream to hope that your pleasant midland hills and fields might begin to become pleasant again in some way or other, even without depopulating them; or that those once lovely valleys of Yorkshire in the "heavy woollen district," with their sweeping hill-sides and noble rivers, should not need the stroke of ruin to make them once more delightful abodes of men, instead of the dog-holes[7] that the Century of Commerce has made them.

---

[1] *degree* Kind.

[2] *cumber* Hinder.

[3] *as ... was* As it needed to be.

[4] *which ... Commerce* Birmingham was (and still is) a major industrial and transportation center.

[5] *Black Country* Area around Staffordshire and Warwickshire blackened by industrial pollution, particularly that of the coal and iron trades; *yonder* Over there.

[6] *base* Morally low; *after ... deluge* Quotation attributed to Louis XV of France (predicting the French Revolution).

[7] *Yorkshire* Region of northern England; *heavy ... district* Major textile center in Yorkshire; *dog-holes* Vile dwelling places.

Well, people will not take the trouble or spend the money necessary to beginning this sort of reform, because they do not feel the evils they live amongst, because they have degraded themselves into something less than men; they are unmanly because they have ceased to have their due share of art.

For again I say that therein rich people have defrauded themselves as well as the poor: you will see a refined and highly educated man nowadays, who has been to Italy and Egypt, and where not, who can talk learnedly enough (and fantastically enough sometimes) about art, and who has at his fingers' ends abundant lore concerning the art and literature of past days, sitting down without signs of discomfort in a house, that with all its surroundings is just brutally vulgar and hideous: all his education has not done more for him than that.

The truth is, that in art, and in other things besides, the laboured education of a few will not raise even those few above the reach of the evils that beset the ignorance of the great mass of the population: the brutality of which such a huge stock has been accumulated lower down, will often show without much peeling through the selfish refinement of those who have let it accumulate. The lack of art, or rather the murder of art, that curses our streets from the sordidness of the surroundings of the lower classes, has its exact counterpart in the dulness and vulgarity of those of the middle classes, and the double-distilled[1] dulness, and scarcely less vulgarity of those of the upper classes.

I say this is as it should be; it is just and fair as far as it goes; and moreover the rich with their leisure are the more like to move if they feel the pinch themselves.

But how shall they and we, and all of us, move? What is the remedy?

What remedy can there be for the blunders of civilisation but further civilisation? You do not by any accident think that we have gone as far in that direction as it is possible to go, do you?—even in England, I mean?

When some changes have come to pass, that perhaps will be speedier than most people think, doubtless education will both grow in quality and in quantity; so that it may be, that as the nineteenth century is to be called the Century of Commerce, the twentieth may be called the Century of Education. But that education does not end when people leave school is now a mere commonplace; and how then can you really educate men who lead the life of machines, who only think for the few hours during which they are not at work, who in short spend almost their whole lives in doing work which is not proper for developing them body and mind in some worthy way? You cannot educate, you cannot civilise men, unless you can give them a share in art.

Yes, and it is hard indeed as things go to give most men that share; for they do not miss it, or ask for it, and it is impossible as things are that they should either miss or ask for it. Nevertheless everything has a beginning, and many great things have had very small ones; and since, as I have said, these ideas are already abroad in more than one form, we must not be too much discouraged at the seemingly boundless weight we have to lift.

After all, we are only bound to play our own parts, and do our own share of the lifting, and as in no case that share can be great, so also in all cases it is called for, it is necessary. Therefore let us work and faint not; remembering that though it be natural, and therefore excusable, amidst doubtful times to feel doubts of success oppress us at whiles,[2] yet not to crush those doubts, and work as if we had them not, is simple cowardice, which is unforgivable. No man has any right to say that all has been done for nothing, that all the faithful unwearying strife of those that have gone before us shall lead us nowhither;[3] that mankind will but go round and round in a circle for ever: no man has a right to say that, and then get up morning after morning to eat his victuals[4] and sleep a nights, all the while making other people toil to keep his worthless life a-going.

Be sure that some way or other will be found out of the tangle, even when things seem most tangled, and be no less sure that some use will then have come of our work, if it has been faithful, and therefore unsparingly careful and thoughtful.

So once more I say, if in any matters civilisation has gone astray, the remedy lies not in standing still, but in more complete civilisation.

---

[1] *double-distilled* Doubly concentrated.

[2] *whiles* Times.

[3] *nowhither* Nowhere.

[4] *victuals* Food.

Now whatever discussion there may be about that often used and often misused word, I believe all who hear me will agree with me in believing from their hearts, and not merely in saying in conventional phrase, that the civilisation which does not carry the whole people with it, is doomed to fall, and give place to one which at least aims at doing so.

We talk of the civilisation of the ancient peoples, of the classical times, well, civilised they were no doubt, some of their folk at least: an Athenian[1] citizen for instance led a simple, dignified, almost perfect life; but there were drawbacks to happiness perhaps in the lives of his slaves: and the civilisation of the ancients was founded on slavery.

Indeed that ancient society did give a model to the world,[2] and showed us for ever what blessings are freedom of life and thought, self-restraint and a generous education: all those blessings the ancient free peoples set forth to the world—and kept them to themselves.

Therefore no tyrant was too base, no pretext too hollow, for enslaving the grandsons of the men of Salamis and Thermopylae:[3] therefore did the descendants of those stern and self-restrained Romans, who were ready to give up everything, and life as the least of things, to the glory of their commonweal, produce monsters of license[4] and reckless folly. Therefore did a little knot of Galilean peasants[5] overthrow the Roman Empire.

Ancient civilisation was chained to slavery and exclusiveness, and it fell; the barbarism that took its place has delivered us from slavery and grown into modern civilisation; and that in its turn has before it the choice of never-ceasing growth, or destruction by that which has in it the seeds of higher growth.

There is an ugly word for a dreadful fact, which I must make bold to use—the residuum:[6] that word since the time I first saw it used, has had a terrible significance to me, and I have felt from my heart that if this residuum were a necessary part of modern civilisation, as some people openly, and many more tacitly, assume that it is, then this civilisation carries with it the poison that shall one day destroy it, even as its elder sister[7] did: if civilisation is to go no further than this, it had better not have gone so far: if it does not aim at getting rid of this misery and giving some share in the happiness and dignity of life to *all* the people that it has created, and which it spends such unwearying energy in creating, it is simply an organised injustice, a mere instrument for oppression, so much the worse than that which has gone before it, as its pretensions are higher, its slavery subtler, its mastery harder to overthrow, because supported by such a dense mass of commonplace well-being and comfort.

Surely this cannot be: surely there is a distinct feeling abroad of this injustice: so that if the residuum still clogs all the efforts of modern civilisation to rise above mere population-breeding and money-making, the difficulty of dealing with it is the legacy, first of the ages of violence and almost conscious brutal injustice, and next of the ages of thoughtlessness, of hurry and blindness; surely all those who think at all of the future of the world are at work in one way or other in striving to rid it of this shame.

That to my mind is the meaning of what we call National Education, which we have begun, and which is doubtless already bearing its fruits, and will bear greater, when all people are educated, not according to the money which they or their parents possess, but according to the capacity of their minds.

What effect that will have upon the future of the arts, I cannot say, but one would surely think a very great effect; for it will enable people to see clearly many things which are now as completely hidden from them as if they were blind in body and idiotic in mind: and this, I say, will act not only upon those who most directly feel the evils of ignorance, but also upon those who feel them indirectly—upon us, the educated: the great wave of rising intelligence, rife with so many natural desires and aspirations, will carry all classes along with it, and force us all to see that many things which

---

[1] *Athenian* Of Athens, the chief city-state of classical Greece.

[2] *model ... world* Democracy.

[3] *Salamis and Thermopylae* Sites of Greek battles.

[4] *commonweal* Common good; *license* Disregard for proper behavior.

[5] *Galilean peasants* Christians.

[6] *residuum* Residue.

[7] *elder sister* Roman Empire.

we have been used to look upon as necessary and eternal evils are merely the accidental and temporary growths of past stupidity, and can be escaped from by due effort, and the exercise of courage, goodwill, and forethought.

And among those evils, I do, and must always, believe will fall that one which last year I told you that I accounted the greatest of all evils, the heaviest of all slaveries; that evil of the greater part of the population being engaged for by far the most part of their lives in work, which at the best cannot interest them, or develop their best faculties, and at the worst (and that is the commonest, too) is mere unmitigated slavish toil, only to be wrung out of them by the sternest compulsion, a toil which they shirk all they can—small blame to them. And this toil degrades them into less than men: and they will some day come to know it, and cry out to be made men again, and art only can do it, and redeem them from this slavery; and I say once more that this is her highest and most glorious end and aim; and it is in her struggle to attain to it that she will most surely purify herself, and quicken her own aspirations towards perfection.

But we—in the meantime we must not sit waiting for obvious signs of these later and glorious days to show themselves on earth, and in the heavens, but rather turn to the commonplace, and maybe often dull work of fitting ourselves in detail to take part in them if we should live to see one of them; or in doing our best to make the path smooth for their coming, if we are to die before they are here.

What, therefore, can we do, to guard traditions of time past that we may not one day have to begin anew from the beginning with none to teach us? What are we to do, that we may take heed to, and spread the decencies of life, so that at the least we may have a field where it will be possible for art to grow when men begin to long for it: what finally can we do, each of us, to cherish some germ of art, so that it may meet with others, and spread and grow little by little into the thing that we need?

Now I cannot pretend to think that the first of these duties is a matter of indifference to you, after my experience of the enthusiastic meeting that I had the honour of addressing here last autumn on the subject of the (so called) restoration of St. Mark's[1] at Venice; you thought, and most justly thought, it seems to me, that the subject was of such moment to art in general, that it was a simple and obvious thing for men who were anxious on the matter to address themselves to those who had the decision of it in their hands; even though the former were called Englishmen, and the latter Italians; for you felt that the name of lovers of art would cover those differences: if you had any misgivings, you remembered that there was but one such building in the world, and that it was worth while risking a breach of etiquette, if any words of ours could do anything towards saving it; well, the Italians were, some of them, very naturally, though surely unreasonably, irritated, for a time, and in some of their prints they bade us look at home; that was no argument in favour of the wisdom of wantonly rebuilding St. Mark's facade: but certainly those of us who have not yet looked at home in this matter had better do so speedily, late and over late though it be: for though we have no golden-pictured interiors like St. Mark's Church at home, we still have many buildings which are both works of ancient art and monuments of history: and just think what is happening to them, and note, since we profess to recognise their value, how helpless art is in the Century of Commerce! In the first place, many and many a beautiful and ancient building is being destroyed all over civilised Europe as well as in England, because it is supposed to interfere with the convenience of the citizens, while a little forethought might save it without trenching on that convenience;[2] but even apart from that, I say that if we are not prepared to put up with a little inconve-

---

[1] *St. Mark's* Eleventh-century basilica; Venice's most famous church.

[2] [Morris's note] As I corrected these sheets for the press, the case of two such pieces of destruction is forced upon me: first, the remains of the Refectory of Westminster Abbey [dining room of the famous Gothic cathedral in London], with the adjacent Ashburnham House [residence located on the grounds of Westminster Abbey], a beautiful work, probably by Inigo Jones [noted British architect (1573–1652)]; and second, Magdalen Bridge at Oxford [eighteenth-century bridge spanning the River Cherwell just east of Oxford, widened in 1882]. Certainly this seems to mock my hope of the influence of education on the Beauty of Life; since the first scheme of destruction is eagerly pressed forward by the authorities of Westminster School, the second scarcely opposed by the resident members of the University of Oxford.

nience in our lifetimes for the sake of preserving a monument of art which will elevate and educate, not only ourselves, but our sons, and our sons' sons, it is vain and idle of us to talk about art—or education either. Brutality must be bred of such brutality.

The same thing may be said about enlarging, or otherwise altering for convenience's sake, old buildings still in use for something like their original purposes: in almost all such cases it is really nothing more than a question of a little money for a new site: and then a new building can be built exactly fitted for the uses it is needed for, with such art about it as our own days can furnish; while the old monument is left to tell its tale of change and progress, to hold out example and warning to us in the practice of the arts: and thus the convenience of the public, the progress of modern art, and the cause of education, are all furthered at once at the cost of a little money.

Surely if it be worth while troubling ourselves about the works of art of to-day, of which any amount almost can be done, since we are yet alive, it is worth while spending a little care, forethought, and money in preserving the art of bygone ages, of which (woe worth the while!) so little is left, and of which we can never have any more, whatever good-hap[1] the world may attain to.

No man who consents to the destruction or the mutilation of an ancient building has any right to pretend that he cares about art; or has any excuse to plead in defence of his crime against civilisation and progress, save sheer brutal ignorance.

But before I leave this subject I must say a word or two about the curious invention of our own days called Restoration, a method of dealing with works of bygone days which, though not so degrading in its spirit as downright destruction, is nevertheless little better in its results on the condition of those works of art; it is obvious that I have no time to argue the question out to-night, so I will only make these assertions:

That ancient buildings, being both works of art and monuments of history, must obviously be treated with great care and delicacy: that the imitative art of to-day is not, and cannot be the same thing as ancient art, and cannot replace it; and that therefore if we superimpose this work on the old, we destroy it both as art and as a record of history: lastly, that the natural weathering of the surface of a building is beautiful, and its loss disastrous.

Now the restorers hold the exact contrary of all this: they think that any clever architect to-day can deal off-hand successfully with the ancient work; that while all things else have changed about us since (say) the thirteenth century, art has not changed, and that our workmen can turn out work identical with that of the thirteenth century; and, lastly, that the weather-beaten surface of an ancient building is worthless, and to be got rid of wherever possible.

You see the question is difficult to argue, because there seem to be no common grounds between the restorers and the anti-restorers: I appeal therefore to the public, and bid them note, that though our opinions may be wrong, the action we advise is not rash: let the question be shelved awhile: if, as we are always pressing on people, due care be taken of these monuments, so that they shall not fall into disrepair, they will be always there to "restore" whenever people think proper and when we are proved wrong; but if it should turn out that we are right, how can the "restored" buildings be restored? I beg of you therefore to let the question be shelved, till art has so advanced among us, that we can deal authoritatively with it, till there is no longer any doubt about the matter.

Surely these monuments of our art and history, which, whatever the lawyers may say, belong not to a coterie, or to a rich man here and there, but to the nation at large, are worth this delay: surely the last relics of the life of the "famous men and our fathers that begat us"[2] may justly claim of us the exercise of a little patience.

It will give us trouble no doubt, all this care of our possessions: but there is more trouble to come; for I must now speak of something else, of possessions which should be common to all of us, of the green grass, and the leaves, and the waters, of the very light and air of heaven, which the Century of Commerce has been too busy to pay any heed to. And first let me remind you that I am supposing every one here present professes to care about art.

Well, there are some rich men among us whom we oddly enough call manufacturers, by which we mean

---

[1] *good-hap* Good fortune.

[2] *coterie* Exclusive group; *famous … us* Cf. Ecclesiasticus 44.1.

capitalists who pay other men to organise manufacturers; these gentlemen, many of whom buy pictures and profess to care about art, burn a deal of coal: there is an Act[1] in existence which was passed to prevent them sometimes and in some places from pouring a dense cloud of smoke over the world, and, to my thinking, a very lame and partial Act it is: but nothing hinders these lovers of art from being a law to themselves, and making it a point of honour with them to minimise the smoke nuisance as far as their own works are concerned; and if they don't do so, when mere money, and even a very little of that, is what it will cost them, I say that their love of art is a mere pretence: how can you care about the image of a landscape when you show by your deeds that you don't care for the landscape itself? or what right have you to shut yourself up with beautiful form and colour when you make it impossible for other people to have any share in these things?

Well, and as to the smoke Act itself: I don't know what heed you pay to it in Birmingham,[2] but I have seen myself what heed is paid to it in other places; Bradford[3] for instance: though close by them at Saltaire[4] they have an example which I should have thought might have shamed them; for the huge chimney there which serves the acres of weaving and spinning sheds of Sir Titus Salt[5] and his brothers is as guiltless of smoke as an ordinary kitchen chimney. Or Manchester:[6] a gentleman of that city told me that the smoke Act was a mere dead letter there: well, they buy pictures in Manchester and profess to wish to further the arts: but you see it must be idle pretence as far as their rich people are concerned: they only want to talk about it, and have themselves talked of.

I don't know what you are doing about this matter here; but you must forgive my saying, that unless you are beginning to think of some way of dealing with it, you are not beginning yet to pave your way to success in the arts.

Well, I have spoken of a huge nuisance, which is a type of the worst nuisances of what an ill-tempered man might be excused for calling the Century of Nuisances, rather than the Century of Commerce. I will now leave it to the consciences of the rich and influential among us, and speak of a minor nuisance which it is in the power of every one of us to abate, and which, small as it is, is so vexatious, that if I can prevail on a score of you to take heed to it by what I am saying, I shall think my evening's work a good one. Sandwich-papers[7] I mean—of course you laugh: but come now, don't you, civilised as you are in Birmingham, leave them all about the Lickey hills[8] and your public gardens and the like? If you don't I really scarcely know with what words to praise you. When we Londoners go to enjoy ourselves at Hampton Court,[9] for instance, we take special good care to let everybody know that we have had something to eat: so that the park just outside the gates (and a beautiful place it is) looks as if it had been snowing dirty paper. I really think you might promise me one and all who are here present to have done with this sluttish[10] habit, which is the type of many another in its way, just as the smoke nuisance is. I mean such things as scrawling one's name on monuments, tearing down tree boughs, and the like.

I suppose 'tis early days in the revival of the arts to express one's disgust at the daily increasing hideousness of the posters with which all our towns are daubed.[11] Still we ought to be disgusted at such horrors, and I think make up our minds never to buy any of the articles so advertised. I can't believe they can be worth much if they need all that shouting to sell them.

Again, I must ask what do you do with the trees on a site that is going to be built over? do you try to save them, to adapt your houses at all to them? do you

---

1. *Act* Law.

2. [Morris's note] Since perhaps some people may read these words who are not of Birmingham, I ought to say that it was authoritatively explained at the meeting to which I addressed these words, that in Birmingham the law is strictly enforced.

3. *Bradford* City in north-central England known for its textile production.

4. *Saltaire* Another northern industrial town.

5. *Sir Titus Salt* Owner of important textile company in Bradford, and founder of Saltaire (1803–1876).

6. *Manchester* Large industrial city in the north of England.

7. *Sandwich-papers* Wrappers.

8. *Lickey hills* Wooded hills near Birmingham.

9. *Hampton Court* English royal palace and its surrounding parks and grounds.

10. *sluttish* Dirty.

11. *daubed* Covered.

understand what treasures they are in a town or a suburb? or what a relief they will be to the hideous dog-holes which (forgive me!) you are probably going to build in their places? I ask this anxiously, and with grief in my soul, for in London and its suburbs we always[1] begin by clearing a site till it is as bare as the pavement: I really think that almost anybody would have been shocked, if I could have shown him some of the trees that have been wantonly murdered in the suburb in which I live (Hammersmith[2] to wit), amongst them some of those magnificent cedars, for which we along the river used to be famous once.

But here again see how helpless those are who care about art or nature amidst the hurry of the Century of Commerce.

Pray do not forget, that any one who cuts down a tree wantonly or carelessly, especially in a great town or its suburbs, need make no pretence of caring about art. What else can we do to help to educate ourselves and others in the path of art, to be on the road to attaining an *Art made by the people and for the people as a joy to the maker and the user?*

Why, having got to understand something of what art was, having got to look upon its ancient monuments as friends that can tell us something of times bygone, and whose faces we do not wish to alter, even though they be worn by time and grief: having got to spend money and trouble upon matters of decency, great and little; having made it clear that we really do care about nature even in the suburbs of a big town—having got so far, we shall begin to think of the houses in which we live.

For I must tell you that unless you are resolved to have good and rational architecture, it is, once again, useless your thinking about art at all.

I have spoken of the popular arts, but they might all be summed up in that one word Architecture; they are all parts of that great whole, and the art of house-building begins it all: if we did not know how to dye or to weave; if we had neither gold, nor silver, nor silk; and no pigments to paint with, but half-a-dozen ochres and

umbers, we might yet frame a worthy art that would lead to everything, if we had but timber, stone, and lime,[3] and a few cutting tools to make these common things not only shelter us from wind and weather, but also express the thoughts and aspirations that stir in us. Architecture would lead us to all the arts, as it did with earlier men: but if we despise it and take no note of how we are housed, the other arts will have a hard time of it indeed.

Now I do not think the greatest of optimists would deny that, taking us one and all, we are at present housed in a perfectly shameful way, and since the greatest part of us have to live in houses already built for us, it must be admitted that it is rather hard to know what to do, beyond waiting till they tumble about our ears.

Only we must not lay the fault upon the builders, as some people seem inclined to do: they are our very humble servants, and will build what we ask for; remember, that rich men are not obliged to live in ugly houses, and yet you see they do; which the builders may be well excused for taking as a sign of what is wanted.

Well, the point is, we must do what we can, and make people understand what we want them to do for us, by letting them see what we do for ourselves.

Hitherto, judging us by that standard, the builders may well say, that we want the pretence of a thing rather than the thing itself; that we want a show of petty luxury if we are unrich, a show of insulting stupidity if we are rich: and they are quite clear that as a rule we want to get something that shall look as if it cost twice as much as it really did.

You cannot have Architecture on those terms: simplicity and solidity are the very first requisites of it: just think if it is not so: How we please ourselves with an old building by thinking of all the generations of men that have passed through it! do we not remember how it has received their joy, and borne their sorrow, and not even their folly has left sourness upon it? it still looks as kind to us as it did to them. And the converse of this we ought to feel when we look at a newly-built house if it were as it should be: we should feel a pleasure in thinking how he who had built it had left a piece of

---

[1] [Morris's note] Not *quite* always: in the little colony at Bedford Park, Chiswick [suburb of London], as many trees have been left as possible, to the boundless advantage of its quaint and pretty architecture.

[2] *Hammersmith* At the time a suburb of London.

[3] *ochers* Shades of orange-yellow; *umbers* Shades of brown; *lime* Limestone, used as mortar in construction.

his soul behind him to greet the new-comers one after another long and long after he was gone— but what sentiment can an ordinary modern house move in us, or what thought—save a hope that we may speedily forget its base ugliness?

But if you ask me how we are to pay for this solidity and extra expense, that seems to me a reasonable question; for you must dismiss at once as a delusion the hope that has been sometimes cherished, that you can have a building which is a work of art, and is therefore above all things properly built, at the same price as a building which only pretends to be this: never forget when people talk about cheap art in general, by the way, that all art costs time, trouble, and thought, and that money is only a counter to represent these things.

However, I must try to answer the question I have supposed put, how are we to pay for decent houses?

It seems to me that, by a great piece of good luck, the way to pay for them is by doing that which alone can produce popular art among us: living a simple life, I mean. Once more I say that the greatest foe to art is luxury, art cannot live in its atmosphere.

When you hear of the luxuries of the ancients, you must remember that they were not like our luxuries, they were rather indulgence in pieces of extravagant folly than what we to-day call luxury; which perhaps you would rather call comfort: well I accept the word, and say that a Greek or Roman of the luxurious time would stare astonished could he be brought back again, and shown the comforts of a well-to-do middle-class house.

But some, I know, think that the attainment of these very comforts is what makes the difference between civilisation and uncivilisation, that they are the essence of civilisation. Is it so indeed? Farewell my hope then!—I had thought that civilisation meant the attainment of peace and order and freedom, of goodwill between man and man, of the love of truth and the hatred of injustice, and by consequence the attainment of the good life which these things breed, a life free from craven fear, but full of incident: that was what I thought it meant, not more stuffed chairs and more cushions, and more carpets and gas, and more dainty meat and drink—and therewithal[1] more and sharper differences between class and class.

If that be what it is, I for my part wish I were well out of it, and living in a tent in the Persian desert, or a turf hut on the Iceland hill-side. But however it be, and I think my view is the true view, I tell you that art abhors that side of civilisation, she cannot breathe in the houses that lie under its stuffy slavery.

Believe me, if we want art to begin at home, as it must, we must clear our houses of troublesome superfluities that are for ever in our way: conventional comforts that are no real comforts, and do but make work for servants and doctors: if you want a golden rule that will fit everybody, this is it:

"*Have nothing in your houses that you do not know to be useful or believe to be beautiful.*"

And if we apply that rule strictly, we shall in the first place show the builders and such-like servants of the public what we really want, we shall create a demand for real art, as the phrase goes; and in the second place, we shall surely have more money to pay for decent houses.

Perhaps it will not try your patience too much if I lay before you my idea of the fittings necessary to the sitting-room of a healthy person: a room, I mean, in which he would not have to cook in much, or sleep in generally, or in which he would not have to do any very litter-making manual work.

First a book-case with a great many books in it: next a table that will keep steady when you write or work at it: then several chairs that you can move, and a bench that you can sit or lie upon: next a cupboard with drawers: next, unless either the book-case or the cupboard be very beautiful with painting or carving, you will want pictures or engravings, such as you can afford, only not stop-gaps, but real works of art on the wall; or else the wall itself must be ornamented with some beautiful and restful pattern: we shall also want a vase or two to put flowers in, which latter you must have sometimes, especially if you live in a town. Then there will be the fireplace of course, which in our climate is bound to be the chief object in the room.

That is all we shall want, especially if the floor be good; if it be not, as, by the way, in a modern house it is pretty certain not to be, I admit that a small carpet which can be bundled out of the room in two minutes will be useful, and we must also take care that it is beautiful, or it will annoy us terribly.

---

[1] *dainty* Refined; *therewithal* Along with that.

Now unless we are musical, and need a piano (in which case, as far as beauty is concerned, we are in a bad way), that is quite all we want: and we can add very little to these necessaries without troubling ourselves, and hindering our work, our thought, and our rest.

If these things were done at the least cost for which they could be done well and solidly, they ought not to cost much; and they are so few, that those that could afford to have them at all, could afford to spend some trouble to get them fitting and beautiful: and all those who care about art ought to take great trouble to do so, and to take care that there be no sham art amongst them, nothing that it has degraded a man to make or sell. And I feel sure, that if all who care about art were to take this pains, it would make a great impression upon the public.

This simplicity you may make as costly as you please or can, on the other hand: you may hang your walls with tapestry instead of whitewash or paper; or you may cover them with mosaic, or have them frescoed[1] by a great painter: all this is not luxury, if it be done for beauty's sake, and not for show: it does not break our golden rule: *Have nothing in your houses which you do not know to be useful or believe to be beautiful.*

All art starts from this simplicity; and the higher the art rises, the greater the simplicity. I have been speaking of the fittings of a dwelling-house—a place in which we eat and drink, and pass familiar hours; but when you come to places which people want to make more specially beautiful because of the solemnity or dignity of their uses, they will be simpler still, and have little in them save the bare walls made as beautiful as may be. St. Mark's at Venice has very little furniture in it, much less than most Roman Catholic churches: its lovely and stately mother St. Sophia of Constantinople[2] had less still, even when it was a Christian church: but we need not go either to Venice or Stamboul[3] to take note of

that: go into one of our own mighty Gothic naves (do any of you remember the first time you did so?) and note how the huge free space satisfies and elevates you, even now when window and wall are stripped of ornament: then think of the meaning of simplicity, and absence of encumbering gew-gaws.[4]

Now after all, for us who are learning art, it is not far to seek what is the surest way to further it; that which most breeds art is art; every piece of work that we do which is well done, is so much help to the cause; every piece of pretence and half-heartedness is so much hurt to it. Most of you who take to the practice of art can find out in no very long time whether you have any gifts for it or not: if you have not, throw the thing up,[5] or you will have a wretched time of it yourselves, and will be damaging the cause by laborious pretence: but if you have gifts of any kind, you are happy[6] indeed beyond most men; for your pleasure is always with you, nor can you be intemperate in the enjoyment of it, and as you use it, it does not lessen, but grows: if you are by chance weary of it at night, you get up in the morning eager for it; or if perhaps in the morning it seems folly to you for a while, yet presently, when your hand has been moving a little in its wonted[7] way, fresh hope has sprung up beneath it and you are happy again. While others are getting through the day like plants thrust into the earth, which cannot turn this way or that but as the wind blows them, you know what you want, and your will is on the alert to find it, and you, whatever happens, whether it be joy or grief, are at least alive.

Now when I spoke to you last year, after I had sat down I was half afraid that I had on some points said too much, that I had spoken too bitterly in my eagerness; that a rash word might have discouraged some of you; I was very far from meaning that: what I wanted to do, what I want to do to-night is to put definitely before you a cause for which to strive.

That cause is the Democracy of Art, the ennobling of daily and common work, which will one day put hope and pleasure in the place of fear and pain, as the

---

[1] *tapestry* Hangings of rich weave; *whitewash* White paint; *paper* Wallpaper; *frescoed* Covered by paintings that are executed on wet plaster.

[2] *St. Sophia … Constantinople* Famous sixth-century CE basilica commonly regarded as one of the world's most important and impressive buildings.

[3] *Stamboul* Capital of Byzantine Empire, renamed Constantinople by Constantine I in the fourth century CE.

[4] *gew-gaws* Decorative baubles.

[5] *throw … up* Give it up.

[6] *happy* Fortunate.

[7] *wonted* Accustomed.

forces which move men to labour and keep the world a-going.

If I have enlisted any one in that cause, rash as my words may have been, or feeble as they may have been, they have done more good than harm; nor do I believe that any words of mine can discourage any who have joined that cause or are ready to do so: their way is too clear before them for that, and every one of us can help the cause whether he be great or little.

I know indeed that men, wearied by the pettiness of the details of the strife, their patience tried by hope deferred, will at whiles, excusably enough, turn back in their hearts to other days, when if the issues were not clearer, the means of trying them were simpler; when, so stirring were the times, one might even have atoned for many a blunder and backsliding by visibly dying for the cause. To have breasted the Spanish pikes at Leyden, to have drawn sword with Oliver:[1] that may well seem to us at times amidst the tangles of today a happy fate: for a man to be able to say, I have lived like a fool, but now I will cast away fooling for an hour, and die like a man—there is something in that certainly: and yet 'tis clear that few men can be so lucky as to die for a cause, without having first of all lived for it. And as this is the most that can be asked from the greatest man that follows a cause, so it is the least that can be taken from the smallest.

So to us who have a Cause at heart, our highest ambition and our simplest duty are one and the same thing: for the most part we shall be too busy doing the work that lies ready to our hands, to let impatience for visibly great progress vex us much; but surely since we are servants of a Cause, hope must be ever with us, and sometimes perhaps it will so quicken[2] our vision that it will outrun the slow lapse of time, and show us the victorious days when millions of those who now sit in darkness will be enlightened by an *Art made by the people and for the people, a joy to the maker and the user*.
—1882

---

[1] *pikes* Spears; *Oliver* Oliver Cromwell (1599–1658), British military commander and revolutionary leader of the Commonwealth (1649–53).

[2] *quicken* Enliven.

from *News from Nowhere*

CHAPTER 1
DISCUSSION AND BED

Up at the League, says a friend, there had been one night a brisk conversational discussion, as to what would happen on the Morrow of the Revolution,[3] finally shading off into a vigorous statement by various friends of their views on the future of the fully-developed new society.

Says our friend: Considering the subject, the discussion was good-tempered; for those present being used to public meetings and after-lecture debates, if they did not listen to each other's opinions (which could scarcely be expected of them), at all events did not always attempt to speak all together, as is the custom of people in ordinary polite society when conversing on a subject which interests them. For the rest, there were six persons present, and consequently six sections of the party were represented, four of which had strong but divergent Anarchist[4] opinions. One of the sections, says our friend, a man whom he knows very well indeed, sat almost silent at the beginning of the discussion, but at last got drawn into it, and finished by roaring out very loud, and damning all the rest for fools; after which befell a period of noise, and then a lull, during which the aforesaid section, having said good-night very amicably, took his way home by himself to a western suburb,[5] using the means of travelling which civilization has forced upon us like a habit. As he sat in that vapour-bath of hurried and discontented humanity, a carriage of the underground railway, he, like others, stewed discontentedly, while in self-reproachful mood he turned over the many excellent and conclusive arguments which, though they lay at his fingers' ends,[6] he had forgotten in the just past discussion. But this frame of mind he was so used to, that it didn't last him long,

---

[3] *League* Socialist League, socialist political party founded in 1885; *Morrow of the Revolution* Day following a socialist revolution.

[4] *Anarchist* Characteristic of anarchism, the political doctrine that all forms of government should be abolished.

[5] *western suburb* Hammersmith, at the time a suburb of London.

[6] *at … ends* At the tips of his fingers, i.e., easily within reach of his memory and therefore easily employed.

and after a brief discomfort, caused by disgust with himself for having lost his temper (which he was also well used to), he found himself musing on the subject-matter of discussion, but still discontentedly and unhappily. "If I could but see a day of it," he said to himself; "if I could but see it!"

As he formed the words, the train stopped at his station, five minutes' walk from his own house, which stood on the banks of the Thames,[1] a little way above an ugly suspension bridge. He went out of the station, still discontented and unhappy, muttering "If I could but see it! If I could but see it!" but had not gone many steps towards the river before (says our friend who tells the story) all that discontent and trouble seemed to slip off him.

It was a beautiful night of early winter, the air just sharp enough to be refreshing after the hot room and the stinking railway carriage. The wind, which had lately turned a point or two north of west, had blown the sky clear of all cloud save a light fleck or two which went swiftly down the heavens. There was a young moon halfway up the sky, and as the home-farer caught sight of it, tangled in the branches of a tall old elm, he could scarce bring to his mind the shabby London suburb where he was, and he felt as if he were in a pleasant country place—pleasanter, indeed, than the deep country was as he had known it.

He came right down to the river-side, and lingered a little, looking over the low wall to note the moonlit river, near upon high water, go swirling and glittering up to Chiswick Eyot:[2] as for the ugly bridge below, he did not notice it or think of it, except when for a moment (says our friend) it struck him that he missed the row of lights down stream. Then he turned to his house door and let himself in; and even as he shut the door to,[3] disappeared all remembrance of that brilliant logic and foresight which had so illuminated the recent discussion; and of the discussion itself there remained no trace, save a vague hope, that was now become a pleasure, for days of peace and rest, and cleanness and smiling goodwill.

---

[1] *Thames* River in southern England, and its chief commercial waterway.

[2] *Chiswick Eyot* Island in the Thames, near Hammersmith.

[3] *shut … to* Closed the door completely.

In this mood he tumbled into bed, and fell asleep after his wont,[4] in two minutes' time; but (contrary to his wont) woke up again not long after in that curiously wide-awake condition which sometimes surprises even good sleepers; a condition under which we feel all our wits preternaturally sharpened, while all the miserable muddles we have ever got into, all the disgraces and losses of our lives, will insist on thrusting themselves forward for the consideration of those sharpened wits.

In this state he lay (says our friend) till he had almost begun to enjoy it: till the tale of his stupidities amused him, and the entanglements before him, which he saw so clearly, began to shape themselves into an amusing story for him.

He heard one o'clock strike, then two and then three; after which he fell asleep again. Our friend says that from that sleep he awoke once more, and afterwards went through such surprising adventures that he thinks that they should be told to our comrades, and indeed the public in general, and therefore proposes to tell them now. But, says he, I think it would be better if I told them in the first person, as if it were myself who had gone through them; which, indeed, will be the easier and more natural to me, since I understand the feelings and desires of the comrade of whom I am telling better than any one else in the world does.

CHAPTER 2
A MORNING BATH

Well, I awoke, and found that I had kicked my bed-clothes off; and no wonder, for it was hot and the sun shining brightly. I jumped up and washed and hurried on my clothes, but in a hazy and half-awake condition, as if I had slept for a long, long while, and could not shake off the weight of slumber. In fact, I rather took it for granted that I was at home in my own room than saw that it was so.

When I was dressed, I felt the place so hot that I made haste to get out of the room and out of the house; and my first feeling was a delicious relief caused by the fresh air and pleasant breeze; my second, as I began to gather my wits together, mere measureless wonder: for it was winter when I went to bed the last night, and

---

[4] *wont* Customary practice.

now, by witness of the river-side trees, it was summer, a beautiful bright morning seemingly of early June. However, there was still the Thames sparkling under the sun, and near high water, as last night I had seen it gleaming under the moon.

I had by no means shaken off the feeling of oppression, and wherever I might have been should scarce have been quite conscious of the place; so it was no wonder that I felt rather puzzled in despite of[1] the familiar face of the Thames. Withal[2] I felt dizzy and queer; and remembering that people often got a boat and had a swim in mid-stream, I thought I would do no less. It seems very early, quoth I to myself, but I daresay I shall find someone at Biffin's to take me. However, I didn't get as far as Biffin's, or even turn to my left thitherward,[3] because just then I began to see that there was a landing-stage[3] right before me in front of my house: in fact, on the place where my next-door neighbour had rigged one up, though somehow it didn't look like that either. Down I went on to it, and sure enough among the empty boats moored to it lay a man on his sculls in a solid-looking tub of a boat clearly meant for bathers.[4] He nodded to me, and bade me good-morning as if he expected me, so I jumped in without any words, and he paddled away quietly as I peeled[5] for my swim. As we went, I looked down on the water, and couldn't help saying—

"How clear the water is this morning!"

"Is it?" said he; "I didn't notice it. You know the flood-tide[6] always thickens it a bit."

"H'm," said I, "I have seen it pretty muddy even at half-ebb."[7]

He said nothing in answer, but seemed rather astonished; and as he now lay just stemming the tide, and I had my clothes off, I jumped in without more ado.[8] Of course when I had my head above water again I turned towards the tide, and my eyes naturally sought for the bridge, and so utterly astonished was I by what I saw, that I forgot to strike out, and went spluttering under water again, and when I came up made straight for the boat; for I felt that I must ask some questions of my waterman, so bewildering had been the half-sight I had seen from the face of the river with the water hardly out of my eyes; though by this time I was quit[9] of the slumbrous and dizzy feeling, and was wide-awake and clear-headed.

As I got in up the steps which he had lowered, and he held out his hand to help me, we went drifting speedily up towards Chiswick;[10] but now he caught up the sculls and brought her head round again, and said—

"A short swim, neighbour; but perhaps you find the water cold this morning, after your journey. Shall I put you ashore at once, or would you like to go down to Putney[11] before breakfast?"

He spoke in a way so unlike what I should have expected from a Hammersmith waterman, that I stared at him, as I answered, "Please to hold her a little; I want to look about me a bit."

"All right," he said; "it's no less pretty in its way here than it is off Barn Elms;[12] it's jolly everywhere this time in the morning. I'm glad you got up early; it's barely five o'clock yet."

If I was astonished with my sight of the river banks, I was no less astonished at my waterman, now that I had time to look at him and see him with my head and eyes clear.

He was a handsome young fellow, with a peculiarly pleasant and friendly look about his eyes,—an expression which was quite new to me then, though I soon became familiar with it. For the rest, he was dark-haired and berry-brown of skin, well-knit and strong, and obviously used to exercising his muscles, but with

[1] *in despite of* In spite of.

[2] *Withal* Moreover.

[3] *thitherward* In that direction (i.e. toward Biffin's); *landing-stage* Landing platform for passengers and goods from water crafts.

[4] *sculls* Oars; *bathers* Swimmers, water–bathers.

[5] *peeled* Stripped.

[6] *flood-tide* Incoming tide.

[7] *half-ebb* Period when return tide is half completed.

[8] *stemming* Making progress against; *ado* Ceremony.

[9] *quit* Rid.

[10] *Chiswick* Suburb, but now a borough, of London.

[11] *Putney* At the time a suburb of London, on the south bank of the Thames.

[12] *Barn Elms* Town near Putney named for a sixteenth-century manor house.

nothing rough or coarse[1] about him, and clean as might be. His dress was not like any modern work-a-day[2] clothes I had seen, but would have served very well as a costume for a picture of fourteenth-century life: it was of dark blue cloth, simple enough, but of fine web,[3] and without a stain on it. He had a brown leather belt round his waist, and I noticed that its clasp was of damascened[4] steel beautifully wrought. In short, he seemed to be like some specially manly and refined young gentleman, playing waterman for a spree,[5] and I concluded that this was the case.

I felt that I must make some conversation; so I pointed to the Surrey bank, where I noticed some light plank stages[6] running down the foreshore, with windlasses at the landward end of them, and said, "What are they doing with those things here? If we were on the Tay,[7] I should have said that they were for drawing the salmon nets; but here—"

"Well," said he, smiling, "of course that is what they *are* for. Where there are salmon, there are likely to be salmon-nets, Tay or Thames; but of course they are not always in use; we don't want salmon *every* day of the season."

I was going to say, "But is this the Thames?" but held my peace in my wonder, and turned my bewildered eyes eastward to look at the bridge again, and thence to the shores of the London river; and surely there was enough to astonish me. For though there was a bridge across the stream and houses on its banks, how all was changed from last night! The soap-works with their smoke-vomiting chimneys were gone; the engineer's works gone; the lead-works gone; and no sound of rivetting and hammering came down the west wind

---

[1] *coarse* Common, lacking refinement.

[2] *work-a-day* Everyday.

[3] *web* Fabric.

[4] *damascened* Ornamented with designs in silver or gold.

[5] *spree* Bout of carefree activity.

[6] *Surrey* County in southeastern England on the Thames; *plank stages* Wooden platforms for fishing.

[7] *Tay* Scottish river notable for its salmon. Through the nineteenth and much of the twentieth centuries the Thames was far too polluted to support higher forms of marine life.

from Thorneycroft's.[8] Then the bridge! I had perhaps dreamed of such a bridge, but never seen such an one out of an illuminated manuscript; for not even the Ponte Vecchio[9] at Florence came anywhere near it. It was of stone arches, splendidly solid, and as graceful as they were strong; high enough also to let ordinary river traffic through easily. Over the parapet showed quaint and fanciful little buildings, which I supposed to be booths or shops, beset with painted and gilded vanes and spirelets. The stone was a little weathered, but showed no marks of the grimy sootiness which I was used to on every London building more than a year old. In short, to me a wonder of a bridge.

The sculler noted my eager astonished look, and said, as if in answer to my thoughts—

"Yes, it *is* a pretty bridge, isn't it? Even the up-stream bridges, which are so much smaller, are scarcely daintier, and the down-stream ones are scarcely more dignified and stately."

I found myself saying, almost against my will, "How old is it?"

"Oh, not very old," he said; "it was built or at least opened, in 2003. There used to be a rather plain timber bridge before then."

The date shut my mouth as if a key had been turned in a padlock fixed to my lips; for I saw that something inexplicable had happened, and that if I said much, I should be mixed up in a game of cross questions and crooked answers. So I tried to look unconcerned, and to glance in a matter-of-course way at the banks of the river, though this is what I saw up to the bridge and a little beyond; say as far as the site of the soap-works. Both shores had a line of very pretty houses, low and not large, standing back a little way from the river; they were mostly built of red brick and roofed with tiles, and looked, above all, comfortable, and as if they were, so to say, alive, and sympathetic with the life of the dwellers in them. There was a continuous garden in front of them, going down to the water's edge, in which the flowers were now blooming luxuriantly, and sending delicious waves of summer scent over the eddying stream. Behind the houses, I could see great trees rising,

---

[8] *Thorneycroft's* Factory on the Thames that produced marine equipment.

[9] *Ponte Vecchio* Famous Italian bridge.

mostly planes, and looking down the water there were the reaches[1] towards Putney almost as if they were a lake with a forest shore, so thick were the big trees; and I said aloud, but as if to myself—

"Well, I'm glad that they have not built over Barn Elms."

I blushed for my fatuity as the words slipped out of my mouth, and my companion looked at me with a half smile which I thought I understood; so to hide my confusion I said, "Please take me ashore now: I want to get my breakfast."

He nodded, and brought her head round with a sharp stroke, and in a trice we were at the landing-stage again. He jumped out and I followed him; and of course I was not surprised to see him wait, as if for the inevitable after-piece[2] that follows the doing of a service to a fellow-citizen. So I put my hand into my waistcoat-pocket, and said, "How much?" though still with the uncomfortable feeling that perhaps I was offering money to a gentleman.

He looked puzzled, and said, "How much? I don't quite understand what you are asking about. Do you mean the tide? If so, it is close on the turn now."

I blushed, and said, stammering, "Please don't take it amiss if I ask you; I mean no offence: but what ought I to pay you? You see I am a stranger, and don't know your customs—or your coins."

And therewith I took a handful of money out of my pocket, as one does in a foreign country. And by the way, I saw that the silver had oxydised, and was like a blackleaded stove in colour.

He still seemed puzzled, but not at all offended; and he looked at the coins with some curiosity. I thought, Well after all, he *is* a waterman, and is considering what he may venture to take. He seems such a nice fellow that I'm sure I don't grudge him a little over-payment. I wonder, by the way, whether I couldn't hire him as a guide for a day or two, since he is so intelligent.

Therewith my new friend said thoughtfully:

"I think I know what you mean. You think that I have done you a service; so you feel yourself bound to give me something which I am not to give to a neighbour, unless he has done something special for me. I have heard of this kind of thing; but pardon me for saying, that it seems to us a troublesome and round-about custom; and we don't know how to manage it. And you see this ferrying and giving people casts about the water is my *business*, which I would do for anybody; so to take gifts in connection with it would look very queer. Besides, if one person gave me something, then another might, and another, and so on; and I hope you won't think me rude if I say that I shouldn't know where to stow away so many mementos of friendship."

And he laughed loud and merrily, as if the idea of being paid for his work was a very funny joke. I confess I began to be afraid that the man was mad, though he looked sane enough; and I was rather glad to think that I was a good swimmer, since we were so close to a deep swift stream. However, he went on by no means like a madman:

"As to your coins, they are curious, but not very old; they seem to be all of the reign of Victoria;[3] you might give them to some scantily-furnished museum. Ours has enough of such coins, besides a fair number of earlier ones, many of which are beautiful, whereas these nineteenth century ones are so beastly ugly, ain't they? We have a piece[4] of Edward III,[5] with the king in a ship, and little leopards and fleurs-de-lys[6] all along the gunwale,[7] so delicately worked. You see," he said, with something of a smirk, "I am fond of working in gold and fine metals; this buckle here is an early piece of mine."

No doubt I looked a little shy of him under the influence of that doubt as to his sanity. So he broke off short, and said in a kind voice:

"But I see that I am boring you, and I ask your pardon. For, not to mince matters, I can tell that you *are* a stranger, and must come from a place very unlike England. But also it is clear that it won't do to overdose you with information about this place, and that you had

---

[1] *planes* Species of tree; *reaches* Stretches of river lying between two bends.

[2] *after-piece* Smaller item following the main attraction in an entertainment.

[3] *Victoria* Queen Victoria I (1837–1901).

[4] *piece* Coin.

[5] *Edward III* British king (1327–77).

[6] *fleurs-de-lys* Lilies; heraldic symbol used by French royalty.

[7] *gunwale* Upper edge of a ship's side.

best suck it in little by little. Further, I should take it as very kind in you if you would allow me to be the showman of our new world to you, since you have stumbled on me first. Though indeed it will be a mere kindness on your part, for almost anybody would make as good a guide, and many much better."

There certainly seemed no flavour in him of Colney Hatch;[1] and besides I thought I could easily shake him off if it turned out that he really was mad; so I said:

"It is a very kind offer, but it is difficult for me to accept it, unless—" I was going to say, Unless you will let me pay you properly; but fearing to stir up Colney Hatch again, I changed the sentence into, "I fear I shall be taking you away from your work—or your amusement."

"O," he said, "don't trouble about that, because it will give me an opportunity of doing a good turn to a friend of mine, who wants to take my work here. He is a weaver from Yorkshire,[2] who has rather overdone himself between his weaving and his mathematics, both indoor work, you see; and being a great friend of mine, he naturally came to me to get him some outdoor work. If you think you can put up with me, pray take me as your guide."

He added presently: "It is true that I have promised to go up-stream to some special friends of mine, for the hay-harvest; but they won't be ready for us for more than a week: and besides, you might go with me, you know, and see some very nice people, besides making notes of our ways in Oxfordshire.[3] You could hardly do better if you want to see the country."

I felt myself obliged to thank him, whatever might come of it; and he added eagerly:

"Well, then, that's settled. I will give my friend a call; he is living in the Guest House like you, and if he isn't up yet, he ought to be this fine summer morning."

Therewith he took a little silver bugle-horn from his girdle[4] and blew two or three sharp but agreeable notes on it; and presently from the house which stood on the

site of my old dwelling (of which more hereafter) another young man came sauntering towards us. He was not so well-looking or so strongly made as my sculler friend, being sandy-haired, rather pale, and not stout-built; but his face was not wanting[5] in that happy and friendly expression which I had noticed in his friend. As he came up smiling towards us, I saw with pleasure that I must give up the Colney Hatch theory as to the waterman, for no two madmen ever behaved as they did before a sane man. His dress also was of the same cut as the first man's, though somewhat gayer, the surcoat being light green with a golden spray embroidered on the breast, and his belt being of filigree silver-work.

He gave me good-day very civilly, and greeting his friend joyously, said:

"Well, Dick, what is it this morning? Am I to have my work, or rather your work? I dreamed last night that we were off up the river fishing."

"All right, Bob," said my sculler; "you will drop into my place, and if you find it too much, there is George Brightling on the look out for a stroke of work, and he lives close handy to you. But see, here is a stranger who is willing to amuse me to-day by taking me as his guide about our country-side, and you may imagine I don't want to lose the opportunity; so you had better take to the boat at once. But in any case I shouldn't have kept you out of it for long, since I am due in the hayfields in a few days."

The newcomer rubbed his hands with glee, but turning to me, said in a friendly voice:

"Neighbour, both you and friend Dick are lucky, and will have a good time to-day, as indeed I shall too. But you had better come in with me at once and get something to eat, lest you should forget your dinner in your amusement. I suppose you came into the Guest House after I had gone to bed last night?"

I nodded, not caring to enter into a long explanation which would have led to nothing, and which in truth by this time I should have begun to doubt myself. And we all three turned toward the door of the Guest House.

—1889

[1] *Colney Hatch* London hospital for the insane, established in 1851.

[2] *Yorkshire* Region in northern England.

[3] *Oxfordshire* Country in southeast England.

[4] *girdle* Belt.

[5] *wanting* Lacking.

How I Became A Socialist

I am asked by the Editor to give some sort of a history of the above conversion, and I feel that it may be of some use to do so, if my readers will look upon me as a type of a certain group of people, but not so easy to do clearly, briefly, and truly. Let me, however, try. But first, I will say what I mean by being a Socialist, since I am told that the word no longer expresses definitely and with certainty what it did ten years ago. Well, what I mean by Socialism is a condition of society in which there should be neither rich nor poor, neither master nor master's man, neither idle nor overworked, neither brain-sick brain workers, nor heart-sick hand workers, in a word, in which all men would be living in equality of condition, and would manage their affairs unwastefully, and with the full consciousness that harm to one would mean harm to all—the realization at last of the meaning of the word COMMONWEALTH.

Now this view of Socialism which I hold today, and hope to die holding, is what I began with; I had no transitional period, unless you may call such a brief period of political radicalism during which I saw my ideal clear enough, but had no hope of any realization of it. That came to an end some months before I joined the (then) Democratic Federation,[1] and the meaning of my joining that body was that I had conceived a hope of the realization of my ideal. If you ask me how much of a hope, or what I thought we Socialists then living and working would accomplish towards it, or when there would be effected any change in the face of society, I must say, I do not know. I can only say that I did not measure my hope, nor the joy that it brought me at the time. For the rest, when I took that step I was blankly ignorant of economics; I had never so much as opened Adam Smith, or heard of Ricardo, or of Karl Marx.[2] Oddly enough, I *had* read some of Mill, to wit, those

posthumous papers of his (published, was it, in the *Westminster Review* or the *Fortnightly*?) in which he attacks Socialism in its Fourierist[3] guise. In those papers he put the arguments, as far as they go, clearly and honestly, and the result, so far as I was concerned, was to convince me that Socialism was a necessary change, and that it was possible to bring it about in our own days. Those papers put the finishing touch to my conversion to Socialism. Well, having joined a Socialist body (for the Federation soon became definitely Socialist), I put some conscience into trying to learn the economical side of Socialism, and even tackled Marx, though I must confess that, whereas I thoroughly enjoyed the historical part of *Capital*,[4] I suffered agonies of confusion of the brain over reading the pure economics of that great work. Anyhow, I read what I could, and will hope that some information stuck to me from my reading; but more, I must think, from continuous conversation with such friends as Bax and Hyndman and Scheu,[5] and the brisk course of propaganda meetings which were going on at the time, and in which I took my share. Such finish to what of education in practical Socialism as I am capable of I received afterwards from some of my Anarchist friends, from whom I learned, quite against their intention, that Anarchism was impossible, much as I learned from Mill against *his* intention that Socialism was necessary.

But in this telling how I fell into *practical* Socialism I have begun, as I perceive, in the middle, for in my position of a well-to-do man, not suffering from the

---

[1] *Democratic Federation* The Social Democratic Federation, Britain's first official socialist political party, was founded in 1881.

[2] *Adam Smith* Scottish political economist (1723–90) credited with outlining the foundation of free-market economic theory in his *Wealth of Nations* (1776); *Ricardo* David Ricardo (1772–1823), British free-market economist; *Karl Marx* German economist, philosopher and social revolutionary (1818–33) whose *Das Kapital* (1867) and *The Communist Manifesto* (1848) heavily influenced modern conceptions of socialism.

[3] *Mill* John Stuart Mill (1806–73), highly influential British philosopher and political economist who advocated utilitarianism, a theory holding that the highest ethical goal is to promote the greatest good for the greatest number of people; *Westminster Review* Periodical established in 1824 showcasing the work of progressive intellectuals; *Fortnightly* Periodicals established in 1824 and 1865 respectively, both associated with liberalism; *Fourierist* Characteristic of the social reforms advocated by Charles Fourier (1772–1837), who proposed that society be organized into small, self-sufficient groups of no more than 1,500 people, who would be interdependent in terms of labor, wealth and housing.

[4] *Capital* Marx's *Das Kapital* (1867).

[5] *Bax* Ernest Belfort Bax (1854–1926), British socialist philosopher; *Hyndman* H.H. Hyndman (1842–1921), founder of the Social Democratic Federation; *Scheu* Andreas Scheu (1844–1927), pioneer in the social democratic movement in Austria and co-founder of the Social Democratic Federation.

disabilities which oppress a working man at every step, I feel that I might never have been drawn into the practical side of the question if an ideal had not forced me to seek towards it. For politics as politics, i.e., not regarded as a necessary if cumbersome and disgustful means to an end, would never have attracted me, nor when I had become conscious of the wrongs of society as it now is, and the oppression of poor people, could I have ever believed in the possibility of a *partial* setting right of those wrongs. In other words, I could never have been such a fool as to believe in the happy and "respectable" poor.

If, therefore, my ideal forced me to look for practical Socialism, what was it that forced me to conceive of an ideal? Now, here comes in what I said of my being (in this paper) a type of a certain group of mind.

Before the uprising of *modern* Socialism almost all intelligent people either were, or professed themselves to be, quite contented with the civilization of this century. Again, almost all of these really were thus contented, and saw nothing to do but to perfect the said civilization by getting rid of a few ridiculous survivals of the barbarous ages. To be short, this was the *Whig*[1] frame of mind, natural to the modern prosperous middle-class men, who, in fact, as far as mechanical progress is concerned, have nothing to ask for, if only Socialism would leave them alone to enjoy their plentiful style.

But besides these contented ones there were others who were not really contented, but had a vague sentiment of repulsion to the triumph of civilization, but were coerced into silence by the measureless power of Whiggery.[2] Lastly, there were a few who were in open rebellion against the said Whiggery—a few, say two, Carlyle and Ruskin.[3] The latter, before my days of practical Socialism, was my master towards the ideal aforesaid, and, looking backward, I cannot help saying, by the way, how deadly dull the world would have been twenty years ago but for Ruskin! It was through him that I learned to give form to my discontent, which I must say was not by any means vague. Apart from the

desire to produce beautiful things, the leading passion of my life has been and is hatred of modern civilization. What shall I say of it now, when the words are put into my mouth, my hope of its destruction—what shall I say of its supplanting by Socialism?

What shall I say concerning its mastery of and its waste of mechanical power, its commonwealth so poor, its enemies of the commonwealth so rich, its stupendous organization—for the misery of life! Its contempt of simple pleasures which everyone could enjoy but for its folly? Its eyeless[4] vulgarity which has destroyed art, the one certain solace of labour? All this I felt then as now, but I did not know why it was so. The hope of the past times was gone, the struggles of mankind for many ages had produced nothing but this sordid, aimless, ugly confusion; the immediate future seemed to me likely to intensify all the present evils by sweeping away the last survivals of the days before the dull squalor of civilization had settled down on the world. This was a bad look-out[5] indeed, and, if I may mention myself as a personality and not as a mere type, especially so to a man of my disposition, careless of metaphysics and religion, as well as of scientific analysis, but with a deep love of the earth and the life on it, and a passion for the history of the past of mankind. Think of it! Was it all to end in a counting-house[6] on the top of a cinder-heap,[7] with Podsnap's[8] drawing-room in the offing,[9] and a Whig committee dealing out champagne to the rich and margarine to the poor in such convenient proportions as would make all men contented together, though the pleasure of the eyes was gone from the world, and the place of Homer[10] was to be taken by Huxley?[11] Yet, believe me, in my heart, when I really forced myself to

---

1 *Whig* Liberal.

2 *Whiggery* Whig principles.

3 *Carlyle* Thomas Carlyle (1795–1881), British historian, essayist and political critic; *Ruskin* John Ruskin (1819–1900), British author and art critic.

4 *eyeless* Undiscriminating.

5 *look-out* Outlook, prospective condition.

6 *counting-house* Office.

7 *cinder-heap* Area of refuse from iron production.

8 *Podsnap's* Belonging to Mr. Podsnap, a wealthy character from Charles Dickens's last novel, *Our Mutual Friend* (1865).

9 *in the offing* Likely to happen in the near future.

10 *Homer* Greek epic poet (c. 850 BCE?) to whom two of the most influential Western literary works are attributed—the *Iliad* and the *Odyssey*.

11 *Huxley* Thomas Huxley (1825–1895), Victorian essayist and educator.

look towards the future, that is what I saw in it, and, as far as I could tell, scarce anyone seemed to think it worth while to struggle against such a consummation of civilization. So there I was in for a fine pessimistic end of life, if it had not somehow dawned on me that amidst all this filth of civilization the seeds of a great change, what we others call Social-Revolution, were beginning to germinate. The whole face of things was changed to me by that discovery, and all I had to do then in order to become a Socialist was to hook myself on to the practical movement, which, as before said, I have tried to do as well as I could.

To sum up, then, the study of history and the love and practice of art forced me into a hatred of the civilization which, if tilings were to stop as they are, would turn history into inconsequent nonsense, and make art a collection of the curiosities of the past, which would have no serious relation to the life of the present.

But the consciousness of revolution stirring amidst our hateful modern society prevented me, luckier than many others of artistic perceptions, from crystallizing into a mere railer against "progress" on the one hand, and on the other from wasting time and energy in any of the numerous schemes by which the quasi-artistic of the middle classes hope to make art grow when it has no longer any root, and thus I became a practical Socialist.

A last word or two. Perhaps some of our friends will say, what have we to do with these matters of history and art? We want by means of Social-Democracy to win a decent livelihood, we want in some sort to live, and that at once. Surely anyone who professes to think that the question of art and cultivation must go before that of the knife and fork (and there are some who do propose that) does not understand what art means, or how that its root must have a soil of a thriving and unanxious life. Yet it must be remembered that civilization has reduced the workman to such a skinny and pitiful existence, that he scarcely knows how to frame a desire for any life much better than that which he now endures perforce.[1] It is the province of art to set the true ideal of a full and reasonable life before him, a life to which the perception and creation of beauty, the enjoyment of real pleasure that is, shall be felt to be as necessary to man as his daily bread, and that no man, and no set of men, can be deprived of this except by mere opposition, which should be resisted to the utmost.

—1894

---

[1] *perforce* Inevitably, unavoidably.

IN CONTEXT

William Morris and Edward Burne-Jones

Frederick Mollyer, *William Morris and Edward Burne-Jones with their families* (c. 1880).
Burne-Jones (1833–98) was, with Morris, a key figure in the Arts and Crafts movement and
the most significant of the second generation of Pre-Raphaelite artists.

Morris is standing in the back at the right of the photograph, and Burne-Jones is seated
in the center. Morris's wife Jane (née Burden), the inspiration for and subject of many Pre-
Raphaelite works, is in front of Morris and Burne-Jones; Burne-Jones's father stands at the
rear left.

AUGUSTA WEBSTER
1837 – 1894

Augusta Webster is best known for bold poetic portraits that give dramatic voice to social issues in Victorian culture. Despite the considerable reputation she enjoyed when alive, for nearly a hundred years after her death she went missing from the English canon; the unstinting support of Victorian literary critic Theodore Watts-Gunn, who declared it "a monstrous thing that such a poet as Augusta Webster should be unknown," was not enough to prevent the politics of twentieth-century canon-formation from ignoring Webster. She lacked any powerful connections to secure her reputation, and the genres she favored—longer dramatic monologues and verse poems—do not lend themselves to anthologization. It was not until the 1980s and '90s that feminist scholarship rediscovered Webster.

Born in 1837 to Julia Hume Davies and Vice-Admiral George Davies of the British Navy in Poole, Dorset, Julia Augusta Davies spent her earliest years on board her father's ship, the *Griper*. It is said that Webster learned Greek at a young age to help her brother with his lessons; her mastery of a classical language traditionally reserved for male education may also have been motivated by literary ambitions, anticipating a career which included two translations of Greek plays. Webster attended the Cambridge School of Art and was admitted to the South Kensington Art School where, according to Ray Strachey, she "nearly dashed the prospects of women art students for ever by being expelled for whistling." In 1863 she married Thomas Webster, a fellow and law lecturer at Trinity College in Cambridge. Their only child, Margaret, is memorialized in one of Webster's finest works, the posthumously published sonnet sequence *Mother and Daughter*. While no personal documents exist to shed light on the Websters' marriage, the couple's decision to move to London suggests that it was not conventionally patriarchal; giving up a prestigious position in Cambridge, Webster's husband supported a move which would enable his wife to develop professionally in proximity to some of her literary models, such as Elizabeth Barrett Browning, Robert Browning, and Tennyson.

In London, Webster was poetry reviewer for the *Athenaeum* for a decade, and wrote regular columns for the *Examiner*. At a time when the dominant ideology of the British Medical Association warned against education for women on the grounds that it would sap the vital energy needed for reproduction, Webster campaigned on behalf of women's suffrage and education, becoming one of the first women to be elected to the London School Board.

Webster's writing is rich with social commentary. Her poem "A Castaway," praised by Robert Browning and called "her masterpiece" by Watts-Dunn, presents through the persona of a prostitute a powerful critique of the Victorian "economy of love" (to borrow the phrase of Webster scholar Christine Sutphin). "A Castaway," like "The Happiest Girl in the World" and "Jeanne D'Arc," is written in the poetic genre in which Webster excelled, the dramatic monologue. Two collections of monologues, *Dramatic Studies* (1866) and *Portraits* (1870), mark Webster's most lasting contribution to English poetry. In contrast to the psychological interiors dramatized by Robert Browning in monologues such as "Fra Lippo Lippi," Webster skillfully crafted the monologue to speak to external social circumstances. Webster was able to give voice to a sensual and political potency prohibited Victorian women by speaking through mythological surrogates in "Medea in Athens" and "Circe." While the implied, silent listener addressed within conventional dramatic monologues is often absent from Webster's treatments (leading the *London Review* to describe *Dramatic Studies* as "a set of soliloquies"), her monologues stage a voice whose message is a moving social performance.

The essays on love and marriage that Webster regularly contributed to the *Examiner* were, like most submissions to Victorian periodicals, anonymous. The editor of the *Examiner* held Webster's essay "A Translation and a Transcription" in high esteem, ranking it "the best article which ever appeared in its pages." Webster's first two books, *Blanche Lisle and Other Poems* (1860) and a narrative poem in blank verse entitled *Lilian Gray* (1864), were published under the pseudonym Cecil Home. All subsequent work, ranging from lyrics to verse dramas, appeared under Webster's own name. She even daringly attached her own name to her translations of *The Medea of Euripides* and *The Prometheus Bound of Aeschylus* at a time when scholarship in classical languages was considered to be strictly the province of "gentlemen."

Webster brought something of the unconventional to whatever genre she attempted. Whereas sonnet sequences had traditionally been vehicles for the expression of romantic love, her sonnet sequence *Mother and Daughter* (1894) took the love between a mother and a daughter as its subject.

When she died in 1894 Webster left behind no diaries or family letters, and only scanty evidence of correspondence with Christina Rossetti, Oliver Wendell Holmes, and a few other prominent writers of the day. Her poetic legacy, however, is increasingly regarded as being of very considerable substance.

⌘⌘⌘

A Castaway

Poor little diary, with its simple thoughts,
  Its good resolves, its "Studied French an hour,"
"Read Modern History," "Trimmed up my grey hat,"
"Darned stockings," "Tatted,"[1] "Practiced my new song,"
5 "Went to the daily service," "Took Bess soup,"
"Went out to tea." Poor simple diary!
And did *I* write it? Was I this good girl,
This budding colourless young rose of home?
Did I so live content in such a life,
10 Seeing no larger scope, nor asking it,
Than this small constant round—old clothes to mend,
New clothes to make, then go and say my prayers,
Or carry soup, or take a little walk
And pick the ragged-robins[2] in the hedge?
15 Then, for ambition, (was there ever life
That could forego that?) to improve my mind

And know French better and sing harder songs;
For gaiety, to go, in my best white
Well washed and starched and freshened with new bows,
20 And take tea out to meet the clergyman.
No wishes and no cares, almost no hopes,
Only the young girl's hazed and golden dreams
That veil the future from her.

                                    So long since:
25 And now it seems a jest to talk of me
As if I could be one with her, of me
Who am ... me.

                          And what is that? My looking-glass
Answers it passably; a woman sure,
30 No fiend, no slimy thing out of the pools,
A woman with a ripe and smiling lip
That has no venom in its touch I think,
With a white brow on which there is no brand;
A woman none dare call not beautiful,
35 Not womanly in every woman's grace.

---

[1] *Tatted* Made lace.

[2] *ragged-robin* Common English flower.

Aye, let me feed upon my beauty thus,
Be glad in it like painters when they see
At last the face they dreamed but could not find
Look from their canvas on them, triumph in it,
40 The dearest thing I have. Why, 'tis my all,
Let me make much of it: is it not this,
This beauty, my own curse at once and tool
To snare men's souls (I know what the good say
Of beauty in such creatures), is it not this
45 That makes me feel myself a woman still,
With still some little pride, some little—

                   Stop!
"Some little pride, some little"—Here's a jest!
What word will fit the sense but modesty?
50 A wanton I, but modest!

              Modest, true;
I'm not drunk in the streets, ply not for hire
At infamous corners with my likenesses
Of the humbler kind; yes, modesty's my word—
55 'Twould shape my mouth well too, I think I'll try:
"Sir, Mr. What-you-will, Lord Who-knows-what,
My present lover or my next to come,
Value me at my worth, fill your purse full,
For I am modest; yes, and honour me
60 As though your schoolgirl sister or your wife
Could let her skirts brush mine or talk of me;
For I am modest."

            Well, I flout myself:
But yet, but yet—

              Fie, poor fantastic fool,
65 Why do I play the hypocrite alone,
Who am no hypocrite with others by?
Where should be my "But yet"? I am that thing
Called half a dozen dainty names, and none
70 Dainty enough to serve the turn and hide
The one coarse English worst that lurks beneath:
Just that, no worse, no better.

              And, for me,
I say let no one be above her trade;

75 I own my kindredship with any drab[1]
Who sells herself as I, although she crouch
In fetid garrets and I have a home
All velvet and marqueterie and pastilles,[2]
Although she hide her skeleton in rags
80 And I set fashions and wear cobweb lace:
The difference lies but in my choicer ware,
That I sell beauty and she ugliness;
Our traffic's one—I'm no sweet slaver-tongue
To gloze[3] upon it and explain myself
85 A sort of fractious angel misconceived—
Our traffic's one: I own it. And what then?
I know of worse that are called honourable.
Our lawyers, who with noble eloquence
And virtuous outbursts lie to hang a man,
90 Or lie to save him, which way goes the fee:
Our preachers, gloating on your future hell
For not believing what they doubt themselves:
Our doctors, who sort poisons out by chance
And wonder how they'll answer, and grow rich:
95 Our journalists, whose business is to fib
And juggle truths and falsehoods to and fro:
Our tradesmen, who must keep unspotted names
And cheat the least like stealing that they can:
Our —— all of them, the virtuous worthy men
100 Who feed on the world's follies, vices, wants,
And do their businesses of lies and shams
Honestly, reputably, while the world
Claps hands and cries "good luck," which of their
      trades,
Their honourable trades, barefaced like mine,
105 All secrets brazened out, would show more white?

      And whom do I hurt more than they? as much?
The wives? Poor fools, what do I take from them
Worth crying for or keeping? If they knew
What their fine husbands look like seen by eyes
110 That may perceive there are more men than one!
But, if they can, let them just take the pains
To keep them; 'tis not such a mighty task
To pin an idiot to your apron-string;

---

[1] *drab* Common prostitute.

[2] *marqueterie* Inlaid mosaic work decorating furniture; *pastilles* Aromatic pastes burnt as perfumes.

[3] *gloze* Interpret deceitfully or flatteringly.

And wives have an advantage over us,
115 (The good and blind ones have) the smile or pout
Leaves them no secret nausea at odd times.
Oh, they could keep their husbands if they cared,
But 'tis an easier life to let them go,
And whimper at it for morality.

120   Oh! those shrill carping virtues, safely housed
From reach of even a smile that should put red
On a decorous cheek, who rail at us
With such a spiteful scorn and rancorousness,
(Which maybe is half envy at the heart)
125 And boast themselves so measurelessly good
And us so measurelessly unlike them,
What is their wondrous merit that they stay
In comfortable homes whence not a soul
Has ever thought of tempting them, and wear
130 No kisses but a husband's upon lips
There is no other man desires to kiss—
Refrain in fact from sin impossible?
How dare they hate us so? what have they done,
What borne, to prove them other than we are?
135 What right have they to scorn us—glass-case saints,
Dianas[1] under lock and key—what right
More than the well-fed helpless barn-door fowl
To scorn the larcenous wild-birds?

                              Pshaw, let be!
140 Scorn or no scorn, what matter for their scorn?
I have outfaced my own—that's harder work.
Aye, let their virtuous malice dribble on—
Mock snowstorms on the stage—I'm proof long since:
I have looked coolly on my what and why,
145 And I accept myself.

                         Oh I'll endorse
The shamefullest revilings mouthed at me,
Cry "True! Oh perfect picture! Yes, that's I!"
And add a telling blackness here and there,
150 And then dare swear you, every nine of ten,
My judges and accusers, I'd not change
My conscience against yours, you who tread out
Your devil's pilgrimage along the roads
That take in church and chapel, and arrange

A roundabout and decent way to hell.
155

Well, mine's a short way and a merry one:
So says my pious hash of ohs and ahs,
Choice texts and choicer threats, appropriate names,
(Rahabs and Jezebels)[2] some fierce Tartuffe[3]
160 Hurled at me through the post. We had rare fun
Over that tract[4] digested with champagne.
Where is it? where's my rich repertory
Of insults Biblical?[5] "I prey on souls"—
Only my men have oftenest none I think:
165 "I snare the simple ones"—but in these days
There seem to be none simple and none snared
And most men have their favourite sinnings planned
To do them civilly and sensibly:
"I braid my hair"—but braids are out of date:
170 "I paint my cheeks"—I always wear them pale:
"I—"

                    Pshaw! the trash is savourless today:
One cannot laugh alone. There, let it burn.
What, does the windy dullard think one needs
175 His wisdom dove-tailed on to Solomon's,[6]
His threats out-threatening God's, to teach the news
That those who need not sin have safer souls?
We know it, but we've bodies to save too;
And so we earn our living.

---

[1] *Diana*   Roman goddess of virginity.

[2] *Rahabs and Jezebels*   I.e., harlots. Rahab was a Biblical harlot whose family was saved from the destruction of Jericho because she hid messengers that had been sent by Joshua to spy on the city. (See Joshua 6.17–25). Jezebel was a Phoenician princess who married Ahab, King of Israel. She refused to worship Yahweh, continuing to practice her country's traditional worship instead, and murdered Yahweh's prophets. Her name is often used to denote a cruel, sexually predatory woman. (See 1 Judges 16 and 18).

[3] *Tartuffe*   Hypocritical character who feigned virtue in Molière's 1664 play of that name.

[4] *tract*   Religious pamphlet.

[5] *insults Biblical*   See Ecclesiastes 7.26: "And I find more bitter than death the woman, whose heart is snares and nets, and her hands as bands: whoso pleaseth God shall escape from her; but the sinner shall be taken by her," and 1 Timothy 2.9–10, which advises women to "adorn themselves in modest apparel, with shamefacedness and sobriety; not with braided hair, or gold, or pearls, or costly array; / But (which becometh women professing godliness) with good works."

[6] *Solomon*   Biblical king of Israel who was known for his wisdom.

180   Well lit, tract!
At least you've made me a good leaping blaze.
Up, up, how the flame shoots! and now 'tis dead.
Oh proper finish, preaching to the last—
No such bad omen either; sudden end,
185 And no sad withering horrible old age.
How one would clutch at youth to hold it tight!
And then to know it gone, to see it gone,
Be taught its absence by harsh careless looks,
To live forgotten, solitary, old—
190 The cruellest word that ever woman learns.
Old—that's to be nothing, or to be at best
A blurred memorial that in better days
There was a woman once with such a name.
No, no, I could not bear it: death itself
195 Shows kinder promise ... even death itself,
Since it must come one day—

           Oh this grey gloom!
This rain, rain, rain, what wretched thoughts it brings!
Death: I'll not think of it.

200   Will no one come?
'Tis dreary work alone.

           Why did I read
That silly diary? Now, sing-song, ding-dong,
Come the old vexing echoes back again,
205 Church bells and nursery good-books, back again
Upon my shrinking ears that had forgotten—
I hate the useless memories: 'tis fools' work
Singing the hackneyed° dirge of "better days":   *stale*
Best take Now kindly, give the past good-bye,
210 Whether it were a better or a worse.

    Yes, yes, I listened to the echoes once,
The echoes and the thoughts from the old days.
The worse for me: I lost my richest friend,
And that was all the difference. For the world,
215 I would not have that flight known. How they'd roar:
"What! Eulalie, when she refused us all,
'Ill' and 'away,' was doing Magdalene,[1]

Tears, ashes, and her Bible, and then off
To hide her in a Refuge[2] ... for a week!"

220   A wild whim that, to fancy I could change
My new self for my old because I wished!
Since then, when in my languid days there comes
That craving, like homesickness, to go back
To the good days, the dear old stupid days,
225 To the quiet and the innocence, I know
'Tis a sick fancy and try palliatives.

    What is it? You go back to the old home,
And 'tis not *your* home, has no place for you,
And, if it had, you could not fit you in it.
230 And could I fit me to my former self?
If I had had the wit, like some of us,
To sow my wild-oats into three per cents,[3]
Could I not find me shelter in the peace
Of some far nook where none of them would come,
235 Nor whisper travel from this scurrilous world
(That gloats, and moralizes through its leers)
To blast me with my fashionable shame?
There I might—oh my castle in the clouds!
And where's its rent?—but there, were there a there,
240 I might again live the grave blameless life
Among such simple pleasures, simple cares:
But could they be my pleasures, be my cares?
The blameless life, but never the content—
Never. How could I henceforth be content
245 With any life but one that sets the brain
In a hot merry fever with its stir?
What would there be in quiet rustic days,
Each like the other, full of time to think,
To keep one bold enough to live at all?
250 Quiet is hell, I say—as if a woman
Could bear to sit alone, quiet all day,
And loathe herself and sicken on her thoughts.

    They tried it at the Refuge, and I failed:
I could not bear it. Dreary hideous room,
255 Coarse pittance, prison rules, one might bear these

---

[1] *doing Magdalene* Becoming a reformed prostitute, so called after Mary Magdalene of the New Testament, one of Jesus's disciples. The houses in Victorian England to which prostitutes could come to reform were known as "Magdalene houses."

[2] *Refuge* Shelter.

[3] *three per cents* British government stocks, which returned three percent interest annually.

And keep one's purpose; but so much alone,
And then made faint and weak and fanciful
By change from pampering to half-famishing—
Good God, what thoughts come! Only one week more
260 And 'twould have ended: but in one day more
I must have killed myself. And I loathe death,
The dreadful foul corruption with who knows
What future after it.

                              Well, I came back,
265 Back to my slough.[1] Who says I had my choice?
Could I stay there to die of some mad death?
And if I rambled out into the world
Sinless but penniless, what else were that
But slower death, slow pining shivering death
270 By misery and hunger? Choice! what choice
Of living well or ill? could I have that?
And who would give it me? I think indeed
If some kind hand, a woman's—I hate men—
Had stretched itself to help me to firm ground,
275 Taken a chance and risked my falling back,
I could have gone my way not falling back:
But, let her be all brave, all charitable,
How could she do it? Such a trifling boon—
A little work to live by, 'tis not much—
280 And I might have found will enough to last:
But where's the work? More seamstresses than shirts;
And defter hands at white work[2] than are mine
Drop starved at last: dressmakers, milliners,
Too many too they say; and then their trades
285 Need skill, apprenticeship. And who so bold
As hire me for their humblest drudgery?
Not even for scullery[3] slut; not even, I think,
For governess although they'd get me cheap.
And after all it would be something hard,
290 With the marts for decent women overfull,
If I could elbow in and snatch a chance
And oust some good girl so, who then perforce
Must come and snatch her chance among our crowd.

            Why, if the worthy men who think all's done
295 If we'll but come where we can hear them preach,

Could bring us all, or any half of us,
Into their fold, teach all us wandering sheep,
Or only half of us, to stand in rows
And baa them hymns and moral songs, good lack,[4]
300 What would they do with us? what could they do?
Just think! with were't but half of us on hand
To find work for ... or husbands. Would they try
To ship us to the colonies for wives?[5]

            Well, well, I know the wise ones talk and talk:
305 "Here's cause, here's cure": "No, here it is, and here":
And find society to blame, or law,
The Church, the men, the women, too few schools,
Too many schools, too much, too little taught:
Somewhere or somehow someone is to blame:
310 But I say all the fault's with God Himself
Who puts too many women in the world.
We ought to die off reasonably and leave
As many as the men want, none to waste.
Here's cause; the woman's superfluity:
315 And for the cure, why, if it were the law,
Say, every year, in due percentages,
Balancing them with males as the times need,
To kill off female infants, 'twould make room;
And some of us would not have lost too much,
320 Losing life ere we know what it *can* mean.

            The other day I saw a woman weep
Beside her dead child's bed: the little thing
Lay smiling, and the mother wailed half mad,
Shrieking to God to give it back again.
325 I could have laughed aloud: the little girl
Living had but her mother's life to live;
There she lay smiling, and her mother wept
To know her gone!

                        My mother would have wept.

330 Oh, mother, mother, did you ever dream,
You good grave simple mother, you pure soul

---

1   *slough* State of moral degradation.

2   *white work* White-thread embroidery on white cloth.

3   *scullery* Room, adjoining the kitchen, in which dishes were washed.

4   *good lack* A polite exclamation.

5   *ship ... wives* Reference to Sir Sidney Herbert's proposal to send half a million "surplus" women, such as those driven to prostitution by a lack of employment, to the colonies, where there was a shortage of women from whom to choose for settlers who wished to marry.

No evil could come nigh, did you once dream
In all your dying cares for your lone girl
Left to fight out her fortune helplessly
335 That there would be *this* danger?—for *your* girl,
Taught by you, lapped in a sweet ignorance,
Scarcely more wise of what things sin could be
Than some young child a summer six months old,
Where in the north the summer makes a day,
340 Of what is darkness … darkness that will come
Tomorrow suddenly. Thank God at least
For this much of my life, that when you died,
That when you kissed me dying, not a thought
Of this made sorrow for you, that I too
345 Was pure of even fear.

                              Oh yes, I thought,
Still new in my insipid treadmill life,
(My father so late dead), and hopeful still,
There might be something pleasant somewhere in it,
350 Some sudden fairy come, no doubt, to turn
My pumpkin to a chariot, I thought then
That I might plod and plod and drum the sounds
Of useless facts into unwilling ears,
Tease children with dull questions half the day
355 Then con dull answers in my room at night
Ready for next day's questions, mend quill pens
And cut my fingers, add up sums done wrong
And never get them right; teach, teach, and teach—
What I half knew, or not at all—teach, teach
360 For years, a lifetime—*I*!

                              And yet, who knows?
It might have been, for I was patient once,
And willing, and meant well; it might have been
Had I but still clung on in my first place—
365 A safe dull place, where mostly there were smiles
But never merry-makings; where all days
Jogged on sedately busy, with no haste;
Where all seemed measured out, but margins broad:
A dull home but a peaceful, where I felt
370 My pupils would be dear young sisters soon,
And felt their mother take me to her heart,
Motherly to all lonely harmless things.
But I must have a conscience, must blurt out
My great discovery of my ignorance!

375 And who required it of me? And who gained?
What did it matter for a more or less
The girls learnt in their schoolbooks, to forget
In their first season?[1] We did well together:
They loved me and I them: but I went off
380 To housemaid's pay, six crossgrained[2] brats to teach,
Wrangles and jangles, doubts, disgrace … then this;
And they had a perfection found for them,
Who has all ladies' learning in her head
Abridged and scheduled, speaks five languages,
385 Knows botany and conchology[3] and globes,
Draws, paints, plays, sings, embroiders, teaches all
On a patent method never known to fail:
And now they're finished and, I hear, poor things,
Are the worst dancers and worst dressers out.[4]
390 And where's their profit of those prison years
All gone to make them wise in lesson-books?
Who wants his wife to know weeds' Latin names?
Who ever chose a girl for saying dates?
Or asked if she had learned to trace a map?

395   Well, well, the silly rules this silly world
Makes about women! This is one of them.
Why must there be pretence of teaching them
What no one ever cares that they should know,
What, grown out of the schoolroom, they cast off
400 Like the schoolroom pinafore,[5] no better fit
For any use of real grown-up life,
For any use to her who seeks or waits
The husband and the home, for any use,
For any shallowest pretence of use,
405 To her who has them? Do I not know this,
I, like my betters, that a woman's life,
Her natural life, her good life, her one life,
Is in her husband, God on earth to her,
And what she knows and what she can and is
410 Is only good as it brings good to him?

---

[1] *first season* The London social season, when Parliament is in session and everyone of social importance is in the city.

[2] *crossgrained* Difficult to manage.

[3] *conchology* The study of sea-shells.

[4] *out* I.e., appearing in society. Young girls did not attend public social functions, so it was said that they "came out" when they became old enough to do so.

[5] *pinafore* Garment worn by little girls.

Oh God, do I not know it? I the thing
Of shame and rottenness, the animal
That feeds men's lusts and preys on them, I, I,
Who should not dare to take the name of wife
415 On my polluted lips, who in the word
Hear but my own reviling, I know that.
I could have lived by that rule, how content:
My pleasure to make him some pleasure, pride
To be as he would have me, duty, care,
420 To fit all to his taste, rule my small sphere
To his intention; then to lean on him,
Be guided, tutored, loved—no not that word,
That *loved* which between men and women means
All selfishness, all cloying talk, all lust,
425 All vanity, all idiocy—not loved,
But cared for. I've been loved myself, I think,
Some once or twice since my poor mother died,
But *cared for*, never—that's a word for homes,
Kind homes, good homes, where simple children come
430 And ask their mother is this right or wrong,
Because they know she's perfect, cannot err;
Their father told them so, and he knows all,
Being so wise and good and wonderful,
Even enough to scold even her at times
435 And tell her everything she does not know.
Ah the sweet nursery logic!

Fool! thrice fool!
Do I hanker after that too? Fancy me
Infallible nursery saint, live code of law!
440 Me preaching! teaching innocence to be good!
A mother!

Yet the baby thing that woke
And wailed an hour or two, and then was dead,
Was mine, and had he lived … why then my name
445 Would have been mother. But 'twas well he died:
I could have been no mother, I, lost then
Beyond his saving. Had he come before
And lived, come to me in the doubtful days
When shame and boldness had not grown one sense,
450 For his sake, with the courage come of him,
I might have struggled back.

But how? But how?

His father would not then have let me go:
His time had not yet come to make an end
455 Of my "forever" with a hireling's fee
And civil light dismissal. None but him
To claim a bit of bread of if I went,
Child or no child: would he have given it me?
He! no; he had not done with me. No help,
460 No help, no help. Some ways can be trodden back,
But never our way, we who one wild day
Have given goodbye to what in our deep hearts
The lowest woman still holds best in life,
Good name—good name though given by the world
465 That mouths and garbles with its decent prate,
And wraps it in respectable grave shams,
And patches conscience partly by the rule
Of what one's neighbour thinks, but something more
By what his eyes are sharp enough to see.
470 How I could scorn it with its Pharisees,[1]
If it could not scorn me: but yet, but yet—
Oh God, if I could look it in the face!

Oh I am wild, am ill, I think, tonight:
Will no one come and laugh with me? No feast,
475 No merriment tonight. So long alone!
Will no one come?

At least there's a new dress
To try, and grumble at—they never fit
To one's ideal. Yes, a new rich dress,
480 With lace like this too, that's a soothing balm
For any fretting woman, cannot fail;
I've heard men say it … and they know so well
What's in all women's hearts, especially
Women like me.

No help! no help! no help!
485 How could it be? It was too late long since—
Even at the first too late. Whose blame is that?
There are some kindly people in the world,
But what can *they* do? If one hurls oneself
Into a quicksand, what can be the end,
490 But that one sinks and sinks? Cry out for help?
Ah yes, and, if it came, who is so strong
To strain from the firm ground and lift one out?

---

1 *Pharisees* I.e., hypocrites.

And how, so firmly clutching the stretched hand
495 As death's pursuing terror bids, even so,
How can one reach firm land, having to foot
The treacherous crumbling soil that slides and gives
And sucks one in again? Impossible path!
No, why waste struggles, I or anyone?
500 What is must be. What then? I where I am,
Sinking and sinking; let the wise pass by
And keep their wisdom for an apter use,
Let me sink merrily as I best may.

Only, I think my brother—I forgot;
505 He stopped his brotherhood some years ago—
But if he had been just so much less good
As to remember mercy. Did he think
How once I was his sister, prizing him
As sisters do, content to learn for him
510 The lesson girls with brothers all must learn,
To do without?

I have heard girls lament
That doing so without all things one would,
But I saw never aught to murmur at,
515 For men must be made ready for their work
And women all have more or less their chance
Of husbands to work for them, keep them safe
Like summer roses in soft greenhouse air
That never guess 'tis winter out of doors:
520 No, I saw never aught to murmur at,
Content with stinted fare and shabby clothes
And cloistered silent life to save expense,
Teaching myself out of my borrowed books,
While he for some one pastime (needful, true,
525 To keep him of his rank; 'twas not his fault)
Spent in a month what could have given me
My teachers for a year.

'Twas no one's fault:
For could he be launched forth on the rude sea
530 Of this contentious world and left to find
Oars and the boatman's skill by some good chance?
'Twas no one's fault: yet still he might have thought
Of our so different youths and owned at least
'Tis pitiful when a mere nerveless girl
535 Untutored must put forth upon that sea,

Not in the woman's true place, the wife's place,
To trust a husband and be borne along,
But impotent blind pilot to herself.

Merciless, merciless—like the prudent world
540 That will not have the flawed soul prank[1] itself
With a hoped second virtue, will not have
The woman fallen once lift up herself ...
Lest she should fall again. Oh how his taunts,
His loathing fierce reproaches, scarred and seared
545 Like branding iron hissing in a wound!
And it was true—*that* killed me: and I felt
A hideous hopeless shame burn out my heart,
And knew myself forever that he said,
That which I was—Oh it was true, true, true.

550 No, not true then. I was not all that then.
Oh, I have drifted on before mad winds
And made ignoble shipwreck; not today
Could any breeze of heaven prosper me
Into the track again, nor any hand
555 Snatch me out of the whirlpool I have reached;
But then?

Nay, he judged very well: he knew
Repentance was too dear a luxury
For a beggar's buying, knew it earns no bread—
560 And knew me a too base and nerveless thing
To bear my first fault's sequel and just die.
And how could he have helped me? Held my hand,
Owned me for his, fronted the angry world
Clothed with my ignominy? Or maybe
565 Taken me to his home to damn him worse?
What did I look for? for what less would serve
That he could do, a man without a purse?
He meant me well, he sent me that five pounds,
Much to him then; and, if he bade me work
570 And never vex him more with news of me,
We both knew him too poor for pensioners.
I see he did his best; I could wish now
Sending it back I had professed some thanks.

But there! I was too wretched to be meek:
575 It seemed to me as if he, everyone,

---

[1] *prank* Dress up, adorn.

The whole great world, were guilty of my guilt,
Abettors and avengers: in my heart
I gibed them back their gibings; I was wild.

I see clear now and know one has one's life
580 In hand at first to spend or spare or give
Like any other coin; spend it, or give,
Or drop it in the mire, can the world see
You get your value for it, or bar off
The hurrying of its marts to grope it up
585 And give it back to you for better use?
And if you spend or give, that is your choice;
And if you let it slip, that's your choice too,
You should have held it firmer. Yours the blame,
And not another's, not the indifferent world's
590 Which goes on steadily, statistically,
And count by censuses not separate souls—
And if it somehow needs to its worst use
So many lives of women, useless else,
It buys us of ourselves; we could hold back,
595 Free all of us to starve, and some of us,
(Those who have done no ill, and are in luck)
To slave their lives out and have food and clothes
Until they grow unserviceably old.

Oh, I blame no one—scarcely even myself.
600 It was to be: the very good in me
Has always turned to hurt; all I thought right
At the hot moment, judged of afterwards,
Shows reckless.

Why, look at it, had I taken
605 The pay my dead child's father offered me
For having been its mother, I could then
Have kept life in me—many have to do it,
That swarm in the back alleys, on no more,
Cold sometimes, mostly hungry, but they live—
610 I could have gained a respite trying it,
And maybe found at last some humble work
To eke the pittance out. Not I, forsooth,
I must have spirit, must have womanly pride,
Must dash back his contemptuous wages, I
615 Who had not scorned to earn them, dash them back
The fiercer that he dared to count our boy
In my appraising: and yet now I think

I might have taken it for my dead boy's sake;
It would have been *his* gift.

620   But I went forth
With my fine scorn, and whither did it lead?
Money's the root of evil do they say?
Money is virtue, strength: money to me
Would then have been repentance: could I live
625 Upon my idiot's pride?

Well, it fell soon.
I had prayed Clement might believe me dead,
And yet I begged of him—That's like me too,
Beg of him and then send him back his alms!
630 What if he gave as to a whining wretch
That holds her hand and lies? I am less to him
Than such a one; her rags do him no wrong,
But I, I wrong him merely that I live,
Being his sister. Could I not at least
635 Have still let him forget me? But 'tis past:
And naturally he may hope I am long dead.

Good God! to think that we were what we were
One to the other … and now!

He has done well;
640 Married a sort of heiress, I have heard,
A dapper little madam dimple cheeked
And dimple brained, who makes him a good wife—
No doubt she'd never own but just to him,
And in a whisper, she can even suspect
645 That we exist, we other women things:
What would she say if she could learn one day
She has a sister-in-law? So he and I
Must stand apart till doomsday.

But the jest,
650 To think how she would look! Her fright, poor thing!
The notion! I could laugh outright … or else,
For I feel near it, roll on the ground and sob.

Well, after all, there's not much difference
Between the two sometimes.

655   Was that the bell?

Someone at last, thank goodness. There's a voice,
And that's a pleasure. Whose though? Ah, I know.
Why did she come alone, the cackling goose?
Why not have brought her sister? She tells more
And titters less. No matter; half a loaf

660

Is better than no bread.

                                    Oh, is it you?
Most welcome, dear: one gets so moped alone.
—1870, 1893

ALGERNON CHARLES SWINBURNE
<u>1837 – 1909</u>

Victorian poet and critic Algernon Swinburne was physically slight, but he had a powerful personality, and he left behind a vast literary output. Much of his writing, however, on topics such as incest, cannibalism, sadomasochism, and necrophilia, was too outrageous for "respectable" Victorian tastes. Although he was born into a distinguished family of British aristocracy, Swinburne's opinions on politics, religion, and sexuality were offensive enough to have earned him the nickname "Swineborn" in *Punch* magazine. Swinburne's poetry, however, was also metrically innovative, musical, and often erudite. Oscar Wilde claimed him as his literary master but said of Swinburne's writing, "Words seem to dominate him. Alliteration tyrannizes over him. Mere sound often becomes his lord. He is so eloquent that whatever he touches becomes unreal." This "diffuseness" was, according to T.S. Eliot, one of his "glories." Although few have disputed the musicality of Swinburne's poetry, some critics have accused him of being vague and soporific.

Algernon Swinburne was born in 1837 into a highly respectable aristocratic family. His father, Admiral Charles Henry Swinburne, was the son of a baronet, and his mother, Lady Jane, was the daughter of an earl. Raised a devout Anglo-Catholic, Swinburne read profusely and acquired an intimate knowledge of the Bible, as well as a proficiency in French and Italian. His early years at Eton, however, were troubled ones; as a result of disciplinary problems, he was removed from the school before he graduated. After private tutoring, he entered Balliol College at Oxford in 1856. During his first two years there, Swinburne excelled in the Classics and won a scholarship for French and Italian; his unruliness got the better of him again, and he was forced to leave Balliol without a degree. He nevertheless made many important friends at Oxford, including Benjamin Jowett (then master of Balliol) and the Pre-Raphaelites Edward Burne-Jones, William Morris, and Dante Gabriel Rossetti (with whom he lived in London after Rossetti's wife, Elizabeth Siddall, died).

London saw the best and the worst of Swinburne. During the 1860s, he gained notoriety for his wild, drunken revelries and experiments with flagellation, as much as for the publication of two important works, *Atalanta in Calydon* (1865) and *Poems and Ballads* (1866). The classical Greek tragic form of the verse-play *Atalanta* and its concentration on fate and divine intervention belied the long poem's modern revolt against religious institutions and its sympathy, instead, with the "holy spirit of man." While Victorians might have been expected to rail against Swinburne's chastisement of religious orthodoxy, the lyrical and mellifluous tragedy held many in its sway, and won accolades from reviewers. John Ruskin said that it was the "grandest thing ever done by a youth—though he is a Demoniac youth," and Tennyson wrote to Swinburne praising the metrical creativity of *Atalanta*.

Poems and Ballads, on the other hand, had the public (Ruskin included) up in arms. In such poems as "The Triumph of Time," "Dolores, "The Leper," "Hymn to Prosperine," and "Laus Veneris," Swinburne explored themes of sexual perversion, paganism, and moral and spiritual decay. One reviewer said the author was an "unclean, fiery imp from the pit," while another, referring to

Swinburne's association with the Aesthetes, called him the "libidinous laureate of a pack of satyrs." Amid this outcry, the publishing house withdrew the book from publication, angering Swinburne and prompting his eloquent riposte in *Notes on Poems and Reviews. Poems and Ballads* was re-released shortly afterward by another publisher.

Swinburne's notoriety continued into the late 1860s and 1870s, as he cultivated his image as a "scandalous poet," to use his own words. He wrote at a feverish rate—even though his alcoholism was by then prompting seizures and blackouts—and produced such works as *A Song of Italy* (1867), a defense of Italian liberation; *Ave Atque Vale* (1868), an elegy to Baudelaire; the brilliant essay *William Blake* (1868); and *Songs Before Sunrise* (1871), which continued the theme of spiritual and political revolution. By the end of the 1870s, however, Swinburne was near death, his nerves destroyed by alcohol, and his body depleted from overwork. Luckily, in 1879, his friend Theodore Watts-Dunton took him to his house in Putney and helped nurse him back to health. There Swinburne lived in quiet solitude for the remaining 30 years of his life, writing and publishing prolifically, and finally succumbing to pneumonia in 1909.

In those final decades, Swinburne won the respect of many Victorians. Although the *Guardian* noted upon his death that his verse could be "careless, trivial, or inharmonious," the newspaper also acknowledged that "the greatest poet lately living is dead … and we cannot doubt that much of his poetry will live by virtue of its exquisite music."

⌘ ⌘ ⌘

The Triumph of Time

Before our lives divide forever,
  While time is with us and hands are free
(Time, swift to fasten and swift to sever
    Hand from hand, as we stand by the sea),
5 I will say no word that a man might say
Whose whole life's love goes down in a day;
For this could never have been; and never,
    Though the gods and the years relent, shall be.

Is it worth a tear, is it worth an hour
10   To think of things that are well outworn?
Of fruitless husk and fugitive flower,
    The dream foregone and the deed forborne?
Though joy be done with and grief be vain,
Time shall not sever us wholly in twain;°   *two*
15 Earth is not spoilt for a single shower;
    But the rain has ruined the ungrown corn.

It will grow not again, this fruit of my heart,
    Smitten with sunbeams, ruined with rain.

The singing seasons divide and depart,
20   Winter and summer depart in twain.
It will grow not again, it is ruined at root,
The bloodlike blossom, the dull red fruit;
Though the heart yet sickens, the lips yet smart,
    With sullen savour of poisonous pain.

25 I have given no man of my fruit to eat;
    I trod the grapes, I have drunken the wine.
Had you eaten and drunken and found it sweet,
    This wild new growth of the corn and vine,
This wine and bread without lees° or leaven,   *sediment*
30 We had grown as gods, as the gods in heaven,
Souls fair to look upon, goodly to greet,
    One splendid spirit, your soul and mine.

In the change of years, in the coil of things,
    In the clamour and rumour of life to be,
35 We, drinking love at the furthest springs,
    Covered with love as a covering tree,
We had grown as gods, as the gods above,
Filled from the heart to the lips with love,

Held fast in his hands, clothed warm with his wings,
    O love, my love, had you loved but me!
40

We had stood as the sure stars stand, and moved
    As the moon moves, loving the world; and seen
Grief collapse as a thing disproved,
    Death consume as a thing unclean.
45 Twain halves of a perfect heart, made fast
Soul to soul while the years fell past;
Had you loved me once, as you have not loved;
    Had the chance been with us that has not been.

I have put my days and dreams out of mind,
50   Days that are over, dreams that are done.
Though we seek life through, we shall surely find
    There is none of them clear to us now, not one.
But clear are these things; the grass and the sand,
Where, sure as the eyes reach, ever at hand,
55 With lips wide open and face burnt blind,
    The strong sea-daisies feast on the sun.

The low downs lean to the sea; the stream,
    One loose thin pulseless tremulous vein,
Rapid and vivid and dumb as a dream,
60   Works downward, sick of the sun and the rain;
No wind is rough with the rank rare flowers;
The sweet sea, mother of loves and hours,
Shudders and shines as the grey winds gleam,
    Turning her smile to a fugitive pain.

65 Mother of loves that are swift to fade,
    Mother of mutable winds and hours.
A barren mother, a mother-maid,
    Cold and clean as her faint salt flowers.
I would we twain were even as she,
70 Lost in the night and the light of the sea,
Where faint sounds falter and wan beams wade,
    Break, and are broken, and shed into showers.

The loves and hours of the life of a man,
    They are swift and sad, being born of the sea,
75 Hours that rejoice and regret for a span,
    Born with a man's breath, mortal as he;
Loves that are lost ere they come to birth,
Weeds of the wave, without fruit upon earth.

I lose what I long for, save what I can,
80   My love, my love, and no love for me!

It is not much that a man can save
    On the sands of life, in the straits of time,
Who swims in sight of the great third wave
    That never a swimmer shall cross or climb.
85 Some waif washed up with the strays and spars[1]
That ebb-tide shows to the shore and the stars;
Weed from the water, grass from a grave,
    A broken blossom, a ruined rhyme.

There will no man do for your sake, I think,
90   What I would have done for the least word said.
I had wrung life dry for your lips to drink,
    Broken it up for your daily bread:
Body for body and blood for blood,
As the flow of the full sea risen to flood
95 That yearns and trembles before it sink,
    I had given, and lain down for you, glad and dead.

Yea, hope at highest and all her fruit,
    And time at fullest and all his dower,
I had given you surely, and life to boot,
100   Were we once made one for a single hour.
But now, you are twain, you are cloven apart,
Flesh of his flesh, but heart of my heart;
And deep in one is the bitter root,
    And sweet for one is the lifelong flower.

105 To have died if you cared I should die for you, clung
    To my life if you bade me, played my part
As it pleased you—these were the thoughts that stung,
    The dreams that smote with a keener dart
Than shafts of love or arrows of death;
110 These were but as fire is, dust, or breath,
Or poisonous foam on the tender tongue
    Of the little snakes that eat my heart.

I wish we were dead together today,
    Lost sight of, hidden away out of sight,
115 Clasped and clothed in the cloven clay,
    Out of the world's way, out of the light,
Out of the ages of worldly weather,

---

[1] *spars* Pieces of wood.

Forgotten of all men altogether,
　As the world's first dead, taken wholly away,
120　　Made one with death, filled full of the night.

How we should slumber, how we should sleep,
　Far in the dark with the dreams and the dews
And dreaming, grow to each other, and weep,
　Laugh low, live softly, murmur and muse;
125 Yea, and it may be, struck through by the dream,
Feel the dust quicken and quiver, and seem
Alive as of old to the lips, and leap
　Spirit to spirit as lovers use.

Sick dreams and sad of a dull delight;
130　For what shall it profit when men are dead
To have dreamed, to have loved with the whole soul's
　　might,
　To have looked for day when the day was fled?
Let come what will, there is one thing worth,
To have had fair love in the life upon earth:
135 To have held love safe till the day grew night,
　While skies had colour and lips were red.

Would I lose you now? would I take you then,
　If I lose you now that my heart has need?
And come what may after death to men,
140　What thing worth this will the dead years breed?
Lose life, lose all; but at least I know,
O sweet life's love, having loved you so,
Had I reached you on earth, I should lose not again,
　In death nor life, nor in dream or deed.

145 Yea, I know this well: were you once sealed mine,
　Mine in the blood's beat, mine in the breath,
Mixed into me as honey in wine,
　Not time, that sayeth and gainsayeth,°　　*contradicts*
Nor all strong things had severed us then;
150 Not wrath of gods, nor wisdom of men,
Nor all things earthly, nor all divine,
　Nor joy nor sorrow, nor life nor death.

I had grown pure as the dawn and the dew,
　You had grown strong as the sun or the sea,
155 But none shall triumph a whole life through:
　For death is one, and the fates are three.

At the door of life, by the gate of breath,
There are worse things waiting for men than death;
Death could not sever my soul and you,
160　As these have severed your soul from me.

You have chosen and clung to the chance they sent you,
　Life sweet as perfume and pure as prayer.
But will it not one day in heaven repent you?
　Will they solace you wholly, the days that were?
165 Will you lift up your eyes between sadness and bliss,
Meet mine, and see where the great love is,
And tremble and turn and be changed? Content you;
　The gate is strait;° I shall not be there.　　*locked*

But you, had you chosen, had you stretched hand,
170　Had you seen good such a thing were done,
I too might have stood with the souls that stand
　In the sun's sight, clothed with the light of the sun;
But who now on earth need care how I live?
Have the high gods anything left to give,
175 Save dust and laurels and gold and sand?
　Which gifts are goodly; but I will none.

O all fair lovers about the world,
　There is none of you, none, that shall comfort me.
My thoughts are as dead things, wrecked and whirled
180　Round and round in a gulf of the sea;
And still, through the sound and the straining stream,
Through the coil and chafe, they gleam in a dream,
The bright fine lips so cruelly curled,
　And strange swift eyes where the soul sits free.

185 Free, without pity, withheld from woe,
　Ignorant; fair as the eyes are fair.
Would I have you change now, change at a blow,
　Startled and stricken, awake and aware?
Yea, if I could, would I have you see
190 My very love of you filling me,
And know my soul to the quick, as I know
　The likeness and look of your throat and hair?

I shall not change you. Nay, though I might,
　Would I change my sweet one love with a word?
195 I had rather your hair should change in a night,
　Clear now as the plume of a black bright bird;

Your face fail suddenly, cease, turn grey,
Die as a leaf that dies in a day.
I will keep my soul in a place out of sight,
200   Far off, where the pulse of it is not heard.

Far off it walks, in a bleak blown space,
    Full of the sound of the sorrow of years.
I have woven a veil for the weeping face,
    Whose lips have drunken the wine of tears;
205 I have found a way for the failing feet,
A place for slumber and sorrow to meet;
There is no rumour about the place,
    Nor light, nor any that sees or hears.

I have hidden my soul out of sight, and said
210   "Let none take pity upon thee, none
Comfort thy crying: for lo, thou art dead,
    Lie still now, safe out of sight of the sun.
Have I not built thee a grave, and wrought
Thy grave-clothes on thee of grievous thought
215 With soft spun verses and tears unshed,
    And sweet light visions of things undone?

"I have given thee garments and balm and myrrh,
    And gold, and beautiful burial things.
But thou, be at peace now, make no stir;
220   Is not thy grave as a royal king's?
Fret not thyself though the end were sore;
Sleep, be patient, vex me no more.
Sleep; what hast thou to do with her?
    The eyes that weep, with the mouth that sings?"

225 Where the dead red leaves of the years lie rotten,
    The cold old crimes and the deeds thrown by,
The misconceived and the misbegotten,
    I would find a sin to do ere I die,
Sure to dissolve and destroy me all through,
230 That would set you higher in heaven, serve you
And leave you happy, when clean forgotten,
    As a dead man out of mind, am I.

Your lithe hands draw me, your face burns through me,
    I am swift to follow you, keen to see;
235 But love lacks might to redeem or undo me;
    As I have been, I know I shall surely be;

"What should such fellows as I do?" Nay,
My part were worse if I chose to play;
For the worst is this after all; if they knew me,
240   Not a soul upon earth would pity me.

And I play not for pity of these; but you,
    If you saw with your soul what man am I,
You would praise me at least that my soul all through
    Clove to you, loathing the lives that lie;
245 The souls and lips that are bought and sold,
The smiles of silver and kisses of gold,
The lapdog loves that whine as they chew,
    The little lovers that curse and cry.

There are fairer women, I hear; that may be;
250   But I, that I love you and find you fair,
Who are more than fair in my eyes if they be,
    Do the high gods know or the great gods care?
Though the swords in my heart for one were seven,
Would the iron hollow of doubtful heaven,
255 That knows not itself whether night-time or day be,
    Reverberate words and a foolish prayer?

I will go back to the great sweet mother,
    Mother and lover of men, the sea.
I will go down to her, I and none other,
260   Close with her, kiss her and mix her with me;
Cling to her, strive with her, hold her fast:
O fair white mother, in days long past
Born without sister, born without brother,
    Set free my soul as thy soul is free.

265 O fair green-girdled mother of mine,
    Sea, that art clothed with the sun and the rain,
Thy sweet hard kisses are strong like wine,
    Thy large embraces are keen like pain.
Save me and hide me with all thy waves,
270 Find me one grave of thy thousand graves,
Those pure cold populous graves of thine
    Wrought without hand in a world without stain.

I shall sleep, and move with the moving ships,
    Change as the winds change, veer in the tide;
275 My lips will feast on the foam of thy lips,
    I shall rise with thy rising, with thee subside;

Sleep, and not know if she be, if she were,
Filled full with life to the eyes and hair,
As a rose is fulfilled to the roseleaf tips
280   With splendid summer and perfume and pride.

This woven raiment° of nights and days,   *garment*
    Were it once cast off and unwound from me,
Naked and glad would I walk in thy ways,
    Alive and aware of thy ways and thee;
285 Clear of the whole world, hidden at home,
Clothed with the green and crowned with the foam,
A pulse of the life of thy straits and bays,
    A vein in the heart of the streams of the sea.

Fair mother, fed with the lives of men,
290   Thou art subtle and cruel of heart, men say.
Thou hast taken, and shalt not render again;
    Thou art full of thy dead, and cold as they.
But death is the worst that comes of thee;
Thou art fed with our dead, O mother, O sea,
295 But when hast thou fed on our hearts? or when,
    Having given us love, hast thou taken away?

O tender-hearted, O perfect lover,
    Thy lips are bitter, and sweet thine heart.
The hopes that hurt and the dreams that hover,
300   Shall they not vanish away and apart?
But thou, thou art sure, thou art older than earth;
Thou art strong for death and fruitful of birth;
Thy depths conceal and thy gulfs discover;
    From the first thou wert; in the end thou art.

305 And grief shall endure not forever, I know.
    As things that are not shall these things be;
We shall live through seasons of sun and of snow,
    And none be grievous as this to me.
We shall hear, as one in a trance that hears,
310 The sound of time, the rhyme of the years;
Wrecked hope and passionate pain will grow
    As tender things of a springtide sea.

Sea-fruit that swings in the waves that hiss,
    Drowned gold and purple and royal rings.
315 And all time past, was it all for this?
    Times unforgotten, and treasures of things?

Swift years of liking and sweet long laughter,
That wist° not well of the years thereafter   *know*
Till love woke, smitten at heart by a kiss,
320   With lips that trembled and trailing wings?

There lived a singer in France of old
    By the tideless dolorous midland sea.
In a land of sand and ruin and gold
    There shone one woman, and none but she.
325 And finding life for her love's sake fail,
Being fain to see her, he bade set sail,
Touched land, and saw her as life grew cold,
    And praised God, seeing; and so died he.

Died, praising God for his gift and grace:
330   For she bowed down to him weeping, and said
"Live"; and her tears were shed on his face
    Or ever the life in his face was shed.
The sharp tears fell through her hair, and stung
Once, and her close lips touched him and clung
335 Once, and grew one with his lips for a space;
    And so drew back, and the man was dead.

O brother, the gods were good to you.
    Sleep, and be glad while the world endures.
Be well content as the years wear through;
340   Give thanks for life, and the loves and lures;
Give thanks for life, O brother, and death,
For the sweet last sound of her feet, her breath,
For gifts she gave you, gracious and few,
    Tears and kisses, that lady of yours.

345 Rest, and be glad of the gods; but I,
    How shall I praise them, or how take rest?
There is not room under all the sky
    For me that knows not of worst or best,
Dream or desire of the days before,
350 Sweet things or bitterness, any more.
Love will not come to me now though I die,
    As love came close to you, breast to breast.

I shall never be friends again with roses;
    I shall loathe sweet tunes, where a note grown strong
355 Relents and recoils, and climbs and closes,
    As a wave of the sea turned back by song.

There are sounds where the soul's delight takes fire,
Face to face with its own desire;
A delight that rebels, a desire that reposes;
360   I shall hate sweet music my whole life long.

The pulse of war and passion of wonder,
The heavens that murmur, the sounds that shine,
The stars that sing and the loves that thunder,
The music burning at heart like wine,
365 An armed archangel whose hands raise up
All senses mixed in the spirit's cup
Till flesh and spirit are molten in sunder—
These things are over, and no more mine.

These were a part of the playing I heard
370   Once, ere my love and my heart were at strife;
Love that sings and hath wings as a bird,
Balm of the wound and heft of the knife.
Fairer than earth is the sea, and sleep
Than overwatching of eyes that weep,
375 Now time has done with his one sweet word,
The wine and leaven of lovely life.

I shall go my ways, tread out my measure,
Fill the days of my daily breath
With fugitive things not good to treasure,
380   Do as the world doth, say as it saith;
But if we had loved each other—O sweet,
Had you felt, lying under the palms of your feet,
The heart of my heart, beating harder with pleasure
To feel you tread it to dust and death—

385 Ah, had I not taken my life up and given
All that life gives and the years let go,
The wine and honey, the balm and leaven,
The dreams reared high and the hopes brought low?
Come life, come death, not a word be said;
390 Should I lose you living, and vex you dead?
I never shall tell you on earth; and in heaven,
If I cry to you then, will you hear or know?
—1866

Itylus[1]

Swallow, my sister, O sister swallow,
How can thine heart be full of the spring?
A thousand summers are over and dead.
What hast thou found in the spring to follow?
5   What hast thou found in thine heart to sing?
What wilt thou do when the summer is shed?

O swallow, sister, O fair swift swallow,
Why wilt thou fly after spring to the south,
The soft south whither thine heart is set?
10 Shall not the grief of the old time follow?
Shall not the song thereof cleave to thy mouth?
Hast thou forgotten ere I forget?

Sister, my sister, O fleet sweet swallow,
Thy way is long to the sun and the south;
15   But I, fulfilled of my heart's desire,
Shedding my song upon height, upon hollow,
From tawny body and sweet small mouth
Feed the heart of the night with fire.

I the nightingale all spring through,
20   O swallow, sister, O changing swallow,
All spring through till the spring be done,
Clothed with the light of the night on the dew,
Sing, while the hours and the wild birds follow,
Take flight and follow and find the sun.

25 Sister, my sister, O soft light swallow,
Though all things feast in the spring's guest chamber,
How hast thou heart to be glad thereof yet?
For where thou fliest I shall not follow,
Till life forget and death remember,
30   Till thou remember and I forget.

---

[1] *Itylus* In Greek mythology, son of Tereus, the King of Thrace, and Procne. After Tereus raped Procne's sister Philomela and cut out her tongue to silence her, Procne murdered her son, cut up his flesh, and served him to Tereus as an act of vengeance. The gods then transformed Procne into a nightingale and Philomela into a swallow.

Swallow, my sister, O singing swallow,
    I know not how thou hast heart to sing.
        Hast thou the heart? is it all past over?
Thy lord the summer is good to follow,
35   And fair the feet of thy lover the spring:
        But what wilt thou say to the spring thy lover?

O swallow, sister, O fleeting swallow,
    My heart in me is a molten ember
        And over my head the waves have met.
40 But thou wouldst tarry or I would follow,
    Could I forget or thou remember,
        Couldst thou remember and I forget.

O sweet stray sister, O shifting swallow,
    The heart's division divideth us.
45   Thy heart is light as a leaf of a tree;
But mine goes forth among sea-gulfs hollow
    To the place of the slaying of Itylus,
        The feast of Daulis,[1] the Thracian sea.

O swallow, sister, O rapid swallow,
50   I pray thee sing not a little space.
        Are not the roofs and the lintels wet?
The woven web that was plain to follow,
    The small slain body, the flowerlike face,
        Can I remember if thou forget?

55 O sister, sister, thy first-begotten!
    The hands that cling and the feet that follow,
        The voice of the child's blood crying yet.
Who hath remembered me? who hath forgotten?
    Thou hast forgotten, O summer swallow,
60   But the world shall end when I forget.
—1866

---

[1] *feast of Daulis* Feast at which Tereus unwittingly ate Itylus's flesh.

Hymn to Proserpine[2]
(*After the Proclamation in Rome of the Christian Faith*[3])

Vicisti, Galilæ[4]

I have lived long enough, having seen one thing, that love hath an end;
Goddess and maiden and queen, be near me now and befriend.
Thou art more than the day or the morrow, the seasons that laugh or that weep;
For these give joy and sorrow; but thou, Proserpina, sleep.
5 Sweet is the treading of wine, and sweet the feet of the dove;
But a goodlier gift is thine than foam of the grapes or love.
Yea, is not even Apollo,[5] with hair and harpstring of gold,
A bitter God to follow, a beautiful God to behold?
I am sick of singing: the bays burn deep and chafe: I am fain
10 To rest a little from praise and grievous pleasure and pain.
For the Gods we know not of, who give us our daily breath,
We know they are cruel as love or life, and lovely as death.
O Gods dethroned and deceased, cast forth, wiped out in a day!
From your wrath is the world released, redeemed from your chains, men say.

---

[2] *Proserpine* In Roman mythology, daughter of Jupiter and Ceres and wife of Pluto, King of the underworld, who stole her from her mother.

[3] *Proclamation ... Faith* Roman Emperor Constantine the Great legalized the Christian faith when he proclaimed the Edict of Milan in 313 CE.

[4] *Vicisti, Galilæ* Latin: "Thou hast conquered, Galilee," said to be the dying words in 363 of Julian the Apostate, half-brother of Constantine the Great. Julian eventually became emperor after the deaths of Constantine I and II; he was a pagan who opposed instituting Christianity as the state religion (as it was eventually proclaimed by Emperor Theodosius in 380).

[5] *Apollo* Greek sun god; also god of the arts.

15   New Gods are crowned in the city; their flowers have
       broken your rods;
   They are merciful, clothed with pity, the young
       compassionate Gods.
   But for me their new device is barren, the days are bare;
   Things long past over suffice, and men forgotten that
       were.
   Time and the Gods are at strife; ye dwell in the midst
       thereof,
20   Draining a little life from the barren breasts of love.
   I say to you, cease, take rest; yea, I say to you all, be at
       peace,
   Till the bitter milk of her breast and the barren bosom
       shall cease.
   Wilt thou yet take all, Galilean? but these thou shalt
       not take,
   The laurel, the palms and the pæan,[1] the breast of the
       nymphs in the brake;[2]
25   Breasts more soft than a dove's that tremble with
       tenderer breath;
   And all the wings of the Loves,[3] and all the joy before
       death;
   All the feet of the hours that sound as a single lyre,
   Dropped and deep in the flowers, with strings that
       flicker like fire.
   More than these wilt thou give, things fairer than all
       these things?
30   Nay, for a little we live, and life hath mutable wings.
   A little while and we die; shall life not thrive as it may?
   For no man under the sky lives twice, outliving his day.
   And grief is a grievous thing, and a man hath enough
       of his tears:
   Why should he labour, and bring fresh grief to
       blacken his years?
35   Thou hast conquered, O pale Galilean; the world has
       grown grey from thy breath;
   We have drunken of things Lethean,[4] and fed on the
       fullness of death.
   Laurel is green for a season, and love is sweet for a day;

---

1 *pæan* Hymn of praise.

2 *brake* Ferns.

3 *Loves* Cupids or other gods representing sexual love.

4 *Lethean* Of the Greek mythological river Lethe in Hades (the
underworld), the waters of which cause the dead to forget the past;
also called the "River of Oblivion."

   But love grows bitter with treason, and laurel outlives
       not May.
   Sleep, shall we sleep after all? for the world is not
       sweet in the end;
40   For the old faiths loosen and fall, the new years ruin
       and rend.
   Fate is a sea without shore, and the soul is a rock that
       abides;
   But her ears are vexed with the roar and her face with
       the foam of the tides.
   O lips that the live blood faints in, the leavings of
       racks and rods!
   O ghastly glories of saints, dead limbs of gibbeted
       Gods!
45   Though all men abase them before you in spirit, and
       all knees bend,
   I kneel not neither adore you, but standing, look to
       the end.
   All delicate days and pleasant, all spirits and sorrows
       are cast
   Far out with the foam of the present that sweeps to
       the surf of the past:
   Where beyond the extreme sea-wall, and between the
       remote sea-gates,
50   Waste water washes, and tall ships founder, and deep
       death waits:
   Where, mighty with deepening sides, clad about with
       the seas as with wings,
   And impelled of invisible tides, and fulfilled of
       unspeakable things,
   White-eyed and poisonous-finned, shark-toothed and
       serpentine-curled,
   Rolls, under the whitening wind of the future, the
       wave of the world.
55   The depths stand naked in sunder behind it, the
       storms flee away;
   In the hollow before it the thunder is taken and
       snared as a prey;
   In its sides is the north-wind bound; and its salt is of
       all men's tears;
   With light of ruin, and sound of changes, and pulse of
       years:
   With travail of day after day, and with trouble of hour
       upon hour;

60 And bitter as blood is the spray; and the crests are as
    fangs that devour:

And its vapour and storm of its steam as the sighing of
    spirits to be;

And its noise as the noise in a dream; and its depth as
    the roots of the sea:

And the height of its heads as the height of the utmost
    stars of the air:

And the ends of the earth at the might thereof
    tremble, and time is made bare.

65 Will ye bridle the deep sea with reins, will ye chasten
    the high sea with rods?

Will ye take her to chain her with chains, who is older
    than all ye Gods?

All ye as a wind shall go by, as a fire shall ye pass and
    be past;

Ye are Gods, and behold, ye shall die, and the waves
    be upon you at last.

In the darkness of time, in the deeps of the years, in
    the changes of things,

70 Ye shall sleep as a slain man sleeps, and the world shall
    forget you for kings.

Though the feet of thine high priests tread where thy
    lords and our forefathers trod,

Though these that were Gods are dead, and thou
    being dead art a God,

Though before thee the throned Cytherean[1] be fallen,
    and hidden her head,

Yet thy kingdom shall pass, Galilean, thy dead shall go
    down to thee dead.

75 Of the maiden thy mother men sing as a goddess with
    grace clad around;

Thou art throned where another was king; where
    another was queen she is crowned.

Yea, once we had sight of another: but now she is
    queen, say these.

Not as thine, not as thine was our mother, a blossom
    of flowering seas,

Clothed round with the world's desire as with
    raiment, and fair as the foam,

80 And fleeter than kindled fire, and a goddess, and
    mother of Rome.

For thine came pale and a maiden, and sister to
    sorrow; but ours,

Her deep hair heavily laden with odour and colour of
    flowers,

White rose of the rose-white water, a silver splendour,
    a flame,

Bent down unto us that besought her, and earth grew
    sweet with her name.

85 For thine came weeping, a slave among slaves, and
    rejected; but she

Came flushed from the full-flushed wave, and
    imperial, her foot on the sea.

And the wonderful waters knew her, the winds and
    the viewless ways,

And the roses grew rosier, and bluer the sea-blue
    stream of the bays.

Ye are fallen, our lords, by what token? we wist[2] that
    ye should not fall.

90 Ye were all so fair that are broken; and one more fair
    than ye all.

But I turn to her still, having seen she shall surely
    abide in the end;

Goddess and maiden and queen, be near me now and
    befriend.

O daughter of earth, of my mother, her crown and
    blossom of birth,

I am also, I also, thy brother; I go as I came unto earth.

95 In the night where thine eyes are as moons are in
    heaven, the night where thou art,

Where the silence is more than all tunes, where sleep
    overflows from the heart,

Where the poppies[3] are sweet as the rose in our world,
    and the red rose is white,

And the wind falls faint as it blows with the fume of
    the flowers of the night.

And the murmur of spirits that sleep in the shadow of
    Gods from afar

100 Grows dim in thine ears and deep as the deep dim
    soul of a star,

In the sweet low light of thy face, under heavens
    untrod by the sun,

---

[1] *throned Cytherean* Venus, Roman goddess of love and beauty
(Aphrodite in Greek mythology), who was born of the foam of the
sea and, according to some accounts, came ashore on the Greek
island of Cythera.

[2] *wist* Know.

[3] *poppies* Flowers representing sleep, sacred to Proserpine.

Let my soul with their souls find place, and forget
    what is done and undone.
Thou art more than the Gods who number the days
    of our temporal breath;
For these give labour and slumber; but thou,
    Proserpina, death.
105 Therefore now at thy feet I abide for a season in
    silence. I know
I shall die as my fathers died, and sleep as they sleep;
    even so.
For the glass of the years is brittle wherein we gaze for
    a span;
A little soul for a little bears up this corpse which is
    man.[1]
So long I endure, no longer; and laugh not again,
    neither weep.
110 For there is no God found stronger than death; and
    death is a sleep.
—1866

The Leper[2]

Nothing is better, I well think,
    Than love; the hidden well-water
Is not so delicate to drink:
    This was well seen of me and her.

5 I served her in a royal house;
    I served her wine and curious meat.
For will to kiss between her brows,
    I had no heart to sleep or eat.

Mere scorn God knows she had of me,
10   A poor scribe, nowise great or fair,
Who plucked his clerk's hood back to see
    Her curled-up lips and amorous hair.

I vex my head with thinking this.
    Yea, though God always hated me,

15 And hates me now that I can kiss
    Her eyes, plait° up her hair to see   *braid*
How she then wore it on the brows,
    Yet am I glad to have her dead
Here in this wretched wattled[3] house
20   Where I can kiss her eyes and head.

Nothing is better, I well know,
    Than love; no amber in cold sea
Or gathered berries under snow:
    That is well seen of her and me.

25 Three thoughts I make my pleasure of:
    First I take heart and think of this:
That knight's gold hair she chose to love,
    His mouth she had such will to kiss.

Then I remember that sundawn
30   I brought him by a privy[4] way
Out at her lattice, and thereon
    What gracious words she found to say.

(Cold rushes for such little feet—
    Both feet could lie into my hand.
35 A marvel was it of my sweet
    Her upright body could so stand.)

"Sweet friend, God give you thank and grace;
    Now am I clean and whole of shame,
Nor shall men burn me in the face
40   For my sweet fault that scandals them."

I tell you over word by word.
    She, sitting edgewise on her bed,
Holding her feet, said thus. The third,
    A sweeter thing than these, I said.

45 God, that makes time and ruins it
    And alters not, abiding God,
Changed with disease her body sweet,
    The body of love wherein she abode.

---

[1] [Swinburne's note] ψυχάριον εἶ βαστάζον νεκρόν.—Epictetus [Greek: "You are a little soul, carrying around a corpse."]

[2] *The Leper* In an early version of this poem, Swinburne attached an endnote in an attempt to deceive the public into believing that it was based on a true story, *Grandes Chroniques de France*, 1505.

[3] *wattled* Built out of intertwining twigs and mud.

[4] *privy* Here, private, secluded.

Love is more sweet and comelier
50   Than a dove's throat strained out to sing.
All they spat out and cursed at her
    And cast her forth for a base thing.

They cursed her, seeing how God had wrought
    This curse to plague her, a curse of his.
55 Fools were they surely, seeing not
    How sweeter than all sweet she is.

He that had held her by the hair,
    With kissing lips blinding her eyes,
Felt her bright bosom, strained and bare,
60   Sigh under him, with short mad cries

Out of her throat and sobbing mouth
    And body broken up with love,
With sweet hot tears his lips were loth°   *averse*
    Her own should taste the savour of,

65 Yea, he inside whose grasp all night
    Her fervent body leapt or lay,
Stained with sharp kisses red and white,
    Found her a plague to spurn away.

I hid her in this wattled house,
70   I served her water and poor bread.
For joy to kiss between her brows
    Time upon time I was nigh dead.

Bread failed; we got but well-water
    And gathered grass with dropping seed;
75 I had such joy of kissing her,
    I had small care to sleep or feed.

Sometimes when service made me glad
    The sharp tears leapt between my lids,
Falling on her, such joy I had
80   To do the service God forbids.

"I pray you let me be at peace,
    Get hence, make room for me to die."
She said that: her poor lip would cease,
    Put up to mine, and turn to cry.

85 I said, "Bethink yourself how love
    Fared in us twain, what either did;
Shall I unclothe my soul thereof?
    That I should do this, God forbid."

Yea, though God hateth us, he knows
90   That hardly in a little thing
Love faileth of the work it does
    Till it grow ripe for gathering.

Six months, and now my sweet is dead
    A trouble takes me; I know not
95 If all were done well, all well said,
    No word or tender deed forgot.

Too sweet, for the least part in her,
    To have shed life out by fragments; yet,
Could the close mouth catch breath and stir,
100   I might see something I forget.

Six months, and I sit still and hold
    In two cold palms her cold two feet.
Her hair, half grey half ruined gold,
    Thrills me and burns me in kissing it.

105 Love bites and stings me through, to see
    Her keen face made of sunken bones.
Her worn-off eyelids madden me,
    That were shot through with purple once.

She said, "Be good with me; I grow
110   So tired for shame's sake, I shall die
If you say nothing": even so.
    And she is dead now, and shame put by.

Yea, and the scorn she had of me
    In the old time, doubtless vexed her then.
115 I never should have kissed her. See
    What fools God's anger makes of men!

She might have loved me a little too,
    Had I been humbler for her sake.
But that new shame could make love new
120   She saw not—yet her shame did make.

I took too much upon my love,
    Having for such mean service done
Her beauty and all the ways thereof,
    Her face and all the sweet thereon.

125 Yea, all this while I tended her,
    I know the old love held fast his part,
I know the old scorn waxed heavier,
    Mixed with sad wonder, in her heart.

It may be all my love went wrong—
130   A scribe's work writ awry and blurred,
Scrawled after the blind evensong[1]—
    Spoilt music with no perfect word.

But surely I would fain have done
    All things the best I could. Perchance
135 Because I failed, came short of one,
    She kept at heart that other man's.

I am grown blind with all these things:
    It may be now she hath in sight
Some better knowledge; still there clings
140   The old question. Will not God do right?
    —1866

A Forsaken Garden

In a coign° of the cliff between lowland and   *wedge*
    highland,
    At the sea-down's edge between windward and lee,
Walled round with rocks as an inland island,
    The ghost of a garden fronts the sea.
5 A girdle of brushwood and thorn encloses
    The steep square slope of the blossomless bed
Where the weeds that grew green from the graves of
    its roses
    Now lie dead.

The fields fall southward, abrupt and broken,
10   To the low last edge of the long lone land.
If a step should sound or a word be spoken,

Would a ghost not rise at the strange guest's hand?
So long have the grey bare walks lain guestless,
    Through branches and briars if a man make way,
15 He shall find no life but the sea-wind's, restless
    Night and day.

The dense hard passage is blind and stifled
    That crawls by a track none turn to climb
To the strait° waste place that the years have   *narrow*
    rifled
20   Of all but the thorns that are touched not of time.
The thorns he spares when the rose is taken;
    The rocks are left when he wastes the plain.
The wind that wanders, the weeds wind-shaken,
    These remain.

25 Not a flower to be pressed of the foot that falls not;
    As the heart of a dead man the seed-lots are dry;
From the thicket of thorns whence the nightingale
    calls not,
    Could she call, there were never a rose to reply.
Over the meadows that blossom and wither
30   Rings but the note of a sea-bird's song;
Only the sun and the rain come hither
    All year long.

The sun burns sere and the rain dishevels
    One gaunt bleak blossom of scentless breath.
35 Only the wind here hovers and revels
    In a round where life seems barren as death.
Here there was laughing of old, there was weeping,
    Haply, of lovers none ever will know,
Whose eyes went seaward a hundred sleeping
40   Years ago.

Heart handfast in heart as they stood, "Look thither,"
    Did he whisper? "look forth from the flowers to
    the sea;
For the foam-flowers endure when the rose-blossoms
    wither,
    And men that love lightly may die—but we?"
45 And the same wind sang and the same waves
    whitened,

---

[1] *evensong* Evening prayers.

And or ever the garden's last petals were shed,
In the lips that had whispered, the eyes that had
    lightened,
    Love was dead.

Or they loved their life through, and then went whither?
50   And were one to the end—but what end who knows?
Love deep as the sea as a rose must wither,
    As the rose-red seaweed that mocks the rose.
Shall the dead take thought for the dead to love them?
    What love was ever as deep as a grave?
55 They are loveless now as the grass above them
    Or the wave.

All are at one now, roses and lovers,
    Not known of the cliffs and the fields and the sea.
Not a breath of the time that has been hovers
60   In the air now soft with a summer to be.
Not a breath shall there sweeten the seasons hereafter
    Of the flowers or the lovers that laugh now or weep,
When as they that are free now of weeping and
      laughter
    We shall sleep.

65 Here death may deal not again forever;
    Here change may come not till all change end.
From the graves they have made they shall rise up
      never,
    Who have left nought living to ravage and rend.
Earth, stones, and thorns of the wild ground growing,
70   While the sun and the rain live, these shall be;
Till a last wind's breath upon all these blowing
    Roll the sea.

Till the slow sea rise and the sheer cliff crumble,
    Till terrace and meadow the deep gulfs drink,
75 Till the strength of the waves of the high tides humble
    The fields that lessen, the rocks that shrink,
Here now in his triumph where all things falter,
    Stretched out on the spoils that his own hand
      spread,
As a god self-slain on his own strange altar,
80   Death lies dead.
—1876

The Ballad of Villon and Fat Madge

'Tis no sin for a man to labour in his vocation.—FALSTAFF [1]
The night cometh, when no man can work. [2]

What though the beauty I love and serve be cheap,
    Ought you to take me for a beast or fool?
All things a man could wish are in her keep;
    For her I turn swashbuckler in love's school.
5   When folk drop in, I take my pot [3] and stool
And fall to drinking with no more ado.
I fetch them bread, fruit, cheese, and water, too;
    I say all's right so long as I'm well paid;
"Look in again when your flesh troubles you,
10   Inside this brothel where we drive our trade."

But soon the devil's among us flesh and fell, [4]
    When penniless to bed comes Madge my whore;
I loathe the very sight of her like hell.
    I snatch gown, girdle, surcoat, all she wore,
15   And tell her, these shall stand against her score.
She grips her hips with both hands, cursing God,
Swearing by Jesus' body, bones, and blood,
    That they shall not. Then I, no whit dismayed,
Cross her cracked nose with some stray shiver of wood
20   Inside this brothel where we drive our trade.

When all's made up she drops me a windy word,
    Bloat like a beetle puffed and poisonous:
Grins, thumps my pate, and calls me dickey-bird, [5]
    And cuffs me with a fist that's ponderous.
25   We sleep like logs, being drunken both of us;
Then when we wake her womb begins to stir;
To save her seed she gets me under her
    Wheezing and shining, flat as planks are laid:
And thus she spoils me for a whoremonger
30   Inside this brothel where we drive our trade.

Blow, hail or freeze, I've bread here baked rent-free!

---

[1] *'Tis no sin ... vocation* From Shakespeare's *1 Henry IV* 1.2.

[2] *The night ... work* From John 9.4.

[3] *pot* Drinking vessel, usually for ale.

[4] *flesh and fell* Phrase meaning flesh and skin, or the complete covering of the body; from Shakespeare's *King Lear* 5.3.

[5] *dickey-bird* Any one of a number of small songbirds.

Whoring's my trade, and my whore pleases me;
    Bad cat, bad rat; we're just the same if weighed.
We that love filth, filth follows us, you see;
35 Honour flees from us, as from here we flee
    Inside this brothel where we drive our trade.
  —1910

Anactoria[1]

τίνος αὖ τὺ πειθοῖ
μὰψ σαγηνεύσας φιλότατα ;[2]—SAPPHO

My life is bitter with thy love; thine eyes
Blind me, thy tresses burn me, thy sharp sighs
Divide my flesh and spirit with soft sound,
And my blood strengthens, and my veins abound.
5 I pray thee sigh not, speak not, draw not breath;
Let life burn down, and dream it is not death.
I would the sea had hidden us, the fire
(Wilt thou fear that, and fear not my desire?)
Severed the bones that bleach, the flesh that cleaves,
10 And let our sifted ashes drop like leaves.
I feel thy blood against my blood: my pain
Pains thee, and lips bruise lips, and vein stings vein.
Let fruit be crushed on fruit, let flower on flower,
Breast kindle breast, and either burn one hour.
15 Why wilt thou follow lesser loves? are thine
Too weak to bear these hands and lips of mine?
I charge thee for my life's sake, O too sweet
To crush love with thy cruel faultless feet,
I charge thee keep thy lips from hers or his,
20 Sweetest, till theirs be sweeter than my kiss:
Lest I too lure, a swallow for a dove,

Erotion or Erinna[3] to my love.
I would my love could kill thee; I am satiated
With seeing thee live, and fain would have thee dead.
25 I would earth had thy body as fruit to eat,
And no mouth but some serpent's found thee sweet.
I would find grievous ways to have thee slain,
Intense device, and superflux of pain;
Vex thee with amorous agonies, and shake
30 Life at thy lips, and leave it there to ache;
Strain out thy soul with pangs too soft to kill,
Intolerable interludes, and infinite ill;
Relapse and reluctation° of the breath,   *resistance*
Dumb tunes and shuddering semitones of death.
35 I am weary of all thy words and soft strange ways,
Of all love's fiery nights and all his days,
And all the broken kisses salt as brine
That shuddering lips make moist with waterish wine,
And eyes the bluer for all those hidden hours
40 That pleasure fills with tears and feeds from flowers,
Fierce at the heart with fire that half comes through,
But all the flowerlike white stained round with blue;
The fervent underlid, and that above
Lifted with laughter or abashed with love;
45 Thine amorous girdle,[4] full of thee and fair,
And leavings of the lilies in thine hair.
Yea, all sweet words of thine and all thy ways,
And all the fruit of nights and flower of days,
And stinging lips wherein the hot sweet brine
50 That Love was born of burns and foams like wine,[5]
And eyes insatiable of amorous hours,
Fervent as fire and delicate as flowers,
Coloured like night at heart, but cloven through
Like night with flame, dyed round like night with blue,
55 Clothed with deep eyelids under and above—
Yea, all thy beauty sickens me with love;
Thy girdle empty of thee and now not fair,
And ruinous lilies in thy languid hair.
Ah, take no thought for Love's sake; shall this be,
60 And she who loves thy lover not love thee?

---

[1] *Anactoria* One of the lovers of Sappho, a Greek lyric poet of the sixth century BCE. Swinburne once said: "Judging even from the mutilated fragments fallen within our reach from the broken altar of her sacrifice of song, I for one have always agreed with all Grecian tradition in thinking Sappho to be beyond all question and comparison the very greatest poet that ever lived. Aeschylus is the greatest poet who was also a prophet; Shakespeare is the best dramatist who was also a poet, but Sappho is simply nothing less—as she certainly is nothing more—than the greatest poet who ever was at all."

[2] τίνος ... φιλότατα Greek: "Whom shall I make to give thee room in her heart's love?"

[3] *Erotion* Greek man's name; *Erinna* Greek woman's name; Sappho had a student (who may have also been a lover) named Erinna.

[4] *girdle* I.e., belt. Here, symbol of Aphrodite, the Greek goddess of love.

[5] *Love ... wine* Aphrodite was born out of the foam of the sea.

Sweet soul, sweet mouth of all that laughs and lives,
Mine is she, very mine; and she forgives.
For I beheld in sleep the light that is
In her high place in Paphos,[1] heard the kiss
65 Of body and soul that mix with eager tears
And laughter stinging through the eyes and ears;
Saw Love, as burning flame from crown to feet,
Imperishable, upon her storied seat;
Clear eyelids lifted toward the north and south,
70 A mind of many colours, and a mouth
Of many tunes and kisses; and she bowed,
With all her subtle face laughing aloud,
Bowed down upon me, saying, "Who doth thee wrong,
Sappho?" but thou—thy body is the song,
75 Thy mouth the music; thou art more than I,
Though my voice die not till the whole world die;
Though men that hear it madden; though love weep,
Though nature change, though shame be charmed to
    sleep.
Ah, wilt thou slay me lest I kiss thee dead?
80 Yet the queen laughed from her sweet heart and said:
"Even she that flies shall follow for thy sake,
And she shall give thee gifts that would not take,
Shall kiss that would not kiss thee" (yea, kiss me)
"When thou wouldst not"—when I would not kiss thee!
85 Ah, more to me than all men as thou art,
Shall not my songs assuage her at the heart?
Ah, sweet to me as life seems sweet to death,
Why should her wrath fill thee with fearful breath?
Nay, sweet, for is she God alone? hath she
90 Made earth and all the centuries of the sea,
Taught the sun ways to travel, woven most fine
The moonbeams, shed the starbeams forth as wine,
Bound with her myrtles, beaten with her rods,
The young men and the maidens and the gods?
95 Have we not lips to love with, eyes for tears,
And summer and flower of women and of years?
Stars for the foot of morning, and for noon
Sunlight, and exaltation of the moon;
Waters that answer waters, fields that wear

100 Lilies, and languor of the Lesbian[2] air?
Beyond those flying feet of fluttered doves,
Are there not other gods for other loves?
Yea, though she scourge thee, sweetest, for my sake,
Blossom not thorns and flowers not blood should
    break.
105 Ah that my lips were tuneless lips, but pressed
To the bruised blossom of thy scourged white breast!
Ah that my mouth for Muses'[3] milk were fed
On the sweet blood thy sweet small wounds had bled!
That with my tongue I felt them, and could taste
110 The faint flakes from thy bosom to the waist!
That I could drink thy veins as wine, and eat
Thy breasts like honey! that from face to feet
Thy body were abolished and consumed,
And in my flesh thy very flesh entombed!
115 Ah, ah, thy beauty! like a beast it bites,
Stings like an adder, like an arrow smites.
Ah sweet, and sweet again, and seven times sweet
The paces and the pauses of thy feet!
Ah sweeter than all sleep or summer air
120 The fallen fillets° fragrant from thine hair!   *hair ribbons*
Yea, though their alien kisses do me wrong,
Sweeter thy lips than mine with all their song;
Thy shoulders whiter than a fleece of white,
And flower-sweet fingers, good to bruise or bite
125 As honeycomb of the inmost honey-cells,
With almond-shaped and roseleaf-coloured shells,
And blood like purple blossom at the tips
Quivering; and pain made perfect in thy lips
For my sake when I hurt thee; O that I
130 Durst crush thee out of life with love, and die,
Die of thy pain and my delight, and be
Mixed with thy blood and molten into thee!
Would I not plague thee dying overmuch?
Would I not hurt thee perfectly? not touch
135 Thy pores of sense with torture, and make bright,
Thine eyes with bloodlike tears and grievous light
Strike pang from pang as note is struck from note,

---

[1] *Paphos* Island on which, according to some accounts, Aphrodite came ashore after her birth.

[2] *Lesbian* Of the Greek island of Lesbos, where Sappho and Anactoria lived; the common usage of the term "lesbian" is derived from the name of the island and harks back to Sappho's love of women.

[3] *Muses* Nine daughters of Zeus and Mnemosyne, each of whom presided over and provided inspiration for an aspect of learning or the arts.

Catch the sob's middle music in thy throat,
Take thy limbs living, and new-mould with these
140 A lyre of many faultless agonies?
Feed thee with fever and famine and fine drouth,°   *drought*
With perfect pangs convulse thy perfect mouth,
Make thy life shudder in thee and burn afresh,
And wring thy very spirit through the flesh?
145 Cruel? but love makes all that love him well
As wise as heaven and crueller than hell.
Me hath love made more bitter toward thee
Than death toward man; but were I made as he
Who hath made all things to break them one by one,
150 If my feet trod upon the stars and sun
And souls of men as his have always trod,
God knows I might be crueller than God.
For who shall change with prayers or thanksgivings
The mystery of the cruelty of things?
155 Or say what God above all gods and years
With offering and blood-sacrifice of tears,
With lamentation from strange lands, from graves
Where the snake pastures, from scarred mouth of slaves
From prison, and from plunging prows of ships
160 Through flamelike foam of the sea's closing lips—
With thwartings of strange signs, and wind-blown hair
Of comets, desolating the dim air,
When darkness is made fast with seals and bars,
And fierce reluctance of disastrous stars,
165 Eclipse, and sound of shaken hills, and wings
Darkening, and blind inexpiable things—
With sorrow of labouring moons, and altering light
And travail of the planets of the night,
And weeping of the weary Pleiads[1] seven,
170 Feeds the mute melancholy lust of heaven?
Is not his incense bitterness, his meat
Murder? his hidden face and iron feet
Hath not man known, and felt them on their way
Threaten and trample all things and every day?
175 Hath he not sent us hunger? who hath cursed
Spirit and flesh with longing? filled with thirst
Their lips who cried unto him? who bade exceed
The fervid will, fall short the feeble deed,
Bade sink the spirit and the flesh aspire,
180 Pain animate the dust of dead desire,

And life yield up her flower to violent fate?
Him would I reach, him smite, him desecrate,
Pierce the cold lips of God with human breath,
And mix his immortality with death.
185 Why hath he made us? what had all we done
That we should live and loathe the sterile sun,
And with the moon wax paler as she wanes,
And pulse by pulse feel time grow through our veins?
Thee too the years shall cover; thou shalt be
190 As the rose born of one same blood with thee,
As a song sung, as a word said, and fall
Flower-wise, and be not any more at all,
Nor any memory of thee anywhere;
For never Muse has bound above thine hair
195 The high Pierian[2] flower whose graft outgrows
All summer kinship of the mortal rose
And colour of deciduous days, nor shed
Reflex and flush of heaven about thine head,
Nor reddened brows made pale by floral grief
200 With splendid shadow from that lordlier leaf.
Yea, thou shalt be forgotten like spilt wine,
Except these kisses of my lips on thine
Brand them with immortality; but me—
Men shall not see bright fire nor hear the sea,
205 Nor mix their hearts with music, nor behold
Cast forth of heaven, with feet of awful gold
And plumeless wings that make the bright air blind,
Lightning, with thunder for a hound behind
Hunting through fields unfurrowed and unsown,
210 But in the light and laughter, in the moan
And music, and in grasp of lip and hand
And shudder of water that makes felt on land
The immeasurable tremor of all the sea,
Memories shall mix and metaphors of me.
215 Like me shall be the shuddering calm of night,
When all the winds of the world for pure delight
Close lips that quiver and fold up wings that ache;
When nightingales are louder for love's sake,
And leaves tremble like lute-strings or like fire;
220 Like me the one star swooning with desire
Even at the cold lips of the sleepless moon,
As I at thine; like me the waste white noon,
Burnt through with barren sunlight; and like me

---

[1]   *Pleiads*   Seven daughters of Atlas, who were changed into doves and later a constellation of stars after fleeing from Orion, the hunter.

[2]   *Pierian*   From Pieria, Greek district said to be the home of the Muses.

The land-stream and the tide-stream in the sea.
225 I am sick with time as these with ebb and flow,
And by the yearning in my veins I know
The yearning sound of waters; and mine eyes
Burn as that beamless fire which fills the skies
With troubled stars and travailing things of flame;
230 And in my heart the grief consuming them
Labours, and in my veins the thirst of these,
And all the summer travail of the trees
And all the winter sickness; and the earth,
Filled full with deadly works of death and birth,
235 Sore spent with hungry lusts of birth and death,
Has pain like mine in her divided breath;
Her spring of leaves is barren, and her fruit
Ashes; her boughs are burdened, and her root
Fibrous and gnarled with poison; underneath
240 Serpents have gnawn it through with tortuous teeth
Made sharp upon the bones of all the dead,
And wild birds rend her branches overhead.
These, woven as raiment° for his word and   clothing
    thought,
These hath God made, and me as these, and wrought
245 Song, and hath lit it at my lips; and me
Earth shall not gather though she feed on thee.
As a shed tear shalt thou be shed; but I—
Lo, earth may labour, men live long and die,
Years change and stars, and the high God devise
250 New things, and old things wane before his eyes
Who wields and wrecks them, being more strong than
    they—
But, having made me, me he shall not slay.
Nor slay nor satiate, like those herds of his
Who laugh and live a little, and their kiss
255 Contents them, and their loves are swift and sweet,
And sure death grasps and gains them with slow feet,
Love they or hate they, strive or bow their knees—
And all these ends he hath his will of these.
Yea, but albeit he slay me, hating me—
260 Albeit he hide me in the deep dear sea
And cover me with cool wan foam, and ease
This soul of mine as any soul of these,
And give me water and great sweet waves, and make
The very sea's name lordlier for my sake,
265 The whole sea sweeter—albeit I die indeed
And hide myself and sleep and no man heed,

Of me the high God hath not all his will.
Blossom of branches, and on each high hill
Clear air and wind, and under in clamorous vales
270 Fierce noises of the fiery nightingales,
Buds burning in the sudden spring like fire,
The wan washed sand and the waves' vain desire,
Sails seen like blown white flowers at sea, and words
That bring tears swiftest, and long notes of birds
275 Violently singing till the whole world sings—
I Sappho shall be one with all these things,
With all high things forever; and my face
Seen once, my songs once heard in a strange place,
Cleave to men's lives, and waste the days thereof
280 With gladness and much sadness and long love.
Yea, they shall say, earth's womb has borne in vain
New things, and never this best thing again;
Borne days and men, borne fruits and wars and wine,
Seasons and songs, but no song more like mine.
285 And they shall know me as ye who have known me here,
Last year when I loved Atthis,[1] and this year
When I love thee; and they shall praise me, and say
"She hath all time as all we have our day,
Shall she not live and have her will"—even I?
290 Yea, though thou diest, I say I shall not die.
For these shall give me of their souls, shall give
Life, and the days and loves wherewith I live,
Shall quicken me with loving, fill with breath,
Save me and serve me, strive for me with death.
295 Alas, that neither moon nor snow nor dew
Nor all cold things can purge me wholly through,
Assuage me nor allay me nor appease,
Till supreme sleep shall bring me bloodless ease;
Till time wax faint in all his periods;
300 Till fate undo the bondage of the gods,
And lay, to slake and satiate me all through,
Lotus and Lethe[2] on my lips like dew,
And shed around and over and under me
Thick darkness and the insuperable° sea.   unconquerable
—1866

---

[1] *Atthis* The subject of a number of Sappho's poems.

[2] *Lotus* In Greek mythology, plant whose fruit produced a blissful state of forgetfulness when eaten; *Lethe* Greek mythological river in Hades, sometimes called "the waters of oblivion" as those who drank from it forgot the past.

WALTER PATER
1839 – 1894

Known as the leader of the nineteenth-century Aesthetic Movement, the unassuming and reserved critic and theorist Walter Pater was somewhat surprised at the influence his writings commanded because of their advocacy of "art for art's sake." (The phrase *"l'art pour l'art"* was first coined in 1818 by the French philosopher Victor Cousins, who in turn based his theory on Kantian notions of art and beauty.) In the famous conclusion to his collection of essays, *Studies in the History of the Renaissance* (1873), Pater repeated in altered form words he had written in 1868 in his essay, "Poems by William Morris" (1868):

> What we have to do is to be for ever curiously testing new opinions and courting new impressions, never acquiescing in a facile orthodoxy of Comte or Hegel, or of our own. … Great passions may give us this quickened sense of life, ecstasy and sorrow of love, the various forms of enthusiastic activity, disinterested or otherwise, which come naturally to many of us. Only be sure it is passion—that it does yield you this fruit of a quickened, multiplied consciousness. Of such wisdom, the poetic passion, the desire of beauty, the love of art for its sake, has most. For art comes to you proposing frankly to give nothing but the highest quality to your moments as they pass, and simply for those moments' sake.

Without specifically advocating hedonism, Pater was reacting against the prevailing moral aesthetic (articulated compellingly by Carlyle, Ruskin, and Arnold) that charged the artist with ethical responsibilities. The response was in some quarters embarrassingly positive; so influential was this essay upon such "decadents" of the 1890s as Oscar Wilde that Pater withdrew the controversial conclusion from the book's second printing. He allowed it to be reprinted in subsequent editions, while making slight alterations "which bring it closer to my original meaning."

The events of Walter Horatio Pater's early life did not give any indication of the effect his work would eventually have upon Victorian aesthetics. Born in London, Pater lost his father, Dr. Richard Glode Pater, at a young age, and moved with his siblings and mother, Maria Hill Pater, to Enfield. At the age of 13, the year before his mother died, Pater entered the King's School in Canterbury and five years later entered Queen's College, Oxford, where, to his disappointment, he graduated in 1862 with only second class honors. After tutoring for two years (Gerard Manley Hopkins was among his students), Pater became a fellow at Brasenose College. He remained a teacher at Oxford for most of his life. Soon after his appointment, Pater began publishing his critical essays, beginning with "Coleridge's Writings," in which he spoke of abandoning his faith in the High Church for the "religion of art." Previously influenced by Ruskin's *Modern Painters*, Pater began to rethink his notions of ideal beauty upon reading about the classical scholar Johann Winckelmann (1717–68). He set out these thoughts in his essay "Winckelmann," published in the *Westminster Review* in 1867.

In 1873, the essay on Winckelmann and essays on Botticelli, Michelangelo, Leonardo da Vinci, and others, were collected in *The Renaissance*. Pater's preface and conclusion attracted much attention, setting out as they did his Epicurean theories. The "Preface" defines the work of the aesthetic critic:

> The aesthetic critic ... regards all objects with which he has to do, all works of art, and the fairer forms of nature and human life, as powers or forces producing pleasurable sensations, each of a more or less peculiar or unique kind .... What is important ... is not that the critic should possess a correct abstract definition of beauty for the intellect, but a certain kind of temperament, the power of being deeply moved by the presence of beautiful objects. To him all periods, types, schools of taste, are in themselves equal.

For many, Pater's subjective vision of art, literature, and music—and indeed of one's responsibility to enjoy life—appeared self-indulgent and even amoral. The book, however, with its rich and eloquent prose style, established him as an important critic and placed him at the center of a school of aesthetes that included Wilde, Swinburne, and Arthur Symons.

Possibly as a result of the controversy over *The Renaissance*, Pater was passed over for a proctorship at Oxford, and thereafter, although his lectures were popular, he was never considered for important positions at the university. He did, however, continue to publish articles and reviews, and worked on a novel, *Marius the Epicurean* (1885), which brought together his philosophies on art and religion, expanding in fictional form the ideas from the "Conclusion" to his first book. In 1887 he published *Imaginary Portraits*, a series of essays on intellectually and artistically rebellious people; in 1889 *Appreciations: With an Essay on Style*; and in 1893 a group of lectures, *Plato and Platonism*. His literary style was so meticulous and eloquent that decades after his death in 1894, Yeats reprinted Pater's description of the *Mona Lisa* in verse form as the opening piece in the *Oxford Book of Modern Verse* (1936). This style, along with his theories of aesthetics, influenced not only Yeats but many modernists, most notably Virginia Woolf and Ezra Pound.

Pater died suddenly, at Oxford, on 30 July 1894, at the age of 54. He is buried at Oxford's Holywell Cemetery.

⌘ ⌘ ⌘

from *The Renaissance: Studies in Art and Poetry*

PREFACE

Many attempts have been made by writers on art and poetry to define beauty in the abstract, to express it in the most general terms, to find a universal formula for it. The value of these attempts has most often been in the suggestive and penetrating things said by the way. Such discussions help us very little to enjoy what has been well done in art or poetry, to discriminate between what is more and what is less excellent in them, or to use words like beauty, excellence, art, poetry, with a more precise meaning than they would otherwise have. Beauty, like all other qualities presented to human experience, is relative; and the definition of it becomes unmeaning and useless in proportion to its abstractness. To define beauty, not in the most abstract, but in the most concrete terms possible, to find, not a universal formula for it, but the formula which expresses most adequately this or that special manifestation of it, is the aim of the true student of aesthetics.

"To see the object as in itself it really is,"[1] has been justly said to be the aim of all true criticism whatever; and in aesthetic criticism the first step towards seeing

---

[1] *"To see ... really is"* From Matthew Arnold's *The Function of Criticism at the Present Time* (1865).

one's object as it really is, is to know one's own impression as it really is, to discriminate it, to realize it distinctly. The objects with which aesthetic criticism deals—music, poetry, artistic and accomplished forms of human life—are indeed receptacles of so many powers or forces; they possess, like the products of nature, so many virtues or qualities. What is this song or picture, this engaging personality presented in life or in a book, to *me*? What effect does it really produce on me? Does it give me pleasure? and if so, what sort or degree of pleasure?

How is my nature modified by its presence, and under its influence? The answers to these questions are the original facts with which the aesthetic critic has to do; and, as in the study of light, of morals, of number, one must realise such primary data for oneself, or not at all. And he who experiences these impressions strongly, and drives directly at the discrimination and analysis of them, has no need to trouble himself with the abstract question what beauty is in itself, or what its exact relation to truth or experience—metaphysical questions, as unprofitable as metaphysical questions elsewhere. He may pass them all by as being, answerable or not, of no interest to him.

The aesthetic critic, then, regards all the objects with which he has to do, all works of art, and the fairer forms of nature and human life, as powers or forces producing pleasurable sensations, each of a more or less peculiar and unique kind. This influence he feels, and wishes to explain, analyzing it, and reducing it to its elements. To him, the picture, the landscape, the engaging personality in life or in a book, *La Gioconda*, the hills of Carrara, Pico of Mirandola,[1] are valuable for their virtues, as we say, in speaking of a herb, a wine, a gem, for the property each has of affecting one with a special, a unique, impression of pleasure. Our education becomes complete in proportion as our susceptibility to these impressions increases in depth and variety. And the function of the aesthetic critic is to distinguish, analyze, and separate from its adjuncts, the virtue by which a picture, a

landscape, a fair personality in life or in a book, produces this special impression of beauty or pleasure, to indicate what the source of that impression is, and under what conditions it is experienced. His end is reached when he has disengaged that virtue, and noted it, as a chemist notes some natural element, for himself and others; and the rule for those who would reach this end is stated with great exactness in the words of a recent critic of Sainte-Beuve: *De se borner à connaître de près les belles choses, et à s'en nourrir en exquis amateurs, en humanistes accomplis.*[2]

What is important, then, is not that the critic should possess a correct abstract definition of beauty for the intellect, but a certain kind of temperament, the power of being deeply moved by the presence of beautiful objects. He will remember always that beauty exists in many forms. To him all periods, types, schools of taste, are in themselves equal. In all ages there have been some excellent workmen, and some excellent work done. The question he asks is always: In whom did the stir, the genius, the sentiment of the period find itself? where was the receptacle of its refinement, its elevation, its taste? "The ages are all equal," says William Blake, "but genius is always above its age."[3]

Often it will require great nicety to disengage this virtue from the commoner elements with which it may be found in combination. Few artists, not Goethe or Byron[4] even, work quite cleanly, casting off all *débris*, and leaving us only what the heat of their imagination has wholly fused and transformed. Take, for instance, the writings of Wordsworth. The heat of his genius, entering into the substance of his work, has crystallised a part, but only a part, of it; and in that great mass of verse there is much which might well be forgotten. But scattered up and down it, sometimes fusing and transforming entire compositions, like the *Stanzas on Resolu-*

---

[1] *La Gioconda* The painting the *Mona Lisa* (1506) by Leonardo da Vinci, the subject of chapter six of Pater's *The Renaissance*; *Carrara* Region in Italy, center of the marble industry; *Pico of Mirandola* Italian Neoplatonist philosopher (1463–94), the subject of chapter two of *The Renaissance*.

[2] *De se borner … accomplis* Quotation by French literary critic Charles Augustin Sainte-Beuve (1804–69): "To restrict themselves with knowing beautiful things thoroughly and to nourish themselves by these, as do perceptive amateurs and accomplished humanists."

[3] *"The ages … age"* From Blake's annotations to *The Works of Sir Joshua Reynolds* (1798).

[4] *Goethe … Byron* Goethe Johann Wolfgang von Goethe (1749–1832), German novelist, playwright, and natural philosopher; *Byron* George Gordon Lord Byron (1788–1824), English Romantic poet.

tion and Independence, and the *Ode on the Recollections of Childhood*,[1] sometimes, as if at random, depositing a fine crystal here or there, in a matter it does not wholly search through and transform, we trace the action of his unique, incommunicable faculty, that strange, mystical sense of a life in natural things, and of man's life as a part of nature, drawing strength and colour and character from local influences, from the hills and streams, and from natural sights and sounds. Well! that is the *virtue*, the active principle in Wordsworth's poetry; and then the function of the critic of Wordsworth is to follow up that active principle, to disengage it, to mark the degree in which it penetrates his verse.

The subjects of the following studies are taken from the history of the *Renaissance*, and touch what I think the chief points in that complex, many-sided movement. I have explained in the first of them what I understand by the word, giving it a much wider scope than was intended by those who originally used it to denote only that revival of classical antiquity in the fifteenth century which was but one of many results of a general excitement and enlightening of the human mind, of which the great aim and achievements of what, as Christian art, is often falsely opposed to the Renaissance, were another result. This outbreak of the human spirit may be traced far into the middle age itself, with its qualities already clearly pronounced, the care for physical beauty, the worship of the body, the breaking down of those limits which the religious system of the middle age imposed on the heart and the imagination. I have taken as an example of this movement, this earlier Renaissance within the middle age itself, and as an expression of its qualities, two little compositions in early French, not because they constitute the best possible expression of them, but because they help the unity of my series, inasmuch as the Renaissance ends also in France, in French poetry, in a phase of which the writings of Joachim du Bellay[2] are in many ways the most perfect illustration; the Renaissance thus putting

forth in France an aftermath, a wonderful later growth, the products of which have to the full that subtle and delicate sweetness which belongs to a refined and comely decadence; just as its earliest phases have the freshness which belongs to all periods of growth in art, the charm of *ascêsis*,[3] of the austere and serious girding of the loins in youth.

But it is in Italy, in the fifteenth century, that the interest of the Renaissance mainly lies—in that solemn fifteenth century which can hardly be studied too much, not merely for its positive results in the things of the intellect and the imagination, its concrete works of art, its special and prominent personalities, with their profound aesthetic charm, but for its general spirit and character, for the ethical qualities of which it is a consummate type.

The various forms of intellectual activity which together make up the culture of an age, move for the most part from different starting points, and by unconnected roads. As products of the same generation they partake indeed of a common character, and unconsciously illustrate each other; but of the producers themselves, each group is solitary, gaining what advantage or disadvantage there may be in intellectual isolation. Art and poetry, philosophy and the religious life, and that other life of refined pleasure and action in the open places of the world, are each of them confined to its own circle of ideas, and those who prosecute either of them are generally little curious of the thoughts of others. There come, however, from time to time, eras of more favorable conditions, in which the thoughts of men draw nearer together than is their wont, and the many interests of the intellectual world combine in one complete type of general culture. The fifteenth century in Italy is one of these happier eras; and what is sometimes said of the age of Pericles is true of that of Lorenzo:[4] it is an age productive in personalities, many-sided, centralised, complete. Here, artists and philosophers and those whom the action of the world has elevated and made keen, do not live in isolation, but breathe a

---

[1] *Stanzas ... Childhood* Two poems by Wordsworth. The exact titles are "Resolution and Independence" (1807) and "Ode: Intimations of Immortality from Recollections of Early Childhood" (1803–06).

[2] *Joachim du Bellay* French poet (c. 1522–60) and subject of chapter eight of *The Renaissance*.

[3] *ascêsis* Asceticism; defined by Pater in his essay "Style" (1888) as "Self-restraint, a skillful economy of means."

[4] *Pericles* Athenian statesman and great patron of the arts of the fifth century BCE; *Lorenzo* Lorenzo de Medici, an Italian prince and art patron of the fifteenth century AD.

common air, and catch light and heat from each other's thoughts. There is a spirit of general elevation and enlightenment in which all alike communicate. It is the unity of this spirit which gives unity to all the various products of the Renaissance; and it is to this intimate alliance with mind, this participation in the best thoughts which that age produced, that the art of Italy in the fifteenth century owes much of its grave dignity and influence.

I have added an essay on Winckelmann,[1] as not incongruous with the studies which precede it, because Winckelmann, coming in the eighteenth century, really belongs in spirit to an earlier age. By his enthusiasm for things of the intellect and the imagination for their own sake, by his Hellenism, his lifelong struggle to attain to the Greek spirit, he is in sympathy with the humanists of an earlier century. He is the last fruit of the Renaissance, and explains in a striking way its motive and tendencies.

—1873

CONCLUSION [2]

Ἀέγει που Ἡράκλειτος ὅτι πάντα χωρεῖ
καὶ οὐδὲν μένει[3]

To regard all things and principles of things as inconstant modes or fashions has more and more become the tendency of modern thought. Let us begin with that which is without—our physical life. Fix upon it in one of its more exquisite intervals, the moment, for instance, of delicious recoil from the flood of water in summer heat. What is the whole physical life in that moment but a combination of natural elements to which science gives their names? But these elements, phosphorus and lime and delicate fibres, are present not in the human body alone; we detect them in places most remote from it. Our physical life is a perpetual motion of them—the passage of the blood, the wasting and repairing of the lenses of the eye, the modification of the tissues of the brain by every ray of light and sound—processes which science reduces to simpler and more elementary forces. Like the elements of which we are composed, the action of these forces extends beyond us; it rusts iron and ripens corn. Far out on every side of us those elements are broadcast, driven by many forces; and birth and gesture and death and the springing of violets from the grave[4] are but a few out of ten thousand resultant combinations. That clear, perpetual outline of face and limb is but an image of ours, under which we group them—a design in a web, the actual threads of which pass out beyond it. This at least of flame-like our life has, that it is but the concurrence, renewed from moment to moment, of forces parting sooner or later on their ways.

Or if we begin with the inward world of thought and feeling, the whirlpool is still more rapid, the flame more eager and devouring. There it is no longer the gradual darkening of the eye and fading of colour from the wall—the movement of the shoreside, where the water flows down indeed, though in apparent rest—but the race of the midstream, a drift of momentary acts of sight and passion and thought. At first sight experience seems to bury us under a flood of external objects, pressing upon us with a sharp and importunate reality, calling us out of ourselves in a thousand forms of action. But when reflexion begins to act upon those objects they are dissipated under its influence; the cohesive force seems suspended like a trick of magic; each object is loosed into a group of impressions—colour, odour, texture—in the mind of the observer. And if we continue to dwell in thought on this world, not of objects in the solidity with which language invests them, but of impressions unstable, flickering, inconsistent, which burn and are extinguished with our consciousness of them, it contracts still further; the whole scope of

---

[1] *Winckelmann* Johann Joachim Winckelmann (1717–68), German classical scholar and art historian, the subject of chapter 9 of *The Renaissance*.

[2] [Pater's note] This brief "Conclusion" was omitted in the second edition of this book, as I conceived it might possibly mislead some of those young men into whose hands it might fall. On the whole, I have thought it best to reprint it here, with some slight changes which bring it closer to my original meaning. I have dealt more fully in *Marius the Epicurean* with the thoughts suggested by it.

[3] Ἀέγει ... μένει Greek (Pater's translation): "Heraclitus says, 'All things give way; nothing remains!'" From Plato's *Cratylus* (360 BCE). Heraclitus (c. 500 BCE), Greek philosopher.

[4] *birth ... grave* Cf. Shakespeare's *Hamlet* 5.1.238–40: "Lay her i' the earth: / And from her fair and unpolluted flesh / May violets spring!"

observation is dwarfed to the narrow chamber of the individual mind. Experience, already reduced to a swarm of impressions, is ringed round for each one of us by that thick wall of personality through which no real voice has ever pierced on its way to us, or from us to that which we can only conjecture to be without. Every one of those impressions is the impression of the individual in his isolation, each mind keeping as a solitary prisoner its own dream of a world. Analysis goes a step farther still, and assures us that those impressions of the individual mind to which, for each one of us, experience dwindles down, are in perpetual flight; that each of them is limited by time, and that as time is infinitely divisible, each of them is infinitely divisible also; all that is actual in it being a single moment, gone while we try to apprehend it, of which it may ever be more truly said that it has ceased to be than that it is. To such a tremulous wisp constantly reforming itself on the stream, to a single sharp impression, with a sense in it, a relic more or less fleeting, of such moments gone by, what is real in our life fines itself down. It is with this movement, with the passage and dissolution of impressions, images, sensations, that analysis leaves off—that continual vanishing away, that strange, perpetual weaving and unweaving of ourselves.

Philosophiren, says Novalis, *ist dephlegmatisiren vivificiren*.[1] The service of philosophy, of speculative culture, towards the human spirit is to rouse, to startle it into sharp and eager observation. Every moment some form grows perfect in hand or face; some tone on the hills or the sea is choicer than the rest; some mood of passion or insight or intellectual excitement is irresistibly real and attractive for us—for that moment only. Not the fruit of experience, but experience itself, is the end. A counted number of pulses only is given to us of a variegated, dramatic life. How may we see in them all that is to be seen in them by the finest senses? How shall we pass most swiftly from point to point, and be present always at the focus where the greatest number of vital forces unite in their purest energy?

To burn always with this hard, gemlike flame, to maintain this ecstasy, is success in life. In a sense it might even be said that our failure is to form habits, for, after all, habit is relative to a stereotyped world, and meantime it is only the roughness of the eye that makes any two persons, things, situations, seem alike. While all melts under our feet, we may well catch at any exquisite passion, or any contribution to knowledge that seems by a lifted horizon to set the spirit free for a moment, or any stirring of the senses, strange dyes, strange colours, and curious odours, or work of the artist's hands, or the face of one's friend. Not to discriminate every moment some passionate attitude in those about us, and in the brilliancy of their gifts some tragic dividing of forces on their ways, is, on this short day of frost and sun, to sleep before evening. With this sense of the splendour of our experience and of its awful brevity, gathering all we are into one desperate effort to see and touch, we shall hardly have time to make theories about the things we see and touch. What we have to do is to be forever curiously testing new opinions and courting new impressions, never acquiescing in a facile orthodoxy of Comte, or of Hegel,[2] or of our own. Philosophical theories or ideas, as points of view, instruments of criticism, may help us to gather up what might otherwise pass unregarded by us. "Philosophy is the microscope of thought."[3] The theory or idea or system which requires of us the sacrifice of any part of this experience, in consideration of some interest into which we cannot enter, or some abstract theory we have not identified with ourselves, or what is only conventional, has no real claim upon us.

One of the most beautiful passages in the writings of Rousseau is that in the sixth book of the *Confessions*, where he describes the awakening in him of the literary sense. An undefinable taint of death had always clung about him, and now in early manhood he believed himself smitten by mortal disease. He asked himself how he might make as much as possible of the interval that remained; and he was not biased by anything in his previous life when he decided that it must be by intellectual excitement, which he found just then in the

---

[1] *Philosophiren … vivificiren* German: "To philosophize is to cast off apathy, to come alive." Novalis is the pseudonym of German poet Friederich von Hardenberg (1772–1801).

[2] *Comte* French philosopher Auguste Comte (1798–1857); *Hegel* German philosopher Georg Wilhelm Friedrich Hegel (1770–1831).

[3] *"Philosophy … thought"* From Victor Hugo's *Les Misérables* (1862) 2.2.

clear, fresh writings of Voltaire. Well! we are all *condamnés*, as Victor Hugo says: we are all under sentence of death but with a sort of indefinite reprieve—*les hommes sont tous condamnés à mort avec des sursis indéfinis*:[1] we have an interval, and then our place knows us no more. Some spend this interval in listlessness, some in high passions, the wisest, at least among "the children of this world,"[2] in art and song. For our one chance lies in expanding that interval, in getting as many pulsations as possible into the given time. Great passions may give us this quickened sense of life, ecstasy and sorrow of love, the various forms of enthusiastic activity, disinterested or otherwise, which come naturally to many of us. Only be sure it is passion—that it does yield you this fruit of a quickened, multiplied consciousness. Of this wisdom, the poetic passion, the desire of beauty, the love of art for art's sake, has most, for art comes to you professing frankly to give nothing but the highest quality to your moments as they pass, and simply for those moments' sake.

—1868

Leonardo da Vinci, *The Last Supper* (1498).

"On the damp wall of the refectory, oozing with mineral salts, Leonardo painted the *Last Supper*. A hundred anecdotes were told about it, his retouchings and delays. They show him refusing to work except at the moment of invention, scornful of whoever thought that art was a work of mere industry and rule, often coming the whole length of Milan to give a single touch. He painted it, not in fresco, where all must be impromptu, but in oils, the new method which he had been one of the first to welcome, because it allowed of so many afterthoughts, so refined a working out of perfection. It turned out that on a plastered wall no process could have been less durable."

from *The Renaissance*

---

[1]   *les hommes ... indéfinis*   From Victor Hugo's *Le dernier jour d'un condamné* (1829).

[2]   *"the children of this world"*   From Luke 16.8: "The children of this world are in their generation wiser than the children of light."

Giorgione, *The Pastoral Concert* (1508–09).

"It is to the law or condition of music, as I said, that all art like this is really aspiring; and, in the school of Giorgione, the perfect moments of music itself, the making or hearing of music, song or its accompaniment, are themselves prominent as subjects. On that background of the silence of Venice, so impressive to the modern visitor, the world of Italian music was then forming. In choice of subject, as in all besides, the *Concert* of the Pitti Palace is typical of everything that Giorgione, himself an admirable musician, touched with his influence; and in sketch or finished picture, in various collections, we may follow it through many intricate variations—men fainting at music; music heard at the poolside while people fish, or mingled with the sound of the pitcher in the well, or heard across running water, or among the flocks; the tuning of instruments; people with intent faces, as if listening, like those described by Plato in an ingenious passage of the *Republic*, to detect the smallest interval of musical sound, the smallest undulation in the air, or feeling for music in thought on a stringless instrument, ear and finger refining themselves infinitely, in the appetite for sweet sound; a momentary touch of an instrument in the twilight, as one passes through some unfamiliar room, in a chance company."   from *The Renaissance*

Thomas Hardy
1840 – 1928

Hardy was born in 1840 in Dorset, where much of his fiction was later set. A frail child, he did not attend the local school until the age of eight. However, his ill health fostered his love of reading. In his walks in the area, Hardy also came into contact with the local farmers and laborers, whose hardship and poverty deeply touched him. At the age of 15, he was apprenticed to a local architect, a career that would sustain him until he became established as a writer.

In 1862 Hardy moved to London to work with another architect. Always driven, he would rise at five in the morning to complete three or four hours of reading—in Homer, the Greek Testament,

the Renaissance poets—before going to the office. On his return from work, he would often stay up reading and writing until midnight. It was during this time that he began writing poetry and short stories. Although he submitted many pieces to various magazines and the editors often wrote that he showed promise, his work was consistently rejected. The hectic schedule that Hardy was following caused his health to deteriorate, and he was forced to return to the countryside in 1867 to recuperate. In Dorchester, he worked as an architect during the day and wrote in his spare time. It was in the course of his employment that he met his first wife, Emma Gifford. He had been sent to St. Juliot to draw plans for a church restoration, and Emma was the sister-in-law of the rector. The two struck up a close friendship and Emma was very support-ive of his writing. With Emma's encouragement, Hardy published his first novel *Desperate Remedies* (1871). The novel, which has much in common with sensation fiction, a popular sub-genre of the 1860s, met with mixed reviews, but he continued to write. *Under the Greenwood Tree*, published in 1872, brought him popular acclaim.

In his early novels, Hardy began to include real places from the Dorset area, renamed Wessex—and to be praised for his portrayal of the countryside and the people of the region. *A Pair of Blue Eyes* appeared in 1873, and mirrored his own courtship with Emma. The two were married in 1874. That year also saw the publication of *Far from the Madding Crowd*, the first of what are now regarded as his classic novels. It depicts the life and loves of Bathsheba Everdene, and provides a convincing portrait of rural life. The novel also includes one of Hardy's "fallen women"; the case of Fanny Robin, who is seduced and eventually dies in a workhouse, shocked many readers. Despite this, the novel was very popular, and allowed him to give up his architectural work and concentrate solely on writing.

The Return of the Native, published in 1878, was also very successful. All of Hardy's novels were by now appearing in serialized form in monthly family magazines—a development which affected both the way that he wrote and the content of his fiction. Like most serialized writers, Hardy incorporated a steady flow of incidents in his novels; he was catering to an audience that needed to be encouraged to keep reading and buy the next issue. The "family" nature of the magazines often led his editors (one of whom was Leslie Stephen, the father of Virginia Woolf) to caution him to tone down the racier scenes and rewrite large sections. Because of the strict morality that dominated editorial policy, for example, Hardy could not state explicitly that some of his characters might have been involved in extra-marital activities. Instead, such situations are written vaguely and readers are left to decide for themselves whether something illicit has taken place.

Serialization also affected the form of Hardy's next major novel, *The Mayor of Casterbridge* (1886), which appeared weekly rather than monthly; it is the most rapidly paced of all his novels. The novel exhibits Hardy's penchant for the tragic and macabre. Michael Henchard, a country laborer, sells his wife and daughter after a bout of drinking. He subsequently becomes wealthy and is elected mayor before his past catches up with him; he eventually dies impoverished on the outskirts of town. The fact that Hardy built the novel on a carefully allusive structure based on the story of Saul and David from the Hebrew scriptures to explore the passage of an older England into modernity indicates his life-long sense of life's ironies and of the wrenching changes in nineteenth-century English life.

Censure of Hardy's depiction of "immoral" subject matter reached its peak with the publication of his next two major novels, *Tess of the d'Urbervilles* (1891) and *Jude the Obscure* (1895). In the first of these, the aristocratic Alec d'Urberville forces himself upon Tess, who then bears his illegitimate child. Both the "seduction" itself and Tess's attempt to have the illegitimate child baptized shocked readers. Tess eventually marries Angel Clare but is forced back into a relationship with d'Urberville when Clare discovers the truth about her past and abandons her. Her husband eventually forgives her, but she kills d'Urberville and is hanged for it. Hardy rewrote many of the novel's explicit or controversial sections for serialization in *Longman's Magazine*, but when the novel was published as a complete volume, the controversial sections were restored.

Jude the Obscure depicts the thwarted life of Jude Fawley, a village mason who dreams of attending university but whose hopes are derailed by romantic entanglements—first with Arabella Dunn and later with Sue Bridehead—and by the deadening exclusions of class-conscious English society of the later nineteenth century. Some have seen Bridehead as a proto-feminist, respecting her intelligence and authority and her fear of and disdain for marriage. Hardy's own marriage was on shaky ground at the time, and his wife Emma attempted to halt the publication of the novel. Publication went forward, but criticism of the book was swift and cruel. The Bishop of Wakefield, for one, said he had "bought one of Mr. Hardy's novels, but was so disgusted with its insolence and indecency" that he "threw it into the fire." Unfavorable and uncomprehending responses to *Jude* encouraged Hardy to give up fiction; this was the last novel which he wrote.

Throughout his earlier writing life, Hardy also produced numerous stories. Like his novels, these are frequently rooted in the details of traditional rural and small town life, although they often touch on highly contemporary issues. Also like his novels, they often take in the broad sweep of his characters' lives, which are typically subject to remorseless twists of fate; the gods may haunt his texts, but no God is there. Ongoing tensions between the city and the countryside, the educated and the uneducated, and the rich and the poor frequently contribute to the tragedy that lies at the heart of the life of a typical Hardy character, although these material factors frequently combine with a more philosophically grounded pessimism.

From the mid-1890s, Hardy concentrated on composing poetry, continuing in *Wessex Poems* (1898) his portrayal of the region he had made famous in the novels. The long poem *The Dynasts* (1904–08) detailed the Napoleonic Wars. The death of Emma in 1912, and Hardy's subsequent remorse for what had become of their relationship, resulted in some of his finest poetry and love poems, which appeared in *Satires of Circumstance* (1914). Hardy remarried in 1914; his second wife, Florence, is listed as the author of a two-volume biography that appeared in 1928 and 1930, but it has since been established that Hardy wrote the work himself. Hardy was awarded the Order of Merit in 1910 and the Gold Medal of the Royal Society of Literature in 1912. When he died in 1928, his ashes were interred in Poets' Corner at Westminster Abbey, but his heart was buried with Emma in Stinsford, in southern England.

⌘ ⌘ ⌘

The Son's Veto

I

To the eyes of a man viewing it from behind, the nut-brown hair was a wonder and a mystery. Under the black beaver hat, surmounted by its tuft of black feathers, the long locks, braided and twisted and coiled like the rushes of a basket, composed a rare, if somewhat barbaric, example of ingenious art. One could understand such weavings and coiling being wrought to last intact for a year, or even a calendar month; but that they should be all demolished regularly at bedtime, after a single day of permanence, seemed a reckless waste of successful fabrication.

And she had done it all herself, poor thing. She had no maid, and it was almost the only accomplishment she could boast of. Hence the unstinted pains.

She was a young invalid lady—not so very much of an invalid—sitting in a wheeled chair, which had been pulled up in the front part of a green enclosure, close to a band-stand, where a concert was going on, during a warm June afternoon. It had place in one of the minor parks or private gardens that are to be found in the suburbs of London, and was the effort of a local association to raise money for some charity. There were worlds within worlds in the great city, and though nobody outside the immediate district had ever heard of the charity, or the band, or the garden, the enclosure was filled with an interested audience sufficiently informed of all these.

As the trains proceeded many of the listeners observed the chaired lady, whose back hair, by reason of her prominent position, so challenged inspection. Her face was not easily discernible, but the aforesaid cunning tress-weavings, the white ear and poll,[1] and the curve of a cheek which was neither flaccid nor sallow, were signals that led to the expectation of good beauty in front. Such expectations are not infrequently disappointed as soon as the disclosure comes; and in the present case, when the lady, by a turn of the head, at length revealed herself, she was not so handsome as the people behind her had supposed, and even hoped—they did not know why.

For one thing (alas! the commonness of this complaint), she was less young than they had fancied her to be. Yet attractive her face unquestionably was, and not at all sickly. The revelation of its details came each time she turned to talk to a boy of twelve or thirteen who stood beside her, and the shape of whose hat and jacket implied that he belonged to a well-known public school.[2] The immediate by-standers could hear that he called her "Mother."

When the end of the programme was reached, and the audience withdrew, many chose to find their way out by passing at her elbow. Almost all turned their heads to take a full and near look at the interesting woman, who remained stationary in the chair till the way should be clear enough for her to be wheeled out without obstruction. As if she expected their glances, and did not mind gratifying their curiosity, she met the eyes of several of her observers by lifting her own, showing these to be soft, brown, and affectionate orbs, a little plaintive in their regard.

She was conducted out of the garden, and passed along the pavement till she disappeared from view, the school-boy walking beside her. To inquiries made by some persons who watched her away, the answer came that she was the second wife of the incumbent of a neighbouring parish, and that she was lame. She was generally believed to be a woman with a story—an innocent one, but a story of some sort or other.

In conversing with her on their way home the boy who walked at her elbow said that he hoped his father had not missed them.

"He have been so comfortable these last few hours that I am sure he cannot have missed us," she replied.

"*Has,* dear mother—not *have*!" exclaimed the

---

[1]　*poll* Nape of the neck.

[2]　*public school* In England, private school.

public-school boy, with an impatient fastidiousness that was almost harsh. "Surely you know that by this time!"

His mother hastily adopted the correction, and did not resent his making it, or retaliate, as she might well have done, by bidding him to wipe that crumby mouth of his, whose condition had been caused by surreptitious attempts to eat a piece of cake without taking it out of the pocket wherein it lay concealed. After this the pretty woman and the boy went onward in silence.

That question of grammar bore upon her history, and she fell into reverie, of a somewhat sad kind to all appearance. It might have been assumed that she was wondering if she had done wisely in shaping her life as she had shaped it, to bring out such a result as this.

In a remote nook in North Wessex, forty miles from London, near the thriving county-town of Aldbrickham, there stood a pretty village with its church and parsonage, which she knew well enough, but her son had never seen. It was her native village, Gaymead, and the first event bearing upon her present situation had occurred at that place when she was only a girl of nineteen.

How well she remembered it, that first act in her little tragi-comedy, the death of her reverend husband's first wife. It happened on a spring evening, and she who now and for many years had filled that first wife's place was then parlor-maid in the parson's house.

When everything had been done that could be done, and the death was announced, she had gone out in the dusk to visit her parents, who were living in the same village, to tell them the sad news. As she opened the white swing-gate and looked towards the trees which rose westward, shutting out the pale light of the evening sky, she discerned, without much surprise, the figure of a man standing in the hedge, though she roguishly exclaimed, as a matter of form, "Oh Sam, how you frightened me!"

He was a young gardener of her acquaintance. She told him the particulars of the late event, and they stood silent, these two young people, in that elevated, calmly philosophic mind which is engendered when a tragedy has happened close at hand, and has not happened to the philosophers themselves. But it had its bearings upon their relations.

"And will you stay on now at the Vicarage, just the same?" asked he.

She had hardly thought of that. "Oh yes—I suppose," she said. "Everything will be just as usual, I imagine."

He walked beside her towards her mother's. Presently his arm stole round her waist. She gently removed it; but he placed it there again, and she yielded the point. "You see, dear Sophy, you don't know that you'll stay on; you may want a home; and I shall be ready to offer one some day, though I may not be ready just yet."

"Why, Sam, how can you be so fast? I've never even said I liked 'ee; and it is all your own doing, coming after me."

"Still, it is nonsense to say I am not to have a try at you, like the rest." He stooped to kiss her a farewell, for they had reached her mother's door.

"No, Sam; you sha'nt!" she cried, putting her hand over his mouth. "You ought to be more serious on such a night as this." And she bade him adieu without allowing him to kiss her or to come indoors.

The vicar just left a widower was at this time a man about forty years of age, of good family, and childless. He had led a secluded existence in this college living, partly because there were no resident landowners; and his loss now intensified his habit of withdrawal from outward observation. He was still less seen than heretofore, kept himself still less in time with the rhythm and racket of the movements called progress in the world without. For many months after his wife's decease the economy of his household remained as before; the cook, the house maid, the parlor-maid, and the man out-of-doors performed their duties or left them undone, just as nature prompted them—the vicar knew not which. It was then represented to him that his servants seemed to have nothing to do in his small family of one. He was struck with the truth of this representation, and decided to cut down his establishment. But he was forestalled by Sophy, the parlor-maid, who said one evening that she wished to leave him.

"And why?" said the parson.

"Sam Hobson has asked me to marry him, sir."

"Well—do you want to marry?"

"Not much. But it would be a home for me. And we have heard that one of us will have to leave."

A day or two after she said: "I don't want to leave just yet, sir, if you don't wish it. Sam and I have quarreled."

He looked at her. He had hardly ever observed her before, though he had been frequently conscious of her soft presence in the room. What a kitten-like, flexuous, tender creature she was! She was the only one of the servants with whom he came into immediate and continuous relation. What should he do if Sophy were gone?

Sophy did not go, but one of the others did, and things proceeded quietly again.

When Mr. Twycott, the vicar, was ill, Sophy brought up his meals to him, and she had no sooner left the room one day than he heard a noise on the stairs. She had slipped down with the tray, and so twisted her foot that she could not stand. The village surgeon was called in; the vicar got better, but Sophy was incapacitated for a long time; and she was informed that she must never again walk much or engage in any occupation which required her to stand long on her feet. As soon as she was comparatively well she spoke to him alone. Since she was forbidden to walk and bustle about, and, indeed could not do so, it became her duty to leave. She could very well work at something sitting down, and she had an aunt, a seamstress.

The parson had been very greatly moved by what she had suffered on his account, and he exclaimed, "No, Sophy; lame or not lame, I cannot let you go. You must never leave me again."

He came close to her, and, though she could never exactly tell how it happened, she became conscious of his lips upon her cheek. He then asked her to marry him. Sophy did not exactly love him, but she had a respect for him which almost amounted to veneration. Even if she had wished to get away from him she hardly dared refuse a personage so reverend and august in her eyes, and she assented forthwith to be his wife.

Thus it happened that one fine morning, when the doors of the church were naturally open for ventilation, and the singing birds fluttered in and alighted on the tie-beams of the rood, there was a marriage-service at the communion rails which hardly a soul knew of. The parson and a neighbouring curate had entered at one door, and Sophy at another, followed by two necessary persons, whereupon in a short time there emerged a newly-made husband and wife.

Mr. Twycott knew perfectly well that he had committed social suicide by this step, despite Sophy's spotless character, and he had taken his measures accordingly. An exchange of livings had been arranged with an acquaintance who was incumbent of a church in the south of London, and as soon as possible the couple removed thither, abandoning their pretty country home with trees and shrubs and glebe[1] for a narrow, dusty house in a long, straight street, and their fine peal of bells for the wretchedest one-tongue clangor that ever tortured mortal ears. It was all on her account. They were, however, away from every one who had known her former position, and also under less observation from without than they would have had to put up with in any country parish.

Sophy the woman was as charming a partner as a man could possess, though Sophy the lady had her deficiencies. She showed a natural aptitude for little domestic refinements, so far as related to things and manners; but in what is called culture she was less intuitive. She had now been married more than fourteen years, and her husband had taken much trouble with her education; but she still held confused ideas on the use of "was" and "were", which did not beget a respect for her among the few acquaintances she made. Her great grief in this relation was that her only child, on whose education no expense had been or would be spared, was now old enough to perceive these deficiencies in his mother, and not only to see them but to feel irritated at their existence.

Thus she lived on in the city, and wasted hours in braiding her beautiful hair, till her once apple cheeks waned to pink of the very faintest. Her foot had never regained its natural strength after the accident, and she was mostly obliged to avoid walking altogether. Her husband had grown to like London for its freedom and its domestic privacy; but he was twenty years his Sophy's senior, and had latterly been seized with a serious illness. On this day, however, he had seemed to be well enough to justify her accompanying her son Randolph to the concert.

---

[1] *glebe* Land granted to clergyman.

2

The next time we get a glimpse of her is when she appears in the mournful attire of a widow.

Mr. Twycott had never rallied, and now lay in a well-packed cemetery to the south of the great city, where, if all the dead it contained had stood erect and alive, not one would have known him or recognized his name. The boy had dutifully followed him to the grave, and was now again at school.

Throughout these changes Sophy had been treated like the child she was in nature though not in years. She was left with no control over anything that had been her husband's beyond her modest personal income. In his anxiety lest her inexperience should be overreached he had safeguarded with trustees all he possibly could. The completion of the boy's course at the public school, to be followed in due time by Oxford and ordination, had been all provisioned and arranged, and she really had nothing to occupy her in the world but to eat and drink, and make a business of indolence, and go on weaving and coiling the nut-brown hair, merely keeping a home open for the son whenever he came to her during vacations.

Foreseeing his probable decease long years before her, her husband in his lifetime had purchased for her use a semi-detached villa in the same long, straight road whereon the church and parsonage faced, which was to be hers as long as she chose to live in it. Here she now resided, looking out upon the fragment of lawn in front, and through the railings at the ever-flowing traffic; or, bending forward over the window-sill on the first floor, stretching her eyes far up and down the vista of sooty trees, hazy air, and drab house façades, along which echoed the noises common to a suburban main thoroughfare.

Somehow, her boy, with his aristocratic school-knowledge, his grammar, and his aversions, was losing those wide infantile sympathies, extending as far as to the sun and moon themselves, with which he, like other children, had been born, and which his mother, a child of nature herself, had loved in him; he was reducing their compass to a population of a few thousand wealthy and titled people, the mere veneer of a thousand million or so of others who did not interest him at all. He drifted further and further away from her. Sophy's *milieu* being a suburb of minor tradesmen and under-clerks, and her almost only companions the two servants of her own house, it was not surprising that after her husband's death she soon lost the little artificial tastes she had acquired from him, and became—in her son's eyes—a mother whose mistakes and origin it was his painful lot as a gentleman to blush for. As yet he was far from being man enough—if he ever would be—to rate these sins of hers at their true infinitesimal value beside the yearning fondness that welled up and remained penned in her heart till it should be more fully accepted by him, or by some other person or thing. If he had lived at home with her he would have had all of it; but he seemed to require so very little in present circum-stances, and it remained stored.

Her life became insupportably dreary; she could not take walks, and had no interest in going for drives, or, indeed, in traveling anywhere. Nearly two years passed without an event, and still she looked on that suburban road, thinking of the village in which she had been born, and whither she would have gone back—oh, how gladly!—even to work in the fields.

Taking no exercise, she often could not sleep, and would rise in the night or early morning and look out upon the then vacant thoroughfare, where the lamps stood like sentinels waiting for some procession to go by. An approximation to such a procession was indeed made every early morning about one o'clock, when the country vehicles passed up with loads of vegetables for Covent Garden market. She often saw them creeping along at this silent and dusky hour—wagon after wagon, bearing green bastions of cabbages nodding to their fall, yet never falling; walls of baskets enclosing masses of beans and pease; pyramids of snow-white turnips, swaying howdahs[1] of mixed produce—creeping along behind aged night-horses, who seemed ever patiently wondering between their hollow coughs why they had always to work at that still hour when all other sentient creatures were privileged to rest. Wrapped in a cloak, it was soothing to watch and sympathize with them when depression and nervousness hindered sleep, and to see how the fresh green-stuff brightened to life as it came opposite the lamp, and how the sweating animals steamed and shone with their miles of travel.

They had an interest, almost a charm, for Sophy, these semi-rural people and vehicles moving in an urban

[1] *howdahs*   Seats carried by elephants.

atmosphere, leading a life quite distinct from that of the daytime toilers on the same road. One morning a man who accompanied a wagon-load of potatoes gazed rather hard at the house fronts as he passed, and with a curious emotion she thought his form was familiar to her. She looked out for him again. His being an old-fashioned conveyance with a yellow front, it was easily recognizable, and on the third night after she saw it a second time. The man alongside was, as she had fancied, Sam Hobson, formerly gardener at Gaymead, who would at one time have married her.

She had occasionally thought of him, and wondered if life in a cottage with him would not have been a happier lot than the life she had accepted. She had not thought of him passionately, but her now dismal situation lent an interest to his resurrection—a tender interest which it is impossible to exaggerate. She went back to bed, and began thinking. When did these market-gardeners, who traveled up to town so regularly at one or two in the morning, come back? She dimly recollected seeing their empty wagons, hardly noticeable among the ordinary day-traffic, passing down at some hour before noon.

It was only April, but that morning, after breakfast, she had the window opened, and sat looking out, the feeble sun shining full upon her. She affected to sew, but her eyes never left the street. Between ten and eleven the desired wagon, now unladen, reappeared on its return journey. But Sam was not looking round him then, and drove on in a reverie.

"Sam!" cried she.

Turning with a start, his face lighted up. He called to him a little boy to hold the horse, alighted, and came and stood under her window.

"I can't come down easily, Sam, or I would!" she said. "Did you know I lived here?"

"Well, Mrs. Twycott, I knew you lived along here somewhere. I have often looked out for 'ee."

He briefly explained his own presence on the scene. He had long since given up his gardening in the village near Aldbrickham, and was now manager at a market-gardener's on the south side of London, it being part of his duty to go up to Covent Garden with wagon-loads of produce two or three times a week. In answer to her curious inquiry, he admitted that he had come to this particular district because he had seen in the Aldbrick-

Hobson came and stood under her window.[1]

ham paper a year or two before the announcement of the death in South London of the aforetime vicar of Gaymead, which had revived an interest in her dwelling-place that he could not extinguish, leading him to hover about the locality till his present post had been secured.

They spoke of their native village in dear old North Wessex, the spots in which they had played together as children. She tried to feel that she was a dignified personage now, that she must not be too confidential with Sam. But she could not keep it up, and the tears hanging in her eyes were indicated in her voice.

"You are not happy, Mrs. Twycott, I'm afraid," he said.

"Oh, of course not! I lost my husband only the year before last."

---

[1] The illustrations that appear here and on page 621 accompanied "The Son's Veto" when it was first published in the *Illustrated London News*, 1 December 1891.

"Ah! I meant in another way. You'd like to be home again!"

"This is my home—for life. The house belongs to me. But I understand"—She let it out then.

"Yes, Sam. I long for home—*our* home! I *should* like to be there, and never leave it, and die there." But she remembered herself. "That's only a momentary feeling. I have a son, you know, a dear boy. He's at school now."

"Somewhere handy, I suppose? I see there's lots of 'em along this road."

"Oh no! Not in one of these wretched holes! At a public school—one of the most distinguished in England."

"Chok' it all! of course! I forgot, ma'am, that you've been a lady for so many years."

"No, I am not a lady," she said, sadly. "I never shall be. But he's a gentleman, and that makes it—oh, how difficult for me!"

3

The acquaintance thus oddly reopened proceeded apace. She often looked out to get a few words with him by night or by day. Her sorrow was that she could not accompany her one old friend on foot a little way, and talk more freely than she could do while he paused before the house. One night, at the beginning of June, when she was again on the watch after an absence of some days from the window, he entered the gate and said, softly, "Now, wouldn't some air do you good? I've only half a load this morning. Why not ride up to Covent Garden with me? There's a nice seat on the cabbages, where I've spread a sack. You can be home again in a cab before anybody is up."

She refused at first, and then, trembling with excitement, hastily finished her dressing, and wrapped herself up in cloak and veil, afterwards sidling downstairs by the aid of the handrail, in a way she could adopt on an emergency. When she had opened the door she found Sam on the step, and he lifted her bodily on his strong arm across the little forecourt into his vehicle. Not a soul was visible or audible in the infinite length of the straight, flat highway, with its ever-waiting lamps converging to points in each direction. The air was fresh as country air at this hour, and the stars shone, except to the north-eastward, where there was a whitish light—

the dawn. Sam carefully placed her in the seat and drove on.

They talked as they had talked in old days, Sam pulling himself up now and then, when he thought himself too familiar. More than once she said with misgiving that she wondered if she ought to have indulged in the freak. "But I am so lonely in my house," she added, "and this makes me so happy!"

"You must come again, dear Mrs. Twycott. There is no time o' day for taking the air like this."

It grew lighter and lighter. The sparrows became busy in the streets, and the city waxed denser around them. When they approached the river it was day, and on the bridge they beheld the full blaze of morning sunlight in the direction of St. Paul's, the river glistening towards it, and not a craft stirring.

Near Covent Garden he put her into a cab, and they parted, looking into each other's faces like the very old friends they were. She reached home without adventure, limped to the door, and let herself in with her latch-key unseen.

The air and Sam's presence had revived her; her cheeks were quite pink—almost beautiful. She had something to live for in addition to her son. A woman of pure instincts, she knew there had been nothing really wrong in the journey, but supposed it conventionally to be very wrong indeed.

Soon, however, she gave way to the temptation of going with him again, and on this occasion their conversation was distinctly tender, and Sam said he never should forget her, notwithstanding that she had served him rather badly at one time. After much hesitation he told her of a plan it was in his power to carry out, and one he should like to take in hand, since he did not care for London work; it was to set up as a master gardener down at Aldbrickham, the county-town of their native place. He knew of an opening—a shop kept by aged people who wished to retire.

"And why don't you do it, then, Sam?" she asked, with a slight heart-sinking.

"Because I'm not sure if—you'd join me. I know you wouldn't—couldn't! Such a lady as ye've been so long, you couldn't be a wife to a man like me."

"I hardly suppose I could!" she assented, also frightened at the idea.

"If you could," he said, eagerly, "you'd on'y have to sit in the back parlor and look through the glass partition when I was away sometimes—just to keep an eye on things. The lameness wouldn't hinder that. I'd keep you as genteel as ever I could, dear Sophy—if I might think of it," he pleaded.

"Sam, I'll be frank," she said, putting her hand on his. "If it were only myself I would do it, and gladly, though everything I possess would be lost to me by marrying again."

"I don't mind that. It's more independent."

"That's good of you, dear, dear Sam. But there's something else. I have a son. I almost fancy when I am miserable sometimes that he is not really mine, but one I hold in trust for my late husband. He seems to belong so little to me personally, so entirely to his dead father. He is so much educated and I so little that I do not feel dignified enough to be his mother. Well, he would have to be told."

"Yes. Unquestionably." Sam saw her thought and her fear. "Still, you can do as you like, Sophy—Mrs. Twycott," he added. "It is not you who are the child, but he."

"Ah, you don't know! Sam, if I could, I would marry you, some day. But you must wait awhile, and let me think."

It was enough for him, and he was blithe at their parting. Not so she. To tell Randolph seemed impossible. She could wait till he had gone up to Oxford, when what she did would affect his life but little. But would he ever tolerate the idea? And if not, could she defy him?

She had not told him a word when the yearly cricket-match came on at Lord's[1] between the public schools, though Sam had already gone back to Aldbrickham. Mrs. Twycott felt stronger than usual. She went to the match with Randolph, and was able to leave her chair and walk about occasionally. The bright idea occurred to her that she could casually broach the subject while moving round among the spectators, when the boy's spirits were high with interest in the game, and he would weigh domestic matters as feathers in the scale

beside the day's victory. They promenaded under the lurid July sun, this pair, so wide apart, yet so near, and Sophy saw the large proportion of boys like her own, in their broad white collars and dwarf hats, and all around the rows of great coaches under which was jumbled the débris of luxurious luncheons—bones, pie-crusts, champagne-bottles, glasses, plates, napkins, and the family silver; while on the coaches sat the proud fathers and mothers; but never a poor mother like her. If Randolph had not appertained to these, had not centred all his interests in them, had not cared exclusively for the class they belonged to, how happy would things have been! A great huzza at some small performance with the bat burst from the multitude of relatives, and Randolph jumped wildly into the air to see what had happened. Sophy fetched up the sentence that had been already shaped; but she could not get it out. The occasion was, perhaps, an inopportune one. The contrast between her story and the display of fashion to which Randolph had grown to regard himself as akin would be fatal. She awaited a better time.

It was on an evening when they were alone in their plain suburban residence, where life was not blue but brown, that she ultimately broke silence, qualifying her announcement of a probable second marriage by assuring him that it would not take place for a long time to come, when he would be living quite independently of her.

The boy thought the idea a very reasonable one, and asked if she had chosen anybody. She hesitated; and he seemed to have a misgiving. He hoped his step-father would be a gentleman, he said.

"Not what you call a gentleman," she answered, timidly. "He'll be much as I was before I knew your father;" and by degrees she acquainted him with the whole. The youth's face remained fixed for a moment; then he flushed, leaned on the table, and burst into passionate tears.

His mother went up to him, kissed all of his face that she could get at, and patted his back as if he were still the baby he once had been, crying herself the while. When he had somewhat recovered from his paroxysm he went hastily to his own room and fastened the door.

Parleyings were attempted through the key-hole, outside which she waited and listened. It was long

---

[1] *yearly cricket-match … Lord's* Lord's cricket ground in London has been the site of an annual cricket match between two of the most prestigious public schools in England, Eton and Harrow, since 1805.

before he would reply, and when he did it was to say sternly at her from within: "I am ashamed of you! It will ruin me! A miserable boor! a churl! a clown! It will degrade me in the eyes of all the gentlemen of England!"

"Say no more—perhaps I am wrong! I will struggle against it!" she cried, miserably.

Before Randolph left her that summer a letter arrived from Sam to inform her that he had been unexpectedly fortunate in obtaining the shop. He was in possession; it was the largest in the town, combining fruit with vegetables, and he thought it would form a home worthy even of her some day. Might he not run up to town to see her?

She met him by stealth, and said he must still wait for her final answer. The autumn dragged on, and when Randolph was home at Christmas for the holidays she broached the matter again. But the young gentleman was inexorable.

It was dropped for months; renewed again; abandoned under his repugnance; again attempted, and thus the gentle creature reasoned and pleaded till four or five long years had passed. Then the faithful Sam revived his suit with some peremptoriness. Sophy's son, now an undergraduate, was down from Oxford one Easter, when she again opened the subject. As soon as he was ordained, she argued, he would have a home of his own, wherein she, with her bad grammar and her ignorance, would be an encumbrance to him. Better obliterate her as much as possible.

He showed a more manly anger now, but would not agree. She on her side was more persistent, and he had doubts whether she could be trusted in his absence. But by indignation and contempt for her taste he completely maintained his ascendancy; and finally taking her before a little cross and shrine that he had erected in his bedroom for his private devotions, there bade her kneel, and swear that she would not wed Samuel Hobson without his consent. "I owe this to my father!" he said.

The poor woman swore, thinking he would soften as soon as he was ordained and in full swing of clerical work. But he did not. His education had by this time sufficiently ousted his humanity to keep him quite firm; though his mother might have led an idyllic life with her faithful fruiterer and green-grocer, and nobody have been anything the worse in the world.

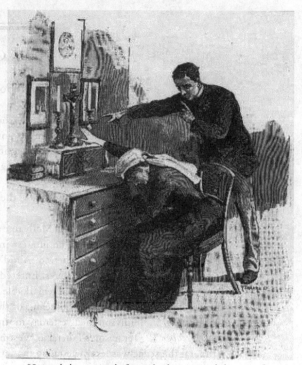

He made her swear before a little cross and shrine in his bed-room that she would not wed Samuel Hobson without his consent.

Her lameness became more confirmed as time went on, and she seldom or never left the house in the long southern thoroughfare, where she seemed to be pining her heart away. "Why mayn't I say to Sam that I'll marry him? Why mayn't I?" she would murmur plaintively to herself when nobody was near.

Some four years after this date a middle-aged man was standing at the door of the largest fruiterer's shop in Aldbrickham. He was the proprietor, but to-day, instead of his usual business attire, he wore a neat suit of black; and his window was partly shuttered. From the railway station a funeral procession was seen approaching; it passed his door and went out of the town towards the village of Gaymead. The man, whose eyes were wet, held his hat in his hand as the vehicles moved by; while from the mourning coach a young smooth-shaven priest in a high waistcoat looked black as a cloud at the shopkeeper standing there.

—DECEMBER 1891.

IN CONTEXT

Hardy's Notebooks and Memoranda

Hardy's notebooks and memoranda for the years during which "The Son's Veto" and other short stories were written contain an interesting mixture of observations on daily life, reflections on broader issues, and thoughts regarding the writing of fiction. The following entries, for example, give a vivid sense of aspects of Hardy's life in the autumn of 1892:

"*End of September*. In London. This is the time to realize London as an old city, all the pulsing excitements of May being absent."

"Drove home from dining with McIlvaine at the Café Royal, behind a horse who had no interest in me, was going a way he had no interest in going, and was whipped on by a man who had no interest in me, or the horse, or the way. Amid this string of compulsions reached home."

"*October*. At Great Fawley, Berks. Entered a ploughed vale which might be called the Valley of Brown Melancholy. The silence is remarkable …. Though I am alive with the living I can only see the dead here, and am scarcely conscious of the happy children at play."

"*October 7*. Tennyson died yesterday morning."

"*October 12*. Tennyson's funeral in Westminster Abbey. The music was sweet impressive, but as a funeral the scene was less penetrating than a plain country interment would have been."

Hardy's notations regarding specific stories are generally unrevealing (e.g., "January 13th. *The Fiddler of the Reels* posted to Messrs Scribner, New York," "December [no date]. Found and touched up a short story called 'An Imaginative Woman'.") They do include, however, several interesting comments about writing in general. On 24 October 1892, for example, Hardy reflected that "the best tragedy—highest tragedy in short—is that of the *worthy* encompassed by the *inevitable*. The tragedies of immoral and worthless people are not of the best." Three months later he made a note that is of particular relevance to his own fiction writing:

"*February 23*. A story must be exceptional enough to justify its telling. We tale-tellers are all Ancient Mariners, and none of us is warranted in stopping Wedding Guests (in other words, the hurrying public) unless he has something more unusual to relate than the ordinary experience of every average man and woman.

"The whole secret of fiction and the drama—in the constructional part—lies in the adjustment of things unusual to things eternal and universal. The writer who knows exactly how exceptional, and how non-exceptional, his events should be made, possesses the key to the art."

(The quotations from Hardy's notebooks and memoranda are as reproduced in Florence Hardy, *The Life of Thomas Hardy, Volume 2: The Later Years of Thomas Hardy, 1892–1928* [London: Macmillan, 1930] 13, 15, 26, 15–16.)

MATHILDE BLIND
1841 – 1896

"Englishwomen," Mathilde Blind once complained, "have not followed the spontaneous impulses of nature." Such spontaneity, Blind believed, was as essential to composing great poetry as it was to living a fulfilling life. In Blind's own compositions, as one might expect, the poet does not hesitate to put forth her own "impulsive" and highly controversial views. Blind challenged the intellects and sensibilities of her Victorian readers with poems such as *The Ascent of Man* (1889), an epic re-writing of Darwinian evolution, and *The Heather on Fire* (1886), a detailed investigation into the brutal Highland Clearances of the 1830s. Her 1891 volume of dramatic monologues, *Dramas in Miniature*, confronted discrimination against women in Victorian culture head-on.

Blind was born Mathilde Cohen in Manheim, Germany. After her father's death, her mother married the radical political activist Karl Blind, who was soon to be exiled from Germany following the revolutions of 1848. The Blind family eventually settled in England, and their London home became a meeting place for other radicals exiled from the continent, including Karl Marx and Giuseppe Mazzini. Blind's revolutionary instincts thus evolved from the example of her parents and their friends. In an 1891 essay on Mazzini, to whom Blind had dedicated her first volume of poetry, she wrote that the Italian revolutionary "considered the evolution of society as an upward movement," and that he believed we must all work "to transform nature." Blind herself dedicated much of her life's work to practical, rather than what she considered idealistic, ends, and she was committed in particular to improving the lives of women. (She eventually left her sizable estate to Newnham College, Cambridge, which had been founded in 1871 to provide higher education for women.)

Given Blind's desire to fuse the political with the poetic, Percy Shelley was an obvious model for the young writer. Shelley, wrote Blind, had used poetry to engage "the internal workings of the human mind, the mighty questions of religion, of the development of humanity, of the hidden laws of nature." Romantic language and imagery inflect much of Blind's work, even as she articulates a skepticism, a wariness of the Romantic project, that marks her as a poet of the Victorian era. Many of her lyrics gesture to an ideal of one sort or another—sympathy with the natural world, for example —only to reveal the impossibility of accomplishing such grand aspirations.

Her social circle was gilded with Pre-Raphaelite painters, poets, and critics, including Ford Madox Brown, Algernon Swinburne, and William Michael Rossetti, and she moved comfortably within various *fin de siècle* literary crowds. In addition to several volumes of poetry, Blind regularly contributed essays and reviews to important journals such as the *Athenaeum*, the *Westminster Review*, and *Fraser's*. In 1883 she published the first full-length biography of George Eliot, whom Blind considered an intellectual and artistic model, and in 1886 she composed her sole novel, *Tarantella*. As does so much of her poetry, *Tarantella* features a pure-hearted and romantic heroine, Mina Lichtenfeld, who suffers at the hands of a hard and uncaring world; just prior to her death, Mina "apprehend[s] the terrible and sinister side of nature …" and feels "in her direst need, but a pitiless indifference that added to her desolation."

Blind died on 26 November 1896, after several years of respiratory troubles. As an artist she was among the most politically vocal of her time, and her poetry still communicates the energy of her commitment to active, practical engagement with the world.

⌘ ⌘ ⌘

The Russian Student's Tale

The midnight sun with phantom glare
　Shone on the soundless thoroughfare
Whose shuttered houses, closed and still,
Seemed bodies without heart or will;
5　Yea, all the stony city lay
Impassive in that phantom day,
As amid livid wastes of sand
The sphinxes of the desert stand.

And we, we two, turned night to day,
10　As, whistling many a student's lay,
We sped along each ghostly street,
With girls whose lightly tripping feet
Well matched our longer, stronger stride,
In hurrying to the water-side.
15　We took a boat; each seized an oar,
Until on either hand the shore
Slipped backwards, as our voices woke
Far echoes, mingling like a dream
With swirl and tumult of the stream.
20　On—on—away, beneath the ray
Of midnight in the mask of day;
By great wharves where the masts at peace
Look like the ocean's barren trees;
Past palaces and glimmering towers,
25　And gardens fairy-like with flowers,
And parks of twilight green and closes,
The very Paradise of roses.
The waters flow; on, on we row,
Now laughing loud, now whispering low;
30　And through the splendour of the white
Electrically glowing night,
Wind-wafted from some perfumed dell,
Tumultuously there loudly rose
Above the Neva's surge and swell,[1]
35　With amorous ecstasies and throes,
And lyric spasms of wildest wail,
The love-song of a nightingale.

I see her still beside me. Yea,
As if it were but yesterday,

---

[1] *Neva's surge and swell* St. Petersburg, the setting for Blind's
poem, sits at the mouth of the Neva River.

40　I see her—see her as she smiled;
Her face that of a little child
For innocent sweetness undefiled;
And that pathetic flower-like blue
Of eyes which, as they look at you,
45　Seemed yet to stab your bosom through.
I rowed, she steered; oars dipped and flashed,
The broadening river roared and splashed,
So that we hardly seemed to hear
Our comrades' voices, though so near;
50　Their faces seeming far away,
As still beneath that phantom day
I looked at her, she smiled at me!
And then we landed—I and she.

There's an old Café in the wood;
55　A student's haunt on summer eves,
Round which responsive poplar leaves
Quiver to each æolian mood
Like some wild harp a poet smites
On visionary summer nights.
60　I ordered supper, took a room
Green-curtained by the tremulous gloom
Of those fraternal poplar trees
Shaking together in the breeze;
My pulse, too, like a poplar tree,
65　Shook wildly as she smiled at me.
Eye in eye, and hand in hand,
Awake amid the slumberous land,
I told her all my love that night—
How I had loved her at first sight;
70　How I was hers, and seemed to be
Her own to all eternity.
And through the splendour of the white
Electrically glowing night,
Wind-wafted from some perfumed dell,
75　Tumultuously there loudly rose
Above the Neva's surge and swell
With amorous ecstasies and throes,
And lyric spasms of wildest wail,
The love-song of a nightingale.

80　I see her still beside me. Yea,
As if it were but yesterday,
I hear her tell with cheek aflame

Her ineradicable shame—
So sweet flower in such vile hands!
85 Oh, loved and lost beyond recall!
Like one who hardly understands,
I heard the story of her fall.
The odious barter of her youth,
Of beauty, innocence and truth,
90 Of all that honest women hold
Most sacred—for the sake of gold.
A weary seamstress, half a child,
Left unprotected in the street,
Where, when so hungry, you would meet
95 All sorts of tempters that beguiled.
Oh, infamous and senseless clods,
Basely to taint so pure a heart,
And make a maid fit for the gods
A creature of the common mart!
100 She spoke quite simply of things vile—
Of devils with an angel's face;
It seemed the sunshine of her smile
Must purify the foulest place.
She told me all—she would be true—
105 Told me things too sad, too bad;
And, looking in her eyes' clear blue
My passion nearly drove me mad!
I tried to speak, but tried in vain;
A sob rose to my throat as dry
110 As ashes—for between us twain
A murdered virgin seemed to lie.
And through the splendour of the white
Electrically glowing night,
Wind-wafted from some perfumed dell,
115 Tumultuously there loudly rose
Above the Neva's surge and swell,
With amorous ecstasies and throes,
And lyric spasms of wildest wail,
The love-song of a nightingale.

120 Poor craven creature! What was I,
To sit in judgment on her life,
Who dared not make this child my wife,
And lift her up to love's own sky?
This poor lost child we all—yes, all—
125 Had helped to hurry to her fall,
Making a social leper of

God's creature consecrate to love.
I looked at her—she smiled no more;
She understood it all before
130 A syllable had passed my lips;
And like a horrible eclipse,
Which blots the sunlight from the skies,
A blankness overspread her eyes—
The blankness as of one who dies.
135 I knew how much she loved me—knew
How pure and passionately true
Her love for me, which made her tell
What scorched her like the flames of hell.
And I, I loved her too, so much,
140 So dearly, that I dared not touch
Her lips that had been kissed in sin;
But with a reverential thrill
I took her work-worn hand and thin,
And kissed her fingers, showing still
145 Where needle-pricks had marred the skin.
And, ere I knew, a hot tear fell,
Scalding the place which I had kissed,
As between clenching teeth I hissed
Our irretrievable farewell.
150 And through the smoldering glow of night,
Mixed with the shining morning light
Wind-wafted from some perfumed dell,
Above the Neva's surge and swell,
With lyric spasms, as from a throat
155 Which dying breathes a faltering note,
There faded o'er the silent vale
The last sob of a nightingale.
—1891

A Mother's Dream

I

The snow was falling thick and fast
On Christmas Eve;
Across the heath the distant blast
Wailed wildly like a soul in grief,
5 A waste soul or a windy leaf
Whirled round and round without reprieve,
    And lost at last.

2

Lisa woke shivering from her sleep
　　At break of day,
10 And felt her flesh begin to creep.
"My child, my child!" she cried; "now may
Our blessed Lord, whose hand doth stay
The wild-fowl on their trackless way,
　　Thee guard and keep."[1]

3

15 "Dreams! dreams!" she to herself did say,
　　And shook with fright.
"I saw her plainly where I lay
Fly past me like a flash of light;
Fly out into the wintry night,
20 Out in the snow as snowy white,
　　Far, far away.

4

"Her cage hung empty just above
　　Your chair, ma mie;[2]
Empty as is my heart of love
25 Since you, my child, dwell far from me—
Dwell in the convent over sea;
All of you left to love Marie,
　　Your darling dove."

5

Hark to that fond, familiar coo!
30 　　Oh, joy untold!
It falls upon her heart like dew.
There safely perching as of old,
The dove is calling through the cold
And ghastly dawn o'er wood and wold,[3]
35 　　"Coo-whoo! Coo-whoo!"

6

The snow fell softly, flake by flake,
　　This Christmas Day,

And whitened every bush and brake;[4]
And o'er the hills so ashen gray
40 The wind was wailing far away,
Was wailing like a child astray
　　Whose heart must break.

7

"I miss my child," she wailed; "I miss
　　Her everywhere!
45 That's why I have such dreams as this.
I miss her step upon the stair,
I miss her laughter in the air,
I miss her bonnie face and hair,
　　And oh—her kiss!

8

50 "Christmas! Last Christmas, oh how fleet,
　　With lark-like trill,
She danced about on fairy feet!
Her eyes clear as a mountain rill,
Where the blue sky is lingering still;
55 Her rosebud lips the dove would bill
　　For something sweet.

9

"My dove! my dear! my undefiled!
　　Oh, heavy doom!
My life has left me with the child.
60 She was a sunbeam in my room,
She was a rainbow on the gloom,
She was the wild rose on a tomb
　　Where weeds run wild.

10

"And yet—'tis better thus! 'Tis best,
65 　　They tell me so.
Yes, though my heart is like a nest,
Whence all the little birds did go—
And empty nest that's full of snow—
Let me take all the wail and woe,
70 　　So she be blest.

---

[1] wild fowl … Thee guard and keep Perhaps a reference to Psalm 91.2–3, "My God, in whom I trust, / For he will deliver you from the snare of the fowler and from the deadly pestilence."

[2] ma mie Literally, "my crumb"; that is, the little part of me, the crumb that fell from the loaf.

[3] wold Here, open countryside.

[4] brake Fern, bracken.

11

"Let me take all the sin and shame,
    And weep for two,
That she may bear no breath of blame.
'Sin—sin!' they say; what sin had you,
75 Pure as the dawn upon the dew?
Child—robbed of a child's rightful due,
    Her father's name.

12

"I gave her life to live forlorn!
    Oh, let that day
80 Be darkness wherein I was born!
Let not God light it, let no ray
Shine on it; let it turn away
Its face, because my sin must weigh
    Her down with shame.

13

85 "I? I? Was I the sinner? I,
    Not he, they say,
Who told me, looking eye in eye,
We'd wed far North where grand and gray
His fair ancestral castle lay,
90 Amid the woods of Darnaway—[1]
    And told a lie.

14

"But I was young; and in my youth
    I simply thought
That English gentlemen spoke truth,
95 Even to a Norman[2] maid, who wrought
The blush-rose shells the tide had brought
To fairy toys which children bought
    Before my booth.

15

"'Those fairy fingers,' he would say,
100   'With shell-pink nails,
Shall shame the pearls of Darnaway!'
And in his yacht with swelling sails

We flew before the favoring gales,
Where leagues on leagues his woods and vales
105   Stretched dim and gray.

16

"Grim rose his castle o'er the wood;
    Its hoary halls
Frowned o'er the Findhorn's roaring flood;[3]
Where, winged with spray and water-galls,°   rainbows
110 The headlong torrent leaps and falls
In thunder through its tunnelled walls,
    Streaked as with blood."

17

It all came back in one wild flash
    Of cruel light,
115 And memory smote her like a lash:—
The foolish trust, the fond delight,
The helpless rage, the fevered flight,
The feet that dragged on through the night,
    The torrent's splash.

18

The long, long sickness bred of lies
120   And lost belief;
The short, sharp pangs and shuddering sighs;
The new-born babe, that in her grief
Bore her wrecked spirit such relief
125 As the dove-carried olive-leaf
    To Noah's eyes.[4]

19

It all came back, and lit her soul
    With lurid flame;
How she—she—she—from whom he stole
130 Her virgin love and honest name—
Must, for the ailing child's sake, tame
Her pride, and take—oh, shame of shame!—
    His lordship's dole.

---

[1] *woods of Darnaway* Darnaway Castle, in northern Scotland.

[2] *Norman* Native of Normandy, in north-western France.

[3] *Findhorn's roaring flood* Findhorn Bay, near Darnaway Castle.

[4] *dove-carried … eyes* Genesis 8.11, "And the dove came back to him in the evening, and lo, in her mouth a freshly plucked olive leaf; so Noah knew that the waters had subsided from the earth."

20

Like one whom grief hath driven wild,
135   She cried again,
"My snowdrop shall not be defiled,
Nor catch the faintest soil or stain,
Reared in the shadow of my pain!
How should a guilty mother train
140   A guiltless child?

21

"You shall be spotless, you!" said she,
        "Whate'er my woe;
Even as the snow on yonder lea.
You shall be spotless!" Faint and low,
145 The wind in dying seemed to blow,
To breathe across the hills of snow,
        "Marie! Marie!"

22

A voice was calling far away,
        O'er fields and fords,
150 Across the Channel veiled and gray;
A voice was calling without words,
Touching her nature's deepest chords;
Drawing her, drawing her as with cords—
        She might not stay.

23

155 Uprose the sun and still and round,
        Shorn of his heat,
Glared bloodshot o'er the frosty ground,
As down the shuttered village street
Fast, fast walked Lisa, and her feet
160 Left black tracks in earth's winding-sheet
        And made no sound.

24

Then on, on, by the iron way—
        With whistling scream—
Piercing hard rocks like potter's clay,
165 She flashed as in a shifting dream
Through flying town, o'er flowing stream,
Borne on by mighty wings of steam,
        Away, away.

25

A sound of wind, and in the air
170   The sea-gull's screech,
And waves lap-lapping everywhere;
A rush of ropes and volleyed speech,
And white cliffs sinking out of reach,
Then rising on the rival beach,
175   Boulogne-sur-Mer.[1]

26

Above the ramparts on the hill,
        Whence like a chart
It saw the low land spreading chill,
Within its cloistered walls apart
180 The Convent of the Sacred Heart
Rose o'er the noise of street and mart,
        Serenely still.

27

Above the unquiet sea it rose,
        A quiet nest,
185 Severed from earthly wants and woes.
There might the weary find his rest;
There might the pilgrim cease his quest;
There might the soul with guilt oppressed
        Implore repose.

28

The day was done, the sun dropped low
190   Behind the mill
That swung within its blood-red glow;
And up the street and up the hill
Lisa walked fast and faster still,
195 Her sable shadow lengthening chill
        Across the snow.

29

Hark! heavenly clear, with holy swell,
        She hears elate
The greeting of the vesper bell,[2]

---

[1] *white cliffs … Boulogne-sur-Mer* Lisa sails across the English
Channel from the "white cliffs" of Dover, England, to Boulogne-sur-
Mer, on the coast of northern France.

[2] *vesper bell* Bell that calls the devout—here the nuns—to evening
prayer.

200 And, knocking at the convent gate,
Sighs, "Here she prays God early and late;
Walled in from love, walled in from hate;
　　All's well! All's well!"

30

A sweat broke from her every pore,
205 　　And yet she smiled,
As, stumbling through the clanging door,
She faced a nun of aspect mild.
Like some starved wolf's her eyes gleamed wild:
"My child!" she gasped; "I want my child."
210 　　And nothing more.

31

The nun looked at her, shocked to see
　　The violent sway
Of love's unbridled agony;
And calmly queried on the way,
215 "Your child, Madame? What child, I pray?"
Still, still the mother could but say,
　　"Marie! Marie!"

32

The nun in silence bowed her head,
　　And then aloud,

220 "Christ Jesus knows our needs," she said.
"Madame, far from the sinful crowd,
The maiden to the Lord you vowed;
There is no safeguard like a shroud—
　　Your child is dead.

33

225 "Upon the night Christ saw the light
　　She passed away,
As snow will when the sun shines bright.
We heard her moaning where she lay,
'Come, mother, come, while yet you may;'
230 Then like a dove, at break of day,
　　Her soul took flight."

34

As from a blow the mother fell,
　　No moan made she;
They bore her to the little cell:
235 There in her coffin lay Marie,
Spotless as snow upon the lea,
Beautiful exceedingly:
　　All's well! All's well!
　　　　—1891

GERARD MANLEY HOPKINS
1844 – 1889

The Victorian priest and poet Gerard Manley Hopkins lived only 45 years, but his work spans three eras of literary history. A Romantic in his notions of the beauty and power of the natural world and of the importance of the imagination and the individual's connection with nature, Hopkins shared some affinities with Keats and other poets of the Romantic period. He also shared affinities with the Victorian Pre-Raphaelites, and like them was very influenced by the writings of John Ruskin. But because his poems and letters, in which he outlined his innovative poetic theories, were not published until 1918, some 30 years after his death, he is sometimes grouped with such Modernists as T.S. Eliot and Ezra Pound. Indeed these poets were influenced by Hopkins's experimental verse, with its unconventional syntax, dense alliteration, and "sprung rhythm" (the term Hopkins coined to describe his unique metric style).

Hopkins was born in Essex of affluent parents and showed promise as a scholar from an early age, but he was clearly also talented in music and the visual arts. His early schooling was at Highgate, where he studied under, and formed a lifelong friendship with, the Pre-Raphaelite poet R.W. Dixon. Hopkins went on to study classics at Oxford, where he became known as the "Star of Balliol [College]" and was educated by such luminaries as Benjamin Jowett and Walter Pater. While Pater's aestheticism was indeed an influence on Hopkins's artistic philosophies, no one at Oxford had a greater impact on him than did John Henry Newman. A convert to Roman Catholicism who later became a Cardinal, Newman was one of the leaders of the "Oxford Movement" of the 1830s and early 1840s, a Tractarian movement (because of the "Tracts for the Times" that Newman and others wrote) that called for the Church of England to recognize points of communion with the Roman Catholic Church.

Hopkins's conversion to Roman Catholicism in 1866 estranged him from his devout Anglican parents, who wrote "terrible" letters to try to dissuade him from his decision to become a Jesuit priest. He replied to his father's concerns by saying: "I am surprised you shd. say fancy and aesthetic tastes have led me to my present state of mind: these wd. be better satisfied in the Church of England, for bad taste is always meeting one in the accessories of Catholicism." Hopkins served the Catholic Church for the rest of his life, and for many of those years he renounced his own poetry, burning much of it in the belief that, with the exception of sermons, authorship was not becoming for a priest. It was obvious, however, that he did not cease thinking about the techniques of writing, as his journals and letters, many written to his Oxford friend and poet (later Poet Laureate) Robert Bridges, attest.

After a famous shipwreck in 1875, Hopkins's superiors encouraged him to write of the fate of five Franciscan nuns, exiled from Germany by the Falk Laws, who had drowned in the disaster. In the long ode *The Wreck of the Deutschland* he began experimenting with the rhythms he had been thinking about for so long. According to Hopkins, every object in the natural world has a unique and fluid identity, or "inscape," an essence that comprises its form and its meaning. Hopkins also coined the term "instress" to describe the way in which objects or people perceive "inscape." Instress is a powerful burst of energy that allows an observer to penetrate and experience the object's essence. Poetry, for Hopkins, is instress, and that which it seeks to penetrate is the divine.

In creating a poetic sound that would present the inscape of objects and of speech itself, Hopkins was inspired by the rhythms of Welsh nursery rhymes and Old English poetry. "Sprung rhythm" was the result, a syntactically disjunctive, highly alliterative, and densely rhyming style that reconfigured the nature of stresses and line length. The poems in this style that followed *Deutschland*—among them the famous "God's Grandeur"—often aimed to celebrate the spiritual and the divine. Notably, Hopkins added the dedication "*To Christ our Lord*" to "The Windhover."

Hopkins continued to write poetry, but his duties as a priest took priority. He served from 1877 to 1879 in various parishes in Sheffield, Oxford, and London, and then went on to fulfill demanding duties in the dreary slums of Manchester, Liverpool, and Glasgow. In 1881 he began teaching at Stonyhurst College in Lancashire, and in 1884 was appointed Professor of Greek and Latin at University College in Dublin. Hopkins disliked both his duties at this university and the city itself, which was still recovering from the Great Famine. Years of illness and depression followed, combined with doubts about his ability to give himself completely to God. During these years of angst, Hopkins composed what are now called his "terrible sonnets," among them "Carrion Comfort" and "No Worst, There is None," named for their themes of anguish and desolation.

Hopkins was not to live long in Ireland; he contracted typhoid fever and died in 1889 at the age of 45. Robert Bridges edited a volume of his poetry, *The Poems of Gerard Manley Hopkins*, and released it to the public thirty years after Hopkins's death, presumably waiting until the world was ready to hear the sound of the poet who acknowledged his "oddness" by saying: "The effect of studying masterpieces is to make me admire and do otherwise." Although his output was relatively small, the poet who "did otherwise" made an enormous impact on the literary world, and has influenced several generations of poets.

⌘ ⌘ ⌘

God's Grandeur

The world is charged with the grándeur of God.
　　It will flame out, like shining from shook foil;[1]
It gathers to a greatness, like the ooze of oil
Crushed.[2] Why do men then now not reck°　　*regard*　10
　　his rod?
5　Generátions have trod, have trod, have trod;
　　And all is seared with trade; bleared, smeared, with
　　　toil;
And wears man's smudge and shares man's smell:
　　the soil
Is bare now, nor can foot feel, being shod.

Ánd, for° all this, náture is never spent;　　*despite*
　　There lives the dearest freshness deep down things;
And though the last lights off the black West went
　　Oh, morning, at the brown brink eastward,
　　　springs—
Because the Holy Ghost óver the bent
　　World broods with warm breast and with ah!
　　　bright wings.
—1918 (WRITTEN 1877)

[1] [Hopkins's note] I mean foil in its sense of leaf or tinsel. ...Shaken goldfoil gives off broad glares like sheet lightning and also, and this is true of nothing else, owing to its zigzag dints and creasings and network of small many cornered facets, a sort of fork lightning too.

[2] *oil / Crushed* I.e., as olive oil.

The Wreck of the Deutschland[1]

December 6. 7.1875
*To the happy memory of five Franciscan nuns, exiles by
the Falck Laws,[2] drowned between midnight and
morning of December 7*

PART THE FIRST

1

Thou mastering me
God! giver of breath and bread;
Wórld's stránd,° swáy of the séa;   shore
Lord of living and dead;
5 Thou hast bóund bónes and véins in me, fástened
me flésh,
And áfter it álmost únmade, what with dréad,
Thy doing: and dost thou touch me afresh?
Óver agáin I féel thy fínger and find thée.

2

I did say yes
10 O at líghtning and láshed ród;
Thou heardst me, truer than tongue, confess
Thy terror, O Christ, O God;
Thou knówest the wálls, áltar and hour and níght:
The swoon of a heart that the sweep and the hurl
of thee trod
15 Hárd dówn with a horror of height:
And the midriff astrain with leaning of, laced with fire
of stress.

3

The frown of his face
Before me, the hurtle of hell
Behind, where, where was a, where was a
place?—
20 I whirled out wings that spell

And fled with a fling of the heart to the heart of
the Host.—[3]
My heart, but you were dovewinged, I can tell,
Cárrier-wítted, I am bóld to bóast,
To flash from the flame to the flame then, tower from
the grace to the grace.

4

25 I am sóft síft
In an hourglass—at the wall
Fast, but mined with a motion, a drift,
And it crowds and it combs to the fall;
I stéady as a wáter in a wéll, to a póise, to a páne,
30 But roped with, always, all the way down from the
tall
Fells or flanks of the voel,[4] a vein
Of the góspel próffer, a préssure, a prínciple, Christ's
gíft.

5

I kiss my hand
To the stars, lovely-asunder
35 Starlight, wafting him out of it; and
Glow, glory in thunder;
Kiss my hand to the dappled-with-damson[5] west:
Since, thóugh he is únder the wórld's spléndour
and wónder,
His mýstery múst be instréssed,[6] stressed;
40 For I greet him the days I meet him, and bless when I
understand.

6

Not out of his bliss
Springs the stress felt
Nor first from heaven (and few know this)
Swings the stroke dealt—
45 Stroke and a stress that stars and storms deliver,

---

[1] *The Wreck of the Deutschland* The *Deutschland*, a German ship,
ran aground on a shoal off the coast of England in December 1875.
With the lifeboats of the ship stripped away by the storm, five nuns
drowned in her hold. As they awaited death, their leader reportedly
called out "O Christ, come quickly!"

[2] *Falck Laws* Anti-Catholic German legislation.

[3] *Host* The consecrated bread of the Holy Eucharist, which
represents the Body of Christ.

[4] *Fells* Pastures; *voel* Mountain.

[5] *damson* Dark purple.

[6] *instréssed* The word, invented by Hopkins, means imbued with
that force which sustains the uniqueness of an object, or the essential
quality of a thing.

That guilt is hushed by, hearts are flushed by and
    melt—
    But it rídes tíme like ríding a ríver
(And here the faithful waver, the faithless fable and
    miss).

7

        It dates from day
50   Of his going in Galilee;
    Warm-laid grave of a womb-life grey;
      Manger, maiden's knee;
The dense and the driven Passion, and frightful
    sweat:
    Thence the discharge of it, there its swelling to be,
55   Though félt befóre, though in high flood
      yét—
What none would have known of it, only the heart,
    being hard at bay,

8

        Is out with it! Oh,
    We lash with the best or worst
    Word last! How a lush-kept plush-capped sloe[1]
60   Will, mouthed to flesh-burst,
Gush!—flush the man, the being with it, sour or
    sweet
    Brim, in a flásh, fúll!—Híther then, lást or fírst,
    To hero of Calvary, Christ's feet—
Never ask if méaning it, wánting it, wárned of
    it—mén gó.

9

65   Be adored among men,
    God, three-numberèd form;
    Wring thy rebel, dogged in den,
      Man's malice, with wrecking and storm.
Beyónd sáying swéet, past télling of tóngue,
70   Thou art lightning and love, I found it, a winter
    and warm;
    Father and fondler of heart thou hast wrung:
Hast thy dark descending and most art merciful then.

10

        With an anvil-ding

---

[1] *sloe* Fruit of the blackthorn.

    And with fire in him forge thy will
75   Or rather, rather then, stealing as Spring
      Through him, melt him but master him
      still:
    Whether át ónce, as ónce at a crásh Pául,
    Or as Áustin,[2] a língering-óut swéet skíll,
    Make mercy in all of us, out of us all
80 Mástery, bút be adóred, bút be adóred King.

PART THE SECOND

11

    "Some find me a swórd; sóme
    The flánge° and the ráil; fláme,   *rim*
    Fang, or flood" goes Death on drum,
      And stórms búgle his fáme.
5   But *wé* dréam we are róoted in éarth—Dúst!
Flesh falls within sight of us: we, though our
    flower the same,
    Wave with the meadow, forget that there must
The sóur scýthe crínge, and the bléar sháre cóme.

12

    —On Saturday sailed from Bremen,
10   American-outward-bound,
    Take settler and seamen, tell men with
      women,
      Two hundred souls in the round—
    O Father, nor under thy feathers[3] nor ever as
    guessing
The goal was a shoal, of a fourth the doom to be
    drowned;
15   Yet *did* the dark side of the bay of thy blessing
Not vault them, the million of rounds of thy mercy
    not reeve[4] even them in?

13

      Into the snows she sweeps,
    Hurling the Haven behind,

---

[2] *Paul … Áustin* St. Paul, whose conversion in an instant on the
road to Damascus (Acts 9.1–19) was very different from the
conversion over many years of St. Augustine (354–430 CE).

[3] *under thy feathers* Reference to Psalm 91.4: "He will cover you
with His feathers, and under His wings you will find refuge."

[4] *reeve* Nautical term: to lace up with ropes.

The Deutschland, on Sunday; and so the sky
        keeps,
20   For the infinite air is unkind,
And the sea flint-flake, black-backed in the regular
        blow,
Sitting Eastnortheast, in cursed quarter, the wind;
          Wiry and white-fiery and whírlwind-swivellèd
          snów
Spins to the widow-making unchilding unfathering
        deeps.

                              14

25   She drove in the dark to leeward,
          She struck—not a reef or a rock
But the combs of a smother of sand: night
        drew her
        Dead to the Kentish Knock;[1]
And she beat the bank down with her bows and
        the ride of her keel;
30   The breakers rolled on her beam with ruinous
        shock;
          And, canvass and compass, the whorl and the
          wheel
Idle for ever to waft her or wind her with, these she
        endūred.

                              15

          Hope had grown grey hairs,
          Hope had mourning on,
35   Trénched with téars, cárved with cáres,
          Hope was twelve hours gone;
And frightful a nightfall folded rueful a day
Nor rescue, only rocket and lightship,[2] shone,
        And lives at last were washing away:
40 To the shrouds they took,—they shook in the hurling
        and horrible airs.

                              16

          One stirred from the rigging to save
          The wild woman-kind below,
        With a rope's end round the man, handy and
        brave—
          He was pitched to his death at a blow,

45 For all his dreadnought° breast and braids   *fearless*
          of thew:°   *muscle*
They could téll him for hóurs, dándled the tó and
        the fró
        Through the cobbled foam-fleece. What could
        he do
With the burl of the fóuntains of aír, búck and the
        flóod of the wave?

                              17

          They fought with God's cold—
50   And they could not, and fell to the deck
(Crushed them) or water (and drowned them)
        or rolled
        With the searomp over the wreck.
Night roared, with the heartbreak hearing a
        heartbroke rabble,
The woman's wailing, the crying of child without
        check—
55   Till a líoness aróse bréasting the bábble,
A próphetess tówered in the túmult, a virginal tóngue
        tóld.

                              18

          Ah, touched in your bower of bone,
          Are you! turned, for an exquisite smart,
        Have you! make words break from me here all
        alone,
60   Do you!—móther of béing in me, héart.
O unteachably after evil, but uttering truth,
Why, tears! is it? tears; such a melting, a
        madrigal° start!   *song*
        Never-eldering revel and river of youth,
What can it be, this glee? the good you have there of
        your own?

                              19

65   Sister, a sister calling
          A master, her master and mine!—
        And the inboard seas run swirling and hawling;
          The rash smart sloggering brine
Blinds her; but shé that wéather sees óne thing,
        óne;
70 Has óne fetch[3] ín her: she réars hersélf to divíne

---

[1] *Kentish Knock* Sandbank near the mouth of the Thames River.

[2] *lightship* Floating warning light.

[3] *fetch* Solution.

Éars, and the cáll of the táll nún
    To the mén in the tóps and the táckle rode óver the
    stórm's brawling.

20

    She was first of a five and came
      Of a coifèd sisterhood.[1]
75   (O Deutschland, double a desperate name!
      O wórld wíde of its góod!
    But Gertrude, lily, and Luther,[2] are two of a town,
    Chríst's líly, and béast of the wáste wóod:
      From life's dáwn it is dráwn dówn,
80 Ábel is Cáin's brother and bréasts they have súcked
    the sáme.)

21

    Loathed for a love men knew in them,
      Banned by land of their birth,
    Rhíne refúsed them, Thámes would rúin
      them;
      Surf, snow, river and earth
85 Gnashed: but thou art above, thou Orion of light;
    Thy unchancelling poising palms were weighing
      the worth,
      Thou mártyr-máster: in thý síght
Storm flákes were scróll-leaved flówers, lily
    shówers—sweet héaven was astréw in them.

22

    Five! the finding and sake
90   And cipher of suffering Christ.
    Márk, the márk is of mán's máke
      And the word of it Sacrificed,
    But he scores it in scarlet himself on his own
    bespoken,
      Before-time-taken, dearest prizèd and priced—
95   Stigma, signal, cinquefoil[3] token
For léttering of the lámb's fléece, rúddying of the
    róse-fláke.

---

[1] *coifèd sisterhood* Reference to the nuns' veils.

[2] *Gertrude ... Luther* Hopkins contrasts St. Gertrude the Great (1256–1301), the first nun's namesake, with Martin Luther (1483–1546) the Protestant reformer, whose doctrinal descendants enacted the laws that exiled the nuns. St. Gertrude is thought to have been born in the town of Eiselben, the birthplace of Luther.

[3] *cinquefoil* Five-leaved plant.

23

    Joy fall to thee, father Francis,
      Drawn to the Life that died;
    With the gnarls of the nails in thee, niche of
      the lance, his
100   Lovescape crucified
    And seal of his seraph-arrival! and these thy
    daughters
    And five-livèd and leavèd favour and pride,
      Are sísterly séaled in wíld wáters,
To bathe in his fall-gold mercies, to breathe in his all-
    fire glances.

24

105   Away in the loveable west,
      On a pastoral forehead of Wales,
    I was under a roof here, I was at rest,
      And they the prey of the gales;
    She to the black-about air, to the breaker, the
    thickly
110 Falling flakes, to the throng that catches and
    quails,
      Was calling "O Christ, Christ, come quickly":
The cross to her she calls Christ to her, christens her
    wild-worst Best.

25

    The majesty! what did she mean?
      Breathe, arch and original Breath.
115 Is it lóve in her of the béing as her lóver had
      béen?
      Breathe, body of lovely Death.
    They were élse-mínded then, áltogéther, the mén
Wóke thee with a *We are périshing* in the wéather
    of Gennésaréth.[4]
      Or ís it that she críed for the crówn thén,
120 The keener to come at the comfort for feeling the
    combating keen?

26

    For how to the heart's cheering
      The down-dugged ground-hugged grey

---

[4] *Gennésaréth* Sea of Galilee. In Matthew 8.23–27, Jesus and his disciples are caught in a boat during a storm on the Sea of Galilee. His disciples cry out in fear, and Jesus calms the storm.

Hovers off, the jay-blue heavens appearing
　　Of pied and peeled May!
125 Blue-beating and hoary-glow height; or night, still
　　higher,
　　With bélled fíre and the móth-soft Mílky Wáy.
　　What bý your méasure is the héaven of desire,
The tréasure never éyesight gót, nor was éver guessed
　　whát for the héaring?

27

　　Nó, but it was nót thése.
130 　　The jáding and the jár of the cárt,
　　Time's tásking, it is fáthers that ásking for éase
　　Of the sódden-with-its-sórrowing héart,
　　Not danger, electrical-horror; then, further, it finds
　　The appéaling of the Pássion is ténderer in práyer
　　apárt:
135 　　Other, I gather, in measure her mind's
Búrden, in wínd's búrly and béat of endrágonèd séas.

28

　　But how shall I ... Make me room there;
　　Reach me a ... Fancy, come faster—
　　Strike you the sight of it? look at it loom there,
140 　　Thing that she ... There then! the Master,
Ipse,° the ónly one, Chríst, Kíng, Héad:　　　*Himself*
　　He was to cure the extremity where he had cast
　　her;
　　Do, deal, lord it with living and dead;
Let him ride, her pride, in his triumph, despatch and
　　have done with his doom there.

29

145 　　Ah! thére was a héart right!
　　There was single eye!
　　Réad the unshápeable shóck níght
　　And knew the who and the why;
　　Wording it how but by him that present and past,
150 　　Heaven and earth are word of, worded by?—
　　The Símon-Péter of a sóul! to the blást
Tárpéïan-fast,[1] but a blówn béacon of líght.

30

　　Jésu, héart's líght,
　　Jésu, máid's són,
155 　　Whát was the féast fóllowed the níght
　　Thou hadst glóry of thís nún?—
Féast of the óne wóman without stáin.
For so conceivèd, so to conceive thee is done;
　　But here was heart-throe, birth of a brain,
160 Wórd, that héard and képt thee and úttered thee
　　óutríght.

31

　　Well, shé has thée for the pain, for the
　　Pátience; but píty of the rést of them!
　　Heart, go and bleed at a bitterer vein for the
　　Comfortless unconfessed of them—
165 No not uncomforted: lovely-felicitous Providence,
Finger of a ténder of, O of a féathery délicacy, the
　　bréast of the
　　Maiden could obey so, be a bell to, ring óf it,
　　and
Stártle the poor shéep back! is the shópwrack then a
　　hárvest, does témpest carry the gráin for thee?

32

　　I admire thee, máster of the tídes,
170 　　Of the Yóre-flood,[2] of the yéar's fáll;
　　The recúrb and the recóvery of the gúlf's sídes,
　　The girth of it and the whárf of it and the
　　wáll;
　　Stánching, quénching ócean of a mótionable mínd;
　　Gróund of béing and gránite of it: pást áll
175 　　Grásp Gód, thróned behínd
Déath, with a sóvereignty that héeds but hídes, bódes
　　but abídes;

33

　　With a mércy that oútrides
　　The all of water, an ark
　　For the lístener; for the língerer with a lóve
　　glídes
180 　　Lówer than déath and the dárk;
　　A véin for the vísiting of the pást-prayer, pént in
　　príson,

---

[1] *Tárpéïan-fast* In the Roman Republic, convicted criminals were executed by being thrown off the Tarpeian Rock.

[2] *Yóre-flood* Ancient flood (i.e., the Biblical flood).

The-last-breath penitent spirits—the uttermost
    mark
    Our passion-plungèd giant risen,
The Christ of the Father compassionate, fetched in
    the storm of his strides.

34

185   Now burn, new born to the world,
          Double-naturèd name,
      The heaven-flúng, heart-fléshed, máiden-fúrled
      Míracle-in-Máry-of-fláme,
    Mid-numberèd he in three of the thunder-throne!
190   Not a dóomsday dázzle in his cóming nor dárk as
        he cáme;
      Kind, but róyally recláiming his ówn;
A released shówer, let flásh to the shire, not a
    líghtning of fíre hard húrled.

35

          Dáme, at óur dóor
          Drówned, and among óur shóals,
195   Remémber us in the róads, the heaven-háven
        of the rewárd:
      Our kíng back, Oh, upon Énglish sóuls!
Let him éaster in us, be a dáyspring to the dímness
    of us, be a crímson-cresseted[1] east,
More bríghtening her, ráre-dear Britain, as his
    réign rólls,
Príde, rose, prínce, hero of us, hígh-príest,
200   Oür héart's charity's héarth's fíre, oür thóughts'
    chivalry's thróng's Lórd.
    —1918 (WRITTEN 1875–76)]

The Windhover:[2]
to Christ our Lord

I caught this morning morning's minion, king-
    dom of daylight's dauphin,[3] dapple-dáwn-drawn
    Falcon, in his riding

---

[1] *cresseted* Lit by a cresset, a type of oil lamp.

[2] *Windhover* Another name for a kestrel, a small falcon that
appears to hover in the wind.

[3] *dauphin* Title of the eldest son of the King of France—the heir.

    Of the rólling level úndernéath him steady air, and
      striding
High there, how he rung upon the rein of a
    wimpling° wing   *rippling*
5 In his écstasy! then off, off forth on swing,
    As a skate's heel sweeps smooth on a bow-bend:
      the hurl and gliding
    Rebuffed the bíg wind. My heart in hiding
Stírred for a bird,—the achieve of, the mástery of the
    thing!

Brute beauty and valour and act, oh, air, pride, plŭme,
    here
10   Buckle! AND the fire that breaks from thee then, a
    billion
Tímes told lovelier, more dangerous, O my
    chevalier!°   *horseman*

    No wŏnder of it: shéer plód makes plóugh down
      síllion°   *furrows*
Shíne, and blue-bleak embers, ah my dear,
    Fall, gáll themsélves, and gásh gŏld-vermílion.
    —1918 (WRITTEN 1877)

Pied[4] Beauty

G lóry be to God for dappled things—
    For skies of couple-colour as a brinded° cow; *spotted*
      For rose-moles all in stipple upon trout that
      swim;
Fresh-firecoal chestnut-fálls;[5] fínches' wings;
    Lándscape plotted and pieced—fold,° fallow, and
      plough;   *pasture*
      And áll trádes, their gear and tackle and
      trim.°   *equipment*

Áll things counter,° original, spáre,° stránge; *contrary / rare*
    Whatever is fickle, frecklèd (who knows how?)
      With swíft, slów; sweet, soŭr; adázzle, dím;
10 He fathers-forth whose beauty is pást chánge:
              Práise hím.
    —1918 (WRITTEN 1877)

---

[4] *Pied* Multicolored.

[5] *Fresh … fálls* Freshly fallen, brightly colored chestnuts.

Felix Randal

Félix Rándal the fárrier,[1] O is he déad then? my
  dúty all énded,
Who have watched his mould of man, big-bóned and
  hardy-handsome
Pining, píning, till time when reason rámbled in it
  and some
Fatal four disorders, fléshed there, all contended?

5 Síckness bróke him. Impatient, he cursed at first, but
  mended
Being anointed[2] and all; though a heavenlier heart
  began some
Mónths éarlier, since I had our swéet repríeve and
  ránsom[3]
Téndered to him. Áh well, God rést him áll road
  éver[4] he offénded!

This séeing the síck endéars them tó us, us tóo it
  endéars.
10 My tongue had taught thee comfort, touch had
  quenched thy tears,
Thy tears that touched my heart, child, Félix, poor
  Felix Randal;

How far from then forethought of, all thy more
  boisterous years,
When thou at the random[5] grim fórge, pówerful
  amídst péers,
Didst fettle° for the great grey drayhorse[6] his bright
  and battering sandal!   *prepare*
—1918 (WRITTEN 1880)

1 *férrier* One who shoes horses.
2 *anointed* As in the sacrament of Extreme Unction, performed for the dying.
3 *had our swéet repríeve and ránsom* I.e., had received Holy Communion.
4 *all road éver* However.
5 *random* Roughly built.
6 *drayhorse* Powerful horse used for drawing a sled.

Spring and Fall: to a Young Child

Márgarét, áre you gríeving
  Over Goldengrove unleaving?
Leáves, like the thíngs of mán, you
With your fresh thoughts care for, can you?
5 Ah! ás the héart grows ólder
It will come to such sights colder
By and by, nor spare a sigh
Though worlds of wanwood leafmeal[7] lie;
And yet you *will* weep and know why.
10 Now no matter, child, the name:
Sórrow's spríngs áre the sáme.
Nor mouth had, no nor mind, expressed
What héart héard of, ghóst° guéssed: *spirit*
It ís the blíght mán was bórn for,
15 It is Margaret you mourn for.
—1918 (WRITTEN 1880)

[As kingfishers catch fire]

As kingfishers catch fire, dragonflies draw flame;
  As tumbled over rim in roundy wells
  Stones ring; like each tucked° string tells, each
    hung bell's   *plucked*
Bow swung finds tongue to fling out broad its name;
5 Each mortal thing does one thing and the same:
  Deals out that being indoors each one dwells;
  Selves—goes its self; *myself* it speaks and spells,
Crying *What I do is me: for that I came.*

I say more: the just man justices;
10 Keeps grace: that keeps all his goings graces;
Ácts in God's eye what in God's eye he is—

  Chríst. For Christ plays in ten thousand places,
Lovely in limbs, and lovely in eyes not his
  To the Father through the features of men's faces.
—1918 (WRITTEN 1879–82)

7 *wanwood leafmeal* Decaying wood and leaves.

[No worst, there is none]

No worst, there is none. Pitched past pitch of grief,
    More pangs will, schooled at forepangs, wilder wring.
Comforter, where, where is your comforting?
Mary, mother of us, where is your relief?
My cries heave, herds-long; huddle in a main, a chief—
Woe, world-sorrow; on an áge-old ánvil wínce and
    síng—
Then lull, then leave off. Fury had shrieked "No ling-
Ering! Let me be fell:° force[1] I must be brief."   *fierce*
O the mind, mind has mountains; cliffs of fall
Frightful, sheer, no-man-fathomed. Hold them cheap
May who ne'er hung there. Nor does long our small
Durance deal with that steep or deep. Here! creep,
Wretch, under a comfort serves in a whirlwind: all
Life death does end and each day dies with sleep.
—1918 (WRITTEN 1884–85)

[I wake and feel the fell[2] of dark, not day]

I wake and feel the fell of dark, not day
    What hours, O what black hours we have spent
This night! what sights you, heart, saw, ways you went!
And more must, in yet longer light's delay.

With witness I speak this. But where I say
Hours I mean years, mean life. And my lament
Is cries countless, cries like dead letters sent
To dearest him that lives alas! away.

I am gall, I am heartburn. God's most deep decree
Bitter would have me taste: my taste was me;
Bones built in me, flesh filled, blood brimmed the
    curse.

Selfyeast of spirit a dull dough sours. I see
The lost are like this, and their scourge to be
As I am mine, their sweating selves; but worse.
—1918

[Not, I'll not, carrion[3] comfort]

Not, I'll not, carrion comfort, Despair, not feast on
    thee;
Not untwist—slack they may be—these last strands of
    man
In me ór, most weary, cry *I can no more.* I can;
Can something, hope, wish day come, not choose not
    to be.

But ah, but O thou terrible, why wouldst thou rude
    on me[4]
Thy wring-world right foot rock? lay a lionlimb
    against me? scan
With darksome devouring eyes my bruisèd bones? and
    fan,
O in turns of tempest, me heaped there; me frantic to
    avoïd thee and flee?

Why? That my chaff might fly; my grain lie, sheer and
    clear.
Nay in all that toil, that coil,° since (seems) I kissed
    the rod,   *tumult*
Hand rather, my heart lo! lapped strength, stole joy,
    would laugh, cheer.
Cheer whóm though? The hero whose héaven-
    handling flúng me, fóot tród
Me? or mé that fóught him? O which one? is it éach
    one? That níght, that yéar
Of now done darkness I wretch lay wrestling with (my
    God!) my God.
—1918

That Nature is a Heraclitean Fire[5] and of the Comfort of the Resurrection

Cloud-puffball, torn tufts, tossed pillows | flaunt
    forth, then chevy° on an air—   *race*

---

[1] *force* Perforce, or out of necessity.

[2] *fell* Bitterness; also an animal hide, used as a covering.

[3] *carrion* Dead flesh.

[4] *rude on me* Roughly against me.

[5] *Heraclitean Fire* Heraclitus (c. 535–475 BCE), a Greek philosopher, taught that everything is derived from fire, and therefore in a
constant state of change.

Built thoroughfare: heaven-roysterers,[1] in gay-gangs | they throng; they glitter in marches.
Down roughcast,[2] down dazzling whitewash, | wherever an elm arches,
Shivelights[3] and shadowtackle[4] in long | lashes lace, lance, and pair.
5   Delightfully the bright wind boisterous | ropes, wrestles, beats earth bare
Of yestertempest's creases; in pool and rut peel parches
Squandering ooze to squeezed | dough, crúst, dust; stánches,° stárches   *reinforces*
Squadroned masks and manmarks | treadmire toil there
Fóotfretted in it. Million-fuelèd, | nature's bonfire burns on.
10 But quench her bonniest, dearest | to her, her clearest-selvèd spark
Mán, how fást his fíredint, | his mark on mind, is gone!
Bóth are in an ŭnfáthomable, áll is in an enórmous dárk
Drowned. O pity and indig | nation! Manshape, that shone
Sheer off, disseveral,° a star, death blots black out; nor mark   *separate*
15   Is any of him at all so stark
But vastness blurs and time | beats level. Enough! the Resurrection,
A héart's-clarion! Awáy grief's gásping, | joyless days, dejection.
              Across my foundering deck shone
A beacon, an eternal beam. | Flesh fade, and mortal trash
20 Fáll to the residuary worm; | world's wildfire, leave but ash:

              In a flash, at a trumpet crash,
I am all at once what Christ is, | since he was what I am, and
This Jack,° jóke, poor pótsherd,[5] | patch,[6] matchwood,° immortal diamond,   *fellow / kindling*
              Is immortal diamond.
—1918 (WRITTEN 1888)

[Thou art indeed just, Lord]

Justus quidem tu es, Domine, si disputem tecum: verumtamen justa loquar ad te: Quare via impiorum prosperatur? etc.[7]

Thou art indeed just, Lord, if I contend
   With thee; but, sir, so what I plead is just.
 Whý do sínners' ways prosper? and why must
Dísappóintment all I endeavour end?
5   Wert thou my enemy, O thou my friend,
How wouldst thou worse, I wonder, than thou dost
Defeat, thwart me? Oh, the sots° and thralls   *drunkards*
      of lust
Do in spare hours more thrive than I that spend,
Sir, life upon thy cause. See, banks and brakes°   *thickets*
10 Now, leavèd how thick! lacèd they are again
With fretty chervil,[8] look, and fresh wind shakes
Them; birds build—but not I build; no, but strain,
Time's eunuch, and not breed one work that wakes.
Mine, O thou lord of life, send my roots rain.
—1918 (WRITTEN 1889)

---

[1] *roysterers* Noisy party-goers.

[2] *roughcast* Wall plastering made of lime and gravel.

[3] *Shivelights* Strips of light.

[4] *shadowtackle* Shadows which resemble a ship's rigging.

[5] *potsherd* Piece of broken pottery.

[6] *patch* Simpleton.

[7] *Justus … prosperatur* Latin: "You are always righteous, O Lord, when I bring a case before you. Yet I would speak with you about your justice: why does the way of the wicked prosper?" (Jeremiah 12.1).

[8] *fretty chervil* Interlaced leaves and stems of a garden herb.

In Context

The Growth of "The Windhover"

Manuscript copies of Hopkins's poems open a remarkable window on his unique approach to poetic rhythm—and to poetic composition; "The Windhover" is a particularly interesting example.

The first page reproduced here (headed "Another version") is entirely in Hopkins's hand, and probably dates from 1877. The second dates from 1883; it is from an album of "fair copy" transcriptions of Hopkins's (often not very legible) manuscripts that was prepared by his friend and mentor, the poet Robert Bridges, and then corrected by Hopkins in 1884. According to Hopkins scholar Norman H. Mackenzie, the corrections and revisions here in Hopkins's handwriting include the addition of ": to Christ our Lord" to the title; the alteration of "o air" to "oh, air"; the replacement of the ampersand with the word "AND" in line 10; the addition of stress marks in lines two, 3, 12, and 14; the addition of a "slur" between "the" and "hurl" in line 6, and the addition of seven "outrides" (as Hopkins termed the curved marks below the line).

Adding marks to indicate particularly strong stresses and adding "slurs" and "outrides" were among the many ways Hopkins endeavored to direct the reading of his poems according to the principles of what he termed "sprung rhythm" (see the Glossary at the back of this volume for a definition). The meaning of the "slur" mark is fairly straightforward; it indicates where two syllables should be compressed together so as to be pronounced as one—much as in this case an apostrophe might be used to do (*th'hurl*). The "outride" denotes a much less familiar concept, and it may be best to quote Hopkins directly here. At one point he writes that "the outride under one or more syllables makes them extrametrical: a slight pause follows as if the voice were silently making its way back to the highroad of the verse." Elsewhere he describes syllables so marked as "hangers or outriders," meaning "one, two or three slack syllables added to a foot and not counted in the nominal scanning. They are so called because they seem to hang below the line or ride forward or backward from it in another dimension than the line itself, according to a principle needless to explain here."

When entering corrections and revisions in 1884 Hopkins also added at lower right the date and place of the poem's original composition. The marginal notes, however, were evidently added by Bridges when he transcribed them; "= A", for example, indicates that the hyphen Bridges has added to line 6 is taken from an early manuscript of the poem (referred to as manuscript A).

The Windhover (Another version) – to Christ our Lord.

I caught this morning morning's minion, kingdom of daylight's dauphin, dapple-dawn-drawn Falcon, in his riding   [and striding
    Of the rolling level underneath him steady air, &
High there
: Oh how he hung upon the rein of a wimpling wing
In his ecstacy! then off, ; off forth on swing,
    As a skate's heel sweeps smooth on a bow-bend:
the hurl and gliding
    Rebuffed the big: wind . my heart in hiding
: Stirred for a bird — for the mastery of the thing!
the achieve of

: Brute beauty and valour and act, oh air, pride, plume,
here   [then, a billion
    Buckle! And the fire that breaks from thee
: Times told lovelier, more dangerous, O my
chevalier!

    No wonder of it: sheer; plod makes plough down
sillion
: Shine, and blue-bleak embers, ah my dear,
    Fall, gall themselves, and gash: gold-vermilion.

(8)

The Windhover: to Christ our Lord

~

I caught this morning morning's minion, king-
dom of daylight's dauphin, dapple-dawn-drawn Falcon, in his riding
Of the rolling, level underneath him steady air, & striding
High there, how he rung upon the rein of a wimpling wing
In his ecstacy! then off, off forth on swing,
As a skate's heel sweeps smooth on a bow-bend: the hurl & gliding   — A
Rebuffed the big wind. My heart in hiding
Stirred for a bird, — for the achieve of, the mastery of the thing!   , A, A.

Brute beauty & valour & act, oh, air, pride, plume, here
Buckle! AND the fire that breaks from thee then, a billion
Times told lovelier, more dangerous, o my chevalier!
No wonder of it: sheer plód makes plough down sillion
Shine, & blue-bleak embers, ah my dear,
Fall, gall themselves, & gash gold-vermilion.

~   St. Beuno's - May 30 1877

from *Journal* 1870–1874

[*"Inscape" and "Instress"*]

[April 15] The white violets are broader and smell; the blue, scentless and finer made, have sharper whelking[1] and a more winged recoil in the leaves.

Take a *few* primroses in a glass and the instress[2] of—brilliancy, sort of starriness: I have not the right word—so simple a flower gives is remarkable. It is, I think, due to the strong swell given by the deeper yellow middle.

"The young lambs bound As to the tabour's sound."[3]

They toss and toss: it is as if it were the earth that flung them, not themselves. It is the pitch of graceful agility when we think that.

April 16—Sometimes they rest a little space on the hind legs and the fore-feet drop curling in on the breast, not so liquidly as we see it in the limbs of foals though.

Bright afternoon; clear distances; Pendle[4] dappled with tufted shadow; west wind; interesting clouding, flat and lying in the warp of the heaved but the pieces with rounded outline and dolphin-backs showing in places and all was at odds and at Z's, one piece with another. Later beautifully delicate crisping. Later rippling....

April 21—We have had other such afternoons, one today—the sky a beautiful grained blue, silky lingering clouds in flat-bottomed loaves, others a little browner in ropes or in burly-shouldered ridges swanny and lustrous, more in the Zenith[5] stray packs of a sort of violet paleness. White-rose cloud formed fast, not in the same density—some caked and swimming in a wan white-ness, the rest soaked with the blue and like the leaf of a flower held against the light and diapered out by the worm or veining of deeper blue between rosette and rosette. Later / moulding, which brought rain: in perspective it was vaulted in very regular ribs with fretting between: but these are not ribs; they are a "wracking" install made of these two realities—the frets, which are scarves of rotten cloud bellying upwards and drooping at their ends and shaded darkest at the brow or tropic where they double to the eye, and the whiter field of sky showing between: the illusion looking down the "wagon" is complete. These swaths of fretted cloud move in rank, not in file.

April 22—But such a lovely damasking in the sky as today I never felt before. The blue was charged with simple instress, the higher, zenith sky earnest and frowning, lower more light and sweet. High up again, breathing through woolly coats of cloud or on the quains[6] and branches of the flying pieces it was the true exchange of crimson, nearer the earth / against the sun / it was turquoise, and in the opposite south-western bay below the sun it was like clear oil but just as full of colour, shaken over with slanted flashing "travellers," all in flight, stepping one behind the other, their edges tossed with bright ravelling,[7] as if white napkins were thrown up in the sun but not quite at the same moment so that they were all in a scale down the air falling one after the other to the ground. ...

[May 9] This day and May 11 the bluebells in the little wood between the College[8] and the highroad and in one of the Hurst Green[9] cloughs.[10] In the little wood / opposite the light / they stood in blackish spreads or sheddings like the spots on a snake. The heads are then like thongs and solemn in grain and grape-colour. But in the clough / through the light / they came in falls of sky-colour washing the brows and slacks of the ground

---

[1] *whelking* Ridges.

[2] *instress* Hopkins's own term, meaning the force or energy which sustains an inscape, which is the individual or essential quality of a thing.

[3] *"The ... sound."* From William Wordsworth's *Ode: Intimations of Immortality*, line 20–21; *tabour's* Drum's.

[4] *Pendle* Pendle Hill in Lancashire, England.

[5] *Zenith* Point in the sky directly overhead.

[6] *quains* Angles (Hopkins's own term).

[7] *ravelling* Frayed edges.

[8] *College* Stonyhurst College, the seminary where Hopkins studied, in Lancashire, England.

[9] *Hurst Green* Village in Blackburn, Lancashire, England.

[10] *cloughs* Ravines.

with vein-blue, thickening at the double, vertical themselves and the young grass and brake fern combed vertical, but the brake struck the upright of all this with light winged transomes.[1] It was a lovely sight.—The bluebells in your hand baffle you with their inscape, made to every sense: if you draw your fingers through them they are lodged and struggle / with a shock of wet heads; the long stalks rub and click and flatten to a fan on one another like your fingers themselves would when you passed the palms hard across one another, making a brittle rub and jostle like the noise of a hurdle strained by leaning against; then there is the faint honey smell and in the mouth the sweet gum when you bite them. But this is easy, it is the eye they baffle. They give one a fancy of panpipes and of some wind instrument with stops—a trombone perhaps. The overhung necks—for growing they are little more than a staff with a simple crook but in water, where they stiffen, they take stronger turns, in the head like sheephooks[2] or, when more waved throughout, like the waves riding through a whip that is being smacked—what with these overhung necks and what with the crisped ruffled bells dropping mostly on one side and the gloss these have at their footstalks they have an air of the knights at chess. Then the knot or "knoop" of buds some shut, some just gaping, which makes the pencil of the whole spike, should be noticed: the inscape of the flower most finely carried out in the siding of the axes, each striking a greater and greater slant, is finished in these clustered buds, which for the most part are not straightened but rise to the end like a tongue and this and their tapering and a little flattening they have made them look like the heads of snakes.

[July 19, 1872] Stepped into a barn of ours, a great shadowy barn, where the hay had been stacked on either side, and looking at the great rudely arched timber-frames—principals(?) and tie-beams, which make them look like bold big *As* with the cross-bar high up—I thought how sadly beauty of inscape was unknown and buried away from simple people and yet how near at hand it was if they had eyes to see it and it could be called out everywhere again …

After the examinations we went for our holiday out to Douglas in the Isle of Man. Aug. 3—At this time I had first begun to get hold of the copy of Scotus[3] on the Sentences in the Baddely library and was flush with a new stroke of enthusiasm. It may come to nothing or it may be a mercy from God. But just then when I took in any inscape of the sky or sea I thought of Scotus …

Aug. 10—I was looking at high waves. The breakers always are parallel to the coast and shape themselves to it except where the curve is sharp however the wind blows. They are rolled out by the shallowing shore just as a piece of putty between the palms whatever its shape runs into a long roll. The slant ruck[4] or crease one sees in them shows the way of the wind. The regularity of the barrels surprised and charmed the eye; the edge behind the comb or crest was as smooth and bright as glass. It may be noticed to be green behind and silver white in front: the silver marks where the air begins, the pure white is foam, the green / solid water. Then looked at to the right or left they are scrolled over like mouldboards[5] or feathers or jibsails seen by the edge. It is pretty to see the hollow of the barrel disappearing as the white combs on each side run along the wave gaining ground till the two meet at a pitch and crush and overlap each other.

About all the turns of the scaping[6] from the break and flooding of wave to its run out again I have not yet satisfied myself. The shores are swimming and the eyes have before them a region of milky surf but it is hard for them to unpack the huddling and gnarls of the water and law out the shapes and the sequence of the running: I catch however the looped or forked wisp made by every big pebble the backwater runs over—if it were clear and smooth there would be a network from their overlapping, such as can in fact be seen on smooth sand after the tide is out; then I saw it run browner, the foam dwindling and twitched into long chains of suds, while

---

[1] *transomes* Crossbeams.

[2] *sheephooks* Shepherds' crooks.

[3] *Scotus* Duns Scotus (c. 1266–1308), Scottish-born theologian and philosopher. In his *Lectura*, he analyzes Thomas Lombard's *Sentences*.

[4] *ruck* Ridge.

[5] *mouldboards* Boards attached to plows, used to form furrows.

[6] *scaping* Hopkins's term for a reflection or impression of the individual quality of a thing or action.

the strength of the backdraught shrugged the stones together and clocked them one against another …

April 8 [1873]—The ashtree growing in the corner of the garden was felled. It was lopped first: I heard the sound and looking out and seeing it maimed there came at that moment a great pang and I wished to die and not to see the inscapes of the world destroyed any more. …

July 23—To Beaumont: it was the rector's day. It was a lovely day: shires-long of pearled cloud under cloud, with a grey stroke underneath marking each row; beautiful blushing yellow in the straw of the uncut rye fields, the wheat looking white and all the ears making a delicate and very true crisping along the top and with just enough air stirring for them to come and go gently; then there were fields reaping. All this I would have looked at again in returning but during dinner I talked too freely and unkindly and had to do penance going home. One field I saw from the balcony of the house behind an elmtree, which it threw up, like a square of pale goldleaf, as it might be, catching the light.
(WRITTEN 1871–73)

from *Letter to Robert Bridges*

St. Giles's, Oxford.
25 February 1879

… No doubt my poetry errs on the side of oddness. I hope in time to have a more balanced and Miltonic[1] style. But as air, melody, is what strikes me most of all in music and design in painting, so design, pattern or what I am in the habit of calling "inscape" is what I above all aim at in poetry. Now it is the virtue of design, pattern, or inscape to be distinctive and it is the virtue of distinctiveness to become queer. This vice I cannot have escaped …
(WRITTEN 1879)

Author's Preface[2]

The poems in this book are written some in Running Rhythm, the common rhythm in English use, some in Sprung Rhythm, and some in a mixture of the two. And those in the common rhythm are some counterpointed,[3] some not.

Common English rhythm, called Running Rhythm above, is measured by feet[4] of either two or three syllables and (putting aside the imperfect feet at the beginning and end of lines and also some unusual measures in which feet seem to be paired together and double or composite feet to arise) never more or less.

Every foot has one principal stress or accent, and this or the syllable it falls on may be called the Stress of the foot and the other part, the one or two unaccented syllables, the Slack. Feet (and the rhythms made out of them) in which the stress comes first are called Falling Feet and Falling Rhythms, feet and rhythm in which the slack comes first are called Rising Feet and Rhythms, and if the stress is between two slacks there will be Rocking Feet and Rhythms. These distinctions are real and true to nature; but for purposes of scanning it is a great convenience to follow the example of music and take the stress always first, as the accent or the chief accent always comes first in a musical bar. If this is done there will be in common English verse only two possible feet—the so-called accentual Trochee[5] and Dactyl,[6] and correspondingly only two possible uniform rhythms, the so-called Trochaic and Dactylic. But they may be mixed and then what the Greeks called a Logaoedic Rhythm[7] arises. These are the facts and according to these the scanning of ordinary regularly-written English verse is very simple indeed and to bring in other principles is here unnecessary.

---

[1]   *Miltonic*   In the manner of John Milton (1608–74), English poet.

[2]   *Author's Preface*   Prefatory to accompany Hopkins's manuscript poems.

[3]   *counterpointed*   Containing two types of rhythm in a line of verse.

[4]   *feet*   Metrical units.

[5]   *Trochee*   Metrical foot consisting of an accented syllable followed by an unaccented syllable.

[6]   *Dactyl*   Metrical foot consisting of an accented syllable followed by two unaccented syllables.

[7]   *Logaoedic Rhythm*   Rhythm in which dactyls are combined with trochees.

But because verse written strictly in these feet and by these principles will become same and tame the poets have brought in licences and departures from rule to give variety, and especially when the natural rhythm is rising, as in the common ten-syllable or five-foot verse, rhymed or blank. These irregularities are chiefly Reversed Feet and Reversed or Counterpoint Rhythm, which two things are two steps or degrees of licence in the same kind. By a reversed foot I mean the putting the stress where, to judge by the rest of the measure, the slack should be and the slack where the stress, and this is done freely at the beginning of a line and, in the course of a line, after a pause; only scarcely ever in the second foot or place and never in the last, unless when the poet designs some extraordinary effect; for these places are characteristic and sensitive and cannot well be touched. But the reversal of the first foot and of some middle foot after a strong pause is a thing so natural that our poets have generally done it, from Chaucer down, without remark and it commonly passes unnoticed and cannot be said to amount to a formal change of rhythm, but rather is that irregularity which all natural growth and motion shows. If however the reversal is repeated in two feet running, especially so as to include the sensitive second foot, it must be due either to great want of ear or else is a calculated effect, the super-inducing or *mounting* of a new rhythm upon the old; and since the new or mounted rhythm is actually heard and at the same time the mind naturally supplies the natural or standard foregoing rhythm, for we do not forget what the rhythm is that by rights we should be hearing, two rhythms are in some manner running at once and we have something answerable to counterpoint in music, which is two or more strains of tune going on together, and this is Counterpoint Rhythm. Of this kind of verse Milton is the great master and the choruses of *Samson Agonistes*[1] are written throughout in it—but with the disadvantage that he does not let the reader clearly know what the ground-rhythm is meant to be and so they have struck most readers as merely irregular. And in fact if you counterpoint throughout, since only one of the counter rhythms is actually heard, the other is really destroyed or cannot come to exist, and what is written is one rhythm only and probably Sprung Rhythm, of which I now speak.

Sprung Rhythm, as used in this book, is measured by feet of from one to four syllables, regularly, and for particular effects any number of weak or slack syllables may be used. It has one stress, which falls on the only syllable, if there is only one, or, if there are more, then scanning as above, on the first, and so gives rise to four sorts of feet, a monosyllable and the so-called accentual Trochee, Dactyl, and the First Paeon.[2] And there will be four corresponding natural rhythms; but nominally the feet are mixed and any one may follow any other. And hence Sprung Rhythm differs from Running Rhythm in having or being only one nominal rhythm, a mixed or "logaoedic" one, instead of three, but on the other hand in having twice the flexibility of foot, so that any two stresses may either follow one another running or be divided by one, two, or three slack syllables. But strict Sprung Rhythm cannot be counterpointed. In Sprung Rhythm, as in logaoedic rhythm generally, the feet are assumed to be equally long or strong and their seeming inequality is made up by pause or stressing.

Remark also that it is natural in Sprung Rhythm for the lines to be *rove over*, that is for the scanning of each line immediately to take up that of the one before, so that if the first has one or more syllables at its end the other must have so many the less at its beginning; and in fact the scanning runs on without break from the beginning, say, of a stanza to the end and all the stanza is one long strain, though written in lines asunder.

Two licences are natural to Sprung Rhythm. The one is rests, as in music; but of this an example is scarcely to be found in this book, unless in the *Echos*, second line. The other is *hangers* or *outrides*, that is one, two, or three slack syllables added to a foot and not counting in the nominal scanning. They are so called because they seem to hang below the line or ride forward or backward from it in another dimension than the line itself, according to a principle needless to explain here. These outriding half feet or hangers are marked by a loop underneath them, and plenty of them will be found.

[1] *Samson Agonistes* Dramatic poem published by Milton in 1671.

[2] *Paeon* Metrical foot consisting of one stressed and three unstressed syllables.

The other marks are easily understood, namely accents, where the reader might be in doubt which syllable should have the stress; slurs, that is loops *over* syllables, to tie them together into the time of one; little loops at the end of a line to show that the rhyme goes on to the first letter of the next line; what in music are called pauses ⌢, to show that the syllable should be dwelt on; and twirls ~, to mark reversed or counterpointed rhythm.

Note on the nature and history of Sprung Rhythm — Sprung Rhythm is the most natural of things. For (1) it is the rhythm of common speech and of written prose, when rhythm is perceived in them. (2) It is the rhythm of all but the most monotonously regular music, so that in the words of choruses and refrains and in songs written closely to music it arises. (3) It is found in nursery rhymes, weather saws, and so on; because, however these may have been once made in running rhythm, the terminations having dropped off by the change of language, the stresses come together and so

the rhythm is sprung. (4) It arises in common verse when reversed or counterpointed, for the same reason.

But nevertheless in spite of all this and though Greek and Latin lyric verse, which is well known, and the old English verse seen in "Pierce Ploughman"[1] are in sprung rhythm, it has in fact ceased to be used since the Elizabethan age, Greene[2] being the last writer who can be said to have recognized it. For perhaps there was not, down to our days, a single, even short, poem in English in which sprung rhythm is employed—not for single effects or in fixed places—but as the governing principle of the scansion. I say this because the contrary has been asserted: if it is otherwise the poem should be cited. . . .
　　—1883

---

[1] *"Pierce Ploughman"* I.e., *Piers Plowman*, by William Langland (written c. 1360–99).

[2] *Greene* Robert Greene (1558–92).

"MICHAEL FIELD"
KATHARINE BRADLEY AND EDITH COOPER
1848 – 1914   1862 – 1913

In May 1884, a volume of two plays by an unknown author, Michael Field, was published to critical acclaim. One reviewer wrote in *The Spectator*: "We know nothing of the author, but we have found a wealth of surprises in the strength, the simplicity, and the terseness of the imaginative feeling.... [The work] has the true poetic voice of fire in it. If this is the work of a young author, it is the work of the highest possible promise." The two authors who had taken the pen name "Michael Field," Katharine Bradley (her first name is spelled various ways, but she signed her name "Katharine") and Edith Cooper, had wished to receive the serious criticism accorded to male authors and also to conceal their relationship as lovers. The authors' identities did become widely known during their lifetimes, but "Michael" (Bradley) and "Field" (Cooper), as they called themselves, continued to collaborate on many books of plays and poetry, sometimes as "Michael Field," sometimes under other pseudonyms.

Bradley's father, a tobacco manufacturer, died in 1848, when she was two. Her mother educated her at home, and she later attended Newnham College, the new women's college at Cambridge. When her older sister, Emma, married James Cooper, the family stayed together with the married couple in Kenilworth, near Birmingham in central England. Bradley's mother died when she was twenty-two, and not long afterward Emma also passed away. Bradley stayed on to help raise her sister's children, Amy and Edith; Edith was then six years old. Katharine and her niece Edith shared a love of literature and writing, evident from the time Edith was young, and the two later attended Bristol University together.

Bradley wrote one volume of poetry on her own in 1875 (*The New Minnesinger*, published under the pseudonym Arran Leigh), but thereafter published only in collaboration with Cooper. A stanza from their poem "It was Deep April" describes their moment of decision: "The world was on us, pressing sore; / My love and I took hands and swore, / Against the world, to be / Poets and lovers evermore." The two eventually wrote some 30 plays and 11 volumes of poetry together in such a close collaboration that they later claimed in their journals that when they reviewed their work they could not distinguish who had written what. When their first collaborative work was published, the plays *Callirrhoë* and *Fair Rosamund*, they sent a copy to Robert Browning and revealed their true identities. Browning loved their work and became a close friend, but unfortunately he let slip to the public the authorship of the plays, a move that Bradley wrote back to tell him would "dwarf and enfeeble our work.... We cannot be stifled in drawing room conventionalities."

But even after their identities were exposed, Bradley and Cooper did not allow themselves to be stifled. They lived and traveled together and wrote poems about love between women; their first joint volume of poetry was inspired by Henry Wharton's translation of the ancient Greek Sappho's fragments of poetry, in which her love object was a woman. Their 1889 volume *Long Ago* was called by the journal *The Academy* "one of the most exquisite lyrical productions of the latter half of the nineteenth century."

For nearly half a century, Bradley and Cooper kept a journal that they called *Works and Days*, in which they described their daily lives and their abiding love for each other: "closer married" than the

Brownings, they said, because they also shared an artistic partnership. The younger Cooper was the first to die, of cancer, in 1913; eight months later Bradley died of the same disease.

The Magdalen

Timoteo Viti[1]

This tender sylph[2] of a maid
   Is the Magdalen—this figure lone:
Her attitude is swayed
By the very breath she breathes,
5 The prayer of her being that takes no voice.
Boulders, the grass enwreathes,
Arch over her as a cave
That of old an earthquake clave
   And filled with stagnant gloom:
10 Yet a woman has strength to choose it for her room.

Her long, fair hair is allowed
   To wander in its thick simpleness;
The graceful tresses crowd
Unequal, yet close enough
15 To have woven about her neck and breast
A wimple of golden stuff.
Though the rock behind is rude,
The sweetness of solitude
   Is on her face, the soft
20 Withdrawal that in wildflowers we have loved so oft.

Her mantle is scarlet red
   In folds of severe resplendency;
Her hair beneath is spread
Full length; from its lower flakes
25 Her feet come forth in their naked charm:
A wind discreetly shakes
The scarlet raiment,° the hair.   *dress*

Her small hands, a tranquil pair,
   Are laid together; her book
30 And cup of ointment furnish scantily her nook.

She is happy the livelong day,
Yet her thoughts are often with the past;
Her sins are done away,

---

[1] *The Magdalen Timoteo Viti* Painting of the Biblical Mary Magdalene by Renaissance painter Timoteo Viti (reproduced here as an illustration).

[2] *sylph* Slight, graceful woman.

They can give her no annoy.
35   She is white—oh! infinitely clean
And her heart throbs with joy;
Besides, there is joy in heaven
That her sins are thus forgiven;
And she thinks till even-fall°   *dusk*
40   Of the grace, the strangeness, the wonder of it all.

She is shut from fellowship;
How she loved to mingle with her friends!
To give them eyes and lip;
She lived for their sake alone;
45   Not a braid of her hair, not a rose
Of her cheek was her own:
And she loved to minister
To any in want of her,
All service was so sweet:
50   Now she must stand all day on lithe, unsummoned feet.

Among the untrodden weeds
And moss she is glad to be remote;
She knows that when God needs
From the sinning world relief,
55   He will find her thus with the wild bees,
The doves and the plantain leaf,
Waiting in a perfect peace
For His kingdom's sure increase,
Waiting with a deeper glow
60   Of patience every day, because He tarrieth so.

By her side the box of nard[1]
Unbroken … God is a great way off;
She loves Him: it is hard
That she may not now even spread
65   The burial spice, who would gladly keep
The tomb where He lay dead,
As it were her rocky cave;

And fold the linen and lave°   *wash*
The napkin that once bound
70   His head; no place for her pure arts is longer found.

And these are the things that hurt;
For the rest she gives herself no pain:
She wears no camel shirt,
She uses nor scourge, nor rod;
75   But bathes her fair body in the well
And keeps it pure for God:
The beauty, that He hath made
So bright, she guards in the shade,
For, as an angel's dress,
80   Spotless she must preserve her newborn loveliness.

Day by day and week by week,
She lives and muses and makes no sound;
She has no words to speak
The joy that her desert brings:
85   In her heart there is a song
And yet no song she sings.
Since the word *Rabboni*[2] came
Straightway at the call of her name
And the Master reproved,
90   It seems she has no choice—her lips have never moved.

She stole away when the pale
Light was trembling on the garden ground
And others told the tale,
Christ was risen; she roamed the wide,
95   Fearful countries of the wilderness
And many a riverside,
Till she found her destined grot,°   *grotto*
South, in France, a woody spot,
Where she is often glad,
100   Musing on those great days when she at first grew sad.
—1892

---

[1]   *nard* Ointment made from the aromatic plant of the same name.

[2]   *Rabboni* Hebrew: master, teacher.

La Gioconda[1]

Leonardo Da Vinci

Historic, sidelong, implicating eyes;
A smile of velvet's lustre on the cheek;
Calm lips the smile leads upward; hand that lies
Glowing and soft, the patience in its rest
5   Of cruelty that waits and doth not seek
For prey; a dusky forehead and a breast
Where twilight touches ripeness amorously:
Behind her, crystal rocks, a sea and skies
Of evanescent blue on cloud and creek;
10 Landscape that shines suppressive of its zest
For those vicissitudes by which men die.
—1892

A girl

A girl,
  Her soul a deep-wave pearl
Dim, lucent of all lovely mysteries;
    A face flowered for heart's ease,
5   A brow's grace soft as seas
    Seen through faint forest trees:
    A mouth, the lips apart,
Like aspen leaflets trembling in the breeze
From her tempestuous heart.
10 Such: and our souls so knit,
I leave a page half-writ—
    The work begun
Will be to heaven's conception done,
    If she come to it.
—1893

It was deep April, and the morn

It was deep April, and the morn
  Shakespeare was born;[2]
The world was on us, pressing sore;
My Love and I took hands and swore,
5   Against the world, to be
Poets and lovers evermore,
To laugh and dream on Lethe's[3] shore
To sing to Charon[4] in his boat,
Heartening the timid souls afloat;
10 Of judgment never to take heed,
But to those fast-locked souls to speed,
Who never from Apollo fled,
Who spent no hour among the dead;
    Continually
      With them to dwell,
15 Indifferent to heaven and hell.
—1893

---

1   *La Gioconda* Da Vinci's painting, the *Mona Lisa*.

2   *morn ... was born* It is traditional to celebrate Shakespeare's birthday on 23 April, St. George's Day.

3   *Lethe* In Greek mythology, a river in Hades (the underworld), the waters of which cause the dead to forget the past.

4   *Charon* Greek mythological ferryman of the underworld who transports the souls of the dead across the River Styx.

To Christina Rossetti

Lady, we would behold thee moving bright
  As Beatrice or Matilda[1] mid the trees,
Alas! thy moan was as a moan for ease
And passage through cool shadows to the night:
⁵ Fleeing from love, hadst thou not poet's right
To slip into the universe? The seas
Are fathomless to rivers drowned in these,
And sorrow is secure in leafy light.
Ah, had this secret touched thee, in a tomb
¹⁰ Thou hadst not buried thy enchanting self,
As happy Syrinx[2] murmuring with the wind,
Or Daphne,[3] thrilled through all her mystic bloom,
From safe recess as genius or as elf,
Thou hadst breathed joy in earth and in thy kind.
—1896

---

[1] *Beatrice* From Dante's *Divine Comedy*, Book 3, *Paradise*: a woman who personifies love and acts as Dante's guide through Paradise; *Matilda* From Book 2, *Purgatory*: a beautiful virgin who meets Dante in the Garden of Eden and leads him to the river Lethe to wash away his sins.

[2] *Syrinx* In Greek mythology, the nymph Syrinx turned herself into a bed of reeds in order to escape Pan's advances.

[3] *Daphne* In Greek mythology, the nymph Daphne fled from the god Apollo's advances and was transformed into a laurel tree in her escape.

ROBERT LOUIS STEVENSON
1850 – 1894

Due in part to his belief in romance rather than realism and in part to the success of *Treasure Island* and *Kidnapped*, Robert Louis Stevenson was once considered primarily a writer of adventure fiction for children. His large body of work has been re-evaluated in the past half century, however. His most famous novel, the science-fiction thriller *The Strange Case of Dr. Jekyll and Mr. Hyde*, has now taken a place among the canonical works of late Victorian literature. Stevenson's interest in the nature of good and evil lends this short novel a provocative moral complexity that has captivated the interest of a wide audience, with some readers viewing the book as a critique of Victorian double standards, others looking to the myth of the *doppelgänger*, or spiritual double, to explain the wicked Mr. Hyde, and still others adopting Freudian theories of the ego and the id to explain the two incarnations of Dr. Jekyll. Although he was long fascinated by the duality of the human psyche, in later years Stevenson turned to the concerns of his adopted country, Samoa, for subject matter, writing about the evils of imperialism and the damage done by foreign merchants. In all he wrote over 50 books in the course of his short life.

Stevenson's life was adventurous, but most of his travels were undertaken in search of respite from his ailments, which he wrote about in so much detail that he was once described as a "connoisseur of disease." He was an only child, born in Edinburgh in 1850 to Margaret Balfour, the daughter of a clergyman, and Thomas Stevenson, a well-known engineer for the Board of Northern Lighthouses. When he was young Stevenson contracted tuberculosis, and he remained frail ever after. He was put under the care of a nurse, who stimulated his interest in literature by reading to him everything from the Bible to serial adventure novels. Even as a child, he began spinning the raw material of these tales into stories of his own. In *Memories and Portraits* (1887), Stevenson said: "All through my boyhood and youth, I was known and pointed out for the pattern of an idler; and yet I was always busy on my own private end, which was to learn to write. I kept always two books in my pocket, one to read, one to write in. As I walked, my mind was busy fitting what I saw with appropriate words."

Stevenson continued writing in university, even though he was there initially to take an engineering degree and thereby continue the family tradition of his father and grandfather. He found himself uninterested in the profession, and switched to law, but after he had been called to the bar he decided to defy his father and pursue a career in writing. Stevenson began his legendary peregrinations soon after graduation; his first full-length published works, *An Inland Voyage* (1878) and *Travels with a Donkey in the Cévennes* (1879), record his travels through France. Both books found an enthusiastic audience. Two years later Stevenson published *Virginibus Puerisque*, a collection of essays previously published in *Macmillan's*, *Cornhill*, and *London* magazines. Many of these essays display the same gentle humor and wit that appears in the letters Stevenson wrote to his friends and family.

On one of his trips to France Stevenson met his future wife, Fanny Osbourne, an American who was then married, his elder by two years and the mother of two. He followed her to California, where she obtained a divorce, and the two were married in 1880. It was for his stepson Lloyd's pleasure that Stevenson created *Treasure Island* (1883), the "boy's story" of a man who procures a secret map and sets out alongside Long John Silver in a quest for hidden treasure. *Kidnapped* (1886) and its sequel *Catriona* (1893) were equally successful. 1886 also saw the publication of Stevenson's most enduring work of fiction, *The Strange Case of Dr. Jekyll and Mr. Hyde*, whose mystery concerns Dr. Jekyll's development of a drug that enables him to separate the good and bad parts of his nature. In these stories Stevenson was the romancer, eschewing the domestic realism that had defined the English novel as written by Dickens and George Eliot, with its complex focus on the home and the good woman who gives it moral definition. "This is a poison bad world for the romancer, this Anglo-Saxon world," he wrote; "I usually get out of it by not having any women in it at all." Later he would add: "Beware of realism; it is the devil."

Stevenson also enjoyed success as a poet and as a writer of short stories. The enormously popular *A Child's Garden of Verses* (1885) included many poems written in his Scottish dialect. His first collection of short stories, *New Arabian Nights* (1882), includes "The Pavilion on the Links," which Arthur Conan Doyle called "the very model of dramatic narrative." According to Doyle, the story is "the high-water mark of [Stevenson's] genius, … enough in itself, without another line, to give a man a permanent place among the great storytellers of the race." *The Merry Men and Other Tales and Fables* was published in 1887, and *Island Nights' Entertainment* in 1893. The latter deals largely with the problems of imperialism in the South Sea islands; "The Beach of Falesà," for instance, concerns discord between colonial merchants and native islanders. Stevenson had come to live in Samoa after searching the South Seas for a more salubrious climate than that of his Scottish homeland. (He left Scotland in 1887 after his father's death, but he continued to express deep longing for it in his final years.)

Stevenson came to love Samoa profoundly. After his death from a cerebral hemorrhage in 1894, his many island friends carried his remains up Mt. Vaea to bury him as he had requested in his poem "Requiem," which also provided the epitaph engraved on his tombstone. Stevenson was in his prime at the time of his death, at work on *Weir of Hermiston* (1896)—a book that, although unfinished, is regarded by many as a masterpiece.

⌘ ⌘ ⌘

Requiem

Under the wide and starry sky
   Dig the grave and let me lie.
Glad did I live and gladly die,
   And I laid me down with a will.

5   This be the verse you 'grave for me:
   Here he lies where he longed to be;
Home is the sailor, home from the sea,
   And the hunter home from the hill.[1]
—1879

---

[1] *Home … hill*   These final two lines are engraved on Stevenson's tombstone.

from *A Child's Garden of Verses*

Whole Duty of Children

A child should always say what's true
   And speak when he is spoken to,
And behave mannerly at table;
   At least as far as he is able.

Looking Forward

When I am grown to man's estate
I shall be very proud and great,
And tell the other girls and boys
Not to meddle with my toys.

The Land of Nod

From breakfast on through all the day
At home among my friends I stay,
But every night I go abroad
Afar into the land of Nod.

5   All by myself I have to go,
With none to tell me what to do—
All alone beside the streams
And up the mountain-sides of dreams.

The strangest things are there for me,
10   Both things to eat and things to see,
And many frightening sights abroad
Till morning in the land of Nod.

Try as I like to find the way,
I never can get back by day,
15   Nor can remember plain and clear
The curious music that I hear.

Good and Bad Children

Children, you are very little,
And your bones are very brittle;
If you would grow great and stately,
You must try to walk sedately.

5   You must still be bright and quiet,
And content with simple diet;
And remain, through all bewild'ring,
Innocent and honest children.

10   Happy hearts and happy faces,
Happy play in grassy places—
That was how, in ancient ages,
Children grew to kings and sages.

But the unkind and the unruly,
And the sort who eat unduly,
15   They must never hope for glory—
Theirs is quite a different story!

Cruel children, crying babies,
All grew up as geese and gabies,
Hated, as their age increases,
20   By their nephews and their nieces.

Foreign Children

Little Indian, Sioux or Crow,
Little frosty Eskimo,
Little Turk or Japanee,
Oh! don't you wish that you were me?

5   You have seen the scarlet trees
And the lions over seas;
You have eaten ostrich eggs,
And turned the turtles off their legs.

Such a life is very fine,
10   But it's not so nice as mine:
You must often, as you trod,
Have wearied *not* to be abroad.

You have curious things to eat,
I am fed on proper meat;
15   You must dwell beyond the foam,
But I am safe and live at home.
Little Indian, Sioux or Crow,
Little frosty Eskimo,
Little Turk or Japanee,
20   Oh! don't you wish that you were me?
—1885

The Pavilion on the Links

CHAPTER 1

Tells how I camped in Graden Sea-Wood, and beheld a light in the pavilion

I was a great solitary when I was young. I made it my pride to keep aloof and suffice for my own entertainment; and I may say that I had neither friends nor acquaintances until I met that friend who became my wife and the mother of my children. With one man only was I on private terms; this was R. Northmour, Esquire, of Graden-Easter, in Scotland. We had met at college; and though there was not much liking between us, nor even much intimacy, we were so nearly of a humour that we could associate with ease to both. Misanthropes, we believed ourselves to be; but I have thought since that we were only sulky fellows. It was scarcely a companionship, but a co-existence in unsociability. Northmour's exceptional violence of temper made it no easy affair for him to keep the peace with anyone but me; and as he respected my silent ways, and let me come and go as I pleased, I could tolerate his presence without concern. I think we called each other friends.

When Northmour took his degree and I decided to leave the university without one, he invited me on a long visit to Graden-Easter; and it was thus that I first became acquainted with the scene of my adventures. The mansion house of Graden stood in a bleak stretch of country some three miles from the shore of the German Ocean. It was as large as a barrack; and as it had been built of a soft stone, liable to consume in the eager air of the seaside, it was damp and draughty within and half ruinous without. It was impossible for two young men to lodge with comfort in such a dwelling. But there stood in the northern part of the estate, in a wilderness of links and blowing sandhills, and between a plantation and the sea, a small pavilion or belvedere,[1] of modern design, which was exactly suited to our wants; and in this hermitage, speaking little, reading much, and rarely associating except at meals, Northmour and I spent four

tempestuous winter months. I might have stayed longer; but one March night there sprang up between us a dispute, which rendered my departure necessary. Northmour spoke hotly, I remember, and I suppose I must have made some tart rejoinder. He leaped from his chair and grappled me; I had to fight, without exaggeration, for my life; and it was only with a great effort that I mastered him, for he was near as strong in body as myself, and seemed filled with the devil. The next morning, we met on our usual terms; but I judged it more delicate to withdraw; nor did he attempt to dissuade me.

It was nine years before I revisited the neighbourhood. I travelled at that time with a tilt cart,[2] a tent, and a cooking-stove, tramping all day beside the wagon, and at night, whenever it was possible, gipsying in a cove of the hills, or by the side of a wood. I believe I visited in this manner most of the wild and desolate regions both in England and Scotland; and, as I had neither friends nor relations, I was troubled with no correspondence, and had nothing in the nature of headquarters, unless it was the office of my solicitors, from whom I drew my income twice a year. It was a life in which I delighted; and I fully thought to have grown old upon the march, and at last died in a ditch.

It was my whole business to find desolate corners, where I could camp without the fear of interruption; and hence being in another part of the same shire, I bethought me suddenly of the Pavilion on the Links. No thoroughfare passed within three miles of it. The nearest town, and that was but a fisher village, was at a distance of six or seven. For ten miles of length, and from a depth varying from three miles to half a mile, this belt of barren country lay along the sea. The beach, which was the natural approach, was full of quicksands. Indeed I may say there is hardly a better place of concealment in the United Kingdom. I determined to pass a week in the Sea-Wood of Graden-Easter, and making a long stage, reached it about sundown on a wild September day.

The country, I have said, was mixed sandhill and links; *links* being a Scottish name for sand which has ceased drifting and become more or less solidly covered with turf. The pavilion stood on an even space; a little

---

[1] *belvedere* Pavilion or tower with a view.

[2] *tilt cart* Cart which can be tilted to empty out contents.

behind it, the wood began in a hedge of elders huddled together by the wind; in front, a few tumbled sandhills stood between it and the sea. An outcropping of rock had formed a bastion for the sand, so that there was here a promontory in the coastline between two shallow bays; and just beyond the tides, the rock again cropped out and formed an islet of small dimensions but strikingly designed. The quicksands were of great extent at low water, and had an infamous reputation in the country. Close in shore, between the islet and the promontory, it was said that they would swallow a man in four minutes and a half; but there may have been little ground for this precision. The district was alive with rabbits, and haunted by gulls which made a continual piping above the pavilion. On summer days the outlook was bright and even gladsome; but at sundown in September, with a high wind, and a heavy surf rolling in close along the links, the place told of nothing but dead mariners and sea disasters. A ship beating to windward on the horizon, and a huge truncheon of wreck half buried in the sands at my feet, completed the innuendo of the scene.

The pavilion—it had been built by the last proprietor, Northmour's uncle, a silly and prodigal virtuoso—presented little signs of age. It was two stories in height, Italian in design, surrounded by a patch of garden in which nothing had prospered but a few coarse flowers; and looked, with its shuttered windows, not like a house that had been deserted, but like one that had never been tenanted by man. Northmour was plainly from home; whether, as usual, sulking in the cabin of his yacht, or in one of his fitful and extravagant appearances in the world of society, I had, of course, no means of guessing. The place had an air of solitude that daunted even a solitary like myself; the wind cried in the chimneys with a strange and wailing note; and it was with a sense of escape, as if I were going indoors, that I turned away and driving my cart before me entered the skirts of the wood.

The Sea-Wood of Graden had been planted to shelter the cultivated fields behind, and check the encroachments of the blowing sand. As you advanced into it from coastward, elders were succeeded by other hardy shrubs; but the timber was all stunted and bushy; it led a life of conflict; the trees were accustomed to swing there all night long in fierce winter tempests; and

even in early spring, the leaves were already flying, and autumn was beginning, in this exposed plantation. Inland the ground rose into a little hill, which, along with the islet, served as a sailing mark for seamen. When the hill was open of the islet to the north, vessels must bear well to the eastward to clear Graden Ness and the Graden Bullers.[1] In the lower ground, a streamlet ran among the trees, and, being dammed with dead leaves and clay of its own carrying, spread out every here and there, and lay in stagnant pools. One or two ruined cottages were dotted about the wood; and, according to Northmour, these were ecclesiastical foundations, and in their time had sheltered pious hermits.

I found a den, or small hollow, where there was a spring of pure water; and there, clearing away the brambles, I pitched the tent, and made a fire to cook my supper. My horse I picketed farther in the wood, where there was a patch of sward.[2] The banks of the den not only concealed the light of my fire, but sheltered me from the wind, which was cold as well as high.

The life I was leading made me both hardy and frugal. I never drank but water, and rarely ate anything more costly than oatmeal; and I required so little sleep, that, although I rose with the peep of day, I would often lie long awake in the dark or starry watches of the night. Thus in Graden Sea-Wood, although I fell thankfully asleep by eight in the evening, I was awake again before eleven with a full possession of my faculties, and no sense of drowsiness or fatigue. I rose and sat by the fire, watching the trees and clouds tumultuously tossing and fleeing overhead, and hearkening to the wind and rollers along the shore, till at length, growing weary of inaction, I quitted the den, and strolled towards the borders of the wood. A young moon, buried in mist, gave a faint illumination to my steps; and the light grew brighter as I walked forth into the links. At the same moment, the wind, smelling salt of the open ocean and carrying particles of sand, struck me with its full force, so that I had to bow my head.

When I raised it again to look about me, I was aware of a light in the pavilion. It was not stationary; but passed from one window to another, as though someone

---

[1] *Ness* Headland; *Bullers* Rocky coves.

[2] *sward* Meadow.

were reviewing the different apartments with a lamp or candle. I watched it for some seconds in great surprise. When I had arrived in the afternoon the house had been plainly deserted; now it was as plainly occupied. It was my first idea that a gang of thieves might have broken in and be now ransacking Northmour's cupboards, which were many and not ill supplied. But what should bring thieves to Graden-Easter? And, again, all the shutters had been thrown open, and it would have been more in the character of such gentry to close them. I dismissed the notion, and fell back upon another. Northmour himself must have arrived, and was now airing and inspecting the pavilion.

I have said that there was no real affection between this man and me; but, had I loved him like a brother, I was then so much in love with solitude that I should nonetheless have shunned his company. As it was, I turned and ran for it; and it was with genuine satisfaction that I found myself safely back beside the fire. I had escaped an acquaintance; I should have one more night in comfort. In the morning, I might either slip away before Northmour was abroad, or pay him as short a visit as I chose.

But when morning came, I thought the situation so diverting that I forgot my shyness. Northmour was at my mercy; I arranged a good practical jest, though I knew well that my neighbour was not the man to jest with in security; and, chuckling beforehand over its success, took my place among the elders at the edge of the wood, whence I could command the door of the pavilion. The shutters were all once more closed, which I remember thinking odd; and the house, with its white walls and green Venetians,[1] looked spruce and habitable in the morning light. Hour after hour passed, and still no sign of Northmour. I knew him for a sluggard in the morning; but, as it drew on towards noon, I lost my patience. To say the truth, I had promised myself to break my fast in the pavilion, and hunger began to prick me sharply. It was a pity to let the opportunity go by without some cause for mirth; but the grosser appetite prevailed, and I relinquished my jest with regret, and sallied from the wood.

The appearance of the house affected me, as I drew near, with disquietude. It seemed unchanged since last evening; and I had expected it, I scarce knew why, to wear some external signs of habitation. But no: the windows were all closely shuttered, the chimneys breathed no smoke, and the front door itself was closely padlocked. Northmour, therefore, had entered by the back; this was the natural, and, indeed, the necessary conclusion; and you may judge of my surprise when, on turning the house, I found the back door similarly secured.

My mind at once reverted to the original theory of thieves; and I blamed myself sharply for my last night's inaction. I examined all the windows on the lower story, but none of them had been tampered with; I tried the padlocks, but they were both secure. It thus became a problem how the thieves, if thieves they were, had managed to enter the house. They must have got, I reasoned, upon the roof of the outhouse[2] where Northmour used to keep his photographic battery; and from thence, either by the window of the study or that of my old bedroom, completed their burglarious entry. I followed what I supposed was their example; and, getting on the roof, tried the shutters of each room. Both were secure; but I was not to be beaten; and, with a little force, one of them flew open, grazing, as it did so, the back of my hand. I remember, I put the wound to my mouth, and stood for perhaps half a minute licking it like a dog, and mechanically gazing behind me over the waste links and the sea; and, in that space of time, my eye made note of a large schooner yacht some miles to the northeast. Then I threw up the window and climbed in.

I went over the house, and nothing can express my mystification. There was no sign of disorder, but, on the contrary, the rooms were unusually clean and pleasant. I found fires laid, ready for lighting; three bedrooms prepared with a luxury quite foreign to Northmour's habits, and with water in the ewers and the beds turned down; a table set for three in the dining room; and an ample supply of cold meats, game and vegetables on the pantry shelves. There were guests expected, that was plain; but why guests, when Northmour hated society? And, above all, why was the house thus stealthily

---

[1] *Venetians* Probably Venetian shutters, constructed like Venetian blinds.

[2] *outhouse* Outbuilding for storage.

prepared at dead of night? and why were the shutters closed and the doors padlocked?

I effaced all traces of my visit, and came forth from the window feeling sobered and concerned.

The schooner yacht was still in the same place; and it flashed for a moment through my mind that this might be the *Red Earl* bringing the owner of the pavilion and his guests. But the vessel's head was set the other way.

Chapter 2

Tells of the nocturnal landing from the yacht

I returned to the den to cook myself a meal, of which I stood in great need, as well as to care for my horse, whom I had somewhat neglected in the morning. From time to time I went down to the edge of the wood; but there was no change in the pavilion, and not a human creature was seen all day upon the links. The schooner in the offing was the one touch of life within my range of vision. She, apparently with no set object, stood off and on or lay to, hour after hour; but as the evening deepened, she drew steadily nearer. I became more convinced that she carried Northmour and his friends, and that they would probably come ashore after dark; not only because that was of a piece with the secrecy of the preparations, but because the tide would not have flowed sufficiently before eleven to cover Graden Floe and the other sea-quags[1] that fortified the shore against invaders.

All day the wind had been going down, and the sea along with it; but there was a return towards sunset of the heavy weather of the day before. The night set in pitch dark. The wind came off the sea in squalls, like the firing of a battery of cannon; now and then there was a flaw[2] of rain, and the surf rolled heavier with the rising tide. I was down at my observatory among the elders, when a light was run up to the masthead of the schooner, and showed she was closer in than when I had last seen her by the dying daylight. I concluded that this must be a signal to Northmour's associates on shore;

[1] *sea-quags* Muddy or swampy shorelines.

[2] *flaw* Burst.

and, stepping forth into the links, looked around me for something in response.

A small footpath ran along the margin of the wood, and formed the most direct communication between the pavilion and the mansion house; and, as I cast my eyes to that side, I saw a spark of light, not a quarter of a mile away, and rapidly approaching. From its uneven course it appeared to be the light of a lantern carried by a person who followed the windings of the path, and was often staggered and taken aback by the more violent squalls. I concealed myself once more among the elders, and waited eagerly for the newcomer's advance. It proved to be a woman; and, as she passed within half a rod of my ambush, I was able to recognise the features. The deaf and silent old dame, who had nursed Northmour in his childhood, was his associate in this underhand affair.

I followed her at a little distance, taking advantage of the innumerable heights and hollows, concealed by the darkness, and favoured not only by the nurse's deafness, but the uproar of the wind and surf. She entered the pavilion, and, going at once to the upper story, opened and set a light in one of the windows that looked towards the sea. Immediately afterwards the light at the schooner's masthead was run down and extinguished. Its purpose had been attained, and those on board were sure that they were expected. The old woman resumed her preparations; although the other shutters remained closed, I could see a glimmer going to and fro about the house; and a gush of sparks from one chimney after another soon told me that the fires were being kindled. Northmour and his guests, I was now persuaded, would come ashore as soon as there was water on the floe. It was a wild night for boat service; and I felt some alarm mingle with my curiosity as I reflected on the danger of the landing. My old acquaintance, it was true, was the most eccentric of men; but the present eccentricity was both disquieting and lugubrious to consider. A variety of feelings thus led me towards the beach, where I lay flat on my face in a hollow within six feet of the track that led to the pavilion. Thence, I should have the satisfaction of recognising the arrivals, and, if they should prove to be acquaintances, greeting them as soon as they had landed.

Some time before eleven, while the tide was still dangerously low, a boat's lantern appeared close in shore; and, my attention being thus awakened, I could perceive another still far to seaward, violently tossed, and sometimes hidden by the billows. The weather, which was getting dirtier as the night went on, and the perilous situation of the yacht upon a lee-shore, had probably driven them to attempt a landing at the earliest possible moment.

A little afterwards, four yachtsmen carrying a very heavy chest, and guided by a fifth with a lantern, passed close in front of me as I lay, and were admitted to the pavilion by the nurse. They returned to the beach, and passed me a third time with another chest, larger but apparently not so heavy as the first. A third time they made the transit; and on this occasion one of the yachtsmen carried a leather portmanteau,[1] and the others a lady's trunk and carriage bag. My curiosity was sharply excited. If a woman were among the guests of Northmour, it would show a change in his habits and an apostasy[2] from his pet theories of life, well calculated to fill me with surprise. When he and I dwelt there together, the pavilion had been a temple of misogyny. And now, one of the detested sex was to be installed under its roof. I remembered one or two particulars, a few notes of daintiness and almost of coquetry which had struck me the day before as I surveyed the preparations in the house; their purpose was now clear, and I thought myself dull not to have perceived it from the first.

While I was thus reflecting a second lantern drew near me from the beach. It was carried by a yachtsman whom I had not yet seen, and who was conducting two other persons to the pavilion. These two persons were unquestionably the guests for whom the house was made ready; and, straining eye and ear, I set myself to watch them as they passed. One was an unusually tall man, in a travelling hat slouched over his eyes, and a Highland cape closely buttoned and turned up so as to conceal his face. You could make out no more of him than that he was, as I have said, unusually tall, and walked feebly with a heavy stoop. By his side, and either clinging to him or giving him support—I could not

make out which—was a young, tall, and slender figure of a woman. She was extremely pale; but in the light of the lantern her face was so marred by strong and changing shadows, that she might equally well have been as ugly as sin or as beautiful as I afterwards found her to be.

When they were just abreast of me, the girl made some remark which was drowned by the noise of the wind.

"Hush!" said her companion; and there was something in the tone with which the word was uttered that thrilled and rather shook my spirits. It seemed to breathe from a bosom labouring under the deadliest terror; I have never heard another syllable so expressive; and I still hear it again when I am feverish at night, and my mind runs upon old times. The man turned towards the girl as he spoke; I had a glimpse of much red beard and a nose which seemed to have been broken in youth; and his light eyes seemed shining in his face with some strong and unpleasant emotion.

But these two passed on and were admitted in their turn to the pavilion.

One by one, or in groups, the seamen returned to the beach. The wind brought me the sound of a rough voice crying, "Shove off!" Then, after a pause, another lantern drew near. It was Northmour alone.

My wife and I, a man and a woman, have often agreed to wonder how a person could be, at the same time, so handsome and so repulsive as Northmour. He had the appearance of a finished gentleman; his face bore every mark of intelligence and courage, but you had only to look at him, even in his most amiable moment, to see that he had the temper of a slave captain. I never knew a character that was both explosive and revengeful to the same degree; he combined the vivacity of the south with the sustained and deadly hatreds of the north; and both traits were plainly written on his face, which was a sort of danger signal. In person he was tall, strong, and active; his hair and complexion very dark; his features handsomely designed, but spoiled by a menacing expression.

At that moment he was somewhat paler than by nature; he wore a heavy frown; and his lips worked, and he looked sharply round as he walked, like a man besieged with apprehensions. And yet I thought he had a look of

---

[1] *portmanteau* Large suitcase.

[2] *apostasy* Renunciation of values.

triumph underlying all, as though he had already done much, and was near the end of an achievement.

Partly from a scruple of delicacy—which I dare say came too late—partly from the pleasure of startling an acquaintance, I desired to make my presence known to him without delay.

I got suddenly to my feet, and stepped forward.

"Northmour!" said I.

I have never had so shocking a surprise in all my days. He leaped on me without a word; something shone in his hand; and he struck for my heart with a dagger. At the same moment I knocked him head over heels. Whether it was my quickness, or his own uncertainty, I know not; but the blade only grazed my shoulder, while the hilt and his fist struck me violently on the mouth.

I fled, but not far. I had often and often observed the capabilities of the sandhills for protracted ambush or stealthy advances and retreats; and, not ten yards from the scene of the scuffle, plumped down again upon the grass. The lantern had fallen and gone out. But what was my astonishment to see Northmour slip at a bound into the pavilion, and hear him bar the door behind him with a clang of iron!

He had not pursued me. He had run away. Northmour, whom I knew for the most implacable and daring of men, had run away! I could scarce believe my reason; and yet in this strange business, where all was incredible, there was nothing to make a work about in an incredibility more or less. For why was the pavilion secretly prepared? Why had Northmour landed with his guests at dead of night, in half a gale of wind, and with the floe scarce covered? Why had he sought to kill me? Had he not recognised my voice? I wondered. And, above all, how had he come to have a dagger ready in his hand? A dagger, or even a sharp knife, seemed out of keeping with the age in which we lived; and a gentleman landing from his yacht on the shore of his own estate, even although it was at night and with some mysterious circumstances, does not usually, as a matter of fact, walk thus prepared for deadly onslaught. The more I reflected, the further I felt at sea. I recapitulated the elements of mystery, counting them on my fingers: the pavilion secretly prepared for guests; the guests landed

at the risk of their lives and to the imminent peril of the yacht; the guests, or at least one of them, in undisguised and seemingly causeless terror; Northmour with a naked weapon; Northmour stabbing his most intimate acquaintance at a word; last, and not least strange, Northmour fleeing from the man whom he had sought to murder, and barricading himself, like a hunted creature, behind the door of the pavilion.

Here were at least six separate causes for extreme surprise; each part and parcel with the others, and forming all together one consistent story. I felt almost ashamed to believe my own senses.

As I thus stood transfixed with wonder, I began to grow painfully conscious of the injuries I had received in the scuffle; skulked round among the sandhills; and, by a devious path, regained the shelter of the wood. On the way, the old nurse passed again within several yards of me, still carrying her lantern, on the return journey to the mansion-house of Graden. This made a seventh suspicious feature in the case. Northmour and his guests, it appeared, were to cook and do the cleaning for themselves, while the old woman continued to inhabit the big empty barrack among the policies.[1] There must surely be great cause for secrecy, when so many inconveniences were confronted to preserve it.

So thinking, I made my way to the den. For greater security, I trod out the embers of the fire, and lit my lantern to examine the wound upon my shoulder. It was a trifling hurt, although it bled somewhat freely, and I dressed it as well as I could (for its position made it difficult to reach) with some rag and cold water from the spring. While I was thus busied, I mentally declared war against Northmour and his mystery. I am not an angry man by nature, and I believe there was more curiosity than resentment in my heart. But war I certainly declared; and, by way of preparation, I got out my revolver, and, having drawn the charges, cleaned and reloaded it with scrupulous care. Next I became preoccupied about my horse. It might break loose, or fall to neighing, and so betray my camp in the Sea-Wood. I determined to rid myself of its neighbourhood; and long before dawn I was leading it over the links in the direction of the fisher village.

---

[1] *policies* Planted lands surrounding a building on an estate.

Chapter 3

Tells how I became acquainted with my wife

For two days I skulked round the pavilion, profiting by the uneven surface of the links. I became an adept in the necessary tactics. These low hillocks and shallow dells, running one into another, became a kind of cloak of darkness for my enthralling, but perhaps dishonourable, pursuit. Yet, in spite of this advantage, I could learn but little of Northmour or his guests.

Fresh provisions were brought under cover of darkness by the old woman from the mansion-house. Northmour and the young lady, sometimes together, but more often singly, would walk for an hour or two at a time on the beach beside the quicksand. I could not but conclude that this promenade was chosen with an eye to secrecy; for the spot was open only to the sea-ward. But it suited me not less excellently; the highest and most accidented of the sandhills immediately adjoined; and from these, lying flat in a hollow, I could overlook Northmour or the young lady as they walked.

The tall man seemed to have disappeared. Not only did he never cross the threshold, but he never so much as showed face at a window; or, at least, not so far as I could see; for I dared not creep forward beyond a certain distance in the day, since the upper floor commanded the bottoms of the links; and at night, when I could venture farther, the lower windows were barricaded as if to stand a siege. Sometimes I thought the tall man must be confined to bed, for I remembered the feebleness of his gait; and sometimes I thought he must have gone clear away, and that Northmour and the young lady remained alone together in the pavilion. The idea, even then, displeased me.

Whether or not this pair were man and wife, I had seen abundant reason to doubt the friendliness of their relation.

Although I could hear nothing of what they said, and rarely so much as glean a decided expression on the face of either, there was a distance, almost a stiffness, in their bearing which showed them to be either unfamiliar or at enmity. The girl walked faster when she was with Northmour than when she was alone; and I conceived that any inclination between a man and a woman would

rather delay than accelerate the step. Moreover, she kept a good yard free of him, and trailed her umbrella, as if it were a barrier, on the side between them. Northmour kept sidling closer; and, as the girl retired from his advance, their course lay at a sort of diagonal across the beach, and would have landed them in the surf had it been long enough continued. But, when it was imminent, the girl would unostentatiously change sides and put Northmour between her and the sea. I watched these manoeuvres, for my part, with high enjoyment and approval, and chuckled to myself at every move.

On the morning of the third day, she walked alone for some time, and I perceived, to my great concern, that she was more than once in tears. You will see that my heart was already interested more than I supposed. She had a firm yet airy motion of the body, and carried her head with unimaginable grace; every step was a thing to look at, and she seemed in my eyes to breathe sweetness and distinction.

The day was so agreeable, being calm and sunshiny, with a tranquil sea, and yet with a healthful piquancy and vigour in the air, that, contrary to custom, she was tempted forth a second time to walk. On this occasion she was accompanied by Northmour, and they had been but a short while on the beach, when I saw him take forcible possession of her hand. She struggled, and uttered a cry that was almost a scream. I sprang to my feet, unmindful of my strange position; but, ere I had taken a step, I saw Northmour bareheaded and bowing very low, as if to apologise; and dropped again at once into my ambush. A few words were interchanged; and then, with another bow, he left the beach to return to the pavilion. He passed not far from me, and I could see him, flushed and lowering, and cutting savagely with his cane among the grass. It was not without satisfaction that I recognised my own handiwork in a great cut under his right eye, and a considerable discoloration round the socket.

For some time the girl remained where he had left her, looking out past the islet and over the bright sea. Then with a start, as one who throws off preoccupation and puts energy again upon its mettle, she broke into a rapid and decisive walk. She also was much incensed by what had passed. She had forgotten where she was. And I beheld her walk straight into the borders of the quicksand where it is most abrupt and dangerous. Two or three steps farther and her life would have been in serious jeopardy, when I slid down the face of the sandhill, which is there precipitous, and, running half-way forward, called to her to stop.

She did so, and turned round. There was not a tremor of fear in her behaviour, and she marched directly up to me like a queen. I was barefoot, and clad like a common sailor, save for an Egyptian scarf round my waist; and she probably took me at first for someone from the fisher village, straying after bait. As for her, when I thus saw her face to face, her eyes set steadily and imperiously upon mine, I was filled with admiration and astonishment, and thought her even more beautiful than I had looked to find her. Nor could I think enough of one who, acting with so much boldness, yet preserved a maidenly air that was both quaint and engaging; for my wife kept an old-fashioned precision of manner through all her admirable life—an excellent thing in woman, since it sets another value on her sweet familiarities.

"What does this mean?" she asked.

"You were walking," I told her, "directly into Graden Floe."

"You do not belong to these parts," she said again. "You speak like an educated man."

"I believe I have a right to that name," said I, "although in this disguise."

But her woman's eye had already detected the sash.

"Oh!" she said; "your sash betrays you."

"You have said the word *betray*," I resumed. "May I ask you not to betray me? I was obliged to disclose myself in your interest; but if Northmour learned my presence it might be worse than disagreeable for me."

"Do you know," she asked, "to whom you are speaking?"

"Not to Mr. Northmour's wife?" I asked, by way of answer.

She shook her head. All this while she was studying my face with an embarrassing intentness. Then she broke out:

"You have an honest face. Be honest like your face, sir, and tell me what you want and what you are afraid of. Do you think I could hurt you? I believe you have far more power to injure me! And yet you do not look

unkind. What do you mean—you, a gentleman—by skulking like a spy about this desolate place? Tell me," she said, "who is it you hate?"

"I hate no one," I answered; "and I fear no one face to face. My name is Cassilis—Frank Cassilis. I lead the life of a vagabond for my own good pleasure. I am one of Northmour's oldest friends; and three nights ago, when I addressed him on these links, he stabbed me in the shoulder with a knife."

"It was you!" she said.

"Why he did so," I continued, disregarding the interruption, "is more than I can guess, and more than I care to know. I have not many friends, nor am I very susceptible to friendship; but no man shall drive me from a place by terror. I had camped in Graden Sea-Wood ere he came; I camp in it still. If you think I mean harm to you or yours, madam, the remedy is in your hand. Tell him that my camp is in the Hemlock Den, and tonight he can stab me in safety while I sleep."

With this I doffed my cap to her, and scrambled up once more among the sandhills. I do not know why, but I felt a prodigious sense of injustice, and felt like a hero and a martyr; while, as a matter of fact, I had not a word to say in my defence, nor so much as one plausible reason to offer for my conduct. I had stayed at Graden out of a curiosity natural enough, but undignified; and though there was another motive growing in along with the first, it was not one which, at that period, I could have properly explained to the lady of my heart.

Certainly, that night, I thought of no one else; and, though her whole conduct and position seemed suspicious, I could not find it in my heart to entertain a doubt of her integrity. I could have staked my life that she was clear of blame, and, though all was dark at the present, that the explanation of the mystery would show her part in these events to be both right and needful. It was true, let me cudgel my imagination as I pleased, that I could invent no theory of her relations to Northmour; but I felt nonetheless sure of my conclusion because it was founded on instinct in place of reason, and, as I may say, went to sleep that night with the thought of her under my pillow.

Next day she came out about the same hour alone, and, as soon as the sandhills concealed her from the pavilion, drew nearer to the edge, and called me by name in guarded tones. I was astonished to observe that she was deadly pale, and seemingly under the influence of strong emotion.

"Mr. Cassilis!" she cried; "Mr. Cassilis!"

I appeared at once, and leaped down upon the beach. A remarkable air of relief overspread her countenance as soon as she saw me.

"Oh!" she cried, with a hoarse sound, like one whose bosom has been lightened of weight. And then, "Thank God, you are still safe!" she added; "I knew, if you were, you would be here." (Was not this strange? So swiftly and wisely does Nature prepare our hearts for these great lifelong intimacies, that both my wife and I had been given a presentiment on this the second day of our acquaintance. I had even then hoped that she would seek me; she had felt sure that she would find me.) "Do not," she went on swiftly, "do not stay in this place. Promise me that you will sleep no longer in that wood. You do not know how I suffer; all last night I could not sleep for thinking of your peril."

"Peril?" I repeated. "Peril from whom? From Northmour?"

"Not so," she said. "Did you think I would tell him after what you said?"

"Not from Northmour?" I repeated. "Then how? From whom? I see none to be afraid of."

"You must not ask me," was her reply, "for I am not free to tell you. Only believe me, and go hence—believe me, and go away quickly, quickly, for your life!"

An appeal to his alarm is never a good plan to rid oneself of a spirited young man. My obstinacy was but increased by what she said, and I made it a point of honour to remain. And her solicitude for my safety still more confirmed me in the resolve.

"You must not think me inquisitive, madam," I replied; "but, if Graden is so dangerous a place, you yourself perhaps remain here at some risk."

She only looked at me reproachfully. "You and your father——" I resumed; but she interrupted me almost with a gasp.

"My father! How do you know that?" she cried. "I saw you together when you landed," was my answer; and I do not know why, but it seemed satisfactory to both of us, as indeed it was the truth. "But," I continued, "you need have no fear from me. I see you have

some reason to be secret, and, you may believe me, your secret is as safe with me as if I were in Graden Floe. I have scarce spoken to anyone for years; my horse is my only companion, and even he, poor beast, is not beside me. You see, then, you may count on me for silence. So tell me the truth, my dear young lady, are you not in danger?"

"Mr. Northmour says you are an honourable man," she returned, "and I believe it when I see you. I will tell you so much; you are right; we are in dreadful, dreadful danger, and you share it by remaining where you are."

"Ah!" said I; "you have heard of me from Northmour? And he gives me a good character?"

"I asked him about you last night," was her reply. "I pretended," she hesitated, "I pretended to have met you long ago, and spoken to you of him. It was not true; but I could not help myself without betraying you, and you had put me in a difficulty. He praised you highly."

"And—you may permit me one question—does this danger come from Northmour?" I asked.

"From Mr. Northmour?" she cried. "Oh, no; he stays with us to share it."

"While you propose that I should run away?" I said. "You do not rate me very high."

"Why should you stay?" she asked. "You are no friend of ours."

I know not what came over me, for I had not been conscious of a similar weakness since I was a child, but I was so mortified by this retort that my eyes pricked and filled with tears, as I continued to gaze upon her face.

"No, no," she said, in a changed voice; "I did not mean the words unkindly."

"It was I who offended," I said; and I held out my hand with a look of appeal that somehow touched her, for she gave me hers at once, and even eagerly. I held it for awhile in mine, and gazed into her eyes. It was she who first tore her hand away, and, forgetting all about her request and the promise she had sought to extort, ran at the top of her speed, and without turning, till she was out of sight. And then I knew that I loved her, and thought in my glad heart that she—she herself—was not indifferent to my suit.[1] Many a time she has denied it in after days, but it was with a smiling and not a serious

---

[1] *suit* Courtship.

denial. For my part, I am sure our hands would not have lain so closely in each other if she had not begun to melt to me already. And, when all is said, it is no great contention, since, by her own avowal, she began to love me on the morrow.

And yet on the morrow very little took place. She came and called me down as on the day before, upbraided me for lingering at Graden, and, when she found I was still obdurate, began to ask me more particularly as to my arrival. I told her by what series of accidents I had come to witness their disembarkation, and how I had determined to remain, partly from the interest which had been wakened in me by Northmour's guests, and partly because of his own murderous attack. As to the former, I fear I was disingenuous, and led her to regard herself as having been an attraction to me from the first moment that I saw her on the links. It relieves my heart to make this confession even now, when my wife is with God, and already knows all things, and the honesty of my purpose even in this; for while she lived, although it often pricked my conscience, I had never the hardihood to undeceive her. Even a little secret, in such a married life as ours, is like the rose-leaf which kept the Princess from her sleep.[1]

From this the talk branched into other subjects, and I told her much about my lonely and wandering existence; she, for her part, giving ear, and saying little. Although we spoke very naturally, and latterly on topics that might seem indifferent, we were both sweetly agitated. Too soon it was time for her to go; and we separated, as if by mutual consent, without shaking hands, for both knew that, between us, it was no idle ceremony. The next, and that was the fourth day of our acquaintance, we met in the same spot, but early in the morning, with much familiarity and yet much timidity on either side.

When she had once more spoken about my danger—and that, I understood, was her excuse for coming—I, who had prepared a great deal of talk during the night, began to tell her how highly I valued her kind interest, and how no one had ever cared to hear about my life, nor had I ever cared to relate it, before yester-

day. Suddenly she interrupted me, saying with vehemence:

"And yet, if you knew who I was, you would not so much as speak to me!" I told her such a thought was madness, and, little as we had met, I counted her already a dear friend; but my protestations seemed only to make her more desperate. "My father is in hiding!" she cried.

"My dear," I said, forgetting for the first time to add "young lady," "what do I care? If he were in hiding twenty times over, would it make one thought of change in you?" "Ah, but the cause!" she cried, "the cause! It is—" she faltered for a second—"it is disgraceful to us!"

CHAPTER 4

Tells in what a startling manner I learned that I was not alone in Graden Sea-Wood

This was my wife's story, as I drew it from her among tears and sobs. Her name was Clara Huddlestone: it sounded very beautiful in my ears; but not so beautiful as that other name of Clara Cassilis, which she wore during the longer and, I thank God, the happier portion of her life. Her father, Bernard Huddlestone, had been a private banker in a very large way of business. Many years before, his affairs becoming disordered, he had been led to try dangerous, and at last criminal, expedients to retrieve himself from ruin. All was in vain; he became more and more cruelly involved, and found his honour lost at the same moment with his fortune. About this period, Northmour had been courting his daughter with great assiduity, though with small encouragement; and to him, knowing him thus disposed in his favour, Bernard Huddlestone turned for help in his extremity. It was not merely ruin and dishonour, nor merely a legal condemnation, that the unhappy man had brought on his head. It seems he could have gone to prison with a light heart. What he feared, what kept him awake at night or recalled him from slumber into frenzy, was some secret, sudden, and unlawful attempt upon his life. Hence, he desired to bury his existence and escape to one of the islands in the South Pacific, and it was in Northmour's yacht, the *Red Earl*, that he designed to go. The yacht picked them up clandestinely upon the coast of Wales, and had once more deposited them at Graden,

---

[1] *rose-leaf ... sleep* Stevenson may be referring to Hans Christian Andersen's fairytale "The Princess and the Pea."

till she could be refitted and provisioned for the longer voyage. Nor could Clara doubt that her hand had been stipulated as the price of passage. For, although Northmour was neither unkind nor discourteous, he had shown himself in several instances somewhat overbold in speech and manner.

I listened, I need not say, with fixed attention, and put many questions as to the more mysterious part. It was in vain. She had no clear idea of what the blow was, nor of how it was expected to fall. Her father's alarm was unfeigned and physically prostrating, and he had thought more than once of making an unconditional surrender to the police. But the scheme was finally abandoned, for he was convinced that not even the strength of our English prisons could shelter him from his pursuers. He had had many affairs with Italy, and with Italians resident in London, in the later years of his business; and these last, as Clara fancied, were somehow connected with the doom that threatened him. He had shown great terror at the presence of an Italian seaman on board the *Red Earl,* and had bitterly and repeatedly accused Northmour in consequence. The latter had protested that Beppo (that was the seaman's name) was a capital fellow and could be trusted to the death; but Mr. Huddlestone had continued ever since to declare that all was lost, that it was only a question of days, and that Beppo would be the ruin of him yet.

I regarded the whole story as the hallucination of a mind shaken by calamity. He had suffered heavy loss by his Italian transactions; and hence the sight of an Italian was hateful to him, and the principal part in his nightmare would naturally enough be played by one of that nation.

"What your father wants," I said, "is a good doctor and some calming medicine."

"But Mr. Northmour?" objected your mother. "He is untroubled by losses, and yet he shares in this terror." I could not help laughing at what I considered her simplicity.

"My dear," said I, "you have told me yourself what reward he has to look for. All is fair in love, you must remember; and if Northmour foments your father's terrors, it is not at all because he is afraid of any Italian man, but simply because he is infatuated with a charming English woman."

She reminded me of his attack upon myself on the night of the disembarkation, and this I was unable to explain. In short, and from one thing to another, it was agreed between us, that I should set out at once for the fisher village, Graden-Wester, as it was called, look up all the newspapers I could find, and see for myself if there seemed any basis of fact for these continued alarms. The next morning, at the same hour and place, I was to make my report to Clara. She said no more on that occasion about my departure; nor indeed, did she make it a secret that she clung to the thought of my proximity as something helpful and pleasant; and, for my part, I could not have left her, if she had gone upon her knees to ask it.

I reached Graden-Wester before ten in the forenoon; for in those days I was an excellent pedestrian, and the distance, as I think I have said, was little over seven miles; fine walking all the way upon the springy turf. The village is one of the bleakest on that coast, which is saying much: there is a church in a hollow, a miserable haven in the rocks, where many boats have been lost as they returned from fishing; two or three score of stone houses arranged along the beach and in two streets, one leading from the harbour, and another striking out from it at right angles; and, at the corner of these two, a very dark and cheerless tavern, by way of principal hotel.

I had dressed myself somewhat more suitably to my station in life, and at once called upon the minister in his little manse[1] beside the graveyard. He knew me, although it was more than nine years since we had met; and when I told him that I had been long upon a walking tour, and was behind with the news, readily lent me an armful of newspapers, dating from a month back to the day before. With these I sought the tavern, and, ordering some breakfast, sat down to study the "Huddlestone Failure."

It had been, it appeared, a very flagrant case. Thousands of persons were reduced to poverty; and one in particular had blown out his brains as soon as payment was suspended. It was strange to myself that, while I read these details, I continued rather to sympathise with Mr. Huddlestone than with his victims; so complete already was the empire of my love for my wife. A price was naturally set upon the banker's head; and, as the

---

[1]   *manse* Cleric's house.

case was inexcusable and the public indignation thoroughly aroused, the unusual figure of £750 was offered for his capture. He was reported to have large sums of money in his possession. One day, he had been heard of in Spain; the next, there was sure intelligence that he was still lurking between Manchester and Liverpool, or along the border of Wales; and the day after, a telegram would announce his arrival in Cuba or Yucatan. But in all this there was no word of an Italian, nor any sign of mystery.

In the very last paper, however, there was one item not so clear. The accountants who were charged to verify the failure had, it seemed, come upon the traces of a large number of thousands, which figured for some time in the transactions of the house of Huddlestone; but which came from nowhere, and disappeared in the same mysterious fashion. It was only once referred to by name, and then under the initials "X. X."; but it had plainly been floated for the first time into the business at a period of great depression some six years ago. The name of a distinguished Royal personage had been mentioned by rumour in connection with this sum. "The cowardly desperado"—such, I remember, was the editorial expression—was supposed to have escaped with a large part of this mysterious fund still in his possession.

I was still brooding over the fact, and trying to torture it into some connection with Mr. Huddlestone's danger, when a man entered the tavern and asked for some bread and cheese with a decided foreign accent. "*Siete Italiano*?"[1] said I.

"*Si, signor*,"[2] was his reply.

I said it was unusually far north to find one of his compatriots; at which he shrugged his shoulders, and replied that a man would go anywhere to find work. What work he could hope to find at Graden-Wester, I was totally unable to conceive; and the incident struck so unpleasantly upon my mind, that I asked the landlord, while he was counting me some change, whether he had ever before seen an Italian in the village. He said he had once seen some Norwegians, who had been shipwrecked on the other side of Graden Ness and rescued by the lifeboat from Cauldhaven.

"No!" said I; "but an Italian, like the man who has just had bread and cheese."

"What?" cried he, "yon blackavised[3] fellow wi' the teeth? Was he an I-talian? Weel, yon's the first that ever I saw, an' I dare say he's like to be the last."

Even as he was speaking, I raised my eyes, and, casting a glance into the street, beheld three men in earnest conversation together, and not thirty yards away. One of them was my recent companion in the tavern parlour; the other two, by their handsome, sallow features and soft hats, should evidently belong to the same race. A crowd of village children stood around them, gesticulating and talking gibberish in imitation. The trio looked singularly foreign to the bleak dirty street in which they were standing, and the dark grey heaven that overspread them; and I confess my incredulity received at that moment a shock from which it never recovered. I might reason with myself as I pleased, but I could not argue down the effect of what I had seen, and I began to share in the Italian terror.

It was already drawing towards the close of the day before I had returned the newspapers at the manse, and got well forward on to the links on my way home. I shall never forget that walk. It grew very cold and boisterous; the wind sang in the short grass about my feet; thin rain showers came running on the gusts; and an immense mountain range of clouds began to arise out of the bosom of the sea. It would be hard to imagine a more dismal evening; and whether it was from these external influences, or because my nerves were already affected by what I had heard and seen, my thoughts were as gloomy as the weather.

The upper windows of the pavilion commanded a considerable spread of links in the direction of Graden-Wester. To avoid observation, it was necessary to hug the beach until I had gained cover from the higher sandhills on the little headland, when I might strike across, through the hollows, for the margin of the wood. The sun was about setting; the tide was low, and all the quicksands uncovered; and I was moving along, lost in unpleasant thought, when I was suddenly thunderstruck to perceive the prints of human feet. They ran parallel to my own course, but low down upon the beach instead of along the border of the turf; and, when I

---

[1] *Siete Italiano?* Italian: Are you Italian?

[2] *Si, signor* Italian: Yes, sir.

[3] *blackavised* Dark complexioned.

examined them, I saw at once, by the size and coarseness of the impression, that it was a stranger to me and to those in the pavilion who had recently passed that way. Not only so; but from the recklessness of the course which he had followed, steering near to the most formidable portions of the sand, he was as evidently a stranger to the country and to the ill-repute of Graden beach.

Step by step I followed the prints; until, a quarter of a mile further, I beheld them die away into the south-eastern boundary of Graden Floe. There, whoever he was, the miserable man had perished. One or two gulls, who had, perhaps, seen him disappear, wheeled over his sepulchre with their usual melancholy piping. The sun had broken through the clouds by a last effort, and coloured the wide level of quicksands with a dusky purple. I stood for some time gazing at the spot, chilled and disheartened by my own reflections, and with a strong and commanding consciousness of death. I remember wondering how long the tragedy had taken, and whether his screams had been audible at the pavilion. And then, making a strong resolution, I was about to tear myself away, when a gust fiercer than usual fell upon this quarter of the beach, and I saw now, whirling high in air, now skimming lightly across the surface of the sands, a soft, black, felt hat, somewhat conical in shape, such as I had remarked already on the heads of the Italians.

I believe, but I am not sure, that I uttered a cry. The wind was driving the hat shoreward, and I ran round the border of the floe to be ready against its arrival. The gust fell, dropping the hat for awhile upon the quicksand, and then, once more freshening, landed it a few yards from where I stood. I seized it with the interest you may imagine. It had seen some service; indeed, it was rustier than either of those I had seen that day upon the street. The lining was red, stamped with the name of the maker, which I have forgotten, and that of the place of manufacture, Venedig. This (it is not yet forgotten) was the name given by the Austrians to the beautiful city of Venice, then, and for long after, a part of their dominions.

The shock was complete. I saw imaginary Italians upon every side; and for the first, and, I may say, for the last time in my experience, became overpowered by what is called panic terror. I knew nothing, that is, to be

afraid of, and yet I admit that I was heartily afraid; and it was with a sensible reluctance that I returned to my exposed and solitary camp in the Sea-Wood.

There I ate some cold porridge which had been left over from the night before, for I was disinclined to make a fire; and, feeling strengthened and reassured, dismissed all these fanciful terrors from my mind, and lay down to sleep with composure.

How long I may have slept it is impossible for me to guess; but I was awakened at last by a sudden, blinding flash of light into my face. It woke me like a blow. In an instant I was upon my knees. But the light had gone as suddenly as it came. The darkness was intense. And, as it was blowing great guns from the sea and pouring with rain, the noises of the storm effectually concealed all others.

It was, I dare say, half a minute before I regained my self-possession. But for two circumstances, I should have thought I had been awakened by some new and vivid form of nightmare. First, the flap of my tent, which I had shut carefully when I retired, was now unfastened; and, second, I could still perceive, with a sharpness that excluded any theory of hallucination, the smell of hot metal and of burning oil. The conclusion was obvious. I had been awakened by someone flashing a bull's-eye lantern in my face.

It had been but a flash, and away. He had seen my face, and then gone. I asked myself the object of so strange a proceeding, and the answer came pat. The man, whoever he was, had thought to recognise me, and he had not. There was yet another question unsolved; and to this, I may say, I feared to give an answer; if he had recognised me, what would he have done?

My fears were immediately diverted from myself, for I saw that I had been visited in a mistake; and I became persuaded that some dreadful danger threatened the pavilion. It required some nerve to issue forth into the black and intricate thicket which surrounded and overhung the den; but I groped my way to the links, drenched with rain, beaten upon and deafened by the gusts, and fearing at every step to lay my hand upon some lurking adversary. The darkness was so complete that I might have been surrounded by an army and yet none the wiser, and the uproar of the gale so loud that my hearing was as useless as my sight.

For the rest of the night, which seemed interminably long, I patrolled the vicinity of the pavilion, without seeing a living creature or hearing any noise but the concert of the wind, the sea, and the rain. A light in the upper story filtered through a cranny in the shutter, and kept me company till the approach of dawn.

CHAPTER 5

Tells of an interview between Northmour, Clara, and myself

With the first peep of day, I retired from the open to my old lair among the sandhills, there to await the coming of my wife. The morning was grey, wild, and melancholy; the wind moderated before sunrise, and then went about, and blew in puffs from the shore; the sea began to go down, but the rain still fell without mercy. Over all the wilderness of links there was not a creature to be seen. Yet I felt sure the neighbourhood was alive with skulking foes. The light that had been so suddenly and surprisingly flashed upon my face as I lay sleeping, and the hat that had been blown ashore by the wind from over Graden Floe, were two speaking signals of the peril that environed Clara and the party in the pavilion.

It was, perhaps, half-past seven, or nearer eight, before I saw the door open, and that dear figure come towards me in the rain. I was waiting for her on the beach before she had crossed the sandhills.

"I have had such trouble to come!" she cried. "They did not wish me to go walking in the rain."

"Clara," I said, "you are not frightened!"

"No," said she, with a simplicity that filled my heart with confidence. For my wife was the bravest as well as the best of women; in my experience I have not found the two go always together, but with her they did; and she combined the extreme of fortitude with the most endearing and beautiful virtues.

I told her what had happened; and, though her cheek grew visibly paler, she retained perfect control over her senses.

"You see now that I am safe," said I in conclusion. "They do not mean to harm me; for, had they chosen, I was a dead man last night."

She laid her hand upon my arm.

"And I had no presentiment!" she cried.

Her accent thrilled me with delight. I put my arm about her, and strained her to my side; and, before either of us was aware, her hands were on my shoulders and my lips upon her mouth. Yet up to that moment no word of love had passed between us. To this time I remember the touch of her cheek, which was wet and cold with the rain; and many a time since, when she has been washing her face, I have kissed it again for the sake of that morning on the beach. Now that she is taken from me, and I finish my pilgrimage alone, I recall our old loving kindness and the deep honesty and affection which united us, and my present loss seems but a trifle in comparison.

We may have thus stood for some seconds—for time passes quickly with lovers—before we were startled by a peal of laughter close at hand. It was not natural mirth, but seemed to be affected in order to conceal an angrier feeling. We both turned, though I still kept my left arm about Clara's waist; nor did she seek to withdraw herself; and there, a few paces off upon the beach, stood Northmour, his head lowered, his hands behind his back, his nostrils white with passion.

"Ah! Cassilis!" he said, as I disclosed my face.

"That same," said I; for I was not at all put about.

"And so, Miss Huddlestone," he continued slowly but savagely, "this is how you keep your faith to your father and to me? This is the value you set upon your father's life? And you are so infatuated with this young gentleman that you must brave ruin, and decency, and common human caution——"

"Miss Huddlestone——" I was beginning to interrupt him, when he, in his turn, cut in brutally——

"You hold your tongue," said he; "I am speaking to that girl."

"That girl, as you call her, is my wife," said I; and my wife only leaned a little nearer, so that I knew she had affirmed my words.

"Your what?" he cried. "You lie!"

"Northmour," I said, "we all know you have a bad temper, and I am the last man to be irritated by words. For all that, I propose that you speak lower, for I am convinced that we are not alone."

He looked round him, and it was plain my remark had in some degree sobered his passion. "What do you mean?" he asked.

I only said one word: "Italians."

He swore a round oath, and looked at us, from one to the other.

"Mr. Cassilis knows all that I know," said my wife.

"What I want to know," he broke out, "is where the devil Mr. Cassilis comes from, and what the devil Mr. Cassilis is doing here. You say you are married: that I do not believe. If you were, Graden Floe would soon divorce you; four minutes and a half, Cassilis; I keep my private cemetery for my friends."

"It took somewhat longer," said I, "for that Italian."

He looked at me for a moment half daunted, and then, almost civilly, asked me to tell my story. "You have too much the advantage of me, Cassilis," he added. I complied, of course; and he listened, with several ejaculations, while I told him how I had come to Graden; that it was I whom he had tried to murder on the night of landing; and what I had subsequently seen and heard of the Italians.

"Well," said he, when I had done, "it is here at last; there is no mistake about that. And what, may I ask, do you propose to do?"

"I propose to stay with you and lend a hand," said I.

"You are a brave man," he returned, with a peculiar intonation.

"I am not afraid," said I.

"And so," he continued, "I am to understand that you two are married? And you stand up to it before my face, Miss Huddlestone?"

"We are not yet married," said Clara; "but we shall be as soon as we can."

"Bravo!" cried Northmour. "And the bargain? D——n it, you're not a fool, young woman; I may call a spade a spade with you. How about the bargain? You know as well as I do what your father's life depends upon. I have only to put my hands under my coat-tails and walk away, and his throat would be cut before the evening."

"Yes, Mr. Northmour," returned Clara, with great spirit; "but that is what you will never do. You made a bargain that was unworthy of a gentleman; but you are a gentleman for all that, and you will never desert a man whom you have begun to help."

"Aha!" said he. "You think I will give my yacht for nothing? You think I will risk my life and liberty for love of the old gentleman; and then, I suppose, be best man at the wedding, to wind up? Well," he added, with an odd smile, "perhaps you are not altogether wrong. But ask Cassilis here. *He* knows me. Am I a man to trust? Am I safe and scrupulous? Am I kind?"

"I know you talk a great deal, and sometimes, I think, very foolishly," replied Clara, "but I know you are a gentleman, and I am not in the least afraid."

He looked at her with a peculiar approval and admiration; then, turning to me, "Do you think I would give her up without a struggle, Frank?" said he. "I tell you plainly, you look out. The next time we come to blows——"

"Will make the third," I interrupted, smiling.

"Aye, true; so it will," he said. "I had forgotten. Well, the third time's lucky."

"The third time, you mean, you will have the crew of the *Red Earl* to help," I said.

"Do you hear him?" he asked, turning to my wife.

"I hear two men speaking like cowards," said she. "I should despise myself either to think or speak like that. And neither of you believes one word that you are saying, which makes it the more wicked and silly."

"She's a trump!" cried Northmour. "But she's not yet Mrs. Cassilis. I say no more. The present is not for me."

Then my wife surprised me.

"I leave you here," she said suddenly. "My father has been too long alone. But remember this: you are to be friends, for you are both good friends to me."

She has since told me her reason for this step. As long as she remained, she declares that we two would have continued to quarrel; and I suppose that she was right, for when she was gone we fell at once into a sort of confidentiality.

Northmour stared after her as she went away over the sandhill.

"She is the only woman in the world!" he exclaimed with an oath. "Look at her action."

I, for my part, leaped at this opportunity for a little further light.

"See here, Northmour," said I; "we are all in a tight place, are we not?"

"I believe you, my boy," he answered, looking me in the eyes, and with great emphasis. "We have all hell upon us, that's the truth. You may believe me or not, but I'm afraid of my life."

"Tell me one thing," said I. "What are they after, these Italians? What do they want with Mr. Huddlestone?"

"Don't you know?" he cried. "The black old scamp had *carbonaro*[1] funds on a deposit—two hundred and eighty thousand; and of course he gambled it away on stocks. There was to have been a revolution in the Tridentino, or Parma; but the revolution is off, and the whole wasp's nest is after Huddlestone. We shall all be lucky if we can save our skins."

"The *carbonari!*" I exclaimed; "God help him indeed!"

"Amen!" said Northmour. "And now, look here: I have said that we are in a fix; and, frankly, I shall be glad of your help. If I can't save Huddlestone, I want at least to save the girl. Come and stay in the pavilion; and, there's my hand on it, I shall act as your friend until the old man is either clear or dead. But," he added, "once that is settled, you become my rival once again, and I warn you—mind yourself."

"Done!" said I; and we shook hands.

"And now let us go directly to the fort," said Northmour; and he began to lead the way through the rain.

Chapter 6

Tells of my introduction to the tall man

We were admitted to the pavilion by Clara, and I was surprised by the completeness and security of the defences. A barricade of great strength, and yet easy to displace, supported the door against any violence from without; and the shutters of the dining room, into which I was led directly, and which was feebly illuminated by a lamp, were even more elaborately fortified. The panels were strengthened by bars and crossbars; and these, in their turn, were kept in position by a system of braces and struts, some abutting on the floor, some on

the roof, and others, in fine,[2] against the opposite wall of the apartment. It was at once a solid and well-designed piece of carpentry; and I did not seek to conceal my admiration.

"I am the engineer," said Northmour. "You remember the planks in the garden? Behold them!"

"I did not know you had so many talents," said I.

"Are you armed?" he continued, pointing to an array of guns and pistols, all in admirable order, which stood in line against the wall or were displayed upon the sideboard.

"Thank you," I returned; "I have gone armed since our last encounter. But, to tell you the truth, I have had nothing to eat since early yesterday evening."

Northmour produced some cold meat, to which I eagerly set myself, and a bottle of good Burgundy, by which, wet as I was, I did not scruple to profit. I have always been an extreme temperance man[3] on principle; but it is useless to push principle to excess, and on this occasion I believe that I finished three quarters of the bottle. As I ate, I still continued to admire the preparations for defence.

"We could stand a siege," I said at length.

"Ye—es," drawled Northmour, "a very little one, perhaps. It is not so much the strength of the pavilion I misdoubt; it is the double danger that kills me. If we get to shooting, wild as the country is someone is sure to hear it, and then—why, then it's the same thing, only different, as they say, caged by law, or killed by *carbonari*. There's the choice. It is a devilish bad thing to have the law against you in this world, and so I tell the old gentleman upstairs. He is quite of my way of thinking."

"Speaking of that," said I, "what kind of person is he?"

"Oh, he?" cried the other; "he's a rancid fellow as far as he goes. I should like to have his neck wrung tomorrow by all the devils in Italy. I am not in this affair for him. You take me? I made a bargain for Missy's hand and I mean to have it too."

"That, by the way," said I, "I understand. But how will Mr. Huddlestone take my intrusion?"

"Leave that to Clara," returned Northmour.

---

1   *carbonaro*   Member of an Italian secret political society, formed in the early nineteenth century with the intention of ousting the occupying French forces and forming a republic in Italy.

2   *in fine*   In conclusion.

3   *temperance man*   One who abstains from drinking alcoholic beverages.

I could have struck him in the face for this coarse familiarity; but I respected the truce, as, I am bound to say, did Northmour, and so long as the danger continued not a cloud arose in our relation. I bear him this testimony with the most unfeigned satisfaction; nor am I without pride when I look back upon my own behaviour. For surely no two men were ever left in a position so invidious and irritating.

As soon as I had done eating, we proceeded to inspect the lower floor. Window by window we tried the different supports, now and then making an inconsiderable change, and the strokes of the hammer sounded with startling loudness through the house. I proposed, I remember, to make loopholes,[1] but he told me they were already made in the windows of the upper story. It was an anxious business, this inspection, and left me downhearted. There were two doors and five windows to protect, and, counting Clara, only four of us to defend them against an unknown number of foes. I communicated my doubts to Northmour, who assured me, with unmoved composure, that he entirely shared them.

"Before morning," said he, "we shall all be butchered and buried in Graden Floe. For me, that is written."

I could not help shuddering at the mention of the quicksand, but reminded Northmour that our enemies had spared me in the wood.

"Do not flatter yourself," said he. "Then you were not in the same boat with the old gentleman; now you are. It's the floe for all of us, mark my words."

I trembled for Clara; and just then her dear voice was heard calling us to come upstairs. Northmour showed me the way, and, when he had reached the landing, knocked at the door of what used to be called *My Uncle's Bedroom,* as the founder of the pavilion had designed it especially for himself.

"Come in, Northmour; come in, dear Mr. Cassilis," said a voice from within.

Pushing open the door, Northmour admitted me before him into the apartment. As I came in I could see the daughter slipping out by the side door into the study, which had been prepared as her bedroom. In the bed, which was drawn back against the wall, instead of standing, as I had last seen it, boldly across the window,

sat Bernard Huddlestone, the defaulting banker. Little as I had seen of him by the shifting light of the lantern on the links, I had no difficulty in recognising him for the same. He had a long and sallow countenance, surrounded by a long red beard and side-whiskers. His broken nose and high cheekbones gave him somewhat the air of a Kalmuck[2] and his light eyes shone with the excitement of a high fever. He wore a skullcap of black silk; a huge Bible lay open before him on the bed, with a pair of gold spectacles in the place, and a pile of other books lay on the stand by his side. The green curtains lent a cadaverous shade to his cheek; and, as he sat propped on pillows, his great stature was painfully hunched, and his head protruded till it overhung his knees. I believe if he had not died otherwise, he must have fallen a victim to consumption in the course of but a very few weeks.

He held out to me a hand, long, thin, and disagreeably hairy.

"Come in, come in, Mr. Cassilis," said he. "Another protector—ahem!—another protector. Always welcome as a friend of my daughter's, Mr. Cassilis. How they have rallied about me, my daughter's friends! May God in heaven bless and reward them for it!"

I gave him my hand, of course, because I could not help it; but the sympathy I had been prepared to feel for Clara's father was immediately soured by his appearance, and the wheedling, unreal tones in which he spoke.

"Cassilis is a good man," said Northmour, "worth ten."

"So I hear," cried Mr. Huddlestone eagerly; "so my girl tells me. Ah, Mr. Cassilis, my sin has found me out, you see! I am very low, very low, but I hope equally penitent. We must all come to the throne of grace at last, Mr. Cassilis. For my part, I come late indeed, but with unfeigned humility, I trust."

"Fiddle-de-dee!" said Northmour roughly.

"No, no, dear Northmour!" cried the banker. "You must not say that; you must not try to shake me. You forget, my dear, good boy, you forget I may be called this very night before my Maker."

His excitement was pitiful to behold; and I felt myself grow indignant with Northmour, whose infidel

---

[1] *loopholes* Holes through which shots can be fired.

[2] *Kalmuck* Member of the Mongolian tribe of the Kalmyk in southwestern Russia.

opinions I well knew, and heartily derided, as he continued to taunt the poor sinner out of his humour of repentance.

"Pooh, my dear Huddlestone!" said he. "You do yourself injustice. You are a man of the world inside and out, and were up to all kinds of mischief before I was born. Your conscience is tanned like South American leather—only you forgot to tan your liver, and that, if you will believe me, is the seat of the annoyance."

"Rogue, rogue! bad boy!" said Mr. Huddlestone, shaking his finger. "I am no precisian,[1] if you come to that; I always hated a precisian; but I never lost hold of something better through it all. I have been a bad boy, Mr. Cassilis; I do not seek to deny that; but it was after my wife's death, and you know, with a widower, it's a different thing: sinful—I won't say no, but there is a gradation, we shall hope. And talking of that—Hark!" he broke out suddenly, his hand raised, his fingers spread, his face racked with interest and terror. "Only the rain, bless God!" he added, after a pause, and with indescribable relief.

For some seconds he lay back among the pillows like a man near to fainting; then he gathered himself together, and, in somewhat tremulous tones, began once more to thank me for the share I was prepared to take in his defence.

"One question, sir," said I, when he had paused. "Is it true that you have money with you?"

He seemed annoyed by the question, but admitted with reluctance that he had a little.

"Well," I continued, "it is their money they are after, is it not? Why not give it up to them?"

"Ah!" replied he, shaking his head, "I have tried that already, Mr. Cassilis; and alas! that it should be so, but it is blood they want."

"Huddlestone, that's a little less than fair," said Northmour. "You should mention that what you offered them was upwards of two hundred thousand short. The deficit is worth a reference; it is for what they call a cool sum, Frank. Then, you see, the fellows reason in their clear Italian way; and it seems to them, as indeed it seems to me, that they may just as well have both while they are about it—money and blood together, by George, and no more trouble for the extra pleasure."

"Is it in the pavilion?" I asked.

"It is; and I wish it was in the bottom of the sea instead," said Northmour; and then suddenly—"What are you making faces at me for?" he cried to Mr. Huddlestone, on whom I had unconsciously turned my back. "Do you think Cassilis would sell you?"

Mr. Huddlestone protested that nothing had been further from his mind.

"It is a good thing," retorted Northmour in his ugliest manner. "You might end by wearying us. What were you going to say?" he added, turning to me.

"I was going to propose an occupation for the afternoon," said I. "Let us carry that money out, piece by piece, and lay it down before the pavilion door. If the *carbonari* come, why, it's theirs at any rate."

"No, no," cried Mr. Huddlestone; "it does not, it cannot belong to them! It should be distributed pro rata[2] among all my creditors."

"Come, now, Huddlestone," said Northmour, "none of that."

"Well, but my daughter," moaned the wretched man.

"Your daughter will do well enough. Here are two suitors, Cassilis and I, neither of us beggars, between whom she has to choose. And as for yourself, to make an end of arguments, you have no right to a farthing, and, unless I'm much mistaken, you are going to die."

It was certainly very cruelly said; but Mr. Huddlestone was a man who attracted little sympathy; and, although I saw him wince and shudder, I mentally endorsed the rebuke; nay, I added a contribution of my own.

"Northmour and I," I said, "are willing enough to help you to save your life, but not to escape with stolen property."

He struggled for awhile with himself, as though he were on the point of giving way to anger, but prudence had the best of the controversy.

"My dear boys," he said, "do with me or my money what you will. I leave all in your hands. Let me compose myself."

---

[1] *precisian* Puritan, or one who is overly strict and rigid in moral matters.

[2] *pro rata* Latin: proportionately.

And so we left him, gladly enough I am sure. The last that I saw, he had once more taken up his great Bible, and with tremulous hands was adjusting his spectacles to read.

CHAPTER 7

Tells how a word was cried through the pavilion window

The recollection of that afternoon will always be graven on my mind. Northmour and I were persuaded that an attack was imminent; and if it had been in our power to alter in any way the order of events, that power would have been used to precipitate rather than delay the critical moment. The worst was to be anticipated; yet we could conceive no extremity so miserable as the suspense we were now suffering. I have never been an eager, though always a great, reader; but I never knew books so insipid as those which I took up and cast aside that afternoon in the pavilion. Even talk became impossible, as the hours went on. One or other was always listening for some sound, or peering from an upstairs window over the links. And yet not a sign indicated the presence of our foes.

We debated over and over again my proposal with regard to the money; and had we been in complete possession of our faculties, I am sure we should have condemned it as unwise; but we were flustered with alarm, grasped at a straw, and determined, although it was as much as advertising Mr. Huddlestone's presence in the pavilion, to carry my proposal into effect.

The sum was part in specie,[1] part in bank paper, and part in circular notes, payable to the name of James Gregory. We took it out, counted it, enclosed it once more in a despatch-box belonging to Northmour, and prepared a letter in Italian which he tied to the handle. It was signed by both of us under oath, and declared that this was all the money which had escaped the failure of the house of Huddlestone. This was, perhaps, the maddest action ever perpetrated by two persons professing to be sane. Had the despatch-box fallen into other hands than those for which it was intended, we stood criminally convicted on our own written testimony; but, as I have said, we were neither of us in a condition to judge soberly, and had a thirst for action that drove us to do something, right or wrong, rather than endure the agony of waiting. Moreover, as we were both convinced that the hollows of the links were alive with hidden spies upon our movements, we hoped that our appearance with the box might lead to a parley,[2] and, perhaps, a compromise.

It was nearly three when we issued from the pavilion. The rain had taken off; the sun shone quite cheerfully. I have never seen the gulls fly so close about the house or approach so fearlessly to human beings. On the very doorstep one flapped heavily past our heads, and uttered its wild cry in my very ear.

"There is an omen for you," said Northmour, who like all freethinkers was much under the influence of superstition. "They think we are already dead."

I made some light rejoinder, but it was with half my heart; for the circumstance had impressed me.

A yard or two before the gate, on a patch of smooth turf, we set down the despatch-box, and Northmour waved a white handkerchief over his head. Nothing replied. We raised our voices, and cried aloud in Italian that we were there as ambassadors to arrange the quarrel; but the stillness remained unbroken save by the seagulls and the surf. I had a weight at my heart when we desisted, and I saw that even Northmour was unusually pale. He looked over his shoulder nervously, as though he feared that someone had crept between him and the pavilion door.

"By God," he said in a whisper, "this is too much for me!" I replied in the same key: "Suppose there should be none, after all!"

"Look there," he returned, nodding with his head, as though he had been afraid to point.

I glanced in the direction indicated; and there, from the northern corner of the Sea-Wood, beheld a thin column of smoke rising steadily against the now cloudless sky.

"Northmour," I said (we still continued to talk in whispers), "it is not possible to endure this suspense. I prefer death fifty times over. Stay you here to watch the pavilion; I will go forward and make sure, if I have to walk right into their camp."

---

[1] *specie* Coin.

[2] *parley* Discussion.

He looked once again all around him with puckered eyes, and then nodded assentingly to my proposal.

My heart beat like a sledgehammer as I set out walking rapidly in the direction of the smoke; and though up to that moment I had felt chill and shivering, I was suddenly conscious of a glow of heat over all my body. The ground in this direction was very uneven; a hundred men might have lain hidden in as many square yards about my path. But I had not practised the business in vain, chose such routes as cut at the very root of concealment, and, by keeping along the most convenient ridges, commanded several hollows at a time. It was not long before I was rewarded for my caution. Coming suddenly onto a mound somewhat more elevated than the surrounding hummocks, I saw, not thirty yards away, a man bent almost double, and running as fast as his attitude permitted, along the bottom of a gully. I had dislodged one of the spies from his ambush. As soon as I sighted him, I called loudly both in English and Italian; and he, seeing concealment was no longer possible, straightened himself out, leaped from the gully, and made off as straight as an arrow for the borders of the wood.

It was none of my business to pursue; I had learned what I wanted—that we were beleaguered and watched in the pavilion; and I returned at once, and walking as nearly as possible in my old footsteps, to where Northmour awaited me beside the despatch-box. He was even paler than when I had left him, and his voice shook a little.

"Could you see what he was like?" he asked.

"He kept his back turned," I replied.

"Let us go into the house, Frank. I don't think I'm a coward, but I can stand no more of this," he whispered.

All was still and sunshiny about the pavilion as we turned to re-enter it; even the gulls had flown in a wider circuit, and were seen flickering along the beach and sandhills; and this loneliness terrified me more than a regiment under arms. It was not until the door was barricaded that I could draw a full inspiration and relieve the weight that lay upon my bosom. Northmour and I exchanged a steady glance; and I suppose each made his own reflections on the white and startled aspect of the other.

"You were right," I said. "All is over. Shake hands, old man, for the last time."

"Yes," replied he, "I will shake hands; for, as sure as I am here, I bear no malice. But, remember, if, by some impossible accident, we should give the slip to these blackguards, I'll take the upper hand of you by fair or foul."

"Oh," said I, "you weary me."

He seemed hurt, and walked away in silence to the foot of the stairs, where he paused.

"You do not understand me," said he, "I am not a swindler, and I guard myself; that is all. It may weary you or not, Mr. Cassilis, I do not care a rush; I speak for my own satisfaction, and not for your amusement. You had better go upstairs and court the girl; for my part, I stay here."

"And I stay with you," I returned. "Do you think I would steal a march, even with your permission?"

"Frank," he said, smiling, "it's a pity you are an ass, for you have the makings of a man. I think I must be *fey*[1] today; you cannot irritate me, even when you try. Do you know," he continued softly, "I think we are the two most miserable men in England, you and I? we have got on to thirty without wife or child, or so much as a shop to look after—poor, pitiful, lost devils, both! And now we clash about a girl! As if there were not several millions in the United Kingdom! Ah, Frank, Frank, the one who loses his throw, be it you or me, he has my pity! It were better for him—how does the Bible say?—that a millstone were hanged about his neck and he were cast into the depth of the sea.[2] Let us take a drink," he concluded suddenly, but without any levity of tone.

I was touched by his words, and consented. He sat down on the table in the dining room, and held up the glass of sherry to his eye.

"If you beat me, Frank," he said, "I shall take to drink. What will you do if it goes the other way?"

"God knows," I returned.

"Well," said he, "here is a toast in the meantime: '*Italia irredenta*!'"[3]

---

[1]   *fey*   Destined to die.

[2]   *millstone ... sea*   Cf. Mark 9.42 and Luke 17.2.

[3]   *irredenta*   Italian: unredeemed (i.e., Italy is under another country's rule).

The remainder of the day was passed in the same dreadful tedium and suspense. I laid the table for dinner, while Northmour and Clara prepared the meal together in the kitchen. I could hear their talk as I went to and fro, and was surprised to find it ran all the time upon myself. Northmour again bracketed us together, and rallied Clara on a choice of husbands; but he continued to speak of me with some feeling, and uttered nothing to my prejudice unless he included himself in the condemnation. This awakened a sense of gratitude in my heart, which combined with the immediateness of our peril to fill my eyes with tears. After all, I thought—and perhaps the thought was laughably vain—we were here three very noble human beings to perish in defence of a thieving banker.

Before we sat down to table, I looked forth from an upstairs window. The day was beginning to decline; the links were utterly deserted; the despatch-box still lay untouched where we had left it hours before.

Mr. Huddlestone, in a long yellow dressing-gown, took one end of the table, Clara the other, while Northmour and I faced each other from the sides. The lamp was brightly trimmed; the wine was good; the viands,[1] although mostly cold, excellent of their sort. We seemed to have agreed tacitly; all reference to the impending catastrophe was carefully avoided; and, considering our tragic circumstances, we made a merrier party than could have been expected. From time to time, it is true, Northmour or I would rise from the table and make a round of the defences; and on each of these occasions Mr. Huddlestone was recalled to a sense of his tragic predicament, glanced up with ghastly eyes, and bore for an instant on his countenance the stamp of terror. But he hastened to empty his glass, wiped his forehead with his handkerchief, and joined again in the conversation.

I was astonished at the wit and information he displayed. Mr. Huddlestone's was certainly no ordinary character; he had read and observed for himself; his gifts were sound; and, though I could never have learned to love the man, I began to understand his success in business, and the great respect in which he had been held before his failure. He had, above all, the talent of society; and though I never heard him speak but on this one and most unfavourable occasion, I set him down among the most brilliant conversationalists I ever met. He was relating with great gusto, and seemingly no feeling of shame, the manoeuvres of a scoundrelly commission merchant whom he had known and studied in his youth, and we were all listening with an odd mixture of mirth and embarrassment, when our little party was brought abruptly to an end in the most startling manner.

A noise like that of a wet finger on the windowpane interrupted Mr. Huddlestone's tale; and in an instant we were all four as white as paper, and sat tongue-tied and motionless round the table.

"A snail," I said at last; for I had heard that these animals make a noise somewhat similar in character.

"Snail be d—d!" said Northmour. "Hush!"

The same sound was repeated twice at regular intervals; and then a formidable voice shouted through the shutters the Italian word "*Traditore*!"[2]

Mr. Huddlestone threw his head in the air; his eyelids quivered; next moment he fell insensible below the table. Northmour and I had each run to the armoury and seized a gun. Clara was on her feet with her hand at her throat.

So we stood waiting, for we thought the hour of attack was certainly come; but second passed after second, and all but the surf remained silent in the neighbourhood of the pavilion.

"Quick," said Northmour; "upstairs with him before they come."

CHAPTER 8

Tells the last of the tall man

Somehow or other, by hook and crook, and between the three of us, we got Bernard Huddlestone bundled upstairs and laid upon the bed in *My Uncle's Room*. During the whole process, which was rough enough, he gave no sign of consciousness, and he remained, as we had thrown him, without changing the position of a finger. His daughter opened his shirt and began to wet his head and bosom; while Northmour and I ran to the window. The weather continued clear; the moon, which was now about full, had risen and shed a very clear light

---

[1] *viands* Foods.

[2] *Traditore* Italian: traitor.

upon the links; yet, strain our eyes as we might, we could distinguish nothing moving. A few dark spots, more or less, on the uneven expanse were not to be identified; they might be crouching men, they might be shadows; it was impossible to be sure.

"Thank God," said Northmour, "Aggie is not coming tonight."

Aggie was the name of the old nurse; he had not thought of her till now; but that he should think of her at all, was a trait that surprised me in the man.

We were again reduced to waiting. Northmour went to the fireplace and spread his hands before the red embers, as if he were cold. I followed him mechanically with my eyes, and in so doing turned my back upon the window. At that moment a very faint report was audible from without, and a ball shivered a pane of glass, and buried itself in the shutter two inches from my head. I heard Clara scream; and though I whipped instantly out of range and into a corner, she was there, so to speak, before me, beseeching to know if I were hurt. I felt that I could stand to be shot at every day and all day long, with such marks of solicitude for a reward; and I continued to reassure her, with the tenderest caresses and in complete forgetfulness of our situation, till the voice of Northmour recalled me to myself.

"An airgun," he said. "They wish to make no noise." I put Clara aside, and looked at him. He was standing with his back to the fire and his hands clasped behind him; and I knew by the black look on his face, that passion was boiling within. I had seen just such a look before he attacked me, that March night, in the adjoining chamber; and, though I could make every allowance for his anger, I confess I trembled for the consequences. He gazed straight before him; but he could see us with the tail of his eye, and his temper kept rising like a gale of wind. With regular battle awaiting us outside, this prospect of an internecine strife within the walls began to daunt me.

Suddenly, as I was thus closely watching his expression and prepared against the worst, I saw a change, a flash, a look of relief, upon his face. He took up the lamp which stood beside him on the table, and turned to us with an air of some excitement.

"There is one point that we must know," said he. "Are they going to butcher the lot of us, or only Huddlestone? Did they take you for him, or fire at you for your own *beaux yeux*?"[1]

"They took me for him, for certain," I replied. "I am near as tall, and my head is fair."

"I am going to make sure," returned Northmour; and he stepped up to the window, holding the lamp above his head, and stood there, quietly affronting death, for half a minute.

Clara sought to rush forward and pull him from the place of danger; but I had the pardonable selfishness to hold her back by force.

"Yes," said Northmour, turning coolly from the window; "it's only Huddlestone they want."

"Oh, Mr. Northmour!" cried Clara, but found no more to add, the temerity she had just witnessed seeming beyond the reach of words.

He, on his part, looked at me, cocking his head, with a fire of triumph in his eyes; and I understood at once that he had thus hazarded his life, merely to attract Clara's notice, and depose me from my position as the hero of the hour. He snapped his fingers.

"The fire is only beginning," he said. "When they warm up to their work, they won't be so particular."

A voice was now heard hailing us from the entrance. From the window we could see the figure of a man in the moonlight; he stood motionless, his face uplifted to ours, and a rag of something white on his extended arm; and as we looked right down upon him, though he was a good many yards distant on the links, we could see the moonlight glitter on his eyes.

He opened his lips again, and spoke for some minutes on end, in a key so loud that he might have been heard in every corner of the pavilion, and as far away as the borders of the wood. It was the same voice that had already shouted "*Traditore!*" through the shutters of the dining room; this time it made a complete and clear statement. If the traitor "Oddlestone" were given up, all others should be spared; if not, no one should escape to tell the tale.

"Well, Huddlestone, what do you say to that?" asked Northmour, turning to the bed.

Up to that moment the banker had given no sign of life, and I, at least, had supposed him to be still lying in a faint; but he replied at once, and in such tones as I

---

[1]   *beaux yeux*   French: beautiful eyes.

have never heard elsewhere, save from a delirious patient, adjured and besought us not to desert him. It was the most hideous and abject performance that my imagination can conceive.

"Enough," cried Northmour; and then he threw open the window, leaned out into the night, and in a tone of exultation, and with a total forgetfulness of what was due to the presence of a lady, poured out upon the ambassador a string of the most abominable raillery both in English and Italian, and bade him be gone where he had come from. I believe that nothing so delighted Northmour at that moment as the thought that we must all infallibly perish before the night was out.

Meantime the Italian put his flag of truce into his pocket, and disappeared, at a leisurely pace, among the sandhills.

"They make honourable war," said Northmour. "They are all gentlemen and soldiers. For the credit of the thing, I wish we could change sides—you and I, Frank, and you too, Missy my darling—and leave that being on the bed to someone else. Tut! Don't look shocked! We are all going post to what they call eternity, and may as well be above-board while there's time. As far as I'm concerned, if I could first strangle Huddlestone and then get Clara in my arms, I could die with some pride and satisfaction. And as it is, by God, I'll have a kiss!"

Before I could do anything to interfere, he had rudely embraced and repeatedly kissed the resisting girl. Next moment I had pulled him away with fury, and flung him heavily against the wall. He laughed loud and long, and I feared his wits had given way under the strain, for even in the best of days he had been a sparing and a quiet laugher.

"Now, Frank," said he, when his mirth had somewhat appeased, "it's your turn. Here's my hand. Goodbye; farewell!" Then, seeing me stand rigid and indignant, and holding Clara to my side—"Man!" he broke out, "are you angry? Did you think we were going to die with all the airs and graces of society? I took a kiss; I'm glad I had it; and now you can take another if you like, and square accounts."

I turned from him with a feeling of contempt which I did not seek to dissemble.

"As you please," said he. "You've been a prig in life;

a prig you'll die."

And with that he sat down in a chair, a rifle over the knee, and amused himself with snapping the lock; but I could see that his ebullition of light spirits (the only one I ever knew him to display) had already come to an end, and was succeeded by a sullen, scowling humour.

All this time our assailants might have been entering the house, and we been none the wiser; we had in truth almost forgotten the danger that so imminently overhung our days. But just then Mr. Huddlestone uttered a cry, and leaped from the bed.

I asked him what was wrong.

"Fire!" he cried. "They have set the house on fire!" Northmour was on his feet in an instant, and he and I ran through the door of communication with the study. The room was illuminated by a red and angry light. Almost at the moment of our entrance, a tower of flame arose in front of the window, and, with a tingling report, a pane fell inwards on the carpet. They had set fire to the lean-to outhouse, where Northmour used to nurse his negatives.

"Hot work," said Northmour. "Let us try in your old room."

We ran thither in a breath, threw up the casement, and looked forth. Along the whole back wall of the pavilion piles of fuel had been arranged and kindled; and it is probable they had been drenched with mineral oil, for, in spite of the morning's rain, they all burned bravely. The fire had taken a firm hold already on the outhouse, which blazed higher and higher every moment; the back door was in the centre of a red-hot bonfire; the eaves we could see, as we looked upward, were already smouldering, for the roof overhung, and was supported by considerable beams of wood. At the same time, hot, pungent, and choking volumes of smoke began to fill the house. There was not a human being to be seen to right or left.

"Ah, well!" said Northmour, "here's the end, thank God."

And we returned to *My Uncle's Room*. Mr. Huddlestone was putting on his boots, still violently trembling, but with an air of determination such as I had not hitherto observed. Clara stood close by him, with her cloak in both hands ready to throw about her shoulders, and a strange look in her eyes, as if she were half hopeful, half doubtful of her father.

"Well, boys and girls," said Northmour, "how about a sally? The oven is heating; it is not good to stay here and be baked; and, for my part, I want to come to my hands with them and be done."

"There is nothing else left," I replied. And both Clara and Mr. Huddlestone, though with a very different intonation, added, "Nothing."

As we went downstairs the heat was excessive, and the roaring of the fire filled our ears; and we had scarce reached the passage before the stairs window fell in, a branch of flame shot brandishing through the aperture, and the interior of the pavilion became lit up with that dreadful and fluctuating glare. At the same moment we heard the fall of something heavy and inelastic in the upper story. The whole pavilion, it was plain, had gone alight like a box of matches, and now not only flamed sky-high to land and sea, but threatened with every moment to crumble and fall in about our ears.

Northmour and I cocked our revolvers. Mr. Huddlestone, who had already refused a firearm, put us behind him with a manner of command.

"Let Clara open the door," said he. "So, if they fire a volley, she will be protected. And in the meantime stand behind me. I am the scapegoat; my sins have found me out."

I heard him, as I stood breathless by his shoulder, with my pistol ready, pattering off prayers in a tremulous, rapid whisper; and I confess, horrid as the thought may seem, I despised him for thinking of supplications in a moment so critical and thrilling. In the meantime, Clara, who was dead white, but still possessed her faculties, had displaced the barricade from the front door. Another moment, and she had pulled it open. Firelight and moonlight illuminated the links with confused and changeful lustre, and far away against the sky we could see a long trail of glowing smoke.

Mr. Huddlestone, filled for the moment with a strength greater than his own, struck Northmour and myself a backhander in the chest; and while we were thus for the moment incapacitated from action, lifting his arms above his head like one about to dive, he ran straight forward out of the pavilion.

"Here am I!" he cried—"Huddlestone! Kill me, and spare the others!"

His sudden appearance daunted, I suppose, our hidden enemies; for Northmour and I had time to recover, to seize Clara between us, one by each arm, and to rush forth to his assistance, ere anything further had taken place. But scarce had we passed the threshold when there came near a dozen reports and flashes from every direction among the hollows of the links. Mr. Huddlestone staggered, uttered a weird and freezing cry, threw up his arms over his head, and fell backward on the turf.

"*Traditore*! *Traditore*!" cried the invisible avengers. And just then, a part of the roof of the pavilion fell in, so rapid was the progress of the fire. A loud, vague, and horrible noise accompanied the collapse, and a vast volume of flame went soaring up to heaven. It must have been visible at that moment from twenty miles out at sea, from the shore at Graden-Wester, and far inland from the peak of Graystiel, the most eastern summit of the Caulder Hills. Bernard Huddlestone, although God knows what were his obsequies, had a fine pyre at the moment of his death.

CHAPTER 9

Tells how Northmour carried out his threat

I should have the greatest difficulty to tell you what followed next after this tragic circumstance. It is all to me, as I look back upon it, mixed, strenuous, and ineffectual, like the struggles of a sleeper in a nightmare. Clara, I remember, uttered a broken sigh and would have fallen forward to earth, had not Northmour and I supported her insensible body. I do not think we were attacked; I do not remember even to have seen an assailant; and I believe we deserted Mr. Huddlestone without a glance. I only remember running like a man in a panic, now carrying Clara altogether in my own arms, now sharing her weight with Northmour, now scuffling confusedly for the possession of that dear burden. Why we should have made for my camp in the Hemlock Den, or how we reached it, are points lost forever to my recollection. The first moment at which I became definitely sure, Clara had been suffered to fall against the outside of my little tent, Northmour and I were tumbling together on the ground, and he, with contained ferocity, was striking for my head with the butt of his revolver. He had already twice wounded me on the scalp; and it is to the consequent loss of blood that I am tempted to attribute the sudden clearness of my mind.

I caught him by the wrist.

"Northmour," I remember saying, "you can kill me afterwards. Let us first attend to Clara."

He was at that moment uppermost. Scarcely had the words passed my lips, when he had leaped to his feet and ran towards the tent; and the next moment, he was straining Clara to his heart and covering her unconscious hands and face with his caresses.

"Shame!" I cried. "Shame to you, Northmour!"

And, giddy though I still was, I struck him repeatedly upon the head and shoulders.

He relinquished his grasp, and faced me in the broken moonlight.

"I had you under, and let you go," said he; "and now you strike me! Coward!"

"You are the coward," I retorted. "Did she wish your kisses while she was still sensible of what she wanted? Not she! And now she may be dying; and you waste this precious time, and abuse her helplessness. Stand aside, and let me help her."

He confronted me for a moment, white and menacing; then suddenly he stepped aside.

"Help her then," said he.

I threw myself on my knees beside her, and loosened, as well as I was able, her dress and corset; but while I was thus engaged, a grasp descended on my shoulder.

"Keep your hands off her," said Northmour fiercely. "Do you think I have no blood in my veins?"

"Northmour," I cried, "if you will neither help her yourself, nor let me do so, do you know that I shall have to kill you?"

"That is better!" he cried. "Let her die also, where's the harm? Step aside from that girl! and stand up to fight."

"You will observe," said I, half rising, "that I have not kissed her yet."

"I dare you to," he cried.

I do not know what possessed me; it was one of the things I am most ashamed of in my life, though, as my wife used to say, I knew that my kisses would be always welcome were she dead or living; down I fell again upon my knees, parted the hair from her forehead, and, with the dearest respect, laid my lips for a moment on that cold brow. It was such a caress as a father might have given; it was such a one as was not unbecoming from a man soon to die to a woman already dead.

"And now," said I, "I am at your service, Mr. Northmour."

But I saw, to my surprise, that he had turned his back upon me.

"Do you hear?" I asked.

"Yes," said he, "I do. If you wish to fight, I am ready. If not, go on and save Clara. All is one to me."

I did not wait to be twice bidden; but, stooping again over Clara, continued my efforts to revive her. She still lay white and lifeless; I began to fear that her sweet spirit had indeed fled beyond recall, and horror and a sense of utter desolation seized upon my heart. I called her by name with the most endearing inflections; I chafed and beat her hands; now I laid her head low, now supported it against my knee; but all seemed to be in vain, and the lids still lay heavy on her eyes.

"Northmour," I said, "there is my hat. For God's sake bring some water from the spring."

Almost in a moment he was by my side with the water.

"I have brought it in my own," he said. "You do not grudge me the privilege?"

"Northmour," I was beginning to say, as I laved[1] her head and breast; but he interrupted me savagely.

"Oh, you hush up!" he said. "The best thing you can do is to say nothing."

I had certainly no desire to talk, my mind being swallowed up in concern for my dear love and her condition; so I continued in silence to do my best towards her recovery, and, when the hat was empty, returned it to him, with one word—"More." He had, perhaps, gone several times upon this errand, when Clara re-opened her eyes.

"Now," said he, "since she is better, you can spare me, can you not? I wish you a goodnight, Mr. Cassilis."

And with that he was gone among the thicket. I made a fire, for I had now no fear of the Italians, who had even spared all the little possessions left in my encampment; and, broken as she was by the excitement and the hideous catastrophe of the evening, I managed,

---

[1] *laved* Bathed.

in one way or another—by persuasion, encouragement, warmth, and such simple remedies as I could lay my hand on—to bring her back to some composure of mind and strength of body.

Day had already come, when a sharp "Hist!" sounded from the thicket. I started from the ground; but the voice of Northmour was heard adding, in the most tranquil tones: "Come here, Cassilis, and alone; I want to show you something."

I consulted Clara with my eyes, and, receiving her tacit permission, left her alone, and clambered out of the den. At some distance off I saw Northmour leaning against an elder; and, as soon as he perceived me, he began walking seaward. I had almost overtaken him as he reached the outskirts of the wood.

"Look," said he, pausing.

A couple of steps more brought me out of the foliage. The light of the morning lay cold and clear over that well-known scene. The pavilion was but a blackened wreck; the roof had fallen in, one of the gables had fallen out; and, far and near, the face of the links was cicatrised[1] with little patches of burnt furze.[2] Thick smoke still went straight upwards in the windless air of the morning, and a great pile of ardent cinders filled the bare walls of the house, like coals in an open grate. Close by the islet a schooner yacht lay to, and a well-manned boat was pulling vigorously for the shore.

"The *Red Earl*!" I cried. "The *Red Earl* twelve hours too late!"

"Feel in your pocket, Frank. Are you armed?" asked Northmour.

I obeyed him, and I think I must have become deadly pale. My revolver had been taken from me.

"You see I have you in my power," he continued. "I disarmed you last night while you were nursing Clara; but this morning—here—take your pistol. No thanks!" he cried, holding up his hand. "I do not like them; that is the only way you can annoy me now."

He began to walk forward across the links to meet the boat, and I followed a step or two behind. In front of the pavilion I paused to see where Mr. Huddlestone had fallen; but there was no sign of him, nor so much as

a trace of blood.

"Graden Floe," said Northmour.

He continued to advance till we had come to the head of the beach.

"No farther, please," said he. "Would you like to take her to Graden House?"

"Thank you," replied I; "I shall try to get her to the minister's at Graden-Wester."

The prow of the boat here grated on the beach, and a sailor jumped ashore with a line in his hand.

"Wait a minute, lads!" cried Northmour; and then lower and to my private ear: "You had better say nothing of all this to her," he added.

"On the contrary!" I broke out, "she shall know everything that I can tell."

"You do not understand," he returned, with an air of great dignity. "It will be nothing to her; she expects it of me. Goodbye!" he added, with a nod.

I offered him my hand.

"Excuse me," said he. "It's small, I know; but I can't push things quite so far as that. I don't wish any sentimental business, to sit by your hearth a white-haired wanderer, and all that. Quite the contrary: I hope to God I shall never again clap eyes on either one of you."

"Well, God bless you, Northmour!" I said heartily.

"Oh, yes," he returned.

He walked down the beach; and the man who was ashore gave him an arm on board, and then shoved off and leaped into the bows himself. Northmour took the tiller; the boat rose to the waves, and the oars between the thole-pins[3] sounded crisp and measured in the air. They were not yet halfway to the *Red Earl*, and I was still watching their progress, when the sun rose out of the sea.

One word more, and my story is done. Years after, Northmour was killed fighting under the colours of Garibaldi for the liberation of the Tyrol.[4]

—1880

---

[1]   *cicatrised*   Scarred.

[2]   *furze*   Coniferous shrubs.

[3]   *thole-pins*   Pegs that support oars for rowing.

[4]   *Garibaldi … Tyrol*   Giuseppe Garibaldi (1807–82), a member of the *carbonari*, battled for years for the unification of Italy; one battle was fought unsuccessfully in the Tyrol against the Austrian occupiers.

OSCAR WILDE
1854 — 1900

For his epigrammatic genius, his challenges to bourgeois sensibilities, and his dazzling essays, dramas, and other writings, Oscar Wilde has been both reverenced and reviled for more than a century. Notorious for his flamboyance and wit before he had ever published a word, Wilde established himself in the literary world with his sole novel, *The Picture of Dorian Gray*, and even more with such sparkling social comedies as *An Ideal Husband* and *The Importance of Being Earnest*. He was a vocal advocate of aestheticism; Wilde saw in art the possibility for a life beyond the day-to-day monotony of ordinary existence. The "aesthetic movement," he writes, "produced certain colours, subtle in their loveliness and fascinating in their almost mystical tone. They were, and are, our reaction against the crude primaries of a doubtless more respectable but certainly less cultivated age."

Wilde began his life as Oscar Fingal O'Flahertie Wills Wilde. His parents, themselves no strangers to controversy, were Lady Jane Francesca Elgee and Dr. (later Sir) William Wilde. Both were accomplished writers. William, an ear and eye surgeon, wrote a book on medical and literary institutions in Austria and another about his voyage to North Africa and the Middle East. He achieved fame for his work on the Irish Census, for which he conducted a groundbreaking demographic study of the Great Famine, earning a knighthood in 1864. His reputation was somewhat tainted, however, by his womanizing; he fathered three children out of wedlock. Lady Wilde was also a prominent figure. Born Jane Frances Agnes Elgee, she adopted the more Italian-sounding "Francesca" to reinforce the family's claim that they were descended from Dante Alighieri (truth never stood in the way of a good Wilde family story). Lady Wilde took yet another name, "Speranza," when she published poems in *The Nation*, a weekly Dublin newspaper published by an anti-British revolutionary group called the Young Irelanders.

Wilde grew up in the colorful environment of his mother's famous salon, where she hosted leading Dublin artists and writers. Once when Wilde returned from college, he invited a friend to Lady Wilde's weekly "conversazione," saying: "I want to introduce you to my mother. We have founded a society for the suppression of virtue." Wilde was a brilliant student at Trinity College, graduating in 1874 with the Berkeley Gold Medal for Classics and receiving a scholarship to study at Oxford. Before long, he was celebrated at Oxford's Magdalen College for his wit, decadence, and ostentatious appearance. He was most influenced in his academic years by two rivals at Oxford, John Ruskin and Walter Pater. From Ruskin, perhaps the most influential art critic of the century, Wilde took counsel on what the older scholar believed to be the spiritual, ethical, and moral nature of art. From Pater, who was already infamous following the publication of his *Studies in the History of the Renaissance* (1873), Wilde picked up elements of aestheticism he would eventually transform into his own theories of art. Wilde would later describe Pater's *Renaissance* as "the holy writ of beauty."

After winning the Newdigate prize for poetry and graduating with first class honors, Wilde moved to London and began his career as a divisive public figure. He was known, for example, for a formal jacket, called his "cello coat," that he wore to the opening of the Grosvenor Gallery in 1877, and for being more generally a poster-boy of the emerging aesthetic movement. By the time he published a book of poems in 1881, he had already become the butt of many caricatures in *Punch* magazine; he had taken to modeling his look on the character of Bunthorne in Gilbert and Sullivan's satirical comic opera *Patience*. For the next few years Wilde delivered lectures in the United States and Great Britain about the aesthetic movement, for which he had ambitious plans: "I want to make this artistic movement the basis for a new civilization." In Boston he voiced some of the ideas about art and life for which he would best be known: "The supreme object of life is to live. Few people live. It is true life only to realize one's own perfection, to make one's every dream a reality. Even this is possible."

In 1884 Wilde married Constance Lloyd, with whom he would have two sons, Cyril and Vyvyan. From 1887 to 1889 he edited *Woman's World*, a popular magazine. Through the late 1880s, Wilde wrote reviews of many of his most famous contemporaries, including the painter James Whistler and the poets D.G. Rossetti, William Morris, Algernon Swinburne, and others. He was also at work on the volume that would ultimately constitute the most thorough account of his aesthetic philosophy, *Intentions* (1891), which included the essays "The Decay of Lying" and "The Critic as Artist." The essays argue for the paramount importance of art in human life: "[Art's] are ... the great archetypes of which things that have existence are but unfinished copies." Rather than artists copying from the world about them, writes Wilde, we as individuals interpret the world *through art*, through the "archetypes" presented to us by works of art. Hence "[T]here may have been fogs for centuries in London," but "no one saw them .... till Art had invented them." The early 1890s also saw the publication of Wilde's novel, *The Picture of Dorian Gray*, which both puts forward Wilde's aesthetic beliefs and suggests some of the dangers of a life given over to aesthetic consumption.

Wilde was clearly at his very best in the early 1890s. In addition to *Intentions* and *Dorian Gray*, Wilde penned a string of brilliant social comedies, including *Lady Windermere's Fan* (1892), *A Woman of No Importance* (1893), and *An Ideal Husband* (1895). His final comedy was his masterpiece of farce, *The Importance of Being Earnest*; it first played in 1895 to wildly enthusiastic crowds at the St. James Theatre in London. Success came to an end only through Wilde's ill-fated affair with a young aristocrat, Lord Alfred Douglas ("Bosie"). Douglas's father, the mentally-unstable Marquis of Queensbury, was infuriated by the relationship, and in 1895 he publicly accused Wilde of sodomy. Convinced he had to defend his own and Douglas's honor, Wilde sued the Marquis for libel. After Wilde failed in his suit against Queensbury, the government used evidence from the trial to launch a criminal investigation against Wilde because homosexuality was a criminal offence. Wilde was found guilty of "gross indecency" and sentenced to two years of imprisonment with hard labor.

Prison left Wilde financially and emotionally broken. The horrid conditions of late-Victorian prison life—including a poor diet, enforced silence, and physically-taxing labor—were especially difficult to handle. From prison Wilde wrote a moving autobiographical letter to Bosie, later entitled *De Profundis*, that accuses the younger man of heartless and selfish behavior. (Bosie had treated Wilde poorly all along, and he abandoned Wilde during his imprisonment.) Even from his cell, however, Wilde wrote of seeing "new developments in Art and Life." Upon his release he composed "The Ballad of Reading Gaol " (1898), a heartfelt indictment of the prison system and capital punishment, as well as a meditation on the universal characteristics of human nature.

Wilde's last years were spent in Italy and France. He seems never to have recovered fully from his prison experience, and by late in 1900 he was quite ill. He died and was buried in Paris before the year ended; the immediate cause of his death has never been conclusively established. In 1995 a window in the Poets' Corner of Westminster Abbey was dedicated in his honor.

⌘⌘⌘

Impression du Matin [1]

The Thames nocturne of blue and gold [2]
  Changed to a harmony in gray:
    A barge with ochre-coloured hay
Dropped from the wharf: and chill and cold

5   The yellow fog came creeping down
      The bridges, till the houses' walls
      Seemed changed to shadows and St. Paul's
Loomed like a bubble o'er the town.

Then suddenly arose the clang
10   Of waking life; the streets were stirred
      With country wagons: and a bird
Flew to the glistening roofs and sang.

But one pale woman all alone,
      The daylight kissing her wan hair,
15   Loitered beneath gas lamps' flare,
With lips of flame and heart of stone.
                                    —1881

E Tenebris [3]

Come down, O Christ, and help me! Reach thy hand,
  For I am drowning in a stormier sea
    Than Simon on thy lake of Galilee: [4]
The wine of life is spilt upon the sand,
5 My heart is as some famine-murdered land
      Whence all good things have perished utterly,
      And well I know my soul in Hell must lie
If I this night before God's throne should stand.
"He sleeps perchance, or rideth to the chase,
10   Like Baal, when his prophets howled that name
      From morn to noon on Carmel's smitten height." [5]
Nay, peace, I shall behold, before the night,
    The feet of brass, [6] the robe more white than flame,
The wounded hands, the weary human face.
                                    —1881

---

from *The Critic as Artist* [7]

ERNEST.   ... [S]urely, the higher you place the creative artist, the lower must the critic rank.

GILBERT.   Why so?

ERNEST.   Because the best that he can give us will be but

---

[1] *Impression du Matin*   French: impression of the morning.

[2] *gold* Cf. James McNeill Whistler's series of paintings, the "Nocturnes." Two of the most famous of these are "Nocturne in Blue and Gold: Old Battersea Bridge" and "Nocturne in Black and Gold: the Falling Rocket," both of which were painted in the 1870s. These and other similar paintings were important precursors of the movement that came to be known as Impressionism; painters such as Claude Monet and Edgar Degas, like Whistler, strove to capture the transitory effects of light both on the landscape and on human figures. Much as Wilde was moved to write his own "impressions" in verse (this is one of several Wilde poems that include the word "impression" in their title), he did not respond positively to Whistler's radical experiments with impressions on canvas. His response to "Nocturne in Black and Gold: the Falling Rocket" on seeing it exhibited at the Grosvenor Gallery in 1877 was to call it "worth looking at for about as long as one looks at a real rocket, that is, for something less than a quarter of a minute." This judgement concurred with that of the famous art critic John Ruskin (who had been a teacher of Wilde's at Oxford). Ruskin criticized Whistler for "flinging a pot of paint in the public's face" with works such as "Nocturne in Black and Gold: the Falling Rocket"—an insult for which Whistler sued him in a famous trial. (Whistler won the case, but was awarded only one farthing in damages and had to pay the costs of the trial, which contributed to his eventual bankruptcy.)

[3] *E Tenebris* Latin: out of the darkness.

[4] *Simon ... Galilee* In Matthew 14.24–31, Simon Peter, one of the twelve apostles, nearly drowns in a storm at sea when Christ bids him to walk across the water to him. Christ reaches out his hand and saves him, saying "O thou of little faith, wherefore didst thou doubt?"

[5] *"He sleeps ... height"* In 1 Kings 18.19–40, Elijah mocks the priests of Baal (who had called upon their God all day in vain) by saying, "either he is talking, or he is pursuing, or he is in a journey, or peradventure he sleepeth, and must be awaked." Here the speaker imagines a similar voice taunting him.

[6] *feet of brass* Revelation 1.13–16 describes a vision of the Son of man in which his feet are "like unto fine brass."

[7] *The Critic as Artist* In this dialogue, the two men debate the merits of art criticism. Earlier, Ernest had questioned the usefulness of criticism, asking, "Why should the artist be troubled by the shrill clamour of criticism? Why should those who cannot create take it upon themselves to estimate the value of creative work?" In response, Gilbert argued that criticism is itself an art, that "there is no fine art without self-consciousness, and self-consciousness and the critical spirit are one," and, furthermore, that it is "very much more difficult to talk about a thing than to do it."

an echo of rich music, a dim shadow of clear-outlined form. It may, indeed, be that life is chaos, as you tell me that it is; that its martyrdoms are mean and its heroisms ignoble; and that it is the function of Literature to create, from the rough material of actual existence, a new world that will be more marvellous, more enduring, and more true than the world that common eyes look upon, and through which common natures seek to realize their perfection. But surely, if this new world has been made by the spirit and touch of a great artist, it will be a thing so complete and perfect that there will be nothing left for the critic to do. I quite understand now, and indeed admit most readily, that it is far more difficult to talk about a thing than to do it. But it seems to me that this sound and sensible maxim, which is really extremely soothing to one's feelings, and should be adopted as its motto by every Academy of Literature all over the world, applies only to the relations that exist between Art and Life, and not to any relations that there may be between Art and Criticism.

GILBERT.   But, surely, Criticism is itself an art. And just as artistic creation implies the working of the critical faculty, and, indeed, without it cannot be said to exist at all, so Criticism is really creative in the highest sense of the word. Criticism is, in fact, both creative and independent.

ERNEST.   Independent?

GILBERT.   Yes; independent. Criticism is no more to be judged by any low standard of imitation or resemblance than is the work of poet or sculptor. The critic occupies the same relation to the work of art that he criticizes as the artist does to the visible world of form and colour, or the unseen world of passion and of thought. He does not even require for the perfection of his art the finest materials. Anything will serve his purpose. And just as out of the sordid and sentimental amours of the silly wife of a small country doctor in the squalid village of Yonville-l'Abbaye, near Rouen, Gustave Flaubert was able to create a classic and make a masterpiece of style,[1] so, from subjects of little or no importance, such as the pictures in this year's Royal Academy, or in any year's Royal Academy for that matter, Mr. Lewis Morris's poems, M. Ohnet's novels, or the plays of Mr. Henry

Arthur Jones,[2] the true critic can, if it be his pleasure so to direct or waste his faculty of contemplation, produce work that will be flawless in beauty and instinct with intellectual subtlety. Why not? Dullness is always an irresistible temptation for brilliancy, and stupidity is the permanent *Bestia Trionfans*[3] that calls wisdom from its cave. To an artist so creative as the critic, what does subject matter signify? No more and no less than it does to the novelist and the painter. Like them, he can find his motives everywhere. Treatment is the test. There is nothing that has not in it suggestion or challenge.

ERNEST.   But is Criticism really a creative art?

GILBERT.   Why should it not be? It works with materials, and puts them into a form that is at once new and delightful. What more can one say of poetry? Indeed, I would call criticism a creation within a creation. For just as the great artists, from Homer and Aeschylus down to Shakespeare and Keats,[4] did not go directly to life for their subject-matter, but sought for it in myth, and legend, and ancient tale, so the critic deals with materials that others have, as it were, purified for him, and to which imaginative form and colour have been already added. Nay, more, I would say that the highest Criticism, being the purest form of personal impression, is in its way more creative than creation, as it has least reference to any standard external to itself, and is, in fact, its own reason for existing, and, as the Greeks would put it, in itself, and to itself, an end. Certainly, it is never trammelled by any shackles of verisimilitude. No ignoble considerations of probability, that cowardly concession to the tedious repetitions of domestic or public life, affect it ever. One may appeal from fiction unto fact. But from the soul there is no appeal.

ERNEST.   From the soul?

---

[1]   *masterpiece of style*   I.e., Flaubert's *Madame Bovary*.

[2]   *Mr. Lewis Morris*   Popular Anglo-Welsh poet; *M. Ohnet* Georges Ohnet, nineteenth-century French novelist, many of whose works were successfully dramatized; *Mr. Henry Arthur Jones* Innovative playwright of the late nineteenth century.

[3]   *Bestia Trionfans*   Latin: triumphant beast. From the title of sixteenth-century philosopher Giordano Bruno's allegory *Spacio della Bestia Trionfante* (*Expulsion of the Triumphant Beast*).

[4]   *Homer*   Greek poet to whom the authorship of *The Iliad* and *The Odyssey* is attributed (?850 BCE); *Shakespeare* William Shakespeare, English poet and playwright (1564–1616); *Keats* John Keats, English poet (1795–1821).

GILBERT.   Yes, from the soul. That is what the highest criticism really is, the record of one's own soul. It is more fascinating than history, as it is concerned simply with oneself. It is more delightful than philosophy, as its subject is concrete and not abstract, real and not vague. It is the only civilized form of autobiography, as it deals not with the events, but with the thoughts of one's life; not with life's physical accidents of deed or circumstance, but with the spiritual moods and imaginative passions of the mind. I am always amused by the silly vanity of those writers and artists of our day who seem to imagine that the primary function of the critic is to chatter about their second-rate work. The best that one can say of most modern creative art is that it is just a little less vulgar than reality, and so the critic, with his fine sense of distinction and sure instinct of delicate refinement, will prefer to look into the silver mirror or through the woven veil, and will turn his eyes away from the chaos and clamour of actual existence, though the mirror be tarnished and the veil be torn. His sole aim is to chronicle his own impressions. It is for him that pictures are painted, books written, and marble hewn into form.

ERNEST.   I seem to have heard another theory of Criticism.

GILBERT.   Yes: it has been said by one whose gracious memory we all revere, and the music of whose pipe once lured Proserpina from her Sicilian fields, and made those white feet stir, and not in vain, the Cumnor cowslips, that the proper aim of Criticism is to see the object as in itself it really is.[1] But this is a very serious error, and takes no cognizance of Criticism's most perfect form, which is in its essence purely subjective, and seeks to reveal its own secret and not the secret of another. For the highest Criticism deals with art not as expressive but as impressive purely.

ERNEST.   But is that really so?

GILBERT.   Of course it is. Who cares whether Mr. Ruskin's views on Turner[2] are sound or not? What does it matter? That mighty and majestic prose of his, so fervid and so fiery-coloured in its noble eloquence, so rich in its elaborate symphonic music, so sure and certain, at its best, in subtle choice of word and epithet, is at least as great a work of art as any of those wonderful sunsets that bleach or rot on their corrupted canvases in England's Gallery;[3] greater indeed, one is apt to think at times, not merely because its equal beauty is more enduring, but on account of the fuller variety of its appeal, soul speaking to soul in those long-cadenced lines, not through form and colour alone, though through these, indeed, completely and without loss, but with intellectual and emotional utterance, with lofty passion and with loftier thought, with imaginative insight, and with poetic aim; greater, I always think, even as Literature is the greater art.

—1890

from *The Decay of Lying*[4]

CYRIL.   ... [I]n order to avoid making any error I want you to tell me briefly the doctrines of the new aesthetics.

VIVIAN.   Briefly, then, they are these. Art never expresses anything but itself. It has an independent life, just as Thought has, and develops purely on its own lines. It is not necessarily realistic in an age of realism, nor spiritual in an age of faith. So far from being the creation of its time, it is usually in direct opposition to it, and the only history that it preserves for us is the history of its own progress. Sometimes it returns upon its footsteps, and

---

[1] *it has ... really is*   Matthew Arnold, whose poem *Thyrsis* attempts to summon the goddess Proserpine from the pastoral landscape of Sicily to the Cumnor hills of England. Arnold discusses the aim of criticism in his essay *The Function of Criticism at the Present Time*.

[2] *Turner*   English landscape painter Joseph Mallord William Turner. Cf. John Ruskin's *Modern Painters*.

[3] *England's Gallery*   The Tate Gallery in London, upon which a major bequest of Turner's paintings was bestowed in 1856.

[4] *"The Decay of Lying"*   In this Platonic dialogue, Wilde sets out a new theory of aesthetics through the conversation of two characters, Vivian and Cyril (named after Wilde's two sons). Vivian, prompted by Cyril's questioning, has been reading from his essay in progress, called "The Decay of Lying," which explores and confirms Plato's claim in *The Republic* that art is falsehood, yet challenges his assertion that art is a mere imitation of life, and that the lies of art are morally repugnant. On the contrary, Vivian celebrates the lies of art, declaring, "if something cannot be done to check, or at least modify, our monstrous worship of facts, Art will become sterile and Beauty will pass from the land." At the heart of this work is a challenge to the Victorian adherence to realism and advocacy of faithful imitation of nature.

revives some antique form, as happened in the archaistic movement of late Greek Art, and in the Pre-Raphaelite movement of our own day. At other times it entirely anticipates its age, and produces in one century work that it takes another century to understand, to appreciate, and to enjoy. In no case does it reproduce its age. To pass from the art of a time to the time itself is the great mistake that all historians commit.

The second doctrine is this. All bad art comes from returning to Life and Nature and elevating them into ideals. Life and Nature may sometimes be used as part of Art's rough material, but before they are of any real service to art they must be translated into artistic conventions. The moment Art surrenders its imaginative medium it surrenders everything. As a method Realism is a complete failure, and the two things that every artist should avoid are modernity of form and modernity of subject matter. To us, who live in the nineteenth century, any century is a suitable subject for art except our own. The only beautiful things are the things that do not concern us. It is, to have the pleasure of quoting myself, exactly because Hecuba is nothing to us that her sorrows are so suitable a motive for a tragedy.[1] Besides, it is only the modern that ever becomes old-fashioned. M. Zola[2] sits down to give us a picture of the Second Empire. Who cares for the Second Empire now? It is out of date. Life goes faster than Realism, but Romanticism is always in front of Life.

The third doctrine is that Life imitates Art far more than Art imitates Life. This results not merely from Life's imitative instinct, but from the fact that the self-conscious aim of Life is to find expression, and that Art offers it certain beautiful forms through which it may realize that energy. It is a theory that has never been put forward before, but it is extremely fruitful, and throws an entirely new light upon the history of Art.

It follows, as a corollary from this, that external Nature also imitates Art. The only effects that she can show us are effects that we have already seen through poetry, or in paintings. This is the secret of Nature's charm, as well as the explanation of Nature's weakness.

The final revelation is that Lying, the telling of beautiful untrue things, is the proper aim of Art. But of this I think I have spoken at sufficient length. And now let us go out on the terrace, where "droops the milk-white peacock like a ghost,"[3] while the evening star "washes the dusk with silver."[4] At twilight nature becomes a wonderfully suggestive effect, and is not without loveliness, though perhaps its chief use is to illustrate quotations from the poets. Come! We have talked long enough.
—1889

Preface to *The Picture of Dorian Gray*[5]

The artist is the creator of beautiful things.

To reveal art and conceal the artist is art's aim. The critic is he who can translate into another medium or a new material his impression of beautiful things.

The highest as the lowest form of criticism is a mode of autobiography.

Those who find ugly meanings in beautiful things are corrupt without being charming. This is a fault.

Those who find beautiful meanings in beautiful things are cultivated. For these there is hope.

They are the elect to whom beautiful things mean only beauty.

There is no such thing as a moral or an immoral book. Books are well written, or badly written. That is all.

The nineteenth century dislike of Realism is the rage of Caliban[6] seeing his own face in a glass.

The nineteenth century dislike of Romanticism is the rage of Caliban not seeing his own face in a glass.

---

[1]   *Hecuba ... tragedy*   Hecuba, Queen of Troy when that city was conquered by the Greeks, saw her husband and her sons murdered. In Shakespeare's *Hamlet*, one of the players performing for Hamlet recites an emotional monologue on the terrible fate of Hecuba, prompting Hamlet to wonder, "What's Hecuba to him, or he to Hecuba, / That he should weep for her?" (2.2.)

[2]   *M. Zola*   (Monsieur) Émile Zola, French novelist (1840–1902).

[3]   *"droops ... ghost"*   From "The Princess" by Alfred Lord Tennyson.

[4]   *"washes ... silver"*   From "To the Evening Star" by William Blake.

[5]   *Preface*   Published in 1891, the year after the novel's first appearance, this preface was a response to the charges of immorality leveled at the novel by numerous critics.

[6]   *Caliban*   The "monster" of Shakespeare's *The Tempest*, Caliban is a native of the island and has been enslaved by Prospero.

The moral life of man forms part of the subject matter of the artist, but the morality of art consists in the perfect use of an imperfect medium.

No artist desires to prove anything. Even things that are true can be proved.

No artist has ethical sympathies. An ethical sympathy in an artist is an unpardonable mannerism of style.

No artist is ever morbid. The artist can express everything.

Thought and language are to the artist instruments of an art.

Vice and virtue are to the artist materials for an art.

From the point of view of form, the type of all the arts is the art of the musician.

From the point of view of feeling, the actor's craft is the type.

All art is at once surface and symbol.

Those who go beneath the surface do so at their peril.

Those who read the symbol do so at their peril.

It is the spectator, and not life, that art really mirrors.

Diversity of opinion about a work of art shows that the work is new, complex, and vital.

When critics disagree the artist is in accord with himself.

We can forgive a man for making a useful thing as long as he does not admire it. The only excuse for making a useless thing is that one admires it intensely.

All art is quite useless.

—1891

The Importance of Being Earnest
A Trivial Comedy for Serious People

THE PERSONS IN THE PLAY

John Worthing, J.P.[1]
Algernon Moncrieff
Rev. Canon Chasuble, D.D.[2]
Merriman, *Butler*
Lane, *Manservant*
Lady Bracknell

Hon.[3] Gwendolen Fairfax
Cecily Cardew
Miss Prism, *Governess*

THE SCENES IN THE PLAY

ACT 1.   Algernon Moncrieff's Flat in Half-Moon Street,[4] W.
ACT 2.   The Garden at the Manor House, Woolton.[5]
ACT 3.   Drawing-Room at the Manor House, Woolton.

TIME: The Present.

ACT 1

SCENE

(*Morning-room in Algernon's flat in Half-Moon Street. The room is luxuriously and artistically furnished. The sound of a piano is heard in the adjoining room.*)

(*Lane is arranging afternoon tea on the table, and after the music has ceased, Algernon enters.*)

ALGERNON.   Did you hear what I was playing, Lane?

LANE.   I didn't think it polite to listen, sir.

ALGERNON.   I'm sorry for that, for your sake. I don't play accurately—any one can play accurately—but I play with wonderful expression. As far as the piano is concerned, sentiment is my forte. I keep science for Life.

LANE.   Yes, sir.

ALGERNON.   And, speaking of the science of Life, have you got the cucumber sandwiches[6] cut for Lady Bracknell?

LANE.   Yes, sir. (*Hands them on a salver.[7]*)

ALGERNON.   (*Inspects them, takes two, and sits down on the sofa.*) Oh! ... by the way, Lane, I see from your book

---

[1]   *J.P.*   Justice of the Peace.

[2]   *D.D.*   Doctor of Divinity.

[3]   *Hon.*   I.e., The Honorable. The honorific in this case designates the daughter of a peer below the rank of Earl.

[4]   *Half-Moon Street*   Street located in a fashionable area of London.

[5]   *Woolton*   A fictional location.

[6]   *cucumber sandwiches*   Small sandwiches of cucumber on thinly-sliced bread, a staple of afternoon tea in polite English society.

[7]   *salver*   Serving tray, typically silver.

that on Thursday night, when Lord Shoreman and Mr.
Worthing were dining with me, eight bottles of champagne are entered as having been consumed.

LANE.   Yes, sir; eight bottles and a pint.

ALGERNON.   Why is it that at a bachelor's establishment the servants invariably drink the champagne? I ask merely for information.

LANE.   I attribute it to the superior quality of the wine, sir. I have often observed that in married households the champagne is rarely of a first-rate brand.

ALGERNON.   Good heavens! Is marriage so demoralising as that?

LANE.   I believe it is a very pleasant state, sir. I have had very little experience of it myself up to the present. I have only been married once. That was in consequence of a misunderstanding between myself and a young person.

ALGERNON.   (*Languidly.*) I don't know that I am much interested in your family life, Lane.

LANE.   No, sir; it is not a very interesting subject. I never think of it myself.

ALGERNON.   Very natural, I am sure. That will do, Lane, thank you.

LANE.   Thank you, sir. (*Lane goes out.*)

ALGERNON.   Lane's views on marriage seem somewhat lax. Really, if the lower orders don't set us a good example, what on earth is the use of them? They seem, as a class, to have absolutely no sense of moral responsibility.

(*Enter Lane.*)

LANE.   Mr. Ernest Worthing.

(*Enter Jack. Lane goes out.*)

ALGERNON. How are you, my dear Ernest? What brings you up to town?

JACK.   Oh, pleasure, pleasure! What else should bring one anywhere? Eating as usual, I see, Algy!

ALGERNON.   (*Stiffly.*) I believe it is customary in good society to take some slight refreshment at five o'clock. Where have you been since last Thursday?

JACK.   (*Sitting down on the sofa.*) In the country.

ALGERNON.   What on earth do you do there?

JACK.   (*Pulling off his gloves.*) When one is in town[1] one amuses oneself. When one is in the country one amuses other people. It is excessively boring.

ALGERNON.   And who are the people you amuse?

JACK.   (*Airily.*) Oh, neighbours, neighbours.

ALGERNON.   Got nice neighbours in your part of Shropshire?

JACK.   Perfectly horrid! Never speak to one of them.

ALGERNON.   How immensely you must amuse them! (*Goes over and takes sandwich.*) By the way, Shropshire is your county, is it not?

JACK.   Eh? Shropshire? Yes, of course. Hallo! Why all these cups? Why cucumber sandwiches? Why such reckless extravagance in one so young? Who is coming to tea?

ALGERNON.   Oh! merely Aunt Augusta and Gwendolen.

JACK.   How perfectly delightful!

ALGERNON.   Yes, that is all very well; but I am afraid Aunt Augusta won't quite approve of your being here.

JACK.   May I ask why?

ALGERNON.   My dear fellow, the way you flirt with Gwendolen is perfectly disgraceful. It is almost as bad as the way Gwendolen flirts with you.

JACK.   I am in love with Gwendolen. I have come up to town expressly to propose to her.

ALGERNON.   I thought you had come up for pleasure? … I call that business.

JACK.   How utterly unromantic you are!

ALGERNON.   I really don't see anything romantic in proposing. It is very romantic to be in love. But there is nothing romantic about a definite proposal. Why, one may be accepted. One usually is, I believe. Then the excitement is all over. The very essence of romance is uncertainty. If ever I get married, I'll certainly try to forget the fact.

JACK.   I have no doubt about that, dear Algy. The Divorce Court was specially invented for people whose memories are so curiously constituted.

ALGERNON.   Oh! there is no use speculating on that subject. Divorces are made in Heaven—(*Jack puts out his hand to take a sandwich. Algernon at once interferes.*) Please don't touch the cucumber sandwiches. They are ordered specially for Aunt Augusta. (*Takes one and eats it.*)

---

[1]   *in town*   In London.

JACK. Well, you have been eating them all the time.

ALGERNON. That is quite a different matter. She is my aunt. (*Takes plate from below.*) Have some bread and butter. The bread and butter is for Gwendolen. Gwendolen is devoted to bread and butter.

JACK. (*Advancing to table and helping himself.*) And very good bread and butter it is too.

ALGERNON. Well, my dear fellow, you need not eat as if you were going to eat it all. You behave as if you were married to her already. You are not married to her already, and I don't think you ever will be.

JACK. Why on earth do you say that?

ALGERNON. Well, in the first place girls never marry the men they flirt with. Girls don't think it right.

JACK. Oh, that is nonsense!

ALGERNON. It isn't. It is a great truth. It accounts for the extraordinary number of bachelors that one sees all over the place. In the second place, I don't give my consent.

JACK. Your consent!

ALGERNON. My dear fellow, Gwendolen is my first cousin. And before I allow you to marry her, you will have to clear up the whole question of Cecily. (*Rings bell.*)

JACK. Cecily! What on earth do you mean? What do you mean, Algy, by Cecily! I don't know any one of the name of Cecily.

(*Enter Lane.*)

ALGERNON. Bring me that cigarette case Mr. Worthing left in the smoking-room the last time he dined here.

LANE. Yes, sir.

(*Lane goes out.*)

JACK. Do you mean to say you have had my cigarette case all this time? I wish to goodness you had let me know. I have been writing frantic letters to Scotland Yard about it. I was very nearly offering a large reward.

ALGERNON. Well, I wish you would offer one. I happen to be more than usually hard up.

JACK. There is no good offering a large reward now that the thing is found.

(*Enter Lane with the cigarette case on a salver. Algernon takes it at once. Lane goes out.*)

ALGERNON. I think that is rather mean of you, Ernest, I must say. (*Opens case and examines it.*) However, it makes no matter, for, now that I look at the inscription inside, I find that the thing isn't yours after all.

JACK. Of course it's mine. (*Moving to him.*) You have seen me with it a hundred times, and you have no right whatsoever to read what is written inside. It is a very ungentlemanly thing to read a private cigarette case.

ALGERNON. Oh! it is absurd to have a hard and fast rule about what one should read and what one shouldn't. More than half of modern culture depends on what one shouldn't read.

JACK. I am quite aware of the fact, and I don't propose to discuss modern culture. It isn't the sort of thing one should talk of in private. I simply want my cigarette case back.

ALGERNON. Yes; but this isn't your cigarette case. This cigarette case is a present from some one of the name of Cecily, and you said you didn't know any one of that name.

JACK. Well, if you want to know, Cecily happens to be my aunt.

ALGERNON. Your aunt!

JACK. Yes. Charming old lady she is, too. Lives at Tunbridge Wells. Just give it back to me, Algy.

ALGERNON. (*Retreating to back of sofa.*) But why does she call herself little Cecily if she is your aunt and lives at Tunbridge Wells? (*Reading.*) "From little Cecily with her fondest love."

JACK. (*Moving to sofa and kneeling upon it.*) My dear fellow, what on earth is there in that? Some aunts are tall, some aunts are not tall. That is a matter that surely an aunt may be allowed to decide for herself. You seem to think that every aunt should be exactly like your aunt! That is absurd! For Heaven's sake give me back my cigarette case. (*Follows Algernon round the room.*)

ALGERNON. Yes. But why does your aunt call you her uncle? "From little Cecily, with her fondest love to her dear Uncle Jack." There is no objection, I admit, to an aunt being a small aunt, but why an aunt, no matter what her size may be, should call her own nephew her uncle, I can't quite make out. Besides, your name isn't Jack at all; it is Ernest.

JACK. It isn't Ernest; it's Jack.

ALGERNON. You have always told me it was Ernest. I have introduced you to every one as Ernest. You answer to the name of Ernest. You look as if your name was Ernest. You are the most earnest-looking person I ever saw in my life. It is perfectly absurd your saying that your name isn't Ernest. It's on your cards. Here is one of them. (*Taking it from case.*) "Mr. Ernest Worthing, B. 4, The Albany." I'll keep this as a proof that your name is Ernest if ever you attempt to deny it to me, or to Gwendolen, or to any one else. (*Puts the card in his pocket.*)

JACK. Well, my name is Ernest in town and Jack in the country, and the cigarette case was given to me in the country.

ALGERNON. Yes, but that does not account for the fact that your small Aunt Cecily, who lives at Tunbridge Wells, calls you her dear uncle. Come, old boy, you had much better have the thing out at once.

JACK. My dear Algy, you talk exactly as if you were a dentist. It is very vulgar to talk like a dentist when one isn't a dentist. It produces a false impression.

ALGERNON. Well, that is exactly what dentists always do. Now, go on! Tell me the whole thing. I may mention that I have always suspected you of being a confirmed and secret Bunburyist; and I am quite sure of it now.

JACK. Bunburyist? What on earth do you mean by a Bunburyist?

ALGERNON. I'll reveal to you the meaning of that incomparable expression as soon as you are kind enough to inform me why you are Ernest in town and Jack in the country.

JACK. Well, produce my cigarette case first.

ALGERNON. Here it is. (*Hands cigarette case.*) Now produce your explanation, and pray make it improbable. (*Sits on sofa.*)

JACK. My dear fellow, there is nothing improbable about my explanation at all. In fact it's perfectly ordinary. Old Mr. Thomas Cardew, who adopted me when I was a little boy, made me in his will guardian to his grand-daughter, Miss Cecily Cardew. Cecily, who addresses me as her uncle from motives of respect that you could not possibly appreciate, lives at my place in the country under the charge of her admirable governess, Miss

Prism.

ALGERNON. Where in that place in the country, by the way?

JACK. That is nothing to you, dear boy. You are not going to be invited … I may tell you candidly that the place is not in Shropshire.

ALGERNON. I suspected that, my dear fellow! I have Bunburyed all over Shropshire on two separate occasions. Now, go on. Why are you Ernest in town and Jack in the country?

JACK. My dear Algy, I don't know whether you will be able to understand my real motives. You are hardly serious enough. When one is placed in the position of guardian, one has to adopt a very high moral tone on all subjects. It's one's duty to do so. And as a high moral tone can hardly be said to conduce very much to either one's health or one's happiness, in order to get up to town I have always pretended to have a younger brother of the name of Ernest, who lives in the Albany, and gets into the most dreadful scrapes. That, my dear Algy, is the whole truth pure and simple.

ALGERNON. The truth is rarely pure and never simple. Modern life would be very tedious if it were either, and modern literature a complete impossibility!

JACK. That wouldn't be at all a bad thing.

ALGERNON. Literary criticism is not your forte, my dear fellow. Don't try it. You should leave that to people who haven't been at a University. They do it so well in the daily papers. What you really are is a Bunburyist. I was quite right in saying you were a Bunburyist. You are one of the most advanced Bunburyists I know.

JACK. What on earth do you mean?

ALGERNON. You have invented a very useful younger brother called Ernest, in order that you may be able to come up to town as often as you like. I have invented an invaluable permanent invalid called Bunbury, in order that I may be able to go down into the country whenever I choose. Bunbury is perfectly invaluable. If it wasn't for Bunbury's extraordinary bad health, for instance, I wouldn't be able to dine with you at Willis's to-night, for I have been really engaged to Aunt Augusta for more than a week.

JACK. I haven't asked you to dine with me anywhere to-night.

ALGERNON. I know. You are absurdly careless about

sending out invitations. It is very foolish of you. Nothing annoys people so much as not receiving invitations.

JACK.   You had much better dine with your Aunt Augusta.

ALGERNON.   I haven't the smallest intention of doing anything of the kind. To begin with, I dined there on Monday, and once a week is quite enough to dine with one's own relations. In the second place, whenever I do dine there I am always treated as a member of the family, and sent down[1] with either no woman at all, or two. In the third place, I know perfectly well whom she will place me next to, to-night. She will place me next Mary Farquhar, who always flirts with her own husband across the dinner-table. That is not very pleasant. Indeed, it is not even decent … and that sort of thing is enormously on the increase. The amount of women in London who flirt with their own husbands is perfectly scandalous. It looks so bad. It is simply washing one's clean linen in public. Besides, now that I know you to be a confirmed Bunburyist I naturally want to talk to you about Bunburying. I want to tell you the rules.

JACK.   I'm not a Bunburyist at all. If Gwendolen accepts me, I am going to kill my brother, indeed I think I'll kill him in any case. Cecily is a little too much interested in him. It is rather a bore. So I am going to get rid of Ernest. And I strongly advise you to do the same with Mr. … with your invalid friend who has the absurd name.

ALGERNON.   Nothing will induce me to part with Bunbury, and if you ever get married, which seems to me extremely problematic, you will be very glad to know Bunbury. A man who marries without knowing Bunbury has a very tedious time of it.

JACK.   That is nonsense. If I marry a charming girl like Gwendolen, and she is the only girl I ever saw in my life that I would marry, I certainly won't want to know Bunbury.

ALGERNON.   Then your wife will. You don't seem to realise, that in married life three is company and two is none.

JACK.   (Sententiously.) That, my dear young friend, is the theory that the corrupt French Drama has been propounding for the last fifty years.

ALGERNON.   Yes; and that the happy English home has proved in half the time.

JACK.   For heaven's sake, don't try to be cynical. It's perfectly easy to be cynical.

ALGERNON.   My dear fellow, it isn't easy to be anything nowadays. There's such a lot of beastly competition about. (The sound of an electric bell is heard.) Ah! that must be Aunt Augusta. Only relatives, or creditors, ever ring in that Wagnerian[2] manner. Now, if I get her out of the way for ten minutes, so that you can have an opportunity for proposing to Gwendolen, may I dine with you to-night at Willis's?

JACK.   I suppose so, if you want to.

ALGERNON.   Yes, but you must be serious about it. I hate people who are not serious about meals. It is so shallow of them.

(Enter Lane.)

Lady Bracknell and Miss Fairfax.

(Algernon goes forward to meet them. Enter Lady Bracknell and Gwendolen.)

LADY BRACKNELL.   Good afternoon, dear Algernon, I hope you are behaving very well.

ALGERNON.   I'm feeling very well, Aunt Augusta.

LADY BRACKNELL.   That's not quite the same thing. In fact the two things rarely go together. (Sees Jack and bows to him with icy coldness.)

ALGERNON.   (To Gwendolen.) Dear me, you are smart!

GWENDOLEN.   I am always smart! Am I not, Mr. Worthing?

JACK.   You're quite perfect, Miss Fairfax.

GWENDOLEN.   Oh! I hope I am not that. It would leave no room for developments, and I intend to develop in many directions.

(Gwendolen and Jack sit down together in the corner.)

LADY BRACKNELL.   I'm sorry if we are a little late, Algernon, but I was obliged to call on dear Lady Har-

---

[1]   sent down   I.e., sent from the drawing-room (typically upstairs) down to the dining-room (typically on a lower floor).

[2]   Wagnerian   Suggesting the music of German composer Richard Wagner (1813–83), known for dramatic, stirring compositions such as Tannhäuser, Lohergrin, and Der Ring des Nibelungen.

bury. I hadn't been there since her poor husband's death. I never saw a woman so altered; she looks quite twenty years younger. And now I'll have a cup of tea, and one of those nice cucumber sandwiches you prom-ised me.

ALGERNON.   Certainly, Aunt Augusta. (*Goes over to tea-table.*)

LADY BRACKNELL. Won't you come and sit here, Gwendolen?

GWENDOLEN.   Thanks, mamma, I'm quite comfortable where I am.

ALGERNON.   (*Picking up empty plate in horror.*) Good heavens! Lane! Why are there no cucumber sandwiches? I ordered them specially.

LANE. (*Gravely.*) There were no cucumbers in the market this morning, sir. I went down twice.

ALGERNON.   No cucumbers!

LANE.   No, sir. Not even for ready money.

ALGERNON.   That will do, Lane, thank you.

LANE.   Thank you, sir. (*Goes out.*)

ALGERNON.   I am greatly distressed, Aunt Augusta, about there being no cucumbers, not even for ready money.

LADY BRACKNELL.   It really makes no matter, Algernon. I had some crumpets with Lady Harbury, who seems to me to be living entirely for pleasure now.

ALGERNON.   I hear her hair has turned quite gold from grief.

LADY BRACKNELL.   It certainly has changed its colour. From what cause I, of course, cannot say. (*Algernon crosses and hands tea.*) Thank you. I've quite a treat for you to-night, Algernon. I am going to send you down with Mary Farquhar. She is such a nice woman, and so attentive to her husband. It's delightful to watch them.

ALGERNON.   I am afraid, Aunt Augusta, I shall have to give up the pleasure of dining with you to-night after all.

LADY BRACKNELL.   (*Frowning.*) I hope not, Algernon. It would put my table completely out. Your uncle would have to dine upstairs. Fortunately he is accustomed to that.

ALGERNON.   It is a great bore, and, I need hardly say, a terrible disappointment to me, but the fact is I have just had a telegram to say that my poor friend Bunbury is very ill again. (*Exchanges glances with Jack.*) They seem to think I should be with him.

LADY BRACKNELL.   It is very strange. This Mr. Bunbury seems to suffer from curiously bad health.

ALGERNON.   Yes; poor Bunbury is a dreadful invalid.

LADY BRACKNELL.   Well, I must say, Algernon, that I think it is high time that Mr. Bunbury made up his mind whether he was going to live or to die. This shilly-shallying with the question is absurd. Nor do I in any way approve of the modern sympathy with invalids. I consider it morbid. Illness of any kind is hardly a thing to be encouraged in others. Health is the primary duty of life. I am always telling that to your poor uncle, but he never seems to take much notice … as far as any improvement in his ailment goes. I should be much obliged if you would ask Mr. Bunbury, from me, to be kind enough not to have a relapse on Saturday, for I rely on you to arrange my music for me. It is my last recep-tion, and one wants something that will encourage conversation, particularly at the end of the season when every one has practically said whatever they had to say, which, in most cases, was probably not much.

ALGERNON.   I'll speak to Bunbury, Aunt Augusta, if he is still conscious, and I think I can promise you he'll be all right by Saturday. Of course the music is a great difficulty. You see, if one plays good music, people don't listen, and if one plays bad music people don't talk. But I'll run over the programme I've drawn out, if you will kindly come into the next room for a moment.

LADY BRACKNELL.   Thank you, Algernon. It is very thoughtful of you. (*Rising, and following Algernon.*) I'm sure the programme will be delightful, after a few expurgations. French songs I cannot possibly allow. People always seem to think that they are improper, and either look shocked, which is vulgar, or laugh, which is worse. But German sounds a thoroughly respectable language, and indeed, I believe is so. Gwendolen, you will accompany me.

GWENDOLEN. Certainly, mamma.

(*Lady Bracknell and Algernon go into the music-room, Gwendolen remains behind.*)

JACK. Charming day it has been, Miss Fairfax.

GWENDOLEN. Pray don't talk to me about the weather, Mr. Worthing. Whenever people talk to me about the weather, I always feel quite certain that they mean something else. And that makes me so nervous.

430 JACK. I do mean something else.

GWENDOLEN. I thought so. In fact, I am never wrong.

JACK. And I would like to be allowed to take advantage of Lady Bracknell's temporary absence …

GWENDOLEN. I would certainly advise you to do so.
435 Mamma has a way of coming back suddenly into a room that I have often had to speak to her about.

JACK. (*Nervously.*) Miss Fairfax, ever since I met you I have admired you more than any girl … I have ever met since … I met you.

440 GWENDOLEN. Yes, I am quite well aware of the fact. And I often wish that in public, at any rate, you had been more demonstrative. For me you have always had an irresistible fascination. Even before I met you I was far from indifferent to you. (*Jack looks at her in amaze-*
445 *ment.*) We live, as I hope you know, Mr. Worthing, in an age of ideals. The fact is constantly mentioned in the more expensive monthly magazines, and has reached the provincial[1] pulpits, I am told; and my ideal has always been to love some one of the name of Ernest. There is
450 something in that name that inspires absolute confidence. The moment Algernon first mentioned to me that he had a friend called Ernest, I knew I was destined to love you.

JACK. You really love me, Gwendolen?

455 GWENDOLEN. Passionately!

JACK. Darling! You don't know how happy you've made me.

GWENDOLEN. My own Ernest!

JACK. But you don't really mean to say that you couldn't
460 love me if my name wasn't Ernest?

GWENDOLEN. But your name is Ernest.

JACK. Yes, I know it is. But supposing it was something else? Do you mean to say you couldn't love me then?

GWENDOLEN. (*Glibly.*) Ah! that is clearly a metaphysical
465 speculation, and like most metaphysical speculations has very little reference at all to the actual facts of real life, as we know them.

JACK. Personally, darling, to speak quite candidly, I don't much care about the name of Ernest … I don't

470 think the name suits me at all.

GWENDOLEN. It suits you perfectly. It is a divine name. It has a music of its own. It produces vibrations.

JACK. Well, really, Gwendolen, I must say that I think there are lots of other much nicer names. I think Jack,
475 for instance, a charming name.

GWENDOLEN. Jack? … No, there is very little music in the name Jack, if any at all, indeed. It does not thrill. It produces absolutely no vibrations … I have known several Jacks, and they all, without exception, were more
480 than usually plain. Besides, Jack is a notorious domesticity for John! And I pity any woman who is married to a man called John. She would probably never be allowed to know the entrancing pleasure of a single moment's solitude. The only really safe name is Ernest.

485 JACK. Gwendolen, I must get christened at once—I mean we must get married at once. There is no time to be lost.

GWENDOLEN. Married, Mr. Worthing?

JACK. (*Astounded.*) Well … surely. You know that I love
490 you, and you led me to believe, Miss Fairfax, that you were not absolutely indifferent to me.

GWENDOLEN. I adore you. But you haven't proposed to me yet. Nothing has been said at all about marriage. The subject has not even been touched on.

495 JACK. Well … may I propose to you now?

GWENDOLEN. I think it would be an admirable opportunity. And to spare you any possible disappointment, Mr. Worthing, I think it only fair to tell you quite frankly before-hand that I am fully determined to accept
500 you.

JACK. Gwendolen!

GWENDOLEN. Yes, Mr. Worthing, what have you got to say to me?

JACK. You know what I have got to say to you.

505 GWENDOLEN. Yes, but you don't say it.

JACK. Gwendolen, will you marry me? (*Goes on his knees.*)

GWENDOLEN. Of course I will, darling. How long you have been about it! I am afraid you have had very little
510 experience in how to propose.

JACK. My own one, I have never loved any one in the world but you.

GWENDOLEN. Yes, but men often propose for practice. I know my brother Gerald does. All my girl-friends tell

---

[1] *provincial* "Province" does not indicate a formal British jurisdiction; "the provinces" is a colloquial term for all areas of the country that are some distance from London.

515 me so. What wonderfully blue eyes you have, Ernest! They are quite, quite, blue. I hope you will always look at me just like that, especially when there are other people present. (*Enter Lady Bracknell.*)

LADY BRACKNELL. Mr. Worthing! Rise, sir, from this
520 semi-recumbent posture. It is most indecorous.

GWENDOLEN. Mamma! (*He tries to rise; she restrains him.*) I must beg you to retire. This is no place for you. Besides, Mr. Worthing has not quite finished yet.

LADY BRACKNELL. Finished what, may I ask?

525 GWENDOLEN. I am engaged to Mr. Worthing, mamma.

(*They rise together.*)

LADY BRACKNELL. Pardon me, you are not engaged to any one. When you do become engaged to some one, I, or your father, should his health permit him, will inform you of the fact. An engagement should come on
530 a young girl as a surprise, pleasant or unpleasant, as the case may be. It is hardly a matter that she could be allowed to arrange for herself … And now I have a few questions to put to you, Mr. Worthing. While I am making these inquiries, you, Gwendolen, will wait for
535 me below in the carriage.

GWENDOLEN. (*Reproachfully.*) Mamma!

LADY BRACKNELL. In the carriage, Gwendolen!

(*Gwendolen goes to the door. She and Jack blow kisses to each other behind Lady Bracknell's back. Lady Bracknell looks vaguely about as if she could not understand what the noise was. Finally turns round.*)

Gwendolen, the carriage!

GWENDOLEN. Yes, mamma. (*Goes out, looking back at
540 Jack.*)

LADY BRACKNELL. (*Sitting down.*) You can take a seat, Mr. Worthing. (*Looks in her pocket for note-book and pencil.*)

JACK. Thank you, Lady Bracknell, I prefer standing.

545 LADY BRACKNELL. (*Pencil and note-book in hand.*) I feel bound to tell you that you are not down on my list of eligible young men, although I have the same list as the dear Duchess of Bolton has. We work together, in fact. However, I am quite ready to enter your name, should

550 your answers be what a really affectionate mother requires. Do you smoke?

JACK. Well, yes, I must admit I smoke.

LADY BRACKNELL. I am glad to hear it. A man should always have an occupation of some kind. There are far
555 too many idle men in London as it is. How old are you?

JACK. Twenty-nine.

LADY BRACKNELL. A very good age to be married at. I have always been of opinion that a man who desires to get married should know either everything or nothing.
560 Which do you know?

JACK. (*After some hesitation.*) I know nothing, Lady Bracknell.

LADY BRACKNELL. I am pleased to hear it. I do not approve of anything that tampers with natural igno-
565 rance. Ignorance is like a delicate exotic fruit; touch it and the bloom is gone. The whole theory of modern education is radically unsound. Fortunately in England, at any rate, education produces no effect whatsoever. If it did, it would prove a serious danger to the upper
570 classes, and probably lead to acts of violence in Gros-venor Square.[1] What is your income?

JACK. Between seven and eight thousand a year.

LADY BRACKNELL. (*Makes a note in her book.*) In land, or in investments?

575 JACK. In investments, chiefly.

LADY BRACKNELL. That is satisfactory. What between the duties[2] expected of one during one's lifetime, and the duties exacted from one after one's death, land has ceased to be either a profit or a pleasure. It gives one
580 position, and prevents one from keeping it up. That's all that can be said about land.

JACK. I have a country house with some land, of course, attached to it, about fifteen hundred acres, I believe; but I don't depend on that for my real income. In fact, as far
585 as I can make out, the poachers are the only people who make anything out of it.

LADY BRACKNELL. A country house! How many bed-rooms? Well, that point can be cleared up afterwards. You have a town house, I hope? A girl with a simple,
590 unspoiled nature, like Gwendolen, could hardly be expected to reside in the country.

---

[1] *Grosvenor Square* Located in a fashionable part of central London.

[2] *duties* Taxes.

JACK. Well, I own a house in Belgrave Square, but it is let by the year to Lady Bloxham. Of course, I can get it back whenever I like, at six months' notice.

595 LADY BRACKNELL. Lady Bloxham? I don't know her.

JACK. Oh, she goes about very little. She is a lady considerably advanced in years.

LADY BRACKNELL. Ah, nowadays that is no guarantee of respectability of character. What number in Belgrave 600 Square?

JACK. 149.

LADY BRACKNELL. (*Shaking her head.*) The unfashionable side. I thought there was something. However, that could easily be altered.

605 JACK. Do you mean the fashion, or the side?

LADY BRACKNELL. (*Sternly.*) Both, if necessary, I presume. What are your politics?

JACK. Well, I am afraid I really have none. I am a Liberal Unionist.[1]

610 LADY BRACKNELL. Oh, they count as Tories. They dine with us. Or come in the evening, at any rate. Now to minor matters. Are your parents living?

JACK. I have lost both my parents.

LADY BRACKNELL. To lose one parent, Mr. Worthing, 615 may be regarded as a misfortune; to lose both looks like carelessness. Who was your father? He was evidently a man of some wealth. Was he born in what the Radical papers call the purple of commerce,[2] or did he rise from the ranks of the aristocracy?

620 JACK. I am afraid I really don't know. The fact is, Lady Bracknell, I said I had lost my parents. It would be nearer the truth to say that my parents seem to have lost me … I don't actually know who I am by birth. I was … well, I was found.

625 LADY BRACKNELL. Found!

JACK. The late Mr. Thomas Cardew, an old gentleman of a very charitable and kindly disposition, found me, and gave me the name of Worthing, because he happened to have a first-class ticket for Worthing in his pocket at the time. Worthing is a place in Sussex. It is a 630 seaside resort.

LADY BRACKNELL. Where did the charitable gentleman who had a first-class ticket for this seaside resort find you?

635 JACK. (*Gravely.*) In a hand-bag.

LADY BRACKNELL. A hand-bag?

JACK. (*Very seriously.*) Yes, Lady Bracknell. I was in a hand-bag—a somewhat large, black leather hand-bag, with handles to it—an ordinary hand-bag in fact.

640 LADY BRACKNELL. In what locality did this Mr. James, or Thomas, Cardew come across this ordinary hand-bag?

JACK. In the cloak-room at Victoria Station. It was given to him in mistake for his own.

LADY BRACKNELL. The cloak-room at Victoria Station?

645 JACK. Yes. The Brighton line.

LADY BRACKNELL. The line is immaterial. Mr. Worthing, I confess I feel somewhat bewildered by what you have just told me. To be born, or at any rate bred, in a hand-bag, whether it had handles or not, seems to me to 650 display a contempt for the ordinary decencies of family life that reminds one of the worst excesses of the French Revolution. And I presume you know what that unfortunate movement led to? As for the particular locality in which the hand-bag was found, a cloak-room at a 655 railway station might serve to conceal a social indiscretion— has probably, indeed, been used for that purpose before now—but it could hardly be regarded as an assured basis for a recognised position in good society.

JACK. May I ask you then what you would advise me to 660 do? I need hardly say I would do anything in the world to ensure Gwendolen's happiness.

LADY BRACKNELL. I would strongly advise you, Mr. Worthing, to try and acquire some relations as soon as possible, and to make a definite effort to produce at any 665 rate one parent, of either sex, before the season[3] is quite over.

JACK. Well, I don't see how I could possibly manage to do that. I can produce the hand-bag at any moment. It is in my dressing-room at home. I really think that 670 should satisfy you, Lady Bracknell.

LADY BRACKNELL. Me, sir! What has it to do with me?

---

[1] *Liberal Unionist* The Liberal Unionists, who in 1886 had broken away from the Liberal party in reaction to Prime Minister William Gladstone's support for Irish Home Rule, occupied the political center between the two large parties, the Liberals and the Conservatives.

[2] *Was he born … the purple of commerce* I.e., was he born into a wealthy merchant or trading family. (The color purple is traditionally associated with royalty.)

[3] *the season* The London social season, which ran while Parliament was sitting. Many wealthy families spent the rest of the year at their country homes.

You can hardly imagine that I and Lord Bracknell would dream of allowing our only daughter—a girl brought up with the utmost care—to marry into a cloak-room, and form an alliance with a parcel? Good morning, Mr. Worthing!

(*Lady Bracknell sweeps out in majestic indignation.*)

JACK. Good morning! (*Algernon, from the other room, strikes up the Wedding March. Jack looks perfectly furious, and goes to the door.*) For goodness' sake don't play that ghastly tune, Algy. How idiotic you are!

(*The music stops and Algernon enters cheerily.*)

ALGERNON. Didn't it go off all right, old boy? You don't mean to say Gwendolen refused you? I know it is a way she has. She is always refusing people. I think it is most ill-natured of her.

JACK. Oh, Gwendolen is as right as a trivet.[1] As far as she is concerned, we are engaged. Her mother is perfectly unbearable. Never met such a Gorgon[2] ... I don't really know what a Gorgon is like, but I am quite sure that Lady Bracknell is one. In any case, she is a monster, without being a myth, which is rather unfair ... I beg your pardon, Algy, I suppose I shouldn't talk about your own aunt in that way before you.

ALGERNON. My dear boy, I love hearing my relations abused. It is the only thing that makes me put up with them at all. Relations are simply a tedious pack of people, who haven't got the remotest knowledge of how to live, nor the smallest instinct about when to die.

JACK. Oh, that is nonsense!

ALGERNON. It isn't!

JACK. Well, I won't argue about the matter. You always want to argue about things.

ALGERNON. That is exactly what things were originally made for.

JACK. Upon my word, if I thought that, I'd shoot myself ... (*A pause.*) You don't think there is any chance of Gwendolen becoming like her mother in about a hundred and fifty years, do you, Algy?

ALGERNON. All women become like their mothers. That is their tragedy. No man does. That's his.

JACK. Is that clever?

ALGERNON. It is perfectly phrased! and quite as true as any observation in civilized life should be.

JACK. I am sick to death of cleverness. Everybody is clever nowadays. You can't go anywhere without meeting clever people. The thing has become an absolute public nuisance. I wish to goodness we had a few fools left.

ALGERNON. We have.

JACK. I should extremely like to meet them. What do they talk about?

ALGERNON. The fools? Oh! about the clever people, of course.

JACK. What fools!

ALGERNON. By the way, did you tell Gwendolen the truth about your being Ernest in town, and Jack in the country?

JACK. (*In a very patronising manner.*) My dear fellow, the truth isn't quite the sort of thing one tells to a nice, sweet, refined girl. What extraordinary ideas you have about the way to behave to a woman!

ALGERNON. The only way to behave to a woman is to make love to her, if she is pretty, and to some one else, if she is plain.

JACK. Oh, that is nonsense.

ALGERNON. What about your brother? What about the profligate Ernest?

JACK. Oh, before the end of the week I shall have got rid of him. I'll say he died in Paris of apoplexy.[3] Lots of people die of apoplexy, quite suddenly, don't they?

ALGERNON. Yes, but it's hereditary, my dear fellow. It's a sort of thing that runs in families. You had much better say a severe chill.

JACK. You are sure a severe chill isn't hereditary, or anything of that kind?

ALGERNON. Of course it isn't!

JACK. Very well, then. My poor brother Ernest is carried off suddenly, in Paris, by a severe chill. That gets rid of him.

---

[1] *as right as a trivet* Proverbial expression indicating stability (a trivet is a three-footed stand or support).

[2] *Gorgon* In Greek mythology the three Gorgons are sisters who have repulsive features (including snakes growing out of their heads instead of hair); anyone who looks at them turns into stone.

[3] *apoplexy* Stroke.

750 ALGERNON. But I thought you said that … Miss Cardew was a little too much interested in your poor brother Ernest? Won't she feel his loss a good deal?

JACK. Oh, that is all right. Cecily is not a silly romantic girl, I am glad to say. She has got a capital appetite, goes
755 on long walks, and pays no attention at all to her lessons.

ALGERNON. I would rather like to see Cecily.

JACK. I will take very good care you never do. She is excessively pretty, and she is only just eighteen.

ALGERNON. Have you told Gwendolen yet that you
760 have an excessively pretty ward who is only just eighteen?

JACK. Oh! one doesn't blurt these things out to people. Cecily and Gwendolen are perfectly certain to be extremely great friends. I'll bet you anything you like
765 that half an hour after they have met, they will be calling each other sister.

ALGERNON. Women only do that when they have called each other a lot of other things first. Now, my dear boy, if we want to get a good table at Willis's, we really must
770 go and dress. Do you know it is nearly seven?

JACK. (*Irritably.*) Oh! It always is nearly seven.

ALGERNON. Well, I'm hungry.

JACK. I never knew you when you weren't …

ALGERNON. What shall we do after dinner? Go to a
775 theatre?

JACK. Oh no! I loathe listening.

ALGERNON. Well, let us go to the Club?

JACK. Oh, no! I hate talking.

ALGERNON. Well, we might trot round to the Empire[1]
780 at ten?

JACK. Oh, no! I can't bear looking at things. It is so silly.

ALGERNON. Well, what shall we do?

JACK. Nothing!

ALGERNON. It is awfully hard work doing nothing.
785 However, I don't mind hard work where there is no definite object of any kind.

(*Enter Lane.*)

LANE. Miss Fairfax.

(*Enter Gwendolen. Lane goes out.*)

ALGERNON. Gwendolen, upon my word!

GWENDOLEN. Algy, kindly turn your back. I have
790 something very particular to say to Mr. Worthing.

ALGERNON. Really, Gwendolen, I don't think I can allow this at all.

GWENDOLEN. Algy, you always adopt a strictly immoral attitude towards life. You are not quite old enough to do
795 that. (*Algernon retires to the fireplace.*)

JACK. My own darling!

GWENDOLEN. Ernest, we may never be married. From the expression on mamma's face I fear we never shall. Few parents nowadays pay any regard to what their
800 children say to them. The old-fashioned respect for the young is fast dying out. Whatever influence I ever had over mamma, I lost at the age of three. But although she may prevent us from becoming man and wife, and I may marry some one else, and marry often, nothing that
805 she can possibly do can alter my eternal devotion to you.

JACK. Dear Gwendolen!

GWENDOLEN. The story of your romantic origin, as related to me by mamma, with unpleasing comments, has naturally stirred the deeper fibres of my nature. Your
810 Christian name has an irresistible fascination. The simplicity of your character makes you exquisitely incomprehensible to me. Your town address at the Albany[2] I have. What is your address in the country?

JACK. The Manor House, Woolton, Hertfordshire.

(*Algernon, who has been carefully listening, smiles to himself, and writes the address on his shirt-cuff. Then picks up the Railway Guide.*)

815 GWENDOLEN. There is a good postal service, I suppose? It may be necessary to do something desperate. That of course will require serious consideration. I will communicate with you daily.

JACK. My own one!

820 GWENDOLEN. How long do you remain in town?

JACK. Till Monday.

GWENDOLEN. Good! Algy, you may turn round now.

ALGERNON. Thanks, I've turned round already.

GWENDOLEN. You may also ring the bell.

825 JACK. You will let me see you to your carriage, my own darling?

---

[1] *the Empire* Theater that often featured risqué variety shows.

[2] *the Albany* Fashionable men's club in London.

GWENDOLEN. Certainly.

JACK. (*To Lane, who now enters.*) I will see Miss Fairfax out.

830 LANE. Yes, sir. (*Jack and Gwendolen go off.*)

(*Lane presents several letters on a salver to Algernon. It is to be surmised that they are bills, as Algernon, after looking at the envelopes, tears them up.*)

ALGERNON. A glass of sherry, Lane.

LANE. Yes, sir.

ALGERNON. To-morrow, Lane, I'm going Bunburying.

LANE. Yes, sir.

835 ALGERNON. I shall probably not be back till Monday. You can put up my dress clothes, my smoking jacket, and all the Bunbury suits …

LANE. Yes, sir. (*Handing sherry.*)

ALGERNON. I hope to-morrow will be a fine day, Lane.

840 LANE. It never is, sir.

ALGERNON. Lane, you're a perfect pessimist.

LANE. I do my best to give satisfaction, sir.

(*Enter Jack. Lane goes off.*)

JACK. There's a sensible, intellectual girl! the only girl I ever cared for in my life. (*Algernon is laughing immoder-*
845 *ately.*) What on earth are you so amused at?

ALGERNON. Oh, I'm a little anxious about poor Bunbury, that is all.

JACK. If you don't take care, your friend Bunbury will get you into a serious scrape some day.

850 ALGERNON. I love scrapes. They are the only things that are never serious.

JACK. Oh, that's nonsense, Algy. You never talk anything but nonsense.

ALGERNON. Nobody ever does.

(*Jack looks indignantly at him, and leaves the room. Algernon lights a cigarette, reads his shirt-cuff, and smiles.*)

ACT DROP

ACT 2

SCENE

(*Garden at the Manor House. A flight of grey stone steps leads up to the house. The garden, an old-fashioned one, full of roses. Time of year, July. Basket chairs, and a table covered with books, are set under a large yew-tree. Miss Prism discovered seated at the table. Cecily is at the back watering flowers.*)

MISS PRISM. (*Calling.*) Cecily, Cecily! Surely such a utilitarian occupation as the watering of flowers is rather Moulton's duty than yours? Especially at a moment when intellectual pleasures await you. Your German
5 grammar is on the table. Pray open it at page fifteen. We will repeat yesterday's lesson.

CECILY. (*Coming over very slowly.*) But I don't like German. It isn't at all a becoming language. I know perfectly well that I look quite plain after my German
10 lesson.

MISS PRISM. Child, you know how anxious your guardian is that you should improve yourself in every way. He laid particular stress on your German, as he was leaving for town yesterday. Indeed, he always lays stress on your
15 German when he is leaving for town.

CECILY. Dear Uncle Jack is so very serious! Sometimes he is so serious that I think he cannot be quite well.

MISS PRISM. (*Drawing herself up.*) Your guardian enjoys the best of health, and his gravity of demeanour is
20 especially to be commended in one so comparatively young as he is. I know no one who has a higher sense of duty and responsibility.

CECILY. I suppose that is why he often looks a little bored when we three are together.

25 MISS PRISM. Cecily! I am surprised at you. Mr. Worthing has many troubles in his life. Idle merriment and triviality would be out of place in his conversation. You must remember his constant anxiety about that unfortunate young man his brother.

30 CECILY. I wish Uncle Jack would allow that unfortunate young man, his brother, to come down here sometimes. We might have a good influence over him, Miss Prism. I am sure you certainly would. You know German, and geology, and things of that kind influence a man very
35 much. (*Cecily begins to write in her diary.*)

MISS PRISM. (*Shaking her head.*) I do not think that even I could produce any effect on a character that according to his own brother's admission is irretrievably weak and vacillating. Indeed I am not sure that I would desire to
40 reclaim him. I am not in favour of this modern mania for turning bad people into good people at a moment's notice. As a man sows so let him reap.[1] You must put away your diary, Cecily. I really don't see why you should keep a diary at all.

45 CECILY. I keep a diary in order to enter the wonderful secrets of my life. If I didn't write them down, I should probably forget all about them.

MISS PRISM. Memory, my dear Cecily, is the diary that we all carry about with us.

50 CECILY. Yes, but it usually chronicles the things that have never happened, and couldn't possibly have happened. I believe that Memory is responsible for nearly all the three-volume novels that Mudie sends us.[2]

MISS PRISM. Do not speak slightingly of the three-
55 volume novel, Cecily. I wrote one myself in earlier days.

CECILY. Did you really, Miss Prism? How wonderfully clever you are! I hope it did not end happily? I don't like novels that end happily. They depress me so much.

MISS PRISM. The good ended happily, and the bad
60 unhappily. That is what Fiction means.

CECILY. I suppose so. But it seems very unfair. And was your novel ever published?

MISS PRISM. Alas! no. The manuscript unfortunately was abandoned. (*Cecily starts.*) I use the word in the
65 sense of lost or mislaid. To your work, child, these speculations are profitless.

CECILY. (*Smiling.*) But I see dear Dr. Chasuble coming up through the garden.

MISS PRISM. (*Rising and advancing.*) Dr. Chasuble! This
70 is indeed a pleasure.

(*Enter Canon Chasuble.*)

CHASUBLE. And how are we this morning? Miss Prism, you are, I trust, well?

CECILY. Miss Prism has just been complaining of a slight headache. I think it would do her so much good to have
75 a short stroll with you in the Park, Dr. Chasuble.

MISS PRISM. Cecily, I have not mentioned anything about a headache.

CECILY. No, dear Miss Prism, I know that, but I felt instinctively that you had a headache. Indeed I was
80 thinking about that, and not about my German lesson, when the Rector came in.

CHASUBLE. I hope, Cecily, you are not inattentive.

CECILY. Oh, I am afraid I am.

CHASUBLE. That is strange. Were I fortunate enough to
85 be Miss Prism's pupil, I would hang upon her lips. (*Miss Prism glares.*) I spoke metaphorically.—My metaphor was drawn from bees. Ahem! Mr. Worthing, I suppose, has not returned from town yet?

MISS PRISM. We do not expect him till Monday after-
90 noon.

CHASUBLE. Ah yes, he usually likes to spend his Sunday in London. He is not one of those whose sole aim is enjoyment, as, by all accounts, that unfortunate young man his brother seems to be. But I must not disturb
95 Egeria and her pupil any longer.

MISS PRISM. Egeria? My name is Lætitia, Doctor.

CHASUBLE. (*Bowing.*) A classical allusion merely, drawn from the Pagan authors.[3] I shall see you both no doubt at Evensong?[4]

100 MISS PRISM. I think, dear Doctor, I will have a stroll with you. I find I have a headache after all, and a walk might do it good.

CHASUBLE. With pleasure, Miss Prism, with pleasure. We might go as far as the schools and back.

105 MISS PRISM. That would be delightful. Cecily, you will read your Political Economy in my absence. The chapter on the Fall of the Rupee you may omit. It is somewhat too sensational. Even these metallic problems have their melodramatic side.[5]

---

1 *As a man sows so let him reap* Galatians 6.7: "whatsoever a man soweth, that shall he also reap."

2 *nearly all ... Mudie sends us* Commercial lending libraries of the time, such as Mudie's, specialized in lending novels that were published in three volumes.

3 *A classical allusion ... pagan authors* In Roman mythology, the nymph Egeria taught Numa, the second King of Rome, the lessons of wisdom and law which he then used to found the institutions of Rome.

4 *Evensong* The evening service in the Anglican church (and various other Christian denominations).

5 *The chapter ... melodramatic side* The rupee (India's currency) declined dramatically in the early 1890s as a result of a variety of disasters, including an outbreak of plague.

(*Goes down the garden with Dr. Chasuble.*)

110 CECILY. (*Picks up books and throws them back on table.*) Horrid Political Economy! Horrid Geography! Horrid, horrid German!

(*Enter Merriman with a card on a salver.*)

MERRIMAN. Mr. Ernest Worthing has just driven over from the station. He has brought his luggage with him.

115 CECILY. (*Takes the card and reads it.*) "Mr. Ernest Worthing, B. 4, The Albany, W." Uncle Jack's brother! Did you tell him Mr. Worthing was in town?

MERRIMAN. Yes, Miss. He seemed very much disap-
120 pointed. I mentioned that you and Miss Prism were in the garden. He said he was anxious to speak to you privately for a moment.

CECILY. Ask Mr. Ernest Worthing to come here. I suppose you had better talk to the housekeeper about a room for him.

125 MERRIMAN. Yes, Miss.

(*Merriman goes off.*)

CECILY. I have never met any really wicked person before. I feel rather frightened. I am so afraid he will look just like every one else. (*Enter Algernon, very gay and debonair.*) He does!

130 ALGERNON. (*Raising his hat.*) You are my little cousin Cecily, I'm sure.

CECILY. You are under some strange mistake. I am not little. In fact, I believe I am more than usually tall for my age. (*Algernon is rather taken aback.*) But I am your
135 cousin Cecily. You, I see from your card, are Uncle Jack's brother, my cousin Ernest, my wicked cousin Ernest.

ALGERNON. Oh! I am not really wicked at all, cousin Cecily. You mustn't think that I am wicked.

140 CECILY. If you are not, then you have certainly been deceiving us all in a very inexcusable manner. I hope you have not been leading a double life, pretending to be wicked and being really good all the time. That would be hypocrisy.

145 ALGERNON. (*Looks at her in amazement.*) Oh! Of course I have been rather reckless.

CECILY. I am glad to hear it.

ALGERNON. In fact, now you mention the subject, I have been very bad in my own small way.

150 CECILY. I don't think you should be so proud of that, though I am sure it must have been very pleasant.

ALGERNON. It is much pleasanter being here with you.

CECILY. I can't understand how you are here at all. Uncle Jack won't be back till Monday afternoon.

155 ALGERNON. That is a great disappointment. I am obliged to go up by the first train on Monday morning. I have a business appointment that I am anxious ... to miss!

CECILY. Couldn't you miss it anywhere but in London?

160 ALGERNON. No: the appointment is in London.

CECILY. Well, I know, of course, how important it is not to keep a business engagement, if one wants to retain any sense of the beauty of life, but still I think you had better wait till Uncle Jack arrives. I know he wants to
165 speak to you about your emigrating.

ALGERNON. About my what?

CECILY. Your emigrating. He has gone up to buy your outfit.

ALGERNON. I certainly wouldn't let Jack buy my outfit.
170 He has no taste in neckties at all.

CECILY. I don't think you will require neckties. Uncle Jack is sending you to Australia.[1]

ALGERNON. Australia! I'd sooner die.

CECILY. Well, he said at dinner on Wednesday night,
175 that you would have to choose between this world, the next world, and Australia.

ALGERNON. Oh, well! The accounts I have received of Australia and the next world are not particularly encouraging. This world is good enough for me, cousin Cecily.

180 CECILY. Yes, but are you good enough for it?

ALGERNON. I'm afraid I'm not that. That is why I want you to reform me. You might make that your mission, if you don't mind, cousin Cecily.

CECILY. I'm afraid I've no time, this afternoon.

185 ALGERNON. Well, would you mind my reforming myself this afternoon?

CECILY. It is rather Quixotic of you. But I think you should try.

ALGERNON. I will. I feel better already.

---

1 *Australia* A former penal colony, at the time still considered to be largely composed of wilderness.

190 CECILY. You are looking a little worse.

ALGERNON. That is because I am hungry.

CECILY. How thoughtless of me. I should have remembered that when one is going to lead an entirely new life, one requires regular and wholesome meals. Won't you

195 come in?

ALGERNON. Thank you. Might I have a buttonhole[1] first? I never have any appetite unless I have a buttonhole first.

CECILY. A Maréchal Niel?[2] (*Picks up scissors.*)

200 ALGERNON. No, I'd sooner have a pink rose.

CECILY. Why? (*Cuts a flower.*)

ALGERNON. Because you are like a pink rose, Cousin Cecily.

CECILY. I don't think it can be right for you to talk to

205 me like that. Miss Prism never says such things to me.

ALGERNON. Then Miss Prism is a short-sighted old lady. (*Cecily puts the rose in his buttonhole.*) You are the prettiest girl I ever saw.

CECILY. Miss Prism says that all good looks are a snare.

210 ALGERNON. They are a snare that every sensible man would like to be caught in.

CECILY. Oh, I don't think I would care to catch a sensible man. I shouldn't know what to talk to him about.

(*They pass into the house. Miss Prism and Dr. Chasuble return.*)

215 MISS PRISM. You are too much alone, dear Dr. Chasuble. You should get married. A misanthrope I can understand—a womanthrope,[3] never!

CHASUBLE. (*With a scholar's shudder.*) Believe me, I do not deserve so neologistic a phrase. The precept as well

220 as the practice of the Primitive Church[4] was distinctly against matrimony.

MISS PRISM. (*Sententiously.*) That is obviously the reason why the Primitive Church has not lasted up to the present day. And you do not seem to realize, dear

---

[1] *buttonhole* Boutonniere, flower for one's lapel.

[2] *Maréchal Niel* Variety of yellow rose.

[3] *misanthrope … womanthrope* The correct word for someone who hates women is a "misogynist"; a "misanthrope" is someone who hates all humanity.

[4] *Primitive Church* Early Christian church.

225 Doctor, that by persistently remaining single, a man converts himself into a permanent public temptation. Men should be more careful; this very celibacy leads weaker vessels astray.

CHASUBLE. But is a man not equally attractive when

230 married?

MISS PRISM. No married man is ever attractive except to his wife.

CHASUBLE. And often, I've been told, not even to her.

MISS PRISM. That depends on the intellectual sympa-

235 thies of the woman. Maturity can always be depended on. Ripeness can be trusted. Young women are green. (*Dr. Chasuble starts.*) I spoke horticulturally. My metaphor was drawn from fruits. But where is Cecily?

CHASUBLE. Perhaps she followed us to the schools.

(*Enter Jack slowly from the back of the garden. He is dressed in the deepest mourning, with crepe hatband and black gloves.*)

240 MISS PRISM. Mr. Worthing!

CHASUBLE. Mr. Worthing?

MISS PRISM. This is indeed a surprise. We did not look for you till Monday afternoon.

JACK. (*Shakes Miss Prism's hand in a tragic manner.*) I

245 have returned sooner than I expected. Dr. Chasuble, I hope you are well?

CHASUBLE. Dear Mr. Worthing, I trust this garb of woe does not betoken some terrible calamity?

JACK. My brother.

250 MISS PRISM. More shameful debts and extravagance?

CHASUBLE. Still leading his life of pleasure?

JACK. (*Shaking his head.*) Dead!

CHASUBLE. Your brother Ernest dead?

JACK. Quite dead.

255 MISS PRISM. What a lesson for him! I trust he will profit by it.

CHASUBLE. Mr. Worthing, I offer you my sincere condolence. You have at least the consolation of knowing that you were always the most generous and forgiv-

260 ing of brothers.

JACK. Poor Ernest! He had many faults, but it is a sad, sad blow.

CHASUBLE. Very sad indeed. Were you with him at the end?

JACK.   No. He died abroad; in Paris, in fact. I had a telegram last night from the manager of the Grand Hotel.

CHASUBLE.   Was the cause of death mentioned?

JACK.   A severe chill, it seems.

MISS PRISM.   As a man sows, so shall he reap.

CHASUBLE.   (*Raising his hand.*) Charity, dear Miss Prism, charity! None of us are perfect. I myself am peculiarly susceptible to draughts. Will the interment take place here?

JACK.   No. He seems to have expressed a desire to be buried in Paris.

CHASUBLE.   In Paris! (*Shakes his head.*) I fear that hardly points to any very serious state of mind at the last. You would no doubt wish me to make some slight allusion to this tragic domestic affliction next Sunday. (*Jack presses his hand convulsively.*) My sermon on the meaning of the manna in the wilderness[1] can be adapted to almost any occasion, joyful, or, as in the present case, distressing. (*All sigh.*) I have preached it at harvest celebrations, christenings, confirmations,[2] on days of humiliation and festal days. The last time I delivered it was in the Cathedral, as a charity sermon on behalf of the Society for the Prevention of Discontent among the Upper Orders. The Bishop, who was present, was much struck by some of the analogies I drew.

JACK.   Ah! that reminds me, you mentioned christenings I think, Dr. Chasuble? I suppose you know how to christen all right? (*Dr. Chasuble looks astounded.*) I mean, of course, you are continually christening, aren't you?

MISS PRISM.   It is, I regret to say, one of the Rector's most constant duties in this parish. I have often spoken to the poorer classes on the subject. But they don't seem to know what thrift is.

CHASUBLE.   But is there any particular infant in whom you are interested, Mr. Worthing? Your brother was, I believe, unmarried, was he not?

JACK.   Oh yes.

MISS PRISM.   (*Bitterly.*) People who live entirely for pleasure usually are.

JACK.   But it is not for any child, dear Doctor. I am very fond of children. No! the fact is, I would like to be christened myself, this afternoon, if you have nothing better to do.

CHASUBLE.   But surely, Mr. Worthing, you have been christened already?

JACK.   I don't remember anything about it.

CHASUBLE.   But have you any grave doubts on the subject?

JACK.   I certainly intend to have. Of course I don't know if the thing would bother you in any way, or if you think I am a little too old now.

CHASUBLE.   Not at all. The sprinkling, and, indeed, the immersion of adults is a perfectly canonical practice.

JACK.   Immersion!

CHASUBLE.   You need have no apprehensions. Sprinkling is all that is necessary, or indeed I think advisable. Our weather is so changeable. At what hour would you wish the ceremony performed?

JACK.   Oh, I might trot round about five if that would suit you.

CHASUBLE.   Perfectly, perfectly! In fact I have two similar ceremonies to perform at that time. A case of twins that occurred recently in one of the outlying cottages on your own estate. Poor Jenkins the carter,[3] a most hard-working man.

JACK.   Oh! I don't see much fun in being christened along with other babies. It would be childish. Would half-past five do?

CHASUBLE.   Admirably! Admirably! (*Takes out watch.*) And now, dear Mr. Worthing, I will not intrude any longer into a house of sorrow. I would merely beg you not to be too much bowed down by grief. What seem to us bitter trials are often blessings in disguise.

MISS PRISM.   This seems to me a blessing of an extremely obvious kind.

(*Enter Cecily from the house.*)

CECILY.   Uncle Jack! Oh, I am pleased to see you back. But what horrid clothes you have got on! Do go and change them.

---

[1] *manna in the wilderness* See Exodus 16.

[2] *christenings, confirmations* Whereas a christening formally admits a person to the Christian church through baptism (usually as an infant), in many Christian denominations a person's standing as a full member of the church must be confirmed at a later ceremony (typically as a young adult).

[3] *carter* Cart driver.

345 MISS PRISM.   Cecily!
CHASUBLE.   My child! my child!

(*Cecily goes towards Jack; he kisses her brow in a melancholy manner.*)

CECILY.   What is the matter, Uncle Jack? Do look happy! You look as if you had toothache, and I have got such a surprise for you. Who do you think is in the dining-
350 room? Your brother!
JACK.   Who?
CECILY.   Your brother Ernest. He arrived about half an hour ago.
JACK.   What nonsense! I haven't got a brother.
355 CECILY.   Oh, don't say that. However badly he may have behaved to you in the past he is still your brother. You couldn't be so heartless as to disown him. I'll tell him to come out. And you will shake hands with him, won't you, Uncle Jack? (*Runs back into the house.*)
360 CHASUBLE.   These are very joyful tidings.
MISS PRISM.   After we had all been resigned to his loss, his sudden return seems to me peculiarly distressing.
JACK.   My brother is in the dining-room? I don't know what it all means. I think it is perfectly absurd.

(*Enter Algernon and Cecily hand in hand. They come slowly up to Jack.*)

365 JACK.   Good heavens! (*Motions Algernon away.*)
ALGERNON.   Brother John, I have come down from town to tell you that I am very sorry for all the trouble I have given you, and that I intend to lead a better life in the future. (*Jack glares at him and does not take his
370 hand.*)
CECILY.   Uncle Jack, you are not going to refuse your own brother's hand?
JACK.   Nothing will induce me to take his hand. I think his coming down here disgraceful. He knows perfectly
375 well why.
CECILY.   Uncle Jack, do be nice. There is some good in every one. Ernest has just been telling me about his poor invalid friend Mr. Bunbury whom he goes to visit so often. And surely there must be much good in one who is kind to an invalid, and leaves the pleasures of London
380 to sit by a bed of pain.

JACK.   Oh! he has been talking about Bunbury, has he?
CECILY.   Yes, he has told me all about poor Mr. Bunbury, and his terrible state of health.
385 JACK.   Bunbury! Well, I won't have him talk to you about Bunbury or about anything else. It is enough to drive one perfectly frantic.
ALGERNON.   Of course I admit that the faults were all on my side. But I must say that I think that Brother John's
390 coldness to me is peculiarly painful. I expected a more enthusiastic welcome, especially considering it is the first time I have come here.
CECILY.   Uncle Jack, if you don't shake hands with Ernest I will never forgive you.
395 JACK.   Never forgive me?
CECILY.   Never, never, never!
JACK.   Well, this is the last time I shall ever do it. (*Shakes hands with Algernon and glares.*)
CHASUBLE.   It's pleasant, is it not, to see so perfect a
400 reconciliation? I think we might leave the two brothers together.
MISS PRISM.   Cecily, you will come with us.
CECILY.   Certainly, Miss Prism. My little task of reconciliation is over.
405 CHASUBLE.   You have done a beautiful action to-day, dear child.
MISS PRISM.   We must not be premature in our judgments.
CECILY.   I feel very happy.

(*They all go off except Jack and Algernon.*)

410 JACK.   You young scoundrel, Algy, you must get out of this place as soon as possible. I don't allow any Bunburying here.

(*Enter Merriman.*)

MERRIMAN.   I have put Mr. Ernest's things in the room next to yours, sir. I suppose that is all right?
415 JACK.   What?
MERRIMAN.   Mr. Ernest's luggage, sir. I have unpacked it and put it in the room next to your own.
JACK.   His luggage?
MERRIMAN.   Yes, sir. Three portmanteaus, a dressing-
420 case, two hat-boxes, and a large luncheon-basket.

ALGERNON.   I am afraid I can't stay more than a week this time.

JACK.   Merriman, order the dog-cart[1] at once. Mr. Ernest has been suddenly called back to town.

425 MERRIMAN.   Yes, sir. (*Goes back into the house.*)

ALGERNON.   What a fearful liar you are, Jack. I have not been called back to town at all.

JACK.   Yes, you have.

ALGERNON.   I haven't heard any one call me.

430 JACK.   Your duty as a gentleman calls you back.

ALGERNON.   My duty as a gentleman has never interfered with my pleasures in the smallest degree.

JACK.   I can quite understand that.

ALGERNON.   Well, Cecily is a darling.

435 JACK.   You are not to talk of Miss Cardew like that. I don't like it.

ALGERNON.   Well, I don't like your clothes. You look perfectly ridiculous in them. Why on earth don't you go up and change? It is perfectly childish to be in deep
440 mourning for a man who is actually staying for a whole week with you in your house as a guest. I call it grotesque.

JACK.   You are certainly not staying with me for a whole week as a guest or anything else. You have got to leave
445 … by the four-five train.

ALGERNON.   I certainly won't leave you so long as you are in mourning. It would be most unfriendly. If I were in mourning you would stay with me, I suppose. I should think it very unkind if you didn't.

450 JACK.   Well, will you go if I change my clothes?

ALGERNON.   Yes, if you are not too long. I never saw anybody take so long to dress, and with such little result.

JACK.   Well, at any rate, that is better than being always over-dressed as you are.

455 ALGERNON.   If I am occasionally a little over-dressed, I make up for it by being always immensely over-educated.

JACK.   Your vanity is ridiculous, your conduct an outrage, and your presence in my garden utterly absurd.
460 However, you have got to catch the four-five, and I hope you will have a pleasant journey back to town. This Bunburying, as you call it, has not been a great

---

[1] *dog-cart*   Small horse-drawn carriage in which the occupants would sit back-to-back; a box for conveying hunting dogs was also typically part of the contraption.

success for you. (*Goes into the house.*)

ALGERNON.   I think it has been a great success. I'm in
465 love with Cecily, and that is everything.

(*Enter Cecily at the back of the garden. She picks up the can and begins to water the flowers.*)

But I must see her before I go, and make arrangements for another Bunbury. Ah, there she is.

CECILY.   Oh, I merely came back to water the roses. I thought you were with Uncle Jack.

470 ALGERNON.   He's gone to order the dog-cart for me.

CECILY.   Oh, is he going to take you for a nice drive?

ALGERNON.   He's going to send me away.

CECILY.   Then have we got to part?

ALGERNON.   I am afraid so. It's a very painful parting.

475 CECILY.   It is always painful to part from people whom one has known for a very brief space of time. The absence of old friends one can endure with equanimity. But even a momentary separation from anyone to whom one has just been introduced is almost unbearable.

480 ALGERNON.   Thank you.

(*Enter Merriman.*)

MERRIMAN.   The dog-cart is at the door, sir.

(*Algernon looks appealingly at Cecily.*)

CECILY.   It can wait, Merriman for … five minutes.

MERRIMAN.   Yes, Miss.

(*Exit Merriman.*)

ALGERNON.   I hope, Cecily, I shall not offend you if I
485 state quite frankly and openly that you seem to me to be in every way the visible personification of absolute perfection.

CECILY.   I think your frankness does you great credit, Ernest. If you will allow me, I will copy your remarks
490 into my diary. (*Goes over to table and begins writing in diary.*)

ALGERNON.   Do you really keep a diary? I'd give anything to look at it. May I?

CECILY. Oh no. (*Puts her hand over it.*) You see, it is simply a very young girl's record of her own thoughts and impressions, and consequently meant for publication. When it appears in volume form I hope you will order a copy. But pray, Ernest, don't stop. I delight in taking down from dictation. I have reached "absolute perfection." You can go on. I am quite ready for more.

ALGERNON. (*Somewhat taken aback.*) Ahem! Ahem!

CECILY. Oh, don't cough, Ernest. When one is dictating one should speak fluently and not cough. Besides, I don't know how to spell a cough. (*Writes as Algernon speaks.*)

ALGERNON. (*Speaking very rapidly.*) Cecily, ever since I first looked upon your wonderful and incomparable beauty, I have dared to love you wildly, passionately, devotedly, hopelessly.

CECILY. I don't think that you should tell me that you love me wildly, passionately, devotedly, hopelessly. Hopelessly doesn't seem to make much sense, does it?

ALGERNON. Cecily!

(*Enter Merriman.*)

MERRIMAN. The dog-cart is waiting, sir.

ALGERNON. Tell it to come round next week, at the same hour.

MERRIMAN. (*Looks at Cecily, who makes no sign.*) Yes, sir.

(*Merriman retires.*)

CECILY. Uncle Jack would be very much annoyed if he knew you were staying on till next week, at the same hour.

ALGERNON. Oh, I don't care about Jack. I don't care for anybody in the whole world but you. I love you, Cecily. You will marry me, won't you?

CECILY. You silly boy! Of course. Why, we have been engaged for the last three months?

ALGERNON. For the last three months?

CECILY. Yes, it will be exactly three months on Thursday.

ALGERNON. But how did we become engaged?

CECILY. Well, ever since dear Uncle Jack first confessed to us that he had a younger brother who was very wicked and bad, you of course have formed the chief topic of conversation between myself and Miss Prism. And of course a man who is much talked about is always very attractive. One feels there must be something in him, after all. I daresay it was foolish of me, but I fell in love with you, Ernest.

ALGERNON. Darling! And when was the engagement actually settled?

CECILY. On the 14th of February last. Worn out by your entire ignorance of my existence, I determined to end the matter one way or the other, and after a long struggle with myself I accepted you under this dear old tree here. The next day I bought this little ring in your name, and this is the little bangle with the true lover's knot I promised you always to wear.

ALGERNON. Did I give you this? It's very pretty, isn't it?

CECILY. Yes, you've wonderfully good taste, Ernest. It's the excuse I've always given for your leading such a bad life. And this is the box in which I keep all your dear letters. (*Kneels at table, opens box, and produces letters tied up with blue ribbon.*)

ALGERNON. My letters! But, my own sweet Cecily, I have never written you any letters.

CECILY. You need hardly remind me of that, Ernest. I remember only too well that I was forced to write your letters for you. I wrote always three times a week, and sometimes oftener.

ALGERNON. Oh, do let me read them, Cecily?

CECILY. Oh, I couldn't possibly. They would make you far too conceited. (*Replaces box.*) The three you wrote me after I had broken off the engagement are so beautiful, and so badly spelled, that even now I can hardly read them without crying a little.

ALGERNON. But was our engagement ever broken off?

CECILY. Of course it was. On the 22nd of last March. You can see the entry if you like. (*Shows diary.*) "To-day I broke off my engagement with Ernest. I feel it is better to do so. The weather still continues charming."

ALGERNON. But why on earth did you break it off? What had I done? I had done nothing at all. Cecily, I am very much hurt indeed to hear you broke it off. Particularly when the weather was so charming.

CECILY. It would hardly have been a really serious engagement if it hadn't been broken off at least once. But I forgave you before the week was out.

ALGERNON. (*Crossing to her, and kneeling.*) What a

perfect angel you are, Cecily.

CECILY. You dear romantic boy. (*He kisses her, she puts her fingers through his hair.*) I hope your hair curls naturally, does it?

ALGERNON. Yes, darling, with a little help from others.

CECILY. I am so glad.

ALGERNON. You'll never break off our engagement again, Cecily?

CECILY. I don't think I could break it off now that I have actually met you. Besides, of course, there is the question of your name.

ALGERNON. Yes, of course. (*Nervously.*)

CECILY. You must not laugh at me, darling, but it had always been a girlish dream of mine to love some one whose name was Ernest. (*Algernon rises, Cecily also.*) There is something in that name that seems to inspire absolute confidence. I pity any poor married woman whose husband is not called Ernest.

ALGERNON. But, my dear child, do you mean to say you could not love me if I had some other name?

CECILY. But what name?

ALGERNON. Oh, any name you like—Algernon—for instance …

CECILY. But I don't like the name of Algernon.

ALGERNON. Well, my own dear, sweet, loving little darling, I really can't see why you should object to the name of Algernon. It is not at all a bad name. In fact, it is rather an aristocratic name. Half of the chaps who get into the Bankruptcy Court are called Algernon. But seriously, Cecily … (*Moving to her*) … if my name was Algy, couldn't you love me?

CECILY. (*Rising.*) I might respect you, Ernest, I might admire your character, but I fear that I should not be able to give you my undivided attention.

ALGERNON. Ahem! Cecily! (*Picking up hat.*) Your Rector here is, I suppose, thoroughly experienced in the practice of all the rites and ceremonials of the Church?

CECILY. Oh, yes. Dr. Chasuble is a most learned man. He has never written a single book, so you can imagine how much he knows.

ALGERNON. I must see him at once on a most important christening—I mean on most important business.

CECILY. Oh!

ALGERNON. I shan't be away more than half an hour.

CECILY. Considering that we have been engaged since February the 14th, and that I only met you to-day for the first time, I think it is rather hard that you should leave me for so long a period as half an hour. Couldn't you make it twenty minutes?

ALGERNON. I'll be back in no time.

(*Kisses her and rushes down the garden.*)

CECILY. What an impetuous boy he is! I like his hair so much. I must enter his proposal in my diary.

(*Enter Merriman.*)

MERRIMAN. A Miss Fairfax has just called to see Mr. Worthing. On very important business, Miss Fairfax states.

CECILY. Isn't Mr. Worthing in his library?

MERRIMAN. Mr. Worthing went over in the direction of the Rectory some time ago.

CECILY. Pray ask the lady to come out here; Mr. Worthing is sure to be back soon. And you can bring tea.

MERRIMAN. Yes, Miss. (*Goes out.*)

CECILY. Miss Fairfax! I suppose one of the many good elderly women who are associated with Uncle Jack in some of his philanthropic work in London. I don't quite like women who are interested in philanthropic work. I think it is so forward of them.

(*Enter Merriman.*)

MERRIMAN. Miss Fairfax.

(*Enter Gwendolen. Exit Merriman.*)

CECILY. (*Advancing to meet her.*) Pray let me introduce myself to you. My name is Cecily Cardew.

GWENDOLEN. Cecily Cardew? (*Moving to her and shaking hands.*) What a very sweet name! Something tells me that we are going to be great friends. I like you already more than I can say. My first impressions of people are never wrong.

CECILY. How nice of you to like me so much after we have known each other such a comparatively short time. Pray sit down.

GWENDOLEN. (*Still standing up.*) I may call you Cecily,

may I not?

CECILY. With pleasure!

GWENDOLEN. And you will always call me Gwendolen, won't you?

660 CECILY. If you wish.

GWENDOLEN. Then that is all quite settled, is it not?

CECILY. I hope so. (*A pause. They both sit down together.*)

GWENDOLEN. Perhaps this might be a favourable opportunity for my mentioning who I am. My father is

665 Lord Bracknell. You have never heard of Papa, I suppose?

CECILY. I don't think so.

GWENDOLEN. Outside the family circle, Papa, I am glad to say, is entirely unknown. I think that is quite as it

670 should be. The home seems to me to be the proper sphere for the man. And certainly once a man begins to neglect his domestic duties he becomes painfully effeminate, does he not? And I don't like that. It makes men so very attractive. Cecily, Mamma, whose views on

675 education are remarkably strict, has brought me up to be extremely short-sighted; it is part of her system; so do you mind my looking at you through my glasses?

CECILY. Oh! not at all, Gwendolen. I am very fond of being looked at.

680 GWENDOLEN. (*After examining Cecily carefully through a lorgnette.*) You are here on a short visit, I suppose.

CECILY. Oh no! I live here.

GWENDOLEN. (*Severely.*) Really? Your mother, no doubt, or some female relative of advanced years, resides

685 here also?

CECILY. Oh no! I have no mother, nor, in fact, any relations.

GWENDOLEN. Indeed?

CECILY. My dear guardian, with the assistance of Miss

690 Prism, has the arduous task of looking after me.

GWENDOLEN. Your guardian?

CECILY. Yes, I am Mr. Worthing's ward.

GWENDOLEN. Oh! It is strange he never mentioned to me that he had a ward. How secretive of him! He grows

695 more interesting hourly. I am not sure, however, that the news inspires me with feelings of unmixed delight. (*Rising and going to her.*) I am very fond of you, Cecily; I have liked you ever since I met you! But I am bound to state that now that I know that you are Mr. Worth-

700 ing's ward, I cannot help expressing a wish you were—

well, just a little older than you seem to be—and not quite so very alluring in appearance. In fact, if I may speak candidly—

CECILY. Pray do! I think that whenever one has anything

705 unpleasant to say, one should always be quite candid.

GWENDOLEN. Well, to speak with perfect candour, Cecily, I wish that you were fully forty-two, and more than usually plain for your age. Ernest has a strong upright nature. He is the very soul of truth and honour.

710 Disloyalty would be as impossible to him as deception. But even men of the noblest possible moral character are extremely susceptible to the influence of the physical charms of others. Modern, no less than Ancient History, supplies us with many most painful examples of what I

715 refer to. If it were not so, indeed, History would be quite unreadable.

CECILY. I beg your pardon, Gwendolen, did you say Ernest?

GWENDOLEN. Yes.

720 CECILY. Oh, but it is not Mr. Ernest Worthing who is my guardian. It is his brother—his elder brother.

GWENDOLEN. (*Sitting down again.*) Ernest never mentioned to me that he had a brother.

CECILY. I am sorry to say they have not been on good

725 terms for a long time.

GWENDOLEN. Ah! that accounts for it. And now that I think of it I have never heard any man mention his brother. The subject seems distasteful to most men. Cecily, you have lifted a load from my mind. I was

730 growing almost anxious. It would have been terrible if any cloud had come across a friendship like ours, would it not? Of course you are quite, quite sure that it is not Mr. Ernest Worthing who is your guardian?

CECILY. Quite sure. (*A pause.*) In fact, I am going to be

735 his.

GWENDOLEN. (*Inquiringly.*) I beg your pardon?

CECILY. (*Rather shy and confidingly.*) Dearest Gwendolen, there is no reason why I should make a secret of it to you. Our little county newspaper is sure to chronicle

740 the fact next week. Mr. Ernest Worthing and I are engaged to be married.

GWENDOLEN. (*Quite politely, rising.*) My darling Cecily, I think there must be some slight error. Mr. Ernest Worthing is engaged to me. The announcement will

745 appear in the *Morning Post* on Saturday at the latest.

CECILY. (*Very politely, rising.*) I am afraid you must be under some misconception. Ernest proposed to me exactly ten minutes ago. (*Shows diary.*)

750 GWENDOLEN. (*Examines diary through her lorgnette carefully.*) It is certainly very curious, for he asked me to be his wife yesterday afternoon at 5.30. If you would care to verify the incident, pray do so. (*Produces diary of her own.*) I never travel without my diary. One should always have something sensational to read in the train.

755 I am so sorry, dear Cecily, if it is any disappointment to you, but I am afraid I have the prior claim.

CECILY. It would distress me more than I can tell you, dear Gwendolen, if it caused you any mental or physical anguish, but I feel bound to point out that since Ernest

760 proposed to you he clearly has changed his mind.

GWENDOLEN. (*Meditatively.*) If the poor fellow has been entrapped into any foolish promise I shall consider it my duty to rescue him at once, and with a firm hand.

CECILY. (*Thoughtfully and sadly.*) Whatever unfortunate

765 entanglement my dear boy may have got into, I will never reproach him with it after we are married.

GWENDOLEN. Do you allude to me, Miss Cardew, as an entanglement? You are presumptuous. On an occasion of this kind it becomes more than a moral duty to speak

770 one's mind. It becomes a pleasure.

CECILY. Do you suggest, Miss Fairfax, that I entrapped Ernest into an engagement? How dare you? This is no time for wearing the shallow mask of manners. When I see a spade I call it a spade.

775 GWENDOLEN. (*Satirically.*) I am glad to say that I have never seen a spade. It is obvious that our social spheres have been widely different.

(*Enter Merriman, followed by the footman. He carries a salver, table cloth, and plate stand. Cecily is about to retort. The presence of the servants exercises a restraining influence, under which both girls chafe.*)

MERRIMAN. Shall I lay tea here as usual, Miss?

CECILY. (*Sternly, in a calm voice.*) Yes, as usual.

(*Merriman begins to clear table and lay cloth. A long pause. Cecily and Gwendolen glare at each other.*)

780 GWENDOLEN. Are there many interesting walks in the vicinity, Miss Cardew?

CECILY. Oh! yes! a great many. From the top of one of the hills quite close one can see five counties.

GWENDOLEN. Five counties! I don't think I should like

785 that; I hate crowds.

CECILY. (*Sweetly.*) I suppose that is why you live in town?

(*Gwendolen bites her lip, and beats her foot nervously with her parasol.*)

GWENDOLEN. (*Looking round.*) Quite a well-kept garden this is, Miss Cardew.

790 CECILY. So glad you like it, Miss Fairfax.

GWENDOLEN. I had no idea there were any flowers in the country.

CECILY. Oh, flowers are as common here, Miss Fairfax, as people are in London.

795 GWENDOLEN. Personally I cannot understand how anybody manages to exist in the country, if anybody who is anybody does. The country always bores me to death.

CECILY. Ah! This is what the newspapers call agricultural

800 depression,[1] is it not? I believe the aristocracy are suffering very much from it just at present. It is almost an epidemic amongst them, I have been told. May I offer you some tea, Miss Fairfax?

GWENDOLEN. (*With elaborate politeness.*) Thank you.

805 (*Aside.*) Detestable girl! But I require tea!

CECILY. (*Sweetly.*) Sugar?

GWENDOLEN. (*Superciliously.*) No, thank you. Sugar is not fashionable any more. (*Cecily looks angrily at her, takes up the tongs and puts four lumps of sugar into the*

810 *cup.*)

CECILY. (*Severely.*) Cake or bread and butter?

GWENDOLEN. (*In a bored manner.*) Bread and butter, please. Cake is rarely seen at the best houses nowadays.

CECILY. (*Cuts a very large slice of cake, and puts it on the*

815 *tray.*) Hand that to Miss Fairfax.

---

[1] *agricultural depression* The British economy in general was in depression from 1873 until the mid-1890s; the agricultural sector was depressed from 1875 until the mid-1890s.

(*Merriman does so, and goes out with footman. Gwendolen drinks the tea and makes a grimace. Puts down cup at once, reaches out her hand to the bread and butter, looks at it, and finds it is cake. Rises in indignation.*)

GWENDOLEN. You have filled my tea with lumps of sugar, and though I asked most distinctly for bread and butter, you have given me cake. I am known for the gentleness of my disposition, and the extraordinary
820 sweetness of my nature, but I warn you, Miss Cardew, you may go too far.

CECILY. (*Rising.*) To save my poor, innocent, trusting boy from the machinations of any other girl there are no lengths to which I would not go.

825 GWENDOLEN. From the moment I saw you I distrusted you. I felt that you were false and deceitful. I am never deceived in such matters. My first impressions of people are invariably right.

CECILY. It seems to me, Miss Fairfax, that I am trespass-
830 ing on your valuable time. No doubt you have many other calls of a similar character to make in the neighbourhood.

(*Enter Jack.*)

GWENDOLEN. (*Catching sight of him.*) Ernest! My own Ernest!

835 JACK. Gwendolen! Darling! (*Offers to kiss her.*)

GWENDOLEN. (*Draws back.*) A moment! May I ask if you are engaged to be married to this young lady? (*Points to Cecily.*)

JACK. (*Laughing.*) To dear little Cecily! Of course not!
840 What could have put such an idea into your pretty little head?

GWENDOLEN. Thank you. You may! (*Offers her cheek.*)

CECILY. (*Very sweetly.*) I knew there must be some misunderstanding, Miss Fairfax. The gentleman whose
845 arm is at present round your waist is my guardian, Mr. John Worthing.

GWENDOLEN. I beg your pardon?

CECILY. This is Uncle Jack.

GWENDOLEN. (*Receding.*) Jack! Oh!

(*Enter Algernon.*)

850 CECILY. Here is Ernest.

ALGERNON. (*Goes straight over to Cecily without noticing any one else.*) My own love! (*Offers to kiss her.*)

CECILY. (*Drawing back.*) A moment, Ernest! May I ask you—are you engaged to be married to this young lady?

855 ALGERNON. (*Looking round.*) To what young lady? Good heavens! Gwendolen!

CECILY. Yes! to good heavens, Gwendolen, I mean to Gwendolen.

ALGERNON. (*Laughing.*) Of course not! What could
860 have put such an idea into your pretty little head?

CECILY. Thank you. (*Presenting her cheek to be kissed.*) You may.

(*Algernon kisses her.*)

GWENDOLEN. I felt there was some slight error, Miss Cardew. The gentleman who is now embracing you is
865 my cousin, Mr. Algernon Moncrieff.

CECILY. (*Breaking away from Algernon.*) Algernon Moncrieff! Oh!

(*The two girls move towards each other and put their arms round each other's waists as if for protection.*)

CECILY. Are you called Algernon?

ALGERNON. I cannot deny it.

870 CECILY. Oh!

GWENDOLEN. Is your name really John?

JACK. (*Standing rather proudly.*) I could deny it if I liked. I could deny anything if I liked. But my name certainly is John. It has been John for years.

875 CECILY. (*To Gwendolen.*) A gross deception has been practised on both of us.

GWENDOLEN. My poor wounded Cecily!

CECILY. My sweet wronged Gwendolen!

GWENDOLEN. (*Slowly and seriously.*) You will call me
880 sister, will you not? (*They embrace. Jack and Algernon groan and walk up and down.*)

CECILY. (*Rather brightly.*) There is just one question I would like to be allowed to ask my guardian.

GWENDOLEN. An admirable idea! Mr. Worthing, there
885 is just one question I would like to be permitted to put to you. Where is your brother Ernest? We are both engaged to be married to your brother Ernest, so it is a

matter of some importance to us to know where your brother Ernest is at present.

890 JACK. (*Slowly and hesitatingly.*) Gwendolen—Cecily—it is very painful for me to be forced to speak the truth. It is the first time in my life that I have ever been reduced to such a painful position, and I am really quite inexperienced in doing anything of the kind. However, I will

895 tell you quite frankly that I have no brother Ernest. I have no brother at all. I never had a brother in my life, and I certainly have not the smallest intention of ever having one in the future.

CECILY. (*Surprised.*) No brother at all?

900 JACK. (*Cheerily.*) None!

GWENDOLEN. (*Severely.*) Had you never a brother of any kind?

JACK. (*Pleasantly.*) Never. Not even of an kind.

GWENDOLEN. I am afraid it is quite clear, Cecily, that

905 neither of us is engaged to be married to any one.

CECILY. It is not a very pleasant position for a young girl suddenly to find herself in. Is it?

GWENDOLEN. Let us go into the house. They will hardly venture to come after us there.

910 CECILY. No, men are so cowardly, aren't they?

(*They retire into the house with scornful looks.*)

JACK. This ghastly state of things is what you call Bunburying, I suppose?

ALGERNON. Yes, and a perfectly wonderful Bunbury it is. The most wonderful Bunbury I have ever had in my

915 life.

JACK. Well, you've no right whatsoever to Bunbury here.

ALGERNON. That is absurd. One has a right to Bunbury anywhere one chooses. Every serious Bunburyist knows that.

920 JACK. Serious Bunburyist! Good heavens!

ALGERNON. Well, one must be serious about something, if one wants to have any amusement in life. I happen to be serious about Bunburying. What on earth you are serious about I haven't got the remotest idea. About

925 everything, I should fancy. You have such an absolutely trivial nature.

JACK. Well, the only small satisfaction I have in the whole of this wretched business is that your friend Bunbury is quite exploded. You won't be able to run

930 down to the country quite so often as you used to do, dear Algy. And a very good thing too.

ALGERNON. Your brother is a little off colour, isn't he, dear Jack? You won't be able to disappear to London quite so frequently as your wicked custom was. And not

935 a bad thing either.

JACK. As for your conduct towards Miss Cardew, I must say that your taking in a sweet, simple, innocent girl like that is quite inexcusable. To say nothing of the fact that she is my ward.

940 ALGERNON. I can see no possible defence at all for your deceiving a brilliant, clever, thoroughly experienced young lady like Miss Fairfax. To say nothing of the fact that she is my cousin.

JACK. I wanted to be engaged to Gwendolen, that is all.

945 I love her.

ALGERNON. Well, I simply wanted to be engaged to Cecily. I adore her.

JACK. There is certainly no chance of your marrying Miss Cardew.

950 ALGERNON. I don't think there is much likelihood, Jack, of you and Miss Fairfax being united.

JACK. Well, that is no business of yours.

ALGERNON. If it was my business, I wouldn't talk about it. (*Begins to eat muffins.*) It is very vulgar to talk about

955 one's business. Only people like stock-brokers do that, and then merely at dinner parties.

JACK. How can you sit there, calmly eating muffins when we are in this horrible trouble, I can't make out. You seem to me to be perfectly heartless.

960 ALGERNON. Well, I can't eat muffins in an agitated manner. The butter would probably get on my cuffs. One should always eat muffins quite calmly. It is the only way to eat them.

JACK. I say it's perfectly heartless your eating muffins at

965 all, under the circumstances.

ALGERNON. When I am in trouble, eating is the only thing that consoles me. Indeed, when I am in really great trouble, as any one who knows me intimately will tell you, I refuse everything except food and drink. At

970 the present moment I am eating muffins because I am unhappy. Besides, I am particularly fond of muffins. (*Rising.*)

JACK. (*Rising.*) Well, that is no reason why you should eat them all in that greedy way. (*Takes muffins from*

975 *Algernon.*)

ALGERNON.   (*Offering tea-cake.*) I wish you would have tea-cake instead. I don't like tea-cake.

JACK.   Good heavens! I suppose a man may eat his own muffins in his own garden.

980 ALGERNON.   But you have just said it was perfectly heartless to eat muffins.

JACK.   I said it was perfectly heartless of you, under the circumstances. That is a very different thing.

ALGERNON.   That may be. But the muffins are the same.

(*He seizes the muffin-dish from Jack.*)

985 JACK.   Algy, I wish to goodness you would go.

ALGERNON.   You can't possibly ask me to go without having some dinner. It's absurd. I never go without my dinner. No one ever does, except vegetarians and people like that. Besides I have just made arrangements with

990 Dr. Chasuble to be christened at a quarter to six under the name of Ernest.

JACK.   My dear fellow, the sooner you give up that nonsense the better. I made arrangements this morning with Dr. Chasuble to be christened myself at 5:30, and

995 I naturally will take the name of Ernest. Gwendolen would wish it. We can't both be christened Ernest. It's absurd. Besides, I have a perfect right to be christened if I like. There is no evidence at all that I have ever been christened by anybody. I should think it extremely

1000 probable I never was, and so does Dr. Chasuble. It is entirely different in your case. You have been christened already.

ALGERNON.   Yes, but I have not been christened for years.

1005 JACK.   Yes, but you have been christened. That is the important thing.

ALGERNON.   Quite so. So I know my constitution can stand it. If you are not quite sure about your ever having been christened, I must say I think it rather dangerous

1010 your venturing on it now. It might make you very unwell. You can hardly have forgotten that some one very closely connected with you was very nearly carried off this week in Paris by a severe chill.

JACK.   Yes, but you said yourself that a severe chill was

1015 not hereditary.

ALGERNON.   It usen't to be, I know—but I daresay it is

now. Science is always making wonderful improvements in things.

JACK.   (*Picking up the muffin-dish.*) Oh, that is nonsense;

1020 you are always talking nonsense.

ALGERNON.   Jack, you are at the muffins again! I wish you wouldn't. There are only two left. (*Takes them.*) I told you I was particularly fond of muffins.

JACK.   But I hate tea-cake.

1025 ALGERNON.   Why on earth then do you allow tea-cake to be served up for your guests? What ideas you have of hospitality!

JACK.   Algernon! I have already told you to go. I don't want you here. Why don't you go!

1030 ALGERNON.   I haven't quite finished my tea yet! and there is still one muffin left. (*Jack groans, and sinks into a chair. Algernon still continues eating.*)

ACT DROP

ACT 3

SCENE

(*Morning-room at the Manor House. Gwendolen and Cecily are at the window, looking out into the garden.*)

GWENDOLEN.   The fact that they did not follow us at once into the house, as any one else would have done, seems to me to show that they have some sense of shame left.

5 CECILY.   They have been eating muffins. That looks like repentance.

GWENDOLEN.   (*After a pause.*) They don't seem to notice us at all. Couldn't you cough?

CECILY.   But I haven't got a cough.

10 GWENDOLEN.   They're looking at us. What effrontery!

CECILY.   They're approaching. That's very forward of them.

GWENDOLEN.   Let us preserve a dignified silence.

CECILY.   Certainly. It's the only thing to do now.

(*Enter Jack followed by Algernon. They whistle some dreadful popular air from a British Opera.*)

15 GWENDOLEN.   This dignified silence seems to produce

an unpleasant effect.

CECILY. A most distasteful one.

GWENDOLEN. But we will not be the first to speak.

CECILY. Certainly not.

20 GWENDOLEN. Mr. Worthing, I have something very particular to ask you. Much depends on your reply.

CECILY. Gwendolen, your common sense is invaluable. Mr. Moncrieff, kindly answer me the following question. Why did you pretend to be my guardian's brother?

25 ALGERNON. In order that I might have an opportunity of meeting you.

CECILY. (To Gwendolen.) That certainly seems a satisfactory explanation, does it not?

GWENDOLEN. Yes, dear, if you can believe him.

30 CECILY. I don't. But that does not affect the wonderful beauty of his answer.

GWENDOLEN. True. In matters of grave importance, style, not sincerity is the vital thing. Mr. Worthing, what explanation can you offer to me for pretending to 35 have a brother? Was it in order that you might have an opportunity of coming up to town to see me as often as possible?

JACK. Can you doubt it, Miss Fairfax?

GWENDOLEN. I have the gravest doubts upon the 40 subject. But I intend to crush them. This is not the moment for German scepticism.[1] (Moving to Cecily.) Their explanations appear to be quite satisfactory, especially Mr. Worthing's. That seems to me to have the stamp of truth upon it.

45 CECILY. I am more than content with what Mr. Moncrieff said. His voice alone inspires one with absolute credulity.

GWENDOLEN. Then you think we should forgive them?

CECILY. Yes. I mean no.

50 GWENDOLEN. True! I had forgotten. There are principles at stake that one cannot surrender. Which of us should tell them? The task is not a pleasant one.

CECILY. Could we not both speak at the same time?

GWENDOLEN. An excellent idea! I nearly always speak at 55 the same time as other people. Will you take the time from me?

CECILY. Certainly.

---

[1] *German scepticism* According to the school of philosophy deriving from Immanuel Kant, we do not always perceive the true state of things-in-themselves.

(Gwendolen beats time with uplifted finger.)

GWENDOLEN and CECILY (Speaking together.) Your Christian names are still an insuperable barrier. That is 60 all!

JACK and ALGERNON (Speaking together.) Our Christian names! Is that all? But we are going to be christened this afternoon.

GWENDOLEN. (To Jack.) For my sake you are prepared 65 to do this terrible thing?

JACK. I am.

CECILY. (To Algernon.) To please me you are ready to face this fearful ordeal?

ALGERNON. I am!

70 GWENDOLEN. How absurd to talk of the equality of the sexes! Where questions of self-sacrifice are concerned, men are infinitely beyond us.

JACK. We are. (Clasps hands with Algernon.)

CECILY. They have moments of physical courage of 75 which we women know absolutely nothing.

GWENDOLEN. (To Jack.) Darling!

ALGERNON. (To Cecily.) Darling! (They fall into each other's arms.)

(Enter Merriman. When he enters he coughs loudly, seeing the situation.)

MERRIMAN. Ahem! Ahem! Lady Bracknell!

80 JACK. Good heavens!

(Enter Lady Bracknell. The couples separate in alarm. Exit Merriman.)

LADY BRACKNELL. Gwendolen! What does this mean?

GWENDOLEN. Merely that I am engaged to be married to Mr. Worthing, Mamma.

LADY BRACKNELL. Come here. Sit down. Sit down 85 immediately. Hesitation of any kind is a sign of mental decay in the young, of physical weakness in the old. (Turns to Jack.) Apprised, sir, of my daughter's sudden flight by her trusty maid, whose confidence I purchased by means of a small coin, I followed her at once by a 90 luggage train. Her unhappy father is, I am glad to say, under the impression that she is attending a more than usually lengthy lecture by the University Extension

Scheme on the Influence of a permanent income on Thought. I do not propose to undeceive him. Indeed I have never undeceived him on any question. I would consider it wrong. But of course, you will clearly understand that all communication between yourself and my daughter must cease immediately from this moment. On this point, as indeed on all points, I am firm.

JACK.   I am engaged to be married to Gwendolen, Lady Bracknell!

LADY BRACKNELL.   You are nothing of the kind, sir. And now, as regards Algernon! … Algernon!

ALGERNON.   Yes, Aunt Augusta.

LADY BRACKNELL.   May I ask if it is in this house that your invalid friend Mr. Bunbury resides?

ALGERNON.   (*Stammering.*) Oh! No! Bunbury doesn't live here. Bunbury is somewhere else at present. In fact, Bunbury is dead.

LADY BRACKNELL.   Dead! When did Mr. Bunbury die? His death must have been extremely sudden.

ALGERNON.   (*Airily.*) Oh! I killed Bunbury this afternoon. I mean poor Bunbury died this afternoon.

LADY BRACKNELL.   What did he die of?

ALGERNON.   Bunbury? Oh, he was quite exploded.

LADY BRACKNELL.   Exploded! Was he the victim of a revolutionary outrage? I was not aware that Mr. Bunbury was interested in social legislation. If so, he is well punished for his morbidity.

ALGERNON.   My dear Aunt Augusta, I mean he was found out! The doctors found out that Bunbury could not live, that is what I mean—so Bunbury died.

LADY BRACKNELL.   He seems to have had great confidence in the opinion of his physicians. I am glad, however, that he made up his mind at the last to some definite course of action, and acted under proper medical advice. And now that we have finally got rid of this Mr. Bunbury, may I ask, Mr. Worthing, who is that young person whose hand my nephew Algernon is now holding in what seems to me a peculiarly unnecessary manner?

JACK.   That lady is Miss Cecily Cardew, my ward.

(*Lady Bracknell bows coldly to Cecily.*)

ALGERNON.   I am engaged to be married to Cecily, Aunt Augusta.

LADY BRACKNELL.   I beg your pardon?

CECILY.   Mr. Moncrieff and I are engaged to be married, Lady Bracknell.

LADY BRACKNELL.   (*With a shiver, crossing to the sofa and sitting down.*) I do not know whether there is anything peculiarly exciting in the air of this particular part of Hertfordshire, but the number of engagements that go on seems to me considerably above the proper average that statistics have laid down for our guidance. I think some preliminary inquiry on my part would not be out of place. Mr. Worthing, is Miss Cardew at all connected with any of the larger railway stations in London? I merely desire information. Until yesterday I had no idea that there were any families or persons whose origin was a Terminus.

(*Jack looks perfectly furious, but restrains himself.*)

JACK.   (*In a clear, cold voice.*) Miss Cardew is the granddaughter of the late Mr. Thomas Cardew of 149 Belgrave Square, S.W.; Gervase Park, Dorking, Surrey; and the Sporran, Fifeshire, N.B.

LADY BRACKNELL.   That sounds not unsatisfactory. Three addresses always inspire confidence, even in tradesmen. But what proof have I of their authenticity?

JACK.   I have carefully preserved the Court Guides[1] of the period. They are open to your inspection, Lady Bracknell.

LADY BRACKNELL.   (*Grimly.*) I have known strange errors in that publication.

JACK.   Miss Cardew's family solicitors are Messrs. Markby, Markby, and Markby.

LADY BRACKNELL.   Markby, Markby, and Markby? A firm of the very highest position in their profession. Indeed I am told that one of the Mr. Markbys is occasionally to be seen at dinner parties. So far I am satisfied.

JACK.   (*Very irritably.*) How extremely kind of you, Lady Bracknell! I have also in my possession, you will be pleased to hear, certificates of Miss Cardew's birth, baptism, whooping cough, registration, vaccination, confirmation, and the measles; both the German and the English variety.

---

[1] *Court Guides*   Directory of names and addresses of those members of the nobility, gentry, and society who have been presented at court.

LADY BRACKNELL.   Ah! A life crowded with incident, I see; though perhaps somewhat too exciting for a young girl. I am not myself in favour of premature experiences. (*Rises, looks at her watch.*) Gwendolen! the time approaches for our departure. We have not a moment to lose. As a matter of form, Mr. Worthing, I had better ask you if Miss Cardew has any little fortune?

JACK.   Oh! about a hundred and thirty thousand pounds in the Funds. That is all. Goodbye, Lady Bracknell. So pleased to have seen you.

LADY BRACKNELL.   (*Sitting down again.*) A moment, Mr. Worthing. A hundred and thirty thousand pounds! And in the Funds! Miss Cardew seems to me a most attractive young lady, now that I look at her. Few girls of the present day have any really solid qualities, any of the qualities that last, and improve with time. We live, I regret to say, in an age of surfaces. (*To Cecily.*) Come over here, dear. (*Cecily goes across.*) Pretty child! your dress is sadly simple, and your hair seems almost as Nature might have left it. But we can soon alter all that. A thoroughly experienced French maid produces a really marvellous result in a very brief space of time. I remember recommending one to young Lady Lancing, and after three months her own husband did not know her.

JACK.   And after six months nobody knew her.

LADY BRACKNELL.   (*Glares at Jack for a few moments. Then bends, with a practised smile, to Cecily.*) Kindly turn round, sweet child. (*Cecily turns completely round.*) No, the side view is what I want. (*Cecily presents her profile.*) Yes, quite as I expected. There are distinct social possibilities in your profile. The two weak points in our age are its want of principle and its want of profile. The chin a little higher, dear. Style largely depends on the way the chin is worn. They are worn very high, just at present. Algernon!

ALGERNON.   Yes, Aunt Augusta!

LADY BRACKNELL.   There are distinct social possibilities in Miss Cardew's profile.

ALGERNON.   Cecily is the sweetest, dearest, prettiest girl in the whole world. And I don't care twopence about social possibilities.

LADY BRACKNELL.   Never speak disrespectfully of Society, Algernon. Only people who can't get into it do that. (*To Cecily.*) Dear child, of course you know that Algernon has nothing but his debts to depend upon.

But I do not approve of mercenary marriages. When I married Lord Bracknell I had no fortune of any kind. But I never dreamed for a moment of allowing that to stand in my way. Well, I suppose I must give my consent.

ALGERNON.   Thank you, Aunt Augusta.

LADY BRACKNELL.   Cecily, you may kiss me!

CECILY.   (*Kisses her.*) Thank you, Lady Bracknell.

LADY BRACKNELL.   You may also address me as Aunt Augusta for the future.

CECILY.   Thank you, Aunt Augusta.

LADY BRACKNELL.   The marriage, I think, had better take place quite soon.

ALGERNON.   Thank you, Aunt Augusta.

CECILY.   Thank you, Aunt Augusta.

LADY BRACKNELL.   To speak frankly, I am not in favour of long engagements. They give people the opportunity of finding out each other's character before marriage, which I think is never advisable.

JACK.   I beg your pardon for interrupting you, Lady Bracknell, but this engagement is quite out of the question. I am Miss Cardew's guardian, and she cannot marry without my consent until she comes of age. That consent I absolutely decline to give.

LADY BRACKNELL. Upon what grounds may I ask? Algernon is an extremely, I may almost say an ostentatiously, eligible young man. He has nothing, but he looks everything. What more can one desire?

JACK.   It pains me very much to have to speak frankly to you, Lady Bracknell, about your nephew, but the fact is that I do not approve at all of his moral character. I suspect him of being untruthful.

(*Algernon and Cecily look at him in indignant amazement.*)

LADY BRACKNELL.   Untruthful! My nephew Algernon? Impossible! He is an Oxonian.[1]

JACK.   I fear there can be no possible doubt about the matter. This afternoon during my temporary absence in London on an important question of romance, he obtained admission to my house by means of the false pretence of being my brother. Under an assumed name he drank, I've just been informed by my butler, an

---

1   *Oxonian*   One who has attended Oxford University.

entire pint bottle of my Perrier-Jouet, Brut, '89; wine I
was specially reserving for myself. Continuing his
disgraceful deception, he succeeded in the course of the
afternoon in alienating the affections of my only ward.
He subsequently stayed to tea, and devoured every
single muffin. And what makes his conduct all the more
heartless is, that he was perfectly well aware from the
first that I have no brother, that I never had a brother,
and that I don't intend to have a brother, not even of
any kind. I distinctly told him so myself yesterday
afternoon.

LADY BRACKNELL. Ahem! Mr. Worthing, after careful
consideration I have decided entirely to overlook my
nephew's conduct to you.

JACK.   That is very generous of you, Lady Bracknell. My
own decision, however, is unalterable. I decline to give
my consent.

LADY BRACKNELL.   (*To Cecily.*) Come here, sweet child.
(*Cecily goes over.*) How old are you, dear?

CECILY. Well, I am really only eighteen, but I always
admit to twenty when I go to evening parties.

LADY BRACKNELL. You are perfectly right in making
some slight alteration. Indeed, no woman should ever be
quite accurate about her age. It looks so calculating …
(*In a meditative manner.*) Eighteen, but admitting to
twenty at evening parties. Well, it will not be very long
before you are of age and free from the restraints of
tutelage. So I don't think your guardian's consent is,
after all, a matter of any importance.

JACK.   Pray excuse me, Lady Bracknell, for interrupting
you again, but it is only fair to tell you that according to
the terms of her grandfather's will Miss Cardew does
not come legally of age till she is thirty-five.

LADY BRACKNELL.   That does not seem to me to be a
grave objection. Thirty-five is a very attractive age.
London society is full of women of the very highest
birth who have, of their own free choice, remained
thirty-five for years. Lady Dumbleton is an instance in
point. To my own knowledge she has been thirty-five
ever since she arrived at the age of forty, which was
many years ago now. I see no reason why our dear
Cecily should not be even still more attractive at the age
you mention than she is at present. There will be a large
accumulation of property.

CECILY. Algy, could you wait for me till I was thirty-
five?

ALGERNON. Of course I could, Cecily. You know I
could.

CECILY. Yes, I felt it instinctively, but I couldn't wait all
that time. I hate waiting even five minutes for anybody.
It always makes me rather cross. I am not punctual
myself, I know, but I do like punctuality in others, and
waiting, even to be married, is quite out of the question.

ALGERNON. Then what is to be done, Cecily?

CECILY. I don't know, Mr. Moncrieff.

LADY BRACKNELL. My dear Mr. Worthing, as Miss
Cardew states positively that she cannot wait till she is
thirty-five—a remark which I am bound to say seems to
me to show a somewhat impatient nature— I would beg
of you to reconsider your decision.

JACK.   But my dear Lady Bracknell, the matter is entirely
in your own hands. The moment you consent to my
marriage with Gwendolen, I will most gladly allow your
nephew to form an alliance with my ward.

LADY BRACKNELL. (*Rising and drawing herself up.*) You
must be quite aware that what you propose is out of the
question.

JACK.   Then a passionate celibacy is all that any of us can
look forward to.

LADY BRACKNELL.   That is not the destiny I propose for
Gwendolen. Algernon, of course, can choose for himself. (*Pulls out her watch.*) Come, dear, (*Gwendolen rises*)
we have already missed five, if not six, trains. To miss
any more might expose us to comment on the platform.

(*Enter Dr. Chasuble.*)

CHASUBLE. Everything is quite ready for the christenings.

LADY BRACKNELL. The christenings, sir! Is not that
somewhat premature?

CHASUBLE. (*Looking rather puzzled, and pointing to Jack
and Algernon.*) Both these gentlemen have expressed a
desire for immediate baptism.

LADY BRACKNELL. At their age? The idea is grotesque
and irreligious! Algernon, I forbid you to be baptized. I
will not hear of such excesses. Lord Bracknell would be
highly displeased if he learned that that was the way in
which you wasted your time and money.

345 CHASUBLE. Am I to understand then that there are to be
no christenings at all this afternoon?

JACK. I don't think that, as things are now, it would be
of much practical value to either of us, Dr. Chasuble.

CHASUBLE. I am grieved to hear such sentiments from
350 you, Mr. Worthing. They savour of the heretical views
of the Anabaptists,[1] views that I have completely
refuted in four of my unpublished sermons. However,
as your present mood seems to be one peculiarly
secular, I will return to the church at once. Indeed, I
355 have just been informed by the pew-opener[2] that for
the last hour and a half, Miss Prism has been waiting
for me in the vestry.

LADY BRACKNELL. (*Starting.*) Miss Prism! Did I hear
you mention a Miss Prism?

360 CHASUBLE. Yes, Lady Bracknell. I am on my way to join
her.

LADY BRACKNELL. Pray allow me to detain you for a
moment. This matter may prove to be one of vital
importance to Lord Bracknell and myself. Is this Miss
365 Prism a female of repellent aspect, remotely connected
with education?

CHASUBLE. (*Somewhat indignantly.*) She is the most
cultivated of ladies, and the very picture of respectability.

370 LADY BRACKNELL. It is obviously the same person. May
I ask what position she holds in your household?

CHASUBLE. (*Severely.*) I am a celibate, madam.

JACK. (*Interposing.*) Miss Prism, Lady Bracknell, has
been for the last three years Miss Cardew's esteemed
375 governess and valued companion.

LADY BRACKNELL. In spite of what I hear of her, I must
see her at once. Let her be sent for.

CHASUBLE. (*Looking off.*) She approaches; she is nigh.

(*Enter Miss Prism hurriedly.*)

MISS PRISM. I was told you expected me in the vestry,

---

[1] *heretical views … Anabaptists* Although Anabaptists, members of
a Protestant sect that rejects Anglican doctrine, believe in baptism,
they reject the Anglican custom of baptizing infants. Dr. Chasuble
is suggesting that Jack is heretical in denying the value of baptism in
the Anglican church.

[2] *pew-opener* One assigned to open the doors of pews for privileged
churchgoers.

380 dear Canon. I have been waiting for you there for an
hour and three-quarters.

(*Catches sight of Lady Bracknell, who has fixed her with a
stony glare. Miss Prism grows pale and quails. She looks
anxiously round as if desirous to escape.*)

LADY BRACKNELL. (*In a severe, judicial voice.*) Prism!
(*Miss Prism bows her head in shame.*) Come here, Prism!
(*Miss Prism approaches in a humble manner.*) Prism!
385 Where is that baby? (*General consternation. The Canon
starts back in horror. Algernon and Jack pretend to be
anxious to shield Cecily and Gwendolen from hearing the
details of a terrible public scandal.*) Twenty-eight years
ago, Prism, you left Lord Bracknell's house, Number
390 104, Upper Grosvenor Street, in charge of a perambulator that contained a baby of the male sex. You never
returned. A few weeks later, through the elaborate
investigations of the Metropolitan police, the perambulator was discovered at midnight, standing by itself in a
395 remote corner of Bayswater. It contained the manuscript
of a three-volume novel of more than usually revolting
sentimentality. (*Miss Prism starts in involuntary indignation.*) But the baby was not there! (*Every one looks at
Miss Prism.*) Prism! Where is that baby? (*A pause.*)

400 MISS PRISM. Lady Bracknell, I admit with shame that I
do not know. I only wish I did. The plain facts of the
case are these. On the morning of the day you mention,
a day that is for ever branded on my memory, I prepared
as usual to take the baby out in its perambulator. I had
405 also with me a somewhat old, but capacious hand-bag in
which I had intended to place the manuscript of a work
of fiction that I had written during my few unoccupied
hours. In a moment of mental abstraction, for which I
never can forgive myself, I deposited the manuscript in
410 the bassinette, and placed the baby in the hand-bag.

JACK. (*Who has been listening attentively.*) But where did
you deposit the hand-bag?

MISS PRISM. Do not ask me, Mr. Worthing.

JACK. Miss Prism, this is a matter of no small impor-
415 tance to me. I insist on knowing where you deposited
the hand-bag that contained that infant.

MISS PRISM. I left it in the cloak-room of one of the
larger railway stations in London.

JACK. What railway station?

MISS PRISM. (*Quite crushed.*) Victoria. The Brighton line. (*Sinks into a chair.*)

JACK.   I must retire to my room for a moment. Gwendolen, wait here for me.

GWENDOLEN.   If you are not too long, I will wait here for you all my life.

(*Exit Jack in great excitement.*)

CHASUBLE. What do you think this means, Lady Bracknell?

LADY BRACKNELL.   I dare not even suspect, Dr. Chasuble. I need hardly tell you that in families of high position strange coincidences are not supposed to occur. They are hardly considered the thing.

(*Noises heard overhead as if some one was throwing trunks about. Every one looks up.*)

CECILY. Uncle Jack seems strangely agitated.

CHASUBLE. Your guardian has a very emotional nature.

LADY BRACKNELL. This noise is extremely unpleasant. It sounds as if he was having an argument. I dislike arguments of any kind. They are always vulgar, and often convincing.

CHASUBLE. (*Looking up.*) It has stopped now. (*The noise is redoubled.*)

LADY BRACKNELL. I wish he would arrive at some conclusion.

GWENDOLEN. This suspense is terrible. I hope it will last.

(*Enter Jack with a hand-bag of black leather in his hand.*)

JACK.   (*Rushing over to Miss Prism.*) Is this the handbag, Miss Prism? Examine it carefully before you speak. The happiness of more than one life depends on your answer.

MISS PRISM. (*Calmly.*) It seems to be mine. Yes, here is the injury it received through the upsetting of a Gower Street omnibus[1] in younger and happier days. Here is the stain on the lining caused by the explosion of a temperance beverage,[2] an incident that occurred at Leamington. And here, on the lock, are my initials. I had forgotten that in an extravagant mood I had had them placed there. The bag is undoubtedly mine. I am delighted to have it so unexpectedly restored to me. It has been a great inconvenience being without it all these years.

JACK. (*In a pathetic voice.*) Miss Prism, more is restored to you than this hand-bag. I was the baby you placed in it.

MISS PRISM. (*Amazed.*) You?

JACK. (*Embracing her.*) Yes … mother!

MISS PRISM. (*Recoiling in indignant astonishment.*) Mr. Worthing! I am unmarried!

JACK. Unmarried! I do not deny that is a serious blow. But after all, who has the right to cast a stone against one who has suffered? Cannot repentance wipe out an act of folly? Why should there be one law for men, and another for women? Mother, I forgive you. (*Tries to embrace her again.*)

MISS PRISM. (*Still more indignant.*) Mr. Worthing, there is some error. (*Pointing to Lady Bracknell.*) There is the lady who can tell you who you really are.

JACK. (*After a pause.*) Lady Bracknell, I hate to seem inquisitive, but would you kindly inform me who I am?

LADY BRACKNELL. I am afraid that the news I have to give you will not altogether please you. You are the son of my poor sister, Mrs. Moncrieff, and consequently Algernon's elder brother.

JACK. Algy's elder brother! Then I have a brother after all. I knew I had a brother! I always said I had a brother! Cecily,—how could you have ever doubted that I had a brother? (*Seizes hold of Algernon.*) Dr. Chasuble, my unfortunate brother. Miss Prism, my unfortunate brother. Gwendolen, my unfortunate brother. Algy, you young scoundrel, you will have to treat me with more respect in the future. You have never behaved to me like a brother in all your life.

ALGERNON. Well, not till to-day, old boy, I admit. I did my best, however, though I was out of practice. (*Shakes hands.*)

GWENDOLEN. (*To Jack.*) My own! But what own are you? What is your Christian name, now that you have

---

[1] *Gower Street omnibus* Public horse-drawn bus on a route in central London.

[2] *temperance beverage* Non-alcoholic drink. (The temperance movement aimed to prohibit all alcoholic beverages.)

495 become some one else?

JACK.   Good heavens! … I had quite forgotten that point. Your decision on the subject of my name is irrevocable, I suppose?

GWENDOLEN.   I never change, except in my affections.

500 CECILY.   What a noble nature you have, Gwendolen!

JACK.   Then the question had better be cleared up at once. Aunt Augusta, a moment. At the time when Miss Prism left me in the hand-bag, had I been christened already?

505 LADY BRACKNELL.   Every luxury that money could buy, including christening, had been lavished on you by your fond and doting parents.

JACK.   Then I was christened! That is settled. Now, what name was I given? Let me know the worst.

510 LADY BRACKNELL.   Being the eldest son you were naturally christened after your father.

JACK.   (*Irritably.*) Yes, but what was my father's Christian name?

LADY BRACKNELL.   (*Meditatively.*) I cannot at the present
515 moment recall what the General's Christian name was. But I have no doubt he had one. He was eccentric, I admit. But only in later years. And that was the result of the Indian climate, and marriage, and indigestion, and other things of that kind.

520 JACK.   Algy! Can't you recollect what our father's Christian name was?

ALGERNON.   My dear boy, we were never even on speaking terms. He died before I was a year old.

JACK.   His name would appear in the Army Lists[1] of the
525 period, I suppose, Aunt Augusta?

LADY BRACKNELL.   The General was essentially a man of peace, except in his domestic life. But I have no doubt his name would appear in any military directory.

JACK.   The Army Lists of the last forty years are here.
530 These delightful records should have been my constant study. (*Rushes to bookcase and tears the books out.*) M. Generals … Mallam, Maxbohm, Magley, what ghastly names they have—Markby, Migsby, Mobbs, Moncrieff! Lieutenant 1840, Captain, Lieutenant-Colonel, Colo-
535 nel, General 1869, Christian names, Ernest John. (*Puts book very quietly down and speaks quite calmly.*) I always told you, Gwendolen, my name was Ernest, didn't I? Well, it is Ernest after all. I mean it naturally is Ernest.

LADY BRACKNELL.   Yes, I remember now that the
540 General was called Ernest, I knew I had some particular reason for disliking the name.

GWENDOLEN.   Ernest! My own Ernest! I felt from the first that you could have no other name!

JACK.   Gwendolen, it is a terrible thing for a man to find
545 out suddenly that all his life he has been speaking nothing but the truth. Can you forgive me?

GWENDOLEN.   I can. For I feel that you are sure to change.

JACK.   My own one!

550 CHASUBLE.   (*To Miss Prism.*) Laetitia! (*Embraces her.*)

MISS PRISM.   (*Enthusiastically.*) Frederick! At last!

ALGERNON.   Cecily! (*Embraces her.*)   At last!

JACK.   Gwendolen! (*Embraces her.*)   At last!

LADY BRACKNELL.   My nephew, you seem to be display-
555 ing signs of triviality.

JACK.   On the contrary, Aunt Augusta, I've now realized for the first time in my life the vital Importance of Being Earnest.

TABLEAU

—1895

---

[1] *Army Lists* | Directories of officers.

In Context

Wilde and "The Public"

Interview with Oscar Wilde, *St. James Gazette*, January 1895

I found Mr. Oscar Wilde (writes a Representative) making ready to depart on a short visit to Algiers, and reading—of course, nothing so obvious as a time-table, but a French newspaper which contained an account of the first night of *The Ideal Husband*[1] and its author's appearance after the play.

"How well the French appreciate these brilliant willful moments in an artist's life," remarked Mr. Wilde, handing me the article as if he considered the interview already at an end.

"Does it give you any pleasure," I inquired, "to appear before the curtain after the production of your plays?"

"None whatsoever. No artist finds any interest in seeing the public. The public is very much interested in seeing an artist. Personally, I prefer the French custom, according to which the name of the dramatist is announced to the public by the oldest actor in the piece."

"Would you advocate," I asked, "this custom in England?"

"Certainly. The more the public is interested in artists, the less it is interested in art. The personality of the artist is not a thing the public should know anything about. It is too accidental." Then, after a pause—

"It might be more interesting if the name of the author were announced by the *youngest* actor present."

"It is only in deference, then, to the imperious mandate of the public that you have appeared before the curtain?"

"Yes; I have always been very good-natured about that. The public has always been so appreciative of my work I felt it would be a pity to spoil its evening."

"I notice some people have found fault with the character of your speeches."

"Yes, the old-fashioned idea was that the dramatist should appear and merely thank his kind friends for their patronage and presence. I am glad to say I have altered all that. The artist cannot be degraded into the servant of the public. While I have always recognized the cultured appreciation that actors and audience have shown for my work, I have equally recognized that humility is for the hypocrite, modesty for the incompetent. Assertion is at once the duty and privilege of the artist."

"To what do you attribute, Mr. Wilde, the fact that so few men of letters besides yourself have written plays for public presentation?"

"Primarily the existence of an irresponsible censorship. The fact that my *Salomé* cannot be performed is sufficient to show the folly of such an institution. If painters were obliged to show their pictures to clerks at Somerset House, those who think in form and colour would adopt some other mode of expression. If every novel had to be submitted to a police magistrate, those whose passion is fiction would seek some new mode of realization. No art ever survived censorship; no art ever will."

"And secondly?"

"Secondly to the rumour persistently spread abroad by journalists for the last thirty years, that the duty of the dramatist was to please the public. The aim of art is no more to give pleasure than to give

---

[1] *The Ideal Husband*   I.e., Wilde's play *An Ideal Husband*. The play, which had opened on 3 January 1895, was currently enjoying a very successful run at the Haymarket Theatre.

pain. The aim of art is to be art. As I said once before, the work of art is to dominate the spectator—the spectator is not to dominate art."

"You admit no exceptions?"

"Yes. Circuses where it seems the wishes of the public might be reasonably carried out."

"Do you think," I inquired, "that French dramatic criticism is superior to our own?"

"It would be unfair to confuse French dramatic criticism with English theatrical criticism. The French dramatic critic is always a man of culture and generally a man of letters. In France poets like Gautier[1] have been dramatic critics. In England they are drawn from a less distinguished class. They have neither the same capacities nor the same opportunities. They have all the moral qualities, but none of the artistic qualifications. For the criticism of such a complex mode of art as the drama the highest culture is necessary. No one can criticize drama who is not capable of receiving impressions from the other arts also."

"You admit they are sincere?"

"Yes; but their sincerity is little more than stereotyped stupidity. The critic of the drama should be versatile as the actor. He should be able to change his mood at will and should catch the colour of the moment."

"At least they are honest?"

"Absolutely. I don't believe there is a single dramatic critic in London who would deliberately set himself to misrepresent the work of any dramatist—unless, of course, he personally disliked the dramatist, or had some play of his own he wished to produce at the same theatre, or had an old friend among the actors, or some natural reasons of that kind. I am speaking, however, of London dramatic critics. In the provinces both audience and critics are cultured. In London it is only the audience who are cultured."

"I fear you do not rate our dramatic critics very highly, Mr. Wilde; but, at all events, they are incorruptible?"

"In a market where there are no bidders."

"Still their memories stand them in good stead," I pleaded.

"The old talk of having seen Macready[;][2] that must be a very painful memory. The middle-aged boast that they can recall *Diplomacy*:[3] hardly a pleasant reminiscence."

"You deny them, then, even a creditable past?"

"They have no past and no future, and are incapable of realizing the colour of the moment that finds them at the play."

"What do you propose should be done?"

"They should be pensioned off, and only allowed to write on politics or theology or bimetallism, or some subject easier than art."

"In fact," I said, carried away by Mr. Wilde's aphorisms, "they should be seen and not heard."

"The old should neither be seen nor heard," said Mr. Wilde with some emphasis.

"You said the other day there were only two dramatic critics in London. May I ask—"

"They must have been greatly gratified by such an admission from me; but I am bound to say that since last week I have struck one of them from the list."

"Whom have you left in?"

"I think I had better not mention his name. It might make him too conceited. Conceit is the privilege of the creative."

"How would you define ideal dramatic criticism?"

---

[1] *Gautier*   Théophile Gautier (1811–72), French poet, novelist, and dramatist.

[2] *Macready*   William Charles Macready (1793–1873), English actor and theater manager.

[3] *Diplomacy*   An English adaptation of the French play *Dora* (1878), by Victorien Sardou (1831–1908).

"As far as my work is concerned[,] unqualified appreciation."

"And whom have you omitted?"

"Mr. William Archer, of the *World*."[1]

"What do you chiefly object to in his article?"

"I object to nothing in the article, but I grieve at everything in it. It is bad taste in him to write of me by my Christian name, and he need not have stolen his vulgarisms from the *National Observer* in its most impudent and impotent days."

"Mr. Archer asked whether[,] if it was agreeable to you to be hailed by your Christian name when the enthusiastic spectators called you before the curtain."

"To be so addressed by enthusiastic spectators is as great a compliment as to be written of by one's Christian name is in a journalist bad manners. Bad manners make a journalist."

"Do you think French actors, like French criticism, superior to our own?"

"The English actors act quite as well; but they act best between the lines. They lack the superb elocution of the French—so clear, so cadenced, and so musical. A long sustained speech seems to exhaust them. At the Théâtre Français we go to listen, to an English theatre we go to look. There are, of course, exceptions. Mr. George Alexander, Mr. Lewis Waller, Mr. Forbes Robertson, and others I might mention, have superb voices and know how to use them. I wish I could say the same of the critics; but in the case of the literary drama in England there is too much of what is technically known as 'business.' Yet there is more than one of our English actors who is capable of producing a wonderful dramatic effect by aid of a monosyllable and two cigarettes."

For a moment Mr. Wilde was silent, and then added, "Perhaps, after all, that is acting."

"But are you satisfied with the interpreters of *The Ideal Husband*?"

"I am charmed with all of them. Perhaps they are a little too fascinating. The stage is the refuge of the too fascinating."

"Have you heard it said that all the characters in your play talk as you do?"

"Rumours of that kind have reached me from time to time," said Mr. Wilde, lighting a cigarette, "and I should fancy that some such criticism has been made. The fact is that it is only in the last few years that the dramatic critic has had the opportunity of seeing plays written by anyone who has a mastery of style. In the case of a dramatist, also an artist, it is impossible not to feel that the work of art, to be a work of art, must be dominated by the artist. Every play of Shakespeare is dominated by Shakespeare. Ibsen and Dumas[2] dominate their works. My works are dominated by myself."

"Have you ever been influenced by any of your predecessors?"

"It is enough for me to state definitely, and I hope once for all, that not a single dramatist in this century has ever in the smallest degree influenced me. Only two have interested me."

"And they are?"

"Victor Hugo and Maeterlinck"[3]

"Other writers surely have influenced your other works?"

"Setting aside the prose and poetry of Greek and Latin authors, the only writers who have influenced me are Keats, Flaubert, and Walter Pater;[4] and before I came across them I had already

---

[1] *Mr. William ... World*   For Archer's criticism of Wilde, see "*An Ideal Husband*," *The World*, 9 January 1895, 26–27.

[2] *Ibsen*   Norwegian playwright Henrik Ibsen (1828–1906); *Dumas*   French author and playwright Alexandre Dumas *fils* (1824–95).

[3] *Maeterlinck*   Maurice Maeterlinck (1862–1949), Belgian poet and playwright who was awarded the Nobel Prize for Literature in 1911.

[4] *Keats ... Pater   Keats*   John Keats, English poet (1795–1821); *Flaubert*   French novelist Gustave Flaubert (1821–80), celebrated author of *Madame Bovary* (1867); *Walter Pater*   English critic and scholar; he had reviewed some of Wilde's works.

gone more than halfway to meet them. Style must be in one's soul before one can recognize it in others."

"And do you consider *The Ideal Husband* the best of your plays?"

A charming smile crossed Mr. Wilde's face.

"Have you forgotten my classical expression—that only mediocrities improve? My three plays are to each other, as a wonderful young poet has beautifully said,

as one white rose
On one green stalk to another one.

They form a perfect cycle, and in their delicate sphere complete both life and art."

"Do you think that the critics will understand your new play,[1] which Mr. George Alexander has secured?"

"I hope not."

"I dare not ask, I suppose, if it will please the public?"

"When a play that is a work of art is produced on the stage, what is being tested is not the play, but the stage; when a play that is *not* a work of art is produced on the stage, what is being tested is not the play, but the public."

"What sort of play are we to expect?"

"It is exquisitely trivial, a delicate bubble of fancy, and it has its philosophy."

"Its philosophy!"

"That we should treat all the trivial things of life very seriously, and all the serious things of life with sincere and studied triviality."[2]

"You have no leanings towards realism?"

"None whatever. Realism is only a background; it cannot form an artistic motive for a play that is to be a work of art."

"Still I have heard you congratulated on your pictures of London society."

"If Robert Chiltern, the Ideal Husband, were a common clerk, the humanity of his tragedy would be none the less poignant. I have placed him in the higher ranks of life merely because that is the side of social life with which I am best acquainted. In a play dealing with actualities to write with ease one must write with knowledge."

"Then you see nothing suggestive of treatment in the tragedies of everyday existence?"

"If a journalist is run over by a four-wheeler in the Strand, an incident I regret to say I have never witnessed, it suggests nothing to me from a dramatic point of view. Perhaps I am wrong; but the artist must have his limitations."

"Well," I said, rising to go, "I have enjoyed myself immensely."

"I was sure you would," said Mr. Wilde. "But tell me how you manage your interviews."

"Oh, Pitman," I said carelessly.

"Is that your name? It's not a very *nice* name."

Then I left.

---

[1] *new play*   *The Importance of Being Earnest*, which opened on 14 February 1895.

[2] *It is ... philosophy*   The full title of the play is *The Importance of Being Earnest: A Trivial Comedy For Serious People.*

IN CONTEXT

The First Wilde Trial (1895)

The following is an excerpt from the transcripts of the cross examination of Wilde by Edward Carson, the attorney defending the Marquess of Queensberry in the libel action[1] Wilde had brought against him.

Portrait of Oscar Wilde at the time of his trial, by Henri de Toulouse-Lautrec.

from The Transcripts of the Trial

CARSON.   You stated that your age was thirty-nine. I think you are over forty. You were born on 16th October 1854?

WILDE.   I have no wish to pose as being young. I am thirty-nine or forty. You have my certificate and that settles the matter.

CARSON.   But being born in 1854 makes you more than forty?

WILDE.   Ah! Very well.

CARSON.   What age is Lord Alfred Douglas?

WILDE.   Lord Alfred Douglas is about twenty-four, and was between twenty and twenty-one years of age when I first knew him. Down to the time of the interview in Tite Street, Lord Queensberry was friendly. I did not receive a letter on 3rd April in which Lord Queensberry desired that my acquaintance with his son should cease. After the interview I had no doubt that such was Lord Queensberry's desire. Notwithstanding Lord Queensberry's protest, my intimacy with Lord Alfred

---

[1] *Marquess ... libel action* The Marquess of Queensberry, offended at the close friendship Wilde had formed with his son, Lord Alfred Douglas, had left a card at Wilde's club addressed to "Oscar Wilde posing as a sodomnite [sic]." Wilde felt that he had little choice but to prosecute, or to become publicly known as a man who was unable to deny such a charge. It was this prosecution which eventually led to his imprisonment and the exile of Lord Alfred Douglas.

Douglas has continued down to the present moment.

CARSON.   You have stayed with him at many places?

WILDE.   Yes.

CARSON.   At Oxford? Brighton on several occasions? Worthing?

WILDE.   Yes.

CARSON.   You never took rooms for him?

WILDE.   No.

CARSON.   Were you at other places with him?

WILDE.   Yes; at Cromer and at Torquay.

CARSON.   And in various hotels in London?

WILDE.   Yes; at one in Albemarle Street, and in Dover Street, and at the Savoy.

CARSON.   Did you ever take rooms yourself in addition to your house in Tite Street?

WILDE.   Yes; at 10 and 11 St. James's Place. I kept the rooms from the month of October 1893 to the end of March 1894. Lord Alfred Douglas has stayed in those chambers, which are not far from Piccadilly. I have been abroad with him several times and even lately to Monte Carlo. With reference to the writings which have been mentioned, it was not at Brighton, in 20 King's Road, that I wrote my article for *The Chameleon*.[1] I observed that there were also contributions from Lord Alfred Douglas, but these were not written at Brighton. I have seen them. I thought them exceedingly beautiful poems. One was "In Praise of Shame" and the other "Two Loves."

CARSON.   These loves. They were two boys?

WILDE.   Yes.

CARSON.   One boy calls his love "true love," and the other boy calls his love "shame"?

WILDE.   Yes.

CARSON.   Did you think that made any improper suggestion?

WILDE.   No, none whatever.

CARSON.   You read "The Priest and the Acolyte"?

WILDE.   Yes.

CARSON.   You have no doubt whatever that that was an improper story?

WILDE.   From the literary point of view it was highly improper. It is impossible for a man of literature to judge it otherwise; by literature, meaning treatment, selection of subject, and the like. I thought the treatment rotten and the subject rotten.

CARSON.   You are of opinion, I believe, that there is no such thing as an immoral book?

WILDE.   Yes.

CARSON.   May I take it that you think "The Priest and the Acolyte" was not immoral?

WILDE.   It was worse; it was badly written.

CARSON.   Was not the story that of a priest who fell in love with a boy who served him at the altar, and was discovered by the rector in the priest's room, and a scandal arose?

WILDE.   I have read it only once, in last November, and nothing will induce me to read it again. I don't care for it. It doesn't interest me.

CARSON.   Do you think the story blasphemous?

WILDE.   I think it violated every artistic canon of beauty.

CARSON.   That is not an answer?

WILDE.   It is the only one I can give.

---

[1]   *The Chameleon*   Oxford undergraduate magazine, of which there was only one issue, that of December 1894 to which Wilde refers. In this issue Wilde's "Phrases and Philosophies for the Use of the Young" appeared, as well as an anonymous story about male homosexuality (actually written not by Wilde but by the editor), called "The Priest and the Acolyte." Though Wilde was not the author, the mere fact that a piece signed by him appeared juxtaposed to this story proved damaging to his reputation.

CARSON.   I want to see the position you pose in?

WILDE.   I do not think you should say that.

CARSON.   I have said nothing out of the way. I wish to know whether you thought the story blasphemous?

WILDE.   The story filled me with disgust. The end was wrong.

CARSON.   Answer the question, sir. Did you or did you not consider the story blasphemous?

WILDE.   I thought it disgusting.

CARSON.   I am satisfied with that. You know that when the priest in the story administers poison to the boy, he uses the words of the sacrament of the Church of England?

WILDE.   That I entirely forgot.

CARSON.   Do you consider that blasphemous?

WILDE.   I think it is horrible. "Blasphemous" is not a word of mine.

[*Carson then read the following passage from "The Priest and the Acolyte."*]:

Just before the consecration the priest took a tiny phial from the pocket of his cassock, blessed it, and poured the contents into the chalice.

When the time came for him to receive from the chalice, he raised it to his lips, but did not taste of it.

He administered the sacred wafer to the child, and then he took his hand; he turned towards him; but when he saw the light in the beautiful face he turned again to the crucifix with a low moan. For one instant his courage failed him; then he turned to the little fellow again, and held the chalice to his lips:

"The Blood of our Lord Jesus Christ, which was shed for thee, preserve thy body and soul unto everlasting life."

CARSON.   Do you approve of those words?

WILDE.   I think them disgusting, perfect twaddle.

CARSON.   I think you will admit that anyone who would approve of such an article would pose as guilty of improper practices?

WILDE.   I do not think so in the person of another contributor to the magazine. It would show very bad literary taste. I strongly objected to the whole story. I took no steps to express disapproval of *The Chameleon* because I think it would have been beneath my dignity as a man of letters to associate myself with an Oxford undergraduate's productions. I am aware that the magazine may have been circulated among the undergraduates of Oxford. I do not believe that any book or work of art ever had any effect whatever on morality.

CARSON.   Am I right in saying that you do not consider the effect in creating morality or immorality?

WILDE.   Certainly, I do not.

CARSON.   So far as your works are concerned, you pose as not being concerned about morality or immorality?

WILDE.   I do not know whether you use the word "pose" in any particular sense.

CARSON.   It is a favorite word of your own?

WILDE.   Is it? I have no pose in this matter. In writing a play or a book, I am concerned entirely with literature—that is, with art. I aim not at doing good or evil, but in trying to make a thing that will have some quality of beauty.

CARSON.   Listen, sir. Here is one of the "Phrases and Philosophies for the Use of the Young" which you contributed: "Wickedness is a myth invented by good people to account for the curious attractiveness of others." You think that true?

WILDE.   I rarely think that anything I write is true.

CARSON.   Did you say "rarely"?

WILDE.   I said "rarely." I might have said "never"—not true in the actual sense of the word.

CARSON.   "Religions die when they are proved to be true." Is that true?

WILDE.   Yes; I hold that. It is a suggestion towards a philosophy of the absorption of religions by science, but it is too big a question to go into now.

CARSON.   Do you think that was a safe axiom to put forward for the philosophy of the young?

WILDE.   Most stimulating.

CARSON.   "If one tells the truth, one is sure, sooner or later, to be found out"?

WILDE.   That is a pleasing paradox, but I do not set very high store on it as an axiom.

CARSON.   Is it good for the young?

WILDE.   Anything is good that stimulates thought in whatever age.

CARSON.   Whether moral or immoral?

WILDE.   There is no such thing as morality or immorality in thought. There is immoral emotion.

CARSON.   "Pleasure is the only thing one should live for"?

WILDE.   I think that the realization of oneself is the prime aim of life, and to realize oneself through pleasure is finer than to do so through pain. I am, on that point, entirely on the side of the ancients—the Greeks. It is a pagan idea.

CARSON.   "A truth ceases to be true when more than one person believes in it"?

WILDE.   Perfectly. That would be my metaphysical definition of truth; something so personal that the same truth could never be appreciated by two minds.

CARSON.   "The condition of perfection is idleness: the aim of perfection is youth"?

WILDE.   Oh, yes; I think so. Half of it is true. The life of contemplation is the highest life, and so recognized by the philosopher.

CARSON.   "There is something tragic about the enormous number of young men there are in England at the present moment who start life with perfect profiles, and end by adopting some useful profession"?

WILDE.   I should think that the young have enough sense of humour.

CARSON.   You think that is humourous?

WILDE.   I think it is an amusing paradox, an amusing play on words.

CARSON.   What would anyone say would be the effect of "Phrases and Philosophies" taken in connection with such an article as "The Priest and the Acolyte"?

WILDE.   Undoubtedly it was the idea that might be formed that made me object so strongly to the story. I saw at once that maxims that were perfectly nonsensical, paradoxical, or anything you like, might be read in conjunction with it.

CARSON.   After the criticisms that were passed on *Dorian Gray*, was it modified a good deal?

WILDE.   No. Additions were made. In one case it was pointed out to me—not in a newspaper or anything of that sort, but by the only critic of the century whose opinion I set high, Mr. Walter Pater—that a certain passage was liable to misconstruction, and I made an addition.

CARSON.   This is in your introduction to *Dorian Gray*: "There is no such thing as a moral or an immoral book. Books are well written, or badly written." That expresses your view?

WILDE.   My view on art, yes.

CARSON.   Then I take it that no matter how immoral a book may be, if it is well written, it is, in your opinion, a good book?

WILDE.   Yes, if it were well written so as to produce a sense of beauty, which is the highest sense of which a human being can be capable. If it were badly written, it would produce a sense of disgust.

CARSON.   Then a well-written book putting forward perverted moral views may be a good book?

WILDE.   No work of art ever puts forward views. Views belong to people who are not artists.

CARSON.   A perverted novel might be a good book?

WILDE.   I don't know what you mean by a "perverted" novel.

CARSON.   Then I will suggest *Dorian Gray* as open to the interpretation of being such a novel?

WILDE.   That could only be to brutes and illiterates. The views of Philistines on art are incalculably stupid.

CARSON.   An illiterate person reading *Dorian Gray* might consider it such a novel?

WILDE.   The views of illiterates on art are unaccountable. I am concerned only with my view of art. I don't care twopence what other people think of it.

CARSON.   The majority of persons would come under your definition of Philistines and illiterates?

WILDE.   I have found wonderful exceptions.

CARSON.   Do you think that the majority of people live up to the position you are giving us?

WILDE.   I am afraid they are not cultivated enough.

CARSON.   Not cultivated enough to draw the distinction between a good book and a bad book?

WILDE.   Certainly not.

CARSON.   The affection and love of the artist of *Dorian Gray* might lead an ordinary individual to believe that it might have a certain tendency?

WILDE.   I have no knowledge of the views of ordinary individuals.

CARSON.   You did not prevent the ordinary individual from buying your book?

WILDE.   I have never discouraged him.

[*Carson then read a long passage from Chapter 1 of* The Picture of Dorian Gray *(from "The story is simply this ..." to "I must see Dorian Gray".)*]

CARSON.   Now I ask you, Mr. Wilde, do you consider that that description of the feeling of one man towards a youth just grown up was a proper or an improper feeling?

WILDE.   I think it is the most perfect description of what an artist would feel on meeting a beautiful personality that was in some way necessary to his art and life.

CARSON.   You think that is a feeling a young man should have towards another?

WILDE.   Yes, as an artist.

[*Carson then read a long passage from Chapter 9 of* The Picture of Dorian Gray *(from "Let us sit down, Dorian" to "You are made to be worshipped").*]

CARSON.   Do you mean to say that that passage describes the natural feeling of one man towards another?

WILDE.   It would be the influence produced by a beautiful personality.

CARSON.   A beautiful person?

WILDE.   I said a "beautiful personality." You can describe it as you like. Dorian Gray's was a most remarkable personality.

CARSON.   May I take it that you, as an artist, have never known the feeling described here?

WILDE.   I have never allowed any personality to dominate my art.

CARSON.   Then you have never known the feeling you described?

WILDE.   No. It is a work of fiction.

CARSON.   So far as you are concerned you have no experience as to its being a natural feeling?

WILDE.   I think it is perfectly natural for any artist to admire intensely and love a young man. It is an incident in the life of almost every artist.

CARSON.   But let us go over it phrase by phrase. "I quite admit that I adored you madly." What do you say to that? Have you ever adored a young man madly?

WILDE.   No, not madly; I prefer love—that is a higher form.

CARSON.   Never mind about that. Let us keep down to the level we are at now?

WILDE.   I have never given adoration to anybody except myself. (*Loud laughter.*)

CARSON.   I suppose you think that a very smart thing?

WILDE.   Not at all.

CARSON.   Then you have never had that feeling?

WILDE.   No. The whole idea was borrowed from Shakespeare, I regret to say—yes, from Shakespeare's sonnets.

CARSON.   I believe you have written an article to show that Shakespeare's sonnets were suggestive of unnatural vice?

WILDE.   On the contrary I have written an article to show that they are not.[1] I objected to such a perversion being put upon Shakespeare.

CARSON.   "I have adored you extravagantly"?

WILDE.   Do you mean financially?

CARSON.   Oh, yes, financially! Do you think we are talking about finance?

WILDE.   I don't know what you are talking about.

CARSON.   Don't you? Well, I hope I shall make myself very plain before I have done. "I was jealous of everyone to whom you spoke." Have you ever been jealous of a young man?

WILDE.   Never in my life.

CARSON.   "I wanted to have you all to myself." Did you ever have that feeling?

WILDE.   No; I should consider it an intense nuisance, an intense bore.

CARSON.   "I grew afraid that the world would know of my idolatry." Why should he grow afraid that the world should know of it?

WILDE.   Because there are people in the world who cannot understand the intense devotion, affection, and admiration that an artist can feel for a wonderful and beautiful personality. These are the conditions under which we live. I regret them.

CARSON.   These unfortunate people, that have not the high understanding that you have, might put it down to something wrong?

WILDE.   Undoubtedly; to any point they chose. I am not concerned with the ignorance of others.

CARSON.   In another passage Dorian Gray receives a book. Was the book to which you refer a moral book?

WILDE.   Not well written, but it gave me an idea.

CARSON.   Was not the book you have in mind of a certain tendency?

WILDE.   I decline to be cross-examined upon the work of another artist. It is an impertinence and a vulgarity.

[*Wilde then stated the book Carson referred to was* A Rebours, *by J.K. Huysmans; and, following an appeal by Sir Edward Clarke, Wilde's attorney, the judge ruled against further reference to it. Carson then read a long passage from Chapter 12 of* The Picture of Dorian Gray *(from "… I think it right that you should know the most dreadful things are being said about you in London" to "Dorian, your reputation is infamous … ").*]

CARSON.   Does not this passage suggest a charge of unnatural vice?

WILDE.   It describes Dorian Gray as a man of very corrupt influence, though there is no statement as to the nature of the influence. But as a matter of fact I do not think that one person influences another, nor do I think there is any bad influence in the world.

[1]   *an article … not*   Cf. "The Portrait of Mr. W.H." first published in *Blackwood's Edinburgh Magazine*, 146.885 (July 1889), and then again in a limited edition in 1921.

CARSON.   A man never corrupts a youth?

WILDE.   I think not.

CARSON.   Nothing could corrupt him?

WILDE.   If you are talking of separate ages.

CARSON.   No, sir, I am talking common sense.

WILDE.   I do not think one person influences another.

CARSON.   You don't think that flattering a young man, making love[1] to him, in fact, would be likely to corrupt him?

WILDE.   No.

CARSON.   Where was Lord Alfred Douglas staying when you wrote that letter to him?

WILDE.   At the Savoy; and I was at Babbacombe, near Torquay.

CARSON.   It was a letter in answer to something he had sent you?

WILDE.   Yes, a poem.

CARSON.   Why should a man of your age address a boy nearly twenty years younger as "My own boy"?

WILDE.   I was fond of him. I have always been fond of him.

CARSON.   Do you adore him?

WILDE.   No, but I have always liked him. I think it is a beautiful letter. It is a poem. I was not writing an ordinary letter. You might as well cross-examine me as to whether *King Lear* or a sonnet of Shakespeare was proper.

CARSON.   Apart from art, Mr. Wilde?

WILDE.   I cannot answer apart from art.

CARSON.   Suppose a man who was not an artist had written this letter, would you say it was a proper letter?

WILDE.   A man who was not an artist could not have written that letter.

Carson.   Why?

WILDE.   Because nobody but an artist could write it. He certainly could not write the language unless he were a man of letters.

CARSON.   I can suggest, for the sake of your reputation, that there is nothing very wonderful in this "red rose-leaf lips of yours"?

WILDE.   A great deal depends on the way it is read.

CARSON.   "Your slim gilt soul walks between passion and poetry." Is that a beautiful phrase?

WILDE.   Not as you read it, Mr. Carson. You read it very badly.

CARSON.   I do not profess to be an artist; and when I hear you give evidence, I am glad I am not—

SIR EDWARD CLARKE.   I don't think my friend should talk like that. (*To witness*) Pray, do not criticize my friend's reading again.

CARSON.   Is that not an exceptional letter?

WILDE.   It is unique, I should say.

CARSON.   Was that the ordinary way in which you carried on your correspondence?

WILDE.   No; but I have often written to Lord Alfred Douglas, though I never wrote to another young man in the same way.

CARSON.   Have you often written letters in the same style as this?

WILDE.   I don't repeat myself in style.

CARSON.   Here is another letter which I believe you also wrote to Lord Alfred Douglas. Will you read it?

---

[1] *making love*   Until the 1960s this expression was generally used to refer to the process of wooing or courtship, not to any physical act of lovemaking.

WILDE.   No; I decline. I don't see why I should.

CARSON.   Then I will.

> Savoy Hotel,
> Victoria Embankment, London.
> Dearest of all Boys,
> Your letter was delightful, red and yellow wine to me; but I am sad and out of sorts. Bosie,[1] you must not make scenes with me. They kill me, they wreck the loveliness of life. I cannot see you, so Greek and gracious, distorted with passion. I cannot listen to your curved lips saying hideous things to me. I would sooner——than have you bitter, unjust, hating.... I must see you soon. You are the divine thing I want, the thing of grace and beauty; but I don't know how to do it. Shall I come to Salisbury? My bill here is £49 for a week. I have also got a new sitting-room.... Why are you not here, my dear, my wonderful boy? I fear I must leave—no money, no credit, and a heart of lead.
> Your own Oscar.…

Is that an ordinary letter?

WILDE.   Everything I write is extraordinary. I do not pose as being ordinary, great heavens! Ask me any question you like about it.

CARSON.   Is it the kind of letter a man writes to another?

WILDE.   It was a tender expression of my great admiration for Lord Alfred Douglas. It was not, like the other, a prose poem.

---

[1]   *Bosie*   Lord Alfred Douglas's nickname.

VERNON LEE
1856 – 1935

Vernon Lee was the author of some fifty books of fiction, philosophical and intellectual criticism, and art history, but her reputation now rests mainly on her stories of the fantastic and her first novel, *Miss Brown*. Walter Pater once called her one of "the very few best critical writers of all time"; among her other admirers were Robert Browning, Henry James, and George Bernard Shaw, all of whom recognized her intellectual prowess.

Violet Paget (Vernon Lee was her pen name) was born in Boulogne, France, in 1856. Her father, Henry Ferguson Paget, was a former Polish soldier who fled to Paris during the 1848 Warsaw uprising. He worked as a tutor, eventually marrying the mother of one of his students, and soon afterward the couple had their own child, Violet. They moved frequently, settling briefly in Germany, Switzerland, and Italy, so the children received schooling in many different languages. In Nice, France, when she was ten, Lee forged a friendship with an American child, John Singer Sargent, and the two prophesied correctly that he would become a famous painter and she a writer.

Lee's parents recognized that their daughter was intellectually gifted, and they encouraged her scholarship. Her first article was published when she was just thirteen. At the age of twenty-four she published her first book, *Studies of the Eighteenth Century in Italy* (1880), a scholarly monograph that received considerable acclaim. On her move from Florence to London after its publication, she joined a literary and intellectual circle that included Browning and Pater. Although initially very supportive of her writing, Pater cooled somewhat for a time after Lee published *Miss Brown* in 1884. The novel was viewed by many as a thinly-veiled *roman à clef* in which Lee satirized the Pre-Raphaelites (such as Dante Gabriel Rossetti) and Aesthetes (Oscar Wilde). Even Henry James, who was a fan of her writing, said to Lee, "You have impregnated all those people too much with the sexual, the basely erotic preoccupation: your hand was too violent, the touch of life is lighter."

Lee wrote prolifically during the following two decades. Chief among her publications was *Euphorion: Being Studies of the Antique and the Medieval in the Renaissance* (1884), a study of Italian art and culture that the American journal *The Nation* called "clever with the cleverness of precocious and presumptuous youth, lively and amusing even in its pretentiousness." Lee furthered her aesthetic theories in her work with her close friend, artist Clementina (Kit) Anstruther-Thomson. The two collaborated on *Beauty and Ugliness and other Studies in Psychological Aesthetics* (1912), which Lee followed with *The Beautiful: An Introduction to Psychological Aesthetics* (1913). On her own Lee also published *The Handling of Words and other Studies in Literary Psychology* (1923), an analytical study that anticipated a number of later twentieth-century trends in theory and criticism.

Lee's interest in and knowledge of other cultures yielded seven volumes of travel essays, including *The Enchanted Woods, and Other Essays on the Genius of Place* (1905), a book she described as a "pilgrimage through the open and hidden ways where, without any noisy calling, the *Genus Loci* [spirit of the place]" met her. Her travel writing was much admired by Aldous Huxley and Edith Wharton, and by a member of the Bloomsbury group, Desmond MacCarthy, who would declare that there was "no doubt [that] Vernon Lee will be read by posterity, for her work is a rare combination of intellectual curiosity and imaginative sensibility." Lee also wrote popular works of fiction, including the short story collections *Hauntings: Fantastic Stories* (1890) and *Pope Jacynth and Other Fantastic Tales* (1904), and the play *Ariadne in Mantua: A Romance in Five Acts* (1903). A later satirical play, *The Ballet of the Nations: A Present-day Morality* (1915), was disparaged by many who objected to its anti-war position.

    Lee's popularity and influence were already waning when she died in Florence in 1935. That same year she had complained to a friend that she felt like "an alien, having no ties, either of nation, blood, class or profession." In a biography (1964), Peter Gunn described her as "a shadowy figure, at the most perhaps only a vaguely remembered name; a name, however, which recalls to an older generation a literary craftsman and polemicist of undoubted importance in her day ... one of the most brilliant and gifted women of her time ... a writer and a talker who both stimulated and irritated her contemporaries." Recently there has been a marked revival of critical interest in her work.

⌘ ⌘ ⌘

The Virgin of the Seven Daggers

I

In a grass-grown square of the city of Grenada,[1] with the snows of the Sierra[2] staring down on it all winter, and the sunshine glaring on its coloured tiles all summer, stands the yellow free-stone Church of Our Lady of the Seven Daggers. Huge garlands of pears and melons hang, carved in stone, about the cupolas and windows; and monstrous heads with laurel wreaths and epaulets burst forth from all the arches. The roof shines barbarically, green, white, and brown, above the tawny stone; and on each of the two balconied and staircased belfries, pricked up like ears above the building's monstrous front, there sways a weathervane, figuring a heart transfixed with seven long-hilted daggers. Inside, the church presents a superb example of the pompous, pedantic, and contorted Spanish architecture of the reign of Philip IV.[3]

On colonnade is hoisted colonnade, pilasters climb upon pilasters, bases and capitals jut out, double and threefold, from the ground, in midair and near the ceiling; jagged lines everywhere as of spikes for exhibit-

ing the heads of traitors; dizzy ledges as of mountain precipices for dashing to bits Morisco rebels;[4] line warring with line and curve with curve; a place in which the mind staggers bruised and half-stunned. But the grandeur of the church is not merely terrific—it is also gallant and ceremonious: everything on which labor can be wasted is labored, everything on which gold can be lavished is gilded; columns and architraves curl like the curls of a peruke;[5] walls and vaultings are flowered with precious marbles and fretted with carving and gilding like a gala dress; stone and wood are woven like lace; stucco is whipped and clotted like pastry cooks' cream and crust; everything is crammed with flourishes like a tirade by Calderon, or a sonnet by Gongora.[6] A golden retablo closes the church at the end; a black and white rood screen, of jasper[7] and alabaster, fences it in the middle; while along each aisle hang chandeliers as for a ball; and paper flowers are stacked on every altar.

Amidst all this gloomy yet festive magnificence, and surrounded, in each minor chapel, by a train of waxen Christs with bloody wounds and spangled loincloths,

---

[1] *Granada* City in Spain, location of the palace-citadel of the Alhambra, constructed by the founder of the Nasrid kingdom, Mohammed ibn Yusaf ben Nasr, in the mid-thirteenth century.

[2] *Sierra* I.e., the Sierra Nevada mountain range in Andalusia, Spain.

[3] *Philip IV* King of Spain and Portugal (1605–65).

[4] *Morisco rebels* Muslim freedom fighters of the Morisco Rebellion (1568–71), a revolt against the Christian suppression of Islamic religion, culture, and trade.

[5] *peruke* Wig.

[6] *Calderon* Pedro Calderón de la Barca, prolific Spanish playwright of the seventeenth century (called Spain's Golden Age); *Gongora* Luis de Góngora y Argote, poet of the same era.

[7] *retablo* Frame enclosing a religious painting above the altar of a church; *rood* Here, large wooden crucifix; *jasper* Opaque quartz.

and madonnas of lesser fame weeping beady tears and carrying bewigged infants, thrones the great Madonna of the Seven Daggers.

Is she seated or standing? 'Tis impossible to decide. She seems, beneath the gilded canopy and between the twisted columns of jasper, to be slowly rising, or slowly sinking, in a solemn court curtsy, buoyed up by her vast farthingale.[1] Her skirts bulge out in melon-shaped folds, all damasked with minute heart's-ease,[2] and brocaded with silver roses; the reddish shimmer of the gold wire, the bluish shimmer of the silver floss, blending into a strange melancholy hue without a definite name. Her body is cased like a knife in its sheath, the mysterious russet and violet of the silk made less definable still by the network of seed pearl, and the veils of delicate lace which fall from head to waist. Her face, surmounting rows upon rows of pearls, is made of wax, white with black glass eyes and a tiny coral mouth; she stares steadfastly forth with a sad and ceremonious smile. Her head is crowned with a great jeweled crown; her slippered feet rest on a crescent moon, and in her right hand she holds a lace pocket-handkerchief. In her bodice, a little clearing is made among the brocade and the seed pearl, and into this are stuck seven gold-hilted knives.

Such is Our Lady of the Seven Daggers; and such her church.

One winter afternoon, more than two hundred years ago, Charles the Melancholy being King of Spain and the New World, there chanced to be kneeling in that church, already empty and dim save for the votive lamps, and more precisely on the steps before the Virgin of the Seven Daggers, a cavalier[3] of very great birth, fortune, magnificence, and wickedness, Don[4] Juan Gusman del Pulgar, Count of Miramor. "O great Madonna, star of the sea, tower of ivory, ungathered flower, cedar of Lebanon, Empress of Heaven"—thus prayed that devout man of quality—"look down benignly on thy knight and servant, accounted judiciously one of the greatest men of this kingdom, in wealth and

honours, fearing neither the vengeance of foes, nor the rigour of laws, yet content to stand foremost among thy slaves. Consider that I have committed every crime without faltering, both murder, perjury, blasphemy, and sacrilege, yet have I always respected thy name, nor suffered any man to give greater praise to other Madonnas, neither her of Good Counsel, nor her of Swift Help, nor our Lady of Mount Carmel, nor our Lady of St. Luke of Bologna in Italy, nor our Lady of the Slipper of Famagosta, in Cyprus, nor our Lady of the Pillar of Saragossa, great Madonnas every one, and revered throughout the world for their powers, and by most men preferred to thee; yet has thy servant, Juan Gusman del Pulgar, ever asserted, with words and blows, their infinite inferiority to thee.

"Give me, therefore, O Great Madonna of the Seven Daggers, Snow Peak untrodden of the Sierras, O Sea unnavigated of the tropics, O Gold Ore unhandled by the Spaniard, O New Minted Doubloon[5] unpocketed by the Jew,[6] give unto me therefore, pray thee, the promise that thou wilt save me ever from the clutches of Satan, as thou hast wrested me ever on earth from the King, Alguazils[7] and the Holy Office's[8] delatours,[9] and let me never burn in eternal fire in punishment of my sins. Neither think that I ask too much, for I swear to be provided always with absolution[10] in all rules, whether by employing my own private chaplain or using violence thereunto to any monk, priest, canon, dean, bishop, cardinal, or even the Holy Father[11] himself.

"Grant me this boon, O Burning Water and Cooling Fire, O Sun that shineth at midnight, and Galaxy that resplendeth at noon—grant me this boon, and I

[1] *farthingale* Hooped petticoat.
[2] *heart's-ease* Pansy.
[3] *cavalier* Knight.
[4] *Don* Title for a Spanish noblemen.

[5] *Doubloon* Gold coin.
[6] *unpocketed by the Jew* Remarks such as this, which we now consider racist and offensive, were casually made at this time. Jews were frequently associated with the lending of money (for centuries one of the few occupations they were not restricted from entering) and thus with pressing to be paid amounts owed.
[7] *Alguazils* Government officials.
[8] *Holy Office* At this time, the Spanish Inquisition, a legally constituted court founded for the suppression of heresy.
[9] *delatours* Informers.
[10] *absolution* Forgiveness of sins through the sacrament of Confession.
[11] *Holy Father* The Pope.

will assert always with my tongue and my sword, in the face of His Majesty and at the feet of my latest love, that although I have been beloved of all the fairest women of the world, high and low, both Spanish, Italian, German, French, Dutch, Flemish, Jewish, Saracen,[1] and Gypsy, to the number of many hundreds, and by seven ladies, Dolores, Fatma, Catalina, Elvira, Violante, Azahar, and Sister Seraphita, for each of whom I broke a commandment and took several lives (the last, moreover, being a cloistered nun, and therefore a case of inexpiable sacrilege), despite all this I will maintain before all men and all the Gods of Olympus that no lady was ever so fair as our Lady of the Seven Daggers of Grenada."

The church was filled with ineffable fragrance, exquisite music, among which Don Juan seemed to recognize the voice of Syphax, His Majesty's own soprano singer, murmured amongst the cupolas, and the Virgin of the Seven Daggers, slowly dipped in her lace and silver brocade hoop, rising as slowly again to her full height, and inclined her white face imperceptibly towards her jeweled bosom.

The Count of Miramor clasped his hands in ecstasy to his breast; then he rose, walked quickly down the aisle, dipped his fingers in the black marble holy water stoop, threw a sequin[2] to the beggar who pushed open the leathern curtain, put his black hat covered with black feathers on his head, dismissed a company of bravos and guitar players who awaited him in the square, and, gathering his black cloak about him, went forth, his sword tucked under his arm, in search of Baruch, the converted Jew of the Albaycin.[3]

Don Juan Gusman del Pulgar, Count of Miramor, Grandee of the First Class, Knight of Calatrava, and of the Golden Fleece, and Prince of the Holy Roman Empire, was thirty-two and a great sinner. This cavalier was tall, of large bone, his forehead low and cheekbones high, chin somewhat receding, aquiline nose, white complexion, and black hair; he wore no beard, but mustachios cut short over the lip and curled upwards at the corners leaving the mouth bare; and his hair flat, parted through the middle and falling nearly to his shoulders. His clothes, when bent on business or pleasure, were most often of black satin, slashed with black. His portrait has been painted by Domingo Zurbaran of Seville.[4]

2

All the steeples of Grenada seemed agog with bell-ringing; the big bell on the Tower of the Sail[5] clanging irregularly into the more professional tinklings and roarings, under the vigorous but flurried pulls of the elderly damsels, duly accompanied by their well-ruffed duennas,[6] who were ringing themselves a husband or the newly begun year, according to the traditions of the city. Green garlands decorated the white glazed balconies, and banners with the arms of Castile and Aragon,[7] and the pomegranate of Grenada, waved or drooped alongside the hallowed palm branches over the carved escutcheons[8] on the doors. From the barracks arose a practising of fifes and bugles; and from the little wine shops on the outskirts of the town a sound of guitar strumming and castanets. The coming day was a very solemn feast for the city, being the anniversary of its liberation from the rule of the Infidels.[9]

But although all Grenada felt festive, in anticipation of the grand bullfight of the morrow, and the grand burning of heretics and relapses in the square of Bibrambla,[10] Don Juan Gusman del Pulgar, Count of Miramor, was fevered with intolerable impatience, not for the following day but for the coming and tediously lagging night.

[1] *Saracen* Muslim.
[2] *sequin* Turkish coin.
[3] *Albaycin* Neighborhood of Granada that encompasses the Alhambra.
[4] *Domingo Zurbaran of Seville* Perhaps a reference to painter Francisco de Zurbarán of Seville (1598–1664).
[5] *Tower of the Sail* The Torre de la Vela, or Tower of the Sail, at the Alhambra.
[6] *duennas* Chaperones.
[7] *Castile and Aragon* Spanish kingdoms.
[8] *escutcheons* Shields bearing coats of arms.
[9] *Infidels* The Moors, who ruled southern Spain until 1492. In the Spanish Inquisition of 1480–1834, the Roman Catholic majority in Spain conducted a violent campaign to root out "unbelievers," in the course of which they expelled or killed large numbers of Spanish Muslims and Jews.
[10] *Bibrambla* Large open square where hundreds of people visit and congregate in central Granada.

Not, however, for the reason which had made him a thousand times before upbraid the Sun God, in true poetic style, for showing so little of the proper anxiety to hasten the happiness of one of the greatest cavaliers of Spain. The delicious heart-beating with which he had waited, sword under his cloak, for the desired rope to be lowered from a mysterious window, or the muffled figure to loom from round a corner; the fierce joy of awaiting, with a band of gallant murderers, some inconvenient father, or brother, or husband on his evening stroll; the rapture even, spiced with awful sacrilege, of stealing in amongst the lemon trees of that cloistered court, after throwing the Sister Portress[1] to tell-tale in the convent well—all, and even this, seemed to him trumpery and mawkish.

Don Juan sprang from the great bed, covered and curtained with dull, blood-coloured damask, on which he had been lying dressed, vainly courting sleep, beneath a painted hermit, black and white in his lantern-jawedness, fondling a handsome skull. He went to the balcony, and looked out of one of its glazed windows. Below a marble goddess shimmered among the myrtle hedges and the cypresses of the tiled garden, and the pet dwarf of the house played at cards with the chaplain, the chief bravo, and a threadbare poet who was kept to make the odes and sonnets required in the course of his master's daily courtships.

"Get out of my sight, you lazy scoundrels, all of you!" cried Don Juan, with a threat and an oath alike terrible to repeat, which sent the party, bowing and scraping as they went, scattering their cards, and pursued by his lordship's jack-boots, guitar, and missal.[2]

Don Juan stood at the window rapt in contemplation of the towers of the Alhambra, their tips still reddened by the departing sun, their bases already lost in the encroaching mists, on the hill yon side of the river.

He could just barely see it, that Tower of the Cypresses, where the magic hand held the key engraven on the doorway, about which, as a child, his nurse from the Morisco village of Andarax had told such marvellous stories of hidden treasures and slumbering infantas.[3] He stood long at the window, his lean, white hands clasped on the rail as on the handle of his sword, gazing out with knit brows and clenched teeth, and that look which made men hug the wall and drop aside on his path.

Ah, how different from any of his other loves! The only one, decidedly, at all worthy of lineage as great as his, and a character as magnanimous. Catalina, indeed, had been exquisite when she danced, and Elvira was magnificent at a banquet, and each had long possessed his heart, and had cost him, one many thousands of doubloons for a husband, and the other the death of a favourite fencing master, killed in a fray with her relations. Violante had been a Venetian worthy of Titian,[4] for whose sake he had been imprisoned beneath the ducal palace, escaping only by the massacre of three jailers; for Fatma, the Sultana of the King of Fez, he had well nigh been impaled, and for shooting the husband of Dolores he had very nearly been broken on the wheel; Azahar, who was called so because of her cheeks like white jessamine, he had carried off at a church door, out of the arms of her bridegroom—without counting that he had cut down her old father, a Grandee of the First Class; and as to Sister Seraphita—ah! she had seemed worthy of him, and Seraphita had nearly come up to his idea of an angel.

But oh, what had any of these ladies cost him compared with what he was about to risk tonight? Letting alone the chance of being roasted by the Holy Office (after all, he had already run that, and the risk of more serious burning hereafter also, in the case of Sister Seraphita), what if the business proved a swindle of that Jewish hound, Baruch?—Don Juan put his hand on his dagger and his black mustachios bristled up at the bare thought—letting alone the possibility of imposture (though who could be so bold as to venture to impose upon him?) the adventure was full of dreadful things. It was terrible, after all, to have to blaspheme the Holy Catholic Apostolic Church, and all her saints, and inconceivably odious to have to be civil to that dog of a

---

[1] *Sister Portress* Nun who keeps the convent gates; the door-keeper.

[2] *jack-boots* Above-the-knee boots worn by the cavalry; *missal* Book that contains the service of the Mass.

[3] *infantas* Daughters of the king and queen; princesses.

[4] *Titian* Renaissance Venetian painter Tiziano Vecellio (c. 1490–1576), commonly known as Titian.

Mahomet[1] of theirs; also, he had not much enjoyed a previous experience of calling up devils, who had smelled most vilely of brimstone and asafœtida,[2] besides using most impolite language; and he really could not stomach that Jew Baruch, whose trade among others consisted in procuring for the archbishop a batch of renegade Moors, who were solemnly dressed in white and baptized afresh every year. It was odious that this fellow should even dream of obtaining the treasure buried under the Tower of the Cypresses.

Then there were the traditions of his family, descended in direct line from the Cid,[3] and from that Fernan del Pulgar[4] who had nailed the Ave Maria[5] to the Mosque; and half his other ancestors were painted with their foot on a Moor's discollated[6] head, much resembling a hairdresser's block, and their very title, Miramor, was derived from a castle which had been built in full Moorish territory to stare the Moor out of countenance.

But, after all, this only made it more magnificent, more delicious, more worthy of so magnanimous and high-born a cavalier…. "Ah, princess … more exquisite than Venus, more noble than Juno, and infinitely more agreeable than Minerva …"[7] sighed Don Juan at his window. The sun had long since set, making a trail of blood along the distant river reach, among the sere spider-like poplars, turning the snows of Mulhacen[8] a livid, bluish blood-red, and leaving all along the lower slopes of the Sierra wicked russet stains, as of the rust of blood upon marble. Darkness had come over the world, save where some illuminated courtyard or window suggested preparations for next day's revelry; the air was piercingly cold, as if filled with minute snowflakes from the mountains. The joyful singing had ceased; and from a neighbouring church there came only a casual death toll, executed on a cracked and lugubrious bell. A shudder ran through Don Juan. "Holy Virgin of the Seven Daggers, take me under thy benign protection," he murmured mechanically.

A discreet knock aroused him.

"The Jew Baruch—I mean his worship, Senor Don Bonaventura," announced the page.

3

The Tower of the Cypresses, destroyed in our times by the explosion of a powder magazine, formed part of the inner defenses of the Alhambra. In the middle of its horseshoe arch was engraved a huge hand holding a flag-shaped key, which was said to be that of the subterranean and enchanted palace; and the two great cypress trees, uniting their shadows into one tapering cone of black, were said to point, under a given position of the moon, to the exact spot where the wise King Yahya, of Cordova, had judiciously buried his jewels, his plate, and his favourite daughter many hundred years ago.

At the foot of this tower, and in the shade of the cypresses, Don Juan ordered his companion to spread out his magic paraphernalia. From a neatly packed basket, beneath which he had staggered up the steep hillside in the moonlight, the learned Jew produced a book, a variety of lamps, some packets of frankincense, a pound of dead man's fat, the bones of a stillborn child who had been boiled by the witches, a live cock that had never crowed, a very ancient toad, and sundry other rarities, all of which he proceeded to dispose in the latest necromantic[9] fashion, while the Count of Miramor mounted guard, sword in hand. But when the fire was laid, the lamps lit, and the first layer of ingredients had already been placed in the cauldron; nay, when he had even borrowed Don Juan's embroidered pocket-handkerchief to envelop the cock that had never crowed, Baruch the Jew suddenly flung himself down before his

[1] *Mahomet* The prophet Mohammed, who founded Islam. Don Juan's characterization of Mohammed is highly offensive to modern ears; Lee clearly intends this speech to add to the reader's understanding of the viciousness of Don Juan's character.

[2] *asafœtida* Plant gum used as a medicine and spice.

[3] *the Cid* Rodrigo Diaz, otherwise known as "El Cid" (the chief), Spanish knight who fought against the Moors in the 11th century.

[4] *Fernan del Pulgar* Spanish historian and author (c. 1430–92).

[5] *Ave Maria* Roman Catholic prayer to Mary, the mother of Jesus Christ.

[6] *discollated* Cut off.

[7] *Venus* Roman goddess of love; *Juno* Queen of the Roman gods; *Minerva* Roman goddess of war. The three goddesses, in their Greek identities of Aphrodite, Hera and Athena, famously competed for the title of the most beautiful goddess, setting in motion the train of events that would culminate in the Trojan War.

[8] *Mulhacen* Mulhacén, the highest mountain in Continental Spain.

[9] *necromantic* Using sorcery.

patron and implored him to desist from the terrible enterprise for which they had come.

"I have come hither," wailed the Jew, "lest your lordship should possibly entertain doubts of my obligingness. I have run the risk of being burned alive in the Square of Bibrambla tomorrow morning before the bullfight; I have imperiled my eternal soul and laid out large sums of money in the purchase of the necessary ingredients, all of which are abomination in the eyes of a true Jew—I mean of a good Christian;[1] but now I implore your lordship to desist. You will see things so terrible that to mention them is impossible; you will be suffocated by the vilest stenches, and shaken by earthquakes and whirlwinds, besides having to listen to imprecations of the most horrid sort; you will have to blaspheme our Holy Mother Church and invoke Mahomet—may he roast everlastingly in hell; you will infallibly go to hell yourself in due course; and all this for the sake of a paltry treasure of which it will be most difficult to dispose to the pawnbrokers; and of a lady, about whom, thanks to my former medical position in the harem of the Emperor of Tetuan, I may assert with confidence that she is fat, ill-favoured, stained with henna, and most disagreeably redolent of camphor...."

"Peace, villain!" cried Don Juan, snatching him by the throat and pulling him violently onto his feet. "Prepare thy messes and thy stinks, begin thy antics, and never dream of offering advice to a cavalier like me. And remember, one other word against her royal highness, my bride, against the princess whom her own father has been keeping three hundred years for my benefit, and by the Virgin of the Seven Daggers, thou shalt be hurled into yonder precipice; which, by the way, will be a very good move, in any case, when thy services are no longer required." So saying, he snatched from Baruch's hand the paper of responses, which the necromancer had copied out from his book of magic; and began to study it by the light of a supernumerary[2] lamp.

"Begin!" he cried. "I am ready, and thou, great Virgin of the Seven Daggers, guard me!"

"Jab, jam, jam—Credo in Grilgoth, Astaroth et Rappatun; trish, trash, trum," began Baruch in faltering tones, as he poked a flame-tipped reed under the cauldron.

"Patapol, Valde Patapol," answered Don Juan from his paper of responses.

The flame of the cauldron leaped up with a tremendous smell of brimstone. The moon was veiled, the place was lit up crimson, and a legion of devils with the bodies of apes, the talons of eagles, and the snouts of pigs suddenly appeared in the battlements all round.

"Credo," again began Baruch; but the blasphemies he gabbled out, and which Don Juan indignantly echoed, were such as cannot possibly be recorded. A hot wind rose, whirling a desertful of burning sand that stung like gnats; the bushes were on fire, each flame turned into a demon like a huge locust or scorpion, who uttered piercing shrieks and vanished, leaving a choking atmosphere of melted tallow.

"Fal lal Polychronicon Nebuzaradon," continued Baruch. "Leviathan! Esto nobis!" answered Don Juan. The earth shook, the sound of millions of gongs filled the air, and a snowstorm enveloped everything like a shuddering cloud. A legion of demons, in the shape of white elephants, but with snakes for their trunks and tails, and the bosoms of fair women, executed a frantic dance round the cauldron, and, holding hands, balanced on their hind legs.

At this moment the Jew uncovered the Black Cock who had never crowed before.

"Osiris! Apollo! Balshazar!" he cried, and flung the cock with superb aim into the boiling cauldron. The cock disappeared; then rose again, shaking his wings, and clawing the air, and giving a fearful piercing crow.

"O Sultan Yahya, Sultan Yahya," answered a terrible voice from the bowels of the earth.

Again the earth shook; streams of lava bubbled from beneath the cauldron, and a flame, like a sheet of green lightning, leaped up from the fire. As it did so a colossal shadow appeared on the high palace wall, and the great hand, shaped like a glover's sign, engraven on the outer arch of the tower gateway, extended its candle-shaped fingers, projected a wrist, an arm to the elbow, and turned slowly in a secret lock the flag-shaped key engraven on the inside vault of the portal.

The two necromancers fell on their faces, utterly stunned.

1 *true... Christian* This speech is meant to imply that Baruch is not truly converted to Christianity.

2 *supernumerary* Extra.

The first to revive was Don Juan, who roughly brought the Jew back to his senses. The moon made serene daylight. There was no trace of earthquake, volcano, or simoon;[1] and the devils had disappeared without traces; only the circle of lamps was broken through, and the cauldron upset among the embers. But the great horseshoe portals of the tower stood open; and, at the bottom of a dark corridor, there shone a speck of dim light.

"My lord," cried Baruch, suddenly grown bold, and plucking Don Juan by the cloak, "we must now, if you please, settle a trifling business matter. Remember that the treasure was to be mine provided the Infanta were yours. Remember also, that the smallest indiscretion on your part, such as may happen to a gay young cavalier, will result in our being burned, with the batch of heretics and relapses, in Bibrambla tomorrow, immediately after high Mass and just before people go to early dinner, on account of the bullfight."

"Business! Discretion! Bibrambla! Early dinner!" exclaimed the Count of Miramor. "Thinkest thou I shall ever go back to Grenada and its frumpish women once I am married to my Infanta, or let thee handle my late father-in-law, King Yahya's treasure! Execrable renegade, take the reward of thy blasphemies." And having rapidly run him through the body, he pushed Baruch into the precipice hard by. Then, covering his left arm with his cloak, and swinging his bare sword horizontally in his right hand, he advanced into the darkness of the tower.

4

Don Juan Gusman del Pulgar plunged down a narrow corridor, as black as the shaft of a mine, following the little speck of reddish light which seemed to advance before him. The air was icy damp and heavy with a vague choking mustiness, which Don Juan imagined to be the smell of dead bats. Hundreds of these creatures fluttered all round; and hundreds more, apparently hanging head downwards from the low roof, grazed his face with their claws, their damp furry coats, and clammy leathern wings. Underfoot, the ground was slippery with innumerable little snakes, who, instead of being crushed, just wriggled under the thread. The

corridor was rendered even more gruesome by the fact that it was a strongly inclined plane, and that one seemed to be walking straight into a pit.

Suddenly a sound mingled itself with that of his footsteps, and of the drip-drop of water from the roof, or, rather, detached itself as a whisper from it.

"Don Juan, Don Juan," it murmured.

"Don Juan, Don Juan," murmured the walls and roof a few yards farther—a different voice this time.

"Don Juan Gusman del Pulgar!" a third voice took up, clearer and more plaintive than the others.

The magnanimous cavalier's blood began to run cold, and icy perspiration to clot his hair. He walked on nevertheless.

"Don Juan," repeated a fourth voice, a little buzz close to his ear.

But the bats set up a dreadful shrieking which drowned it.

He shivered as he went; it seemed to him he had recognized the voice of the jasmine-cheeked Azahar, as she called on him from her deathbed.

The reddish speck had meanwhile grown large at the bottom of the shaft, and he had understood that it was not a flame but the light of some place beyond. Might it be hell? he thought. But he strode on nevertheless, grasping his sword and brushing away the bats with his cloak.

"Don Juan! Don Juan!" cried the voices issuing faintly from the darkness. He began to understand that they tried to detain him; and he thought he recognized the voices of Dolores and Fatma, his dead mistresses.

"Silence, you sluts!" he cried. But his knees were shaking, and great drops of sweat fell from his hair on to his cheek.

The speck of light had now become quite large, and turned from red to white. He understood that it represented the exit from the gallery. But he could not understand why, as he advanced, the light, instead of being brighter, seemed filmed over and fainter.

"Juan, Juan," wailed a new voice at his ear. He stood still half a second; a sudden faintness came over him.

"Seraphita," he murmured—"it is my little nun Seraphita." But he felt that she was trying to call him back.

---

[1] *simoon*   Extremely hot desert wind.

"Abominable witch!" he cried. "Avaunt!"[1]

The passage had grown narrower and narrower; so narrow that now he could barely squeeze along beneath the clammy walls, and had to bend his head lest he should hit the ceiling with its stalactites of bats.

Suddenly there was a great rustle of wings, and a long shriek. A night bird had been startled by his tread and had whirled on before him, tearing through the veil of vagueness that dimmed the outer light. As the bird tore open its way, a stream of dazzling light entered the corridor: it was as if a curtain had suddenly been drawn.

"Too-hoo! Too-hoo!" shrieked the bird, and Don Juan, following its flight, brushed his way through the cobwebs of four centuries and issued, blind and dizzy, into the outer world.

5

For a long while the Count of Miramor stood dazed and dazzled, unable to see anything save the whirling flight of the owl, which circled in what seemed a field of waving, burning red. He closed his eyes; but through the singed lids he still saw that waving red atmosphere, and the black creature whirling about him.

Then, gradually, he began to perceive and comprehend: lines and curves arose shadowy before him, and the faint plash of waters cooled his ringing ears.

He found that he was standing in a lofty colonnade, with a deep tank at his feet, surrounded by high hedges of flowering myrtles, whose jade-coloured water held the reflection of Moorish porticos, shining orange in the sunlight, of high walls covered with shimmering blue and green tiles, and of a great red tower, raising its battlements into the cloudless blue. From the tower waved two flags, a white one and one of purple with a gold pomegranate. As he stood there, a sudden breath of air shuddered through the myrtles, wafting their fragrance towards him; the fountain began to bubble; and the reflection of the porticos and hedges and tower to vacillate in the jade-green water, furling and unfurling like the pieces of a fan; and, above, the two banners unfolded themselves slowly, and little by little began to stream in the wind.

Don Juan advanced. At the farther end of the tank a peacock was standing by the myrtle hedge, immovable as if made of precious enamels; but as Don Juan went by, the short blue-green feathers of his neck began to ruffle; he moved his tail, and, swelling himself out, he slowly unfolded it in a dazzling wheel. As he did so, some blackbirds and thrushes in gilt cages hanging within an archway, began to twitter and to sing.

From the court of the tank, Don Juan entered another and smaller court, passing through a narrow archway. On its marble steps lay three warriors, clad in long embroidered surcoats[2] of silk, beneath which gleamed their armour, and wearing on their heads strange helmets of steel mail,[3] which hung loose on to their gorgets[4] and were surmounted by gilded caps; beneath them—for they had seemingly leaned on them in their slumbers—lay round targes or shields, and battle-axes of Damascus work. As he passed they began to stir and breathe heavily. He strode quickly by, and at the entrance of the smaller court, from which issued a delicious scent of full-blown Persian roses, another sentinel was leaning against a column, his hands clasped round his lance, his head bent on his breast. As Don Juan passed he slowly raised his head, and opened one eye, then the other. Don Juan rushed past, a cold sweat on his brow.

Low beams of sunlight lay upon the little inner court, in whose midst, surrounded by rose hedges, stood a great basin of alabaster, borne on four thickset pillars; a skin, as of ice, filmed over the basin; but, as if someone should have thrown a stone onto a frozen surface, the water began to move and to trickle slowly into the other basin below.

"The waters are flowing, the nightingales singing," murmured a figure which lay by the fountain, grasping, like one just awakened, a lute that lay by his side. From the little court Don Juan entered a series of arched and domed chambers, whose roofs were hung as with icicles of gold and silver, or encrusted with mother-of-pearl constellations that twinkled in the darkness, while the walls shone with patterns that seemed carved of ivory and pearl and beryl and amethyst where the sunbeam grazed them, or imitated some strange sea caves, filled

[1] *Avaunt!*   Go away!

[2] *surcoats*   Richly decorated coats.

[3] *mail*   Rings or plates.

[4] *gorgets*   Armored collars.

with flitting colours, where the shadow rose fuller and higher. In these chambers Don Juan found a number of sleepers, soldiers and slaves, black and white, all of whom sprang to their feet and rubbed their eyes and made obeisance as he went. Then he entered a long passage, lined on either side by a row of sleeping eunuchs, dressed in robes of honour, each leaning, sword in hand, against the wall, and of slave girls with stuff of striped silver about their loins, and sequins at the end of their long hair, and drums and timbrels[1] in their hands.

At regular intervals stood great golden cressets,[2] in which burned sweet-smelling wood, casting a reddish light over the sleeping faces. But as Don Juan approached, the slaves inclined their bodies to the ground, touching it with their turbans, and the girls thumped on their drums and jingled the brass bells of their timbrels. Thus he passed on from chamber to chamber till he came to a great door formed of stars of cedar and ivory studded with gold nails, and bolted by a huge gold bolt, on which ran mystic inscriptions. Don Juan stopped. But, as he did so, the bolt slowly moved in its socket, retreating gradually, and the immense portals swung slowly back, each into its carved hinge column.

Behind them was disclosed a vast circular hall, so vast that you could not possibly see where it ended, and filled with a profusion of lights, wax candles held by rows and rows of white maidens, and torches held by rows and rows of white-robed eunuchs, and cressets burning upon lofty stands, and lamps dangling from the distant vault, through which here and there entered, blending strangely with the rest, great beams of white daylight. Don Juan stopped short, blinded by this magnificence, and as he did so the fountain in the midst of the hall arose and shivered its cypress-like crest against the topmost vault, and innumerable voices of exquisite sweetness burst forth in strange, wistful chants, and instruments of all kinds, both such as are blown and such as are twanged and rubbed with a bow, and such as are shaken and thumped, united with the voices and filled the hall with sound, as it was already filled with light.

Don Juan grasped his sword and advanced. At the extremity of the hall a flight of alabaster steps led up to a dais or raised recess, overhung by an archway whose stalactites shone like beaten gold, and whose tiled walls glistened like precious stones. And on the dais, on a throne of sandalwood and ivory, encrusted with gems and carpeted with the product of the Chinese loom,[3] sat the Moorish Infanta, fast asleep.

To the right and the left, but on a step beneath the princess, stood her two most intimate attendants, the Chief Duenna and the Chief Eunuch, to whom the prudent King Yahya had entrusted his only child during her sleep of four hundred years. The Chief Duenna was habited in a suit of sad-coloured violet weeds,[4] with many modest swathings of white muslin round her yellow and wrinkled countenance. The Chief Eunuch was a portly negro, of a fine purple hue, with cheeks like an allegorical wind,[5] and a complexion as shiny as a well-worn door-knocker: he was enveloped from top to toe in marigold-coloured robes, and on his head he wore a towering turban of embroidered cashmere.

Both these great personages held, beside their especial insignia of office, namely, a Mecca rosary in the hand of the Duenna, and a silver wand in the hand of the Eunuch, great fans of white peacock's tails wherewith to chase away from their royal charge any ill-advised fly. But at this moment all the flies in the place were fast asleep, and the Duenna and the Eunuch also. And between them, canopied by a parasol of white silk on which were embroidered, in figures which moved like those in dreams, the histories of Jusuf and Zuleika,[6] of Solomon and the Queen of Sheba, and of many other famous lovers, sat the Infanta, erect, but veiled in gold-starred gauzes, as an unfinished statue is veiled in the roughness of the marble.

Don Juan walked quickly between the rows of prostrate slaves, and the singing dancing girls, and those holding tapers and torches; and stopped only at the very foot of the throne steps.

"Awake!" he cried. "My princess, my bride, awake!"

A faint stir arose in the veils of the muffled form; and Don Juan felt his temples throb, and, at the same

---

[1] *timbrels* Tambourines.

[2] *cressets* Vessels that hold combustible materials, for light.

[3] *product … loom* I.e., silk.

[4] *weeds* Clothes.

[5] *cheeks … wind* I.e., puffed out, as if ready to blow.

[6] *Jusuf and Zuleika* Subjects of a love story written by Sufi author Jami (c. 1490).

time, a deathly coldness steal over him.

"Awake!" he repeated boldly. But instead of the Infanta, it was the venerable Duenna who raised her withered countenance and looked round with a startled jerk, awakened not so much by the voices and instruments as by the tread of a masculine boot. The Chief Eunuch also awoke suddenly; but with the grace of one grown old in the antechamber of kings he quickly suppressed a yawn, and, laying his hand on his embroidered vest, made a profound obeisance.

"Verily," he remarked, "Allah (who alone possesses the secrets of the universe) is remarkably great, since he not only—"

"Awake, awake, princess!" interrupted Don Juan ardently, his foot on the lowest step of the throne.

But the Chief Eunuch waved him back with his wand, continuing his speech—"since he not only gave unto his servant King Yahya (may his shadow never be less!) power and riches far exceeding that of any of the kings of the earth or even of Solomon the son of David—"

"Cease, fellow!" cried Don Juan, and pushing aside the wand and the negro's dimpled chocolate hand, he rushed up the steps and flung himself at the foot of the veiled Infanta, his rapier clanging strangely as he did so.

"Unveil, my beloved, more beautiful than Oriana, for whom Amadis wept in the Black Mountain, than Gradasilia whom Felixmarte sought on the winged dragon, than Helen of Sparta who fired the towers of Troy, than Calixto whom Jove was obliged to change into a female bear, than Venus herself on whom Paris bestowed the fatal apple. Unveil and arise, like the rosy Aurora from old Tithonus'[1] couch, and welcome the knight who has confronted every peril for thee, Juan Gusman del Pulgar, Count of Miramor, who is ready, for thee, to confront every other peril of the world or of hell; and to fix upon thee alone his affections, more roving hitherto than those of Prince Galaor or of the many-shaped god Proteus!"

A shiver ran through the veiled princess. The Chief Eunuch gave a significant nod, and waved his white wand thrice. Immediately a concert of voices and instruments, as numerous as those of the forces of the air when mustered before King Solomon, filled the vast hall. The dancing girls raised their tambourines over their heads and poised themselves on tiptoe. A wave of fragrant essences passed through the air filled with the spray of innumerable fountains. And the Duenna, slowly advancing to the side of the throne, took in her withered fingers the topmost fold of shimmering gauze, and, slowly gathering it backwards, displayed the Infanta unveiled before Don Juan's gaze.

The breast of the princess heaved deeply; her lips opened with a little sigh, and she languidly raised her long-fringed lids, then cast down her eyes on the ground and resumed the rigidity of a statue. She was most marvellously fair. She sat on the cushions of the throne with modestly crossed legs; her hands, with nails tinged violet with henna, demurely folded in her lap. Through the thinness of her embroidered muslins shone the magnificence of purple and orange vests, stiff with gold and gems, and all subdued into a wondrous opalescent radiance. From her head there descended on either side of her person a diaphanous veil of shimmering colours, powdered over with minute glittering spangles. Her breast was covered with rows and rows of the largest pearls, a perfect network reaching from her slender throat to her waist, among which flashed diamonds embroidered in her vest.

Her face was oval, with the silver pallor of the young moon; her mouth, most subtly carmined,[2] looked like a pomegranate flower among tuberoses, for her cheeks were painted white, and the orbits of her great long-fringed eyes were stained violet. In the middle of each cheek, however, was a delicate spot of pink, in which an exquisite art had painted a small pattern of pyramid shape, so naturally that you might have thought that a real piece of embroidered stuff was decorating the maiden's countenance. On her head she wore a high tiara of jewels, the ransom of many kings, which sparkled and blazed like a lit-up altar. The eyes of the princess were decorously fixed on the ground.

Don Juan stood silent in ravishment.

"Princess!" he at length began.

But the Chief Eunuch laid his wand gently on his shoulder.

---

[1] *Oriana … Tithonus* Don Juan alludes to numerous love stories from romance, epic and myth.

[2] *carmined* Rubbed with crimson pigment.

"My Lord," he whispered, "it is not etiquette that your Magnificence should address her Highness in any direct fashion; let alone the fact that her Highness does not understand the Castilian tongue, nor your Magnificence the Arabic. But through the mediumship of this most respectable lady, her Discretion the Principal Duenna, and my unworthy self, a conversation can be carried on equally delicious and instructive to both parties."

"A plague upon the old brute!" thought Don Juan; but he reflected upon what had never struck him before, that they had indeed been conversing, or attempting to converse, in Spanish, and that the Castilian spoken by the Chief Eunuch was, although correct, quite obsolete, being that of the sainted King Ferdinand. There was a whispered consultation between the two great dignitaries; and the Duenna approached her lips to the Infanta's ear. The princess moved her pomegranate lips in a faint smile, but without raising her eyelids, and murmured something which the ancient lady whispered to the Chief Eunuch, who bowed thrice in answer. Then turning to Don Juan with most mellifluous tones, "Her Highness the Princess," he said, bowing thrice as he mentioned her name, "is, like all princesses, but to an even more remarkable extent, endowed with the most exquisite modesty. She is curious, therefore, despite the superiority of her charms—so conspicuous even to those born blind—to know whether your Magnificence does not consider her the most beautiful thing you have ever beheld."

Don Juan laid his hand upon his heart with an affirmative gesture more eloquent than any words.

Again an almost invisible smile hovered about the pomegranate mouth, and there was a murmur and a whispering consultation.

"Her Highness," pursued the Chief Eunuch blandly, "has been informed by the judicious instructors of her tender youth, that cavaliers are frequently fickle, and that your Lordship in particular has assured many ladies in succession that each was the most beautiful creature you had ever beheld. Without admitting for an instant the possibility of a parallel, she begs your Magnificence to satisfy her curiosity on the point. Does your Lordship consider her as infinitely more beautiful than the Lady Catalina?"

Now Catalina was one of the famous seven for whom Don Juan had committed a deadly crime.

He was taken aback by the exactness of the Infanta's information; he was rather sorry they should have told her about Catalina.

"Of course," he answered hastily; "pray do not mention such a name in her Highness's presence."

The princess bowed imperceptibly.

"Her Highness," pursued the Chief Eunuch, "still actuated by the curiosity due to her high birth and tender youth, is desirous of knowing whether your Lordship considers her far more beautiful than the Lady Violante?"

Don Juan made an impatient gesture. "Slave! Never speak of Violante in my princess's presence!" he exclaimed, fixing his eyes upon the tuberose cheeks and the pomegranate mouth which bloomed among that shimmer of precious stones.

"Good. And may the same be said to apply to the ladies Dolores and Elvira?"

"Dolores and Elvira and Fatma and Azahar," answered Don Juan, greatly provoked at the Chief Eunuch's want of tact, "and all the rest of womankind."

"And shall we add also, than Sister Seraphita of the Convent of Santa Isabel la Real?"

"Yes," cried Don Juan, "than Sister Seraphita, for whom I committed the greatest sin which can be committed by living man."

As he said these words, Don Juan was about to fling his arms about the princess and cut short this rather too elaborate courtship.

But again he was waved back by the white wand.

"One question more, only one, my dear Lord," whispered the Chief Eunuch. "I am most concerned at your impatience, but the laws of etiquette and the caprices of young princesses *must* go before everything, as you will readily admit. Stand back, I pray you."

Don Juan felt sorely inclined to thrust his sword through the yellow bolster of the great personage's vest; but he choked his rage, and stood quietly on the throne steps, one hand on his heart, the other on his sword-hilt, the boldest cavalier in all the kingdom of Spain.

"Speak, speak!" he begged.

The princess, without moving a muscle of her exquisite face, or unclosing her flower-like mouth, murmured some words to the Duenna, who whispered them mysteriously to the Chief Eunuch.

At this moment also the Infanta raised her heavy eyelids, stained violet with henna, and fixed upon the cavalier a glance long, dark, and deep, like that of the wild antelope.

"Her Highness," resumed the Chief Eunuch, with a sweet smile, "is extremely gratified with your Lordship's answers, although, of course, they could not possibly have been at all different. But there remains yet another lady—"

Don Juan shook his head impatiently.

"Another lady concerning whom the Infanta desires some information. Does your Lordship consider her more beautiful also than the Virgin of the Seven Daggers?"

The place seemed to swim about Don Juan. Before his eyes rose the throne, all vacillating in its splendour, and on the throne the Moorish Infanta with the triangular patterns painted on her tuberose cheeks, and the long look in her henna'd eyes; and the image of her was blurred, and imperceptibly it seemed to turn into the effigy, black and white in her stiff puce frock and seed-pearl stomacher,[1] of the Virgin of the Seven Daggers staring blankly into space.

"My Lord," remarked the Chief Eunuch, "methinks that love has made you somewhat inattentive, a great blemish in a cavalier, when answering the questions of a lovely princess. I therefore venture to repeat: do you consider her more beautiful than the Virgin of the Seven Daggers?"

"Do you consider her more beautiful than the Virgin of the Seven Daggers?" repeated the Duenna, glaring at Don Juan.

"Do you consider me more beautiful than the Virgin of the Seven Daggers?" asked the princess, speaking suddenly in Spanish, or, at least, in language perfectly intelligible to Don Juan. And, as she spoke the words, all the slave-girls and eunuchs and singers and players, the whole vast hallful, seemed to echo the same question.

The Count of Miramor stood silent for an instant; then raising his hand and looking around him with quiet decision, he answered in a loud voice:

"No!"

"In that case," said the Chief Eunuch, with the politeness of a man desirous of cutting short an embarrassing silence, "in that case I am very sorry it should be my painful duty to intimate to your Lordship that you must undergo the punishment usually allotted to cavaliers who are disobliging to young and tender princesses."

So saying, he clapped his black hands, and, as if by magic, there arose at the foot of the steps a gigantic Berber of the Rif,[2] his brawny sunburned limbs left bare by a scanty striped shirt fastened round his waist by a wisp of rope, his head shaven blue except in the middle, where, encircled by a coronet of worsted rag, there flamed a topknot of dreadful orange hair.

"Decapitate that gentleman," ordered the Chief Eunuch in his most obliging tones. Don Juan felt himself collared, dragged down the steps, and forced into a kneeling posture on the lowest landing, all in the twinkling of an eye.

From beneath the bronzed left arm of the ruffian he could see the milk white of the alabaster steps, the gleam of an immense scimitar,[3] the mingled blue and yellow of the cressets and tapers, the daylight filtering through the constellations in the dark cedar vault, the glitter of the Infanta's diamonds, and, of a sudden, the twinkle of the Chief Eunuch's eye.

Then all was black, and Don Juan felt himself, that is to say, his own head, rebound three times like a ball upon the alabaster steps.

6

It had evidently all been a dream—perhaps a delusion induced by the vile fumigations of that filthy ruffian of a renegade Jew. The infidel dogs had certain abominable drugs which gave them visions of paradise and hell when smoked or chewed—nasty brutes that they were—and this was some of their devilry. But he should pay for it, the cursed old graybeard, the Holy Office should keep him warm, or a Miramor was not a Miramor. For Don Juan forgot, or disbelieved, not only that he himself had been beheaded by a Rif Berber the evening before, but that he had previously run poor Baruch through the

---

[1]   *stomacher*   Jeweled chest covering.

[2]   *Berber*   Member of a tribe of North Africa, in this case from the Rif district in Morocco.

[3]   *scimitar*   Curved sword.

body and hurled him down the rocks near the Tower of the Cypresses.

This confusion of mind was excusable on the part of the cavalier. For, on opening his eyes, he had found himself lying in a most unlikely resting place, considering the time and season, namely, a heap of old bricks and rubbish, half-hidden in withered reeds and sprouting weeds, on a ledge of the precipitous hillside that descends into the River Darro. Above him rose the dizzy red-brick straightness of the tallest tower of the Alhambra, pierced at its very top by an arched and pillared window, and scantily overgrown with the roots of a dead ivy tree. Below, at the bottom of the precipice, dashed the little Darro, brown and swollen with melted snows, between its rows of leafless poplars; beyond it, the roofs and balconies and orange trees of the older part of Grenada; and above that, with the morning sunshine and mists fighting among its hovels, its square belfries and great masses of prickly pear and aloe, the Albaycin, whose highest convent tower stood out already against a sky of winter blue. The Albaycin—that was the quarter of that villain Baruch, who dared to play practical jokes on grandees of Spain of the very first class.

This thought caused Don Juan to spring up, and, grasping his sword, to scramble through the sprouting elder-bushes and the heaps of broken masonry, down to the bridge over the river.

It was a beautiful winter morning, sunny, blue, and crisp through the white mists; and Don Juan sped along as with wings to his feet, for having remembered that it was the anniversary of the Liberation, and that he, as descendant of Fernan Perez del Pulgar, would be expected to carry the banner of the city at High Mass in the Cathedral, he had determined that his absence from the ceremony should raise no suspicions of his ridiculous adventure. For ridiculous it had been—and the sense of its being ridiculous filled the generous breast of the Count of Miramor with a longing to murder every man, woman, or child he encountered as he sped through the streets. "Look at his Excellency the Count of Miramor; look at Don Juan Gusman del Pulgar! He's been made a fool of by old Baruch the renegade Jew!" he imagined everybody to be thinking.

But, on the contrary, no one took the smallest notice of him. The muleteers, driving along their beasts laden with heather and myrtle for the bakehouse ovens, allowed their loads to brush him as if he had been the merest errand-boy; the stout black housewives, going to market with their brass braziers tucked under their cloaks, never once turned round as he pushed them rudely on the cobbles; nay, the very beggars, armless and legless and shameless, who were alighting from their go-carts and taking up their station at the church doors, did not even extend a hand towards the passing cavalier. Before a popular barber's some citizens were waiting to have their topknots plaited into tidy tails, discussing the while the olive harvest, the price of spart-grass[1] and the chances of the bull-ring. This, Don Juan expected, would be a fatal spot, for from the barber's shop the news must go about that Don Juan del Pulgar, hatless and covered with mud, was hurrying home with a discomfited countenance, ill-befitting the hero of so many nocturnal adventures. But, although Don Juan had to make his way right in front of the barber's, not one of the clients did so much as turn his head, perhaps out of fear of displeasing so great a cavalier. Suddenly, as Don Juan hurried along, he noticed for the first time, among the cobbles and the dry mud of the street, large drops of blood, growing larger as they went, becoming an almost uninterrupted line, then, in the puddles, a little red stream. Such were by no means uncommon vestiges in those days of duels and town broils;[2] besides, some butcher or early sportsman, a wild boar on his horse, might have been passing.

But somehow or other this track of blood exerted an odd attraction over Don Juan; and unconsciously to himself, instead of taking the shortcut to his palace, he followed it along some of the chief streets of Grenada. The bloodstains, as was natural, led in the direction of the great hospital, founded by St. John of God, to which it was customary to carry the victims of accidents and street fights. Before the monumental gateway, where St. John of God knelt in effigy before the Madonna, a large crowd was collected, above whose heads oscillated the black-and-white banners of a mortuary confraternity, and the flame and smoke of their torches. The street was blocked with carts, and with riders rising in their stirrups to look over the crowd, and even by gaily

---

[1]　*spart-grass*　Spanish broom, or rushes.

[2]　*broils*　Battles.

trapped mules and gilded coaches, in which veiled ladies were anxiously questioning their lackeys and outriders. The throng of idle and curious citizens, of monks and brothers of mercy, reached up the steps and right into the cloistered court of the hospital.

"Who is it?" asked Don Juan, with his usual masterful manner pushing his way into the crowd. The man whom he addressed, a stalwart peasant with a long tail pinned under his hat, turned round vaguely, but did not answer.

"Who is it?" repeated Don Juan louder.

But no one answered, although he accompanied the question with a good push, and even a thrust with his sheathed sword.

"Cursed idiots! Are you all deaf and dumb that you cannot answer a cavalier?" he cried angrily, and taking a portly priest by the collar he shook him roughly.

"Jesus Maria Joseph!" exclaimed the priest; but turning round he took no notice of Don Juan, and merely rubbed his collar, muttering, "Well, if the demons are to be allowed to take respectable canons by the collar, it *is* time that we should have a good witch-burning."

Don Juan took no heed of his words, but thrust onward, upsetting, as he did so, a young woman who was lifting her child to let it see the show. The crowd parted as the woman fell, and people ran to pick her up, but no one took any notice of Don Juan. Indeed, he himself was struck by the way in which he passed through its midst, encountering no opposition from the phalanx of robust shoulders and hips.

"Who is it?" asked Don Juan again.

He had got into a clearing of the crowd. On the lowest step of the hospital gate stood a little knot of black penitents, their black linen cowls flung back on their shoulders, and of priests and monks muttering together. Some of them were beating back the crowd, others snuffing their torches against the paving-stones, and letting the wax drip off their tapers. In the midst of them, with a standard of the Virgin at its head, was a light wooden bier, set down by its bearers. It was covered with coarse black serge, on which were embroidered in yellow braid a skull and crossbones, and the monogram I.H.S.[1] Under the bier was a little red pool.

"Who is it?" asked Don Juan one last time; but instead of waiting for an answer, he stepped forward, sword in hand, and rudely pulled aside the rusty black pall.

On the bier was stretched a corpse dressed in black velvet, with lace cuffs and collar, loose boots, buff gloves, and a blood-clotted dark matted head, lying loose half an inch above the mangled throat.

Don Juan Gusman del Pulgar stared fixedly.

It was himself.

The church into which Don Juan had fled was that of the Virgin of the Seven Daggers. It was deserted, as usual, and filled with chill morning light, in which glittered the gilded cornices and altars, and gleamed, like pools of water, the many precious marbles. A sort of mist seemed to hang about it all and dim the splendour of the high altar.

Don Juan del Pulgar sank down in the midst of the nave; not on his knees, for (O horror!) he felt that he had no longer any knees, nor indeed any back, any arms, or limbs of any kind, and he dared not ask himself whether he was still in possession of a head: his only sensations were such as might be experienced by a slowly trickling pool, or a snow-wreath in process of melting, or a cloud fitting itself on to a flat surface of rock.

He was disembodied. He now understood why no one had noticed him in the crowd, why he had been able to penetrate through its thickness, and why, when he struck people and pulled them by the collar and knocked them down, they had taken no more notice of him than of a blast of wind. He was a ghost. He was dead. This was the afterlife; and he was infallibly within a few minutes of hell.

"O Virgin, Virgin of the Seven Daggers," he cried with hopeless bitterness, "is this the way you recompense my faithfulness? I have died unshriven,[2] in the midst of mortal sin, merely because I would not say you were less beautiful than the Moorish Infanta; and is this all my reward?"

But even as he spoke these words an extraordinary miracle took place. The white winter light broke into wondrous iridescences; the white mist collected into

---

[1] *I.H.S.*   Represents the Greek abbreviation of the word Jesus.

[2] *unshriven* Without the sacrament of Confession and the accompanying forgiveness of sins.

shoals of dim palm-bearing angels; the cloud of stale incense, still hanging over the high altar, gathered into fleecy balls, which became the heads and backs of well-to-do cherubs; and Don Juan, reeling and fainting, felt himself rise, higher and higher, as if borne up on clusters of soap bubbles. The cupola began to rise and expand; the painted clouds to move and blush a deeper pink; the painted sky to recede and turn into deep holes of real blue. As he was borne upwards, the allegorical virtues in the lunettes began to move and brandish their attributes; the colossal stucco angels on the cornices to pelt him with flowers no longer of plaster of Paris; the place was filled with delicious fragrance of incense, and with sounds of exquisitely played lutes and viols, and of voices, among which he distinctly recognized Syphax, His Majesty's chief soprano. And, as Don Juan floated upwards through the cupola of the church, his heart suddenly filled with a consciousness of extraordinary virtue; the gold transparency at the top of the dome expanded; its rays grew redder and more golden, and there burst from it at last a golden moon crescent, on which stood, in her farthingale of puce and her

stomacher of seed-pearl, her big black eyes fixed mildly upon him, the Virgin of the Seven Daggers.

"Your story of the late noble Count of Miramor, Don Juan Gusman del Pulgar," wrote Don Pedro Calderon de la Barca, in March 1666, to his friend, the Archpriest Morales, at Grenada, "so veraciously revealed in a vision to the holy prior of St. Nicholas, is indeed such as must touch the heart of the most stubborn. Were it presented in the shape of a play, adorned with graces of style and with flowers of rhetoric, it would be indeed (with the blessing of heaven) well calculated to spread the glory of our holy church. But alas, my dear friend, the snows of age are as thick on my head as the snows of winter upon your Mulhacen; and who knows whether I shall ever be able to write again ?"

The forecast of the illustrious dramatic poet proved, indeed, too true; and hence it is that unworthy modern hands have sought to frame the veracious and moral history of Don Juan and the Virgin of the Seven Daggers.

—1889

SIR ARTHUR CONAN DOYLE
_1859 – 1930_

Britritish Detective Sherlock Holmes is so renowned that his fame outstrips that of his creator, Sir Arthur Conan Doyle. Conan Doyle wrote many other sorts of fiction, as well as books on history, war, and supernatural subjects, and although some were very successful, they never roused the interest generated by the man with the deerstalker cap, calabash pipe, and magnifying glass, who solved crimes using "elementary" deductions, abetted by the faithful Dr. Watson. When Conan Doyle grew bored with his creation and tried to kill off Holmes and his evil nemesis Professor Moriarty, his reading public wore arm bands to display their mourning, and publishers offered such enormous sums to have Holmes revived that Conan Doyle eventually succumbed to pressure and brought his character back to life.

For Conan Doyle, life began in Edinburgh, Scotland, in 1859. His father, Charles Altamont Doyle, was a civil servant with artistic aspirations, but alcoholism and epilepsy eventually caused him to be institutionalized. Conan Doyle's mother, Mary Foley Doyle, encouraged her son's voluminous appetite for books and his literary aspirations, even though unrelieved poverty made educating her ten children a financial struggle. When Conan Doyle came of age, he studied medicine at Edinburgh University—where he met Dr. Joseph Bell, the man who became the model for Sherlock Holmes—and earned his medical degree in 1881. During a subsequent medical stint in Southsea near Portsmouth, where his practice was undemanding and left him ample spare time, he began writing; he devoted himself to it full-time beginning in 1891.

Conan Doyle's first Sherlock Holmes adventure, _A Study in Scarlet_, was written in Southsea and published in the 1887 _Beeton Christmas Annual._ After he had published his second Holmes story, _The Sign of the Four_, in _Lippincott's Magazine_ in 1890, _The Strand Magazine_ began featuring "The Adventures of Sherlock Holmes." (The illustrations by Sidney Paget that accompany "The Adventure of the Speckled Band," below are from its original publication in _The Strand_ in 1892.) In an age of great scientific discovery, the public became captivated by Holmes's cool, rational, almost superhuman reasoning skills, but readers also responded to his all-too-human problems, such as his fear of emotional ties and his cocaine habit. Conan Doyle created other memorable characters in such books as _Micah Clarke_ (1889) and _The Lost World_ (1912), but none attained Holmes's cachet, much to Conan Doyle's chagrin. In 1891 he complained that the Sherlock Holmes adventures held back his writing career: "I'm thinking of slaying Holmes," he said in a letter to his mother, "He takes my mind from better things."

Whether or not these other "things" were better, Conan Doyle penned much fine work alongside his Sherlock Holmes adventures, including the historical novel _The White Company_ (1891) and _The Poison Belt_ (1913). He also adapted some of his Holmes stories, such as "The Speckled Band," for the stage. After serving in the Boer War in South Africa, he was knighted in recognition of two treatises he had written in support of the war. In the final decades of his life, most notably after the death of his son in World War I, Conan Doyle became immersed in spiritualism and the occult, writing and lecturing extensively on the subject.

After returning from an exhaustive lecture tour in 1929, Conan Doyle suffered a heart attack. He never regained his health and he died in 1930. He is buried in the rose garden at Windlesham, his home in Sussex, where he had lived with his second wife (his first wife had died in 1906) and children.

⌘ ⌘ ⌘

The Adventure of the Speckled Band

In glancing over my notes of the seventy odd cases in which I have during the last eight years studied the methods of my friend Sherlock Holmes, I find many tragic, some comic, a large number merely strange, but none commonplace; for, working as he did rather for the love of his art than for the acquirement of wealth, he refused to associate himself with any investigation which did not tend towards the unusual, and even the fantastic. Of all these varied cases, however, I cannot recall any which presented more singular features than that which was associated with the well-known Surrey family of the Roylotts of Stoke Moran. The events in question occurred in the early days of my association with Holmes, when we were sharing rooms as bachelors, in Baker Street. It is possible that I might have placed them upon record before, but a promise of secrecy was made at the time, from which I have only been freed during the last month by the untimely death of the lady to whom the pledge was given. It is perhaps as well that the facts should now come to light, for I have reasons to know there are widespread rumours as to the death of Dr. Grimesby Roylott which tend to make the matter even more terrible than the truth.

It was early in April, the year '83, that I woke one morning to find Sherlock Holmes standing, fully dressed, by the side of my bed. He was a late riser as a rule, and, as the clock on the mantelpiece showed me that it was only a quarter past seven, I blinked up at him in some surprise, and perhaps just a little resentment, for I was myself regular in my habits.

"Very sorry to knock you up,[1] Watson," said he, "but it's the common lot this morning. Mrs. Hudson has

been knocked up, she retorted upon me, and I on you."

"What is it, then? A fire?"

"No, a client. It seems that a young lady has arrived in a considerable state of excitement, who insists upon seeing me. She is waiting now in the sitting room. Now, when young ladies wander about the metropolis at this hour of the morning, and knock sleepy people up out of their beds, I presume that it is something very pressing which they have to communicate. Should it prove to be an interesting case, you would, I am sure, wish to follow it from the outset. I thought at any rate that I should call you, and give you the chance."

"My dear fellow, I would not miss it for anything."

I had no keener pleasure than in following Holmes in his professional investigations, and in admiring the rapid deductions, as swift as intuitions, and yet always founded on a logical basis, with which he unravelled the problems which were submitted to him. I rapidly threw on my clothes, and was ready in a few minutes to accompany my friend down to the sitting room. A lady dressed in black and heavily veiled, who had been sitting in the window, rose as we entered.

"Good morning, madam," said Holmes cheerily. "My name is Sherlock Holmes. This is my intimate friend and associate, Dr. Watson, before whom you can speak as freely as before myself. Ha, I am glad to see that Mrs. Hudson has had the good sense to light the fire. Pray draw up to it, and I shall order you a cup of hot coffee, for I observe that you are shivering."

"It is not cold which makes me shiver," said the woman in a low voice, changing her seat as requested.

"What then?"

"It is fear, Mr. Holmes. It is terror." She raised her veil as she spoke, and we could see that she was indeed in a pitiable state of agitation, her face all drawn and grey, with restless, frightened eyes, like those of some

---

[1] *knock you up* I.e., "wake you up with a knock at the door." (This usage remains current in some parts of Britain.)

hunted animal. Her features and figure were those of a woman of thirty, but her hair was shot with premature grey, and her expression was weary and haggard. Sherlock Holmes ran her over with one of his quick, all-comprehensive glances.[1]

"She raised her veil."

"You must not fear," said he soothingly, bending forward and patting her forearm. "We shall soon set matters right, I have no doubt. You have come in by train this morning, I see."

"You know me, then?"

"No, but I observe the second half of a return ticket in the palm of your left glove. You must have started early, and yet you had a good drive in a dog-cart, along heavy roads, before you reached the station."

The lady gave a violent start, and stared in bewilderment at my companion.

"There is no mystery, my dear madam," said he, smiling. "The left arm of your jacket is spattered with mud in no less than seven places. The marks are perfectly fresh. There is no vehicle save a dog-cart which throws up mud in that way, and then only when you sit on the left-hand side of the driver."

"Whatever your reasons may be, you are perfectly correct," said she. "I started from home before six, reached Leatherhead at twenty past, and came in by the first train to Waterloo. Sir, I can stand this strain no

longer, I shall go mad if it continues. I have no one to turn to—none, save only one, who cares for me, and he, poor fellow, can be of little aid. I have heard of you, Mr. Holmes; I have heard of you from Mrs. Farintosh, whom you helped in the hour of her sore need. It was from her that I had your address. Oh, sir, do you not think you could help me too, and at least throw a little light through the dense darkness which surrounds me? At present it is out of my power to reward you for your services, but in a month or two I shall be married, with the control of my own income, and then at least you shall not find me ungrateful."

Holmes turned to his desk, and unlocking it, drew out a small casebook which he consulted.

"Farintosh," said he. "Ah, yes, I recall the case; it was concerned with an opal tiara. I think it was before your time, Watson. I can only say, madam, that I shall be happy to devote the same care to your case as I did to that of your friend. As to reward, my profession is its reward; but you are at liberty to defray whatever expenses I may be put to, at the time which suits you best. And now I beg that you will lay before us everything that may help us in forming an opinion upon the matter."

"Alas!" replied our visitor. "The very horror of my situation lies in the fact that my fears are so vague, and my suspicions depend so entirely upon small points, which might seem trivial to another, that even he to whom of all others I have a right to look for help and advice looks upon all that I tell him about it as the fancies of a nervous woman. He does not say so, but I can read it from his soothing answers and averted eyes. But I have heard, Mr. Holmes, that you can see deeply into the manifold wickedness of the human heart. You may advise me how to walk amid the dangers which encompass me."

"I am all attention, madam."

"My name is Helen Stoner, and I am living with my stepfather, who is the last survivor of one of the oldest Saxon families in England, the Roylotts of Stoke Moran, on the western border of Surrey."

Holmes nodded his head. "The name is familiar to me," said he.

"The family was at one time among the richest in England, and the estate extended over the borders into Berkshire in the north, and Hampshire in the west. In

---

[1] *She raised her veil ... glances*   The illustration of this scene is by Sidney Paget; it accompanied the story's original publication in *The Strand Magazine* in 1892. Paget's eight other original illustrations are also included in these pages.

the last century, however, four successive heirs were of a dissolute and wasteful disposition, and the family ruin was eventually completed by a gambler, in the days of the Regency.[1] Nothing was left save a few acres of ground and the two-hundred-year-old house, which is itself crushed under a heavy mortgage. The last squire dragged out his existence there, living the horrible life of an aristocratic pauper; but his only son, my stepfather, seeing that he must adapt himself to the new conditions, obtained an advance from a relative, which enabled him to take a medical degree, and went out to Calcutta, where, by his professional skill and his force of character, he established a large practice. In a fit of anger, however, caused by some robberies which had been perpetrated in the house, he beat his native butler to death, and narrowly escaped a capital sentence. As it was, he suffered a long term of imprisonment, and afterwards returned to England a morose and disappointed man.

"When Dr. Roylott was in India he married my mother, Mrs. Stoner, the young widow of Major-General Stoner, of the Bengal Artillery. My sister Julia and I were twins, and we were only two years old at the time of my mother's re-marriage. She had a considerable sum of money, not less than a thousand a year, and this she bequeathed to Dr. Roylott entirely whilst we resided with him, with a provision that a certain annual sum should be allowed to each of us in the event of our marriage. Shortly after our return to England my mother died—she was killed eight years ago in a railway accident near Crewe. Dr. Roylott then abandoned his attempts to establish himself in practice in London, and took us to live with him in the ancestral house at Stoke Moran. The money which my mother had left was enough for all our wants, and there seemed no obstacle to our happiness.

"But a terrible change came over our stepfather about this time. Instead of making friends and exchanging visits with our neighbours, who had at first been overjoyed to see a Roylott of Stoke Moran back in the old family seat, he shut himself up in his house, and seldom came out save to indulge in ferocious quarrels

with whoever might cross his path. Violence of temper approaching to mania has been hereditary in the men of the family, and in my stepfather's case it had, I believe, been intensified by his long residence in the tropics. A series of disgraceful brawls took place, two of which ended in the police-court, until at last he became the terror of the village, and the folks would fly at his approach, for he is a man of immense strength, and absolutely uncontrollable in his anger.

"He hurled the blacksmith over a parapet."

"Last week he hurled the local blacksmith over a parapet[2] into a stream and it was only by paying over all the money that I could gather together that I was able to avert another public exposure. He had no friends at all save the wandering gypsies, and he would give these vagabonds leave to encamp upon the few acres of bramble-covered land which represent the family estate, and would accept in return the hospitality of their tents, wandering away with them sometimes for weeks on end. He has a passion also for Indian animals, which are sent over to him by a correspondent, and he has at this moment a cheetah and a baboon, which wander freely over his grounds, and are feared by the villagers almost as much as their master.

---

[1] the Regency   I.e., 1810–20, the period in which George, Prince of Wales, acted as regent for his father, George III, who was incapacitated by mental illness.

[2] parapet   Stone embankment.

"You can imagine from what I say that my poor sister Julia and I had no great pleasure in our lives. No servant would stay with us, and for a long time we did all the work of the house. She was but thirty at the time of her death, and yet her hair had already begun to whiten, even as mine has."

"Your sister is dead, then?"

"She died just two years ago, and it is of her death that I wish to speak to you. You can understand that, living the life which I have described, we were little likely to see anyone of our own age and position. We had, however, an aunt, my mother's maiden sister, Miss Honoria Westphail, who lives near Harrow, and we were occasionally allowed to pay short visits at this lady's house. Julia went there at Christmas two years ago, and met there a half-pay Major[1] of Marines, to whom she became engaged. My stepfather learned of the engagement when my sister returned, and offered no objection to the marriage; but within a fortnight of the day which had been fixed for the wedding, the terrible event occurred which has deprived me of my only companion."

Sherlock Holmes had been leaning back in his chair with his eyes closed, and his head sunk in a cushion, but he half opened his lids now, and glanced across at his visitor.

"Pray be precise as to details," said he.

"It is easy for me to be so, for every event of that dreadful time is seared into my memory. The manor house is, as I have already said, very old, and only one wing is now inhabited. The bedrooms in this wing are on the ground floor, the sitting rooms being in the central block of the buildings. Of these bedrooms, the first is Dr. Roylott's, the second my sister's, and the third my own. There is no communication between them, but they all open out into the same corridor. Do I make myself plain?"

"Perfectly so."

"The windows of the three rooms open out upon the lawn. That fatal night Dr. Roylott had gone to his room early, though we knew that he had not retired to rest, for my sister was troubled by the smell of the strong Indian cigars which it was his custom to smoke. She left her room, therefore, and came into mine, where she sat for some time, chatting about her approaching wedding.

At eleven o'clock she rose to leave me, but she paused at the door and looked back. 'Tell me, Helen,' said she, 'have you ever heard anyone whistle in the dead of the night?'

"'Never,' said I.

"'I suppose that you could not possibly whistle yourself in your sleep?'

"'Certainly not. But why?'

"'Because during the last few nights I have always, about three in the morning, heard a low clear whistle. I am a light sleeper, and it has awakened me. I cannot tell where it came from—perhaps from the next room, perhaps from the lawn. I thought that I would just ask you whether you had heard it.'

"'No, I have not. It must be those wretched gypsies in the plantation.'

"'Very likely. And yet if it were on the lawn I wonder that you did not hear it also.'

"'Ah, but I sleep more heavily than you.'

"'Well, it is of no great consequence, at any rate,' she smiled back at me, closed my door, and a few moments later I heard her key turn in the lock."

"Indeed," said Holmes. "Was it your custom always to lock yourselves in at night?"

"Always."

"And why?"

"I think that I mentioned to you that the doctor kept a cheetah and a baboon. We had no feeling of security unless our doors were locked."

"Her face blanched with terror."

[1] *half-pay Major* When retired or not in service, officers were paid half their wages.

"Quite so. Pray proceed with your statement."

"I could not sleep that night. A vague feeling of impending misfortune impressed me. My sister and I, you will recollect, were twins, and you know how subtle are the links which bind two souls which are so closely allied. It was a wild night. The wind was howling outside, and the rain was beating and splashing against the windows. Suddenly, amidst all the hubbub of the gale, there burst forth the wild scream of a terrified woman. I knew that it was my sister's voice. I sprang from my bed, wrapped a shawl round me, and rushed into the corridor. As I opened my door I seemed to hear a low whistle, such as my sister described, and a few moments later a clanging sound, as if a mass of metal had fallen. As I ran down the passage my sister's door was unlocked, and revolved slowly upon its hinges. I stared at it horror-stricken, not knowing what was about to issue from it. By the light of the corridor lamp I saw my sister appear at the opening, her face blanched with terror, her hands groping for help, her whole figure swaying to and fro like that of a drunkard. I ran to her and threw my arms round her, but at that moment her knees seemed to give way and she fell to the ground. She writhed as one who is in terrible pain, and her limbs were dreadfully convulsed. At first I thought that she had not recognized me, but as I bent over her she suddenly shrieked out in a voice which I shall never forget, 'O, my God! Helen! It was the band! The speckled band!' There was something else which she would fain have said, and she stabbed with her finger into the air in the direction of the doctor's room, but a fresh convulsion seized her and choked her words. I rushed out, calling loudly for my stepfather, and I met him hastening from his room in his dressing gown. When he reached my sister's side she was unconscious, and though he poured brandy down her throat, and sent for medical aid from the village, all efforts were in vain, for she slowly sank and died without having recovered her consciousness. Such was the dreadful end of my beloved sister."

"One moment," said Holmes; "are you sure about this whistle and metallic sound? Could you swear to it?"

"That was what the county coroner asked me at the inquiry. It was my strong impression that I heard it, and yet among the crash of the gale, and the creaking of an old house, I may possibly have been deceived."

"Was your sister dressed?"

"No, she was in her nightdress. In her right hand was found the charred stump of a match, and in her left a matchbox."

"Showing that she had struck a light and looked about her when the alarm took place. That is important. And what conclusions did the coroner come to?"

"He investigated the case with great care, for Dr. Roylott's conduct had long been notorious in the county, but he was unable to find any satisfactory cause of death. My evidence showed that the door had been fastened upon the inner side, and the windows were blocked by old-fashioned shutters with broad iron bars, which were secured every night. The walls were carefully sounded, and were shown to be quite solid all round, and the flooring was also thoroughly examined, with the same result. The chimney is wide, but is barred up by four large staples. It is certain, therefore, that my sister was quite alone when she met her end. Besides, there were no marks of any violence upon her."

"How about poison?"

"The doctors examined her for it, but without success."

"What do you think that this unfortunate lady died of, then?"

"It is my belief that she died of pure fear and nervous shock, though what it was which frightened her I cannot imagine."

"Were there gypsies in the plantation at the time?"

"Yes, there are nearly always some there."

"Ah, and what did you gather from this allusion to a band—a speckled band?"

"Sometimes I have thought that it was merely the wild talk of delirium, sometimes that it may have referred to some band of people, perhaps to these very gypsies in the plantation. I do not know whether the spotted handkerchiefs which so many of them wear over their heads might have suggested the strange adjective which she used."

Holmes shook his head like a man who is far from being satisfied.

"These are very deep waters," said he; "pray go on with your narrative."

"Two years have passed since then, and my life has

been until lately lonelier than ever. A month ago, however, a dear friend, whom I have known for many years, has done me the honour to ask my hand in marriage. His name is Armitage—Percy Armitage—the second son of Mr. Armitage, of Crane Water, near Reading. My stepfather has offered no opposition to the match, and we are to be married in the course of the spring. Two days ago some repairs were started in the west wing of the building, and my bedroom wall has been pierced, so that I have had to move into the chamber in which my sister died, and to sleep in the very bed in which she slept. Imagine, then, my thrill of terror when last night, as I lay awake, thinking over her terrible fate, I suddenly heard in the silence of the night the low whistle which had been the herald of her own death. I sprang up and lit the lamp, but nothing was to be seen in the room. I was too shaken to go to bed again, however, so I dressed, and as soon as it was daylight I slipped down, got a dog-cart at the Crown Inn, which is opposite, and drove to Leatherhead, from whence I have come on this morning, with the one object of seeing you and asking your advice."

"You have done wisely," said my friend. "But have you told me all?"

"Yes, all."

"Miss Stoner, you have not. You are screening your stepfather."

"Why, what do you mean?"

For answer Holmes pushed back the frill of black lace which fringed the hand that lay upon our visitor's knee. Five little livid spots, the marks of four fingers and a thumb, were printed upon the white wrist.

"You have been cruelly used," said Holmes.

The lady coloured deeply, and covered over her injured wrist. "He is a hard man," she said, "and perhaps he hardly knows his own strength."

There was a long silence, during which Holmes leaned his chin upon his hands and stared into the crackling fire.

"This is very deep business," he said at last. "There are a thousand details which I should desire to know before I decide upon our course of action. Yet we have not a moment to lose. If we were to come to Stoke Moran today, would it be possible for us to see over these rooms without the knowledge of your stepfather?"

"As it happens, he spoke of coming into town today upon some most important business. It is probable that he will be away all day, and that there would be nothing to disturb you. We have a housekeeper now, but she is old and foolish, and I could easily get her out of the way."

"Excellent. You are not averse to this trip, Watson?"

"By no means."

"Then we shall both come. What are you going to do yourself?"

"I have one or two things which I would wish to do now that I am in town. But I shall return by the twelve o'clock train, so as to be there in time for your coming."

"And you may expect us early in the afternoon. I have myself some small business matters to attend to. Will you not wait and breakfast?"

"No, I must go. My heart is lightened already since I have confided my trouble to you. I shall look forward to seeing you again this afternoon." She dropped her thick black veil over her face, and glided from the room.

"And what do you think of it all, Watson?" asked Sherlock Holmes, leaning back in his chair.

"It seems to me to be a most dark and sinister business."

"Dark enough and sinister enough."

"Yet if the lady is correct in saying that the flooring and walls are sound, and that the door, window, and chimney are impassable, then her sister must have been undoubtedly alone when she met her mysterious end."

"What becomes, then, of these nocturnal whistles, and what of the very peculiar words of the dying woman?"

"I cannot think."

"When you combine the ideas of whistles at night, the presence of a band of gypsies who are on intimate terms with this old doctor, the fact that we have every reason to believe that the doctor has an interest in preventing his stepdaughter's marriage, the dying allusion to a band, and finally, the fact that Miss Helen Stoner heard a metallic clang, which might have been caused by one of those metal bars which secured the shutters falling back into their place, I think there is good ground to think that the mystery may be cleared along these lines."

"But what, then, did the gypsies do?"

"I cannot imagine."

"I see many objections to any such a theory."

"And so do I. It is precisely for that reason that we are going to Stoke Moran this day. I want to see whether the objections are fatal, or if they may be explained away. But what, in the name of the devil!"

The ejaculation had been drawn from my companion by the fact that our door had been suddenly dashed open, and that a huge man framed himself in the aperture. His costume was a peculiar mixture of the professional and of the agricultural, having a black top hat, a long frock-coat, and a pair of high gaiters,[1] with a hunting-crop swinging in his hand. So tall was he that his hat actually brushed the crossbar of the doorway, and his breadth seemed to span it across from side to side. A large face, seared with a thousand wrinkles, burned yellow with the sun, and marked with every evil passion, was turned from one to the other of us, while his deep-set, bile-shot eyes, and the high thin fleshless nose, gave him somewhat the resemblance to a fierce old bird of prey.

"Which of you is Holmes?"

"Which of you is Holmes?" asked this apparition.

"My name, sir, but you have the advantage of me," said my companion quietly.

"I am Dr. Grimesby Roylott, of Stoke Moran."

"Indeed, Doctor," said Holmes blandly. "Pray take a seat."

"I will do nothing of the kind. My stepdaughter has been here. I have traced her. What has she been saying to you?"

"It is a little cold for the time of the year," said Holmes.

"What has she been saying to you?" screamed the old man furiously.

"But I have heard that the crocuses promise well," continued my companion imperturbably.

"Ha! You put me off, do you?" said our new visitor, taking a step forward, and shaking his hunting crop. "I know you, you scoundrel! I have heard of you before. You are Holmes the meddler."

My friend smiled.

"Holmes the busybody!"

His smile broadened.

"Holmes the Scotland Yard jack-in-office."[2]

Holmes chuckled heartily. "Your conversation is most entertaining," said he. "When you go out close the door, for there is a decided draught."

"I will go when I have had my say. Don't you dare to meddle with my affairs. I know that Miss Stoner has been here—I traced her! I am a dangerous man to fall foul of! See here." He stepped swiftly forward, seized the poker, and bent it into a curve with his huge brown hands.

"See that you keep yourself out of my grip," he snarled, and hurling the twisted poker into the fireplace, he strode out of the room.

"He seems a very amiable person," said Holmes, laughing. "I am not quite so bulky, but if he had remained I might have shown him that my grip was not much more feeble than his own." As he spoke he picked up the steel poker, and with a sudden effort straightened it out again.

"Fancy his having the insolence to confound me with the official detective force! This incident gives zest to our investigation, however, and I only trust that our little friend will not suffer from her imprudence in

---

[1]   *gaiters*   Coverings of cloth or leather for the lower legs.

[2]   *jack-in-office*   Insolent minor official.

allowing this brute to trace her. And now, Watson, we shall order breakfast, and afterwards I shall walk down to Doctors' Commons,[1] where I hope to get some data which may help us in this matter."

It was nearly one o'clock when Sherlock Holmes returned from his excursion. He held in his hand a sheet of blue paper, scrawled over with notes and figures.

"I have seen the will of the deceased wife," said he. "To determine its exact meaning I have been obliged to work out the present prices of the investments with which it is concerned. The total income, which at the time of the wife's death was little short of £1,100, is now through the fall in agricultural prices not more than £750. Each daughter can claim an income of £250, in case of marriage. It is evident, therefore, that if both girls had married this beauty would have had a mere pittance, while even one of them would cripple him to a serious extent. My morning's work has not been wasted, since it has proved that he has the very strongest motives for standing in the way of anything of the sort. And now, Watson, this is too serious for dawdling, especially as the old man is aware that we are interesting ourselves in his affairs, so if you are ready we shall call a cab and drive to Waterloo. I should be very much obliged if you would slip your revolver into your pocket. An Eley's No. 2[2] is an excellent argument with gentlemen who can twist steel pokers into knots. That and a toothbrush are, I think, all that we need."

At Waterloo we were fortunate in catching a train for Leatherhead, where we hired a trap[3] at the station inn, and drove for four or five miles through the lovely Surrey lanes. It was a perfect day, with a bright sun and a few fleecy clouds in the heavens. The trees and wayside hedges were just throwing out their first green shoots, and the air was full of the pleasant smell of the moist earth. To me at least there was a strange contrast between the sweet promise of the spring and this sinister quest upon which we were engaged. My companion sat in front of the trap, his arms folded, his hat pulled down over his eyes, and his chin sunk upon his breast, buried in the deepest thought.

Suddenly, however, he started, tapped me on the shoulder, and pointed over the meadows.

"Look there!" said he.

A heavily timbered park stretched up in a gentle slope, thickening into a grove at the highest point. From amidst the branches there jutted out the grey gables and high roof-tree[4] of a very old mansion.

"Stoke Moran?" said he.

"Yes, sir, that be the house of Dr. Grimesby Roylott," remarked the driver.

"There is some building going on there," said Holmes; "that is where we are going."

"There's the village," said the driver, pointing to a cluster of roofs some distance to the left; "but if you want to get to the house, you'll find it shorter to go over this stile,[5] and so by the footpath over the fields. There it is, where the lady is walking."

"And the lady, I fancy, is Miss Stoner," observed Holmes, shading his eyes. "Yes, I think we had better do as you suggest."

"We got off, paid our fare."

We got off, paid our fare, and the trap rattled back on its way to Leatherhead.

"I thought it as well," said Holmes, as we climbed the stile, "that this fellow should think we had come here as architects, or on some definite business. It may stop his gossip. Good afternoon, Miss Stoner. You see

---

[1] *Doctors' Commons* Buildings that housed the association of Doctors of Civil Law in London.

[2] *Eley's No. 2* Holmes is likely referring to a small but powerful pistol called a "Webley No. 2," which could be loaded with cartridges made by the ammunition manufacturer Eley.

[3] *trap* Small, two-wheeled carriage.

[4] *roof-tree* Ridge pole.

[5] *stile* Set of steps passing over a fence.

that we have been as good as our word."

Our client of the morning had hurried forward to meet us with a face which spoke her joy. "I have been waiting so eagerly for you," she cried, shaking hands with us warmly. "All has turned out splendidly. Dr. Roylott has gone to town, and it is unlikely that he will be back before evening."

"We have had the pleasure of making the doctor's acquaintance," said Holmes, and in a few words he sketched out what had occurred. Miss Stoner turned white to the lips as she listened.

"Good heavens!" she cried, "he has followed me, then."

"So it appears."

"He is so cunning that I never know when I am safe from him. What will he say when he returns?"

"He must guard himself, for he may find that there is someone more cunning than himself upon his track. You must lock yourself from him tonight. If he is violent, we shall take you away to your aunt's at Harrow. Now, we must make the best use of our time, so kindly take us at once to the rooms which we are to examine."

The building was of grey, lichen-blotched stone, with a high central portion, and two curving wings, like the claws of a crab, thrown out on each side. In one of these wings the windows were broken and blocked with wooden boards, while the roof was partly caved in, a picture of ruin. The central portion was in little better repair, but the right-hand block was comparatively modern, and the blinds in the windows, with the blue smoke curling up from the chimneys, showed that this was where the family resided. Some scaffolding had been erected against the end wall, and the stonework had been broken into, but there were no signs of any workmen at the moment of our visit. Holmes walked slowly up and down the ill-trimmed lawn, and examined with deep attention the outsides of the windows.

"This, I take it, belongs to the room in which you used to sleep, the centre one to your sister's, and the one next to the main building to Dr. Roylott's chamber?"

"Exactly so. But I am now sleeping in the middle one."

"Pending the alterations, as I understand. By the way, there does not seem to be any very pressing need for repairs at that end wall."

"There were none. I believe that it was an excuse to move me from my room."

"Ah! that is suggestive. Now, on the other side of this narrow wing runs the corridor from which these three rooms open. There are windows in it, of course?"

"Yes, but very small ones. Too narrow for anyone to pass through."

"As you both locked your doors at night, your rooms were unapproachable from that side. Now, would you have the kindness to go into your room, and to bar your shutters."

Miss Stoner did so, and Holmes, after a careful examination through the open window, endeavoured in every way to force the shutter open, but without success. There was no slit through which a knife could be passed to raise the bar. Then with his lens[1] he tested the hinges, but they were of solid iron, built firmly into the massive masonry. "Hum!" said he, scratching his chin in some perplexity, "my theory certainly presents some difficulties. No one could pass these shutters if they were bolted. Well, we shall see if the inside throws any light upon the matter."

A small side door led into the white-washed corridor from which the three bedrooms opened. Holmes refused to examine the third chamber, so we passed at once to the second, that in which Miss Stoner was now sleeping, and in which her sister had met her fate. It was a homely[2] little room, with a low ceiling and a gaping fireplace, after the fashion of old country houses. A brown chest of drawers stood in one corner, a narrow white-counterpaned bed in another, and a dressing-table on the left-hand side of the window. These articles, with two small wicker-work chairs, made up all the furniture in the room, save for a square of Wilton carpet[3] in the centre. The boards round and the panelling of the walls were brown, worm-eaten oak, so old and discoloured that it may have dated from the original building of the house. Holmes drew one of the chairs into a corner and

[1] *lens* Magnifying glass.
[2] *homely* Simple, unsophisticated.
[3] *Wilton carpet* Brand of carpet made in Wilton, England.

sat silent, while his eyes travelled round and round and up and down, taking in every detail of the apartment.

"Where does that bell communicate with?" he asked at last, pointing to a thick bell-rope which hung down beside the bed, the tassel actually lying upon the pillow.

"It goes to the housekeeper's room."

"It looks newer than the other things?"

"Yes, it was only put there a couple of years ago."

"Your sister asked for it, I suppose?"

"No, I never heard of her using it. We used always to get what we wanted for ourselves."

"Indeed, it seemed unnecessary to put so nice a bell-pull there. You will excuse me for a few minutes while I satisfy myself as to this floor." He threw himself down upon his face with his lens in his hand, and crawled swiftly backwards and forwards, examining minutely the cracks between the boards. Then he did the same with the woodwork with which the chamber was panelled. Finally he walked over to the bed and spent some time in staring at it, and in running his eye up and down the wall. Finally he took the bell-rope in his hand and gave it a brisk tug.

"Why, it's a dummy," said he.

"Won't it ring?"

"No, it is not even attached to a wire. This is very interesting. You can see now that it is fastened to a hook just above where the little opening of the ventilator is."

"How very absurd! I never noticed that before."

"Very strange!" muttered Holmes, pulling at the rope. "There are one or two very singular points about this room. For example, what a fool a builder must be to open a ventilator in another room, when, with the same trouble, he might have communicated with the outside air!"

"That is also quite modern," said the lady.

"Done about the same time as the bell-rope," remarked Holmes.

"Yes, there were several little changes carried out about that time."

"They seem to have been of a most interesting character—dummy bell-ropes, and ventilators which do not ventilate. With your permission, Miss Stoner, we shall now carry our researches into the inner apartment."

Dr. Grimesby Roylott's chamber was larger than that of his stepdaughter, but was as plainly furnished. A camp bed, a small wooden shelf full of books, mostly of a technical character, an armchair beside the bed, a plain wooden chair against the wall, a round table, and a large iron safe were the principal things which met the eye. Holmes walked slowly round and examined each and all of them with the keenest interest.

"What's in here?" he asked, tapping the safe.

"My stepfather's business papers."

"Oh! you have seen inside, then?"

"Only once, some years ago. I remember that it was full of papers."

"There isn't a cat in it, for example?"

"No. What a strange idea!"

"Well, look at this!" He took up a small saucer of milk which stood on the top of it.

"Well, look at this."

"No; we don't keep a cat. But there is a cheetah and a baboon."

"Ah, yes, of course! Well, a cheetah is just a big cat, and yet a saucer of milk does not go very far in satisfying its wants, I daresay. There is one point which I should wish to determine." He squatted down in front of the wooden chair, and examined the seat of it with the greatest attention.

"Thank you. That is quite settled," said he, rising and putting his lens in his pocket. "Hullo! Here is something interesting!"

The object which had caught his eye was a small dog lash hung on one corner of the bed. The lash, however, was curled upon itself, and tied so as to make a loop of whipcord.

"What do you make of that, Watson?"

"It's a common enough lash. But I don't know why it should be tied."

"That is not quite so common, is it? Ah, me! It's a wicked world, and when a clever man turns his brain to crime it is the worst of all. I think that I have seen enough now, Miss Stoner, and, with your permission, we shall walk out upon the lawn."

I had never seen my friend's face so grim, or his brow so dark, as it was when we turned from the scene of this investigation. We had walked several times up and down the lawn, neither Miss Stoner nor myself liking to break in upon his thoughts before he roused himself from his reverie. "It is very essential, Miss Stoner," said he, "that you should absolutely follow my advice in every respect."

"I shall most certainly do so."

"The matter is too serious for any hesitation. Your life may depend upon your compliance."

"I assure you that I am in your hands."

"In the first place, both my friend and I must spend the night in your room."

Both Miss Stoner and I gazed at him in astonishment.

"Yes, it must be so. Let me explain. I believe that that is the village inn over there?"

"Yes, that is the Crown."

"Very good. Your windows would be visible from there?"

"Certainly."

"You must confine yourself to your room, on pretence of a headache, when your stepfather comes back. Then when you hear him retire for the night, you must open the shutters of your window, undo the hasp, put your lamp there as a signal to us, and then withdraw with everything which you are likely to want into the room which you used to occupy. I have no doubt that, in spite of the repairs, you could manage there for one night."

"Oh, yes, easily."

"The rest you will leave in our hands."

"But what will you do?"

"We shall spend the night in your room, and we shall investigate the cause of this noise which has disturbed you."

"I believe, Mr. Holmes, that you have already made up your mind," said Miss Stoner, laying her hand upon my companion's sleeve.

"Perhaps I have."

"Then for pity's sake tell me what was the cause of my sister's death."

"I should prefer to have clearer proofs before I speak."

"You can at least tell me whether my own thought is correct, and if she died from some sudden fright."

"Good-bye, and be brave."

"No, I do not think so. I think that there was probably some more tangible cause. And now, Miss Stoner, we must leave you, for if Dr. Roylott returned and saw us, our journey would be in vain. Goodbye, and be brave, for if you will do what I have told you, you may rest assured that we shall soon drive away the dangers that threaten you."

Sherlock Holmes and I had no difficulty in engaging a bedroom and sitting room at the Crown Inn. They were on the upper floor, and from our window we could command a view of the avenue gate, and of the inhabited wing of Stoke Moran Manor House. At dusk we saw Dr. Grimesby Roylott drive past, his huge form looming up beside the little figure of the lad who drove him. The boy had some slight difficulty in undoing the heavy iron gates, and we heard the hoarse roar of the doctor's voice, and saw the fury with which he shook his clenched fists at him. The trap drove on, and a few minutes later we saw a sudden light spring up among the trees as the lamp was lit in one of the sitting rooms.

"Do you know, Watson," said Holmes, as we sat together in the gathering darkness, "I have really some scruples as to taking you tonight. There is a distinct element of danger."

"Can I be of assistance?"

"Your presence might be invaluable."

"Then I shall certainly come."

"It is very kind of you."

"You speak of danger. You have evidently seen more in these rooms than was visible to me."

"No, but I fancy that I may have deduced a little more. I imagine that you saw all that I did."

"I saw nothing remarkable save the bell-rope, and what purpose that could answer I confess is more than I can imagine."

"You saw the ventilator, too?"

"Yes, but I do not think that it is such a very unusual thing to have a small opening between two rooms. It was so small that a rat could hardly pass through."

"I knew that we should find a ventilator before ever we came to Stoke Moran."

"My dear Holmes!"

"Oh, yes, I did. You remember in her statement she said that her sister could smell Dr. Roylott's cigar. Now, of course that suggests at once that there must be a communication between the two rooms. It could only be a small one, or it would have been remarked upon at the coroner's inquiry. I deduced a ventilator."

"But what harm can there be in that?"

"Well, there is at least a curious coincidence of dates. A ventilator is made, a cord is hung, and a lady who sleeps in the bed dies. Does not that strike you?"

"I cannot as yet see any connection."

"Did you observe anything very peculiar about that bed?"

"No."

"It was clamped to the floor. Did you ever see a bed fastened like that before?"

"I cannot say that I have."

"The lady could not move her bed. It must always be in the same relative position to the ventilator and to the rope—for so we may call it, since it was clearly never meant for a bell-pull."

"Holmes," I cried, "I seem to see dimly what you are hitting at. We are only just in time to prevent some subtle and horrible crime."

"Subtle enough and horrible enough. When a doctor does go wrong he is the first of criminals. He has nerve and he has knowledge. Palmer and Pritchard[1] were among the heads of their profession. This man strikes even deeper, but I think, Watson, that we shall be able to strike deeper still. But we shall have horrors enough before the night is over; for goodness' sake let us have a quiet pipe, and turn our minds for a few hours to something more cheerful."

About nine o'clock the light among the trees was extinguished, and all was dark in the direction of the Manor House. Two hours passed slowly away, and then, suddenly, just at the stroke of eleven, a single bright light shone out right in front of us.

"That is our signal," said Holmes, springing to his feet; "it comes from the middle window."

As we passed out he exchanged a few words with the landlord, explaining that we were going on a late visit to an acquaintance, and that it was possible that we might spend the night there. A moment later we were out on

[1] *Palmer and Pritchard* Both men were doctors who, in unrelated cases, were executed in the mid-1800s for murdering people using poison.

the dark road, a chill wind blowing in our faces, and one yellow light twinkling in front of us through the gloom to guide us on our sombre errand. There was little difficulty in entering the grounds, for unrepaired breaches gaped in the old park wall. Making our way among the trees, we reached the lawn, crossed it, and were about to enter through the window, when out from a clump of laurel bushes there darted what seemed to be a hideous and distorted child, who threw itself on the grass with writhing limbs, and then ran swiftly across the lawn into the darkness.

"My God!" I whispered, "did you see it?"

Holmes was for the moment as startled as I. His hand closed like a vice upon my wrist in his agitation. Then he broke into a low laugh, and put his lips to my ear.

"It is a nice household," he murmured, "that is the baboon."

I had forgotten the strange pets which the doctor affected. There was a cheetah, too; perhaps we might find it upon our shoulders at any moment. I confess that I felt easier in my mind when, after following Holmes's example and slipping off my shoes, I found myself inside the bedroom. My companion noiselessly closed the shutters, moved the lamp on to the table, and cast his eyes round the room. All was as we had seen it in the daytime. Then creeping up to me and making a trumpet of his hand, he whispered into my ear again so gently that it was all that I could do to distinguish the words:

"The least sound would be fatal to our plans."

I nodded to show that I had heard.

"We must sit without a light. He would see it through the ventilator."

I nodded again.

"Do not go to sleep; your very life may depend upon it. Have your pistol ready in case we should need it. I will sit on the side of the bed, and you in that chair."

I took out my revolver and laid it on the corner of the table. Holmes had brought up a long thin cane, and this he placed upon the bed beside him. By it he laid the box of matches and the stump of a candle. Then he turned down the lamp and we were left in darkness.

How shall I ever forget that dreadful vigil? I could not hear a sound, not even the drawing of a breath, and yet I knew that my companion sat open-eyed, within a few feet of me, in the same state of nervous tension in which I was myself. The shutters cut off the least ray of light, and we waited in absolute darkness. From outside came the occasional cry of a night bird, and once at our very window a long drawn, cat-like whine, which told us that the cheetah was indeed at liberty. Far away we could hear the deep tones of the parish clock, which boomed out every quarter of an hour. How long they seemed, those quarters! Twelve o'clock, and one, and two, and three, and still we sat waiting silently for whatever might befall.

Suddenly there was the momentary gleam of a light up in the direction of the ventilator, which vanished immediately, but was succeeded by a strong smell of burning oil and heated metal. Someone in the next room had lit a dark lantern.[1] I heard a gentle sound of movement, and then all was silent once more, though the smell grew stronger. For half an hour I sat with straining ears. Then suddenly another sound became audible—a very gentle, soothing sound, like that of a small jet of steam escaping continually from a kettle. The instant that we heard it, Holmes sprang from the bed, struck a match, and lashed furiously with his cane at the bell-pull.

"Holmes lashed furiously."

"You see it, Watson?" he yelled. "You see it?"

But I saw nothing. At the moment when Holmes struck the light I heard a low, clear whistle, but the

---

[1]   *dark lantern*   Lantern with a slide so that its light can be hidden.

sudden glare flashing into my weary eyes made it impossible for me to tell what it was at which my friend lashed so savagely. I could, however, see that his face was deadly pale, and filled with horror and loathing.

He had ceased to strike, and was gazing up at the ventilator, when suddenly there broke from the silence of the night the most horrible cry to which I have ever listened. It swelled up louder and louder, a hoarse yell of pain and fear and anger all mingled in the one dreadful shriek. They say that away down in the village, and even in the distant parsonage, that cry raised the sleepers from their beds. It struck cold to our hearts, and I stood gazing at Holmes, and he at me, until the last echoes of it had died away into the silence from which it rose.

"What can it mean?" I gasped.

"It means that it is all over," Holmes answered. "And perhaps, after all, it is for the best. Take your pistol, and we shall enter Dr. Roylott's room."

With a grave face he lit the lamp, and led the way down the corridor. Twice he struck at the chamber door without any reply from within. Then he turned the handle and entered, I at his heels, with the cocked pistol in my hand.

"He made neither sound nor motion."

It was a singular sight which met our eyes. On the table stood a dark lantern with the shutter half open, throwing a brilliant beam of light upon the iron safe, the door of which was ajar. Beside this table, on the wooden chair, sat Dr. Grimesby Roylott, clad in a long grey dressing gown, his bare ankles protruding beneath, and his feet thrust into red heelless Turkish slippers. Across

his lap lay the short stock with the long lash which we had noticed during the day. His chin was cocked upwards, and his eyes were fixed in a dreadful rigid stare at the corner of the ceiling. Round his brow he had a peculiar yellow band, with brownish speckles, which seemed to be bound tightly round his head. As we entered he made neither sound nor motion.

"The band! The speckled band!" whispered Holmes.

I took a step forward. In an instant his strange headgear began to move, and there reared itself from among his hair the squat diamond-shaped head and puffed neck of a loathsome serpent.

"It is a swamp adder!" cried Holmes—"the deadliest snake in India. He has died within ten seconds of being bitten. Violence does, in truth, recoil upon the violent, and the schemer falls into the pit which he digs for another. Let us thrust this creature back into its den, and we can then remove Miss Stoner to some place of shelter, and let the county police know what has happened."

As he spoke he drew the dog whip swiftly from the dead man's lap, and throwing the noose round the reptile's neck, he drew it from its horrid perch, and, carrying it at arm's length, threw it into the iron safe, which he closed upon it.

Such are the true facts of the death of Dr. Grimesby Roylott, of Stoke Moran. It is not necessary that I should prolong a narrative which has already run to too great a length, by telling how we broke the sad news to the terrified girl, how we conveyed her by the morning train to the care of her good aunt at Harrow, of how the slow process of official inquiry came to the conclusion that the doctor met his fate while indiscreetly playing with a dangerous pet. The little which I had yet to learn of the case was told me by Sherlock Holmes as we travelled back next day.

"I had," said he, "come to an entirely erroneous conclusion, which shows, my dear Watson, how dangerous it always is to reason from insufficient data. The presence of the gypsies, and the use of the word 'band,' which was used by the poor girl, no doubt, to explain the appearance which she had caught a horrid glimpse of by the light of her match, were sufficient to put me upon an entirely wrong scent. I can only claim the merit that I instantly reconsidered my position when, however, it became clear to me that whatever danger threatened an occupant of the room could not come either from the window or the door. My attention was speedily drawn, as I have already remarked to you, to this ventilator, and to the bell-rope which hung down to the bed. The discovery that this was a dummy, and that the bed was clamped to the floor, instantly gave rise to the suspicion that the rope was there as a bridge for something passing through the hole, and coming to the bed. The idea of a snake instantly occurred to me, and when I coupled it with my knowledge that the doctor was furnished with a supply of creatures from India, I felt that I was probably on the right track. The idea of using a form of poison which could not possibly be discovered by any chemical test was just such a one as would occur to a clever and ruthless man who had had an Eastern training. The rapidity with which such a poison would take effect would also, from his point of view, be an advantage. It would be a sharp-eyed coroner indeed who could distinguish the two little dark punctures which would show where the poison fangs had done their work. Then I thought of the whistle. Of course, he must recall the snake before the morning light revealed it to the victim. He had trained it, probably by the use of the milk which we saw, to return to him when summoned. He would put it through the ventilator at the hour that he thought best, with the certainty that it would crawl down the rope, and land on the bed. It might or might not bite the occupant, perhaps she might escape every night for a week, but sooner or later she must fall a victim.

"I had come to these conclusions before ever I had entered his room. An inspection of his chair showed me that he had been in the habit of standing on it, which, of course, would be necessary in order that he should reach the ventilator. The sight of the safe, the saucer of milk, and the loop of whipcord were enough to finally dispel any doubts which may have remained. The metallic clang heard by Miss Stoner was obviously caused by her father hastily closing the door of his safe upon its terrible occupant. Having once made up my mind, you know the steps which I took in order to put the matter to the proof. I heard the creature hiss, as I have no doubt that you did also, and I instantly lit the light and attacked it."

"With the result of driving it through the ventilator."

"And also with the result of causing it to turn upon its master at the other side. Some of the blows of my cane came home, and roused its snakish temper, so that it flew upon the first person it saw. In this way I am no doubt indirectly responsible for Dr. Grimesby Roylott's death, and I cannot say that it is likely to weigh very heavily upon my conscience."

—1892

AMY LEVY
1861 — 1889

Amy Levy was practically unknown in the twentieth century until the 1993 publication of her *Complete Novels and Selected Writings* helped to rescue her work from obscurity. With a recent biography and the republication of her most famous book, *Reuben Sachs*, a satirical novel set in London's Jewish community, she is now recognized as one of the talented "New Woman" authors—the feminist writers of late-Victorian England.

Levy, the daughter of Isabelle Levin and Lewis Levy, a stockbroker, grew up in a large, Anglo-Jewish, middle-class household in London. Intelligent and well educated, she began writing poetry at an early age, publishing her first work, "Ida Grey: A Story of Woman's Sacrifice," in a feminist journal at the age of thirteen. Contributions of poems, essays, and stories to many other journals followed, among them *The Cambridge Review*, *The Jewish Chronicle* and the *Pall Mall Gazette*. In 1879 Levy became the first Jewish woman to attend Cambridge University, where she studied at Newnham College. She left the university without taking her exams when, in 1881, she had published her first book of poetry, *Xantippe, and Other Verse*. The title poem is a defense of the wife of Socrates, who was much maligned for her outspokenness and intelligence. The volume, which quickly sold out, was followed by two more books of poems, many of the lyrics of which concentrated on melancholic and depressive themes; *A Minor Poet and Other Poems* appeared in 1884, and *A London Plane-Tree and Other Verse* was published posthumously in 1889. In an 1886 article in *The Jewish Chronicle*, Levy criticized literary depictions of Jewish characters, saying that no one had as yet portrayed Jews with all their "surprising virtues and no less surprising vices." From this idea was born her most influential work, which was, ironically, criticized by *The Jewish Chronicle* and members of the Jewish community as being anti-Semitic. The novel *Reuben Sachs* (1888) proved to be very popular, notwithstanding its portrayal of, as one reviewer called it, "the less than refined aspects of Jewish society." Oscar Wilde praised the novel, saying: "Its directness, its uncompromising truths, its depth of feeling, and above all, its absence of any single superfluous word, make it, in some sort, a classic. Like all her best work it is sad, but the sadness is by no means morbid. The strong undertone of moral earnestness, never preached, gives a stability and force to the vivid portraiture, and prevents the satiric touches from degenerating into mere malice. Truly, the book is an achievement."

Yet Levy did not emphasize only Jewish themes. In *The Romance of a Shop*, published a couple of months earlier in 1888, she writes of the determination of a family of orphaned sisters to support themselves by opening a photographic studio. The short novel gives a vivid picture of the challenges facing independent, working, "new women" and the relatively uncharted territory they face when attempting to integrate the demands of self-employment and of romantic relationships.

Levy moved in literary and artistic circles, counting among her friends Olive Schreiner (author of *The Story of an African Farm*), Beatrix Potter (author and political activist), Eleanor Marx (daughter of Karl and later a translator of Levy's poetry into German), and Vernon Lee (the *nom de plume* of author Violet Paget), for whom she was said to harbor a deep passion. She wrote a number of short essays, largely on literary matters (such as recent American fiction, and the poet James Thomson) or on Jewish issues, often seeking to explain to a gentile readership such topics as Jewish humor or contemporary middle-class Jewish women.

Levy's writings often betray her self-conscious status as an outsider, and they reveal a fascination with others who felt themselves to be outsiders, whether by race or gender. She suffered intense periods of depression that she called "the great-devil that lyeth ever in wait in the recesses of my heart." There is speculation that the press's negative reaction to *Reuben Sachs*, combined with Levy's health problems, contributed to her suicide (by charcoal gas inhalation) at the age of 27. But the difficulties experienced by a woman in the Victorian era living an independent literary life and being attracted to other women may also have been factors.

⌘ ⌘ ⌘

Xantippe[1] *(A Fragment)*

What, have I waked again? I never thought
　To see the rosy dawn, or ev'n this grey,
Dull, solemn stillness, ere the dawn has come.
The lamp burns low; low burns the lamp of life:
5　The still morn stays expectant, and my soul,
All weighted with a passive wonderment,
Waiteth and watcheth, waiteth for the dawn.
Come hither, maids; too soundly have ye slept
That should have watched me; nay, I would not chide—
10　Oft have I chidden, yet I would not chide
In this last hour—now all should be at peace.
I have been dreaming in a troubled sleep
Of weary days I thought not to recall;
Of stormy days, whose storms are hushed long since;
15　Of gladsome days, of sunny days; alas!
In dreaming, all their sunshine seemed so sad,
As though the current of the dark To-Be
Had flowed, prophetic, through the happy hours.
And yet, full well, I know it was not thus;
20　I mind me sweetly of the summer days,
When, leaning from the lattice, I have caught
The fair, far glimpses of a shining sea:
And nearer, of tall ships which thronged the bay,
And stood out blackly from a tender sky

25　All flecked with sulphur, azure, and bright gold;
And in the still, clear air have heard the hum
Of distant voices; and methinks there rose
No darker fount° to mar or stain the joy　　*fountain*
Which sprang ecstatic in my maiden breast
30　Than just those vague desires, those hopes and fears,
Those eager longings, strong, though undefined,
Whose very sadness makes them seem so sweet.
What cared I for the merry mockeries
Of other maidens sitting at the loom?
35　Or for sharp voices, bidding me return
To maiden labour? Were we not apart—
I and my high thoughts, and my golden dreams,
My soul which yearned for knowledge, for a tongue
That should proclaim the stately mysteries
40　Of this fair world, and of the holy gods?
Then followed days of sadness, as I grew
To learn my woman-mind had gone astray,
And I was sinning in those very thoughts—
For maidens, mark, such are not woman's thoughts—
45　(And yet, 'tis strange, the gods who fashion us
Have given us such promptings)....

　　　　　　　　　　　　　　Fled the years,
Till seventeen had found me tall and strong,
And fairer, runs it, than Athenian maids
50　Are wont to seem; I had not learnt it well—
My lesson of dumb patience—and I stood
At Life's great threshold with a beating heart,
And soul resolved to conquer and attain....
Once, walking 'thwart° the crowded marketplace,　　*across*
55　With other maidens, bearing in the twigs,

---

[1] *Xantippe* Wife of Socrates, ancient Greek philosopher (469–399 BCE) who devoted his life to the study and teaching of ethics and moral behavior; Socrates was later executed for corrupting the youth and interfering with the religion of Athens. Xantippe was criticized for being headstrong.

White doves for Aphrodite's sacrifice,[1]
I saw him, all ungainly and uncouth,
Yet many gathered round to hear his words,
Tall youths and stranger-maidens—Sokrates—
60 I saw his face and marked it, half with awe,
Half with a quick repulsion at the shape....
The richest gem lies hidden furthest down,
And is the dearer for the weary search;
We grasp the shining shells which strew the shore,
65 Yet swift we fling them from us; but the gem
We keep for aye° and cherish. So a soul,   *forever*
Found after weary searching in the flesh
Which half repelled our senses, is more dear,
For that same seeking, than the sunny mind
70 Which lavish Nature marks with thousand hints
Upon a brow of beauty. We are prone
To overweigh such subtle hints, then deem,
In after disappointment, we are fooled....
And when, at length, my father told me all,
75 That I should wed me with great Sokrates,
I, foolish, wept to see at once cast down
The maiden image of a future love,
Where perfect body matched the perfect soul.
But slowly, softly did I cease to weep;
80 Slowly I 'gan to mark the magic flash
Leap to the eyes, to watch the sudden smile
Break round the mouth, and linger in the eyes;
To listen for the voice's lightest tone—
Great voice, whose cunning modulations seemed
85 like to the notes of some sweet instrument.
So did I reach and strain, until at last
I caught the soul athwart the grosser flesh.
Again of thee, sweet Hope, my spirit dreamed!
I, guided by his wisdom and his love,
90 Led by his words, and counselled by his care,
Should lift the shrouding veil from things which be,
And at the flowing fountain of his soul
Refresh my thirsting spirit....
                                    And indeed,
95 In those long days which followed that strange day
When rites and song, and sacrifice and flow'rs,
Proclaimed that we were wedded, did I learn,

In sooth,° a-many lessons; bitter ones   *truth*
Which sorrow taught me, and not love inspired,
100 Which deeper knowledge of my kind impressed
With dark insistence on reluctant brain—
But that great wisdom, deeper, which dispels
Narrowed conclusions of a half-grown mind,
And sees athwart the littleness of life
105 Nature's divineness and her harmony,
Was never poor Xantippe's....
                                    I would pause
And would recall no more, no more of life,
Than just the incomplete, imperfect dream
110 Of early summers, with their light and shade,
Their blossom-hopes, whose fruit was never ripe;
But something strong within me, some sad chord
Which loudly echoes to the later life,
Me to unfold the after-misery
115 Urges, with plaintive wailing in my heart.
Yet, maidens, mark; I would not that ye thought
I blame my lord departed, for he meant
No evil, so I take it, to his wife.
'Twas only that the high philosopher,
120 Pregnant with noble theories and great thoughts,
Deigned not to stoop to touch so slight a thing
As the fine fabric of a woman's brain—
So subtle as a passionate woman's soul.
I think, if he had stooped a little, and cared,
125 I might have risen nearer to his height,
And not lain shattered, neither fit for use
As goodly household vessel, nor for that
Far finer thing which I had hoped to be....
Death, holding high his retrospective lamp,
130 Shows me those first, far years of wedded life,
Ere I had learnt to grasp the barren shape
Of what the Fates[2] had destined for my life.
Then, as all youthful spirits are, was I
Wholly incredulous that Nature meant
135 So little, who had promised me so much.
At first I fought my fate with gentle words,
With high endeavours after greater things;
Striving to win the soul of Sokrates,
Like some slight bird, who sings her burning love
140 To human master, till at length she finds
Her tender language wholly misconceived,

---

[1] *White doves ... sacrifice* Aphrodite is the Greek goddess of love;
white doves, Aphrodite's favorite birds, were sacrificed during her
festival.

[2] *Fates* Three Greek goddesses of destiny.

And that same hand whose kind caress she sought,
With fingers flippant flings the careless corn....
I do remember how, one summer's eve,
He, seated in an arbour's leafy shade,
Had bade me bring fresh wine-skins....

                        As I stood
Ling'ring upon the threshold, half concealed
By tender foliage, and my spirit light
With draughts of sunny weather, did I mark
An instant the gay group before mine eyes.
Deepest in shade, and facing where I stood,
Sat Plato,[1] with his calm face and low brows
Which met above the narrow Grecian eyes,
The pale, thin lips just parted to the smile,
Which dimpled that smooth olive of his cheek.
His head a little bent, sat Sokrates,
With one swart° finger raised admonishing,   *dark-skinned*
And on the air were borne his changing tones.
Low lounging at his feet, one fair arm thrown
Around his knee (the other, high in air
Brandished a brazen amphor,° which yet rained   *wine vessel*
Bright drops of ruby on the golden locks
And temples with their fillets of the vine),
Lay Alkibiades the beautiful.[2]
And thus, with solemn tone, spake Sokrates:
"This fair Aspasia, which our Perikles
Hath brought from realms afar, and set on high[3]
In our Athenian city, hath a mind,
I doubt not, of a strength beyond her race;
And makes employ of it, beyond the way
Of women nobly gifted: woman's frail—
Her body rarely stands the test of soul;
She grows intoxicate with knowledge; throws
The laws of custom, order, 'neath her feet,
Feasting at life's great banquet with wide throat."
Then sudden, stepping from my leafy screen,
Holding the swelling wine-skin o'er my head,

With breast that heaved, and eyes and cheeks aflame,
Lit by a fury and a thought, I spake:
"By all great powers around us! can it be
That we poor women are empirical?[4]
That gods who fashioned us did strive to make
Beings too fine, too subtly delicate,
With sense that thrilled response to ev'ry touch
Of nature's, and their task is not complete?
That they have sent their half-completed work
To bleed and quiver here upon the earth?
To bleed and quiver, and to weep and weep,
To beat its soul against the marble walls
Of men's cold hearts, and then at last to sin!"
I ceased, the first hot passion stayed and stemmed
And frighted by the silence: I could see,
Framed by the arbour foliage, which the sun
In setting softly gilded with rich gold,
Those upturned faces, and those placid limbs;
Saw Plato's narrow eyes and niggard° mouth,   *stingy*
Which half did smile and half did criticise,
One hand held up, the shapely fingers framed
To gesture of entreaty—"Hush, I pray,
Do not disturb her; let us hear the rest;
Follow her mood, for here's another phase
Of your black-browed Xantippe...."

                        Then I saw
Young Alkibiades, with laughing lips
And half-shut eyes, contemptuous shrugging up
Soft, snowy shoulders, till he brought the gold
Of flowing ringlets round about his breasts.
But Sokrates, all slow and solemnly,
Raised, calm, his face to mine, and sudden spake:
"I thank thee for the wisdom which thy lips
Have thus let fall among us: prithee[5] tell
From what high source, from what philosophies
Didst cull the sapient° notion of thy words?"   *astute*
Then stood I straight and silent for a breath,
Dumb, crushed with all that weight of cold contempt;
But swiftly in my bosom there uprose
A sudden flame, a merciful fury sent
To save me; with both angry hands I flung
The skin upon the marble, where it lay

---

[1] *Plato* Greek philosopher and student of Socrates (427–347 BCE).

[2] *Alkibiades the beautiful* The statesman Alcibiades (c. 450–404 BCE) was once a student of Socrates; his outstanding beauty was said to contrast with that of Socrates.

[3] *Aspasia ... set on high* Pericles, a statesman in ancient Athens, divorced his wife and married his lover, Aspasia, a woman of great education and intellect, who influenced the writings of many philosophers, including Socrates, Plato, and Cicero.

[4] *that we ... empirical* I.e., that we rely on experience rather than theory.

[5] *prithee* Please.

Spouting red rills° and fountains on the white; *rivulets*
Then, all unheeding faces, voices, eyes,
I fled across the threshold, hair unbound—
White garment stained to redness—beating heart
225 Flooded with all the flowing tide of hopes
Which once had gushed out golden, now sent back
Swift to their sources, never more to rise....
I think I could have borne the weary life,
The narrow life within the narrow walls,
230 If he had loved me; but he kept his love
For this Athenian city and her sons;
And, haply, for some stranger-woman, bold
With freedom, thought, and glib philosophy....
Ah me! the long, long weeping through the nights,
235 The weary watching for the pale-eyed dawn
Which only brought fresh grieving: then I grew
Fiercer, and cursed from out my inmost heart
The Fates which marked me an Athenian maid.
Then faded that vain fury; hope died out;
240 A huge despair was stealing on my soul,
A sort of fierce acceptance of my fate,—
He wished a household vessel—well 'twas good,
For he should have it! He should have no more
The yearning treasure of a woman's love,
245 But just the baser treasure which he sought.
I called my maidens, ordered out the loom,
And spun unceasing from the morn till eve;
Watching all keenly over warp and woof,[1]
Weighing the white wool with a jealous hand.
250 I spun until, methinks, I spun away
The soul from out my body, the high thoughts
From out my spirit; till at last I grew
As ye have known me,—eye exact to mark
The texture of the spinning; ear all keen
255 For aimless talking when the moon is up,
And ye should be a-sleeping; tongue to cut
With quick incision, 'thwart the merry words
Of idle maidens....
                        Only yesterday
260 My hands did cease from spinning; I have wrought
My dreary duties, patient till the last.
The gods reward me! Nay, I will not tell
The after years of sorrow; wretched strife
With grimmest foes—sad Want and Poverty;—

265 Nor yet the time of horror, when they bore
My husband from the threshold; nay, nor when
The subtle weed had wrought its deadly work.[2]
Alas! alas! I was not there to soothe
The last great moment; never any thought
270 Of her that loved him—save at least the charge,
All earthly, that her body should not starve....
You weep, you weep; I would not that ye wept;
Such tears are idle; with the young, such grief
Soon grows to gratulation, as, "her love
275 Was withered by misfortune; mine shall grow
All nurtured by the loving," or, "her life
Was wrecked and shattered—mine shall smoothly sail."
Enough, enough. In vain, in vain, in vain!
The gods forgive me! Sorely have I sinned
280 In all my life. A fairer fate befall
You all that stand there....
                              Ha! the dawn has come;
I see a rosy glimmer—nay! it grows dark;
Why stand ye so in silence? throw it wide,
285 The casement, quick; why tarry?—give me air—
O fling it wide, I say, and give me light!
—1881

Magdalen

All things I can endure, save one.
The bare, blank room where is no sun;
The parcelled hours; the pallet hard;
The dreary faces here within;
5 The outer women's cold regard;
The Pastor's iterated "sin"—
These things could I endure, and count
No overstrained, unjust amount;
No undue payment for such bliss—
10 Yea, all things bear, save only this:
That you, who knew what thing would be,
Have wrought this evil unto me.
It is so strange to think on still—
That you, that *you* should do me ill!
15 Not as one ignorant or blind,

---

[1] *warp and woof* Cross threads in a weaving.

[2] *Nor ... work* Socrates was condemned to die by suicide, which was accomplished by his drinking a cup of poison made from hemlock.

But seeing clearly in your mind
How this must be which now has been,
Nothing aghast at what was seen.
Now that the tale is told and done,
20 It is so strange to think upon.

You were so tender with me, too!
One summer's night a cold blast blew,
Closer about my throat you drew
The half-slipped shawl of dusky blue.
25 And once my hand, on a summer's morn,
I stretched to pluck a rose; a thorn
Struck through the flesh and made it bleed
(A little drop of blood indeed!)
Pale grew your cheek; you stooped and bound
30 Your handkerchief about the wound;
Your voice came with a broken sound;
With the deep breath your breast was riven;
I wonder, did God laugh in Heaven?

How strange, that *you* should work my woe!
35 How strange! I wonder, do you know
How gladly, gladly I had died
(And life was very sweet that tide)
To save you from the least, light ill?
How gladly I had borne your pain.
40 With one great pulse we seemed to thrill,—
Nay, but we thrilled with pulses twain.°   two

Even if one had told me this,
"A poison lurks within your kiss,
Gall that shall turn to night his day":
45 Thereon I straight had turned away—
Ay, though my heart had cracked with pain—
And never kissed your lips again.

At night, or when the daylight nears,
I hear the other women weep;
50 My own heart's anguish lies too deep

For the soft rain and pain of tears.
I think my heart has turned to stone.
A dull, dead weight that hurts my breast;
Here, on my pallet-bed alone,
55 I keep apart from all the rest.
Wide-eyed I lie upon my bed,
I often cannot sleep all night;
The future and the past are dead,
There is no thought can bring delight.
60 All night I lie and think and think;
If my heart were not made of stone,
But flesh and blood, it needs must shrink
Before such thoughts. Was ever known
A woman with a heart of stone?

65 The doctor says that I shall die.
It may be so, yet what care I?
Endless reposing from the strife,
Death do I trust no more than life.
For one thing is like one arrayed,
70 And there is neither false nor true;
But in a hideous masquerade
All things dance on, the ages through.
And good is evil, evil good;
Nothing is known or understood
75 Save only Pain. I have no faith
In God or Devil, Life or Death.

The doctor says that I shall die.
You, that I knew in days gone by,
I fain would see your face once more,
80 Con° well its features o'er and o'er;   study
And touch your hand and feel your kiss,
Look in your eyes and tell you this:
That all is done, that I am free;
That you, through all eternity,
85 Have neither part nor lot in me.
    —1884

RUDYARD KIPLING
1865 – 1936

The name "Rudyard Kipling" evokes images of the Raj in India, a time when Britannia ruled the waves and the sun never set on the British Empire. Indeed his life spanned most of the duration of British Colonial Office rule in India (1858–1947). Kipling, for many years considered England's unofficial poet laureate, was a strong proponent of imperialism; he believed it was Britain's duty to govern and civilize colonized lands. Though he was also capable of offering serious critiques of empire—and though he acknowledged that colonized people were "captives"— Kipling gave frequent voice to his belief that the British were in India to serve the native people. His famous 1899 poem, "The White Man's Burden," published in *McClure's Magazine*, aroused a storm of controversy, coming out at a time when many people were beginning to question the right of imperialist powers to subjugate foreigners. Nevertheless, for more than a half century Kipling's poems, short stories, and novels were wildly popular in India, Great Britain, and the United States, and in 1907 the Nobel Foundation honored him "in consideration of the power of observation, originality of imagination, virility of ideas and remarkable talent for narration which characterize the creations of this world-famous author." Thus Kipling became the first British writer to be awarded the Nobel Prize for Literature.

Kipling was named after Rudyard Lake in England, but he was born in Bombay (now Mumbai), India. Both his father, John Lockwood Kipling, professor of architectural sculpture at the University of Bombay, and his mother, Alice Macdonald, were children of Methodist ministers. Macdonald and her sisters were all associated with distinguished people—one sister married the neoclassical painter Sir Edward Poynter; another was the mother of Stanley Baldwin, who became Prime Minister of England in 1923; and another was the wife of the Pre-Raphaelite painter Sir Edward Burne-Jones. Kipling spent his first six years with his parents, learning the languages of his Indian friends and imbibing the cultural wealth of India. Of his school years, however, Kipling would say in his autobiography that his only happy moments were spent at the Burne-Jones home. Like many children of expatriates, he and his sister were sent to England for their education, where they spent five miserable years with severe, Calvinist foster parents in a home that Kipling would later call the House of Desolation. In 1878 he transferred to a boarding school in Devon (depicted in *Stalky and Co.*), which was also brutal at times, but where he acquired his schoolboy ethos (the sense of loyalty to and camaraderie with his peers so evident in his work) and began to write in earnest.

Upon graduation, Kipling moved back to India, working first as a newspaper journalist for the *Civil and Military Gazette* in Lahore (now part of Pakistan) and then as an editor of *Pioneer* in Allahabad. Many of the poems and stories he wrote during that time were collected in *Departmental Ditties* (1886) and *Plain Tales from the Hills* (1888), in which Kipling wrote about the moral and psychological difficulties of integrating Indian and British cultures. The Indian Railway Library also published some of Kipling's stories, such as *The Phantom Rickshaw* and *Wee Willie Winkie* (1888), in booklet form. By the time he returned to England in 1889, Kipling was a well-established author in India and had become very popular in Britain as well. The English public loved his "tales of the exotic," which took them to worlds they could scarcely imagine and introduced them to cultures they would likely never experience first-hand.

Kipling published several collections of short stories and poems in the early 1890s; the volume *Barrack-Room Ballads and Other Verses* (1892), which included such well-known poems as "Mandalay" and "Gunga Din," went into more than 50 editions in the 30 years following. Two early novels, *The Light that Failed* (1891) and *The Naulahka* (1892), did not fare as well. Nevertheless, in this period Kipling acquired a reputation as a spokesman for the people. With lyrics often inspired by street ballads and music hall ditties, he wrote using everyday language and expressed the thoughts of soldiers and other working people.

In 1892 Kipling married an American, Caroline Balestier, and the couple settled in Vermont. Although Kipling was unhappy in the United States, he wrote some of his most esteemed works during his five-year stay there, including *The Jungle Book* (1894), *The Second Jungle Book* (1895), and *Captains Courageous* (1897). On a return trip to the United States in 1899, Josephine, one of the three Kipling children, died. Another child, John, died in action in World War I; Kipling dealt with his grief by writing a history of his son's regiment, *The Irish Guards in the Great War*, published in 1923.

The family eventually settled in Sussex, England, but Kipling continued to travel the world as a newspaper correspondent. He covered the Boer War in South Africa in 1899 and returned to the region annually thereafter, staying in a house given to him by Cecil Rhodes, the famous British imperialist and business magnate. Kipling's own imperialist political sentiments were disseminated widely at the turn of the century, most notably in the London *Times*, which published "Recessional," composed in honor of Queen Victoria's Diamond Jubilee, and "The White Man's Burden." The latter poem was soon afterward countered in the London magazine *Truth* with a poem by Henry Labouchère, which changed Kipling's opening refrain from "Take up the white man's burden," to "Pile on the brown man's burden." Amid the controversy that ensued, a letter to the editor was published that read: "There is something almost sickening in this 'imperial' talk of assuming and bearing burdens for the good of others. They are never assumed or held where they are not found to be of material advantage or ministering to honor or glory." Kipling himself suggested that his poem offered neither a noble call to arms nor a justification for colonization, but rather a warning of the costs involved on both sides of imperialist missions abroad.

Kipling's least controversial and best-loved novel appeared in 1901. *Kim* is a picaresque adventure tale of a British beggar boy, the orphaned son of an Irish soldier. Raised in Lahore by an opium-addicted, half-caste woman, Kim O'Hare comes to believe he is destined for greatness and eventually travels through India with a holy man in search of his glorious future. In 1907, the Nobel committee said that in *Kim* "there is an elevated diction as well as a tenderness and charm. ... In sketching a personality he makes clear, almost in his first words, the peculiar traits of that person's character and temper. ... [Kipling is] capable of reproducing with astounding accuracy the minutest detail from real life."

In the decades following his Nobel Prize, Kipling's literary output dwindled somewhat amid controversy over his politics and grief over the loss of two of his three children. Even former admirers, such as W.B. Yeats and T.S. Eliot, began to be critical of Kipling's unwavering allegiance to British imperialism. Nevertheless, the last half century has seen a resurgence of interest in his work.

Sir Ian Hamilton said that Kipling's death in January 1936 (two days before the death of Kipling's friend, King George V) placed "a full stop to the period when war was a romance and the expansion of our Empire a duty." When his ashes were interred in Poets' Corner of Westminster Abbey, Kipling's pallbearers included the then-prime minister of England, a field marshal, and the admiral of the fleet; the poem "Recessional" was sung as a hymn. Kipling's unfinished autobiography, *Something of Myself*, was published posthumously a year after his death.

⌘ ⌘ ⌘

Gunga Din

You may talk o' gin and beer
When you're quartered safe out 'ere,
An' you're sent to penny-fights° an' Aldershot[1] it;   *skirmishes*
But when it comes to slaughter
5 You will do your work on water,
An' you'll lick the bloomin' boots of 'im that's got it.
Now in Injia's sunny clime,
Where I used to spend my time
A-servin' of 'Er Majesty the Queen,
10 Of all them blackfaced crew
The finest man I knew
Was our regimental bhisti,° Gunga Din.   *water carrier*
          He was "Din! Din! Din!
     "You limpin' lump o' brick-dust, Gunga Din!
15   "Hi! Slippy *hitherao*![2]
          "Water, get it! *Panee lao*,[3]
     "You squidgy-nosed old idol, Gunga Din."

The uniform 'e wore
Was nothin' much before,
20 An' rather less than 'arf o' that be'ind,
For a piece o' twisty rag
An' a goatskin water bag
Was all the field equipment 'e could find.
When the sweatin' troop train lay
25 In a sidin' through the day,
Where the 'eat would make your bloomin' eyebrows crawl,
We shouted "Harry By!"[4]
Till our throats were bricky-dry,
Then we wopped 'im 'cause 'e couldn't serve us all.
30   It was "Din! Din! Din!
     "You 'eathen, where the mischief 'ave you been?
          "You put some *juldee*[5] in it

"Or I'll *marrow*[6] you this minute
     "If you don't fill up my helmet, Gunga Din!"

35 'E would dot an' carry one[7]
Till the longest day was done;
An' 'e didn't seem to know the use o' fear.
If we charged or broke or cut,
You could bet your bloomin' nut,
40 'E'd be waitin' fifty paces right flank rear.
With 'is mussick° on 'is back,   *waterbag*
'E would skip with our attack,
An' watch us till the bugles made "Retire,"
An' for all 'is dirty 'ide
45 'E was white, clear white, inside
When 'e went to tend the wounded under fire!
          It was "Din! Din! Din!"
     With the bullets kickin' dust spots on the green.
          When the cartridges ran out,
50   You could hear the front ranks shout,
     "Hi! ammunition mules an' Gunga Din!"

I shan't forgit the night
When I dropped be'ind the fight
With a bullet where my belt plate should 'a' been.
55 I was chokin' mad with thirst,
An' the man that spied me first
Was our good old grinnin,' gruntin' Gunga Din.
'E lifted up my 'ead,
An' he plugged me where I bled,
60 An' 'e guv me 'arf-a-pint o' water green.
It was crawlin' and it stunk,
But of all the drinks I've drunk,
I'm gratefullest to one from Gunga Din.
          It was "Din! Din! Din!
65   "'Ere's a beggar with a bullet through 'is spleen;
          "'E's chawin' up the ground,
          "An' 'e's kickin' all around:
     "For Gawd's sake git the water, Gunga Din!"

---

[1] *Aldershot*   Town southwest of London, site of a military training center.

[2] *Slippy hitherao*   I.e., *idhar ao*. Urdu: Come here!

[3] *Panee lao*   Urdu: Bring water.

[4] *Harry By*   I.e., *arré bhai!* Urdu: in this context, Hey, you!

[5] *julee*   I.e., *juldee karo*. Urdu: Hurry!

[6] *marrow*   I.e., *maro*. Urdu: hit.

[7] *dot an' carry one*   From mathematics: calculate.

'E carried me away
70   To where a dooli° lay,   stretcher
An' a bullet come an' drilled the beggar clean.
'E put me safe inside,
An' just before 'e died,
"I 'ope you liked your drink," sez Gunga Din.
75   So I'll meet 'im later on
At the place where 'e is gone—
Where it's always double drill and no canteen.
'E'll be squattin' on the coals
Givin' drink to poor damned souls,
80   An' I'll get a swig in hell from Gunga Din!
        Yes, Din! Din! Din!
     You Lazarushian[1]-leather Gunga Din!
        Though I've belted you and flayed you,
        By the livin' Gawd that made you,
85   You're a better man than I am, Gunga Din!
        —1890

The Widow at Windsor[2]

'Ave you 'eard o' the Widow at Windsor
With a hairy gold crown on 'er 'ead?
She 'as ships on the foam—she 'as millions at 'ome,
An' she pays us poor beggars in red.[3]
5   (Ow, poor beggars in red!)
There's 'er nick[4] on the cavalry 'orses,
   There's 'er mark[5] on the medical stores—
An' 'er troopers° you'll find with a fair wind be'ind   troop-ships
   That takes us to various wars.
10   (Poor beggars!—barbarious wars!)
     Then 'ere's to the Widow at Windsor,
        An 'ere's to the stores an' the guns,
     The men an' the 'orses what makes up the
                forces
        O' Missis Victorier's sons.

        (Poor beggars! Victorier's sons!)
15
Walk wide o' the Widow at Windsor,
   For 'alf o' Creation she owns:
We 'ave bought 'er the same with the sword an' the flame,
   An' we've salted it down with our bones.
20   (Poor beggars!—it's blue with our bones!)
Hands off o' the sons o' the Widow,
   Hands off o' the goods in 'er shop,
For the kings must come down an' the emperors frown
   When the Widow at Windsor says "Stop!"
25   (Poor beggars!—we're sent to say "Stop!")
     Then 'ere's to the lodge o' the Widow,
        From the pole to the tropics it runs—
     To the lodge that we tile with the rank an' the file,
        An' open in form with the guns.
30   (Poor beggars!—it's always they guns!)

We 'ave 'eard o' the Widow at Windsor,
   It's safest to leave 'er alone:
For 'er sentries we stand by the sea an' the land
   Wherever the bugles are blown.
35   (Poor beggars!—an' don't we get blown!)
Take 'old o' the Wings o' the Mornin',[6]
   An' flop round the earth till you're dead;
But you won't get away from the tune that they play
   To the bloomin' old rag over'ead.
40   (Poor beggars!—it's 'ot over'ead!)
     Then 'ere's to the sons o' the Widow,
        Wherever, 'owever they roam.
     'Ere's all they desire, an' if they require
        A speedy return to their 'ome.
45   (Poor beggars! they'll never see 'ome!)
        —1890

Recessional[7]

God of our fathers, known of old,
Lord of our far-flung battle-line,

---

[1] *Lazarushian*   Cf. Luke 16; the good Lazarus was a leper/beggar.

[2] *The Widow at Windsor*   Queen Victoria, who, upon losing her husband in 1861, went into permanent mourning. (See the "In Context" section below for more information.)

[3] *red*   Red coats of British soldiers.

[4] *'er nick*   Mark distinguishing animals as belonging to the queen.

[5] *'er mark*   "V.R.I.," the Queen's identification mark.

[6] *Wings of the Mornin'*   From Psalm 139.9–10: "If I take the wings of the morning, and dwell in the uttermost parts of the sea; / Even there shall thy hand lead me, and thy right hand shall hold me."

[7] *Recessional*   Hymn written for Queen Victoria's sixtieth anniversary Jubilee.

Beneath whose awful Hand we hold
    Dominion over palm and pine—
5 Lord God of Hosts, be with us yet,
    Lest we forget[1]—lest we forget!

The tumult and the shouting dies;
    The captains and the kings depart:
Still stands Thine ancient sacrifice,
10   An humble and a contrite heart.[2]
Lord God of Hosts, be with us yet,
    Lest we forget—lest we forget!

Far-called, our navies melt away;
    On dune and headland sinks the fire:
15 Lo, all our pomp of yesterday
    Is one with Nineveh and Tyre![3]
Judge of the nations, spare us yet,
    Lest we forget—lest we forget!

If, drunk with sight of power, we loose
20   Wild tongues that have not Thee in awe,
Such boastings as the Gentiles use,
    Or lesser breeds without the law[4]—
Lord God of Hosts, be with us yet,
    Lest we forget—lest we forget!

25 For heathen heart that puts her trust
    In reeking tube and iron shard,
All valiant dust that builds on dust,
    And guarding, calls not Thee to guard,
For frantic boast and foolish word—
30 Thy mercy on Thy people, Lord!
    —1897

---

[1] *Lest we forget* Cf. Deuteronomy 4.9: "[T]ake heed to thyself, and keep thy soul diligently, lest thou forget the things which thine eyes have seen, and lest they depart from thy heart all the days of thy life; but teach them thy sons, and thy sons' sons."

[2] *contrite heart* Cf. Psalms 51.17: "The sacrifices of God are a broken spirit: a broken and a contrite heart."

[3] *Nineveh and Tyre* Ruined cities that were once capitals of empires.

[4] *Gentiles ... law* Cf. Romans 2.14: "For when the Gentiles, which have not the law, do by nature the things contained in the law, these, having not the law, are a law unto themselves."

The White Man's Burden

THE UNITED STATES AND THE PHILIPPINE ISLANDS[5]

Take up the White Man's burden—
    Send forth the best ye breed—
Go bind your sons to exile
    To serve your captives' need;
5 To wait in heavy harness
    On fluttered folk and wild—
Your new-caught, sullen peoples,
    Half devil and half child.

Take up the White Man's burden—
10   In patience to abide,
To veil the threat of terror
    And check the show of pride;
By open speech and simple,
    An hundred times made plain.
15 To seek another's profit,
    And work another's gain.

Take up the White Man's burden—
    The savage wars of peace—
Fill full the mouth of Famine
20   And bid the sickness cease;
And when your goal is nearest
    The end for others sought,
Watch Sloth and heathen Folly
    Bring all your hope to nought.

25 Take up the White Man's burden—
    No tawdry rule of kings,
But toil of serf and sweeper—
    The tale of common things.
The ports ye shall not enter,
30   The roads ye shall not tread,
Go make them with your living,
    And mark them with your dead!

---

[5] *United States and the Philippine Islands* Response to the American takeover of the Philippines after the Spanish American War of 1898. (See the "In Context" section below for more information.)

Take up the White Man's burden—
    And reap his old reward:
35 The blame of those ye better,
    The hate of those ye guard—
The cry of hosts ye humour
    (Ah, slowly!) toward the light:—
"Why brought ye us from bondage,
40   "Our loved Egyptian night?"

Take up the White Man's burden—
    Ye dare not stoop to less—
Nor call too loud on Freedom
    To cloak your weariness;
45 By all ye cry or whisper,
    By all ye leave or do,
The silent, sullen peoples
    Shall weigh your gods and you.

Take up the White Man's burden—
50 Have done with childish days—
The lightly proffered laurel,[1]
    The easy, ungrudged praise.
Comes now, to search your manhood
    Through all the thankless years,
55 Cold-edged with dear-bought wisdom,
    The judgment of your peers!
—1899

If—[2]

If you can keep your head when all about you
  Are losing theirs and blaming it on you,
If you can trust yourself when all men doubt you,
    But make allowance for their doubting too;
5 If you can wait and not be tired by waiting,
    Or being lied about, don't deal in lies,
Or being hated, don't give way to hating,
    And yet don't look too good, nor talk too wise:

10 If you can dream—and not make dreams your master;
    If you can think—and not make thoughts your aim;
If you can meet with Triumph and Disaster
    And treat those two impostors just the same;
If you can bear to hear the truth you've spoken
    Twisted by knaves to make a trap for fools,
15 Or watch the things you gave your life to, broken,
    And stoop and build 'em up with worn out tools:

If you can make one heap of all your winnings
    And risk it on one turn of pitch-and-toss,[3]
And lose, and start again at your beginnings
20   And never breathe a word about your loss;
If you can force your heart and nerve and sinew
    To serve your turn long after they are gone,
And so hold on when there is nothing in you
    Except the Will which says to them: "Hold on!"

25 If you can talk with crowds and keep your virtue,
    Or walk with kings—nor lose the common touch,
If neither foes nor loving friends can hurt you,
    If all men count with you, but none too much;
If you can fill the unforgiving minute
30   With sixty seconds' worth of distance run,
Yours is the earth and everything that's in it,
    And—which is more—you'll be a man, my son!
—1910

The Story of Muhammad Din

"Who is the happy man? He that sees in his own house at home little children crown with dust, leaping and falling and crying."

Munichandra, translated by Professor Peterson

The polo-ball was an old one, scarred, chipped, and dinted. It stood on the mantlepiece among the pipe-stems which Imam Din, *khitmatgar*,[4] was cleaning for me.

"Does the heaven-born want this ball?" said Imam Din deferentially.

---

[1] *laurel* Leaves of the bay laurel tree are a symbol of victory.

[2] *If* Among other possibilities, this poem may have been written in celebration of Dr. Leander Starr Jameson. Jameson launched the failed Jameson Raid of British troops against the Boers in South Africa in 1895, which ultimately led to the Boer War (1899–1902). Jameson went on to serve as Premier of the Cape Colony from 1904–08.

[3] *pitch-and-toss* Coin tossing game.

[4] *khitmatgar* I.e., *khitmat-ghar*. Urdu: one who serves the household; houseboy.

The heaven-born set no particular store by it; but of what use was a polo-ball to a *khitmatgar*?

"By Your Honor's favor, I have a little son. He has seen this ball, and desires it to play with. I do not want it for myself."

No one would for an instant accuse portly old Imam Din of wanting to play with polo-balls. He carried out the battered thing into the verandah; and there followed a hurricane of joyful squeaks, a patter of small feet, and the *thud-thud-thud* of the ball rolling along the ground. Evidently the little son had been waiting outside the door to secure his treasure. But how had he managed to see that polo-ball?

Next day, coming back from office half an hour earlier than usual, I was aware of a small figure in the dining room—a tiny, plump figure in a ridiculously inadequate shirt which came, perhaps, halfway down the tubby stomach. It wandered round the room, thumb in mouth, crooning to itself as it took stock of the pictures. Undoubtedly this was the "little son."

He had no business in my room, of course; but was so deeply absorbed in his discoveries that he never noticed me in the doorway. I stepped into the room and startled him nearly into a fit. He sat down on the ground with a gasp. His eyes opened, and his mouth followed suit. I knew what was coming, and fled, followed by a long, dry howl which reached the servants' quarters far more quickly than any command of mine had ever done. In ten seconds Imam Din was in the dining room. Then despairing sobs arose, and I returned to find Imam Din admonishing the small sinner who was using most of his shirt as a handkerchief.

"This boy," said Imam Din, judicially, "is a *budmash*,[1] a big *budmash*. He will, without doubt, go to the *jail-khana*[2] for his behavior." Renewed yells from the penitent, and an elaborate apology to myself from Imam Din.

"Tell the baby," said I, "that the *Sahib*[3] is not angry, and take him away." Imam Din conveyed my forgiveness to the offender, who had now gathered all his shirt round his neck, stringwise, and the yell subsided into a

sob. The two set off for the door. "His name," said Imam Din, as though the name were part of the crime, "is Muhammad Din, and he is a *budmash*." Freed from present danger, Muhammad Din turned round, in his father's arms, and said gravely: "It is true that my name is Muhammad Din, *Tahib*,[4] but I am not a *budmash*. I am a *man*!"

From that day dated my acquaintance with Muhammad Din. Never again did he come into my dining room, but on the neutral ground of the compound, we greeted each other with much state, though our conversation was confined to "*Talaam, Tahib*"[5] from his side, and "*Salaam, Muhammad Din*" from mine. Daily on my return from office, the little white shirt, and the fat little body used to rise from the shade of the creeper-covered trellis where they had been hid; and daily I checked my horse here, that my salutation might not be slurred over or given unseemly.

Muhammad Din never had any companions. He used to trot about the compound, in and out of the castor-oil bushes, on mysterious errands of his own. One day I stumbled upon some of his handiwork far down the ground. He had half buried the polo-ball in dust, and stuck six shrivelled old marigold flowers in a circle round it. Outside that circle again, was a rude square, traced out in bits of red brick alternating with fragments of broken china; the whole bounded by a little bank of dust. The *bhisti*[6] from the well-curb[7] put in a plea for the small architect, saying that it was only the play of a baby and did not much disfigure my garden.

Heaven knows that I had no intention of touching the child's work then or later; but, that evening, a stroll through the garden brought me unawares full on it; so that I trampled, before I knew, marigold-heads, dust-bank, and fragments of broken soap-dish into confusion past all hope of mending. Next morning I came upon Muhammad Din crying softly to himself over the ruin I had wrought. Someone had cruelly told him that the *Sahib* was very angry with him for spoiling the garden,

---

[1] *budmash* Bad character; rascal.

[2] *jail-khana* Prison/jail.

[3] *Sahib* Title of respect (like "Sir"), used formerly by the natives of India in addressing Europeans.

[4] *Tahib* I.e., Sahib; Muhammad Din has a lisp.

[5] *Talaam Tahib* Muhammad Din lips out "Salaam, Sahib," "Peace be upon you, Sir"—an East Indian and Pakistani salutation.

[6] *bhisti* Also spelled "bheestie"; servant who carries water from the well.

[7] *well-curb* Border around a well.

and had scattered his rubbish using bad language the while. Muhammad Din labored for an hour at effacing every trace of the dust-bank and pottery fragments, and it was with a tearful and apologetic face that he said, "*Talaam Tahib*," when I came home from the office. A hasty inquiry resulted in Imam Din informing Muhammad Din that by my singular favor he was permitted to disport himself as he pleased. Whereat the child took heart and fell to tracing the ground-plan of an edifice which was to eclipse the marigold-polo-ball creation.

For some months, the chubby little eccentricity revolved in his humble orbit among the castor-oil bushes and in the dust; always fashioning magnificent palaces from stale flowers thrown away by the bearer, smooth water-worn pebbles, bits of broken glass, and feathers pulled, I fancy, from my fowls—always alone and always crooning to himself.

A gayly-spotted seashell was dropped one day close to the last of his little buildings; and I looked that Muhammad Din should build something more than ordinarily splendid on the strength of it. Nor was I disappointed. He meditated for the better part of an hour, and his crooning rose to a jubilant song. Then he began tracing in dust. It would certainly be a wondrous palace, this one, for it was two yards long and a yard broad in ground-plan. But the palace was never completed.

Next day there was no Muhammad Din at the head of the carriage-drive, and no "*Talaam Tahib*" to welcome my return. I had grown accustomed to the greeting, and its omission troubled me. Next day, Imam Din told me that the child was suffering slightly from fever and needed quinine. He got the medicine, and an English doctor.

"They have no stamina, these brats," said the doctor, as he left Imam Din's quarters.

A week later, though I would have given much to have avoided it, I met on the road to the Mussalman[1] burying-ground Imam Din, accompanied by one other friend, carrying in his arms, wrapped in a white cloth, all that was left of little Muhammad Din.

—1886

---

[1] *Mussalman* Muslim.

The Mark of the Beast[2]

Your gods and my gods—do you or I know which are the stronger?
NATIVE PROVERB

East of Suez, some hold, the direct control of providence ceases, man being there handed over to the power of the gods and devils of Asia, and the Church of England providence only exercising an occasional and modified supervision in the case of Englishmen.

This theory accounts for some of the more unnecessary honors of life in India: it may be stretched to explain my story.

My friend Strickland of the police, who knows as much of the natives as is good for any man, can bear witness to the facts of the case. Dumoise, our doctor, also saw what Strickland and I saw. The inference which he drew from the evidence was entirely incorrect. He is dead now; he died, in a rather curious manner, which has been elsewhere described.

When Fleete came to India he owned a little money and some land in the Himalayas, near a place called Dharmsala. Both properties had been left him by an uncle, and he came out to finance them. He was a big, heavy, genial, and inoffensive man. His knowledge of natives was, of course, limited, and he complained of the difficulties of the language.

He rode in from his place in the hills to spend New Year in the station,[3] and he stayed with Strickland. On New Year's Eve there was a big dinner at the club, and the night was excusably wet. When men foregather from the uttermost ends of the Empire, they have a right to be riotous. The Frontier had sent down a contingent o' Catch-'em-Alive-O's[4] who had not seen twenty white faces a year, and were used to ride fifteen miles to dinner at the next fort at the risk of a Khyberee bullet[5] where

---

[2] *Mark of the Beast* According to Revelations 16.2, those who had this mark were devil worshipers: "[T]here fell a noisome and grievous sore upon the men which had the mark of the beast, and upon them which worshiped his image."

[3] *station* Colonial outpost.

[4] *Catch-'em-Alive-O's* Slang regimental name.

[5] *Khyberee bullet* Bullet fired from the gun of a denizen of the Khyber Pass, which runs through northern Afghanistan, Pakistan, and India, and was the scene of many British battles.

there drinks should lie. They profited by their new security, for they tried to play pool with a curled-up hedgehog found in the garden, and one of them carried the marker round the room in his teeth. Half a dozen planters had come in from the south and were talking "horse"[1] to the Biggest Liar in Asia, who was trying to cap all their stories at once. Everybody was there, and there was a general closing up of ranks and taking stock of our losses in dead or disabled that had fallen during the past year. It was a very wet night, and I remember that we sang "Auld Lang Syne" with our feet in the Polo Championship Cup, and our heads among the stars, and swore that we were all dear friends. Then some of us went away and annexed Burma, and some tried to open up the Sudan and were opened up by Fuzzies in that cruel scrub outside Suakim,[2] and some found stars and medals, and some were married, which was bad, and some did other things which were worse, and the others of us stayed in our chains and strove to make money on insufficient experiences.

Fleete began the night with sherry and bitters, drank champagne steadily up to the dessert, then raw, rasping Capri with all the strength of whisky, took Benedictine with his coffee, four or five whiskies and sodas to improve his pool strokes, beer and bones at half-past two, winding up with old brandy. Consequently, when he came out, at half past three in the morning, into fourteen degrees of frost, he was very angry with his horse for coughing and tried to leapfrog into the saddle. The horse broke away and went to his stables; so Strickland and I formed a Guard of Dishonour to take Fleete home.

Our road lay through the bazaar, close to a little temple of Hanuman, the Monkey god, who is a leading divinity worthy of respect. All gods have good points, just as have all priests. Personally, I attach much importance to Hanuman, and am kind to his people—the great gray apes of the hills. One never knows when one may want a friend.

---

[1] *talking "horse"* Bragging.

[2] *Sudan … Suakim* In 1884 the British were involved in a campaign to seize control of Sudan from the Egyptian occupiers and the Sudanese Mahdis; *Fuzzies* "Fuzzy-wuzzies" was the British nickname for the Beja tribe that was fighting with the Mahdis against the British and Egyptians; *Suakim* Red Sea port, site of an 1884 Beja massacre of Egyptians.

There was a light in the temple, and as we passed, we could hear voices of men chanting hymns. In a native temple, the priests rise at all hours of the night to do honour to their god. Before we could stop him, Fleete dashed up the steps, patted two priests on the back, and was gravely grinding the ashes of his cigar butt into the forehead of the red stone image of Hanuman. Strickland tried to drag him out, but he sat down and said solemnly:

"Shee that? Mark of the B—beasht! I made it. Ishn't it fine?"

In half a minute the temple was alive and noisy, and Strickland, who knew what came of polluting gods, said that things might occur. He, by virtue of his official position, long residence in the country, and weakness for going among the natives, was known to the priests and he felt unhappy. Fleete sat on the ground and refused to move. He said that "good old Hanuman" made a very soft pillow.

Then, without any warning, a Silver Man[3] came out of a recess behind the image of the god. He was perfectly naked in that bitter, bitter cold, and his body shone like frosted silver, for he was what the Bible calls "a leper as white as snow."[4] Also he had no face, because he was a leper of some years' standing and his disease was heavy upon him. We two stooped to haul Fleete up, and the temple was filling and filling with folk who seemed to spring from the earth, when the Silver Man ran in under our arms, making a noise exactly like the mewing of an otter, caught Fleete round the body and dropped his head on Fleete's breast before we could wrench him away. Then he retired to a corner and sat mewing while the crowd blocked all the doors.

The priests were very angry until the Silver Man touched Fleete. That nuzzling seemed to sober them.

At the end of a few minutes' silence one of the priests came to Strickland and said, in perfect English, "Take your friend away. He has done with Hanuman, but Hanuman has not done with him." The crowd gave room and we carried Fleete into the road.

---

[3] *Silver Man* Possibly a Hindu "Sadhu," a holy man, who would traditionally cover his naked body with ash.

[4] *"a leper as white as snow"* From 2 Kings 5.27: "The leprosy therefore of Naaman shall cleave unto thee, and unto thy seed for ever. And he went out from his presence a leper as white as snow."

Strickland was very angry. He said that we might all three have been knifed, and that Fleete should thank his stars that he had escaped without injury.

Fleete thanked no one. He said that he wanted to go to bed. He was gorgeously drunk.

We moved on, Strickland silent and wrathful, until Fleete was taken with violent shivering fits and sweating. He said that the smells of the bazaar were overpowering, and he wondered what slaughterhouses were permitted so near English residences. "Can't you smell the blood?" said Fleete.

We put him to bed at last, just as the dawn was breaking, and Strickland invited me to have another whisky and soda. While we were drinking he talked of the trouble in the temple, and admitted that it baffled him completely. Strickland hates being mystified by natives, because his business in life is to overmatch them with their own weapons. He has not yet succeeded in doing this, but in fifteen or twenty years he will have made some small progress.

"They should have mauled us," he said, "instead of mewing at us. I wonder what they meant. I don't like it one little bit."

I said that the managing committee of the temple would in all probability bring a criminal action against us for insulting their religion. There was a section of the Indian Penal Code which exactly met Fleete's offence. Strickland said he only hoped and prayed that they would do this. Before I left I looked into Fleete's room, and saw him lying on his right side, scratching his left breast. Then I went to bed cold, depressed, and unhappy, at seven o'clock in the morning.

At one o'clock I rode over to Strickland's house to inquire after Fleete's head. I imagined that it would be a sore one. Fleete was breakfasting and seemed unwell. His temper was gone, for he was abusing the cook for not supplying him with an underdone chop. A man who can eat raw meat after a wet night is a curiosity. I told Fleete this and he laughed.

"You breed queer mosquitoes in these parts," he said. "I've been bitten to pieces, but only in one place."

"Let's have a look at the bite," said Strickland. "It may have gone down since this morning."

While the chops were being cooked, Fleete opened his shirt and showed us, just over his left breast, a mark, the perfect double of the black rosettes—the five or six irregular blotches arranged in a circle—on a leopard's hide. Strickland looked and said, "It was only pink this morning. It's grown black now."

Fleete ran to a glass.

"By jove!" he said, "this is nasty. What is it?"

We could not answer. Here the chops came in, all red and juicy, and Fleete bolted three in a most offensive manner. He ate on his right grinders only, and threw his head over his right shoulder as he snapped the meat. When he had finished, it struck him that he had been behaving strangely for he said apologetically, "I don't think I ever felt so hungry in my life. I've bolted like an ostrich."

After breakfast Strickland said to me, "Don't go. Stay here, and stay for the night."

Seeing that my house was not three miles from Strickland's, this request was absurd. But Strickland insisted, and was going to say something when Fleete interrupted by declaring in a shamefaced way that he felt hungry again. Strickland sent a man to my house to fetch over my bedding and a horse, and we three went down to Strickland's stables to pass the hours until it was time to go out for a ride. The man who has a weakness for horses never wearies of inspecting them; and when two men are killing time in this way they gather knowledge and lies the one from the other.

There were five horses in the stables, and I shall never forget the scene as we tried to look them over. They seemed to have gone mad. They reared and screamed and nearly tore up their pickets; they sweated and shivered and lathered and were distraught with fear. Strickland's horses used to know him as well as his dogs, which made the matter more curious. We left the stable for fear of the brutes throwing themselves in their panic. Then Strickland turned back and called me. The horses were still frightened, but they let us "gentle" and make much of them, and put their heads in our bosoms.

"They aren't afraid of *us*" said Strickland. "D'you know, I'd give three months' pay if Outrage here could talk."

But Outrage was dumb and could only cuddle up to his master and blow out his nostrils, as is the custom of horses when they wish to explain things but can't. Fleete came up when we were in the stalls, and as soon as the horses saw him, their fright broke out afresh. It was all that we could do to escape from the place unkicked. Strickland said, "They don't seem to love you, Fleete." "Nonsense," said Fleete, "my mare will follow me like a dog." He went to her; she was in a loose-box; but as he slipped the bars she plunged, knocked him down, and broke away into the garden. I laughed, but Strickland was not amused. He took his moustache in both fists and pulled at it till it nearly came out. Fleete, instead of going off to chase his property, yawned, saying that he felt sleepy. He went to house to lie down, which was a foolish way of spending New Year's Day.

Strickland sat with me in the stables and asked if I had noticed anything peculiar in Fleete's manner. I said that he ate his food like a beast, but that this might have been the result of living alone in the hills out of the reach of society as refined and elevating as ours for instance. Strickland was not amused. I do not think that he listened to me, for his next sentence referred to the mark on Fleete's breast, and I said that it might have been caused by blister-flies, or that it was possibly a birthmark newly born and now visible for the first time. We both agreed that it was unpleasant to look at, and Strickland found occasion to say that I was a fool.

"I can't tell you what I think now," said he, "because you would call me a madman; but you must stay with me for the next few days, if you can. I want you to watch Fleete, but don't tell me what you think till I have made up my mind."

"But I am dining out tonight," I said.

"So am I," said Strickland, "and so is Fleete. At least if he doesn't change his mind."

We walked about the garden smoking, but saying nothing—because we were friends, and talking spoils good tobacco—till our pipes were out. Then we went to wake up Fleete. He was wide awake and fidgeting about his room.

"I say, I want some more chops," he said. "Can I get them?"

We laughed and said, "Go and change. The ponies will be round in a minute."

"All right," said Fleete. "I'll go when I get the chops—underdone ones, mind."

He seemed to be quite in earnest. It was four o'clock, and we had had breakfast at one; still, for a long time, he demanded those underdone chops. Then he changed into riding clothes and went out into the verandah. His pony—the mare had not been caught—would not let him come near. All three horses were unmanageable—mad with fear—and finally Fleete said that he would stay at home and get something to eat. Strickland and I rode out wondering. As we passed the temple of Hanuman, the Silver Man came out and mewed at us.

"He is not one of the regular priests of the temple," said Strickland. "I think I should peculiarly like to lay my hands on him."

There was no spring in our gallop on the racecourse that evening. The horses were stale, and moved as though they had been ridden out.

"The fright after breakfast has been too much for them," said Strickland.

That was the only remark he made through the remainder of the ride. Once or twice I think he swore to himself; but that did not count.

We came back in the dark at seven o'clock, and saw that there were no lights in the bungalow. "Careless ruffians my servants are!" said Strickland.

My horse reared at something on the carriage drive, and Fleete stood up under its nose.

"What are you doing, grovelling about the garden?" said Strickland.

But both horses bolted and nearly threw us. We dismounted by the stables and returned to Fleete, who was on his hands and knees under the orange bushes.

"What the devil's wrong with you?" said Strickland.

"Nothing, nothing in the world," said Fleete, speaking very quickly and thickly. "I've been gardening—botanising you know. The smell of the earth is delightful. I think I'm going for a walk—a long walk—all night."

Then I saw that there was something excessively out of order somewhere, and I said to Strickland, "I am not dining out."

"Bless you!" said Strickland. "Here, Fleete, get up. You'll catch fever there. Come in to dinner and let's have the lamps lit. We'll all dine at home."

Fleete stood up unwillingly, and said, "No lamps— no lamps. It's much nicer here. Let's dine outside and have some more chops—lots of 'em and under-done—bloody ones with gristle."

Now a December evening in Northern India is bitterly cold, and Fleete's suggestion was that of a maniac.

"Come in," said Strickland sternly. "Come in at once."

Fleete came, and when the lamps were brought, we saw that he was literally plastered with dirt from head to foot. He must have been rolling in the garden. He shrank from the light and went to his room. His eyes were horrible to look at. There was a green light behind them, not in them, if you understand, and the man's lower lip hung down.

Strickland said, "There is going to be trouble—big trouble—tonight. Don't you change your riding things."

We waited and waited for Fleete's reappearance, and ordered dinner in the meantime. We could hear him moving about his own room, but there was no light there. Presently from the room came the long-drawn howl of a wolf.

People write and talk lightly of blood running cold and hair standing up and things of that kind. Both sensations are too horrible to be trifled with. My heart stopped as though a knife had been driven through it, and Strickland turned as white as the tablecloth.

The howl was repeated, and was answered by another howl far across the fields.

That set the gilded roof on the horror. Strickland dashed into Fleete's room. I followed, and we saw Fleete getting out of the window. He made beast noises in the back of his throat. He could not answer us when we shouted at him. He spat.

I don't quite remember what followed, but I think that Strickland must have stunned him with the long boot-jack or else I should never have been able to sit on his chest. Fleete could not speak, he could only snarl, and his snarls were those of a wolf, not of a man. The human spirit must have been giving way all day and have died out with the twilight. We were dealing with a beast that had once been Fleete.

The affair was beyond any human and rational experience. I tried to say "Hydrophobia,"[1] but the word wouldn't come, because I knew that I was lying.

We bound this beast with leather thongs of the punkah rope,[2] and tied its thumbs and big toes together, and gagged it with a shoehorn, which makes a very efficient gag if you know how to arrange it. Then we carried it into the dining room, and sent a man to Dumoise, the doctor, telling him to come over at once. After we had despatched the messenger and were drawing breath, Strickland said, "It's no good. This isn't any doctor's work." I, also, knew that he spoke the truth.

The beast's head was free, and it threw it about from side to side. Anyone entering the room would have believed that we were curing a wolf's pelt. That was the most loathsome accessory of all.

Strickland sat with his chin in the heel of his fist, watching the beast as it wriggled on the ground, but saying nothing. The shirt had been torn open in the scuffle and showed the black rosette mark on the left breast. It stood out like a blister.

In the silence of the watching we heard something without[3] mewing like a she-otter. We both rose to our feet, and, I answer for myself, not Strickland, felt sick—actually and physically sick. We told each other, as did the men in *Pinafore*, that it was the cat.[4]

Dumoise arrived, and I never saw a little man so unprofessionally shocked. He said that it was a heart-rending case of hydrophobia, and that nothing could be

[1] *"Hydrophobia"* Aversion to water, a symptom of rabies.

[2] *punkah rope* Cord used to manipulate a punkah, or suspended cloth used as a fan.

[3] *without* Outside.

[4] *Pinafore ... cat* Cf. Gilbert and Sullivan's comic opera *H.M.S. Pinafore*, in which some sailors unwittingly mistake the sound of a whip (a cat-o'-nine-tails) for that of a cat.

done. At least any palliative measures would only prolong the agony. The beast was foaming at the mouth. Fleete, as we told Dumoise, had been bitten by dogs once or twice. Any man who keeps half a dozen terriers must expect a nip now and again. Dumoise could offer no help. He could only certify that Fleete was dying of hydrophobia. The beast was then howling, for it had managed to spit out the shoehorn. Dumoise said that he would be ready to certify to the cause of death, and that the end was certain. He was a good little man, and he offered to remain with us; but Strickland refused the kindness. He did not wish to poison Dumoise's New Year. He would only ask him not to give the real cause of Fleete's death to the public.

So Dumoise left, deeply agitated; and as soon as the noise of the cartwheels had died away, Strickland told me, in a whisper, his suspicions. They were so wildly improbable that he dared not say them out aloud; and I, who entertained all Strickland's beliefs, was so ashamed of owning to them that I pretended to disbelieve.

"Even if the Silver Man had bewitched Fleete for polluting the image of Hanuman, the punishment could not have fallen so quickly."

As I was whispering this the cry outside the house rose again, and the beast fell into a fresh paroxysm of struggling till we were afraid that the thongs that held it would give way.

"Watch!" said Strickland. "If this happens six times I shall take the law into my own hands. I order you to help me."

He went into his room and came out in a few minutes with the barrels of an old shotgun, a piece of fishing line, some thick cord, and his heavy wooden bedstead. I reported that the convulsions had followed the cry by two seconds in each case, and the beast seemed perceptibly weaker.

Strickland muttered, "But he can't take away the life! He can't take away the life!"

I said, though I knew that I was arguing against myself, "It may be a cat. It must be a cat. If the Silver Man is responsible, why does he dare to come here?"

Strickland arranged the wood on the hearth, put the gun barrels into the glow of the fire, spread the twine on the table and broke a walking stick in two. There was one yard of fishing line, gut, lapped with wire, such as is used for mahseer[1] fishing, and he tied the two ends together in a loop.

Then he said, "How can we catch him? He must be taken alive and unhurt."

I said that we must trust in providence, and go out softly with polo sticks into the shrubbery at the front of the house. The man or animal that made the cry was evidently moving round the house as regularly as a night-watchman. We could wait in the bushes till he came by and knock him over. Strickland accepted this suggestion, and we slipped out from a bathroom window into the front verandah and then across the carriage drive into the bushes.

In the moonlight we could see the leper coming round the corner of the house. He was perfectly naked, and from time to time he mewed and stopped to dance with his shadow. It was an unattractive sight, and thinking of poor Fleete, brought to such degradation by so foul a creature, I put away all my doubts and resolved to help Strickland from the heated gun barrels to the loop of twine—from the loins to the head and back again—with all tortures that might be needful.

The leper halted in the front porch for a moment and we jumped out on him with the sticks. He was wonderfully strong, and we were afraid that he might escape or be fatally injured before we caught him. We had an idea that lepers were frail creatures, but this proved to be incorrect. Strickland knocked his legs from under him and I put my foot on his neck. He mewed hideously, and even through my riding boots I could feel that his flesh was not the flesh of a clean man.

He struck at us with his hand and feet stumps. We looped the lash of a dog whip round him, under the armpits, and dragged him backwards into the hall and so into the dining room where the beast lay. There we tied him with trunk straps. He made no attempt to escape, but mewed.

---

[1]   *mahseer*   Carp of a type found in Malaysia, in the Himalayas.

When we confronted him with the beast the scene was beyond description. The beast doubled backwards into a bow as though he had been poisoned with strychnine, and moaned in the most pitiable fashion. Several other things happened also, but they cannot be put down here.

"I think I was right," said Strickland. "Now we will ask him to cure this case."

But the leper only mewed. Strickland wrapped a towel round his hand and took the gun barrels out of the fire. I put the half of the broken walking stick through the loop of fishing line and buckled the leper comfortably to Strickland's bedstead. I understood then how men and women and little children can endure to see a witch burnt alive, for the beast was moaning on the floor, and though the Silver Man had no face, you could see horrible feelings passing through the slab that took its place, exactly as waves of heat play across red hot iron—gun barrels for instance.

Strickland shaded his eyes with his hands for a moment and we got to work. This part is not to be printed.

* * * * *

The dawn was beginning to break when the leper spoke. His mewings had not been satisfactory up to that point. The beast had fainted from exhaustion and the house was very still. We unstrapped the leper and told him to take away the evil spirit. He crawled to the beast and laid his hand upon the left breast. That was all. Then he fell face down and whined, drawing in his breath as he did so.

We watched the face of the beast, and saw the soul of Fleete coming back into the eyes. Then a sweat broke out on the forehead and the eyes—they were human eyes—closed. We waited for an hour but Fleete still slept. We carried him to his room and bade the leper go, giving him the bedstead, and the sheet on the bedstead to cover his nakedness, the gloves and the towels with which we had touched him, and the whip that had been hooked round his body. He put the sheet about him and went out into the early morning without speaking or mewing.

Strickland wiped his face and sat down. A night gong, far away in the city, made seven o'clock.

"Exactly four-and-twenty hours!" said Strickland. "And I've done enough to ensure my dismissal from the service, besides permanent quarters in a lunatic asylum. Do you believe that we are awake?"

The red hot gun barrel had fallen on the floor and was singeing the carpet. The smell was entirely real.

That morning at eleven we two together went to wake up Fleete. We looked and saw that the black leopard rosette on his chest had disappeared. He was very drowsy and tired, but as soon as he saw us, he said,

"Oh! Confound you fellows. Happy New Year to you. Never mix your liquors. I'm nearly dead."

"Thanks for your kindness, but you're over time," said Strickland. "Today is the morning of the second. You've slept the clock round with a vengeance."

The door opened, and little Dumoise put his head in. He had come on foot, and fancied that we were laying out Fleete.

"I've brought a nurse," said Dumoise. "I suppose that she can come in for … what is necessary."

"By all means," said Fleete cheerily, sitting up in bed. "Bring on your nurses."

Dumoise was dumb. Strickland led him out and explained that there must have been a mistake in the diagnosis. Dumoise remained dumb and left the house hastily. He considered that his professional reputation had been injured, and was inclined to make a personal matter of the recovery.

Strickland went out too. When he came back, he said that he had been to call on the Temple of Hanuman to offer redress for the pollution of the god, and had been solemnly assured that no white man had ever touched the idol and that he was an incarnation of all the virtues labouring under a delusion. "What do you think?" said Strickland.

I said, "'There are more things …'"[1]

But Strickland hates that quotation. He says that I have worn it threadbare.

---

[1] *There are more things …*   From Shakespeare's *Hamlet* 1.5: "There are more things in heaven and earth, Horatio, / Than are dreamt of in your philosophy."

One other curious thing happened which frightened me as much as anything in all the night's work. When Fleete was dressed he came into the dining room and sniffed. He had a quaint trick of moving his nose when he sniffed. "Horrid doggy smell, here," said he. "You should really keep those terriers of yours in better order. Try sulphur, Strick."

But Strickland did not answer. He caught hold of the back of a chair, and, without warning, went into an amazing fit of hysterics. It is terrible to see a strong man overtaken with hysteria. Then it struck me that we had fought for Fleete's soul with the Silver Man in that room, and had disgraced ourselves as Englishmen forever, and I laughed and gasped and gurgled just as shamefully as Strickland, while Fleete thought that we

had both gone mad. We never told him what we had done.

Some years later, when Strickland had married and was a churchgoing member of society for his wife's sake, we reviewed the incident dispassionately, and Strickland suggested that I should put it before the public.

I cannot myself see that this step is likely to clear up the mystery, because, in the first place, no one will believe a rather unpleasant story, and, in the second, it is well known to every right-minded man that the gods of the heathen are stone and brass, and any attempt to deal with them otherwise is justly condemned.

—1891

In Context

Victoria and Albert

Queen Victoria was widowed when Prince Albert died on 14 December 1861. His partnership with the Queen had been an extraordinarily successful one—as a professional partnership as well as in family life. For many years after his death the Queen was a recluse, so much so that the public began to lose patience with and sympathy for Victoria in her mourning. It was not until the early 1870s that the Queen began to re-emerge. As she did so she gradually regained public favor, and by the time Kipling's "The Widow at Windsor" was published in 1890 she was widely revered. Her 60th Anniversary Jubilee in 1897—for which Kipling composed "Recessional"—was a massive national celebration.

Frederick Shuckard's painting of an idealized 18-year-old Princess Victoria receiving
news of her accession to the throne in 1837.

Queen Victoria and Prince Albert in the early
1850s. (Photograph by Roger Fenton.)

Queen Victoria in mourning, 1867.

Queen Victoria with John Brown, a servant who had been personal ghillie (the term applied to the attendant to a Highland Chief) to Prince Albert and who later served Queen Victoria; Brown is credited with helping to bring the Queen out from seclusion. (Photo by W & D Downy.)

The Queen with Princess Beatrice, Princess Victoria, and great-granddaughter Alice, 1867. (Photographer unknown.)

Queen Victoria in the Golden Jubilee procession, 1897.

Victoria holding the future Edward VIII on the occasion of his baptism;
her sons Edward (later Edward VII) and George (later George V) are in the background.

IN CONTEXT

The "White Man's Burden" in the Philippines

The Philippine Islands had long been a Spanish colony, but Spain's defeat in 1898 at the hands of American Admiral George Dewey during the Spanish-American War was followed by an agreement ceding the islands to the United States for $20 million. Local forces (under Emilio Agninaldo) had been rebelling against the Spanish, and, expecting the American victory to lead to liberation, declared a republic. The Americans, however, deciding that the natives were not ready for independence, ruthlessly suppressed the insurrection of Agninaldo's forces (which continued until 1905). Not until 1946 was the Republic of the Philippines granted full independence. The American annexation of the islands in 1899 was widely popular in the United States, but a significant minority loudly protested the expression of American imperialism that was the occasion for Kipling's famous poem. Following are excerpts from the platform adopted by one American organization at their founding meeting in Chicago, 17 October 1899.

Platform of the American Anti-Imperialist League

We hold that the policy known as imperialism is hostile to liberty and tends toward militarism, an evil from which it has been our glory to be free. We regret that it has become necessary in the land of Washington and Lincoln to reaffirm that all men, of whatever race or color, are entitled to life, liberty, and the pursuit of happiness. We maintain that governments derive their just powers from the consent of the governed. We insist that the subjugation of any people is "criminal aggression" and open disloyalty to the distinctive principles of our government.

We earnestly condemn the policy of the present national administration in the Philippines. It seeks to extinguish the spirit of 1776 in those islands. We deplore the sacrifice of our soldiers and sailors, whose bravery deserves admiration even in an unjust war. We denounce the slaughter of the Filipinos as a needless horror. We protest against the extension of American sovereignty by Spanish methods.

We demand the immediate cessation of the war against liberty, begun by Spain and continued by us. We urge that Congress be promptly convened to announce to the Filipinos our purpose to concede to them the independence for which they have so long fought and which of right is theirs.

The United States have always protested against the doctrine of international law which permits the subjugation of the weak by the strong. A self-governing state cannot accept sovereignty over an unwilling people. The United States cannot act upon the ancient heresy that might makes right.

Imperialists assume that with the destruction of self-government in the Philippines by American hands, all opposition here will cease. This is a grievous error. Much as we abhor the war of "criminal aggression" in the Philippines, greatly as we regret that the blood of the Filipinos is on American hands, we more deeply resent the betrayal of American institutions at home. The real firing line is not in the suburbs of Manila. The foe is of our own household. The attempt of 1861 was to divide the country. That of 1899 is to destroy its fundamental principles and noblest ideals.

Whether the ruthless slaughter of the Filipinos shall end next month or next year is but an incident in a contest that must go on until the Declaration of Independence and the Constitution of the United States are rescued from the hands of their betrayers. Those who dispute about standards of value while the Republic is undermined will be listened to as little as there who would wrangle about the small economies of the household while the house is on fire. The training of a great people for a century, the aspiration for liberty of a vast immigration are forces that will hurl aside those who in the delirium of conquest seek to destroy the character of our institutions.

We deny that the obligation of all citizens to support their Government in times of grave national peril applies to the present situation. If an administration may with impunity ignore the issues upon which it was chosen, deliberately create a condition of war anywhere on the face of the globe, debauch the civil service for spoils to promote the adventure, organize a truth suppressing censorship and demand of all citizens a suspension of judgement and their unanimous support while it chooses to continue the fighting, representative government itself is imperiled.

We propose to contribute to the defeat of any person or party that stands for the forcible subjugation of any people. We shall oppose for reelection all who in the White House or in Congress betray American liberty in pursuit of un-American gains. We still hope that both of our great political parties will support and defend the Declaration of Independence in the closing campaign of the century.

We hold, with Abraham Lincoln, that "no man is good enough to govern another man without that other's consent. When the white man governs himself, that is self-government, but when he governs himself and also governs another man, that is more than self-government—that is despotism." "Our reliance is in the love of liberty which God has planted in us. Our defense is in the spirit which prizes liberty as the heritage of all men in all lands. Those who deny freedom to others deserve it not for themselves, and under a just God cannot long retain it."

We cordially invite the co-operation of all men and women who remain loyal to the Declaration of Independence and the Constitution of the United States.

RACE, EMPIRE, AND A WIDER WORLD
CONTEXTS

In the Victorian era colonies in the British Empire were divided into two broad categories. In one category were crown colonies ruled by governments with no direct responsibility to the people they ruled, but only to the Foreign Office and the home country as a whole. The vast majority of the populace in such colonies did not share in the history, religion, or traditions of England or other European cultures, and were brown or black in color; in this category were the bulk of British possessions in Africa, Asia, and the Caribbean. In areas of the Empire where emigration from Britain and other European nations had created a majority or a substantial minority of a population sharing the cultural and racial makeup of "the old country," on the other hand, responsible government became the norm. Under the terms of Imperial arrangements in the latter category, administration was still overseen by British authority, but governments with a substantial degree of real power were elected by and responsible to the local populace, and were composed of local leaders rather than temporary appointees from abroad. Canada, the Australian colonies, and New Zealand were prominent in this second category.

India was in many ways a special case, with local hereditary rulers in some cases maintaining considerable authority under an umbrella of British rule over the subcontinent, and with Imperial rule complicated both by the existence of the India Office as a separate government department in Britain, and by the authority wielded (until 1858) by the East India Company. The latter was the last such entity to hold substantial power in a British colony. In the seventeenth century, the East India Company, the Hudson's Bay Company, and the Royal Africa Company were among the commercial entities given royal charters, empowering them not only to trade commercially in particular parts of the globe but also to exercise political authority over the local people. Beginning in the eighteenth century, such authority began to be transferred to government of a more conventional sort.

Throughout the history of the British Empire various notions of "Empire" competed with one another. Perhaps the least complicated was the notion that Empire should be based purely on the commercial interests of the Imperial power. It was this notion that was foremost in the minds of many commercial adventurers staking out an Imperial claim—but also in the minds of many "little Englanders" in the nineteenth century who did not necessarily have any desire to abandon the Empire as a whole, but felt it would be expedient and appropriate to "cut loose" colonies that were perceived to represent a net drain on Britain's resources, financial and otherwise. For others, though, the Empire was a vital symbol of the nation's importance in the world—and of its "greatness" (a word in which power and morality came to be inextricably entangled). Finally, there were those whose notions of Empire were shaped by a hope and a confidence that Britain would improve the lot of her subject peoples—improve their economic conditions, certainly, but also bring to them literacy and an appropriate level of education, what were perceived to be the benefits of Christianity, and a broader set of cultural benefits, as well. It is easy to be cynical about this last set of ideas, and there was surely much in these "enlightened" notions of Empire that was hypocritical, patronizing, and racist. That there was also frequently some kernel of altruism in the "enlightened imperialism" of the likes of William Gladstone or David Livingstone, however, is difficult to doubt, even as it must now be plain to all how horrifically misguided such impulses often were.

There was no pretense made that the greatest of horrors endured by subject peoples under British imperialism was a civilizing mission. After a long struggle, outright slavery had been abolished in all British possessions in 1833, but in certain British colonies in the Caribbean, practices tantamount to slavery continued for decades thereafter—prompting incidents such as the uprising against British Governor Edward Eyre in Jamaica in 1865. Nor was there anything civilizing in the unspeakable atrocities meted out during the suppression of the Indian mutiny in 1857–58, or the brutal treatment accorded the aboriginal peoples of Australia, New Zealand, and (to a somewhat lesser extent) Canada; all these represented Imperialism stripped of any veneer of civilization.

The feelings of cultural and racial superiority on which rationalizations of the subjugation of other peoples were founded took a variety of forms. The sort of anthropological theorizing that Adam Smith and other eighteenth-century thinkers had engaged in was comparatively benign, and remained popular throughout the nineteenth century. According to this way of thinking, other peoples were not inherently inferior; they were simply at a less fully advanced stage of social and economic organization than were European peoples. An anthropological "stages of development" approach often led to an assumption by the British and other Europeans of a "childish" mentality among peoples elsewhere in the globe, but it also left room for the moral anthropology of Rousseau and others that ascribed to the "noble savage" the attribute of an innocence largely lost to "higher" stages of civilization. (It is this view with which Charles Dickens takes vehement issue in the essay from *Household Words* excerpted in this section.)

Although this approach was widely held throughout the Victorian era, pseudo-scientific claims of a biological sort were increasingly made. According to many making such claims, other peoples were not at a lower stage of development (from which they could, with assistance, be raised over the course of time to the level of Europeans); rather they were inherently, biologically inferior, and it would thus always be appropriate to treat them as creatures of a lower order.

Through most of the twentieth century little direct attention was paid to the attitudes of leading Victorian literary figures towards these issues, and it came to be widely assumed that writers who had deplored, for example, the brutality of conditions for workers in industry in England would also have deplored oppression and brutality overseas. As Edward Said and others were instrumental in demonstrating, in the late twentieth-century, however, this was simply not the case. While John Stuart Mill and some others did indeed hold what we now acknowledge to be relatively enlightened views on the subject of race and culture, the list of those espousing views which today can only be described as racist (tellingly, neither the word "racialist" or the word "racist" is recorded as having been used before the twentieth century) is a long one, and includes such major figures as Thomas Carlyle, William Thackeray, John Ruskin, and Walter Bagehot. It is difficult to read the pronouncements of many of these figures on such matters without feeling a sense of revulsion. Again, though, we should be wary of presuming ourselves to be at a moral pinnacle; it may well be that in another 150 years we will look back on the views that predominate in our own time—our willingness to ignore genocide so long as it is happening in faraway lands, for example—with as much revulsion as we feel toward the racism of many of the great Victorians.

⌘ ⌘ ⌘

from Frances Trollope, *Domestic Manners of the Americans* (1832)

> The novelist Frances Trollope's account of her visit to the United States features a number of reflections on the direction taken by the American character in the decades since America became independent from Britain.

from CHAPTER 1: ENTRANCE OF THE MISSISSIPPI

On the 4th of November, 1827, I sailed from London, accompanied by my son and two daughters; and after a favourable, though somewhat tedious voyage, arrived on Christmas-day at the mouth of the Mississippi.

The first indication of our approach to land was the appearance of this mighty river pouring forth its muddy mass of waters, and mingling with the deep blue of the Mexican Gulf. The shores of this river are so utterly flat, that no object upon them is perceptible at sea, and we gazed with pleasure on the muddy ocean that met us, for it told us we were arrived, and seven weeks of sailing had wearied us; yet it was not without a feeling like regret that we passed from the bright blue waves, whose varying aspect had so long furnished our chief amusement, into the murky stream which now received us.

Large flights of pelicans were seen standing upon the long masses of mud which rose above the surface of the waters, and a pilot came to guide us over the bar, long before any other indication of land was visible.

I never beheld a scene so utterly desolate as this entrance of the Mississippi. Had Dante seen it, he might have drawn images of another Bolgia[1] from its horrors. One only object rears itself above the eddying waters; this is the mast of a vessel long since wrecked in attempting to cross the bar, and it still stands, a dismal witness of the destruction that has been, and a boding prophet of that which is to come.

By degrees bulrushes of enormous growth become visible, and a few more miles of mud brought us within

sight of a cluster of huts called the Balize, by far the most miserable station that I ever saw made the dwelling of man, but I was told that many families of pilots and fishermen lived there.

For several miles above its mouth, the Mississippi presents no objects more interesting than mud banks, monstrous bulrushes, and now and then a huge crocodile luxuriating in the slime. Another circumstance that gives to this dreary scene an aspect of desolation, is the incessant appearance of vast quantities of drift wood, which is ever finding its way to the different mouths of the Mississippi. Trees of enormous length, sometimes still bearing their branches, and still oftener their uptorn roots entire, the victims of the frequent hurricane, come floating down the stream. Sometimes several of these, entangled together, collect among their boughs a quantity of floating rubbish, that gives the mass the appearance of a moving island, bearing a forest, with its roots mocking the heavens; while the dishonoured branches lash the tide in idle vengeance: this, as it approaches the vessel, and glides swiftly past, looks like the fragment of a world in ruins.

from CHAPTER 3: COMPANY ON BOARD THE STEAM BOAT

The weather was warm and bright, and we found the guard of the boat, as they call the gallery that runs round the cabins, a very agreeable station; here we all sat as long as light lasted, and sometimes wrapped in our shawls, we enjoyed the clear bright beauty of American moonlight long after every passenger but ourselves had retired. We had a full complement of passengers on board. The deck, as is usual, was occupied by the Kentucky flat-boat men, returning from New Orleans, after having disposed of the boat and cargo which they had conveyed thither, with no other labour than that of steering her, the current bringing her down at the rate of four miles an hour. We had about two hundred of these men on board, but the part of the vessel occupied by them is so distinct from the cabins, that we never saw them, except when we stopped to take in wood; and then they ran, or rather sprung and vaulted over each other's heads to the shore, whence they all assisted in carrying wood to supply the steam engine; the performance of this duty being a stipulated part of the pay-

---

[1]   *Dante*   Italian poet Dante Alighieri (1265–1321), author of the epic poem *The Divine Comedy*, composed of three sections describing Heaven (*Paradiso*), Purgatory (*Purgatorio*), and Hell (*Inferno*); *Bolgia* Level of Hell in Dante's *Inferno*.

ment of their passage.

From the account given by a man servant we had on board, who shared their quarters, they are a most disorderly set of persons, constantly gambling and wrangling, very seldom sober, and never suffering a night to pass without giving practical proof of the respect in which they hold the doctrines of equality, and community of property. The clerk of the vessel was kind enough to take our man under his protection, and assigned him a berth in his own little nook; but as this was not inaccessible, he told him by no means to detach his watch or money from his person during the night. Whatever their moral characteristics may be, these Kentuckians are a very noble-looking race of men; their average height considerably exceeds that of Europeans, and their countenances, excepting when disfigured by red hair, which is not unfrequent, extremely handsome.

The gentlemen in the cabin (we had no ladies) would certainly neither, from their language, manners, nor appearance, have received that designation in Europe; but we soon found their claim to it rested on more substantial ground, for we heard them nearly all addressed by the titles of general, colonel, and major. On mentioning these military dignities to an English friend some time afterwards, he told me that he too had made the voyage with the same description of company, but remarking that there was not a single captain among them; he made the observation to a fellow-passenger, and asked how he accounted for it. "Oh, sir, the captains are all on deck," was the reply.

… I know it is equally easy and invidious[1] to ridicule the peculiarities of appearance and manner in people of a different nation from ourselves; we may, too, at the same moment, be undergoing the same ordeal in their estimation; and, moreover, I am by no means disposed to consider whatever is new to me as therefore objectionable; but, nevertheless, it was impossible not to feel repugnance to many of the novelties that now surrounded me.

The total want of all the usual courtesies of the table, the voracious rapidity with which the viands[2] were seized and devoured, the strange uncouth phrases and pronunciation; the loathsome spitting, from the contamination of which it was absolutely impossible to protect our dresses; the frightful manner of feeding with their knives, till the whole blade seemed to enter into the mouth; and the still more frightful manner of cleaning the teeth afterwards with a pocket knife, soon forced us to feel that we were not surrounded by the generals, colonels, and majors of the old world; and that the dinner hour was to be any thing rather than an hour of enjoyment.

The little conversation that went forward while we remained in the room, was entirely political, and the respective claims of Adams and Jackson[3] to the presidency were argued with more oaths and more vehemence than it had ever been my lot to hear. Once a colonel appeared on the verge of assaulting a major, when a huge seven-foot Kentuckian gentleman horse-dealer, asked of the heavens to confound them both, and bade them sit still and be d——d. We too thought we should share this sentence; at least sitting still in the cabin seemed very nearly to include the rest of it, and we never tarried[4] there a moment longer than was absolutely necessary to eat.

from CHAPTER 34: RETURN TO NEW YORK—CONCLUSION

… Nothing could be more beautiful than our passage down the Hudson on the following day, as I thought of some of my friends in England, dear lovers of the picturesque; … not even a moving panoramic view, gliding before their eyes for an hour together, in all the scenic splendour of Drury Lane, or Covent Garden,[5] could give them an idea of it. They could only see one side at a time. The change, the contrast, the ceaseless variety of beauty, as you skim from side to side, the liquid smoothness of the broad mirror that reflects the scene, and most of all, the clear bright air through which

---

[1] *invidious* Tending to incite ill-feeling or unpopularity against others.

[2] *viands* Food.

[3] *Adams* John Quincy Adams (1767–1848) won a controversial majority in the American election of 1824 by joining forces with third candidate Henry Clay, whom he later named Secretary of State; *Jackson* Andrew Jackson (1767–1845) contested Adams's government and went on to win the 1829 election.

[4] *tarried* Delayed, prolonged.

[5] *Drury Lane* Street in London, England, location of the famous theater of that name; *Covent Garden* Theater and entertainment district in central London, England.

you look at it; all this can only be seen and believed by crossing the Atlantic.

As we approached New York the burning heat of the day relaxed, and the long shadows of evening fell coolly on the beautiful villas we passed. I really can conceive nothing more exquisitely lovely than this approach to the city. The magnificent boldness of the Jersey shore on the one side, and the luxurious softness of the shady lawns on the other, with the vast silvery stream that flows between them, altogether form a picture which may well excuse a traveller for saying, once and again, that the Hudson River can be surpassed in beauty by none on the outside of Paradise.

It was nearly dark when we reached the city, and it was with great satisfaction that we found our comfortable apartments in Hudson Street unoccupied; and our pretty, kind (Irish) hostess willing to receive us again. We passed another fortnight there; and again we enjoyed the elegant hospitality of New York, though now it was offered from beneath the shade of their beautiful villas. In truth, were all America like this fair city, and all, no, only a small proportion of its population like the friends we left there, I should say, that the land was the fairest in the world.

It is a matter of historical notoriety that the original stock of the white population now inhabiting the United States, were persons who had banished themselves, or were banished from the mother country. The land they found was favourable to their increase and prosperity; the colony grew and flourished. Years rolled on, and the children, the grand-children, and the great grand-children of the first settlers, replenished the land, and found it flowing with milk and honey. That they should wish to keep this milk and honey to themselves, is not very surprising. What did the mother country do for them? She sent them out gay and gallant officers to guard their frontier; the which they thought they could guard as well themselves; and then she taxed their tea. Now, this was disagreeable; and to atone for it, the distant colony had no great share in her mother's grace and glory. It was not from among them that her high and mighty were chosen; the rays which emanated from that bright sun of honour, the British throne, reached them but feebly. They knew not, they cared not, for her

kings nor her heroes; their thriftiest trader was their noblest man; the holy seats of learning were but the cradles of superstition; the splendour of the aristocracy, but a leech that drew their "golden blood." The wealth, the learning, the glory of Britain, was to them nothing; the having their own way every thing. Can any blame their wish to obtain it? Can any lament that they succeeded? …

As long as their governments are at peace with each other, the individuals of every nation in Europe make it a matter of pride, as well as of pleasure, to meet each other frequently, to discuss, compare, and reason upon their national varieties, and to vote it a mark of fashion and good taste to imitate each other in all the external embellishments of life.

The consequence of this is most pleasantly perceptible at the present time, in every capital of Europe. The long peace has given time for each to catch from each what was best in customs and manners, and the rapid advance of refinement and general information has been the result.

To those who have been accustomed to this state of things, the contrast upon crossing to the new world is inconceivably annoying; and it cannot be doubted that this is one great cause of the general feeling of irksomeness, and fatigue of spirits, which hangs upon the memory while recalling the hours passed in American society.

A single word indicative of doubt, that any thing, or every thing, in that country is not the very best in the world, produces an effect which must be seen and felt to be understood. If the citizens of the United States were indeed the devoted patriots they call themselves, they would surely not thus encrust themselves in the hard, dry, stubborn persuasion, that they are the first and best of the human race, that nothing is to be learnt, but what they are able to teach, and that nothing is worth having, which they do not possess.

The art of man could hardly discover a more effectual antidote to improvement, than this persuasion; and yet I never listened to any public oration, or read any work, professedly addressed to the country, in which they did not labour to impress it on the minds of the people.

from Thomas Babington Macaulay, "Minute on Indian Education" (1835)

> In this 1835 speech, Macaulay, then a member of the Council of India, argued that the sum set aside by the British Parliament for the education of Indian citizens should be used to teach the English language and the scientific and cultural advancements of Britain, rather than to promote the study of India's native cultures and languages. In the paragraphs immediately preceding this excerpt, Macaulay put forward the claim that the people of India should not be taught in any of their native languages, as the various dialects are "poor and rude," and "contain neither literary nor scientific information." In addition, he asserted, the historical, philosophical, and literary achievements of works written in European languages far surpassed their Sanskrit and Arabic equivalents.

from "Minute on Indian Education"

… How, then, stands the case? We have to educate a people who cannot at present be educated by means of their mother-tongue. We must teach them some foreign language. The claims of our own language it is hardly necessary to recapitulate. It stands pre-eminent even among the languages of the west. It abounds with works of imagination not inferior to the noblest which Greece has bequeathed to us; with models of every species of eloquence; with historical compositions, which, considered merely as narratives, have seldom been surpassed, and which, considered as vehicles of ethical and political instruction, have never been equalled; with just and lively representations of human life and human nature; with the most profound speculations on metaphysics, morals, government, jurisprudence,[1] and trade; with full and correct information respecting every experimental science which tends to preserve the health, to increase the comfort, or to expand the intellect of man. Whoever knows that language has ready access to all the vast intellectual wealth which all the wisest nations of the earth have created and hoarded in the course of ninety generations. It may safely be said that the literature now extant in that language is of far greater value than all the literature which three hundred years ago was extant in all the languages of the world together. Nor is this all. In India, English is the language spoken by the ruling class. It is spoken by the higher class of natives at the seats of government. It is likely to become the language of commerce throughout the seas of the East. It is the language of two great European communities which are rising, the one in the south of Africa, the other in Australasia; communities which are every year becoming more important, and more closely connected with our Indian Empire. Whether we look at the intrinsic value of our literature, or at the particular situation of this country, we shall see the strongest reason to think that, of all foreign tongues, the English tongue is that which would be the most useful to our native subjects.

The question now before us is simply whether, when it is in our power to teach this language, we shall teach languages in which, by universal confession, there are no books on any subject which deserve to be compared to our own; whether, when we can teach European science, we shall teach systems which, by universal confession, whenever they differ from those of Europe, differ for the worse; and whether, when we can patronize sound philosophy and true history, we shall countenance, at the public expense, medical doctrines which would disgrace an English farrier,[2] astronomy which would move laughter in girls at an English boarding-school, history abounding with kings thirty feet high, and reigns thirty thousand years long, and geography made up of seas of treacle and seas of butter.

We are not without experience to guide us. History furnishes several analogous cases, and they all teach the same lesson. There are in modern times, to go no further, two memorable instances of a great impulse given to the mind of a whole society—of prejudices overthrown, of knowledge diffused, of taste purified, of arts and sciences planted in countries which had recently been ignorant and barbarous.

The first instance to which I refer is the great revival of letters among the western nations at the close of the fifteenth, and the beginning of the sixteenth, century. At that time almost everything that was worth reading was contained in the writings of the ancient Greeks and Romans. Had our ancestors acted as the Committee of

---

[1] *jurisprudence* Law.

[2] *farrier* One who shoes or cares for horses.

Public Instruction has hitherto acted;[1] had they neglected the language of Cicero and Tacitus;[2] had they confined their attention to the old dialects of our own island; had they printed nothing, and taught nothing at the universities, but chronicles in Anglo-Saxon, and romances in Norman-French, would England have been what she now is? What the Greek and Latin were to the contemporaries of More and Ascham,[3] our tongue is to the people of India. The literature of England is now more valuable than that of classical antiquity. I doubt whether the Sanskrit literature be as valuable as that of our Saxon and Norman progenitors. In some departments—in history, for example—I am certain that it is much less so.

Another instance may be said to be still before our eyes. Within the last hundred and twenty years, a nation which had previously been in a state as barbarous as that in which our ancestors were before the crusades, has gradually emerged from the ignorance in which it was sunk, and has taken its place among civilized communities—I speak of Russia. There is now in that country a large educated class, abounding with persons fit to serve the state in the highest functions, and in no wise inferior to the most accomplished men who adorn the best circles of Paris and London. There is reason to hope that this vast empire, which in the time of our grandfathers was probably behind the Punjab, may, in the time of our grandchildren, be pressing close on France and Britain in the career of improvement. And how was this change effected? Not by flattering national prejudices; not by feeding the mind of the young Muscovite[4] with old women's stories which his rude fathers had believed; not by filling his head with lying legends about St.

Nicholas;[5] not by encouraging him to study the great question, whether the world was or was not created on the 13th of September; not by calling him "a learned native," when he has mastered all these points of knowledge: but by teaching him those foreign languages in which the greatest mass of information had been laid up, and thus putting all that information within his reach. The languages of Western Europe civilized Russia. I cannot doubt that they will do for the Hindu what they have done for the Tartar.[6] …

It is impossible for us, with our limited means, to attempt to educate the body of the people. We must at present do our best to form a class who may be interpreters between us and the millions whom we govern; a class of persons, Indian in blood and colour, but English in taste, in opinions, in morals, and in intellect. To that class we may leave it to refine the vernacular dialects of the country, to enrich those dialects with terms of science borrowed from the Western nomenclature, and to render them by degrees fit vehicles for conveying knowledge to the great mass of the population.

from Report of a Speech by William Charles Wentworth, Australian Legislative Council (1844)

In 1844 the aboriginal populace in Australia probably still outnumbered that of the whites. Official policy called for "amity and kindness" and forbade "any unnecessary interruption" of aboriginal existence, but, as the excerpt below suggests, attitudes towards native peoples that prevailed were often brutally harsh.

He could not see if the whites in this colony were to go out into the land and possess it, that the Government had much to do with them. No doubt there would be battles between the settlers and the border tribes; but they might be settled without the aid of the Government. The civilized people had come in and the savage must go back. They must go on progressing until their dominancy was established, and therefore he could

---

[1] *Committee … acted* The Committee of Public Instruction had hitherto used the allocated funds solely for promoting the study of Arabic and Sanskrit literature and for encouraging those "learned natives" who studied the science, religions, and histories of their native cultures.

[2] *Cicero* Roman orator of the first century BCE; *Tacitus* First-century CE author of two works of Roman history, *Histories* and *Annals*.

[3] *More* Sir Thomas More (1478–1535), English politician and humanist scholar, author of *Utopia*; *Ascham* Roger Ascham (1515–68), Latin Secretary to Edward VI, Mary I, and Elizabeth I.

[4] *Muscovite* Resident of Moscow.

[5] *St. Nicholas* Patron saint of sailors, revered in Christian Orthodox tradition.

[6] *Tartar* Here, Russian.

think that no measure was wise or merciful to the blacks which clothed them with a degree of seeming protection, which their position would not allow them to maintain.... It was not the policy of a wise Government to attempt the perpetuation of the aboriginal race of New South Wales.... They must give way before the arms, aye! even the diseases of civilized nations—they must give way before they attain the power of those nations.

from William H. Smith, *Smith's Canadian Gazetteer* (1846)

> Smith states in his preface that he was "induced to undertake the task" of writing his gazetteer by the "great ignorance" which he found to exist respecting the province of Canada West (now Ontario), "not only amongst persons in Great Britain, or newly arrived emigrants, but even amongst many of those who had been for years resident in the country." The gazetteer includes information on all towns and geographical areas in the province. The following excerpts are taken from the section of general reflections with which the work concludes.

It is most extraordinary, so long as Canada has been settled, that its great natural advantages should still be so little known; that so many persons who are either compelled by necessity to emigrate, or who do so from choice, should continue to pass it by and go on to the west of the United States, or otherwise emigrate to the more distant colonies of the Cape, New South Wales, or New Zealand and yet such is the case....

In what respects will the advocates of emigration to the United States pretend to say that any portion of that country is superior to Canada. Is it in the climate? A tree may be judged of by its fruits, and very many of the native Canadians, in point of robust appearance and complexion, might be taken for English emigrants. Will any one venture to make the same assertion respecting a native of Ohio, Indiana, Illinois, or Missouri? And of what avail is it that the climate will grow cotton and tobacco, if the settler neither has the strength to cultivate them, nor a market in which to dispose of them, when grown? In the winter and spring of 1841–2, pork (a staple article of the State) was selling in Illinois, at from a dollar to a dollar and a half per 100 lbs.; and at that price it was almost impossible to obtain cash for it; wheat at a quarter dollar, and Indian corn from five to ten cents per bushel; butter, fifteen and sixteen pounds for a dollar; fowls, half a dollar per dozen; and other farming produce in proportion. At such prices farming could not be very profitable. A man certainly might live cheaply, and cram himself with bacon and corn bread till he brought on bilious fever;[1] but he could *make nothing* of what he raised. And a farmer having a fat ox, has even been known after killing it, to take from it the hide and tallow, and drag the carcass into the woods to be devoured by the wolves; finding from the small price the beef would fetch, that it was more profitable to do so than to sell the whole animal!

Is it from the nature of the government, that the States are so much more desirable as a place of residence—where the only law is mob law, and the bowie knife is the constant companion of the citizens, and is used even in the halls of legislature themselves? Or is New Zealand much to be preferred, where the settler in taking his morning ramble, to acquire an appetite for his breakfast, frequently receives a "settler" himself, and instead of returning to his morning's meal, is roasted for the breakfast of some native chief, and his interesting family. Canada, on the contrary, suffers under none of these disadvantages and annoyances. The government and constitution of the country are English; the laws English; the climate is fine and healthy; the Indians are tolerably civilized, none of them at any rate are cannibals, and few of them are even thieves; and bowie knives are not "the fashion." The settler, unless he has been guilty of the folly of planting himself down beyond the bounds of civilization and of roads, may always command a fair price and cash for whatever he can raise—he need never be beyond the reach of medical attendance, churches, and schools—he can obtain as much land as he need wish to purchase, at a fair and moderate rate—he knows that whatever property he acquires is as secure as if he had it in England—his landed property, if he possesses any, is gradually increasing in value—and if he is only moderately careful and industrious, he need have no anxiety for the future—his sons, growing up in and with the country, and as they grow, acquiring a

---

[1] *bilious fever* Over-secretion of bile, causing indigestion.

knowledge of the country and its customs, and the various modes of doing business in it, if steady, will have no difficulty in succeeding in any business they may select, or may be qualified for.

Much has been written on the subject of emigration, and many speculations entered into as to *who* are the proper persons to emigrate? The only answer that can be given to this question is—*those who are obliged to do so.* Let no person who is doing *well* at home, no matter what may be his profession or occupation, emigrate with the expectation of doing *better*,—let him not leave his home and travel over the world, in search of advantages which he may not find elsewhere. But those who are *not* doing well, who find it difficult to struggle against increasing competition, who fear the loss in business of what little property they possess, or who find it difficult with an increasing family to keep up appearances as they have been accustomed to do, and find it necessary to make a change—all these may safely emigrate, with a fair prospect of improving their condition. Persons of small, independent incomes may live cheaply in Canada, particularly in the country, and enjoy many comforts, and even luxuries, that were not within their reach at home. Retired military men do not generally make good settlers. They usually, when they leave the army, sell out, instead of retiring on half pay; and when they emigrate they are apt to squander their property in purchasing land and in building, till at length they come to a stand for want of the means to proceed, frequently with their buildings half-finished, from being planned on too large a scale; although, if they had been asked in the commencement how they intended to *live* when the ready money was expended, they would have been unable to give an intelligible answer. If they succeed in getting some government office, the emoluments[1] of which are sufficient for their support, they will manage to get along very well; otherwise they will sink gradually lower and lower, and their children are apt to get into idle and dissipated habits. The idle and inactive life to which they have been accustomed while in the army, particularly during these "piping times of peace,"[2]

[1]   *emoluments*   Salary, remuneration.

[2]   *piping ... peace*   See William Shakespeare's *Richard III* 1.1.24: "Why, I, in this weak piping time of peace, / Have no delight to pass away the time."

totally incapacitates them for making good settlers in the backwoods. *A lounger, unless independent, has no business in Canada.* Naval officers, on the contrary, make settlers of a very different character. They have been accustomed, when on service, to a life of activity; and if they have been long on service, they have generally seen a great deal of the world—they have their half-pay to fall back on, which fortunately for them they cannot sell—and they generally make very excellent settlers. Lawyers are not wanted: Canada swarms with them; and they multiply in the province so fast, that the demand is not by any means equal to the supply. Medical men may find many openings in the country, where they will have no difficulty in making a tolerable living; but they will have to work hard for it, having frequently to ride fifteen, twenty-five, or even thirty miles to see a patient! And in the towns, the competition is as great as in England....

Carlyle, Mill, and "The Negro Question"

In the wake of the abolition of slavery in all British possessions in 1837, and of the ending of the preferential tariff on sugar in 1846, plantation owners in the British West Indies complained vociferously about their situation, arguing that they were placed in the unfair position of having to compete against sugar produced in countries such as Brazil where slavery was still permitted. Amongst the many in Britain who supported their arguments was Thomas Carlyle, who sets out his position in the essay excerpted below. Shortly thereafter, John Stuart Mill delivered a stinging reply, also excerpted below. Carlyle reprinted a revised version of the essay in 1853 under the more incendiary title "Occasional Discourse on the Nigger Question."[3] In the 1860s the two also disagreed publicly over the Eyre

[3]   *more incendiary ... Nigger Question*   From the late sixteenth century into the eighteenth, the term "nigger" was generally used in a more or less neutral fashion, and rarely in a way that directly expressed hostility towards blacks. In the late eighteenth and early nineteenth centuries the word began to be used more and more frequently to express contempt. An example from the same period at which Carlyle was writing is Hartley Coleridge's 1849 complaint against turning Othello "into a rank wooly-pated, thick-lipped nigger."

rebellion (an uprising in Jamaica against the oppressive conditions under which black Jamaicans were forced to work, which became a *cause célèbre* in England when the rebellion was suppressed, with extraordinary brutality, by Governor Edward John Eyre).

from Thomas Carlyle, "Occasional Discourse on the Negro Question," *Fraser's Magazine* (1849)

West Indian affairs, as we all know, and some of us know to our cost, are in a rather troublous condition this good while. In regard to West Indian affairs, however, Lord John Russell[1] is able to comfort us with one fact, indisputable where so many are dubious, that the negroes are all very happy and doing well. A fact very comfortable indeed. West Indian whites, it is admitted, are far enough from happy; West Indian colonies not unlike sinking wholly into ruin; at home, too, the British whites are rather badly off—several millions of them hanging on the verge of continual famine—and, in single towns, many thousands of them very sore put to it, at this time ... to live at all—these, again, are uncomfortable facts; and they are extremely extensive and important ones. But ... how pleasant to have always this fact to fall back upon; our beautiful black darlings are at last happy; with little labor except to the teeth, *which*, surely, in those excellent horse-jaws of theirs, will not fail!

Exeter Hall,[2] my philanthropic friends, has had its way in this matter. The twenty millions, a mere trifle, despatched with a single dash of the pen, are paid; and, far over the sea, we have a few black persons rendered extremely "free" indeed. Sitting yonder, with their beautiful muzzles up to the ears in pumpkins, imbibing sweet pulps and juices; the grinder and incisor teeth ready for every new work, and the pumpkins cheap as grass in those rich climates; while the sugar crops rot round them, uncut, because labor cannot be hired. ... A state of matters lovely to contemplate, in these emancipated epochs of the human mind, which has earned us, not only the praises of Exeter Hall, and loud, long-eared hallelujahs of laudatory psalmody[3] from the friends of freedom everywhere, but lasting favor (it is hoped) from the heavenly powers themselves; which may, at least, justly appeal to the heavenly powers, and ask them, if ever, in terrestrial procedure, they saw the match of it! Certainly, in the past history of the human species, it has no parallel; nor, one hopes, will it have in the future. ...

Truly, my philanthropic friends, Exeter Hall philanthropy is wonderful; and the social science ... which finds the secret of this universe in "supply and demand," and reduces the duty of human governors to that of letting men alone, is also wonderful. A dreary, desolate and, indeed, quite abject and distressing one; what we might call, by way of eminence, the *dismal science*.[4] These two, Exeter Hall philanthropy and the Dismal Science, led by any sacred cause of black emancipation, or the like, to fall in love and make a wedding of it—will give birth to progenies and prodigies: dark extensive moon-calves, unnameable abortions, wide-coiled monstrosities, such as the world has not seen hitherto!...

My philanthropic friends, can you discern no fixed headlands in this wide-weltering[5] deluge of benevolent twaddle and revolutionary grapeshot that has burst forth on us—no sure bearings at all? Fact and nature, it seems to me, say a few words to us, if, happily, we have still an ear for fact and nature. Let us listen a little, and try. And first, with regard to the West Indies, it may be laid down as a principle, which no eloquence in Exeter Hall, or Westminster Hall,[6] or elsewhere, can invalidate or hide, except for a short time only, that no black man, who will not work according to what ability the gods have given him for working, has the smallest right to eat pumpkin, or to any fraction of land that will grow

---

[1] *Lord John Russell* Russell (1792–1878) was British Prime Minister from 1846 to 1852 and from 1865 to 1866.

[2] *Exeter Hall* Exeter Hall, on the Strand, in London, was built in 1830 to serve as a meeting place for a variety of religious groups, benevolent associations, and other charitable institutions.

[3] *psalmody* Singing of psalms.

[4] *dismal science* This famous phrase describing the science now known as economics has often been cited as first used by Carlyle in his "Latter Day Pamphlet" (1850), rather than in the present essay.

[5] *wide-weltering* State of turmoil, often used to describe the sea.

[6] *Westminster Hall* Location of British Parliament.

pumpkin, however plentiful such land may be, but has an indisputable and perpetual *right* to be compelled, by the real proprietors of said land, to do competent work for his living. This is the everlasting duty of all men, black or white, who are born into this world. To do competent work, to labor honestly according to the ability given them; for that, and for no other purpose, was each one of us sent into this world; and woe is to every man who by friend or by foe, is prevented from fulfilling this, the end of his being....

The idle black man in the West Indies had, not long since, the right, and will again, under better form, if it please Heaven, have the right (actually the first "right of man" for an indolent person) to be *compelled* to work as he was fit, and to *do* the Maker's will, who had constructed him with such and such prefigurements of capability....

And now observe, my friends, it was not Black Quashee,[1] or those he represents, that made those West India islands what they are, or can, by any hypothesis, be considered to have the right of growing pumpkins there. For countless ages, since they first mounted oozy on the back of earthquakes, from their dark bed in the ocean deeps, and reeking, saluted the tropical sun, and ever onward, till the European white man first saw them, some three short centuries ago, those islands had produced mere jungle, savagery, poison reptiles and swamp malaria till the white European first saw them, they were, as if not yet created; their noble elements of cinnamon—sugar, coffee, pepper, black and gray, lying all asleep, waiting the white Enchanter, who should say to them, awake! Till the end of human history, and the sounding of the trump of doom, they might have lain so, had Quashee, and the like of him, been the only artists in the game. Swamps, fever-jungles, man-eating caribs, rattle-snakes, and reeking waste and putrefaction: this had been the produce of them under the incompetent caribal[2] (what we call cannibal) possessors till that time; and Quashee knows, himself, whether ever he could have introduced an improvement. Him, had he, by a miraculous chance, been wafted thither, the caribals

would have eaten, rolling him as a fat morsel under their tongue—for him, till the sounding of the trump of doom, the rattlesnakes and savageries would have held on their way. It was not he, then—it was another than he! ... Quashee, if he will not help in bringing out the spices, will get himself made a slave again (which state will be a little less ugly than his present one), and with beneficent whip, since other methods avail not, will be compelled to work. ... The gods are long-suffering; but the law, from the beginning, was, He that will not work shall perish from the earth—and the patience of the gods has limits!

Before the West Indies could grow a pumpkin for any negro, how much European heroism had to spend itself in obscure battle; to sink, in mortal agony, before the jungles, the putrescences and waste savageries could become arable, and the devils be, in some measure, chained there! The West Indies grow pineapples, and sweet fruits, and spices; we hope they will, one day, grow beautiful, heroic human lives too, which is surely the ultimate object they were made for; beautiful souls and brave; sages, poets, what not—making the earth nobler round them, as their kindred from of old have been doing; ... heroic white men, worthy to be called old Saxons, browned with a mahogany tint in those new climates and conditions. But under the soil of Jamaica, before it could even produce spices, or any pumpkin, the bones of many thousand British men had to be laid....

Already one hears of black *Adscripti glebae*;[3] which seems a promising arrangement, one of the first to suggest itself in such a complicacy. It appears the Dutch blacks, in Java, are already a kind of *Adscripts*, after the manner of the old European serfs; bound by royal authority, to give so many days of work a year. Is not this something like a real approximation; the first step toward all manner of such? Wherever, in British territory, there exists a black man, and needful work to the just extent is not to be got out of him, such a law, in defect of better, should be brought to bear upon said black man!...

---

[1] *Quashee* African first name, used by some eighteenth- and nineteenth-century writers to stand for all black people.

[2] *caribal* Insulting combination of "Carib," indigenous person of the West Indies, and "cannibal."

[3] *Adscripti glebae* Latin: permanently tied to the land; serf.

from John Stuart Mill, "The Negro Question,"
Fraser's Magazine (1850)

To the Editor of *Fraser's Magazine*

Sir:

Your last month's number contains a speech against the "rights of Negroes," the doctrines and spirit of which ought not to pass without remonstrance. The author issues his opinions, or rather ordinances, under imposing auspices no less than those of the "immortal gods." "The Powers," "the Destinies," announce, through him, not only what *will* be, but what *shall* be done; what they "have decided upon, passed their eternal act of Parliament for." This is speaking "as one having authority"; but authority from whom? If by the quality of the message we may judge of those who sent it, not from any powers to whom just or good men acknowledge allegiance. This so-called "eternal act of Parliament" is no new law, but the old law of the strongest—a law against which the great teachers of mankind have in all ages protested—it is the law of force and cunning; the law that whoever is more powerful than an other, is "born lord" of that other, the other being born his "servant," who must be "compelled to work" for him by "beneficent whip," if "other methods avail not." I see nothing divine in this injunction. If "the gods" will this, it is the first duty of human beings to resist such gods. Omnipotent these "gods" are *not*, for powers which demand *human* tyranny and injustice cannot accomplish their purpose unless human beings cooperate. The history of human improvement is the record of a struggle by which inch after inch of ground has been wrung from these maleficent[1] powers, and more and more of human life rescued from the iniquitous[2] dominion of the law of might. Much, very much of this work still remains to do; but the progress made in it is the best and greatest achievement yet performed by mankind, and it was hardly to be expected at this period of the world that we should be enjoined, by way of a great reform in human affair, to begin *un*doing it.

… I must first set my anti-philanthropic opponent right on a matter of fact. He entirely misunderstands the great national revolt of the conscience of this country against slavery and the slave-trade if he supposes it to have been an affair of sentiment. It depended no more on humane feelings than any cause which so irresistibly appealed to them must necessarily do: Its first victories were gained while the lash yet ruled uncontested in the barrack-yard, and the rod in schools, and while men were still hanged by dozens for stealing to the value of forty shillings. It triumphed because it was the cause of justice; and, in the estimation of the great majority of its supporters, of religion. Its originators and leaders were persons of a stern sense of moral obligation, who, in the spirit of the religion of their time, seldom spoke much of benevolence and philanthropy, but often of duty, crime, and sin. For nearly two centuries had negroes, many thousands annually, been seized by force or treachery and carried off to the West Indies to be worked to death, literally to death; for it was the received maxim, the acknowledged dictate of good economy, to wear them out quickly and import more. In this fact every other possible cruelty, tyranny, and wanton oppression was by implication included. And the motive on the part of the slave-owners was the love of gold; or, to speak more truly, of vulgar and puerile ostentation. I have yet to learn that anything more detestable than this has been done by human beings towards human beings in any part of the earth….

After fifty years of toil and sacrifice, the object was accomplished, and the negroes, freed from the despotism of their fellow-beings, were left to themselves, and to the chances which the arrangements of existing society provide for those who have no resource but their labour. These chances proved favorable to them, and, for the last ten years, they afford the unusual spectacle of a labouring class whose labour bears so high a price that they can exist in comfort on the wages of a comparatively small quantity of work. This, to the ex-slave-owners, is an inconvenience; but I have not yet heard that any of them has been reduced to beg his bread, or even to dig for it, as the negro, however scandalously he enjoys himself, still must…. If the [plantation owners] cannot continue to realize their large incomes without more labourers, let them find them, and bring them from where they can best be procured, only not by force. Not so, thinks your anti-philanthropic contribu-

---

[1] *maleficent* Harmful, evil.

[2] *iniquitous* Unjust, unrighteous.

tor. That negroes should exist, and enjoy existence, on so little work, is a scandal, in his eyes, worse than their former slavery. It must be put a stop to at any price. He does not "wish to see" them slaves again "if it can be avoided"; but "decidedly" they "will have to be servants," "servants to the whites," "compelled to labour," and "not to go idle another minute." "Black Quashee," "up to the ears in pumpkins," and "working about half an hour a day," is to him the abomination of abominations.

. . . To give it a rational meaning, it must first be known what he means by work. Does work mean everything which people *do*? No; or he would not reproach people with doing no work. Does it mean laborious exertion? No; for many a day spent in killing game, includes more muscular fatigue than a day's ploughing. Does it mean *useful* exertion? But your contributor always scoffs at the idea of utility. Does he mean that all persons ought to earn their living? But some earn their living by doing nothing, and some by doing mischief; and the negroes, whom he despises, still do earn by labour the "pumpkins" they consume and the finery they wear.

Work, I imagine, is not a good in itself. There is nothing laudable in work for work's sake. To work voluntarily for a worthy object is laudable; but what constitutes a worthy object? On this matter, the oracle of which your contributor is the prophet[1] has never yet been prevailed on to declare itself. He revolves in an eternal circle round the idea of work, as if turning up the earth, or driving a shuttle or a quill, were ends in themselves, and the ends of human existence. Yet, even in the case of the most sublime service to humanity, it is not because it is work that it is worthy; the worth lies in the service itself, and in the will to render it—the noble feelings of which it is the fruit; and if the nobleness of will is proved by other evidence than work, as for instance by danger or sacrifice, there is the same worthiness. While we talk only of work, and not of its object, we are far from the root of the matter; or, if it may be called the root, it is a root without flower or fruit.

In the present case, it seems, a noble object means

"spices."———"The gods wish, besides pumpkins, that spices and valuable products be grown in their West Indies"———the "noble elements of cinnamon, sugar, coffee, pepper black and gray," "things far nobler than pumpkins." Why so? Is what supports life inferior in dignity to what merely gratifies the sense of taste? Is it the verdict of the "immortal gods" that pepper is noble, freedom (even freedom from the lash) contemptible? But spices lead "towards commerces, arts, polities, and social developments." Perhaps so; but of what sort? When they must be produced by slaves, the "polities and social developments" they lead to are such as the world, I hope, will not choose to be cursed with much longer.

The worth of work does not surely consist in its leading to other work, and so on to work upon work without end. On the contrary, the multiplication of work, for purposes not worth caring about, is one of the evils of our present condition. When justice and reason shall be the rule of human affairs, one of the first things to which we may expect them to be applied is the question. How many of the so-called luxuries, conveniences, refinements, and ornaments of life, are *worth* the labour which must be undergone as the condition of producing them? The beautifying of existence is as worthy and useful an object as the sustaining of it; but only a vitiated[2] taste can see any such result in those fopperies[3] of so-called civilization, which myriads of hands are now occupied and lives wasted in providing. In opposition to the "gospel of work," I would assert the gospel of leisure, and maintain that human beings *cannot* rise to the finer attributes of their nature compatibly with a life filled with labour. I do not include under the name labour such work, if work it be called, as is done by writers and afforders of "guidance," an occupation which, let alone the vanity of the thing, cannot be called by the same name with the real labour, the exhausting, stiffening, stupefying toil of many kinds of agricultural and manufacturing labourers. To reduce very greatly the quantity of work required to carry on existence is as needful as to distribute it more equally; and the progress of science, and the increasing ascendency of justice and good sense, tend to this result.

[1] *prophet* With the publication of *Past and Present* in 1843, Carlyle began to be considered a visionary, even a prophetic voice, of social and cultural commentary in England.

[2] *vitiated* Corrupted.

[3] *fopperies* Here, useless consumer goods.

There is a portion of work rendered necessary by the fact of each person's existence: no one could exist unless work, to a certain amount, were done either by or for him. Of this each person is bound, in justice, to perform his share; and society has an incontestable right to declare to every one, that if he work not, at this work of necessity, neither shall he eat. Society has not enforced this right, having in so far postponed the rule of justice to other considerations. But there is an ever-growing demand that it be enforced, so soon as any endurable plan can be devised for the purpose. If this experiment is to be tried in the West Indies, let it be tried impartially; and let the whole produce belong to those who do the work which produces it. We would not have black labourers compelled to grow spices which they do not want, and white proprietors who do not work at all exchanging the spices for houses in Belgrave Square.[1] We would not withhold from the whites, any more than from the blacks, the "divine right" of being compelled to labour. Let them have exactly the same share in the produce that they have in the work. If they do not like this, let them remain as they are, so long as they are permitted, and make the best of supply and demand.

Your contributor's notions of justice and proprietary right are of another kind than these. According to him, the whole West Indies belong to the whites: the negroes have no claim there, to either land or food, but by their sufferance. "It was not Black Quashee, or those he represents, that made those West India islands what they are." I submit, that those who furnished the thews[2] and sinews really had something to do with the matter.

But the great ethical doctrine of the discourse, … than which a doctrine more damnable, I should think, never was propounded by a professed moral reformer, is, that one kind of human beings are born servants to another kind. "You will have to be servants," he tells the negroes, "to those that are born wiser than you, that are born lords of you—servants to the whites, if they are (as what mortal can doubt that they are?) born wiser than you." I do not hold him to the absurd letter of his dictum; it belongs to the mannerism in which he is enthralled like a child in swaddling clothes. By "born wiser," I will suppose him to mean, born more capable

of wisdom: a proposition which, he says, no mortal can doubt, but which, I will make bold to say, that a full moiety[3] of all thinking persons, who have attended to the subject, either doubt or positively deny.

Among the things for which your contributor professes entire disrespect, is the analytical examination of human nature. It is by analytical examination that we have learned whatever we know of the laws of external nature; and if he had not disdained to apply the same mode of investigation to the laws of the formation of character, he would have escaped the vulgar error of imputing every difference which he finds among human beings to an original difference of nature. As well might it be said, that of two trees, sprung from the same stock one cannot be taller than another but from greater vigor in the original seedling. Is nothing to be attributed to soil, nothing to climate, nothing to difference of exposure—has no storm swept over the one and not the other, no lightning scathed it, no beast browsed on it, no insects preyed on it, no passing stranger stripped off its leaves or its bark? If the trees grew near together, may not the one which, by whatever accident, grew up first, have retarded the other's development by its shade? Human beings are subject to an infinitely greater variety of accidents and external influences than trees, and have infinitely more operation in impairing the growth of one another; since those who begin by being strongest, have almost always hitherto used their strength to keep the others weak. What the original differences are among human beings, I know no more than your contributor, and no less; it is one of the questions not yet satisfactorily answered in the natural history of the species. This, however, is well known—that spontaneous improvement, beyond a very low grade—improvement by internal development, without aid from other individuals or peoples—is one of the rarest phenomena in history; and whenever known to have occurred, was the result of an extraordinary combination of advantages; in addition doubtless to many accidents of which all trace is now lost. No argument against the capacity of negroes for improvement, could be drawn from their not being one of these rare exceptions. It is curious, withal, that the earliest known civilization was, we have the strongest reason to believe, a negro civilization. The

---

[1] *Belgrave Square* Fashionable area of London.

[2] *thews* Muscles.

[3] *moiety* Half.

original Egyptians are inferred, from the evidence of their sculptures, to have been a negro race: it was from negroes, therefore, that the Greeks learnt their first lessons in civilization; ... but I again renounce all advantage from facts: [even if it *were* true that] whites [were] born ever so superior in intelligence to the blacks, and competent by nature to instruct and advise them, it would not be the less monstrous to assert that they had therefore a right either to subdue them by force, or circumvent them by superior skill; to throw upon them the toils and hardships of life, reserving for themselves, under the misapplied name of work, its agreeable excitements....

Though we cannot extirpate[1] all pain, we can, if we are sufficiently determined upon it, abolish all tyranny; one of the greatest victories yet gained over that enemy is slave-emancipation and all Europe is struggling, with various success, towards further conquests over it. If, in the pursuit of this, we lose sight of any object equally important; if we forget that freedom is not the only thing necessary for human beings, let us be thankful to any one who points out what is wanting; but let us not consent to turn back. That this country should turn back, in the matter of negro slavery, I have not the smallest apprehension.

There is, however, another place where that tyranny still flourishes, but now for the first time finds itself seriously in danger. At this crisis of American slavery, when the decisive conflict between right and iniquity seems about to commence, your contributor steps in, and flings this missile, loaded with the weight of his reputation, into the abolitionist camp. The words of English writers of celebrity are words of power on the other side of the ocean; and the owners of human flesh, who probably thought they had not an honest man on their side between the Atlantic and the Vistula,[2] will welcome such an auxiliary. Circulated as his dissertation will probably be, by those whose interests profit by it, from one end of the American Union to the other, I hardly know of an act by which one person could have done so much mischief as this may possibly do; and I hold that by thus acting, he has made himself an instru-

ment of what an able writer in the *Inquirer* justly calls "a true work of the devil."[3]

from Henry Mayhew, *London Labour and the London Poor* (1851)

Mayhew's work is known primarily for the sympathetic attention it drew to the plight of poor Londoners. When the poor were not of "English stock," however, Mayhew was decidedly less sympathetic—as the following excerpt from his section on "Hindo Beggars" illustrates.

HINDO BEGGARS

[These] are those spare, snake-eyed Asiatics who walk the streets, coolly dressed in Manchester cottons, or chintz of a pattern commonly used for bed-furniture, to which the resemblance is carried out by the dark, polished colour of the thin limbs which it envelopes. They very often affect to be converts to the Christian religion, and give away tracts; with the intention of entrapping the sympathy of elderly ladies. They assert that they have been high-caste Brahmins,[4] but as untruth, even when not acting professionally, is habitual to them, there is not the slightest dependence to be placed on what they say. Sometimes, in the winter, they "do shallow," that is, stand on the kerb-stone of the pavement, in their thin, ragged clothes, and shiver as with cold and hunger, or crouch against a wall and whine like a whipped animal; at others they turn out with a small, barrel-shaped drum, on which they make a monotonous noise with their fingers, to which music they sing and dance. Or they will "stand pad with a fakement," i.e., wear a placard upon their breasts, that describes them as natives of Madagascar, in distress, converts to Christianity, anxious to get to a seaport where they can work their passage back. This is a favourite artifice with Lascars[5]—

---

[1] *extirpate* To remove, literally pull out roots.

[2] *between the Atlantic and the Vistula* I.e., in Britain or in Continental Europe. (The Vistula is a river in Poland.)

[3] *writer ... devil* From an article responding to Carlyle in *London Inquirer*: "It is a true work of the Devil, the fostering of a tyrannical prejudice."

[4] *Brahmins* Members of the highest Hindu class or caste.

[5] *Lascars* East Indian sailors.

or they will sell lucifers,[1] or sweep a crossing, or do anything where their picturesque appearance, of which they are proud and conscious, can be effectively displayed. They are as cunning as they look, and can detect a sympathetic face among a crowd. They never beg of soldiers, or sailors, to whom they always give a wide berth as they pass them in the streets....

Dickens and Thackeray on the Race Question

Charles Dickens and William Makepeace Thackeray, widely regarded as the two greatest novelists of the age, were also great friends. And, as the excerpts below show, they held similar views on the question of race.

from Charles Dickens, "The Noble Savage," *Household Words* (1853)

To come to the point at once, I beg to say that I have not the least belief in the Noble Savage.[2] I consider him a prodigious nuisance, and an enormous superstition. His calling rum firewater, and me a pale face, wholly fail to reconcile me to him. I don't care what he calls me. I call him a savage, and I call a savage a something highly desirable to be civilised off the face of the earth. I think a mere gent (which I take to be the lowest form of civilisation) better than a howling, whistling, clucking, stamping, jumping, tearing savage. It is all one to me, whether he sticks a fish-bone through his visage, or bits of trees through the lobes of his ears, or bird's feathers in his head; whether he flattens his hair between two boards, or spreads his nose over the breadth of his face, or drags his lower lip down by great weights, or blackens his teeth, or knocks them out, or paints one cheek red and the other blue, or tattoos himself, or oils himself, or rubs his body with fat, or crimps it with knives. Yielding to whichsoever of these agreeable

eccentricities, he is a savage cruel, false, thievish, murderous; addicted more or less to grease, entrails, and beastly customs; a wild animal with the questionable gift of boasting; a conceited, tiresome, bloodthirsty, monotonous humbug.

Yet it is extraordinary to observe how some people will talk about him, as they talk about the good old times; how they will regret his disappearance, in the course of this world's development, from such and such lands where his absence is a blessed relief and an indispensable preparation for the sowing of the very first seeds of any influence that can exalt humanity; how, even with the evidence of himself before them, they will either be determined to believe, or will suffer themselves to be persuaded into believing, that he is something which their five senses tell them he is not.

There was Mr. Catlin,[3] some few years ago, with his Ojibbeway Indians. Mr. Catlin was an energetic, earnest man, who had lived among more tribes of Indians than I need reckon up here, and who had written a picturesque and glowing book about them. With his party of Indians squatting and spitting on the table before him, or dancing their miserable jigs after their own dreary manner, he called, in all good faith, upon his civilised audience to take notice of their symmetry and grace, their perfect limbs, and the exquisite expression of their pantomime; and his civilised audience, in all good faith, complied and admired. Whereas, as mere animals, they were wretched creatures, very low in the scale and very poorly formed; and as men and women possessing any power of truthful dramatic expression by means of action, they were no better than the chorus at an Italian Opera in England—and would have been worse if such a thing were possible.

Mine are no new views of the noble savage. The greatest writers on natural history found him out long ago. Buffon[4] knew what he was, and showed why he is the sulky tyrant that he is to his women, and how it happens (Heaven be praised!) that his race is spare in numbers. For evidence of the quality of his moral

[1] *lucifers* Cheap matches sold by street peddlers.

[2] *Noble Savage* The notion of the "noble savage" is associated with the ideas of the French philosopher Jean-Jacques Rousseau (1712–78), who held that human beings are naturally innocent and good, but become corrupted by civilized society. According to this way of thinking, indigenous peoples were seen as inherently nobler because they were closer to a "state of nature."

[3] *Mr. Catlin* George Catlin (1796–1872), pioneered the Wild West Show, which brought indigenous peoples and cultures from the American West to the American east coast and to Europe.

[4] *Buffon* George-Louis Leclerc, Comte de Buffon (1707–88), French naturalist and mathematician.

nature, pass himself for a moment and refer to his "faithful dog." Has he ever improved a dog, or attached a dog, since his nobility first ran wild in woods, and was brought down (at a very long shot) by Pope?[1] Or does the animal that is the friend of man, always degenerate in his low society?

It is not the miserable nature of the noble savage that is the new thing; it is the whimpering over him with maudlin admiration, and the affecting to regret him, and the drawing of any comparison of advantage between the blemishes of civilisation and the tenor of his swinish life. There may have been a change now and then in those diseased absurdities, but there is none in him.

Think of the Bushmen.[2] Think of the two men and the two women who have been exhibited about England for some years. Are the majority of persons—who remember the horrid little leader of that party in his festering bundle of hides, with his filth and his antipathy to water, and his straddled legs, and his odious eyes shaded by his brutal hand, and his cry of "Qu-u-u-u-aaa!" (Bosjesman[3] for something desperately insulting I have no doubt)—conscious of an affectionate yearning towards that noble savage, or is it idiosyncratic in me to abhor, detest, abominate, and abjure him? I have no reserve on this subject, and will frankly state that, setting aside that stage of the entertainment when he counterfeited the death of some creature he had shot, by laying his head on his hand and shaking his left leg—at which time I think it would have been justifiable homicide to slay him—I have never seen that group sleeping, smoking, and expectorating round their brazier, but I have sincerely desired that something might happen to the charcoal smouldering therein, which would cause the immediate suffocation of the whole of the noble strangers.

There is at present a party of Zulu Kaffirs[4] exhibiting at the St. George's Gallery, Hyde Park Corner, London. These noble savages are represented in a most agreeable manner; they are seen in an elegant theatre, fitted with appropriate scenery of great beauty, and they are described in a very sensible and unpretending lecture, delivered with a modesty which is quite a pattern to all similar exponents. Though extremely ugly, they are much better shaped than such of their predecessors as I have referred to; and they are rather picturesque to the eye, though far from odoriferous to the nose. What a visitor left to his own interpretings and imaginings might suppose these noblemen to be about, when they give vent to that pantomimic expression which is quite settled to be the natural gift of the noble savage, I cannot possibly conceive; for it is so much too luminous for my personal civilisation that it conveys no idea to my mind beyond a general stamping, ramping, and raving, remarkable (as everything in savage life is) for its dire uniformity. But let us—with the interpreter's assistance, of which I for one stand so much in need—see what the noble savage does in Zulu Kaffirland.

The noble savage sets a king to reign over him, to whom he submits his life and limbs without a murmur or question, and whose whole life is passed chin deep in a lake of blood; but who, after killing incessantly, is in his turn killed by his relations and friends, the moment a grey hair appears on his head. All the noble savage's wars with his fellow-savages (and he takes no pleasure in anything else) are wars of extermination—which is the best thing I know of him, and the most comfortable to my mind when I look at him. He has no moral feelings of any kind, sort, or description; and his "mission" may be summed up as simply diabolical.

The ceremonies with which he faintly diversifies his life are, of course, of a kindred nature. If he wants a wife he appears before the kennel of the gentleman whom he has selected for his father-in-law, attended by a party of male friends of a very strong flavour, who screech and whistle and stamp an offer of so many cows for the young lady's hand. The chosen father-in-law—also supported by a high-flavoured party of male friends—screeches, whistles, and yells (being seated on the ground, he can't stamp) that there never was such a daughter in the market as his daughter, and that he must have six more cows. The son-in-law and his select circle of backers screech, whistle, stamp, and yell in reply, that they will give three more cows. The father-in-law (an old deluder, overpaid at the beginning) accepts

---

[1] *Pope* Alexander Pope (1688–1744), British poet.

[2] *Bushmen* European name for peoples of the Kalahari desert.

[3] *Bosjesman* Language of the "Bushmen."

[4] *Kaffirs* Derogatory term for Africans.

four, and rises to bind the bargain. The whole party, the young lady included, then falling into epileptic convulsions, and screeching, whistling, stamping, and yelling together—and nobody taking any notice of the young lady (whose charms are not to be thought of without a shudder)—the noble savage is considered married, and his friends make demoniacal leaps at him by way of congratulation.

When the noble savage finds himself a little unwell, and mentions the circumstance to his friends, it is immediately perceived that he is under the influence of witchcraft. A learned personage, called an Imyanger or Witch Doctor, is immediately sent for to Nooker the Umtargartie, or smell out the witch. The male inhabitants of the kraal[1] being seated on the ground, the learned doctor, got up like a grizzly bear, appears, and administers a dance of a most terrific nature, during the exhibition of which remedy he incessantly gnashes his teeth, and howls:—"I am the original physician to Nooker the Umtargartie. Yow yow yow! No connexion with any other establishment. Till till till! All other Umtargarties are feigned Umtargarties, Boroo Boroo! but I perceive here a genuine and real Umtargartie, Hoosh Hoosh Hoosh! in whose blood I, the original Imyanger and Nookerer, Blizzerum Boo! will wash these bear's claws of mine. O yow yow yow!" All this time the learned physician is looking out among the attentive faces for some unfortunate man who owes him a cow, or who has given him any small offence, or against whom, without offence, he has conceived a spite. Him he never fails to Nooker as the Umtargartie, and he is instantly killed. In the absence of such an individual, the usual practice is to Nooker the quietest and most gentlemanly person in company. But the nookering is invariably followed on the spot by the butchering.

Some of the noble savages in whom Mr. Catlin was so strongly interested, and the diminution of whose numbers, by rum and smallpox, greatly affected him, had a custom not unlike this, though much more appalling and disgusting in its odious details.

The women being at work in the fields, hoeing the Indian corn, and the noble savage being asleep in the shade, the chief has sometimes the condescension to come forth, and lighten the labour by looking at it. On these occasions, he seats himself in his own savage chair, and is attended by his shield-bearer: who holds over his head a shield of cowhide—in shape like an immense mussel shell fearfully and wonderfully, after the manner of a theatrical supernumerary. But lest the great man should forget his greatness in the contemplation of the humble works of agriculture, there suddenly rushes in a poet, retained for the purpose, called a Praiser. This literary gentleman wears a leopard's head over his own, and a dress of tigers' tails; he has the appearance of having come express on his hind legs from the Zoological Gardens; and he incontinently strikes up the chief's praises, plunging and tearing all the while. There is a frantic wickedness in this brute's manner of worrying the air, and gnashing out, "O what a delightful chief he is! O what a delicious quantity of blood he sheds! O how majestically he laps it up! O how charmingly cruel he is! O how he tears the flesh of his enemies and crunches the bones! O how like the tiger and the leopard and the wolf and the bear he is! O, row row row row, how fond I am of him!" which might tempt the Society of Friends to charge at a hand-gallop into the Swartz-Kop location and exterminate the whole kraal.

When war is afoot among the noble savages—which is always—the chief holds a council to ascertain whether it is the opinion of his brothers and friends in general that the enemy shall be exterminated. On this occasion, after the performance of an Umsebcuza, or war song,—which is exactly like all the other songs, the chief makes a speech to his brothers and friends, arranged in single file. No particular order is observed during the delivery of this address, but every gentleman who finds himself excited by the subject, instead of crying "Hear, hear!" as is the custom with us, darts from the rank and tramples out the life, or crushes the skull, or mashes the face, or scoops out the eyes, or breaks the limbs, or performs a whirlwind of atrocities on the body, of an imaginary enemy. Several gentlemen becoming thus excited at once, and pounding away without the least regard to the orator, that illustrious person is rather in the position of an orator in an Irish House of Commons. But, several of these scenes of savage life bear a strong generic resemblance to an Irish election, and I think would be

---

[1] *kraal* A community of indigenous people in southern or central Africa, typically dwelling in huts surrounded by a stockade.

extremely well received and understood at Cork.[1]

In all these ceremonies the noble savage holds forth to the utmost possible extent about himself; from which (to turn him to some civilised account) we may learn, I think, that as egotism is one of the most offensive and contemptible littlenesses a civilised man can exhibit, so it is really incompatible with the interchange of ideas; inasmuch as if we all talked about ourselves we should soon have no listeners, and must be all yelling and screeching at once on our own separate accounts: making society hideous. It is my opinion that if we retained in us anything of the noble savage, we could not get rid of it too soon. But the fact is clearly otherwise. Upon the wife and dowry question, substituting coin for cows, we have assuredly nothing of the Zulu Kaffir left. The endurance of despotism is one great distinguishing mark of a savage always. The improving world has quite got the better of that too. In like manner, Paris is a civilised city, and the Théâtre Français a highly civilised theatre; and we shall never hear, and never have heard in these later days (of course) of the Praiser THERE. No, no, civilised poets have better work to do. As to Nookering Umtargarties, there are no pretended Umtargarties in Europe, and no European powers to Nooker them; that would be mere spydom, subordination, small malice, superstition, and false pretence. And as to private Umtargarties, are we not in the year eighteen hundred and fifty-three, with spirits rapping at our doors?

To conclude as I began. My position is, that if we have anything to learn from the Noble Savage, it is what to avoid. His virtues are a fable; his happiness is a delusion; his nobility, nonsense.

We have no greater justification for being cruel to the miserable object, than for being cruel to a WILLIAM SHAKESPEARE or an ISAAC NEWTON; but he passes away before an immeasurably better and higher power than ever ran wild in any earthly woods, and the world will be all the better when his place knows him no more.

from William Makepeace Thackeray, Letters to Mrs. Carmichael-Smyth

To Mrs. Carmichael-Smyth, 26 January 1853

... I don't believe Blacky *is* my man and my brother, though God forbid I should own him or flog him, or part him from his wife and children. But the question is a much longer [one than] is set forth in Mrs. Stowe's philosophy:[2] and I shan't speak about it, till I know it, or till it's my business, or I think I can do good.

To Mrs. Carmichael-Smyth, 13 February 1853

... They are not my men and brethren,[3] these strange people with retreating foreheads, with great obtruding lips and jaws: with capacities for thought, pleasure, endurance quite different to mine. They are not suffering as you are impassioning yourself for their wrongs as you read Mrs. Stowe, they are grinning and joking in the sun; roaring with laughter as they stand about the streets in squads; very civil, kind and gentle, even winning in their manner when you accost them at gentlemen's houses, where they do all the service. But they don't seem to me to be the same as white men, any more than asses are the same animals as horses; I don't mean this disrespectfully, but simply that there is such a difference of colour, habits, conformation of brains, that we must acknowledge it, and can't by any rhetorical phrase get it over; Sambo[4] is not my man and my brother; the very aspect of his face is grotesque and inferior.... As soon as the cheap substitute is found, depend on it the Planter, who stoutly pleads humanity now as the one of the reasons why he can't liberate his people, will get rid of them quickly enough; & the price of the slave-goods will fall so that owners won't care to hold such an unprofitable & costly stock.

---

[1] *Several gentlemen ... Cork* Dickens is displaying his prejudice against the Irish, who had historically been held, by many Englishmen and women, to have been "savages."

[2] *Mrs. Stowe's philosophy* Reference to Harriet Beecher Stowe's anti-slavery novel, *Uncle Tom's Cabin* (1852).

[3] *They are ... brethren* Reference to abolitionist materials that featured a slave in chains accompanied by the caption "Am I not a man and your brother?"

[4] *Sambo* Common slave name which became a derogatory term for any black person.

Conservatives, Liberals, and Empire

The following excerpts from speeches by Liberal Prime Minister William Gladstone, Conservative Prime Minister Benjamin Disraeli, and businessman, mining magnate, politician, and colonizer Cecil Rhodes provide three different perspectives on the attitudes taken by Britain's two main political parties towards issues of Empire in the second half of the nineteenth century.

from William Gladstone, "Our Colonies" (1855)

But an idea far more important and effective to a far greater extent has been the idea that the colonies ought to be maintained for the purpose of establishing an exclusive trade, the whole profit of which should be confined to the mother country, and should be enjoyed by the mother country. This was in fact the basis of the modern colonial system of Europe. I do not speak now of the political system, but it was the basis of the commercial laws of the countries which had colonies: that the industry of the colonists, instead of having a fair field and equal favour given to it, was attempted to be made entirely subservient to the interests and the profit of the mother country. It was placed in an unfair position. People were told in fact that they might go to the colonies, but that whatever they produced in the colonies must be sent to the British market—nay, that it must be sent in British vessels to the British market—nay, that whatever was produced must be sent to the British market in British vessels and in the state of raw produce, because if sent in other vessels, although it were sent better and cheaper, it would not be for the interest of the British shipowner, and if sent in a manufactured state it would not be for the interest of the British manufacturer....

Now, as I repudiate any and all of these reasons for desiring the possession of colonies, it is but fair that I should endeavour to state why I think colonies are desirable for a country circumstanced as England is. I have stated, that I do not think them desirable simply to puff up our reputation, apart from the basis and substance on which it rests. It is plain that they are not to be desired for revenue, because they do not yield it. It is plain that they are not to be desired for trading monopoly, because that we have entirely abandoned. It is plain they are not to be desired for patronage, properly so called, within their limits, because they will not allow us to exercise patronage, and I am bound to say, I do not think the public men of this country have any desire so to exercise it. With respect to territory, it is perfectly plain that mere extension of territory is not a legitimate object of ambition, unless you can show that you are qualified to make use of that territory for the purposes for which God gave the earth to man. Why then are colonies desirable? In my opinion, and I submit it to you with great respect, they are desirable both for the material and for the moral and social results which a wise system of colonisation is calculated to produce. As to the first, the effect of colonisation undoubtedly is to increase the trade and employment of the mother country. Take the case of the emigrant going across the Atlantic. Why does he go across the Atlantic? Because he expects—and in general he is the best judge of his own interests—to get better wages across the Atlantic than he can get at home. If he goes across the Atlantic to get better wages, he leaves in the labour market at home fewer persons than before, and consequently raises the rate of wages at home by carrying himself away from the competition with his fellows. By going to the colony and supplying it with labour he likewise creates a demand for capital there, and by this means he creates a trade between the colony and the mother country. The capital and labour thus employed in the colony raise and export productions, for which commodities are wanted in return....

But I do not concede that the material benefit of colonies is the only consideration which we are able to plead. Their moral and social advantage is a very great one. If we are asked why, on these grounds, it is desirable that colonies should be founded and possessed, I answer by asking another question—Why is it desirable that your population at home should increase? Why is it that you rejoice, always presuming that the increase of population goes hand in hand with equally favourable or more favourable conditions of existence for the mass of the people—why is it that you rejoice in an increase of population at home? Because an increase of population is an increase of power, an increase of strength and stability to the state, and because it multiplies the number of people who, as we hope, are living under good laws, and belong to a country to which it is an honour and an advantage to belong. That is the great moral benefit that attends the foundation of British colonies. We think that our country is a country blessed with laws and a constitution that are eminently beneficial to mankind, and if so, what can be more to be desired than that we should have the means of reproducing in different portions of the globe something as like as may be to that country which we honour and revere? I think it is in a work by Mr. Roebuck that the expression is used, "that the object of colonisation is the creation of so many happy Englands." It is the reproduction of the image and likeness of England—the reproduction of a country in which liberty is reconciled with order, in which ancient institutions stand in harmony with popular freedom, and a full recognition of popular rights, and in which religion and law have found one of their most favoured homes....

from Benjamin Disraeli, "Conservative and Liberal Principles" (1872)

Gentlemen, there is another and second great object of the Tory party. If the first is to maintain the institutions of the country, the second is, in my opinion, to uphold the Empire of England. If you look to the history of this country since the advent of Liberalism—forty years ago—you will find that there has been no effort so continuous, so subtle, supported by so much energy, and carried on with so much ability and acumen, as the attempts of Liberalism to effect the disintegration of the Empire of England.

And, gentlemen, of all its efforts, this is the one which has been the nearest to success. Statesmen of the highest character, writers of the most distinguished ability, the most organised and efficient means, have been employed in this endeavour. It has been proved to all of us that we have lost money by our colonies. It has been shown with precise, with mathematical demonstra-

tion, that there never was a jewel in the Crown of England that was so truly costly as the possession of India. How often has it been suggested that we should at once emancipate ourselves from this incubus.[1] Well, that result was nearly accomplished. When those subtle views were adopted by the country under the plausible plea of granting self-government to the colonies, I confess that I myself thought that the tie was broken. Not that I for one object to self-government. I cannot conceive how our distant colonies can have their affairs administered except by self-government. But self-government, in my opinion, when it was conceded, ought to have been conceded as part of a great policy of Imperial consolidation. It ought to have been accompanied by an Imperial tariff, by securities for the people of England for the enjoyment of the unappropriated lands which belonged to the Sovereign as their trustee, and by a military code which should have precisely defined the means and the responsibilities by which the colonies should be defended, and by which, if necessary, this country should call for aid from the colonies themselves. It ought, further, to have been accompanied by the institution of some representative council in the metropolis, which would have brought the colonies into constant and continuous relations with the Home Government. All this, however, was omitted because those who advised that policy—and I believe their convictions were sincere—looked upon the colonies of England, looked even upon our connection with India, as a burden upon this country, viewing everything in a financial aspect, and totally passing by those moral and political considerations which make nations great, and by the influence of which alone men are distinguished from animals.

Well, what has been the result of this attempt during the reign of Liberalism for the disintegration of the Empire? It has entirely failed. But how has it failed? Through the sympathy of the colonies with the Mother Country. They have decided that the Empire shall not be destroyed, and in my opinion no minister in this country will do his duty who neglects any opportunity

---

[1] *incubus* Mythical demon said to rape sleeping women, and in so doing to drain their life force to sustain itself. Figuratively, an evil that drains vital energy.

THE RHODES COLOSSUS
STRIDING FROM CAPE TOWN TO CAIRO.

Cecil Rhodes (1858–1902), nowadays best known for having endowed the Rhodes Scholarships for study at Oxford University, was the leading Briton in Southern Africa in the late nineteenth century—and a leading backer of the extension of British commercial and political interests in Africa as a whole. (The statue of the Colossus in the ancient city of Rhodes to which this cartoon alludes is said to have straddled the entrance to the harbor.)

of reconstructing as much as possible our Colonial Empire, and of responding to those distant sympathies which may become the source of incalculable strength and happiness to this land....

from Cecil Rhodes, Speech Delivered in Cape Town, 18 July 1899

And, sir, my people have changed. I speak of the English people, with their marvellous common sense, coupled with their powers of imagination—all thoughts of a Little England are over. They are tumbling over each other, Liberals and Conservatives, to show which side are the greatest and most enthusiastic Imperialists. The people have changed, and so do all the parties, just like the Punch and Judy show[1] at a country fair. The people have found out that England is small, and her trade is large, and they have also found out that other people are taking their share of the world, and enforcing hostile tariffs. The people of England are finding out that "trade follows the flag,"[2] and they have all become Imperialists. They are not going to part with any territory. And the bygone ideas of nebulous republics are over. The English people intend to retain every inch of land they have got, and perhaps, sir, they intend to secure a few more inches. ...

from David Livingstone, "Cambridge Lecture Number 1" (1858)

The following excerpts are from a speech delivered at Cambridge University by the famous missionary; it was received with extended cheering.

When I went to Africa about seventeen years ago I resolved to acquire an accurate knowledge of the native tongues; and as I continued, while there, to speak generally in the African languages, the result is that I am not now very fluent in my own; but if you will excuse my imperfections under that head, I will endeavour to give you as clear an idea of Africa as I can....

My object in going into the country south of the desert was to instruct the natives in a knowledge of Christianity, but many circumstances prevented my living amongst them more than seven years, amongst which were considerations arising out of the slave system carried on by the Dutch Boers. I resolved to go into the country beyond, and soon found that, for the purposes of commerce, it was necessary to have a path to the sea. I might have gone on instructing the natives in religion, but as civilization and Christianity must go on together, I was obliged to find a path to the sea, in order that I should not sink to the level of the natives. The chief was overjoyed at the suggestion, and furnished me with twenty-seven men, and canoes, and provisions, and presents for the tribes through whose country we had to pass. We might have taken a shorter path to the sea than that to the north, and then to the west, by which we went; but along the country by the shorter route, there is an insect called the tsetse, whose bite is fatal to horses, oxen, and dogs, but not to men or donkeys. You seem to think there is a connexion between the two. The habitat of that insect is along the shorter route to the sea. The bite of it is fatal to domestic animals, not immediately, but certainly in the course of two or three months; the animal grows leaner and leaner, and gradually dies of emaciation: a horse belonging to Gordon Cumming died of a bite five or six months after it was bitten.

On account of this insect, I resolved to go to the north, and then westwards to the Portuguese settlement of Loanda. Along the course of the river which we passed, game was so abundant that there was no difficulty in supplying the wants of my whole party: antelopes were so tame that they might be shot from the canoe. But beyond 14 degrees of south latitude the natives had guns, and had themselves destroyed the game, so that I and my party had to live on charity. The people, however, in that central region were friendly and hospitable: but they had nothing but vegetable productions: the most abundant was the cassava, which, however nice when made into tapioca pudding, resembles in its more primitive condition nothing so much as a mess of laundress's starch. There was a desire in the

---

[1] *Punch and Judy show* Puppet show involving Mr. Punch and his wife Judy.

[2] *trade ... flag* Popular dictum of the period, meant to encourage colonization.

David Livingstone, 1864 (photo by Thomas Annan).

various villages through which we passed to have intercourse with us, and kindness and hospitality were shown us; but when we got near the Portuguese settlement of Angola the case was changed, and payment was demanded for every thing. But I had nothing to pay with. Now the people had been in the habit of trading with the slavers, and so they said I might give one of my men in payment for what I wanted. When I shewed them that I could not do this, they looked upon me as an interloper, and I was sometimes in danger of being murdered.

As we neared the coast, the name of England was recognized, and we got on with ease. Upon one occasion, when I was passing through the parts visited by slave-traders, a chief who wished to shew me some kindness offered me a slave-girl: upon explaining that I had a little girl of my own, whom I should not like my

own chief to give to a black man, the chief thought I was displeased with the size of the girl, and sent me one a head taller. By this and other means I convinced my men of my opposition to the principle of slavery; and when we arrived at Loanda I took them on board a British vessel, where I took a pride in showing them that those countrymen of mine and those guns were there for the purpose of putting down the slave-trade. They were convinced from what they saw of the honesty of Englishmen's intentions; and the hearty reception they met with from the sailors made them say to me, "We see they are your countrymen, for they have hearts like you." On the journey, the men had always looked forward to reaching the coast: they had seen Manchester prints and other articles imported therefrom, and they could not believe they were made by mortal hands. On reaching the sea, they thought that they had come to the end of the world. They said, "We marched along with our father, thinking the world was a large plain without limit; but all at once the land said 'I am finished, there is no more of me'"; and they called themselves the true old men—the true ancients—having gone to the end of the world. On reaching Loanda, they commenced trading in firewood, and also engaged themselves at sixpence a day in unloading coals, brought by a steamer for the supply of the cruiser lying there to watch the slave-vessels. On their return, they told their people "we worked for a whole moon, carrying away the stones that burn." By the time they were ready to go back to their own country, each had secured a large bundle of goods. On the way back, however, fever detained them, and their goods were all gone, leaving them on their return home, as poor as when they started....

A prospect is now before us of opening Africa for commerce and the Gospel. Providence has been preparing the way, for even before I proceeded to the Central basin it had been conquered and rendered safe by a chief named Sebituane, and the language of the Bechuanas made the fashionable tongue, and that was one of the languages into which Mr. Moffat had translated the Scriptures. Sebituane also discovered Lake Ngami some time previous to my explorations in that part. In going back to that country my object is to open up traffic along the banks of the Zambesi, and also to preach the Gospel. The natives of Central Africa are very desirous of trading, but their only traffic is at present in slaves, of which the poorer people have an unmitigated horror; it is therefore most desirable to encourage the former principle, and thus open a way for the consumption of free productions, and the introduction of Christianity and commerce. By encouraging the native propensity for trade, the advantages that might be derived in a commercial point of view are incalculable; nor should we lose sight of the inestimable blessings it is in our power to bestow upon the unenlightened African, by giving him the light of Christianity. Those two pioneers of civilization—Christianity and commerce—should ever be inseparable; and Englishmen should be warned by the fruits of neglecting that principle as exemplified in the result of the management of Indian affairs. By trading with Africa, also, we should at length be independent of slave labour, and thus discountenance

practices so obnoxious to every Englishman.

Though the natives are not absolutely anxious to receive the Gospel, they are open to Christian influences. Among the Bechuanas the Gospel was well received. These people think it a crime to shed a tear, but I have seen some of them weep at the recollection of their sins when God had opened their hearts to Christianity and repentance....

I beg to direct your attention to Africa; I know that in a few years I shall be cut off in that country, which is now open; do not let it be shut again! I go back to Africa to try to make an open path for commerce and Christianity; do you carry out the work which I have begun. I LEAVE IT WITH YOU!

Eliza M., "Account of Cape Town," *King William's Town Gazette* (1863)

The following account (brought to light by M.J. Daymond et al. and the Women Writing Africa Project[1]) is one of the most remarkable literary descriptions we have of the world of nineteenth-century British colonialism from the point of view of one of the colonized. King William's Town was a small town some 500 miles east of Cape Town, and Eliza M., as she was identified in the *King William's Town Gazette*, had attended school at St. Matthews Mission in the area. As Daymond et al. suggest, such a piece as this would in all likelihood have "been written as a school exercise." It would have been published, they speculate, "partly because its naiveté was amusing to the whites, but also because it was proof of the civilizing policies of the missionaries. It was translated from Xhosa into English by an unknown translator." What may have seemed "amusing naiveté" to nineteenth-century settlers is more likely to strike the modern reader as a style of elemental freshness.

We left East London on the Sunday, while it was raining; the sea was fighting very much, and there were soldiers going to England and their wives. On the

---

[1] *Women Writing Africa Project*   M.J. Daymond et al., eds., *Women Writing Africa: The Southern Region* (New York: The Feminist Press, 2003), 98–104.

Tuesday we arrived at Algoa Bay, and boats came to fetch the people who were going there, and other people came in. The ship went off the same day. A great wind blew, and I thought myself that if it had been another ship, it would not have been able to go on, but in its going, it kept twisting about, it did not go straight, but it went well on the day of our arrival, for the wind was good. We arrived on the Friday. While I was in the ship, I forgot I was on the water, it was like a house inside, but outside it was not like a house. There is everything that is kept at home; there were fowls and sheep and pigs, and slaughtering every day. I kept looking at the thing which makes the ship go. There are two horses inside, made of iron, which make it go; and when I looked inside, it was very frightful. There are many bedrooms inside. The ship we were in is named the *Norman*, it is a steamer. It was unpleasant when nothing appeared, but when we left the Bay, we saw the mountains till we got to the Cape. One mountain is called the Lion's Head, and another is called Green Point, and I myself saw those mountains. That which is called the Lion's Head, is like a lion asleep. And another mountain above the town is that called Table Mountain; nevertheless it is not like a table, still that name is proper for it.

Before I came into the town, my heart said, "this place is not large," but when I entered it, I wondered, and was afraid. Oh, we slept that day. I have forgotten to relate something I saw the day I arrived. I saw black people, and I thought they were our kind, but they are not; they are Slams, called in English, Malays. Also, I was astonished at their large hats, pointed at the top, and large below. I saw some making baskets of reeds, and I wished I knew how to do it. On the Saturday evening, we went to a shop to buy butter and bread. At night lights were hung up throughout the whole town. I had thought we were going to walk in the darkness. I have not yet seen houses built with grass, like those we live in, they are high beautiful houses. The roads where people walk, are very fine. I have not yet seen a dirty, muddy place in the whole town. On the Sunday, bells sounded; there is one big one, and other small ones; we went to service in the great church.

Early on the Monday, wagons came about to sell things. Really people here get these things for nothing from their owners. A person can get men's trousers for three shilling each, yet in other places a person can never get them for that money. You can get three pairs of stockings for a shilling, a child's cap for a penny; you can get a width of a dress for threepence, if it is five widths, it is a shilling and threepence. There are little wagons, the man who drives the horses sits behind, the proprietor does nothing, he sits so.

Another thing. The shoes of the Malays astonished me. There is a heel, and yonder on before a piece of wood sticks out, and they put it between their toes, and so make a clattering like the Germans. As things are to be got for such little money, how cheap must they be in England!

On Friday I saw a man riding in a wagon, there was a barrel inside and a cross-bar, and the water came out there. I don't know how it came out. It watered the new road, which is being made. And on Tuesday I saw people working at slates, taking off their ends—it was a great heap; the people who were at work were four. On the day of our arrival, a house was burnt, the people escaped, but I don't know whether the goods escaped. There are carts which go every day, carrying earth to throw on the road which is being mended, drawn by one horse.

There is a house where there are all kinds of beasts, and there are figures of black people, as if they were alive; their blackness is very ugly; also the bones of a man when he is dead, and birds and elephants, and lions, and tigers and sea-shells. I was afraid of those people, and the skeleton. There is also an ape holding Indian Corn, and there are monkeys.

In the evening we went out again, we went to the houses of the Malays; we went to see their decorations, for they were rejoicing because their days of fasting were ended. They were very beautiful; they had made flowers of paper, you would never think they were made of paper. We went for the sole purpose of seeing these works. They made a great noise, singing as they walked; you would laugh to see the children dancing outside and clapping their hands.

There are also wagons there for the sale of fish. The proprietors sound a thing like a horn to announce that he who wishes to buy let him buy. There are others for collecting dust-heaps, they ring a bell. There are vehicles to convey two people, he who drives the horses, and he who sits inside. In some there are windows and lights lit at night: those windows are two.

There are not many trees in the town; in some places there are not many at all, but in one place it is like the bush; it is pleasant underneath the trees; there are stools to sit on when a person is tired. That path is very long; I saw two Newfoundland dogs. I did not know that I should ever come to see them when I heard them spoken of. They are dogs with large heads and great long ears; the hair is like sheep's wool, and they have great claws; they are suited to assist people. It seemed as if they could swallow me without chewing; I was very much afraid, but one was not very big, it was about the size of the dogs of black people, when it barks, it says so with a great voice. Also, I saw sheep rather unlike others, in the tail here it was very large, the head was small, and the body was large and fat.

I have forgotten to mention something which I ought to have said before; when I came out of the ship and walked on land the earth seemed to move, and when I entered a house, it seemed to imitate the sailing of a ship, and when I lay down it seemed to move.

I saw an ox-wagon here, but I had not imagined that I should see a wagon.

We go to a very large beautiful Church; I don't forget the people who sing, the English; the prayers are said with thin voices as if it were singing; but the chief thing done is singing frequently, all the while there is continually singing, and then sitting. There is a Kafir school here; I went one day, they were reading; they can read well; there are also carpenters &c.

There is another place besides that which I said is like the bush, and in that place there are trees and flowers, and two fountains; a thing is stuck in, and the water comes out above. I saw the date-tree when it is young; it is one leaf, yet when it is grown, it is a very large tree. In that place there are wild birds, doves are there, and those birds which the English call canaries, and a very beautiful bird, its tail is long, its bill is red.

Yesterday the soldiers had sports, the music-band played, and when they finished playing they fired. They were many, and they fired together. And as we were walking, they fired; I was very much startled and afraid. And to-day they are playing the music. It seems to-day it exceeds in sweetness, I mean its sound.

There came a person here who is a Kafir. I rejoiced very much when I heard that he too was one. He asked me what I had come to do here; I said "I am only travelling." He asked whether I was a prisoner, and I said "No." He said he was very glad, he had thought I was a prisoner. I told him that I was going away again, and he said "May you go in peace, the Lord preserve you well till you arrive whence you came." I never saw a person like him of such kindness; he said he had come here to learn, he came from where I did; but I should not have known him to be a Kafir, and he did not know that I was one.

There are creatures which are eaten; they come from the sea, their name is called crawfish, they are frightful in appearance, yet their flesh is very fine and white.

The person of this house is a dyer of clothes, the white he makes red, and the red green, and the brown he makes black. I saw the wood with which they dye. Soap is cut in pieces, and put in water, and heated and boiled well, and continually stirred. This thing—dyeing clothes, is a great work. Water is even in the house; I don't know where it comes from, a person turns a thing, and fresh water comes out as if it were of a river.

There are also carts for selling meat, and for selling bread. I saw the fire-wagon, I did nothing but wonder. I did not know that it was such a big thing. It is long, with many wheels, they are not so large as those of an ox-wagon; people sit in places inside. The wheels run on metal; I say I could do nothing but wonder very much. I had not thought that it was such a great thing. And when it is about to proceed it says "Sh!" I don't know whether it is the boiling of the water; it hastens exceedingly, a person would be unable to notice it well, yet now some people say that this is a small one which I have seen. If it treads on anything, it must smash it, it is a very great thing. I shall never forget it. Where I saw it, the place was fenced on both sides, and I beheld it from the outside. I entered it another week after I had seen it; we went to Somerset West and slept one night. In the morning we returned by it: when I was inside, the earth seemed to move; it is pleasant to ride inside. I end now although this is not all the news about it. When I was in it, I saw a sugar plant; it is not a large plant, it is short with red flowers. I saw other trees at Somerset West which I had never seen before.

One day I saw people going to a burial, the carriages were black, but that people should wear black clothes is done also among the natives where a person has died; there were stuck up black feathers, and on the graves were placed stones with writing; the name of the person was written, and the years of his age, and the year in which he died.

I have seen to-day another thing which I did not know of, that thing which is said to be always done by white people in this month of May. They make themselves black people, they smear themselves with something black, with red patches on the cheeks; a thing is made with evergreens, and a man is put inside, and two people carry it, and another man carries a pan, and goes begging for money.

Another thing which I saw during the past month, was people going to the Governor's house—little chiefs, and chiefs of the soldiers, some had hats with red and white feathers, and silver coats, and gold swords, and the bishop went too. I heard it said that they were going to hear the things which were about to be spoken by people who had come from Graham's Town, King William's Town, Beaufort, and other places; it was said that these people were going to speak of the state of those towns and the doings of the people who live there. I do not say that those coats were really of gold, I say there was gold on some parts of them, on the arms and the back.

Also I have seen the fruit of the tree which the English call the chestnut; I did not see what the tree is like, the fruit is nice, the outside of it is hard; when you eat it it is sweet and edible like the potato, you can roast it or boil it. There is another fruit called Banana in English, it also is a nice fruit; it is not boiled or roasted, it is eaten like other fruits. There is a great white sweet potato, it is called Sweet Potato; those potatoes are very large, I had never seen them before, they are nearly all long: I do not know whether they are the potatoes named "Medicine" by the Fingoes.

I am puzzled to know how to begin to relate what was done yesterday, but I will try. Yesterday was said to be the wedding-day of the Great Son of Victoria, but it was not really the day of his marriage, for he has been married some time. The thing first done was arranging the children of the schools and I was there too. All walked in threes, going from one street to another. When we left the school-house we took up our station on an open piece of ground, other people climbed on the houses, and others looked on from below. On one house where we were standing there was the figure of a man like a king, a red cloth was put as if it were held by him, it is called in English a flag. Amongst all of us there were flags of different beautiful kinds; we stood there a great while, till we saw a multitude of soldiers and their officers and little chiefs and different sorts of people: one set wore clothes all alike, another had different clothes and ancient hats which were worn by the people of that time. All these now went in front, a very long line, then followed the ranks of another school, and we came after them. When we had finished going through many streets, we went to stand in another open spot of ground. All the time we were walking we were singing the song of Victoria. And there we saw the Governor and his wife; we all saluted. Although it seems that I have written a great deal I have not yet wondered at the things done at night, but let me finish those of the day. We were given food. We saw boats going along with people inside and boys wearing red clothes; there followed one with an old man, his hairs were long and white. There was a woman at his side wearing short clothes. Other boats followed with people in them, all the time they were appearing the drum and trumpets were sounded. I don't know how I shall make myself understood. I never saw such a beautiful thing; some of the men wore short dresses and short coats, and others wore short trousers like those of the French. All these things were red. When we had finished walking we went to stand in an open piece of ground, then we all went home. I do not know if any other things were done.

We went out again in the evening to see the fireworks. First we went into the gardens, where there were what I shall call candles; but nevertheless they are not called so in English. They were lights put inside little red and green glasses—When I was at a distance I thought they were little round things, all these were hung up and fastened in the trees,—there were some large ones and there were others not put in glasses.

We walked and went to a great crowd of people, we could not tell what we should do to see that which we came to see. There we saw a tall man with a high hat, I did not understand how it was made, and another man wearing women's clothes continually playing with that tall man. All these things have their names in English, some were called *Punch & Judy*, *Spectre*, *Father of the Doomed Arm-chair*, or the *Maid, the Murderer and the Midnight Avenger*,[1] and many other plays besides these. We passed on from that woman and man and went to see white people smeared with soot, they went into a house made of a tent where there were stools, and two came out and spoke to the people saying, "Ladies and gentlemen, come in and see what we have got here inside." Some went in and others did not, afterwards they opened that the people might see; there were black people sitting on chairs and singing. So we left; at the entrance of the garden there was written in letters of fire, "GOD bless Albert and Alexandra." In another place there were other things of fire, that place is called in English the Parade, where there was a thing like a light-house, on all sides there were candles. Some people sent up fire from Table Mountain, others from Green Point, others sent up fire in the midst of the town, it went up and came down again.

Besides these things there was another thing done, an ox was baked whole, the legs were not removed, only the inside and the hoofs. Many tables were set underneath the trees; that ox was intended for the poor people.

I am going to end now; I am very glad that I was brought here to see things which I never thought I should see.

There is another thing which has lately taken place, the birthday of Queen Victoria. Two balloons were made, no one went in them, there were only lights. That sort is called fire-balloons. The first was sent up; it rose very high till it was like a star: I did not see it again where it went. The other reappeared, it did not rise high like the first, it burnt, and fire came down like two stars.

I saw where newspapers are printed; four people were at work. I do not know what I shall say to tell about it. There is a thing which folds the papers and another thing which continually receives them. It made us sleepy.

E.M.
Translator unknown

---

[1]   *Spectre ... Avenger*   Popular plays of the period.

from Agnes Macdonald, "By Car and Cowcatcher," *Murray's Magazine* (1887)

The essay from which the passages below are excerpted describes Macdonald's trip across Canada by train with her husband, Canadian Prime Minister Sir John A. Macdonald.

... The description of a cow-catcher is less easy. To begin with, it is misnamed, for it catches no cows at all. Sometimes, I understand, it throws up on the buffer-beam whatever maimed or mangled animal it has struck, but in most cases it clears the line by shoving forward, or tossing aside, any removable obstruction. It is best described as a sort of barred iron beak, about six feet long, projecting close over the track in a V shape, and attached to the buffer-beam by very strong bolts. It is sometimes sheathed with thin iron plates in winter, and acts then as a small snow-plough.

Behold me now, enthroned on the candle-box, with a soft felt hat well over my eyes, and a linen carriage-cover tucked round me from waist to foot. Mr. E.[2] had seated himself on the other side of the headlight. He had succumbed to the inevitable, ceased further expostulation, disclaimed all responsibility, and, like the jewel of a Superintendent he was, had decided on sharing my peril! I turn to him, peeping round the headlight, with my best smile. "This is *lovely*," I triumphantly announce, seeing that a word of comfort is necessary, "*quite lovely*; I shall travel on this cowcatcher from summit to sea!"

Mr. Superintendent, in his turn, peeps round the headlight and surveys me with solemn and resigned surprise. "I—suppose—you—will," he says slowly, and I see that he is hoping, at any rate, that I shall live to do it!

With a mighty snort, a terribly big throb, and shrieking whistle, No. 374 moves slowly forward. The very small population of Laggan have all come out to see. They stand in the hot sunshine, and shade their eyes as the stately engine moves on. "It is an awful thing to do!" I hear a voice say, as the little group lean forward; and for a moment I feel a thrill that is very like fear; but

---

[2]   *Mr. E.*   John M. Egan, general superintendent of the western division of the Canadian Pacific Railroad at the time.

it is gone at once, and I can think of nothing but the novelty, the excitement, and the fun of this mad ride in glorious sunshine and intoxicating air, with magnificent mountains before and around me, their lofty peaks smiling down on us, and never a frown on their grand faces!

The pace quickens gradually, surely, swiftly, and then we are rushing up to the summit. We soon stand on the "Great Divide"—5300 feet above sea-level—between the two great oceans. As we pass, Mr. E. by a gesture, points out a small river (called Bath Creek, I think) which, issuing from a lake on the narrow summit-level, winds near the track. I look, and lo! the water, flowing *eastward* towards the Atlantic side, turns in a moment as the Divide is passed, and pours *westward* down the Pacific slope!

Another moment and a strange silence has fallen round us. With steam shut off and brakes down, the 60-ton engine, by its own weight and impetus alone, glides into the pass of the Kicking Horse River, and begins a descent of 2800 feet in twelve miles. We rush onward through the vast valley stretching before us, bristling with lofty forests, dark and deep, that, clinging to the mountain side, are reared up into the sky. The river, widening, grows white with dashing foam, and rushes downwards with tremendous force. Sunlight flashes on glaciers, into gorges, and athwart[1] huge, towering masses of rock crowned with magnificent tree crests that rise all round us of every size and shape. Breathless—almost awe-stricken—but with a wild triumph in my heart, I look from farthest mountain peak, lifted high before me, to the shining pebbles at my feet! Warm wind rushes past; a thousand sunshine colours dance in the air. With a firm right hand grasping the iron stanchion, and my feet planted on the buffer beam, there was not a yard of that descent in which I faltered for a moment.

If I had, then assuredly in the wild valley of the Kicking Horse River, on the western slope of the Rocky Mountains, a life had gone out that day! I did not think of danger, or remember what a giddy post I had. I could only gaze at the glaciers that the mountains held so closely, 5000 feet above us, at the trace of snow avalanches which had left a space a hundred feet wide massed with torn and prostrate trees; on the shadows that played over the distant peaks; and on a hundred rainbows made by the foaming, dashing river, which swirls with tremendous rapidity down the gorge on its way to the Columbia in the valley below....

Halted at Palliser. The Chief and his friends walked up to the cow-catcher to make a morning call. I felt a little "superior" and was rather condescending. Somewhat flushed with excitement, but still anxious to be polite, I asked "would the Chief step up and take a drive?" To the horror of the bystanders he carelessly consented, and in another moment had taken the place of Mr. E., the latter seating himself at our feet on the buffer-beam. There was a general consternation among our little group of friends and the few inhabitants of Palliser—the Chief rushing through the flats of the Columbia on a cow-catcher! and, worse still, possibly even among the wild Selkirk Mountains—those mountains of which scarcely three years before, in his charming book, "From Old Westminster to New," my friend Mr. Sandford Fleming[2] had said, "no one had been through the western slope of the Selkirks"! Every one is horrified. It is a comfort to the other occupant of the buffer to find some one else wilful, and as we steamed away towards Donald, at the eastern base of the Selkirks, I felt not so bad after all!...

---

[1] *athwart* Run across in oblique direction.

[2] *Sanford Fleming* Canadian engineer and inventor (1827–1915).

THE AESTHETIC MOVEMENT

From the Victorian *fin de siècle* to the early twentieth century, Aestheticism inspired poets, painters, playwrights, and innumerable others to reconsider the purpose of literature and art. Also known as "art for art's sake," the movement represented a break from the view that the arts must have a moral, social, or religious function. Aestheticism affirmed instead the autonomy of art and the belief that beauty and its appreciation are justifiable ends in themselves. Influenced in England by the writings of Walter Pater and a circle of young avant-garde writers at Oxford, leading Aesthetes such as Algernon Charles Swinburne and Oscar Wilde rejected the limits imposed on art by utilitarianism and conventional Victorian ethics and religion, and created in their place a body of literature determined to be uninhibited by the bourgeois standards of the day.

The term "aesthetics," derived from the Greek word for sense perception (*aesthesis*), was first used in 1750 by the German philosopher Alexander Baumgarten (1714–62) to describe "the science of sensitive knowing." All subsequent considerations of aesthetics maintain to some degree this concern with the "sensitive" origins of knowledge, and in particular the subjective experience by which individuals come to appreciate works of art. French philosopher Victor Cousin (1792–1867) later coined the phrase "*l'art pour l'art*," building on Kant's notion of disinterestedness in aesthetic judgment to proclaim that "the beautiful cannot be the way to what is useful, or to what is good, or to what is holy; it leads only to itself." In 1835, French author Théophile Gautier (1811–72) further developed the idea of "art for art's sake" in the preface to his novel *Mademoiselle de Maupin*: "nothing is truly beautiful except that which can serve for nothing; whatever is useful is ugly."

Aestheticism as defined by these writers emerged most powerfully in France through Charles Baudelaire's 1857 volume of poetry, *Les Fleurs du Mal* ("The Flowers of Evil"), which employed a language of symbolism to suggest "correspondences" among sounds, scents, and colors ("Les parfums, les couleurs et les sons se répondent"). On the other side of the English Channel a group of young artists who called themselves the "Pre-Raphaelite Brotherhood" advanced similar ideas through both poetry and painting. Originating in 1848 as seven men—Dante Gabriel Rossetti (who was also a poet), John Everett Millais, William Holman Hunt, James Collinson, Frederic George Stephens, Thomas Woolner, and critic William Michael Rossetti—the Pre-Raphaelite Brotherhood set the stage for the Aesthetic Movement in England. With their attention to fine detail, symbolism, and brilliant use of color, the Pre-Raphaelites aimed to excite the senses of the spectator, to create a unique aesthetic experience through a combination of sense impressions.

British Aestheticism was effectively inaugurated as a movement in 1868 when Walter Pater published an unsigned essay on William Morris's poetry in the *Westminster Review*. Pater, who taught at Oxford, encouraged the constant pursuit of passionate experience, and especially the sort of passion that might come of reading literature or viewing works of art. When Pater republished his review of Morris as part of his 1873 *Studies in the History of the Renaissance*, it prompted a tidal wave of reaction, both for and against Aestheticism. "Great passions," Pater wrote, "may give us [a] quickened sense of life, ecstasy and sorrow of love, the various forms of enthusiastic activity." Pater valued above all "the poetic passion, the desire for beauty, the love of art for art's sake," precisely insofar as art might be separated from politics, ethics, and religion. The beauty of art, in other words, arises from its autonomy, from the moments of pleasure that arise "simply for those moments' sake."

It was precisely because Aestheticism wanted to dissociate art from politics, ethics, and religion that critics saw it as a danger to British culture and society. A writer for *Blackwood's Edinburgh Magazine* worried in 1895 that a "wave of unrest" was passing over the world due in part to those authors who, following Pater's advice, sought "for new thrills and sensations." Critics took to characterizing this unrest as "decadence," a term that in many minds became synonymous with Aestheticism. In an 1893 *Harper's* magazine essay entitled "The Decadent Movement in Literature," Arthur Symons, once a pupil of Walter Pater and a self-proclaimed Aesthete, launched an attack on the Decadent Movement, calling it a "new and beautiful and interesting disease," epitomized by an "intense self-consciousness, a restless curiosity in research, an oversubtilizing refinement upon refinement, a spiritual and moral perversity." The German social theorist Max Nordau used many of the same terms to describe the Decadents—"diseased … immoral … anti-social"—but with the goal of illustrating the ways in which Aestheticism had led to what he called, in the title of his 1892 work, *Degeneration*, a deterioration of Western society and culture.

When Aestheticism wasn't being decried for its immorality, it was often the subject of parody. Gilbert and Sullivan's 1881 operetta *Patience* featured an Aesthetic poet, Bunthorne, whom Oscar Wilde himself took for a model (his career as the most prominent of Aesthetes was just getting under way), and the magazine *Punch* relentlessly parodied the Aesthetes, characterizing them as narcissistic, self-serving dandies. Authors such as Swinburne and Wilde ignored the derision of the critics and consciously dressed the part of dandies, donning clothes of flamboyant colors and wearing plumes, velvet jackets, and knee breeches. The movement became increasingly associated with sensuous beauty and the decorative arts, and for a time sales of blue china and peacock feathers, objects of the sort appreciated by the Aesthetes, soared, while the public clamored for books on decorating ideas. In the arts, Aestheticism found expression in the paintings of Edward Burne-Jones and James McNeill Whistler and in the erotic illustrations of Aubrey Beardsley, many of which were published in *The Yellow Book*, a *fin de siècle* quarterly of the arts and literature that was a vehicle for Aesthetic works. The movement also influenced architecture and design, inspiring the ornate and decorative motifs of the Art Nouveau movement as well as, paradoxically, the devotion to simplicity and handcrafted work of the Arts and Crafts Movement (exemplified by the works of the William Morris Company and the Scottish architect and designer Charles Rennie Mackintosh). Among the literary Aesthetes were George Meredith, Lionel Johnson, Ernest Dowson, Max Beerbohm, and George Moore. Recent scholarship has added to this list several women writers of the *fin de siècle*, including "Lucas Malet" (Mary St. Leger Kingsley Harrison), Alice Meynell, "Vernon Lee" (Violet Paget), "Michael Field" (Katherine Bradley and Edith Cooper), and Mona Caird.

Although the Aesthetic Movement seemed to expire with the celebrated and humiliating trial of Oscar Wilde on charges of homosexuality, its after-effects were felt in the writing of such twentieth-century literary figures as William Butler Yeats and Henry James. More important, perhaps, Aestheticism helped break the Victorian loyalty to realism and moral aestheticism. Aestheticism's opposition to traditional forms, its concern with the self and individuality, and above all its principle of aesthetic autonomy, permanently altered the production and reception of art in Britain and elsewhere.

⌘⌘⌘

"MICHAEL FIELD"

KATHARINE BRADLEY (1848–1914) AND EDITH COOPER (1862–1913)

"Michael Field" was the pseudonym used by Katharine Bradley and her niece Edith Cooper, who together published eight volumes of poetry and numerous tragedies. The two women, who were also lovers, disguised their identity for fear that the truth would influence the reception of their work. A larger selection of their work appears under a separate author entry elsewhere in this volume; two poems whose themes relate strongly to those of the Aesthetes appear below.

From Baudelaire[1]

There shall be beds full of light odours blent,
  Divans, great couches, deep, profound as tombs,
And, frown for us, in light magnificent,
  Over the flower-stand there shall droop strange blooms.

5   Careful of their last flame declining,
  As two vast torches our two hearts shall flare,
And our two spirits in their double shining
  Reflect the double lights enchanted there.

One night—a night of mystic blue, of rose,
10 A look will pass supreme from me, from you,
Like a long sob, laden with long adieux.

And, later on, an angel will unclose
  The door, and, entering joyously, re-light
The tarnished mirrors and the flames blown to the night.
  —1908

The Poet

Within his eyes are hung lamps of the sanctuary:
  A wind, from whence none knows, can set in
      sway
And spill their light by fits; but yet their ray
Returns, deep-boled,[2] to its obscurity.

5   The world as from a dullard[3] turns annoyed
To stir the days with show or deeds or voices;
But if one spies him justly one rejoices,
With silence that the careful lips avoid.

He is a plan, a work of some strange passion
10 Life has conceived apart from Time's harsh drill,
A thing it hides and cherishes to fashion.

---

[1] *Baudelaire* French poet and critic Charles Baudelaire (1821–67), whose volume of poetry *Les Fleurs du Mal* (1857) established a symbolic correspondence between sensory images of sound, scent, and color.

[2] *deep-boled* I.e., having deep apertures. A bole is a recess in the wall of a castle, etc., for admitting light.

[3] *dullard* Stupid or dull person.

At odd bright moments to its secret will:
Holy and foolish, ever set apart,
He waits the leisure of his god's free heart.
  —1908

JOHN DAVIDSON (1857–1909)

Poet, playwright, and novelist John Davidson spent his early life in Scotland before moving to London, where his work as a journalist provided him with a wealth of material for his poetry. Davidson remained marginal to the Aesthetic Movement, with which he had an ambivalent relationship. His poetry often relied upon deep philosophical enquiries into the nature of human existence and the pursuit of desire. He was unique among his contemporaries in his exploration of Nietzsche's poetic theories, and his deeply ironic tone, compelling urban images, and expressions of scientific materialism had an effect on many of the poets who followed him.

A Northern Suburb

Nature selects the longest way,
  And winds about in tortuous grooves;
A thousand years the oaks decay;
  The wrinkled glacier hardly moves.

5   But here the whetted fangs of change
  Daily devour the old demesne°—   district
The busy farm, the quiet grange,°   country-house
  The wayside inn, the village green.

In gaudy yellow brick and red,
10 With rooting pipes, like creepers rank,
The shoddy terraces o'erspread
  Meadow, and garth,[4] and daisied bank.

With shelves for rooms the houses crowd,
  Like draughty cupboards in a row—
15 Ice-chests when wintry winds are loud,
  Ovens when summer breezes blow.

---

[4] *garth* Yard; garden.

Roused by the fee'd° policeman's knock,   *hired*
    And sad that day should come again,
Under the stars the workmen flock
20   In haste to reach the workmen's train.

For here dwell those who must fulfil
    Dull tasks in uncongenial spheres,
Who toil through dread of coming ill,
    And not with hope of happier years—

25 The lowly folk who scarcely dare
    Conceive themselves perhaps misplaced,
Whose prize for unremitting care
    Is only not to be disgraced.
    —1897

CONSTANCE NADEN (1858–89)

Poet and philosopher Constance Naden was well
educated in a range of sciences, including botany,
chemistry, physics, and zoology. Her poetry demonstrates a particular interest in natural selection and
evolutionary ethics, as well as a deep religious skepticism. Neither of the two volumes of poetry that
Naden published in her lifetime received much
notice, but those who reviewed her work praised it
highly. One reviewer named her, Elizabeth Barrett
Browning, and Christina Rossetti as the three finest
female poets, while another described her second
collection of poetry as displaying "both culture and
courage—culture in its use of language, courage in
its choice of subject matter." By 1887, Naden had
stopped writing poetry, choosing to focus instead on
her philosophical writing.

Illusions

Not in the heavens alone is Truth renowned;
    Sad human hearts, that seem to love her less,
Even in mutiny her power confess:
    We speak in fables, and are compassed round
5 With poesy, distilling song from sound,
    Colour from light, and hope from happiness;

Subliming weakness, yearning, and distress,
To that high faith wherewith our life is crowned.

All fair deceits are prophets of the truth,
10 E'en as the desert mirage tells a tale
Of palms and wells, real, though far away:
The star-bright hopes that light the world's dim youth
Are not too brilliant, but too silvery pale,
To sparkle still, when dawns the golden day.
    —1881

ERNEST DOWSON (1867–1900)

Dowson was a central figure of the Aesthetic Movement, and moved frequently in the London literary
society of Lionel Johnson, Richard Le Gallienne,
Oscar Wilde, Walter Pater, and Aubrey Beardsley,
while contributing to most of the Aesthetic magazines of the time. Influenced by Charles Swinburne,
classical Latin poets such as Horace, and the French
symbolist Verlaine, Dowson also drew upon Roman
Catholic liturgy in some poems. (He was received
into the Church around 1891.) Throughout his
work he demonstrates a technical mastery of the
language and a lyrical, mellifluous style.

Nuns of the Perpetual Adoration

Calm, sad, secure; behind high convent walls,
    These watch the sacred lamp, these watch and pray:
And it is one with them when evening falls,
    And one with them the cold return of day.

5 These heed not time; their nights and days they make
    Into a long, returning rosary,
Whereon their lives are threaded for Christ's sake;
    Meekness and vigilance and chastity.

A vowed patrol, in silent companies,
10 Life-long they keep before the living Christ.
In the dim church, their prayers and penances
    Are fragrant incense to the Sacrificed.

Outside, the world is wild and passionate;
    Man's weary laughter and his sick despair

15 Entreat at their impenetrable gate:
    They heed no voices in their dream of prayer.

They saw the glory of the world displayed;
    They saw the bitter of it, and the sweet;
They knew the roses of the world should fade,
20   And be trod under by the hurrying feet.

Therefore they rather put away desire,
    And crossed their hands and came to sanctuary;—
And veiled their heads and put on coarse attire:
    Because their comeliness was vanity.

25 And there they rest; they have serene insight
    Of the illuminating dawn to be:
Mary's sweet Star[1] dispels for them the night,
    The proper darkness of humanity.

Calm, sad, secure; with faces worn and mild:
30   Surely their choice of vigil is the best?
Yea! for our roses fade, the world is wild;
    But there, beside the altar, there, is rest.
        —1891

To One in Bedlam[2]

With delicate, mad hands, behind his sordid bars,
    Surely he hath his posies, which they tear and
        twine;
Those scentless wisps of straw, that miserably line
His strait, caged universe, whereat the dull world stares,

5 Pedant and pitiful. O, how his rapt gaze wars
With their stupidity! Know they what dreams divine
Lift his long, laughing reveries like enchaunted wine,
And make his melancholy germane to the stars?

O lamentable brother! if those pity thee,
10 Am I not fain° of all thy lone eyes promise me;   *glad*
Half a fool's kingdom, far from men who sow and reap,
All their days, vanity? Better than mortal flowers,
Thy moon-kissed roses seem: better than love or sleep,
The star-crowned solitude of thine oblivious hours.
    —1892

Spleen
For Arthur Symons[3]

I was not sorrowful, I could not weep,
    And all my memories were put to sleep.

I watched the river grow more white and strange,
All day till evening I watched it change.

5 All day till evening I watched the rain
Beat wearily upon the window pane.

I was not sorrowful, but only tired
Of everything that ever I desired.

Her lips, her eyes, all day became to me
10 The shadow of a shadow utterly.

All day mine hunger for her heart became
Oblivion, until the evening came,

And left me sorrowful, inclined to weep,
With all my memories that could not sleep.
    —1896

---

[1] *Mary's sweet Star* I.e., Jesus; the star of Bethlehem, that announced his birth, is used here as a metaphor for Jesus.

[2] *Bedlam* I.e., London's Hospital of St. Mary of Bethlehem, a public asylum for the mentally ill. The term came to be used to refer to any asylum.

[3] *Spleen* Melancholy; ill-humor. (According to medieval physiology, the spleen was the source of these emotions.) *Arthur Symons* Literary scholar and editor (1865–1945) who established himself as a leading writer of the Aesthetic Movement. Some of Dowson's work was published in Symon's short-lived Aesthetic magazine *The Savoy* (1896).

LIONEL JOHNSON (1867–1902)

Johnson, like his close friend Ernest Dowson, was central to the poetic movements of the 1890s. He was tutored at Oxford by Walter Pater and had close relationships with W.B. Yeats and Arthur Symons. His poems display a sensitivity to beauty, despite their often brooding tone, and frequently take literary themes as their topics. (Johnson was also a renowned scholar and critic.) His work also occasionally demonstrates religious anxiety— Johnson's Roman Catholic faith was a central part of his life, but he most likely struggled with homosexual desires. Johnson suffered from the effects of alcoholism throughout his adult life, and eventually died from complications of this disease.

Plato[1] in London
To Campbell Dodgson[2]

The pure flame of one taper fall
   Over the old and comely page:
No harsher light disturb at all
This converse with a treasured sage.
5   Seemly, and fair, and of the best,
         If Plato be our guest,
            Should things befall.

Without, a world of noise and cold:
Here, the soft burning of the fire.
10   And Plato walks, where heavens unfold,
About the home of his desire.
From his own city of high things,
         He shows to us, and brings,
            Truth of fine gold.

15   The hours pass; and the fire burns low;
The clear flame dwindles into death:
Shut then the book with care; and so,
Take leave of Plato, with hushed breath:
A little, by the falling gleams,

20   Tarry the gracious dreams;
            And they too go.

Lean from the window to the air:
Hear London's voice upon the night!
Thou hast held converse with things rare:
25   Look now upon another sight!
The calm stars, in their living skies:
         And then, these surging cries,
            This restless glare!

That starry music, starry fire,
30   High above all our noise and glare:
The image of our long desire,
The beauty, and the strength, are there.
And Plato's thought lives, true and clear,
         In as august a sphere:
35   Perchance, far higher.
—1889

The Dark Angel

Dark Angel, with thine aching lust
   To rid the world of penitence:
Malicious Angel, who still dost
My soul such subtile violence!

5   Because of thee, no thought, no thing,
Abides for me undesecrate:
Dark Angel, ever on the wing,
Who never reachest me too late!

When music sounds, then changest thou
10   Its silvery to a sultry fire:
Nor will thine envious heart allow
Delight untortured by desire.

Through thee, the gracious Muses[3] turn
To Furies,[4] O mine Enemy!

---

[1] *Plato*   Greek philosopher (427?–347 BCE).

[2] *Campbell Dodgson*   Museum curator, art historian, and renowned scholar (1867–1948).

[3] *Muses*   In classical mythology, the nine daughters of Zeus and Mnemosyne, each of whom presided over and provided inspiration for an aspect of the arts and sciences.

[4] *Furies*   Three winged deities of classical mythology who pursued and punished the doers of unavenged crimes, and who were terrifying in their appearance and behavior.

15   And all the things of beauty burn
      With flames of evil ecstasy.

      Because of thee, the land of dreams
      Becomes a gathering place of fears:
      Until tormented slumber seems
20   One vehemence of useless tears.

      When sunlight glows upon the flowers,
      Or ripples down the dancing sea:
      Thou, with thy troop of passionate powers,
      Beleaguerest, bewilderest, me.

25   Within the breath of autumn woods,
      Within the winter silences:
      Thy venomous spirit stirs and broods,
      O Master of impieties!

      The ardour of red flame is thine,
30   And thine the steely soul of ice:
      Thou poisonest the fair design
      Of nature, with unfair device.

      Apples of ashes, golden bright;
      Waters of bitterness, how sweet!
35   O banquet of a foul delight,
      Prepared by thee, dark Paraclete![1]

      Thou art the whisper in the gloom,
      The hinting tone, the haunting laugh:
      Thou art the adorner of my tomb,
40   The minstrel of mine epitaph.

      I fight thee, in the Holy Name!
      Yet, what thou dost, is what God saith:
      Tempter! should I escape thy flame,
      Thou wilt have helped my soul from Death:

45   The second Death, that never dies,
      That cannot die, when time is dead:
      Live Death, wherein the lost soul cries,
      Eternally uncomforted.
      Dark Angel, with thine aching lust!

50   Of two defeats, of two despairs:
      Less dread, a change to drifting dust,
      Than thine eternity of cares.

      Do what thou wilt, thou shalt not so,
      Dark Angel! triumph over me:
55   *Lonely, unto the Lone I go;*
      Divine, to the Divinity.
      —1893, 1894

The Darkness
To the Rev. Fr. Dover, S.J.

Master of spirits! hear me: King of souls!
I kneel before Thine altar, the long night,
Besieging Thee with penetrable prayers;
And all I ask, light from the Face of God.
5   Thy darkness Thou hast given me enough,
      The dark clouds of Thine angry majesty:
      Now give me light! I cannot always walk
      Surely beneath the full and starless night.
      Lighten me, fallen down, I know not where,
10   Save, to the shadows and the fear of death.
      Thy Saints in light see light, and sing for joy:
      Safe from the dark, safe from the dark and cold.
      But from my dark comes only doubt of light:
      Disloyalty, that trembles to despair.
15   Now bring me out of night, and with the sun
      Clothe me, and crown me with Thy seven stars,
      Thy spirits in the hollow of Thine hand.
      Thou from the still throne of Thy tabernacle[2]
      Wilt come to me in glory, O Lord God!
20   Thou wilt, I doubt Thee not: I worship Thee
      Before Thine holy altar, the long night.
      Else have I nothing in the world, but death:
      Thine hounding winds rush by me day and night,
      Thy seas roar in mine ears: I have no rest,
25   No peace, but am afflicted constantly,
      Driven from wilderness to wilderness.
      And yet Thou hast a perfect house of light,
      Above the four great winds, an house of peace:

---

[1] *Paraclete* Comforter; advocate (a title usually given to the Holy Spirit).

[2] *tabernacle* Dwelling place (of God).

Its beauty of the crystal and the dew,
30 Guard Angels and Archangels, in their hands
The blade of a sword shaken. Thither bring
Thy servant: when the black night falls on me,
With bitter voices tempting in the gloom,
Send out Thine armies, flaming ministers,
35 And shine upon the night: for what I would,

I cannot, save these help me. O Lord God!
Now, when my prayers upon Thine altar lie,
When Thy dark anger is too hard for me:
Through vision of Thyself, through flying fire,
40 Have mercy, and give light, and stablish me!
—1897, 1889

CHARLOTTE MEW
1869 - 1928

Although Virginia Woolf once called her "the world's greatest living poetess," Charlotte Mew has never achieved the fame once predicted for her. She published over sixty poems and many short stories in journals and in her own three volumes. Many of her works evoke the deaths of those close to her, unrequited love, and insanity, while others deal with isolation, loneliness, and sorrow. Thomas Hardy, who became a close friend after discovering her work, called Mew "far and away the best living woman poet—who will be read when others are forgotten." Hardy's prediction may turn out to be prescient after all; Mew's poetry has recently begun again to spark interest.

Mew was born in London to Fred Mew, an architect, and Anna Maria Marden Kendall, who bore seven children but lost three in infancy when Charlotte was young. Two other siblings were eventually consigned to asylums for the mentally ill, and the threat of insanity left its pall over both Charlotte and her sister Anne, who vowed never to marry for fear of perpetuating the family history of schizophrenia. The family tragedies eventually played themselves out in Mew's poems and short stories, which are also informed by a sense of rebelliousness and of the terrible poverty suffered by the family for much of her life.

Mew first came to the public's attention in 1894, when her short story "Passed" appeared in *The Yellow Book*, but it was with the publication of her poem "The Farmer's Bride" in a 1912 edition of *The Nation* that she arrived on London's literary scene. The poem is written from the point of view and in the dialect of a farmer, whose wife tries unsuccessfully to flee from him at the beginning of the marriage. She does warm to her husband, who longs for her throughout his life. Mew wrote in a letter after the publication of her first volume of poetry, *The Farmer's Bride* (1916), that she strove to present "not only the cry but the gesture and the accent … calling up witnesses to the real thing!" She became known as the eccentric author with the short hair who wore men's suits and smoked and swore, but who also wrote exquisite poems full of despair and pathos. The suffering in her poetry often mirrored the "real thing" of her life, with its unrequited love for Ella D'Arcy, an editor of *The Yellow Book*, and later for the novelist May Sinclair, who was said to have spurned Mew cruelly.

After her sister Anne—her only remaining family member and the one with whom she had lived her entire life—died of cancer in 1927, Mew fell into a deep depression and began suffering delusions. Following the death of Thomas Hardy in 1928 she checked herself into a nursing home, where she committed suicide a few months later by swallowing disinfectant.

⌘ ⌘ ⌘

The Farmer's Bride

He asked life of thee, and thou gavest him a long life:
even forever and ever.[1]

Three summers since I chose a maid,
  Too young maybe—but more's to do
At harvest-time than bide and woo.
  When us was wed she turned afraid
5 Of love and me and all things human;
  Like the shut of a winter's day.
Her smile went out, and 'twasn't a woman—
  More like a little frightened fay.°   *fairy*
    One night, in the fall, she runned away.

10 "Out 'mong the sheep, her be," they said,
  Should properly have been abed;
But sure enough she wasn't there
Lying awake with her wide brown stare.
So over seven-acre field and up-along across the down
15 We chased her, flying like a hare
  Before our lanterns. To Church-Town
    All in a shiver and a scare
  We caught her, fetched her home at last
  And turned the key upon her, fast.

20 She does the work about the house
  As well as most, but like a mouse:
    Happy enough to chat and play
With birds and rabbits and such as they,
  So long as men-folk keep away.
25 "Not near, not near!" her eyes beseech
When one of us comes within reach.
  The women say that beasts in stall
  Look round like children at her call.
  I've hardly heard her speak at all.

30 Shy as a leveret,° swift as he,   *young hare*
Straight and slight as a young larch tree,
Sweet as the first wild violets, she,
To her wild self. But what to me?

The short days shorten and the oaks are brown,
35 The blue smoke rises to the low grey sky,
One leaf in the still air falls slowly down,
  A magpie's spotted feathers lie
On the black earth spread white with rime,
The berries redden up to Christmas-time.
40 What's Christmas-time without there be
  Some other in the house than we!

She sleeps up in the attic there
  Alone, poor maid. 'Tis but a stair
Betwixt us. Oh! my God! the down,
45 The soft young down of her, the brown,
  The brown of her—her eyes, her hair, her hair!
—1912

Madeleine[2] In Church

Here, in the darkness, where this plaster saint
  Stands nearer than God stands to our distress,
And one small candle shines, but not so faint
  As the far lights of everlastingness
5 I'd rather kneel than over there, in open day
  Where Christ is hanging, rather pray
    To something more like my own clay,

---

[1] *He asked ... ever* From Psalms 21.4.

[2] *Madeleine* "Madeleine" is an alternate spelling for Magdalene, and an allusion to the Biblical Mary Magdalene. Although nowhere in the Bible is Mary Magdalene named a prostitute, that has been a frequent historical speculation. Hence "Magdalene" has become an epithet for a prostitute or for a woman whose sexual behavior is unconventional.

Not too divine;
For, once, perhaps my little saint
10   Before he got his niche and crown,
Had one short stroll about the town;
It brings him closer, just that taint
And anyone can wash the paint
Off our poor faces, his and mine!
15 Is that why I see Monty now? equal to any saint, poor boy, as good as gold,
But still, with just the proper trace
Of earthliness on his shining wedding face;
And then gone suddenly blank and old
The hateful day of the divorce:
20 Stuart got his, hands down, of course
Crowing like twenty cocks and grinning like a horse:
But Monty took it hard. All said and done I liked him best—
He was the first, he stands out clearer than the rest.
It seems too funny all we other rips°   *worthless people*
25   Should have immortal souls; Monty and Redge quite damnably
Keep theirs afloat while we go down like scuttled ships.
It's funny too, how easily we sink,
One might put up a monument, I think
To half the world and cut across it "Lost at Sea!"
30 I should drown Jim, poor little sparrow, if I netted him tonight—
No, it's no use this penny light—
Or my poor saint with his tin-pot crown—
The trees of Calvary[1] are where they were,
When we are sure that we can spare
35   The tallest, let us go and strike it down
And leave the other two still standing there.
I, too, would ask him to remember me
If there were any paradise beyond this earth that I could see.[2]

Oh! quiet Christ who never knew
40   The poisonous fangs that bite us through
And make us do the things we do,
See how we suffer and fight and die,
How helpless and how low we lie,
God holds You, and You hang so high,
45   Though no one looking long at You,
Can think You do not suffer too,
But, up there, from your still, starlighted tree
What can You know, what can You really see
Of this dark ditch, the soul of me!

---

[1] *trees of Calvary* I.e., crucifixes. Christ was crucified with two criminals at Calvary.

[2] *I, too … could see* See Luke 23.39–43.

50   We are what we are: when I was half a child I could not sit
Watching black shadows on green lawns and red carnations burning in the sun,
                        Without paying so heavily for it
That joy and pain, like any mother and her unborn child were almost one.
                        I could hardly bear
55   The dreams upon the eyes of white geraniums in the dusk,
                The thick, close voice of musk,
            The jessamine° music on the thin night air,   *jasmine*
            Or, sometimes, my own hands about me anywhere—
The sight of my own face (for it was lovely then) even the scent of my own hair,
60   Oh! there was nothing, nothing that did not sweep to the high seat
            Of laughing gods, and then blow down and beat
My soul into the highway dust, as hoofs do the dropped roses of the street.
                I think my body was my soul,
                And when we are made thus
65   Who shall control
            Our hands, our eyes, the wandering passion of our feet,
                Who shall teach us
To thrust the world out of our heart; to say, till perhaps in death,
                When the race is run,
70   And it is forced from us with our last breath
                "Thy will be done"?[1]
If it is Your will that we should be content with the tame, bloodless things,
        As pale as angels smirking by, with folded wings.
            Oh! I know virtue, and the peace it brings!
75   The temperate, well-worn smile
        The one man gives you, when you are evermore his own:
        And afterwards the child's, for a little while,
            With its unknowing and all-seeing eyes
        So soon to change, and make you feel how quick
80   The clock goes round. If one had learned the trick—
                (How does one though?) quite early on,
        Of long green pastures under placid skies,
        One might be walking now with patient truth.
What did we ever care for it, who have asked for youth,
85   When, oh! my God! this is going or has gone?

            There is a portrait of my mother, at nineteen,
        With the black spaniel, standing by the garden seat,
        The dainty head held high against the painted green
And throwing out the youngest smile, shy, but half haughty and half sweet.
90   Her picture then: but simply Youth, or simply Spring
                To me today: a radiance on the wall,
                So exquisite, so heartbreaking a thing

---

[1] *Thy will be done* The Lord's Prayer, from Matthew 6.10.

Beside the mask that I remember, shrunk and small,
Sapless and lined like a dead leaf,
95   All that was left of oh! the loveliest face, by time and grief!

And in the glass, last night, I saw a ghost behind my chair—
Yet why remember it, when one can still go moderately gay—?
Or could—with any one of the old crew,
But oh! these boys! the solemn way
100   They take you, and the things they say—
This "I have only as long as you"
When you remind them you are not precisely twenty-two—
Although at heart perhaps—God! if it were
Only the face, only the hair!
105   If Jim had written to me as he did today
A year ago—and now it leaves me cold—
I know what this means, old, old, *old!*
Et avec ça—mais on a vécu, tout se paie.[1]

That is not always true: there was my mother—(well at least the dead are free!)
110   Yoked to the man that Father was; yoked to the woman I am, Monty too;
The little portress at the convent school, stewing in hell so patiently;
The poor, fair boy who shot himself at Aix. And what of me—and what of me?
But I, I paid for what I had, and they for nothing. No, one cannot see
How it shall be made up to them in some serene eternity.
115   If there were fifty heavens God could not give us back the child who went or never came;
Here, on our little patch of this great earth, the sun of any darkened day,
Not one of all the starry buds hung on the hawthorn trees of last year's May,
No shadow from the sloping fields of yesterday;
For every hour they slant across the hedge a different way,
120   The shadows are never the same.

"Find rest in Him"[2] One knows the parsons' tags—
Back to the fold, across the evening fields, like any flock of baaing sheep:
Yes, it may be, when He has shorn, led us to slaughter, torn the bleating soul in us to rags,
For so He giveth His belovèd sleep.[3]
125   Oh! He will take us stripped and done,
Driven into His heart. So we are won:
Then safe, safe are we? in the shelter of His everlasting wings—
I do not envy Him his victories. His arms are full of broken things.

---

[1] *Et avec … paie* French: And with this—in living, everything has its cost.
[2] *Find rest in Him* From Matthew 11.29.
[3] *For so … sleep* From Psalms 127.2.

But I shall not be in them. Let Him take
130   The finer ones, the easier to break.
And they are not gone, yet, for me, the lights, the colours, the perfumes,
      Though now they speak rather in sumptuous rooms,
        In silks and in gemlike wines;
    Here, even, in this corner where my little candle shines
135   And overhead the lancet-window glows
     With golds and crimsons you could almost drink
To know how jewels taste, just as I used to think
There was the scent in every red and yellow rose
        Of all the sunsets. But this place is grey,
140   And much too quiet. No one here,
         Why, this is awful, this is fear!
          Nothing to see, no face,
Nothing to hear except your heart beating in space
      As if the world was ended. Dead at last!
145   Dead soul, dead body, tied together fast.
These to go on with and alone, to the slow end:
No one to sit with, really, or to speak to, friend to friend:
      Out of the long procession, black or white or red
Not one left now to say "Still I am here, then see you, dear, lay here your head."
150   Only the doll's house looking on the park
   Tonight, all nights, I know, when the man puts the lights out, very dark.
With, upstairs, in the blue and gold box of a room, just the maids' footsteps overhead,
Then utter silence and the empty world—the room—the bed—
      The corpse! No, not quite dead, while this cries out in me,
155   But nearly: very soon to be
       A handful of forgotten dust—
     There must be someone. Christ! there must,
      Tell me there *will* be some one. Who?
    If there were no one else, could it be You?

160   How old was Mary out of whom You cast
So many devils?[1] Was she young or perhaps for years
She had sat staring, with dry eyes, at this and that man going past
   Till suddenly she saw You on the steps of Simon's house[2]
    And stood and looked at You through tears.[3]
165   I think she must have known by those
    The thing, for what it was that had come to her.
    For some of us there is a passion, I suppose

---

1 *How old ... devils* See Luke 8.2 and Mark 16.9.

2 *Simon's house* I.e., Simon the Pharisee.

3 *Till suddenly ... tears* See Luke 7.37–50 for the Biblical account of the story that follows, in which one unnamed woman "who was a sinner" washed Christ's feet with her tears, dried them with her hair, and anointed them with perfume.

So far from earthly cares and earthly fears
That in its stillness you can hardly stir
170   Or in its nearness, lift your hand,
So great that you have simply got to stand
Looking at it through tears, through tears.
Then straight from these there broke the kiss,
          I think You must have known by this
175   The thing for what it was, that had come to You:
          She did not love You like the rest,
It was in her own way, but at the worst, the best,
          She gave You something altogether new.
     And through it all, from her, no word,
180   She scarcely saw You, scarcely heard:
Surely You knew when she so touched You with her hair,
          Or by the wet cheek lying there,
And while her perfume clung to You from head to feet all through the day
     That You can change the things for which we care,
185   But even You, unless You kill us, not the way.

          This, then was peace for her, but passion too.
     I wonder was it like a kiss that once I knew,
          The only one that I would care to take
     Into the grave with me, to which if there were afterwards, to wake.
190   Almost as happy as the carven dead
     In some dim chancel[1] lying head by head
We slept with it, but face to face, the whole night through—
One breath, one throbbing quietness, as if the thing behind our lips was endless life,
          Lost, as I woke, to hear in the strange earthly dawn, his "Are you there?"
195   And lie still, listening to the wind outside, among the firs.

     So Mary chose the dream of Him for what was left to her of night and day,
It is the only truth: it is the dream in us that neither life nor death nor any other thing can
          away:
     But if she had not touched Him in the doorway of the dream could she have cared so much?
     She was a sinner, we are what we are: the spirit afterwards, but first, the touch.

200   And He has never shared with me my haunted house beneath the trees
Of Eden and Calvary, with its ghosts that have not any eyes for tears,
And the happier guests who would not see, or if they did, remember these,
          Though they lived there a thousand years.
          Outside, too gravely looking at me, He seems to stand,
205   And looking at Him, if my forgotten spirit came
               Unwillingly back, what could it claim
               Of those calm eyes, that quiet speech,

---

[1] *chancel* Area surrounding a church's altar.

Breaking like a slow tide upon the beach,
    The scarred, not quite human hand?—
210 Unwillingly back to the burden of old imaginings
    When it has learned so long not to think, not to be,
Again, again it would speak as it has spoken to me of things
    That I shall not see!

I cannot bear to look at this divinely bent and gracious head:
215 When I was small I never quite believed that He was dead:
    And at the Convent school I used to lie awake in bed
Thinking about His hands.[1] It did not matter what they said,
He was alive to me, so hurt, so hurt! And most of all in Holy Week[2]
    When there was no one else to see
220 I used to think it would not hurt me too, so terribly,
    If He had ever seemed to notice me
    Or, if, for once, He would only speak.

—1916

Passed

Like souls that meeting pass,
And passing never meet again.

Let those who have missed a romantic view of London in its poorest quarters—and there will romance be found—wait for a sunset in early winter. They may turn north or south, towards Islington or Westminster, and encounter some fine pictures and more than one aspect of unique beauty. This hour of pink twilight has its monopoly of effects. Some of them may never be reached again.

On such an evening in mid-December, I put down my sewing and left tame glories of firelight (discoverers of false charm) to welcome, as youth may, the contrast of keen air outdoors to the glow within.

My aim was the perfection of a latent appetite, for I had no mind to content myself with an apology for hunger, consequent on a warmly passive afternoon.

The splendid cold of fierce frost set my spirit dancing. The road rung hard underfoot, and through

the lonely squares woke sharp echoes from behind. This stinging air assailed my cheeks with vigorous severity. It stirred my blood grandly, and brought thought back to me from the warm embers just forsaken, with an immeasurable sense of gain.

But after the first delirium of enchanting motion, destination became a question. The dim trees behind the dingy enclosures were beginning to be succeeded by rows of flaring gas jets, displaying shops of new aspect and evil smell. Then the heavy walls of a partially demolished prison reared themselves darkly against the pale sky.

By this landmark I recalled—alas that it should be possible—a church in the district, newly built by an infallible architect, which I had been directed to seek at leisure. I did so now. A row of cramped houses, with the unpardonable bow window, projecting squalor into prominence, came into view. Robbing these even of light, the portentous walls stood a silent curse before them. I think they were blasting the hopes of the sad dwellers beneath them—if hope they had—to despair. Through spattered panes faces of diseased and dirty children leered into the street. One room, as I passed, seemed full of them. The window was open; their wails and maddening requirements sent out the mother's cry. It was thrown back to her, mingled with her children's

---

[1] *His hands* Christ's hands were nailed to the cross on which He was crucified.

[2] *Holy Week* Week of the Christian calendar in which the events of Christ's passion, death, and resurrection are commemorated.

screams, from the pitiless prison walls.

These shelters struck my thought as travesties—perhaps they were not—of the grand place called home.

Leaving them I sought the essential of which they were bereft. What withheld from them, as poverty and sin could not, a title to the sacred name?

An answer came, but interpretation was delayed. Theirs was not the desolation of something lost, but of something that had never been. I thrust off speculation gladly here, and fronted Nature free.

Suddenly I emerged from the intolerable shadow of the brickwork, breathing easily once more. Before me lay a roomy space, nearly square, bounded by three-storey dwellings, and transformed, as if by quick mechanism, with colours of sunset. Red and golden spots wavered in the panes of the low scattered houses round the bewildering expanse. Overhead a faint crimson sky was hung with violet clouds, obscured by the smoke and nearing dusk.

In the centre, but towards the left, stood an old stone pump, and some few feet above it irregular lamps looked down. They were planted on a square of paving railed in by broken iron fences, whose paint, now discoloured, had once been white. Narrow streets cut in five directions from the open roadway. Their lines of light sank dimly into distance, mocking the stars' entrance into the fading sky. Everything was transfigured in the illuminated twilight. As I stood, the dying sun caught the rough edges of a girl's uncovered hair, and hung a faint nimbus[1] round her poor desecrated face. The soft circle, as she glanced toward me, lent it the semblance of one of those mystically pictured faces of some medieval saint.

A stillness stole on, and about the square dim figures hurried along, leaving me stationary in existence (I was thinking fancifully), when my medieval saint demanded "who I was a-shoving of?" and dismissed me, not unkindly, on my way. Hawkers[2] in a neighbouring alley were calling, and the monotonous ting-ting of the muffin bell[3] made an audible background to the picture. I left it, and then the glamour was already passing. In a

little while darkness possessing it, the place would reassume its aspect of sordid gloom.

There is a street not far from there, bearing a name that quickens life within one, by the vision it summons of a most peaceful country, where the broad roads are but pathways through green meadows, and your footstep keeps the time to a gentle music of pure streams. There the scent of roses, and the first pushing buds of spring, mark the seasons, and the birds call out faithfully the time and manner of the day. Here Easter is heralded by the advent in some squalid mart of air-balls[4] on Good Friday; early summer and late may be known by observation of that unromantic yet authentic calendar in which alley-tors, tip-cat, whip- and peg-tops, hoops and suckers,[5] in their courses mark the flight of time.

Perhaps attracted by the incongruity, I took this way. In such a thoroughfare it is remarkable that satisfied as are its public with transient substitutes for literature, they require permanent types (the term is so far misused it may hardly be further outraged) of art. Pictures, so-called, are the sole departure from necessity and popular finery which the prominent wares display. The window exhibiting these aspirations was scarcely more inviting than the fishmonger's next door, but less odoriferous, and I stopped to see what the ill-reflecting lights would show. There was a typical selection. Prominently, a large chromo[6] of a girl at prayer. Her eyes turned upwards, presumably to heaven, left the gazer in no state to dwell on the elaborately bared breasts below. These might rival, does wax-work attempt such beauties, any similar attraction of Marylebone's[7] extensive show. This personification of pseudo-purity was sensually diverting, and consequently marketable.

My mind seized the ideal of such a picture, and turned from this prostitution of it sickly away. Hurriedly I proceeded, and did not stop again until I had passed the low gateway of the place I sought.

Its forbidding exterior was hidden in the deep twilight and invited no consideration. I entered and swung back the inner door. It was papered with memo-

---

1   *nimbus*   Halo.

2   *Hawkers*   Street sellers.

3   *muffin bell*   Bell of a street seller of baked goods.

4   *air-balls*   Inflated balls; toys.

5   *alley-tors ... suckers*   Various children's toys.

6   *chromo*   Chromolithograph; color picture produced through the use of lithographic stones.

7   *Marylebone*   District in London.

rial cards, recommending to mercy the unprotesting spirits of the dead. My prayers were requested for the "repose of the soul of the Architect of that church, who passed away in the True Faith—December—1887." Accepting the assertion, I counted him beyond them, and mentally entrusted mine to the priest for those who were still groping for it in the gloom.

Within the building, darkness again forbade examination. A few lamps hanging before the altar struggled with obscurity.

I tried to identify some ugly details with the great man's complacent eccentricity, and failing, turned toward the street again. Nearly an hour's walk lay between me and my home. This fact and the atmosphere of stuffy sanctity about the place, set me longing for space again, and woke a fine scorn for aught but air and sky. My appetite, too, was now an hour ahead of opportunity. I sent back a final glance into the darkness as my hand prepared to strike the door. There was no motion at the moment, and it was silent; but the magnetism of human presence reached me where I stood. I hesitated, and in a few moments found what sought me on a chair in the far corner, flung face downwards across the seat. The attitude arrested me. I went forward. The lines of the figure spoke unquestionable despair.

Does speech convey intensity of anguish? Its supreme expression is in form. Here was human agony set forth in meagre lines, voiceless, but articulate to the soul. At first the forcible portrayal of it assailed me with the importunate strength of beauty. Then the Thing stretched there in the obdurate darkness grew personal and banished delight. Neither sympathy nor its vulgar substitute, curiosity, induced my action as I drew near. I was eager indeed to be gone. I wanted to ignore the almost indistinguishable being. My will cried: Forsake it!—but I found myself powerless to obey. Perhaps it would have conquered had not the girl swiftly raised herself in quest of me. I stood still. Her eyes met mine. A wildly tossed spirit looked from those ill-lighted windows, beckoning me on. Mine pressed towards it, but whether my limbs actually moved I do not know, for the imperious summons robbed me of any consciousness save that of necessity to comply.

Did she reach me, or was our advance mutual? It cannot be told. I suppose we neither know. But we met, and her hand, grasping mine, imperatively dragged me into the cold and noisy street.

We went rapidly in and out of the flaring booths, hustling little staggering children in our unpitying speed, I listening dreamily to the concert of hoarse yells and haggling whines which struck against the silence of our flight. On and on she took me, breathless and without explanation. We said nothing. I had no care or impulse to ask our goal. The fierce pressure of my hand was not relaxed a breathing space; it would have borne me against resistance could I have offered any, but I was capable of none. The streets seemed to rush past us, peopled with despair.

Weirdly lighted faces sent blank negations to a spirit of question which finally began to stir in me. Here, I thought once vaguely, was the everlasting No![1]

We must have journeyed thus for more than half an hour and walked far. I did not detect it. In the eternity of supreme moments time is not. Thought, too, fears to be obtrusive and stands aside.

We gained a door at last, down some blind alley out of the deafening thoroughfare. She threw herself against it and pulled me up the unlighted stairs. They shook now and then with the violence of our ascent; with my free hand I tried to help myself up by the broad and greasy balustrade. There was little sound in the house. A light shone under the first door we passed, but all was quietness within.

At the very top, from the dense blackness of the passage, my guide thrust me suddenly into a dazzling room. My eyes rejected its array of brilliant light. On a small chest of drawers three candles were guttering, two more stood flaring in the high window ledge, and a lamp upon a table by the bed rendered these minor illuminations unnecessary by its diffusive glare. There were even some small Christmas candles dropping coloured grease down the wooden mantelpiece, and I

[1]   everlasting No!   See Thomas Carlyle's *Sartor Resartus* (1833), in which the protagonist suffers a loss of faith: "Thus had the Everlasting No (*das ewige Nein*) pealed authoritatively through all the recesses of my being, of my me; and then was it that my whole me stood up, in native God-created majesty, and with emphasis recorded its protest.... The Everlasting No had said: 'Behold, thou art fatherless, outcast, and the universe is mine (the Devil's).'"

noticed a fire had been made, built entirely of wood. There were bits of an inlaid work box or desk, and a chair rung, lying half burnt in the grate. Some peremptory demand for light had been, these signs denoted, unscrupulously met. A woman lay upon the bed, half clothed, asleep. As the door slammed behind me the flames wavered and my companion released my hand. She stood beside me, shuddering violently, but without utterance.

I looked around. Everywhere proofs of recent energy were visible. The bright panes reflecting back the low burnt candles, the wretched but shining furniture, and some odd bits of painted china, set before the sputtering lights upon the drawers, bore witness to a provincial intolerance of grime. The boards were bare, and marks of extreme poverty distinguished the whole room. The destitution of her surroundings accorded ill with the girl's spotless person and well-tended hands, which were hanging tremulously down.

Subsequently I realized that these deserted beings must have first fronted the world from a sumptuous stage. The details in proof of it I need not cite. It must have been so.

My previous apathy gave place to an exaggerated observation. Even some pieces of a torn letter, dropped off the quilt, I noticed, were of fine texture, and inscribed by a man's hand. One fragment bore an elaborate device in colours. It may have been a club crest or coat of arms. I was trying to decide which, when the girl at length gave a cry of exhaustion or relief, at the same time falling into a similar attitude to that she had taken in the dim church. Her entire frame became shaken with tearless agony or terror. It was sickening to watch. She began partly to call or moan, begging me, since I was beside her, wildly, and then with heartbreaking weariness, "to stop, to stay." She half rose and claimed me with distracted grace. All her movements were noticeably fine.

I pass no judgement on her features; suffering for the time assumed them, and they made no insistence of individual claim.

I tried to raise her, and kneeling, pulled her reluctantly towards me. The proximity was distasteful. An alien presence has ever repelled me. I should have pitied the girl keenly perhaps a few more feet away. She clung to me with ebbing force. Her heart throbbed painfully close to mine, and when I meet now in the dark streets others who have been robbed, as she has been, of their great possession, I have to remember that.

The magnetism of our meeting was already passing, and, reason asserting itself, I reviewed the incident dispassionately, as she lay like a broken piece of mechanism in my arms. Her dark hair had come unfastened and fell about my shoulder. A faint white streak of it stole through the brown. A gleam of moonlight strays thus through a dusky room. I remember noticing, as it was swept with her involuntary motions across my face, a faint fragrance which kept recurring like a subtle and seductive sprite, hiding itself with fairy cunning in the tangled maze.

The poor girl's mind was clearly travelling a devious way. Broken and incoherent exclamations told of a recently wrung promise, made to whom, or of what nature, it was not my business to conjecture or inquire.

I record the passage of a few minutes. At the first opportunity I sought the slumberer on the bed. She slept well; hers was a long rest; there might be no awakening from it, for she was dead. Schooled in one short hour to all surprises, the knowledge made me simply richer by a fact. Nothing about the sternly set face invited horror. It had been, and was yet, a strong and, if beauty be not confined to youth and colour, a beautiful face.

Perhaps this quiet sharer of the convulsively broken silence was thirty years old. Death had set a firmness about the finely controlled features that might have shown her younger. The actual years are of little matter; existence, as we reckon time, must have lasted long. It was not death, but life that had planted the look of disillusion there. And romance being over, all goodbyes to youth are said. By the bedside, on a roughly constructed table, was a dearly bought bunch of violets. They were set in a blue bordered teacup, and hung over in wistful challenge of their own diviner hue. They were foreign, and their scent probably unnatural, but it stole very sweetly round the room. A book lay face downwards beside them—alas for parochial energies, not of a religious type—and the torn fragments of the destroyed letter had fallen on the black binding.

A passionate movement of the girl's breast against

mine directed my glance elsewhere. She was shivering, and her arms about my neck were stiffly cold. The possibility that she was starving missed my mind. It would have found my heart. I wondered if she slept, and dared not stir, though I was by this time cramped and chilled. The vehemence of her agitation ended, she breathed gently, and slipped finally to the floor.

I began to face the need of action and recalled the chances of the night. When and how I might get home was a necessary question, and I listened vainly for a friendly step outside. None since we left it had climbed the last flight of stairs. I could hear a momentary vibration of men's voices in the room below. Was it possible to leave these suddenly discovered children of peace and tumult? Was it possible to stay?

This was Saturday, and two days later I was bound for Scotland; a practical recollection of empty trunks was not lost in my survey of the situation. Then how, if I decided not to forsake the poor child, now certainly sleeping in my arms, were my anxious friends to learn my whereabouts, and understand the eccentricity of the scheme?

Indisputably, I determined, something must be done for the half-frantic wanderer who was pressing a tiring weight against me. And there should be some kind hand to cover the cold limbs and close the wide eyes of the breathless sleeper, waiting a comrade's sanction to fitting rest.

Conclusion was hastening to impatient thought, when my eyes let fall a fatal glance upon the dead girl's face. I do not think it had changed its first aspect of dignified repose, and yet now it woke in me a sensation of cold dread. The dark eyes unwillingly open reached mine in an insistent stare. One hand lying out upon the coverlid, I could never again mistake for that of temporarily suspended life. My watch ticked loudly, but I dared not examine it, nor could I wrench my sight from the figure on the bed. For the first time the empty shell of being assailed my senses. I watched feverishly, knowing well the madness of the action, for a hint of breathing, almost stopping my own.

Today, as memory summons it, I cannot dwell without reluctance on this hour of my realization of the thing called Death.

A hundred fancies, clothed in mad intolerable terrors, possessed me, and had not my lips refused it outlet, I should have set free a cry, as the spent child beside me had doubtless longed to do, and failed, ere, desperate, she fled.

My gaze was chained; it could not get free. As the shapes of monsters of ever varying and increasing dreadfulness flit through one's dreams, the images of those I loved crept round me, with stark yet well-known features, their limbs borrowing death's rigid outline, as they mocked my recognition of them with soundless semblances of mirth. They began to wind their arms about me in fierce embraces of burning and supernatural life. Gradually the contact froze. They bound me in an icy prison. Their hold relaxed. These creatures of my heart were restless. The horribly familiar company began to dance at intervals in and out a ring of white gigantic bedsteads, set on end like tombstones, each of which framed a huge and fearful travesty of the sad set face that was all the while seeking vainly a pitiless stranger's care. They vanished. My heart went home. The dear place was desolate. No echo of its many voices on the threshold or stair. My footsteps made no sound as I went rapidly up to a well-known room. Here I besought the mirror for the reassurance of my own reflection. It denied me human portraiture and threw back cold glare. As I opened mechanically a treasured book, I noticed the leaves were blank, not even blurred by spot or line; and then I shivered—it was deadly cold. The fire that but an hour or two ago it seemed I had forsaken for the winter twilight, glowed with slow derision at my efforts to rekindle heat. My hands plunged savagely into its red embers, but I drew them out quickly, unscathed and clean. The things by which I had touched life were nothing. Here, as I called the dearest names, their echoes came back again with the sound of an unlearned language. I did not recognize, and yet I framed them. What was had never been!

My spirit summoned the being who claimed mine. He came, stretching out arms of deathless welcome. As he reached me my heart took flight. I called aloud to it, but my cries were lost in awful laughter that broke to my bewildered fancy from the hideously familiar shapes which had returned and now encircled the grand form of him I loved. But I had never known him. I beat my breast to wake there the wonted pain of tingling joy. I called past experience with unavailing importunity to bear witness the man was wildly dear to me. He was not. He left me with bent head a stranger, whom I would not if I could recall.

For one brief second, reason found me. I struggled to shake off the phantoms of despair. I tried to grasp while it yet lingered the teaching of this never-to-be-forgotten front of death. The homeless house with its indefensible bow window stood out from beneath the prison walls again. What had this to do with it? I questioned. And the answer it had evoked replied, "Not the desolation of something lost, but of something that had never been."

The half-clad girl of the wretched picture shop came into view with waxen hands and senseless symbolism. I had grown calmer, but her doll-like lips hissed out the same half-meaningless but pregnant words. Then the nights of a short life when I could pray, years back in magical childhood, sought me. They found me past them—without the power.

Truly the body had been for me the manifestation of the thing called soul. Here was my embodiment bereft. My face was stiff with drying tears. Sickly I longed to beg of an unknown God a miracle. Would He but touch the passive body and breathe into it the breath even of transitory life.

I craved but a fleeting proof of its ever possible existence. For to me it was not, would never be, and had never been.

The partially relinquished horror was renewing dominance. Speech of any incoherence or futility would have brought mental power of resistance. My mind was fast losing landmarks amid the continued quiet of the living and the awful stillness of the dead. There was no sound, even of savage guidance, I should not then have welcomed with glad response.

"The realm of silence," says one of the world's great teachers,[1] "is large enough beyond the grave."

I seemed to have passed life's portal, and my soul's small strength was beating back the noiseless gate. In my extremity, I cried, "O God! for man's most bloody war shout, or Thy whisper!" It was useless. Not one dweller

in the crowded tenements broke his slumber or relaxed his labour in answer to the involuntary prayer.

And may the "Day of Account[2] of Words" take note of this! Then, says the old fable, shall the soul of the departed be weighed against an image of truth. I tried to construct in imagination the form of the dumb deity who should bear down the balances for me. Soundlessness was turning fear to madness. I could neither quit nor longer bear company the grim presence in that room. But the supreme moment was very near.

Long since, the four low candles had burned out, and now the lamp was struggling fitfully to keep alight. The flame could last but a few moments. I saw it, and did not face the possibility of darkness. The sleeping girl, I concluded rapidly, had used all available weapons of defiant light.

As yet, since my entrance, I had hardly stirred, steadily supporting the burden on my breast. Now, without remembrance of it, I started up to escape. The violent suddenness of the action woke my companion. She staggered blindly to her feet and confronted me as I gained the door.

Scarcely able to stand, and dashing the dimness from her eyes, she clutched a corner of the drawers behind her for support. Her head thrown back, and her dark hair hanging round it, crowned a grandly tragic form. This was no poor pleader, and I was unarmed for fight. She seized my throbbing arm and cried in a whisper, low and hoarse, but strongly audible: "For God's sake, stay here with me."

My lips moved vainly. I shook my head.

"For God in heaven's sake"—she repeated, swaying, and turning her burning, reddened eyes on mine— "don't leave me now."

I stood irresolute, half stunned. Stepping back, she stooped and began piecing together the dismembered letter on the bed. A mute protest arrested her from a cold sister's face. She swept the action from her, crying, "No!" and bending forward suddenly, gripped me with fierce force.

"Here! Here!" she prayed, dragging me passionately back into the room.

The piteous need and wild entreaty—no, the vision of dire anguish—was breaking my purpose of flight. A

[1] one of the world's great teachers   George Eliot, nom de plume of Mary Anne Evans (1819–80), English novelist and woman of letters. The quotation comes from a letter to Georgiana Burne-Jones.

[2] Day of Account   See 1 Corinthians 3.13.

fragrance that was to haunt me stole between us. The poor little violets put in their plea. I moved to stay. Then a smile—the splendour of it may never be reached again—touched her pale lips and broke through them, transforming, with divine radiance, her young and blurred and never-to-be-forgotten face. It wavered, or was it the last uncertain flicker of the lamp that made me fancy it? The exquisite moment was barely over when darkness came. Then light indeed forsook me. Almost ignorant of my own intention, I resisted the now trembling figure, indistinguishable in the gloom, but it still clung. I thrust it off me with unnatural vigour.

She fell heavily to the ground. Without a pause of thought I stumbled down the horrible unlighted stairs. A few steps before I reached the bottom my foot struck a splint off the thin edge of one of the rotten treads. I slipped, and heard a door above open and then shut. No other sound. At length I was at the door. It was ajar. I opened it and looked out. Since I passed through it first the place had become quite deserted. The inhabitants were, I suppose, all occupied elsewhere at such an hour on their holiday night. The lamps, if there were any, had not been lit. The outlook was dense blackness. Here too the hideous dark pursued me and silence held its sway. Even the children were screaming in more enticing haunts of gaudy squalor. Some, whose good angels perhaps had not forgotten them, had put themselves to sleep. Not many hours ago their shrieks were deafening. Were these too in conspiracy against me? I remembered vaguely hustling some of them with unmeant harshness in my hurried progress from the church. Dumb the whole place seemed, and it was, but for the dim stars aloft quite dark. I dared not venture across the threshold, bound by pitiable cowardice to the spot. Alas for the unconscious girl upstairs. A murmur from within the house might have sent me back to her. Certainly it would have sent me, rather than forth into the empty street. The faintest indication of humanity had recalled me. I waited the summons of a sound. It came.

But from the deserted, yet not so shamefully deserted, street. A man staggering home by aid of friendly railings, set up a drunken song. At the first note I rushed towards him, pushing past him in wild departure, and on till I reached the noisome and flaring thoroughfare,

a haven where sweet safety smiled. Here I breathed joy, and sped away without memory of the two lifeless beings lying alone in that shrouded chamber of desolation, and with no instinct to return.

My sole impulse was flight, and the way, unmarked in the earlier evening, was unknown. It took me some minutes to find a cab, but the incongruous vehicle, rudely dispersing the haggling traders in the roadway, came at last, and carried me from the distorted crowd of faces and the claims of pity to peace.

I lay back shivering, and the wind crept through the rattling glass in front of me. I did not note the incalculable turnings that took me home.

My account of the night's adventure was abridged and unsensational. I was pressed neither for detail nor comment, but accorded a somewhat humorous welcome which bade me say farewell to dying horror, and even let me mount boldly to the once death-haunted room.

Upon its threshold I stood and looked in, half believing possible the greeting pictured there under the dead girl's influence, and I could not enter. Again I fled, this time to kindly light, and heard my brothers laughing noisily with a friend in the bright hall.

A waltz struck up in the room above as I reached them. I joined the impromptu dance, and whirled the remainder of that evening gladly away.

Physically wearied, I slept. My slumber had no break in it. I woke only to the exquisite joys of morning, and lay watching the early shadows creep into the room. Presently the sun rose. His first smile greeted me from the glass before my bed. I sprang up disdainful of that majestic reflection, and flung the window wide to meet him face to face. His splendour fell too on one who had trusted me, but I forgot it. Not many days later the same sunlight that turned my life to laughter shone on the saddest scene of mortal ending, and, for one I had forsaken, lit the ways of death. I never dreamed it might. For the next morning the tragedy of the past night was a distant one, no longer intolerable.

At twelve o'clock, conscience suggested a search. I acquiesced, but did not move. At half-past, it insisted on one, and I obeyed. I set forth with a determination of success and no clue to promise it. At four o'clock, I admitted the task hopeless and abandoned it. Duty could ask no more of me, I decided, not wholly dissatisfied that failure forbade more difficult demands. As I passed it on my way home, some dramatic instinct impelled me to re-enter the unsightly church.

I must almost have expected to see the same prostrate figure, for my eyes instantly sought the corner it had occupied. The winter twilight showed it empty. A service was about to begin. One little lad in violet skirt and goffered[1] linen was struggling to light the benediction tapers, and a troop of schoolchildren pushed past me as I stood facing the altar and blocking their way. A grey-clad sister of mercy was arresting each tiny figure, bidding it pause beside me, and with two firm hands on either shoulder, compelling a ludicrous curtsey, and at the same time whispering the injunction to each hurried little personage—"always make a reverence to the altar." "Ada, come back!" and behold another unwilling bob! Perhaps the good woman saw her Master's face behind the tinsel trappings and flaring lights. But she forgot His words. The saying to these little ones that has rung through centuries commanded liberty and not allegiance. I stood aside till they had shuffled into seats, and finally kneeling stayed till the brief spectacle of the afternoon was over.

Towards its close I looked away from the mumbling priest, whose attention, divided between inconvenient millinery and the holiest mysteries, was distracting mine.

Two girls holding each other's hands came in and stood in deep shadow behind the farthest rows of high-backed chairs by the door. The younger rolled her head from side to side; her shifting eyes and ceaseless imbecile grimaces chilled my blood. The other, who stood praying, turned suddenly (the place but for the flaring altar lights was dark) and kissed the dreadful creature by her side. I shuddered, and yet her face wore no look of loathing nor of pity. The expression was a divine one of habitual love.

She wiped the idiot's lips and stroked the shaking hand in hers, to quiet the sad hysterical caresses she would not check. It was a page of gospel which the old man with his back to it might never read. A sublime and ghastly scene.

Up in the little gallery the grey-habited nuns were singing a long Latin hymn of many verses, with the refrain "Oh! Sacred Heart!" I buried my face till the last vibrating chord of the accompaniment was struck. The organist ventured a plagal cadence.[2] It evoked no "amen." I whispered one, and an accidentally touched note shrieked disapproval. I repeated it. Then I spit upon the bloodless cheek of duty, and renewed my quest. This time it was for the satisfaction of my own tingling soul.

I retook my unknown way. The streets were almost empty and thinly strewn with snow. It was still falling. I shrank from marring the spotless page that seemed outspread to challenge and exhibit the defiling print of man. The quiet of the muffled streets soothed me. The neighbourhood seemed lulled into unwonted rest.

Black little figures lurched out of the white alleys in twos and threes. But their childish utterances sounded less shrill than usual, and sooner died away.

Now in desperate earnest I spared neither myself nor the incredulous and dishevelled people whose aid I sought.

Fate deals honestly with all. She will not compromise though she may delay. Hunger and weariness at length sent me home, with an assortment of embellished negatives ringing in my failing ears.

I had almost forgotten my strange experience, when, some months afterwards, in late spring, the wraith of that winter meeting appeared to me. It was past six o'clock, and I had reached, ignorant of the ill-chosen hour, a notorious thoroughfare in the western part of this glorious and guilty city. The place presented to my unfamiliar eyes a remarkable sight. Brilliantly lit windows, exhibiting dazzling wares, threw into prominence the human mart.

This was thronged. I pressed into the crowd. Its steady and opposite progress neither repelled nor sanctioned my admittance. However, I had determined on a purchase, and was not to be baulked by the unforeseen. I made it, and stood for a moment at the shop door preparing to break again through the rapidly thickening throng.

Up and down, decked in frigid allurement, paced the insatiate daughters of an everlasting king. What fair

---

[1] *goffered* Frilly.

[2] *plagal cadence* Type of chord progression, alternatively called the amen cadence.

messengers, with streaming eyes and impotently craving arms, did they send afar off ere they thus "increased their perfumes and debased themselves even unto hell"?[1] This was my question. I asked not who forsook them, speaking in farewell the "hideous English of their fate."[2]

I watched coldly, yet not inapprehensive of a certain grandeur in the scene. It was Virtue's very splendid Dance of Death.

A sickening confusion of odours assailed my senses; each essence a vile enticement, outraging Nature by a perversion of her own pure spell.

A timidly protesting fragrance stole strangely by. I started at its approach. It summoned a stinging memory. I stepped forward to escape it, but stopped, confronted by the being who had shared, by the flickering lamplight and in the presence of that silent witness, the poor little violet's prayer.

The man beside her was decorated with a bunch of sister flowers to those which had taken part against him, months ago, in vain. He could have borne no better badge of victory. He was looking at some extravagant trifle in the window next the entry I had just crossed. They spoke, comparing it with a silver case he turned over in his hand. In the centre I noticed a tiny enamelled shield. The detail seemed familiar, but beyond identity. They entered the shop. I stood motionless, challenging memory, till it produced from some dim corner of my brain a hoarded "No."

The device now headed a poor strip of paper on a dead girl's bed. I saw a figure set by death, facing starvation, and with ruin in torn fragments in her hand. But what place in the scene had I? A brief discussion next me made swift answer.

They were once more beside me. The man was speaking; his companion raised her face; I recognized its outline—its true aspect I shall not know. Four months since it wore the mask of sorrow, it was now but one of the pages of man's immortal book. I was conscious of the matchless motions which in the dim church had first attracted me.

She was clothed, save for a large scarf of vehemently brilliant crimson, entirely in dull vermilion. The two shades might serve as symbols of divine and earthly passion. Yet does one ask the martyr's colour, you name it "Red" (and briefly thus her garment): no distinctive hue. The murderer and the prelate too may wear such robes of office. Both are empowered to bless and ban.

My mood was reckless. I held my hands out, craving mercy. It was my bitter lot to beg. My warring nature became unanimously suppliant, heedless of the debt this soul might owe me—of the throes to which I left it, and of the discreditable marks of mine it bore. Failure to exact regard I did not entertain. I waited, with exhaustless fortitude, the response to my appeal. Whence it came I know not. The man and woman met my gaze with a void incorporate stare. The two faces were merged into one avenging visage—so it seemed. I was excited. As they turned towards the carriage waiting them, I heard a laugh, mounting to a cry. It rang me to an outraged Temple. Sabbath bells peal sweeter calls, as once this might have done.

I knew my part then in the despoiled body, with its soul's tapers long blown out.

Wheels hastened to assail that sound, but it clanged on. Did it proceed from some defeated angel? or the woman's mouth? or mine? God knows!

—1894

---

[1] *"increased ... hell"* See Isaiah 57.9.

[2] *"hideous ... fate"* From Chapter 37 of George Meredith's *The Egoist* (1879).

READING POETRY

WHAT IS A POEM?

Most of us know what a poem is when we see one. Still, even poets find it difficult to define a poem, or poetry. In a lecture on "The Name and Nature of Poetry" (1933), the English poet A.E. Housman stated that he could "no more define poetry than a terrier can define a rat"; however, he added, "we both recognize the object by the symptoms which it provokes in us." Housman knew he was in the presence of poetry if he experienced a shiver down the spine, or "a constriction of the throat and a precipitation of water to the eyes." Implicit in Housman's response is a recognition that we have to go beyond mere formal characteristics—stanzas, rhymes, rhythms—if we want to know what poetry is, or why it differs from prose. Poetry both represents and *creates* emotions in a highly condensed way. Therefore, any definition of the genre needs to consider, as much as possible, the impact of poetry on us as readers or listeners.

Worth consideration too is the role of the listener or reader not only as passive recipient of a poem, but also as an active participant in its performance. Poetry is among other things the locus for a communicative exchange. A section below deals with the sub-genre of performance poetry, but in a very real sense all poetry is subject to performance. Poems are to be read aloud as well as on the page, and both in sensing meaning and in expressing sound the reader plays a vital role in bringing a poem to life, no matter how long dead its author may be; as W.H. Auden wrote memorably of his fellow poet W.B. Yeats, "the words of a dead man / Are modified in the guts of the living."

For some readers, poetry is, in William Wordsworth's phrase, "the breath and finer spirit of all knowledge" ("Preface" to the *Lyrical Ballads*). They look to poetry for insights into the nature of human experience, and expect elevated thought in carefully-wrought language. In contrast, other readers distrust poetry that seems moralistic or didactic. "We hate poetry that has a palpable design upon us," wrote John Keats to his friend J.H. Reynolds; rather, poetry should be "great & unobtrusive, a thing which enters into one's soul, and does not startle it or amaze it with itself but with its subject." The American poet Archibald MacLeish took Keats's idea a step further: in his poem "Ars Poetica" he suggested that "A poem should not mean / But be." MacLeish was not suggesting that a poem should lack meaning, but rather that meaning should inhere in the poem's expressive and sensuous qualities, not in some explicit statement or versified idea.

Whatever we look for in a poem, the infinitude of forms, styles, and subjects that make up the body of literature we call "poetry" is, in the end, impossible to capture in a definition that would satisfy all readers. All we can do, perhaps, is to agree that a poem is a discourse that is characterized by a heightened attention to language, form, and rhythm, by an expressiveness that works through figurative rather than literal modes, and by a capacity to stimulate our imagination and arouse our feelings.

THE LANGUAGE OF POETRY

To speak of "the language of poetry" implies that poets make use of a vocabulary that is somehow different from the language of everyday life. In fact, all language has the capacity to be "poetic," if by poetry we understand a use of language to which some special importance is attached. The ritualistic utterances of religious ceremonies sometimes have this force; so do the skipping rhymes of children in the schoolyard. We can distinguish such uses of language from the kind of writing we find in, say, a computer user's manual: the author of the manual can describe a given function in a variety of ways, whereas the magic of the skipping rhyme can be invoked only by getting the right words in the right order. So with the poet: he or she chooses particular words in a particular order; the *way* the poet speaks is as important to our understanding as what is said. This doesn't mean that an instruction manual couldn't have poetic qualities—indeed, modern poets have created "found" poems from even less likely materials—but it does mean that in poetry there is an intimate relation amongst language, form, and meaning, and that the writer deliberately structures and manipulates language to achieve very particular ends.

THE BEST WORDS IN THE BEST ORDER

Wordsworth provides us with a useful example of the way that poetry can invest quite ordinary words with a high emotional charge:

> No motion has she now, no force,
> She neither hears nor sees;
> Rolled round in earth's diurnal course
> With rocks, and stones, and trees.

To paraphrase the content of this stanza from "A Slumber Did My Spirit Seal," "she" is dead and buried. But the language and structures used here give this prosaic idea great impact. For example, the regular iambic meter of the two last lines conveys something of the inexorable motion of the earth and of Lucy embedded in it; the monosyllabic last line is a grim reminder of her oneness with objects in nature; the repeated negatives in the first two lines drive home the irreparable destructiveness of death; the alliteration in the third and fourth lines gives a tangible suggestion of roundness, circularity, repetition in terms of the earth's shape and motion, suggesting a cycle in which death is perhaps followed by renewal. Even the unusual word "diurnal" (which would not have seemed so unusual to Wordsworth's readers) seems "right" in this context; it lends more weight to the notion of the earth's perpetual movement than its mundane synonym "daily" (which, besides, would not scan here). It is difficult to imagine a change of any kind to these lines; they exemplify another attempted definition of poetry, this time by Wordsworth's friend Samuel Taylor Coleridge: "the best words in the best order" (*Table Talk*, 1827).

POETIC DICTION AND THE ELEVATED STYLE

Wordsworth's diction in the "Lucy" poem cited above is a model of clarity; he has chosen language that, in its simplicity and bluntness, conveys the strength of the speaker's feelings far more strongly than an elaborate description of grief in more conventionally "poetic" language might have done. Wordsworth, disturbed by what he felt was a deadness and artificiality in the poetry of his day, sought to "choose incidents and situations from common life" and to describe them in "a selection of language really used by men" ("Preface" to *Lyrical Ballads*). His plan might seem an implicit reproach of the "raised" style, the elevated diction of epic poetry we associate with John Milton's *Paradise Lost*:

> Anon out of the earth a fabric huge
> Rose like an exhalation, with the sound
> Of dulcet symphonies and voices sweet,

Built like a temple, where pilasters round
Were set, and Doric pillars overlaid
With golden architrave; nor did there want
Cornice or frieze, with bossy sculptures graven;
The roof was fretted gold.

(*Paradise Lost* I.710–17)

At first glance this passage, with its Latinate vocabulary and convoluted syntax, might seem guilty of inflated language and pretentiousness. However, Milton's description of the devils' palace in Hell deliberately seeks to distance us from its subject in order to emphasize the scale and sublimity of the spectacle, far removed from ordinary human experience. In other words, language and style in *Paradise Lost* are well adapted to suit a particular purpose, just as they are in "A Slumber Did My Spirit Seal," though on a wholly different scale. Wordsworth criticized the poetry of his day, not because of its elevation, but because the raised style was too often out of touch with its subject; in his view, the words did not bear any significant relation to the "truths" they were attempting to depict.

"PLAIN" LANGUAGE IN POETRY

Since Wordsworth's time, writers have been conscious of a need to narrow the apparent gap between "poetic" language and the language of everyday life. In much of the poetry of the past century, especially free verse, we can observe a growing approximation to speech—even to conversation—in the diction and rhythms of poetry. This may have something to do with the changed role of the poet, who today has discarded the mantle of teacher or prophet that was assumed by poets of earlier times, and who is ready to admit all fields of experience and endeavor as appropriate for poetry. The modern poet looks squarely at life, and can often find a provoking beauty in even the meanest of objects.

We should not assume, however, that a greater concern with the "ordinary," with simplicity, naturalness, and clarity, means a reduction in complexity or suggestiveness. A piece such as Stevie Smith's "Mother, Among the Dustbins," for all the casual and playful domesticity of some of its lines, skilfully evokes a range of emotions and sense impressions defying simple paraphrase.

IMAGERY, SYMBOLISM, AND FIGURES OF SPEECH

The language of poetry is grounded in the objects and phenomena that create sensory impressions. Sometimes the poet renders these impressions quite literally, in a series of *images* that seek to recreate a scene in the reader's mind:

Only a man harrowing clods
In a slow silent walk
With an old horse that stumbles and nods
Half asleep as they stalk.

Only thin smoke without flame
From the heaps of couch-grass;
Yet this will go onward the same
Though Dynasties pass.

Yonder a maid and her wight
Come whispering by:
War's annals will cloud into night
Ere their story die.
(Thomas Hardy, "In Time of 'The Breaking of Nations'")

Here, the objects of everyday life are re-created with sensory details designed to evoke in us the sensations or responses felt by the speaker viewing the scene. At the same time, the writer invests the objects with such significance that the poem's meaning extends beyond the literal to the symbolic: that is, the images come to stand for something much larger than the objects they represent. Hardy's poem moves from the presentation of stark images of rural life to a sense of their timelessness. By the last stanza we see the ploughman, the burning grass, and the maid and her companion as symbols of recurring human actions and motives that defy the struggles and conflicts of history.

IMAGISM

The juxtaposition of clear, forceful images is associated particularly with the Imagist movement that flourished at the beginning of the twentieth century. Its chief representatives (in their early work) were the American poets H.D. and Ezra Pound, who defined an image as "that which represents an intellectual and emotional complex in an instant of time." Pound's two-line poem "In a Station of the Metro" provides a good example of the Imagists' goal of representing emotions or impressions through the use of concentrated images:

The apparition of these faces in the crowd,
Petals on a wet, black bough.

As in a Japanese *haiku,* a form that strongly influenced the Imagists, the poem uses sharp, clear, concrete details to evoke both a sensory impression and the emotion or the atmosphere of the scene. Though the Imagist movement itself lasted only a short time (from about 1912 to 1917), it had a far-reaching influence on modern poets such as T. S. Eliot, and William Carlos Williams.

FIGURES OF SPEECH

Imagery often works together with figurative expression to extend and deepen the meaning or impact of a poem. "Figurative" language means language that is metaphorical, not literal or referential. Through "figures of speech" such as metaphor and simile, metonymy, synecdoche, and personification, the writer may alter the ordinary, denotative meanings of words in order to convey greater force and vividness to ideas or impressions, often by showing likenesses between unlike things.

With *simile,* the poet makes an explicit comparison between the subject (called the *tenor*) and another object or idea (known as the *vehicle*), using "as" or "like":

It is a beauteous evening, calm and free,
The holy time is quiet as a Nun
Breathless with adoration. ...

In this opening to a sonnet, Wordsworth uses a visual image of a nun in devout prayer to convey in concrete terms the less tangible idea of evening as a "holy time." The comparison also introduces an emotional dimension, conveying something of the feeling that the scene induces in the poet. The simile can thus illuminate and expand meaning in a compact way. The poet may also extend the simile to elaborate at length on any points of likeness.

In *metaphor*, the comparison between tenor and vehicle is implied: connectives such as "like" are omitted, and a kind of identity is created between the subject and the term with which it is being compared. Thus in John Donne's "The Good-Morrow," a lover asserts the endless joy that he and his beloved find in each other:

> My face in thine eye, thine in mine appears,
> And true plain hearts do in the faces rest;
> Where can we find two better hemispheres,
> Without sharp north, without declining west?

Here the lovers are transformed into "hemispheres," each of them a half of the world not subject to the usual natural phenomena of wintry cold ("sharp north") or the coming of night ("declining west"). Thus, they form a perfect world in balance, in which the normal processes of decay or decline have been arrested. Donne renders the abstract idea of a love that defies change in pictorial and physical terms, making it more real and accessible to us. The images here are all the more arresting for the degree of concentration involved; it is not merely the absence of "like" or "as" that gives the metaphor such direct power, but the fusion of distinct images and emotions into a new idea.

Personification is the figure of speech in which the writer endows abstract ideas, inanimate objects, or animals with human characteristics. In other words, it is a type of implied metaphorical comparison in which aspects of a non-human subject are compared to the feelings, appearance, or actions of a human being. In the second stanza of his ode "To Autumn," Keats personifies the concept of autumnal harvesting in the form of a woman, "sitting careless on a granary floor, / Thy hair soft-lifted by the winnowing wind." Personification may also help to create a mood, as when Thomas Gray attributes human feelings to a hooting owl in "Elegy Written in a Country Church-Yard"; using such words as "moping" and "complain," Gray invests the bird's cries with the quality of human melancholy:

> … from yonder ivy-mantled tow'r
> The moping owl does to the moon complain
> Of such, as wand'ring near her secret bow'r,
> Molest her ancient solitary reign.

In his book *Modern Painters* (1856), the English critic John Ruskin criticized such attribution of human feelings to objects in nature. Calling this device the "pathetic fallacy," he objected to what he saw as an irrational distortion of reality, producing "a falseness in all our impressions of external things." Modern criticism, with a distrust of any notions of an objective "reality," tends to use Ruskin's term as a neutral label simply to describe instances of extended personification of natural objects.

Apostrophe, which is closely related to personification, has the speaker directly addressing a non-human object or idea as if it were a sentient human listener. Blake's "The Sick Rose," Shelley's "Ode to the West Wind" and his ode "To a Sky-Lark" all employ apostrophe, personifying the object addressed. Keats's "Ode on a Grecian Urn" begins by apostrophizing the urn ("Thou still unravish'd bride of quietness"), then addresses it in a series of questions and reflections through which the speaker attempts to unravel the urn's mysteries.

Apostrophe also appeals to or addresses a person who is absent or dead. W. H. Auden's lament "In Memory of W. B. Yeats" apostrophizes both the earth in which Yeats is to be buried ("Earth, receive an honoured guest") and the dead poet himself ("Follow, poet, follow right / To the bottom of the night …"). Religious prayers offer an illustration of the usefulness of apostrophe, since they are direct appeals from an earth-bound supplicant to an invisible god. The suggestion of strong emotion associated with such appeals is a common feature of apostrophe in poetry also, especially poetry with a religious theme, like Donne's "Holy Sonnets" (e.g., "Batter My Heart, Three-Personed God").

Metonymy and *synecdoche* are two closely related figures of speech that further illustrate the power of metaphorical language to convey meaning more intensely and vividly than is possible with prosaic statement. *Metonymy* (from the Greek, meaning "change of name") involves referring to an object or concept by substituting the name of another object or concept with which it is usually associated: for example, we might speak of "the Crown" when we mean the monarch, or describe the U.S. executive branch as "the White House." When the writer uses only part of something to signify the whole, or an individual to represent a class, we have an instance of *synecdoche*. T. S. Eliot provides an example in "The Love Song of J. Alfred Prufrock" when a crab is described as "a pair of ragged claws." Similarly, synecdoche is present in Milton's contemptous term "blind mouths" to describe the "corrupted clergy" he attacks in "Lycidas."

Dylan Thomas employs both metonymy and synecdoche in his poem "The Hand That Signed the Paper":

The hand that signed the paper felled a city;
Five sovereign fingers taxed the breath,
Doubled the globe of dead and halved a country;
These five kings did a king to death.

The mighty hand leads to a sloping shoulder,
The finger joints are cramped with chalk;
A goose's quill has put an end to murder
That put an end to talk.

The hand that signed the treaty bred a fever,
And famine grew, and locusts came;
Great is the hand that holds dominion over
Man by a scribbled name.

The five kings count the dead but do not soften
The crusted wound nor stroke the brow;
A hand rules pity as a hand rules heaven;
Hands have no tears to flow.

The "hand" of the poem is evidently a synecdoche for a great king who enters into treaties with friends and foes to wage wars, conquer kingdoms, and extend his personal power—all at the expense of his suffering subjects. The "goose quill" of the second stanza is a metonymy, standing for the pen used to sign the treaty or the death warrant that brings the war to an end.

Thomas's poem is an excellent example of the power of figurative language, which, by its vividness and concentrated force, can add layers of meaning to a poem, make abstract ideas concrete, and intensify the poem's emotional impact.

THE POEM AS PERFORMANCE: WRITER AND PERSON

Poetry is always dramatic. Sometimes the drama is explicit, as in Robert Browning's monologues, in which we hear the voice of a participant in a dialogue; in "My Last Duchess" we are present as the Duke reflects on the portrait of his late wife for the benefit of a visitor who has come to negotiate on behalf of the woman who is to become the Duke's next wife. Or we listen with amusement and pity as the dying Bishop addresses his venal and unsympathetic sons and tries to bargain with them for a fine burial ("The Bishop Orders His Tomb at St. Praxed's"). In such poems, the notion of a speaking voice is paramount: the speaker is a personage in a play, and the poem a means of conveying plot and character.

Sometimes the drama is less apparent, and takes the form of a plea, or a compliment, or an argument addressed to a silent listener. In Donne's "The Flea" we can infer from the poem the situation that has called it forth: a lover's advances are being rejected by his beloved, and his poem is an argument intended to overcome her reluctance by means of wit and logic. We can see a similar example in Marvell's "To His Coy Mistress": here the very shape of the poem, its three-paragraph structure, corresponds to the stages of the speaker's argument as he presents an apparently irrefutable line of reasoning. Much love poetry has this kind of background as its inspiration; the yearnings or lamentations of the lover are part of an imagined scene, not merely versified reflections about an abstraction called "love."

Meditative or reflective poetry can be dramatic too. Donne's "Holy Sonnets" are pleas from a tormented soul struggling to find its god; Tennyson's "In Memoriam" follows the agonized workings of a mind tracing a path from grief and anger to acceptance and renewed hope.

We should never assume that the speaker, the "I" of the poem, is simply a voice for the writer's own views. The speaker in W. H. Auden's "To an Unknown Citizen," presenting a summary of the dead citizen's life, appears to be an official spokesperson for the society which the citizen served ("Our report on his union"; "Our researchers ..." etc.). The speaker's words are laudatory, yet we perceive immediately that Auden's own views of this society are anything but approving. The speaker seems satisfied with the highly regimented nature of his society, one in which every aspect of the individual's life is under scrutiny and subject to correction. The only things necessary to the happiness of the "Modern Man," it seems, are "A phonograph, a radio, a car, and a frigidaire." The tone here is subtly ironic, an irony created by the gap between the imagined speaker's perception and the real feelings of the writer.

PERFORMANCE POETRY

Poetry began as an oral art, passed on in the form of chants, myths, ballads, and legends recited to an audience of listeners rather than readers. Even today, the dramatic qualities of a poem may extend beyond written text. "Performance poets" combine poetry and stagecraft in presenting their work to live audiences. Dramatic uses of voice, rhythm, body movement, music, and sometimes other visual effects make the "text" of the poem multi-dimensional. For example, Edith Sitwell's poem-sequence *Façade* (1922) was originally set to music: Sitwell read from behind a screen, while a live orchestra played. This performance was designed to enhance the verbal and rhythmic qualities of her poetry:

Beneath the flat and paper sky
The sun, a demon's eye
Glowed through the air, that mask of glass;
All wand'ring sounds that pass

Seemed out of tune, as if the light
Were fiddle-strings pulled tight.
The market-square with spire and bell
Clanged out the hour in Hell.
        (from *Façade*)

By performing their poetry, writers can also convey cultural values and traditions. The cultural aspect of performance is central to Black poetry, which originates in a highly oral tradition of folklore and storytelling. From its roots in Africa, this oral tradition has been manifested in the songs and stories of slaves, in spirituals, in the jazz rhythms of the Twenties and the Thirties and in the rebelliousness of reggae and of rap. Even when it remains "on the page," much Black poetry written in the oral tradition has a compelling rhythmic quality. The lines below from Linton Kwesi Johnson's "Mi Revalueshanary Fren," for example, blur the line between spoken poetry and song. Johnson often performs his "dub poetry" against reggae or hip-hop musical backings.

yes, people powa jus a showa evry howa
an evrybady claim dem democratic
but some a wolf an some a sheep
an dat is problematic

The chorus of Johnson's poems, with its constant repetitions, digs deeply into the roots of African song and chant. Its performance qualities become clearer when the poem is read aloud:

Husak
e ad to go
Honnicka
e ad to go
Chowcheskhu
e ad to go
Just like apartied
will av to go

To perform a poem is one way to see and hear poetry as multi-dimensional, cultural, historical, and often also political. Performance is also another way to discover how poetic "meaning" can be constructed in the dynamic relation between speaker and listener.

TONE: THE SPEAKER'S ATTITUDE

In understanding poetry, it is helpful to imagine a poem as having a "voice." The voice may be close to the poet's own, or that of an imagined character, a *persona* adopted by the poet. The tone of the voice will reveal the speaker's attitude to the subject, thus helping to shape our understanding and response. In speech we can indicate our feelings by raising or lowering our voices, and we can accompany words with physical actions. In writing, we must try to convey the tonal inflections of the speaking voice through devices of language and rhythm, through imagery and figures of speech, and through allusions and contrasts.

THE IRONIC TONE

Housman's poem "Terence, This Is Stupid Stuff" offers a useful example of ways in which manipulating tone can reinforce meaning. When Housman, presenting himself in the poem as "Terence," imagines himself to be criticized for writing gloomy poems, his response to his critics takes the form of an ironic alternative: perhaps they should stick to drinking ale:

> Oh, many a peer of England brews
> Livelier liquor than the Muse,
> And malt does more than Milton can
> To justify God's ways to man.

The tone here is one of heavy scorn. The speaker is impatient with those who refuse to look at the realities of life and death, and who prefer to take refuge in simple-minded pleasure. The ludicrous comparisons, first between the brewers who have been made peers of England and the classical Muse of poetry, then between malt and Milton, create a sense of disproportion and ironic tension; the explicit allusion to *Paradise Lost* ("To justify God's ways to man") helps to drive home the poet's bitter recognition that his auditors are part of that fallen world depicted by Milton, yet unable or unwilling to acknowledge their harsh condition. The three couplets that follow offer a series of contrasts: in each case, the first line sets up a pleasant expectation and the second dashes it with a blunt reminder of reality:

> Ale, man, ale's the stuff to drink
> For fellows whom it hurts to think:
> Look into the pewter pot
> To see the world as the world's not.
> And faith, 'tis pleasant till 'tis past:
> The mischief is that 'twill not last.

These are all jabs at the "sterling lads" who would prefer to lie in "lovely muck" and not think about the way the world is. Housman's sardonic advice is all the more pointed for its sharp and ironic tone.

POETIC FORMS

In poetry, language is intimately related to form, which is the structuring of words within identifiable patterns. In prose we speak of phrases, sentences, and paragraphs; in poetry, we identify structures by lines, stanzas, or complete forms such as the sonnet or the ode (though poetry in complete or blank verse has paragraphs of variable length, not formal stanzas: see below).

Rightly handled, the form enhances expression and meaning, just as a frame can define and enhance a painting or photograph. Unlike the photo frame, however, form in poetry is an integral part of the whole work. At one end of the scale, the term "form" may describe the *epic,* the lengthy narrative governed by such conventions as division into books, a lofty style, and the interplay between human and supernatural characters. At the other end lies the *epigram*, a witty and pointed saying whose distinguishing characteristic is its brevity, as in Alexander Pope's famous couplet,

> I am his Highness' dog at Kew;
> Pray tell me sir, whose dog are you?

Between the epic and the epigram lie many other poetic forms, such as the sonnet, the ballad, or the ode. "Form" may also describe stanzaic patterns like *couplets* and *quatrains*.

"FIXED FORM" POEMS

The best-known poetic form is probably the sonnet, the fourteen-line poem inherited from Italy (the word itself is from the Italian *sonetto*, little song or sound). Within those fourteen lines, whether the poet chooses the "Petrarchan" rhyme scheme or the "English" form (see below in the section on "Rhyme"), the challenge is to develop an idea or situation that must find its statement and its resolution within the strict confines of the sonnet frame. Typically, there is an initial idea, description, or statement of feeling, followed by a "turn" in the thought that takes the reader by surprise, or that casts the situation in an unexpected light. Thus in Sonnet 130, "My Mistress' Eyes Are Nothing Like the Sun," William Shakespeare spends the first three quatrains apparently disparaging his lover in a series of unfavorable comparisons—"If snow be white, why then her breasts are dun"—but in the closing couplet his point becomes clear:

> And yet, by heaven, I think my love as rare
> As any she belied with false compare.

In other words, the speaker's disparaging comparisons have really been parodies of sentimental clichés which falsify reality; his mistress has no need of the exaggerations or distortions of conventional love poetry.

Other foreign forms borrowed and adapted by English-language poets include the *ghazal* and the *pantoum*. The *ghazal*, strongly associated with classical Urdu literature, originated in Persia and Arabia and was brought to the Indian subcontinent in the twelfth century. It consists of a series of couplets held together by a refrain, a simple rhyme scheme (a/a, b/a, c/a, d/a…), and a common rhythm, but only loosely related in theme or subject. Some English-language practitioners of the form have captured the epigrammatic quality of the ghazal, but most do not adhere to the strict pattern of the classical form.

The *pantoum*, based on a Malaysian form, was imported into English poetry via the work of nineteenth-century French poets. Typically it presents a series of quatrains rhyming *abab*, linked by a pattern of repetition in which the second and fourth lines of a quatrain become the first and third lines of the stanza that follows. In the poem's final stanza, the pattern is reversed: the second line repeats the third line of the first stanza, and the last line repeats the poem's opening line, thus creating the effect of a loop.

Similar to the pantoum in the circularity of its structure is the *villanelle*, originally a French form, with five *tercets* and a concluding *quatrain* held together by only two rhymes (aba, aba, aba, aba, aba, abaa) and by a refrain that repeats the first line at lines 6, 12, and 18, while the third line of the first tercet reappears as lines 9, 15, and 19. With its interlocking rhymes and elaborate repetitions, the villanelle can create a variety of tonal effects, ranging from lighthearted parody to the sonorous and earnest exhortation of Dylan Thomas's "Do Not Go Gentle Into That Good Night."

STANZAIC FORMS

Recurring formal groupings of lines within a poem are usually described as "stanzas." Both the recurring and the formal aspects of stanzaic forms are important; it is a common misconception to think that any group of lines in a poem, if it is set off by line spaces, constitutes a stanza. If such a group of lines is not patterned as one of a recurring group sharing similar formal characteristics, however, then it may be more appropriate to refer to such irregular groupings in the way we do for prose—as paragraphs. A ballad is typically divided into stanzas; a prose poem or a poem written in free verse, on the other hand, will rarely be divided into stanzas.

A stanza may be identified by the number of lines and the patterns of rhyme repeated in each grouping. One of the simpler traditional forms is the *ballad stanza*, with its alternating four and three-foot lines and its *abcb* rhyme scheme. Drawing on this form's association with medieval ballads and legends, Keats produces the eerie mystery of "La Belle Dame Sans Merci":

> I saw pale kings and princes too,
> Pale warriors, death-pale were they all;
> They cried—"La Belle Dame sans Merci
> Hath thee in thrall!"

Such imitations are a form of literary allusion; Keats uses a traditional stanza form to remind us of poems like "Sir Patrick Spens" or "Barbara Allen" to dramatize the painful thralldom of love by placing it within a well-known tradition of ballad narratives with similar forms and themes.

The four-line stanza, or *quatrain*, may be used for a variety of effects: from the elegiac solemnity of Gray's "Elegy Written in a Country Churchyard" to the apparent lightness and simplicity of some of Emily Dickinson's poems. Tennyson used a rhyming quatrain to such good effect in *In Memoriam* that the form he employed (four lines of iambic tetrameter rhyming *abba*) is known as the "In Memoriam stanza."

Other commonly used forms of stanza include the *rhyming couplet, terza rima, ottava rima, rhyme royal*, and the *Spenserian stanza*. Each of these is a rhetorical unit within a longer whole, rather like a paragraph within an essay. The poet's choice among such forms is dictated, at least in part, by the effects that each may produce. Thus the *rhyming couplet* often expresses a complete statement within two lines, creating a sense of density of thought, of coherence and closure; it is particularly effective where the writer wishes to set up contrasts, or to achieve the witty compactness of epigram:

> Of all mad creatures, if the learn'd are right,
> It is the slaver kills, and not the bite.
> A fool quite angry is quite innocent:
> Alas! 'tis ten times worse when they repent.

> (from Pope, "Epistle to Dr. Arbuthnot")

Ottava rima, as its Italian name implies, is an eight-line stanza, with the rhyme scheme *abababcc*. Like the sonnet, it is long enough to allow the development of a single thought in some detail and complexity, with a concluding couplet that may extend the central idea or cast it in a wholly unexpected light. W.B. Yeats uses this stanza form in "Sailing to Byzantium" and "Among Schoolchildren." Though much used by Renaissance poets, it is particularly associated with George Gordon, Lord Byron's *Don Juan*, in which the poet exploits to the full its potential for devastating irony and bathos. It is long enough to allow the development of a single thought in some detail and complexity; the concluding couplet can then, sonnet-like, turn that thought upon its head, or cast it in a wholly unexpected light:

Sagest of women, even of widows, she
        Resolved that Juan should be quite a paragon,
And worthy of the noblest pedigree
        (His sire was of Castile, his dam from Aragon).
Then for accomplishments of chivalry,
        In case our lord the king should go to war again,
He learned the arts of riding, fencing, gunnery,
        And how to scale a fortress—or a nunnery.

(Don Juan I.38)

FREE VERSE

Not all writers want the order and symmetry—some might say the restraints and limitations—of traditional forms, and many have turned to *free verse* as a means of liberating their thoughts and feelings. Deriving its name from the French "vers libre" made popular by the French Symbolistes at the end of the nineteenth century, free verse is characterized by irregularity of metre, line length, and rhyme. This does not mean that it is without pattern; rather, it tends to follow more closely than other forms the unforced rhythms and accents of natural speech, making calculated use of spacing, line breaks, and "cadences," the rhythmic units that govern phrasing in speech.

Free verse is not a modern invention. Milton was an early practitioner, as was Blake; however, it was the great modern writers of free verse—first Walt Whitman, then Pound, Eliot, and William Carlos Williams (interestingly, all Americans, at least originally)—who gave this form a fluidity and flexibility that could free the imagination to deal with any kind of feeling or experience. Perhaps because it depends so much more than traditional forms upon the individual intuitions of the poet, it is the form of poetic structure most commonly found today. The best practitioners recognize that free verse, like any other kind of poetry, demands clarity, precision, and a close connection between technique and meaning.

PROSE POETRY

At the furthest extreme from traditional forms lies poetry written in prose. Contradictory as this label may seem, the two have much in common. Prose has at its disposal all the figurative devices available to poetry, such as metaphor, personification, or apostrophe; it may use structuring devices such as verbal repetition or parallel syntactical structures; it can draw on the same tonal range, from pathos to irony. The difference is that prose poetry accomplishes its ends in sentences and paragraphs, rather than lines or stanzas. First given prominence by the French poet Charles Baudelaire (*Petits Poèmes en prose*, 1862), the form is much used to present fragments of heightened sensation, conveyed through vivid or impressionistic description. It draws upon such prosaic forms as journal entries, lists, even footnotes. Prose poetry should be distinguished from "poetic prose," which may be found in a variety of settings (from the King James Bible to the fiction of Jeanette Winterson); the distinction—which not all critics would accept—appears to lie in the writer's intention.

Christian Bok's *Eunoia* is an interesting example of the ways in which a writer of prose poetry may try to balance the demands of each medium. *Eunoia* is an avowedly experimental work in which each chapter is restricted to the use of a single vowel. The text is governed by a series of rules described by the author in an afterword; they include a requirement that all chapters "must allude to the art of writing. All sentences must accent internal rhyme through the use of syntactical parallelism. The text must exhaust the lexicon for each vowel, citing at least 98% of the available repertoire...." Having imposed such constraints upon the language and form of the work, Bok then sets himself the task of showing that "even under such improbable conditions of duress, language can still express an uncanny, if not sublime, thought." The result is a surrealistic narrative that blends poetic and linguistic devices to almost hypnotic effect.

THE POEM AS A MATERIAL OBJECT

Both free verse and prose poetry pay attention in different ways to the poem as a living thing on the printed page. But the way in which poetry is presented in material form is an important part of the existence of almost any form of poetry. In the six volumes of this anthology the material form of the poem is highlighted by the inclusion of a number of facsimile reproductions of poems of other eras in their earliest extant material form.

RHYTHM AND SCANSION

When we read poetry, we often become aware of a pattern of rhythm within a line or set of lines. The formal analysis of that rhythmic pattern, or "metre," is called *scansion*. The verb "to scan" may carry different meanings, depending upon the context: if the *critic* "scans" a line, he or she is attempting to determine the metrical pattern in which it is cast; if the *line* "scans," we are making the observation that the line conforms to particular metrical rules. Whatever the context, the process of scansion is based on the premise that a line of verse is built on a pattern of stresses, a recurring set of more or less regular beats established by the alternation of light and heavy accents in syllables and words. The rhythmic pattern so distinguished in a given poem is said to be the "metre" of that poem. If we find it impossible to identify any specific metrical pattern, the poem is probably an example of free verse.

QUANTITATIVE, SYLLABIC, AND ACCENTUAL-SYLLABIC VERSE

Although we owe much of our terminology for analyzing or describing poetry to the Greeks and Romans, the foundation of our metrical system is quite different from theirs. They measured a line of verse by the duration of sound ("quantity") in each syllable, and by the combination of short and long syllables. Such poetry is known as *quantitative* verse.

Unlike Greek or Latin, English is a heavily accented language. Thus poetry of the Anglo-Saxon period, such as *Beowulf*, was *accentual:* that is, the lines were based on a fixed number of accents, or stresses, regardless of the number of syllables in the line:

> Oft Scyld Scefing   sceapena þreatum
> monegum maegþum   meodosetla ofteah.

Few modern poets have written in the accentual tradition. A notable exception was Gerard Manley Hopkins, who based his line on a pattern of strong stresses that he called "sprung rhythm." Hopkins experimented with rhythms and stresses that approximate the accentual quality of natural speech; the result is a line that is emphatic, abrupt, even harsh in its forcefulness:

> I caught this morning morning's minion, kingdom of daylight's dauphin, dapple-dawn-drawn
>   Falcon, in his riding

> Of the rolling level underneath him steady air ....
>
>   (from "The Windhover")

Under the influence of French poetry, following the Norman invasion of the eleventh century, English writers were introduced to *syllabic* prosody: that is, poetry in which the number of syllables is the determining factor in the length of any line, regardless of the number of stresses or their placement. A few modern writers have successfully produced syllabic poetry.

However, the accentual patterns of English, in speech as well as in poetry, were too strongly ingrained to disappear. Instead, the native accentual practice combined with the imported syllabic conventions to produce the *accentual-syllabic* line, in which the writer works with combinations of stressed and unstressed syllables in lines of equal syllabic length. Geoffrey Chaucer was the first great writer to employ the accentual-syllabic line in English poetry:

> Ther was also a Nonne, a Prioresse,
> That of hir smiling was ful simple and coy.
> Hir gretteste ooth was but by sainté Loy,
> And she was clepéd Madame Eglantine.
>
>   (from *The Canterbury Tales*)

The fundamental pattern here is the ten-syllable line (although the convention of sounding the final "e" at the end of a line in Middle English verse sometimes produces eleven syllables). Each line contains five stressed syllables, each of which alternates with one or two unstressed syllables. This was to become the predominant metre of poetry in English until the general adoption of free verse in the twentieth century.

IDENTIFYING POETIC METER

Conventionally, meter is established by dividing a line into roughly equal parts, based on the rise and fall of the rhythmic beats. Each of these divisions, conventionally marked by a bar, is known as a "foot," and within the foot there will be a combination of stressed and unstressed syllables, indicated by the prosodic symbols / (stressed) and x (unstressed).

> I know | that I | shall meet | my fate
> Somewhere | among | the clouds | above ...
>
>   (from *Yeats*, "An Irish Airman Foresees His Death")

To describe the meter used in a poem, we must first determine what kind of foot predominates, and then count the number of feet in each line. To describe the resultant meter we use terminology borrowed from classical prosody. In identifying the meter of English verse we commonly apply the following labels:

iambic (x /): a foot with one weak stress followed by one strong stress

>   ("Look home | ward, Ang | el, now, | and melt | with ruth")

trochaic (/ x): strong followed by weak

>   ("Ty | ger! Ty | ger! bur | ning bright")

anapaestic (x x /): two weak stresses, followed by a strong

("I have passed | with a nod | of the head")

dactylic (/ x x): strong stress followed by two weak

("Hickory | dickory | dock")

spondaic (/ /): two strong stresses

("If hate | killed men,| Brother | Lawrence,
   God's blood,| would not | mine kill | you?")

We also use classical terms to describe the number of feet in a line. Thus, a line with one foot is *monometer*; with two feet, *dimeter*; three feet, *trimeter*; four feet, *tetrameter*; five feet, *pentameter*; and six feet, *hexameter*.

Scansion of the two lines from Yeats's "Irish Airman" quoted above shows that the predominant foot is iambic (x /), that there are four feet to each line, and that the poem is therefore written in *iambic tetrameters*. The first foot of the second line, however, may be read as a trochee ("Somewhere"); the variation upon the iambic norm here is an example of *substitution*, a means whereby the writer may avoid the monotony that would result from adhering too closely to a set rhythm. We very quickly build up an expectation about the dominant meter of a poem; the poet will sometimes disturb that expectation by changing the beat, and so through substitution create a pleasurable tension in our awareness.

The prevailing meter in English poetry is iambic, since the natural rhythm of spoken English is predominantly iambic. Nonetheless, poets may employ other rhythms where it suits their purpose. Thus W.H. Auden can create a solemn tone by the use of a trochaic meter(/ x):

Earth, receive an honoured guest;
William Yeats is laid to rest;
Let the Irish vessel lie
Emptied of its poetry.

The same meter may be much less funereal, as in Ben Jonson's song *"To Celia"*:

Come, my Celia, let us prove,
While we may, the sports of love.
Time will not be ours forever;
He, at length, our good will sever.

The sense of greater pace in this last example derives in part from the more staccato phrasing, and also from the greater use of monosyllabic words. A more obviously lilting, dancing effect is obtained from anapaestic rhythm (x x /):

I sprang to the stirrup, and Joris, and he;
I galloped, Dirck galloped, we galloped all three.
"Good speed!" cried the watch, as the gatebolts undrew;
"Speed!" echoed the wall to us galloping through.
        (from *Browning*, "How They Brought the Good News from Ghent to Aix")

Coleridge wittily captured the varying effects of different meters in "Metrical Feet: Lesson for a Boy," which the poet wrote for his sons, and in which he marked the stresses himself:

> Trochee trips from long to short;
> From long to long in solemn sort
> Slow Spondee stalks; strong foot! yet ill able
> Ever to come up with Dactyl trisyllable.
> Iambics march from short to long:—
> With a leap and a bound the swift Anapaests throng....

A meter which often deals with serious themes is unrhymed iambic pentameter, also known as *blank verse*. This is the meter of Shakespeare's plays, notably his great tragedies; it is the meter, too, of Milton's *Paradise Lost*, to which it lends a desired sonority and magnificence; and of Wordsworth's "Lines Composed a Few Miles above Tintern Abbey," where the flexibility of the meter allows the writer to move by turns from description, to narration, to philosophical reflection.

RHYME, CONSONANCE, ASSONANCE, AND ALLITERATION

Perhaps the most obvious sign of poetic form is rhyme: that is, the repetition of syllables with the same or similar sounds. If the rhyme words are placed at the end of the line, they are known as *end-rhymes*. The opening stanza of Housman's "To an Athlete Dying Young" has two pairs of end-rhymes:

> The time you won your town the *race*
> We chaired you through the market-*place*;
> Man and boy stood cheering *by*,
> And home we brought you shoulder-*high*.

Words rhyming within a line are *internal rhymes*, as in the first and third lines of this stanza from Coleridge's "The Rime of the Ancient Mariner":

> The fair breeze *blew*, the white foam *flew*
> The furrow followed free;
> We were the *first* that ever *burst*
> Into that silent sea.

When, as is usually the case, the rhyme occurs in a stressed syllable, it is known as a *masculine rhyme*; if the rhyming word ends in an unstressed syllable, it is referred to as *feminine*. The difference is apparent in the opening stanzas of Alfred Tennyson's poem "The Lady of Shalott," where the first stanza establishes the basic iambic meter with strong stresses on the rhyming words:

> On either side the river *lie*
> Long fields of barley and of *rye*,
> That clothe the wold and meet the *sky*;
> And through the field the road runs *by*
> To many-towered Camelot ...

In the second stanza Tennyson changes to trochaic lines, ending in unstressed syllables and feminine rhymes:

> Willows whiten, aspens *quiver*,
> Little breezes dusk and *shiver*
> Through the wave that runs *forever*
> By the island in the *river*
> Flowing down to Camelot.

Not only does Tennyson avoid monotony here by his shift to feminine rhymes, he also darkens the mood by using words that imply a contrast with the bright warmth of day—"quiver," "dusk," "shiver"—in preparation for the introduction of the "silent isle" that embowers the Lady.

NEAR RHYMES

Most of the rhymes in "The Lady of Shalott" are exact, or "*perfect*" rhymes. However, in the second of the stanzas just quoted, it is evident that "forever" at the end of the third line is not a "perfect" rhyme; rather, it is an instance of "*near*" or "*slant*" rhyme. Such "*imperfect*" rhymes are quite deliberate; indeed, two stanzas later we find the rhyming sequence "early," "barley," "cheerly," and "clearly," followed by the rhymes "weary," "airy," and "fairy." As with the introduction of feminine rhymes, such divergences from one dominant pattern prevent monotony and avoid a too-mechanical sing-song effect.

More importantly, near-rhymes have an oddly unsettling effect, perhaps because they both raise and frustrate our expectation of a perfect rhyme. Their use certainly gives added emphasis to the words at the end of these chilling lines from Wilfred Owen's "*Strange Meeting*":

> For by my glee might many men have laughed,
> And of my weeping something had been left,
> Which must die now. I mean the truth untold,
> The pity of war, the pity war distilled.
> Now men will go content with what we spoiled,
> Or, discontent, boil bloody, and be spilled.

CONSONANCE AND ASSONANCE

In Owen's poem, the near-rhymes "laughed / left" and "spoiled / spilled" are good examples of *consonance*, which pairs words with similar consonants but different intervening vowels. Other examples from Owen's poem include "groined / groaned," "hall / Hell," "years / yours," and "mystery / mastery."

Related to consonance as a linking device is *assonance*, the echoing of similar vowel sounds in the stressed syllables of words with differing consonants (lane/hail, penitent/reticence). A device favored particularly by descriptive poets, it appears often in the work of the English Romantics, especially Shelley and Keats, and their great Victorian successor Tennyson, all of whom had a good ear for the musical quality of language. In the following passage, Tennyson makes effective use of repeated "o" and "ow" sounds to suggest the soft moaning of the wind as it spreads the seed of the lotos plant:

> The Lotos blooms below the barren peak,
> The Lotos blows by every winding creek;

All day the wind breathes low with mellower tone;
  Through every hollow cave and alley lone
  Round and round the spicy downs the yellow Lotos dust is blown.

(from "The Lotos-Eaters")

ALLITERATION

Alliteration connects words which have the same initial consonant. Like consonance and rhyme, alliteration adds emphasis, throwing individual words into strong relief, and lending force to rhythm. This is especially evident in the work of Gerard Manley Hopkins, where alliteration works in conjunction with the heavy stresses of *sprung rhythm*:

Brute beauty and valour and act, oh, air, pride, plume, here
  Buckle! AND the fire that breaks from thee then, a billion
  Times told lovelier, more dangerous, O my chevalier!

(from "The Windhover")

Like assonance, alliteration is useful in descriptive poetry, reinforcing an impression or mood through repeated sounds:

Thou on whose stream, 'mid the steep sky's commotion,
  Loose clouds like Earth's decaying leaves are shed,
  Shook from the tangled boughs of Heaven and Ocean ....

(from Percy Shelley, "Ode to the West Wind")

The repetition of "s" and "sh" sounds conveys the rushing sound of a wind that drives everything before it. This effect is also an example of *onomatopoeia*, a figure of speech in which the sound of the words seems to echo the sense.

RHYME AND POETIC STRUCTURE

Rhyme may play a central role in the structure of a poem. This is particularly apparent in the *sonnet* form, where the expression of the thought is heavily influenced by the poet's choice of rhyme-scheme. The "English" or "Shakespearean" sonnet has three quatrains rhyming *abab, cdcd, efef,* and concludes with a rhyming couplet, *gg.* This pattern lends itself well to the statement and restatement of an idea, as we find, for example, in Shakespeare's sonnet "That time of year thou mayst in me behold." Each of the quatrains presents an image of decline or decay—a tree in winter, the coming of night, a dying fire; the closing couplet then relates these images to the thought of an impending separation and attendant feelings of loss.

    The organization of the "Italian" or "Petrarchan" sonnet, by contrast, hinges on a rhyme scheme that creates two parts, an eight-line section (the *octave*) typically rhyming *abbaabba,* and a concluding six-line section (the *sestet*) rhyming *cdecde* or some other variation. In the octave, the writer describes a thought or feeling; in the sestet, the writer may elaborate upon that thought, or may introduce a sudden "turn" or change of direction. A good example of the Italian form is Donne's "Batter My Heart, Three-Personed God."

The rhyming pattern established at the beginning of a poem is usually followed throughout; thus the opening sets up an expectation in the reader, which the poet may sometimes play on by means of an unexpected or surprising rhyme. This is especially evident in comic verse, where peculiar or unexpected rhymes can contribute a great deal to the comic effect:

> I shoot the Hippopotamus
> with bullets made of platinum,
> Because if I use leaden ones
> his hide is sure to flatten 'em.
>
> (*Hilaire Belloc,* "The Hippopotamus")

Finally, one of the most obvious yet important aspects of rhyme is its sound. It acts as a kind of musical punctuation, lending verse an added resonance and beauty. And as anyone who has ever had to learn poetry by heart will testify, the sound of rhyme is a powerful aid to memorization and recall, from helping a child to learn numbers—

> One, two,
> Buckle my shoe,
> Three, four,
> Knock at the door—

—to selling toothpaste through an advertising jingle in which the use of rhyme drives home the identity of a product:

> You'll wonder where the yellow went,
> When you brush your teeth with Pepsodent.

OTHER FORMS WITH INTERLOCKING RHYMES

Other forms besides the sonnet depend upon rhyme for their structural integrity. These include the *rondeau*, a poem of thirteen lines in three stanzas, with two half lines acting as a refrain, and having only two rhymes. The linking effect of rhyme is also essential to the three-line stanza called *terza rima*, the form chosen by Shelley for his "Ode to the West Wind," where the rhyme scheme (*aba, bcb, cdc* etc.) gives a strong sense of forward movement. But a poet need not be limited to particular forms to use interlocking rhyme schemes.

THE POET'S TASK

The poet's task, in Sir Philip Sidney's view, is to move us to virtue and well-doing by coming to us with

words set in delightful proportion, either accompanied with, or prepared for, the well-enchanting skill of music; and with a tale forsooth he cometh unto you, with a tale which holdeth children from play, and old men from the chimney corner; and pretending no more, doth intend the winning of the mind from wickedness to virtue: even as the child is often brought to take most wholesome things by hiding them in such other as have a pleasant taste.

(The Defence of Poesy, 1593)

Modern poets have been less preoccupied with the didactic or moral force of poetry, its capacity to win the mind to virtue; nonetheless, like their Renaissance counterparts, they view poetry as a means to understanding, a point of light in an otherwise dark universe. To Robert Frost, a poem "begins in delight and ends in wisdom":

It begins in delight, it inclines to the impulse, it assumes direction with the first line laid down, it runs a course of lucky events, and ends in a clarification of life—not necessarily a great clarification, such as sects and cults are founded on, but in a momentary stay against confusion.

("The Figure a Poem Makes," *Collected Poems,* 1939)

Rhyme and metre are important tools at the poet's disposal, and can be valuable aids in developing thought as well as in creating rhythmic or musical effects. However, the technical skills needed to turn a good line or create metrical complexities should not be confused with the ability to write good poetry. Sidney wryly observes in his *Defence of Poesy* that "there have been many excellent poets that never versified, and now swarm many versifiers that need never answer to the name of poets....it is not rhyming and versing that maketh a poet, no more than a long gown maketh an advocate." Technical virtuosity may arouse our admiration, but something else is needed to bring that "constriction of the throat and … precipitation of water to the eyes" that A.E. Housman speaks about. What that "something" is will always elude definition, and is perhaps best left for readers and listeners to determine for themselves through their own encounters with poetry.

COUNTIES
OF BRITAIN
AND IRELAND

THE BRITISH ISLES

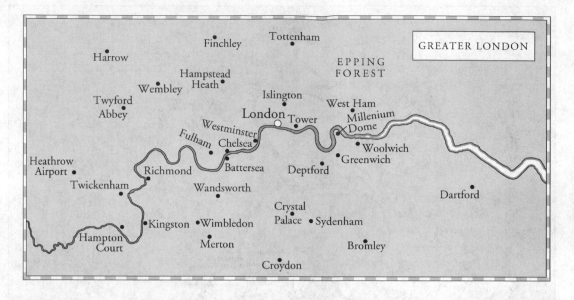

GREATER LONDON

Harrow
Finchley
Tottenham
EPPING
FOREST
Hampstead
Heath
Wembley
Islington
Twyford
Abbey
London
Tower
West Ham
Millenium
Dome
Westminster
Woolwich
Fulham
Chelsea
Greenwich
Heathrow
Airport
Battersea
Deptford
Richmond
Twickenham
Wandsworth
Dartford
Crystal
Palace
Kingston
Wimbledon
Sydenham
Hampton
Court
Merton
Bromley
Croydon

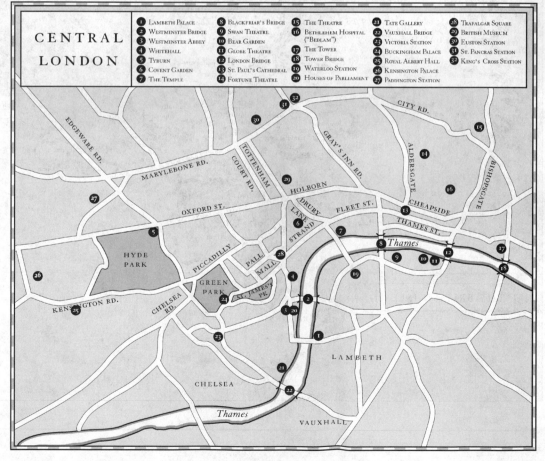

CENTRAL
LONDON

1 LAMBETH PALACE
2 WESTMINSTER BRIDGE
3 WESTMINSTER ABBEY
4 WHITEHALL
5 TYBURN
6 COVENT GARDEN
7 THE TEMPLE

8 BLACKFRIAR'S BRIDGE
9 SWAN THEATRE
10 BEAR GARDEN
11 GLOBE THEATRE
12 LONDON BRIDGE
13 ST. PAUL'S CATHEDRAL
14 FORTUNE THEATRE

15 THE THEATRE
16 BETHLEHEM HOSPITAL
("BEDLAM")
17 THE TOWER
18 TOWER BRIDGE
19 WATERLOO STATION
20 HOUSES OF PARLIAMENT

21 TATE GALLERY
22 VAUXHALL BRIDGE
23 VICTORIA STATION
24 BUCKINGHAM PALACE
25 ROYAL ALBERT HALL
26 KENSINGTON PALACE
27 PADDINGTON STATION

28 TRAFALGAR SQUARE
29 BRITISH MUSEUM
30 EUSTON STATION
31 ST. PANCRAS STATION
32 KING'S CROSS STATION

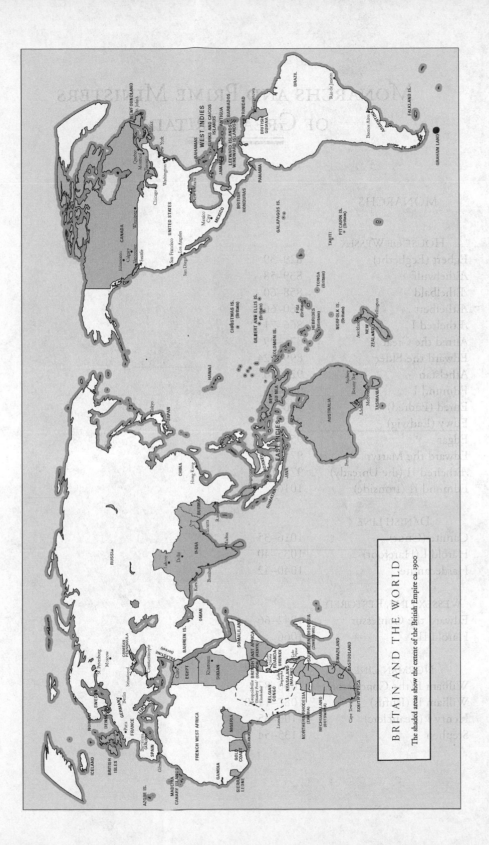

BRITAIN AND THE WORLD

The shaded areas show the extent of the British Empire ca. 1900

Monarchs and Prime Ministers of Great Britain

MONARCHS

House of Wessex

Egbert (Ecgberht)	829–39
Æthelwulf	839–58
Æthelbald	858–60
Æthelbert	860–66
Æthelred I	866–71
Alfred the Great	871–99
Edward the Elder	899–924
Athelstan	924–40
Edmund I	940–46
Edred (Eadred)	946–55
Edwy (Eadwig)	955–59
Edgar	959–75
Edward the Martyr	975–78
Æthelred II (the Unready)	978–1016
Edmund II (Ironside)	1016

Danish Line

Canute (Cnut)	1016–35
Harold I (Harefoot)	1035–40
Hardecanute	1040–42

Wessex Line, Restored

Edward the Confessor	1042–66
Harold II	1066

Norman Line

William I (the Conqueror)	1066–87
William II (Rufus)	1087–1100
Henry I (Beauclerc)	1100–35
Stephen	1135–54

MONARCHS

PLANTAGENET, ANGEVIN LINE

Henry II	1154–89
Richard I (Coeur de Lion)	1189–99
John (Lackland)	1199–1216
Henry III	1216–72
Edward I (Longshanks)	1272–1307
Edward II	1307–27
Edward III	1327–77
Richard II	1377–99

PLANTAGENET, LANCASTRIAN LINE

Henry IV	1399–1413
Henry V	1413–22
Henry VI	1422–61

Henry VIII

PLANTAGENET, YORKIST LINE

Edward IV	1461–83
Edward V	1483
Richard III	1483–85

HOUSE OF TUDOR

Henry VII	1485–1509
Henry VIII	1509–47
Edward VI	1547–53
Mary I	1553–58
Elizabeth I	1558–1603

HOUSE OF STUART

James I	1603–25
Charles I	1625–49

(The Commonwealth)	1649–60
Oliver Cromwell	1649–58
Richard Cromwell	1658–59

Mary I

MONARCHS

HOUSE OF STUART, RESTORED

Charles II	1660–85
James II	1685–88

HOUSE OF ORANGE AND STUART

William III and Mary II	1689–94
William III	1694–1702

HOUSE OF STUART

Anne	1702–14

HOUSE OF BRUNSWICK, HANOVER LINE

George I	1714–27
George II	1727–60
George III	1760–1820

George, Prince of Wales,
Prince Regent

PRIME MINISTERS

George III

Sir Robert Walpole (Whig)	1721–42
Earl of Wilmington (Whig)	1742–43
Henry Pelham (Whig)	1743–54
Duke of Newcastle (Whig)	1754–56
Duke of Devonshire (Whig)	1756–57
Duke of Newcastle (Whig)	1757–62
Earl of Bute (Tory)	1762–63
George Grenville (Whig)	1763–65
Marquess of Rockingham (Whig)	1765–66
William Pitt the Elder (Earl of Chatham) (Whig)	1766–68
Duke of Grafton (Whig)	1768–70
Frederick North (Lord North) (Tory)	1770–82
Marquess of Rockingham (Whig)	1782
Earl of Shelburne (Whig)	1782–83
Duke of Portland	1783
William Pitt the Younger (Tory)	1783–1801
Henry Addington (Tory)	1801–04
William Pitt the Younger (Tory)	1804–06
William Wyndham Grenville (Baron Grenville) (Whig)	1806–07

MONARCHS

George, Prince of Wales,   1811–20
  Prince Regent
George IV   1820–30

William IV   1830–37

Victoria   1837–1901

Victoria

HOUSE OF SAXE-COBURG-GOTHA

Edward VII   1901–10

HOUSE OF WINDSOR

George V   1910–36

PRIME MINISTERS

Duke of Portland (Whig)	1807–09
Spencer Perceval (Tory)	1809–12
Earl of Liverpool (Tory)	1812–27
George Canning (Tory)	1827
Viscount Goderich (Tory)	1827–28
Duke of Wellington (Tory)	1828–30
Earl Grey (Whig)	1830–34
Viscount Melbourne (Whig)	1834
Sir Robert Peel (Tory)	1834–35
Viscount Melbourne (Whig)	1835–41
Sir Robert Peel (Tory)	1841–46
Lord John Russell (later Earl) (Liberal)	1846–52
Earl of Derby (Con.)	1852
Earl of Aberdeen (Tory)	1852–55
Viscount Palmerston (Lib.)	1855–58
Earl of Derby (Con.)	1858–59
Viscount Palmerston (Lib.)	1859–65
Earl Russell (Liberal)	1865–66
Earl of Derby (Con.)	1866–68
Benjamin Disraeli (Con.)	1868
William Gladstone (Lib.)	1868–74
Benjamin Disraeli (Con.)	1874–80
William Gladstone (Lib.)	1880–85
Marquess of Salisbury (Con.)	1885–86
William Gladstone (Lib.)	1886
Marquess of Salisbury (Con.)	1886–92
William Gladstone (Lib.)	1892–94
Earl of Rosebery (Lib.)	1894–95
Marquess of Salisbury (Con.)	1895–1902
Arthur Balfour (Con.)	1902–05
Sir Henry Campbell-Bannerman (Lib.)	1905–08
Herbert Asquith (Lib.)	1908–15
Herbert Asquith (Lib.)	1915–16

MONARCHS			PRIME MINISTERS	
			Andrew Bonar Law (Con.)	1922–23
			Stanley Baldwin (Con.)	1923–24
			James Ramsay MacDonald (Labour)	1924
			Stanley Baldwin (Con.)	1924–29
			James Ramsay MacDonald (Labour)	1929–31
			James Ramsay MacDonald (Labour)	1931–35
			Stanley Baldwin (Con.)	1935–37
Edward VIII		1936	Neville Chamberlain (Con.)	1937–40
George VI		1936–52	Winston Churchill (Con.)	1940–45
			Winston Churchill (Con.)	1945
			Clement Attlee (Labour)	1945–51
			Sir Winston Churchill (Con.)	1951–55
Elizabeth II		1952–	Sir Anthony Eden (Con.)	1955–57
			Harold Macmillan (Con.)	1957–63
			Sir Alex Douglas-Home (Con.)	1963–64
			Harold Wilson (Labour)	1964–70
			Edward Heath (Con.)	1970–74
			Harold Wilson (Labour)	1974–76
			James Callaghan (Labour)	1976–79
			Margaret Thatcher (Con.)	1979–90
			John Major (Con.)	1990–97
			Tony Blair (Labour)	1997–

Glossary of Terms

Accent: the natural emphasis (stress) speakers place on a syllable.

Accentual Verse: poetry in which a line is measured only by the number of accents or stresses, not by the number of syllables.

Accentual-Syllabic Verse: the most common metrical system in traditional English verse, in which a line is measured by the number of syllables and by the pattern of accented (stressed) and unaccented (unstressed) syllables.

Aesthetes: members of a late nineteenth-century movement that valued "art for art's sake"—for its purely aesthetic qualities, as opposed to valuing art for the moral content it may convey, for the intellectual stimulation it may provide, or for a range of other qualities.

Alexandrine: a line of verse that is 12 syllables long. In English verse, the alexandrine is always an iambic hexameter: that is, it has six iambic feet. The most-often quoted example is the second line in a couplet from Alexander Pope's "Essay on Criticism" (1711): "A needless Alexandrine ends the song / That, like a wounded snake, drags its slow length along." See also *Spenserian stanza*.

Allegory: a narrative with both a literal meaning and secondary, often symbolic meaning or meanings. Allegory frequently employs personification to give concrete embodiment to abstract concepts or entities, such as feelings or personal qualities. It may also present one set of characters or events in the guise of another, using implied parallels for the purposes of satire or political comment, as in John Dryden's poem "Absalom and Achitophel."

Alliteration: the grouping of words with the same initial consonant (e.g., "break, blow, burn, and make me new"). The repetition of sound acts as a connector. See also *assonance* and *consonance*.

Alliterative Verse: poetry that employs alliteration of stressed syllables in each line as its chief structural principle.

Allusion: a reference, often indirect or unidentified, to a person, thing, or event. A reference in one literary work to another literary work, whether to its content or its form, also constitutes an allusion.

Ambiguity: an "opening" of language created by the writer to allow for multiple meanings or differing interpretations. In literature, ambiguity may be deliberately employed by the writer to enrich meaning; this differs from any unintentional, unwanted, ambiguity in non-literary prose.

Amphibrach: a metrical foot with three syllables, the second of which is stressed: x / x (e.g., sensation).

Analogy: a broad term that refers to our processes of noting similarities among things or events. Specific forms of analogy in poetry include *simile* and *metaphor* (see below).

Anapaest: a metrical foot containing two unstressed syllables followed by one stressed syllable: xx/ (e.g., underneath, intervene).

Anglican Church / Church of England: formed after Henry VIII's break with Rome in the 1530s, the Church of England had acquired a permanently Protestant cast by the 1570s. There has remained considerable variation within the Church, however, with distinctions often drawn among High Church, Broad Church, and Latitudinarian. At one extreme High Church Anglicans (some of whom prefer to be known as "Anglo-Catholics") prefer relatively elaborate church rituals not dissimilar in form to those of the Roman Catholic Church and place considerable emphasis on church hierarchy, while in the other direction Latitudinarians prefer relatively informal religious services and tend far more towards egalitarianism.

Antistrophe: from Greek drama, the chorus's countermovement or reply to an initial movement (strophe). See *ode* below.

Apostrophe: a figure of speech (a trope; see figures of speech below) in which a writer directly addresses an object—or a dead or absent person—as if the imagined audience were actually listening.

Archetype: in literature and mythology, a recurring idea, symbol, motif, character, or place. To some scholars and psychologists, an archetype represents universal human thought-patterns or experiences.

Assonance: the repetition of identical or similar vowel sounds in stressed syllables in which the surrounding consonants are different: for example, "shame" and "fate"; "gale" and "cage"; or the long "i" sounds in "Beside the pumice isle..."

Aubade: a lyric poem that greets or laments the arrival of dawn.

Ballad: a folk song, or a poem originally recited to an audience, which tells a dramatic story based on legend or history.

Ballad Stanza: a quatrain with alternating four-stress and three-stress lines, rhyming *abcb*. A variant is "common measure," in which the alternating lines are strictly iambic, and rhyme *abab*.

Ballade: a fixed form most commonly characterized by only three rhymes, with an 8-line stanza rhyming *ababbcbc* and an envoy rhyming *bcbc*. Both Chaucer and Dante Gabriel Rossetti ("Ballad of the Dead Ladies") adopted this form.

Baroque: powerful and heavily ornamented in style. "Baroque" is a term from the history of visual art and of music that is sometimes also used to describe certain literary styles, such as that of Richard Crashaw.

Bathos: an anticlimactic effect brought about by a writer's descent from an elevated subject or tone to the ordinary or trivial.

Benedictine Rule: set of instructions for monastic communities, composed by Saint Benedict of Nursia (died c. 457).

Blank Verse: unrhymed lines written in iambic pentameter, a form introduced to English verse by Henry Howard, Earl of Surrey, in his translation of parts of Virgil's *Aeneid* in 1547.

Bombast: inappropriately inflated or grandiose language.

Broadside: individual sheet of paper printed on only one side. From the sixteenth through to the eighteenth centuries broadsides of a variety of different sorts (e.g., ballads, political tracts, short satires) were sold on the streets.

Broken Rhyme: in which a multi-syllable word is split at the end of a line and continued onto the next, to allow an end-rhyme with the split syllable.

Burlesque: satire of a particularly exaggerated sort, particularly that which ridicules its subject by emphasising its vulgar or ridiculous aspects.

Caesura: a pause or break in a line of verse occurring where a phrase, clause, or sentence ends, and indicated in scansion by the mark ll. If it occurs in the middle of the line, it is known as a "medial" caesura.

Canon: in literature, those works that are commonly accepted as possessing authority or importance. In practice, "canonical" texts or authors are those that are discussed most frequently by scholars and taught most frequently in university courses.

Canto: a sub-section of a long (usually epic) poem.

Canzone: a short song or poem, with stanzas of equal length and an envoy.

Carpe Diem: Latin (from Horace) meaning "seize the day." The idea of enjoying the moment is a common one in Renaissance love poetry. See, for example, Marvell's "To His Coy Mistress."

Catalexis: the omission of unstressed syllables from a line of verse (such a line is referred to as "catalectic"). In iambic verse it is usually the first syllable of the line that is omitted; in trochaic, the last. For example, in the first stanza of Housman's "To an Athlete Dying Young" the third line is catalectic: i.e., it has dropped the first, unstressed syllable called for by the poem's iambic tetrameter form: "The time you won your town the race / We chaired you through the market-place; / Man and boy stood cheering by, / And home we brought you shoulder-high."

Catharsis: the arousal through the performance of a dramatic tragedy of "emotions of pity and fear" to a point where "purgation" or "purification" occurs and the feelings are released or transformed. The concept was developed by Aristotle in his *Poetics* from an ancient Greek medical concept, and adapted by him into an aesthetic principle.

Chiasmus: a figure of speech (a scheme) that reverses word order in successive parallel clauses. If the word order is A-B-C in the first clause, it becomes C-B-A in the second: for example, Donne's line "She is all states, and all princes, I" ("The Sun Rising") incorporates this reversal (though with an ellipsis).

Classical: originating in or relating to ancient Greek or Roman culture. As commonly conceived, *classical* implies a strong sense of formal order. The term *neoclassical* is often used with reference to literature of the Restoration and eighteenth century that was strongly influenced by ancient Greek and Roman models.

Closet Drama: a play (typically in verse) written for private performance. The term came into use in the first half of the nineteenth century.

Colored Narrative: alternative term for *free indirect discourse*.

Comedy: as a literary term, used originally to denote that class of ancient Greek drama in which the action ends happily. More broadly the term has been used to describe a wide variety of literary forms of a more or less light-hearted character.

Commedia dell'arte: largely improvised comic performances conducted by masked performers and involving considerable physical activity. The genre of *commedia dell'arte* originated in Italy in the sixteenth century; it was influential throughout Europe for more than two centuries thereafter.

Commonwealth: from the fifteenth century, a term roughly equivalent to the modern "state," but tending to emphasize the commonality of interests among all citizens. In the seventeenth century Britain was named a commonwealth under Oliver Cromwell. In the twentieth century, the term came to be applied to associations of many nations; the British Commonwealth became the successor to the British Empire.

Conceit: an unusually elaborate metaphor or simile that extends beyond its original tenor and vehicle, sometimes becoming a "master" analogy for the entire poem (see, for example, Donne's "The Flea," and Robert Frost's sonnet "She is as in a field a silken tent"). Ingenious or fanciful images and comparisons were especially popular with the metaphysical poets of the seventeenth century, giving rise to the term "metaphysical conceit."

Concrete Poetry: an experimental form, most popular during the 1950s and 60s, in which the printed type itself forms a visual image of the poem's key words or ideas. See also *pattern poetry, assonance*.

Connotation: the implied, often unspoken meaning(s) of a given word, as distinct from its denotation, or literal meaning. Connotations may have highly emotional undertones and are usually culturally specific.

Conservative Party: See *Political Parties*.

Consonance: the pairing of words with similar initial and ending consonants, but with different vowel sounds (live/love, wander/wonder). See also *alliteration*.

Convention: aesthetic approach, technique, or practice accepted as characteristic and appropriate for a particular form. It is a convention of certain sorts of plays, for example, that the characters speak in blank verse, of other sorts of plays that characters speak in rhymed couplets, and of still other sorts of dramatic performances that characters frequently break into song to express their feelings.

Couplet: a pair of rhyming lines, usually in the same meter. If they form a complete unit of thought and are grammatically complete, the lines are known as a closed couplet. See also *heroic couplet* below.

Dactyl: a metrical foot containing one strong stress followed by two weak stresses: / xx (e.g., muttering, helplessly). A minor form known as "double dactyls" makes use of this meter for humorous purposes, e.g., "Jiggery pokery" or "Higgledy Piggledy."

Denotation: See *connotation* above.

Devolution: process through which a degree of political power was transferred in the late twentieth and early twenty-first centuries from the British government to assemblies in Scotland and in Wales.

Dialogue: words spoken by characters to one another. (When a character is addressing him or her self or the audience directly, the words spoken are referred to as a *monologue*.)

Diction: word choice. Whether the diction of a literary work (or of a literary character) is colloquial, conversational, formal, or of some other type contributes significantly to the tone of the text as well as to characterization.

Didacticism: aesthetic approach emphasizing moral instruction.

Dimeter: a poetic line containing two metrical feet.

Dirge: a song or poem that mourns someone's death. See also *elegy* and *lament* below.

Disestablishmentarianism: movement opposing an official state-supported religion, in particular the Church of England in that role.

Dissonance: harsh, unmusical sounds or rhythms which poets may use deliberately to achieve certain effects.

Dramatic Irony: this form of irony occurs when the audience's reception of a speech by a character on the stage is affected by the possession by the audience of information not available to the character.

Dramatic Monologue: a lyric poem that takes the form of an utterance by a single person addressing a silent listener. The speaker may be an historical personage (as in some of Robert Browning's dramatic monologues), a figure drawn from myth or legend (as in some of Tennyson's), or an entirely imagined figure, as in Webster's "A Castaway."

Dub Poetry: a form of protest poetry originating in Jamaica, with its roots in dance rhythms, especially reggae, and often accompanied in performance by drums and music. See also *rap* and *hip-hop*.

Duple Foot: A duple foot of poetry has two syllables. The possible duple forms are iamb (in which the stress is on the second of the two syllables), trochee (in which the stress is on the first of the two syllables), spondee (in which both are stressed equally), and pyrrhic (in which both syllables are unstressed).

Eclogue: now generally used simply as an alternative name for a pastoral poem. In classical times and in the early modern period, however, an *eclogue* (or *idyll*) was a specific type of pastoral poem—a dialogue or dramatic monologue involving rustic characters. (The other main sub-genre of the pastoral was the *georgic*.)

Elegiac Stanza: a quatrain of iambic pentameters rhyming *abab*, often used in poems meditating on death or sorrow. The best-known example is Thomas Gray's "Elegy Written in a Country Churchyard."

Elegy: a poem which formally mourns the death of a particular person (e.g., Tennyson's "In Memoriam") or in which the poet meditates on other serious subjects (e.g., Gray's "Elegy"). See also *dirge*.

Elision: omitting or suppressing a letter or an unstressed syllable at the beginning or end of a word, so that a line of verse may conform to a given metrical scheme. For example, the three syllables at the beginning of Shakespeare's sonnet 129 are reduced to two by the omission of the first vowel: "Th' expense of spirit in a waste of shame." See also *syncope*.

Ellipsis: the omission of a word or words necessary for the complete grammatical construction of a sentence, but not necessary for our understanding of the sentence.

End-Rhyme: See *rhyme*.

End-stopped: a line of poetry is said to be end-stopped when the end of the line coincides with a natural pause in the syntax, such as the conclusion of a sentence; e.g., in this couplet from Pope's "Essay on Criticism," both lines are end-stopped: "A little learning is a dangerous thing; / Drink deep, or taste not the Pierian spring." Compare this with *enjambement*.

Enjambement: the "running-on" of the sense from one line of poetry to the next, with no pause created by punctuation or syntax. (The more commonly found alternative is referred to as an *end-stopped line*.)

Envoy (Envoi):   a stanza or half-stanza that forms the conclusion of certain French poetic forms, such as the *sestina* or the *ballade*. It often sums up or comments upon what has gone before.

Epic: a lengthy narrative poem, often divided into books and sub-divided into cantos. It generally celebrates heroic deeds or events, and the style tends to be lofty and grand. Examples in English include Spenser's *The Faerie Queene* and Milton's *Paradise Lost*.

Epic Simile: an elaborate simile, developed at such length that the vehicle of the comparison momentarily displaces the primary subject with which it is being compared.

Epigram: a very short poem, sometimes in closed couplet form, characterized by pointed wit.

Epigraph: a quotation placed at the beginning of a discourse to indicate or foreshadow the theme.

Epiphany: a moment at which matters of significance are suddenly illuminated for a literary character (or for the reader), typically triggered by something small and seemingly of little import. The term first came into wide currency in connection with the fiction of James Joyce.

Episodic Plot: plot comprising a variety of episodes that are only loosely connected by threads of story material (as opposed to plots that present one or more continually unfolding narratives where successive episodes build one on another).

Epithalamion: a poem celebrating a wedding. The best-known example in English is probably Edmund Spenser's "Epithalamion" (1595).

Eulogy: text expressing praise, especially for a distinguished person recently deceased.

Euphemism: mode of expression through which aspects of reality considered to be vulgar, crudely physical, or unpleasant are referred to indirectly rather than named explicitly. A variety of euphemisms exist for the processes of urination and defecation; *passed away* is often used as a euphemism for *died*. (The word *euphemism* has the same root as *Euphuism* (see below), but has taken on a different meaning.)

Euphony: pleasant, musical sounds or rhythms—the opposite of dissonance.

Euphuism: In the late sixteenth century John Lyly published a prose romance, *Euphues*, which employed a style that featured long sentences filled with balanced phrases and clauses, many of them adding little to the content. This highly mannered style was popular in the court of Elizabeth I for a few years following the publication of Lyly's famous work, and the style became known as *Euphuism*.

European Union: (EU) Group of nations formed in 1993 as the successor to the European Economic Community (Common Market). Britain first applied for membership in the latter in 1961; at first its efforts to join were blocked by the French government, but in 1973 Prime Minister Edward Heath successfully negotiated Britain's entry into the group. Britain has resisted some moves towards full integration with the European community, in particular retaining its own currency when other European nations adopted the Euro on 1 January 2002.

Exchequer: In earlier eras, the central royal financial office, responsible for receiving and keeping track of crown revenues. In later eras, part of the bureaucracy equivalent to the Ministry of Finance in Canada or the Treasury in the United States (the modern post of Chancellor of the Exchequer is equivalent to the American post of Secretary of the Treasury, the Canadian post of Minister of Finance or the Australian post of Treasurer).

Exposition: the setting out of material in an ordered form, either in speech or in writing. In a play those parts of the action that do not occur on stage but are rather recounted by the characters are frequently described as being presented in exposition. Similarly, when the background narrative is filled in near the beginning of a novel, such material is often described as having been presented in exposition. Somewhat confusingly, however, the term "expository prose" is usually used with reference not to fiction but to the setting forth of arguments or descriptions in the context of essays or other works of prose non-fiction.

Eye-Rhyme: See *rhyme* below.

Feminine Ending: the ending of a line of poetry on an "extra," and, especially, on an unstressed syllable. See, for example, the first line of Keat's "Ode on a Grecian Urn": "A thing of beauty is a joy forever," a line of iambic pentameter in which the final foot is an amphibrach rather than an iamb.

Feminine Rhyme: See *rhyme* below.

Figures of Speech: deliberate, highly concentrated uses of language to achieve particular purposes or effects on an audience. There are two kinds of figures: schemes and tropes. Schemes involve changes in word-sound and word-order, such as *alliteration* and *chiasmus*. Tropes play on our understandings of words to extend, alter, or transform meaning, as in *metaphor* and *personification*.

First-Person Narrative: narrative recounted using *I* and *me*. See also *narrative perspective*.

Fixed Forms: the term applied to a number of poetic forms and stanzaic patterns, many derived from French models, such as *ballade, rondeau, sestina, triolet*, and *villanelle*. Other "fixed forms" include the *sonnet, rhyme royal, haiku*, and *ottava rima*.

Folio: largest of several sizes of book page commonly used in the first few centuries after the introduction of the printing press. A folio size results from sheets of paper of at least 14 inches by 20 inches being folded in half (a folio page size will thus be at least 7 inches by 10 inches). When the same sheet is folded twice a quarto is produced, and when it is folded 3 times an octavo.

Foot: a unit of a line of verse which contains a particular combination of stressed and unstressed syllables. Dividing a line into metrical feet (*iambs, trochees*, etc.), then counting the number of feet per line, is part of *scansion*. See also *meter*.

Franklin: in the late medieval period, a landholder of free status, but ranking below the gentry.

Free Indirect Discourse: in prose fiction, commentary in which a seemingly objective and omniscient narrative voice assumes the point of view of one or more characters. When we hear through the third person narrative voice of Jane Austen's *Pride and Prejudice*, for example, that Mr. Darcy "was the proudest, most disagreeable man in the world, and every body hoped that he would never come there again," the narrative voice has assumed the point of view of "every body" in the community; we as readers are not meant to take it that Mr. Darcy is indeed the most disagreeable man in the world. Similarly, in the following passage from the same novel, we are likely to take it to read it as being the view of the character Charlotte that marriage is "the only honourable provision for well-educated young women of small fortune," not to take it to be an objective statement of perceived truth on the part of the novel's third person narrative voice:

> [Charlotte's] reflections were in general satisfactory. Mr. Collins to be sure was neither sensible nor agreeable; his society was irksome, and his attachment to her must be imaginary. But still he would be her husband. Without thinking highly either of men or of matrimony, marriage had always been her object; it was the only honourable provision for well-educated young women of small fortune, and however uncertain of giving happiness, must be their pleasantest preservative from want.

The term free indirect discourse may also be applied to situations in which it may not be entirely clear if the thoughts expressed emanate from the character, the narrator, or some combination of the two. (In the above-quoted passage expressing Charlotte's thoughts, indeed, some might argue that the statement concerning marriage should be taken as the expression of a belief that the narrative voice shares, at least in part.)

Free Verse: poetry that does not follow any regular meter, line length, or rhyming scheme. In many respects, though, free verse follows the complex natural "rules" and rhythmic patterns (or cadences) of speech.

Gaelic: Celtic language, variants of which are spoken in Ireland and Scotland.

Genre: a particular literary form. The concept of genre may be used with different levels of generality. At the most general, poetry, drama, and prose fiction are distinguished as separate genres. At a lower level of generality various sub-genres are frequently distinguished, such as (within drama) comedy and tragedy, or, at a still lower level of generality, Elizabethan domestic tragedy, Edwardian drawing-room comedy, and so on.

Georgic: (from Virgil's *Georgics*) a poem that celebrates the natural wealth of the countryside and advises how to cultivate and live in harmony with it. Pope's *Windsor Forest* and James Thomson's *Seasons* are classed as georgics. They were often said to make up, with eclogues, the two alliterative forms of pastoral poetry.

Ghazal: derived from Persian and Indian precedents, the ghazal presents a series of thoughts in closed couplets joined by a simple rhyme-scheme: *ab bb cb eb fb*, etc.

Gothic: in architecture and the visual arts, a term used to describe styles prevalent from the twelfth to the fourteenth centuries, but in literature a term used to describe work with a sinister or grotesque tone that seeks to evoke a sense of terror on the part of the reader or audience. Gothic literature originated as a genre in the eighteenth century with works such as Horace Walpole's *The Castle of Otranto*. To some extent the notion of the medieval itself then carried with it associations of the dark and the grotesque, but from the beginning an element of intentional exaggeration (sometimes verging on self-parody) attached itself to the genre. The Gothic trend of youth culture that began in the late twentieth century is less clearly associated with the medieval, but shares with the various varieties of Gothic literature (from Walpole in the eighteenth century, to Bram Stoker in the early twentieth, to Stephen King and Anne Rice in the late twentieth) a fondness for the sensational and the grotesque, as well as a propensity to self-parody.

Guilds: non-clerical associations that arose in the late Anglo-Saxon period, devoted both to social purposes (such as the organization of feasts for the members) and to piety. In the later medieval period guilds developed strong associations with particular occupations.

Haiku: a Japanese form, using three unrhymed lines of five, seven, and five syllables. Conventionally, it uses precise, concentrated images to suggest states of feeling.

Heptameter: a line containing seven metrical feet.

Heroic Couplet: a pair of rhymed iambic pentameters, so called because the form was much used in seventeenth and eighteenth-century poems and plays on heroic subjects.

Hexameter: a line containing six metrical feet.

Home Rule: movement dedicated to making Ireland politically independent from Britain.

Horatian Ode: inspired by the work of the Roman poet Horace, an ode that is usually calm and meditative in tone, and homostrophic (i.e., having regular stanzas) in form. Keats's odes are English examples.

House of Commons: elected legislative body, in Britain currently consisting of six hundred and fifty-nine members of Parliament. See also *Parliament*.

House of Lords: the "Upper House" of the British Houses of Parliament. Since the nineteenth century the House of Lords has been far less powerful than the elected House of Commons. The House of Lords is currently made up of both hereditary peers (Lords whose title is passed on from generation to generation) and life peers. As a result of legislation enacted by the Labour government of Tony Blair, the role of hereditary peers in Parliament is being phased out.

Humors: The four humors were believed in until the sixteenth and seventeenth centuries to be elements in the makeup of all humans; a person's temperament was thought to be determined by the way in which the humors were combined. When the *choleric* humor was dominant, the person would tend towards anger; when the *sanguine* humor was dominant, towards pleasant affability; when the *phlegmatic* humor was dominant, towards a cool and calm attitude and/or a lack of feeling or enthusiasm; and when the *melancholic* humor was dominant, towards withdrawal and melancholy.

Hymn: a song whose theme is usually religious, in praise of divinity. Literary hymns may praise more secular subjects.

Hyperbole: a *figure of speech* (a trope) that deliberately exaggerates or inflates meaning to achieve particular effects, such as the irony in A.E. Housman's claim (from "Terence, this is stupid stuff") that "malt does more than Milton can / To justify God's ways to man."

Iamb: the most common metrical foot in English verse, containing one unstressed syllable followed by a stressed syllable: x / (e.g., between, achieve).

Idyll: traditionally, a short pastoral poem that idealizes country life, conveying impressions of innocence and happiness.

Image: the recreation in words of objects perceived by the senses, sometimes thought of as "pictures," although other senses besides sight are involved. Besides this literal application, the term also refers more generally to the descriptive effects of figurative language, especially in *metaphor* and *simile*.

Imagism: a poetic movement that was popular mainly in the second decade of the twentieth century. The goal of Imagist poets (such as H.D. and Ezra Pound in their early work) was to represent emotions or impressions through highly concentrated imagery.

In Memoriam Stanza: a four-line stanza in iambic tetrameter, rhyming *abba*: the type of stanza used by Tennyson in *In Memoriam*.

Incantation: a chant or recitation of words that are believed to have magical power. A poem can achieve an "incantatory" effect through a compelling rhyme scheme and other repetitive patterns.

Interlocking Rhyme: See *rhyme*.

Internal Rhyme: See *rhyme*.

Irony: a subtle form of humor in which a statement is understood to convey a quite different (and often entirely opposite) meaning. A writer achieves this by carefully making sure that the statement occurs in a context which undermines or twists the statement's "literal" meaning. *Hyperbole* and *litotes* are often used for ironic effect. *Sarcasm* is a particularly strong or crude form of irony (usually spoken), in which the meaning is conveyed largely by the tone of voice adopted; something said sarcastically is meant clearly to imply its opposite.

Labour Party: See *Political Parties*.

Lament: a poem which expresses profound regret or grief either because of a death, or because of the loss of a former, happier state.

Language Poetry: a movement that defies the usual lyric and narrative conventions of poetry, and that challenges the structures and codes of everyday language. Often seen as both politically and aesthetically subversive, its roots lie in the works of modernist writers like Ezra Pound and Gertrude Stein.

Liberal Party: See *Political Parties*.

Litotes: a *figure of speech* (a trope) in which a writer deliberately uses understatement to highlight the importance of an argument, or to convey an ironic attitude.

Liturgical Drama: drama based on and/or incorporating text from the liturgy—the text recited during religious services.

Lollard: member of the group of radical Christians that took its inspiration from the ideas of John Wyclif (c. 1330–84). The Lollards, in many ways precursors of the Protestant Reformation, advocated making the Bible available to all, and dedication to the principles of evangelical poverty in imitation of Christ.

Luddites: protestors against the mechanization of industry on the grounds that it was leading to the loss of employment and to an increase in poverty. In the years 1811 to 1816 there were several Luddite protests in which machines were destroyed.

Lyric: a poem, usually short, expressing an individual speaker's feelings or private thoughts. Originally a song performed with accompaniment on a lyre, the lyric poem is often noted for musicality of rhyme and rhythm. The lyric genre includes a variety of forms, including the *sonnet*, the *ode*, the *elegy*, the *madrigal*, the *aubade*, the *dramatic monologue,* and the *hymn*.

Madrigal: a lyric poem, usually short and focusing on pastoral or romantic themes. A madrigal is often set to music.

Masculine Ending: a metrical line ending on a stressed syllable. *Masculine Rhyme*: see *rhyme*.

Masque: an entertainment typically combining music and dance, with a limited script, extravagant costumes and sets, and often incorporating spectacular special effects. Masques, which were performed before court audiences in the early seventeenth century, often focused on royal themes and frequently drew on classical mythology.

Mass: Within Christianity, a church service that includes the sacrament of the Eucharist (Holy Communion), in which bread and wine are consumed which are believed by those of many Christian denominations to have been transubstantiated into the body and blood of Christ. Anglicans (Episcopalians) are more likely to believe the bread and wine merely symbolizes the body and blood.

Melodrama: originally a term used to describe nineteenth-century-plays featuring sensational story lines and a crude separation of characters into moral categories, with the pure and virtuous pitted against evil villains. Early melodramas employed background music throughout the action of the play as a means of heightening the emotional response of the audience. By extension, certain sorts of prose fictions or poems are often described as having melodramatic elements.

Metaphor: a *figure of speech* (in this case, a trope) in which a comparison is made or identity is asserted between two unrelated things or actions without the use of "like" or "as." The primary subject is known as the *tenor*; to illuminate its nature, the writer links it to wholly different images, ideas, or actions referred to as the *vehicle*. Unlike a *simile*, which is a direct comparison of two things, a metaphor "fuses" the separate qualities of two things, creating a new idea. For example, Shakespeare's "Let slip the dogs of war" is a metaphorical statement. The tenor, or primary subject, is "war"; the vehicle of the metaphor is the image of hunting dogs released from their leash. The line fuses the idea of war with the qualities of ravening bloodlust associated with hunting dogs.

Metaphysical Poets: a group of seventeenth-century English poets, notably Donne, Cowley, Marvell, and Herbert, who employed unusual difficult imagery and *conceits* (see above) in order to develop intellectual and religious themes. The term was first applied to these writers to mark as far-fetched their use of philosophical and scientific ideas in a poetic context.

Meter: the pattern of stresses, syllables, and pauses that constitutes the regular rhythm of a line of verse. The meter of a poem written in the English accentual-syllabic tradition is determined by identifying the stressed and unstressed syllables in a line of verse, and grouping them into recurring units known as feet. See *accent, accentual-syllabic, caesura, elision*, and *scansion*. For some of the better known meters, see *iamb, trochee, dactyl, anapaest*, and *spondee*. See also *monometer, dimeter, trimeter, tetrameter, pentameter*, and *hexameter*.

Methodist: Protestant denomination formed in the eighteenth century as part of the religious movement led by John and Charles Wesley. Originally a movement within the Church of England, Methodism entailed enthusiastic evangelism, a strong emphasis on free will, and a strict regimen of Christian living.

Metonymy: a *figure of speech* (a trope), meaning "change of name," in which a writer refers to an object or idea by substituting the name of another object or idea closely associated with it: for example, the substitution of "crown" for monarchy, "the press" for journalism, or "the pen" for writing. *Synecdoche* (see below) is a kind of metonymy.

Mock-heroic: a style applying the elevated diction and vocabulary of epic poetry to low or ridiculous subjects. An example is Alexander Pope's "The Rape of the Lock."

Monologue: words spoken by a character to him or herself or to an audience directly.

Monometer: a line containing one metrical foot.

Mood: This can describe the writer's attitude, implied or expressed, towards the subject (see *tone* below); or it may refer to the atmosphere that a writer creates in a passage of description or narration.

Motif: an idea, image, action, or plot element that recurs throughout a literary work, creating new levels of meaning and strengthening structural coherence. The term is taken from music, where it describes recurring melodies or themes. See also *theme*.

Narrative Perspective: in fiction, the point of view from which the story is narrated. A first-person narrative is recounted using *I* and *me*, whereas a third person narrative is recounted using *he, she, they*, and so on. When a narrative is written in the third person and the narrative voice evidently "knows" all that is being done and thought, the story is typically described as being recounted by an "omniscient narrator."

Neoclassical: adapted from or substantially influenced by the cultures of ancient Greece and Rome. The term *neoclassical* is often used to describe the ideals of Restoration and eighteenth-century writers and artists who looked to ancient Greek and Roman civilization for models.

Nobility: privileged class, the members of which are distinguished by the holding of titles. Dukes, Marquesses, Earls, Viscounts, and Barons (in that order of precedence) are all holders of hereditary titles—that is to say, in the British patrilineal tradition, titles passed on from generation to generation to the eldest son. The title of Baronet, also hereditary, was added to this list by James I. Holders of non-hereditary titles include Knights and Dames.

Nonconformist: general term used to describe one who does subscribe to the Church of England.

Nonsense Verse: light, humorous poetry which contradicts logic, plays with the absurd, and invents words for amusing effects. Lewis Carroll is one of the best-known practitioners of nonsense verse.

Octave: also known as "octet," the first eight lines in an Italian/Petrarchan sonnet, rhyming *abbaabba*. See also *sestet* and *sonnet*.

Octosyllabic: a line of poetry with eight syllables, as in iambic tetrameter.

Ode: originally a classical poetic form, used by the Greeks and Romans to convey serious themes. English poetry has evolved three main forms of ode: the Pindaric (imitative of the odes of the Greek poet Pindar); the Horatian (modeled on the work of the Roman writer Horace); and the irregular ode.

The Pindaric ode was an irregular stanza in English, has a tripartite structure of "strophe," "antistrophe," and "epode" (meaning turn, counterturn, and stand), modeled on the songs and movements of the Chorus in Greek drama. The Horatian ode is more personal, reflective, and literary, and employs a pattern of repeated stanzas. The irregular ode, as its name implies, avoids a recurrent stanza pattern, and is sometimes irregular in line length also (see, for example, Wordsworth's "Ode: Intimations of Immortality").

Onomatopoeia: a *figure of speech* (a scheme) in which a word "imitates" a sound, or in which the sound of a word seems to reflect its meaning.

Ottava Rima: an 8-line stanza, usually in iambic pentameter, with the rhyme scheme *abababcc*. For an example, see Byron's *Don Juan*, or Yeats's "Sailing to Byzantium."

Oxymoron: a *figure of speech* (a trope) in which two words whose meanings seem contradictory are placed together, a paradox: for example, the phrase "darkness visible," from Milton's *Paradise Lost*.

Paean: a triumphant, celebratory song, often associated with a military victory.

Pale: in the medieval period, term for a protective zone around a fortress. As of the year 1500 three of these had been set up to guard frontiers of territory controlled by England—surrounding Calais in France, Berwick-upon-Tweed on the Scottish frontier, and Dublin in Ireland. The Dublin Pale was the largest of the three, and the term remained in use for a longer period there.

Pantoum: a poem in linked quatrains that rhyme *abab*. The second and fourth lines of one stanza are repeated as the first and third lines of the stanza that follows. In the final stanza the pattern is reversed: the second line repeats the third line of the first stanza, the fourth and final line repeats the first line of the first stanza.

Parliament: in Britain, the legislative body, comprising both the House of Commons and the House of Lords. Since the eighteenth century, the most powerful figure in the British government has been the Prime Minister rather than the monarch, the House of Commons has been the dominant body in Parliament, and members of the House of Commons have been organized in political parties. Since the mid-nineteenth century the effective executive in the British Parliamentary system has been the Cabinet, each member of which is typically in charge of a department of government. Unlike the American system, the British Parliamentary system (sometimes called the "Westminster system," after the location of the Houses of Parliament) brings together the executive and legislative functions of government, with the Prime Minister leading the government party in the House of Commons as well as directing the cabinet. By convention it is understood that the House of Lords will not contravene the wishes of the House of Commons in any fundamental way, though the "Upper House," as it is often referred to, may sometimes modify or reject legislation.

Parody: a close, usually mocking imitation of a particular literary work, or of the well-known style of a particular author, in order to expose or magnify weaknesses. Parody is a form of satire—that is, humor that may ridicule and scorn its object.

Pastiche: a discourse which borrows or imitates other writers' characters, forms, style, or ideas. Unlike a parody, a pastiche is usually intended as a compliment to the original writer.

Pastoral: in general, pertaining to country life; in prose, drama, and poetry, a stylized type of writing that idealizes the lives and innocence of country people, particularly shepherds and shepherdesses. Also see *eclogue, georgic, idyll*, above.

Pastoral Elegy: a poem in which the poet uses the pastoral style to lament the death of a friend, usually represented as a shepherd. Milton's "Lycidas" provides a good example of the form, including its use of such conventions as an invocation of the muse and a procession of mourners.

Pathetic Fallacy: a form of personification in which inanimate objects are given human emotions: for example, rain clouds "weeping." The word "fallacy" in this connection is intended to suggest the distortion of reality or the false emotion that may result from an exaggerated use of personification.

Pathos: the emotional quality of a discourse; or the ability of a discourse to appeal to our emotions. It is usually applied to the mood conveyed by images of pain, suffering, or loss that arouse feelings of pity or sorrow in the reader.

Pattern Poetry: a predecessor of modern concrete poetry, in which the shape of the poem on the page is intended to suggest or imitate an aspect of the poem's subject. George Herbert's "Easter Wings" is an example of pattern poetry.

Penny Dreadful: Victorian term for a cheap and poorly produced work of short fiction, usually of a sensational nature.

Pentameter: a line of verse containing five metrical feet.

Performance Poetry: poetry composed primarily for oral performance, often very theatrical in nature. See also *dub poetry* and *rap*.

Persona: the assumed identity or "speaking voice" that a writer projects in a discourse. The term "persona" literally means "mask." Even when a writer speaks in the first person, we should be aware that the attitudes or opinions we hear may not necessarily be those of the writer in real life.

Personification: a *figure of speech* (a trope), also known as "prosopopoeia," in which a writer refers to inanimate objects, ideas, or animals as if they were human, or creates a human figure to represent an abstract entity such as Philosophy or Peace.

Petrarchan Sonnet: the earliest form of the sonnet, also known as the Italian sonnet, with an 8-line octave and a 6-line sestet. The Petrarchan sonnet traditionally focuses on love and descriptions of physical beauty.

Phoneme: a linguistic term denoting the smallest unit of sound that it is possible to distinguish. The words *fun* and *phone* each have three phonemes, though one has three letters and one has five. (Each makes up a single syllable.)

Pindaric: See *ode*.

Plot: the organization of story materials within a literary work. The order in which story material is presented (especially causes and consequences); the inclusion of elements that allow or encourage the reader or audience to form expectations as to what is likely to happen; the decision to present some story material through exposition rather than in more extended form as part of the main action of the narrative—all these are matters of plotting.

Political Parties: The party names "Whig" and "Tory" began to be used in the late seventeenth century; before that time members of the House of Commons acted individually or through shifting and very informal factions. At first the Whigs and Tories had little formal organization either, but by the mid-eighteenth century parties had acknowledged leaders, and the leader of the party with the largest number of members in the House of Commons had begun to be recognized as the Prime Minister. The Tories evolved into the modern Conservative Party, and the Whigs into the Liberal Party. In the late nineteenth century the Labour Party was formed in an effort to provide better representation in Parliament for the working class, and since the 1920s Labour and the Conservatives have alternated as the party of government, with the Liberals reduced to third-party status. (Since 1988, when the Liberals merged with a breakaway faction from Labour known as the Social Democrats, this third party has been named the Liberal Democrats.)

Pre-Raphaelites: originally a group of Victorian artists and writers, formed in 1848. Their goal was to revive what they considered the simpler, fresher, more natural art that existed before Raphael (1483-1520). The poet Dante Gabriel Rossetti was one of the founders of the group.

Presbyterian: term applied to a group of Protestants (primarily English and Scottish) who advocated replacing the traditional hierarchical church in which bishops and archbishops governed lower level members of the clergy with a system in which all presbyters (or ministers) would be equal. The Presbyterians, originally led by John Knox, were strongly influenced by the ideas of John Calvin.

Prose Poem: a poetic discourse that uses prose formats (e.g., it may use margins and paragraphs rather than line breaks or stanzas) yet is written with the kind of attention to language, rhythm and cadence that characterizes verse.

Prosody: the study and analysis of meter, rhythm, rhyme, stanzaic pattern, and other devices of versification.

Protagonist: the central character in a literary work.

Prothalamion: a wedding song; a term coined by the poet Edmund Spenser, adapted from "epithalamion" (see above).

Public School: See *schools* below.

Pun: a play on words, in which a word with two or more distinct meanings, or two words with similar sounds, may create humorous ambiguities. Also known as *paranomasia*.

Puritan: term, originally applied only in a derogatory fashion but later widely accepted as descriptive, referring to those in England who favored religious reforms that went beyond those instituted as part of the Protestant Reformation, or, more generally, who were more forceful and uncompromising in pressing for religious purity both within the Church and in society as a whole.

Pyrrhic: a metrical foot containing two weak stresses: xx.

Quadrivium: group of four academic subjects (arithmetic, astronomy, geometry, and music) that made up part of the university coursework in the Middle Ages. There were studied after the more basic subjects of the *Trivium.*

Quantitative Meter: a metrical system used by Greek and Roman poets, in which a line of verse was measured by the "quantity," or length of sound of each syllable. A foot was measured in terms of syllables classed as long or short.

Quantity: duration of syllables in poetry. The line "There is a Garden in her face" (the first line from the poem of the same name by Thomas Campion) is characterized by the short quantities of the syllables. The last line of Thomas Hardy's "During Wind and Rain" has the same number of syllables as the line by Campion, but the quantities of the syllables are much longer—in other words, the line take much longer to say: "Down their carved names the rain drop ploughs."

Quatrain: a four-line stanza, usually rhymed.

Quintet: a five-line stanza. Sometimes given as *quintain.*

Rap: originally coined to describe informal conversation, "rap" now usually describes a style of performance poetry in which a poet will chant rhymed verse, sometimes improvised and usually with musical accompaniment that has a heavy beat.

Realism: as a literary term, the presentation through literature of material closely resembling real life. As notions both of what constitutes "real life" and of how it may be most faithfully represented in literature have varied widely, "realism" has taken a variety of meanings. The term *naturalistic* has sometimes been used a synonym for *realistic*; *naturalism* originated in the nineteenth century as a term denoting a form of realism focusing in particular on grim, unpleasant, or ugly aspects of the real.

Refrain: one or more words or lines repeated at regular points throughout a poem, often at the end of each stanza or group of stanzas. Sometimes a whole stanza may be repeated to create a refrain, like the chorus in a song.

Reggae: a style of heavily-rhythmic music from the West Indies with lyrics that are colloquial in language and often anti-establishment in content and flavor. First popularized in the 1960s and 1970s, reggae has had a lasting influence on performance poetry, rap, and dub.

Rhetoric: in classical Greece and Rome, the art of persuasion and public speaking. From the Middle Ages onwards, the study of rhetoric gave greater attention to style, particularly figures of speech. Today in poetics, the term rhetoric may encompass not only figures of speech, but also the persuasive effects of forms, sounds and word choices.

Rhyme: the repetition of identical or similar sounds, usually in pairs and generally at the ends of metrical lines.

   End-rhyme: a rhyming word or syllable at the end of a line.

   Eye Rhyme: rhyming that pairs words whose spellings are alike but whose pronunciations are different. for example, though/slough.

Feminine Rhyme: a two-syllable (also known as "double") rhyme. The first syllable is stressed and the second unstressed: for example, hasty/tasty. See also *triple rhyme* below.

Interlocking Rhyme: the repetition of rhymes from one stanza to the next, creating links that add to the poem's continuity and coherence. Examples may be found in Shelley's use of *terza rima* in "Ode to the West Wind" and in Dylan Thomas's villanelle "Do Not Go Gentle Into That Good Night."

Internal Rhyme: the placement of rhyming words within lines so that at least two words in a line rhyme with each other.

Masculine Rhyme: a correspondence of sound between the final stressed syllables at the end of two or more lines, as in grieve/leave, arr-ive/sur-vive.

Slant Rhyme: an imperfect or partial rhyme (also known as "near" or "half" rhyme) in which the final consonants of stressed syllables match but the vowel sounds do not. E.g., spoiled / spilled, taint / stint.

Triple Rhyme: a three-syllable rhyme in which the first syllable of each rhyme-word is stressed and the other two unstressed (e.g., lottery / coterie).

True Rhyme: a rhyme in which everything but the initial consonant matches perfectly in sound and spelling.

Rhyme Royal: a stanza of seven iambic pentameters, with a rhyme-scheme of *ababbcc*. This is also known as the Chaucerian stanza, as Chaucer was the first English poet to use this form. See also *septet*.

Rhythm: in speech, the arrangement of stressed and unstressed syllables creates units of sound. In song or verse, these units usually form a regular rhythmic pattern, a kind of beat, described in prosody as *meter*.

Romanticism: a major social and cultural movement, originating in Europe, that shaped much of Western artistic thought in the late eighteenth and nineteenth centuries. Opposing the ideal of controlled, rational order of the Enlightenment, Romanticism emphasizes the importance of spontaneous self-expression, emotion, and personal experience in producing art. In Romanticism, the "natural" is privileged over the conventional or the artificial.

Rondeau: a fifteen-line poem, generally octosyllabic, with only two rhymes throughout its three stanzas, and an unrhymed refrain at the end of the ninth and fifteenth lines, repeating part of the opening line.

Sarcasm: See *irony*.

Satire: literary work designed to make fun of or seriously criticize its subject. According to many literary theories of the Renaissance and neoclassical periods, the ridicule through satire of a certain sort of behavior may function for the reader or audience as a corrective of such behavior.

Scansion: the formal analysis of patterns of rhythm and rhyme in poetry. Each line of verse will have a certain number of fairly regular "beats" consisting of alternating stressed and unstressed syllables. To "scan" a poem is to count the beats in each line, to mark stressed and unstressed syllables and indicate their combination into "feet," to note pauses, and to identify rhyme schemes with letters of the alphabet.

Scheme: See *figures of speech*.

Schools: In the sixteenth and seventeenth centuries the different forms of school in England included Cathedral schools (often founded with a view to the education of members of the choir); grammar schools (often founded by towns or by guilds, and teaching a much broader curriculum than the modern sense of "grammar" might suggest, private schools, operated by private individuals out of private residences; and public schools, which (like the private schools and the grammar schools) operated independent of any church authority, but unlike the grammar schools and private schools were organized as independent charities, and often offered free education. Over the centuries certain of these public schools, while remaining not-for-profit institutions, began to accept fee-paying students and to adopt standards that made them more and more exclusive. In the eighteenth and nineteenth century attendance at such prestigious public boarding schools as Eton, Westminster, and Winchester had become almost exclusively the preserve of the upper classes; by the nineteenth century such "public" schools were the equivalent of private schools in North America. Though a few girls attended some early grammar schools, the greater part of this educational system was for boys only. Though a number of individuals of earlier periods were concerned to increase the number of private schools for girls, the movement to create a parallel girls' system of public schools and grammar schools dates from the later nineteenth century.

Septet: a stanza containing seven lines.

Serf: in the medieval period, a person of unfree status, typically engaged in working the land.

Sestet: a six-line stanza that forms the second grouping of lines in an Italian / Petrarchan sonnet, following the octave. See *sonnet* and *sestina*.

Sestina: an elaborate unrhymed poem with six 6-line stanzas and a 3-line envoy.

Shire: originally a multiple estate; since the late medieval period a larger territory forming an administrative unit—also referred to as a county.

Simile: a *figure of speech* (a trope) which makes an explicit comparison between a particular object and another object or idea that is similar in some (often unexpected) way. A simile always uses "like" or "as" to signal the connection. Compare with *metaphor* above.

Sonnet: a highly structured lyric poem, which normally has fourteen lines of iambic pentameter. We can distinguish four major variations of the sonnet.

Italian/Petrarchan: named for the 14th-century Italian poet Petrarch, has an octave rhyming *abbaabba*, and a sestet rhyming *cdecde*, or *cdcdcd* (other arrangements are possible here). Usually, a turn in argument takes place between octave and sestet.

Miltonic: developed by Milton and similar to the Petrarchan in rhyme scheme, but eliminating the turn after the octave, thus giving greater unity to the poem's structure of thought.

Shakespearean: often called the English sonnet, this form has three quatrains and a couplet. The quatrains rhyme internally but do not interlock: *abab cdcd efef gg*. The turn may occur after the second quatrain, but is usually revealed in the final couplet. Shakespeare's sonnets are the best-known examples of this form.

Spenserian: after Edmund Spenser, who developed the form in his sonnet cycle *Amoretti*. This sonnet form has three quatrains linked through interlocking rhyme, and a separately rhyming couplet: *abab bcbc cdcd ee*.

Speaker: in the late medieval period, a member of the Commons in Parliament who spoke on behalf of that entire group. (The Commons first elected a Speaker in 1376.) In later eras the role of Speaker became one of chairing debates in the House of Commons and arbitrating disputes over matters of procedure.

Spenserian Stanza: a nine-line stanza, with eight iambic pentameters and a concluding alexandrine, rhyming *ababbcbcc*.

Spondee: a metrical foot containing two strong stressed syllables: // (e.g., blind mouths).

Sprung Rhythm: a modern variation of accentual verse, created by the English poet Gerard Manley Hopkins, in which rhythms are determined largely by the number of strong stresses in a line, without regard to the number of unstressed syllables. Hopkins felt that sprung rhythm more closely approximated the natural rhythms of speech than did conventional poetry.

Stanza: any lines of verse that are grouped together in a poem and separated from other similarly-structured groups by a space. In metrical poetry, stanzas share metrical and rhyming patterns; however, stanzas may also be formed on the basis of thought, as in irregular odes. Conventional stanza forms include the *tercet*, the *quatrain*, *rhyme royal*, the *Spenserian stanza*, the *ballad stanza*, and *ottava rima*.

Stream of Consciousness: narrative technique that attempts to convey in prose fiction a sense of the progression of the full range of thoughts and sensations occurring within a character's mind. Twentieth-century pioneers in the use of the stream of consciousness technique include Dorothy Richardson, Virginia Woolf, and James Joyce.

Stress: See *accent*.

Strophe: the first stanza in a Pindaric ode. This is followed by an *antistrophe* (see above), which presents the same metrical pattern and rhyme scheme, and finally by an *epode*, differing in meter from the preceding stanzas. Upon completion of this "triad," the entire sequence can recur. *Strophe* may also describe a stanza or other subdivision in other kinds of poem.

Sublime: a concept, most popular in eighteenth-century England, of the qualities of grandeur, power, and awe that may be inherent in or produced by undomesticated nature or great art. The sublime was thought of as higher and loftier than something that is merely beautiful.

Subplot: a line of story that is subordinate to the main storyline of a narrative. (Note that properly speaking a subplot is a category of story material, not of plot.)

Substitution: a deliberate change from the dominant pattern of stresses in a line of verse to create emphasis or variation. Thus the first line of Shakespeare's sonnet "'Shall I compare thee to a summer's day?' is decidedly iambic in meter (x / x / x / x / x /), whereas the second line substitutes a trochee (/ x) in the opening foot: "Thou art more lovely and more temperate."

Subtext: implied or suggested meaning of a passage of text, or of an entire work.

Syllabic Verse: poetry in which the length of a line is measured solely by the number of syllables, regardless of accents or patterns of stress.

Syllable: vocal sound or group of sounds forming a unit of speech; a syllable may be formed with a single effort of articulation. Some syllables consist of a single phoneme (e.g., the word *I*, or the first syllable in the word *u*-ni-ty) but others may be made up of several phonemes (as with one-syllable words such as *lengths*, *splurged*, and *through*). By contrast, the much shorter words *ago*, *any*, and *open* each have two syllables.

Symbol: a word, image, or idea that represents something more, or other, than for what it at first appears to stand. Like metaphor, the symbol extends meaning; but while the tenor and vehicle of metaphor are bound in a specific relationship, a symbol may have a range of connotations. For example, the image of a rose may call forth associations of love, passion, transience, fragility, youth and beauty, among others. Depending upon the context, such an image could be interpreted in a variety of ways, as in Blake's lyric, "The Sick Rose." Though this power of symbolic representation characterizes all language, poetry most particularly endows the concrete imagery evoked through language with a larger meaning. Such meaning is implied rather than explicitly stated; indeed, much of the power of symbolic language lies in the reader's ability to make meaningful sense of it.

Syncope: in poetry, the dropping of a letter or syllable from the middle of a word, as in "trav'ler." Such a contraction allows a line to stay within a metrical scheme. See also *catalexis* and *elision*.

Synecdoche: a kind of *metonymy* in which a writer substitutes the name of a part of something to signify the whole: for example, "sail" for ship or "hand" for a member of the ship's crew.

Tercet: a group, or stanza, of three lines, often linked by an interlocking rhyme scheme as in *terza rima*. See also *triplet*.

Terza Rima: an arrangement of tercets interlocked by a rhyme scheme of *aba bcb cdc ded*, etc., and ending with a couplet that rhymes with the second-last line of the final tercet (for example, *efe, ff*). See, for example, Percy Shelley's "Ode to the West Wind."

Tetrameter: a line of poetry containing four metrical feet.

Theme: the governing idea of a discourse, conveyed through the development of the subject, and through the recurrence of certain words, sounds, or metrical patterns. See also *motif*.

Third-Person Narrative: See *narrative perspective*.

Tone: the writer's attitude toward a given subject or audience, as expressed though an authorial persona or "voice." Tone can be projected through particular choices of wording, imagery, figures of speech, and rhythmic devices. Compare *mood*.

Tories: See *Political Parties*.

Tragedy: in the traditional definition originating in discussions of ancient Greek drama, a serious narrative recounting the downfall of the protagonist. More loosely, the term has been applied to a wide variety of literary forms in which the tone is predominantly a dark one and the narrative does not end happily.

Transcendentalism: a philosophical movement that influenced such Victorian writers as Thomas Carlyle and Robert Browning. Also a mode of Romantic thought, Transcendentalism places the supernatural and the natural within one great Unity and believes that each individual person embodies aspects of the divine.

Trimeter: a line of poetry containing three metrical feet.

Triolet: a French form in which the first line appears three times in a poem of only eight lines. The first line is repeated at lines 4 and 7; the second line is repeated in line 8. The triolet has only two rhymes: *abaaabab*.

Triple Foot: poetic foot of three syllables. The possible varieties of triple foot are the anapest (in which two unstressed syllables are followed by a stressed syllable), the dactyl (in which a stressed syllable is followed by two unstressed lines), and the mollossus (in which all three syllables are stressed equally). English poetry tends to use duple rhythms far more frequently than triple rhythms.

Triplet: a group of three lines with the same end-rhyme, much used by eighteenth-century poets to vary or punctuate the flow of couplets. See also *tercet*.

Trivium: group of three academic subjects (dialectic, grammar, and rhetoric) that were part of the university curriculum in the Middle Ages. Their study precedes that of the more advanced subjects of the *quadrivium*.

Trochee: a metrical foot containing one strong stress followed by one weak stress: / x (heaven, lover).

Trope: any figure of speech that plays on our understandings of words to extend, alter, or transform "literal" meaning. Common tropes include *metaphor*, *simile*, *personification*, *hyperbole*, *metonymy*, *oxymoron*, *synecdoche*, and *irony*. See also *figures of speech*, above.

Turn (Italian "volta"): the point in a *sonnet* where the mood or argument changes. The turn may occur between the octave and sestet, i.e., after the eighth line, or in the final couplet, depending on the kind of sonnet.

Unities: Many literary theorists of the late sixteenth through late eighteenth centuries held that a play should ideally be presented as representing a single place, and confining the action to a single day and a single dominant event. They disapproved of plots involving gaps or long periods of time, shifts in place, or subplots. These concepts, which came to be referred to as the unities of space, time, and action, were based on a misreading of classical authorities (principally of Aristotle).

Vers de societé: French: literally, "verse about society." The term originated with poetry written by aristocrats and upper-middle-class poets that specifically disavows the ambition of creating "high art" while treating the concerns of their own group in verse forms that demonstrate a high degree of formal control (e.g., artful rhymes, surprising turns of diction).

Vers libre (French):   See *free verse* above.

Verse: a general term for works of poetry, usually referring to poems that incorporate some kind of metrical structure. The term may also describe a line of poetry, though more frequently it is applied to a stanza.

Villanelle: a poem usually consisting of 19 lines, with five 3-line stanzas (tercets) rhyming *aba*, and a concluding quatrain rhyming *abaa*. The first and third lines of the first tercet are repeated at fixed intervals throughout the rest of the poem. See, for example, Dylan Thomas's "Do Not Go Gentle Into That Good Night."

Whigs: See *Political Parties*.

Workhouse: public institution in which the poor were provided with a minimal level of sustenance and with lodging in exchange for work performed. Early workhouses were typically administered by individual parishes. In 1834 a unified system covering all of England and Wales was put into effect.

Zeugma: a *figure of speech* (trope) in which one word links or "yokes" two others in the same sentence, often to comic or ironic effect. For example, a verb may govern two objects, as in Pope's line "Or stain her honour, or her new brocade."

Permissions Acknowledgments

Illustration Credits

Index of First Lines

Index of Authors and Titles